AN EXEGETICAL SUMMARY OF
EPHESIANS

AN EXEGETICAL SUMMARY OF EPHESIANS

Second Edition

Glen H. Graham

SIL International

Second Edition
© 1997, 2008 by SIL International

Library of Congress Catalog Card Number: 2008923534
ISBN: 978-155671-208-1

Printed in the United States of America

All Rights Reserved
No part of this publication may be reproduced, stored in a retrieval system, or transmitted in any form or by any means without the express permission of SIL International. However, brief excerpts, generally understood to be within the limits of fair use, may be quoted without written permission.

Copies of this and other publications
of SIL International may be obtained from

International Academic Bookstore
SIL International
7500 West Camp Wisdom Road
Dallas, TX 75236-5699, USA

Voice: 972-708-7404
Fax: 972-708-7363
academic_books@sil.org
www.ethnologue.com

PREFACE

Exegesis is concerned with the interpretation of a text. Exegesis of the New Testament involves determining the meaning of the Greek text. Translators must be especially careful and thorough in their exegesis of the New Testament in order to accurately communicate its message in the vocabulary, grammar, and literary devices of another language. Questions occurring to translators as they study the Greek text are answered by summarizing how scholars have interpreted the text. This is information that should be considered by translators as they make their own exegetical decisions regarding the message they will communicate in their translations.

The Semi-Literal Translation

As a basis for discussion, a semi-literal translation of the Greek text is given so that the reasons for different interpretations can best be seen. When one Greek word is translated into English by several words, these words are joined by hyphens. There are a few times when clarity requires that a string of words joined by hyphens have a separate word, such as 'not' (μή), inserted in their midst. In this case, the separate word is surrounded by spaces between the hyphens. When alternate translations of a Greek word are given, these are separated by slashes.

The Text

Variations in the Greek text are noted under the heading TEXT. The base text for the summary is the text of the fourth revised edition of *The Greek New Testament,* published by the United Bible Societies, which has the same text as the twenty-sixth edition of the *Novum Testamentum Graece* (Nestle-Aland). The versions that follow different variations are listed without evaluating their choices.

The Lexicon

The meaning of a key word in context is the first question to be answered. Words marked with a raised letter in the semi-literal translation are treated separately under the heading LEXICON. First, the lexicon form of the Greek word is given. Within the parentheses following the Greek word is the location number where, in the author's judgment, this word is defined in the *Greek-English Lexicon of the New Testament Based on Semantic Domains* (Louw and Nida 1988). When a semantic domain includes a translation of the particular verse being treated, **LN** in bold type indicates that specific translation. If the specific reference for the verse is listed in *A Greek-English Lexicon of the New Testament and Other Early Christian Literature* (Bauer, Arndt, Gingrich, and Danker 1979), the outline location and page number is given. Then English equivalents of the Greek word are given to show how it is translated by commentators who offer their own translations of the whole text and, after a semicolon, all the versions in the list of abbreviations for translations. When reference is made to "all versions," it refers to only the versions in the list of translations. Sometimes further comments are made about the meaning of the word or the significance of a verb's tense, voice, or mood.

The Questions

Under the heading QUESTION, a question is asked that comes from examining the Greek text under consideration. Typical questions concern the identity of an implied actor or object of an event word, the antecedent of a pronominal reference, the connection indicated by a relational word, the meaning of a genitive construction, the meaning of figurative language, the function of a rhetorical question, the identification of an ambiguity, and the presence of implied information that is needed to understand the passage correctly. Background information is also considered for a proper understanding of a passage. Although not all implied information and background information is made explicit in a translation, it is important to consider it so that the translation will not be stated in such a way that prevents a reader from arriving at the proper interpretation. The question is answered with a summary of what commentators have said. If there are contrasting differences of opinion, the different interpretations are numbered and the commentaries that support each are listed. Differences that are not treated by many of the commentaries often are not numbered, but are introduced with a contrastive 'Or' at the beginning of the sentence. No attempt has been made to select which interpretation is best.

In listing support for various statements of interpretation, the author is often faced with the difficult task of matching the different terminologies used in commentaries with the terminology he has adopted. Sometimes he can only infer the position of a commentary from incidental remarks. This book, then, includes the author's interpretation of the views taken in the various commentaries. General statements are followed by specific statements, which indicate the author's understanding of the pertinent relationships, actors, events, and objects implied by that interpretation.

The Use of This Book

This book does not replace the commentaries that it summarizes. Commentaries contain much more information about the meaning of words and passages. They often contain arguments for the interpretations that are taken and they may have important discussions about the discourse features of the text. In addition, they have information about the historical, geographical, and cultural setting. Translators will want to refer to at least four commentaries as they exegete a passage. However, since no one commentary contains all the answers translators need, this book will be a valuable supplement. It makes more sources of exegetical help available than most translators have access to. Even if they had all the books available, few would have the time to search through all of them for the answers.

When many commentaries are studied, it soon becomes apparent that they frequently disagree in their interpretations. That is the reason why so many answers in this book are divided into two or more interpretations. The reader's initial reaction may be that all of these different interpretations complicate exegesis rather than help it. However, before translating a passage, a translator needs to know exactly where there is a problem of interpretation and what the exegetical options are.

Acknowledgments

Robin Thurman made available his preliminary study of this book. Richard C. Blight edited this volume for its content and presentation. Faith Blight has carefully edited the material to prepare it for publication.

ABBREVIATIONS AND BIBLIOGRAPHY

COMMENTARIES AND REFERENCE BOOKS

AB   Barth, Markus. *Ephesians*. The Anchor Bible, vols. 34, 34A. Garden City, NY: Doubleday & Company, 1974.

Ag   Aglen. "The Psalms." *Ellicott's Commentary on the Whole Bible*, vol. 4. (note)d. Reprint. Grand Rapids, Mich.: Zondervan, 1954.

Alf   Alford, Henry. "Ephesians." In vol 3 of *The Greek Testament*. 1874. Revised by Everett F. Harrison. Chicago: Moody Press, 1958.

Alf-ed   Supplementary notes to the above by Everett F. Harrison.

Ba   Barnes, Albert. *Notes on the New Testament*. Nd. Reprint. Grand Rapids, Mich.: Baker, 1972.

BAGD   Bauer, Walter. *A Greek-English Lexicon of the New Testament and Other Early Christian Literature*. Translated and adapted from the 5th ed., 1958 by William F. Arndt and F. Wilbur Gingrich. 2d English ed. revised and augmented by F. Wilbur Gingrich and Frederick W. Danker. Chicago: University of Chicago Press, 1979.

BB   Barth, Markus, and Helmut Blanke. *Colossians*. The Anchor Bible, vol. 34B. Garden City, NY: Doubleday, 1994.

BD   Blass, F., and A. Debrunner. *A Greek Grammar of the New Testament and Other Early Christian Literature*. A translation and revision of the ninth-tenth German edition incorporating supplementary notes by A. Debrunner. Translated by Robert W. Funk. Chicago: University of Chicago Press, 1961.

Bu   Bullinger, E. W. *Figures of Speech Used in the Bible*. 1898. Reprint. Grand Rapids, Mich.: Baker, 1968.

Cal   Calvin, John. *Calvin's Commentaries*, vol. 12 Nd. Reprint. Wilmington, Delaware: Associated Publishers and Authors, Nd.

Can   Candlish, James S. *The Epistle of Paul to the Ephesians*. Edinburgh: T. & T. Clark, 1901.

CBC   Thompson, G. H. P. *The Letters of Paul to the Ephesians to the Colossians and to Philemon*. The Cambridge Bible Commentary. Cambridge: Cambridge University Press, 1967.

Da   Dahood, Mitchell. *Psalms II, 51-100*. The Anchor Bible, vol. 17. 3rd ed. Garden City, NY: Doubleday, 1983.

Del   Delitzsch, Franz. *Biblical Commentary on the Psalms*, vol. 2. Translated from the German 2nd edition by Francis Bolton. Biblical Commentary on the Old Testament by C. F. Keil and F. Delitzsch. Nd. Reprint. Grand Rapids, Mich.: Eerdmans, 1959.

ABBREVIATIONS AND BIBLIOGRAPHY

DNTT   Brown, Colin, ed. *The New International Dictionary of New Testament Theology*. Translated, with additions and revisions, from *Theologisches Begriffslexikon zum Neuen Testament*, edited by Lothar Coenen, Erich Beyreuther, and Hans Bietenhard. Grand Rapids, Mich.: Zondervan, 1975.

Ds   Deismann, Adolf. *Light from the Ancient East*. 4th ed. Translated by Lionel R. M. Strachan. New York: Harper, 1922.

Ds2   Deismann, Adolf. *Paul. A Study in Social and Religious History*. Translated by William E. Wilson. 2nd ed revised and enlarged. 1927. Reprint. New York: Harper, 1957.

Ds3   Deismann, Adolf. *Bible Studies*. 2nd. ed. Translated by Alexander Grieve. Edinburgh: T. & T. Clark, 1903.

Ea   Eadie, John. *A Commentary on the Greek Text of the Epistle of Paul to the Ephesians*. Edited by W. Young. 1883. Reprint. Grand Rapids, Mich.: Baker, 1979.

EBC   Wood, A. Skevington. "Ephesians." In vol. 11 of *The Expositor's Bible Commentary*, edited by Frank E. Gabelein. Grand Rapids, Mich.: Zondervan, 1978.

ECWB   Barry, Alfred. Nd. "The Epistle of Paul the Apostle to the Ephesians," In vol. 8 of *Ellicott's Commentary on the Whole Bible*. Nd. Reprint. Grand Rapids, Mich.: Zondervan, 1954.

EGT   Salmond, S. D. F. "The Epistle to the Ephesians," In vol. 3 of *The Expositor's Greek Testament*, edited by W. Robertson Nicoll. Nd. Reprint. Grand Rapids, Mich.: Eerdmans, 1970.

El   Ellicott, Charles J. *St. Paul's Epistle to the Ephesians*. 5th ed. London: Longmans, Green and Co., 1884.

Fd   Field, Frederick. *Notes on the Translation of the New Testament*. Cambridge: University Press, 1899.

Gd   Goodwin, Thomas. *Exposition of Ephesians, Chapter 1 to 2:10*. Before 1679. Reprint. Grand Rapids, Mich.: Sovereign Grace Book Club, 1958; distributed by Zondervan Publishing House.

HG   Robertson, A. T. *A Grammar of the Greek New Testament in the Light of Historical Research*. Nashville, Tenn.: Broadman, 1934.

Ho   Hodge, Charles. *A Commentary on the Epistle to the Ephesians*. 1856. Reprint. Grand Rapids, Mich.: Eerdmans, 1950.

IB   Beare, Francis W. "The Epistle to the Ephesians." Exposition by Theodore O. Wedel. In vol 10 of *The Interpreter's Bible*. New York and Nashville, Tenn.: Abingdon, 1953.

ICC   Abbott, T. K. *A Critical and Exegetical Commentary on the Epistles to the Ephesians and to the Colossians*. The International Critical Commentary on the Holy Scriptures of the Old and New Testaments. 1897. Reprint. Edinburgh: T. & T. Clark, 1897.

IDB   Buttrick, George Arthur, ed. *The Interpreter's Dictionary of the Bible*. 4 vols. with Supplementary Volume edited by Keith Crim. Nashville, Tenn.: Abingdon, 1962.

ISBE	Orr, James, ed. *The International Standard Bible Encyclopaedia*. 5 vols. Grand Rapids, Mich.: Eerdmans, 1939.
ISBE2	Bromiley, Geoffrey W., ed. *The International Standard Bible Encyclopedia*. 4 vols. Fully revised. Grand Rapids, Mich.: Eerdmans, 1979.
Kid	Kidner, Derek. *Psalms 1-72. An Introduction and Commentary on Books 1 and 2 of the Psalms*. The Tyndale Old Testament Commentaries. Downers Grove, Ill.: Inter-Varsity, 1973.
Leu	Leupold, H. C. *Exposition of the Psalms*. Columbus, Ohio: Wartburg, 1959.
LJ	Lloyd-Jones, D. Martin. Individually titled volumes on the exposition of Ephesians. 8 vols. Grand Rapids, Mich.: Baker, 1972–82.
LN	Louw, Johannes P., and Eugene A. Nida. *Greek-English Lexicon of the New Testament Based on Semantic Domains*. 2 vols. New York: United Bible Societies, 1988.
Lns	Lenski, R. C. H. *The Interpretation of St. Paul's Epistles to the Galatians, to the Ephesians, and to the Philippians*. Minneapolis, Minn.: Augsburg, 1937.
Lt	Lightfoot, J. B. *Notes on the Epistles of St. Paul*. 1895. Reprint. Grand Rapids, Mich.: Zondervan, 1957.
Mac	Maclaren, Alexander. "The Psalms." In vol. 3 of *The Expositor's Bible*, edited by W. Robertson Nicoll. 1903. Reprint. Grand Rapids, Mich.: Baker, 1982.
MM	Moulton, James Hope, and George Milligan. *The Vocabulary of the Greek Testament Illustrated from the Papyri and Other Non-Literary Sources*. 1914–1929. Reprint. Grand Rapids, Mich.: Eerdmans, 1957.
MNTC	Scott, E. F. *The Epistles of Paul to the Colossians, to Philemon and to the Ephesians*. Moffatt's New Testament Commentary. London: Hodder and Stoughton, 1930.
Mo	Moule, C. F. D. *An Idiom Book of New Testament Greek*. 2nd ed. Cambridge: Cambridge University Press, 1959.
Mou	Moulton, James Hope. *Prolegomena*. A Grammar of New Testament Greek, vol. 1. 3rd ed. Edinburgh: T. and T. Clark, 1908.
MT	Burton, Ernest De Witt. *Syntax of the Moods and Tenses in New Testament Greek*. 3rd ed. Edinburgh: T. & T. Clark, 1898.
My	Meyer, Heinrich August Wilhelm. "Critical and Exegetical Handbook to the Epistle to the Ephesians." In vol. 7 of *Meyer's Commentary on the New Testament*. Translated from the 4th German edition by Maurice J. Evans and the translation revised and edited by William P. Dickson. With a preface, translation of references and supplementary notes to the American edition by Henry E. Jacobs. New York: Funk & Wagnalls, 1884.
My-ed	Supplementary notes to the above by Henry E. Jacobs.

NCBC	Mitton, C. Leslie. *Ephesians*. The New Century Bible Commentary. Grand Rapids, Mich.: Eerdmans, 1973.
NIC	Bruce, F. F. *The Epistles to the Colossians, to Philemon, and to the Ephesians*. The New International Commentary on the New Testament. Grand Rapids, Mich.: Eerdmans, 1984.
NTC	Hendriksen, William. *Exposition of Ephesians*. New Testament Commentary. Grand Rapids, Mich.: Baker, 1967.
Pf	Pfitzner, Victor C. *Paul and the Agon Motif. Traditional Athletic Imagery in the Pauline Literature*. Supplements to Novum Testamentum, vol. 16. Leiden: E. J. Brill, 1967.
Rob	Robinson, J. Armitage. *Commentary on Ephesians*. 2nd ed. 1904. Reprint. Grand Rapids, Mich.: Kregel, 1979.
Si	Simpson, E. K. "Commentary on the Epistle to the Ephesians." In *Commen-tary on the Epistles to the Ephesians and the Colossians*, by E. K. Simpson and F. F. Bruce. The New International Commentary on the New Testament. Grand Rapids, Mich.: Eerdmans, 1957.
Si-ed	Supplementary footnotes to the above by F. F. Bruce.
Sp	Spurgeon, C. H. *The Treasury of David*. 6 vols. Nd. Reprint. London and Edinburgh: Marshall, Morgan and Scott, 1950.
St	Stott, John R. W. *God's New Society: The Message of Ephesians*. Downers Grove, Ill.: Inter-Varsity, 1979.
TD	Kittel, Gerhard, and Gerhard Friedrich, eds. *Theological Dictionary of the New Testament*. 10 vols. Translated and edited by Geoffrey W. Bromiley. Grand Rapids, Mich.: Eerdmans, 1964–1976.
TH	Bratcher, Robert G., and Eugene A. Nida. *A Translator's Handbook on Paul's Letter to the Ephesians*. New York: United Bible Societies, 1982.
TNTC	Foulkes, Francis. *The Epistle of Paul to the Ephesians*. The Tyndale New Testament Commentaries. Grand Rapids, Mich.: Eerdmans, 1956.
Tu	Turner, Nigel. *Syntax*. Vol. 3. of *A Grammar of New Testament Greek*. Edinburgh: T. & T. Clark, 1963.
Tu2	Turner, Nigel. *Grammatical Insights into the Greek New Testament*. Edinburgh: T. & T. Clark, 1965.
Tu3	Turner, Nigel. *Style*. Vol. 4 of *A Grammar of New Testament Greek*. Edinburgh: T. & T. Clark, 1976.
WBC	Lincoln, Andrew T. *Ephesians*. Word Biblical Commentary. Dallas, Texas: Word, 1990.
We	Westcott, Brooke Foss. *Saint Paul's Epistle to the Ephesians*. 1906. Reprint. Minneapolis, Minn.: Klock and Klock, 1983.
WeBC	Carter, Charles W. "The Epistle of Paul to the Ephesians," In vol. 5 of *The Wesleyan Bible Commentary*. Grand Rapids, Mich.: Eerdmans, 1965.

Wei   Weiser, Artur. *The Psalms*. Translated by Herbert Hartwell. The Old Testament Library. Philadelphia: Westminister, 1962.

RECOMMENDATIONS

Barth (AB) in his "Comments" sections and Lincoln (WBC) in his "Form/Structure/Setting" sections provide valuable information on the structure of discourse levels which could not be included in this summary. They also provide background information and arguments, pro and con, for alternative interpretations. Eadie (Ea) also provides information on various interpretations. A shorter commentary, published too late to be included in this summary, but literally crammed with exegetical information relevant to the Bible translator, is Leon Morris' *Expository Reflections on the Letter to the Ephesians* (Grand Rapids, Mich.: Baker, 1994, 217 pp.)

GREEK TEXT AND TRANSLATIONS

GNT   The Greek New Testament. Edited by B. Aland, K Aland, J. Karavidopoulos, C. Martini, and B. Metzger. 4th ed. London, New York: United Bible Societies, 1993.
KJV   The Holy Bible. Authorized (or King James) Version, 1611.
NAB   The New American Bible. Camden, New Jersey: Thomas Nelson, 1971.
NASB The New American Standard Bible. Nashville, Tenn.: Holman, 1977.
NIV   The Holy Bible, New International Version. Grand Rapids, Mich.: Zondervan, 1984.
NJB   The New Jerusalem Bible. Garden City, New York: Doubleday, 1985.
NRSV The Holy Bible: New Revised Standard Version. New York: Oxford University Press, 1989.
REB   The Revised English Bible. Oxford: Oxford University Press and Cambridge University Press, 1989.
TEV   Good News Bible, Today's English Version. 2d ed. New York: American Bible Society, 1992.
TNT   The Translator's New Testament. London: British and Foreign Bible Society, 1973.

GRAMMATICAL TERMS

act.	active	opt.	optative
fut.	future	pass.	passive
impera.	imperative	perf.	perfect
indic.	indicative	pres.	present
infin.	infinitive	subj.	subjunctive
mid.	middle		

EXEGETICAL SUMMARY OF EPHESIANS

DISCOURSE UNIT: 1:1–6:21. Commentaries differ as to the purpose of the book. Most list one or more of the following: to prepare the church in the doctrine of grace [Gd], for arising heresies of the time [AB, Can, Ea, Gd, My], including incipient gnosticism [AB, NCBC]; to promote unity among Jewish and Gentile elements in the church [AB, CBC, Ho, MNTC, NCBC, Rob]; to expound God's aim in salvation [Alf, EGT, My, TH, TNTC] out of a sense of thankfulness for the good state of the church [Ea, Lns]; to provide the moral precepts for the church given in ch. 4-6 [Can]; and to guard against the teaching that moralism resulted in salvation [NCBC]. It consists of two almost equal parts (ch. 1–3 and 4–6) [AB, Alf, Can, EGT, Gd, MNTC, NTC, WBC, WeBC], one doctrinal, the other hortatory [AB, Alf, ECWB, EGT, Gd, MNTC, WeBC], intimately tied together [AB, ECWB, EGT, MNTC] by the theme of unity which pervades the book [ECWB, MNTC]. The ἀμήν 'amen' at the end of 3:21 and the change to direct exhortation at the beginning of 4:1 are the clear division markers [WBC].

DISCOURSE UNIT: 1:1–23 [Alf, NTC, TNTC; NASB]. The topic is the blessings of redemption [NASB], adoration of the Church for its eternal foundation in Christ [NTC], praise to the Father whose will is to sum up all things in Christ [Alf].

DISCOURSE UNIT: 1:1–2 [AB, Alf, Ba, Can, CBC, Ea, ECWB, EGT, Ho, IB, ICC, Lns, MNTC, My, NIC, NTC, Rob, Si, St, TH, TNTC, WBC, WeBC; NAB, NIV, NJB, REB, TEV]. All who comment about this discourse unit agree that it forms the salutation or greeting portion of the letter. The normal Greek letter began with a fairly stereotyped formula: A to B: greetings. Paul has expanded each element and has filled it with Christian meaning [CBC, EBC, EGT, LJ, Lns, MNTC, NCBC, St, TH, TNTC, WBC, WeBC].

1:1 **Paul, an-apostle[a] of-Christ Jesus by[b] (the) will[c] of-God,**

TEXT—Some manuscripts reverse the order of 'Christ Jesus' to 'Jesus Christ'. GNT does not mention this alternative. The order 'Jesus Christ' is followed only by KJV and NAB.

LEXICON—a. ἀπόστολος (LN 53.74) (BAGD 3. p. 99): 'apostle' [AB, BAGD, El, LN, Lns, NIC, NTC, Rob, WBC, We; all versions], 'envoy' [Can], 'delegate' [EGT], 'special messenger' [LN]. Here it refers to the special office of apostle, restricted to the twelve and Paul [AB, LN, Lns, NIC, NTC].

b. διά with genitive object (LN 89.76) (BAGD A.III.1.d. p. 180): 'by' [AB, BAGD, El, LN, Rob, WBC; all versions], 'through' [LN, Lns, NIC, NTC, We], 'by means of' [BAGD, LN]. It is used here to denote the efficient cause [BAGD].

c. θέλημα (LN 30.59) (BAGD 2.b. p. 354): 'will' [BAGD, El, LN, Lns, NIC, NTC, Rob, WBC, We; all versions], 'decision' [AB]. This is the subjective aspect of the rule of God's will, i.e., the action of willing or desiring [Alf, BAGD, Cal, Si, WeBC].

QUESTION—How are the nouns related in the genitive construction ἀπόστολος Χριστοῦ Ἰησοῦ 'apostle of Christ Jesus'?

1. The noun in the genitive acts as subject of the action noun it modifies [Can, ICC, Lns, WeBC; REB]: Paul is an apostle who is sent by Christ Jesus.
2. This is a possessive genitive [Alf, Ea, EGT, El, Gd]: Paul is an apostle who belongs to Christ Jesus. This implies that he serves his owner, Christ [El].

QUESTION—What relationship is indicated by διά 'by'?

It indicates the source of [ECWB] or the cause for his being an apostle [BAGD, Ea, NCBC; probably all versions]: I am an apostle because God willed me to be. This implies that God appointed him [AB, Alf, Cal, CBC, Ea, EGT, Gd, Lns, WBC, We] through Christ [Gd, Ho].

to-the saints^a the-(ones) being in Ephesus and/even^b faithful/believing^c in^d Christ Jesus,

TEXT—Some manuscripts omit ἐν Ἐφέσῳ 'in Ephesus'. In this case the article would be joined with the following words, 'the ones being also faithful' (a construction similar to the NRSV margin reading) which a number of commentators see as being an awkward grammatical construction [AB, BD, CBC, ECWB, EGT, HG, ICC, Lns, MNTC, Mou, NCBC, NIC, NTC, Si, TH, TNTC, WBC, We]. Some think this is an encyclical epistle and Paul left a blank for the name of the city in which the person doing the public reading would pronounce the city name as he read the epistle to the church [CBC, ECWB, EGT, LJ, NCBC, NIC, NTC, Rob, TH, TNTC, We, WeBC], but there are no extant examples of this practice from antiquity [WBC]. Some indicate their doubt about including it by enclosing the words in brackets [AB, El, ICC, NIC, Rob, We; NAB] or by means of marginal notes [NASB, NIV, NRSV, REB, TEV, TNT]. GNT gives the phrase a C rating, indicating a consideralbe degree of doubt about including it. The reading ἐν Ἐφέσῳ 'in Ephesus' is accepted by Alf, Ba, BD, Cal, Ea, El, Gd, HG, Ho, Lns, MNTC, Mou, My; KJV and NRSV. It is rejected by Can, CBC, ECWB, IB, ICC, LJ, NCBC, NIC, NTC, Rob, TH, TNTC, WBC, We, WeBC, NAB, and NJB. NTC believes that it was added to a later copy by the apostle himself.

LEXICON—a. ἅγιος (LN 11.27): 'holy'. The plural form is translated as a substantive: 'saints' [AB, BAGD, El, Lns, NIC, NTC, Rob, WBC, We; KJV, NASB, NIV, NRSV], 'holy ones' [NAB], 'God's people' [LN; REB, TEV, TNT], 'God's holy people' [NJB]. This term is the normal designation for Christians [Alf, Cal, CBC, Ea, EBC, ECWB, El, Ho, LJ, Lns, Rob, St, TH, TNTC, We] and has the primary sense of being consecrated or separated to God [AB, Alf, BAGD, CBC, ECWB, EGT, Ho, LJ, Lns, NCBC, NTC, We, WeBC].

b. καί (LN 89.92): 'and' [El, LN, Lns, NTC, Rob, We; KJV, NASB, NRSV], 'also' [WBC], 'even' [though a possible translation, no translation adopted this], not explicit [AB, NIC; NAB, NIV, NJB, REB, TEV, TNT].
   c. πιστός (LN 31.86, 31.87) (BAGD 2. p. 665): 'faithful' [AB, El, LN, Rob, WBC, We; NASB, NJB, NRSV, TEV, TNT]. The adjective is also translated as a substantive: 'the faithful' [KJV, NIV, REB], 'believers' [BAGD, Lns, NIC, NTC; NAB].
   d. ἐν with dative object (LN 89.119): 'in' [El, LN, Lns, NIC, NTC, Rob, WBC, We; NAB, NASB, NIV, NJB, NRSV], 'incorporate in' [REB], 'in union with' [LN; TEV], '(who) belong to' [TNT], 'to' [AB].

QUESTION—What relationship is indicated by καί 'and/even'?

Presumably those who translate καί as 'and' do not intend to imply that two groups are being spoken of. It functions as 'even/namely'. The occurrence of the article before ἁγίοις 'saints' and its omission before πιστοῖς 'faithful/ believing' supports this, showing both adjectives belong to the same persons [Alf, ECWB, Lns]. Various ways of joining the two designations are used: to the saints, who are faithful [MNTC; NASB, NRSV, TEV]; to God's faithful people [TNT]; to the saints, believers [NIC; NAB]; to the saints, to the faithful [REB]; to the saints, the faithful [NIV].

QUESTION—What area of meaning is intended by πιστός 'faithful, believing'?

1. This means the attribute of being faithful [AB, ECWB, EGT, ICC, LJ, Lt, Mo, NCBC, TH, We, WeBC; all versions except NAB]: the ones who are faithful. They are faithful in respect to their Christian profession [AB, ECWB, EGT, LJ, NCBC, TH, TNTC, WeBC].
2. This means the state of believing [Alf, Ba, BAGD (2. p. 665), Cal, Can, CBC, Ds2, Ea, El, Ho, IB, Lns, My, NIC, NTC, St, WBC; NAB]: the ones who believe. They believe in Christ [Ba, BAGD, Ds2, Ea, El, Lns, My].
3. Both meanings are included [Gd, Rob, TNTC]: faithful believers in Christ Jesus.

QUESTION—To what is the phrase ἐν Χριστῷ 'in Christ' connected?

1. The phrase is connected to both ἁγίοις 'saints' and πιστοῖς 'faithful/believing (ones)' [ECWB, Gd, Ho, ICC, LJ, Lns, NTC, WBC, We; TNT]: to the saints and faithful/believing (ones) who are in Christ Jesus. This is evident from the pattern observed in the greeting in the parallel Col. 1:2 as well as in 1 Thess. 1:1 [Gd].
2. The phrase is connected only with πιστοῖς 'faithful/believing (ones)' [AB, Alf, Ba, Cal, Can, Ea, EGT, El, IB, Lt, My, NCBC, NIC, Rob, TH, TNTC; NRSV]: and to the faithful/believing (ones) in Christ Jesus. The phrase 'faithful in Christ Jesus' completes the description of the 'saints' and states what their state and condition is [El].

QUESTION—What relationship is indicated by ἐν 'in'?
1. This indicates union with Christ [CBC, EGT, El, Gd, LJ, Lns, NIC, NTC, TNTC, WBC, We, WeBC; REB, TEV]: to the faithful ones/ believers who are in union with Christ.
2. This indicates ownership [TNT]: to the faithful ones/believers who belong to Christ; to Christ's faithful people.
3. This indicates the object of their believing [Alf, Can, Ea, ECWB, El, IB, My]: to those who believe in Christ.
4. This indicates the area within which they are faithful [AB, NIC]: to those who are faithful to Christ.

1:2 grace[a] to-you and peace[b] from God our Father and (the/our) Lord Jesus Christ.

LEXICON—a. χάρις (LN 25.89, 88.66) (BAGD 2.c. p. 877): 'grace' [AB, BAGD, El, LN, Lns, NIC, NTC, Rob, WBC, We; all versions], 'kindness' [LN], 'favor' [BAGD, LN].
b. εἰρήνη (LN 22.42) (BAGD 2. p. 227): 'peace' [AB, BAGD, El, LN, Lns, NIC, NTC, Rob, WBC, We; all versions], 'tranquility' [LN].

QUESTION—What is the significance of this clause?
These words constitute a prayer-wish [WBC]. Coming from an apostle, the words are the equivalent of an OT priestly blessing [Gd].

QUESTION—What is meant by εἰρήνη 'peace'?
1. It indicates peace between people and God [CBC, El, Gd, LJ, St, WBC, WeBC]. As a result of this peace, there is a feeling of tranquility or a state of spiritual well being [AB, BAGD, Ea, Ho, LJ, NCBC, WeBC]. In greetings it corresponds to the Hebrew *shalom* 'welfare, health, wholeness, salvation', which was a wish for the messianic peace [BAGD, DNTT, Ea, Gd, LJ, TD, WBC, WeBC]. Εἰρήνη 'peace', together with χάρις 'grace', represent the major themes of Ephesians [WBC].
2. It indicates peace between people and refers to unity among the members of the local church [St, TH].

QUESTION—What relationship is indicated by καί 'and'?
It indicates that both God, our Father, and our Lord Jesus Christ are the ones who act in grace and give peace [AB, Can, CBC, Ea, EBC, Gd, IB, ICC, LJ, NCBC, Si, St, WeBC].

DISCOURSE UNIT: 1:3–3:21 [Alf, Ba, EBC, My, NCBC, NIC, TH, WBC, WeBC; NJB, TEV]. This half of the letter emphasizes doctrine, while the latter half emphasizes practical matters. The topic is Christian doctrine [Ba, EBC], the doctrine of the Church [Alf, WeBC], the privileges Christians have [NCBC], adoration [NTC], the blessedness of their membership in the one holy church [Lns], the new humanity [NIC], exposition [TH].

DISCOURSE UNIT: 1:3–14 [AB, Ba, Can, EBC, El, Ho, IB, Lns, MNTC, NCBC, NIC, NTC, Rob, Si, St, TD, TH, TNTC, WBC, We; NAB, NIV, NJB, TEV]. The topic is doxology [Lns, Rob], praise [AB, Can, EBC, El, NIC,

TNTC, WBC], thanksgiving [MNTC, NCBC, TH]. This unit is one long, involved sentence in Greek and is built up around the phrase ἐν Χριστῷ 'in Christ' [EBC, Lns, MNTC] which, with its parallel forms, occurs about a dozen times. A classic feature of the section are the structures involved with the use of the prepositions ἐν 'in', κατά 'according to', εἰς 'into/for' [AB, TD], ἀπό 'from', πρό 'before', and διά 'through' [AB]. Efforts to divide 1:3–14 on the basis of strophes, as having been taken from an ancient hymn, fail through lack of objective criteria and lack of agreement between the various proposals [WBC].

DISCOURSE UNIT: 1:3–8 [EGT, ICC]. The topic is praise to God for the blessings of salvation [EGT, ICC].

DISCOURSE UNIT: 1:3–6 [Alf, CBC, ECWB, NIC, WeBC]. The topic is praise to God for election and adoption [NIC], Christian sonship [CBC, ECWB], the Father's plan and purpose for the Church [WeBC].

1:3 Blessed[a] (be/is) the God and/even Father of-our Lord Jesus Christ,

LEXICON—a. εὐλογητός (LN 33.362) (BAGD p. 322): 'blessed' [AB, BAGD, El, Lns, NTC, TH, WBC; KJV, NASB, NJB, NRSV, REB], 'praised' [BAGD; NAB], 'praise' [NIV]. This is also translated as an active verb: 'to give thanks to' [TEV, TNT]. It pertains to the worthiness of God to be praised [Lt]. Many of the commentators mention the fact that God blesses men in a different way than men bless him—God's beneficial gift to men versus men's praise to God.

QUESTION—What is the significance of εὐλογητός 'blessed' as the first word of this sentence?

As the first word in the sentence, εὐλογητός 'blessed' is emphasized [Ea, My; implied by EGT]. It is emphasized by the occurrence of the cognate εὐλογήσας 'who has blessed' in the next clause [Bu, Lns], and also by the fact that this cognate is used with a different meaning [Bu].

QUESTION—What is the implied verb in this clause?

1. This is a statement about God [AB, Ba, Cal, CBC, DNTT, Ea, EBC, EGT, Gd, ICC, LJ, LN (33.362), Lt, NCBC, NTC, Si, TNTC]: God is worthy to be praised. This is not in conflict with the following interpretations, since it implies that the readers or all people should therefore praise him [NTC].
2. This is an exhortation for the readers to praise God [Alf, Can, El, Rob, WBC, We; all versions]. Most indicate this by supplying the hortatory verb 'be' [Rob, WBC, We; KJV, NAB, NASB, NIV, NJB, NRSV, REB]: blessed/praised be God; may God be praised. The exhortation is also translated as a cohortative [TEV, TNT]: let us praise God. 'Blessed be' implies that blessing or praise is due God by man [Rob, We].

QUESTION—What does the genitive phrase τοῦ κυρίου ἡμῶν Ἰησοῦ Χριστοῦ 'of our Lord Jesus Christ' modify and what relationship is indicated by καί 'and/even'?
1. The genitive phrase modifies both words, θεός 'God' and πατήρ 'Father', requiring that the καί function as a coordinate 'and' [Alf, Ea, EGT, Gd, HG, Ho, LJ, Lns, Lt, NCBC, NTC, Rob, TH, We; all versions except NJB]: praise be to the one who is both the God of Christ and also the Father of Christ.
2. The genitive phrase modifies only the word πατήρ 'Father' and καί functions as 'even' [AB, BAGD (I.1.a. p. 391), El, My, TD, WBC; NJB]: praise be to God, even the one who is the Father of Christ.

the (one) having-blessed[a] us with[b] every[c] spiritual[d] blessing[e] in the heavenly (places)[f]

LEXICON—a. aorist act. participle of εὐλογέω (LN **88.69**) (BAGD 3. p. 322): 'to bless' [AB, BAGD, El, LN, Lns, NIC, NTC, Rob, TH, WBC, We; all versions except NAB, REB], 'to bestow on' [NAB], 'to confer on' [REB], 'to provide with benefits' [BAGD], 'to act kindly toward' [**LN**]. The aorist tense sums up all the many blessings of the past [Lns], or indicates that the blessing was done once for all [ECWB, LJ] in the actual historical [Alf] past act of redemption [El], the fulfillment of the election and predestination spoken of in the next verse [ECWB, Ho, ICC, Lt, TNTC]. The act of God in history is what is in focus here and not just the indication of purpose in God's mind [Lt].
b. ἐν with dative object (LN 89.5) (BAGD III.1.a. p. 260): 'with' [AB, El, Lns, NIC, NTC, Rob, TH, WBC; KJV, NASB, NIV, NJB, NRSV, TNT], 'in' [We], 'with regard to' [LN]. This is also translated as a phrase: 'by giving' [TEV]. Some indicate this relationship by making the phrase the object of the preceding verb which they translate as 'to bestow/to confer' [NAB, REB]. This usage of the preposition occurs with things and introduces the instrument or means [BAGD].
c. πᾶς (LN 58.28, 59.23) (BAGD 1.a.β. p. 631): 'every' [El, LN, Lns, NIC, NTC, TH, WBC; all versions except KJV, NJB], 'every kind of' [BAGD], 'all sorts of' [BAGD], 'full' [AB]. This is also translated: 'all' [El, Rob, We; KJV, NJB], and thus requires that the singular noun it modifies be translated in the plural: all the blessings. Some commentators explain that πᾶς 'every' individualizes the many blessings which make up the sum total [Lns, TH, TNTC]: every blessing. Another stresses that the effect of πᾶς on the singular noun εὐλογία 'blessing' is to make it a composite of many individual blessings [AB]: the full blessing, the epitome of blessing. Others say it includes everything belonging to the class designated by the noun it occurs with: 'every kind of/all sorts of' [Alf, BAGD, DNTT, We].
d. πνευματικός (LN **12.21, 26.10**) (BAGD 2.a.β. p. 679): 'spiritual' [AB, BAGD, LN (**12.21, 26.10**), Lns, NIC, NTC, Rob, TH, WBC, We; all versions], 'pertaining to the Spirit' [BAGD, LN (12.21)], 'from the Spirit'

[LN (**12.21**)], 'of the Spirit' [El]. It means something derived from the Spirit [LN (12.21)], or something that pertains to the spiritual nature of a person [LN (26.10)].
  e. εὐλογία (LN 88.70) (BAGD 3.b.α. p. 323): 'blessing' [AB, BAGD, El, LN, Lns, NIC, NTC, Rob, TH, WBC, We; all versions], 'benefit' [LN]. It is bestowed by God or Christ [BAGD], or by the Spirit [LN (12.21)].
  f. ἐπουράνιος (LN 1.12): 'heavenly'. The plural form is translated 'heavenlies' [TH], 'heavens' [AB; NAB], 'heaven' [BAGD; NJB], 'heavenly places' [Lns, NTC, Rob; KJV, NASB, NRSV], 'heavenly realms' [NIC, WBC; NIV, REB], 'heavenly world' [TEV], 'supernatural world' [TNT], 'heavenly order' [We], 'heavenly regions' [El]. This term is essentially equivalent to a semantic compound in that it combines a semantic element of 'heaven' as a celestial abode with another semantic element indicating location or relationship [LN, TD]. Therefore it can be translated as 'in heaven' [LN, TD] or 'pertaining to heaven' [LN]. Used as a substantive, the term is a periphrasis for 'heaven' [BAGD, DNTT, Gd, TD].

QUESTION—What relationships are indicated by the use of the participle εὐλογήσας 'having blessed'?

The attributive participle is nonrestrictive, making a statement about God [Ba, Ea, EGT; TEV]: who has blessed us. It implicitly gives one of the reasons why God is to be praised [Ba, Cal, Ea, EGT, LJ, Lt; TEV]. This participle also receives emphasis from being cognate in form with εὐλογητός 'blessed (be)' but having a different meaning: who has richly blessed us [Bu]. (Cognate forms of this word occur three times in this verse.)

QUESTION—To whom does ἡμᾶς 'us' refer?

It is inclusive, referring to Paul and the Ephesian readers [Can, Ea, Lns], i.e., the people to whom Paul was writing. He probably does not imply that other Christians did not also receive God's blessings and many refer this pronoun to all Christians generally [Alf, Ba, Can, ECWB, EGT, El, Gd, My, NCBC, NTC, Rob, We].

QUESTION—What is meant by πνευματικῇ 'spiritual'?
  1. This refers to the Holy Spirit and means that he produced the blessings [BAGD, Ea, EBC, ECWB, El, Gd, Ho, LJ, LN (**12.21**), MNTC, My, WBC]: God, the Father, blessed us with blessings produced by the Holy Spirit's work in us.
  2. This means that the blessings relate to the spiritual sphere rather than being material things [CBC, IB, ICC, Lt, We, WeBC]: God blessed us with blessings which are spiritual in nature. It relates to the nature of the blessings, rather than the source [ICC, Lt, WeBC], transcendental, belonging to the realm of the eternal, the imperishable, the divine [IB].
  3. This means that the blessings affect the Christians' spirits [AB, Can, EGT, Lns]: God blessed us in regards to our spirits.

QUESTION—What are the blessings?

The blessings are: the development of the character as described in the list under the fruit of the Spirit (Gal. 5:22–23) [EGT, My]; God's saving activity in Christ [WBC], that is, the topics of the following verses, the blessings of election, adoption, redemption, and forgiveness [Ea, ECWB, Gd, NIC, NTC, Rob, St, TH]; the work of God, consisting of his decision, acts, and revelation, which was culminated in the impartation of the Holy Spirit to both Jews and Gentiles and the changes in them which this effected [AB]; all the spiritual blessings of salvation which the Spirit applies to us now [Gd, LJ]; all blessings, both material and spiritual, with the fullness of eternal life reserved in Christ in trust for us being the crowning one [Si]; only spiritual blessings, since material blessings are not part of God's covenant with the Christian [Lt].

QUESTION—What is meant by τοῖς ἐπουρανίοις 'the heavenlies'?

1. This refers to heaven, where God is [AB, Alf, Ba, BAGD, Can, ECWB, EGT, El, Gd, LJ, Lns, Lt, My, My-ed, NTC, Si (probably), TD, WBC, WeBC]: God blessed us with every spiritual blessing that is connected with heaven, or God blessed us with every spiritual blessing which pertains to states or qualities found in heaven [Ba, My-ed, WBC], and may be considered to come from heaven [EGT, My, NTC]. This interpretation focuses upon the source of the blessings (as actually coming from the location of heaven, from Christ who is in heaven) as well as upon their nature or character (such as are actually enjoyed in heaven itself). The phrase only occurs in Ephesians (1:3, 20; 2:6; 3:10; 6:12) [ECWB, LJ, Lt, WeBC], and in the other occurrences in this book, the local sense also is meant [ECWB, LJ, Lt, My, WBC, WeBC]. This interpretation also incorporates the meaning found in interpretation 2 below [Gd, WBC].

2. This refers to the supernatural realm in which believers live even while living in the earthly realm [Cal, CBC, Ho, IB, ICC, MNTC, NCBC, NIC, Rob, St, TH, TNTC, We; TNT]: God blessed us in respect to our living in the supernatural world with every spiritual blessing. This interpretation focuses only upon the nature of the blessings.

in[a] Christ,

LEXICON—a. ἐν with dative object (LN 89.119): 'in' [AB, El, LN, Lns, NIC, NTC, Rob, TH, WBC, We; all versions except TEV], 'in union with' [LN; TEV].

QUESTION—What is the meaning of ἐν 'in' and what relationship is indicated by it?

This word indicates a spiritual connection with Christ [Alf, Can, CBC, Ea, ECWB, EGT, El, Gd, Ho, IB, ICC, LJ, LN (89.119), Lns, Lt, My, NCBC, NTC, Rob, Si, TH, WBC, We, WeBC; TEV]: in union with Christ.

1. It indicates the reason why God blessed us [Can, EGT, Ho, IB, NTC, TH]: God blessed us because we are in union with Christ.

2. It indicates the means or agency by which God blessed us [Ba, CBC, Ea, ICC, NCBC, WBC]: God united us to Christ and so provided the way to bless us.

1:4 as/because[a] he-chose[b] us in[c] him before (the) foundation[d] of-(the)-world

LEXICON—a. καθώς (LN 64.14, 89.34) (BAGD 3. p. 391): 'as' [AB, NIC], 'just as' [LN (64.14), NTC; NASB, NRSV], 'even as' [El, Lns, TH, WBC, We], 'according as' [Rob; KJV], 'for' [NIV], 'thus' [NJB], 'since, in so far as' [BAGD], 'inasmuch as, because' [LN (89.34)]; not explicit [NAB, REB, TEV, TNT].

b. aorist mid. indic. of ἐκλέγομαι (LN 30.86, 30.92) (BAGD 3.c. p. 242): 'to choose' [AB, BAGD, El, LN (30.86, 30.92), NIC, Rob, TH, WBC, We; all versions], 'to select' [BAGD, LN (30.86)], 'to elect' [Lns, NTC]. The middle voice indicates that God chose us for himself [Alf, BAGD, Can, ECWB, EGT, El, ICC, Lns, Lt, NTC, Si-ed, We]: he chose us to be his people.

c. ἐν with dative object (LN 89.119): 'in' [AB, El, LN, Lns, NIC, NTC, Rob, TH, WBC, We; all versions except TEV], 'through our union with' [TEV].

d. καταβολή (LN 42.37) (BAGD 1. p. 409): 'foundation' [AB, BAGD, El, Lns, NIC, NTC, Rob, TH, WBC, We; KJV, NASB, NRSV, REB], 'creation' [LN; NIV, TNT]. This is also translated as a verb: 'to begin' [NAB], 'to be made' [NJB, TEV].

QUESTION—What relationship is indicated by καθώς 'as/because'?

1. This indicates that the spiritual blessings are in conformity with God's decree that preceded them [Ba, Can, ICC, Lns, Lt, Rob, We; KJV, NASB, NRSV]. The spiritual blessings are dependent upon our relation to Christ [Can, Lns]: it was in Christ that he blessed us, just as it was in Christ that he chose us. Just as he chose us in eternity past, so he has also blessed us in Christ in time [Lns, NTC, We]. The blessings we have received through Christ conforms to the fact that God has chosen Christ to be both the foundation and goal of our salvation [TD].

2. This indicates the reason God blessed us (1:3) [BAGD, Cal, ECWB, El, Ho, LJ, NCBC, NTC, WBC; NIV]: he blessed us because he chose us. The writer is saying that God has blessed believers both because and to the extent that he elected them [WBC]. Καθώς 'as/because' is joined to the whole of the statement from 1:4 through 1:14. It introduces the whole statement [LJ, Rob]. The blessing in 1:3 is a general reference to all of God's blessings, and this is the reason for blessing us [Ho]. Some keep the wording of 'in conformity with the fact', but speak of it functioning as the reason [EGT, My].

3. This specifies what the blessings are [Alf, TH; perhaps NJB]: he blessed us, in that he chose us. Although translating this connection as 'thus', the note in NJB identifies this choice of us as the first blessing, the second being predestination, 1:5.

QUESTION—What was involved in God's choice?

God chose us out from the mass of mankind [Alf, Cal, Can, Ea, EBC, EGT, El, Gd, ICC, LJ, Lns, My, NTC, We]. This does not imply that we were more worthy than others [Cal, LJ, NCBC, NIC, NTC, St, TH].

QUESTION—What relationship is indicated by ἐν 'in'?
1. It indicates the reason he chose us [Alf, Ea, EGT, El, Gd, Ho, ICC, LJ, Lt, My, NIC, St, TH].
   1.1 God chose us because Christ made it possible for God to accept us [EGT, My, NIC, St]: he chose us because of what Christ had done to redeem us.
   1.2 God chose us because Christ is our federal head, or representative in place of Adam [Alf, Ea, El, Gd, Ho, ICC, Lt]: he chose us because Christ became our representative; he chose us because he considered us to be one with Christ. The actual cause of God's choosing us is God's own good pleasure (1:5–6), but Christ was chosen (1 Pet. 1:20) as our federal head and we were chosen in him [Gd].
2. It indicates agency [NCBC]: God, through his agent Christ, chose us.

QUESTION—What time is indicated by the phrase πρὸ καταβολῆς κόσμου 'before the foundation of the world'?
It indicates that the choice was made independently of time or temporal circumstances, that is, from eternity past [Alf, Ba, Cal, Can, DNTT, Ea, EBC, ECWB, EGT, Gd, Ho, ISBE2, Lt, My, NCBC, NIC, NTC, Rob, St, TD, TH, TNTC, WBC, We, WeBC].

(that) we be holy[a] and without-blemish/blameless[b] before[c] him
LEXICON—a. ἅγιος (LN 53.46, 88.24) (BAGD 1.b.α. p. 9): 'holy' [AB, BAGD, El, LN (88.24), Lns, NIC, NTC, Rob, WBC, We; all versions except REB], 'consecrated to God' [BAGD], 'dedicated' [LN (53.46)], 'his people' [REB].
   b. ἄμωμος (LN **88.34**) (BAGD 2.a. p. 48): 'without blemish' [We; REB, TNT], 'blemishless' [Lns], 'blameless' [AB, BAGD, El, LN, NIC, Rob, WBC; NAB, NASB, NIV, NRSV], 'without blame' [KJV], 'faultless' [LN, NTC; NJB], 'without fault' [LN; TEV], 'perfect' [LN].
   c. κατενώπιον with the genitive object (LN **90.20**) (BAGD b. p. 421): 'before' [AB, BAGD, El, Lns, NIC, NTC, Rob, WBC, We; KJV, NASB, NJB, NRSV, TEV], 'in (his) sight' [**LN**; NAB, NIV, REB, TNT], 'in the opinion of, in the judgment of' [LN].

QUESTION—What relationship is indicated by the use of the infinitive εἶναι 'to be'?
This indicates the purpose or goal of the preceding verb [Alf, Ba, BAGD, Ea, EBC, ECWB, EGT, El, Gd, ICC, LJ, Lns, My, NCBC, NIC, NTC, Rob, TNTC, WBC, We, WeBC]: he chose us in order that we should be holy and without blemish before him.

QUESTION—What is referred to in the use of the expression ἁγίους καὶ ἀμώμους 'holy and without blemish'?
The reference is to our sanctification [all commentaries except My]. Another view is that the reference is to our justification by faith, i.e. imputed or forensic righteousness. The occurrence of εἶναι 'to be' as opposed to

γίνομαι 'to become' and the whole context of 3:5–7 is decisive for this interpretation [My].

QUESTION—What is the difference between ἅγιος 'holy' and ἄμωμος 'without blemish/blameless'?

They are virtually synonyms [Ea, TH]. Some distinguish between them by making 'holy' to be a positive aspect and 'without blemish' a negative aspect [Alf, Ea, EBC, ECWB, El, ICC, LJ, My, NIC, TH, TNTC, WBC, WeBC], the positive being consecration to God and the negative, freedom from fault [DNTT, Ea, EBC, ECWB, NIC, TNTC] or the positive being inward consecration to God, the negative being external conduct or complete obedience [CBC, LJ, WBC]. 'Unblemished' may also be understood as fitness for holiness [Lt].

QUESTION—What is meant by ἄμωμος 'without blemish/blameless'?
1. This is a live metaphor referring to the Jewish sacrificial system [AB, CBC, EBC, ECWB, Lt, NTC, TH, TNTC, We; REB, TNT]: as a sacrificial animal is unblemished so you are to be unblemished before him. The ground of comparison is the absence of imperfection needed in order to be accepted by God.
2. This is a dead metaphor and is better rendered as 'blameless' [Alf, Ba, BAGD, Ea, EGT, El, Gd, Ho, ICC, LJ, LN (**88.34**), My, NCBC, NIC, Rob, WBC, WeBC; KJV, NAB, NASB, NIV, NRSV, TEV]: you are to be blameless. One commentator prefers this etymological interpretation because there is no direct or indirect sacrificial allusion in this passage [El].

QUESTION—What is the time reference for the believer to be seen as holy and unblemished before God?
1. This focuses on the present time, the believer's sanctification in this life [AB, Alf, CBC, ECWB, EGT, Ho, MNTC, St, TH, TNTC, WBC, We]: we were chosen so that we might live our lives holy and unblemished in God's sight (not to mention our final, eternal, holy state). The wording is adopted from Col. 1:22 where there is no clear connection with the Parousia and refers to believers' present lives [WBC].
2. This focuses on the believers' final state in heaven [Gd, ICC, LJ, My-ed, NTC, Si]: the ultimate purpose of his choosing us was that we might finally stand before him with a holy, unblemished, righteousness. However great the inherent righteousness of the believer (sanctification) is even in its perfected stage, it is incomparable to the imputed righteousness of the Redeemer [My-ed].
3. The reference is to the whole concept of sanctification, without special focus on either present or future states, but including both [Cal, Can, Ea, Lns, NIC, WeBC].

in[a] love,[b]

LEXICON—a. ἐν with dative object (LN 89.26, 89.80): 'in' [El, Lns, NIC, NTC, Rob, TH, WBC, We; KJV, NASB, NIV, NJB, NRSV], 'because of'

[LN (89.26); TEV, TNT], 'on account of, by reason of' [LN (89.26)], 'with' [LN (89.80)]. This preposition is also joined with ἀγάπη 'love' and translated as a verbal phrase (see next entry below).
  b. ἀγάπη (LN 25.43) (BAGD I.2.a. p. 5): 'love' [AB, BAGD, El, LN, Lns, NIC, NTC, Rob, TH, WBC, We; all versions except NAB, REB, TNT]. This is also translated as a verb: 'to love' [TNT]. The phrase ἐν ἀγάπῃ 'in love' is also translated as a verbal phrase: 'to live by love' [AB], 'to be full of love' [NAB, REB].

QUESTION—To what is this phrase connected, and what relationship is indicated by ἐν 'in'?
  1. It is connected with the preceding clauses and refers to our love [AB, Alf, Cal, CBC, EGT, Gd, Ho, LJ, Lns, Lt, NIC, Rob, TD, TNTC, WBC, We; KJV, NAB, NRSV, REB]. The object of our love is other people [TNTC], and also love for God [Lns].
    1.1 It is connected with ἐξελέξατο 'he chose' and indicates a purpose for which God chose us [AB; NAB, REB]: he chose us in order that we should be holy and unblemished and in order that we be full of love for others.
    1.2 It is connected with εἶναι ἡμᾶς ἁγίους καὶ ἀμώμους 'that we should be holy and unblemished' [Alf, Cal, CBC, EGT, Gd, Ho, LJ, Lns, Lt, NIC, Rob, TD, TNTC, WBC, We; KJV, NRSV]: he chose us in order that we should be holy and unblemished in loving others. 'In love' indicates the essence of what being holy and unblemished is [Alf, Cal, EGT, Gd, Ho, LJ], a characteristic or manifestation of being holy and unblemished [CBC, NIC, TD, WBC], an accompanying circumstance of being holy and unblemished [TNTC], and/or the climax of the divine intention for our being holy and unblemished [Gd, LJ, Rob, WBC].
  2. It is connected with the following participle προορίσας 'predestining' in 1:5 and refers to God's love for the people he chose [Ba, Can, Ea, EBC, ECWB, El, ICC, My, NTC, St, TH, WeBC; NASB, NIV, TEV, TNT]: in his love for us, he destined us to be his sons. It is assumed, with this interpretation, that the phrase is emphatic by position [El]. It gives the reason he destined us [EBC, My, NTC, St, TH; TEV, TNT]: because God loved us, he destined us to be his sons.

1:5 predestining[a] us to adoption[b] through[c] Jesus Christ to himself,

LEXICON—a. aorist act. masc. participle of προορίζω (LN **30.84**) (BAGD p. 709): 'to predestine' [BAGD, TH, WBC; NAB, NASB, NIV, REB], 'to predestinate' [Lns; KJV], 'to destine' [NRSV], 'to already have decided' [**LN**; TEV], 'to set apart' [TNT], 'to mark out beforehand' [NJB], 'to foreordain' [El, NIC, NTC, Rob, We], 'to predesignate' [AB], 'to decide upon beforehand' [BAGD, LN], 'to determine ahead of time' [LN]. The prefix προ- 'before' indicates that the event will occur after the time of its decree [Can, ECWB, EGT, El, Lns, My, TH].

b. υἱοθεσία (LN **35.53**) (BAGD 2. p. 833): 'adoption' [BAGD, El, LN, Lns], 'adoption of sons' [Rob], 'adoption of children' [KJV], 'adoption as (his) children' [NRSV], 'adoption as sons' [NTC, We; NASB], 'adoption as (his own) sons' [WBC]. Some translate this noun as a verbal phrase: 'to adopt (us) to be (his) children' [**LN**], 'to be/become (his) adopted sons' [NAB, NJB, TNT], 'to be adopted as (his) sons' [NIV], 'to be adopted as (his) children' [REB], 'to make (us his) children' [TEV], 'to become (his) children' [AB], 'to be instated as (his) sons' [NIC]. The action involved is a formal and legal one [LN]. In a religious sense, it means to be accepted by God as his sons [BAGD].

c. διά with the genitive object (LN 89.76, 90.4): 'through' [AB, El, LN, Lns, NIC, NTC, Rob, WBC, We; all versions except KJV], 'by' [LN; KJV].

QUESTION—What relationship is indicated by the use of the participial form προορίσας 'predestining'?

1. It indicates the reason for choosing us [Ho, ICC, Lt, NCBC, We]: he chose us to be holy because he had predestined us to be adopted as his sons. This predestinating is logically prior to choosing us, but not necessarily earlier in time [EGT, ICC, LJ, Lt].
2. It indicates the manner in which he chose us [EGT, Lns, My, TH]: he chose us to be holy by predestinating us to be adopted. The action of the participle is simultaneous with that of the main verb ἐξελέξατο 'he chose' [EGT, Lns, My].
3. It indicates an explanation [Can, ECWB, Gd, LJ, MNTC, WBC] or a restatement [NTC, TNTC], but with a slightly different phase of the truth contained in ἐξελέξατο 'he chose' [Ea]: he chose us to be holy, that is, he predestinated us to be adopted. The action of the participle is coincident with that of the main verb [Ea, LJ, NTC].

QUESTION—What is the difference between predestinating us and choosing us (1:4)?

The election or choosing is in reference to the persons so chosen, including the mass from which they came, while predestination or foreordination refers to the end or purpose pre-appointed for them [Can, Ea, ECWB, EGT, El, Gd, LJ, TNTC].

QUESTION—What metaphor is intended by υἱοθεσίαν 'adoption'?

1. This makes a comparison with the contemporary customs of adopting a person [CBC, Ds2, EBC, EGT, ICC, IDB, ISBE, LJ, MNTC, Si, St, TH, TNTC, WBC, WeBC]: God adopts us as sons like a man adopts another man who was not born into his family. The ground of comparison is giving the rights and privileges of a son to one who formerly did not have them. The nonfigurative statement is: God accepted us as his children.
2. The metaphor does not come from any human custom of adoption [Lns, NIC, NTC], on the contrary it might have come from God's deliverance of Israel from bondage in Egypt [My, NIC, Rob, We].

QUESTION—What is the significance in the use of a word containing the term υἱός 'son' here?

Υἱός 'son', as opposed to τέκνον 'child', suggests the idea of adoption to privilege or rank [DNTT, Ds2, LJ, We], not of nature [DNTT, LJ, We]. In the legal documents of the time, υἱοθεσία 'adoption' is inextricably bound up with terms designating 'inheritance' and 'testament' or 'will' [Ds2].

QUESTION—What relationship is indicated by διά 'through'?

This indicates the means or agency by which the adoption is made possible [Alf, Cal, Can, CBC, Ea, ECWB, EGT, Gd, HG, Ho, LJ, Lns, Lt, MNTC, My, NCBC, NIC, NTC, Rob, TH, TNTC, WBC, WeBC]: God adopted us by means of what Jesus Christ did to make it possible. Jesus atoned for our sins so that we could be adopted [LJ, NTC]. We become members of God's family by union with the Son of God [NIC].

QUESTION—What is meant by εἰς αὐτόν 'to him' and to what is it connected?

The person referred to is God the Father [all commentaries except Gd, WeBC]. Some think it refers to Christ [Gd, WeBC]. Most commentaries connect it with υἱοθεσίαν 'adoption', but one connects it with προορίσας 'predestining' as well, on the basis of scriptural analogy [Gd]. It most naturally refers back to the subject of προορίσας 'predestining' and so is parallel to κατενώπιον αὐτοῦ 'before him' of the previous clause [WBC].

1. Special emphasis is put on the words [AB, Ea, Gd, WBC]: they are his and no one else's children [AB]. Adoption is through Christ, but we find its ultimate enjoyment and blessing in God; it is to *himself* that he adopts us [Cal, Ea, EGT, WBC], or unites us [El].
2. Apparently there is no special emphasis in the words [Ho, ICC, My]: they mean no more than 'his sons' [ICC; NAB, NIV, NRSV, REB, TEV, TNT], and should not be made to carry the meaning of union with God [ICC]. The words carry no more force than 'with reference to (God)' [Ho, My].

according-to/because-of[a] the pleasure/purpose[b] of his will,[c]

LEXICON—a. κατά with accusative object (LN 89.8) (BAGD II.5.a.δ. p. 407): 'according to' [AB, El, Lns, NIC, NTC, Rob, TH, We; KJV, NASB, NRSV], 'in accordance with' [LN, WBC; NIV], 'such was' [NAB, NJB, TNT], 'this was' [REB, TEV], 'because of' [BAGD].
  b. εὐδοκία (LN 25.88) (BAGD 2. p. 319): 'pleasure' [TH; NAB, NIV, REB, TEV, TNT], 'what pleases' [LN], 'favor' [BAGD], 'good pleasure' [BAGD, El, Lns, NIC, NTC, Rob, WBC, We; KJV, NJB, NRSV], 'kind intention' [NASB]. This noun is also translated as an adjective modifying θελήματος 'will': 'favorable' [AB].
  c. θέλημα (LN **30.59**) (BAGD 2. p. 354): 'will' [BAGD, El, LN, Lns, NIC, NTC, Rob, TH, WBC, We; KJV, NAB, NASB, NIV, NRSV, REB], 'purpose' [**LN**; NJB, TEV, TNT], 'intent, plan' [LN], 'decision' [AB].

QUESTION—What relationship is indicated by κατά 'according to'?
1. This indicates conformity to or the measure or standard of the preceding participle [AB, Alf, Ea, El, Lns, My, WBC; KJV, NASB, NIV, NRSV]: his destining us to be adopted conformed to the measure or standard of what he was pleased/purposed to do.
2. This indicates the reason for the preceding participle [BAGD, Cal, Can, EBC, ECWB, EGT, Gd, Ho, MNTC, NIC (probably), NTC, Rob]: he destined us to be adopted because he was pleased/purposed to do so. This can be inferred from the first interpretation also.
3. This is a comment on the preceding participle [NCBC; NAB, NJB, REB, TEV, TNT]: he predestined us to be adopted—such was the good pleasure of his will.

QUESTION—What area of meaning is intended by εὐδοκία 'pleasure/ purpose' and how is this word to be related to the genitive construction τοῦ θελήματος αὐτοῦ 'of his will'?
1. Εὐδοκία focuses on the delight God felt in making this decision [AB, Alf, Ba, Cal, Can, CBC, Ea, EBC, EGT, Gd, ISBE, LN (30.59), Lns, MM, NTC, Si, TD, WBC, WeBC; all versions except NASB]: according to what pleased him, that is, doing what he willed.
2. Εὐδοκία focuses on the purpose God had in mind [DNTT, ECWB, El, Ho, ICC, Lt, NIC, Rob, TNTC, We; NASB]: according to the purpose that he had in so willing. The focus is on God as the actor and not on the objects toward which/whom satisfaction is felt, therefore 'purpose' is the preferred meaning here [El, Ho, ICC].

1:6 to[a] (the) praise[b] of-(the)-glory[c] of-his grace[d]

LEXICON—a. εἰς with accusative object (LN 89.48, 89.57): 'to' [El, NTC, Rob, WBC, We; KJV, NASB, NIV, NJB, NRSV], 'for' [Lns, NIC, TH], 'in order that' [REB], 'in order to' [LN (89.57)], 'that' [NAB, TNT], 'so that' [AB], 'so that as a result' [LN (89.48)]. This has also been conflated with ἔπαινος 'praise' and translated as an imperative: 'let us praise' [TEV].
b. ἔπαινος (LN **33.354**) (BAGD 1.b. p. 281): 'praise' [BAGD, El, LN, NIC, NTC, Rob, TH, WBC, We; all versions except NAB, TEV, TNT]. This noun has also been combined with the following noun in the genitive δόξης 'of glory' and translated as a hyphenated, compound noun: 'Glory-Praise' [Lns]. This noun has also been translated as a verb: 'let us praise' [TEV], 'to praise' [NAB], 'to be praised' [AB], 'to truly value' [TNT].
c. δόξα (LN 87.23) (BAGD 1.a. p. 203): 'glory' [AB, El, LN, Lns, NTC, Rob, TH, WBC, We; KJV, NASB, NJB, REB], 'greatness' [LN], 'brightness, splendor, radiance' [BAGD]. This noun is also translated as an adjective: 'glorious' [NIC; NAB, NIV, NRSV, TEV, TNT].
d. χάρις (LN 88.66) (BAGD 2.a. p. 877): 'grace' [AB, BAGD, El, LN, Lns, NIC, NTC, Rob, TH, WBC, We; KJV, NASB, NIV, NJB, NRSV, TEV],

'gift' [TNT], 'favor' [BAGD; NAB], 'gracious gift' [REB], 'goodwill, gracious care, help' [BAGD], 'kindness' [LN].

QUESTION—What relationship is indicated by εἰς 'to'?
1. This indicates purpose or contemplated result [Alf, Ba, Cal, Can, Ea, EBC, ECWB, EGT, El, Gd, Ho, ICC, LJ, MNTC, NCBC, NIC, NTC, Rob, WBC, We; NAB, REB, TNT; and probably KJV, NASB, NIV, NJB, NRSV].
    1.1 This gives the purpose or goal for predestining us to be adopted [Alf, Cal, Ea, EGT, El, Gd, IB, My, NCBC (probably), NIC, WBC; NAB, NIV, NRSV, REB]: God predestined us to be adopted in order that his grace be praised.
    1.2 This gives the purpose for choosing us [MNTC, Rob]: God chose us in order that his grace be praised.
    1.3 This gives the purpose of both choosing and predestinating us [Ba, Ho, NTC] (inasmuch as Can, EBC, ECWB, LJ, and Lt speak of this as the purpose of salvation, they are judged to support this position also): God has chosen us and predestined us to adoption as sons in order that his grace might be praised.
2. This indicates result [Lns, TH]: God destined us to be adopted. As a result his grace is praised. Probably the imperative translation 'let us praise' [TEV] indicates result also.

QUESTION—Who are the ones who praise God's grace?
Many commentators think that it is redeemed mankind who praises God's grace [Ba, EGT, Ho, IB, ICC, Lns, Lt, MNTC, NCBC, NTC, TNTC], especially the Ephesians [Lns]. Others think that it is not just redeemed mankind who have received his grace that are to praise him, but all who observe his work of grace in his saints [Alf, CBC, Ea, ECWB, LJ, WBC (probably)] including the world of unconverted men [CBC, LJ].

QUESTION—How are the three nouns related in the double genitive construction εἰς ἔπαινον δόξης τῆς χάριτος αὐτοῦ 'the praise of the glory of his grace'?
1. The object of praise is the second genitive in the construction. 'Glory' modifies 'grace' [Ba, Bu, Can, MNTC, NCBC, WBC, We; NAB, NIV, NRSV, TEV, TNT]: to the praise of his glorious grace. The focus then comes on the word 'grace' in the genitive construction 'glory of his grace'. The focus for praise is not simply on God's glory but on his grace [WBC].
2. The object of praise is the first genitive in the construction. The focus is on the word 'glory' in the genitive construction 'glory of his grace' [AB, Alf, BD, Ea, ECWB, El, Gd, HG, Ho, ICC, LJ, Mo, My, Tu]: to the praise of how glorious his grace is. Δόξης 'of glory' is a pure substantive and specifies that peculiar quality of the χάρις 'grace' which forms the subject of praise [El].

3. The focus is on the word 'praise', with 'glory' modifying it, and the object of praise is God's grace [Cal, Lns, NIC]: to the glorious praise of his grace.

QUESTION—What aspect of God's grace does χάρις specify here?

Χάρις 'grace' has to do with the manifestation of God's love here [Gd, WBC] because election and predestination are concerned with God's primary decrees concerning the believer's appointed destiny without reference to the intervening sinful state [Gd]. The grace highlighted in this verse refers to the blessing of salvation, the whole subject of this *berakah* 'blessing' section. Χάρις 'grace' is seen as the principle of God's redemptive activity [WBC].

of-which he-highly-favored[a] us in[b] the (one) having-been-loved,[c]

- TEXT—Instead of ἧς 'of which', some manuscripts have ἐν ᾗ 'in/with which'. AB, Alf, BAGD, Ea, EGT, GNT, ICC, Lns, Lt, My, NIC, NTC, Rob, WBC, We; NASB, NIV, and TEV support ἧς 'of which'. Those supporting the reading ἐν ᾗ 'in/with which' are Ba (apparently), Can, El, Ho (probably); KJV. If ἐν ᾗ 'in/with which' is chosen, the preceding occurrence of χάρις 'grace' will cause ἐν ᾗ 'in which' to portray the state within which (rather than the means by which) God has manifested his favor [El].
- LEXICON—a. aorist act. indic. of χαριτόω (LN **88.66**) (BAGD p. 879): 'to favor highly' [BAGD, WBC], 'to bless' [BAGD], 'to bestow favor upon' [BAGD; NAB], 'to bestow grace on' [El], 'to freely bestow' [NIC, Rob, We; NASB, NRSV], 'to graciously bestow' [NTC], 'to graciously grant' [Lns], 'to graciously confer' [REB], 'to graciously show' [**LN**], 'to freely give' [NIV, TNT] 'to generously give' [TH], 'to give a free gift' [TEV], 'to pour out' [AB], 'to show kindness, to manifest graciousness toward' [LN], 'to make (us) accepted' [KJV]. This is also translated as a possessive noun phrase: 'his free gift' [NJB].
  b. ἐν with dative object (LN 89.119): 'in' [AB, El, LN, Lns, NIC, NTC, Rob, TH, WBC, We; all versions], 'in union with, joined closely to' [LN].
  c. perf. pass. masc. participle of ἀγαπάω (LN 25.43) (BAGD 1.d. p. 5): 'to be loved'. This is translated as a substantive: 'the/his Beloved' [El, NTC, Rob, TH, WBC, We; KJV, NAB, NASB, NJB, NRSV, REB], 'the one loved (by God)' [BAGD], 'the One he loves' [NIV], 'his beloved Son' [AB; TNT], 'his dear Son' [TEV], 'Beloved One' [Lns, NIC]. The passive form suggests in every case some special manifestation of love [We].

QUESTION—What is the significance of the occurrence of the same root in both the noun χάριτος 'grace' and the verb ἐχαρίτωσεν 'he favored'?

The fact that both the noun and the verb forms of this root occur in the verse makes this a cognate construction and so serves to emphasize the concept of grace [WBC], giving the meaning of an abundant amount of grace [AB, Ea, IB, Lt, NTC, Rob, WeBC]. One commentator apparently feels the manner of the gift is in view rather than the quantity, rendering it 'graciously granted' [Lns].

30   EPHESIANS 1:6

QUESTION—What relationship is indicated by ἐν 'in'?
1. It stands for our union with Christ [AB, Alf, Ba (probably), Ea, ECWB, EGT, El, Gd, Ho, IB, LJ, Lns, Lt, MNTC, NIC, Rob (probably), Si, TD, WBC, We]: God has highly favored us with his grace, we who are in union with Christ. Christ, as 'the Beloved' is the primary recipient of God's love, and we, as united with him, receive this love as undeserved grace. Christ himself is the embodiment of God's grace [AB, EGT, LJ, MNTC].
2. It indicates the means by which we receive God's grace [NCBC, NTC, TH]: God highly favored us with his grace by means of Christ whom he loves. These commentators indicate that it is Christ who earned this grace for us.

DISCOURSE UNIT: 1:7–10 [CBC, ECWB, NIC, WeBC]. The topic is praise to God for redemption and final reconciliation.

1:7 in[a] whom we-have[b] the redemption[c] through[d] his blood,[e]

LEXICON—a. ἐν with dative object (LN 89.119): 'in' [AB, El, LN, Lns, NIC, NTC, Rob, TH, WBC, We; KJV, NAB, NASB, NIV, NJB, NRSV, REB], 'in union with, joined closely to' [LN]. Not explicit [TEV, TNT].
  b. pres. act. indic. of ἔχω (LN 90.65): 'to have' [El, LN, Lns, NIC, NTC, Rob, TH, WBC, We; KJV, NASB, NIV, NRSV], 'to possess' [AB], 'to gain' [NJB], 'to experience' [LN]. This is also translated as a passive: 'to be secured' [REB]. The phrase ἔχομεν ἀπολύτρωσιν 'we have redemption' is translated 'to be set free' [LN (**37.128**); TEV, TNT], 'to be redeemed' [NAB]. The present tense makes a sudden transition from long past events, before creation, to the benefits of Christ's death which his people enjoy in the present age [AB, Can, Ea, EBC, Gd, NIC]. This puts emphasis [El] on the 'redemption' here being a present possession rather than something belonging to the future [EGT, Gd, NCBC].
  c. ἀπολύτρωσις (LN **37.128**) (BAGD 2.a. p. 96): 'redemption' [BAGD, El, NIC, NTC, Rob, TH, WBC, We; KJV, NASB, NIV, NRSV], 'the state of being redeemed' [BAGD], 'ransoming' [Lns], 'release' [REB], 'freedom' [AB; NJB], 'acquittal' [BAGD], 'liberation, deliverance' [LN]. This is also translated in verbal form: 'to be redeemed' [NAB], 'to be set free' [LN; TEV, TNT].
  d. διά with genitive object (LN 89.76): 'through' [AB, BAGD, El, LN, Lns, NIC, NTC, Rob, TH, WBC, We; all versions except TEV], 'by' [LN; TEV], 'by means of' [BAGD, LN].
  e. αἷμα (LN 23.107) (BAGD 2.b. p. 23): 'blood' [BAGD, El, ICC, Lns, NIC, NTC, Rob, TH, WBC, We; KJV, NAB, NASB, NIV, NJB, NRSV, TEV], 'the shedding of blood' [AB; REB], 'death' [LN; TNT], 'violent death' [LN].

QUESTION—How does this clause relate to the preceding verse?
1. This specifies what was bestowed upon us by his gracious act [Ea, EBC, My, TNTC, WBC]: God favored us with his grace; specifically, Christ

EPHESIANS 1:7

redeemed us. This is an elaboration on the grace bestowed upon believers in terms of some of the present benefits of salvation [WBC].
2. This gives the grounds or reason for the statement in the last verse that God has acted in grace towards us and his actions are designed for and worthy of praise [TEV]: God is worthy of such praise because he has redeemed us in Christ (the beloved). This appears to be the reason TEV begins this verse with 'for'.
3. The repetition of the phrase ἐν ᾧ 'in whom' marks the transition to another part of his theme [AB, Can, IB, Lns, MNTC, NIC, NTC]: to the death of Christ on the cross [AB], the work of Christ for us and the work of the Holy Spirit within us [Can], from the Father's determinations in heaven in eternity past to Christ's work on earth and its effects in the present age [MNTC, NTC].

QUESTION—What is the meaning of ἐν 'in' and what relationship is indicated by it?

The answer to the question in 1:6 concerning ἐν τῷ ἠγαπημένῳ 'in the Beloved' is the same answer here because of the close proximity of the two phrases and the use of the relative pronoun referring back to ἠγαπημένῳ 'the Beloved' [ICC, Lns].

QUESTION—What is the meaning of the metaphor 'redemption'?
1. It refers to the freeing of a slave or captive by the payment of a ransom [Can, DNTT, Ds, Ds2, Ea, EBC, ECWB, EGT, El, Ho, IDB, ISBE, ISBE2, LJ, Lns, Lt, My, NCBC, NIC, NTC, Si, Si-ed, St, WeBC]. The comparison is: Christ has redeemed us by dying for us like a slave is redeemed by the payment of a ransom. The point of comparison is the freeing of someone from the power of someone or something by doing what is required to free him. The nonfigurative statement would be: we are saved by Christ's dying for us. Suggestions about what we are freed from are: being liable for the punishment due our sins [ECWB, EGT, LJ, Lt, My, NTC, WeBC], God's anger [My], the power of sin [NTC, WeBC].
2. There is metaphor here, but the idea of a price or ransom paid for the freedom gained is not present [CBC, DNTT, IB, ICC, LN (**37.128**) (probably), TD (probably), TH, TNTC, WBC].
2.1 The metaphor is that of the release of a slave from the state of slavery [CBC, ICC, TD (probably)]. The comparison is: as a slave is released from slavery so Christ has released us from slavery to our sins. The point of the comparison is the freeing of a person from a state of slavery. The nonfigurative statement would be: we have been saved, or, we have been given freedom. What we have been delivered from is the power of sin [CBC, ICC, LN, TD].
2.2 The metaphor is taken from the redemption of Israel from Egypt [IB, TH, WBC] as well as other instances of the redemption of people and property in the Old Testament, sometimes with no accompanying idea of payment of a price [TNTC, WBC]. The basic idea of the word, then,

is the setting free of a person or thing formerly owned by one party but which has come into the hands of another. The comparison is: as people or property were restored to the hands of their rightful owners so Christ has freed us from the dominion of sin and restored us to God. The point of the comparison is not only freedom from the dominion of another, but restoration to the previous state of ownership or family. The nonfigurative statement would be: God has freed us and restored us to himself.

3. There is (apparently) no metaphor involved [AB], the word simply means 'freedom'.

QUESTION—What relationship does the phrase διὰ τοῦ αἵματος αὐτοῦ 'through his blood' have to the phrase ἐν ᾧ 'in whom'?

The phrase διὰ τοῦ αἵματος αὐτοῦ 'through his blood' is a more precise definition of ἐν ᾧ 'in whom' [Alf, El, Ho, My]. The ἐν 'in' points to the method in which redemption become ours—in union with Christ, while the διά 'through' points to the instrumental connection, the means of provision, that the death of Christ has to our redemption. We are redeemed by means of his blood [Alf, Ba, BAGD, Cal, Ea, EGT, El, Ho, MNTC, My, NIC, TH, WBC, We].

QUESTION—What figure of speech is indicated by αἷμα 'blood'?

The commentaries are somewhat divided in their terminology here, whether a violent death is in view or a sacrificial one. The interpretations are not necessarily exclusive of each other since the sacrifice of animals involved violence done to them.

1. This is a metonymy in which blood stands for a violent death since it is a prominent aspect of such a death [Bu, Cal, MNTC, TD; TEV, TNT]: by his being killed.
2. It is a metaphor based on the Jewish sacrificial system [AB, Alf, Ba, BAGD, CBC, DNTT, Ea, ECWB, EGT, Gd, IB, ICC, LJ, Lns, My, NIC, NTC, Rob, TD, TH, TNTC, WBC]. The comparison is: Christ offered his blood to God like a priest offers an animal's blood to God to obtain forgiveness for the Jew. The point of comparison is the death required by the one effecting the atonement of sin. The nonfigurative statement would be: his death obtained our forgiveness. In supplying 'death', 'blood' is also taken as a metonymy. By using the term αἷμα 'blood' rather than θάνατος 'death' Paul obviously had the idea of expiation and propitiation in his mind as well as the idea of deliverance from bondage that ἀπολύτρωσις 'redemption' contains [Alf, ECWB, LJ].
3. It includes both of the preceding meanings [EBC].

the forgiveness[a] of-trespasses,[b] according-to[c] the riches[d] of-his grace[e]

LEXICON—a. ἄφεσις (LN 40.8) (BAGD 2 p. 125): 'forgiveness' [AB, BAGD, El, LN, NIC, NTC, Rob, TH, WBC, We; KJV, NASB, NIV, NJB, NRSV], 'remission' [Lns], 'pardon, cancellation (of a debt)' [BAGD]. This noun is also translated as a verb: 'to be forgiven' [NAB, REB, TEV,

TNT]. It is important to note that the focus of the meaning of this word is upon the guilt of the one who does wrong and not on the wrongful deed itself. The guilt, therefore is removed, but the deed itself can never be undone [LN].
b. παράπτωμα (LN 88.297) (BAGD 2.b. p. 621): 'trespass' [Lns, NIC, NTC, Rob, WBC, We; NASB, NRSV], 'sin' [BAGD, LN, TH; all versions except NASB, NRSV], 'lapse' [AB], 'transgression' [El, LN].
c. κατά with accusative object (LN 89.8): 'according to' [El, Lns, NIC, NTC, Rob, TH, We; KJV, NASB, NRSV], 'in accordance with' [LN, WBC; NIV], 'in relation to' [LN], 'so' [NAB]. This is also translated as beginning a new sentence: 'In the richness of his grace' [REB], 'Such are/is' [AB; NJB], with exclamatory force in conjunction with the following noun πλοῦτος 'riches': 'how (great/abundantly rich is)' [TEV, TNT].
d. πλοῦτος (LN **78.15**) (BAGD 2. p. 674): 'riches' [AB, El, Lns, NTC, Rob, We; KJV, NASB, NIV, NRSV], 'richness' [WBC; NJB, REB], 'wealth' [BAGD, NIC, TH], 'abundance' [BAGD], 'abundant, abundantly' [LN], 'abundantly rich' [TNT], 'great' [LN; TEV]. This is also conflated with the following verb ἐπερίσσευσεν 'he lavished': 'immeasurably generous' [NAB]. It is used figuratively of that which God or Christ possesses in unlimited abundance [BAGD].
e. χάρις: 'grace'. See this word at 1:6.

QUESTION—How is the phrase τὴν ἄφεσιν τῶν παραπτωμάτων 'the forgiveness of trespasses' related to the preceding context?

It is in apposition to the word ἀπολύτρωσις 'redemption' [Cal, Can, El, Ho, ICC, LJ, My, NCBC, TD, TH, TNTC, WBC, We; TEV] and specifies the essential character of redemption [El] or the aspect of redemption that is in focus [Cal, Can, Ho, ICC, LJ, My, NCBC, TD, TH, TNTC, We; TEV]: we have redemption, that is, we have forgiveness of trespasses. It also specifies the manner in which redemption is obtained [Cal, WBC] or the result of redemption [Gd].

QUESTION—How is παράπτωμα 'trespass' different from ἁμαρτία 'sin'?
1. Παράπτωμα 'trespass' focuses on an individual act of sin while ἁμαρτία 'sin' is the more general word [Ea, EBC, EGT, El, My, WBC, We]. This term has the connotation of a positive commission of sin, a trespass, transgression, or act of disobedience [El, WBC].
2. There is no significant difference between the two words in this passage [AB, NIC, TH].

QUESTION—To what does κατά 'according to' refer?
1. This refers to redemption [Alf, BAGD, Cal, Ho, ICC, Lt, MNTC, My, TH, WBC]: in redeeming us, God acted in accordance with his grace. This served to demonstrate how great this grace was [EGT, Ho].
2. This refers to forgiveness [CBC, Gd, NCBC, NTC, Si, TNTC, WeBC]: in forgiving us, God acted in accordance with his grace. However, since

forgiveness explains redemption, there is little difference in meaning between these interpretations. LJ seems to hold both interpretations.

QUESTION—How are the two nouns related in the genitive construction τὸ πλοῦτος τῆς χάριτος αὐτοῦ 'the riches of his grace'?

'Riches' indicates the degree of his grace. But commentators differ as to which is the prominent word in the construction. If it is a Hebraism, as some hold, then χάριτος 'grace' is the prominent word [Ba, CBC, TH, WBC]: his rich grace. Τὸ πλοῦτος 'the riches' here and ἐπερίσσευσεν 'he lavished' in the following relative clause (1:8), with their connotations of abundance and extravagance, help to make the notion of grace emphatic and at the same time give the impression that words fail to describe the inexhaustible resources of God's giving [WBC]. Others deny it is a Hebraism and interpret πλοῦτος 'riches' as the prominent word [Bu, Cal, Ea, ECWB, EGT, El, Gd, ICC, LJ, Lt, My, NIC, NTC, Rob, Si, TNTC, We; NIV, NJB, REB, TEV, TNT]: the richness of his grace.

QUESTION—What aspect of God's grace does χάρις 'grace' refer to here?

Χάρις 'grace' refers to God's mercy here because redemption and forgiveness of sins has reference to the believer's sinful state [Gd].

1:8 which he lavished[a] on us, in[b] all wisdom[c] and insight,[d]

LEXICON—a. aorist act. indic. of περισσεύω (LN 59.54) (BAGD 2.a. p. 651): 'to lavish' [AB, TH, WBC; NASB, NIV, NRSV, REB], 'to shower upon' [NJB, TNT], 'to give in large measure' [TEV], 'to be generous' [NAB], 'to abound' [KJV], 'to make abound' [El, Lns, Rob, We], 'to cause to abound, make extremely rich' [BAGD], 'to provide in abundance, provide a great deal of, cause to be abundant' [LN], 'to cause to overflow' [NTC], 'to multiply' [NIC].

b. ἐν with dative object (LN 89.80): 'in' [AB, El, Lns, Rob, TH, We; KJV, NASB, NJB, TEV, TNT], 'in the form of' [NTC], 'with' [LN, NIC, WBC; NIV, NRSV], not explicit [NAB, REB].

c. σοφία (LN 32.32) (BAGD 2. p. 759): 'wisdom' [AB, BAGD, El, LN, Lns, NIC, NTC, Rob, TH, WBC, We; all versions]. It marks the capacity to understand something and therefore the quality of being prudent or acting wisely [LN].

d. φρόνησις (LN **32.30**) (BAGD 2. p. 866): 'insight' [BAGD, NTC, TH, WBC; NASB, NJB, NRSV, REB, TEV], 'understanding' [BAGD, NIC; NIV, TNT], 'prudence' [AB, Rob, We; KJV], 'intelligence' [BAGD, Lns], 'discernment' [El], 'ability to understand' [LN]. This noun is also translated as a verb: 'to understand' [NAB]. This word marks the ability to understand as the result of insight and wisdom [LN].

QUESTION—To what does ἧς 'which' refer?

It refers to χάριτος 'grace' [AB, Alf, Ba, Bu, Can, Ea, EBC, ECWB, EGT, El, HG, Ho, ICC, LN (**59.54**), Lns, Lt, MNTC, My, NIC, NTC, Rob, WBC, We].

QUESTION—To what is the phrase ἐν πάσῃ σοφίᾳ καὶ φρονήσει 'in all wisdom and insight' connected and to whom are these attributes referred?
1. This phrase is connected with the preceding verb ἐπερίσσευσεν 'he lavished' [AB, Alf, Ba, Cal, Can, EBC, ECWB, EGT, El, Gd, Ho, IB, ICC, LJ, Lns, Lt, MNTC, My, NIC, NTC, Rob, TNTC, WBC, We; KJV, NIV, NJB, REB].
  1.1 This refers to some of the qualities God gave to us when he acted in grace toward us [Cal, Can, CBC, EBC, ECWB, EGT, El, Gd, Ho, IB, ICC, LJ, Lns, Lt, MNTC, My, NIC, NTC, Rob, TNTC, WBC, We; KJV, REB]: God lavished his grace upon us, and this included giving us wisdom and insight. The main idea of the context is the knowledge which the Christian is given [Lt], and the parallel passage, Col. 1:9 [El, Lt, WBC] as well as Col. 3:16 [Lt], support this interpretation [El, Lt, WBC].
  1.2 This refers to qualities God exercised in lavishing grace upon us [Alf, Si]: God, using all his wisdom and insight, lavished his grace upon us. While Col. 1:9 may support the previous interpretation, here Paul's purpose is theocentric throughout, describing the purpose of the ages as decreed by God and incapable of frustration [Si].
2. The phrase is connected to the following participle γνωρίσας 'making known' [Ea; NAB, NASB, NRSV, TEV, TNT].
  2.1 This refers to qualities God exercised [Ea; NASB, NRSV, TEV, TNT]: using all his wisdom and insight, God made known to us the mystery.
  2.2 This refers to qualities God gave us [NAB]: God made known the mystery, giving us all wisdom and insight.
QUESTION—What is the force of πᾶς 'all' in this phrase?
Most of the commentators who comment on this support the interpretation that this phrase refers to the believer's exercise of these virtues. They hold that πᾶς 'all' is always used in literature in an extensive sense: 'all kinds of' or 'every kind of'. It is never used intensively: 'the highest form of'. These commentators have trouble applying πᾶς 'all' to God's attribute, since, idiomatically, it implies a limitation of wisdom and insight such as only men could be said to have, suggesting, as it does, growth from the partial to the complete [EBC]. One commentator applies this phrase to God's use of these qualities and feels that πᾶς 'all' is inferentially intensive as well as being extensive [Ea]. It means 'full' or 'perfect' [Cal].
QUESTION—What is the difference between the two qualities, σοφία 'wisdom' and φρόνησις 'insight'?
1. There is no significant difference in meaning between the terms σοφία 'wisdom' and φρόνησις 'insight' [AB, MNTC, NCBC, TH, WBC]: God has given us practical wisdom with respect to the mystery of his will. Both terms denote the knowledge of how to do something [AB]. Paul prefers the use of doublets rather than just using one single word [NCBC].
2. This is a generic-specific doublet so there is a difference between the two terms that should be preserved in translation [Can, Ea, EBC, ECWB,

EGT, El, Gd, Ho, IB, ICC, Lns, Lt, My, NTC, Rob, Si, TNTC, We, WeBC]: God has not only given us insight into the nature of the mystery of his will, but the ability to apply it in right action. Σοφία 'wisdom' is often joined to another word which is a partial manifestation of it [ECWB]. Σοφία 'wisdom' is the understanding of the nature of a thing, a knowledge of first principles, while φρόνησις 'insight' is the result of spiritual σοφία 'wisdom' [El], the application of this knowledge in operation [Si], i.e., to behavior or right action [Can, Ea, EBC, ECWB, EGT, El, IB, ICC, Lns, Lt, My, Rob, TNTC, We, WeBC]; 'wisdom' is the revelation God has given in the gospel and 'insight' is the spiritual discernment that comes from the apprehension of this [Ho]; 'wisdom' is the ability to apply knowledge to best advantage, while 'insight' is the application of this ability in respect to the will of God [NTC]; 'wisdom' is the ability to understand and believe saving truth and 'insight' the ability to see its application in obedient living [Gd].

1:9 making known[a] to-us the mystery[b] of-his will,[c]

LEXICON—a. aorist act. participle of γνωρίζω (LN 28.26) (BAGD 1. p. 163): 'to make known' [AB, BAGD, El, LN, Lns, NIC, NTC, Rob, TH, WBC, We; all versions except NAB], 'to reveal' [BAGD]. This participle is also conjoined with the phrase ἐν πάσῃ σοφίᾳ καὶ φρονήσει 'in all wisdom and insight' in 1:8 and translated 'has given wisdom to understand' [NAB].

b. μυστήριον (LN 28.77) (BAGD 2. p. 530): 'mystery' [BAGD, El, LN, Lns, NIC, NTC, Rob, TH, WBC, We; KJV, NAB, NASB, NIV, NJB, NRSV], 'secret' [AB, BAGD, LN; TNT], 'secret plan' [TEV]. This noun is also translated as an adjective: 'secret (purpose)' [REB].

c. θέλημα: 'will'. See this word at 1:5.

QUESTION—What relationship is indicated by the use of the participle γνωρίσας 'making known'?

1. This indicates the grounds for stating that God lavished his grace [TNTC]: he lavished his grace on us in all wisdom and insight because he made known to us the mystery of his will.
2. This indicates the means by which he lavished his grace [EGT, Gd, Ho, Lns, My, TH]: he lavished his grace on us in all wisdom and insight by making known to us the mystery of his will.
3. This explains or specifies the preceding statement [Alf, Ea, El, IB, ICC, Lt, NTC, Rob, We]: he lavished his grace on us in all wisdom and insight, that is, he made known to us the mystery of his will.

QUESTION— To whom does ἡμῖν 'to us' refer?

It is inclusive and refers to Christians generally [Alf, Can, EBC, EGT, My, NTC, WBC].

QUESTION—What is the relationship between the two nouns in the genitive construction τὸ μυστήριον τοῦ θελήματος αὐτοῦ 'mystery of his will'?
1. 'Mystery' describes the contents of what God wills [Alf, Cal, Ea, EBC, EGT, El, Gd, ICC, Lns, My, TH, WBC]: the mystery/revelation of what God willed.
2. This is a figure of speech called hypallage, in which the noun in the genitive is the modified word rather than the reverse [Bu]: his secret purpose.

QUESTION—What is the mystery?
'Mystery' means a truth that was not known until it was made known by God [AB, Alf, Ba, Can, Ea, EBC, ECWB, EGT, Gd, Ho, ICC, LJ, Lns, Lt, My, NCBC, NIC, TH, TNTC, WBC]. A better equivalent in English would be 'a revealed secret', and therefore 'a revelation' [AB, Alf, Can, DNTT, Ea, EGT, Ho, ICC, LN (28.77), MNTC, Rob, St, TH, TNTC, WBC, We] or the object of revelation [TD]. Most commentators state that the mystery is the special purpose God has in mind for the whole created universe as seen in the next verse [Can, DNTT, Ea, EBC, Ho, IB, ICC, Lt, MNTC, NCBC, NIC, NTC, Rob, St, TD, TH, TNTC, WeBC]. Some state it more inclusively as the carrying out of the plan of salvation or redemption [Alf, BAGD, EGT, El, LJ, My, WBC] or the whole gospel [Lns] in the last times [WBC]. A few cite the inclusion of the Gentiles among the redeemed as a particular aspect of the mystery that is in focus [Ba, Cal, DNTT, ICC]. One seems to define the content of the mystery only as God's love for mankind [AB], another, as God's will to save sinners [Gd].

according-to[a] his good pleasure/purpose[b]

LEXICON—a. κατά with accusative object: 'according to'. See this word at 1:5.
b. εὐδοκία: 'good pleasure'. See this word at 1:5 concerning the interpretation of its meaning.

QUESTION—What relationship is indicated by κατά 'according to'?
1. This relates to the preceding participle γνωρίσας 'making known' [Alf, Can, Ea, EBC, ECWB, EGT, El, Gd, Ho, ICC, Lns, Lt, My, NTC, TH, WBC; KJV, NASB, NIV, NJB, REB, TEV].
1.1 This indicates the reason for God's action of 'making known' [EBC, EGT, Gd]: he made known to us the mystery of his will because he purposed/was pleased to do so. His purpose or pleasure was the motive for making known to us the mystery of his will.
1.2 This gives the norm or standard by which God acted [Alf, ECWB, El, Lns, My, WBC]: he made known to us the mystery of his will and this action of making known was in accordance with or corresponded to his purpose or pleasure.
2. This, along with the following clause, serves to function as the grounds or reason for the decision given in 1:10 [AB, MNTC]: because God set his favor on him, Christ will administer the fullness of the times, that all things may be united in Christ.

3. A few seem to relate κατά 'according to' to μυστήριον 'mystery' [TNTC; TEV, TNT], not translating κατά but placing the words εὐδοκίαν αὐτοῦ 'his good pleasure' in apposition with μυστήριον 'mystery': the mystery of his will, that is, the purpose/pleasure which he, etc.

which he-purposed[a] in[b] him/himself
LEXICON—a. aorist mid. indic. of προτίθεμαι, προτίθημι (LN **30.62**) (BAGD 2.b. p. 722): 'to purpose' [El, LN, Lns, Rob, TH, WBC, We; KJV, NASB, NIV], 'to determine beforehand' [NJB, REB], 'to plan' [BAGD, NIC], 'to plan beforehand' [LN], 'to intend' [BAGD, LN], 'to set forth' [NRSV], 'to decide' [TEV], 'to set' [AB; TNT]. This is also translated as a verbal clause: 'to cherish the purpose for one's self' [NTC], 'to decree a plan' [NAB].
  b. ἐν with dative object (LN 90.6): 'in' [El, LN (**30.62**), Lns, NIC, NTC, Rob, TH, WBC, We; all versions except TEV], 'by' [LN], 'by means of' [TEV], 'upon' [AB].

QUESTION—To whom does αὐτῷ 'him/himself' refer and what relationship is indicated by ἐν 'in'?
  1. This refers to Christ [AB, Can, EBC, IB, LN (**30.62**), Lns, Lt, NCBC, NIC, NTC, Si-ed, TH, WBC, We; NAB, NIV, NJB, NRSV, REB, TEV] though some translate only 'him'. It refers to Christ because the middle voice of the verb itself already incorporates the reflexive idea of 'in/for himself' [Lns, NTC, We]. Two commentators think that ἐν 'in' indicates the means by which God will accomplish his plan [TH; TEV]: which he purposed (to accomplish) by means of Christ. The remainder leave the preposition ambiguous.
  2. The pronoun is taken as equivalent to ἑαυτῷ 'in himself' and refers to God [Ba, Cal, Ea, ECWB, EGT, El, Gd, Ho, My]: which he himself purposed. Here, the connection with προέθετο 'he purposed' is so immediate that the reflexive form alone seems the only possibility [El]. The text is speaking of the purposes of God, i.e. what was in his mind, and while God is the planner, Christ's role was to carry it out [Ea, EGT, My]. The repetition of ἐν τῷ Χριστῷ 'in Christ' in the next clause forbids the reference to Christ here. To take it as referring to Christ is to introduce tautology into this passage [Ho].

1:10 for[a] an administration/plan[b] of-the fullness[c] of-the times,[d]
LEXICON—a. εἰς with accusative object (LN 89.57): 'for' [Lns, Rob, TH, WBC; NJB], 'unto' [We], 'that' [AB; KJV], 'with a view to' [NASB], 'for the purpose of, in order to' [LN], 'as' [NRSV], 'in regard of' [El], not explicit [TEV, TNT]. This is also conjoined with the noun οἰκονομία 'administration' and translated as an infinitive of purpose: 'to be administered' [NIC], 'to be put into effect' [NTC; NIV, REB], 'to be carried out' [NAB].

b. οἰκονομία (LN 30.68) (BAGD 2.b. p. 559): 'administration' [Lns, TH, WBC; NASB], 'arrangement, order' [BAGD], 'dispensation' [El, Rob, We; KJV], 'plan' [BAGD, LN; NAB, NRSV, TEV, TNT], 'purpose, scheme, arrangement' [LN]. This is also translated as a verb: 'to administer' [AB], 'to be administered' [NIC], 'to be put into effect' [NTC; NIV, REB], 'to be carried out' [NAB], 'to act upon' [NJB]. This noun denotes a plan which involves a set of arrangements. In the NT it refers to God's plan for bringing salvation to mankind within the course of history [LN].

c. πλήρωμα (LN 67.69) (BAGD 5. p. 672): 'fullness' [BAGD, El, Lns, NIC, NTC, Rob, TH, WBC, We; KJV, NAB, NASB, NRSV], 'the state of being full' [BAGD], 'fulfillment' [AB], 'end, completion' [LN]. This is also translated as a verbal phrase: 'to complete when it is right to' [TEV], 'to fulfill when the right time should come' [TNT], 'to run its course' [NJB], 'to reach fulfillment' [NIV], 'to be ripe' [REB].

d. καιρός (LN 67.145) (BAGD 4. p. 395): 'time' [WBC; NAB, NRSV, REB, TEV, TNT], 'times' [El, NIC, NTC, Rob, TH; KJV, NASB, NIV, NJB], 'time-seasons' [Lns], 'days' [AB], 'seasons' [We], 'the time of crisis, the last times' [BAGD], 'age, era' [LN]. This usage of the word probably carries the implication of the relation of a period of time to a particular state of affairs [LN].

QUESTION—What relationship is indicated by εἰς 'for'?
1. It indicates the purpose of the preceding verb προέθετο 'he purposed' [AB, Alf, Ba, ECWB, EGT, El, Gd, Lns, Lt, MNTC, NTC, Rob, Si, WBC; KJV, NAB, NJB, TNT]: God purposed a plan in order to have an administration for uniting all things.
2. It means 'with reference to' or 'in regards to' and indicates what the action of the verb προέθετο 'he purposed' had reference to [Ea, Ho, IB, ICC, My, TNTC; NASB]: God purposed a plan with reference to an administration for uniting all things. (This interpretation does not necessarily exclude purpose, since El translates εἰς 'for' with 'in regards of' but regards it as indicating purpose.)
3. It is connected to τὸ μυστήριον τοῦ θελήματος αὐτοῦ 'the mystery of his will' and shows the purpose of this [NIV]: he has made known to us the mystery of his will to be put into effect in the fullness of the times.
4. It is connected to τὸ μυστήριον τοῦ θελήματος αὐτοῦ 'the mystery of his will' and makes an additional, subordinate statement concerning the phrase [REB, TEV]: he made known to us the mystery of his will, the plan which he will put into effect in the fullness of the times, which is to bring all things together, etc.

QUESTION—What is meant by οἰκονομία 'administration, plan'?
1. It means 'administration', 'stewardship', or 'management' and focuses on the office or the work of the office [AB, Can, EBC, ECWB, Gd, ICC, Lns, MNTC, TH, TNTC, WBC; NAB, NASB, NIV, NJB, TEV, TNT]: he purposed (a plan) for an administration of the fullness of the times. The administrator is God himself [Alf, Cal, ECWB, ICC, LJ, Lt, TH, WBC].

Others say the implied administrator is Christ [AB, DNTT, EGT, Lns]. This fits in with Christ's responsibilities as given elsewhere in Ephesians as well as with his servant role given elsewhere in the NT [AB].
2. It means an 'arrangement', 'dispensation', 'plan', or 'strategy' and focuses on the plan or strategy underlying the office of administration [Ba, BAGD, DNTT, Ea, EGT, El, Ho, IB, LJ, Lt, MNTC, My, NCBC, NIC, NTC, Rob, Si, St, TD, We (probably); KJV, NRSV, REB]: he purposed a plan/strategy concerning the fullness of the times.

QUESTION—What is the relationship between the nouns in the genitive phrase οἰκονομίαν τοῦ πληρώματος τῶν καιρῶν 'administration/plan of the ₍fullness₎ of the times'?
1. 'Fullness of time' gives the quality which characterizes the administration/plan [Cal, CBC, Ea, EGT, El; NASB]: an administration or plan suitable to the fullness of the times. In this usage there is a strong temporal reference so there is only a vague differentiation between this usage and the following [El].
2. 'Fullness of time' indicates when the administration/plan will take place [Alf, Gd, ICC, LJ, Lns, Lt, MNTC, My, NIC, Rob, TH, TNTC; NIV, NJB, TEV, TNT]: an administration or plan which will take effect when the fullness of the times comes. The versions which adopt this interpretation all convert the noun οἰκονομία 'administration/plan' into verbal form.
3. 'Fullness of time' denotes that which is being administered [WBC]: to administer the fullness of the times. God's purpose to make known the mystery of his will embraces the ordering of history so that it culminates in the achievement of his purpose [WBC].

QUESTION—What is the meaning of τοῦ πληρώματος τῶν καιρῶν 'the fullness of the times'?
1. It means the right, fit, or appropriate time, the καιρός 'time, season' giving this sense to the phrase [Cal, Can, CBC, ICC, NCBC, NIC, NTC, TH, TNTC; REB, TEV, TNT]: an administration/plan which will take effect at the appropriate time.
2. It means the completion of the time, the πλήρωμα 'fullness' giving this sense to the phrase [AB, Alf, Ba, BAGD, DNTT, Ea, ECWB, El, Gd, Lns, My, TD, WBC; NIV, NJB]: an administration/plan which will take effect when the time is completed.
3. Both meanings are present in the phrase [EGT, Lt]: an administration/plan which will take effect at the appropriate time, that is when the time is completed.

QUESTION—What is the concept of time which lies behind the use of this phrase?
Distinct successive ages are implied, with the fullness of the times being the final one, or the culminating point of the final one [AB, Ba, Ea, EBC, ECWB, EGT, El, IB, ICC, LJ, Lns, Lt, My, NTC, WBC, We]. Time, here, is not simply the continuous passage of years, days, hours, and seconds, but

time filled with content, or time defined by what happens within it. It is viewed as consisting of successive periods or eras, each filled with significant persons or events and each preparatory toward the outworking of a final culminating purpose [AB, Ea, EGT, IB, ICC, TD, We].

QUESTION—To what does this phrase refer?

1. Reference is to the present age of the gospel or of grace, inaugurated by the first advent of Christ (or by Christ's resurrection and ascension [NTC]) and culminated by the second advent with its time of judgment [Alf, CBC, Ea, ECWB, EGT, El, Gd, IB, ICC (probably), LJ, Lt, My, NCBC, NTC].
2. Reference is to the final age, inaugurated by Christ's second advent and culminating in the uniting of all things in him [AB, Ba, EBC, Ho, WBC (probably)].

to-unite[a] all (things) in[b] Christ,

LEXICON—a. aorist mid. infin. of ἀνακεφαλαιόω (LN **63.8**) (BAGD p. 56): 'to sum up' [BAGD, WBC, We; NASB], 'to summarize' [Lns], 'to gather together in one' [KJV], 'to gather up to a unity' [TNT], 'to gather up again together' [El], 'to gather up in one' [Rob], 'to gather up' [NRSV], 'to be brought into a unity' [REB], 'to bring together' [BAGD, LN, NIC], 'to bring together under one head' [NTC; NIV], 'to bring together (under/with Christ) as head' [NJB, TEV], 'to bring into one (under Christ's) headship' [NAB], 'to be comprehended (under) one head' [AB], 'to head up' [TH]. The term implies some unifying principle as a basis for the gathering together [LN]. Those who comment on the voice of this verb are unanimous in labeling it middle voice. It implies that God is not only the initiator of the action but that he acts in his own interest in this program of uniting everything together in Christ [BAGD, Ea, ECWB, EGT, El, ICC, MNTC, My, NIC]: to sum up/unite/gather together all things to/for himself in Christ.

b. ἐν with dative object (LN 89.119): 'in' [BAGD, El, LN, Lns, NIC, NTC, Rob, TH, WBC, We; KJV, NASB, NRSV, REB, TNT], 'in union with' [LN], 'with' [TEV], 'under' [AB; NAB, NIV, NJB].

QUESTION—What relationship is indicated by the use of the infinitive ἀνακεφαλαιώσασθαι 'to unite'?

1. It is connected with μυστήριον 'mystery' of 1:9 and explains what the mystery consisted of [AB, Ea, IB, NTC, St, TH, WBC]: (making known to us) the mystery of his will, that is, to unite/bring under one head all things. This infinitive gives the main point of the clause which begins with γνωρίσας 'having made known' [WBC]. This infinitive phrase is a quotation from some source giving the kernel and highlight of the section (1:3-14), as well as functioning as an explanation of the mystery [AB].
2. The phrase is connected to οἰκονομία 'administration' [EGT, El, ICC, Lns, MNTC, My, Rob]. While not dependent upon προέθετο 'he

purposed', it is an epexegetical infinitive defining the nature and purpose of the preceding statement [El].
- 2.1 It indicates the purpose of the 'administration' [EGT, ICC, Lns, MNTC] or its intended result [EGT, Lt]: for an administration of the fullness of the times, in order that he might unite/bring under one head all things. It is the epexegetical infinitive in the particular aspect of *consequence* or *contemplated result* [EGT].
- 2.2 It explains 'administration' [My, Rob]: for an administration of the fullness of the times, that is, to unite/bring under one head all things, etc.
3. It is connected to κατὰ τὴν εὐδοκίαν αὐτοῦ 'according to his good pleasure' (v. 9) [Alf]: according to his good pleasure to sum up all things. With this construction the words ἣν…καιρῶν 'which… of the times' are parenthetical.

QUESTION—What is meant by the infinitive ἀνακεφαλαιώσασθαι 'to unite'?
1. It means 'to sum up', 'to summarize', or 'to gather together' and therefore 'to unite' [Alf, Ba, Cal, NCBC, NIC, Rob; KJV, NASB, NRSV, REB]: to sum up, gather together, or unite all things in Christ.
2. It means 'to bring under' or 'to unite under one head' [AB, Can, Ho, IB (possibly), LN (**63.8**), Lns (probably), Lt, NTC, St, TD, TH, TNTC; NAB, NIV, NJB, TEV, TNT]: to bring all things under the headship of Christ.
3. It means 'to renew' or 'to restore' [DNTT, Ea, EBC, ECWB, EGT, El, Gd, LJ, MNTC, My, Si, WBC; NJB (note)]: to renew all things in Christ or to reunite or bring together again all things in Christ. The preposition ἀνά- 'up/again' signifies repetition [Ea, El, Gd, Ho, LJ, MNTC, My]: to sum up again or to reunite all things in Christ. The preposition indicates a restoration of harmony with Christ as the point of the reintegration. In doing this it necessarily implies the state of the universe previous to the entrance of sin and the fall of man [WBC].

QUESTION—What is the time reference of the event specified by this infinitive?

A few commentators think that the event specified by ἀνακεφαλαιώσασθαι 'to unite' has its inception and foundation in the incarnation, the atonement, or the exaltation and enthronement of Christ [AB, Ea, LJ, Lt, My, Si, WBC]. Accordingly, some commentators regard this event as having already occurred [Cal, CBC, Ea, ECWB, Ho, Lns, NTC, WBC], and take it as the basis for Christ's present governing of heaven and earth [Ea, NTC]. Most, however, understand the context as having to do with God's ultimate purpose, and they focus upon the action in relation to its culmination [EGT, LJ, NIC, Si] and speak of the event as belonging to the eschatological future [Ba, EBC, EGT, IB, LJ, Lt, My, NCBC, NIC, Si, St, TNTC, We].

QUESTION—To what does τὰ πάντα 'all things' refer?
1. 'All things' refers to everything and everyone that has been created, things physical and spiritual, living and material [AB, Alf, Ba, BAGD, Can, Ea, EBC, EGT, El, Gd, IB, ICC, Lns, MNTC, My, NCBC, NTC, Rob, St, TH, TNTC, WBC, We; NAB (note), REB, TEV, TNT]: to unite everyone and

everything ever created in Christ. Some feel, however, that beings are what is mainly in view [Can, Gd]. Some feel the use of the neuter gender points to a generalized meaning [Ea, El].
2. 'All things' refers to the heavenly beings and human beings, referred to in the appositional phrase following [NJB (note)]: to unite all heavenly beings and people in Christ.
3. 'All things' refers only to those human beings who have been redeemed [Ho, NIC]: to unite all redeemed mankind in Christ.

QUESTION—What is meant by ἐν τῷ Χριστῷ 'in Christ'?
'In Christ' means that all things are to be united under Christ's rule [AB, Ba, LJ, Lns, TNTC; NAB, NJB, TEV] or power [NCBC]. The whole universe is to be united with him as its point of focus [IB, WBC].

the (things) in[a] the heavens[b] and the (things) on[c] the earth[d]

LEXICON—a. ἐπί with dative object (LN 83.9, 83.23) (BAGD II.1.a.α. p. 286): 'in' [AB, BAGD, El, Lns, NIC, NTC, Rob, TH, WBC, We; all versions].
  b. οὐρανός (LN 1.11): 'heaven' [AB, El, LN, NIC, TH, WBC; KJV, NIV, NRSV, REB, TEV, TNT], 'heavens' [Lns, NTC, Rob, We; NAB, NASB, NJB].
  c. ἐπί with genitive object (LN 83.46): 'on' [El, LN, Lns, NIC, NTC, Rob, TH, WBC; KJV, NAB, NIV, NJB, NRSV, REB, TEV], 'upon' [AB, LN, We; NASB]. The two occurrences of ἐπί are conflated: 'in heaven and earth' [TNT].
  d. γῆ (LN 1.39): 'earth' [AB, El, LN, Lns, NIC, NTC, Rob, TH, WBC, We; all versions], 'world' [LN].

QUESTION—What does the phrase τὰ ἐπὶ τοῖς οὐρανοῖς 'the things in the heavens' mean?
It refers to the holy inhabitants of other worlds [Ba, ECWB (probably)], the angels [Cal, Gd, LJ, Si], the principalities and powers that the writer speaks of later in this epistle [Can, Gd, WBC]; the supernatural forces of evil [CBC]; the more distant and higher spheres of creation [Ea], God [NCBC], or redeemed saints who are now in heaven [Ho].

QUESTION—What does the phrase τὰ ἐπὶ τῆς γῆς 'the things on the earth' mean?
It refers to the redeemed saints on earth [Ba, Cal, Ho, Si]; redeemed believers (who are subordinated to Christ) and the unredeemed (who are subjugated by Christ) [Alf]; redeemed men as well as the rest of the created world [Gd, LJ].

in[a] him.

LEXICON—a. ἐν with dative object (LN 89.119): 'in' [El, LN, Lns, NIC, NTC, Rob, TH, We; all versions except TEV], 'under' [AB], 'in union with' [LN; TEV].

QUESTION—To what is this phrase connected?
  1. It is connected with the preceding clause [AB, Alf, Ea, EGT, El, TH, TNTC, WBC; KJV, TNT]: to unite all things in Christ, the things in the

heavens and the things on the earth—*in him*. The phrase serves to reassert with emphasis the ἐν τῷ Χριστῷ 'in the Christ' in this verse [Ea, WBC]. Attaching it to the previous phrase makes this phrase parallel to the phrase τὰ πάντα ἐν τῷ Χριστῷ 'all things in Christ' with which it is in apposition. It is also in harmony with the structural pattern of the epistle in which ἐν 'in' phrases conclude sections, while relative clauses with ἐν ᾧ 'in whom' alternate with aorist participles to begin new stretches of syntax (here 1:11, 12) [WBC]. The phrase also serves as a transition to the next verse by serving as the nearer reference to the following 'in whom' phrase [Ea, El].

2. While referring back to the ἐν τῷ Χριστῷ 'in the Christ' of 1:10, it is connected to the following verb, ἐκληρώθημεν 'we were chosen' [LJ, Lns, MNTC, My, NIC, NTC, Rob, St, We; NAB, NASB, NIV, NJB, NRSV, REB, TEV (assuming these versions conflate the second ἐν ᾧ 'in whom' phrase with this phrase)]: in him (also) we were chosen. This phrase is also emphatic by position, with this connection [Rob, St, We]. Its occurrence here emphasizes Christ's role as the reconciler (v. 10) [St].

DISCOURSE UNIT: 1:11–14 [CBC, ECWB, LJ, My, NIC, Rob, St, WeBC]. The one long Greek sentence, 1:3–14, is divided here because of a semantic change of theme. The topic is praise for the assurance of the believer's heritage [NIC], the scope of the blessings [CBC, St], the joint heritage of Jew and Gentile [Rob], praise for the salvation appropriated by Jew and Gentile [My], election by predestination of both Jew and Gentile [ECWB], inauguration of the Church by the Spirit [WeBC], the Church as an illustration of God's cosmic plan [LJ].

1:11 In[a] whom also/indeed[b] we-were-chosen[c]

LEXICON—a. ἐν with dative object (LN 89.119): 'in' [AB, El, LN, Lns, NTC, Rob, TH, WBC, We; KJV], 'through' [TNT]. Conflated with the previous ἐν 'in' phrase (at end of 1:10) [NIC; NAB, NASB, NIV, NJB, NRSV, REB, TEV].

b. καί (LN 89.93, 91.12): 'also' [El, LN (89.93), Lns, NTC, Rob, TH, WBC, We; KJV, NASB, NIV, NRSV], 'too' [NIC], 'indeed' [LN (91.12); REB], 'and' [AB; NJB, TEV], not explicit [NAB, TNT].

c. aorist pass. indic. of κληρόω (LN **30.105**) (BAGD 1. p. 435): 'to be chosen' [BAGD, LN, MM; NAB, NIV], 'to be appointed by lot' [BAGD], 'to be given a lot' [Lns], 'to be appropriated' [AB], 'to be selected' [TH], 'to be appointed' [WBC], 'to be chosen as (his) inheritance' [El], 'to be chosen to be (his) people' [TNT], 'to be chosen as (God's) portion' [Rob], 'to be claimed (by God) as (his) portion' [NIC], 'to be made (God's) portion' [We], 'to be given a share in the heritage' [REB], 'to receive a heritage' [NJB], 'to be made heirs' [NTC], 'to obtain an inheritance' [KJV, NASB, NRSV]. This is also translated as an active verb with God as subject: 'to choose (us) to be his own people' [TEV].

EPHESIANS 1:11

QUESTION—What relationship is indicated by ἐν 'in'?
1. It indicates the reason for the following clause [My]: because of our union with Christ, God chose us.
2. It indicates the means for the following clause [Cal, LJ, St, WBC; TNT]: by means of our union with Christ, God chose us. It is through being in this cosmic Christ in whom all things are summed up that God's choice has fallen on them [WBC].

QUESTION—To what is καί 'also/indeed' connected and what is its meaning here?
1. It is translated as a simple connective [NJB, TEV]: and it is in him that we have been chosen.
2. It is joined to the verb ἐκληρώθημεν 'we were chosen' and means 'also' or 'too' [Alf, Cal, Ea, EBC, EGT, El, Ho, ICC, LJ, Lns, My, NIC, NTC, Rob, WBC, We; NIV, NRSV]: in whom we were also chosen; or, it was in him too that we were chosen. With either of these meanings καί 'also/too' seems to specify an additional action which God has caused to happen to us in our union with Christ [EGT]. One commentator joins it to the implied pronoun 'we' in this verb: in Christ we also (in addition to others) were chosen [Lns].
    2.1 Καί 'also' makes the being chosen an addition to the action of God making known to us the secret of his grace (1:9) [Alf, EGT, Ho, LJ].
    2.2 Καί 'also' makes the being chosen an addition to the cardinal blessings specified in the previous verses [MNTC (probably), NTC].
    2.3 Καί 'also' makes the being chosen an addition to our being chosen out in 1:4 [El].
    2.4 Καί 'also actually' makes the being chosen an addition to the purpose expressed in 1:9–10, the being chosen [My].
3. It is joined to ἐν ᾧ 'in whom' and intensifies it [REB]: in Christ indeed we have been chosen.

QUESTION—To whom does the 'we' refer in the verb ἐκληρώθημεν 'we were chosen'?
1. This 'we' is used in an exclusive sense (excluding the people written to) and refers to Jews of which Paul was one [AB, DNTT, Gd, Ho, IB, ICC, MNTC, TH, TNTC, We, WeBC; NAB (note), NJB (note), TNT]. The reference is to Israel under the Old Testament economy, ideally considered [IB, MNTC, TNTC, WeBC; NJB (note)] or to Jewish Christians as a continuation of the people of God under the OT economy (and into which believing Gentiles, the following 'you' references, were later added) [AB, Cal, DNTT, ECWB, Ho, ICC, LJ, Si, TH; NAB (note)].
2. This 'we' is used in an exclusive sense, and refers to Christians who believed in Christ prior to the Ephesians' conversion [Ba, NCBC]: in whom we, who were Christians before you, were chosen.
3. This 'we' is inclusive (including the Ephesian readers) and refers to all Christians everywhere [Alf, CBC, Ea, EGT, El, Lns, NIC, NTC, Rob, St,

WBC, We]: in whom all us Christians were chosen. The change to ὑμεῖς 'you' in 1:13 then becomes a matter of focus, not of contrast [NTC].

QUESTION—What is meant by ἐκληρώθημεν 'we were chosen'?
1. The verb means 'to be appointed by lot/to be given a lot/allotment' [BAGD, LJ, Lns, WBC], the following reference to predestination, eliminating the idea of chance [ICC, though following interpretation 3]: in whom we were given a lot (by God).
2. The verb is taken with the infinitive purpose clause εἰς τὸ εἶναι ἡμᾶς εἰς ἔπαινον δόξης αὐτοῦ 'that we should be to the praise of his glory' in the next verse, which gives the verb the meaning here of 'to be chosen/ appointed' [BAGD, TD; NAB, NIV]: in whom we are chosen/ appointed...to be/live to the praise of his glory. The verb with this construction gives Christians their life's goal [TD].
3. The verb means 'to be given a share or heritage or an inheritance' [Ba, Cal, DNTT, Ea, EBC, Gd, Ho, ICC, MNTC, My, NCBC, NTC, Si; KJV, NASB, NRSV, REB]: in whom we were given (our) heritage.
4. The verb means 'to be chosen or appropriated as (God's) property/ inheritance' [AB, Alf, Can, ECWB, EGT, El, IB, NIC, Rob, St, TNTC, WeBC; NJB (note), TEV, TNT]: in whom we became God's people/inheritance. The background of this interpretation is the OT teaching that Israel was God's inheritance (Deut. 4:20; 9:29; 32:9), a teaching which Paul applies to the church in Ephesians (1:14, 18). With this interpretation, the preceding ἐν ᾧ 'in whom' refers to the price that was paid for the redemption necessary for this inheritance to take place [AB].

being-predestined[a] according-to/because-of[b] (the) purpose[c]

LEXICON—a. aorist pass. participle of προορίζω (LN 30.84) (BAGD p. 709): 'to be predestined' [BAGD, TH, WBC; NAB, NASB, NIV], 'to be predestinated' [Lns; KJV], 'to be destined' [NRSV], 'to be decided upon beforehand' [BAGD, LN], 'to be marked out beforehand' [NJB], 'to be determined ahead of time, to be decided upon ahead of time' [LN], 'to be decreed' [REB], 'to be foreordained' [El, NIC, NTC, Rob, We], 'to be designated' [AB], 'to be set apart' [TNT]. This is also translated as a clause indicating grounds of a previous action (probably ἐκληρώθημεν 'we were chosen'): 'based on what he had decided from the very beginning' [TEV].
b. κατά with accusative object (LN 89.8) (BAGD II.5.a.δ. p. 407): 'according to' [BAGD, El, Lns, NIC, NTC, Rob, TH, We; KJV, NASB, NIV, NRSV], 'in accordance with' [LN, WBC], 'under' [NJB], 'in' [REB], 'for' [NAB, TNT], 'because of' [BAGD; TEV]. This is also translated as 'as' in conjunction with the translation of the noun πρόθεσις 'purpose' as a verb [AB].
c. πρόθεσις (LN **30.63**) (BAGD 2.b. p. 706): 'purpose' [AB, BAGD, El, **LN**, Lns, NIC, NTC, Rob, TH, We; KJV, NASB, NRSV, TEV], 'design' [BAGD; REB], 'plan' [BAGD, LN, WBC; NIV, NJB, TNT], 'decree'

[NAB], 'resolve, will' [BAGD]. This is also translated as a verb: 'to be resolved (by God)' [AB].

QUESTION—What is the relationship of the aorist passive participle προορισθέντες 'being predestined' to the verb ἐκληρώθημεν 'we were chosen'?

Most translate it ambiguously as circumstantial [El, Lns, NIC, NTC, Rob, TH, WBC, We; KJV, NASB, NIV, NJB, NRSV]: having been predestined. A few make it the reason for being chosen or receiving an inheritance [EBC, EGT, Gd; NAB, REB, TEV]: because we were predestined. Two make it coordinate with the verb [AB; TNT]: we were chosen and predestined in the Messiah. Another commentator seems to regard the sequence ἐκληρώθημεν προορισθέντες 'we were chosen having been predestined' as the equivalent of an hendiadys: we were foreordained to be his heritage [Can]. Others state the participle indicates the means of the choosing or receiving a heritage [IB, LJ]: by being predestined. The participle is added to the verb to exclude any idea of chance [ICC]. It is an elaboration of the verb [WBC].

QUESTION—To what is κατά 'according to' attached and what relationship does it indicate ?

1. It indicates the agreement of his predestining with his purpose [Alf, Can, EGT, El, Ho, Lns, My, NIC, NTC, Rob, TH, TNTC, WBC, We; KJV, NASB, NIV, NJB, NRSV, REB]: what he predestined was what he had purposed. Κατά 'according to' states concord or correspondence and the noun to which it is attached states the standard of the correspondence [Lns]. Briefly, the general doctrine of the divine purpose is this, that whatever God does in time, he has purposed to do from eternity [Can].
2. It indicates the cause of their predestination [Gd]: God predestined us because of his own purpose.
3. It indicates the agreement of his action of choosing with his purpose [IB, NCBC, St]: God chose us according to his purpose.
4. It indicates the reason for his action of choosing [TEV]: God chose us because of his own purpose.
5. It indicates the agreement of both his choosing and predestining with his purpose [AB]: as resolved by him who carries out all things, we were first designated and appropriated.

of-the (one) working[a] all (things) according-to[b] the counsel[c] of-his will[d]

LEXICON—a. pres. act. participle of ἐνεργέω (LN 42.3) (BAGD 2. p. 265): 'to work' [BAGD, El, LN, Lns, NIC, Rob, We; KJV, NASB], 'to effect (something)' [BAGD], 'to be at work' [REB], 'to work out' [NIV], 'to accomplish' [NTC, TH; NRSV], 'to carry out' [AB, WBC], 'to guide' [NJB] 'to administer' [NAB], 'to shape (the course of events)' [TNT]. This is also translated as a passive: '(all things) are done' [TEV].
  b. κατά with accusative object (LN 89.8): 'according to' [Lns, NIC, NTC, Rob, TH, WBC; NAB, NRSV, TEV], 'in conformity with' [NIV], 'after' [AB, El, We; KJV, NASB], 'to' [TNT], not explicit [REB]. This is also

translated as 'as' in conjunction with the translation of βουλή 'counsel' as a verb: 'as (he decides)' [NJB].

c. βουλή (LN 30.57) (BAGD 2.b. p.145): 'counsel' [El, Lns, NIC, NTC, Rob, We; KJV, NAB, NASB, NRSV], 'purpose' [BAGD, LN, WBC; NIV, REB], 'plan' [LN; TEV], 'ends' [TNT], 'decision' [AB, BAGD, TH], 'intention' [LN], 'resolution' [BAGD]. This is also translated as a verb: 'to decide' [NJB].

d. θέλημα (LN 30.59) (BAGD 2.b. p. 354): 'will' [AB, BAGD, El, LN, Lns, NIC, NTC, Rob, TH, WBC, We; all versions except TEV, TNT], 'decision' [TEV], 'purpose, plan' [LN]. This is also translated as a verbal adjective modifying βουλή 'purpose': '(his own) appointed ends' [TNT].

QUESTION—To what does τὰ πάντα 'all things' refer?

Although some mention that others have taken this to be restricted to the things that pertain to salvation, none of the commentaries consulted here, except possibly LJ and Lns, took such a view. This phrase is taken to encompass everything there is in existence [Alf, Ba, Ea, EGT, Gd, Ho, IB, ISBE2, My, NTC]. One commentator relates it primarily to God's governing of the universe [NIC], which would seem to agree with the view of another that the phrase must be restricted to effects and results only [Lns, although he does not allow the phrase to denote objects as it does in 1:10].

QUESTION—Is there any distinction between βουλή 'counsel' and θέλημα 'will'?

While these two terms are most often used interchangeably, with no distinction between them, the commentators who commented on their use in this passage agree that Paul intended to make a distinction between them here. Several commentators note that scholars take diametrically opposing viewpoints on the distinctions between these two terms [DNTT, EGT, ICC, TD], but the commentators used in this summary seem to agree on the following basic distinction: βουλή 'counsel, decision' denotes the specific action of the more general term θέλημα 'will'. Θέλημα is the sovereign volition, based upon the divine desire, the activity of will in general [AB, Alf, Ba, Can, DNTT, Ea, EGT, El, Gd, Ho, ICC, Lns, MNTC, My, NCBC, NIC, NTC, Rob, WBC, We]. The effect is to show that while God's decisions are sovereign, proceeding from him alone, they are not necessarily arbitrary, but have a reason and a gracious purpose behind them, intelligently arrived at, even if they are not understood by man's finite mind [Ba, Can, ECWB, EGT, ICC, Lns, NTC, We].

QUESTION—What is the focus of the word βουλή 'counsel, decision'?

1. The focus of βουλή is on the deliberative process involved in the decision making [Alf, ECWB, EGT, Gd, ICC, LJ, Lns; NJB]: according to the deliberation of his will, or, as he decides by his own will [NJB].

2. The focus of βουλή is upon the result of deliberation, the decision made [Ba, Can, Ea, LN (30.57), TH, TNTC, WBC, We; NIV]: according to the decision of his will. Βουλή 'counsel/decision' signifies 'purpose' in the sense of 'decisive resolve' [WBC].

DISCOURSE UNIT: 1:12–14 [ICC]. The theme is that formerly the Jews had the promise of the Messiah, and now the Gentiles are partaking of those blessings and have received the earnest of their inheritance by being sealed with the Holy Spirit.

1:12 so-that we be to (the) praise[a] of his glory[b]

LEXICON—a. ἔπαινος (LN 33.354) (BAGD 1.b. p. 281): 'praise' [AB, BAGD, El, LN, NIC, NTC, Rob, TH, WBC, We; KJV, NASB, NIV, NJB, NRSV], 'approval, recognition' [BAGD]. This is also combined with its modifying noun in the genitive δόξης 'of glory' and translated as a hyphenated compound: 'Glory–Praise' [Lns]. This is also translated as a causative verb: 'to make (men) truly praise' [TNT], 'to cause to be praised' [REB]; as an infinitive following a passive verb: '(we were predestined) to praise (his glory)' [NAB]; and as an exhortation: 'let us praise' [TEV]. See this word at 1:6.

b. δόξα (LN 87.23): 'glory' [AB, El, LN, Lns, NTC, Rob, TH, WBC, We; all versions], 'greatness' [LN]. This is also translated as an adjective modifying 'praise': 'glorious praise' [NIC]. See this word at 1:6.

QUESTION—What is the force of the pronoun ἡμᾶς 'we' in the infinitive phrase εἰς τὸ εἶναι ἡμᾶς 'that we be'?

The pronoun is emphatic [My, We], standing in contrast to the ὑμεῖς 'you' of 1:13 [El] and preparing the way for that pronoun [My]. The question of to whom the pronoun refers is bound up with the interpretation of προηλπικότας 'to be the first to hope'.

QUESTION—What relationship is indicated by εἰς 'so that'?

1. It indicates purpose [AB, Can, El, Gd, HG, Ho, ICC, Lns, MNTC, MT, My, NIC, St, TH, TNTC, Tu, WBC; KJV, NASB, NIV, NJB, NRSV, TNT].

    1.1 This is connected with the main verb of 1:11, ἐκληρώθημεν 'we were chosen' [Can, El, Lns, MNTC, My, TH, WBC; NIV, NJB]: God chose us/gave us an inheritance in order that we may be to the praise of his glory (except NJB who follows ICC in the larger construction).

    1.2 This is connected with προορισθέντες 'being predestined' [Gd, Ho, ICC, NIC]: God predestined us to be for the praise of his glory. ICC significantly departs from the position of the others in the larger construction.

    1.3 This is connected to both the main verb and the participle προορισθέντες 'being predestined' [AB, St; NRSV, TNT]: we were chosen and predestined to be to the praise of his glory.

2. This indicates the result of being chosen [Ea, EGT; TEV]: God chose us, or gave us an inheritance, and consequently we are to be the praise of his glory.

QUESTION—Who are the implied actors who will praise God's glory?

1. The actors are the ones who previously hoped in Christ (however interpreted) [Lns, MNTC, NCBC, TH; NAB, TEV]: in order that we who

previously hoped in Christ should praise his glory; or, let us who previously hoped in Christ praise his glory [TEV].
2. The actors are all who observe God's action of choosing and/or predestinating these people including, of course, those chosen and predestined [Ba, Can, EBC, EGT, Ho, IB, NIC, St, TNTC; REB, TNT; and probably NIV and NRSV]: that we who previously hoped in Christ should be the means/cause of all people praising God's glory. Those praising God's glory may also include the angels [EBC, NIC] and all intelligent creation [IB].

the (ones) having-first-hoped[a] in the Christ.

LEXICON—a. perf. act. participle of προελπίζω (LN **25.60**) (BAGD p. 705): 'to be the first to hope' [BAGD, **LN**, Rob; NAB, NASB, NIV, TEV], 'to be the first to set (our) hope' [AB; NRSV, REB], 'to first place (our) hope' [NIC], 'to first trust' [KJV], 'to hope before/beforehand' [BAGD, El, LN, We], 'to set (our) hopes (on Christ) before (you)' [TNT], 'to center (our) hope beforehand' [NTC], 'to hope in advance' [Lns], 'to put (their) hopes (in Christ) before (he came)' [NJB], 'to have already hoped' [TH, WBC].

QUESTION—To what is this clause connected, to whom does it refer, and how does the interpretation affect the meaning assigned to the bound preposition προ- 'before' in προελπίζω 'to hope before/to be the first to hope'?
1. Paul is talking about all Christians in general and is not distinguishing between Jew and Gentile. In this case the προ- in προελπίζω means 'before having fully attained' or 'already' [CBC, NTC, WBC]: we who hoped in Christ before we have fully attained the inheritance, or, we who have already hoped in Christ.
2. This clause is limited to Paul and the Ephesians only [Lns]. The meaning of προελπίζω is the same as 1 above.
3. This clause refers to Christians who believed in Christ before the Ephesians did, and the force of the προ- is simply prior belief or hope [Ba, Cal, NCBC]: we who believed in Christ before you did.
4. This clause refers to the hopes of the Jewish nation, ideally conceived under the OT economy, as resting in the coming Messiah so that the προ- in προελπίζω has the implied meaning of 'before Christ came' [IB, MNTC, TNTC, We, WeBC; NJB]: we Israelites who first hoped in the promised Messiah before he appeared, or, we Israelites who (historically) had placed hope in the Messiah who was to come.
5. This clause refers to Christian Jews who, because of their messianic heritage, believed in Christ as their promised Messiah [AB, Alf, DNTT, Ea, EBC, ECWB, EGT, El, Gd, Ho, ICC, LJ, My, NIC, Rob, Si, St, TD, TH; NAB (note)].
5.1 The προ- then has the force of having hoped or believed 'before the conversion of the Gentiles' [EBC, Gd, ICC, LJ, NIC, Rob]: we Jews who believed/hoped in the Messiah before you Gentiles did, or, we Jews

who were the first to believe/hope in the Messiah (as opposed to you Gentiles who still had no such hope).

5.2 The προ- then has the force of 'before he appeared' [AB, Alf, ECWB, EGT, El, My]: we Jewish Christians who first had hoped in the (promised) Messiah before he appeared.

QUESTION—What is the significance of the phrase ἐν τῷ Χριστῷ 'in the Christ'?

It indicates the object of their hope [El, WBC]. Some commentators see a distinction in the use of the preposition ἐν 'in' here instead of εἰς 'into/towards'. One states that to have hoped 'in Christ' was a higher characteristic than to have directed hope 'towards Christ', and so designated them as more worthy exponents of praise to God's glory [El]. Another notes only that the phrase indicates the object of their hope, and not that Christ was the one in whom those who hope exist [WBC].

QUESTION—Is the word Χριστός 'Christ' here a name or a title?

A number of those commentators who follow either interpretations 3 or 4 above see Χριστός 'Christ' used in its OT and the Gospels sense of 'Messiah' [AB, Alf, EBC, ECWB, EGT, El, Ho, IB, My, Rob, Si, TH, TNTC, WeBC; NASB (note)]. Most of these see the occurrence of the definite article with Χριστός 'Christ' as indicating such a title. Another, though following another interpretation, also sees significance in the article, but translates it in his comments (1:10) with its literal meaning, 'the Anointed One' [Lns]. Others, who also follow either interpretations 3 or 4, seem to see no more than a name here [ICC, LJ, MNTC, NIC, Rob, We], as do the remaining commentators [Ba, Cal, NCBC, NTC, WBC; and all of the versions in their text].

1:13 In whom also you,

QUESTION—To what verb does the 2nd person nom. plural pronoun ὑμεῖς 'you' act as subject?

1. This is connected with the main verb of the sentence, ἐσφραγίσθητε 'you were sealed' [Ea, ECWB, EGT, El, ICC, Lns, NIC, Rob, TH, WBC; NASB, NJB, NRSV]: in him also you were sealed. The sentence is interrupted by the participle ἀκούσαντες 'having heard' and the noun phrases associated with it, and the following ἐν ᾧ 'in whom' phrase resumes the sentence [EGT, HG]. The sentence is interrupted because the participles ἀκούσαντες 'hearing' and πιστεύσαντες 'believing' form an important preparation for the Christian privilege of being sealed which is stated in the main verb of the sentence [EGT]. This construction thus allows the theme 'in Christ' which governs the whole section 1:3–14 to be emphasized by the second ἐν ᾧ 'in whom' phrase and adds prominence to the participle πιστεύσαντες 'having believed' associated with it [ICC].

2. The participle ἀκούσαντες 'having heard' is translated as a finite verb and ὑμεῖς 'you' is made its subject [NJB, TNT]: in him you too have heard the message of the truth.

3. This ὑμεῖς 'you' has an implied verb, making the following ἐν ᾧ 'in whom' phrase begin a new thought [AB, Alf, Ba, Bu, Cal, Can, EBC, Gd, Ho, IB, My, NTC, TNTC, WBC, We; NAB, NIV, REB, TEV].

3.1 The verb 'to be' is ellipsed and must be supplied here [AB, Alf, EBC, My, NTC, TNTC, WBC; NIV, REB, TEV]: you also (are) in him, or you also were included in him, or you too became incorporate in Christ, or you also became God's people.

3.2 The verb to be supplied is 'to trust' [Ba, Cal; KJV]: you also trusted in him.

3.3 The verb to be supplied is 'to obtain an inheritance' or 'to be made a heritage' from 1:11 [Bu, Can, Gd, Ho, IB]: you also (have obtained an inheritance) in him. The object of Paul's statement is to apply to these Gentiles all that he had previously stated concerning the Jews [Gd]

3.4 The verb to be supplied is 'to chose' from 1:11 [NAB]: you also were chosen in him.

QUESTION—What is meant by καὶ ὑμεῖς 'you also'?

1. Καὶ ὑμεῖς 'you also' serves to shift the attention to the Gentile believers in Ephesus, thus completing the contrast with the ἡμᾶς 'we' of the last verse [AB, Alf, Ba, DNTT, EBC, ECWB, EGT, El, Gd, Ho, IB, ICC, LJ, MNTC, My, NCBC, NIC, Rob, TH, We, WeBC; NAB (note), NJB (note), TNT]: in whom you Gentiles also, as well as we Jews.

2. Καὶ ὑμεῖς 'you also' does not contrast Gentiles with Jews, nor even with the ἡμᾶς 'we' of 1:12 but serves to focus on the Ephesians [Cal, CBC, Lns, NTC, WBC]: in whom you (Ephesian believers) as well as all other believers. The Ephesians were included with all Christians in the ἡμᾶς 'we' of the last verse, but now with ὑμεῖς 'you' here, Paul focuses on the Ephesians particularly [NTC]. The ὑμεῖς 'you' here addresses the readers explicitly and draws them into the blessing which is offered by all believers generally as they are reminded of their reception of the gospel [WBC]. The purpose in changing pronouns is not to contrast Jews and Gentiles here, but gradually to prepare them for that contrast which will begin with 2:11 [NTC].

having-heard[a] the word[b] of-the truth,[c] the gospel[d] of-your salvation,[e]

LEXICON—a. aorist act. participle of ἀκούω (LN 31.56): 'to hear' [AB, El, Lns, NIC, Rob, TH, WBC, We; all versions except NASB], 'to listen to' [LN, NTC; NASB].

b. λόγος (LN 33.98, 33.260) (BAGD 1.b.β. p. 478): 'word' [AB, BAGD, El, LN (33.98), Lns, Rob, TH, WBC, We; KJV, NAB, NIV, NRSV], 'message' [LN (33.98), NIC, NTC; NASB, NJB, REB, TEV, TNT], 'the Christian message' [BAGD], 'what is preached, gospel' (focusing on the content of what is preached about Christ—a highly specialized use of the word in the NT) [LN (33.260)].

c. ἀλήθεια (LN 72.2) (BAGD 2.b. p. 36): 'truth' [BAGD, El, LN, Lns, NIC, NTC, Rob, TH, WBC, We; all versions except TEV]. This is also translated as an adjective modifying λόγος 'word': 'true' [AB; TEV].
d. εὐαγγέλιον (LN 33.217) (BAGD 2.b.α. p. 318): 'gospel' [BAGD, El, LN, Lns, NIC, NTC, Rob, We; KJV, NASB, NIV, NJB, NRSV], 'good news' [BAGD, LN, TH, WBC; REB, TEV, TNT], 'glad tidings' [NAB], 'message' [AB].
e. σωτηρία (LN 21.25, 21.26) (BAGD 2. p. 801): 'salvation' [BAGD, El, LN, Lns, NIC, NTC, Rob, TH, WBC, We; all versions]. This noun is also translated as a verb: 'to save' [AB].

QUESTION—What is the relationship between the participle ἀκούσαντες 'having heard' and the other participle and verb in this sentence, πιστεύσαντες 'having believed' and ἐσφραγίσθητε 'were sealed'?

These all list the distinctive events involved in the Gentiles' conversion and incorporation into the people of God [AB, LJ, WeBC]. The two participles precede and modify the main verb ἐσφραγίσθητε 'you were sealed' so that the sealing is the result of the believing and the believing is the result of the hearing [Ba, ECWB, EGT, LJ, Lns, TH]. These participles are important preparations for the statement of Christian privilege that Paul will make in the main verb [EGT]. These three terms may be related in the following manner: you heard...you believed...and then/so you were sealed [El, LJ, TH].

QUESTION—What relationship is indicated by the use of the participial form ἀκούσαντες 'having heard'?

1. This indicates the temporal circumstance of which main verb is supplied with the phrase ἐν ᾧ καὶ ὑμεῖς 'in whom also you' [Alf, EGT, Gd, My, NIC (probably), TH; KJV, NAB, NASB, NIV, NRSV, REB, TEV]: after having heard, or, when you heard the word of truth.
2. This indicates the means by which the Ephesian Gentiles obtained an inheritance [Ho, IB]: you have obtained an inheritance by having heard the word of truth.

QUESTION—How are the two nouns related in the genitive construction τὸν λόγον τῆς ἀληθείας 'the word of truth'?

1. 'Truth' is an attribute of 'word' [AB, Ba, NCBC; TEV]: the true word.
2. 'The truth' is a substantive which refers to the Christian teaching and describes the content or essence of 'the word' and affirms something about it [Alf, Cal, Ea, EBC, EGT, El, Ho, ICC, My, NTC, Rob, TNTC, WBC]: the word which is truth. It does this as though there were no truth but itself [Cal].
3. 'The truth' is a substantive which refers to the Christian teaching and affirms something about it [Gd, Lns, TH]: the word/message concerning the truth. This is the word of an eminent truth [Gd].

QUESTION—How is the phrase τὸ εὐαγγέλιον τῆς σωτηρίας ὑμῶν 'the gospel of your salvation' related to what precedes it?
It is in apposition to the previous phrase, τὸν λόγον τῆς ἀληθείας 'the word of truth' [AB, Ea, EGT, Ho, ICC, LJ, Lns, MNTC, My, NCBC, NIC, NTC, Rob, TH, TNTC, WBC, WeBC] and serves as a restatement that further defines the word of truth [Ea, EGT, Ho, ICC, MNTC, NCBC, NIC, St, TH, TNTC]. The εὐαγγέλιον 'gospel' defines the λόγος 'word' and σωτηρία ὑμῶν 'your salvation' defines ἀλήθεια 'the truth' [Lns].
QUESTION—How are the two nouns related in the genitive construction τὸ εὐαγγέλιον τῆς σωτηρίας 'the gospel of salvation'?
1. 'Salvation' is the subject matter of 'gospel' [Alf, BAGD, Ea, EGT, El, Gd, ICC, Lns, My, TNTC]: the gospel which tells how you are saved.
2. The gospel is defined by its accomplishment of bringing salvation [AB, Ba, Ho, NTC, TH, WBC]: the gospel which saves you.
QUESTION—What does σωτηρία 'salvation' mean?
It means deliverance from bondage to sin and the flesh, spiritual death, and misery [Can, Ea, WBC], deliverance from sin with possession of the Divine image and enjoyment of the Divine favor as an inheritance [Ea], the participation of Gentiles in the messianic salvation [MNTC, My, We], the present privileges of the Christian: the transformation of human life into joyousness and purposefulness [NCBC], the totality of the Divine blessings offered in the gospel [IB].

in whom/which also having-believed[a]
LEXICON—a. aorist act. participle of πιστεύω (LN 31.102) (BAGD 2.a.ε. or 2.b. p. 661): 'to believe' [BAGD, El, Lns, NIC, NTC, Rob, TH, WBC, We; all versions except NJB, TNT], 'to put one's trust in' [NJB], 'to trust' [BAGD], 'to come to faith' [AB], 'to be a believer, to be a Christian' [LN], 'to become believers' [TNT].
QUESTION—To what does ἐν ᾧ 'in whom/which' refer and to what is it connected?
1. It refers to Christ [AB, Alf, Ba, Can, DNTT, Ea, EBC, EGT, El, Gd, HG, Ho, IB, ICC, LJ, Lns, MNTC, Mou, NIC, NTC, Rob, St, TH, TNTC, WBC, We; KJV, NASB, NIV, NRSV, REB, TEV, TNT]. Supporters of this position think that the symmetry of the passage with its ἐν τῷ Χριστῷ 'in Christ' and ἐν αὐτῷ 'in him' phrases, together with the ἐν ᾧ 'in whom' at the beginning of this verse, argue heavily for a similar interpretation for this phrase.
1.1 This phrase connects with ἐσφραγίσθητε 'you were sealed' [AB, Alf, DNTT, EBC, EGT, El, Gd, HG, Ho, ICC, LJ, Lns, MNTC, Mou, NIC, TNTC, We; KJV, NASB, NIV, REB]: in Christ you were sealed with the Holy Spirit, after/when you believed (the gospel). Since both ἐν ᾧ 'in whom' phrases connect with this verb, the second phrase resumes the train of thought begun by the first [EGT, El, ICC, Rob].

1.2 It connects with πιστεύσαντες 'having believed' and indicates the person in whom they believed [Ba, Ea, IB, NTC, Rob, St, TH; NRSV, TEV, TNT]: when/after (you) believed in Christ, you were sealed with the Holy Spirit.
 2. Ἐν ᾧ should be translated 'in which', because it refers to τὸ εὐαγγέλιον 'the gospel', its closest antecedent, and is the object of πιστεύσαντες 'believed' [My, NCBC; NAB, NJB]: when you heard the gospel in which you believed, you were sealed with the Holy Spirit.

QUESTION—What is the function of the second καί 'also' in this verse?
  1. It is ascensive, connecting with πιστεύσαντες 'having believed', and adds to the first condition of ἀκούσαντες 'having heard' the second and higher condition of πιστεύσαντες 'having believed' [EGT, El].
  2. It connects with an implied ὑμεῖς 'you', referring to the Ephesians as Gentiles [Alf]: in whom (you Gentiles) also, having believed were sealed.
  3. It, together with ἐν ᾧ 'in whom' is a formula which Paul used in 1:7 and previously in this verse to introduce a new blessing [LJ]: in whom also (another blessing he has given you) after you believed you were sealed.

QUESTION—What is the relationship of the aorist participle πιστεύσαντες 'having believed' to the verb ἐσφραγίσθητε 'you were sealed'?
  1. The action of the participle precedes that of the finite verb [Alf, Cal, CBC, Ea, EBC, EGT, El, Gd, Ho, LJ, Lns, My; KJV, NASB, NIV, NRSV, REB, TNT]: after you believed you were sealed, or, when you had believed you were sealed.
  2. The action of the participle is coincident with that of the finite verb [Si-ed, WBC]: in whom, as you believed you were sealed.

you-were-sealed[a] with-the Spirit of-the promise[b] the holy (one),
LEXICON—a. aorist pass. indic. of σφραγίζω (LN 33.484) (BAGD 2.b. p. 796): 'to be sealed' [El, LN, Lns, NIC, NTC, Rob, TH, WBC, We; KJV, NAB, NASB], 'to be sealed with (his) seal' [AB], 'to be marked with a seal' [BAGD, LN; NIV, NRSV], 'to be stamped with a seal' [NJB, REB]. This is also translated actively with God as subject: '(God) put on (his) stamp of ownership' [TEV]. It is also translated according to its function: 'to show that you were his, (you received, etc.)' [TNT].
  b. ἐπαγγελία (LN 33.288) (BAGD 2.a. p. 280): 'promise' [El, LN, NIC, Rob, TH, We; KJV, NASB], 'the promise' [BAGD, Lns], 'the Promise' [NJB]. This is also translated as a verbal adjective: 'the promised (Spirit)' [AB, NTC, WBC; NIV, NRSV, REB], 'the promised (gift)' [TNT], and as an active verb with God as subject: 'to promise' [TEV], and as a passive verb with πνεῦμα 'Spirit' as its subject: 'to have been promised' [NAB]. While the act of promising is always relevant, the focus of the word is upon the content of what is promised [LN].

QUESTION—How is the point of comparison applied in this passage?
  1. The comparison is proof of ownership [Can, DNTT, EGT, IB, ISBE, LN (33.484), Lns, MNTC, NCBC, NIC, St, TD, TH; TEV, TNT]: as an owner

puts his mark on his property, so God has put his Spirit within you to mark you as His own. The nonfigurative statement would be: you are shown to belong to God by having the Holy Spirit come to be present with you.

2. The comparison is proof of authenticity [Bu, Cal, Gd, IB, ISBE2, LJ, NTC, Si]: as an official guaranteed the contents of a document by putting his mark on it, so God has shown you to be a genuine child of His by putting His mark on you by the Holy Spirit who is present with you. The nonfigurative statement would be: you are shown to be a genuine child of God by the fact that God has sent His Holy Spirit to be present with you.

3. The comparison is the security of the item so marked [El, My]: as an owner or official secured an item against theft or tampering by putting his seal on it, so God has secured your future by giving you His Holy Spirit to be present with you. The nonfigurative statement would be: you are kept saved by having the Holy Spirit come to be with you.

4. No single comparison is involved in this metaphor [AB, Ea, EBC, ECWB, Ho, Rob, TNTC, WBC, We, WeBC]. All three are involved [AB, EBC, Ho, Rob, TNTC, We]. Only 1 and 3 are involved [Ea, WBC]. The act of sealing was also a means of preserving the object so marked as the owner's property, so that security and protection of the object are also involved [WBC]. Only 2 and 3 are involved [ECWB].

QUESTION—What is the seal?

1. This is a reference to the rite of baptism [CBC, DNTT, IB, Lns, MNTC]: (the Spirit came upon you and) you were sealed (when/after you were baptized). Proponents cite 1 Cor. 6:11, 12:13; 2 Cor. 1:22; and Col. 2:11 as evidence that baptism was called a seal in the NT and later Christian literature, as was the Jewish rite of circumcision (Rom. 4:11). When the believer is baptized, he ratifies his surrender to Christ and in the moment of baptism the Spirit descends onto the believer and so he is sealed with the Spirit. This is a reference to the specific instance of baptism recorded in Acts 19:1–6 and resulting miraculous manifestation of the Spirit to those Ephesian believers [Ba].

2. This is a reference to the Spirit Himself as both the instrument of sealing and the seal itself [BAGD, Ea, EBC, ECWB, HG, IB, Lns, NIC, St, TD, WBC, We, WeBC]: God set the mark of His Spirit upon you. God is seen as the actor in this case, and the Spirit is the instrument of sealing [HG], the seal itself [IB, Lns, WBC]. For some commentators, this took place at baptism [IB, Lns] or was associated with it [WBC].

3. This is a reference to the activity of the Spirit in the life of the believer [AB, Cal, Can, CBC, DNTT, EGT, El, Gd, LJ, My, NCBC, Si, TNTC]: the Spirit marked you (as God's people) by His activity in your lives, or, God marked you as His own by sending His Spirit to work in your lives. The seal is the hope and assurance that the Spirit imparts to our spirits [EGT, El, Gd, My], the moral qualities which the Spirit imparts to believers [Can, NCBC], the ability of the believer, through the Spirit, to worship

and serve God [AB], the confirmation of the faith—a conviction of the truth that allows no doubt [Cal], a sense of God's love for the believer, given to him through God's word [Gd], a direct, overwhelming testimony of the Spirit to the believer of his sonship [LJ].

QUESTION—Is the attestation implied in sealing for the believer's benefit or for others?

1. It is for the believer himself [Cal, CBC (probably), Ea, EGT, Gd, IB, LJ, My, NTC]: God sealed you with his Holy Spirit (so that you might know in yourselves that you are His). Proponents cite such passages as Rom. 8:16 and 1 Jn. 3:24 on the internal witness of the Spirit as support for this interpretation.
2. It is for others [AB, Rob, We]: God sealed you with his Holy Spirit (so that it would be evident to all that you are His). The attestation is the certification of the Gentile converts to the Jews [Rob]. It is a public attestation of the seal in both the secular and religious worlds [AB].
3. It is for both [Alf, Can, Ho, MNTC, Si, TNTC]: God sealed you with his Holy Spirit (so that both you yourselves and others may know that you are His).

QUESTION—What does τῷ πνεύματι τῆς ἐπαγγελίας τῷ ἁγίῳ 'the Holy Spirit of promise' mean?

1. The reference is to the Spirit, whose coming had been promised in Old Testament times [AB, Alf, Ba, Ea, ECWB, EGT, El, Ho, ICC, LJ, MNTC, My, NCBC, NTC, St, TH, WBC, We, WeBC; NAB, NIV, NJB (note), NRSV, REB, TEV]. Thus the Spirit is the object promised, God being the implied actor: the Holy Spirit who had been promised [NAB], the promised Holy Spirit [NIV, NJB (note), NRSV, REB], the Holy Spirit he had promised [TEV]. For some of the above commentators this incorporates Christ's reiteration of this promise in the NT.
2. The reference is to the Spirit as promised by Christ (Luke 24:49) [CBC, Gd]: the Holy Spirit whom Christ promised. It also indicates the means or the instrument the Spirit uses in his act of sealing—he seals by means of promises made particularly real to the individual believers [Gd].
3. In addition to the above, the phrase may also include the idea of the Spirit in a more active role, the One who guarantees the promise or promises relating to the future [EBC, NIC, TNTC]. The Spirit who brings with Him the promise of future glory [NIC].

QUESTION—What is the force of ἅγιος 'holy', which is not in its usual position relative to πνεῦμα 'Spirit'?

Its position in the phrase puts a solemn emphasis on the pronouncement by whom they were sealed [Alf, Ea, ECWB, EGT, El, ICC, My]: even the Holy Spirit Himself or, by none other than the Holy Spirit Himself. Another view is that the emphasis is restricted more to the idea of the holy nature of the Spirit than as applying to the instrument of their sealing [We]. Reference is to the nature of holiness that characterizes the Person of the Spirit himself, the Spirit's personal holiness [BAGD, Can, EGT, El, My, We]. Reference is not only to the personal nature of the Holy Spirit but to the Spirit's role as the Sanctifier [Ea, ECWB, Gd, Lns, NTC], the act of sealing resulting in sanctification of the life [Gd]. The occurrence of the word 'promise' in this phrase carries with it the implication of the gift of holiness for believers promised by God in the OT [Lns, and perhaps the others holding this interpretation].

1:14 which is a-down-payment[a] of-our inheritance,[b]

TEXT—Instead of ὅ 'which' (neuter case), some manuscripts have ὅς 'who' (masculine). The antecedent is πνεῦμα 'Spirit' which is neuter in form, but the predicate following it (ἀρραβών 'earnest') is masculine, and the case of the relative pronoun could have been attracted to it. GNT chooses the neuter form and gives it a B rating, indicating that this form is almost certain. The commentaries AB, Ea, EBC, EGT, El, Gd, ICC, Lns, My, NIC, Si-ed, and WBC support the masculine reading, while only Alf, Rob, and We support the neuter reading.

LEXICON—a. ἀρραβών (LN **57.170**) (BAGD p. 109): 'deposit/down payment' [BAGD, LN], 'pledge' [BAGD, LN, Lns; NASB, NJB, NRSV, REB], 'first installment' [BAGD, **LN**, NTC], 'guarantee' [AB, LN, NIC, TH, WBC; TEV], 'earnest' [El, Rob, We; KJV], 'installment and pledge' [TNT], 'the pledge...the first payment' [NAB], 'a deposit guaranteeing (our inheritance)' [NIV]. It is the first or initial payment of money or other assets which guarantees the completion of a transaction or pledge [LN].

b. κληρονομία (LN 57.132) (BAGD 3. p. 435): 'inheritance' [El, Lns, NIC, NTC, Rob, TH, WBC, We; KJV, NAB, NASB, NIV, NJB, NRSV, REB], 'possession' [LN], 'salvation' [BAGD], 'what we shall inherit' [AB], 'what is yet to be ours' [TNT], '(we shall receive) what God has promised his people' [TEV].

QUESTION—What is the antecedent of ὅ 'who/which'?

All commentaries used agreed that the antecedent is the neuter πνεῦμα 'Spirit'. Some mentioned the fact that some early commentators, perhaps with regard to strict Classical Greek usage [AB], regarded Χριστός 'Christ' as the antecedent [AB, Ea, El, Gd] (this is also postulated as a reason for the neuter pronoun reading—that it arose as an effort to correct the wrong exegesis of the passage [AB]). But its function as a comment on the last part of the previous verse, as well as the fact that ἀρραβών 'down payment' elsewhere in the NT (parallel passages to this verse) is only used of the Spirit, argues conclusively for πνεῦμα 'Spirit' as antecedent here [AB, DNTT].

QUESTION—What does ἀρραβών 'down payment' mean?

It is a payment by which a person guarantees further payment to the recipient, so that it implies an act which binds the payer to something bigger [AB, Alf, BAGD, Cal, CBC, DNTT, Ea, EBC, ECWB, EGT, Gd, Ho, IB, IDB, ISBE, LJ, LN (**57.170**), Lns, Lt, MM, My, NCBC, NIC, NTC, Rob, Si, St, TD, TH, TNTC, WBC, We]. Almost all the commentators prefer terms such

EPHESIANS 1:14 59

as 'deposit', 'earnest' or 'down payment' as a translation of this word in preference to 'pledge' (which often implies something greater in value given as security for something contracted for which is of lesser value than the pledge [AB]). Some of them point out or imply that it denotes a payment of like kind or quality to what is guaranteed in full later [Bu, Can, Ea, EGT, Gd, Ho, IB, ICC, ISBE, LJ, Lt, MM, NCBC, NTC, Rob, Si, St, TNTC, WBC], so that it is a part of what is to be given in due time. The comparison is: as a partial payment is an earnest or down payment guaranteeing the complete payment of what is promised, so God gives his Spirit to his children as a guarantee that they will receive the full salvation he has promised to them. The point of comparison is the part given as a guarantee of complete fulfillment of what one has promised to give later. The nonfigurative statement is: The fact that the Holy Spirit lives in you/is with you proves conclusively that God will complete his promise to you.

QUESTION—What is meant by κληρονομία 'inheritance'?

The commentators differ in their wording of what the inheritance is here, but not necessarily in the essential concept. Descriptions given are: full and complete participation of life in God's Holy Spirit in our final state [Gd, ICC, MNTC, NCBC, St; NJB (note)], our full salvation or emancipation later to come [BAGD, Can, Ea, Ho, IB, LJ, Lns, NTC, Rob, TD, TH, WBC; NAB], our future life in heaven [Ea, EBC, EGT, Gd, Lns, NCBC], full enjoyment of fellowship with God in the eternal world [MNTC], messianic blessedness [My, TH], immortality [IDB, NIC], everything encompassed in the promise of the Kingdom of God [CBC, DNTT, ECWB, El], our ultimate glory [Can, NTC]. The comparison for this metaphor of inheritance is: as sons ultimately inherit the property of their father, so God has promised His children a heritage. The nonfigurative statement would be: you will receive the full salvation God has promised to you.

until/for[a] (the) redemption[b] of-the possession,[c]

LEXICON— a. εἰς with accusative object (LN 89.57): 'until' [NIC; KJV, NIV], 'unto' [Rob, We], 'toward' [NRSV], 'when' [REB, TNT], 'for' [BAGD, El, Lns, NTC, TH; NJB], 'for the purpose of, in order to' [LN], 'with a view to' [NASB], 'against' [NAB]. This is also translated as an active verb: 'to vouch for' [AB, WBC]; as a dependent clause to indicate purpose: 'and this assures (us) that' [TEV].

b. ἀπολύτρωσις (LN 37.128) (BAGD 2.a. p. 96): 'redemption' [BAGD, El, NIC, NTC, Rob, TH, WBC, We; KJV, NASB, NIV, NRSV], 'the full redemption' [NAB], 'the state of being redeemed' [BAGD], 'liberation' [AB, LN], 'deliverance' [LN], 'freedom' [NJB]. This is also translated as a verb: 'to redeem' [REB], 'to fully redeem' [TNT], 'to ransom' [Lns], 'to give complete freedom' [TEV].

c. περιποίησις (LN 57.62) (BAGD 3. p. 650): 'possession' [BAGD, LN, Lns, TH], 'property' [BAGD, LN], 'purchased possession' [El; KJV], 'ownership' [MM], 'God's possession' [NIC], 'his [God's] possession'

[WBC], 'God's own possession' [NTC, Rob, We; NASB], 'those who are God's possession' [NIV], 'what is his own' [REB], 'those who are his' [TEV], 'God's own people' [AB; NRSV], 'those whom he has made his own' [TNT], 'a people God has made his own' [NAB], 'people whom God has taken for his own' [NJB]. The word stands for that which has been acquired, presumably, with considerable effort [Gd, LN].

QUESTION—What relationship is indicated by εἰς 'until/for'?

1. This preposition is temporal in force and connects this phrase to the immediately preceding one [Ba, Cal, DNTT, Ea, Gd, LJ, NCBC, TNTC, Tu; KJV, REB, TNT].

1.1 It means 'until' [Ba, Cal, DNTT, Ea, Gd, LJ, NCBC, TNTC, Tu; KJV]: the Spirit is the down payment or earnest of our inheritance until the redemption (is completed). Understood in this way, 'until' does not imply that the Spirit will be withdrawn at the completion of the redemption, as no longer needed, but rather that the believer's present enjoyment of Him, in only a measure now as the earnest or down payment, will be absorbed into the fullness of the future inheritance [Ea, Gd].

1.2 It means 'when' [REB, TNT]: The Spirit is the down payment of our inheritance (which we will yet receive) when God fully redeems (His own).

2. This preposition indicates the purpose, either of the immediately preceding phrase or of the main verb ἐσφραγίσθητε 'you were sealed' in the previous verse [AB, Alf, BAGD, EGT, El, Ho, IB, ICC, Lns, MNTC, My, NIC, NTC, Rob, TH, WBC, We; NAB, NASB, NIV, NJB, NRSV, TEV].

2.1 It indicates the purpose for which the Holy Spirit is a down payment [AB, ICC, NTC, WBC, We; NAB, NASB, NIV, NRSV, TEV]: The Holy Spirit is the down payment of our inheritance for/with a view toward/vouching for our (complete) redemption.

2.2 It indicates the purpose for which we were sealed with the Holy Spirit [Alf, BAGD, EGT, El, Ho, Lns, MNTC, My, Rob, TH]: God sealed us with the Holy Spirit for/with a view toward our (complete) redemption.

QUESTION—What does ἀπολύτρωσις 'redemption' mean?

For the meaning of the word and the metaphor involved, see the treatment of this word in 1:7. Nevertheless, there is a difference between the usage in that verse and its occurrence here. Here, according to all the commentaries used, the focus of the word is upon the redemption of the believer in its final, completed stage. Only a few commentators see any implication in this passage of the price paid for this redemption [Gd, Ho, LJ, Lns]. On the other hand, some think that it is impossible to attach any idea of a ransom paid to the word in eschatological passages, of which this is one, since the concept is beyond the view of these passages [TD, and less explicitly Rob]. One commentator objects to translations such as 'to obtain' or 'to acquire' on the grounds that they are inadequate, since ἀπολύτρωσις 'redemption' implies that what is now possessed had previously been lost [MNTC].

QUESTION—How are the two nouns related in the genitive construction ἀπολύτρωσιν τῆς περιποιήσεως 'redemption of the possession'?
1. 'The possession' means 'our possession' and this genitive is epexegetical, explaining what redemption consists of [Ba, DNTT, ICC, LJ, MNTC, NCBC, TD]: the redemption that consists of taking possession of our inheritance [TD].
2. 'The possession' refers to 'God's possession' and this is the object of the event word ἀπολύτρωσιν 'redemption' [AB, Alf, BAGD, Cal, Can, Ea, ECWB, EGT, El, Ho, IB, ISBE, Lns, MM, My, NIC, NTC, Rob, St, TH, TNTC, WBC, We; KJV, NAB, NASB, NIV, NJB, NRSV, REB, TEV, TNT]: redemption of God's possession.

to (the) praise of-his glory.
LEXICON—See this identical phrase in 1:12.
QUESTION—What relationship is indicated by εἰς 'to'?
Though grammatically connected with either ἐσφραγίσθητε 'you were sealed' or ὅ ἐστιν ἀρραβὼν τῆς κληρονομίας ἡμῶν 'who is a down payment of our inheritance', a number of commentaries remark that this phrase shows the purpose of the whole preceding passage, presumably from 1:3 onwards—that all things are to work out for God's praise [Ho, LJ, NCBC, TH, We]. Others see it as concluding the third section of this paragraph, each repetition of this phrase (1:6 and 1:12) marking the end of a stage in Paul's development of this paragraph [Ea, EGT, El, Gd, IB, Lns, My, St, TNTC]. Another sees it as only loosely connected with what has preceded in this verse, but suggests that in completing the process of redemption, God's glory is praised and that the prospect of such a completion of his purposes should call forth a response of praise from his creatures now [WBC]. Others think the first phrase in this verse (εἰς ἀπολύτρωσις 'for redemption') indicates the final goal on man's side, while this one indicates the final goal on God's side [EGT, El, Lns].

DISCOURSE UNIT: 1:15–2:22 [AB, We]. The topic is God's perfect work in salvation.

DISCOURSE UNIT: 1:15–2:10 [Can, IB, Rob]. The topic is thanksgiving for the faith of Paul's readers and his prayer that their enlightenment might continue to increase [Can].

DISCOURSE UNIT: 1:15–23 [AB, Alf, Ba, CBC, Ea, EBC, ECWB, EGT, Ho, LJ, Lns, MNTC, NCBC, NIC, NTC, Rob, St, TNTC, WBC, WeBC; NAB, NASB, NIV, NJB, REB, TEV]. The topic is prayer, but some focus on a certain aspect of the prayer: thanksgiving [NIC, NTC, WBC], a request for knowledge or understanding of the plan of redemption [Alf, Ba, ECWB, Lns, St, TNTC]. Having praised God for having blessed them in Christ (1:3–14), he now prays that God will open their eyes to understand the fullness of this blessing [St].

62   EPHESIANS 1:15

DISCOURSE UNIT: 1:15–19 [CBC, ICC, MNTC, My, NIC, Rob]. The topic is prayer for deeper knowledge [CBC, ICC, MNTC] and thanksgiving and prayer [My, NIC, Rob].

1:15 Because of this,^a I-myself/I-also,^b

LEXICON—a. διὰ τοῦτο: 'because of this' [Lns], 'because of all this' [REB], 'for this reason' [NTC, TH, WBC; NASB, NIV, NRSV, TEV], 'for that reason' [BAGD], 'for this cause' [El, We], 'that is why' [NJB], 'this is why' [TNT], 'therefore' [AB, NIC] 'wherefore' [Rob; KJV], not explicit [NAB].

b. κἀγώ: 'I also' [El, Rob, We; KJV], 'I, too' [Lns, TH; NASB], 'I, for my part' [AB, NIC; NAB], 'I' [BAGD, NTC; NIV, NJB, NRSV, REB, TEV, TNT], conflated with inflected subject of παύομαι 'to cease' in 1:16: 'I' [WBC]. This is the emphatic first person pronoun [WBC].

QUESTION—What relationship is indicated by διὰ τοῦτο 'because of this'?

1. Διὰ τοῦτο 'because of this' refers backwards [Alf, Ea, EBC, EGT, El, Gd, Ho, ICC, LJ, Lns, My, NCBC, NTC, Rob, Si, St, TH, TNTC, WBC, We; NJB, REB]. The following participial phrase is then probably to be taken as a secondary reason or as the temporal circumstance, the occasion, in which he gives thanks. Even if the participial phrase is taken to be temporal, it is implied that it is also a cause.

   1.1 It indicates the result of the whole previous paragraph, 1:3–14 [Gd, ICC, LJ, Lns, NTC, Rob, Si, TH, TNTC; REB]: because of all this, therefore, since hearing of your faith and love, I do not cease to thank God for you [TH; REB]; or, because this salvation is so wonderful, and because I heard of your faith and love, I do not cease to thank God for you. Paul's gratitude is called forth both by the blessings God has bestowed in salvation and the report he has received of these believers' faith and love [NTC], in short, by what God has done for the readers in the salvation he has wrought [TH].

   1.2 It primarily indicates the result of 1:13–14 [Alf, Ea, EBC, EGT, El, Ho, My, NCBC, St, WBC, We]: because you too have heard, believed, and been sealed, therefore, after/because I heard of your faith and love, I do not cease to thank God for you. While the phrase διὰ τοῦτο 'because of this' probably points back to the whole of 1:3–14, more particularly it provides a link with 1:13–14 where the writer has drawn the readers into his blessing of God as he focused on their experience of the gospel [WBC]. The rationale for this interpretation is that thanksgiving and intercession really have reference to the readers (the 'you' of 1:13, 16), and it is at 1:13 where this shift is made [Ea, EGT, El, My].

2. It primarily refers forward to the following clause, making it the cause for the giving of thanks in 1:16 [Cal, MNTC; NAB (probably), NRSV]: Because of this, namely, that I have heard of your faith and love, I never cease giving thanks. If there is any connection to the preceding material it is only as a loose transitional device to material that is to follow, so there

is no strong reference back to the previous section [MNTC]. As in 1 above, this interpretation may also imply a temporal element in the following participial clause [NAB]: since/from the time I heard, I have never stopped giving thanks.

QUESTION—What is the significance of using κἀγώ 'I myself/ I also' instead of the normal ἐγώ 'I'?

1. This is only a transitional device used to shift from 'you' to the first person pronoun 'I' [AB, Alf, Ea, EGT, ICC, MNTC, NCBC, NIC, TNTC; NAB, NIV, NJB, NRSV, REB, TEV, TNT]: that happened to you and I, for my part, give thanks for you; or, you did that (believed in the Lord) and I give thanks for you. It either resumes the first person after the second, going back to ἐκληρώθημεν 'we were made his inheritance' (1:11), or it corresponds to the preceding καὶ ὑμεῖς 'and you' (1:13) [Alf]. It is preferable to take it as corresponding to καὶ ὑμεῖς 'and you' [EGT, El]. The term hints at the union in prayer and praise which existed between the Apostle and his converts [El].
2. This implies that other people besides Paul, either third parties or these readers or both, are giving thanks for the faith of Paul's readers [Ho, Lns, My, We]: you (and perhaps others) thank God for your faith, and I join you in doing so. One commentator also sees an implied contrast between Paul, who as a Jew might have been expected to be jealous for his people's peculiar privileges, and his Gentile readers [We].
3. It is used to focus upon the apostolic authority behind the epistle [WBC]: I, Paul the Apostle.

having-heard[a] the according-to[b] you faith/faithfulness[c] in the Lord Jesus

LEXICON—a. aorist act. participle of ἀκούω (LN 33.212) (BAGD 3.b. p. 32): 'to hear' [AB, El, LN, Lns, NIC, NTC, Rob, TH, WBC, We; all versions], 'to receive news' [LN], 'to learn about' [BAGD].

b. κατά with accusative object (LN 89.8) (BAGD II.7.b. p. 408): 'in accordance with' [LN]. Most combine this preposition with the accusative pronoun ὑμᾶς 'you' and translate this as a possessive pronoun 'your' [BAGD, Lns, NIC, Rob, TH, WBC; KJV, NAB, NIV, NJB, NRSV, REB, TEV]. It is also translated as a verb phrase: 'you have' [TNT], 'shown among you' [AB], or as a relative clause: 'which is/exists among you' [El, NTC, We; NASB].

c. πίστις (LN 31.102) (BAGD 2.b.β. p. 663): 'faith' [BAGD, El, LN, Lns, NIC, NTC, Rob, TH, WBC, We; all versions], 'faithfulness' [AB].

QUESTION—What does ἀκούσας 'having heard' imply about the writer's previous personal contact with these readers?

1. The writer had never previously had any personal contact with them [AB, CBC, IB, ICC, MNTC, NCBC, NIC, Rob, St, TH, TNTC, WBC; NJB], and this is usually cited as proof that Ephesians was either not written by Paul, or that it was not originally written just to the Ephesian congregation, or it addressed only the Gentile element of the Ephesian congrega-

tion who had been converted since Paul left them. In this case, it can be taken to mean that Paul was referring to their conversion [EGT (although supporting the next interpretation)].
2. It only implies the passage of some time since Paul's last contact with them [Alf, Ba, Can, Ea, EBC, EGT, El, Gd, Ho, LJ, Lns, My, NTC, Si]. In this case Paul's having heard of their faith would presumably mean their continued growth in faith.

QUESTION—What is the significance in the use of κατὰ ὑμᾶς 'according to you' instead of the more common ὑμῶν 'your'?
1. This is simply another way of expressing the possessive genitive 'your' and no difference in meaning is intended [BAGD, BD, Cal, CBC, EGT, ICC, My, NIC, Rob, TH, WBC; all versions except NASB, TNT]: having heard of your faith.
2. This form is used to denote the faith of the congregation in an objective manner and with a partitive or distributive sense [AB, Alf, Can, Ea, El, Gd, IB, LJ, Lns, MNTC, NTC, We; NASB, TNT] as opposed to the use of the simple possessive genitive which would have expressed the subjective faith of the individuals [El]: having heard of the faith that exists among you, or, that dwells among you, or, that you have. This form also carries a certain amount of emphasis [Alf, Ea], intensifying the following prayer [Alf].

QUESTION—What is meant by πίστις 'faith/faithfulness'?
1. This refers to the active sense of putting trust or confidence in the Lord [Alf, BAGD, Cal, Ea, ECWB, EGT, El, Gd, Ho, IB, ICC, LJ, Lns, My, NIC, NTC, Rob, Si, St, TH, TNTC, WBC, We, WeBC; all versions]: having heard of your faith in the Lord Jesus, or, having heard of the faith in the Lord Jesus that exists among you. Reference is to constancy in faith rather than to their initial experience of it. The element of the eminency and renown of their faith is also implied [Gd].
2. This refers to the quality of faithfulness, loyalty, or fidelity shown by these saints [AB, CBC, MNTC]: your faithfulness, or the faithfulness that is shown or exists among you. These commentators reject the reading containing τὴν ἀγάπην 'the love' in the following clause. This then makes εἰς πάντας τοὺς ἁγίους 'to all the saints' a second object of πίστις 'faith/faithfulness'. Since πίστις is never linked to ἅγιοι 'saints' in Pauline literature with the meaning of 'faith', it must be taken as 'faithfulness' here [AB, MNTC].
3. Both meanings are present depending upon which of its two objects is considered [Can, TNTC]: having heard that you believe in Christ Jesus and are faithful to the saints. This interprets the article following καὶ 'and/even' as resumptive (if τὴν ἀγάπην 'the love' is rejected as spurious) and thus constituting a second occurrence of πίστις, but with the meaning this time of 'faithfulness'. This is consistent with the fact that Paul sometimes passes from one meaning of the word into the other as seen, for example, in Rom. 3:3 and 1 Thess. 3:2–3 [Can].

QUESTION—What is the meaning of the preposition ἐν 'in' in the phrase ἐν τῷ κυρίῳ Ἰησοῦ 'in the Lord Jesus'?

Most of the commentaries and at least one translation take this in the sense of the grounds or sphere of faith [Ea, Ho, IB, ICC, Lns, MNTC, Mo, My, NIC, TNTC, Tu, WBC, We; TNT] as opposed to the far more common use of πίστις 'faith' with εἰς 'to/toward/into' denoting motion toward something [AB, ICC, MNTC, My, NIC, We]. These commentaries use terms such as 'to lay immovable in' [Ea], 'to rest in' [IB, ICC, My], 'to be grounded in' [Ho], 'to be rooted in' [MNTC], or 'to be grounded and resting in' [We] to express its force. It indicates both the sphere and object of 'faith' [El]. Another view is to take it in a directional sense: 'faithfulness shown to the Lord Jesus' [AB, TH].

QUESTION—Why does Paul use the title κυρίῳ Ἰησοῦ 'Lord Jesus' here, as opposed to Χριστῷ Ἰησοῦ 'Christ Jesus' which he uses in the parallel Col. 1:4?

Only three commentators focus attention on this [Ho, LJ, Lns]. One calls attention to the OT use of κύριος 'Lord' as referring to the Supreme God and feels that with the reference here to Jesus being the object and ground of faith, His deity is in view [Ho]. Another seems to agree, adding that κύριος 'Lord' is soteriological here, and that Ἰησοῦς 'Jesus' was the name he bore on earth. He sees both the heavenly and earthly aspects of Christ's work implied here [Lns].

and the love[a], the (love) towards[b] all the saints[c]

TEXT—Some manuscripts omit τὴν ἀγάπην 'the love' from the text. GNT includes it with a B rating, indicating that the text is almost certain. Most commentaries and translations accept it. It is omitted by Can, IB, MNTC, TNTC, and We.

LEXICON—a. ἀγάπη (LN 25.43) (BAGD I.1.b.β. p. 5): 'love' [AB, BAGD, El, LN, Lns, NIC, NTC, Rob, TH, WBC, We; all versions], 'loving concern' [LN]. See this word at 1:4.

b. εἰς with accusative object (LN 90.41): 'towards' [AB; REB], 'toward' [NIC; NRSV], 'unto' [El, Rob, We; KJV], 'for' [LN, Lns, NTC, TH, WBC; NAB, NASB, NIV, NJB, TEV, TNT].

c. ἅγιος (LN 11.27): 'holy'. The plural is translated as a substantive: 'saints' [AB, El, Lns, NIC, NTC, Rob, TH, WBC, We; KJV, NASB, NIV, NRSV], 'God's people' [LN; REB, TEV, TNT], 'God's holy people' [NJB], 'members of the church' [NAB].

QUESTION—What is the function of the article following τὴν ἀγάπην 'the love'?

Assuming τὴν ἀγάπην 'the love' belongs in the original text, the construction τὴν ἀγάπην τήν 'the love the' serves to carry two movements of thought. First, the quality of love is stated generally, then this second article further defines, and restricts [AB, Alf] love by the quality that is its true Christian characteristic: love for God's people [Ea, El, My], as opposed to love for mankind in general (philanthropy) [AB, Alf, Ho]. Thus the construction does not have the same unity of thought given in the parallel phrase in which πίστις 'faith' occurs [Alf, Ea, El, My]. One commentator believes this construction was used because of the change in prepositions, from ἐν 'in' to εἰς 'towards' [Ea]. The relationship expressed by εἰς (towards all the saints) is not altogether parallel to [IB], nor as intimate as that expressed by ἐν ('in' the Lord), 'faith' having had a better understood foundation [Ea] and begetting 'love' [Ea, EBC, Lns, St]. Assuming τὴν ἀγάπην 'the love' is a later interpolation, then this second article refers back to πίστιν 'faith' and is resumptive of it [Can].

QUESTION—What is the nature of this love?

This word does not denote a warm feeling of affection in its NT usage. Rather it is an attitude of practical concern for the welfare of another person [CBC, NCBC, WBC]. Because it is an attitude of will, it can be commanded as a Christian duty [NCBC].

1:16 I-do-not-cease[a] giving-thanks[b] for[c] you

LEXICON—a. pres. mid. indic. of παύω (παύομαι LN 68.34) (BAGD 2. p. 638): 'to cease' [AB, BAGD, El, LN, Lns, NIC, NTC, Rob, WBC, We; KJV, NASB, NRSV, REB], 'to stop' [TH; NAB, NIV, TEV, TNT], 'to stop (oneself)' [BAGD, LN], 'to fail' [NJB].

b. pres. act. participle of εὐχαριστέω (LN 33.349) (BAGD 2. p. 328): 'to give thanks' [AB, BAGD, El, Lns, NIC, NTC, Rob, TH, WBC, We; KJV, NASB, NIV, NRSV, REB, TEV, TNT], 'to thank' [LN; NAB, NJB]. The focus of the domain in which this usage occurs is upon the communication of an attitude of thankfulness, not upon the attitude itself [LN].

c. ὑπέρ with genitive object (LN 90.24, 89.28): 'for' [AB, El, LN, Lns, NIC, NTC, Rob, TH, WBC, We; all versions], 'concerning' [LN (90.24)], 'because of' [LN (89.28)].

QUESTION—How does this clause connect with the previous material?

This clause contains the principal verb of the sentence and connects to 1:3–14 through the διὰ τοῦτο 'because of this' in 1:15 [Can, Gd].

QUESTION—To what does οὐ παύομαι 'I cease not' connect in the following material?

1. This connects primarily with the participle εὐχαριστῶν 'giving thanks' [AB, Can, Ea, EBC, EGT, Ho, LJ, Lns, MNTC, My, NTC, Rob, St, TH, TNTC, WBC, We; all versions]: I do not cease giving thanks as I (constantly) make mention of you in my prayers. Εὐχαριστῶν 'giving thanks' is the nearest of the two participles and one commentator states that it is more natural to take it with this one [EGT]. Since most commentaries regard μνείαν ποιούμενος 'making mention' as an extension or further direction of εὐχαριστῶν 'giving thanks' (see below), its connection to οὐ παύομαι 'I cease not' is through the first participle. However, three translations seem to stop short of connecting it with μνείαν

ποιούμενος 'making mention' by placing a period after εὐχαριστῶν ὑπὲρ ὑμῶν 'giving thanks for you' [AB; TEV, TNT].

2. This connects primarily with the participial clause μνείαν ποιούμενος 'making mention' [ICC]: in giving thanks I do not cease mentioning you in my prayers. The following ἵνα 'that' clause, which gives the content of Paul's prayer for them, requires μνείαν ποιούμενος 'making mention' to be the principal thought, and therefore οὐ παύομαι 'I cease not' goes with it [ICC].

QUESTION—What is the force of the negativized verb οὐ παύομαι 'I cease not'?

One commentator regards this negation of a negative verb as litotes [TH], which may serve to emphasize the corresponding affirmative idea: I always give thanks, or I constantly give thanks. Another says it is a popular form of hyperbole [My]. The writer does not claim to have given over the whole of his life to thanksgiving but that, in his regular prayer times, he does not forget to give thanks for those to whom he is writing [WBC].

QUESTION—What is the semantic relationship between the participle εὐχαριστῶν 'giving thanks' and the following participial clause μνείαν ποιούμενος 'making mention'?

Most commentators regard the participial clause as the direction the thanksgiving takes [El, Lns, My, We], i.e., it is the mode of the thanksgiving [AB]. One also regards it as a bridge which joins the thanksgiving to the intercession, the content of which is in the following verses [My]. Thus εὐχαριστῶν 'giving thanks' and μνείαν ποιούμενος 'making mention' are not fully synonymous. The first participle blends into the second, so that the thanksgiving ends in prayer. Paul thanks God for what they have enjoyed and asks that they might be given more to enjoy [Ea, NCBC].

making mention/remembrance[a] in my prayers,[b]

LEXICON—a. μνεία (LN 29.18) (BAGD 2. p. 524): 'mention' [BAGD, El, Lns, NTC, Rob, TH, We; KJV, NASB]. This noun is also translated as a verb: 'to remember and mention, to remember to mention' [LN]. This noun is also conflated with the participle ποιούμενος 'making' and translated as a single verb: 'to mention' [AB, NIC; REB], 'to recommend' [NAB], 'to remember' [WBC; NIV, NJB, NRSV, TEV, TNT]. The meaning not only involves remembering, but mentioning a person in prayer. However, it is possible that the prayer would be inaudible [LN].

b. προσευχή (LN 33.178) (BAGD 1. p. 713): 'prayer' [AB, BAGD, El, LN, Lns, NIC, NTC, Rob, TH, WBC, We; all versions].

QUESTION—What relationship is indicated by the use of the participle ποιούμενος 'making'?

1. This participle indicates a circumstance of the previous clause [EGT, Lns, MNTC, My, NTC, TH; NASB, NRSV, REB]: I do not cease giving thanks for you while mentioning you in my prayers.

2. The participle is coordinate with the preceding participle [NJB]: I do not cease giving thanks for you and I do not cease mentioning you in my prayers.
3. The preceding participle εὐχαριστῶν 'giving thanks' gives the circumstance of this participle, and this participle is the complement of the verb 'to cease' [ICC, Tu]: I do not cease, while giving thanks for you, to mention you in my prayers.
4. This participle indicates a temporal circumstance of a following implied verb 'to ask', the contents of which are given in the following ἵνα 'that' clause [AB, Mo, MT, We]: I do not cease giving thanks for you. When mentioning you in my prayers, (I ask) that the God of our Lord Jesus Christ.

QUESTION—What is meant by μνεία 'mention/remembrance'?
1. This means 'mention' [AB, Alf, DNTT, Ds, Ea, EBC, EGT, El, Gd, IB, Lns, MNTC, My, NIC, NTC, Rob, TD, TH, TNTC, WBC; KJV, NAB, NASB, REB]. The writer is indicating that he makes use of what he knows about his readers and their situation to intercede for them [WBC].
2. This means 'recommend' [NAB].
3. this means 'to ask' [IB]. The word includes the idea of intercession and the following clause requires this meaning [IB].
4. This means 'remembrance' [NCBC; NIV, NJB, NRSV, TEV, TNT].

QUESTION—What is the topic of μνεία 'mention/remembrance'?
This must be supplied from the context and is either 'you' [AB, Ba, Can, Ea, EBC, Gd, Lns, NIC, NTC, Rob, St, TH, WBC] or 'your faith and love' [Alf, NCBC], or both [My, We].

1:17 that^a the God of-our Lord Jesus Christ, the Father of-glory,^b

LEXICON—a. ἵνα (LN 91.15) (BAGD I.4. and II.1.a.γ. p. 377): 'that' [AB, El, LN, Lns, NTC, Rob, TH, WBC, We; KJV, NASB, NIV, NRSV, REB], 'namely that/that is' [LN]. Some do not specify this particle but translate by beginning a new sentence here without a relational verb [NIC; NAB, NJB]: 'May the God of…', or supplying a conjunction 'and' with an implied verb: 'and ask' [TEV, TNT].
b. δόξα (LN 87.23): 'glory' [El, LN, Lns, NTC, Rob, TH, WBC, We; KJV, NAB, NASB, NJB, NRSV], 'greatness' [LN]. This noun is also translated as an adjective: 'glorious' [NIV, TEV, TNT], 'all-glorious' [AB, NIC; REB].

QUESTION—What relationship is indicated by ἵνα 'that'?
1. It indicates the content of the preceding verb μνείαν ποιούμενος 'making mention' [IB, ICC, Lns, NIC, Rob]: I do not cease to mention that, etc.
2. It indicates the content of the prayer and implies a verb such as 'I ask' or 'I pray' [AB, BAGD, El, Gd, Mo, MT, NTC, TH, WBC; NIV, NRSV, REB, TEV, TNT]: I remember you in my prayers and I ask that, etc. After verbs of entreaty, ἵνα 'that' may cause the subject of the prayer to become

more prominent than the purpose for making it. The presence of the optative δῴη 'may give' later in the verse which occurs in conjunction with the present tense verb construction of 1:16, supports this interpretation [El].
3. It indicates the purpose of mentioning them [Alf, Ea, EBC, EGT, HG, My]: I do not cease to mention you in order that, etc. Disclosure of the purpose of a prayer automatically implies its content or purport [Alf, Ea].

QUESTION—Why does Paul insert the descriptive phrase ὁ θεὸς τοῦ κυρίου ἡμῶν Ἰησοῦ Χριστοῦ 'the God of our Lord Jesus Christ'?

This title is the NT equivalent of the old Jewish titles 'the God of Abraham, Isaac, and Jacob', 'the God of our fathers', 'the God of Israel', etc. [DNTT, Gd, LJ, TD]. As such, it is a title belonging to the New Covenant which Jesus instituted [Cal, DNTT, Gd, LJ].

QUESTION—What is the relationship between the nouns in the genitive construction ὁ πατὴρ τῆς δόξης 'the Father of glory'?

Several different relationships are reflected among the commentators with some expressing no clear-cut preference for a single choice, so that the following interpretations shade into one another to some extent.
1. Δόξα 'glory' functions as an adjective to πατήρ 'father' [AB, Ba, Can, Ea, EBC, EGT, El, Ho, LJ, MNTC, NCBC, NIC, NTC, TH; NIV, REB, TEV, TNT].
  1.1 Δόξα 'glory' functions as an attributive adjective modifying πατήρ 'father' [AB, Ba, EBC, LJ, MNTC, NCBC, NIC, NTC, TH; NIV, REB, TEV, TNT]: the glorious Father, or, the wonderful Father.
  1.2 Δόξα 'glory' has an adjectival function to πατήρ 'father' but should not be regarded as merely attributive [Ea, EGT, El, Ho, WBC]: the Father who is glorious. Proponents of this interpretation believe a rendering such as 'glorious father' is vague and inadequate, preferring more prominence be given to δόξα 'glory' [EGT, WBC]. To these 'glory' is the characteristic quality of the Father [Ea, EGT, El, WBC].
2. Πατήρ 'father' is the possessor of δόξα 'glory' [EGT, Ho, ICC, Lns, My, TNTC]: the Father to whom glory belongs.
3. Πατήρ 'father' is the source of δόξα 'glory' with the implication that it may be communicated to or given to men [AB, Alf, Can, Gd, LJ, We]: the Father from whom all glory (or revelation) comes, or, the Father who gives glory.

QUESTION—What is the meaning of δόξα 'glory' here?

The commentaries offer a wide range of possible meanings of this word, which are more complementary than mutually exclusive. It denotes God as worthy to be praised and honored [Ba, Ea, EGT], having specific reference to the glory mentioned in the preceding paragraph [Ea, EGT, El, LJ, NTC] as revealed in his works of election, foreordination, redemption, spiritual illumination, and certification [NTC]. It denotes God as the possessor or source of all true glory [ICC, LJ, NIC, Si, TNTC, We], and can be understood to refer to his essential nature, as the summation of all the excellencies, perfections and attributes of God [Alf, EBC, Gd, IB, ISBE, LJ, Lns, MNTC, NTC, TNTC, We], as well as to all his works, creation, providence, and redemption, which are a manifestation of that glory [LJ, TNTC], especially his acts of mercy [EBC]. It frequently [DNTT] or always [TH] implies some visible manifestation of God's power to save [DNTT, EBC, TH]. It denotes the glory which God will finally bestow on men [Alf, Can, Gd, ISBE, LJ]. Δόξα 'glory' has behind it the OT notion of 'weight', or 'glory', the mode of God's being and activity. It denotes the splendor of his divine presence and power. It is also linked with the notion of enlightenment in the next verse, being the power to enlighten. In Pauline literature it is synonymous with 'power' in terms of God's activity [WBC].

may-he-give[a] you a-Spirit/spirit[b] of-wisdom[c] and of-revelation[d]

TEXT—Some difference of opinion exists whether the text here should be amended from δῴη (aorist optative) to read δώῃ (aorist subjunctive). Though no extant manuscripts actually have this particular form of the subjunctive, an alternative subjunctive form does occur in two texts of the Egyptian text type, Codex Vaticanus (B) and the cursive 1739 (EGT lists the cursive 63 as also containing the subjunctive variant).

1. Accept the predominant text form δῴη and regard it as truly optative [Alf, Ea, EBC, EGT, El, HG, Lns, My, Rob]: perhaps he will give you. One commentator feels the optative construction with ἵνα 'that' is used to express a previous desire of Paul's (i.e. Paul's desire did not begin at the point of his writing this) [Alf, Ea] and the optative does not imply any doubt in Paul's mind that his petition will be granted [Ea], but other proponents fail to support this position. Proponents say this is a volative optative expressing a wish for the future [Ea, EBC, HG, Lns, My, Rob] or a hoped-for realization [El].
2. Accept the dominant form δῴη but regard it as functioning as a subjunctive [AB, BD, ICC]: that he may give you. The optative δῴη and subjunctive δώῃ were identical in pronunciation in early Christian times and early copyists could easily have written the optative form since it was often used after ἵνα 'that' to function as a subjunctive [BD].
3. Amend the text to read the subjunctive form δώῃ [BAGD, Mou, MT, Tu], since Greek writers of the early Christian period often used the optative form (δῴη) with ἵνα to express the subjunctive function anyway [Mou, MT, Tu]: that he may give you.

LEXICON—a. aorist act. optative of δίδωμι (LN 57.71) (BAGD p. 192): 'to give' [AB, El, LN, Lns, NIC, NTC, Rob, TH, WBC, We; all versions except NAB, REB], 'to grant' [NAB], 'to confer on (you)' [REB]. The optative verb expresses a conditional, hoped-for realization of the petition [El].

b. πνεῦμα (LN 12.18, 30.6) (BAGD 5.e. p. 677): 'Spirit' [AB, BAGD, El, LN (12.18), NTC, Rob, WBC; NIV, TEV], 'spirit' [Lns, NIC, TH, We;

KJV, NAB, NASB, NJB, NRSV], 'disposition, attitude, way of thinking' [LN (30.6)], 'spiritual gifts' [REB, TNT].

c. σοφία (LN 32.32, 32.37) (BAGD 2. p. 759): 'wisdom' [AB, BAGD, El, LN, Lns, NIC, NTC, Rob, TH, WBC, We; all versions except TEV]. This noun is also translated as a verbal phrase: 'to make one wise' [TEV]. This word may refer to either the capacity for understanding [LN (32.32)], or the content of what is known [LN (32.37)], i.e., 'insight' or 'understanding'.

d. ἀποκάλυψις (LN 28.38) (BAGD 1. p. 92): 'revelation' [AB, BAGD, El, LN, Lns, NIC, NTC, Rob, TH, WBC, We; KJV, NASB, NIV, NRSV], 'disclosure' [BAGD], 'vision' [REB], 'insight' [NAB, TNT], 'perception of what is revealed' [NJB]. This noun is also translated as a verb: 'to reveal (God)' [TEV].

QUESTION—To what or whom does the term πνεῦμα 'Spirit/spirit' refer and how do the words σοφία 'wisdom' and ἀποκάλυψις 'revelation' relate to it?

1. The reference is to the Holy Spirit at work upon the believers' minds, i.e., the Holy Spirit produces the wisdom and revelation [Ba, Cal, Can, Ea, EBC, EGT, Gd, My, NTC, Rob, St, TH, TNTC, WBC, WeBC; NIV, TEV]: that God may give to you the Holy Spirit (who himself makes you) wise and reveals (to you) the knowledge of God. This is a request for the Holy Spirit to be at work, unveiling and giving insights into aspects of the purpose of God in Christ. Such activity could occur privately to individuals or in the corporate assembly as they worshipped [WBC].

2. Πνεῦμα 'Spirit' refers to the Holy Spirit, but the words σοφία 'wisdom' and ἀποκάλυψις 'revelation' refer to the activity of the implied spirit of man which has been recreated [AB, DNTT, Ho, LJ, MNTC]: God will give to you the Holy Spirit (who creates and develops in you a spirit with qualities) of wisdom and illumination. This interpretation may be little different from the first, but commentators assigned here use language which seems to imply more recognition of a human faculty at work in both the elements of 'wisdom' and 'revelation', but the Holy Spirit remains the principal actor. Interpreted in this manner, the words imply the teaching ministry of the church [AB, DNTT].

3. The reference is to the activity of the human disposition or spirit as worked upon by the Holy Spirit, i.e. the human spirit produces the wisdom and revelation [CBC, IB, ICC, Lns, NCBC, NIC, We; NAB, NASB, NJB, NRSV, REB, TNT]: that God may give to you a disposition/spiritual gifts of wisdom and revelation/vision. One commentator feels that the participial clause πεφωτισμένους τοὺς ὀφθαλμοὺς τῆς καρδίας ὑμῶν 'the eyes of your hearts having been enlightened' in the next verse is in apposition to this clause and so is determinative for πνεῦμα here designating the human spirit rather than the Holy Spirit, which the apposition does not fit [Lns].

QUESTION—Since these readers have already been sealed by the Spirit, what is Paul asking for when he prays God might give them 'the Spirit/spirit of wisdom and revelation'?

Paul is asking for a continued bestowal of the Spirit so that they might ever increasingly be enlightened [Ho, LJ, My, NTC], or, Paul is asking God to grace the spirits of the Ephesians with wisdom and revelation so they might come to know God and the gospel contents in the fullest possible manner [CBC, Lns, Si], or, that they might have a greater knowledge of their Divine calling [Cal]. In 1:8, God was praised for supplying, in grace, all wisdom and insight. Now this language is taken up again with a request that the Spirit will continue to communicate to them what is already theirs [WBC]. In any case, what God has already done in their lives must be further strengthened [LJ, Lns, NTC].

QUESTION—To what does σοφία 'wisdom' refer?

While one commentator feels this refers to the sanctified use of the intellectual powers of the human mind, aided by the Spirit of God [Gd], most commentators feel that σοφία refers to a capacity or disposition to receive and understand divine truths that are normally beyond the bounds of human reason. This is an effect of the Holy Spirit [ICC], which results in a humble knowledge of God and a sense of how to live [AB, NCBC]. This is described as spiritual enlightenment [Ho, My], spiritual understanding [EGT, LJ, NIC] or insight [Lns, MNTC], illumination [El], and receptiveness [AB]. Some feel that specific information is given by the Holy Spirit which results in the development of this capacity or disposition [DNTT, LJ, Lns, NTC, Rob, TH, TNTC]. This specific information relates to the doctrines of the gospel [NTC], the nature of divine realities [Lns, TH, TNTC], or, very specifically in this epistle, the mystery of God in Christ as the OT pre-existent Wisdom which is hereafter to be revealed in Christ through the Church [DNTT]. Paul's use of the term combines the OT sense of wisdom as practical knowledge, the ability to choose right conduct, with the understanding of God's activity in Christ and the benefits this brings to believers [WBC].

QUESTION—To what does ἀποκάλυψις 'revelation' refer?

1. This refers to revelation in general [AB, BAGD, DNTT, EBC, Ho]: revelation. Both revelation as objectively given by the Holy Spirit as in prophecy generally, and as subjectively received or attained through the powers of the recreated human spirit is covered in this interpretation.
2. This refers to subjective revelation [Alf (probably), IB, ICC, Lns, MNTC, My, NCBC, St, We, WeBC]: illumination or insight. This is the spiritual insight gained by the renewed human mind or spirit by means of its experience with divine realities, and which may be learned from or taught to other Christians.
3. This refers to objective revelation only [Ba, Can, Ea, EGT, Gd, LJ, NTC, Rob, TH, WBC]: revelation. This is revelation given through the Holy Spirit not necessarily only as extraordinary messages given in a supernatural manner, but in any manner that reveals to us God's mind and will,

such knowledge still regarded as beyond the powers of the renewed human spirit on its own, i.e., it must still be objectively given [Can, Gd, LJ]. Some feel this includes messages given to specially gifted men (prophets) before the writings of the NT had been collected [Ea, EGT]. Another feels it is such revelation as is to be given to ordinary Christians, particularly to those believers less gifted with intellectual powers, and so is not inclusive of the extraordinary revelation given through the apostles and prophets [Gd].

QUESTION—What is revealed by revelation?

A number of suggestions are given: further wisdom and understanding of the secret of God [AB, EBC, EGT, ICC, MNTC, Rob, WeBC]; the character and work of the Redeemer [Ba]; the character, grace, purposes, and working of God [Can, Ea, Ho, NCBC, We]; the gospel [CBC, Lns, My]; the personal knowledge of God [NIC, St, TH]; fresh insight into some aspect of the nature of God [Gd], the will of God [Ba, Can, NTC]; and the disclosure that men are destined to share in the glory and exaltation of Christ [We]. The content of this revelation is suggested by the petition for the threefold enlightenment which follows in 1:18–19 [WBC].

QUESTION—How are the words σοφία 'wisdom' and ἀποκάλυψις 'revelation' related to each other?

1. The words are in a simple coordinate relationship to each other [Alf, Cal, Gd, My, NCBC, NIC, Rob, TNTC, WBC]: wisdom and revelation. The one refers to the giving of insight, the other to an unveiling [WBC].
2. The words are related in a generic-specific relationship [EGT, El, ICC, WeBC]: that he may give to you (a/the) spirit/Spirit of wisdom, (that is) insight into the divine mysteries.
3. The words are in a subjective-objective relationship to each other [AB, Ba, Lns, NTC, TH]: wisdom/insight (to learn divine mysteries) and to reveal/teach them (to others), or, insight that perceives revelation/hidden truth and/together with the granting of revelation (to you).
4. The words are in a cause-result [Lns] or means-result relationship to each other [Ea, ECWB, LJ, We]: wisdom which comes by means of/is the result of revelation.

in[a] a-knowledge[b] of him,

LEXICON—a. ἐν with dative object (LN 89.48, 89.80): 'in' [El, NIC, NTC, Rob, TH, WBC, We; KJV, NASB], '(in order to)' [NAB], 'so that' [AB, LN (89.48); NIV, TEV], 'in connection with' [Lns], 'as (you come to know him)' [NRSV, TNT], 'with, while at the same time' [LN (89.80)], 'with (the knowledge of him) that they bring' [REB]. This preposition is also translated as a verb phrase: 'to bring (you) to' [NJB]. Translations which indicate attendant circumstances may well imply the means by which something is brought about as well [LN (89.80)].

b. ἐπίγνωσις (LN 28.2, 28.18) (BAGD p. 291): 'knowledge' [BAGD, Lns, NIC, Rob, TH, WBC, We; KJV, NASB, REB], 'full knowledge' [El;

NJB], 'clear knowledge' [NTC], 'knowledge about' [LN (28.2)], 'knowledge, definite knowledge, full knowledge, what is known' [LN (28.18)]. Some translate this noun as a verb: 'to know' [AB; TEV], 'to come to know' [NRSV, TNT], 'to know clearly' [NAB], 'to know better' [NIV]. Both subdomains given in LN imply the possession of definite information and subdomain 28.2 may imply a degree of thoroughness or competence as well. This is reflected in remarks of other commentators that this composite noun (ἐπι- preposition acting as prefix intensifier of the noun γνῶσις 'knowledge') means accurate and certain knowledge [Ho, My], or knowledge of a particular subject [AB, TH].

QUESTION—What relationship is indicated by ἐν 'in'?
1. It indicates the purpose or goal of wisdom and revelation [AB, Ba, EBC, LJ, NIC, NTC (probably), TH; NAB, NIV, NJB, TEV]: a spirit of wisdom and revelation so that you may know him.
2. It indicates the sphere within which wisdom and revelation operate [Alf, Ea, EGT, El, Lns, My]: a spirit of wisdom and revelation with regard to/in connection with the knowledge of him.
3. It indicates the means by which wisdom and revelation come [Can, TNTC]: a spirit of wisdom and revelation that comes by/through the knowledge of him.
4. It indicates the means by which the knowledge of God comes [WBC; REB]: a spirit of wisdom and revelation by which there comes the knowledge of him.
5. It indicates that with which wisdom and revelation are accompanied [Ho; TNT]: a spirit of wisdom and revelation together with the knowledge of himself, or, as you come to know him.
6. It indicates the means by which the eyes of the heart are enlightened [ICC]: a spirit of wisdom and revelation by means of which the knowledge of God enlightens the eyes of your hearts.
7. It indicates the substance of the wisdom and revelation [IB]: a spirit of wisdom and revelation, that is, the knowledge of him.

QUESTION—What is meant by ἐπίγνωσις 'knowledge'?
1. The word ἐπίγνωσις is simply a synonym for γνῶσις [DNTT, IDB, St, TD, TNTC, WBC]: the knowledge of him. Hellenistic syncretistic religion used both of these terms in connection with its concern for the communication of esoteric knowledge. It could be that both Colossians and Ephesians use these terms to suggest a contrast with syncretistic philosophy, so that, in this prayer, the use of ἐπίγνωσις 'knowledge' indicates the writer is praying for the genuine article—real knowledge of God. For followers of Paul, ἐπίγνωσις 'knowledge' not only has intellectual overtones, but moral ones as well, which come from the OT background [WBC].
2. The word ἐπίγνωσις has its own distinctive difference from γνῶσις [AB, Alf, Ba, BAGD, Can, Ea, ECWB, EGT, El, Gd, Ho, ISBE, LJ, LN (28.2, 28.18), Lns, My, NIC, NTC, Rob, TH, We; NAB, NIV, NJB, TNT]. Both

subdomains which LN lists indicate that ἐπίγνωσις indicates a more definite degree of knowledge than the simple γνῶσις would carry.
  2.1 It means intensive knowledge [El, Gd, Ho, Lns, My, NTC; NAB]: in the true/certain/clear knowledge of him. It indicates an intimate knowledge gained by communion with God, a knowledge that results in personal holiness [Gd].
  2.2 It means full knowledge [Alf, Ba, Can, Ea, EBC, ECWB, EGT, ICC, ISBE, LJ; NJB]: in the full knowledge of him.
  2.3 It refers to a knowledge which is directed towards a particular subject [AB, BAGD, MNTC, Rob, TH, We; NIV, NRSV, TNT]: in your getting to know him. The force of the prefixed preposition ἐπι- in a large number of compounds is never shown to be intensive, but rather has a directive force. Paul generally uses the term γνῶσις to denote knowledge in the abstract or wider sense, while he uses ἐπίγνωσις where the special object of the knowledge is expressed. Paul freely uses the word, generally following it with the genitive of the object denoting what is to be known [Rob].
QUESTION—To whom does the pronoun αὐτοῦ 'of him' refer?
  1. This refers to God the Father [AB, Alf, Can, Ea, EBC, EGT, El, Gd, Ho, IB, ICC, LJ, Lns, MNTC, My, NIC, NTC, Rob, St, TH, TNTC, WBC, We]: the knowledge of God. Supporters of this interpretation point out that the material of the following verses clearly makes the reference here refer to God the Father [Can, Ea, EGT, IB, ICC, LJ, Lns, My, St, TNTC, We]. Some holding this interpretation mention the knowledge of Christ as a necessary intermediate step to the knowledge of the Father [Gd, LJ, We]. The pronoun indicates that it is as the God of our Lord Jesus Christ and as the Father of Glory that Paul prays that these believers will come to have a greater knowledge [Gd].
  2. This refers to Jesus Christ our Redeemer [Ba, NCBC (possibly)]: the knowledge of Christ.

1:18 having-been-enlightened[a] the eyes[b] of-your heart,[c]
TEXT—Instead of καρδίας 'heart', some manuscripts have διανοίας 'understanding'. GNT does not mention this variant reading. Only KJV supports the reading 'understanding'.
LEXICON—a. perf. pass. participle of φωτίζω (LN 28.36) (BAGD 2.b. p. 873): 'to be enlightened' [BAGD, El, Lns, NIC, Rob, WBC, We; KJV, NASB, NIV, NRSV, REB, TNT], 'to be illumined' [NTC, TH], 'to have light given to, to be shed upon' [BAGD], 'to be opened' [TEV]. The passive verb is also translated actively: 'to enlighten' [NAB, NJB], 'to illumine' [AB], 'to make known' [LN]. This word is one in the sensory domain of seeing, causing to see, or giving light to, which involves a shift to the cognitive domain of making something fully known, evident, or clear [LN]. The perfect passive participle denotes not only an action of God but a status or state already created by that action [AB, IB, Lns,

WBC] and continuing to exist [Lns, WBC]. Though a progressive enlightenment may be involved from the nature of the case [AB, IB], the perfect tense itself here does not carry this meaning [IB]. The perfect tense refers to the illumination of conversion, not baptism [WBC].

b. ὀφθαλμός (LN **32.24**) (BAGD 2. p. 599): 'eyes' [AB, BAGD, El, Lns, NTC, Rob, TH, WBC, We; KJV, NASB, NIV, NJB, NRSV, REB], 'eyesight' [NIC], 'vision' [NAB], 'understanding' [LN]. This noun is also translated as a verb or verb phrase: 'to be able to understand, to come to perceive' [LN], 'to see light' [TEV]. This is a figurative meaning of ὀφθαλμός and stands for the capacity to understand as the result of perception. In this verse it designates a faculty of understanding [DNTT, ISBE, ISBE2, LN] and is not just a reference to perception. Being joined to καρδία 'heart' which denotes the mind, the phrase ὀφθαλμοὺς τῆς καρδίας focuses on the enlightenment of the understanding [My] and means 'the capacity for understanding which the mind has' [LN].

c. καρδία (LN 26.3) (BAGD 1.b.β. p. 403): 'heart' [BAGD, El, LN, Lns, Rob, TH, WBC, We; NASB, NIV, NRSV], 'hearts' [AB, NTC], 'mind' [BAGD, LN; NJB], 'minds' [TEV], 'inner self' [LN], 'understanding' (see TEXT above) [KJV]. Some translate this noun as an adjective: 'inward (eyes)' [REB], 'spiritual (eyesight)' [NIC], 'innermost (vision)' [NAB]. The phrase τοὺς ὀφθαλμοὺς τῆς καρδίας ὑμῶν 'the eyes of your hearts' is translated 'your minds' [TNT]. As used here, this is a figurative extension of the literal meaning 'heart' denoting the seat of the whole inner life [BAGD, ECWB, My, TD], the causative source of a person's psychological or moral life under various aspects [LN, My, TD], the seat of knowledge and understanding as well as of love, conscience, emotions [Cal, My; NJB (note)] and volition [My], especially emphasizing knowledge [My] or the thoughts [BAGD, LN, WBC]. It was regarded as the organ of practical knowledge and wisdom [WBC]. This contrasts with the English usage which is primarily emotive [LN, My]. Καρδία 'heart' is a distributive singular so that, rather than indicating a collective 'heart', the individual 'heart' of each member of the group is meant [Tu].

QUESTION—To what is this clause connected?

1. The words in this participial clause together form an accusative absolute which is to be connected with πνεῦμα σοφίας καὶ ἀποκαλύψεως 'spirit of wisdom and revelation' and gives the intended result of those gifts [Ea, EGT, My]: so that the eyes of your heart have been enlightened. The participle takes its case from the preceding accusative case of the plural noun ὀφθαλμούς 'eyes' [IB, ICC].

2. This is a case of anacoluthon, a disruption from the original course of the sentence, and is connected with, and explanatory of, ὑμῖν 'to you' (1:17) [Alf, El, IB, Rob, Si-ed, WBC, We]. Normally the participle would have taken the dative case yielding the meaning 'the ones having been enlightened', but due to anacoluthon the accusative case occurs together with the

noun in the accusative, 'eyes', this latter being an accusative of respect or nearer definition carrying the sense of 'as to the eyes'. It gives the intended result of the 'spirit of wisdom and revelation' [Alf, El, IB, We]: so that you may be enlightened as to the eyes of your heart.
3. This is an accusatival clause connected to the verb δώῃ 'may give' [AB, Ba, Can, Gd, Ho, ICC, Lns, MNTC, NCBC, NIC, NTC, TD, TH; NASB, NIV, NJB, REB, TEV, TNT].
  3.1 It is understood to be in apposition to πνεῦμα 'spirit', making a restatement or a further description of it [Can, Ho, ICC, LJ, Lns, MNTC, NTC, TD, TH, TNTC]: may give you a spirit/Spirit, i.e., the eyes of your heart having been enlightened. It also gives the immediate effect of the πνεῦμα 'spirit' [ICC]. It states the means by which wisdom and revelation take place [LJ, TH], functioning as a circumstantial clause to do this, or, alternatively it functions as an imperative: 'the eyes of your heart be opened' [TH].
  3.2 It is taken as parallel to πνεῦμα 'spirit/Spirit' and constitutes a second major prayer petition [AB, Gd, NCBC, NIC; NASB, NIV, NJB, REB, TEV, TNT]: and may he also give to you the eyes of the heart which have been enlightened; or, may he also cause the eyes of your heart to be enlightened.
  3.3 This is a parenthetical insertion [Ba; NRSV]: that he give you the Spirit—the eyes of your hearts having been enlightened, so that you may know, etc.; or, that he give you a spirit so that, with the eyes of your heart enlightened, you may know, etc. [NRSV].
QUESTION—What is the meaning of the metaphor 'the eyes of your heart having been enlightened'?
  The expression refers to the ability of the spiritually renewed man's mind to perceive and understand spiritual or ultimate truth [most commentators except CBC and Si, who do not comment on the meaning of the metaphor]. Because the gift in question is that of knowledge or insight, the figure of the eyes is used [EGT, Gd], and because this knowledge is spiritual in nature, the figure of the heart occurs [EGT]. The comparison is as light enables the physical eye to see and thus to act as a guide to the body, so the Spirit of God enables the inner eye, the perceptive faculty of the inner man (καρδία 'heart' or 'mind') to perceive and understand spiritual truth and thus to act as a guide to the spiritual part of man. The point of comparison is the respective cognitive [Gd, My] abilities of the eye and the spiritually renewed mind to perceive and respond to the stimuli each was designed to receive. The nonfigurative statement would be: your mind having been enabled to understand God's truth.

in-order to-know[a] what is the hope[b] of-the calling[c] of-him
LEXICON—a. perf. act. infin. of οἶδα (LN 28.1, 32.4) (BAGD 4. p. 556): 'to know' [El, LN (28.1), NIC, NTC, Rob, TH, WBC, We; KJV, NAB, NASB, NIV, NRSV, REB, TEV, TNT], 'to become aware of' [AB], 'to

get to know' [Lns], 'to come to know/to recognize/to experience' [BAGD], 'to understand' [BAGD, LN (32.4)], 'to comprehend' [LN (32.4)], 'to be able to see' [NJB]. Domain 32 'understand' refers to the processing of information so as to arrive at a correct comprehension or evaluation, while domain 28 'know' involves the possession of information [LN].
- b. ἐλπίς (LN 25.61) (BAGD 2.b. p. 253): 'hope' [AB, BAGD, El, LN, Lns, NIC, NTC, Rob, TH, WBC, We; all versions except NAB], 'great hope' [NAB]. This refers to the object of one's hope [AB, EGT].
- c. κλῆσις (LN **33.312**) (BAGD 1. p. 435): 'calling' [BAGD, El, LN, Lns, NIC, Rob, TH, WBC, We; KJV, NASB], '(his) call' [NJB]. This is also translated as a verb 'to call' [AB, BAGD, **LN**, NTC; NAB, NIV, NRSV, REB, TEV, TNT]. This is an urgent invitation for someone to accept responsibilities for a particular task, and implies a new relationship to the one who is the source of the call [LN].

QUESTION—What relationship is indicated by εἰς 'in order that'?

Εἰς τό with the infinitive indicates here the intended result of the enlightenment [Alf, Ea, EGT, El, HG, Ho, Lns, My, Tu, WeBC].

QUESTION—What is the relationship between the items that Paul prays for them to know (i.e. the items of 1:18b–19a after the infinitive construction)?

Most of the commentaries indicate that these items, each being an indirect question beginning with τίς or τί 'what' [AB, Lns], are three aspects of the knowledge of God which the Apostle wants his reader to know, and each involves the others [Can], but in what way opinions diverge. Most do not deal with the interrelationship very much, perhaps because of the recognized ambiguity of construction [AB]. Several see these aspects listed in order of crescendo [IB, Lns, We], with the whole prayer moving at this point toward the exposition of the last item dealing with the knowledge of the power of God [IB, Lns, TD]. Some understand the final two items, the wealth of the inheritance and the power of God, to be specifications or explanations of the first, the hope of the calling [El, ICC, MNTC]. Others understand that the final item, the power of God, gives the means by which the other two are accomplished [NTC, We]. Another view is that 'the riches of the glory of his inheritance' is the content of 'the hope of his calling', and 'the exceeding greatness of his power toward us' is the basis of 'the riches of the glory of his inheritance' [TD].

QUESTION—What is the relationship between the words in the genitive construction ἡ ἐλπὶς τῆς κλήσεως αὐτοῦ 'the hope of the calling of him'?
1. Τῆς κλήσεως 'of the calling' states the source or origin from which the hope comes [Alf, Ea, Ho, ICC, Lns, Si-ed]: the hope which comes from God's calling you.
2. Τῆς κλήσεως 'of the calling' states the cause of the hope [EGT, El, My, TH, WBC, We]: God's calling of you produces the hope you have.
3. Τῆς κλήσεως 'of the calling' states in what respect God called them [AB, Ba, BAGD, Ho, IB, ICC, LJ, LN (**33.312**), NCBC, NIC, NTC, St, TH;

NAB, NIV, NRSV, REB, TEV, TNT]: the hope to which God has called you.

QUESTION—What is the hope?

The hope is ultimate salvation in Christ [AB, Ba, Can, Ea, WBC], the fact of an eternal life [MNTC]. It is what the Christian expects [EGT], the inheritance mentioned in the next clause [Ea, Lns, TD], the hope of glory [NIC], the assurance of salvation [Gd, LJ], the attainment of full spiritual development [IB]. But the biblical hope denotes both the act of hoping and the idea of the object hoped for [Alf, DNTT], and there is disagreement over which meaning is more in focus here.

1. The focus here is more upon the object hoped for than upon the subjective sense of expectation the person experiences [AB, Ba, Can, Ea, ECWB, IB, ICC, Lns, NIC, Si, WBC]: that you may know the glorious destiny to which he has called you. Growth in the Christian life consists largely in realizing all that is given to us in Christ [Can, IB], which causes the heart to respond to the truth and the Spirit [Ea]. This realization does require special enlightenment to comprehend the truth and glory of what objects are hoped for [Ea].
2. The focus here is upon the sense of expectation in the person hoping [EGT, El, Gd, Ho LJ, Lns, My, NTC, St, TNTC, We]: that you may know what it is to look forward to that which he has called you. The act of hoping is more than just a vague wish, such as the English usage may suggest, but a confident expectation [CBC, DNTT, LJ, NCBC, NTC, Rob, TNTC], linked many times (as in this passage, 1:15) with the other subjective elements of faith and love [DNTT, Lns, My, NCBC, NTC], and that the experience of hoping encourages and animates the Christian [My] and so exerts a sanctifying influence in the Christian's present life [NTC, TNTC]. The object hoped for is given in the next clause—the inheritance [Gd, Ho, LJ, Lns, My, NCBC].
3. Both elements are in focus [Alf, CBC, NCBC, TH]: that you may know the glorious destiny to which he has called you and wait expectantly for it.

QUESTION—What is the κλῆσις 'calling'?

Most commentators that comment on this state or imply that the call is what gives hope its certainty, since it is God's call and rests on his initiative [CBC, Gd, LJ, Rob, TNTC, WBC]. Most commentators relate this call to God's elect, those who are enabled to accept it, calling it the effective or effectual call [AB, Ea, EGT, El, Gd, Ho, LJ, My, NTC, Rob, St, TNTC, WBC, We] or the successful call [Lns] in contrast to the general call to all mankind to repent and turn to him. Two commentators, however, understand it to be the general call to all mankind [TH] or all creation [IB]. In favor of the first interpretation are the facts that in the Epistles (1) the 'called of God' are always those who have become believers [BAGD, DNTT, EGT, Ho, NTC, We] and (2) κλῆσις 'calling' and its verb form are seldom used in any other sense [BAGD, DNTT].

QUESTION—To what time does this calling relate?

Some commentators, in treating it as a concept, focus on its culmination and so seem to relate it to the future [CBC, ICC, My, NCBC] probably because of the ἐλπίς 'hope' which it modifies. Most relate it to the present [AB, Can, Ea, EBC, El, Gd, IB, LJ, NTC, St, WBC, We], the time of each individual's conversion [Can, Ea, ECWB, NTC, Si]. One relates it to past, present, and future [TNTC], and two relate it specifically to eternity past [Rob, WeBC] when the decree to call some to salvation was made.

what (are) the riches[a] of-the glory[b] of-the inheritance[c] of-him in[d] the saints,[e]

LEXICON—a. πλοῦτος (LN **78.15**) (BAGD 2. p. 674): 'riches' [AB, El, Lns, NTC, Rob, WBC, We; KJV, NASB, NIV, NRSV], 'wealth' [BAGD, NIC, TH; NAB, TNT], 'abundance' [BAGD, LN]. This noun is also translated as an adverb: 'very (wonderful inheritance)' [**LN**]; as an adjective: 'great' [LN]. The clause τίς ὁ πλοῦτος 'what (are) the riches' is translated 'how rich is' [NJB, REB, TEV]. This usage of πλοῦτος indicates a high point on any scale and has the implication of value as well as abundance [LN]. See this word at 1:7.

b. δόξα (LN 87.23) (BAGD 1.a. p. 203): 'glory' [BAGD, El, LN, Lns, NTC, Rob, TH, We; KJV, NASB, NJB], 'greatness' [LN]. This noun is also translated as an adjective: 'glorious' [AB, NIC, WBC; NAB, NIV, NRSV, REB, TNT], 'wonderful' [LN (**78.15**); TEV]. This usage of the word describes a state of being great and wonderful [LN]. BAGD lists δόξα in this verse under the category of 'brightness, splendor, radiance'.

c. κληρονομία (LN 57.131, 57.140) (BAGD 3. p. 435): 'inheritance' [El, LN, Lns, NIC, NTC, Rob, TH, WBC, We; KJV, NASB, NIV, NRSV], 'possession' [LN], '(the possession of) salvation' [BAGD], 'heritage to be distributed' [NAB], 'heritage he offers' [NJB], 'blessings he promises' [TEV], 'the share he offers (you) in their inheritance' [REB]. This noun is also translated as a verb: 'to share' [TNT], 'to be inherited' [AB].

d. ἐν with dative object (LN 83.9, 89.5): 'in' [LN (89.5), NIC, Rob, We; KJV, NASB, NIV], 'among' [AB, El, LN (83.9), NTC, TH, WBC; NAB, NJB, NRSV, REB], 'in the case of' [LN (89.5), Lns], 'with regard to' [LN (89.5)], 'with' [LN (83.9); TNT]. One omits 'in' and makes 'saints' the direct object of 'to promise' [TEV].

e. ἅγιος: 'saints'. See this word at 1:15.

QUESTION—What are the relationships within the double genitive construction ὁ πλοῦτος τῆς δόξης τῆς κληρονομίας αὐτοῦ 'the riches of the glory of his inheritance'?

1. Πλοῦτος 'riches' is an attribute of δόξα 'glory' which is an attribute of κληρονομία 'inheritance' [Bu, Can, Ea, EGT, El, Gd, Ho, ICC, LJ, LN (**78.15**), Lns, MNTC, My, NCBC, St, TH, Tu, We; KJV, NAB, NASB, NIV, NJB, NRSV, TEV]: the very glorious inheritance; or, how rich is the glory of his heritage [NJB]. Syntactically πλοῦτος 'riches' is the head of

this phrase, but semantically ὁ πλοῦτος 'the riches' indicates the extent of the δόξα 'glory' and that, in turn, explains the nature of the κληρονομία 'inheritance' [LN (**78.15**)]. The glory of God's inheritance is the honor and beauty of the destiny that awaits his people, and the riches of that glory is the fullness, abundance, and extreme value of that honor and beauty [Can, Gd].

2. Δόξα 'glory' is an attribute of πλοῦτος 'riches' which is an attribute of κληρονομία 'inheritance' [AB, Ba, IB, MNTC (translation), NIC, NTC, WBC; TNT]: the gloriously rich inheritance.

3. Δόξα 'glory' and πλοῦτος 'riches' are both attributes of κληρονομία 'inheritance' [TNTC; REB]: the rich and glorious inheritance.

QUESTION—What is the meaning of the genitive construction τῆς κληρονομίας αὐτοῦ 'the inheritance of him'?

1. This pronoun is possessive and indicates that the inheritance belongs to God [Alf, Can, NIC, Rob, Si, WBC, WeBC]: his inheritance. In this case κληρονομία 'inheritance' is God's people, the people God is saving for himself. This rests upon Old Testament passages such as Deut. 4:30; 32:9; Ps. 28:9 and others where the people of Israel are stated to be God's portion or inheritance [Can, NIC, Rob, WBC]. The prayer then becomes a request that Paul's readers will realize and appreciate what great value God places upon his people [Can, NIC, WeBC].

2. This pronoun gives the source of the inheritance, i.e., it states who gives the inheritance [AB, Ba, CBC, DNTT, Ds2, Ea, EBC, ECWB, EGT, Ho, IB, ICC, LJ, Lns, MNTC, My, NCBC, NTC, St, TD, TH, TNTC, We; NAB, NJB, REB, TEV, TNT]: the inheritance God has promised. In this case κληρονομία 'inheritance' is eternal life in glory in his presence [AB, Ba, DNTT, Ea, EBC, IB, ICC, LJ, Lns, My, St, TNTC, We]. The prayer is that Paul's readers may grasp the glorious reality of what God's promises have in store for them [Ea, LJ, My].

3. The pronoun indicates both possession and source [Gd]. This interpretation assigns a double sense to the inheritance because of its reciprocal effect. God gives himself to them as their inheritance and the glory he receives from this action is his inheritance [Gd].

QUESTION—What is the relationship indicated by the preposition ἐν 'in' and with what is the phrase ἐν τοῖς ἁγίοις 'in the saints' connected?

1. The phrase is connected to κληρονομία 'inheritance' [AB, Alf, Can, Ea, ECWB, Ho, IB, Lns, MNTC, NCBC, NIC, NTC, Rob, St, TNTC, WBC, We; KJV, NASB, NIV, NJB].

1.1 The preposition is translated as 'in' [Can, NIC, Rob, We; KJV, NASB, NIV]: of his inheritance in the saints. With several of these authorities ἐν 'in' has the sense of 'consisting of' [Can, NIC, Rob].

1.2 The preposition means 'in the case of' [Alf, Lns]: of his inheritance in the case of the saints. It refers to what is mentioned as pertaining to them [Lns]. God's fullness is embodied in, and exemplified by, the saints [Alf].

1.3 The preposition is translated as 'among' [AB, Ea, ECWB, Ho, IB, MNTC, NCBC, NTC, St, TNTC, WBC; NJB]: of his inheritance among the saints. With several authorities the sense of 'together with/with' is also implied [NTC, St, TNTC; TNT (who supports 2. below)]: of his inheritance (which you will share) together with all the saints.
2. The phrase is connected to the clause as a whole and ἐν is translated as 'among' [EGT, El, ICC, My, TH; NAB, NRSV, REB, TNT]: what the riches of the glory of his inheritance are among the saints. If the phrase was connected directly to κληρονομία 'inheritance' an article would be required after κληρονομία 'inheritance' [EGT, El] before ἐν 'among' [ICC, My]. Some of these commentators argue that an implied ἐστίν 'is' should be inserted after τίς 'what' in the Greek text and the phrase connected directly to that. This would, in turn, not require the article to occur after κληρονομία 'inheritance' [El, My]. The difference in meaning would be to shift the focus from 'inheritance' to 'riches' [My]: what are the riches…among the saints.

QUESTION—Who or what are τοῖς ἁγίοις 'the saints'?
1. They are God's people—redeemed humanity [AB, Alf, Can, CBC, DNTT, Ea, EBC, ECWB, EGT, El, Gd, Ho, ICC, LJ, Lns, My, NCBC, NIC, NTC, Rob, Si, TD, TH, TNTC, WBC, We, WeBC; NAB, NJB, REB, TEV, TNT]. Interpreting them as God's inheritance, they are the perfected saints—the saints as they will be after their redemption is completed, not as they are in the present life [Alf].
1.1 They are the church [CBC, TD, WBC, WeBC; NAB]. This involves the people of God from both Jews and Gentiles [WBC].
1.2 These are Israel [AB, DNTT]. The inheritance will be obtained by Israel together with Christian believers [AB, DNTT].
2. They are angelic beings [IB (probably), MNTC]. The inheritance will be obtained by all believers as it is found (or exists) among the holy beings that surround God's throne [IB]; or, the Christian brethren will be incorporated into the host of the angelic beings [MNTC].

1:19 and what (is) the exceeding[a] greatness[b] of-the power[c] of-him toward[d] us the (ones) believing[e]

LEXICON—a. pres. act participle of ὑπερβάλλω (LN 78.33) (BAGD p. 840). As a participle of a verb meaning 'to exceed, to surpass' [BAGD], this verb is usually translated as an adjective or an adverb: 'exceeding' [Lns, Rob, TH, We; KJV], 'exceedingly' [LN (**78.2**)], 'surpassing' [BAGD, El, NIC, NTC, WBC; NASB], 'immeasurable' [NAB, NRSV], 'incomparably' [NIV], 'extraordinarily' [NJB], 'extraordinary' [BAGD, LN], 'limitless' [TNT], 'outstanding' [BAGD]. The phrase τί τὸ ὑπερβάλλον μέγεθος 'what exceeding greatness' is translated 'how exceedingly great' [AB], 'how very great' [TEV], 'how vast are the resources' [REB]. The term denotes a degree which greatly exceeds a point on an overt, or implied, scale of extent [LN (78.33)].

b. μέγεθος (LN **78.2**) (BAGD 2. p. 498): 'greatness' [BAGD, El, LN, Lns, NIC, NTC, Rob, TH, WBC, We; KJV, NASB, NRSV], 'to a great degree' [LN], 'resources' [REB], 'scope' [NAB, TNT]. This noun is also translated as an adjective: 'great' [AB, BAGD, **LN**; NIV, NJB, TEV]. The term denotes the upper range on a scale of extent [LN].
c. δύναμις (LN 76.1) (BAGD 1. p. 207): 'power' [AB, BAGD, El, LN, Lns, NIC, NTC, Rob, TH, WBC, We; all versions except NJB], 'power that he has exercised' [NJB]. This denotes the ability to accomplish what is intended [AB, Can, DNTT, EBC, IB, LN]. This is the more general word which, in this verse, expresses the content of the words denoting power in the last part of the verse [IB, Lns, My].
d. εἰς with accusative object (LN 83.13) (BAGD 4.c.β. or 4.g. p. 229): 'toward' [LN (90.59), WBC; NASB], 'to (us)-ward' [El, Rob, We; KJV], 'open to' [REB], 'with respect to' [LN (90.23), NTC], 'for' [Lns; NIV, NJB, NRSV], 'in' [LN, NIC, TH; NAB, TEV, TNT], 'over' [AB]. It indicates the goal in a friendly sense [BAGD].
e. pres. act. participle of πιστεύω (LN 31.102) (BAGD 2.b. p. 661): 'to believe' [BAGD, El, Lns, NIC, NTC, Rob, WBC, We; KJV, NAB, NASB, NIV, NRSV, TEV], 'to trust' [BAGD], 'to have faith' [REB], 'to be a believer, to be a Christian' [LN]. The article and the participle are also translated as a substantive: 'believers' [AB, TH; NJB]. This is also translated as an adverbial clause: '(his power at work in us) once we believe' [TNT]. The present tense indicates a characteristic attitude [EGT, Lns]: who continue to believe. The usage in this subdomain differs from the subdomain 'trust, rely' in that this subdomain has the added semantic component of believing a particular set of truths or trusting a particular person—Christ [BAGD, LN, TH].

QUESTION—What is the time frame to which this verse relates?
1. This verse relates to the present life of the believer as well as to his final perfected state [AB, Alf, Ba, Cal, Can, Ea, Gd, Ho, IB, LJ, NCBC, NIC, Rob, St, TD, TH, TNTC, WBC]: what the exceeding greatness of his power is toward us even in our present life. The modes of the effects of God's power upon the believer's existence will be shown in chapter 2 [AB, Can, Ea, Ho, LJ, NIC, St]. This power will be manifested towards the saints from their conversion until they reach their final inheritance [Ba, LJ, St]. Col. 2:4 [LJ] and 2:12 [Ho] indicate that Paul saw a parallel between Christ's resurrection and the believers' spiritual resurrection. Some commentators particularly mention this verse as applying to the exaltation of Christ over all cosmic powers (1:20-21) and thus nullifying any power these powers have over the believer [CBC, LJ, Lns, TD].
2. This verse relates primarily [El] or exclusively [My] to the future state of the believer [El, ICC, My]: what the exceeding greatness of his power toward us who believe will be when we experience resurrection, etc. The references to 'the hope' and 'inheritance' (1:18) and the following context

84   EPHESIANS 1:19

(1:20–23) indicate that Paul is talking primarily about the power of God that will be manifested in regards to believers at the Second Coming [El].

QUESTION—What is the relationship between the words in the genitive construction ὑπερβάλλον μέγεθος τῆς δυνάμεως 'the exceeding greatness of the power'?

Ὑπερβάλλον 'exceeding' and μέγεθος 'greatness' are two expressions of degree which, while syntactically acting as the head of the phrase, nevertheless modify δύναμις 'power' semantically as expressions of degree [LN (78.2)]. Ὑπερβάλλον 'exceeding' modifies μέγεθος 'greatness' [AB], but semantically surpasses it [TD].

QUESTION—With what is the prepositional phrase εἰς ἡμᾶς 'toward us' connected?

1. It is connected with the whole preceding clause τὸ ὑπερβάλλον μέγεθος τῆς δυνάμεως αὐτοῦ 'the exceeding greatness of his power' [Alf, Ea, EGT, IB, Lns, NCBC, WBC]: the exceeding greatness of his power towards us who believe. Two of these commentators [Ea, IB] confine their remarks only to δύναμις 'power', but this difference from the others is only superficial. The apostle wants these people to know the nature of the power that has been exerted upon them in their conversion. The power works in a certain normal direction; it works on believers as it worked in Christ [Ea].
2. It is connected to an implied ἐστί 'is' following τί 'what' [El, ICC, My]: what the exceeding greatness of his power is toward us who believe. This makes the second and third clauses symmetrical to each other in construction and makes the prepositional phrases ἐν τοῖς ἁγίοις 'in the saints' and εἰς ἡμᾶς 'towards us' parallel to each other [El, ICC].

QUESTION—What is the force of the articular participle τοὺς πιστεύοντας 'who are believing'?

The articular participle is emphatic by nature when used in place of an adjective [Ea], is durative in force and in apposition to ὑμᾶς 'us' [Ea, HG, Lns], describing these people as those who continue in believing [Ea, Lns, TD].

according-to[a] the working[b] of the strength[c] of-the might[d] of-him.

LEXICON—a. κατά with accusative object (LN 89.8): 'according to' [BAGD, El, NIC, Rob, TH, WBC, We; KJV, NRSV], 'in accordance with' [LN; NASB], 'in accord with' [Lns]. This is also translated as a verb phrase: 'to be the same as' [TEV], 'this accords with' [NJB], 'to be like' [NAB, NIV], 'as seen in' [NTC]. This is also translated as a nominal clause: 'this is that same (stupendous power)' [TNT]. This is also conflated with the following noun ἐνέργειαν 'working': '(his mighty strength) was seen at work' [REB].

b. ἐνέργεια (LN 42.3) (BAGD 1. p. 265): 'working' [BAGD, LN, Lns, Rob, TH, WBC, We; KJV, NASB, NIV, NRSV], 'manifestation' [BAGD, NTC], 'operation' [BAGD, El, NIC], 'action' [BAGD], not explicit

[NAB]. This noun is also translated as a verb: 'to be at work' [AB; NJB, REB, TNT], or as a participle: 'working' [TEV]. It refers to the exercise of power, power in operation [Alf, DNTT, Ea, EBC, EGT, Ho, IB, ICC, LJ, Lns, My, NTC, TNTC], and power producing its effect [Can]. It is the actual operation of the power described in the other two synonyms in this phrase [Alf].

- c. κράτος (LN 76.6) (BAGD 3. p. 449): 'strength' [BAGD, Lns; NASB, NJB], 'might' [LN, Rob, TH, We], 'power' [El, LN], 'intensity' [BAGD], not explicit [NAB]. This noun is also translated as an adjective: 'mighty' [AB, NIC, WBC; KJV, NIV, REB, TEV], 'stupendous' [TNT], 'infinite' [NTC], 'great' [NRSV]. This word has the connotation of ruling and exercising authority [DNTT, IB, LN, My, We], of conquering and overcoming resistance [AB, DNTT, Ea, EBC, EGT, El, Ho, IB, ICC, LJ, My, NTC], of the power or strength which is exercised [Can, El, Lns, NTC]. It is the actual measure of ἰσχύς 'might' [Alf] and, as used here, denotes divine might in its supremacy [TD].
- d. ἰσχύς (LN 79.62) (BAGD p. 383): 'might' [BAGD, El, Lns, NTC; NASB], 'strength' [AB, BAGD, LN, NIC, Rob, TH, WBC, We; NAB, NIV, REB, TEV], 'power' [BAGD; KJV, NJB, NRSV, TNT].

QUESTION—What is the significance of the string of synonyms denoting power?

The language is meant to exalt the idea of Divine power which Paul is striving to present [Cal, Ea, Gd] and their accumulation expresses the highest form of power [Gd, Ho]. They express nothing short of the irresistible [Gd] omnipotence of God [Ba, Gd, Ho, IB, LJ].

1. Each term contributes its own individual meaning to Paul's conception of God's power [AB, Alf, Cal, Can, Ea, EBC, EGT, El, Gd, Ho, IB, ICC, LJ, Lns, MNTC, My, Rob, TNTC, We; KJV, NASB, NIV, NJB, REB, TEV]: according to the working of the might of his strength. Paul wants to point out the absolutely unique and superior strength of God exerted in the resurrection of Christ [AB] so he pauses to describe it slowly and analytically in its three different phases, first in its actual operation [Ea] or effect [MNTC], then in its motive power [Ea] or character [MNTC], and finally in its unexhausted might [Ea, MNTC].
2. The effect is rhetorical, intensity of idea being the aim, and each term need not be distinguished from the other [ECWB (probably), NCBC, NTC, TD, TH, WBC, WeBC; NAB, NRSV, TNT]: according to the working of his great strength.

QUESTION—With what is κατὰ τὴν ἐνέργειαν τοῦ κράτους τῆς ἰσχύος αὐτοῦ 'according to the working of the might of his strength' connected?

1. It is connected with the main thought of the preceding clause [AB, Cal, Can, Ea, ECWB, El, Gd, ICC, MNTC, My, TD, WeBC; NIV, TNT]: what is the exceeding greatness of his power towards us…according to the working of the might of his strength. It serves as a definition of the mode of operation of God's power [Ea, El, NTC], or as the ground of knowl-

edge of the preceding point (the exceeding greatness of God's power) [My], or as a demonstration of the efficacy of God's power [Cal, Gd].
2. It is connected with the whole of the preceding clause [Alf, EGT, IB, Lns, NIC, Rob, St, TH, TNTC, We; TEV]: what is the exceeding greatness of his power towards us who are believing according to the working of the might of his strength. This makes the phrase connect with the whole thought of divine power as put forth in the life of believers, not just divine power alone, or of believing alone [IB].
3. It is connected with the articular participle τοὺς πιστεύοντας 'who are believing' [Ho, LJ]: who are believing in virtue of the working of the might of his strength.
4. It is connected with the whole of the preceding three indirect questions [NASB]: These are in accordance with the working of the strength of his might.

QUESTION—What relationship is indicated by κατά 'according to'?
1. It means 'according to' and indicates conformity to a norm or standard [AB, Alf, Ba, BAGD, Cal, Can, Ea, ECWB, EGT, El, Gd, IB, ICC, Lns, MNTC, My, NIC, NTC, Rob, St, TH, WBC, We; NASB, NJB, NRSV]: according to the working of the strength of his might. The measure of this strength is the immeasurable might of the Divine nature [ECWB]. The κατά phrase with its synonyms for power is seen as modal, specifying the nature of the power and defining how the power operates [Ea, EBC, El, NTC, WeBC]. The following verses which are attached to this κατά phrase are variously interpreted as descriptive or illustrative of the measure of this power [AB, Ba, Can, CBC, EBC, EGT, IB, ICC, MNTC, My, TH; NIV, TEV, TNT], as specifying the ground of the knowledge of God's power [My, St (probably), TNTC (probably), We], as specifying the result of God's power [AB (probably), Ea], as specifying the cause or guarantee of God's power acting in or toward ἡμᾶς 'us' [Ba, Lns, NTC], or as providing the evidence of God's power [NCBC, Si, WeBC].
2. It means 'by, in virtue of' and signals that the material in the rest of the chapter forms a cause-result relationship with the articular participle τοὺς πιστεύοντας 'who are believing' [Ho, LJ]: towards us, who are believing in virtue of (as a result of) the working of the strength of his might.

QUESTION—What is the relationship between the genitive nouns κράτος 'strength' and ἰσχύς 'might' ?

Governing genitives usually precede those governed, therefore κράτος 'strength' is the more prominent word here [Tu]. The genitive string is equivalent to τοῦ ἰσχυροῦ κράτους αὐτοῦ 'his mighty strength' [Mo, TD]. Since ἰσχύος 'might' signifies natural strength, the phrase κράτους τῆς ἰσχύος 'strength of the might', the might of that strength, is the utmost extension of it [Gd].

DISCOURSE UNIT: 1:20–23 [MNTC, NIC]. The topic is the power of God shown in the resurrection [NIC] and exaltation [MNTC] of Christ.

1:20 Which he-worked[a] in[b] the Christ

TEXT—Instead of the aorist tense ἐνήργησεν 'he worked', some manuscripts have the perfect tense ενήργηκεν 'he has worked'. GNT has the aorist tense with no indication of the alternative. The perfect tense is supported by AB, Alf, EBC, EGT (probably), IB, ICC, Rob, TH, WBC, We. The aorist tense is supported by Cal, Ea, El, GNT, Lns, My, NIC.

LEXICON—a. aorist (alternate reading—perf.) act. indic. of ἐνεργέω (LN 42.3) (BAGD 2. p. 265): 'to work' [BAGD, El, LN, Lns, Rob, We; KJV], 'to put to work' [NRSV], 'to exert' [AB, NIC, NTC; NIV, TNT], 'to produce, to effect' [BAGD], 'to accomplish' [TH, WBC], 'to bring about' [NASB], 'to exercise' [NJB], 'to show' [NAB], 'to use' [TEV]. This is also conflated with the previous phrase κατὰ τὴν ἐνέργειαν 'according to the working' (1:19) and translated there as 'to be seen at work' [REB].

b. ἐν with dative object (LN 83.13, 89.5): 'in' [AB, El, NIC, NTC, Rob, TH, WBC, We; KJV, NAB, NASB, NIV, NJB, NRSV], 'in the person of' [Lns]. Some make 'Christ' the direct object of 'to raise' and either do not translate ἐν or conflate it with the aorist participle ἐγείρας 'raised' and translate it 'when' with the temporal sense of that participle [REB, TEV, TNT].

QUESTION—To what does the relative pronoun ἥν 'which' refer?

1. It refers to the preceding δυνάμεως 'power' [Ba, Gd, MNTC, NTC, TNTC]: what is the greatness of his power which he worked in Christ. The relative pronoun ἥν 'which' identifies this as the same power which God exercised in raising Christ from among the dead [Gd].
2. It refers to the preceding ἐνέργειαν 'working' [Alf, Cal, Can, Ea, EBC, EGT, El, IB (probably), Lns, My, NIC, Rob, WBC]: according to the working of his strength, which working he worked in Christ. The relative is feminine and modifies the first feminine noun of the preceding κατά 'according to' phrase [Lns].
3. It refers to the preceding ἰσχύος 'strength' [AB, TH; TEV]: according to the working of his strength, which he worked in Christ.

QUESTION—What is the significance of the verb ἐνεργέω 'to work'?

The verb is cognate with the noun ἐνέργεια 'working' in the preceding string of synonyms for power. This construction results in an intensification of meaning [Alf, Cal, Ea].

QUESTION—What relationship is indicated by ἐν 'in'?

1. It indicates the ground or substratum upon which the action takes effect [Ea, El, TD]: which he worked on Christ (as the Messiah). It indicates the objective basis of Christ's fellowship or participation with God [TD].
2. It particularizes the object upon which the action takes effect and means 'in the case of' or 'in the person of' [Ba, Lns, My]: which he worked in the case of Christ. Used in this sense ἐν is a marker of an area of activity which bears some relation to something else [LN (89.5)].

QUESTION—Does Χριστός 'Christ' indicate a name or a title?
1. It indicates a title [AB, Alf, Can, Ea, ECWB, EGT, El, Gd, IB, Lns, We]: the Christ, or, the Messiah. Christ was raised not as an individual but as the representative and head of mankind [Alf, Cal, Can, Ea, ECWB, EGT, El, Gd, IB, LJ]. Both the presence of the definite article with Χριστός and the use of the preposition ἐν 'in' point to this interpretation [EGT]. This passage (1:19–2:10) establishes a direct connection between the resurrection of Christ and the resurrection of the saints [AB, EGT, Gd], almost identical terms being used for the resurrection and enthronement of the saints as for that of Christ [AB].
2. It is a name [Ba, MNTC, NCBC, NIC, NTC, TH, WBC, WeBC; all versions]: Christ.

having-raised[a] him from[b] (the) dead[c]

LEXICON—a. aorist act. participle of ἐγείρω (LN 23.94) (BAGD 1.a.β. p. 214): 'to raise' [AB, BAGD, El, NIC, NTC, Rob, TH, WBC, We; all versions], 'to raise up' [Lns], 'to raise to life, to make live again' [LN].
b. ἐκ with genitive object (LN 90.16): 'from' [AB, El, LN, Lns, NIC, NTC, Rob, TH, WBC, We; all versions].
c. νεκρός (LN 23.121) (BAGD 2.a. p. 535): 'the dead' [AB, BAGD, El, LN, Lns, NIC, NTC, Rob, TH, WBC, We; all versions except TEV, TNT], 'death' [TEV, TNT]. Νεκρός with the preposition ἐκ 'from' and without the article means all the dead, all those in the underworld [BAGD]. It can refer to the state of being dead rather than to being in the midst of dead people: 'death' [Lns; TEV, TNT]. It carries with it the implication of being in a state of death as well as being a companion of the dead [Gd].

QUESTION—What relationships are indicated by the use of the aorist participles ἐγείρας 'having raised' and καθίσας 'having seated'?
1. The participles indicate the temporal circumstances of the preceding verb ἐνήργησεν 'he worked' [AB, Can, Ea, Ho, ICC, My, NCBC, NIC, NTC, TH, WBC; KJV, NASB, NIV, NRSV, REB, TEV, TNT]: which he worked in Christ when he raised him from the dead and seated him, etc.
2. It explains 'the working of his power' [Alf, El, Lns, MNTC, Rob, Si-ed, TH; NAB, NJB]: which he worked in Christ in raising him from the dead and seating him, etc.
3. It indicates the result of the working of his power [Ea, EGT]: which he worked in Christ in that, as a result, he raised him from the dead and seated him, etc.

and having-seated[a] (him) at[b] (the) right[c] of-him in the heavenly (places)[d]

TEXT—Instead of the aorist act. participle form of καθίζω 'to seat', some manuscripts have the finite form of the aorist ἐκάθισεν 'he seated'. GNT does not mention this alternative form. The finite form is selected by: Ea, El, Gd, My, and KJV.

LEXICON—a. aorist act. participle of καθίζω (LN **87.36**) (BAGD 1.a. p. 389): 'to seat' [BAGD, Lns, NIC, TH, WBC; NAB, NASB, NIV, NRSV, TEV], 'to set' [BAGD, El, Rob; KJV], 'to make or cause to sit' [BAGD, NTC, We], 'to have (someone) sit' [BAGD], 'to enthrone' [AB; NJB, REB, TNT]. When used with the phrase ἐν δεξιᾷ 'at (the) right', it is an idiom meaning 'to give a special place of honor to' [LN]. It has the sense of 'to install', or even 'to enthrone' [TD].

b. ἐν with dative object (LN **83.23**) (BAGD I.1.c. p. 258): 'at' [AB, BAGD, LN, Lns, NIC, NTC, Rob, TH, WBC, We; all versions], 'on' [El]. This usage of ἐν designates a position in the immediate vicinity of or in proximity to an object [LN].

c. δεξιά (LN **87.36**) (BAGD 2.a. p. 174): 'right' [Lns, TH], 'right hand' [AB, BAGD, El, LN, NIC, NTC, Rob, WBC, We; all versions except TEV], 'right side' [LN; TEV].

d. ἐπουράνιος (LN **1.12**) (BAGD 2.a.α. p. 306): 'heavenly places' [NTC, Rob; KJV, NASB, NRSV], 'heavenly place' [Lns], 'heaven' [BAGD, LN; NAB, NJB], 'heavens' [AB], 'heavenly realms' [WBC; NIV, REB], 'heavenly realm' [NIC], 'heavenly regions' [El], 'heavenly order' [We], 'heavenly world' [TEV], 'heavenlies' [TH], 'supernatural world' [TNT]. See additional comments on this term at 1:3.

QUESTION—What is the significance of sitting at the right hand or right side?

This is the position of honor [Ba, Can, DNTT, Ea, EGT, Gd, Ho, IB, ISBE2, LN, St, TD, TH]. Others believe that it implies more than just honor. They state it as the position of authority or of both (authority implying the honor attached to it) [AB, Bu, Cal, DNTT, Ea, EBC, El, Ho, IB, IDB, ISBE, ISBE2, LJ, Lns, My, NCBC, NIC, NTC, Si, St, TH, TNTC, WBC, WeBC]. Since this is the right hand or right side of God, the position implies the supreme place of honor and authority in the universe, co-regency with God [Cal, Can, DNTT, Ea, Gd, ISBE2, LJ, Si, TD, WBC], since in the ancient world to sit at the right hand signified equal power and dignity [Cal, DNTT, Gd, TD]. Some commentators point out that when this position was given to the king's son, it implied heirship to the throne [Ba, Gd] and actual enthronement [Gd].

QUESTION—What does ἐν τοῖς ἐπουρανίοις 'in the heavenlies' mean?

1. The phrase is local in force [Alf, Ba, BAGD, DNTT, EGT, El, Gd, IB, ICC, ISBE2, LN (**87.36**), Lns, My, NCBC, TD, WBC]: in heaven. Supporters of this position do not mean to restrict the action to heaven alone, but argue that the terms are local because of the restrictions of the imagery used [El, Gd, IB, WBC]. Some point out that Christ's possession of a physical human body, in itself occupying space, forces a sense of locality to the phrase [Alf, El, Gd, Lns, WBC].

2. The phrase is not to be taken in a local, literal sense, but indicates rather the invisible world [Cal, Can, Ea, ISBE, MNTC, My-ed, NIC, Rob, TNTC]: in the unseen or invisible world. One commentator states it is the sphere of spiritual privilege [ISBE]. Others seem to imply that it stands in contrast to the created universe [Can, My-ed] thus strengthening the sense

1:21 far-above[a] all rule[b] and authority[c] and power[d] and lordship[e]

LEXICON—a. ὑπεράνω with genitive object (LN **87.31**) (BAGD p. 840): 'far above' [**LN**, Lns, NTC, WBC, We; KJV, NASB, NIV, NJB, NRSV, REB], 'high above' [BAGD, NIC; NAB], 'over above' [El], 'above' [AB, Rob, TH], 'considerably superior to' [LN]. This is also translated as a verbal phrase: 'to rule above' [TEV]. One translation extends the force of this preposition to both parts of the verse, translating it for the list of titles as a verbal phrase, 'to rule supreme over', and as 'high above' for the participial clause following them [TNT].

b. ἀρχή (LN **12.44**) (BAGD 3. p. 112): 'rule' [Lns, TH, We; NASB, NIV, NRSV], 'ruler' [BAGD; TNT], 'rulers' [LN], 'heavenly rulers' [TEV], 'principality' [El, NIC, NTC, Rob, WBC; KJV, NAB, NJB], 'government' [AB; REB], 'authority' [BAGD]. This is a supernatural being with reference to the political organization thought to exist among them [BAGD]. This is a reference to governmental authority [ECWB].

c. ἐξουσία (LN **12.44**) (BAGD 4.c.β. p. 278): 'authority' [AB, Lns, NTC, Rob, TH, WBC, We; NASB, NIV, NRSV, REB, TNT], 'authorities' [BAGD, LN; TEV], 'power' [El, NIC; KJV, NAB], 'ruling force' [NJB], 'officials, government' [BAGD]. This refers to the bearers of power and authority—the spirit world's rulers or functionaries [BAGD, DNTT, TD].

d. δύναμις (LN **12.44**) (BAGD 6. p. 208): 'power' [AB, BAGD, Lns, NTC, Rob, TH, WBC, We; NASB, NIV, NJB, NRSV, REB, TNT], 'powers' [LN; TEV], 'might' [El, NIC; KJV] 'virtue' [NAB]. This is a personal supernatural spirit or angel [BAGD]. They are cosmic powers between heaven and earth [DNTT]. This is a reference to the actual rule of a government official [ECWB].

e. κυριότης (LN **12.44, 37.52**) (BAGD 3. p. 461): 'lordship' [Lns, TH; TNT], 'lords' [TEV], 'dominion' [AB, El, NIC, NTC, Rob, WBC, We; KJV, NASB, NIV, NRSV, REB], 'dominions' [BAGD], 'domination' [NAB], 'sovereignty' [NJB], 'forces' [LN (**12.44**)], 'ruling power' [LN (**37.52**)], 'bearers of the ruling power' [BAGD]. This is a supernatural ruling power [LN (**37.52**)] of a special angelic class [BAGD, El, TD]. This has special reference to the moral force of dignity or lordship in which governmental authority is clothed [ECWB].

QUESTION—What relationship does this verse have to the preceding one?

This verse is either an amplification [Can, Ea, El, Gd, TH, TNTC] or an illustration [Ho] of Christ's exaltation and so it is a fuller explanation of the phrase ἐν τοῖς ἐπουρανίοις 'in the heavenly (places)' [El]. It expresses in a more literal manner what the previous verse expressed figuratively. This verse indicates the eminence and universality of Christ's exaltation [Gd].

EPHESIANS 1:21 91

QUESTION—Does the composite form of ὑπεράνω 'far above' have any special force?
1. Yes, the composite form is intensive [Ba, BAGD, Can, Ea, Ho, IB, LN, Lns, NIC, NTC, Si-ed, WBC, We; all versions except TEV, TNT]: far above. This is a composite preposition and the prefix ὑπερ- 'over' may give this word an intensive force over the simple ἄνω 'over' [Ea], such as 'high, far above'.
2. No, it is the equivalent of the simple preposition ὑπέρ 'above' [AB, Alf, EGT, El, HG, ICC, MNTC, My, Rob, TH; TEV, TNT]: above, or, over above.

QUESTION—What is the meaning of πᾶς 'all' here?
It means 'all kinds of' [Alf, DNTT, ECWB] or 'every' in the sense of 'every particular kind' [EGT]. One article in TD regards it as total, absolutely 'all'.

QUESTION—What is the purpose of this list of synonyms?
The purpose of this list of synonyms is to heap synonyms together [Bu, TD] in order to attract the readers' attention and impress the mind and so enhance the force of the passage. These synonyms are joined together by another figure of speech called *polysyndeton*, meaning 'many ands'. This figure tends to heighten the emphasis of the passage by directing attention to each item in the listing, and each of these items consists of a metonymy in which an attribute of power is listed in place of the being who possessed the attribute [Bu]. They are, in fact, names or titles [Bu, Cal], though another commentator states they are abstract nouns [El].

QUESTION—What is the relationship between the members of this list of synonyms?
1. This lists powerful beings in descending order of rank [Alf, Gd, My]: above the highest ranks of rulers and authorities and powers and lordships. However, one commentator implies that the ranks are only two since the second member of each pair explains the first [Alf]: above the highest ranks of rulers, i.e., authorities; and powers, i.e., lordships.
2. This lists different types of authorities probably without strict regard to rank [Bu (probably), Can, Ea, EBC, ECWB, EGT, El, ICC, LN (**12.44**), Lns, NTC, TD (probably), TNTC, WeBC]. In other passages where these terms occur, as in Col. 1:16, the terms occurs in different order, which argues against any assignment or rank to these terms [ECWB]. One commentator believes the first and last members have special reference to government, princedom or lordship, while the middle members refer to prerogative and command, i.e., the being with ἀρχή 'rule' displays ἐξουσία 'authority' and the being with κυριότης 'lordship' wields δύναμις 'power' [Ea]. Others believe each term in the list explains the preceding one: with ἀρχή 'rule' goes the corresponding ἐξουσία 'authority', and with that authority goes the corresponding δύναμις 'power', and with that power, the corresponding κυριότης 'lordship' [Can, Lns]. One commentator adds a fifth member to the list, ὄνομα

'name' so that with 'lordship' goes the corresponding 'name' or 'title' [Lns].

QUESTION—To whom or what does this listing of authorities refer?
1. This refers to both human and supernatural beings [Alf, Ba, Bu (probably), Gd, ICC, IDB, Lns, NIC, WeBC]: far above all beings that have rule and authority and power and lordship.
2. This refers to supernatural beings [AB, BAGD, Cal, Can, CBC, DNTT, Ea, EBC, ECWB, EGT, El, Ho, IDB, ISBE, LJ, LN (**12.44**), MNTC, My, NTC, Rob, St, TD, TH, WBC, We; NJB (note)].
2.1 These are both good angels and evil demonic beings [AB, DNTT, IB, ICC, LJ, NTC, Rob, TH; NJB (note)]: far above all angels, both good and evil, that have rule and authority etc. The principalities and powers (rule and authority) are the supernatural beings which, in Jewish thinking, controlled the totality of mankind's environment [AB, CBC, DNTT].
2.2 These are good angels [Cal, Can, CBC, DNTT, Ea, EBC (probably), EGT, El, Ho, ISBE, MNTC, My]: far above all angels that have rule and authority etc. These are the angels through whom God exercises his power and dominion [Cal], the guardian angels of nations [Can]. The focus is upon the good angels since it would be pointless to Christ's exaltation to say he is superior to human rulers and not properly befitting his position to mention only his superiority to demonic ones. Yet, in making him superior to all angelic authorities, these others would be implied since his position of power is all embracing [Ea].
2.3 These are primarily or only evil angels or demons [LN (**12.44**) (probably), NCBC, St, TD, WBC]: far above all those demonic beings that have rule and authority etc. Elsewhere in the Pauline writings, beings designated by these terms are regarded as having a negative influence over different spheres of human life. In Eph. 6:12 the ἀρχάς 'rulers' and ἐξουσίας 'authorities' are shown to be spiritual powers related to evil and darkness, who dwell in the ἐπουράνια 'heavenlies' [NCBC, TD, WBC], and against whom the Christian must fight.
2.4 This refers to spiritual powers venerated by the Gnostic teachers at Colosse [ECWB, TD, TNTC]: far above all those spirit beings with rule and authority, etc. that you are venerating. While the terminology is all inclusive, Paul's focus, as seen in the epistles of the captivity, may have been upon supernatural beings and may have been occasioned by the semi-Gnostic veneration for them at Colosse [ECWB].

and every name[a] being-named,[b] not only in this age,[c] but also in the coming;[d]

LEXICON—a. ὄνομα (LN 33.126): 'name' [El, LN, Lns, NIC, NTC, Rob, TH, WBC, We; KJV, NAB, NASB, NJB, NRSV], 'title' [AB; NIV, TNT], 'title of sovereignty' [REB].

b. pres. pass. participle of ὀνομάζω (LN 33.127) (BAGD 2. p. 574): 'to be named' [El, Lns, NIC, NTC, Rob, TH, WBC, We; KJV, NASB, NJB, NRSV, TNT], 'to be given a name' [LN], 'to be given a title to' [LN], 'to be given' [NAB, NIV], 'to be bestowed' [AB]. This phrase is also translated as a unit: 'to have a title superior to all titles of authority' [TEV], 'to use a name, to name a name' [BAGD], 'any title of sovereignty that commands allegiance' [REB].

c. αἰών (LN 67.143) (BAGD 2.b. p. 27): 'age' [AB, BAGD, LN, NIC, NTC, TH, WBC, We; NAB, NASB, NIV, NJB, NRSV, REB, TNT], 'era' [LN], 'eon' [Lns], 'world' [El, Rob; KJV, TEV]. The term designates a unit of time as a particular stage or period of history [LN]. It is not a purely temporal term but has a blended temporal, ethical, and quasi-local reference that is best expressed by the English word 'world' [El]. It indicates the world viewed from the standpoint of time, change, and prevalent mood, and therefore 'age' best expresses it [NTC].

d. pres. act. participle of μέλλω (LN 67.62) (BAGD 2. p. 501): 'to come' [AB, BAGD, El, Lns, NIC, NTC, Rob, TH, WBC, We; all versions except TEV], 'the next' [TEV], 'future' [BAGD]. The participle stands absolutely here for the future and the reference is to the age to come which brings the reign of God [BAGD]. The term refers to an event which is to occur at a point of time in the future that is closely related to another event and subsequent to it [LN].

QUESTION—What is the function of καί 'and'?

The καί 'and' introduces a final and comprehensive assertion [Ea, El, My], having the meaning 'and in general' [ICC].

QUESTION—What is the function of the participial clause παντὸς ὀνόματος ὀνομαζομένου 'every name being named'?

This is a further generalization from the preceding list of synonyms [Alf, Ea, EBC, St, WBC] (indicating thereby that the list is not intended to be exhaustive [AB, Gd, WBC]) and provides the transition from it to the idea of the subjugation of all things to Christ in 1:22 [Alf]. The idea is to comprehensively [MNTC] cover all created things by whatever name they are called [Ba, EGT, El, Gd].

QUESTION— What meaning does ὄνομα 'name' carry here?

1. It carries the simple sense of 'name' as personal identity [Cal, CBC, EGT, El, Gd, ICC, MNTC, My, NCBC, St, We].

  1.1 This means all names, both of ordinary and superior beings [EGT, El, ICC, My, St]: every name (of whatever being) named. The idea is to cover any created intelligence whatever [St] or anything in existence, any created object, personal or impersonal, that can be named [EGT, El] or is capable of designation [El].

  1.2 This indicates names of superior or powerful beings and so carries the connotation of honor and dignity [Cal, CBC, Gd, MNTC, NCBC, We]: every name (of whatever dignitary) named. It stands for largeness or

excellence; and ὀνομαζομένου 'to be named' means to have celebrity and praise [Cal, Gd].
2. It denotes more than a personal name and implies a title of honor [AB, Alf, Ba, Can, Ea, EBC, Ho, IB, Lns, NIC, NTC, Rob, TH, TNTC]: every title bestowed. The implication of rank is denoted [Ba, Ea, NIC].

QUESTION—What is the function of the phrase οὐ μόνον ἐν τῷ αἰῶνι τούτῳ ἀλλὰ καὶ ἐν τῷ μέλλοντι 'not only in this age, but also in the coming one'?

This is a further generalization of the preceding participial clause παντὸς ὀνόματος ὀνομαζομένου 'every name named' [Alf, EGT, El] and adds universality to the preceding negation [El, Ho]. Its force is: everything named whether now or hereafter, in the present state of things or the world to come [El]. It is designed to show that Christ's rank is eternal and not just temporal [Cal, ICC].

1:22 and all (things) he-put[a] under[b] his feet

LEXICON—a. aorist act. indic. of ὑποτάσσω (LN 37.31) (BAGD 1.a. p. 848): 'to put' [AB, El, Rob; KJV, NAB, NJB, NRSV, TEV, TNT], 'to place' [WBC; NIV], 'to put in subjection' [We; NASB, REB], 'to range' [Lns], 'to range in subjection' [NTC], 'to subject' [NIC, TH], 'to subject to' [BAGD, LN], 'to bring under control' [LN], 'to subordinate' [BAGD].

b. ὑπό with accusative object (LN 37.8) (BAGD 2.a.α. p. 843): 'under' [AB, BAGD, El, Lns, NTC, Rob, TH, WBC, We; all versions except REB], 'below' [BAGD], 'beneath' [NIC; REB]. The phrase ὑπὸ τοὺς πόδας 'under the feet' is an idiom meaning 'to be under the complete control of someone' [LN].

QUESTION—To what is this clause connected through its main verb ὑπέταξεν 'he put'?

The verb is coordinate with the preceding ἐνήργησεν 'he worked' (1:20) [EGT], as is also the other finite verb in this sentence, ἔδωκεν 'he gave'. Thus the construction is no longer one of subordination but independent and coordinate [EBC, Lns] so that the description of how God's mighty power is demonstrated, begun in 1:20, is continued in this verse and completed in 1:23 [EBC, TH].

QUESTION—What is the meaning of the metaphor 'to put under the feet'?

In both classical Greek and Old Testament times, the foot represented the power exercised by a person, and in the classical tradition in situations of honoring and subjection, the inferior or subordinate addressed himself to the feet of the mighty or the superior. In the OT the foot was often used to depict the suppression, subjection, or enslavement of persons or nations by the conquering power or person [TD]. The comparison is: as the conquering king of old times placed his foot upon the neck of his conquered opponent to humble him and show his power and exaltation over him by force of arms, so God, by his power, has exalted Christ and placed all power in him, placing the whole created universe, including enemies, in subjection to him.

The point of comparison is being put under subjection. The nonfigurative statement is: God has made all things subject to him.
1. This refers to or has the implication of conquering hostile forces [Bu, ECWB, IB, NIC, WeBC]: he made him victorious over all his enemies. The words describe the actual subjugation of all the forces of sin and death [ECWB].
2. This is not limited to the idea of conquest but is broader, referring to having supreme authority [Cal, Ea, EGT, El, Gd, Lns, My, Si, TD, WBC, We]: he subjected all things under him. This is not a repetition of the idea of Christ's honor shown in the preceding verse, but a proclamation of his imperial prerogative [Ea]. It looks at Christ's supreme authority from below, from the standpoint of the object so subjected, whereas previously it had been viewed from above, from the seat of the exalted Lord. Such a presentation is not tautology, but exhaustive and emphatic [My].

QUESTION—What is the meaning of πάντα 'all (things)'?

Πάντα 'all' is a summing up of all that is in the previous verse [Alf], so for some it is restricted to intelligent beings [Alf (probably), ECWB, IB]. For others it refers back to the teaching of the first chapter, seen in especially 1:10, respecting God's cosmic intention for Christ so that it includes the material creation as well [AB, Can, CBC, Ea, LJ, Lns, MNTC, My, NIC, NTC, Rob, Si, TH, TNTC, WBC]. Some commentators feel that while the meaning may embrace the whole of creation, its focus, at least, is upon intelligent beings [Can, Rob]. Others feel all creatures are meant [Cal, EGT, El, Ho, ICC].

and he-gave[a] him (as) head[b] over[c] all (things) to-the church,

LEXICON—a. aorist act. indic. of δίδωμι (LN 37.98, 57.71) (BAGD 5. p. 193): 'to give' [El, LN (57.71), Lns, NIC, NTC, Rob, TH, WBC, We; KJV, NASB, REB, TEV, TNT], 'to make' [NAB, NJB, NRSV], 'to appoint' [AB, BAGD, LN (37.98); NIV].
b. κεφαλή (LN 87.51) (BAGD 2.a. p. 430): 'head' [AB, BAGD, El, LN, Lns, NIC, NTC, Rob, TH, WBC, We; all versions except TEV], 'supreme Lord' [TEV], 'one who is superior to, one who is supreme over' [LN]. It has a figurative meaning denoting superior rank [BAGD]. It involves authority to order or command [Lns].
c. ὑπέρ with accusative object (LN 87.30) (BAGD 2. p. 839): 'over' [AB, El, Lns, NTC, Rob, TH, WBC, We; KJV, NASB, NIV, NRSV, REB, TEV], 'of' [NAB], 'above' [LN; NJB], 'superior to' [LN]. Some translate the phrase 'over all things' as an adjective: 'supreme' [BAGD, NIC; TNT]. (Such a translation may introduce an implied contrast to subordinate 'heads' in the church, which commentators deny is present in the phrase [Alf, Ea, EGT, El, Ho, ICC, My], even one who uses the adjective [Ho].)

QUESTION—What is the meaning of ἔδωκεν 'he gave' and to what is it connected?

The verb is coordinate with ὑπέταξεν 'he subjected' and connected to it by καί 'and' [EGT, Lns, TH].

1. The verb has the simple meaning of 'to give' in this context [Alf, Ea, EBC, EGT, El, Gd, IB, ICC, Lns, My, NIC, NTC, Rob, St, TH, TNTC, WBC, We; KJV, NASB, REB, TEV, TNT]: and gave him to the church as its head. Christ's occupancy of this exalted position is a Divine gift to the church [Ea, EBC, EGT, Gd, IB, ICC, Lns, NIC, TH, WBC], and likewise it is a gift from God to Christ [Gd].
2. The verb has the meaning of 'to appoint' [AB, Ba; NIV], 'to make' [NCBC; NAB, NJB, NRSV], 'to set' [MNTC], or 'to place' [Ho]: and appointed him as head for the church.

QUESTION—What is meant by κεφαλὴν ὑπὲρ πάντα 'head over all things'?

1. Christ's role as head of creation is what is primarily meant here [Alf, Ba, BAGD, Can, Ea, EBC, EGT, IDB, LJ, Lns, MNTC, NCBC, NTC, Si, St, TH, TNTC, WBC, WeBC; TEV]: and gave him to the church as head of all creation. The preceding content of chapter 1 and the original context of Ps. 8:6 show that the author is interested in Christ's universal and cosmic rule [AB, Can]. The idea of Christ's headship over the church is more expressly implied in the next clause (1:23) with its mention of the church as forming Christ's body [EGT, NTC].
2. Christ's role as head of the church is the primary or only meaning here [Cal, CBC, ECWB, Gd, IB, ISBE, ISBE2, NIC, Rob, TD; NAB, TNT]: and gave him to be head of the church over all things. With the insistence on Christ's universal lordship in the previous verse as well as in the previous clause goes the implication that he is the church's Lord also. Here the word κεφαλήν 'head' is not explicitly used to denote Christ's supremacy over the principalities and powers and the rest of creation [NIC].
3. Both roles are in focus [AB, El, Ho, My, We; NJB]: and gave him, head over all creation, as head of the church.

QUESTION—How is the phrase κεφαλὴν ὑπὲρ πάντα 'head over all (things)' connected in this verse?

1. This is given as a statement of role or function [Alf, Ba, Cal, Can, Ea, EGT, Gd, Ho, Lns, My, NIC, NTC, Rob, St, TH, TNTC, WBC, We; KJV, NASB, NIV, REB, TEV, TNT].
1.1 With the infinitive 'to be' added [Ba, Cal, Can (probably), Rob, TNTC, We; KJV, NIV]: and gave him to the church to be head over all creation, or, and gave him to the church to be head over all things.
1.2 With the adverb 'as' added [Alf, Ea, EGT, Ho, Lns, My, NIC, NTC, St, TH, WBC; NASB, REB, TEV, TNT]: and gave him as head over all creation to the church, or, and gave him as supreme head to the church. By the figure of brevity of speech an ellipsed κεφαλήν 'head' stands

before τῇ ἐκκλησίᾳ 'to the church' [My]: and gave him as head of all creation to be head to the church.
2. This stands in apposition to αὐτόν 'him' and implies by the figure of conciseness of speech an ellipsed κεφαλήν 'head' before τῇ ἐκκλησίᾳ 'to the church' [AB, El]: and appointed him, head over all creation, to be head of the church.
3. This is regarded as the object of the verb ἔδωκεν [NAB, NRSV]: and he made him the head over all things for the church.
4. This is regarded as parenthetical [NJB]: and made him, as he is above all things, the head of the Church.

QUESTION—What meaning does the metaphor κεφαλήν 'head' have in this verse?

1. It denotes authority [BAGD, Cal, CBC, Ea, ECWB, EGT, ISBE, ISBE2, LJ, Lns (probably), My, NCBC, NIC, Rob (probably), TNTC, WBC, We]: and he gave him as the highest authority over all things to the church. The metaphor of the head denotes the highest authority [Cal, ISBE2]. This interpretation takes its meaning from the extended meaning of κεφαλή denoting the leading member of a social group, a family or nation for instance. The comparison is: as the head of the family (or nation), the father (or king), wields the highest authority within his social unit, so Christ as the head of all creation, or the church, as the case may be, wields highest authority over creation or the church. The nonfigurative statement would be: and gave him as highest authority over all things to the church.
2. It denotes 'origin' or 'source' [Gd, NIC]: and he gave him as supreme source (of life) to the church. In this case the comparison would be: as the head is the source of life to the body so the church finds its life through its head, Christ. The nonfigurative statement would be: he gave him to the church as its source of life. But NIC states at the beginning of his comments on the following verse that as soon as σῶμα 'body' is mentioned there, a further meaning, interpretation 3 below, is imparted to κεφαλή 'head'.
3. It denotes a mystical, organic union [Ea (probably), EGT, Gd, Ho, IB, LJ, NIC, Si, TD, We]: and he gave him to the church so that it (the church) could be united to him [Ea, EGT, Ho, IB, LJ, NIC, Si, We], or, so that it and all creation could be united to him [TD]. In this interpretation the main ideas expressed are intimate union and communication of life [Gd, Ho, NIC, We]. The church is the body of which Christ is the head, imparting to the body (church) his fullness [Gd, IB, LJ]. The comparison is: as the head is united to the body imparting its life to the body, so Christ is united to the church imparting his life to it. The nonfigurative statement would be: and he gave him to the church so it could be united to him and partake of his life.

QUESTION—What is the force of the dative case in the phrase τῇ ἐκκλησίᾳ 'to the church'?
1. This is the simple dative, denoting the indirect object [AB, Alf, EGT, MNTC, NIC, Rob, Si, St, TH, WBC, We; KJV, NASB, REB, TEV, TNT]: 'to the church'. Paul doesn't think of Christ as supreme over all creation for the benefit of the church, but the other way around [MNTC]. He is the head of the church in order that ultimately he may be the head of everything in existence [Cal, MNTC]. The church is to be the instrument by which he is to exercise universal power [MNTC].
2. This is the benefactive dative [Ba, Ea, EBC, Gd, LJ, NCBC (probably), TNTC; NIV, NRSV]: for the church. God appointed Christ to be supreme ruler of the universe so that all the elements in it work together for the welfare of his church [Ba, Ea, LJ], including all of nature, governments, supernatural beings [Ba, LJ], revolutions, science, and art [Ea]. Thus the church is able to overcome all opposition to it [EBC, LJ, NCBC, TNTC].
3. This is the dative of possession [NAB, NJB]: of the church.

1:23 which is his body,[a]

LEXICON—a. σῶμα (LN 11.34) (BAGD 5. p. 800): 'body' [AB, BAGD, El, LN, Lns, NIC, NTC, Rob, TH, WBC, We; all versions].

QUESTION—How is this clause related to the preceding one?
1. This clause stands in an epexegetical or qualifying relationship to the preceding clause 'gave him to be head over all things to the church', further explaining Christ's relationship to the church [AB, Alf, El, Gd, IB, ICC, My, WBC, We]: which, in fact, is his body. It explains the use and meaning of κεφαλήν 'head' by introducing the corresponding term σῶμα 'body' [El].
2. This clause gives the cause or grounds for the preceding clause [Can, EGT, Lns, NTC]: since it is his body. The clause explains the preceding one by giving the grounds for God's gift of Christ to the church as its head [EGT]. The reason lies in the nature of the church as his body [EGT, Lns].

the fullness[a] **of-the (one) filling/being-filled**[b] **the all (things) in**[c] **all (things).**

LEXICON—a. πλήρωμα (LN 59.32; 59.36) (BAGD 1.b. p. 672): 'fullness' [El, LN (59.32), Lns, NIC, NTC, Rob, TH, WBC, We; KJV, NAB, NASB, NIV, NJB, NRSV, REB], 'completion' [TEV], 'completeness, totality, full measure' [LN (59.32)], 'that which is full of something' [BAGD], 'that which fills, contents' [LN (59.36)]. This noun is also translated as a verb: 'to be completed' [TNT]; or as an adverb: 'full' [AB].
b. pres. mid. or pass. participle of πληρόω (LN 59.33; 59.37; 68.26) (BAGD 1.a. p. 671): 'to fill' [AB, BAGD, El, LN (59.37), NTC, TH, WBC; KJV, NAB, NASB, NIV, NRSV, REB], 'to fill for oneself' [Lns], 'to make full' [BAGD], 'to complete' [LN (68.26); TEV, TNT], 'to make complete' [LN (59.33)], 'to be filled' [NJB], 'to be constantly filled' [NIC], 'to be fulfilled' [Rob], 'to reach one's fullness' [We]. The present tense shows that the process of filling or being filled is continuous [IB, NIC, We]. It

points to the progressive and continuous movement of all things to their final goal in Christ [IB, We]. It expresses the continuity of Christ's filling [WBC] or upholding and governing the universe [My].

c. ἐν with dative object (LN 83.13): 'in' [BAGD, LN, Lns, NTC, Rob, TH, We; KJV, NAB, NASB, NIV, NJB, NRSV, REB], 'with' [El]. The phrase ἐν πᾶσιν 'in all (things)' is translated as a whole: 'totally' [AB, NIC], 'everywhere' [TEV].

QUESTION—What is the purpose of the *paronomasia* and alliteration in this clause?

The writer intended to say something very important in this clause [NCBC, WBC] as the impressive combination of *paronomasia* (use of cognate forms of noun and verb in πλήρωμα 'fullness' and πληρουμένου 'the one filling/being filled') and the alliteration in πάντα 'all things' and πᾶσιν '(in) all things' indicate [WBC], but precisely what he intended to communicate is hard to determine with any certainty [NCBC, WBC].

QUESTION—To what is this clause attached?

1. This clause is in apposition to τῇ ἐκκλησίᾳ 'to the church' of the previous verse [Ba, BAGD, Cal, EBC, ECWB, EGT, Ho, ICC, IDB, ISBE, My, NTC, Si, TD, TH, TNTC, We]: to the church, the fullness of him who, etc. This clause corresponds to and is parallel to the clause 'which is his body' [My], describing further the church as the body of Christ [NTC], more precisely explaining the relation of the church to Christ in nonfigurative language [My].

2. This clause is in apposition to σῶμα 'body' in the previous clause [AB, Alf, Can, CBC, Ea, El, Gd, IB, Lns, MNTC, Rob, St, WBC; NAB, NJB (note), REB]: his body (which is) the fullness of him who, etc. The difference between this and the first interpretation is merely one of construction, there being no substantial difference in meaning.

3. Πλήρωμα 'fullness' is put absolutely in the accusative case, so making the clause a summary of the general idea of the preceding material from 1:20 onwards [NIC]: even him who is the fullness of that (the church) which is being totally filled.

4. This clause is in apposition to αὐτόν 'him' in the previous verse [Mo (possibly), NCBC]: gave to the church him (who) is the fullness of him who etc. One grammar classifies this πλήρωμα 'fullness' clause as possibly an accusative which predicates something of the previous accusative αὐτόν 'him' (Christ) [Mo]. The argument supporting this interpretation is that this passage would then teach much the same thing as Col. 2:9.

QUESTION—What is the meaning of πλήρωμα 'fullness'?

1. The word has a passive sense [AB, Alf, BAGD, CBC, Ea, EBC, EGT, El, ISBE, MNTC, My, NIC, St, TD, TNTC, WBC].

    1.1 It refers to God [Alf] or Christ filling the church [AB, BAGD, CBC, Ea, EBC, EGT, El, ISBE, MNTC, My, NIC, St, TD, TNTC, WBC]: the church (which) is filled by (Christ). In this case Christ fills the church with his presence, power, life, and directions [AB, EGT, St, TD] or,

with all his gifts, graces, and blessing [Alf, El, TD]. The church is the sphere in which he directly exercises his power and the instrument by which his power will extend out to all parts of the universe [MNTC, TD, WBC], it is a microcosm of what all things in existence will finally become [MNTC].
- 1.2 It refers to Christ being filled by God [NCBC]: (Christ) who is filled (by God). In this case the πλήρωμα 'fullness' is the nature of deity.
- 1.3 It refers to the new creation or the members of Christ filling up (constituting) the church [Bu; NJB (note)]: his members fill up the body of Christ.
2. The word has an active sense and refers to the church fulfilling Christ in the sense of completing him [Ba, Cal, Can, ECWB, Gd, Ho, IB, ICC, IDB, Lns, NTC, Rob, Si, TH, We; TEV, TNT (note)]: the church (which) completes (Christ) who fills/is filled by all in all. According to this interpretation, while Christ on his Divine side cannot be said to be lacking in anything, in his role as Messiah and Son of Man, he is seen as incomplete without the corporate body of those who make him such by constituting his kingdom [Gd, IB, NTC, TH], (i.e., a king is not truly a king without a kingdom to rule over [Ba], nor a bridegroom a bridegroom without a bride [NTC]).

QUESTION—Is πληρουμένου 'he who fills/is filled' middle or passive voice and what is the resultant meaning?

1. The participle is middle voice [AB, Alf, Ba, BAGD, Bu, Can, DNTT, Ea, EBC, ECWB, EGT, El, Gd, Ho, ICC, Lns, MNTC, Mo (possibly), My, NTC, Si-ed, St, TD, TH, TNTC, WBC; KJV, NAB, NASB, NIV, NRSV, TEV].
   - 1.1 While middle in form, it is understood as the active form would be [AB, Ba, BAGD, Bu, Can, DNTT, EBC, Gd, Ho, ICC, Mo (possibly), TD, TH, TNTC, WBC; KJV, NAB, NASB, NIV, NRSV, REB, TEV]: he who fills the all in all. Christ completes all things [DNTT, TH], he fills the cosmos in every respect [WBC]. Nothing has existence apart from him and his purposes [DNTT]. This allows τὰ πάντα 'the all things' to be taken naturally as the object of the clause and as designating the cosmos and ἐν πᾶσιν to have its straightforward meaning of 'in all respects, in every way' [WBC].
   - 1.2 The middle voice has a reflexive sense [Alf, Ea, ECWB, EGT, El, HG, Lns, MNTC, My, NTC, Si-ed]: he who fills the all in all for himself. The filling refers to the gifts Christ imparts that are appropriate to the welfare of the universe [Ea], or the filling refers to upholding and governing the universe [My], or it denotes Christ's omnipresence [Si].
2. The participle is passive voice [CBC, IB, NIC, Rob, We; NJB, TNT].
   - 2.1 Christ is fulfilled or made complete by the all in all [IB, Rob, We]: of him who is completed by the all in all. The summing up of the universe in Christ (1:10) is the issue of the divine purposes [Rob, We].

2.2 Christ is filled by God [CBC]: of him who is filled entirely (by God). Christ is part of God's being [CBC].
2.3 The Church is filled by Christ [NIC]: of that which is being constantly and totally filled.
3. Both voices are intended [LJ (probably); TNT (note)]: then he who completes all things will himself by completed (by the church). Paul had both ideas in mind and used the ambiguous form of the participle to express both ideas [TNT note].

QUESTION—What does the phrase τὰ πάντα ἐν πᾶσιν 'all (things) in all (things)' denote?
1. It denotes the same thing that πᾶς 'all' in the previous verses has denoted—the universe and all that is in it [AB, Alf, DNTT, EGT, El, Ho, IB, Lns, MNTC, My, NCBC, NTC, Rob, Si, TD, TH, TNTC, WBC, We; NAB, NIV, REB, TEV]: of him who fills everything there is.
2. It denotes Christ's filling or spiritual governing of the church [Bu, Cal, Gd, NIC]: of him who fills all things (in the church). Two commentators think it refers to all the individual members of the church [Bu, Gd]. Christ fills each member with his Spirit, and through his Spirit extends his influence through all the powers and faculties of their souls. Christ also fills his church corporately [Gd].

QUESTION—What does ἐν 'in' mean, and what is the resultant meaning of the phrase ἐν πᾶσιν 'in all (things)'?
1. The preposition is instrumental in force and means 'with' [Alf, Bu, Can, Ea, EGT, El, Gd, Ho, My]: with all things. In this case ἐν πᾶσιν may mean 'with all (benefits or blessings)' [Bu, Can, Ea, Gd] or 'with everything (it possesses)' [Alf, EGT, El], showing that the universe is maintained and governed by Christ [EGT, My] or God the Father [Alf]. Or, it may also mean 'with his presence', showing that he is present in each being in the universe [Can, Ho].
2. The preposition is adverbial in force and means 'in' [BAGD, Cal, ICC, Lns, MNTC, NTC, TD, WBC; NAB, NIV, NJB (note)]: in all respects or in all ways. The phrase may mean he fills all that exists in all possible respects or ways [BAGD, Lns, TD, WBC; NIV], or he fills the universe in all its parts [MNTC, TD; NAB, REB]. Here also the interpretation is that the universe is dependent upon him for its every need, including his governing it [NTC].
3. The preposition has no meaning on its own, but is understood as part of a phrase (ἐν πᾶσιν 'in all (things)') that is understood idiomatically as meaning 'entirely', or 'totally' [AB, CBC, NIC], or 'everywhere' [TEV].

QUESTION—With all the variables in this final clause in this chapter, what are the interpretative combinations for the clause as a whole that the various commentators adopt?

The combinations occur according to the following outline:

1. The Church is filled (πλήρωμα 'fullness') [AB, Alf, BAGD, Bu, CBC, Ea, EBC, EGT, El, MNTC, My, NIC, St, TD, TNTC, WBC; NJB (note), REB].
1.1 by Christ [AB, CBC, Ea, EBC, EGT, El, MNTC, My, NIC, St, TD, TNTC, WBC].
1.1.1 and Christ fills (πληρουμένου 'the (one) filling/being filled') the universe (τὰ πάντα 'the all (things)') [AB, BAGD, EBC, MNTC, St, TD, TNTC, WBC] totally (ἐν πᾶσιν 'in all (things)') [AB, EBC, TNTC], or in all its parts [MNTC], or in all respects, in every way [BAGD, WBC].
1.1.2 and Christ fills for himself (πληρουμένου 'the (one) filling/being filled') the universe (τὰ πάντα 'the all (things)') [Ea, EGT, El, My] with all things (ἐν πᾶσιν 'in all (things)') [EGT, El, My], or with all blessings [Ea].
1.1.3 and Christ is filled (πληρουμένου 'the (one) filling/being filled') by God with the entire (ἐν πᾶσιν 'in all (things)') fullness (τὰ πάντα 'the all (things)') of God [CBC].
1.1.4 and it (the Church) is being constantly (and totally (ἐν πᾶσιν 'in all (things)')) filled (πληρουμένου 'the (one) filling/being filled') [NIC].
1.2 by God and God fills for himself (πληρουμένου 'the (one) filling/being filled') the universe (τὰ πάντα 'the all (things)') with all things (ἐν πᾶσιν 'in all (things)') [Alf].
1.3 by Christians (or the New Creation), and Christ fills (πληρουμένου 'the (one) filling/being filled') Christians with all spiritual gifts and graces (τὰ πάντα ἐν πᾶσιν 'the all (things) in all (things)') [Bu; NJB (note)].
2. Christ is filled by God (πλήρωμα 'fullness') and God fills (πληρουμένου 'the (one) filling/being filled') the universe (τὰ πάντα 'the all (things)') [NCBC].
3. The church fulfills or completes Christ (πλήρωμα 'fullness') [Ba, Cal, Can, ECWB, Gd, Ho, IB, ICC, Lns, NTC, Rob, Si, TH, We; TEV] or, when the body joins the head (πλήρωμα 'fullness') [TNT]
3.1 and Christ fills (πληρουμένου 'the (one) filling/being filled') the universe (τὰ πάντα 'the all (things)') [Ba, Can, Ho] in all its parts (ἐν πᾶσιν 'in all (things)') [Can, Ho].
3.2 and Christ fills for himself (πληρουμένου 'the (one) filling/being filled') the universe (τὰ πάντα 'the all (things)') [ECWB, ICC, Lns, NTC, Si] in all respects (ἐν πᾶσιν 'in all (things)') [Lns, NTC], or in all [ICC].
3.3 and Christ completes (πληρουμένου 'the (one) filling/being filled') the universe (τὰ πάντα 'the all (things)') everywhere (ἐν πᾶσιν 'in all (things)') [TH; TEV].
3.4 then Christ who completes (πληρουμένου 'the (one) filling/being filled') the universe (τὰ πάντα 'the all (things)') will be completed (πληρουμένου 'the (one) filling/being filled') (by the church) [TNT (note)].

3.5 and Christ fills (πληρουμένου 'the (one) filling/being filled') the church [Cal, Gd] with all graces [Gd] and governs it (τὰ πάντα ἐν πᾶσιν 'the all (things) in all (things)') [Cal].

3.6 and Christ is completed (πληρουμένου 'the (one) filling/being filled') by the universe (τὰ πάντα 'the all (things)') [IB, Rob, We].

DISCOURSE UNIT: 2:1–3:21 [TNTC]. The topic is life in Christ.

DISCOURSE UNIT: 2:1–22 [Alf, ECWB, El, LJ, NTC, WeBC; NASB]. The topic is the glory of the church in its universal scope [NTC] of uniting Jew and Gentile together in Christ [Alf, ECWB, LJ, NTC], a new way of life in Christ [WeBC].

DISCOURSE UNIT: 2:1–10 [AB, Alf, Ba, Ea, EBC, EGT, El, Gd, Ho, ICC, LJ, Lns, MNTC, NCBC, NIC, NTC, Rob, St, TD, TH, TNTC, WBC; NAB, NASB, NIV, NJB, REB, TEV]. The topic is the power of God illustrated by the resurrection of life from the state and condition of the Ephesians before their conversion [Ba, EGT, Gd, Ho, ICC, LJ, MNTC, NTC, Rob]. The topic has shifted from what Paul is praying the Ephesians might know to reminding them of what they once were and of what God has made of them [Lns].

DISCOURSE UNIT: 2:1–7 [ECWB, Gd, My, NIC, Si]. The topic is the giving of new life to men from their death in sin and bondage to Satan [ECWB, My, NIC], the old manhood contrasted with the new [Si].

DISCOURSE UNIT: 2:1–6 [Alf; NJB]. The topic is the power of the Father shown in giving life to us [Alf].

DISCOURSE UNIT: 2:1–3 [AB, Ba, CBC, Gd, Ho, IB, LJ, Lns, NCBC, St, WeBC]. The topic is the common captivity of mankind, both Jew and Gentile, in a state of sin, death, and condemnation before God's power and grace was demonstrated in them by raising them to new life in Christ [AB, Ba, CBC, Gd, Ho, IB, LJ, WeBC].

2:1 And[a] you being dead[b] in-the trespasses[c] and in-the sins[d] of-you,

LEXICON—a. καί (LN 89.92, 89.93): 'and' [Lns, NTC, Rob, WBC, We; KJV, NASB, NJB], 'and also' [El], 'too' [NIC], 'as for' [NIV], 'especially' [AB], not explicit [NAB, NRSV, REB, TEV, TNT].

b. νεκρός (LN **74.28**) (BAGD 1.b.α. p. 534): 'dead' [AB, BAGD, El, LN, Lns, NIC, NTC, Rob, WBC, We; all versions except TEV], 'spiritually dead' [LN; TEV]. It means 'unable to respond to matters pertaining to God' [LN].

c. παράπτωμα (LN 88.297) (BAGD 2.b. p. 621): 'trespass' [El, Lns, NIC, NTC, Rob, WBC, We; KJV, NASB, NRSV], 'transgression' [BAGD, LN; NIV], 'disobedience' [TEV], 'crime' [NJB], 'offense' [TNT], 'sin' [BAGD, LN; NAB, REB], 'lapse' [AB], 'false step' [BAGD]. This word pertains to what a person has done in transgressing the will and law of God through some false step or failure [LN]. Although it often seems to be equivalent in meaning to ἁμαρτία 'sin', it may differ in that 'trespass' focuses more upon unpremeditated violation of God's will and law [LN]. See this word at 1:7.

d. ἁμαρτία (LN 88.289): 'sin' [AB, El, LN, Lns, NIC, NTC, Rob, WBC, We; all versions except NAB, REB], 'offense' [NAB], 'wickedness' [REB].

QUESTION—What relationship is indicated by καί 'and'?

1. The unit introduced by this conjunction is connected in thought, at least, to the statement in 1:19–20 and helps the readers know how great the power of God is that is working in them [AB, Alf, Ba, Can, Ea, EGT, El, Gd, Ho, IB, ICC, LJ, MNTC, My, NIC, Rob, Si, St, WBC]. God's power was demonstrated in Christ's resurrection and exaltation and it has also been demonstrated in the readers' spiritual resurrection.

2. The connection is with the mention of the church in 1:22–23 [NCBC, TNTC, We], with the believers' relation to Christ through the church [Lns], or with the thought of the church as a theme underlying the preceding chapter [NTC, WeBC]. The apostle wants to develop further his doctrine of the church but first he wants to discuss what salvation is to both Jew and Gentile [NCBC, TNTC, WeBC].

3. The connection is with the doctrine of election and redemption through union with Christ of the last chapter [ECWB]. Paul is shifting to the particular application of this doctrine to the Ephesians.

QUESTION—What is the construction that καὶ ὑμᾶς 'and you' imposes on the following verses and with what verb does the accusative pronoun ὑμᾶς 'you' connect?

The sentence begun by καὶ ὑμᾶς 'and you' is long and broken, being variously described as extending through 2:5 [El], 2:7 [Ho, WBC], or 2:10 [Lns, TNTC]. (Alternatively, 2:1–3 are called an incomplete sentence, with a new sentence beginning at v. 4 and extending through 2:7 [TH].) Ὑμᾶς 'you' is in an emphatic position [AB, Alf, Ea, El, MNTC, NTC, St] and since it is in the accusative case, it is evidently intended to be the object of a verb. Paul started off with this plural accusative pronoun intending to join it with συνεζωοποίησεν τῷ χριστῷ 'made alive together with Christ' but was led aside by the relative clauses ἐν αἷς ποτε…'in which formerly…' [Alf, EBC], and ἐν οἷς καὶ ἡμεῖς…'among whom we also…' [Alf], desiring to clear up any misconceptions before proceeding on with his sentence, (1) of how he could speak of them as being dead and (2) not only they but the Jews likewise [Rob]. He then resumes his train of thought in 2:4–5, giving the subject of the sentence in 2:4 (God) [Alf, EGT, El, ICC, My], but the mention of ἡμεῖς 'we' (the Jews) in the second relative clause necessitated his use of the accusative plural pronoun ἡμᾶς 'us' (2:5) rather than ὑμᾶς 'you' as object of the verb he had intended to use in this first verse [Alf, El, ICC, MNTC, My]. It is with this verb (συνεζωοποίησεν 'he made alive together with') that the various commentators here join ὑμᾶς 'you' [AB, Alf, Ba, Bu, Cal, Can, Ea, EBC, ECWB, EGT, El, Ho, IB, ICC, LJ, Lns,

MNTC, My, NCBC, NIC, NTC, Rob, Si, St, TH, TNTC, WBC, We; KJV]. Some cover up this grammatical roughness by duplicating the verb from 2:5 into 2:1 [Ba, Ho, IB, LJ, NCBC, NIC, Si, TNTC, We; KJV]: 'and he made you alive when you were dead in your trespasses and sins'. Some translations make the grammar smoother by treating ὑμᾶς 'you' (accusative case) as if it were the subject (nominative case) and translating the participle ὄντας 'being' as an active verb [TH; NAB, NASB, NIV, NJB, NRSV, REB, TEV, TNT]: 'you were dead in your trespasses and sins'.

QUESTION—Who are the referents of ὑμᾶς 'you'?
1. The referents of ὑμᾶς 'you' are the Ephesians as representative of Gentile believers [AB, Alf, Cal, EBC, ECWB, EGT El, Ho, IB, ICC, LJ, Lns, MNTC, My, NIC, NTC, Rob, Si, St, TD, TH, TNTC, We, WeBC; NJB (note), TNT]: you Ephesians, as Gentiles. Therefore it is resumptive of the 2nd person of 1:13, 15–18 and anticipatory of ὑμεῖς 'you' in 2:11 [EBC].
2. The referents of ὑμᾶς 'you' here are the Ephesians considered as apart from Paul himself [Ba, Bu, Can, CBC, NCBC] or Christians generally [WBC]: you Ephesians. But the ἡμεῖς 'we' of 2:3 includes Paul together with them.

QUESTION—What is meant by νεκρός 'dead'?
The term designates the present spiritual death of unregenerate mankind [all commentators except My]. It refers to the liability to the final, eternal spiritual death [My]. Spiritual death is an inability to respond in faith or obedience to matters relating to God [CBC, Ea, EBC, Gd, ISBE, LN (74.28), NTC, St, TH], being dead to holiness [Ba, Ea] or God [IDB], or a slave to sin [Gd, TD], being alienated from God [Cal, Can, Gd, IB, LJ, Lns, NIC, St, WBC, WeBC], being independent from God [DNTT], being under the power of death [DNTT, ISBE2, TD], ethical [EGT, Si] or moral [ICC] death, moral degeneration and the hardening and insensibility caused by it [NCBC], the lack of any capacity for spiritual activity or development [TNTC] particularly with respect to the purpose for which man was created—to grow into the Divine likeness [We]. The comparison is as a dead body is unable to respond to any stimulus from its environment so the spiritually dead man is unable to respond in a positive manner to God. The point of comparison is insensibility and lack of response. The nonfigurative statement would be: you were unable to respond in any way to God.

QUESTION—What is the difference between παράπτωμα 'trespass' and ἁμαρτία 'sin'?
1. There is no difference in meaning, they form a fully synonymous couplet [AB, EGT, ICC, Lns, My, NCBC, NIC, Si, TD, TNTC, WBC]: your trespasses (which are) sins, or, your sinful trespasses. The repetition of synonyms serves to state the cause of the condition more emphatically [Lns, WBC].
2. There is a difference in meaning that should be preserved in translation [Alf, Can, Ea, EBC, ECWB, El, Ho, LJ, NTC, St, TH]: your trespasses and your sins. Παράπτωμα 'trespass' in the plural indicates various

specific acts of unrighteousness [Can, El, Ho], deviations from the straight and narrow or the true and right [LJ, NTC], failure in visible and special acts [ECWB], sins of a fleshly nature seen as separate and repeated acts [Ea], disobedience to God's law [TH], lapses [EBC]; while ἁμαρτία 'sin' in the plural indicates the actual sins of a more general nature in which the sinful inclination is manifested [Can, Ea, El, Ho, LJ], shortcomings [EBC], inclinations, thoughts, words, and deeds that 'miss the mark' of glorifying God [NTC], universal and positive principles of evil doing [ECWB]. Together the terms indicate sins of every species, however manifested [Ea], and give a comprehensive picture of human evil [St] and the spiritual death of which they give evidence [EBC].

QUESTION—What is the force of the dative case in the phrase τοῖς παραπτώμασιν καὶ ταῖς ἁμαρτίαις ὑμῶν 'in your trespasses and sins'?
  1. The dative case indicates the reason they were spiritually dead [Alf, Cal, Can, DNTT, EGT, El, Ho, IB, LJ, Lns, My, NCBC, NIC, NTC, TH WBC, We, WeBC; NAB, NJB, NRSV, REB, TEV, TNT]: you were dead because of your trespasses and sins.
  2. The dative case indicates the sphere or the accompanying circumstances of the spiritual death [AB, Ea, EBC, ICC, Rob; KJV, NASB, NIV]: you were dead, living in trespasses and sins. It indicates that in which the spiritual death consisted [ICC], i.e., the trespasses and sins denotes more than just the cause, but also describes the state and condition of the death [AB, Ea], as well as the instrument, manifestation, and consequence of it [AB]. It could be said to define the death [Rob].

2:2 in[a] which formerly[b] you-walked,[c] according-to[d] the course/age[e] of-this world,[f]

LEXICON—a. ἐν with dative object (LN 89.5): 'in' [LN, Lns, NIC, NTC, WBC; NASB, NIV, NRSV], 'by' [AB], not explicit [NJB, REB, TEV, TNT], 'with regard to' [LN]. The phrase ἐν αἷς 'in which' is translated 'wherein' [El, Rob, We; KJV], 'as' [NAB].
  b. ποτέ (LN 67.30) (BAGD 1. p. 695): 'formerly' [BAGD, NTC; NASB], 'aforetime' [We], 'once' [BAGD, El, NIC, WBC; NRSV, REB], 'in time past' [Rob; KJV], 'in the past' [AB], 'at one time' [Lns], 'in the past at that time' [TEV], 'there was a time when' [TNT], 'when' [LN], not explicit [NAB]. This is also translated with the verb περιπατέω 'to walk': 'you used to live' [NIV, NJB].
  c. aorist act. indic. of περιπατέω (LN 41.11) (BAGD 2.a.δ. p. 649): 'to walk' [BAGD, El, Lns, NTC, Rob, We; KJV, NASB], 'to live' [BAGD, LN, WBC; NIV, NRSV], 'to make up one's way of life' [NJB], 'to lead one's life' [NIC], 'to behave, to go about doing' [LN], 'to conduct oneself' [BAGD]. This is also translated as a passive verb: 'your steps were bound' [AB]. Some conflate this verb with the preposition κατά 'according to': 'to follow' [REB, TEV], 'to give allegiance to' [NAB]. This is also translated as a noun phrase: 'your whole way of life' [TNT].

The verb means to live or behave according to a customary manner [DNTT, LN, TD]. When used figuratively, the word is almost always more exactly defined by an accompanying dative case or prepositional phrase [BAGD, DNTT, TD]. When used with the preposition ἐν 'in', the preposition indicates the state in which one lives (or in other contexts, ought to live) [BAGD].

d. κατά with accusative object (LN 89.8): 'according to' [El, NIC, Rob, We; KJV, NASB], 'in accordance with' [LN, WBC], 'in relation to' [LN], 'in accord with' [Lns], 'in line with' [NTC]. This preposition is also translated as a verb: 'to follow' [AB; NIV, NRSV], 'to conform to' [TNT], 'to live by' [NJB].

e. αἰών (LN **12.44**) (BAGD 4. p. 28): 'course' [El, NTC, Rob, We; KJV, NASB, NRSV], 'principle' [NJB], 'way' [NIV, REB], 'evil way' [TEV, TNT], 'present age' [NAB], 'eon, aeon' [Lns, NIC], 'Aeon' (as a person) [BAGD], 'supernatural force' [LN]. This noun is also conflated with the following noun, κόσμος 'world' and translated 'world-age' [AB, WBC].

f. κόσμος (LN **12.44**, 41.38) (BAGD 7. p. 446): 'world' [BAGD, El, LN, Lns, NIC, NTC, Rob, We; all versions except NAB, REB], 'present world order' [REB], not explicit [NAB]. This is also conflated with the preceding αἰών 'age' (e. above). The world and everything in it that is hostile to God and wholly opposed to anything divine [BAGD].

QUESTION—To what does the feminine plural relative pronoun αἷς 'which' refer?

Although it agrees in gender only with the nearer, preceding noun, ἁμαρτίαις 'sins', it refers to both of the synonyms [AB, Alf, Ba, Ea, EGT, ICC, Lns, My, NCBC, NIC, NTC, TH, WBC]. The phrase denotes the sphere or environment within which they formerly conducted their lifestyle [Ba, Ea, EGT, El, Gd, Lns, My, NTC, We].

QUESTION—What relationship is indicated by κατά 'according to'?

This indicates the standard or norm by which one conforms [Alf, Ba, Ea, EGT, Gd, Ho, Lns, My, WBC] and qualifies the verb περιεπατήσατε 'you walked' negatively [DNTT, WBC]: you lived in conformity with the standard of this world's ways. The two occurrences of the phrase in this verse mark influences that directed their walk [Can, EGT].

QUESTION—What does αἰῶνα 'age' mean?

1. The word is used either in reference to a Gnostic emanation named Αἰών [IB], or at least in reference to a personal force antagonistic to God [AB, BAGD, LN (**12.44**), NIC, TD, TH] and, either way, becomes a title for Satan [AB, BAGD, IB, LN (**12.44**), NIC, TH]: according to Aion (Satan), the god of this world. This meaning is necessary because αἰών is in apposition with the words ἄρχοντα 'prince' and πνεύματος 'spirit' which refer to personal beings [AB, IB, NIC, TD]. The usual sense of 'age' is hard to accept here, and while 'course' makes good sense, it is cited as not being a natural meaning for αἰών [NIC].

2. The word has a heavy ethical connotation and looks at the world from the standpoint of time and change [Alf, Ba, Bu, Cal, Can, Ea, EBC, ECWB, EGT, El, Gd, Ho, ICC, LJ, Lns, My, NCBC, NTC, Rob, Si, St, TNTC, WBC, We, WeBC; all versions]: according to the course of this world. Αἰών 'age' is put by metonymy for what takes place within its time-span; i.e., the practices, customs, and follies of the world [Bu, Gd]. The word is very close to the English 'spirit of the age' [Ea, EGT, El, Gd, ICC, NCBC, NTC, TNTC]. The word describes the mood of the age [Gd, NTC], the ruling principle governing the world [Ho], the outlook, mentality, and organization of life without God [LJ].

according-to[a] the ruler[b] of-the-authority[c] of-the air,[d]
LEXICON—a. κατά with accusative object (LN 89.8): 'according to' [El, NIC, Rob, We; KJV, NASB], 'in accord with' [Lns], 'in accordance with' [LN, WBC], 'in relation to' [LN], 'in line with' [NTC], 'to' [NAB], 'of' [NIV], not explicit [AB]. This preposition is also translated as a verb: 'to follow' [NRSV], 'to obey' [NJB, REB, TEV], 'to be in subjection to' [TNT].
   b. ἄρχων (LN **12.44**) (BAGD 3. p. 114): 'ruler' [AB, BAGD, LN, Lns, NIC, WBC; NIV, NJB, NRSV, TEV, TNT], 'prince' [BAGD, El, NTC, Rob, We; KJV, NAB, NASB], 'commander' [REB], 'lord' [BAGD].
   c. ἐξουσία (LN **12.44**) (BAGD 4.b. p. 278): 'authority' [Lns], 'power' [Rob, We; KJV, NASB, NRSV], 'spiritual powers' [REB, TEV, TNT], 'kingdom' [BAGD; NIV] 'domain' [BAGD, NIC, NTC], 'empire' [El], 'realm' [WBC], 'supernatural powers' [LN]. This is also translated as a relative clause: 'who dominates' [NJB], or it is conflated with the preceding noun [AB; NAB].
   d. ἀήρ (LN **1.7**) (BAGD p. 20): 'air' [BAGD, El, LN, Lns, NIC, NTC, Rob, WBC, We; all versions except TEV], 'sky' [LN], 'atmosphere' [AB], 'space' [LN; TEV]. The word is used of the kingdom of the air, in which spirit beings live [BAGD]. The region designated by ἀήρ 'air' is the space above the earth but below the heavenly places where God dwells [Can, DNTT, EGT, El, NCBC, NIC, NTC]. Alternatively, it designates the lower atmosphere as contrasted to the αἰθήρ, the 'sky' [IB, IDB].
QUESTION—In what relationship does this κατά 'according to' prepositional phrase stand to the preceding one?
   1. This κατά phrase is in apposition to the preceding one [IB, NIC]: that is, according to the ruler of the authority of the air. This serves to show that the preceding phrase is being used as the title of a supernatural person.
   2. This κατά phrase serves as a climactic parallel to the preceding one [Cal, EGT, El, Gd, Lns, My]: (which in turn operates) according to the ruler of the authority of the air. This phrase is a more intensive description [EGT], reaching deeper into the subject [Cal, Lns] and making explicit [My] the identity of the energizing force behind the first named influence (the first κατά phrase) directing their previously pagan lives [Gd, My].

QUESTION—Who is 'the ruler of the authority of the air'?

The ruler is the devil, Satan [AB, Alf, Ba, Cal, Can, DNTT, Ea, EBC, ECWB, EGT, El, Gd, Ho, IB, IDB, ISBE, ISBE2, LJ, Lns, MNTC, My, NCBC, NIC, NTC, Rob, Si, St, TD, TH, TNTC, WBC, We, WeBC; NJB (note)].

QUESTION—What does ἐξουσία 'authority' mean?

1. Ἐξουσία is a metonymy for a domain or sphere of authority, with 'authority' being put for the domain wherein it is exercised [AB, Ba, BAGD, EGT, El, IB, NIC, NTC, Si, TD, WBC]: the ruler of the domain of the air. The element of evil is implied: the ruler of the evil domain of the air [EGT].
2. Ἐξουσία is a metonymy for the persons ruled [Alf, Bu, Cal, Can, Ea, Gd, Ho, LJ, LN (**1.7**, **12.44**), MNTC, My, Rob, WeBC].
2.1 It refers to the evil spirits, in a collective sense, that are under Satan's authority [Alf, Can, CBC, Ea, ECWB, Gd, Ho, LJ, LN (**1.7**, **12.44**), MNTC, My, Rob, TH, WeBC] and who themselves possess power or spheres of authority [Alf, ECWB, Ho, LN (**1.7**, **12.44**), My, Rob]: the ruler of the evil spirits in the air. Ἐξουσία 'authority', both in the singular and plural forms, is used almost in a technical sense in Ephesians for superhuman powers [ECWB]. The singular number here is used, both with τῆς ἐξουσίας 'of the authority' and τοῦ πνεύματος 'of the spirit', to show the unanimity of the spirit of rebellion that exists among these rebellious spirits. They are all agreed in their sin of opposing God's kingdom [Gd].
2.2 It refers to wicked beings generally, including and focusing upon wicked men [Bu, Cal]: the ruler of wicked people.

QUESTION—What is meant by ἀήρ 'air'?

1. The reference is to the earth's atmosphere [Alf, Can, IB, ICC, MNTC, My, NCBC, Rob, TH, WeBC] or space [LN (**1.7**, **12.44**); TEV] and is entirely literal: ruler of the dominion of the air, or, the ruler of the evil spirits who dwell in or rule over the air. The point of mentioning the air is to emphasize how closely the evil powers crowd in on human life, filling the very atmosphere around us [Alf, IB, We].
2. The reference is to the atmosphere that surrounds the earth, but used as metonymy [AB, Ba, BAGD, EBC, EGT, El, Gd, ISBE2, NIC, NTC, TD, WBC, We].
2.1 The air is put for the evil spirits that dwell or rule there [AB, Ba, BAGD, EBC, EGT, El, Gd, NIC, NTC, TD, WBC, We]: ruler of the domain of the evil spirits (who live in the air).
2.2 The air is put for the region where men live and move [ISBE2]: the ruler of the domain of the evil spirits (who are active in the region where men live).
3. The word is used in a metaphorical sense [Cal, Ea, ECWB, Ho, Si, St].
3.1 It is a metaphor of spiritual darkness [Ho, TD]: the ruler of the evil spirits (whose rule is) spiritual darkness. The connotation of impurity

[DNTT, TD] and cloudiness, dimness, or darkness is always associated with 'the air' [ECWB, Ho, TD]. The comparison is: as the atmosphere is associated with murkiness and darkness so the domain of Satan is one of imposing spiritual darkness on the minds of men. The point of comparison is darkness and its power to conceal and confuse. The nonfigurative statement would be: the ruler of the evil spirits whose rule imposes spiritual confusion and blindness upon the minds of men.

3.2 It is a metaphor of the spiritual environment in which the world lives [Ea, ECWB, Si]: the ruler of the evil spirits (whose influence) surrounds them like the air. The comparison is: as the earth is surrounded by the atmosphere so Satan's hosts form the spiritual environment in which the world lives. The point of comparison is the permeable quality of the atmosphere. The nonfigurative statement would be: the ruler of the evil spirits who completely surround and permeate mankind.

3.3 It is a metaphor expressing the ethereal nature of these unseen evil spirits [Ho, LJ, TNTC], or, of the unseen world in which they operate [St]: The ruler of the unseen evil powers. The comparison is: as air is invisible so are the evil spirits whom Satan rules and controls. The point of comparison is the invisible nature of both the air as such and spiritual beings. The nonfigurative statement would be: the ruler of the unseen, evil, spiritual powers.

of-the-spirit[a] now working[b] in the sons[c] of-disobedience;[d]

LEXICON—a. πνεῦμα (LN 12.37, 30.6) (BAGD 5.g. p. 677): 'spirit' [AB, El, Lns, NIC, NTC, Rob, WBC, We; all versions], 'demon, evil spirit' [LN (12.37)], 'disposition, attitude, way of thinking' [LN (30.6)].

b. pres. act. participle of ἐνεργέω (LN 42.3) (BAGD 1.a. p. 265): 'to work' [BAGD, El, LN, Rob, We; KJV, NASB], 'to be at work' [AB, BAGD, LN, NTC, WBC; NAB, NIV, NJB, NRSV, REB, TNT], 'to operate' [BAGD, Lns, NIC], 'to control' [TEV], 'to be effective' [BAGD]. The meaning of the term is to be engaged in some function or activity with a possible focus upon the force or energy involved [LN].

c. υἱός (LN 58.26) (BAGD 1.c.δ. p. 834): 'son' [BAGD, El, LN, Lns, NTC, Rob, We; NASB], 'children' [LN; KJV], 'people' [LN; TEV], 'men' [AB], 'subjects' [REB], 'those who have the characteristics of' [LN], not explicit [NIC; NAB]. This is also translated as a demonstrative pronoun: 'those who' [WBC; NIV, NJB, NRSV, TNT]. This specifies a kind or class of persons, with the implication that they possess certain derived characteristics [LN]. With the genitive of the thing, it designates one who shares in this thing or is worthy of it, or stands in some other close relationship to it [BAGD].

d. ἀπείθεια (LN **31.107**, 36.23) (BAGD p. 82): 'disobedience' [BAGD, El, Lns, NTC, Rob, We; KJV, NASB]. The phrase τοῖς υἱοῖς τῆς ἀπειθείας 'the sons of disobedience' is translated 'those who are disobedient' [WBC; NIV, NRSV], 'the disobedient' [NIC], 'those who disobey God'

[TNT], 'the people who disobey God' [TEV], 'those who rebel' [NJB], 'the rebellious' [NAB], 'rebellious men' [AB], 'God's rebel subjects' [REB], 'those who refuse to believe' [**LN**]. It designates those who disobey and oppose God [BAGD, DNTT; TEV, TNT].

QUESTION—To what is τοῦ πνεύματος 'of the spirit' connected, and what does it mean?

1. Τοῦ πνεύματος 'of the spirit' is in apposition to τὸν αἰῶνα τοῦ κόσμου τούτου 'the age of this world' (understood in the sense 'spirit of the age') [CBC, WeBC]: according to the spirit of the age, which is the spirit that is now working in, etc. In this case, πνεῦμα 'spirit' is nonpersonal, and is the disposition of mankind subject to evil, supernatural manipulation.

2. Τοῦ πνεύματος 'of the spirit' is in apposition with τὸν ἄρχοντα 'the ruler' [AB, Ba, EBC, IB, NCBC, TH; NAB (note), NIV, NJB, TEV, TNT]: according to the ruler of the authority of the air (who is) the spirit that is now working in, etc. In this case πνεῦμα 'spirit' is a personal spirit, recognized to be Satan.

3. Τοῦ πνεύματος 'of the spirit' is in apposition with ἐξουσία 'authority', and attached to the accusative τὸν ἄρχοντα 'the ruler' by its genitive case [Alf, Can, Ea, ECWB, El, Gd, Ho, ICC, LJ, MNTC, Rob, We]: according to the ruler of the authority, which authority is that host of spirits who are now working in, etc., or, (which authority is) that spirit which is now working in, etc. In this case πνεῦμα 'spirit' is either personal or nonpersonal. If personal, it is the host of Satan's demons viewed collectively [Can, Ea, ECWB, Gd, MNTC, Rob, We]. If nonpersonal, it is the aggregate of the evil principle or influence that proceeds from 'the ruler', Satan and his hosts [Alf, El, Ho, ICC, LJ]. Either way, πνεῦμα 'spirit' serves to explain the preceding ἐξουσία 'authority' [ICC].

4. Τοῦ πνεύματος 'of the spirit' is attached through its genitive case to the accusative τὸν ἄρχοντα 'the ruler', defining it, and is parallel to ἐξουσία 'authority' [EGT, My, St, WBC]: according to the ruler of the authority of the air (and) of the spirit that now works in, etc. Again πνεῦμα 'spirit' may be personal or nonpersonal. If personal, πνεῦμα 'spirit', is an unnamed spirit who has direct control over human affairs [EGT]. If nonpersonal, it is the evil principle or influence that proceeds from Satan [My, St, WBC].

5. Τοῦ πνεύματος 'of the spirit' is the possessive genitive of ἐξουσία 'authority' (understood as 'domain') and in apposition to τὸν ἄρχοντα 'the ruler' [NIC, NTC]: according to the ruler of the domain of the air, (the domain) of the spirit that now works in, etc. Here πνεῦμα is personal—Satan [NTC].

6. Τοῦ πνεύματος 'of the spirit' is in apposition with the preceding genitive τοῦ ἀέρος 'of the air' [Si]: according to the ruler of the domain of the spiritual atmosphere which (atmosphere) is the spirit that now works in, etc. In this case πνεῦμα 'spirit' is also the same as τῶν αἰῶνα τοῦ κόσμου τούτου 'the age of this world' [Si].

112   EPHESIANS 2:2

QUESTION—What is the significance of the word νῦν 'now'?
   This word stands in emphatic [My] contrast to ποτέ 'formerly' at the beginning of the verse [Alf, Ea, EGT, El, ICC, My, WBC]. It stresses that the spirit that formerly worked in the Christian readers is still working at the present time in the unbelieving world of men [Ba, Ea, EGT, El, WBC]. It may point rather to the present rejection of the gospel by unbelievers than to the readers' pre-Christian state [AB].
QUESTION—What is meant by τοῖς υἱοῖς τῆς ἀπειθείας 'in the sons of disobedience'?
   This is a semiticism which serves to characterize something much as an adjective would (but with greater intensity [Bu, Can, El, HG]), or to give an outright definition of it [AB]. The attribute here is ἀπείθεια 'disobedience', not just unbelief but active rebellion [AB, LJ], voluntary disregard of known duty [Can, WBC], active, obstinate, hostile opposition to the will and government of God [Ea, EGT, LJ, We].

2:3 among[a] whom/which also[b] we all lived[c] formerly[d] in[e] the lusts[f] of-our flesh[g]

LEXICON—a. ἐν with dative object (LN 83.9): 'among' [El, LN, Lns, NIC, NTC, WBC, We; KJV, NASB, NIV, NJB, NRSV], 'with' [LN], 'of' [NAB], not explicit [AB]. This preposition is also translated as a verb: 'to be like' [TEV, TNT]. This preposition is also translated in conjunction with its dative object οἷς 'whom/which': 'wherein' [Rob], 'to be of (their number)' [REB].
   b. καί (LN 89.93): 'also' [LN, Lns, NIC, NTC, Rob, WBC, We; KJV, NIV], 'too' [AB; NASB, NJB, REB, TNT], 'in addition' [LN], 'even' [El, LN], 'actually' [TEV], not explicit [NAB, NRSV].
   c. aorist pass. indic. of ἀναστρέφω (LN 41.3) (BAGD 2.b.β. p. 61): 'to live' [BAGD, LN, Lns, NTC, WBC, We; NAB, NASB, NIV, NJB, NRSV, TEV], 'to follow' [AB], 'to indulge' [TNT], 'to have one's conversation' [El, Rob; KJV], 'to lead one's life' [NIC], 'to act, to behave, to conduct oneself' [BAGD, LN]. This is also translated as a passive verb: 'to be ruled' [REB]. When used figuratively, as here, of human conduct the kind of behavior is always more exactly described, here by the prepositional phrase 'in the lusts of the flesh', and so the meaning becomes equivalent to 'to be a slave to physical passion' [BAGD].
   d. ποτέ (LN 67.9) (BAGD 1. p. 695): 'formerly' [BAGD; NASB], 'in the past' [AB], 'in time/times past' [Rob; KJV], 'at one time' [Lns, NIC; NIV], 'once' [BAGD, El, NTC, WBC, We; NAB, NJB, NRSV, REB, TNT], not explicit [TEV]. See this word at 2:2.
   e. ἐν with dative object (LN 89.5): 'in' [AB, El, LN, Lns, NIC, NTC, Rob, WBC, We; KJV, NASB, NRSV], 'by' [NJB, REB], 'at the level of' [NAB], 'according to' [TEV], 'with regard to' [LN]. This preposition is also translated as a verb: 'to gratify' [NIV], not explicit [TNT].

EPHESIANS 2:3   113

f. ἐπιθυμία (LN 25.20) (BAGD 3. p. 293): 'lust' [El, LN, Lns, NTC, Rob, We; KJV, NASB], 'evil desire' [LN], 'passion' [AB, WBC; NRSV], 'craving' [NIV], 'desire' [BAGD, LN, NIC; REB, TEV, TNT], 'inclination' [NJB], not explicit [NAB]. BAGD lists the word as used in a bad sense here, as a desire for something forbidden, and notes that the genitive τῆς σαρκός 'of the flesh' denotes the origin of the desire.

g. σάρξ (LN 26.7) (BAGD 7. p. 744): 'flesh' [BAGD, El, Lns, NTC, Rob, WBC, We; KJV, NAB, NASB, NRSV], 'human nature' [LN], 'lower nature' [TNT], 'sinful nature' [NIV]. This noun is also translated as an adjective modifying the preceding noun, ἐπιθυμία 'lusts': 'natural' [LN; NJB, TEV], 'fleshly' [AB, NIC], 'physical' [REB]. The word may denote the psychological aspect of human nature that contrasts with the spiritual nature, i.e., the part of human nature that is characterized by human reasoning and desires, as contrasted to those aspects of human thought and behavior that relate to God and the spiritual life [LN]. This is the part of man that Paul describes as subject to sin and is its willing instrument [BAGD, LN, NCBC, NIC]. Other commentators state or imply that σάρξ 'flesh', in this occurrence, is a metonymy [Ea] denoting the whole natural man, his inner self in its fallen, natural condition, apart from God and at enmity with him [Alf, Ba, Cal, Can, CBC, Ea, EBC, ECWB, EGT, Gd, Ho, ICC, LJ, Lns, MNTC, My, NIC, NTC, TH, TNTC], or fallen humanity [Ea].

QUESTION—What is the gender of the relative pronoun οἷς 'whom/which' and to what does it refer?

1. It is masculine and refers to the immediately preceding phrase ἐν τοῖς υἱοῖς τῆς ἀπειθείας 'in the sons of disobedience' [AB, Alf, Ba, Cal, Can, Ea, EBC, ECWB, EGT, El, Ho, ICC, LJ, Lns, MNTC, My, NCBC, NIC, NTC, Si, TNTC, WBC; all versions]: we formerly lived among these sons of disobedience.

2. It is neuter and refers back to τοῖς παραπτώμασιν καὶ ταῖς ἁμαρτίαις 'trespasses and sins' in 2:1 [Rob]: we formerly lived in trespasses and sins.

3. It refers to the total characterization of the Gentiles given in the two preceding verses and forms a bridge to a discussion of the Jewish Christians [TH], i.e., it refers to both the ταῖς ἁμαρτίαις ὑμῶν 'your sins' and the Gentiles as τοῖς υἱοῖς τῆς ἀπειθείας 'the sons of disobedience' [Gd]: That was the way we all also lived formerly, or, we Jews formerly lived among the Gentiles and did the same kinds of sins [Gd].

QUESTION—To whom does ἡμεῖς 'we' refer?

1. Paul means to include Jews [Cal, LJ] or Jewish Christians [Alf, Ea, EBC, ECWB, EGT, El, Gd, Lns, NTC, Si, WBC, We, WeBC] in this 'we' as well as his readers, so the reference is inclusive in sense [Alf, Cal, Ea, ECWB, EGT, El, Gd, LJ, Lns, NTC, Si, WBC, We, WeBC]: we all,

Jewish and Gentile believers alike. Paul demonstrates that formerly Jew and Gentile were equal in alienation and sin [ECWB, My].
2. Paul seems to include only himself and his readers in this 'we' [Ba, Can, CBC, NCBC, St; NAB, NASB, NIV, NRSV, TEV]: we. Paul is thinking in terms of the total human condition. There is nothing in the context that indicates he has any racial distinctions in mind [Can]. The addition of 'all' lays particular emphasis upon the identification of the writer with his readers [NCBC].
3. Paul is thinking only of himself and his fellow Jews, so the 'we' is exclusive in sense [AB, Ho, IB, ICC, MNTC, My, NIC, Rob, TD, TH, TNTC; NJB (note), TNT]: all we Jews. When the pronouns 'you' and 'we' are contrasted with each other in this epistle, as here, 'you' means 'you Gentiles' and 'we' means 'we Jews' [Ho, My]. Καὶ ἡμεῖς 'and we' is emphatic here and would be quite unintelligible if it included the ὑμεῖς 'you' (Gentiles) of 2:1, 2.

QUESTION—What is the relationship between περιπατήσατο 'you walked' in the last verse and ἀνεστράφημεν 'we lived' here?

They are practically synonymous [AB, Ds3, Ea, EBC, Lns, NIC, NTC, WBC], but περιπατέω 'to walk' could not have been used in reference to a manner of life among 'the sons of disobedience', and so ἀναστρέφω 'to live' was called for [ICC].

QUESTION—What relationship is indicated by ἐν 'in'?

The verb ἀνεστράφω 'to live' is frequently followed by the preposition ἐν 'in' to denote condition or circumstances [DNTT, Rob].
1. This indicates the sphere in which they once lived [Alf, Ea, EGT, El, Gd, My, NIC, WBC; KJV, NASB, NRSV]: we lived in the midst of, or surrounded by, our fleshly desires.
2. This indicates the standard to which they conformed [NAB, TEV]: we lived according to our fleshly desires.
3. This indicates their characteristic manner of life [AB, EBC, Ho, NIC; NIV, TNT]: we lived fulfilling our fleshly desires.
4. This indicates the means by which they lived [NJB, REB]: we lived by our fleshly desires.

doing[a] the desires[b] of-the flesh[c] and of-the mind,[d]

LEXICON—a. pres. act participle of ποιέω (LN 42.7) (BAGD I.1.c.α. p. 682): 'to do' [AB, BAGD, El, LN, Lns, NIC, Rob, We; REB, TEV, TNT], 'to follow' [NAB, NIV, NRSV], 'to indulge' [NASB], 'to fulfill' [NTC; KJV], 'to carry out' [BAGD, LN, WBC], 'to commit' [BAGD], 'to accomplish' [BAGD, LN], 'to obey' [NJB]. The present tense of the participle makes it durative in force [Lns].

b. θέλημα (LN 25.2) (BAGD 1.c.δ. p. 354): 'desire' [El, LN, NTC, Rob; KJV, NASB, NIV, NRSV], 'wish' [LN, WBC], 'volition' [Lns], 'demand' [NJB], 'will' [NIC, We]. This is also translated as a verb: 'to desire' [BAGD], 'to decide' [AB], 'to suggest' [REB]. The phrase τὰ θελήματα τῆς σαρκὸς καὶ τῶν διανοιῶν 'the desires of the flesh and of the mind' is also translated 'every whim and fancy' [NAB]. This usage has the objective sense of 'what is willed' [BAGD], 'whatever suits the wishes' [TEV], 'whatever is wanted' [TNT]. The plural form refers to the multiplicity of purposes suggested by the 'flesh' and by the many thoughts of the mind [We], and suggests the lack of a settled will [IB].

c. σάρξ (LN 8.4) (BAGD 7. p. 744): 'flesh' [AB, BAGD, El, Lns, NIC, NTC, Rob, WBC, We; KJV, NASB, NRSV], 'body' [LN; TEV, TNT], 'instinct' [REB], 'human self-indulgence' [NJB]. This is also translated as the impersonal possessive pronoun 'its' with reference back to the preceding σάρξ 'flesh' as 'sinful nature' [NIV].

d. διάνοια (LN 26.14) (BAGD 5. p. 187): 'mind' [LN, We; KJV, NASB], 'minds' [NIC, Rob; TEV, TNT], 'thought' [AB, El, WBC; NIV], 'reasoning' [Lns, NTC], 'evil imagination' [REB], 'sense' [BAGD; NRSV], 'impulse' [BAGD], 'whim' [NJB].

QUESTION—What relationship is indicated by the use of the participle ποιοῦντες 'doing'?

The participle describes the action of the finite verb ἀνεστράφημεν 'we lived' [Ea, Lns]. The finite verb describes in general the life of fallen mankind while the participle describes their actual activity [Ea], the way and manner of their life [My], where the 'lusts' of the finite verb clause result in the things willed in the participial clause [Ea, ICC, Lns]. The participle is emphatic in force [My].

QUESTION—What is the relationship between ἐπιθυμίαις 'lusts' of the preceding clause and θελήματα 'desires' in this one?

Ἐπιθυμία 'lust' is desire as impulse, a motion of the will, as seen in the fact that 'lusts of the flesh' and 'desires of the flesh' are exact parallels [TD]. By directing a man's attention, ἐπιθυμίαις 'lusts' can bring him completely under their domination [DNTT], so the θελήματα 'desires' are responses to the ἐπιθυμίαις 'lusts' [Lns]. The plural θελήματα 'desires' denotes various exhibitions and manifestation of the will and is symmetrical with ἐπιθυμίαις 'lusts' and a fuller expansion of it [El]. It intensifies the thought of instability given in ἐπιθυμίαις 'lusts' [IB].

QUESTION—What are the θελήματα 'desires' in this genitive phrase?

They are of two types. Those of the 'flesh' are the animal-like appetites which generate the grosser types of sin: adultery, fornication, murder, drunkenness, etc. The 'desires of the mind' are those that are more mental or emotional in nature [Ea, Ho, LJ] which generate sins of the spiritual type: hatred, wrath, strife, heresies, jealousy, pride, envy, bitterness, covetousness, love of fame, wealth, etc. [Ba, Can, Ea, El, Gd, LJ, NCBC, NIC, St], even a perverted love of beauty or knowledge [Can, LJ].

QUESTION—What is the relationship to each other of the genitives τῆς σαρκός 'of the flesh' and τῶν διανοιῶν 'of the mind'?

1. They are co-equal, indicating two kinds of θελήματα 'desires' [Ea, El, WBC, WeBC]: the desires of the flesh and the desires of the mind. The

fact that the definite article precedes each of the nouns supports this interpretation [Ea, HG].
2. This is a generic-specific relationship [EGT, ICC, NCBC, NIC, NTC]: the desires of the flesh, specifically the desires of the mind. He adds the specific element to indicate that the dictates of the flesh are not simply the physical urges, but include such qualities as pride and self-aggrandizement [NCBC, NIC].
3. These genitives indicate the order in which sinful desires are fulfilled [Gd]: doing the desires that arise in the flesh and are fulfilled by the mind. The desires arise from the corrupt nature of men, the 'flesh', but need the consent of the will and understanding before they can be fulfilled [Gd].
4. This indicates a synonymous doublet [NAB]: every whim and fancy.

QUESTION—What is the difference in meaning between the two occurrences of σάρξ 'flesh' in this verse?
1. There is no difference in meaning [BAGD, Lns; NIV]: we lived in the lusts of our fleshly nature, doing the desires of this nature and of our minds.
2. There is a generic-specific relationship between the two occurrences [Ea, ECWB, Gd, Ho, LJ, St, TH, WBC; NJB, NRSV, REB, TEV, TNT]: We lived in the lusts of our fleshly nature, doing the desires of our natural bodies and of our minds. The genitive construction of the participial clause serves, in effect, to define the 'flesh' of the finite verb clause, so that 'flesh' (first occurrence) is seen to include not only the sensuous part of man ('flesh'—second occurrence), but also the desires generated by the thinking, reasoning part of man, his mind [ECWB, Gd, Ho, LJ, St, TH, TNTC].

QUESTION—What is meant by διανοιῶν 'minds'?
1. This means 'mind' or 'minds' [Cal, Ho, IB, LJ, Rob, St, WeBC; KJV, NASB, TEV, TNT]. Some think the plural form is used to denote the whole thinking and perception principle [Ho, LJ]. Another thinks the plural is used here because its companion word, σάρξ 'flesh', cannot be pluralized when used in this kind of context, so that, in effect, the plural genitive διανοιῶν 'minds' is meant to carry the plural meaning for both [Rob]. Another thinks the plural may denote the sense of unsettledness—a man of many minds [IB].
2. This means the products of the mind, the 'thoughts' or 'reasonings' [AB, Alf, Ba, Can, Ea, EBC, ECWB, EGT, El, Gd, Lns, MNTC, My, NTC, TD, TH, TNTC, WBC, We; NAB, NIV, REB]. Those holding this interpretation usually note the unusual occurrence of the plural form here which they regard as unsuitable for the meaning 'mind' [Alf, Ea, EGT, Lns] and use wording which reflects an opinion that what is in focus here is the products of the mind [Alf, Ba, EBC, Lns, My, NTC, TD, TH, We].

and we-were by-nature^a children^b of-wrath^c as even^d the rest;^e

LEXICON—a. φύσις (LN 58.8) (BAGD 1. p. 869): 'nature' [AB, El, LN, Lns, NIC, NTC, Rob, WBC, We; KJV, NAB, NASB, NIV, NJB, NRSV], 'natural condition' [BAGD; REB, TEV], 'natural endowment' [BAGD]. This noun is also translated as an adverb: 'naturally' [TNT]. The word denotes the nature of something as the result of its natural development or condition [LN].

    b. τέκνον (LN 58.26) (BAGD 2.f.β. p. 808): 'children' [BAGD, El, LN, Lns, NTC, Rob, WBC, We; KJV, NASB, NRSV], 'one who has the characteristics of' [LN], 'objects' [NIV]. The idiom τέκνα ὀργῆς 'children of wrath' means 'to be subject to divine wrath' [BAGD] and so is translated as a whole: 'we were destined to suffer God's anger' [TEV], 'we deserved to suffer God's wrath' [TNT], 'we deserved God's wrath' [NAB], 'we lay under the condemnation of God' [REB], 'we were liable to God's retribution' [NJB], 'we were liable to divine wrath' [NIC], 'we were under the wrath of God' [AB].

    c. ὀργή (LN 38.10) (BAGD 2.b. p. 579): 'wrath' [AB, BAGD, El, Lns, NIC, NTC, Rob, WBC, We; KJV, NAB, NASB, NIV, NRSV, TNT], 'anger' [TEV], 'retribution' [NJB], 'condemnation' [REB], 'judgment' [BAGD], 'punishment' [LN]. It denotes the divine reaction towards evil, but the thought is focused more on the outcome of an angry frame of mind (judgment) than on the emotion [BAGD, LN].

    d. καί (LN 89.93): 'even' [El, LN, Lns, NTC, Rob, We; KJV, NASB], 'too' [TNT], 'in fact' [NIC], not explicit [WBC; NAB, NIV, NRSV, REB, TEV]. This conjunction is also conflated with ὡς 'as': 'as much as' [AB], 'no less than' [NJB].

    e. λοιπός (LN 63.21) (BAGD 2.b.α. p. 480): 'rest' [El, LN, Lns, NTC, Rob, WBC; NAB, NASB, NIV, TNT], 'rest of mankind' [AB, NIC; REB], 'rest of men' [We], 'rest of the world' [NJB], 'others' [BAGD, LN; KJV], 'everyone else' [NRSV, TEV], 'remaining, what remains' [LN].

QUESTION—What is meant by φύσει 'nature'?

    1. This refers to what people are like in their natural condition, innately from birth, prior to the work of regeneration [Alf, Ba, Cal, Can, DNTT, Ea, EGT, El, Gd, Ho, ISBE, LJ, Lns, My-ed, NIC, NTC, Si, St, WBC]: by nature from birth children of wrath. By using the phrase, Paul is implying the doctrine of original sin (there being no direct assertion of it [El, Gd, Ho, WBC]), the propensity to sin inherited from our original ancestor, Adam [Alf, Ba, Cal, Can, DNTT, Ea, EGT, El, Gd, LJ, Lns, NIC, NTC, Si, St, WBC].

    2. This refers to what people are like from habitual practice, apart from God's work of grace [AB, ICC, My, NCBC, Rob, TD, TH (probably), TNTC, We, WeBC]: by nature, as demonstrated from our actions, children of wrath. The context indicates Paul is talking about actual transgressions here, an actually produced state of guilt [My], about a

manner of life lived in this way, not just an inborn propensity to sin, so this passage does not concern the doctrine of original sin [ICC, My, Rob].

QUESTION—What is meant by the Semitic idiom τέκνα ὀργῆς 'children of wrath'?

This means people who are the objects of God's wrath. The reference to God's wrath implies that punishment is due them [DNTT, EGT, El, Gd, Ho, ICC, Lns, MNTC, My, NCBC, NIC, NTC, Rob, St, TH, WBC]. Most regard the punishment to be in the future [BAGD, EGT, Gd, Ho, ICC, Lns, MNTC, NIC, NTC, Rob, St, TH, WBC], or both temporal and eternal [DNTT, My], although some add that men in their natural condition are currently under his wrath without specifying when it actually falls upon them [Ea, NCBC].

QUESTION—What is the implied referent of οἱ λοιποί 'the rest'?

This includes all those who deserve God's punishment—all mankind not included by 'we' [AB, Alf, Ba, Cal, Can, Ea, EBC, ECWB, El, Gd, Ho, ICC, LJ, Lns, MNTC, My, NCBC, NIC, NTC, St, TH, TNTC, WBC, We, WeBC; NJB, NRSV, REB, TEV], though some, who hold 'we' to refer to Jewish Christians, restrict this to Gentiles [DNTT, My; TNT]. One of these understands this to be a typically Jewish disparaging reference to Gentiles [TNTC].

DISCOURSE UNIT: 2:4–10 [AB, CBC, NCBC, St, WeBC]. The topic is the power and effect of God's love [AB, CBC], the change which Christ has made in these Christians [NCBC], and their present state in Christ [WeBC].

DISCOURSE UNIT: 2:4–7 [IB]. The topic is the abundance of God's goodness in bestowing upon us the highest spiritual blessings.

2:4 but/and[a] God, being rich[b] in[c] mercy,[d]

LEXICON—a. δέ (LN 89.87, 89.124): 'but' [AB, El, LN (89.124), NIC, Rob, WBC, We; all versions], 'on the other hand' [LN (89.124)], 'and then' [LN (89.87)], not explicit [Lns, NTC].

b. πλούσιος (LN **59.57**) (BAGD 2. p. 673): 'rich' [AB, BAGD, El, LN, Lns, NIC, NTC, Rob, WBC, We; all versions except TEV], 'so abundant' [**LN**; TEV]. This word denotes that which exists in a large amount, with the implication that it is valuable. It may be interpreted either as degree or extent [LN].

c. ἐν with dative object (LN **89.5**) (BAGD IV. 1.a. p. 261): 'in' [AB, El, **LN**, Lns, NIC, NTC, Rob, WBC, We; all versions except TEV, TNT], 'in the case of, in regard to' [LN], 'as far as it is concerned' [BAGD], not explicit [TEV, TNT].

d. ἔλεος (LN **88.76**) (BAGD 2.b. p. 250): 'mercy' [AB, BAGD, El, **LN**, Lns, NIC, NTC, Rob, WBC, We; all versions except NJB], 'compassion, pity, clemency' [BAGD], 'faithful love' [NJB].

QUESTION—What relationship is indicated by δέ 'but/and'?

1. It indicates a contrast with the material in 2:1–3 [AB, Alf, Can, Ea, EGT, El, Gd, IB, ICC, MNTC, My, St, TNTC, WBC, WeBC; all versions]: we

were by nature children of wrath living in sin, but God made us alive. The construction begun in 2:1, but broken by the intervening material, is resumed here [Alf, Ea, EGT, El, ICC, My, WBC], but in a manner that contrasts the ὀργή 'wrath' of 2:3 with the ἔλεος 'mercy' and ἀγάπη 'love' in this verse [Alf, EGT, El, Gd, WBC].
2. It is not contrastive, but merely resumes the account [Lns, NTC]. Since there is no equivalent word in English, the best way to reflect this anacolouthon construction is to leave the conjunction untranslated [Lns, NTC].

QUESTION—To what is Θεός 'God' attached?

Θεός 'God' is the subject of the verb συνζωοποιέω 'to make alive with' in 2:5 [AB, Cal, Ea, El, Gd, Ho, Lns, My, NCBC, NTC, St, TH, TNTC, WBC].

QUESTION—What relationship is indicated by the use of the participle ὤν 'being'?
1. This indicates a reason why God raised dead sinners to life [Alf, DNTT, Ea, Gd, Ho, IB, ICC, Lns, My, NCBC, NIC, NTC, TH, WBC, We]: because God is rich in mercy, he made us alive. This participial clause contains the general reason, while the following causal clause contains the specific motive for making us alive [Alf, Cal, Ea, Lns, My].
2. This indicates a circumstance in which the raising of dead sinners took place [El]: while being rich in mercy, God made us alive. Even though this is taken grammatically as a circumstance, it is mentioned to show the general principle under which God's love operates.

QUESTION—How is ἔλεος 'mercy' related to the words ἀγάπη 'love' and χάρις 'grace' in this verse and the next?

All three terms are synonyms [ISBE, Lns, WBC]. Χάρις 'grace' and ἔλεος 'mercy' frequently occur together in the NT [ISBE] and may be used interchangeably in places [TD]. The basic word is ἀγάπη 'love' and it is the most comprehensive [Gd, Lns, NTC]. Χάρις 'grace' looks at the freeness of God's love and forgiveness of sins, while ἔλεος 'mercy' looks at love as directed toward misery of sin and its relief [ISBE, ISBE2, Lns, NTC]. Together these three terms, with their modifiers, show Paul is stressing the abundance of God's goodness in 2:4–8 [IB, WBC].

because-of[a] his great[b] love[c] (with) which[d] he-loved[e] us,

LEXICON—a. διά with accusative object (LN 89.26) (BAGD B.II.1. p. 181): 'because of' [El, LN, Lns, NIC, NTC; NAB, NASB, NIV, REB], 'because' [TNT], 'on account of' [LN], 'by reason of' [LN], 'for' [AB, Rob, We; KJV], 'through' [NJB], not explicit [TEV]. With words of emotion and indicating the reason why something happens, the word may be translated 'out of' [BAGD, WBC; NRSV].

b. πολύς (LN 78.3) (BAGD I.1.b.β. p. 688): 'great' [BAGD, El, LN, Lns, NIC, NTC, Rob, WBC, We; KJV, NAB, NASB, NIV, NJB, NRSV, REB], 'so great' [TEV], 'so much' [TNT], 'much' [BAGD, LN], 'all' [AB], 'deep, profound, strong' [BAGD]. This word indicates degree

[BAGD], or, the upper range on a scale of extent. It is probably somewhat less on this scale than the word μέγας 'great' [LN].
   c. ἀγάπη (LN 25.43) (BAGD I.2.a. p. 5): 'love' [AB, BAGD, El, LN, Lns, NIC, NTC, Rob, WBC, We; all versions except TNT], 'loving concern' [LN]. This is also conflated with the following verb: 'to love' [TNT]. See this word at 1:4, 15.
   d. ἥ (LN 92.27): 'with which' [NIC, NTC, WBC; NASB, NJB, NRSV], 'wherewith' [El, Lns, Rob, We; KJV], 'with' [AB]. This is also translated by joining the phrase with the preceding one so that 'which' is omitted: 'his great love for us' [NAB, NIV, REB, TEV], 'God loved us so much' [TNT].
   e. aorist act. indic. of ἀγαπάω (LN 25.43) (BAGD 2. p. 5): 'to love' [AB, El, LN, Lns, NIC, NTC, Rob, WBC, We; KJV, NASB, NJB, NRSV, TNT], 'to regard with affection' [LN], not explicit [NAB, NIV, REB, TEV]. This is an historical [MT] or constative [HG] aorist describing an extended act or state [HG, Mo, MT], though the idea of the verb itself is naturally durative [HG, Mo].
QUESTION—What relationship is indicated by διά 'because of/through'?
   1. It indicates the reason for what follows [Alf, Can, Ea, EGT, El, Ho, Lns, MNTC, My, NTC, WBC; all versions except NJB, TNT]: because of his love, he made us alive, raised us up, and made us sit with Christ. Διά 'because of' plus the accusative case on words of emotion indicates motivation. This clause states the other major motive cited for God's action of saving his people—that of love [WBC].
   2. It indicates the reason for what precedes [Ba, EBC, Gd, ICC, NCBC, St, TH, TNTC; TNT]: God is rich in mercy because he loves us.
   3. It indicates the means by which God brought us to life with Christ [NJB]: through his great love with which he loved us, he brought us to life with Christ.
QUESTION—What is the significance of both the noun and verb forms of 'love' occurring in this verse?
   This is a cognate accusative construction [BD, Ea, EGT, El, HG, ICC, Mo, My, Si-ed, WBC] and serves to convey an idea of intensity or emphasis to the passage [Ea, EGT, El, ICC, TH, WBC].
QUESTION—To whom does ἡμᾶς 'us' refer?
   It includes Paul, and all believers that have been made alive [Alf, Can, Ea, EGT, Gd, Ho, NIC], both Jew and Gentile [AB, Alf, EGT, El, IB, ICC, Lns, My, NIC, TH, TNTC]. It is co-extensive with ἡμεῖς πάντες 'we all' of the preceding verse [Alf, El].

2:5 even/and[a] us being dead[b] in-the trespasses,[c] he-made-alive-together-with[d] the Christ,
LEXICON—a. καί (LN 89.93): 'even' [El, LN, Lns, NIC, WBC, We; KJV, NASB, NIV, NJB, NRSV], 'though' [TNT], 'even though' [NTC, Rob], 'and' [My], 'also' [LN], not explicit [AB; NAB, REB, TEV].

b. νεκρός: 'dead'. See this word at 2:1.

c. παράπτωμα (LN 88.297) (BAGD 2.b. p. 621): 'trespass'. See this word at 2:1.

d. aorist act. indic. of συζωοποιέω (LN **23.95**) (BAGD p. 776): 'to make alive together with' [AB, BAGD, NTC; NASB, NRSV], 'to make alive with' [WBC; NIV], 'to quicken together with' [El, Lns, Rob, We; KJV], 'to bring to life with' [LN; NAB, NJB, REB, TEV], 'to bring to life together with' [NIC], 'to raise to life again with' [TNT], 'to raise to life together with' [LN], 'to cause to live again together with' [LN]. The reference is to people who were dead in their sins, but whom God has made alive together with Christ through union with Christ [BAGD]. The usage here is highly figurative and refers to spiritual existence rather than to a literal resurrection of the body [LN]. The aorist tense here has its proper and characteristic force; that which God did in Christ he did *ipso facto* in all those who are united with him [El].

QUESTION—What relationship is indicated by καί 'even/and'?
1. The καί is intensive in meaning [AB, Alf, Cal, Ea, ECWB, EGT, El, Gd, Ho, ICC, Lns, NIC, We; KJV, NASB, NIV, NJB, NRSV].
    1.1 It is connected to the participle ὄντας 'being' [AB, Alf, Cal, Ea, ECWB, EGT, El, Gd, Ho, ICC, NIC, We; KJV, NASB, NIV, NJB, NRSV]: even when we were dead in our sins. The καί 'even' belongs to and intensifies the state predicated by ὄντας νεκρούς 'being dead' [Alf, EGT, El, Gd] by throwing the νεκρούς 'dead' emphatically forward, heightening the sense of the divine power: it was a power operating upon us even while we were held tightly in the state of death [EGT, El].
    1.2 It is connected to the preceding pronoun ἡμᾶς 'us' of 2:4 [Lns]: he loved even us.
2. The καί is concessive in meaning [NTC, Rob; TNT]: even though we were dead in our sins.
3. The καί is simply copulative here [My]: because of the great love with which he loved us and when we were dead in our sins, he made us alive together with Christ. It joins 'because of the great love with which he loved us' with the further element of our 'being dead in our sins.' Both of these elements, standing side by side, place in full light what God has done.

QUESTION—What relationship is indicated by the use of the participle ὄντας 'being'?
1. The participle indicates a temporal circumstance of the following clause [Alf, Cal, EBC, ECWB, EGT, El, Gd, Ho, ICC, LJ, MNTC, My, NCBC, NIC, TH, WBC, We; all versions except TNT]: when we were dead, God made us alive.
2. The participle indicates a temporal circumstance of the preceding clause [Ba, Can, Lns, TNTC]: God loved us even/while we were dead. Though grammatically connected with the following statement, this participial

clause serves rather to intensify the preceding statement of the love of God [Can].
3. The participle indicates the reason for the following clause [AB]: because we were dead, God made us alive.
4. The participle indicates a concession to the following clause [NTC, Rob; TNT]: although we were dead, God made us alive.

QUESTION—What is the significance of the article with παραπτώμασιν 'sins'?

This article defines these sins as those already mentioned in connection with this state of death (2:1) [AB, EGT], and therefore has the sense of 'our' [Alf, EGT, ICC, My].

QUESTION—What is meant by συνεζωοποίησεν τῷ Χριστῷ 'he made alive together with Christ'?

1. This is a metaphor which refers to spiritual life [Alf, Ba, Can, CBC, Ea, EBC, EGT, El, Gd, Ho, ICC, LJ, LN, Lns, MNTC, NCBC, NIC, Si, St, TH, WBC, WeBC; TEV]: he made us spiritually alive with Christ. The focus is on the present spiritual life [Alf, EGT, El, LJ, NCBC, NIC, WeBC], but this necessarily includes a future physical resurrection also [Alf, Ea, ICC, WBC], since the opposite, spiritual death (2:1), entailed physical death as its consequence [Alf, Ea, ICC]. The life given corresponds in nature to the death suffered [Ea, El, NIC, Si, TH, WeBC]. The readers were made spiritually alive because of their spiritual union with Christ [DNTT, Ea, Gd, Ho, ICC, LJ, MNTC, NCBC, NIC, Si, St, WBC, WeBC (probably)]. Jesus experienced life, resurrection and glorification, and because of our union with him, they are ours as well [Ea, ICC, LJ, NIC, WBC]. When God quickened and raised Christ physically, all his people were ideally raised with him, and as a consequence they, through faith, are actually quickened and raised again [Alf, Ba, Ea, EBC, EGT, LJ, Lns, St, TNTC]. The life they receive is the same that the risen Savior has [Can, Gd, LJ, NIC], so they are 'made alive' not just 'through' him but 'with' him [Can, Gd]. As a metaphor the word compares God's action of making the human spirit (the part of man that responds to God's promptings) alive again to his action of making Christ alive again at his resurrection. The point of comparison is the ability of the body to be conscious of and respond to stimuli in its environment on the physical plane. So spiritual life enables the spirit of a person to be conscious of God and respond to stimuli in the spiritual plane of the 'heavenlies'. The nonfigurative expression would be: by uniting us together with Christ, God enabled our spirits to be responsive to himself.

2. The readers were potentially made physically alive because of their union with Christ when he was resurrected [Cal (probably), My]. The revivification of believers is objectively included in Christ's resurrection [My]. In his convictions, Paul sees this as accomplished because Christ's resurrection is accomplished [Cal, My].

QUESTION—What is the significance of the article before Χριστῷ 'Christ'?

A few believe that this focuses on his official office as Messiah [AB, EGT, Lns, We]. But most translate without the article or otherwise take no notice of this as an official title and seem to consider this as a regular name [Alf, Ba, Cal, Can, CBC, Ea, EBC, ECWB, El, Ho, ICC, LJ, MNTC, My, NCBC, NIC, NTC, Si, St, TH, TNTC, WeBC; all versions].

—by-grace^a you-are having-been-saved^b—

LEXICON—a. χάρις (LN 88.66) (BAGD 2.a. p. 877): 'grace' [AB, BAGD, El, LN, Lns, NIC, NTC, Rob, WBC, We; all versions except NAB], 'favor' [BAGD; NAB], 'gracious care, help' [BAGD], 'kindness/graciousness' [LN], 'goodwill' [BAGD]. This denotes the action of one who volunteers to do something which he is not bound to do [BAGD, Gd] and that generously and freely [Gd]. The 'grace' referred to is that of God, not of Christ [Ea, My]. Its case indicates means [HG] or instrument [Mo, Tu]. See this word at 1:6, 7.

b. perf. pass. participle of σῴζω (LN 21.17) (BAGD 2.b. p. 798): 'to be saved' [AB, El, LN, Lns, NIC, NTC, Rob, WBC, We; all versions]. The biblical use involves two important elements: (1) the deliverance of a person from a situation of danger, and (2) the restoration of a person to health and wholeness [TH]. The perfect tense indicates that their salvation, completed from God's side in the past, has continuing effects for them [AB, Alf, EBC, EGT, El, Gd, ICC, Mou, NCBC, Rob, Si, St, TD, TNTC, WBC, WeBC].

QUESTION—How does this clause relate to its context?

It is a parenthetical comment [AB, Alf, Ba, Can, Ea, ECWB, EGT, Gd, GNT, Ho, IB, ICC, Lns, MNTC, My, NCBC, NIC, Rob, Si, TD, WBC; KJV, NASB, NIV, NRSV] which emphasizes the thought of God's grace [El, Gd, MNTC, My, Si, WBC] (one of the most prominent ideas of the context and of the epistle [Ho]), by putting the word χάρις 'grace' first [EGT, My]. This anticipates the fuller statement to come in 2:8–10 [AB, Can, Ea, EBC, ECWB, Gd, IB, MNTC, NCBC, NIC, Rob, TH, TNTC, WBC, WeBC].

2:6 and he-raised-(us)-together-with^a and seated-(us)-with^b in^c the heavenly^d (places) in^e Christ Jesus,

LEXICON—a. aorist act. indic. of συνεγείρω (LN 23.95) (BAGD 2. p. 786): 'to raise together with' [TNT], 'to raise together' [AB, Rob], 'to raise up together' [Lns; KJV], 'to raise up with' [El, NIC, NTC, WBC, We; NAB, NASB, NIV, NJB, NRSV, TEV], 'to raise up' [REB], 'to raise to life together with' [LN]. The usage here is highly figurative [LN].

b. aorist act. indic. of συγκαθίζω (LN **17.18**) (BAGD 1. p. 773): 'to seat with' [LN, NIC, WBC; NASB, NIV, NRSV], 'to seat together' [Lns, Rob], 'to make to sit with' [El, NTC, We], 'to cause to sit down with' [BAGD, LN], 'to make to sit together' [KJV], 'to give a place with' [NAB, NJB], 'to enthrone with' [REB], 'to enthrone together' [AB], 'to rule with' [TEV], 'to cause to share a place of honor' [TNT].

c. ἐν with dative object (LN 83.13): 'in' [AB, El, LN, Lns, NIC, NTC, Rob, WBC, We; all versions].

d. ἐπουράνιος (LN 1.12) (BAGD 2.a.α. p. 306): 'heavenly' [LN], 'pertaining to heaven' [LN]. The substantive is translated 'heavenly places' [Lns, NTC, Rob; KJV, NASB, NRSV], 'heavenly regions' [El], 'heavenly realm' [NIC], 'heavenly realms' [WBC; NIV, REB], 'heavenly world' [TEV], 'heavenly order' [We], 'supernatural world' [TNT], 'heaven' [BAGD, LN; NJB], 'heavens' [AB; NAB]. See this word at 1:3, 20.

e. ἐν with dative object (LN 89.119): 'in' [AB, El, LN, NIC, NTC, Rob, WBC, We; KJV, NAB, NASB, NIV, NRSV], 'in union with' [LN; REB, TEV], 'joined closely to' [LN], 'one with' [LN], 'in connection with' [Lns], 'because we belong to' [TNT].

QUESTION—What relationship is indicated by καί 'and' beginning this verse?
1. It introduces this verse as explanatory of 2:5a–b, having the sense of 'for' [AB]: For he has in the Messiah Jesus raised us and enthroned us together in the heavens.
2. It introduces an elaboration of συζωοποιέω 'to make alive' under the two aspects of resurrection and glorification (ascension) [ECWB, Ho, MNTC, NIC]: and (in doing so) he raised us up together with him, etc.
3. It introduces further parallels between Christ's physical resurrection and ascension and the believers' resurrection and ascension [Alf, Ba, Cal, Can, IB, LJ, Lns, My, St, TH, WBC, We]: and (further) he raised us up together with him. etc.
4. It resumes the discourse after the interjection of 2:5c [NIV, REB]: And God raised us up with Christ.

QUESTION—How is the verb συνεγείρω 'to raise together with' different from the preceding verb συζωοποιέω 'to make alive together with'?
1. The words are treated synonymously [AB, Ba, MNTC, NCBC, NIC].
2. There is a distinction intended here [Alf, Can, Ea, EGT, Gd, Ho, IB, ICC, LJ, Lns, My, NTC, St, TD, TH, WBC, We]. A step-by-step parallel is being drawn between aspects of Christ's physical resurrection and ascension and believers' spiritual resurrection and ascension. What happened to Christ has also happened to the believer [Gd, IB, LJ, Lns, NTC, TD, TH, WBC, We]. These two words, together with the third, form a climax in the manifested love of God [We].
   2.1 The first verb concerns the moment of giving life, while the second verb is more distinct in its suggestion of physical resurrection [Gd, ICC, We], i.e., the first verb relates to the eternal life presently experienced by believers, while the second and third verbs relate to life in the glory to come.
   2.2 The first verb refers to the imparting of new life, but the second concerns the activity of the new life in resurrection [Can, Ea, LJ, Lns].

2.3 The first verb refers to the resurrection and the second to the ascension (with the third referring to the present session of believers with Christ) [St].

3. There is a generic-specific relationship here [ECWB, TNTC (probably)]. Συζωοποιέω is used generically for eternal life, the believers' salvation. Συνεγείρω specifies an aspect of that eternal life, resurrection (with συγκαθίζω 'to seat together with' specifying a second aspect, ascension and glorification) [ECWB].

QUESTION—What is meant by being raised up together with Christ?
1. This is a metaphor referring primarily to our spiritual life resulting from Christ's physical resurrection [AB, Alf, Ba, Can, CBC, DNTT, Ea, IB, ICC, Lns, NCBC, NIC, Rob, St, TH, WBC, WeBC]: he raised us to spiritual life because Christ was resurrected. The comparison is: just as Christ was resurrected and was active again in a physical sense, so those who believe in him are resurrected and are active in a spiritual sense. The point of comparison is primarily the activity of the new life given in the act of resurrection. The nonfigurative statement would be: God has given us new life and we are active with Christ in the spiritual realm.
2. This refers primarily to the future resurrection resulting from Christ's resurrection [Bu, Cal, El, Gd, ICC, ISBE, My]: he will raise us to everlasting life because Christ was resurrected. The resurrection of the saints, because of their union with Christ [Cal, Gd] or because of the efficacy of God's power [El], is so certain that it is spoken of as already accomplished [Cal, El, Gd, ISBE, My, We].
3. Both present and future aspects are in focus [EBC, ECWB, EGT, NTC]: he raised us to new spiritual life and will raise us up again from physical death because Christ was resurrected.

QUESTION—What is meant by being seated together with Christ?
1. This is a metaphor describing our present spiritual exaltation brought about by Christ's exaltation [AB, Can, CBC, DNTT, Ea, EGT, Ho, IDB, LJ, Lns, NCBC, Rob, St, TD, WBC, WeBC]: and, in a manner of speaking, has spiritually seated us with him in the heavenlies. The comparison is: just as Christ was enthroned so are his people enthroned with him. The point of comparison is the privileges, honor, authority, and function involved in enthronement [AB]. The nonfigurative statement would be: God has given us important work to do with Christ, together with the privileges, honor, authority that go with it.
2. This refers to or focuses on our future exaltation and location [Bu, Cal, El, Gd, My, NIC, Si, TD, We]: and he will seat us with him in the heavenlies. Though future, Paul sees this as already accomplished in Christ's installation at the right hand of God [Bu, Cal, El, Gd, My, NIC, Si, We], and because of the union of the believer with Christ, the believer is presently represented there with Christ [Gd].

3. Both present and future senses are in focus [Alf, Ba, MNTC, NTC]: and he has seated us spiritually and will later completely seat us with him in the heavenlies.

QUESTION—What is meant by ἐν τοῖς ἐπουρανίοις 'in the heavenly places'?
1. The actual locale of heaven is meant [Ba, Cal, DNTT, EGT, El, Gd, ICC, ISBE2, My, NIC, NTC, Si, TD, WBC]: he seated us together with Christ in heaven. This focuses on the spatial aspect of realized eschatology, the believer's present experience of participating in Christ's life and reign in the heavenly realms by virtue of his union with Christ in his exaltation in heaven [WBC].
2. The expression, in this reference, is equivalent to 'the kingdom of heaven' [AB, Can (probably), CBC, Ea, Ho, ISBE, Lns, MNTC, My-ed, Rob, St, TH], or, 'in the presence of God' [NCBC] as a state of existence [ISBE], the sphere of the super-earthly [ISBE]: he has seated us together with Christ in his spiritual kingdom. The verb used with this expression ('to seat') refers to a new function or relationship, not necessarily to a dislocation, so that 'heavenly places' is not an absolute locality where God dwells, but a sphere in which God manifests himself [AB], a higher level of life [CBC], a state of purity, exaltation and favor with God [Ho].

QUESTION—In the phrase ἐν Χριστῷ Ἰησοῦ 'in Christ Jesus', what is meant by ἐν 'in' in connection with the prefix συν- 'with' on the preceding verbs?

The preposition ἐν 'in' defines more precisely what was intended by συν- 'with' [Ea, EGT, El, ICC, Lns, My]: not only together with Christ, but also in vital connection with him. The preposition joins the phrase, not simply to ἐν τοῖς ἐπουρανίοις 'in the heavenly places', but to the two [Alf, El, My, WBC] or three preceding verbs [Ea] as well.

2:7 so-that[a] he-might-show[b] in the coming[c] ages[d]

LEXICON—a. ἵνα (LN 89.59): 'so that' [LN, WBC; NRSV, REB], 'in order that' [Lns, NTC; NASB, NIV], 'that' [El, Rob, We; KJV, NAB], 'in order to' [AB, LN], 'for the purpose of' [LN], 'this was to' [NIC; NJB], 'he did this to' [TEV], 'all this he did that' [TNT].
b. aorist mid. subj. of ἐνδείκνυμι (ἐνδείκνυμαι LN 28.51) (BAGD 1. p. 262): 'to show' [BAGD, LN, NIC, NTC, WBC, We; KJV, NASB, NIV, NJB, NRSV], 'to show forth' [El, Lns, Rob], 'to cause to be known' [LN], 'to display' [NAB, REB], 'to demonstrate' [BAGD, LN; TEV, TNT], 'to prove' [AB]. The middle voice may be taken as a true middle, 'to show for himself' (i.e., for his own glory) [Alf, Can, Ea, El], or as an equivalent to the active voice [EGT, El, ICC, Lns, My].
c. pres. mid. (deponent = active) participle of ἐπέρχομαι (LN 15.83) (BAGD 1.b.α. p. 285): 'to come' [AB, BAGD, El, Lns, NIC, NTC, Rob, WBC, We; all versions except TNT], 'to come to, to arrive' [LN], 'future' [TNT].
d. αἰών (LN 67.143) (BAGD 2.b. p. 27): 'ages' [AB, BAGD, El, LN, NIC, NTC, Rob, WBC, We; all versions except TEV], 'all time' [TEV], 'eons'

[LN, Lns], 'eras' [LN]. This term denotes a unit of time as a particular stage or period of history [LN]. It is also used to denote the coming messianic age [BAGD].

QUESTION—What relationship is indicated by ἵνα 'so that'?

This indicates the purpose of the preceding clauses [AB, Cal, Can, Ea, EBC, EGT, El, Gd, Ho, LJ, Lns, MNTC, My, NCBC, NIC, NTC, Rob, St, TD, TH, TNTC WBC; all versions]. God's purpose in saving men is to demonstrate to succeeding ages the greatness of his grace [Can, Ea]. This is the true and final cause of salvation [Cal]. By placing a full stop at the end of 2:5, some indicate that 2:7 forms the purpose for the clauses of 2:6 only [AB; NAB, NIV, REB, TEV]. Others make it the purpose of the section 2:4–6 [WBC; TNT]. Most regard it as the purpose of the three clauses of 2:5–6. Since the topic of all these clauses is salvation, the sense is not materially affected by the alternatives.

QUESTION—Who are the beings, living in these times, to whom these things will be shown?

1. They are all intelligent creation [Can, Gd, Ho (probably) NIC, NTC (probably), TNTC, WBC], both angels and people [EBC, LJ, Lns]: in order that he may show to all intelligent beings of the coming ages, etc.
2. They are the principalities and powers before mentioned, with particular focus on the future Gentile rulers [AB]: in order that he may show particularly to the Gentile rulers of the coming ages, etc.
3. They are the supernatural insurgent powers of the personalized αἰών 'Aeon' mentioned in 2:2 [TD]: in order that he may show to the spirits of Aeon...
4. They are all people [Ba, Ea]: in order that he may show to people of the coming ages. Like AB and TD, above, Ea also gives the word a connotation of hostility.
5. They are the members of the church [Alf, CBC] or all redeemed mankind [Cal, IB, NCBC]: in order that he may show to all redeemed mankind of the coming ages, etc.

QUESTION—What time period is covered by this term?

1. The time period referred to includes the present age only [AB, Alf, Ea, El, NCBC]: in order that he might show to those who will live in the coming periods of this present age.
2. The time period is the unending period from the time of the first century throughout all the rest of time and eternity [Ba, Cal, EBC, ECWB, Gd, Ho, LJ, MNTC, NIC, NTC]: in order that he might show to those who will live in all the coming ages throughout the rest of time and eternity.
3. The time period is the future age only, the unending period following Christ's second advent [Can (probably), CBC, EGT, IB, ICC, Lns, My, Si, TD, TNTC, Tu3, WBC, WeBC]: in order that he might show to those who will live in all the ages of his future Kingdom.

EPHESIANS 2:7

the exceeding[a] riches[b] of-his grace[c] in[d] kindness[e] toward[f] us in[g] Christ Jesus.

LEXICON—a. pres. act. participle of ὑπερβάλλω (LN **78.33**) (BAGD p. 840): 'to exceed' [Lns, Rob, We; KJV], 'to surpass' [BAGD, El, NIC, NTC, WBC; NASB]. This is also translated as an adjective: 'extraordinary' [BAGD, LN; TEV], 'incomparable' [NIV], 'measureless' [TNT], 'immeasurable' [NRSV], 'great' [NAB], 'outstanding' [BAGD]. It is also translated as an adverb: 'how immense, how great' [REB], 'how extraordinarily' [NJB], 'how infinitely' [AB]. This word indicates a degree which exceeds in an extraordinary way a point on a scale of extent, either overt or implied. In this expression both ὑπερβάλλον 'extraordinarily' and πλοῦτος 'riches, greatness' serve as expressions of degree; ὑπερβάλλον indicating an implied comparison, while πλοῦτος indicates not only a high degree of something, but also value [LN].

b. πλοῦτος (LN 78.15) (BAGD 2. p. 674): 'riches' [El, Lns, NTC, Rob, We; KJV, NASB, NIV, NRSV, TNT], 'richness' [WBC], 'wealth' [NIC; NAB], 'resources' [REB], 'greatness' [LN (**78.33**); TEV], 'a wealth, abundance (of something)' [BAGD]. This is also translated as an adjective: 'rich' [AB; NJB], 'abundant, great' [LN]. This term indicates a high point on any scale and has the implication of abundance as well as of value [LN]. See this word at 1:7, 18.

c. χάρις: 'grace'. See this word at 2:5.

d. ἐν with dative object (LN 89.5): 'in' [El, LN, Lns, NIC, Rob, WBC, We; KJV, NASB, NRSV, TEV], 'with regard to, in the case of' [LN], 'expressed in' [NTC; NIV], 'through' [AB; NJB], 'by' [TNT], 'manifested by' [NAB], 'and how great' [REB].

e. χρηστότης (LN 88.67) (BAGD 2.b. p. 886): 'kindness' [BAGD, El, LN, NIC, NTC, Rob, WBC, We; KJV, NAB, NASB, NIV, NRSV, REB, TNT], 'goodness' [AB, BAGD, Lns; NJB], 'generosity' [BAGD], 'love he showed (us)' [TEV]. The term designates an act beneficial to someone done as an act of kindness [LN].

f. ἐπί with accusative object (LN 84.17, 90.57) (BAGD III. 1. b. ε. p. 289): 'toward(s)' [BAGD, El, LN (84.17), NIC, NTC, Rob, We; KJV, NASB, NJB, NRSV], 'to' [AB, LN (90.57), WBC; NAB, NIV, REB, TNT], 'upon' [Lns], not explicit TEV.

g. ἐν with dative object (LN 89.119): 'in' [AB, El, LN, NIC, NTC, Rob, WBC, We; all versions except KJV], 'in union with, joined closely to' [LN], 'in connection with' [Lns], 'through' [KJV].

QUESTION—What relationship is indicated by ἐν 'in' in the phrase ἐν χρηστότητι 'in kindness'?

    1. It indicates the manner in which God showed his grace to us [Cal, Ea, EGT, El, LJ, Lns]: God kindly showed the riches of his grace to us.

    2. It indicates the means by which God showed his grace to us [Can, Ho, My, TH]: God showed the riches of his grace by being kind to us.

3. It indicates the material of which the display of grace consists [Alf, TNTC]: God showed the riches of his grace which consisted of his kindness to us.
4. It indicates the particular sphere in which his grace was manifested to us [WBC]: The demonstration of the riches of God's grace took place in his kindness to us in all that he accomplished for us in and through Christ.

QUESTION—What is this kindness?

It is not the general providential kindness of God to all men, but the special kindness shown that has its sphere of activity in Christ [Ea, Gd]. It has its source in the preceding χάρις 'grace' and consists in God's actions of forgiving and giving benefits to us [My]. It is God's love and goodness in action [EBC, TNTC, WBC]. It refers to the eschatological consummation of the preceding verbs, the rising again and ruling with Christ in the heavenly world, i.e., the comprehensive fullness of salvation [TD]. It refers to the calling of the Gentiles [Cal].

QUESTION—What group of people is meant by the pronoun ἡμᾶς 'us'?

It refers to the church universal, the Christians who have been and are being saved throughout the ages [AB, Alf, Ba, Can, CBC, EBC, EGT, Gd, Ho, IB, LJ, Lns, MNTC, My, NIC, NTC, Si, TD, TNTC, WBC, We]. Other suggestions are: Paul and the Ephesians [Ea], redeemed Gentiles of Paul's time [Cal], and Christians of Paul's time [NCBC].

QUESTION—What relationship is indicated by ἐν 'in' in the phrase ἐν Χριστῷ Ἰησοῦ 'in Christ Jesus'?

1. It indicates means [Cal, LJ (probably), TH; KJV]: in kindness to us through Christ Jesus. All grace and love and the blessings of salvation are mediated to us through Christ [Cal, LJ].
2. It indicates reason [EGT, Ho, ICC, My]: in kindness to us because of Christ Jesus. Three of these commentators retain the formal translation 'in' [EGT, ICC, My] while the fourth [Ho] uses 'through'.
3. It indicates the sphere of blessing [Ea, El]: in kindness to us in Christ Jesus.
4. It indicates a union or connection to Christ [Lns, NIC]: in kindness to us in union with Christ.

DISCOURSE UNIT: 2:8–10 [Alf, Ba, ECWB, Gd, NCBC, NIC, Rob, Si]. The topic is God's new creation [NIC], a summary of Paul's doctrine of justification (or salvation) by grace [Ba, ECWB, Gd, NCBC, NIC, Si] through faith [ECWB, NCBC, NIC], which is also a summary of 2:1–7.

DISCOURSE UNIT: 2:8–9 [Can, Ho, IB]. The topic is the restatement and amplification of 2:5, salvation by grace. The nature of the unit is that it constitutes a brief parenthesis [IB] explaining the preceding declaration affirmatively and negatively [Ho].

2:8 For[a] by-grace[b] you-are having-been-saved[c] through[d] faith;[e]

TEXT—Instead of διὰ πίστεως 'through faith' some manuscripts have διὰ τῆς πίστεως 'through (the) faith'. GNT does not mention this alternative. Those who accept διὰ πίστεως 'through faith' are AB, BD, EBC, El, GNT, HG, ICC, NIC, Rob, WBC, We. Those who accept διὰ τῆς πίστεως 'through (the) faith' are Alf, Ea, EGT, MNTC (probably), My. The Textus Receptus upon which the KJV is based also supports the article, though KJV and other commentators who accept this reading do not reflect it in their translation. If the anarthrous reading is correct then 'faith' is treated abstractly [Alf, HG]—faith as a quality or principle, but if the reading with the definite article is correct, then the force of the article is best seen as giving 'faith' a subjective quality [Alf, Ea] and being equivalent to a possessive pronoun 'your faith' [Alf, Ea, ICC].

LEXICON—a. γάρ (LN 89.23): 'for' [El, LN, Lns, NTC, Rob, WBC, We; KJV, NASB, NIV, NRSV, REB, TEV], 'because' [LN; NJB], 'I repeat' [NAB], 'Yes!' [TNT], not explicit [AB, NIC].
  b. χάρις: 'grace'. See this word at 2:5, 7.
  c. perf. pass. participle of σῴζω: 'to be saved'. See this word at 2:5.
  d. διά with genitive object (LN 89.76) (BAGD A. III. 1.d. p. 180): 'through' [AB, BAGD, El, LN, Lns, NIC, NTC, Rob, WBC, We; all versions except TNT], 'by means of' [BAGD, LN], 'by' [LN], not explicit [TNT]. This preposition marks the means by which one event makes another event possible [LN]. It denotes here the efficient cause [BAGD] or the immediate means [DNTT] of salvation.
  e. πίστις (LN **31.102**) (BAGD 2.d.α. p. 663): 'faith' [AB, BAGD, El, LN, Lns, NIC, NTC, Rob, WBC, We; all versions except TNT], 'trust' [BAGD, LN], 'confidence' [BAGD]. This noun is also translated as a verb phrase: 'you believed in him' [TNT], 'you have faith' [LN]. The word denotes the Christian faith, to be a believer and follower of Jesus Christ or to be a Christian [LN]. The word denotes true piety or genuine religion [BAGD]. Paul's characteristic use of the word shows that it refers to an attitude of complete openness to God and implies (1) a willingness to receive the benefits which God wants to give us and (2) a readiness to obey God's commands. Here the more passive element seems to be prominent [NCBC]. Jesus Christ [NIC] or God [TH] is the object of this 'faith'.

QUESTION—What relationship is indicated by γάρ 'for'?
  It introduces an inference or general conclusion from the preceding statements [Cal, TNTC]. It tells why mankind can experience the life of heaven and how the love of God is exhibited to all creation so they can learn and wonder [TNTC]. Others restrict this to a confirmation [Can, El, Ho, ICC, My; TNT] of the preceding statement (2:7), explaining the grounds for making that statement [Ea, El, Gd, ICC, My, WBC].

QUESTION—What force do the words τῇ χάριτι 'by grace' have in this clause, especially as relating to the phrase διὰ πίστεως 'through faith'?

By position in the clause the words τῇ χάριτι 'by grace' are given the prominence or emphasis [Ea, EGT, El, ICC, Lns, My, NCBC], more so even than the words διὰ πίστεως 'through faith' [EGT, ICC, My]. The dative case of χάριτι 'by grace' indicates means [HG], so that grace is the objective instrumental and effective cause [Alf, EBC, ECWB, El, Gd, LJ, My, TH], source [Ea, TH], or ground [EGT, Ho, WBC] of salvation as contrasted with the subjective, apprehending medium [Alf, EBC, ECWB, El, Gd, Ho, ICC, LJ, My, WBC], or means or method [DNTT, Ea, EGT, Lns, TH] of salvation shown by διὰ with the genitive πίστεως 'by faith'.

QUESTION—What is meant by διὰ πίστεως 'through faith'?

It serves to further explain the clause τῇ γὰρ χάριτί ἐστε σεσῳσμένοι 'for by grace you are saved' [EGT, El, My]. It indicates that although 'grace' is the sole source of salvation [Ea, Gd, NCBC, TD, TH], 'grace' is not universally, directly, and arbitrarily imposed upon its object [Ea, TH]. It acts through a medium—'faith'. 'Faith' is the means or instrument by which 'grace' becomes effective in salvation [Ea, ECWB, EGT, El, Gd, LJ, Lns, My, TH, WBC]. And this involves no merit or credit on man's part since he does not produce it [AB, Ea, EBC, Gd, Ho, Lns, TD]. Even in relationships strictly on the natural, human level, 'faith' is something that is normally produced in one person by the actions of another [Lns]. Thus 'faith' is only the sinner's reception [Ho, LJ, Lns, WBC] and acquiescence in the goodness and wisdom of God's plan of salvation [Ea, WBC].

and[a] this (is) not of[b] you, of-God (it is) the gift;[c]
- LEXICON—a. καί (LN 89.92; 91.12) (BAGD I.3. p. 393): 'and' [El, LN (89.92), Lns, NIC, NTC, Rob, WBC, We; KJV, NASB, NIV, NRSV], 'and indeed' [BAGD], 'indeed, yet' [LN (91.12)], not explicit [AB; NAB, NJB, REB, TEV, TNT]. As an explicative it joins one word or clause with another word or clause for the purpose of explaining the first word or clause [BAGD]. As ascensive it is a marker of emphasis and involves surprise and unexpectedness [LN (91.12)].
  - b. ἐκ with genitive object (LN 90.16): 'of' [NTC, Rob, We; KJV, NASB,], 'from' [LN, Lns, WBC; NIV], 'because of' [TNT], 'by' [LN], 'by (anything) of' [NJB]. This preposition is also translated with the genitive pronoun ὑμῶν 'of you' as a verb phrase: 'out of your own doing' [AB], 'your own doing' [NAB, NRSV, REB], 'cometh (not) of yourselves' [El], 'does (not) proceed from yourselves' [NIC]. This prepositional phrase is also conflated with the ἐξ ἔργων 'of works' in the next clause and translated as a single unit: 'the result of your own efforts' [TEV]. This is a marker of the source of an activity or state [LN].
  - c. δῶρον (LN 57.84) (BAGD 1. p. 210): 'gift' [AB, BAGD, El, LN, Lns, NIC, NTC, Rob, WBC, We; all versions], 'present' [BAGD, LN].

QUESTION—To what does the neuter pronoun τοῦτο 'this' refer?
1. It refers not to the main topic of salvation but to the subordinate one of 'faith' [Can, Gd, Ho, NTC, Si, We]: and indeed this faith does not even arise from within yourselves as its source. The fact that τοῦτο 'this' is neuter gender and πίστις 'faith' is feminine is no argument against this. Classical Greek also has instances of a neuter gender demonstrative pronoun referring to a substantive of masculine or feminine gender when the idea conveyed by the substantive is referred to in a general way. Here, it refers not to πίστις 'faith' precisely, but to the fact of our exercising faith [NTC]. This interpretation necessitates making this latter half of the verse a parenthesis [Can, Ho] since the phrase beginning the next verse 'not of works' must refer to salvation [Can]. The construction of these statements would therefore be: (2:8) For by grace are you saved through faith (and that not from yourselves, it is a gift of God) (2:9) not of works [Can].
2. It refers to 'you are saved' [Alf, Ba, Cal, CBC, Ea, El, HG, IB, LJ (probably), Lns, MNTC, My] or, much the same thing, to the whole preceding statement involving salvation by grace through faith [AB, EBC, ECWB, EGT, HG, ICC, NCBC, NIC, Rob, St, TH, TNTC, WBC, WeBC]: and this salvation by grace through faith does not take its source from within yourselves. The words καὶ τοῦτο 'and this' introduce the first of two balancing negatives (the second being 2:9) which enforce the positive statement that we have been saved by grace through faith [AB, El, St, TNTC]. To adopt a parenthetical interpretation for this half of the verse is to destroy the parallelism between οὐκ ἐξ ὑμῶν 'not of yourselves' and οὐκ ἐξ ἔργων 'not of works' [Ea, EBC, ICC, My, TNTC] both of which belong to the same flow of discourse [My]. Nor does this interpretation destroy the idea that faith is created in the individual by God. Besides being taught in other passages [Lns, NCBC, St] it is included in this one [AB, EBC, ECWB, St, WBC] because, being a part of salvation, it too must come from God [EBC, NCBC, NIC, WBC].

2:9 **not of[a] works,[b] in-order-that not anyone should-boast,[c]**

LEXICON—a. ἐκ with genitive object (LN 90.16): 'of' [El, NTC, Rob, We; KJV], 'from' [LN, Lns], 'as a result of' [NASB], 'the result of' [NRSV, TEV, TNT], 'as a reward for' [AB], 'a reward for' [NAB, REB], 'by' [WBC; NIV, NJB]. This is also translated as a verb phrase: 'it is (not) based on' [NIC].
b. ἔργον (LN 42.11) (BAGD 1.c.β. p. 308): 'works' [AB, El, Lns, NIC, NTC, Rob, WBC, We; KJV, NASB, NIV, NRSV], 'work done' [REB], 'tasks' [LN (42.42)], 'effort' [TEV], 'act' [LN (42.11)], 'deed' [BAGD, LN (42.11)]. This noun is also translated by a clause: 'anything (that) you have done' [NJB, TNT], 'to accomplish anything' [NAB]. It is used of the deeds of men that exhibit a consistent moral character and implies the deeds commanded by the (Mosaic) law [BAGD].

c. aorist mid. subj. of καυχάομαι (LN 33.368) (BAGD 1. p. 425): 'to boast' [BAGD, El, LN, Lns, NTC, Rob, WBC; KJV, NASB, NIV, NRSV], 'to boast of' [REB], 'to boast about' [TEV, TNT], 'to boast about oneself' [AB], 'to have room for boasting' [NIC], 'to glory' [BAGD, We], 'to pride oneself' [BAGD; NAB], 'to claim credit' [NJB]. The aorist tense gives an ingressive aspect: 'that no one shall ever get to boast' [Lns].

QUESTION—What is meant by ἔργων 'of works'?
1. This has specific reference to the Mosaic law [AB, Alf, CBC, DNTT, Ea, ECWB, ISBE2 (probably), MNTC, TNTC]: not from works of Moses' law.
2. This may include, but is not restricted to, the Mosaic law [Cal, Can (probably), EBC, Ho, IB, ICC, LJ, Lns, My, NCBC, NTC, St, TD (probably), TH, WBC, We, WeBC]: not from any human achievement. This has reference to any deed by which a person might seek to establish himself as meritorious in God's eyes with the intention of attaining salvation thereby [EBC, Ho, IB, LJ, Lns, NCBC, NTC, TH, WeBC]. It stands for human effort in general [IB, WBC].

QUESTION—What relationship is indicated by ἵνα 'in order that'?
1. It indicates purpose [Alf, Ea, EBC, El, My, TD, WBC; KJV, NASB, NRSV]: it is not of works, in order that no one may boast. This need not mean that it was God's main or leading aim in providing salvation by grace, only that it was included in his scheme [Alf, El, TNTC].
2. It indicates result or contemplated result [ICC; NAB, NJB, REB, TNT]: with the result that no one can boast. It is also possible to regard this as the author's reaction to the preceding clauses: so let no one pride himself on it [NAB], or, so there is nothing for anyone to boast of [REB, TNT].

QUESTION—What is meant by 'boasting'?
The English term usually refers to boastful words. But what is really being described is an attitude of mind that lies behind boastful words [IDB, ISBE, ISBE2, MNTC, NCBC]—putting confidence in the flesh [WBC], arrogance [ISBE2], self-congratulation [NCBC] and spiritual pride [IDB, ISBE2, NCBC], or a self-righteous [ISBE, ISBE2, MNTC], self-satisfaction [ISBE2, MNTC].

2:10 For[a] of-him we are a handiwork,[b]

LEXICON—a. γάρ (LN 89.23, 91.1): 'for' [AB, El, LN (89.23), Lns, NTC, Rob, WBC, We; KJV, NASB, NIV, NRSV], 'because' [LN (89.23)], not explicit [LN (91.1), NIC; NAB, NJB, REB, TEV, TNT].
b. ποίημα (LN **42.30**) (BAGD p. 683): 'handiwork' [NTC; NAB, REB], 'workmanship' [El, Lns, NIC, Rob, We; KJV, NASB, NIV], 'work' [BAGD, WBC], 'creation' [BAGD], 'product' [LN], 'work of art' [NJB]. This noun is also translated as a clause: 'what he has made' [AB, BAGD, LN; NRSV, TEV, TNT].

QUESTION—What relationship is indicated by γάρ 'for'?
1. It indicates the grounds for making the statement in 2:8–9 that salvation is not of works [Alf, Cal, Ea, EGT, El, Ho, ICC, My, WBC; REB]: salvation is God's gift and not of works, since we are God's handiwork. We, together with all that we are, are both a product of God's work [WBC]. Good works are shown to be the result of salvation, not its cause [Ea, Ho].
2. It indicates the positive counterpart of the preceding clause [IB]: not of works; to the contrary, we are created for good works.
3. It signals the start of a new sentence [AB, EBC, GNT, NIC; NAB, NASB, NIV, NJB, NRSV, TEV, TNT] concluding the paragraph as a whole [AB, EBC, NIC, Si]: We are his workmanship. This verse is the outcome or conclusion of the whole paragraph 2:1–10 [EBC] standing in contrast to the first three verses [NIC, Si]. It is not a subsidiary postscript to the paragraph; it shows what salvation is for [EBC].

QUESTION—What is the force of αὐτοῦ 'of him, his'?
The pronoun is emphatic by its position at the beginning of the clause [EGT, El, HG, Ho, ICC, Lns, My, NCBC, St, TNTC, Tu, WBC, We]—we are his handiwork and no other's [AB, My, NCBC]—stressing that salvation is God's achievement [St, WBC]. The possessive noun phrase in which the pronoun occurs is one of the points upon which the argument of this verse turns [ICC, My].

QUESTION—What is meant by ποίημα 'handiwork'?
The addition of the clause κτισθέντες ἐν Χριστῷ Ἰησοῦ 'created in Christ Jesus' shows that here its reference is the new birth or new spiritual creation of the Christian [AB, Alf, Ba, Cal, Can, DNTT, Ea, EBC, ECWB, EGT, El, Ho, ICC, IDB, LJ, Lns, MNTC, My, NCBC, NIC, NTC, Rob, Si, St, TD, TH, TNTC, We], though some would not exclude a reference to our first creation as well [Can, ECWB, IB, WBC]. Most commentators simply refer to it as a product of God's work [AB, Cal, Can, DNTT, EGT, El, LJ, Lns, My, NIC, NTC, TD, TH]. Others play up the connotation of 'masterpiece' or 'work of art' [EBC, St; NJB], with God being portrayed as an artist or craftsman [CBC].

created[a] in/by[b] Christ Jesus for[c] good[d] works;[e]

LEXICON—a. aorist pass. participle of κτίζω (LN 42.35) (BAGD p. 455): 'to be created' [AB, BAGD, El, LN, Lns, NIC, NTC, Rob, WBC, We; all versions except TEV, TNT]. This passive voice is also translated actively: 'to create' [TEV, TNT]. The word means to make or create something which has not existed before [LN, TD].
  b. ἐν with dative object (LN 89.119): 'in' [AB, El, LN, NIC, NTC, Rob, WBC, We; all versions except TEV], 'in union with' [LN; TEV], 'in connection with' [Lns], 'joined closely to, one with' [LN].
  c. ἐπί with dative object (LN 89.60) (BAGD II.1.b.ε. p. 287): 'for' [AB, BAGD, El, Lns, NIC, NTC, WBC, We; NASB, NJB, NRSV, REB, TEV, TNT], 'for the purpose of' [LN], 'unto' [Rob; KJV], not explicit [NAB].

EPHESIANS 2:10

    This is also translated as a purpose in connection with a verb: 'to do' [NIV]. This is a marker of purpose and points to the goal of an event or state [BAGD, LN].
  d. ἀγαθός (LN 88.1): 'good' [AB, El, LN, Lns, NIC, NTC, Rob, WBC, We; all versions].
  e. ἔργον (LN 42.11) (BAGD 1.c.β. p. 308): 'works' [AB, El, Lns, NIC, NTC, Rob, WBC, We; KJV, NASB, NIV, NJB, NRSV, TNT], 'deeds' [BAGD, LN; NAB, REB, TEV], 'acts' [LN]. This is used of the deeds of men which exhibit a consistent moral quality and is referred to in a collective sense [BAGD]. See this word at 2:9.

QUESTION—What relationship is indicated by the use of the participle κτισθέντες 'created'?

This explains and limits the preceding noun ποίημα 'handiwork' [Cal, Can, Ea, EGT, El, Ho, ICC, Lns, TH]. We are God's work because we have been created by him [Cal, EGT, Ho]. God's power in the new creation is parallel to the description of power just given, as making alive and raising from the dead, so continuing the theme expressed in 1:19 [Can].

QUESTION—What is meant by the phrase ἐν Χριστῷ Ἰησοῦ 'in Christ Jesus'?

The phrase is emphatic [EBC] and modifies the participle κτισθέντες 'created' defining the creation being spoken of as the new creation, the spiritual rebirth of the Christian [Ea, EBC, ECWB, EGT, Ho, ICC, LJ, Lns]. The preposition ἐν 'in' indicates the means or instrument of this creation [LJ, NCBC, TH, TNTC], but it may carry in addition the meaning of 'union with' so that the new creation is carried out by means of uniting the believer to Christ [CBC, Ea, EGT, Ho, LJ, Lns, NCBC, TH] and his work [CBC, LJ], or, it expresses the fellowship in which the new creation takes place [ICC]. At the same time it presents Christ as the sphere of creation [Ea], the element of life within which this creation has taken place [Lns, My]. In short, the phrase stands for 'God's activity in Christ'. Christ is presented as the mediator of the new creation just as much as he was of the first one (Col. 1:16) [WBC].

QUESTION—What relationship is indicated by ἐπί 'for'?

1. It indicates God's goal or purpose in creating us [Alf, Ba, Cal, Can, DNTT, Ea, EBC, EGT, El, HG, Ho, IB, Mo, My, NCBC, Rob, St, TH]: God created us in Christ Jesus in order that we perform good works.
2. It indicates that the result of God creating us is an ability and obligation on our part to accept and perform these good works [ECWB, ICC, MNTC, TNTC, We]: God created us in Christ Jesus in a condition in which we are obliged to perform the good works he has prepared for us to do. The good works are an inseparable characteristic or condition of the regenerate life [ECWB, ICC, MNTC, TNTC], not just its goal [ICC].

QUESTION—What does Paul mean by 'good works'?

1. The term specifies individual acts which God has prepared for each believer to do [Alf, Can, IB, Si]: created in Christ Jesus to do the

particular good things he has designed each of us to do. The tasks are those related to the particular sphere in which we serve God, tasks that are designed for us and for which we have been designed [Alf, IB, Si].

2. The term is used in a general sense for holiness of life which is incumbent on all Christians [AB, Ba, Cal, Ea, El, Ho, Lns, My, NCBC, NTC, TNTC, WBC, WeBC]: created in Christ Jesus that we all lead lives of holiness. These good works are fruits of regeneration [My, NIC], all the thoughts, words, and deeds through which the righteousness and holiness of the new life manifest themselves [Lns], righteous living [WeBC], acts of love, mercy, and practical help to those in need [NCBC], works which reflect the character and action of God himself [NIC].

3. Both of the above senses are meant [LJ]: created in Christ Jesus to be holy and to do the particular things he has designed us each to do.

which God prepared-beforehand,ᵃ in-order-thatᵇ we-might-walkᶜ in them.

LEXICON—a. aorist act. indic. of προετοιμάζω (LN 77.4) (BAGD p. 705): 'to prepare beforehand' [BAGD, NTC; NASB, NRSV], 'to prepare before' [El, Rob, We], 'to prepare in advance' [LN, Lns, NIC, WBC; NAB, NIV], 'to already prepare' [TEV], 'to already designate' [NJB], 'to make ready in advance' [LN], 'to ordain before' [KJV], 'to design' [REB], 'to plan' [TNT], 'to provide' [AB].

b. ἵνα (LN 89.59): 'in order that' [WBC], 'in order to, for the purpose of' [LN], 'so that' [LN, NIC], 'that' [El, NTC, Rob, We; KJV, NASB], 'for' [Lns; REB, TEV, TNT]. Others unite this particle with the verb περιπατέω 'to walk' to indicate purpose with an infinitive construction [NAB, NIV, NJB, NRSV]. This particle and verb is also translated with adverbial force: 'as our way of life' [AB].

c. aorist act. subj. of περιπατέω: 'to walk'. See this word at 2:2.

QUESTION—How is the relative pronoun οἷς 'which' related to the verb προητοίμασεν 'he prepared beforehand'?

1. It is the object of the verb [AB, Alf, BAGD, Cal, Can, Ea, EBC, ECWB, EGT, El, HG, Ho, IB, Lns, MNTC, My, NIC, NTC, Rob, Si, St, TH, TNTC, WBC, We; NAB, NASB, NIV, NJB, NRSV, REB, TEV, TNT]: God planned these good works beforehand. Οἷς 'which' occurs in the dative case because it refers back to ἔργοις ἀγαθοῖς 'good works' in the previous clause which is in the dative case, so it is attracted to that case from the accusative case which it would normally take as object of the verb [BAGD, El, WBC]. This means that the good works have been prescribed and adapted to us in order that we might walk in them [Alf, Ea, EGT, El, IB, WBC].

2. It is the indirect object of the verb [Ba, ICC, NCBC]: God prepared us beforehand for doing these good works.

QUESTION—What is meant by προητοίμασεν 'he prepared beforehand' and what is its point of reference?

1. This verb has its point of reference in eternity past [AB, Alf, Ba, Cal, Can, Ea, EBC, ECWB, EGT, Ho, My, NCBC (probably), St, WBC]: which God prepared beforehand in his decree in eternity past that we should walk in them. It means 'to prepare before', or 'to place in readiness before', not 'to foreordain' [EGT, El, My]. The prefixed προ- 'before' refers to a period prior to that expressed in κτισθέντες 'created' [Ea, EGT, El, My], but the source of these 'good works' is found in God's eternal decree [EGT, My, NCBC (probably)].
2. The point of reference of this verb is to the time of [ICC, MNTC, NTC] or prior to [El] our new creation: which God prepared at or before our (new) creation that we should walk in them. The capacity to know and do the will of God is given to us with our new life [MNTC, NTC]. One commentator says the προ- manifests primacy rather than priority, meaning that the new creation is the primary thing, with the end in view that the good works are its result [ICC].

QUESTION—What relationship is indicated by ἵνα 'in order that'?

It indicates purpose, 'in order that' or 'so that' [AB, Alf, Ba, Ea, EBC, EGT, El, Ho, LJ, Lns, My, NCBC, NIC, NTC, Rob, St, TH, TNTC, WBC, We; NAB, NASB, NIV, NJB, NRSV, TEV]. A few regard it as epexegetical of 'good works', defining the range of the noun ('duties ('good works') for us to perform' or 'good works as our way of life') [AB, IB, MNTC; REB], but even here, purpose is still implied.

DISCOURSE UNIT: 2:11–3:21 [St]. The topic is the new society.

DISCOURSE UNIT: 2:11–22 [AB, Alf, Ba, Can, Ea, EBC, ECWB, EGT, El, Ho, IB, ICC, LJ, NCBC, NIC, Rob, St, TH, TNTC, WBC, We, WeBC; NAB, NIV, NJB, TEV]. The topic is the call to remembrance of their former, alienated position as Gentiles [AB, Alf, Ba, Can, EGT, Ho, IB, ICC, LJ, WBC] by God's law [LJ], and the reconciliation of the division between Jews and Gentiles [AB, EBC, EGT, Ho, IB, ICC, NIC, TH, TNTC, WBC], by overcoming the obstacle of the law [LJ], which resulted in peace [AB, TH] and unity [Ho, IB, ICC, LJ, NCBC, NIC, St, TH, We] between the two, a new humanity [St, TH].

DISCOURSE UNIT: 2:11–18 [Lns, MNTC, NTC, Rob]. The topic is Paul's exultation over God's glorious church for its universal scope [NTC] in the reconciliation or acceptance of the Gentiles with the Jews [Lns, MNTC, NTC], and the great peace that resulted [Lns].

DISCOURSE UNIT: 2:11–16 [CBC]. The topic is a reminder of their religious-racial past.

DISCOURSE UNIT: 2:11–13 [Ba, ECWB, My, Si, We]. The topic is the drawing of the Gentiles into unity with God from their condition of alienation from God, his covenant and promises [ECWB, Si] and the broad contrast between their past and present condition [Ba, My, We].

DISCOURSE UNIT: 2:11–12 [AB, Alf, Ho, IB, NCBC, NIC, Rob, WeBC]. The topic is a reminder their former relationship as Gentiles [AB, Alf, Ho, IB, NCBC, NIC, Rob, WeBC].

2:11 Therefore[a] remember[b] that formerly[c] you Gentiles[d] in (the) flesh,[e]

LEXICON—a. διό (LN 89.47): 'therefore' [LN, NIC, NTC, WBC; NASB, NIV], 'wherefore' [El, Lns, Rob, We; KJV], 'then' [AB; NJB, REB, TNT], 'so then' [LN; NRSV], 'for this reason' [LN], not explicit [NAB, TEV].
  b. pres. act. imper. of μνημονεύω (LN 29.7) (BAGD 1.c. p. 525): 'to remember' [AB, BAGD, El, LN, Lns, NIC, NTC, Rob, WBC, We; all versions except NJB], 'to recall, to think about again' [LN], 'to keep in mind, to think of' [BAGD], 'to not forget' [NJB]. This does not necessarily imply that the persons have actually forgotten the thing to be remembered [LN].
  c. ποτε: 'formerly'. See this word at 2:2, 3.
  d. ἔθνος (LN 11.37): 'Gentiles' [AB, El, Lns, NIC, NTC, Rob, WBC, We; all versions], 'heathen, pagans' [LN].
  e. σάρξ (LN 8.63, 10.1) (BAGD 7. p. 744): 'flesh' [AB, El, LN (8.63), Lns, NTC, Rob, WBC, We; KJV, NASB], 'race, ethnic group, nation' [LN (10.1)], 'a sinful and unregenerate state' [BAGD]. The phrase ἐν σαρκί 'in the flesh' is translated 'by birth' [NIV, NRSV, TEV], 'as you are by birth' [REB], 'by physical descent' [NJB], 'by natural descent' [NIC]. This is also translated by a clause: 'you had (not) undergone a physical rite' [TNT]. The phrase τὰ ἔθνη ἐν σαρκί 'Gentiles in the flesh' is translated 'men of Gentile stock' [NAB].

QUESTION—What relationship is indicated by διό 'wherefore'?
  1. It indicates an exhortation based on the previous paragraph, 2:1–10 [EBC, EGT, El, ICC, LJ, Lns, My, NTC, WBC, We]: since you were dead in sin and under the control of evil forces and by God's grace were given life, raised up and seated with Christ, and have been given a high and noble calling, therefore remember that, etc. In light of what has been said in 2:1–10 about the change God has wrought in these readers, they are now to further reflect upon their pre-Christian state from another vantage point [WBC]. Since 2:1–10 is a single sentence in the Greek text, the διό 'therefore' refers back to this [EBC], not just to 2:10 [EBC, EGT, El]. It refers back especially to 2:1–7 [ECWB, El] or 2:4–10 [My].
  2. It refers back to the whole of 1:3–2:10 [NCBC, WeBC], but especially to 2:1–10 [WeBC]: since God has given you all these blessings that I have been writing about so far, therefore remember that, etc. The argument for their corporate unity, which Paul is preparing to argue, is based upon the reality of the good things they have already experienced as individual Christians [NCBC]. This new paragraph, 2:11–22, is a recapitulation of all

that the Apostle has said in the earlier part of this chapter, and in general of all that has gone before in the epistle [WeBC].
3. It is regarded as a general connective with no clear antecedent specified [AB, Alf, Ea, Ho, NIC, Rob]: since God has done such great things for you, therefore remember that, etc.

QUESTION—What is meant by μνημονεύετε 'remember'?

Μνημονεύετε 'remember' does not imply a loss of memory [TH]. The readers are only asked to think about [EGT, ICC] and recall their former status in order that a sense of humility [Cal, Ea, Ho] and gratitude [AB, Ba, Ea, EGT, Ho, ICC, My, NIC, Si, TD, TNTC, WBC, WeBC] may arise within them for what God has done for them.

QUESTION—What is the significance of ποτέ 'formerly'?

The word refers to their former status as Gentiles (relative to the religious privileges of Israelites) [Ea, IB, WBC], it does not mean they were formerly Gentiles but now are no longer so. Insofar as the word ἔθνη 'Gentiles' designates a distinction of race, they still were Gentiles [Can, IB].

QUESTION—Is there an ellipsed verb in the nominal clause ὑμεῖς τὰ ἔθνη 'you the Gentiles' (i.e., 'you being/were Gentiles')?

The resumption of ὅτι 'that' and of ποτέ 'formerly' by τῷ καιρῷ ἐκείνῳ 'at that time' in the next verse [Ea, El, ICC, My] together with the position of ποτέ 'formerly' (indicating that τὰ ἔθνη 'the Gentiles' is in apposition to ὑμεῖς 'you') [El, ICC, My] is enough to convince most commentators that there is no ellipsed verb, such as ὄντες 'being' or ἦτε '(you) were', here. A few do insert a verb here [Ba; KJV, NIV, NJB, REB, TNT]. Of these, NIV and NJB are careful to translate in a manner that interprets this construction (by means of an inserted relative clause, 'who are') as descriptive of ὑμεῖς 'you', rather than indicating an event ('you were Gentiles') in addition to the events following the resumptive ὅτι 'that' of the next verse.

QUESTION—What does the presence of the definite article with ἔθνη 'Gentiles' and its absence with σάρξ 'flesh' mean?

The occurrence of the article with ἔθνη 'Gentiles' marks the underprivileged group [EBC] to which these people belonged as a class or category [Alf, Ea, El, ICC, My, We], while its absence with σάρξ 'flesh' unites the phrase ἐν σαρκί 'in (the) flesh' closely with τὰ ἔθνη 'the Gentiles' [Ea], because the phrase makes a predication about the Gentiles [BD], forming one idea [El, ICC, My]: that of the flesh being the ground of their distinction as Gentiles, i.e., those who are Gentiles according to a distinction which exists in the flesh [Rob]. (However, another thinks Paul simply felt the article was not needed here [HG].) Omission of the article with σάρξ 'flesh' prevents any suggestion that there was another class of Gentiles [Rob]. The article with ἔθνη 'Gentiles' is generalizing the address: not 'you Gentiles' but 'you, the Gentiles' [IB].

QUESTION—What is meant by ἐν σαρκί 'in (the) flesh'?

The two occurrences of the phrase in this verse serve to characterize both of the categories of people spoken of in this verse. It marks the basis on which they were either included or excluded from the only Covenant that God had made with men prior to NT times. At the same time it indicates the inadequacy of that Covenant to meet human needs, even in a provisional way, because the basis of the distinction is outwardly: 'in (the) flesh' [We]. The use of the phrase shows that the distinction between Jew and Gentile is only temporary [DNTT] and provisional [TD], holding good only within the earthly human world but not applicable to the spiritual community of Christ's Church [TD, WBC], transitoriness being a particularly characteristic mark of σάρξ 'flesh' [DNTT].

1. It has a literal reference to the flesh of the human body [AB, Alf, Cal, Can, CBC, Ea, EBC, ECWB, EGT, El, Ho, IB, ICC, IDB, ISBE2, Lns, My, NIC, NTC, St, TH, TNTC, We; NASB, TNT]: formerly you Gentiles, as evidenced by your very bodies. It may refer specifically to the uncircumcised part itself [AB (possibly), Ho, IDB, ISBE2, Lns, My, TH].

2. In addition to its literal reference, it is used as a complex figure of speech for their birth (or descent) as Gentiles [Can, EBC, LJ, NCBC, TH; NAB, NJB, NRSV, REB, TEV]: formerly you who were born Gentiles, as evidenced in your very bodies. Σάρξ 'flesh' is a euphemism for that part of the male body upon which the rite of circumcision (or the lack of it in the case of the Gentiles) is performed [TH]. Because circumcision was associated with birth and the Covenant [Can, EBC, LJ, NCBC, TH], this euphemism, itself a synecdoche (the whole being put for the part), becomes metonymy for membership in a group by birth or descent.

3. In addition to its literal reference, it is used figuratively of the superficial mindset against the Gentiles on the part of the Jews [Can, LJ, Lns, MNTC, NCBC, Rob, TNTC, WBC]: formerly you Gentiles, as evidenced in your bodies according to the superficial standards of the Jews. The phrase ἐν σαρκί 'in (the) flesh' underlines the fact that the writer is making an ethnic distinction. It appears to indicate not only that the distinction is based upon a real physical difference, but that from the Christian perspective this distinction is no longer religiously significant. So, in this context, σάρξ 'flesh' has a connotation of inferiority, but it does not have the strong negative ethical sense it had in 2:3 [WBC]. This was a superficial and unspiritual way of thinking on the part of the Jews [TNTC]. The figure is metonymy—'flesh' being put for the type of thinking it produces.

4. It is used figuratively of the lower, unregenerate nature [AB, Ba, BAGD, WeBC]: you formerly unregenerate Gentiles. Here also two commentators still see the literal reference as receiving some focus [AB, WeBC]. Σάρξ 'flesh' has the same evil meaning here as it has in 2:3 [AB]. The figure of speech is synecdoche, 'flesh' being put for the whole unregenerate person—body and spirit.

5. In addition to its literal reference to the physical body, it has figurative references to their birth as Gentiles and to the lower, unregenerate nature

[NIC, Si]: you, born as unregenerate Gentiles, evidenced by your very bodies.

the (ones) being-called[a] (the) Uncircumcision[b] by that being-called[c] (the) Circumcision[d] in (the) flesh[e] made-by-hands,[f]

LEXICON—a. pres. pass. participle of λέγω (LN 33.131) (BAGD II.3. p. 470): 'to be called' [AB, BAGD, El, LN, Lns, NIC, NTC, Rob, WBC, We; KJV, NAB, NASB, NIV, NRSV, REB, TEV], 'to be termed' [NJB]. This passive participle is also translated as an active verb: 'to call' [TNT]. This term designates the usage of an attribute as a name or title in speaking of a person [LN].

b. ἀκροβυστία (LN 11.53) (BAGD 3. p. 33): 'the Uncircumcision' [AB, El, Rob, We], 'Uncircumcision' [KJV, NASB], 'the uncircumcision' [WBC; NRSV], 'uncircumcision' [NIC, NTC] 'the uncircumcised' [BAGD; NJB, REB, TEV, TNT], 'uncircumcised' [LN; NAB, NIV], 'foreskin' [Lns], 'heathenism' [BAGD]. By metonymy [AB], the word is used as a collective for those who are uncircumcised [AB, Cal, DNTT, Ea, LN, Lns, NIC].

c. pres. mid./pass. participle of λέγω (LN 33.131) (BAGD II.3. p. 470): 'to be called' [LN, NTC, Rob, WBC, We; KJV, NRSV], 'to be known' [TNT], 'to call themselves' [AB; NAB, NIV, REB, TEV], 'to speak of themselves' [NJB]. This participle is also translated as an adjective: 'so-called' [BAGD, El, Lns, NIC; NASB]. This term designates the usage of an attribute as a name or title in speaking of a person [LN].

d. περιτομή (LN 53.51) (BAGD 4.a. p. 653): 'the Circumcision' [AB, El, Rob, We; KJV], 'the circumcision' [BAGD, Lns, WBC; NIV, NRSV], 'Circumcision' [NASB], 'circumcision' [LN, NIC, NTC], 'the circumcised' [NJB, REB, TEV, TNT], 'circumcised' [NAB]. This term designates the cutting off of the foreskin of the male genital organ as a religious rite which involves consecration and ethnic identification [LN]. By metonymy [AB] this term is a collective name for the Jews [AB, BAGD, Cal, DNTT, Ea, Lns, NIC, TD, TH].

e. σάρξ (LN 8.63) (BAGD 1. p. 743): 'flesh' [AB, BAGD, El, LN, Lns, NTC, Rob, WBC, We; KJV, NAB, NASB, NRSV], 'body' [NIV, TEV]. This is also translated as an adjective: 'external' [NIC], 'physical (rite/operation)' [NJB, REB, TNT].

f. χειροποίητος (LN 42.32) (BAGD p. 881): 'made by hands' [Rob, WBC, We; KJV], 'handmade' [Lns, NTC], 'handmade operation' [AB], 'done by the hands of men' [NIV], 'manmade' [LN, NIC], 'what men do' [TEV], 'performed by human hands' [NASB], 'performed by hand' [El], 'made by human hands' [BAGD, LN; NRSV], 'brought about by human hands' [BAGD], 'a hand executed rite' [NAB]. This is also translated in conjunction with σάρξ 'flesh': 'physical rite' [REB, TNT], 'physical operation' [NJB].

QUESTION—To what is the articular participle οἱ λεγόμενοι 'the ones being called' related and what is its function?

It begins the participial clause (consisting of the remainder of the verse) which is in apposition to and describes τὰ ἔθνη 'the Gentiles' [Ba, Can, CBC, Ea, EBC, EGT, El, Ho, Lns, My, Rob, TH, TNTC]. This apposition is a brief expansion or digression [EGT, LJ, Rob, TH] which gives the verse its incomplete or anacolouthic character [AB, EGT, Rob, TH], necessitating the repetition of ὅτι 'that' at the beginning of the next verse in order to resume the topic of discussion [AB, Can, EGT, Ho, ICC, Lns, TH, WBC].

QUESTION—To what are the words ἐν σαρκὶ χειροποιήτου 'in (the) flesh, made by hands' connected?

They are Paul's addition to περιτομῆς 'circumcision', used to clarify how he is using the term. The Jews used the noun 'Circumcision' in reference to themselves, but not with the attached words Paul uses [Alf, Ea, ECWB, EGT, El, Lns, My].

QUESTION—Is the meaning of ἐν σαρκί 'in (the) flesh' in this second occurrence the same as in the first?

1. It has the same meaning as in the first occurrence [AB, Alf, Cal, CBC, Ea, ECWB, EGT, El, IB, ICC, LJ, Lns, MNTC, My, NTC, Rob, St, TH, TNTC, WBC, We].
2. It has a different meaning when applied to the Jews than when applied to the Gentiles [Ba, BAGD, Can, EBC, NCBC, NIC, Si, WeBC; NAB, NIV, NJB, NRSV, REB, TEV]. All agree that in respect to the Jews, the phrase denotes the rite of physical circumcision. Disagreement here exists over its meaning in respect to the Gentiles. One group says that in respect to the Gentiles, it had the meaning 'by birth' [Can, EBC, NCBC; NAB, NIV, NJB, NRSV, REB, TEV]. The other group says that it had the meaning 'unregenerate' [Ba, BAGD Si, WeBC]. Another believes that it meant both 'by birth' and 'unregenerate' [NIC].

QUESTION—What is the significance of Paul's use of χειροποίητος 'made by hands'?

The use of this term throws a negative evaluation on the title περιτομῆς 'the circumcision' [My-ed, WBC]. In all its occurrences in the NT [TD], χειροποίητος 'made by hands' stands for work that is of human origin as opposed to the work of God [DNTT, TD, TH]. Therefore, only a relative validity can be attached to the judgment that the circumcised pass upon the Gentiles [Rob, TD]. Because of this contrast, the term implicitly brings to the readers' minds the true circumcision performed by the Holy Spirit in virtue of Christ's death that Paul describes elsewhere (Rom. 2:29, Phil. 3:3, Col. 2:11) [AB, Alf, BAGD, Ea, ECWB, IB, ICC, Si-ed, St, TD, WBC]. It indicates that the distinctions arising from the physical rite of circumcision are purely human [LJ, WBC], that it belongs to the realm of the flesh, the old eon or old creation [AB, TD], and will have to give place to what is done in the new age by the Spirit [AB, Rob].

EPHESIANS 2:12

2:12 that you-were at-that time[a] without[b] Christ,

LEXICON—a. καιρός (LN 67.78) (BAGD 1. p. 394): 'time' [AB, BAGD, El, LN, Lns, NIC, NTC, Rob, WBC, We; all versions except NAB], 'period of time' [LN]. This may also translated in conjunction with the attached demonstrative ἐκεῖνος 'that': 'then' [BAGD], 'in former times' [NAB]. This is an indefinite unit of time. The actual extent of this time must be determined from the context [LN].

b. χωρίς with genitive object (LN 89.120) (BAGD 2.a.α. p. 890): 'without' [BAGD, El, LN, NIC, Rob; KJV, NRSV, TNT], 'apart from' [AB, BAGD, LN, Lns, WBC, We; TEV], 'separate from' [NTC; NASB, NIV, NJB, REB], 'to be separated from' [BAGD], 'no part in' [NAB], 'far from' [BAGD].

QUESTION—How does this verse relate to the context?

Grammatically, this verse is resumptive of the main clause of 2:11: 'Wherefore remember that formerly you Gentiles in the flesh' [AB, Alf, EBC, EGT, WBC]. The beginning ὅτι 'that' of this verse resumes the ὅτι 'that' of that clause after the interruption of the appositional clause of 2:11b [AB, Alf, Ea, EGT, El, Ho, ICC, My, WBC], and the τῷ καιρῷ ἐκείνῳ 'at that time' resumes the ποτέ 'formerly' of that clause [Alf, Ea, EGT, El, Ho, ICC, My, TH, WBC]. Semantically, this verse gives the content of what the writer wants his readers to remember (signaled by the beginning ὅτι 'that') [Can, NCBC]. This verse is also intentionally contrastive in every point with the description of Christian privilege given in 2:19–20 [ECWB].

QUESTION—What is significant about the imperfect verb ἦτε 'you were'?

The imperfect marks the durative aspect of their former state, and contrasts with the aorist ἐγενήθητε 'you have become' in 2:13. They were existing (past durative) in the most deplorable condition, but all at once this ceased and they entered (aorist) an entirely different position [Lns].

QUESTION—What is the frame of reference in the word ἦτε 'you were' and the phrase τῷ καιρῷ ἐκείνῳ 'at that time'?

1. The ἦτε 'you were' refers only to the Gentiles in Ephesus or Asia Minor and the time reference is to the period after Christ's coming to earth as a human [CBC, Lns, MNTC, My, NCBC, NTC, TD, TH (probably), TNTC (probably)]. The τῷ καιρῷ ἐκείνῳ 'at that time' applies to the pre-Christian lifetime of the readers and so refers to a time that was subsequent to the incarnation. This interpretation may require Χριστός in the phrase χωρὶς Χριστοῦ 'without Christ' to be interpreted of the historical Christ [My].

2. The ἦτε 'you were' refers to these Gentiles as representative of all Gentiles throughout history and, as such, the time reference then also embraces the whole Old Testament period since the covenant with Abraham [AB, Cal, Can, Ea, ECWB, EGT, El, Ho, ICC, LJ, St, WBC, WeBC; NAB (note), NJB (note), TNT]. Those who take this interpretation usually understand the phrase χωρὶς Χριστοῦ as having some reference

to Israel's messianic hope [AB, Cal, Ea, EGT, El, Ho, LJ, WeBC; NAB (note), NJB (note), TNT]: 'without the Messiah' [AB; TNT].
- 2.1 This verse, then, presupposes the pre-existence of Christ with Israel in his Old Testament appearances [AB, Can]. This is not to be weakened down to a statement concerning the hope or mere expectation of a Messiah. Even if only ideally conceived, Paul speaks elsewhere of Christ as really existing (Gal. 3:16, Phil. 2:5–7) and of having some type of fellowship with men before he came in the flesh, of actions Christ took toward Israel in its OT history (1 Cor 10:4) [Can].
- 2.2 This verse presupposes only the Old Testament promise of Christ as Messiah and Savior [Cal, Ea, EBC, ECWB, EGT, El, Ho, LJ, NCBC, St, WBC, WeBC]. Christ was the foundation of all the promises, of Israel's hope, and even of Israel as a society [Cal]. These Gentiles did not even have the expectation of a coming Messiah [St].

QUESTION—How do the propositions of this verse relate to each other?
1. The primary predicate is χωρὶς Χριστοῦ 'without Christ', with the remaining predicates having various relationships to it [ECWB, EGT, El, Ho, ICC, LJ, MNTC, My, TNTC, WBC].
- 1.1 The remaining predicates are explanations of the primary predicate [El, ICC, LJ, My, TNTC]: you were without Christ, meaning that you were excluded from the commonwealth of Israel and strangers to the covenants of the promise, having no hope and godless in the world.
- 1.2 The remaining predicates are consequences of the primary predicate [ECWB, EGT, MNTC]: you were without Christ, with the results that, etc.
- 1.3 The final two predicates ἐλπίδα μὴ ἔχοντες 'having no hope' and ἄθεοι ἐν τῷ κόσμῳ 'godless in the world' are results of the preceding predicates [EBC, WBC (probably)]: you were without Christ, excluded from the commonwealth of Israel and strangers to the covenants of the promise, with the results that (you were) having no hope and (were) godless in the world.
- 1.4 This is a chain of effect-cause relationships: each following predicate is the cause of each immediately preceding predicate, so that the primary predicate is the effect or result of the chain [Ho]: you were without Christ because you were excluded from the commonwealth of Israel and (excluded) because (you were) strangers to the covenants of the promise, (and strangers) because (you) were having no hope, and (hopeless) because you were godless in the world.
2. The first predicate is not χωρὶς Χριστοῦ 'without Christ', but ἀπηλλοτριωμένοι τῆς πολιτείας τοῦ Ἰσραήλ 'excluded from the commonwealth of Israel', with χωρὶς Χριστοῦ 'without Christ' as its condition [Lns, Rob] or cause [Ea], and the remaining predicates listing the effects or results [Ea, Lns, Rob].

QUESTION—What is meant by χωρὶς Χριστοῦ 'without Christ'?
1. Paul is focusing upon the lack of knowledge, or personal relationship, or experience of Christ that these former Gentiles had had [Cal, CBC, Ho, IB, Lns, NTC, St, TH, We, WeBC]: at that time you had experienced no personal relationship to Christ. One commentator recognizes a reference to Israel's messianic hope here but states it means more than that and goes on to comment on the believer's personal relationship to Christ [Ho].
2. Paul is contrasting an implied national hope that Israel had with the destitute state in which these former Gentiles had been [AB, Alf, Ba, Can, Ea, ECWB, EGT, El, ICC, LJ, My, NCBC, NIC, Rob, TNTC, WBC]: at that time you had no relationship at all to Christ (such as Israel had to its Messiah).

QUESTION—In what sense is Paul using the term Χριστός 'Christ' here?
1. He is using it as a proper name [Cal, Can, CBC, Ea, ECWB, EGT, Ho, IB, LJ, Lns, MNTC, My, NIC, NTC, Rob, St, TH, TNTC, We; KJV, NASB, NIV, NRSV, REB, TEV]: without Christ. Paul is speaking of Israel's promised Messiah as having appeared in the historical person of Christ Jesus (3:13) [Ea, My, TNTC] and therefore the sense of a proper name is retained.
2. He is using it with the sense of 'Messiah' [AB, Alf, EBC, El, ICC, NCBC, WBC; TNT]: without the Messiah. The term Χριστός was the official designation of the promised Messiah [Ea]. Two factors favoring this interpretation are: (1) The parallel passage in Rom. 9:4–5 where 'Christ after the flesh' occurs in the list of Jewish advantages, meaning the Jewish Messiah; and (2) the similar context here concerning their former relationship to Israel, the name 'Jesus' is added to 'Christ' in 2:13, perhaps to show that it is the Christian Messiah, not the Jewish one, that is there meant [NCBC]. Some retain the translation 'Christ' even though their notes or exposition makes it clear that 'Messiah' is meant [Alf, El, ICC, WBC; NAB, NJB].

having-been excluded-from[a] the commonwealth[b] of Israel and strangers[c] to the covenants[d] of promise,[e]

LEXICON—a. perf. pass. participle of ἀπαλλοτριόω (ἀπαλλοτριόομαι LN 11.75) (BAGD p. 80): 'to be excluded from' [AB, BAGD; NAB, NASB, NIV, NJB, REB, TNT], 'to be separated from' [WBC], 'to be estranged from' [BAGD], 'to be alienated from' [BAGD, Lns, NTC, We], 'to be aliens from' [El, Rob; KJV, NRSV], 'aliens from' [NIC], 'to be foreigners not belonging to' [LN; TEV]. In Eph. 2:12 the perf. passive participle indicates the state of alienation men are in before their reconciliation to God [AB, DNTT, LJ, Lns, TD]. The passive form does not indicate who produced this state [Lns, TH], it only states it as a fact [TH].
  b. πολιτεία (LN **11.67**) (BAGD 2. p. 686): 'commonwealth' [BAGD, El, Lns, NIC, NTC, Rob, WBC, We; KJV, NASB, NRSV, TNT], 'community' [NAB, REB], 'state' [BAGD, LN], 'people' [**LN**], '(God's)

people' [TEV], 'constitution' [MM], 'citizenship' [AB; NIV], 'membership' [NJB]. It is possible that this is not just a socio-political grouping here, but a socio-religious grouping as well, since with the Jewish constituency, religion and ethnic identification were so inextricably bound together [LN].

c. ξένος (LN 11.73) (BAGD 1.b.α. p. 548): 'stranger' [AB, El, LN, NIC, NTC, Rob, We; KJV, NAB, NASB, NRSV, REB, TNT], 'foreigner' [LN, Lns; NIV, TEV], 'alien' [WBC; NJB], 'strange to' [BAGD]. It carries the connotations of enmity [ISBE2, TD], outlawry, and estrangement [TD]. It means 'estranged from, unacquainted with, without interest in' [BAGD]. It refers to someone who belongs to a different socio-political group [LN]. It refers to someone who is estranged from something, unacquainted with it, having no interest in it [BAGD].

d. διαθήκη (LN 34.44) (BAGD 2. p. 183): 'covenants' [AB, El, Lns, NIC, NTC, Rob, WBC, We; all versions except NAB], 'covenant' [LN; NAB], 'pact' [LN]. Normally in secular literature the word for 'testament' or 'will' [MM], in biblical literature this term specifies the verbal content of an agreement between two parties which lays out the reciprocal benefits and responsibilities accruing from it. This agreement, however, is not an agreement in the sense that it is the result of negotiation and compromise [LN, Lns, NTC, TH]. It is the unilateral declaration of the will of one party [BAGD, Lns, MM, NTC, TH], the one initiating the covenantal relationship [LN], the one who has plenary power which the other party may accept or reject, but cannot alter [MM], therefore it is synonymous with such terms as 'decree', 'declaration of purpose', 'set of regulations' [BAGD], 'disposition', or 'arrangement' [MM]. As applied to God's covenants, sometimes the singular and sometimes the plural is used, as here, since God has made his will known on more than one occasion through reaffirmations and amplifications of the original covenant to succeeding generations [AB, Ba, BAGD, Can, CBC, Ea, ECWB, EGT, El, Ho, IB, ICC, Lns, MNTC, My, NCBC, NIC, NTC, Rob, Si, TH, TNTC, We, WeBC].

e. ἐπαγγελία (LN 33.288) (BAGD 2.a. p. 280): 'promise' [AB, BAGD, El, LN, Lns, NIC, NTC, Rob, WBC, We; all versions except NJB, TEV], 'Promise' [NJB], 'promises' [TEV]. This term focuses upon the content of what is promised [LN].

QUESTION—Does the use of the verb ἀπαλλοτριόομαι 'to be excluded from' imply a previous unity of Jew and Gentile?

1. It implies that there was a previous unity of Jew and Gentile in the hope of redemption prior to the apostasy of the nations and establishment of the Jews as a people [Alf, Ea, ECWB, El, ISBE, ISBE2, LJ, TD]: having become aliens to the commonwealth of Israel. Ἀπαλλοτριωμένοι 'excluded' is translated by those holding this interpretation as 'estranged', 'alienated', or 'being aliens' [Alf, Ea, ECWB, El, LJ]. This union, though not historically demonstrable, is nevertheless spiritually true. Both were

once under one spiritual commonwealth of which the Jewish became a subsequent manifestation. The Gentiles lapsed from it and the Jews made theirs invalid [El]. 'Alienated' implies that the covenant with Israel, since it was held in trust for all families of the earth, was the true birthright of humanity. The first covenant in Scripture (Gen. 9:8–17) was with the post-diluvian race and from this all mankind fell [ECWB].

2. It does not imply any previous unity between Jew and Gentile [AB, Can, IB, ICC, Lns, MNTC, My, NCBC, NIC, TH, WBC]: having been excluded from the commonwealth of Israel. While other passages teach a former unity in mankind (Acts 17:26, Rom. 5, 1 Cor. 15), here Paul is not implying that the Gentiles have fallen out of it [AB], but that they are in a state of estrangement or exclusion [AB, Can, Lns]. Never having belonged to Israel, these Gentiles could not be estranged from it, so Paul uses the participle as meaning nothing more than their ethnic status: 'foreigners' [MNTC, My]. The perfect participle only emphasizes the completeness of the separation [Can]. In Eph. 2:19 the expression ξένοι καὶ πάροικοι 'strangers and sojourners' is the authentic interpretation of ἀπαλλοτριωμένοι 'excluded' [AB].

QUESTION—What is meant by πολιτεία 'commonwealth'?

1. It means 'commonwealth' [Alf, Ba, Cal, Can, CBC, Ea, ECWB, EGT, El, Ho, IB, ICC, IDB, ISBE, ISBE2, LJ, Lns, MNTC, My, NCBC, NIC, NTC, Rob, St, WBC, We, WeBC; KJV, NASB, NRSV, TNT]. But those who use this translation refer to it in either of two senses.

   1.1 This refers to the socioreligious community that constituted the state of Israel [BAGD, Cal, Can, CBC, ECWB, Ho, IB, ISBE2, LJ, LN, Lns, MNTC, NCBC, NIC, NTC, Rob, WeBC; NAB, NJB, REB, TEV]: excluded from (membership in) the (Divinely constituted) community of Israel, or, excluded from God's people, Israel.

   1.2 This refers to the principle upon which the state of Israel was formed, its constitution or form of government [Alf, Ba, Ea, EGT, El, ICC, ISBE, MM, My, We]: excluded from (the benefits of) the Divine law or principle that formed Israel. It means here that arrangement or organization by which the worship of the true God was maintained in the world [Ba], the true Divine government [Ea], the OT constitution under which God made himself known to the Jews and entered into relations with them [EGT].

2. This refers to the rights of citizenship in the state of Israel [AB, DNTT, EBC, Mo, TD, TH, TNTC; NIV]: excluded from citizenship in Israel.

QUESTION—Why does Paul use the name Ἰσραήλ 'Israel' here?

Ἰσραήλ 'Israel' is the theocratic name God bestowed upon his people [EGT, El, Ho] and it is the name used when the relationship of this people to God is in view [ICC].

QUESTION—What is the function of the two occurrences of καί 'and' in this verse?

Each links two predicates having a particular relationship to each other [Lns, My], creating two double predicates [Lns], the 'strangers to the covenants of the promises' being a specification of 'excluded from the commonwealth of Israel' and 'without God in the world' being a specification of 'having no hope' [Lns].

QUESTION—What is meant by ξένοι 'strangers'?

The word has the particular meaning of being one who is not a member of a state or city and therefore foreign to it [EGT, IB, NTC, TD, We] and thus possessing none of the rights and privileges of the member [Ba, IB, NTC, TD]. Some commentators maintain or imply that the Gentiles were strangers to the provisions of the covenants that would ultimately affect them [Rob, St], because the original covenant, and its ratification in the other covenants, included in its scope all the families and nations of the earth [Cal, CBC, ECWB, NIC, NTC, We]. Others, however, maintain that the Gentiles were not included in the covenants [TH, WeBC; NJB] until after the first advent of Christ [TNTC].

QUESTION—How are the two nouns related in the genitive construction τῶν διαθηκῶν τῆς ἐπαγγελίας 'the covenants of promise'?

1. 'Promise' states the kind of covenants they were [AB, BAGD, LJ, NCBC, NTC, Si-ed, TH; KJV, NASB, NRSV, TEV]: strangers to the covenants, the ones based on God's promise. The singular ἐπαγγελίας 'promise', in fact, had manifold specifications [AB]. The second noun indicates that promise is the dominant feature of God's successive affirmations in his covenant with his people [Si-ed].
2. 'Promise' specifies the content of the covenants; they are related to a particular promise [Alf, Ba, Cal, Can, CBC, Ea, ECWB, EGT, El, Ho, IB, ICC, Lns, MNTC, My, NIC, St, TNTC, We; NAB, NIV, NJB, REB, TNT]: strangers to the covenants which contained the promise. The singular number of ἐπαγγελίας 'promise' [EGT, El, St] together with the presence of the definite article [Ho, St, TNTC] point to a single, foundational [St, We], well-known [EGT] promise, the singular promise comprising them all [We].

QUESTION—What are the covenants of which Paul is speaking?

Most agree that the covenants Paul has in mind are those deriving from the covenant God made with Abraham and ratified with the other patriarchs who descended from him, as well as other leaders in Israel's history [AB, Ba, BAGD, Can, Ea, ECWB, EGT, El, Ho, IB, ICC, LJ, Lns, MNTC, My, NIC, Rob, St, TH, TNTC, WBC, We; NJB (note)]. A few believe the Mosaic law is specifically in focus [Cal, CBC, NCBC]. Others include it but do not focus upon it [AB, Ea, ECWB, IB, ICC, MNTC, My, Rob, TH, TNTC; NJB (note)] and some specifically disallow the focus on the Law [Alf, Ea, Lns]. One excludes it altogether as not being based on the promise [EGT]. Some would also include covenants with Adam [NCBC] and Noah [ECWB,

NCBC]. One maintains it is the theological covenant of grace, made in eternity past, and that all the biblical covenants were merely reaffirmations of it [NTC].

QUESTION—What is the content of 'the promise'?
1. It is general [LJ, TH], in respect to God's blessings [IB, NIC], friendship [NTC], and help [NCBC]: strangers to the covenants that promised God's blessings.
2. It concerns the Messiah and his kingdom [AB, Ba, Cal, ECWB, EGT, El, Ho, ICC, MNTC, My, TH, WeBC; NJB (note)] and the salvation and other blessings connected with him [Ba, DNTT, Ho, TD; NJB (note)]: strangers to the covenants that promised salvation through the Messiah.
3. It concerns God's promise to Abraham to make from him a great nation [CBC, WBC (probably)]: strangers to the covenants that promised greatness for God's people Israel. It concerns the promises of God's presence, of descendants, and of the land, all of which were essential to the existence of Israel [WBC].

not having[a] hope[b] and without-God[c] in the world.[d]

LEXICON—a. pres. act. participle of ἔχω (LN 57.1, 90.65) (BAGD I.2.e.β. p. 332): 'to have' [BAGD, El, LN, Lns, NTC, Rob, WBC, We; KJV, NASB, NRSV], 'to experience' [LN]. With the negative particle this is translated 'to be bare of' [AB], 'to be bereft' [NIC], 'to be without' [NAB, NIV, NJB], 'to live without' [TEV, TNT], 'yours was a world without' [REB].

b. ἐλπίς (LN 25.59, 25.62) (BAGD 2.b. p. 253): 'hope' [AB, El, LN (25.59), Lns, NIC, NTC, Rob, WBC, We; all versions], 'basis of/for hope' [BAGD, LN (25.62)], 'reason for hope' [LN (25.62)]. The word denotes the looking forward with confidence to that which is good and beneficial, and involves three important elements: an orientation to the future, a desire, and a benefit to be gained [LN (25.59)].

c. ἄθεος (LN **12.2**) (BAGD 1. p. 20): 'without God' [AB, BAGD, El, Lns, NIC, NTC, Rob, WBC, We; all versions], 'being without God' [**LN**], 'godless' [BAGD]. The term denotes the absence of any relationship to God [LN]. In this context the word carries no censure [BAGD].

d. κόσμος (LN 41.38): 'world' [AB, El, LN, Lns, NIC, NTC, Rob, WBC, We; all versions], 'world system' [LN].

QUESTION—Is ἐλπίδα μὴ ἔχοντες 'not having hope' stated from Paul's Christian perspective, or from the perspective of the unregenerated Gentiles?
1. This is a judgment from the Christian perspective of things [AB (probably), ECWB, LJ (probably), Lns, MNTC, My, NIC, TD, WBC]. It is not true that Gentiles had no hopes for the future, but this is an evaluation of such hopes. They are seen as having no hope because it is only Christ among the Gentiles that can produce true hope. This reminder should cause the readers to appreciate all the more the real hope they now enjoy [WBC].

2. This is a judgment from the perspective of the Gentiles themselves [Alf, El, IB, ICC, My, NCBC]. The negative particle μή 'not' reflects the thoughts and feelings of these Gentiles [Alf, El, ICC, My].

QUESTION—What was the content that their ἐλπίς 'hope' lacked?

They had no hope in the Messiah [AB, Cal]. They had no hope of salvation [BAGD, Can, NTC, St] or hope of an afterlife [Ba, DNTT, ECWB, EGT, Lns, MNTC, NCBC, TD]. Paul does not mean to say they did not cherish *any* hope, because this is hardly true of anyone, but that they had no proper ground of hope [Ba, Lns] such as God's promise had enabled Israel to cherish [Can, NTC]. They had no hope because they were shut out of the covenant of promise [Ho, TNTC]. Having no hope of redemption, they were, in the widest sense of the word, hopeless [Ho].

QUESTION—What is meant by ἄθεοι 'without God'?

1. It means they were ignorant of God [Ba, Can, EBC, ECWB, EGT, Ho, ICC, LJ, Lns, MNTC, NCBC, NIC, NTC, St, TH, TNTC]: you were ignorant of God. The word must be taken in the sense of ignorant of God's true nature [MNTC].
2. It means they denied or neglected God [Cal, TD (probably)]: you had denied God. They were idol worshippers, and idolatry is a denial of the true God [Cal]. They were without Christ, opposed to the Law of God, and thus ἄθεοι 'godless' [TD].
3. It means they were forsaken by God [AB, Alf, El, Ho, My, WBC] and they were without God's help [Ea, Lns, My]: you were people whom God had forsaken. The word is to be understood passively as 'forsaken by God'.

QUESTION—To what is the phrase ἐν τῷ κόσμῳ 'in the world' joined?

1. It is joined to ἄθεοι 'without God' [Alf, Ba, Cal, Can, EGT, El, Ho, IB (probably), Lns, My, NIC, NTC, TD, TNTC; KJV, NAB, NASB, NIV, NRSV]: and godless in the world. Standing in contrast with the preceding πολιτείας τοῦ Ἰσραήλ 'commonwealth of Israel' [Alf, Can, Ea, EGT, El, Ho, ICC, My], the combination thus results in the sense 'without God in this *evil* world' [EGT, El].
2. It is joined to both ἐλπίδα μὴ ἔχοντες 'not having hope' and ἄθεοι 'without God' [AB, ECWB, ICC, MNTC, NCBC, Rob, TH; REB, TEV, TNT]: (being) in the world (you were) without hope and without God. Being limited to the world was the hopeless and godless lot of the Gentiles apart from Christ [Rob].
3. It is independent, a separate epithet in its own right [Ea, LJ; NJB]: (you were) without hope, without God, and in the world. The κόσμος 'world' is the entire region beyond the 'commonwealth' and as such is dark, hostile, and under the dominion of Satan. The phrase refers to the whole description and marks the position of ancient heathendom [Ea].

QUESTION—What is meant by κόσμος 'world'?
1. The word denotes the realm of nature, the physical universe, or, the earth, and so has no moral connotation [Ba, IB, MNTC, NCBC, We]: (you were) without God in this physical realm of nature.
2. The word denotes the world system that is in opposition to the influence of God [AB, Alf, Ea, EGT, El, LJ, My, NTC, Rob, WBC]: (you were left) without God in this evil world system. The presence of the article may indicate that Paul has in mind 'that well-known world' which was considered evil and set in opposition to the world to come.

DISCOURSE UNIT: 2:13–22 [NCBC]. The topic is a reminder of the way in which Christ has corrected their former disadvantages by reconciling them to God.

DISCOURSE UNIT: 2:13–20 [WeBC]. The topic is the present concept and prospect of the Ephesian Gentile's salvation.

DISCOURSE UNIT: 2:13–18 [AB, NIC, Rob, St, TH]. The topic is the present access of Gentiles to God [NIC], a portrait of the peacemaking Christ through what he has done [St], a description of the reconciling work of Christ [TH], and the Gentile, now one man with the Jew [Rob].

2:13 But[a] now[b] in[c] Christ Jesus

LEXICON—a. δέ (LN 89.124): 'but' [AB, El, LN, Lns, NIC, NTC, Rob, WBC, We; all versions], 'on the other hand' [LN].
b. νυνί (LN 67.38) (BAGD 1.c. p. 546): 'now' [AB, BAGD, El, LN, Lns, NIC, NTC, Rob, WBC, We; all versions]. An emphatic form of νῦν 'now' [BAGD], this usage of the term marks a point of time that is simultaneous with the event of the discourse itself [LN].
c. ἐν with dative object (LN 89.119): 'in' [El, LN, NIC, NTC, Rob, WBC, We; KJV, NAB, NASB, NIV, NJB, NRSV], 'in union with' [LN; REB, TEV], 'through union with' [TNT], 'one with, joined closely to' [LN], 'in connection with' [Lns], 'in the realm of' [AB]. This is a marker of close personal association [LN].

QUESTION—What relationship is indicated by δέ 'but'?
It indicates a sharp contrast with ποτέ 'formerly' of 2:11 [AB, IB, LJ, NCBC, NTC] and the τῷ καιρῷ ἐκείνῳ 'at that time' of 2:12 [Alf, Ea, EGT, El, ICC, LJ, Lns, My, NTC, WBC] and the phrase ἐν Χριστῷ Ἰησοῦ 'in Christ Jesus' contrasts with (and reverses [WBC]) the χωρὶς Χριστοῦ 'without Christ' of 2:12 [Alf, Can, Ea, EBC, EGT, El, IB, ICC, LJ, Lns, NCBC, NTC, TD, WBC].

QUESTION—To what does the phrase ἐν Χριστῷ Ἰησοῦ 'in Christ Jesus' relate?
1. This phrase relates to the verb phrase ἐγενήθητε ἐγγύς 'you have been brought near' [Can, Ea, Ho, ICC, My, TH, WBC; TEV, TNT]: But now, in Christ Jesus you have been brought near. Some commentators believe the phrase states adverbially the reason for the declaration expressed in

the verb phrase, i.e., because you are in Christ Jesus you have been brought near [Can, Ea, Ho, My, TH, WBC].
2. This phrase relates to the temporal particle νυνί 'now' [EGT, El, Lns; NJB]: But now in Christ Jesus, you have been brought near. The phrase is forefronted for the sake of emphasis [EGT, El].
3. The phrase goes with an implied verb [AB, Cal]: But now (you are included) in Christ Jesus.

you, the (ones) formerly[a] being far off[b]
LEXICON—a. ποτέ: 'formerly'. See this word at 2:2, 3, 11.
  b. μακράν (LN 83.30) (BAGD 1.a.β. p. 487): 'far off' [AB, El, NIC, Rob, WBC; KJV, NAB, NASB, NRSV, REB, TNT], 'so far off' [NJB], 'afar off' [Lns], 'afar' [We], 'far away' [BAGD, LN, NTC; NIV, TEV], 'far, at a distance, some distance away' [LN]. The word is used figuratively here [BAGD].
QUESTION—What is the force of the pronoun ὑμεῖς 'you'?
  The pronoun is emphatic [Lns, St] and is parallel to the emphatic pronoun ὑμεῖς 'you' in 2:11 [St].
QUESTION—What is the purpose of the participial clause ὑμεῖς οἵ ποτε ὄντες μακράν 'you who were once far off'?
  The clause serves to repeat what was stated in 2:12 about their former condition, especially the ἀπηλλοτριωμένοι 'being alienated' and ξένοι 'strangers' [EGT, ICC, LJ, My], and may anticipate and prepare for the metaphorical reference to the dividing wall in the next verse [IB].
QUESTION—What is the metaphor behind the usage of the word μακράν 'far off' and its antonym ἐγγύς 'near'?
  Most regard the terms as taken from Isaiah 57:19 [AB, EGT, IB, ICC, MNTC, My, NCBC, NIC, Rob, Si-ed, TH, We, WeBC; TNT (note)] (with WBC sharply disagreeing on the basis that Isaiah 57:19 does not speak of those far off coming near, and that this OT text is not in view yet in the present verse), which the author will quote in 2:17. In practice, these spatial terms [St] were used, even in OT times, in a metaphorical sense to designate Jews and Gentiles [AB, Ba, CBC, Ea, EBC, EGT, El, Ho, IB, ICC, Lns, NIC, NTC, St, TH, WBC, WeBC; TNT (note)] in the context of proselytism [WBC]. The analogy may have arisen from the fact that Jerusalem was regarded as the city where the temple as the site of the presence of God was located [Ba, Ea, EBC, Ho, NTC, TH]. Since the Gentiles were from lands outside of Israel, they were said to be far from God [Alf, Ba, Ea, EBC, Ho, NTC, TH, WeBC]. When a Gentile became a Jewish proselyte, he was allowed admittance to the court of Israel [AB, Ho, ICC, My, NTC, TH, TNTC] or to God's holy and spiritual community [El, WBC] and so he was said to 'have come near' [AB, Ho, ICC, My, NTC, TH, TNTC, WBC]. So alternatively, the analogy may have arisen from the plan of the Israelite temple with respect to the relative distances of the court of Israel and the court of the Gentiles from the Holy Place itself, the court of the Gentiles

being located the furthest away [IB, LJ]. The comparison is: as Gentiles were located far from God in the spatial sense, so they are far from him in a spiritual and moral sense also. The point of comparison is relative distance, spatially, which the Jews and Gentiles occupied in relation to the place where God's presence was conceived to be. The nonfigurative statement would be: you who once did not know God have come to know him.

were brought[a] near[b] by[c] the blood[d] of-Christ.

LEXICON—a. aorist pass. indic. of γίνομαι (LN 85.7) (BAGD I.4.c. p. 160): 'to be brought' [AB, NIC, NTC; NAB, NASB, NIV, NJB, NRSV, REB, TEV, TNT], 'to be made' [Rob, We; KJV]. This passive verb is also translated as active voice: 'to get to be' [Lns], 'to come' [BAGD, WBC], 'to become' [El]. The verb is placed in its most emphatic position [ICC].

b. ἐγγύς (LN 83.26) (BAGD 1.d. p. 214): 'near' [AB, BAGD, LN, Lns, NIC, WBC, We; NAB, NASB, NIV, NRSV, REB, TEV, TNT], 'nigh' [El, Rob; KJV], 'nearby' [LN, NTC], 'close' [NJB].

c. ἐν (LN 89.76): 'by' [El, LN, NIC, Rob; KJV, NASB, NJB, NRSV, TEV], 'by means of' [LN], 'through' [AB, LN, NTC, WBC; NAB, NIV, REB, TNT], 'in' [We], 'in connection with' [Lns]. This is a marker of the means [LN, Lns, We, WeBC] or instrumentality [Alf, Ea, EGT, El]. Some interpret this preposition as also marking the atmosphere 'in' which the reconciled soul lives [We]. Similarly, others see a usage wherein the guilty party is metaphysically present or represented 'in' the blood of the one making the atonement (Lev. 16:3, Heb. 9:25, 10:19) [Alf (probably), Can].

d. αἷμα (LN 23.107) (BAGD 2.b. p. 23): 'blood' [AB, BAGD, El, Lns, NIC, NTC, Rob, WBC, We; all versions except REB, TNT], 'death' [LN; TNT], 'violent death' [LN]. This noun is also translated by a gerund phrase: 'the shedding of (Christ's) blood' [REB]. This usage is figurative of blood and life as an expiatory sacrifice, which here brings about a fellowship [BAGD].

QUESTION—What relationship does the phrase ἐν τῷ αἵματι τοῦ Χριστοῦ 'in the blood of Christ' have to the previous phrase ἐν Χριστῷ Ἰησοῦ 'in Christ Jesus'?

Most of those who comment on the relationship interpret the phrase ἐν τῷ αἵματι τοῦ Χριστοῦ 'in the blood of Christ' as a further specification or explanation of the first phrase [Can, El, Ho, LJ, My]; i.e., it tells the special way in which believers are brought near [Can].

QUESTION—What is the significance of the mention of the blood?

The 'blood' stands for the sacrificial death of Christ [AB, Ba, BAGD, Can, DNTT, Ho, IDB, ISBE2, LJ, LN, Lns, NCBC, NIC, TNTC, WBC, We, WeBC; TEV]. This consists of a synecdoche, the blood standing for blood-shedding, or the violent death, and then this death standing for the atonement effected by the sacrificial act [Bu]. So the term does not designate the actual blood corpuscles shed [Bu, TD], nor yet the act of sacrifice so much as the effects or merits of the atonement or expiation that the sacrificial act brought about [Bu, TD]. This expiation for the sins of mankind opened the way for all men, Gentile as well as Jew, to approach God [Ba, Can, DNTT, Ho, LJ, Lns, NCBC, NIC, TNTC, We, WeBC].

DISCOURSE UNIT: 2:14–18 [AB, Ba, ECWB, Lns, My, Si, TH, We]. The topic is the work of the Messiah in making peace [Ba, My, Si, We] between Jew and Gentile [My] and man and God [Ba, We], or the perfect unity [ECWB, Lns, TH] and equality of Jew and Gentile with each other in Christ, and the access both have to the Father [ECWB].

2:14 **For[a] he is the peace[b] of-us,**

LEXICON—a. γάρ (LN 89.23, 91.1): 'for' [AB, El, LN (89.23), Lns, NIC, NTC, Rob, TH, WBC, We; all versions except NAB, TNT], 'because' [LN (89.23)].
- b. εἰρήνη (LN 22.42, 25.248) (BAGD 3. p. 227): 'peace' [AB, BAGD, El, LN (22.42, 25.248), Lns, NIC, NTC, Rob, TH, WBC, We; all versions]. This term designates a set of favorable circumstances involving peace and tranquility [LN (22.42)]. This is to be distinguished from the usage which denotes a psychological state (as opposed to a set of circumstances) involving a state of freedom from anxiety and inner turmoil [LN (25.248)]. This designates the peace which will be an essential characteristic of the messianic kingdom, and regarded in Christian thought as nearly synonymous to messianic salvation [BAGD].

QUESTION—What relationship is indicated by γάρ 'for'?
1. It signals the beginning of a new sentence and may be left untranslated [NAB, TNT]: It is he himself who is our peace.
2. It indicates the reason that the previous event happened [Ea]: you were brought near by the blood of Christ because he himself is our peace.
3. It indicates the ground for the previous statement by introducing a confirmation [El, Ho] and illustration [Ho] or explanation of the previous statement [El, Lns, My, WBC]: for he himself is our peace.

QUESTION—What is the significance of the αὐτός 'he himself' in the sentence?

The pronoun indicates strong emphasis: he himself or he alone [AB, Alf, Can, Ea, EBC, EGT, El, IB, ICC, LJ, Lns, My, NCBC, NTC, Rob, Si-ed, St, TH, We]. The pronoun probably indicates not only 'he alone' but also 'he in his own person' [EGT, Rob, TD].

QUESTION—What is meant by ἡ εἰρήνη 'the peace'?

The presence of the definite article with εἰρήνη 'peace' indicates this is the messianic peace predicted in the OT [AB, EGT, El]. It has reference to the 'Prince of peace' in Isa. 9:6 [Alf, Ba, ECWB, EGT, El, NTC, TNTC], as well as being another word taken from Isa. 57:19 [Alf, EGT, Rob, TD] (and as a consequence the sense of salvation is present in it [TD]) which will be quoted more fully in 2:17. The messianic peace involved more than the notion of cessation of war and hostilities and included the ideas of positive well-being and salvation. But the context of Ephesians 2 requires that the primary meaning here be the cessation of hostilities and the resulting situation of unity [WBC]. This indicates that Christ is peace in the *absolute* sense [EGT, My], the essence of peace [El]. In addition, the presence of the defining articular participle ὁ ποιήσας 'who made' in the following clause indicates that εἰρήνη 'peace' is used in some degree as metonymy, so yielding a meaning similar to εἰρηνοποιός 'peacemaker' (the product, 'peace', being put for 'peacemaker') [El], so that Christ is both the essence and the producer of peace [El, WBC]. Peace does not exist separately from him as though having made peace he could leave and it would still exist as a separate achievement [Alf, EGT, TD]. He is its medium and substance [Alf], his own nature being the actual tie of unity between man and man, and man and God [ECWB]. Being the messianic peace, this peace is more of a social and political kind than it is of the individual soul [AB]. It denotes order, the healing of all relationships [TD]. It is that by which a *union* of worship and feeling has been produced between Jews and Gentiles. Now they worship the same God, have the same Savior, have the same hope, and belong to the same family [Ba].

QUESTION—Who are the parties to whom this peace refers?
1. This refers to peace between Jew and Gentile [Ag, Ba, Can, EGT, IB, ICC, Lns, My, WBC; NJB]: He is the peace between us (inclusive of Jews and Gentiles). The next verse shows that the peace is especially between Jew and Gentile [EGT]. 'Peace' in this verse and the next is between Jew and Gentile, while the 'peace' of 2:17 is between man and God [AB].
2. This refers to peace between man and God [CBC]: He is our peace (with God). 'Peace' in the NT is usually the harmony that Jesus brought between man and God. As a result of this, human divisions are broken down and so he has become 'our peace'.
3. This refers to peace between Jew and Gentile and also between man and God [Alf, Cal, Ea, EBC, ECWB, El, Ho, LJ, NCBC, NIC, NTC, St, TD, TNTC, We, WeBC]: He is the peace between Jew and Gentile as well as between ourselves and God. While 2:15 indicates the peace is between Jew and Gentile, 2:17–18 indicates the reference is to man and God as well [El], so the word is to be taken in its widest, comprehensive sense [El, TD].

the (one) having-made[a] both[b] one[c]

LEXICON—a. aorist act. participle of ποιέω (LN 13.9) (BAGD I.1.b.ι. p. 682): 'to make' [El, LN, Lns, NIC, NTC, Rob, TH, WBC, We; all versions except NASB, NJB, NRSV], 'to make (someone or something) into (something)' [AB, BAGD; NASB, NJB, NRSV], 'to cause to be, to bring about' [LN]. This is one of the aorist tenses in this discourse unit which expresses a unique and completed action [AB, EGT (probably)], having specific reference to Christ's death [EGT].

b. ἀμφότεροι (LN 59.25) (BAGD 1. p. 47): 'both' [AB, BAGD, El, LN, NIC, NTC, Rob, TH, WBC, We; KJV], 'two' [NIV, NJB], 'both parts' [Lns], 'both groups' [NASB, NRSV], 'the two of us' [NAB], 'Jews and Gentiles' [TEV, TNT], 'Gentiles and Jews the two' [REB].
c. ἕν (LN 63.4) (BAGD 1.b. p. 230): 'one' [AB, El, LN, NIC, NTC, Rob, TH, WBC, We; all versions except NJB, TEV, TNT], 'one part' [Lns], 'one entity' [NJB], 'one people' [TEV, TNT]. The word designates that which is united as one in contrast to being divided or in consisting of separate parts [BAGD, LN]. This is also conjoined with ποιέω 'to make' and translated as a verb: 'to unite' (the two divisions) [BAGD].

QUESTION—What relationship is indicated by the use of the participle ποιήσας 'having made'?
1. It stands in apposition to αὐτός 'he', further defining it [EGT, El, Lns, MNTC, NIC (probably), NTC, Rob, St, We; KJV, NAB, NASB, NIV]: He himself is our peace, who made the both one.
2. It indicates the reason Christ is our peace [Ho, NCBC; TNT]: He himself is our peace because he made the both one.
3. It indicates the means by which he became our peace [Alf, Cal, Can, Ea (probably), LJ, My, TNTC; TEV]: He himself became our peace by making the both one. Now begins the more precise information telling us how Christ has himself become our peace [My]. In these verses the apostle tells us how he brought peace into being [LJ].

QUESTION—What is the referent of τὰ ἀμφότερα 'the both'?
This refers to the two peoples being discussed in the context—Jews and Gentiles [AB, Alf, Ba, Cal, Can, Ea, EBC, ECWB, EGT, El, Ho, IB, ICC, Lns, MNTC, My NCBC, NIC, NTC, Si, St, TNTC, We, WeBC; NAB (note), NASB, NJB (note), NRSV, REB, TEV, TNT].

QUESTION—What is the significance here of the neuter gender of τὰ ἀμφότερα 'the both' and ἕν 'one'?
The writer is looking at these diverse peoples, abstractly, as parts, elements, things, or units or parties of a new whole [AB, Alf, Ea, EBC, EGT, El, ICC, My, NCBC, Rob, TNTC]. It looks at them as bodies or categories of people [WBC, We]. By generalizing the idea [El, ICC, NCBC, NTC], it serves to express the idea of the *unity* [EGT, MNTC]. The use of the neuter seems to look at the system [We] or the organization of things [NTC, We] in the Jewish and Gentile worlds. In 2:15 he will use the masculine gender to describe them as a new man [AB]. Jew and Gentile are not changed in race nor amalgamated in blood, but they are 'one' as far as privilege and position before God [Ea]. They have been made one in a unity in which both are no longer what they were previously [WBC]. Divisions and distinctions no longer exist as far as their standing before God is concerned. God has made a way for the divided to become one [TNTC].

and the dividing-wall[a] **of-the fence**[b] **having-broken down**[c]**, the enmity**[d] **in**[e] **his flesh**[f]

LEXICON—a. μεσότοιχον (LN **7.62**) (BAGD p. 508): 'dividing wall' [BAGD, LN], 'intervening wall' [LN (**34.39**), NIC], 'middle wall' [El, Lns, Rob, We; KJV], 'partition wall' [MM], 'wall which separates' [**LN**], 'wall' [TH; TEV, TNT], 'barrier' [LN, NTC; NAB, NASB, NIV, NJB, REB]. It is also translated as a gerund modifying 'wall': 'dividing' [AB, WBC; NRSV (probably)]. This is a wall or fence which separates one area from another [LN].

b. φραγμός (LN **34.39**) (BAGD 2. p. 865): 'fence' [BAGD, Lns], 'dividing wall' [NTC; NASB, NIV], 'wall' [AB, BAGD, WBC; NRSV] 'hedge' [BAGD], 'partition' [El, Rob, We; KJV], 'separation' [TH]. This noun is also translated as a relative clause: 'which used to keep (them) apart' [NJB], 'that kept (us) apart' [NAB], 'which/that separates/separated (them/us)' [LN; REB, TEV, TNT], 'which formed a barrier between (us)' [NIC], 'that which separates, that which isolates' [LN]. This term is used as a figurative extension of its meaning of 'fence' [BAGD, LN], designating that which, in interpersonal relationships, serves to separate [LN]; in this case it designates the law which served to separate Jew and Gentile, arousing enmity between them [BAGD].

c. aorist act. participle of λύω (LN **20.53**) (BAGD 3. p. 483): 'to break down' [AB, El, **LN**, NIC, NTC, Rob, WBC, We; all versions except NIV], 'to break up' [BAGD], 'tear down' [BAGD, TH], 'to break to pieces' [LN], 'to destroy' [BAGD, LN, Lns; NIV]. This is another of the aorists in this discourse unit which designates a unique, completed action, and may imply that there was an historical destruction of the obstacle [AB].

d. ἔχθρα (LN 39.10) (BAGD p. 331): 'enmity' [BAGD, El, LN, Lns, Rob, TH, We; KJV, NASB, REB], 'hostility' [NIC, NTC, WBC; NAB, NIV, NJB], 'hatred' [TNT]. This noun is also translated as a phrase: 'the hostility between us' [NRSV]; as a clause: 'he has wiped out all enmity' [AB], 'that kept (them) enemies' [TEV].

e. ἐν with dative object (LN 90.10): 'in' [AB, El, NIC, NTC, Rob, TH, WBC, We; KJV, NAB, NASB, NIV, NJB, NRSV, REB], 'in connection with' [Lns], 'with' [LN; TEV]. This preposition is also translated by a participial phrase expressing means: 'by giving' [TNT].

f. σάρξ (LN 8.4): 'flesh' [AB, El, Lns, NIC, NTC, Rob, TH, WBC, We; KJV, NAB, NASB, NIV, NRSV], 'body' [LN; TEV, TNT], 'physical body' [LN], 'body of flesh and blood' [REB], 'person' [NJB].

QUESTION—What relationship is indicated by καί 'and'?

It is epexegetical, introducing an explanation of how it is that Jew and Gentile are made one [Alf, Ea, EGT, El, ICC, My]: in that he, etc.

QUESTION—How are the nouns related in the genitive construction τὸ μεσότοιχον τοῦ φραγμοῦ 'the dividing wall of the fence'?
1. The noun in the genitive (φραγμοῦ 'of the fence') is identical with or forms an essential part of the modified noun [AB, Alf, BAGD, BD, DNTT, Ea, EBC, EGT, HG, Ho, ICC, Lns, My, NTC, Rob, TD, Tu, WBC, We; KJV, NASB, NIV]: having torn down the dividing wall which forms or consists of the fence.
2. 'Dividing wall' modifies 'fence' [AB, NIC, TH; NRSV]: having torn down the dividing/intervening fence, or the fence which divides or separates.
3. 'Fence' modifies 'dividing wall' [NAB, NJB, REB, TEV, TNT]: the fenced dividing wall, or the wall which fences off.

QUESTION—What is meant by τὸ μεσότοιχον τοῦ φραγμοῦ 'the dividing wall of the fence'?

Μεσότοιχον means a partition inside a house [AB, DNTT, ISBE2]. Φραγμός originally meant a fence or railing erected for protection [AB, ISBE2] rather than separation [AB]. The combination of the two nouns results in a composite sense: it was a wall erected to prevent certain persons from entering into a house or city, and had a connotation of hostility such as a ghetto wall, or the Berlin Wall has for the people of our time [AB]. Alternatively, the combined terms, if they are not a mere pleonasm, convey the sense of a wall erected for both separation and protection [ISBE2].
1. The phrase designates the ceremonial observances or the system of the Mosaic law [Alf, BAGD, Cal, DNTT, EBC, ECWB, El, IB, Lns, MNTC (probably), TD, WBC, We]: having broken down like a dividing wall the Mosaic system of ceremonial observances that separated Jews and Gentiles. Φραγμός 'fence' is the wider of the two in meaning and itself stands for the whole arrangement of the Mosaic law, while the μεσότοιχον 'dividing wall' was only an instrument, the separation itself consequent upon a system of separation [Alf]. That the Jews were to be separated as God's own people was due to the appointment of God. Ceremonial observances were the means by which this separation was accomplished, and out of this separation arose the enmity between Gentile and Jew [Cal, TD, WBC].
2. The phrase designates the enmity caused by the system of Mosaic Law [CBC, Ea, EGT, Ho, LJ, My, NCBC, NTC, Rob (probably), St, TD, TH, TNTC]: having broken down what was like a dividing wall, the enmity that separated Jews and Gentiles. What Paul is really expressing is that the Mosaic legal system, while originally intended as a system of protection for the Israelites against the corruption of heathen idolatry, became the means of Jewish exclusiveness, and hence enmity, in their relation to the Gentiles [EGT, LJ]. That this enmity, or alienation, itself was the wall is shown by the fact that, in what follows, the removal of this enmity and the abolition of the law are distinguished from each other, the latter being the means of the accomplishment of the former [Ho, My].

3. The phrase designates both the system of Mosaic Law and the enmity that arose from it [TD]. The dividing wall is explained by 'the enmity' and the fence is explained by 'the law of the commandments in decrees' beginning in 2:15 [TD].
4. The phrase designates the moral, religious, and social separation that forbade fellowship with Gentiles [ICC]: having broken down what was like a dividing wall, the separation between Jews and Gentiles. The enmity was not the wall of partition, nor was the law alone, though that was its ultimate cause [ICC].
5. The phrase designates the sphere of astral powers separating the heavenly and earthly worlds [TD], or both this sphere of powers and the Mosaic Law [DNTT].

QUESTION—To what is τὴν ἔχθραν 'the enmity' connected?
1. It is in apposition to μεσότοιχον 'dividing wall' and so is also connected to the participle λύσας 'having broken down' [AB, Alf, Can, CBC, Ea, EBC, EGT, El, Ho, ICC (probably), LJ, My, NCBC, NTC, TD, TH; NAB, NIV, NRSV, REB, TEV, TNT]: having broken down the dividing wall of the fence, that is, the enmity.
2. It is in apposition with τὸν νόμον 'the law' in 2:15 and so is also connected with the participle καταργήσας 'having abolished' [Ba, Cal, IB, Lns, MNTC, NIC, Rob, WBC, We; KJV, NASB, NJB]: having abolished the enmity, the law of the commandments. The reason for breaking down the middle wall of partition is now added—to abolish the enmity [Cal].

QUESTION—Who are the parties at enmity?
1. The enmity here is primarily between Jew and Gentile [AB, Ba, Cal, CBC, DNTT, Ea, EBC, ECWB, EGT, Ho, ICC, LJ, Lns, My, My-ed, NCBC, NIC, NTC, Rob, St, TD, TH, TNTC, WBC, We]. It is the apostle's present design not to speak of the enmity of man toward God, but to show first how Jew and Gentile are reconciled [Ea]. It was the principle of Jewish exclusiveness, mandated by the ceremonial ordinances of the Mosaic law, that lay at the root of the enmity between Jew and Gentile [AB, Ba, Cal, ECWB, EGT, LJ, NCBC, NIC, NTC, Rob, St, TNTC], though others feel rather this enmity has its cause in the general enmity of the human heart toward God [Ea, My-ed].
2. The enmity is primarily between man and God [Alf, Can, TD]. This is due to the law pronouncing a curse upon all transgressors [Can]. The real cause of the separation between man and God was the enmity, and in virtue of that was also the inclusive, mediate cause of the separation between Jew and Gentile. When Christ abolished the first enmity, he abolished the second also [Alf].
3. The enmity is between Jew and Gentile as well as between man and God [DNTT, El, TD]. The fall of man brought a two-fold enmity, between themselves and between men and God. The law revealed both of these enmities [DNTT, TD]. It revealed the enmity of man toward God through

the impossibly high standard for men that God demanded [DNTT] (as well as separating Israel from God [TD]), and it revealed the enmity between Jew and Gentile by creating this enmity through separating the Jew from the Gentile [DNTT, El, TD].

QUESTION—To what is ἐν τῇ σαρκὶ αὐτοῦ 'in his flesh' connected?
1. It goes with the participle ποιήσις 'having made' [NRSV]: In his flesh having made the both one.
2. It goes with the participle λύσας 'having broken down' [Alf, Can, DNTT, EGT, El, TH; REB, TEV, TNT (note)]: having broken down by his flesh the dividing wall of the fence. It subjoins this participle as an equally emphatic specification [El].
3. It goes with the participle καταργήσας 'having abolished' in 2:15 [Ba, Cal, DNTT, Ea, EBC, ECWB, Ho, IB, Lns, MNTC, My, NCBC, NIC, NTC, Rob, St, TNTC, WBC, We; KJV, NAB, NASB, NIV, NJB]: having abolished by his flesh the law of the commandments. It is best to take the phrase with καταργήσας 'having abolished' as the means or manner of the abolition [Ea, My]. Paul does not mean to say Christ destroyed the enmity between Jew and Gentile 'by his flesh' [Ho]; what he means to say is Christ 'by his flesh' freed us from the law [Ho, MNTC, NIC, NTC, St].

QUESTION—What is meant by σάρξ 'flesh'?
1. It refers to Christ's incarnation, his human nature [Cal, DNTT, Rob]. The flesh of Christ is that of our common humanity, so that all humanity finds its meeting point in him [Rob]. By assuming a nature common to all, the Son of God has formed in his own body a perfect unity [Cal].
2. It refers to Christ's earthly ministry [CBC, We]. In Christ's earthly ministry, he made no distinctions between the people he helped, whether Jew or non-Jew [CBC].
3. It refers to Christ's crucified body [AB, Alf, Ba, Can, DNTT, Ea, ECWB, EGT, El, Ho, Lns, MNTC, My, NCBC, NIC, NTC, St, TD, TH, WBC, WeBC]. The formula ἐν τῇ σαρκὶ αὐτοῦ 'in his flesh' is a parallel, and perhaps a synonym of the formulae ἐν τῷ αἵματι 'in his blood', ἐν αὐτῷ 'in him', ἐν ἑνὶ σώματι 'in one body', and ἐν ἑνὶ πνεύματι 'in one Spirit' (2:13, 15, 16, 18), the terms 'flesh', 'body', and 'blood' being used elsewhere in Paul's writings as designations of Christ's sacrifice [AB]. The context of the sentence indicates it is Christ's crucifixion alone which is meant here [El, TH]. By dying for us on the cross, Christ became a curse for us, thus releasing us from the curse of the law and making that law powerless [AB, Can, St].
4. It refers to Christ's incarnation and death [TD].
5. It refers to Christ's incarnation, earthly ministry, and death [IB, TNTC]. It refers not to his death alone, but to his participation in the life of humanity. But his death was the climax of his life among men [IB]. So particular focus is upon his death [TNTC].

2:15 the law^a of-the commandments^b in^c decrees^d having abolished,^e

LEXICON—a. νόμος (LN 33.55): 'law' [AB, BAGD, El, Lns, NIC, NTC, Rob, TH, WBC, We; all versions except NASB, NJB, TEV, TNT], 'Law' [LN; NASB, NJB, TNT], 'Jewish Law' [TEV]. This term designates the Law given in the first five books of the OT, the Torah [LN].
  b. ἐντολή (LN 33.330) (BAGD 2.a.γ. p. 269): 'commandment' [AB, BAGD, El, LN, Lns, NIC, NTC, Rob, TH, WBC, We; all versions except NAB, REB], 'command' [NAB], 'rule' [REB], 'order' [BAGD, LN]. This term specifies single commandments within the OT Law [BAGD].
  c. ἐν with dative object (LN **89.141**) (BAGD IV. 3. p. 261): 'in' [LN, Lns, TH], 'consisting in' [BAGD, NIC (alternative translation)], 'consisting of' [LN], 'expressed in' [AB, El, We], 'contained in' [Rob; KJV, NASB], 'with' [LN, NTC; NAB, NIV, NJB, NRSV, REB, TEV, TNT], 'and' [WBC]. The phrase ἐν δόγμασιν 'in decrees' is also translated as a unit: 'ordinances and all' [NIC]. This is a marker denoting that of which something consists [LN]. One of the grammars calls this a marker of attendant circumstances or instrumental [Tu]. Some grammars describe it as a relatively rare predicative [HG, Mou], descriptive usage [Mo]: 'consisting in' [HG, Mo, Mou, Tu], 'containing' [Mo].
  d. δόγμα (LN 33.332) (BAGD 1. p. 201): 'decree' [BAGD, El, LN, Lns; NJB, TNT], 'ordinance' [BAGD, NIC, Rob, We; KJV, NASB, NRSV], 'order' [LN], 'regulation' [WBC; NIV, REB], 'statute' [AB], 'precept' [NAB], 'rule' [TH; TEV], 'requirement' [NTC]. This term specifies an official order or decree [LN]. In the NT this word always means a decree or edict [ISBE]. Joining this term to the two previous lexical items, BAGD translates the whole phrase: the law of commandments consisting in (single) ordinances.
  e. aorist act. participle of καταργέω (LN **76.26**) (BAGD 1.b p. 417): 'to abolish' [AB, El, **LN**, Lns, NIC, NTC, Rob, TH, WBC, We; all versions except NJB, REB], 'to make invalid, to make ineffective' [BAGD], 'to invalidate' [LN], 'to annul' [REB], 'to destroy' [NJB].

QUESTION—What relationship is indicated by the use of the participle καταργήσας 'having abolished'?
  1. It indicates the means of breaking down the dividing wall of the fence [EGT, NTC; NAB (note), NASB, NIV] or τὴν ἔχθραν 'the enmity' [Ea, IB, LJ, NCBC, WBC]: he broke down the dividing wall of the fence by abolishing the law of the commandments in decrees.
  2. It indicates the means of the preceding participial clauses [Lns; NJB]: having made the two into one and having broken down the dividing wall of the fence, the enmity, by abolishing the law.
  3. It indicates an explanation of the preceding verse [My; REB]: he is our peace, for he has abolished the law.
  4. It indicates a second result of giving up his body [TNT]: by giving his own body he has abolished the law of commandments in decrees. The first result was the breaking down of the wall.

QUESTION—What is the meaning of τὸν νόμον τῶν ἐντολῶν ἐν δόγμασιν 'the law of the commandments in decrees'?

All commentators agree that the reference is to the Jewish law as contained in the Torah, the first five books of the OT as given by Moses, though one [Ho] would extend it to include the whole law of God, even that written on heathen hearts. Two commentators say the phrase is an accumulation of synonyms used to graphically describe how all these regulations were swept away by Christ [DNTT, TD]. Another admits this possibility [NCBC]. But generally, the commentators see the phrase as a description of the nature of the law. The Decalogue itself may be specified by τῶν ἐντολῶν 'the commandments' [Alf (probably), TH], or it may specify the whole range of commandments in the law [TH, WBC]. As to its nature, it was a law that consisted in commandments dogmatically [Alf, TD] and dictatorially [My] expressed. The term νόμος 'law' indicates that it was a code sanctioned by supreme legislative authority. The genitive τῶν ἐντολῶν 'of the commandments' indicates the contents of this code [EGT, El, Ho, ICC, Lns, MNTC, My], it being comprised of a prodigious number of individual, minute, varied, formal regulations [DNTT, Ea, EGT]. And the phrase ἐν δόγμασιν 'in decrees' defines the nature of these decrees: as issued under Divine sanction, revealing the immediate will of God [Ea]. It shows the form in which the ἐντολῶν 'commandments' expressed themselves, and operated in the manner of individual, mandatory decrees or ordinances [DNTT, EGT, El, Ho, ICC, Lns, My].

QUESTION—What is meant by καταργέω 'to abolish'?

It means 'to supersede' [Ea], 'to supersede by something better than itself' [ECWB], 'to make void' [Ea], 'to make (completely [TD]) inoperative' [EGT, ISBE, TD], 'to put out of commission' [Lns], 'to put out of use' [TD], 'to make ineffective' [EBC, ISBE, Lns], 'to make powerless' [EBC], 'to invalidate' [EBC], 'to cause to cease' [Ho]. Christ accomplished this by satisfying the demands of the law so that we are judicially free from it [Ho, IDB] and/or by fulfilling the types and shadows of the ceremonial law so that it found its culmination in him [LJ, NTC, St, TNTC].

QUESTION—What part or aspect of this code of law is abolished?

1. The whole of the Mosaic code of law is abolished, both the moral and the ceremonial [Alf, Can, DNTT, EBC, EGT, El, Ho, ICC, IDB, Lns, My, NCBC, TD, TH, WBC, WeBC]. Νόμος 'law' is to be understood in its full sense—the Mosaic Law as a whole [Alf, Can, EBC, EGT, Ho], though this does not prevent a focus here upon the mandatory or ceremonial part [Can, Ho, NCBC].

2. Only the ceremonial aspect of the Mosaic Law is totally abolished [Ba, Cal, Ea, ISBE, LJ, NTC, Rob, St, TNTC]. The word δόγμα 'decree' is Paul's ordinary word for describing the ceremonial law [Cal], in fact the whole phrase τὸν νόμον τῶν ἐντολῶν ἐν δόγμασιν 'the law of the commandments in decrees' is a graphic description of the ceremonial law [Ea]. The laws which were the occasion for the peculiarity of the Jewish

system, and hence the enmity, were not the moral laws, but the ceremonial ones. These were the ones which Christ's death abolished [Ba, Cal, Ea, LJ, NTC, Rob, St], not the moral ones, which are still binding in some respects [Ba, Cal, Ea, LJ, NTC, St]. The moral law has its origin and basis in the Divine nature, and therefore it is unchanging and unchangeable, and binding upon all [Ea].
3. What is abolished is the manner in which the law is to be observed [ECWB, NIC, We] and its validity as a means of condemnation and death for men [NIC]. The law was a system of injunctions to be obeyed to the letter as ordinances [ECWB, NIC, We]. It was this aspect which was abrogated [ECWB, NIC]. It is valid now only as to its spirit [ECWB]. This interpretation is also consistent with interpretation 2, as some there also make this point [Rob, TNTC].
4. Only specific functions of the Mosaic Law are abolished [AB, DNTT]. The distinction between moral law and ceremonial law is not scriptural and is unjustified. Rather, only certain functions of the law were abolished. Primarily, in this context, the abolished function is the one that makes a separation between men on the basis of covenantal distinctions between Jew and non-Jew and, as well, the one that condemns man by inflicting a curse and death upon him [AB]. With the death of Christ, the law with all its commandments and ordinances ceased to be a factor in salvation [DNTT].

in-order-that[a] the two[b] he-might-create[c] in himself into[d] one[e] new[f] man[g]

LEXICON—a. ἵνα (LN 89.59): 'in order that' [Lns, NTC, WBC], 'that' [El, Rob, We; NASB, NRSV, TNT], 'in order to, for the purpose of, so that' [LN]. Most translations combine some kind of purpose expression plus the infinitive of the English verb 'to create' or 'to make' (except AB, which combines the purpose expression 'this was' with the English infinitive 'to make peace'): 'in order to create' [NIC, TH; TEV], 'so as to create' [REB], 'for to make' [KJV], 'his purpose was to create' [NIV, NJB]. Another simply uses the infinitive to express purpose: 'to create' [NAB]. This particle is a marker of purpose for events and states [LN].

b. δύο (LN 60.11): 'two' [AB, El, LN, Lns, NIC, NTC, TH, WBC; all versions except KJV, NAB, NJB, TEV, TNT], 'twain' [Rob, We; KJV], 'the two races' [TEV], 'the two of them' [NJB]. One transforms this into a clause: '(from) us who had been two' [NAB]. Another specifies the referent: 'Jews and Gentiles' [TNT].

c. aorist subj. act. of κτίζω (LN 42.35) (BAGD p. 455): 'to create' [AB, BAGD, LN, Lns, NIC, NTC, Rob, TH, WBC, We; all versions except KJV, NASB], 'to make' [BAGD, El; KJV, NASB].

d. εἰς with accusative object (LN 13.62): 'into' [El, Lns, TH, WBC, We; NASB], 'to' [LN]. Since this use of the preposition denotes a change from one state of existence to another [LN], most translations represent this change by translating ἕνα καινὸν ἄνθρωπον 'one new man' as the direct object of the verb κτίζω 'to create' and attaching an English preposition indicating *source* to τοὺς δύο 'the two', according to this pattern: 'to create out of the two one new man' [AB; NIV, NJB, REB, TEV, TNT], 'to create of the two one new man' [NIC, NTC, Rob; KJV], 'to create from the two one new man' [NAB], 'to create in place of the two one new man' [NRSV].

e. εἷς (LN 60.10) (BAGD 1.b. p. 230): 'one' [BAGD, El, LN, Lns, NIC, NTC, Rob, TH, WBC, We; all versions except NJB, REB], 'single' [AB; NJB, REB]. This represents a single entity in contrast to the parts which make up a whole [BAGD].

f. καινός (LN 58.71) (BAGD 3.b. p. 394): 'new' [AB, BAGD, El, LN, Lns, NIC, NTC, Rob, TH, WBC, We; all versions]. This term denotes that which is new or recent and therefore is usually superior to that which is old [BAGD, DNTT, LN], implying obsolescence in that which it replaces [BAGD]. It denotes that which is new in its own way [DNTT], new in kind [TD].

g. ἄνθρωπος (LN 9.1): 'man' [AB, El, Lns, NTC, Rob, TH, We; KJV, NAB, NASB, NIV], 'Man' [NJB], 'humanity' [NRSV, REB], 'person' [LN, WBC], 'people' [TEV, TNT], 'human being' [LN, NIC], 'individual' [LN].

QUESTION—What relationship is indicated by ἵνα 'in order that'?

῞Ινα 'in order that' introduces the goal or purpose of the abolishing of the law [AB, Alf, Can, Ea, EBC, EGT, El, Ho, Lns, My, NCBC, TD, TH, We; NJB].

1. This purpose is seen in the following two clauses governed by the verbs in the subjunctive mode [Alf, Can, Ea, EBC, EGT, El, Ho, IB, ICC (probably), Lns, My, NCBC, NTC, Rob, TH, TNTC, WBC, We; NJB]: that (1) he might create the two into one new man and (2) he might reconcile the both to God (2:16). For comments of some of these commentators about the epexegetical nature of the second clause, see the relevant section in 2:16.

2. This purpose is seen in the participial clause at the end of 2:15, 'making peace' [AB]: to make peace by creating out of the two one new man.

QUESTION—What is the referent of τοὺς δύο 'the two'?

This is the same as τὰ ἀμφότερα 'the both' in 2:14, the Jewish and Gentile portions of the human race [AB, Alf, Ba, Cal, Can, CBC, Ea, EBC, ECWB, EGT, El, Ho, ICC, LJ, Lns, MNTC, My, My-ed, NCBC, NIC, NTC, St, TD, TH, TNTC, WBC, We; NAB (note), NJB (note), TNT]. Through the use of the masculine gender (as opposed to the neuter gender in 2:14) the discussion here deals with two men, one representing the totality of the Jews and the other the totality of the Gentiles, whom Christ has made into a single new man, the totality of Christians [ICC, Lns, My]. The contrast with τὰ ἀμφότερα 'the both' in 2:14 is instructive. He calls them τοὺς δύο 'the two' to mark their separateness. It is a transition from the systems (expressed in 2:14 by the neuter ἀμφότερα 'both') to the men that live under them.

Expressing the two groups as two individuals shows their corporate unity, as does the passing over of the two individuals into one [We].

QUESTION—What is meant by the phrase ἐν αὐτῷ 'in himself'?

Most see this as indicating union with Christ himself [Cal, Can, CBC, Ea, ECWB, EGT, Ho, LJ, Lns, My, My-ed, NIC, WBC]. Some say it indicates an act of creation that Christ performed within himself [MNTC, WBC]. Christ himself serves as the focus of the new unity [Cal, Can] so that Jew and Gentile meet in a common humanity [CBC, ECWB, NTC]. But 'in himself' is more than an ideal. Jew and Gentile were actually created as one new man; they became a unit by being one with Christ, namely with his blood and his cross [Lns]. The Church is formed in Christ. This happens as a result of her relationship to him. He is her head and she forms his body [LJ]. The unity that was to be brought about in this new creation was to be founded in Christ himself, that is, it is to have its basis of existence [EGT, ICC, My, St] and continuance in him [My, St] as opposed to any other unifying principle. This new unity has its causal and objective basis, as a fact before God, in the death of Christ, because it abolished the law; but as regards the subjects, it is effected subjectively by and in their appropriation of the Spirit [My]. Some see this also as including cause or means: he created one new man by virtue of his death [Ba, Ho], while others discount any idea of means or agency, saying it means 'in himself', 'in his person', not 'through' or 'by himself' [Alf, EGT, El, ICC, My].

QUESTION—Who and what is meant by ἕνα καινὸν ἄνθρωπον 'one new man'?

1. This refers collectively to the Church [AB, Alf, Ba, BAGD, Cal, Can, CBC, Ea, EBC, ECWB, EGT, IB, IDB, ISBE2, LJ, Lns, MNTC, My, My-ed, NIC, Rob, St, TD, TH, TNTC, WBC, We, WeBC] This is the new kind of humanity that Christ created in union with himself, its individual members organically united to one another in a corporate personality with himself as its head [AB, IB, ISBE2, LJ, My-ed, NIC, St, WBC]. The 'new man' here is a different usage from where Paul speaks of the individual Christian's new man in contrast to his previous unregenerated old man [LJ]. Christians are one only because in their *totality* are they the new man, i.e., the new man is not perfectly realized in any single one of them, so that without unity each is only a fragment. Only the entire church can mirror Christ's kingdom [My-ed]. Many call it a third order or race of man [EGT, TH, WBC, WeBC], or a new humanity [CBC, EBC, IB, ISBE2, MNTC, NIC, NTC, St, TH, TNTC; NJB (note), NRSV, REB] but one commentator objects to such terms on the basis that they imply the loss of the different distinctives of the groups comprising the 'new man' [AB].

2. This refers to believers as regenerated men, each individual neither Jew nor Greek, but a new creation [DNTT, EBC, ICC, ISBE, NCBC]. Other Pauline allusions to the 'new man' show that the concept is individualistic. In addition to Jew and Gentile, a third type of person has

now appeared—the Christian [EBC]. It refers to the regenerated believer in the sense that his moral nature has been renovated and built over again [ISBE].
3. This refers to the person of Christ himself as the prototype of the new humanity—the New Adam or, the New Man [TD; NJB (note)]. This New Man is the prototype of the new humanity that God re-created in Christ. He is unique because in him all boundaries between individual groups and the rest of the human race disappear [NJB (note)].

QUESTION—What is implied in the use of the word καινός 'new'?
1. It implies a new order of mankind where all distinctions between Jew and Gentile are done away with in respect to their standing before God [EGT, Ho, LJ, St, TNTC, WBC, WeBC].
2. It implies a new order of mankind as far as unity is concerned, but this does not imply that racial or other distinctions are lost in it [AB, IB, St, TD]. The 'one new man' is not just an amalgamation of the comprising groups. It is a completely new creation [AB, WBC (in support of 1. above)]. But each group is free to contribute its own idiosyncrasies, history, experiences and gifts to the common peace [AB, IB].

making[a] peace[b]

LEXICON—a. pres. act. participle of ποιέω (LN 42.29) (BAGD I.1.b.γ. p. 681): 'to make' [AB, BAGD, El, LN, Lns, NIC, NTC, Rob, TH, WBC, We; KJV, NAB, NIV, NRSV, REB, TEV], 'to establish' [BAGD; NASB], 'to bring' [TNT], 'to bring about' [BAGD], 'to restore' [NJB]. This word denotes the production of something new, implying the use of materials already in existence, as contrasted to κτίζω 'to create' (42.35) [LN].
b. εἰρήνη (LN 22.42) (BAGD 1.b. p. 227): 'peace' [AB, BAGD, El, LN, Lns, NIC, NTC, Rob, TH, WBC, We; all versions], 'harmony' [BAGD].

QUESTION—What relationship is indicated by the use of the participial phrase ποιῶν εἰρήνην 'making peace'?
1. It indicates the result of creating one new man [AB, Can, ECWB, EGT, El, Ho, IB, ICC, LJ, My, NCBC, NIC, NTC, Rob, TH, WBC, We; KJV, NASB, NIV, NRSV, TNT]: he created one new man, thus making peace.
2. It indicates a second purpose for abolishing the law [NAB]: he abolished the law in order to create one new man and to make peace.
3. It indicates the means by which the new creation took place [NJB]: by making peace he created a single new man.

QUESTION—What is the function of the present tense of the participle ποιῶν 'making'?
1. It denotes continuous [AB, Ho, ICC] or repeated (iterative) action [Lns]: that he might create of the two one new man in himself, making a continuous peace, or, constantly making peace. The present participle is used because the effect or operation is a continuous one [AB, Ho]. Christ's great peacemaking goes on constantly as he brings more Gentiles

and Jews into the one sacred body, welding them into one by faith in his atoning blood [Lns].
2. It denotes simultaneous action with the subjunctive verb κτίσῃ 'he might create' [Ea, EGT, El, My]: that he might create of the two in himself one new man, in the process making peace. A present participle is used because the making of peace was that which was to be brought about *in and with* the new creation [My]. The action of the participle covers the entire process, abolition of enmity, abrogation of law, and creation of the new person [Ea, El].

QUESTION—Who are the parties between whom peace is made?
1. This peace is primarily made between Jews and Gentiles [AB, Ba, Cal, Ea, ECWB, EGT, Ho, IB, ICC, ISBE, LJ, My, NCBC, TH, TNTC, WBC]. The words explain αὐτὸς γάρ ἐστιν ἡ εἰρήνη 'for he is our peace' in 2:14 [ICC, Lns]. Making peace is a synonym for reconciling, which notion follows immediately, but the peace at this point is between the two old enemies, Jew and Gentile, not with God [WBC].
2. This peace is primarily made between man and God [Alf].
3. The focus is both on peace between Jews and Gentiles and peace between man and God [El, TD, WeBC].

2:16 and he-might-reconcile[a] the both in[b] one body[c] to-God through[d] the cross,[e]

LEXICON—a. aorist subj. act. of ἀποκαταλλάσσω (LN 40.1) (BAGD p. 92): 'to reconcile' [AB, BAGD, LN, Lns, NIC, NTC, Rob, TH, WBC, We; all versions except TEV, TNT], 'to reconcile again' [El], 'to make things right with one another' [LN], 'to bring back' [TEV, TNT]. This term denotes the re-establishment of proper, friendly, interpersonal relations after the disruption of the same. [LN]. The use of the aorist tense on this verb indicates this action of reconciliation was completed once and forever on the cross [LJ]. Since the word applies to the one addressed, it is a completed fact.
b. ἐν with dative object (LN 89.119): 'in' [AB, El, LN, Lns, NIC, NTC, Rob, TH, WBC, We; all versions except TEV, TNT], 'in union with' [LN], 'as' [TNT]. This is also translated as a verb phrase: 'to unite into' [TEV]. This is a marker of close personal relationship [LN].
c. σῶμα (LN 8.1, 11.34) (BAGD 5. p. 800): 'body' [AB, BAGD, El, LN (8.1), Lns, NIC, NTC, Rob, TH, WBC, We; KJV, NAB, NASB, NRSV, REB, TEV], 'Body' [NJB], 'this body' [NIV], 'people' [TNT], 'congregation, Christian group, church' [LN].
d. διά with genitive object (LN **89.76**) (BAGD A.III.1.a. p. 180): 'through' [AB, BAGD, **LN**, NIC, NTC, TH, WBC, We; NAB, NASB, NIV, NJB, NRSV, REB], 'by means of' [BAGD, LN, Lns; TEV], 'by' [El, LN, Rob; KJV], 'with' [BAGD]. This is also translated as a purpose clause in conjunction with σταυρός 'cross' and ἀποκτείνας τὴν ἔχθραν 'to kill the enmity': 'He died on the cross to put an end to the hatred' [TNT]. This

is a marker denoting the means [BAGD LJ, LN, TH] or instrument [BAGD, NIC] by which one event makes another event possible [LN].
   e. σταυρός (LN 6.27) (BAGD 3. p. 765): 'cross' [AB, BAGD, El, LN, Lns, NIC, NTC, Rob, TH, WBC, We; all versions except TNT]. This is also translated as a clause: 'he died on the cross' [TNT].
QUESTION—What relationship is indicated by καί 'and'?
   1. It is copulative [TH] and epexegetical, indicating a further explanation of the purpose for which the law was abolished [Alf, Ba, Can, Ea, EBC, EGT, El, Ho, LJ, Lns, MNTC, Rob, WBC]: in order that he might create one new man, namely that he might reconcile both to God. It joins this verse to the ἵνα 'in order that' clause of 2:15 as a second [El, Ho], or parallel [Alf, Can, El, TH] purpose, continuing and extending the statement of the purpose of the abolishing of the law [Ba, EGT, LJ, Lns, Rob], and resulting in a statement in regressive order of the Divine procedure [El]. Because this verse contains the primary [Alf, Ba, El], or larger [EGT] purpose for the abolishing of the law, reconciliation with God, the καί 'and' is epexegetic and has the force of 'namely' [Alf]. Another commentator sees it as introducing a separate purpose for abolishing the law [Ea].
   2. It indicates logical sequence [ICC, My, NCBC]: in order that he might create one new man and consequently might reconcile both to God. It continues the sentence, expressing the purpose of the doing away with the law and denotes sequence of thought.
QUESTION—What is the significance of the prefixed preposition ἀπο 'again' in ἀποκαταλλάξῃ 'he might reconcile'?
   1. The prefixed preposition ἀπο 'again' adds the idea of a restoration [Alf, EBC, ECWB, EGT, El, LJ, LN, Lns, Rob, TH; TEV, TNT]: (that) he might again reconcile. The word implies a return to a former, primeval state of the unity of all created beings in Christ [EBC, ECWB, El], a theme found elsewhere in this epistle and also in Colossians [ECWB], as in Eph. 1:10 [EBC]. The fact that the larger reconciliation of man to God comes into focus in this clause is an argument in favor of a restoration of a condition which had been lost [EGT].
   2. The prefixed preposition ἀπο 'again' is only a mild intensification device [AB, Ea, ICC, ISBE2, My, Si-ed]: (that) he might reconcile. The preposition strengthens the notion of reconciliation. This fits the context better than interpreting the prefixed preposition as 'again' [My].
QUESTION—In what direction is the movement of the action of the verb ἀποκαταλλάξῃ '(that) he might reconcile'?
   'To reconcile' is the effecting of peace and union between two parties previously at variance. But neither the Greek nor English terms themselves indicate whether the change made is mutual or one-sided only. Whether the reconciliation made by Christ between God and man results from an inward change on men's part, or from the propitiation of God, or whether both ideas

are included, can only be decided by the context and the analogy of scripture [Ho].
1. It is directed to man [AB, Alf (probably), DNTT, Ds2, IDB, ISBE2, Lns, NIC, TD, TH]: Christ reconciles man to God, i.e., he destroyed man's enmity towards God. Human hostility to God has to be overcome [NIC]. God does not need reconciling to men [ISBE2, Lns, TH], because he is not estranged [ISBE2, TH]; it is not his attitude that needs to be changed [IDB, ISBE2]. Man is made the object of reconciliation because it is his reaction which is now needed [DNTT].
2. It is directed to God [Cal, Ea, Ho]: Christ reconciled God to man, i.e., he destroyed God's enmity toward man. By means of the cross, Christ restored man to favor with God [Cal, Ea]. What is stated in one place, by saying Christ reconciled us to God, is stated in another as Christ propitiating God [Ho]. The attachment of the phrase διὰ τοῦ σταυροῦ 'by the cross' to this clause shows it is the propitiation of God of which the apostle speaks, not of man's hatred for God [Ea].
3. It is bi-directional, the reconciliation being mutual [Can, EGT, ISBE, LJ, St, TD, WBC (probably)]: Christ reconciled God to man and man to God. Ἀποκαταλλάσσω 'to reconcile' and its word-group convey the idea of a change, not primarily of feeling, but of relations, and these are mutual, on the side of God to man and on the side of man to God [EGT, ISBE]. It is clear that there were barriers on both sides [Can]. On the side of God, it is that his 'wrath' has been upon us for our sin, and on man's side, it is our attitude of sin and rebellion towards him [Can, ISBE, St]. Before reconciliation is possible, something has to happen on God's side as well as on our side [LJ]. On God's side, when Christ bore our sin and judgment on the cross, God turned his wrath away from us [ISBE, St]; this has been accomplished [ISBE]. On our side, when we see his great love for us, we turn to him from our sin and rebellion [ISBE, St], and this is the great concern now [ISBE].

QUESTION—What is meant by ἐν ἑνὶ σώματι 'in one body'?
1. It refers to the Church as the 'one new man' just mentioned in 2:15 [Alf, Ba, Cal, Ea, EBC, ECWB, EGT, El, Ho, IB, ICC, LJ, Lns, MNTC, My, NCBC, NTC, Rob, TH, TNTC, WBC; NIV, TEV, TNT]: that he might reconcile both to God, united together in the church through the cross. The occurrence of ἑνί 'one' finds a better explanation in the idea of the unity of Jews and Gentiles in a single humanity than it does as a tautology in reference to Christ's humanity [Ea, Ho, ICC, My], (i.e., how Christ could have had a plurality of bodies is inconceivable even in the abstract! [My]).
2. It refers to Christ's human body as crucified [AB, TD]: that he might reconcile both to God in his own body through the cross. Ἓν σῶμα 'one body' is undoubtedly Christ's body on the cross. It was by undergoing death in this body that Christ slew the enmity and thereby established all men anew, both Jews and Gentiles, as the humanity which is reconciled to

God and which is united to God by him and in him [TD]. The pronominal phrase ἐν αὐτῷ 'in him' in the next clause takes ἐν ἑνὶ σώματι 'in one body' as its antecedent.

3. It refers both to Christ's human body and to the church [Can, CBC; NJB (note)]: that he might reconcile both to God (united together through his crucified body) in the church through the cross. Probably the reference is to both bodies. Those who are reconciled to God must be in vital union with the Savior, who still possesses a human body, now glorified and exalted, and as thus, in his body, they constitute the one spiritual body of which he is the head [Can]. Another agrees with this statement, saying that the two senses of σῶμα 'body' cannot be separated, but choosing to put the accent on Christ's crucified body [TD].

QUESTION—What is meant by σταυρός 'cross'?

It is a reference by metonymy to Christ's death on the cross [AB, ECWB, Ho, ICC, LJ, Lns, NTC, TH, TNTC, WBC], the object being put for what was accomplished upon it. It has the connotations of sacrifice [Cal, LJ, LN (89.76), Lns, WBC, We], a shameful death [AB] and that the person so executed is under God's curse [AB, Lns]. It is the blood-shedding, the life poured out [LJ, Lns]. It suggests God's love to mankind [CBC].

killing[a] the enmity[b] by[c] himself/it.

LEXICON—a. aorist act. participle of ἀποκτείνω (LN **13.44**) (BAGD 2. p. 94): 'to kill' [AB, TH; NJB, REB], 'to slay' [El, Lns, NTC, Rob, We; KJV], 'to put to death' [BAGD, NIC, WBC; NAB, NASB, NIV, NRSV], 'to destroy' [TEV], 'to put an end to' [TNT], 'to do away with, to eliminate' [LN]. This is a figurative extension of the meaning 'to kill'. The word relates to causing the complete cessation of a state [LN].

b. ἔχθρα: 'enmity'. See this word at 2:14.

c. ἐν with dative object (LN 89.76): 'by' [LN; NASB, NIV, REB, TEV], 'by means of' [LN, NTC], 'through' [LN; NRSV], 'in' [AB, Lns, TH, WBC; NJB], not explicit [NAB, TNT]. This is also translated in conjunction with αὐτός 'it': 'thereby' [El, Rob, We; KJV], 'by its means' [NIC]. This is the marker of the means by which one event is made possible by another event [LN].

QUESTION—Why is the verb ἀποκτείνω 'to kill' used here?

The word was probably suggested by the occurrence of σταυρός 'cross' in the last clause [El, My]. It forms a subtle rhetorical device to ascribe to Christ the activity of 'killing', when actually he was the one killed on the cross in order to make life possible [AB, Can, IDB, LJ, LN, NTC, Rob, St, TNTC]. This device involves the use of the verb as a metaphor. The comparison is: just as the sentence of death on the cross resulted in the permanent termination of mortal life in Christ's earthly body, so Christ terminated, just as permanently, the enmity between Jew and Gentile and/or man and God (see interpretation problem below). The point of comparison is the termination of something. The nonfigurative statement would be: Christ terminated the enmity that existed between Jew and Gentile and/or between man and God.

QUESTION—What is the enmity that is killed?
1. It is the enmity between Jews and Gentiles [AB, Cal, CBC, DNTT, Ea, EBC, EGT, El, IB, ICC, ISBE, ISBE2, Lns, My, NCBC, NIC, NTC, Rob, Si, TD, TNTC, WBC; NAB, NRSV, TEV, TNT]: that he might reconcile both to God through the cross, thereby killing the enmity between Jew and Gentile. This enmity is the same as that in 2:14 [Lns, My]. The hostility between people of different races is ended because Christ has reconciled both to God [NCBC, NIC].
2. It is the enmity between man and God [Alf, ECWB, Ho, LJ, St]: that he might reconcile both Jew and Gentile to God through the cross, thereby killing the enmity between man and God. While this is enmity on God's part, it is not hatred, for God is love, but the calm, holy purpose to punish men for their sins. The parallel passage, Col. 1:20–22 indicates clearly that the enmity between God and man is in view [Ho].
3. It is both the enmity between man and God and between Jew and Gentile [Ba, Can, IDB, MNTC, TD]: that he might reconcile both to God through the cross, thereby killing all enmity of whatever sort.

QUESTION—What is the referent of ἐν αὐτῷ 'in himself/it'?
1. It refers to Christ's person and should be translated reflexively [AB, Lns, WBC; NJB]: in his person, or, in himself. Ἐν αὐτῷ 'in himself' is so much like the other phrases 'in him', 'in Christ', previously used in this context that it should not be translated instrumentally in reference to the cross [Lns, WBC]. The phrase is emphatic, 'in union with his own person', and it echoes the αὐτός 'he himself' at the beginning of 2:14 [Lns].
2. It refers to the cross [Alf, Ba, Cal, Can, Ea, EBC, EGT, El, Ho, IB, ICC, LJ, MNTC, My, NIC, NTC, Rob, St, TH, We; all versions except NJB]: in it. It could not refer to σῶμα 'body' because this body was just mentioned as the medium of reconciliation to God whereas, in this clause, it is the enmity between Jews and Gentiles that is in question [ICC].

DISCOURSE UNIT: 2:17–22 [CBC]. The topic is the new place and privilege of the Gentiles as a part of God's people and their place in the spiritual temple.

2:17 And having-come[a] he-proclaimed-the-good-news[b] (of) peace[c] to-you the (ones) far-off[d] and peace to-the (ones) near;[e]

TEXT—Some manuscripts omit the second occurrence of εἰρήνη 'peace' in this verse. GNT does not show this variation in its textual apparatus. Those who do not translate the second occurrence are KJV, NAB, TEV, TNT. Those who accept it feel the repetition lends an appropriate emphasis [Ea, El, ICC, My, WBC] and rhetorical force [EGT], in the form of solemnity [El], to the apostle's words.

LEXICON—a. aorist act. participle of ἔρχομαι (LN 15.81): 'to come' [AB, El, LN, Lns, NIC, NTC, Rob, WBC, We; all versions].

b. aorist mid. indic. of εὐαγγελίζω (LN 33.215) (BAGD 2.a.α. p. 317): 'to proclaim the good news' [AB, NTC; REB], 'to tell the good news, to announce the gospel' [LN], 'to announce the good news of' [NAB], 'to bring the good news of' [NJB], 'to bring as good tidings' [Lns], 'to preach the good news/Good News' [WBC; TEV, TNT], 'to preach the glad tidings' [We], 'to preach' [BAGD, El, Rob; KJV, NASB, NIV], 'to proclaim' [BAGD, NIC; NRSV].

c. εἰρήνη (LN 22.42) (BAGD 3. p. 227): 'peace' [AB, BAGD, El, LN, Lns, NIC, NTC, Rob, WBC, We; all versions], 'tranquility' [LN]. This is the messianic peace as the greatest good and therefore nearly synonymous with messianic salvation [BAGD, DNTT]. As such, the word describes both the content and goal of all Christian preaching, the message itself being called 'the gospel of peace' [DNTT]. See this word at 2:15.

d. μακράν (LN 83.30) (BAGD 1.a.β. p. 487): 'far off' [NIC, WBC, We; NAB, NJB, NRSV, REB, TNT], 'afar off' [El, Lns, Rob; KJV], 'far away' [BAGD, LN, NTC; NASB, NIV], 'far away from God' [TEV], 'far' [AB, LN], 'at a distance, some distance away' [LN]. This denotes a position at a relatively great distance from another position [LN]. The usage is figurative, denoting the Gentiles in contrast to the Jews [BAGD].

e. ἐγγύς (LN 83.26) (BAGD 3. p. 214): 'near' [AB, BAGD, LN, NIC, WBC, We; NAB, NASB, NIV, NJB, NRSV, REB, TNT], 'near to him' [TEV], 'nearby' [LN, Lns, NTC], 'nigh' [El, Rob; KJV]. This denotes a position relatively close to another position [LN]. The usage is figurative [BAGD].

QUESTION—What relationship is indicated by the initial καί 'and'?

1. It indicates a chronological sequence with 2:14–16 [AB, Alf, Ba, Cal, Can, Ea, EBC, ECWB, EGT, El, Ho, ICC, LJ, MNTC, My, St, TNTC, We; NJB (note)]: Christ first made peace and then announced it. The previous verses have shown how Christ made peace [Can, Ea, EGT, ICC, St, We], expounding the starting proposition of 2:14 [Ea], and this one now takes up his proclamation of peace [AB, Can, Ea, EGT, El, Ho, ICC, My, St, We].

2. It indicates a summary or conclusion of 2:14–16 [CBC, NCBC, NTC, TD, TH, WBC; NRSV, REB, TEV]: This means that Christ came and proclaimed the good news. Having dealt with Christ's work of reconciliation, the writer will now use the proselyte terminology of μακράν 'far' and ἐγγύς 'near' and his adaptation of the OT references they bring to mind to summarize the material he has presented in 2:14–16. The καὶ ἐλθών 'and he came' provides a transition to this summarization [WBC]. Since 2:17–18 serve as a conclusion to the preceding material [TH], this καί 'and' may be translated as 'so' [TH; NRSV, REB, TEV] in the sense of 'this means that' [TH].

3. It indicates the result of 2:14–16 [Lns]: By means of abolishing the law, reconciling men to God, and uniting Jew and Gentile into one body, Christ was able to come and proclaim the good news of peace.

EPHESIANS 2:17

QUESTION—To what time and events does ἐλθὼν εὐηγγελίσατο εἰρήνην ὑμῖν 'having come, he proclaimed the good news of peace to you' refer?

It refers to the days of Jesus' earthly ministry [Can, NCBC, TD, WBC]. Preaching was characteristic of the earthly ministry of Jesus and there are several instances recorded of his conversing with Gentiles [NCBC]. It refers to his coming after his resurrection when he greeted them with 'Peace be unto you' and gave the Great Commission to his apostles who carried out this commission through the Spirit [Can, Ho, St]. This 'coming' must refer to Christ's coming in his Spirit (referred to in John 14:18 [EGT, ICC, My, We]), and his mediate preaching through his apostles and others [Alf, EGT, El, ICC, LJ, NIC, TH, We], especially that which resulted in these Gentiles becoming Christians [EGT]. It refers to most of the above in a general way but is not restricted to the NT era [AB, Alf, Ba, ECWB, Ho, MNTC, St, TNTC]. The proclamation of peace is that which he does till the end of the world through his church [ECWB, Ho, St, TNTC]. To try to pin this reference down too specifically to a single event or period of Jesus' or the apostles' ministry might amount to a limitation of its time and place, thus contradicting the universal character of the peace made [AB]. Christ preached to the Jews personally during his ministry on earth. He preached to the Gentiles through his apostles. So this verse teaches that Christ is the author of the system which is adapted to proclaiming peace with God to both [Ba]. The reference has to do with the *purpose* of Christ's coming, that which his work made possible through his church [TNTC].

QUESTION—What is the significance of this OT quote and how does it compare with the original?

The portion of the verse following ἐλθών 'coming' seems to be a composite of perhaps two OT quotes [AB, GNT, NIC, Rob, Si-ed, TNTC, WBC], though the usual citation formula does not occur [AB]. The words εὐηγγελίσατο 'he proclaimed the good news' may come from Isaiah 52:7 [AB, GNT, NIC, Rob, Si-ed, TD, TNTC, WBC]. The bulk of the verse comes from Isaiah 57:19 [AB, Can, CBC, ECWB, LJ, My, NCBC, NIC, Rob, Si-ed, TD, TH, TNTC, WBC], though not an exact quotation from either the Hebrew or LXX [AB, WBC].

QUESTION—To what does εἰρήνη 'peace' refer in this verse?

1. It refers to peace between man and God [Alf, Ba, Cal, Can, ECWB, EGT, Ho, LJ, Lns, NTC, TD, WBC]. This refers to reconciliation with God [Ba] and peace is the inner assurance that all is well because the curse of the law has been borne by Christ's substitutionary atonement [NTC].
2. It refers to peace between Jew and Gentile [DNTT, My, Si, TH]. This interpretation is the only one in keeping with the whole context. This is supported by 2:18, for if both have access to God in one Spirit, both must have received the same message of peace with each other, a necessary historic premise to the unity that now subsists between the two through Christ [My].

3. It refers to both kinds of peace [AB, Ea, NCBC, NIC, TNTC]. The following verse, 2:18, proves this interpretation to be the correct one, for it testifies that both Jews and Gentiles now have access to the Father [AB, Ea]. The peace is presented as given by God *to* those far off and near and as existing *between* them [AB].

QUESTION—What is the significance of the second person plural pronoun ὑμῖν 'to you' being inserted into this OT citation?

The author is said to take up again the second plural pronoun from 2:13 indicating that the material in 2:14–16 has been a parenthetical preparation for this OT citation. This commentator believes it is also an indication that he is not using this citation as a prophecy which is then said to be fulfilled, but only for the terminology he wishes to utilize [WBC].

QUESTION—Why does Paul use the third person type of reference in τοῖς ἐγγύς 'to those near'?

Paul, although a Jew, does not write 'to us near ones' because he is afraid that doing so would uphold the distinctions between Jew and Gentile that he is trying to merge [Alf].

2:18 for/that[a] through[b] him we-have access,[c] the both[d] (of us), in[e] one Spirit, to[f] the Father.

LEXICON—a. ὅτι (LN 89.33): 'for' [LN, NTC, Rob, WBC; KJV, NASB, NIV, NRSV, REB], 'because' [LN, We], 'since' [El], 'in view of the fact that' [LN], 'then' [NJB], 'that' [Lns], not explicit [AB, NIC; NAB, TEV, TNT].

b. διά with genitive object (LN 89.76): 'through' [AB, El, LN, Lns, NIC, NTC, Rob, WBC, We; all versions], 'by means of' [LN]. This is a marker of the means by which one event makes another event possible [LN].

c. προσαγωγή (LN 33.72) (BAGD p. 711): 'access' [BAGD, LN, Lns, NIC, NTC, Rob, WBC, We; KJV, NAB, NASB, NIV, NRSV, REB], 'free access' [AB; NJB], 'approach' [BAGD, LN], 'admission' [El]. The phrase 'to have access' is translated 'to be able to come into the presence of' [TEV], 'to be able to go right into the presence' [TNT]. This denotes the opportunity or right to address someone, and implies the person addressed is higher in rank than the person initiating the approach [LN].

d. ἀμφότεροι (LN 59.25) (BAGD 1. p. 47): 'both' [BAGD, El, LN, NIC, NTC, Rob, WBC, We; all versions except NRSV, TEV, TNT], 'both of us' [Lns; NRSV, TNT], 'two of us' [AB], 'all of us, Jews and Gentiles' [TEV]. This term denotes the totality of two [LN].

e. ἐν with dative object (LN 89.80): 'in' [AB, El, Lns, NIC, NTC, Rob, WBC, We; all versions except KJV, NIV], 'by' [KJV, NIV], 'with' [LN]. This is a marker of attendant circumstances [LN, TH], often with the implication of means [LN].

f. πρός with accusative object (LN 84.18) (BAGD III.1.a. p. 709): 'to' [AB, LN, Lns, NIC, NTC, WBC, We; NAB, NASB, NIV, NJB, NRSV, REB], 'unto' [El, Rob; KJV], 'towards' [BAGD]. This is also conjoined with the translation of προσαγωγή 'access' as a verb: 'to come/go into the presence of' [TEV, TNT].

QUESTION—What relationship is indicated by ὅτι 'for/that'?

1. This indicates the confirmation or proof of the proclamation of the good news of peace [AB, Can, Ea, EGT, El, Ho, ICC, MNTC, My, NCBC, NTC, TH]: he proclaimed the good news of peace as evidenced by the fact that through him we both have access in one Spirit to the Father. The ὅτι 'that' points out the proof [Ea, Ho, ICC, MNTC, My] and result of the proclamation of peace [Ea, NCBC], relating this verse, with its message concerning worship, as a conclusion to all that has been said about peace in 2:14–17 [AB]. It serves to demonstrate the fact that peace has been proclaimed by the fact of our free access to the Father [El, My, TH]. It may be translated as 'since' [Ho].

2. This indicates the reason for the proclamation of the good news of peace being made to both divisions of mankind [Alf, WBC, We]: he proclaimed the good news of peace to those far off and to those near because through him we both have access in one Spirit to the Father. Since both now have access to the Father, the same good news of peace with God can be proclaimed to both [WBC]. The preaching of peace is universally effective because of the common access to the Father, through the Son, by the Spirit [We].

3. This indicates the contents of the proclamation of the good news of peace [Lns]: namely, that through him we both have access in one Spirit to the Father. The fact that Jew and Gentile both now have access to the Father is not the cause of Christ's having preached, but rather the contents of his preaching.

4. Both the content and the confirmation of the message of peace is indicated [Cal]: as evidenced by the fact that through him we both have access in one Spirit to the Father, and which also constitutes that peace. Primarily, this is an argument from the fact, but it must also be viewed as a definition of that peace, given for the sake of wicked men, in order to guard against a sense of false peace.

QUESTION—What relationship is indicated by διά 'through'?

It refers to Christ's mediatorship and intercession [Ba, Ho, LJ, My] and his sacrificial work on the cross [Ba, LJ, NTC]. Believers have access to the Father in the peace secured by the cross of the Son through the agency and work of the Holy Spirit [WeBC]. Christ provides the means of humanity's access to God, and the Holy Spirit is the manner or circumstance in which this right of access is exercised [TH]. One commentator thinks it refers to the victory which Christ won and the knowledge of God which he imparted [MNTC]. Another believes it relates directly to the church's worship of God, stating that when Jews and Gentiles worship God together, it is because of the office fulfilled by Christ and the peace made by him [AB].

QUESTION—What is meant by ἐν ἑνὶ πνεύματι 'in one spirit'?
1. This is a reference to the Holy Spirit [Alf, Ba, Cal, DNTT, Ea, ECWB, EGT, Ho, IB, ICC, IDB, ISBE, ISBE2, LJ, My, NCBC, NIC, NTC, Rob, Si, St, TH, TNTC, WBC, We, WeBC]: we both have access in the one Holy Spirit to the Father. Now being 'one body', the community is animated and indwelt by the 'one Spirit' [NCBC, Rob]. The preposition ἐν 'in' may be understood instrumentally, and translated 'by' [Ho, NTC], the Spirit being the subjective means of man's access to the Father [DNTT, NTC]. However, some commentators object to this [DNTT, EGT, TD] on the grounds that ἐν 'in' here cannot be instrumental with δι' αὐτοῦ 'through him' preceding it [DNTT, TD], arguing for a spatial, local meaning ('in' [EGT, TD] or 'united in' [Alf, El]) with reference to the element in which we have access [EGT, El]. Alternatively, it may mean 'in communion with' [Ea, Ho].
2. This is a reference to the new spirit of unity within redeemed mankind [Lns, MNTC]: we both have access in one united spirit to the Father. Paul is not speaking of the means by which we make our approach to God, but of the new attitude of worship which is now possible for all men. The meaning is 'in one frame of mind' or 'with one heart and soul' [MNTC].
3. This is a reference to the Holy Spirit's work of giving a united spirit to redeemed mankind [AB, Can, Rob]: we both have access by the Holy Spirit in one united spirit to the Father. In the context of the hymn from which this is taken, this may intentionally be part of a Trinitarian reference, of which Ephesians has several [AB]. But, at the same time, it may stand for the work of the Spirit of God upon the human spirit, resulting in the spirit of unity, reconciliation, and peace [AB, Can].

DISCOURSE UNIT: 2:19–22 [AB, Ba, ECWB, Lns, MNTC, My, NIC, NTC, Si, St, TH, We]. The topic is the unity of the church as constituting the household of God [My, NIC, We], the spiritual temple of God [AB, Ba, ECWB, Lns, MNTC, My, NTC, Si, We], the portrait of God's new Society [St].

2:19 Consequently[a] then[b] no-longer[c] are-you strangers[d] and aliens[e]

LEXICON—a. ἄρα (LN 89.46) (BAGD 4. p. 104): 'consequently, as a result' [BAGD, LN], 'accordingly' [Lns], 'so' [BAGD, El, LN, NIC, NTC, Rob, WBC, We; NASB, NRSV, TEV], 'now' [KJV], 'then' [LN]. This is a marker of result presenting an inference from what has preceded [LN]. When it occurs with the following conjunction οὖν 'then', ἄρα expresses the inference and οὖν the transition [BAGD]. This conjunction is also translated in combination with the next conjunction οὖν 'then': 'thus' [REB], 'accordingly' [AB], 'this means that' [NAB], 'consequently' [NIV], 'so' [NJB, TNT].
b. οὖν (LN 89.50): 'then' [BAGD, El, LN, NIC, NTC, Rob, WBC, We; NASB, NRSV, TEV], 'therefore' [LN, Lns; KJV], 'so, consequently, accordingly, so then' [LN]. This is a marker of result and often implies the conclusion of a process of reasoning [LN].

c. οὐκέτι (LN 67.130) (BAGD 1. p. 592): 'no longer' [AB, BAGD, LN, Lns, NIC, NTC, WBC; NAB, NASB, NIV, NJB, NRSV, REB, TNT], 'not any longer' [TEV], 'no more' [BAGD, El, Rob, We; KJV].
d. ξένος: 'strangers'. See this word at 2:12.
e. πάροικος (LN 11.77) (BAGD 2. p. 629): 'aliens' [BAGD, LN, NIC, NTC; NAB, NASB, NIV, NRSV], 'outsiders' [Lns], 'foreigners' [KJV, TNT], 'strangers' [BAGD, LN, WBC; TEV], 'sojourners' [AB, El, Rob, We], 'temporary resident' [LN], 'foreign visitors' [NJB]. This is also combined with the preceding noun, ξένος 'stranger', and translated as hendiadys: 'aliens in a foreign land' [REB]. In Christian literature this term is almost always used as a substantive for one who lives in a place that is not his home [BAGD] or, who lives for a period of time in a place that is not his normal residence [LN]. It is used in a figurative sense of Christians [BAGD].

QUESTION—What is the force of the two conjunctions in the combination ἄρα οὖν 'consequently then'?

The word ἄρα 'consequently' is a conjunction that marks progress in the argument of a discourse and οὖν 'then' is an even stronger conjunction in this respect [Ea, EGT, El], having even a collective sense [EGT, El]. The force of the combination serves to introduce a conclusion or result based upon the previous reasoning [Can, Ea, EBC, EGT, El, Ho, My, St, TH, We]. The phrase ἄρα οὖν 'so then' announces a summarizing statement of the main point the author has been trying to make [AB, LJ, WBC]. This is a deduction from the four 'one' terms upon which the preceding context is focused [LJ, Lns] (the factor of the unity that exists among true Christians being uppermost in the apostle's mind in this new section, the factor of their privilege being also prominent [LJ]), or it is a conclusion that follows directly from the equal privilege that all sons in Christ have in regard to their heavenly Father [We].

QUESTION—What is meant by the phrase ξένοι καὶ πάροικοι 'strangers and aliens'?

1. It is a metaphor referring to two separate entities [Ba, Cal, Can, Ea, EBC, ECWB, EGT, El, Ho, LJ, Lns, MM, My, NCBC, NIC, NTC, Rob, TD, TH, We].

1.1 Ξένοι 'strangers' refers to a foreigner, while πάροικοι 'alien' specifies a foreign national having his residence for a period of time within the country [Cal, Can, EBC, ECWB, EGT, El, IB, Lns, MM, My, NCBC, NIC, NTC, Rob, TD, TH, We]: you are no longer foreigners nor are you resident aliens. It is a comprehensive expression denoting all who were not citizens [EBC, EGT, El, Rob], whether because of natural or territorial demarcations, or because of the lack of civic privileges [EGT, El]. Though ruled by God and included in the messianic promise, they did not participate in the time-hallowed prerogatives of the Israelites [My]. The phrase is a full antithesis to συμπολῖται 'fellow citizens' in the next clause [EBC, El, My, NCBC].

1.2 Ξένοι 'strangers' refers to civil status within a nation, while πάροικοι 'alien' ('sojourner') refers to domestic status in a home [Ba, Ea, Ho]: you are no longer strangers to the nation nor are you sojourners in a home.
1.3 Ξένοι 'strangers' refers to status relative to the family while πάροικοι 'alien' refers to status relative to the nation [LJ]: you are no longer strangers to the family nor are you aliens to the nation.
2. It is a metaphor referring to a single entity [AB, Alf (probably), CBC, ICC, St, TNTC, WBC; REB]. It is in line with the style of this epistle to use two terms, where one would suffice, in order to emphasize the Gentile's previous status as an outsider [WBC].
2.1 Presented in the form of hendiadys [AB, CBC, St (probably); REB]: you are no longer aliens in a foreign land. They were visitors without legal rights [St]. Πάροικος 'alien' etymologically means 'outside the *house*' and this etymology suggests to Paul God's household (οἰκεῖοι) in the next clause which further leads to an elaboration on God's 'house' in 2:20–22 [AB].
2.2 Presented in the form of a generic-specific doublet with focus upon the specific item, the term πάροικοι 'aliens' [Alf (probably), ICC, TNTC (probably)]: you are no longer strangers, that is aliens. These were people who might live alongside them in the same country, but who had nothing more than the most superficial rights of citizenship [TNTC]. Ξένος 'stranger' is 'foreigner' in general while πάροικος is a foreigner dwelling in a state, and not having rights of citizenship [ICC].

but[a] you-are fellow-citizens[b] of-the saints[c] and members-of-(the)-household[d] of God,

LEXICON—a. ἀλλά (LN 89.125): 'but' [AB, El, LN, NIC, NTC, Rob, WBC, We; KJV, NASB, NIV, NRSV, REB], 'on the contrary' [LN, Lns], 'instead' [LN], 'no' [NAB], not explicit [NJB, TEV, TNT]. This is a marker of a more emphatic contrast [LN].

b. συμπολίτης (LN **11.72**) (BAGD p. 780): 'fellow citizen' [AB, BAGD, El, LN, Lns, MM, NIC, NTC, Rob, WBC, We; all versions except NRSV], 'citizen' [NRSV, TEV]. This denotes fellow members of a sociopolitical unit [LN]. It is used figuratively of Gentiles who accept the Christian faith, so becoming Christians, who are πολῖται 'citizens' of the Kingdom of God [BAGD].

c. ἅγιος: 'saints'. See this word at 1:1, 15, 18.

d. οἰκεῖος (LN 10.11) (BAGD 2. p. 556): 'member of the household' [AB, BAGD, NTC, WBC; NAB, NIV, NRSV, REB], 'part of the household' [NJB], 'member of the house' [NIC], 'household' [El, Rob, We; KJV, NASB], 'member of the family' [LN; TEV], 'family member' [Lns], 'relative' [LN], 'intimate, spiritually akin with' [MM]. This noun is also translated as a clause: 'to belong to one's family' [TNT]. This denotes a person who belongs to a particular household or extended family [LN].

Literally, it means 'belonging to the house'. This is a figurative expression denoting Christians [BAGD]. One commentator notes that the primary meaning of the word is 'house' in the sense of 'dwelling place' and only secondarily 'household', 'clan', or 'family'. This fact will account for the use of an architectural metaphor in the remaining verses of the chapter [IB].

QUESTION—What is the reason for the order συμπολῖται τῶν ἁγίων 'fellow citizens with the saints' followed by οἰκεῖοι τοῦ θεοῦ 'members of the household of God'?

Οἰκεῖοι τοῦ θεοῦ 'members of the household of God' further defines συμπολῖται τῶν ἁγίων 'fellow citizens with the saints' [El]. Οἰκεῖοι τοῦ θεοῦ 'members of the household of God' forms the climax to the preceding phrase [El, My]. Together they form the contrast to ξένοι 'strangers' and πάροικοι 'aliens' [My]. This continues the order given in 2:12–18. The two relationships are not really separable. One relationship presupposes and interprets the other [AB].

QUESTION—What is meant by συμπολίτης 'fellow citizen'?

This is a metaphor going back to the commonwealth of Israel in 2:12 [IB, MNTC, St, TNTC]. The saints are viewed as forming a spiritual state [Cal, CBC, Ea, LJ, NCBC, St, TH, WeBC] perhaps on the model of an old Greek city-state [CBC, Ea, LJ, MNTC]. They form its citizenship [Ba, Cal, Can, Ea, IB, LJ, MNTC, NCBC, NIC, NTC, St, We, WeBC].

QUESTION—To whom does ἁγίων 'saints' refer?

1. It refers collectively to the church in the widest sense [Alf, Cal, Can, Ea, EBC, EGT, TNTC, WeBC]: you are fellow citizens with the rest of the members of the Church. These are not saints of any time or any class, but saints of all times and all lands [Cal, Ea, EBC], all the members of the mystical body of Christ [Alf], all who in any sense could be called people of God [TNTC]. Even the angels are included among these 'saints' [Cal].
2. It refers to the Church as now composed of Jew and Gentile Christians united together [El, Ho, ICC, Lns, My, NCBC, NTC, Rob, WBC]: you are fellow citizens with the rest of us Christians.
3. It refers to Israel as the historic community that worshipped God and served him among the nations [AB, St], to spiritual Israel [ECWB, IB, LJ, MNTC, Si-ed, TD, We], or to Jewish Christians [DNTT, NIC]: you are fellow citizens with spiritual Israel/us Jewish Christians.
4. It refers to the angels of heaven [MNTC, TD]: you are fellow citizens with the angels. MNTC gives this as an alternative interpretation to 3 above.

QUESTION—What is meant by the use of the metaphor οἰκεῖος 'members of the household'?

The saints are viewed as forming more than a spiritual polity, they form God's own family, his household [AB, Ba, Cal, Can, CBC, Ea, EBC, ECWB, IB, LJ, My, NCBC, NIC, NTC, St, TNTC, WBC, WeBC], with God filling the role of father, the head of the household [LJ, NCBC, St, WeBC], though one commentator interprets these saints as being the servants of the household, as the immediate retinue of a king, the inner circle [MNTC]. This corresponds with Paul's use of πατήρ 'father' in the previous verse [Can, Lns, Rob, St].

2:20 having-been-built[a] upon[b] the foundation[c] of-the apostles[d] and prophets,[e]

LEXICON—a. aorist pass. participle of ἐποικοδομέω (LN 45.5) (BAGD 1.b. p. 305): 'to be built upon' [AB, BAGD, LN, NIC, NTC, Rob, WBC, We; all versions except NAB, TNT], 'to be built up' [El, Lns]. This is also translated by complex clauses that make explicit more of the metaphor: 'to form a building which rises' [NAB], 'to be part of a building which is being built' [TNT]. The term denotes the construction of something on some specified location [LN]. Used figuratively, the term may denote the beginnings of a congregation as if it were the beginnings of a building [BAGD]. The aorist tense refers to the time they became Christians [ICC, Lns, My, TH, WBC]. God is the agent of the passive verb [AB, LJ, Lns, WBC].

b. ἐπί with dative object (LN 83.46) (BAGD II.1.a.β. p. 287): 'upon' [AB, BAGD, El, LN, Lns, NTC, Rob, We; all versions except NAB, NIV, REB], 'on' [BAGD, LN, NIC, WBC; NAB, NIV, REB]. It may be that the preposition is repeated after the verb in which it forms a compound, in order to emphasize the local idea ('upon') of the preposition. It may also be that the preposition in composition (ἐποικοδομέω 'to be built') has weakened in its force [HG].

c. θεμέλιος (LN 7.41) (BAGD 2.b. p. 356): 'foundation' [AB, BAGD, El, LN, Lns, NIC, NTC, Rob, WBC, We; all versions except NJB], 'foundations' [NJB]. This denotes that upon which a structure is built [LN]. Figuratively, the word denotes the indispensable prerequisites necessary for something to come into existence [BAGD].

d. ἀπόστολος: 'apostle'. See this word at 1:1.

e. προφήτης (LN 53.79) (BAGD 5. p. 724): 'prophet' [AB, BAGD, El, LN, Lns, NIC, NTC, Rob, TH, WBC, We; all versions], 'inspired preacher' [LN]. This term denotes one who proclaims inspired utterances on behalf of God [LN].

QUESTION—What relationship is indicated by the use of the participle ἐποικοδομηθέντες 'having been built upon'?

1. The participle indicates the time when the events in the previous verse took place and it refers to their becoming Christians [ICC, Lns, My, WBC]. It also indicates the reason for the statement of the previous verse [Lns]: because you have been built upon the foundation.

2. It indicates the circumstances or manner of these Gentiles' admission to becoming full members of the Kingdom and of the family of God [Cal, TH]: seeing/in this way you have been built upon the foundation. The participle is dependent upon the main verb ἐστέ 'you are' of the last verse.

It is also possible that a time reference is explicit in this participle, referring to the time when they became Christians [TH].

QUESTION—What is the force of the prefixed preposition ἐπί- in ἐποικοδομηθέντες 'having been built upon'?

It gives the verb the meaning of 'to build up' [Alf, Ea, EGT, El, ICC, My, TD] or 'to build further' [TD], referring to the superstructure which is erected on the foundation. Other commentators, however, say the verb only means 'to build upon' [DNTT, Rob], the prefixed preposition only corresponding to the free preposition (ἐπί 'upon') following the verb [Rob], the prefixed preposition being somewhat weak in Paul's usage [TD]. It also gives prominence to the thought of the foundation *on* which this superstructure rests so the thought in the writer's mind is on the basis of the building [Ea]. Used in the figurative sense as here, the preposition intensifies the sense of fellowship which is contained in the concept of 'building up' [DNTT].

QUESTION—What is the meaning of the metaphor which ἐποικοδομηθέντες 'having been built upon' introduces?

Because of the double meaning of οἶκος 'house' [NTC, Rob], a component of both οἰκεῖος 'household' and ἐποικοδομηθέντες 'having been built' (see lexical entry under οἰκεῖος 'household' in 2:19), Paul can change the metaphor from that of a household or family in the previous verse to that of a building [Alf, Can, CBC, ECWB, LJ, My, NTC, Rob, TH, TNTC, WeBC], particularly to that of a temple [Ba, IB, ISBE2, LJ, Lns, MNTC, Si, St, TD, WBC, WeBC]. This new metaphor expresses vividly the elements of beauty [Ba], cohesion, privilege [LJ], permanence, and stability in the position of these believing Gentiles by comparing them to the stones (implied) comprising the structure [Can, TD, WBC], making them an integral part of the whole structure, not just an annex [Si].

QUESTION—How are the nouns related in the genitive construction τῷ θεμελίῳ τῶν ἀποστόλων καὶ προφητῶν 'the foundation of the apostles and prophets'?

1. The apostles and prophets themselves constitute the foundation, as founders of churches [CBC, MNTC, NCBC, Rob, TD, WBC]: the foundation which consists of the apostles and prophets. The apostles and prophets had been closely associated with Christ in the establishment of the church [NCBC, TD]. According to some, Christ [NCBC, TD] or God [TD] is implied as the one who built the foundation consisting of the apostles and prophets.

2. The doctrine or gospel of which the apostles and prophets are witnesses constitutes the foundation [AB, Ba, DNTT, EBC, ECWB, LJ, Lns, NTC, Si, St, TNTC]: the foundation consisting of the gospel or doctrine given to the apostles and prophets. Some commentators recognize that the apostles and prophets may be considered to be the foundation in a secondary sense [DNTT, ECWB, NTC] and qualify this appositional statement to the effect that it is the apostolic office of teaching and the witness of the

apostles and prophets concerning Christ which is the foundation upon which the church is built rather than the apostles and prophets themselves [AB, Ba, DNTT, EBC, ECWB, Lns, NTC, St, TNTC].

3. The apostles and prophets are the actors in relation to this foundation [Cal, Can, Ea, EGT, El, LN (7.44), My, TH, We; TEV]: the foundation which the apostles and prophets have laid. Christ has already been said to be the one who preached peace (2:17), and the church is never represented as being founded upon a doctrine or testimony, but always upon the person of Christ. Elsewhere those who are united to Christ by genuine faith are represented as forming the foundation (e.g., 1 Cor. 3:10–17; 2 Tim. 2:19), and this appears to be the meaning here [Can, EGT]. Others believe the foundation is the gospel or doctrine which the apostles and prophets proclaimed and by which they established the churches (Rom. 15:20, 1 Cor. 3:10) [Cal, EGT, My, TH, We (probably)].

4. The genitives are possessive, indicating that the apostles and prophets themselves are built upon this foundation [Alf]: having been built upon the same foundation upon which the apostles and prophets are built. The foundation is Jesus Christ, according to 1 Cor. 3:12.

QUESTION—Who are these apostles?

These apostles are restricted to the twelve disciples of Christ and Paul [AB, Lns, NCBC, NTC], at least primarily [Rob]. Others indicate it refers to these plus a few other men who received some special commission from the resurrected Christ [ICC, IDB, LJ, NIC, St, TD, WBC]. Others indicate that it means any of the missionaries of the early church whose ministry it was to found churches [EGT, ISBE, TH (probably)].

QUESTION—Who are these prophets?

1. These are the prophets of the Old Testament [Ba, Cal, Lns, Mo, TD]. The mention of prophets is put by synecdoche for the whole of the Old Testament as forming a part of the divine revelation upon which the church is founded [Ba].

2. These are the prophets of the New Testament church [AB, Alf, Can, CBC, DNTT, Ea, EBC, ECWB, EGT, El, Ho, IB, ICC, ISBE, ISBE2, LJ, MNTC, My, My-ed, NCBC, NIC, NTC, Rob, Si-ed, St, TD, TH, TNTC, Tu, WBC, We, WeBC; NJB (note), TNT]. Elsewhere in this epistle (3:5; 4:11) prophets are listed with apostles as Christian office bearers, so it is natural to understand them as such here [AB, Can, Ea, EBC, ECWB, EGT, El, ICC, ISBE2, MNTC, My, NCBC, NIC, NTC, Rob, Si-ed, TH, TNTC, WBC, We, WeBC]. The prophets were those in the early church who received direct communication from God for the guidance of believers [Can, CBC, Ea, LJ, NCBC, St, TD, WBC].

Christ Jesus himself being (the) cornerstone,[a]

LEXICON—a. ἀκρογωνιαῖος (LN **7.44**) (BAGD p. 33): 'cornerstone' [BAGD, **LN**, Lns, NIC, Rob; all versions except KJV, NAB, NIV], 'chief cornerstone' [El, NTC; KJV, NIV], 'head cornerstone' [We], 'important stone' [LN], 'keystone' [AB, WBC], 'capstone' [BAGD; NAB].

QUESTION—What is the function of αὐτοῦ 'himself' in this clause?

All commentators who comment on this indicate that it refers to Χριστοῦ Ἰησοῦ 'Christ Jesus' [Alf, EGT, El, ICC, Lns, My, WBC], though they report that some older commentators referred it to the 'foundation'. Its function is to give emphasis to Χριστοῦ Ἰησοῦ 'Christ Jesus' in contrast to those who laid the foundations [El, ICC, WBC], thus maintaining the concept of the primary importance of Christ as the one to whom the building owes its existence, strength and increase [EGT].

QUESTION—What is meant by ἀκρογωνιαῖος 'cornerstone'?

1. It is a metaphor based upon the function of a cornerstone [Alf, Ba, BAGD, Bu, Cal, Can, CBC, DNTT, Ea, EBC, ECWB, EGT, El, Ho, ICC, IDB, LJ, LN (7.44), Lns, MM, MNTC, My, NCBC, NIC, NTC, Rob, Si, St, TD, TNTC, We, WeBC; all versions except NAB]: Christ Jesus himself being the cornerstone. Some commentators state that the cornerstone was cut so as to govern the lay of all the walls and crosswalls of the building [Alf, ECWB, LJ, Lns, MM, NCBC, NTC, Si-ed, St, TNTC; TNT (note)]. Its importance was ideal and symbolic, being placed in or on the top tier of the foundation, so as to be seen by all [Lns]. Some maintain that its purpose was more utilitarian, that it was a large stone placed so as to join two walls [Can, Ea, EBC, ECWB, EGT, Ho, IDB], binding them together [Can, Ea, EBC, ECWB, EGT, El, Ho, IDB, LJ, NIC, Rob, TNTC, WeBC; TNT (note)], and supporting the whole building [Ba, Can, Ea, LJ, MNTC, My, NTC, St]. A large cornerstone was placed at each corner of a building, supporting the walls, the reason being that if the stones were small and unstable and settled down, the whole building would be unstable [Ba]. The cornerstones were straight blocks of great length which run up to a corner where they were met by similar stones, the ends of which rested immediately above or below them. One such stone found in the substructures of the Jerusalem temple was over 38 feet long [Rob, St, TH]. Some state or imply that the cornerstone was considered to be a part of the foundation [Ea, El, NCBC, NTC, Rob, St, TD], some stating it was the primary foundation-stone [LJ, MM]. The comparison in the metaphor is: just as a cornerstone occupies the place of honor in the Temple building and determines the lay of the rest of the building, so Christ has the place of ultimate honor in the church and determines its direction. The point of comparison is the position of honor the cornerstone occupies and the support and direction that the cornerstone gives to the building. The nonfigurative statement would be: Christ Jesus holds the ultimate place of honor in the church [EBC, LN (7.44), Lns, TH], supporting and uniting it [LJ] and guiding its growth and character [ECWB, NTC, St].

2. It is a metaphor based upon the function of a keystone [AB, WBC], copestone [IB], (topmost) cornerstone [TD], or capstone [ISBE; NAB]:

Christ Jesus himself being the keystone/capstone. This was a stone used to link together the last tier of stones on a wall [ISBE] or to top an arch [AB]. The reference may be to an arched gate or the crown and centerpiece of a vaulted ceiling [AB]. In either case, the keystone bears all the pressure of the stones forming the arch. Its removal will cause the collapse of the whole [AB, WBC]. The comparison in the metaphor according to this interpretation is: just as a keystone completes and holds a building together, so Christ will complete and support the church. The point of comparison is the role of the keystone in completing and supporting the rest of the structure (the whole structure having been determined beforehand by the shape and strength of the final stone to be inserted). The nonfigurative statement is: God is forming his church, getting it ready for Christ who will join himself to it in a final manner, so completing its organization.

2:21 in[a] whom all[b] (the) building[c] being-fitted-together[d]

TEXT—Some manuscripts include an article following πᾶσα 'all' and before οἰκοδομή 'building'. The addition of the article gives the meaning 'the whole building'. Without the article, the meaning, according to some, could be 'the whole building' or it could be 'every building', implying the existence of more than one building [El, WBC]. See discussion on the meaning below. GNT omits the article with a B rating, indicating that its omission is almost certain. The reading with the definite article is taken by only BD.

LEXICON—a. ἐν with dative object (LN 89.119): 'in' [AB, El, NIC, NTC, Rob, WBC, We; KJV, NASB, NIV, NJB, NRSV, REB], 'in connection with' [Lns], 'in union with' [LN; TNT], 'through' [NAB]. One translation begins a new sentence with this verse, translating the phrase containing this preposition as the subject of an active verb (see d. below): 'He is the one who' [TEV].

b. πᾶς (LN 59.23, 63.2) (BAGD 1.a.ε. p. 631): 'all' [BAGD, El, LN (59.23), Lns, Rob; KJV], 'the whole' [AB, BAGD, LN (63.2), NIC, WBC; NAB, NASB, NIV, NRSV, REB, TEV, TNT], 'the entire' [LN (63.2), NTC], 'every' [NJB], 'each several' [We].

c. οἰκοδομή (LN 7.1, 42.34) (BAGD 2.b. p. 559): 'building' [BAGD, El, LN (7.1), Lns, NTC, Rob, WBC, We; KJV, NASB, NIV, REB, TEV], 'structure' [LN, NIC; NAB, NJB, NRSV], 'edifice' [BAGD], 'construction' [AB, LN (42.34)], 'building process' [TNT]. The word may denote the construction of something where the focus is upon the event of building up or upon the result of such an event [LN (42.34)].

d. pres. pass. participle of συναρμολογέω (συναρμολογέομαι LN **62.1**) (BAGD p. 785): 'to be fitted together' [AB, BAGD; NAB, NASB], 'to be harmoniously fitted together' [NTC], 'to be joined together' [BAGD, **LN**, WBC; NIV, NRSV], 'to be knit together' [NJB], 'to be bonded together' [NIC; REB], 'to be framed together' [Lns], 'to be fitly framed together'

[El, Rob, We; KJV], 'to be brought to perfection' [TNT]. This passive verb is also translated actively: 'to fit together' [**LN**], 'to hold together' [TEV]. It denotes the fitting together of things in a coherent and compatible manner [Ba, LN]. The present tense implies that the process of being fitted together is still going on [Alf, CBC, EGT, El, ICC, My, TH, TNTC, WBC]. The implied agent is the Holy Spirit [LJ], Christ [Ho, NIC], or God [Lns].

QUESTION—What is the meaning of the preposition ἐν 'in' in the phrase ἐν ᾧ 'in whom'?

1. It means 'in union with' or 'in connection with' Christ [Alf, Ea, ECWB, EGT, El, Ho, LJ, Lns, My, NIC, NTC, St, TNTC; TEV, TNT]: in union with whom the whole building is fitted together. It is only by connection with Christ that the building is what it is here declared to be [EGT]. The whole building holds together in him, it is squared and ruled by its unity to him [Alf, Lns, NIC].
2. It means 'by' or 'through', and designates Christ as the agent of the passive participle συναρμολογουμένη 'being fitted together' [TH; NAB, TEV]: through whom the whole building is being fitted together.

QUESTION—What is meant by πᾶσα οἰκοδομή 'all the building'?

1. The meaning is 'the whole building' [AB, Alf, Ba, Cal, Can, CBC, Ea, EBC, ECWB, El, Ho, IB, LJ, Lns, MNTC, Mo, NIC, NTC, Rob, Si-ed, St, TD, TH, TNTC, Tu, WBC; KJV, NAB, NASB, NIV, NRSV, REB, TEV, TNT]: the whole building is being fitted together. The context demands the meaning of a single, whole temple building [Alf, Ea, El, MNTC, NIC, NTC, Rob] for which the mention of the foundation and cornerstone in the previous verse has prepared us [Alf, Ea, NTC].
2. The meaning is 'each/every building' [EGT, HG, ICC, My, NCBC, We, WeBC; NJB]: each individual building is being fitted together. The meaning is that every Christian community is at present being framed and fitted together so that it may form, with other Christian communities, the great mystical Body of Christ which is God's true Temple [EGT, My, NCBC, WeBC]. The picture is that of an extensive group of buildings all in process of construction at different points on a common plan [ICC].

QUESTION—What is meant by οἰκοδομή 'building'?

1. Reference is to the edifice considered concretely [AB, Ba, BAGD, Cal, Can, EGT, El, IDB, My, NCBC, NIC, Si, St, TD, Tu, WBC, We, WeBC; KJV, NAB, NASB, NIV, NJB, NRSV, REB, TEV]: the whole building, being fitted together, etc. Οἰκοδομή 'building' signifies the aggregate of the single parts of the building, the edifice. It cannot signify the parts individually such as the wall, the roof, etc. Only the building as a whole can grow to become the holy Temple [My].
2. Reference is to the building process rather than the building itself [EBC, IB, ICC, Lns, MNTC, NTC, Rob, TNTC; TNT]: all that is being added to what is being built is being fitted together and is growing, etc. The reference is to all that is built after the foundation is laid [Lns (probably),

MNTC]. The absence of the article before οἰκοδομή 'building' implies that the work is still in progress, so the meaning is really 'all building that is being done' [EBC], 'everything that is being built' [TNTC], or 'everything that from time to time is built in' [ICC], or, if the figure is dropped, 'all that God is shaping to his purpose'. With this last gloss, the statement becomes a restatement of 1:10, the movement of all things toward a final unity in Christ, with the added thought that all of God's handiwork is growing into a temple [IB]. By giving this word such an abstract reference, the problem of πᾶς meaning 'the whole' or 'every' is much less acute, there being little difference in meaning in this case [HG, Lns].

QUESTION—What relationship is indicated by the use of the present participle συναρμολογουμένη 'being fitted together'?

The participle precisely defines the function of the cornerstone, that of 'fitting or joining together' [EBC, TNTC].

1. It indicates the means of the growth [Lns, MNTC]: by being framed or fitted together, all that is the building grows into a sanctuary. An inner harmony, unity, and correspondence pervades all that forms the building.
2. It indicates a temporal relationship to the verb αὔξει 'it grows' [My, WBC]: every building, while its framing together takes place in Christ, grows etc. The participle is closely connected to ἐν ᾧ 'in whom'.

QUESTION—What is the meaning of the metaphor in συναρμολογουμένη 'being fitted together'?

This word is a technical term for an ancient building process in which the individual stones being assembled into the building were squared off to fit each other exactly. They were then joined to each other internally with metal pegs held fast with melted lead [AB, Rob, TH; TNT (note)]. This gave the final visible surface of the building the appearance of being a single piece of stone [TNT (note)]. The metaphor teaches that the joining and fitting together of all the elements that make up the church constitutes the process of the growth of the church toward its final condition of holiness [WBC].

1. Assuming the majority view that πᾶσα οἰκοδομή 'all the building' has implied reference to the addition of individual stones (Christians) to the building [Cal, Can, CBC (probably), Ea, Ho, LJ, Lns, MNTC, NTC, Rob, Si, St, TD, TNTC], the metaphor teaches that the gifts and graces of one member of the true church are made supplementary to the gifts and graces of another [Ea], that members of the church are responsible citizens who mutually support and pray for one another [AB], that each individual Christian is in the process of having his character conformed to the image of Christ [LJ], or that believers' unity in the faith is the main part of the symmetry in the building [Cal].
2. Assuming the reference of πᾶσα οἰκοδομή 'all the building' is to local congregations rather than individual believers [EGT, My, NCBC, WeBC], the metaphor teaches that each local congregation is aligned with every other congregation in what it does and stands for in Christ [NCBC].

3. Assuming that the reference of πᾶσα οἰκοδομή 'all the building' is to an abstract generality [IB, ICC], the metaphor may be teaching that God is shaping everything to his own purpose and everything is moving to a final unity in Christ, Eph. 1:10 [IB]. The significance of the abstract construction is not all that clear [AB, IB] but it may be used because more than just Christian believers must be meant [IB].

grows[a] into[b] a holy[c] temple[d] in (the) Lord,
LEXICON—a. pres. act. indic. of αὐξάνω (LN **59.62**) (BAGD 3. p. 121): 'to grow' [AB, BAGD, El, LN, Lns, NIC, NTC, Rob, WBC, We; KJV, NASB, NJB, NRSV, REB], 'to make to grow' [TEV], 'to increase' [BAGD, LN], 'to extend, to increase' [**LN**], 'to rise' [NIV], 'to produce' [TNT], 'to take shape' [NAB]. The present tense indicates that the growth is continuous [Alf, CBC, DNTT, Ea, EBC, EGT, El, ICC, TH, WBC], normal [DNTT, EGT, El], perpetual [DNTT, El], and unconditional [El].
  b. εἰς with accusative object (LN 67.119, 89.48) (BAGD 4.e. p. 229): 'into' [AB, BAGD, Lns, NIC, NTC, Rob, WBC; NASB, NJB, NRSV, REB, TEV], 'unto' [El, We; KJV], 'as' [NAB], 'with the result that' [LN (89.48)], 'so that' [BAGD], 'until (it becomes)' [LN (67.119)], 'to' [BAGD], not explicit [TNT]. This usage of the preposition designates the result of an action or condition [BAGD, LN (89.48)], or it denotes the extent of time continuous up to a given point [LN (67.119)].
  c. ἅγιος (LN 53.46) (BAGD 1.a.β. p. 9): 'holy' [AB, BAGD, El, Lns, NIC, NTC, Rob, WBC, We; all versions except TEV, TNT], 'sacred' [TEV], 'dedicated' [LN; TNT], 'worthy of God, perfect' [BAGD]. This is a term which pertains to being dedicated or consecrated to the service of God [CBC, Ho, LN]. According to 2:22, the presence of God in the temple constitutes its holiness [AB, My].
  d. ναός (LN 7.15) (BAGD 2. p. 533): 'temple' [AB, BAGD, El, LN, Rob, WBC; all versions], 'sanctuary' [LN, Lns, NIC, NTC, We]. This term designates a building in which a deity is worshipped. In the case of the Temple at Jerusalem, it designates the place where God was regarded as dwelling [LN, WBC] as the counterpart of his heavenly abode [WBC]. The usage here is figurative of the Church [BAGD].
QUESTION—What is the meaning of the metaphor in αὔξει 'grows'?
  Biological language is imported into the architectural figure [NIC, TH, WeBC] to liken the building to a living organism [IB, Rob, TNTC, WBC, WeBC]. It stresses the fact that this is a spiritual, living sanctuary [Lns, WeBC]. Other literature of the time also joined these images together in similar fashion [WBC]. Αὔξει 'grows' defines the work of συναρμολογουμένη 'being fitted together' as a growth [Rob]. As stone after stone is fitted in, the edifice grows [Can]. But this growth is not just an increase in size and number but in power and glory, and in a perpetual reformation and maturation [AB]. The comparison is: just as a living organism grows so this building grows. The point of comparison is the increase in size of both living

organisms and buildings under construction. The nonfigurative statement would be: it increases in size and maturity until it is finished and becomes a spiritual organization through which God manifests his presence. This does not imply that God's presence is not manifested in the present state of the church; it is strictly a question of focus upon the end in view [LJ].

QUESTION—What is meant by ναός 'temple'?

When it is distinguished from ἱερόν 'temple', it has special reference to the sanctuary part of the temple, as in the Most Holy Place in the Jerusalem Temple [AB, Ea, LN (7.15), Lns, Rob, TNTC, We] where God was thought to live or be uniquely present [AB, Ea, LN (7.15), NCBC, NTC, Rob, TNTC, We], but sometimes the distinction between the two words is not always intended [BAGD, LN (7.16), TH]. Some commentators call special attention to the distinction between the words [AB, EBC, Lns, Rob, TNTC] and see a special reference to the temple here as the place where God is regarded as living and manifesting his presence [AB, Cal, Ea, Ho, MNTC, NCBC, NTC, Rob, St, We]. Others regard it as simply the holy place where God is worshipped [Can, CBC, NCBC].

QUESTION—What is the meaning of the metaphor in ναός 'temple'?

The metaphor is based upon the concept of the Jerusalem Temple as God's dwelling (see previous question). The Church is to become the larger Incarnation of Christ, a body corresponding to the body he had on earth [MNTC]. The comparison is: just as God dwells in the Temple in Jerusalem, so his goal is to dwell in his Church. The point of comparison is the function of the sanctuary of the temple, the Most Holy Place, as the place peculiarly separated to God as his dwelling place on earth. The nonfigurative statement would be: the church is made fit to be the organization in which God will peculiarly and permanently manifest his presence.

QUESTION—To what is the phrase ἐν κυρίῳ 'in the Lord' attached?

1. It is attached to the whole of the preceding statement concerning 'being fitted together' and 'growing' [EGT]: being fitted together it grows into a holy temple in the Lord.
2. It is attached to the verb αὔξει 'grows' [AB, Cal, Ho, My, Rob (probably), WBC, We]: It grows in union with the Lord. This has in its favor the parallel passage Eph. 4:16 [Ho]. The shift from 'in Christ' ('in whom') to 'in the Lord' marks a transition from presupposition and instrumentality [AB] to the realm of ethics and conduct [AB, Rob].
3. It is attached to the noun phrase ναὸν ἅγιον 'holy temple' [Alf, Can, Ea, EBC, ECWB, El, MNTC, TH; TEV]: a holy temple in the Lord. It cannot be attached to the verb αὔξει 'grows' because this would create a tautology, this growth having already been said to be in Christ the cornerstone [Can, El].
4. It is attached to the adjective ἅγιον 'holy' which immediately precedes it [IB (probably), ICC, Lns; TNT]: holy in the Lord, or, dedicated to the Lord.

QUESTION—Who is referred to by κυρίῳ 'Lord'?
1. It refers to Christ [AB, Alf, Cal, Can, Ea, ECWB, EGT, El, Ho, ICC, Lns, MNTC, Rob, St, TNTC, WBC]. This is the normal reference in the Pauline usage of κύριος 'lord' [ICC]. In the Pauline corpus, what believers are in relation to Christ is designated as ἐν Χριστῷ 'in Christ', what they are to become or do in relation to Christ is stated as ἐν κυρίῳ 'in the Lord' [AB, Rob, WBC].
2. It refers to God the Father [NCBC].

2:22 in whom also you are-being-built-together[a] into[b] a-dwelling-place[c] of-God in[d] (the) Spirit.[e]

LEXICON—a. pres. pass. indic. of συνοικοδομέω (συνοικοδομοῦμαι LN **45.6**) (BAGD 1. p. 791): 'to be built together' [AB, El, LN, Lns, MM, NIC, Rob, WBC, We; KJV, NASB, NIV, NRSV], 'to be built together with' [TEV], 'to be built with' [REB], 'to be built up together' [BAGD, NTC], 'to be built up' [NJB,], 'to be built up with' [TNT], 'to be built' [NAB]. The present tense implies that the building is still going on [EBC, ICC, Lns, TH]. The usage here is figurative [LN, MM]. Christ is the agent as stated in 2:21 [TH]. The prefixed preposition συν- 'with' emphasizes the underlying idea of fellowship which is contained in the idea of building up and shows that this term is to be linked with ἐποικοδομέω 'to build up' in 2:20 [DNTT]. Yet this fellowship is not just with other believers but is between all who are united together to compose this building, Christ, apostles and prophets, and believers [TD].

b. εἰς with accusative object: 'into' [Lns, WBC; NASB, NJB, NRSV, REB, TEV, TNT], 'for' [El, NIC, NTC, Rob, We; KJV], 'so as to be' [AB]. This preposition is also translated as a verb: 'to become' [NIV]. The phrase εἰς κατοικητήριον 'into a dwelling place' is translated 'into this temple, to become a dwelling place' [NAB].

c. κατοικητήριον (κατοίκησις LN **85.70**) (BAGD p. 424): 'dwelling place' [BAGD, LN, NIC, NTC, WBC; NJB, NRSV, TNT], 'dwelling' [AB, LN; NASB, REB], 'habitation' [El, Lns, Rob, We; KJV], 'a place where one dwells' [**LN**], 'temple...dwelling place' [NAB]. This is also translated in conjunction with the following proper noun in the genitive case: 'a dwelling in which God lives' [NIV], 'a place where God lives' [TEV].

d. ἐν with dative object (LN 89.76): 'in' [AB, El, LN, Lns, NIC, NTC, Rob, WBC, We; NAB, NASB, NJB], 'by' [NIV, TNT], 'through' [LN; KJV, TEV]. The phrase ἐν πνεύματι 'in (the) Spirit' is translated as an adjective modifying κατοικητήριον 'dwelling place': 'spiritual' [REB], or as an adverb modifying συνοικοδομεῖσθε 'you are being built together': 'you are built together spiritually' [NRSV].

e. πνεῦμα (LN) (BAGD 5.d.β. p. 677): 'Spirit' [AB, BAGD, El, Lns, NIC, NTC, Rob, WBC, We; all versions except NRSV, REB], 'spiritually' [NRSV], 'spiritual' [REB].

QUESTION—To what is the phrase ἐν ᾧ 'in whom' connected?
1. This refers to back to Χριστοῦ Ἰησοῦ 'Christ Jesus' in 2:20 [AB, Alf, Ba, Cal, Can, ECWB, Ho, ICC, MNTC, NIC, Rob, TH, WBC, We], making this verse parallel to 2:21 [Alf, ECWB, Ho, ICC, MNTC, NIC, Rob, TH, WBC, We]: in whom also you are being built together into a dwelling place of God in the Spirit. It is characteristic of this part of the epistle to string together these relative expressions, all referring to a common antecedent [Alf].
2. This refers back to the immediately preceding κυρίῳ 'Lord' of 2:21 [EGT, El, My]: in which Lord you also are being built together into a dwelling place of God in the Spirit.
3. This refers back to ναὸν ἅγιον 'holy temple' in 2:21 [Ea, NTC]: in which temple you also are being built together for a dwelling place of God in the Spirit. Taking ἐν ᾧ as 'in which' and referring it to the temple keeps the figure homogenous [Ea].

QUESTION—What is the force of the καὶ ὑμεῖς 'you also'?

The reference of ὑμεῖς 'you' is the same as that of 2:13 [EBC, ICC] or 2:19 [Ea]. This applies to these Ephesian, Gentile readers, what was said of the whole body of believers in the previous clause [Ho, MNTC, St, TNTC]. The ascensive and slightly contrasting καί 'also' [El] points to the dignity of their position [EGT, El].

QUESTION—What does συνοικοδομεῖσθε 'you are built together' mean?

This is a metaphor expressing the mutual coordination and support of the reconciled Jews and Gentiles as determined by the context, 2:13–19 [AB]. The sense is 'you are built together with all built in along with you' [Ea, ECWB, Ho, ICC, WBC] (implying that the process of being formed into the church must take place in company with other believers [WBC]), so that the verb has similar meaning and reference as συναρμολογουμένη 'being fitted together' in the previous verse [Ea, WBC]. Other commentators assert that being paralleled by συναρμολουμένη 'being fitted together' in the last clause, the meaning is rather the compact connection of one with another [EGT, El].

QUESTION—What relationship is indicated by εἰς 'into'?
1. It indicates the purpose or goal of the finite verb [Ba, Ea, EBC, MNTC, NTC, Rob, St, WBC, We; KJV, NAB, NIV]: you are built together that you might be a dwelling place.
2. It indicates the result of the finite verb [My]: you are being built together with the result that you will be a dwelling place.

QUESTION—What is meant by εἰς κατοικητήριον 'into a dwelling place'?

This phrase is an explanation of εἰς ναὸν ἅγιον 'for a holy temple' in the last verse [Ba, Ea, EGT, Ho, ICC, MNTC, NCBC, St] and defines the purpose of the holy temple as being a place where God dwells [Ba, Ea, EGT, ICC, MNTC, St]. The term is used frequently in the Septuagint [EBC, Rob, TD, WBC] to denote the Divine resting place, either on earth or in heaven [EBC, Rob, WBC].

QUESTION—To what is the phrase ἐν πνεύματι 'in (the) Spirit' attached?
1. It goes with θεοῦ 'God' [Alf, Can, Ea, EBC, El, Lns, NCBC, NIC, Si, St, TD, TH, TNTC, WBC, We, WeBC], denoting the manner or means of God's powerful presence [AB, Can, Ea, NCBC, WBC]: a dwelling place of God through his Spirit.
2. It goes with the verb συνοικοδομεῖσθε 'you are built' [EGT, Ho, My], denoting the way it is forged into a unit [AB]: you are built together by/in the Spirit.
3. It goes with κατοικητήριον 'dwelling place' [Cal, CBC, ICC, MNTC, TD], revealing the character of the building that is being constructed [AB, MNTC] and may have the meaning 'spiritual' [AB, Cal, CBC, MNTC, NTC, Rob, TD]: a spiritual dwelling place. It points out the superiority of the spiritual building compared to all Jewish and outward services [Cal, MNTC].

QUESTION—What relationship is indicated by ἐν 'in'?
It indicates means [CBC, Ho, NTC, WBC, WeBC] and may be translated 'by' [Ho, St, TNTC, WeBC] or 'by virtue of' [NTC]: by the Spirit. Some think that it denotes both the means and the sphere [EBC, ICC, NCBC, TD]: in the Spirit. God dwells in this building in, with, and by his Spirit [TD].

DISCOURSE UNIT: 3:1–4:24 [AB]. The topic is praise to God for the continuing work of God's revelation to and through his church.

DISCOURSE UNIT: 3:1–21 [Alf, Ba, Can, Ea, ECWB, Ho, IB, LJ, Lns, NTC, TH, We; KJV, NASB, REB]. The topic is the purpose of the church (1) in making known to the principalities and powers in heavenly places [IB, NTC] the wisdom of God [Alf, IB, NTC], the plan of salvation that incorporates the Gentiles [Ba], and (2) in the church learning more and more about God's love [NTC]. Other statements of topic are: Paul's appeal as the prisoner of Christ for the Gentiles [Can], the prayer for the Ephesians' fuller knowledge [ECWB; REB], the account of the apostle's call to the Gentiles and his prayer for the Ephesians' greater spiritual knowledge [Ea].

DISCOURSE UNIT: 3:1–13 [AB, Alf, EBC, ECWB, EGT, El, Ho, IB, Lns, MNTC, NCBC, NTC, Rob, St, TH, TNTC, WBC, We, WeBC; NASB, NIV, NJB, REB, TEV]. The topic is the church as God's mystery revealed in Christ [WeBC], the cosmic significance of the church as God's appointed instrument for the revelation of God's purposes to the spirit beings who rule the higher spheres [IB, NTC, TH], Paul's office and work as Apostle to the Gentiles [Alf, EBC, EGT, WBC; NASB, TEV], the commission God gave to Paul [AB, ECWB, El, Ho, Lns, MNTC, NCBC, TH], explaining the nature of the gospel as God revealed it to Paul [MNTC], and why Paul identifies his personal history with God's call of the Gentiles to salvation [AB, EGT, Lns, St, TH] as the basis for an affirmation of his authority for the obligations he lays upon his readers in the second half of the epistle (chapter 4–6) [TH].

DISCOURSE UNIT: 3:1–12 [Ba]. The topic is the commission to Paul to proclaim the inclusion of the Gentiles in God's plan of salvation.

DISCOURSE UNIT: 3:1–9 [ICC]. The topic is Paul's declaration that the truth of the inclusion of the Gentiles into God's plan of salvation has now been revealed to the apostles and prophets and that he has been especially privileged to make known this mystery to all men.

DISCOURSE UNIT: 3:1–6 [CBC, St, WeBC; NAB]. The topic is the special insight of the apostles and prophets into the revelation of God's secret [CBC], the revelation that was given to Paul [St], the commission to announce God's plan [NAB].

3:1 (For) this reason[a] I, Paul, the prisoner[b] of-Christ Jesus on-behalf-of[c] you the Gentiles[d]—

LEXICON—a. χάριν used as a preposition, with genitive object (LN 89.29, **89.60**) (BAGD 1. or 2. p. 877): 'reason', 'because of, by reason of' [LN (89.29)], 'on account of' [BAGD]. The phrase τούτου χάριν 'this reason' is translated 'for this reason' [AB, BAGD, NIC, NTC, WBC; NASB, NIV, TEV], 'for this cause' [El, Lns, Rob, We; KJV], 'for this purpose' [LN (**89.60**)], 'that is why' [NAB], 'this is why' [TEV, TNT], 'it is because of this' [NJB], 'this is the reason that' [NRSV], 'with this in mind' [REB]. This is a marker of purpose, and points to the goal of an event or state, 'for the purpose of' [LN (**89.60**)]. But in Eph. 3:1 it may well express reason [BAGD, LN (89.60)] with the implication of an underlying purpose [BAGD, LN (89.29)].

b. δέσμιος (LN 37.117) (BAGD p. 176): 'prisoner' [AB, BAGD, El, LN, Lns, NIC, NTC, Rob, WBC, We; all versions].

c. ὑπέρ with genitive object (LN 89.28, 90.36) (BAGD 1.a.ε. p. 838): 'on behalf of' [LN (90.36), We; NAB, NJB], 'in behalf of' [BAGD, Lns], 'for the sake of' [AB, BAGD, LN (90.36), NIC, NTC, WBC; NASB, NIV, NRSV, REB, TEV, TNT], 'for' [BAGD, El, LN (90.36), Rob; KJV], 'because of, in view of' [LN (89.28)].

d. ἔθνος: 'Gentile'. See this word at 2:11.

QUESTION—What is the construction of this verse?
1. This is a nominal sentence with an implied copulative verb εἰμί 'to be' [Ba, Bu, My; NRSV]: For this reason, I, Paul, *am* the prisoner of Christ Jesus for the sake of you Gentiles.
2. This is a broken construction with the phrase ὁ δέσμιος τοῦ Χριστοῦ Ἰησοῦ 'the prisoner of Christ Jesus' in apposition to ἐγὼ Παῦλος 'I, Paul' and the verb that Paul had intended to use here is found later in the context [AB, Alf, Can, CBC, Ea, EBC, ECWB, EGT, El, Ho, ICC, LJ, Lns, MNTC, NCBC, NIC, NTC, Rob, Si, St, TH, TNTC, WBC, We; KJV, NAB, NASB, NIV, NJB, REB, TEV, TNT].
   2.1 The sentence is resumed at 3:14 and the verb Paul had intended to use here belongs to the category of prayer [AB, Alf, CBC, Ea, EBC, ECWB,

EGT, El, Ho, ICC, LJ, Lns, MNTC, NCBC, NIC, NTC, Rob, St, TH, TNTC, WBC, We, WeBC; REB, TEV, TNT]: For this reason, I, Paul, the prisoner of Christ Jesus on behalf of you Gentiles, bow my knees to the Father, etc. Paul's intention is to resume his prayer for the saints (1:15ff.) but this is not carried out immediately [AB, Ea, EBC, Ho, MNTC, NIC, NTC, Rob, St, TNTC, WBC, WeBC]. The sentence begun here at 3:1 will be completed only after an extended parenthesis describing Paul's apostolic ministry [AB, Ea, EBC, LJ, MNTC, NIC, NTC, St, WBC], its basis in the revealed mystery [AB, MNTC, NTC, WeBC], its extension in the church's 'cosmic' service [AB, NTC], and its confirmation in the apostle's suffering and courageous endurance (3:2–13) [AB, Ea, LJ, NTC]. The emphatic repetition of τούτου χάριν 'for this reason' [ECWB, Rob] and the weight and finality of the sentence at 3:14 argues for the resumption of 3:1 there [ECWB].
  2.2 The sentence is resumed at 3:3 with the contents of that verse being what Paul had intended say here [NAB]: For this reason the mystery, as I have briefly written above, was made known by revelation to me, Paul, the prisoner of Christ Jesus on behalf of you Gentiles.
QUESTION—What relationship is indicated by the phrase τούτου χάριν 'for this reason'?
  1. It indicates purpose [LN (**89.60**), My] and refers back to 2:22 [My]: For this purpose, that you may be built into the dwelling of God by means of the Spirit I, Paul, am a prisoner of Christ Jesus.
  2. It indicates reason [AB, Alf, Ba, BAGD, Can, Ea, EBC, EGT, El, Ho, ICC, LJ, Lns, MNTC, NIC, NTC, Rob, TH, TNTC, WBC, We].
  2.1 This refers to everything previously covered in this epistle [NTC, TNTC]: because of the great things God has purposed in Christ, I, Paul bow my knees to the Father.
  2.2 This refers to the whole of chapter 2 [AB, Ea, El, ICC, LJ, Lns]: because God has raised you to life together with Christ, and united you, Jew and Gentile, to form the new spiritual temple, I, Paul, etc.
  2.3 This refers to 2:11–22 [Ba, EBC, Ho, Rob, TH, We], 2:13–22 [Can], or 2:18–22 [WBC]: because God has united Jew and Gentile together in Christ, I, Paul bow my knees to the Father. The preaching of the doctrine that the gospel was to be proclaimed to the Gentiles was the reason Paul was imprisoned [Ba, Can].
  2.4 This refers to 2:22 [Alf]: Because you are being built into a dwelling of God through the Spirit, I, Paul bow my knees to the Father.
  3. It is a loose transitional device used to move on to another point [NCBC].
QUESTION—What is the meaning of the genitive construction ὁ δέσμιος τοῦ Χριστοῦ Ἰησοῦ 'the prisoner of Christ Jesus'?
  1. 'Prisoner' is used in a literal sense [Alf, Ba, Can, DNTT, Ea, EBC, EGT, El, IB, ICC, MNTC, My, NCBC, TH].
  1.1 The genitive specifies the owner of the one who is the prisoner [DNTT]: the prisoner who belongs to Jesus Christ.

1.2 The genitive specifies the originating agent, or the cause of the imprisonment [Alf, Ea, EGT, El, IB, ICC, MNTC, My]: the prisoner because of Christ Jesus. Christ has caused the imprisonment [El, IB, ICC, MNTC].

1.3 The genitive specifies both the cause of the imprisonment and the person benefited by it [Can, NCBC, TH]: the prisoner because of and for the sake of Christ Jesus.

2. 'Prisoner' is used in a metaphorical sense [CBC, Si (probably)]. Paul will not admit he is the prisoner of the Roman Emperor, Nero. He is the captive only of Jesus [CBC, Si] who knows what is best for his cause [Si] and who controls his life [CBC]. The comparison is: just as a prisoner is held captive, I am held captive by Jesus. The point of comparison is the subjection of the life of a prisoner to the will of his captor. The nonfigurative statement would be: The circumstances of my life are totally controlled only by Christ Jesus.

3. The word is to be taken both literally and metaphorically [AB, St, TNTC, WBC, We, WeBC; and probably ECWB, ICC, TD] with the genitive specifying the owner of the prisoner [AB, Ho, LJ, Lns, NIC, NTC, TNTC]: Christ Jesus' prisoner.

QUESTION—What is the meaning of the preposition ὑπέρ 'on behalf of'?

The expression ὑπὲρ ὑμῶν τῶν ἐθνῶν 'on behalf of you Gentiles' is intentionally emphatic [Rob]. The primary meaning is that Paul was imprisoned because of his ministry on behalf of the Gentiles [AB, Alf, Ba, Cal, Ea, EBC, ECWB, EGT, Ho, ICC, LJ, Lns, MNTC, NCBC, NIC, NTC, Rob, Si-ed, St, TH, TNTC, WeBC]. It was Paul's preaching to the Gentiles that aroused the jealousy and hostility of the Jews, leading to his imprisonment [Alf, Cal, CBC, Ea, EBC, ECWB, EGT, Ho, LJ, Lns, MNTC, My, NCBC, NIC, NTC, Rob, Si-ed, St, WBC]. This imprisonment would work out to the benefit of Paul's Gentile readers [AB, Alf, ECWB, EGT, MNTC, My, NIC, TD, TNTC].

DISCOURSE UNIT: 3:2–13 [IB, My, NIC]. The topic is the mystery of Christ [NIC], the nature of Paul's apostleship, concluding in 3:13 with an exhortation to the readers not to be discouraged by Paul's sufferings [My].

DISCOURSE UNIT: 3:2–7 [LJ, NIC]. The topic is Paul's stewardship [NIC], the revelation of the mystery of Christ [LJ].

DISCOURSE UNIT: 3:2–6 [Rob]. The topic is a description of the mystery.

3:2 if[a] indeed you-heard-of the stewardship/plan[b] of-the grace[c] of God the-(one) given to me for[d] you,

LEXICON—a. εἰ (LN 89.65): 'if' [El, LN, Lns, TH, We; KJV, NASB]. The phrase εἴ γε 'if indeed' is translated 'surely' [NTC; NIV, NJB, REB, TEV, TNT], 'I am sure' [NAB], 'have you not (heard)' [NIC], 'inasmuch as' [BAGD], 'for surely' [NTC; NRSV, REB], 'if so be that' [Rob], 'assuming that of course' [WBC].

b. οἰκονομία (LN 30.68, 42.25) (BAGD 1.b. p. 559): 'stewardship' [BAGD, NIC, NTC, WBC; NASB], 'administration' [Lns, TH, We; NIV], 'management, direction' [BAGD], 'ministry' [NAB], 'dispensation' [El, Rob, We; KJV], 'commission' [LN (42.25); NRSV], 'task, responsibility' [LN (42.25)], 'a special responsibility' [TNT], 'purpose, scheme, plan, arrangement' [LN (30.68)]. This noun is also translated as a verb: 'to administer' [AB], 'to entrust' [NJB], 'to design' [REB], 'to do work' [TEV]. This word denotes a task involving organization and management [LN (42.25)] or a plan involving a set of arrangements [LN (30.68)]. See this word at 1:10.

c. χάρις (LN 57.103, 88.66) (BAGD 4. p. 878): 'grace' [AB, El, LN (88.66), Lns, NIC, NTC, Rob, TH, WBC, We; all versions except NAB, TNT], 'goodness' [NAB], 'graciousness, kindness' [LN (88.66)], 'gracious purpose' [TNT], 'favor, gracious deed' [BAGD], 'gift' [BAGD, LN (57.103)] 'gracious gift' [LN (57.103)]. This term denotes showing kindness to someone, implying graciousness on the part of the one showing the kindness [LN]. The word is used to express the exceptional effects produced by God's grace, above and beyond that usually experienced by Christians [BAGD].

d. εἰς with accusative object (LN 90.41): 'for' [LN, Lns, NIC, TH, WBC; NASB, NIV, NRSV], 'on behalf of' [LN], 'to' [AB], 'toward' [El, Rob, We; KJV]. The phrase εἰς ὑμᾶς 'for you' is translated in various ways: 'for your sake' [NJB], 'for your benefit' [NTC; REB], 'in your regard' [NAB], 'for your good' [TEV], 'to tell you' [TNT]. It means 'on your behalf' or 'in your interests' [EBC, MNTC, TH]. The grace was given to Paul for their benefit [EBC, TH, WBC]. According to others, it indicates direction 'to you, toward you' [Alf, Ba, Ea, El], 'to be dispensed in your direction' [Alf], 'to work in you' [El]. One calls it the ethical direction [EGT]. According to others, it means 'in reference to you' [Ho, My].

QUESTION—What do the particles εἴ γε 'if indeed' mean?

1. They express an assumption [AB, Alf, Ba, EBC, ECWB, EGT, El, Ho, IB, LJ, Lns, MNTC, NIC, TH, WBC], or even certainty [Ea, EBC, EGT, El, My, NTC, Rob, TNTC, WBC, We]: as you have heard, or, as you have certainly heard. The Ephesians had heard this and this is a delicate or polite way of reminding them of it [Alf, EGT, El, Ho, Lns, My].

2. They express a degree of doubt [Cal, Can (probably), ICC]: if you have heard. This particle may be used where a writer is practically certain, but a doubt is conceivable [ICC].

QUESTION—To what event or events does the word ἠκούσατε 'you heard' refer?

1. This refers to the messages these readers had heard from Paul's own lips [Alf, Ea, El, We]: as indeed you heard from me when I preached among you.

2. This refers to reports of Paul's ministry that these readers had heard from others who were acquainted with Paul [AB, Can, CBC, IB, ICC, MNTC,

WBC]: if/as indeed you have heard from others who know of my ministry. This and 1:15 are references which indicate that the apostle was known to these readers by reputation only [AB, MNTC].
3. This refers to both of the above [EBC, ECWB, Lns, My, NIC, Rob, TNTC]: as indeed you have heard, either from me or from those acquainted with my ministry. There is a vague generality about the expression which well suits an encyclical letter to the Asiatic churches generally; and probably would not have been used in a letter sent particularly to a church so beloved and well known to him as that of the Ephesians [ECWB, TNTC]. This language is due to the fact that Paul had been absent from the church for some time [Lns, NTC], and in the interval other Gentiles whom Paul had not personally instructed had come into the congregation [Lns].
4. This refers to the matter of the calling of the Gentiles which Paul had not previously discussed with them during his years of ministry among them [Cal]: if, indeed, you heard (since I have not discussed this with you previously).
5. This refers to the event of Paul having been imprisoned [Ba]: assuming you heard of my imprisonment. Paul is concerned that they will be grieved over the fact that he was imprisoned on their account and he wants to assure them that this was by the appointment of God, and was just one part of an eternal purpose.

QUESTION—What is meant by the phrase τὴν οἰκονομίαν τῆς χάριτος τοῦ θεοῦ 'the stewardship/plan of the grace of God'?
1. Οἰκονομία refers to the office or work of a steward or manager [AB, Alf, DNTT, Ho, IB, IDB, ISBE, ISBE2, LJ, Lns, NCBC, NIC, TD, TH, TNTC, WBC, We; NASB] and means 'stewardship' [AB, Ho, IB, NCBC, NIC, TNTC, WBC, We; NASB]. By referring to Paul as an οἰκονόμος 'house-steward, manager', some commentators see a metaphor here [Alf, DNTT, ISBE2, LJ, NCBC].
  1.1 Οἰκονομία 'stewardship' refers to Paul's office of apostleship [Ho, LJ, Lns, TD, TNTC, WBC, We].
    1.1.1 Χάριτος 'of grace' refers to God's gift to Paul of the office of apostle [Ho, Lns]: you heard of the stewardship God gave me, that is, of his gift of being an apostle.
    1.1.2 Χάριτος 'of grace' refers to God being gracious to Paul in choosing him for the office of apostle to the Gentiles [WBC, We]: you heard of the stewardship that God in his grace gave to me.
    1.1.3 Χάριτος 'of grace' refers to both of the above [LJ, TNTC], as well as to other gifts given to Paul [LJ]. The office of apostleship itself was a grace [LJ, TNTC]. But it also includes the idea that when God called a man to be an apostle, by grace he equipped him to be an apostle with certain ordinary and extraordinary gifts [LJ].
  1.2 Οἰκονομία 'stewardship' refers to Paul's stewardship of proclaiming some particular grace given by God [AB, Alf, IB, ISBE2, NCBC, NIC,

TH]: you heard of the stewardship to proclaim God's grace, a stewardship given to me by God. The same grace of God which is given to all the saints was given to Paul the apostle for the sake of all Gentiles. This also involves his assignment as an apostle to serve in the salvation of the Gentiles [AB].

1.2.1 Χάριτος 'of grace' refers to Paul's knowledge of the mystery given to him by revelation [IB]: you heard of the knowledge of the mystery God so graciously gave me to proclaim to you. Χάριτος 'of grace' means that which God out of his grace has bestowed, and as the sequel shows, it means specifically the knowledge of the mystery Paul received by revelation. 'Grace' and 'stewardship' are virtually identical [IB].

1.2.2 Χάριτος 'of grace' refers to Paul's commission to evangelize the Gentiles, viewed as a gift [TH]: you heard how God gave me a special task, the gift of proclaiming salvation to you Gentiles.

1.2.3 Χάριτος 'of grace' refers to God's saving grace as presented in the gospel [Alf, NCBC, NIC]: you heard how God gave me a special task, to proclaim God's gift of salvation.

1.2.4 Χάριτος 'of grace' refers to all three of the above [AB].

2. Οἰκονομία 'plan' refers to an arrangement or plan God made with regard to the salvation of the Gentiles [Ba, Can, Ea, EBC, ECWB, EGT, El, ICC, MNTC, My, NTC, Rob; REB]. All except ICC regard this as a metaphor.

2.1 Χάριτος 'of grace' refers to the grace God showed to Paul in choosing him for the office of apostle to the Gentiles [Ea, EBC, EGT, El, My]: you heard of the plan in which God graciously chose me to be an apostle to you Gentiles. The word refers to the gift of grace that chose Paul [EGT] and qualified him [EGT, El] for the apostolic office, and assisted him in the exercise of that office [El].

2.2 Χάριτος 'of grace' refers to Paul's spiritual gift of evangelizing Gentiles [MNTC]: you heard of the plan in which God gave me, the gift of proclaiming the gospel to you Gentiles. Paul's use of χάρις 'grace' here equates with spiritual gifts, specifically the gift given him for evangelizing the Gentiles [MNTC].

2.3 Χάριτος 'of grace' refers to God's saving grace as presented in the gospel [Can, ECWB, Rob]: you heard of God's plan for graciously giving his salvation to all people, the message of which was given to me. By the grace given to him we understand the revelation of God's Son in him so that Paul might preach Christ to the Gentiles with the message of personal reconciliation to God [Can].

QUESTION—To what is the articular aorist participle τῆς δοθείσης 'which was given' connected?

Most connect this participle to τῆς χάριτος τοῦ θεοῦ 'the grace of God' [AB, Alf, Can, ECWB, EGT, El, Ho, ICC, LJ (probably), Lns, MNTC, My, NCBC, Rob, WBC; NJB, REB]. Others connect it with οἰκονομίαν 'stewardship/plan' [IB, TH; NAB, TEV, TNT; and probably NASB, NIV, NRSV].

3:3 that[a] by[b] revelation[c] the mystery[d] was-made-known[e] to-me,

LEXICON—a. ὅτι (LN 91.15): 'that' [LN, Lns, NIC, TH, WBC; NASB], 'how that' [El, NTC, Rob, We; KJV], 'that is' [LN; NIV], 'namely, namely that' [LN], 'how' [TNT], 'and how' [NRSV], not explicit [NAB, NJB]. Some begin a new sentence here and do not translate this particle [AB; REB, TEV]. This is a marker of identificational and explanatory clauses. Such markers do not enter into the internal syntactic structure of the clauses they mark [LN].

b. κατά with accusative object (LN 89.4, 89.8) (BAGD II.5.a.δ. p. 407): 'by' [AB, BAGD, El, Lns, NIC, NTC, Rob, TH, We; KJV, NASB, NIV, NJB, NRSV, REB], 'according to' [BAGD, WBC], 'in accordance with' [BAGD, LN (89.8)], 'in relation to' [LN (89.4, 89.8)]. Some do not translate κατά, but change ἀποκάλυψις 'revelation' to a verb [NAB, TEV, TNT].

c. ἀποκάλυψις (LN 28.38) (BAGD 2. p. 92): 'revelation' [AB, BAGD, El, LN, Lns, NIC, NTC, Rob, TH, WBC, We; KJV, NASB, NIV, NJB, NRSV, REB], 'disclosure' [BAGD]. Some translate this noun as a verb: 'to be revealed' [NAB], 'to reveal' [TEV, TNT]. The reference must not be limited to one instance of revelation only [AB, LJ, MNTC, My, NTC, WeBC]. See this word at 1:17.

d. μυστήριον (LN 28.77) (BAGD 2. p. 530): 'mystery' [BAGD, El, LN, Lns, NIC, NTC, Rob, WBC, We; KJV, NASB, NIV, NJB, NRSV], 'secret' [AB, BAGD, LN, MM, TH], 'secret plan' [NAB, TEV], 'secret design' [TNT], 'secret purpose' [REB]. See this word at 1:9.

e. aorist pass. indic. of γνωρίζω (LN 28.26) (BAGD 1. p. 163): 'to be made known' [AB, BAGD, El, LN, Lns, NIC, NTC, Rob, TH, WBC, We; NASB, NIV, NRSV, REB], 'to be revealed' [BAGD]. Some translate this passive verb actively: 'to make known' [MM; KJV, NJB, TEV]. Some conflate this verb with the noun ἀποκάλυψις 'revelation' and translate it as a verb: 'to be revealed' [NAB, TNT]. God is the implied actor in this passive verb [My, TH].

QUESTION—What is the function of the particle ὅτι 'that'?

This is an epexegetical particle that introduces an explanation of 3:2 [Alf, Ea, El, ICC, LN (91.15)]: 'if indeed you heard of the administration of the grace of God, (the grace) that was given me for you, namely that by revelation the mystery was made known to me'. Therefore this clause serves as a supplementary accusative to the previous verb ἠκούσατε 'you heard' [Ea], making clear the nature of this administration of χάρις 'grace' [EBC, EGT, El, TH].

QUESTION—What relationship is indicated by κατά 'by'?

1. It indicates the manner in which the revelation was made known [AB, Ea, EGT, El, Ho, ICC, My, We]: God made the mystery known to me by way

EPHESIANS 3:3   199

of revelation. The emphasis obviously falls on the predication of manner [El]. This preposition, with its object, ἀποκάλυψιν 'revelation' in the accusative case, has here an adverbial force [Ea, My] and describes the form which the disclosure of the μυστήριον 'mystery' took [Ea], the manner in which it was made known [EGT, My, We]. The immediacy of communication between God and the writer is emphasized, not the specific means by which this communication was distinct from others [AB].
  2. It indicates that revelation was the norm or standard by which the mystery was made known [BAGD, WBC]: God made the mystery known to me in accordance with the standard set by revelation.
QUESTION—What is meant by μυστήριον 'mystery'?
Refer to 1:9 for the cultural background and connotations of the word. It refers to an eternal decision of God, formerly hidden from men, but which has now been revealed and must be proclaimed to the world [AB, Can, Ea, IDB, ISBE, ISBE2, Lns, St].
  1. It has specific reference to the revealed truth that Gentiles as well as Jews are called to be the people of God and are united together as equal partners in Christ to form the church [AB, Alf, Ba, BAGD, Ea, EBC, EGT, El, Ho, ICC, IDB, ISBE, ISBE2, Lns, My, NCBC, NTC, Rob, St, TH, TNTC, WBC, We, WeBC].
  2. It refers generally to God's plan of redemption through Christ [CBC, IB, LJ].

as[a] I-wrote-before in brief,[b]
LEXICON—a. καθώς (LN 64.14): 'as' [AB, El, NIC, NTC, Rob, TH, WBC, We; KJV, NAB, NASB, NIV, NRSV, TNT], 'even as' [Lns], 'just as' [LN], not explicit [NJB, REB, TEV].
  b. ὀλίγος (LN 67.106) (BAGD 3.b. p. 563): 'brief' [BAGD, LN (67.106), Lns, NIC; NASB]. The phrase ἐν ὀλίγῳ 'in brief' is translated 'briefly' [AB, LN, TH, WBC; NAB, NIV, NJB, TEV, TNT], 'a brief account' [REB], 'in a few words' [El, NTC, Rob, We; KJV, NRSV].
QUESTION—Does this clause introduce parenthetical material?
  1. It begins a parenthesis which extends through the end of 3:4 [ECWB, LJ, Lns, MNTC, We; KJV, NRSV, TEV]. The words are parenthetic, unfolding St. Paul's peculiar endowments compared to the men of old time [We]. The words suggest they were inserted by the author later as he read over what he had dictated [ECWB]. The words in the parenthesis are a subsidiary statement. The main statement is: (v. 3) 'how that by revelation he made known unto me the mystery, (v. 5) which in other ages was not made known unto the sons of men, as it is now revealed unto his holy apostles and prophets by the Spirit; that the Gentiles should be fellow-heirs, and of the same body' [LJ].
  2. It begins a parenthesis which extends through the end of 3:5 [TH]. The thought logically passes from 'the mystery was made known to me' to the

beginning of 3:6 giving the contents of the mystery, 'that the Gentiles are' with 3:3b–5 constituting a digression from the main thought.
3. It is followed by a parenthesis which comprise 3:4–5 [AB, Ea, El, Ho, My, NIC, NTC, Rob, WBC; NAB, NASB, NIV, NJB]. This clause should not be regarded as a parenthesis, inasmuch as the relative ὅ 'which' in 3:5 is connected to ἐν τῷ μυστηρίῳ τοῦ Χριστοῦ 'in the mystery of Christ' at the end of 3:4 [Ea, El, My, NTC, WBC].

QUESTION—To what event does this clause refer?
1. It refers to something written previously in this epistle and so means 'to write above' [AB, Alf, Can, DNTT, Ea, EBC, ECWB, EGT, El, HG, Ho, IB, ICC, LJ, Lns, MNTC, My, NTC, Rob, Si-ed, TD, TH, TNTC, WBC, We, WeBC]: as I have (just) briefly written above. Some refer it to 1:9–10 [Alf, Can, IB], others to the latter half of chapter 2 [Ea, ICC, My, TH, TNTC, We], and others to both [AB, ECWB, EGT, Ho, LJ, MNTC, NCBC, NTC, Si-ed, WBC, WeBC]. The implication is that he is about to speak more fully of something which he has expressed in summary form before [IB].
2. It refers to something written previously in another or other epistles and so means 'to write before' [Cal, CBC]: as I have briefly written before.

3:4 in-accordance-with[a] which, reading (this),

LEXICON—a. πρός with accusative object (LN 89.9) (BAGD III.5.d. p. 710): 'in accordance with' [BAGD, El, LN, WBC], 'according to' [LN, TH], 'in view of' [Lns], 'by reference to' [NIC], not explicit [NJB, NRSV]. One translates this preposition by a participial phrase: 'and by referring to' [NASB]. Some translate the whole phrase πρὸς ὅ 'in accordance with which' by a conjunction: 'whereby' [NTC, Rob, We; KJV], 'and' [REB, TEV], 'then' [NIV], or by an adverb: 'correspondingly' [AB]. Some merely start a new sentence here [NAB, TNT].

QUESTION—What is the function and meaning of πρὸς ὅ 'in accordance with which'?

It refers back to προέγραψα 'I wrote' in the previous clause, or more properly, to the written material to which that verb refers [Alf, EGT, El, ICC, My, NIC, NTC, TD], linking this verse to that clause [Alf, EBC, Ho, My, NIC, NTC]. It has the meaning of 'in reference to which' [Ea; NASB], 'in accordance with which' [El, My, WBC], 'having regard to which' [Rob], or 'looking to which' [IB, Rob, We]. The preposition indicates the standard or measure of Paul's knowledge of the subject [AB, EGT, El, Ho, My] or the standard of evaluation or judgment the readers are to form of the writer's insight into the subject, when they read what he has written [WBC].

QUESTION—What relationship is indicated by the use of the present participle ἀναγινώσκοντες 'reading'?
1. It indicates time [Ea, EBC, El, IB, ICC, My, NIC, NTC, Rob, TNTC, WBC, We; KJV, NAB, NASB]: when, as, while you read, you will gain perception.

2. It indicates means [AB, Ba, Cal, Lns, TH; REB]: by reading, you will gain perception. One translates it as the protasis of a conditional sentence: if you will read, you will gain perception [TEV].

you-are-able to-perceive[a] my understanding[b] in the mystery[c] of-Christ,

LEXICON—a. aorist act. infin. of νοέω (LN 32.2) (BAGD 1.a. p. 540): 'to perceive' [AB, BAGD, El, LN, Lns, NTC, Rob, WBC, We; NJB, NRSV], 'to understand' [BAGD, LN; KJV, NASB, NIV], 'to comprehend' [LN], 'to apprehend' [BAGD], 'to know' [TH], 'to see' [REB], 'to gain insight into' [BAGD, LN], 'to discern' [NIC], 'to learn about' [TEV], 'to realize' [NAB, TNT]. This term denotes the rational reflection or inner contemplation of a matter [BAGD]. It denotes the comprehension of something on the basis of careful thought and consideration [LN].

b. σύνεσις (LN **32.6**) (BAGD 2. p. 788): 'understanding' [BAGD, El, LN, Rob, TH, We; NJB, NRSV, TEV], 'knowledge' [KJV], 'insight' [BAGD, Lns, NIC, NTC, WBC; NASB, NIV], 'what is understood' [LN]. This noun is also translated as a verb: 'to understand' [AB; REB, TNT], or a clause: 'to know what one is talking about' [NAB].

c. μυστήριον: 'mystery'. See this word at 3:3.

QUESTION—How are the nouns related in the genitive construction τῷ μυστηρίῳ τοῦ Χριστοῦ 'the mystery of Christ'?

1. The relationship is one of apposition [AB, Alf, Can, El, Ho, My, NIC, NTC, St, TNTC, WBC]: the mystery which is Christ. The secret is the Messiah: his place with the Father, the various aspects of his preaching, commission and work, his exaltation, etc. [AB, My]. The parallel in Col. 1:27 clearly demonstrates that this is the appositional use of the genitive [Alf, Ho, My]. Others further specify the relationship, saying the genitive identifies [El], defines [NIC] the mystery, or denotes Christ as the content of the mystery [WBC]. Others say that the genitive states not only the substance of the mystery, but also its source (cf. 3. below) [NTC, St].
2. The mystery is about Christ [Cal, Ea, EBC, EGT, ICC, Lns]: the mystery concerning Christ. What he had called the μυστήριον 'mystery' he now calls the μυστήριον τοῦ Χριστοῦ 'mystery about Christ' because it was necessary that this mystery remain hidden until it was revealed by his coming. The calling of the Gentiles was to be fulfilled under the reign of Christ [Cal]. This is the revelation of the long-hidden purpose of God concerning Christ as savior not for the Jews only, but also for the Gentiles [EGT].
3. Christ is the author or source of the mystery [TH; REB]: the mystery which was put into effect by Christ. It is the secret purpose of Christ [REB].

QUESTION—What is this mystery?

1. This μυστήριον 'mystery' again has specific reference to the incorporation of Gentiles along with Jews into the Body of Christ as in the previous verse and in 3:6 [AB, Ba, CBC (probably), Ea, EBC, EGT, ICC,

IDB, ISBE, ISBE2, MNTC, My, NCBC, NIC, NTC, St, TD, TH, TNTC, WBC, We, WeBC]. The phrase should not be interpreted to mean there are other mysteries besides the messianic one. The one 'mystery' is the mystery of Christ. The inclusion of the Gentiles into the body of Christ (and the mystery of Christ in them in Col. 1:27) is not a further mystery added to the mystery of Christ. To speak of the Messiah who includes the Gentiles in his body is to speak about the one revealed secret of God [AB]. The mystery of Christ is Christ, through his Spirit, actually dwelling in the hearts of both Jews and Gentiles, united together in one body, the church [NTC].

2. This μυστήριον 'mystery' has reference to the whole gospel of redemption [Ho, LJ, Lns]. This is the same μυστήριον 'mystery' as in 3:3, but different from the one that will be expounded in 3:6. The reference to the 'mystery of Christ' here in 3:4 is to the *general* 'mystery' of the whole gospel of salvation—what he has already been expounding to these Ephesians. The 'mystery' he will treat in 3:6 is the *particular* 'mystery' of the inclusion of the Gentiles, a truth kept secret from previous generations [LJ]. Two commentators change their interpretation of 'mystery' from 3:3 and state that the mystery here, which incorporates the whole gospel, is somewhat broader in scope than 3:3 [Ho, Lns].

3:5 which in-other[a] generations[b] (was) not made-known[c] to-the sons[d] of-men

LEXICON—a. ἕτερος (LN 58.37) (BAGD 1.b.β. p. 315): 'other' [AB, BAGD, El, LN, Lns, NIC, NTC, Rob, TH, WBC, We; KJV, NASB, NIV], 'former' [NAB, NRSV, REB], 'previous' [NJB], 'past' [TEV], 'earlier' [TNT].

b. γενεά (LN 67.144) (BAGD 3.b. p. 154): 'generation' [AB, El, Lns, NIC, NTC, Rob, TH, WBC, We; NASB, NIV, NJB, NRSV, REB, TNT], 'age' [BAGD, LN; KJV, NAB], 'time' [BAGD; TEV], 'epoch' [LN]. The word denotes a 'period of time' generally [BAGD]. The word denotes an indefinite period of time, but in some contexts dealing with human existence, it denotes a period of time about the length of a generation [LN].

c. aorist pass. indic. of γνωρίζω: 'to be made known'. See this word in 3:3. The actor in this passive verb is God [AB, EGT, My, TH, WBC]. Specifically, the term is used here for God's declaration concerning his secret counsel of salvation [TD].

d. υἱός (LN 9.2) (BAGD 1.c.β. p. 833): 'sons' [AB, BAGD, El, LN, Lns, NTC, Rob, TH, We; KJV, NASB], 'children' [NIC]. Others translate the entire phrase υἱοὶ τῶν ἀνθρώπων 'sons of men' as a unit: 'men' [NAB, NIV], 'humanity' [NJB], 'humankind' [NRSV], 'mankind' [LN; REB, TEV, TNT], 'people' [BAGD, LN, WBC]. The phrase υἱοὶ τῶν ἀνθρώπων 'sons of men' is a Semitic idiom designating human beings and is equivalent in meaning to ἄνθρωπος 'man' in the plural [LN].

QUESTION—What is the referent of the relative pronoun ὅ 'which'?
Some refer it back to μυστήριον 'mystery' of 3:3 [Bu, Ea, Ho, LJ, NIC, NTC, St, We]. Others feel the referent should be the closer μυστηρίῳ τοῦ Χριστοῦ 'mystery of Christ' in the preceding clause [Cal, Lns, NTC], since it includes the mystery concerning the Gentiles [Cal, Lns].

QUESTION—What is the meaning of the phrase ἑτέραις γενεαῖς 'in other generations'?
Most commentators regard this as a temporal phrase [AB, Alf, Cal, Ea, EGT, El, IB, ICC, Lns, Mo, My, NCBC, NIC, NTC, Rob, Si-ed, St, TH, Tu, WBC, We; all versions], most translating it 'in other generations', the dative case giving it a punctiliar sense as a point of time [Mo, Tu]. Two commentators regard it as the indirect object of the passive verb οὐκ ἐγνωρίσθη 'it was not made known' and translate it 'to other generations' (the phrase τοῖς υἱοῖς τῶν ἀνθρώπων 'to the sons of men' being regarded as an explanatory apposition to ἑτέραις γενεαῖς 'in other generations') [ECWB, Ho]. The word γενεά 'generation' signifies here the time occupied by the average length of human life, 'a generation' [Ea, EGT, Ho], or about 33 years [ISBE], (and signifies as well the 'generation' or 'race' itself [EGT, Ho]), the plural form designating a succession of these times [AB, Ea]. To others, a γενεά 'generation' is the period from a man's birth to the birth of his son [IDB], or from his prime to that of his son [ISBE2], as well as standing, collectively, for the people who live in that period [IDB, ISBE2]. Some accept the translation of γενεαῖς as 'ages' [Cal, El, ISBE2, NTC, TD; KJV, NAB]. The phrase stands for all the past ages prior to the one designated by νῦν 'now' [Ea, ICC, My, NCBC, TH, WBC]. The use of the adjective ἑτέραις 'other' suggests the thought of two series of generations, one series before and the other series after the Incarnation [We].

QUESTION—What is meant by the phrase τοῖς υἱοῖς τῶν ἀνθρώπων 'to the sons of men'?
1. This refers to specifically elected servants of God in Old Testament times [AB, Cal]: which in other generations was not made known to God's chosen servants.
2. This was an Old Testament reference to mankind generally [Alf, Ba, Can, CBC, DNTT, Ea, EBC, ECWB, EGT, IB, ICC, WBC]: which in other generations was not made known to mankind. The expression designates the successive band of men whose lives were measured by the previously mentioned passing γενεαί 'generations' [Ea].

as[a] now it-was-revealed[b] to-the holy[c] apostles[d] of-him and prophets[e] by[f] (the) Spirit,[g]

LEXICON—a. ὡς (LN 64.12): 'as' [AB, El, LN, Lns, NIC, NTC, Rob, TH, WBC, We; KJV, NASB, NIV, NJB, NRSV, TNT], 'like' [LN], 'but' [NAB, REB, TEV].

b. aorist pass. indic. of ἀποκαλύπτω (LN 28.38) (BAGD 2. p. 92): 'to be revealed' [AB, BAGD, El, LN, Lns, NIC, NTC, Rob, TH, WBC, We; all versions except TEV, TNT]. This passive verb is also translated as active with 'God' or 'the Spirit' acting as subject: 'to reveal' [TEV, TNT]. This verb denotes the action of causing something to be fully known [LN]. The verb is placed forward in this clause to emphasize it [Lns].

c. ἅγιος (LN 53.46) (BAGD 1.b.α. p. 9): 'holy' [AB, BAGD, El, Lns, NIC, NTC, Rob, TH, WBC, We; all versions], 'dedicated' [LN], 'consecrated to God' [BAGD], 'devout' [LN]. This term denotes something or someone as being dedicated or consecrated to the service of God [LN].

d. ἀπόστολος: 'apostle'. See this word at 2:20.

e. προφήτης: 'prophet'. See this word at 2:20.

f. ἐν with dative object (LN 90.6): 'by' [BAGD, El, LN, NTC, WBC; KJV, NAB, NIV, NRSV, REB, TEV], 'through' [AB, BAGD], 'in' [BAGD, NIC, Rob, TH, We; NASB, NJB], 'in connection with' [Lns]. One indicates agency by making 'Spirit' the subject of ἀποκαλύπτω 'to reveal' and translates this in the active voice: 'the Spirit has now revealed it' [TNT]. This is a marker of agent, and often implies that the agent is used as an instrument [El, LN].

g. πνεῦμα (LN 12.18) (BAGD 5.d.β. p. 677): 'Spirit' [AB, BAGD, El, LN, Lns, NIC, NTC, Rob, WBC, We; all versions except REB], 'spirit' [TH], 'inspiration' [REB].

QUESTION—What is the relationship to each other of the two passive verbs ἐγνωρίσθη 'was made known' and ἀπεκαλύφθη 'was revealed'?

The verbs are synonyms [AB, Can, My, TD], standing in contrast to each other [Can, Ea, EGT, IB, ICC, My, WBC]. Some commentators regard them to be in a generic-specific relationship [Can, Ea, EGT, ICC, My, TD], ἐγνωρίσθη 'was (not) made known' being general and covering all kinds and ways of obtaining knowledge [Can], and ἀπεκαλύφθη 'was revealed' designating the special way of divine illumination [Can, EGT, ICC, My]. Others regard them to be full synonyms here [AB, NIC (probably)], saying the accent is not upon a specific *mode* of conveying information, but upon the fact that a secret is 'made known' to man by God himself [AB]. By some God is seen as the actor in both of these passive verbs [EGT, My, TH, WBC], by others the Spirit is the actor in ἀπεκαλύφθη 'was revealed' [El, Ho; TNT].

QUESTION—What comparison does the particle ὡς 'as' convey?

1. It compares (and contrasts) the state of ignorance with the state of knowledge about the Jew-Gentile unity and equality [AB, Ba, Can, NCBC, NIC, St, WBC], or the universality of the gospel [IB], in previous and present generations: this mystery concerning the fact of Jews and Gentiles being united on an equal basis into one body was not made known in other generations to the sons of men as it has now been revealed. While Paul knew and cited Old Testament anticipations of God's universal grace [Can, NIC], here he is thinking in terms of the broad general contrast of the ages: human ignorance and divine revelation [Can, IB]. This was a radically new revelation [St].

2. It compares the degrees of revelation concerning the place of the Gentiles in God's kingdom in previous and present generations [Alf, Cal, CBC, Ea, EBC, EGT, El, Ho, ICC, LJ, Lns, My, NTC, Si, TNTC, We, WeBC]: this mystery concerning the participation of Gentiles in God's kingdom was not made known in other generations to the sons of men to the same extent as it has now been revealed. The Old Testament prophets knew that some communication of God's grace would be made to the Gentiles [Cal, CBC, Ea, EBC, Ho, LJ, NTC, Si, We], but they had no information on when and, especially, how it would come about [Cal, CBC, Ea].

QUESTION—To whom does the possessive pronoun αὐτοῦ 'his' refer?

1. It refers to God [Ea, EGT, My, TH, WBC; NIV]: to God's holy apostles and prophets. The referent is God, whose action is implied in the passive verbs ἐγνωρίσθη 'was (not) made known' and ἀπεκαλύφθη 'was revealed' [My, TH, WBC]. The source passage, Col. 1:26, supports this [WBC].
2. It refers to Christ [Can, We]: to Christ's holy apostles and prophets. The αὐτοῦ 'his' naturally goes back to Χριστοῦ 'of Christ' in 3:4 [We].

QUESTION—To what is the adjective ἁγίοις 'holy' attached?

1. It goes with ἀποστόλοις 'apostles' [Ea, ECWB, ICC, IDB, TNTC, WBC]. It is primarily the apostles who are designated as the recipients of revelation and who, therefore, deserve to be called 'holy'. The prophets are covered under this only because they are intimately connected with revelation [WBC].
2. It goes with both ἀποστόλοις 'apostles' and προφήταις 'prophets' [AB, Alf, Can, EGT, Ho, IB, Lns, MNTC, My, TH]. The fact that the phrase τοῖς...ἀποστόλοις...καὶ προφήταις 'to the apostles and prophets' is interpreted to refer to these men as a single class or group (making the apostles to also be prophets) argues for attaching ἁγίοις 'holy' to the whole phrase [Lns].

QUESTION—What does the adjective ἁγίοις 'holy' mean here?

1. It has its usual meaning of being set apart or consecrated for service to God [AB, Alf, El, Ho, ICC, Lns, MNTC, My, Rob, Si, TNTC] or as belonging to him [Can, Ea, EGT]. It does not apply to personal character [ECWB, ICC, MNTC] but to official call and privilege [ECWB, El].
2. It means to have a special degree of personal holiness [NCBC] or special reverence [IB, NCBC, NIC, TD, TH, WBC].

QUESTION—Who are these prophets and how are they related to the apostles?

These are the prophets of the New Testament church [AB, Alf, Ba, Cal, Can, CBC, DNTT, Ea, EGT, El, Ho, IB, ICC, IDB, ISBE2, Lns, NIC, Rob, Si, TD, TNTC, WBC; NJB (note)]. This is shown by the fact that προφήταις 'prophets' occurs in the clause governed by νῦν 'now' [Lns]. Since a single article governs both ἀποστόλοις 'apostles' and προφήταις 'prophets', some conclude that both of these offices are united into a single class of people as in 2:20 [HG, Lns]. Others treat 'prophets' as a distinct class of teachers separate from the apostles [Ba, NIC], one noting that the common article here cannot be pressed to make 'apostles and prophets' refer to the same persons [NIC].

3:6 the Gentiles[a] to-be fellow-heirs[b] and members-of-the-same-body[c]

LEXICON—a. ἔθνος: 'Gentiles'. See this word at 3:1.
    b. συγκληρονόμος (LN 57.134) (BAGD p. 774): 'fellow heir' [El, LN, Lns, MM, NIC, Rob; KJV, NASB, NRSV], 'fellow-heir with Israel' [We], 'joint heir' [AB, WBC], 'joint heir with the Jews' [REB], 'heirs together with Israel' [NIV], 'fellow-sharers in the inheritance' [NTC], 'inheriting together with' [BAGD], 'coinheritor' [TH], 'co-heir with the Jews' [NAB], 'one who also receives, receiver' [LN]. This noun is also conflated with the preceding infinitive of εἰμί 'to be' and translated as a verb phrase: 'to have the same inheritance' [NJB], 'to have a part with the Jews' [TEV], 'to share with us Jews in the privileges' [TNT]. This noun denotes one who is designated as the receiver of an unearned gift together with someone else. Heirs of God are those who receive the blessings that God has for his people [LN].
    c. σύσσωμος (LN **11.9**) (BAGD p. 794): 'members of the same body' [NIC; NAB, NRSV, TEV], 'members in the same body' [AB], 'fellow-members of the body' [NTC, Rob; NASB], 'fellow-members of the one body' [We], 'joint members of the body' [WBC], 'members together of one body' [NIV], 'belonging to the same body' [BAGD], 'of the same body' [El; KJV], 'part of the same body' [REB], 'fellow body members' [Lns], 'co-member' [LN], 'concorporate' [TH], 'fellow-slave' [MM]. This noun is also translated as a verb: 'to form the same body' [NJB], 'to share in membership of the body' [TNT]. This term denotes a person who is a member of a group and emphasizes this person's coordinate relationship with other members of that group [LN].

QUESTION—How does Paul use τὰ ἔθνη 'the Gentiles' in this verse?
    1. It is used as synecdoche, the whole being put for the part [Can]: those Gentiles who believe the gospel. The revelation is that the Gentiles really are all that is spoken here of them. What is said in this verse is actually already true of many from among many nations, and these are viewed by Paul as representatives of the whole, while he eagerly anticipates the full realization [Can].
    2. The reference is inclusive of all Gentiles [AB, ECWB (probably)]: all Gentiles. Paul is treating God's intention toward the Gentiles so that there is a note of universalism here, since all the Gentiles come under Messiah's realm, though all may not yet be aware of that fact [AB].

QUESTION—What is the function of the infinitive εἶναι 'to be'?
    1. It explains the contents or meaning of the μυστήριον 'mystery' and should be translated with the indicative mode [AB, Alf, Can, Ea, EBC, ECWB, EGT, El, HG, Ho, ICC, Lns, My, NTC, Rob, Si-ed, TH, WBC, We]: namely, that the Gentiles are fellow heirs. The infinitive is appositional [HG] or epexegetical [Si, WBC], explaining the content of

the μυστήριον 'mystery' [HG]. This objective infinitive [EGT, El] fulfills the function of a sentence beginning with 'that' [AB, Alf, EGT, El, Ho, ICC, Lns, My, NTC, Rob, We] and describes a belief, an utterance, a perception, or an item of information [AB]. A mystery is not a secret design or purpose, but a secret fact [Alf, EGT].
2. It not only explains the content of the μυστήριον 'mystery' [NIC], but expresses the purpose of the revelation of the mystery and should be translated as a subjunctive [NIC; KJV]: that the Gentiles should be fellow heirs, etc.

QUESTION—What is the relationship between συγκληρονόμα 'fellow heirs', σύσσωμα 'members of the same body', and the following συμμέτοχα 'sharers together'?
1. These words are arranged in an order that forms a climax [AB, NTC, We]. Paul wants to make it very clear that God's revealed 'mystery' is not just an alliance of Jew and Gentile, or an agreement to live together in peace, or even a partnership, but it is a complete and permanent spiritual *fusion* of formerly hostile elements into one new organism, with the climaxing result that they are 'fellow-partakers of the promise' [NTC].
2. These words do not form a climax [Ea, ICC], but progressively demonstrate the degree of Gentile participation in the promise [Can, Ea, ECWB, Lns]. No climax is formed, because the final term is no stronger than the second [ICC]. The first term gives the Gentiles title to all the spiritual blessings from God; the next acknowledges them as belonging to the united community of his people; and finally, they are stated to be fellow-partakers of the promise [Can, ECWB].
3. These words are arranged in order so as to emphasize the similarity of ideas in the three terms [IB, LJ, MNTC, NCBC, St, TH, WBC]. The words form a paronomasia in the Greek [IB, LJ, St, TH], which is hard to reproduce in translation [IB, WBC], but 'fellow-heirs', 'fellow-members of the body', and 'fellow-partakers of the promise' gives the idea [LJ, St].
4. The first term forms a general statement and the last two give the particulars of it [EGT, El, My]. The last two epithets restate the first epithet (συγκληρονόμα 'fellow-heirs'), figuratively (σύσσωμα 'members of the same body') and literally (συμμέτοχα 'sharers together') [My].

QUESTION—What is meant by συγκληρονόμα 'fellow heirs'?
It indicates co-heirship [Ea, Ho, My, NCBC, NIC, NTC, St, TD, WBC]. The Gentiles have the same right to the eternal inheritance of messianic bliss as the Jews [Ho, My, NCBC, NIC] or with those who were once Jews [WBC]. The Gentile heirship is based upon the same charter (the promise to Abraham [NIC]) and refers to the same inheritance as does the Jews [Ea, LJ, NIC, St]. The συν- 'together with' prefix does not have reference to Israel or the Jewish people as such. The writer uses these terms to indicate unity within the Church, which is an entirely new entity in which believing Gentiles have been made fully equal joint members, and not a previously

existing one to which they have been added. The reference, therefore, is to believers of Jewish birth, not Israel and her past [WBC].

QUESTION—What is meant by σύσσωμα 'fellow members of the body'?

This indicates a corporate relationship [AB, Ea, EBC, ECWB, El, NIC, Rob, Si-ed, St, TNTC, We, WeBC], concorporate [AB, Ea, Rob, Si-ed, St, WBC], a more initimate association than συγκληρονόμα 'fellow heirs' [Ea]. In relation to the Body, the members are incorporate. In relation to one another, the members are concorporate [Rob].

and sharers-together[a] of-the promise[b] in[c] Christ Jesus through[d] the gospel,[e]

TEXT—Some texts contain variant readings in this verse that are not noted by GNT. The first is the reading αὐτοῦ 'his' following ἐπαγγελίας 'promise' in the Textus Receptus. It is supported by only KJV. The second reading is ἐν τῷ Χριστῷ 'in Christ' of the Textus Receptus, in place of the reading accepted by most commentators, ἐν Χριστῷ Ἰησοῦ 'in Christ Jesus'. This is accepted by only My and KJV.

LEXICON—a. συμμέτοχος (LN **57.8**) (BAGD p. 778): 'sharer together' [NIV, REB], 'sharer' [LN, WBC; NAB, NRSV], 'sharing with someone in something' [BAGD], 'partner' [**LN**], 'partaker' [KJV], 'fellow partaker' [Lns, NTC, Rob, We; NASB], 'joint-partaker' [El, NIC], 'fellow beneficiary' [AB], 'joint-possessor' [MM], 'co-participant' [TH]. This noun is also translated as a verb: 'to share' [TEV, TNT]. The noun is also conflated with the following noun in the genitive, τῆς ἐπαγγελίας 'of the promise': 'to enjoy the same promise' [NJB].

b. ἐπαγγελία (LN 33.288) (BAGD 2.c. p. 280): 'promise' [BAGD, El, LN, Lns, NIC, NTC, Rob, TH, WBC, We; all versions except TEV], 'the promise that God made' [TEV], 'all that is promised' [AB]. This term denotes the content of what is promised [LN].

c. ἐν with dative object (LN 89.5, 89.26, 89.76, 89.119, 90.23): 'in' [AB, El, LN (89.5, 89.119, 90.23), Rob, TH, WBC, We; all versions except REB, TEV, TNT], 'through' [LN (89.76); TEV], 'concerning' [LN (89.5, 90.23)], 'with regard to' [LN (89.5)], 'with respect to' [LN (90.23)], 'connected with' [Lns], 'fulfilled in' [NIC; TNT], '(realized) in' [NTC], 'made in' [REB], 'because of' [LN (89.26)].

d. διά with genitive object (LN 89.76, 90.8): 'through' [AB, El, LN (89.76, 90.8), Lns, NIC, Rob, TH, WBC, We; NAB, NASB, NIV, NJB, NRSV, REB], 'by' [LN (89.76); KJV], 'by means of' [LN (90.8); TEV, TNT], 'with' [LN (90.8)], '(as conveyed) through' [NTC].

e. εὐαγγέλιον: 'gospel'. See this word at 1:13.

QUESTION—What is meant by τῆς ἐπαγγελίας 'the promise'?

1. The reference here is generally to the promises contained in the covenant, the messianic promise of salvation [Alf, CBC, ECWB, EGT, El, Ho, ICC, Lns, MNTC, My, NCBC, NIC, NTC, TD, TH, TNTC, WeBC]: sharers of the promise of salvation. The reference is to messianic salvation in all its length and breadth. The reference should not be restricted to the promise

of the Holy Spirit [Alf, EGT, El, My] even though this was a major feature of the promise [Alf, El], and a sign to the Christian of the fulfillment of the promise of salvation [TD]. The promise made to the Jews was of a better order of things in which God would be better known to them [CBC]. It includes forgiveness of sins, enabling power for the tasks of the present, and a hope for the future [NCBC].

2. The reference here is to the promise of the Holy Spirit [AB, Can, Ea, IB, LJ, We]: sharers together in the promise concerning the Holy Spirit. The promise is the pouring forth of the Spirit and all the results that flow from it—the final resurrection and the coming of the glorious kingdom. The presence of the article here singles out the promise and argues that this is a reference to the Holy Spirit since, in 1:13, Paul had already referred to him under a similar designation and in reference to the inheritance. The Holy Spirit was the one grand distinctive gift or promise given in the new covenant as attested elsewhere by the Apostle (Gal. 3:2, 14) and by Peter, as well (Acts 15:8) [Ea].

QUESTION—To what are the phrases ἐν Χριστῷ Ἰησοῦ 'in Christ Jesus' and διὰ τοῦ εὐαγγελίου 'through the gospel' attached, and what relationship is indicated by the prepositions?

1. Both phrases are attached to τῆς ἐπαγγελίας 'of the promise' [Lns, MNTC, TD, WeBC; NJB, NRSV, TNT].

    1.1 The ἐν 'in' specifies what the promise was about [Lns; TNT] and the διά 'through' indicates means [Lns, MNTC; TNT]: the Gentiles share the same promise fulfilled in Christ through the gospel. The promise is 'in Christ Jesus' as the substance and fulfillment of the promise. Christ is named as the meritorious cause of our salvation while the gospel is given as the instrumental cause [Lns]. The promised salvation has been realized in Christ and is offered through the gospel [MNTC].

    1.2 The ἐν 'in' indicates Christ is the ground or reason of the promise, while διά 'through' indicates that the gospel mediates the promise to the Gentiles [TD]: the Gentiles are sharers of the promise through the gospel because of Christ Jesus. Attached to ἐπαγγελίας 'promise', ἐν 'in' denotes the objective basis of fellowship with God, and the 'gospel' mediates to the Gentiles the benefits of salvation [TD].

2. Both phrases are attached to the whole of the verse, i.e., to the three epithets in this verse [AB, Alf, Cal, Can, CBC, Ea, ECWB, EGT, El, Ho, ICC, My, NCBC, NIC, NTC, St, TNTC, WBC, We]. (Two of these commentators assign 'in Christ Jesus' to the whole verse, but make no statement concerning 'through the gospel' [Cal, CBC]). Were they to be attached to τῆς ἐπαγγελίας 'of the promise', the article would be expected to be repeated [Alf, Ea], but not required [Alf].

    2.1 The prepositions ἐν 'in' and διά 'through' are synonymous [AB, NCBC].

2.1.1 Both indicate the means or instrument of the Gentiles' change of status [AB]: through Christ Jesus and the gospel, the Gentiles are fellow heirs, members of the same body, and sharers together of the promise.

2.1.2 Both indicate the cause for the Gentiles' change of status [NCBC]: because of Christ Jesus and the gospel, the Gentiles are fellow heirs and sharers together of the promise.

2.2 The ἐν 'in' indicates the sphere of inner union [Can, CBC, Ea, ECWB, Ho, ICC, St, TNTC, WBC, We], while the διά 'through' indicates the means or instrument [Can, Ea, ECWB, Ho, St, TNTC, WBC]: in union with Christ Jesus through the gospel, the Gentiles are fellow heirs and sharers together of the promise. By virtue of their union with Christ, the Gentiles are fellow heirs, and of the same body, and partakers of the promise. This is effected or brought about by means of the gospel [Can, Ho, St, We].

2.3 The ἐν 'in' indicates Christ is the objective ground or reason for the Gentiles' change of status [EGT, El, My], while the διά 'through' indicates that acceptance of the gospel is the means or instrument of it [EGT, El, My]: because of Christ Jesus and through the gospel, the Gentiles are fellow heirs and sharers together of the promise.

2.4 The ἐν 'in' indicates the condition under which the Gentiles participate in the promise, while the διά 'through' indicates the gospel as the subjective medium of the Gentiles' change in status, Christ himself being the objective ground of their incorporation [Alf]: since the Gentiles (have believed) in Christ Jesus through the gospel, they are fellow heirs and sharers together of the promise.

3. The phrase διὰ τοῦ εὐαγγελίου 'through the gospel' is attached to the whole verse, ἐν Χριστῷ Ἰησοῦ 'in Christ Jesus' is attached to τῆς ἐπαγγελίας 'of the promise' [TH; NIV, REB, TEV], the ἐν 'in' indicating Christ is the cause of the promise, and the διά 'through' the means of Gentile participation in the community [TH]: through the gospel the Gentiles are fellow heirs and sharers together of the promise (made) in Christ Jesus. The phrase διὰ τοῦ εὐαγγελίου 'through the gospel' could just as well be attached to τῆς ἐπαγγελίας 'of the promise' [TH].

4. The phrase ἐν Χριστῷ Ἰησοῦ 'in Christ Jesus' is attached to the whole verse, and διὰ τοῦ εὐαγγελίου 'through the gospel' is attached to τῆς ἐπαγγελίας 'of the promise' [NAB]: in Christ Jesus the Gentiles are fellow heirs and sharers together of the promise through the gospel.

QUESTION—What is meant by τοῦ εὐαγγελίου 'the gospel'?

In this verse, the meaning of the word focuses not upon a book or doctrine, but upon the act of proclamation [AB, My, NCBC, St, WBC]—preaching [AB, EGT, NTC; NAB], the joyful tidings [Alf, Can].

DISCOURSE UNIT: 3:7–13 [CBC, Rob, St, WeBC; NAB]. The topic is the divine commission that was entrusted to Paul [Rob, St].

3:7 of-which I-became a-servant[a] according-to[b] the gift[c] of-the grace[d] of-God

LEXICON—a. διάκονος (LN 35.20) (BAGD 1.a. p. 184): 'servant' [AB, BAGD, LN, TH, WBC; NIV, NJB, NRSV, TEV, TNT], 'minister' [El, Lns, NIC, NTC, Rob, We; KJV, NAB, NASB, REB].
  b. κατά with accusative object (LN 89.4, 89.8): 'according to' [El, Lns, NIC, NTC, Rob, TH, WBC, We; KJV, NASB, NRSV], 'in accordance with, in relation to' [LN (89.8)], 'through' [AB; NAB], 'by' [NIV, NJB, REB, TEV, TNT], 'in relation to, with regard to' [LN (89.4)]. Κατά marks a specific element as bearing a relation to something else [LN (89.4)] or marks a relation involving similarity of process [LN (89.8)].
  c. δωρεά (LN 57.84) (BAGD p. 210): 'gift' [AB, BAGD, El, LN, Lns, NIC, NTC, Rob, TH, WBC, We; all versions except TNT], 'free gift' [TNT], 'present' [LN].
  d. χάρις: 'grace'. See this word at 3:2.

QUESTION—How does this verse relate to the context?

This verse continues on from 3:6 without a break [TH]. Paul has just mentioned the gospel as the means of the Gentiles' participation in the blessings just described. He now restates his special relationship to that gospel (cf. 3:2) [Cal, Can, EBC, LJ, Lns, MNTC, NTC, WBC] in terms that indicate that it was through the gracious gift [Ba, EBC, LJ, WBC] and calling of God [EBC], due solely to God's initiative and doing and through no honor, merit, or power of his own [AB, Cal, EBC, ICC, LJ]. While the verse is a comment on Paul's relationship to the Gospel, it serves to round off the first major statement about the mystery within this digression, by returning to the thought and language with which he had begun in 3:1–2, so completing the first Greek sentence in the unit [WBC].

QUESTION—What is meant by διάκονος 'servant'?

In contrast to other words used for 'servant', διάκονος denotes a servant in relation to the task he has to perform, rather than a relationship to his master [Can, DNTT]. However, others claim that these distinctions cannot be maintained [EGT, El, ICC, My]. Though it did not designate a servant who performed menial tasks, like δοῦλος 'slave, servant' [AB], still διάκονος had no prestige connected with it [EBC]. In the NT, the term designates one who works for the service of Christ [CBC, DNTT, EBC] and the church [DNTT, EBC], one who serves in the interests of and for the benefit of others [DNTT, LJ, Lns], one who is concerned with the salvation of men [DNTT]. Here, however, is a rare usage in which διάκονος 'servant' occurs with an impersonal object, τοῦ εὐαγελλίου 'the gospel' [TH]. Since this clause is linked by the relative pronoun οὗ 'of which' to τοῦ εὐαγγελίου 'of the gospel', διάκονος designates a 'minister of the gospel [Ho, LJ, We; NAB], one whose business it is to preach the gospel [Can, Ho, My, TH].

QUESTION—What relationship is indicated by κατά 'according to'?

1. It indicates a correspondence to the standard or measure of the grace by which he was made a servant [Alf, Ea, EGT, El, Ho, IB, ICC, Lns, NCBC,

NIC, NTC, Rob, TH, We; KJV, NASB, NRSV]: of which I became a servant according to the gift of the grace of God. Paul fulfills his task 'according to the gift of God's grace which was given' him [NCBC].
2. It indicates the means by which he became a servant [AB, Cal, Can, EBC, LJ, Lns, MNTC, My, St, TNTC; NAB, NIV, NJB, REB, TEV, TNT]: of which I became a servant by means of the gift of the grace of God.

QUESTION—What is the relationship between the nouns in the genitive construction τὴν δωρεὰν τῆς χάριτος τοῦ θεοῦ 'the gift of the grace of God'?
1. The gift is God's grace [AB, Alf, Ea, EBC, EGT, El, Ho, ICC, MNTC, NCBC, NIC (probably), TH; NJB, TNT]: the gift consisting of God's grace. Paul understands 'the gift of grace' as a gift of God's favor [Can], his appointment and equipment for his ministry to the Gentiles [AB, Ea, EBC, EGT, El, Ho, IB, LJ, MNTC, NCBC, NIC, St]. It is not given for his own benefit only, but is for distribution to the Gentiles [AB].
2. 'Grace' describes the manner in which God gave the gift [Ho, Lns, My, TH; NAB, REB, TEV]: the gracious gift. Ho and TH offer this interpretation as an alternative possibility, showing no real preference for either. The article with δωρεάν 'gift' indicates that Paul's office was a special gift to him [Lns].

having-been-given to-me through/according-to[a] the working[b] of-his power.[c]

TEXT—Instead of the participle δοθείσης 'having been given' in the genitive case (modifying τῆς χάριτος 'of the grace'), some manuscripts have it in the accusative case, thus modifying τὴν δωρεάν 'the gift'. GNT does not mention this variant. The accusative case is accepted by Ea, Ho, My, NIC, and KJV.

LEXICON—a. κατά with accusative object (LN 89.8): 'according to' [BAGD, El, Lns, NIC, NTC, Rob, TH, We; NASB], 'in accordance with' [LN], 'for' [AB], 'by' [KJV, NAB, NJB, NRSV, TNT], 'through' [WBC; NIV, TEV], 'so' [REB].
b. ἐνέργεια (LN **42.3**) (BAGD 1. p. 265): 'working' [BAGD, **LN**, NTC, Rob, TH, WBC, We; NASB, NIV, NRSV, TEV, TNT], 'workings' [NJB], 'effectual working' [KJV], 'operation' [BAGD, El, Lns, NIC], 'exercise' [NAB], 'action' [BAGD]. This noun is also translated as a verb: 'to be at work' [AB; REB]. This term denotes being engaged in some function or activity with a possible focus upon the energy or force involved [LN].
c. δύναμις (LN 76.1): 'power' [AB, El, LN, Lns, NIC, NTC, Rob, TH, WBC, We; all versions except REB]. This noun is also translated as an adverb: 'powerfully (at work)' [REB]. This term denotes the potentiality to exert force in order to perform some function [LN]. See this word at 1:19.

QUESTION—To what is the participle δοθείσης 'having been given' linked?
1. It is attached to δωρεάν 'gift' [Ea, Ho, My, NIC]: the gift consisting of God's grace is given to me.

2. It is attached to the genitive χάριτος 'of grace' [AB, Alf, EBC, EGT, El, ICC, Lns, NTC, St, TH, WBC]: the gift consisting of God's grace, which grace was given to me. Logically, the genitive has the advantage over the accusative δωρεάν 'gift', since χάριτος 'of grace' required the further definition of κατὰ τὴν ἐνέργειαν τῆς δυνάμεως αὐτοῦ 'according to the working of his power' more than the δωρεάν 'gift' did [ICC]. Grammatically, the genitive participle is linked to the genitive noun 'grace', but in meaning the participle goes with the whole phrase 'gift of his grace' [TH].

QUESTION—What relationship is indicated by κατά 'according to'?

1. It indicates the means by which the gift was given [Ho, IB, ICC, LJ, Lns, NCBC, St, TH, TNTC; KJV, NAB, NIV, NJB, NRSV, TEV, TNT]: given by the effectual working of his power. It refers to the inward change by which Paul, a malignant opposer of Christ, was instantly changed into an obedient servant. Paul's vocation as an apostle involved his conversion, and his conversion was the effect of God's power [Ho, LJ].
2. It indicates a correspondence to the measure or standard by which the gift was given [AB, BAGD, ECWB, EGT, El, Lns, MNTC, NIC, NTC, Rob, TH, We; NASB, REB]: given according to the working of his power. The preposition has the sense of 'in proportion to' [MNTC]. In fact, what is a 'gift' in its source, is 'effectual working' in its nature [ECWB]. Some commentators also see in this an indication of the manner in which the gift was bestowed [EGT, El]. Another interprets this correspondence in terms of the evidence of the gift: through the gift of God's grace which was given me—for his power is at work—I was made etc. [AB]. Another indicates the idea of measure by interpreting it as introducing an adjectival clause modifying 'gift' [REB]: by God's unmerited gift, so powerfully at work in me.

QUESTION—What is meant by the phrase τὴν ἐνέργειαν τῆς δυνάμεως αὐτοῦ 'the working of his power'?

This indicates a divine force in the soul, energetic and not latent [ECWB]. It is God [TH] or Christ, present in the Spirit [TD], working though Paul [TD, TH], and 'in me' may be implied after 'working' [TH].

1. This is a reference to the change made in Paul by his conversion and commission as an apostle [Ba, Cal, Can, EGT, El, Ho, ICC, LJ, Lns, My]. The following verse (3:8) shows that this refers to the power which God put forth in the conversion of Paul himself and in putting him into the ministry.
2. This is a reference to the power shown in Paul's ministry to the Gentiles [AB, Alf, CBC, IB, MNTC, NCBC, Rob, St, TD, TH, TNTC, WBC]. He had received his ministry by God's grace, he would exercise it by the working of God's power [St]. The reference to δύναμις 'power' is a reference to God himself (Gal. 2:8). This is not an infused grace or power poured into the apostle. It is God himself working through Paul, making him an instrument for diffusing God's grace to the Gentiles [AB].

3. This refers to both of the above [Ea, EBC, NIC, NTC]. Both in his initial call and in the subsequent empowerment which he received throughout his career, the apostle experienced the 'operation' of God's power [NIC].

QUESTION—What is the effect of the genitive use of the synonyms ἐνέργεια 'working' and δύναμις 'power' in this phrase?

Passages in Ephesians, of which this is one, use the accumulation of synonyms in the genitive to give a fuller characterization to what is said [TD], thus indicating the fullness and certainly of this power [NTC]. The use of synonyms here gives a rhetorical effect [NTC, TH]. It shows that this power worked very effectively [Ea]. Paul indicates that the power was given as an energizing strength (ἐνέργεια) operating in his life by the presence of the Holy Spirit [TNTC].

DISCOURSE UNIT: 3:8–13 [NIC]. The topic is the eternal purpose of the Mystery of Christ.

3:8 To me the very-least[a] of-all saints[b] was-given this grace,[c]

LEXICON—a. ἐλάχιστος (LN 87.66) (BAGD 2.b. p. 249): 'very least' [BAGD, NTC, TH, WBC; NASB, NRSV, TNT], 'less than the least' [AB, El, Lns, Rob, We; KJV, NIV, NJB, REB, TEV], 'least' [NAB], 'lessermost' [NIC], 'lowest, least important, last' [LN]. This term has reference to someone or something that is of the lowest status [LN]. The lexicon form is a genuine superlative, while ἐλαχιστότερος, the nominative form of the dative appearing in the text, is a comparative formed on this superlative [Ba, BD, Can, Ea, EGT, HG, Ho, IB, ICC, Lns, MNTC, My, NIC, NTC, Si-ed, St, TD, TH, TNTC] and so becomes an intensive superlative [HG, Rob], one who is less than even the least of saints [Lns].

b. ἅγιος: 'saints'. See this word at 1:15, 18; 2:19.

c. χάρις: 'grace'. See this word at 3:7.

QUESTION—How does this verse relate to the context?

This sentence is appositional to the preceding sentence, as shown by the absence of a connective, the emphatic ἐμοί 'to me', resuming the μοι 'to me' of the last verse, and the repetition of the thought about grace [Lns]. The thought of his having received his ministry through the gracious power of God (3:7) leads the apostle to break his sentence [Rob] to dwell for a moment upon his unworthiness of this high office [Alf, Ea, My, NIC, Rob, Si, TNTC], the emphatic ἐμοί 'to me' [Ea, NTC, Rob] calling attention to the contrast between the high office to which he had been called and his consciousness of his own demerit [Ea], or serving to emphasize that his gospel was the grace of God to the Gentiles [Rob]. The re-occurrence of the passive voice verb ἐδόθη 'was given', referring back to the passive participle of the same verb in the previous statement, also serves to link this verse to the previous one [EBC]. The infinitive εὐαγγελίσασθαι 'to preach (the gospel)' is a reference back to διὰ τοῦ εὐαγγελίου 'through the gospel' in 3:6 [Rob].

QUESTION—What is the meaning of τῷ ἐλαχιστοτέρῳ 'the very least'?
This word is a comparative made from the superlative ἐλάχιστος 'least' [Ba, BD, Can, Ea, EGT, HG, Ho, IB, ICC, Lns, MNTC, My, NIC, NTC, Si, St, TD, TH, TNTC, WBC] and so it is the equivalent of the ungrammatical English words 'smallester' [AB, EBC], 'leaster' [AB, St], or 'more least' [EBC]. 'Less than the least' is a more grammatically acceptable expression which gives the meaning of the word [Can, El, Lns, Mo, My, TH, Tu], though this must be seen as a humble exaggeration, since such a statement is logically impossible [TH]. The purpose of the apostle is not primarily to depreciate himself so much, as to demonstrate that the gift that has done such wonders among the Gentiles, through one so unworthy, must be from God [MNTC].

QUESTION—What consideration causes the apostle to make this statement concerning himself?
1. This remark is called forth primarily by the memory of his past actions as a persecutor of the church [Ba, Cal, ECWB, Ho, ICC, ISBE2, Lns, MNTC, My, NCBC, NIC, NTC, St, TD]. It is not the consciousness of sin in general, in respect of which Paul knew he stood on a level with anyone else, but the deeply humbling consciousness of having persecuted Christ that is the ground of this self abasement [My].
2. This remark is called forth primarily by his consciousness of his own inherent sinfulness [Cal, TNTC]. He confines his attention to what he was in himself apart from the grace of God [Cal].
3. This remark is called forth by both of the above [Can, El].

QUESTION—What is the referent of ἡ χάρις αὕτη 'this grace'?
1. This refers back to the τὴν δωρεὰν τῆς χάριτος τοῦ θεοῦ 'the gift of the grace of God' in 3:7 [Ea, IB, TH, We], as evidenced by the fact that the clause ἐδόθη ἡ χάρις αὕτη 'this grace was given' is a restatement of the articular passive participle τῆς δοθείσης 'which was given' in 3:7 [Cal, TH].
2. This refers to the infinitive clause that follows [El, ICC, WBC], linking it directly with the problem of what that clause is connected with [ICC].

to-proclaim-the-good-news[a] to-the Gentiles[b] (of) the unfathomable[c] riches[d] of-Christ

TEXT—Some manuscripts insert the preposition ἐν 'among' before τοῖς ἔθνεσιν 'the Gentiles' so that the meaning becomes 'among the Gentiles', defining the *sphere* of Paul's ministry rather than the *subjects* of Paul's ministry. GNT does not note this variant reading. This insertion is accepted by Ea, El, and KJV.

LEXICON—a. aorist mid. infin. of εὐαγγελίζω: 'to proclaim the good news'. See this word at 2:17.
  b. ἔθνος: 'Gentiles'. See this word at 3:6.
  c. ἀνεξιχνίαστος (LN 32.23) (BAGD p. 65): 'unfathomable' [AB, BAGD, LN, NIC, NTC; NAB, NASB, NJB, REB], 'incomprehensible,

inscrutable' [BAGD], 'impossible to understand, impossible to comprehend' [LN], 'unsearchable' [El, Rob, WBC, We; KJV, NIV], 'untraceable' [Lns], 'unfindable' [TH], 'infinite' [TEV] 'boundless' [NRSV, TNT]. This term denotes something as being impossible to understand on the basis of careful examination or investigation [LN].

 d. πλοῦτος: 'riches'. See this word at 1:7, 18; 2:7.

QUESTION—To what is this infinitive clause joined?

 1. It is joined to the preceding part of this verse [AB, Alf, Can, Ea, El, HG, ICC, Lns, MNTC, My, NCBC, NIC, NTC, TD, TH, WBC; all versions]: To me was this grace given, namely, to proclaim the good news to the Gentiles, etc. It is in apposition [HG], or partial apposition to [El], and defines the preceding phrase ἡ χάρις αὕτη 'this grace' [AB, El, HG, ICC, Lns, MNTC, My, WBC] showing what ἡ χάρις αὕτη 'this grace' consisted in [AB, ICC, NCBC, TD, WBC]. It gives the purpose of his office [Ea] and it shows the theme and nature of the message he preached [Can].

 2. It is joined with the first part of 3:7, the first part of the present verse being parenthetical [Rob, We]: of which I became a servant according to the gift of the grace of God to proclaim the good news to the Gentiles, etc. (to me, the very least of all saints, was this grace given). The first part of this verse is a parenthetical reflection of the apostle, with the following infinitive clause τοῖς ἔθνεσιν εὐαγγελίσασθαι κ.τ.λ. 'to preach to the Gentiles etc.' going with οὗ ἐγενήθην διάκονος 'of which I became a minister' in 3:7.

QUESTION—What is meant by τὸ ἀνεξιχνίαστον πλοῦτος τοῦ Χριστοῦ 'the unfathomable riches of Christ'?

It refers to all of God's purposes in Christ as set forth in this epistle [Bu], especially chs. 1 and 2 [St], the secrets of God that are only known by divine revelation (3:3) [WeBC]. It refers to the sufficiency and glory that is in the Savior [Ba]. It is Christ Himself [TNTC, WBC]. It denotes the overflowing fullness of every kind of good and blessing [Can, Ea, ICC, LJ], all the saving grace and gifts which belong to Christ [Lns]. It refers to the astonishing and boundless treasures of grace which God is bestowing upon the Gentiles [Cal], the exhaustless, divine fullness of salvation [El, My]. It is the wealth of grace and truth that exist in Christ [ECWB]. It is the truth contained in the gospel [MNTC], its divine grace and glory [NIC]. It is a reference to the fullness of wisdom, righteousness, sanctification and redemption that are all centered in and summed up in Christ [Alf, LJ]. It is the fullness of the Godhead, the plenitude of all the perfections and glories which reside in him, his fullness of grace to pardon, sanctify, and save. In short, it is everything in Christ which can satisfy the soul of a person [Ho]. It is the mark of the future world present in Christ [TD]. There is no more emphatic expression in the NT than this. It shows that the heart of the apostle was full of admiration for the sufficiency and glory that is in the Savior but that he lacked words to express it [Ba]. Yet, for all the glory attributed to Christ by this phrase, in the context this thought is still subordinated to the ministry of the apostle. It is to Paul that this grace has been given to proclaim these glorious riches to the Gentiles [WBC].

QUESTION—What is the meaning of ἀνεξιχνίαστος 'unfathomable'?

This adjective is formed on the noun ἴχνος 'footprint' or 'track' [NIC] and so becomes a metaphor of tracking footprints [Bu, ECWB, EGT, TNTC; TNT (note)], but of being unable to track them completely to their source [TNT (note)]. Others suggest a metaphor involving a treasury [LJ] or area that is trackless [IB, MNTC], unexplorable, too vast to be mapped out and measured [IB, LJ, TH], though not implying that any part is inaccessible [IB]. Others suggest it pictures a reservoir so deep that soundings cannot reach its bottom, and therefore no limit can be placed upon its resources [NCBC, WBC]. It means something that cannot be traced out [Ba, EBC, EGT], or explored, something that is inscrutable, or incomprehensible [Ba, EGT, IB, LJ], something that is infinite [St, TH]. This word describes the riches of Christ as unsearchable in their nature, extent, and application [Alf, El]. They have a depth of meaning that never ceases to cause wonder [CBC], the human intellect being unable to explore them so as to form an adequate conception of them [My]. While they can be seen in part, they can never be wholly measured. They can be enjoyed [ECWB] but can never be exhausted [CBC, ECWB, LJ].

3:9 and[a] to-enlighten[b] all (men) what (is) the plan/stewardship[c] of-the mystery[d] hidden[e] from the ages[f] in[g] God

TEXT—Some manuscripts omit the word πάντας 'all'. GNT includes the word in brackets to show that it is difficult to decide whether or not to include it. It is omitted by ICC, Rob, TNTC, We, NASB, NJB, and REB.

TEXT—Instead of οἰκονομία 'administration', some manuscripts have the word κοινωνία 'fellowship'. Those supporting this reading are: Ba (possibly), Cal and KJV.

LEXICON—a. καί (LN 89.92): 'and' [AB, El, LN, Lns, NIC, NTC, Rob, TH, WBC, We; all versions except TNT]. TNT begins a new sentence here.

b. aorist act. infin. of φωτίζω (LN **28.36**) (BAGD 2.b. or 2.c. p. 873): 'to enlighten' [BAGD (2.b.), Lns, NTC; NAB, TNT], 'to make see' [AB, El; KJV, NRSV, TEV], 'to make plain' [LN, WBC; NIV], 'to make clear' [BAGD (2.c.), TH], 'to make (someone) understand' [NIC], 'to bring to light' [BAGD (2.c.), LN, Rob, We; NASB, REB], 'to throw light' [NJB], 'to give light to, shed light upon' [BAGD (2.b.)], 'to reveal' [BAGD (2.c.), LN]. 'to make known' [**LN**]. This verb denotes the causing of something to be fully known by revealing it clearly and in some detail [LN]. See this word at 1:18.

c. οἰκονομία (LN **30.68**) (BAGD 2.b. p. 559): 'plan' [BAGD, **LN**; NRSV], 'design' [NAB], 'stewardship' [NIC], 'administration' [Lns, NTC, TH, WBC; NASB, NIV], 'arrangement' [BAGD, LN], 'scheme' [LN], 'purpose' [LN], 'dispensation' [El, Rob, We], 'inner workings' [NJB],

'the working out' [TNT]. This noun is also translated as a verb: 'to administer' [AB]. This noun is also conjoined with μυστήριον 'mystery' and translated 'this hidden purpose was to be put into effect' [REB], 'God's secret plan is to be put into effect' [TEV], 'the working out of God's secret design' [TNT]. See this word at 1:10; 3:2.
- d. μυστήριον: 'mystery'. See this word at 1:9; 3:3, 4.
- e. perf. pass. participle of ἀποκρύπτω (LN 28.80) (BAGD p. 93): 'to be hidden' [AB, BAGD, El, Lns, NIC, NTC, Rob, TH, WBC, We; KJV, NAB, NASB, NRSV], 'to be kept hidden' [NIV, NJB], 'to be kept secret' [BAGD, LN], 'to be concealed' [LN], 'to lie concealed' [REB]. This passive verb is also translated actively: 'to keep hidden' [TEV], 'to keep to himself' [TNT]. This verb denotes the causing of something to remain unknown, and carries the implication of concealment and inaccessibility [LN].
- f. αἰών (LN 67.133) (BAGD 4. p. 28): 'ages' [AB, El, Rob, TH], 'all ages' [We], 'all the ages' [NJB], 'all the past ages', [TEV], 'eternity' [NIC], 'all eternity' [TNT], 'the beginning of the world' [KJV], 'Aeons' [BAGD, regarding the Aeons as persons]. The phrase ἀπὸ τῶν αἰώνων 'from the ages' is translated 'from eons on' [Lns], 'for ages' [NTC, WBC; NAB, NASB, NRSV], 'for ages past' [NIV], 'for long ages' [REB], 'since all time, from all ages past, from the beginning of time' [LN].
- g. ἐν with dative object (LN 83.13, 90.6): 'in' [AB, El, LN (83.13), Lns, NIC, NTC, Rob, TH, WBC, We; all versions except REB, TEV, TNT], 'by' [LN (90.6), TH], 'with' [REB]. TEV, TNT omit 'in' and make 'God' the subject of a verb 'to hide' [TEV] or 'to keep' [TNT].

QUESTION—What relationship is indicated by καί 'and'?
1. It indicates an additional purpose or task of the χάρις 'grace' (3:8) given to Paul [Can, Ho, LJ, NCBC, NTC, St, TNTC, WBC, We, WeBC]: this grace was given me in order that the wealth of Christ be proclaimed as good news to the Gentiles and that the plan/stewardship of the mystery might be made known to all.
2. It further defines or specifies the meaning of εὐαγγελίσασθαι τὸ ἀνεξιχνίαστον πλοῦτος τοῦ Χριστοῦ 'to proclaim the good news of the unfathomable riches of Christ' [El, Lns, TD]: this grace was given me in order that the wealth of Christ be proclaimed as good news to the Gentiles, that is, that the plan/stewardship of the mystery might be made known to all. This is an expansion of the foregoing clause both as to the process and as to the persons. The apostle had grace given to him, not only to outwardly preach the gospel, but to inwardly enlighten; and that not only to the Gentiles, but to all [El].

QUESTION—What is the meaning of the infinitive φωτίσαι 'to enlighten'?
The meaning is much the same with either of the following alternatives [EBC, ICC, NTC], since the result of bringing the οἰκονομία 'plan/stewardship' to light is that all men are enabled to see it [ICC, NTC].

Thus, even with interpretation 2, translation will still require an indirect object such as 'to people' [TH].
1. It means 'to enlighten, to make known' [AB, Alf, Ba, BAGD (2.b.), Cal, Can, Ea, EBC, ECWB, EGT, El, Ho, LJ, LN (**28.36**), Lns, MNTC, My, NCBC, NIC, NTC, St, TH, WBC; KJV, NAB, NIV, NRSV, TEV, TNT]: to enlighten all men. Φωτίζω followed by the accusative of the person means to enlighten inwardly, to give spiritual apprehension [Ea]. This area of meaning is required if πάντας 'all' is recognized as the genuine reading (see above) [AB, EGT]. Since the light imparted by the Gospel was knowledge [Ho], some maintain the idea in the word is 'to teach, to instruct' [BAGD, Ho], but others disagree saying φωτίζω 'to enlighten' does not merely refer to the external aspects of Paul's work, the teaching, but to the internal effect upon his hearers, to their apprehension of the material, their spiritual enlightenment as well [Alf, Ea, EGT, El]. It refers to the preaching of the gospel in such a way as to cause men to be unmistakably clear as to its implications [NCBC].
2. It means 'to bring to light' [BAGD (2.c.), IB, ICC, Rob, TNTC, We; NASB, NJB, REB]: to bring to light what is the plan/stewardship of the mystery. This is the meaning required if πάντας 'all' is not genuine [EGT, TNTC] (though one, IB, accepts this meaning while still recognizing the πάντας 'all' as genuine). This word is the natural one to use for the public proclamation of a secret which had been hidden [Rob, TNTC].

QUESTION—Assuming πάντας 'all' to be genuine, to what does it refer?
1. It refers to all men, Jew and Gentile alike [AB, Ba, Cal, Can, Ea, EBC, ECWB, Ho, IB, ICC, LJ, Lns, MNTC, NCBC, NIC, NTC, St, TH, WeBC; KJV, NAB, NIV, NRSV, TEV, TNT]: and to enlighten all men, both Jew and Gentile.
2. It refers only to the previously mentioned Gentiles [EGT, El, My]: and to enlighten all these Gentiles.
3. It refers to the whole of creation [BAGD (2.b.β. p. 633)]: and to enlighten the whole universe. Πάντας 'all' is used in the absolute sense of the whole of creation...Eph. 3:9 [BAGD].

QUESTION—What is the meaning of οἰκονομία 'plan/stewardship' here, and who is the implied actor?
1. The word designates a plan or arrangement, with God as its author [Alf, BAGD, Can, DNTT, Ea, EBC, ECWB, EGT, El, Ho, IB, ICC, LJ, LN (**30.68**), MNTC, My, NCBC, Rob, St, TD, TH, TNTC, WBC, WeBC; NAB, NRSV, REB, TEV, TNT]: to make all men see what God's secret plan is. This is the point on which they were instructed [Ea, EGT, Ho, IB, LJ, NCBC, WeBC]. The subject of enlightenment is how God ordered and arranged his now revealed secret [Can, WBC]. The οἰκονομία 'plan' is a reference back to 1:10 [AB, Alf, El, LJ, NCBC], and so is the law or order which God himself has ordained for the manifestation of the truth

[ECWB, El], the administration or plan of the union of Jews and Gentiles in Christ [Alf, El, ICC, NCBC, WeBC], or their redemption [Ho, LJ].
2. The word designates the office of stewardship with either Christ or Paul administering this office [AB, Lns, NIC, TH (as an alternative)].
2.1 Christ administers this office [AB, TH]: to make all men see how the Messiah administers the secret. In 3:2 Paul has spoken of an administration of God's grace which was given to him to administer. But 3:9 appears to refer back to 1:10 which spoke of the stewardship of Christ. In this book Paul leaves to Christ alone the task of revealing and carrying out the one μυστήριον 'mystery' of God. Therefore it should be made clear that Paul is returning from his subsidiary administration to Christ's original and plenipotentiary administration [AB].
2.2 Paul administers this office [Lns, NIC]: to enlighten all men as to what my stewardship in the secret is. Paul's commission also involved the public demonstration of his stewardship, the stewardship of the long-hidden mystery [NIC].

QUESTION—What is the μυστηρίου 'mystery'?

The meaning of the 'mystery' is the same as in 3:6 [Ea, EBC, EGT, El, ICC, Lns, My], or 1:9 and 3:3–5 [NCBC, TH, TNTC, WBC] because the same course of thought is still pursued [Ea].

QUESTION—What is meant by the articular perfect passive participle τοῦ ἀποκεκρυμμένου 'which has been hidden'?

The word suggests a positive act of concealment and that the mystery was in existence in times past, but was unknown because it had been purposely hid from view, as a part of God's dispensation of the matter [Can, EBC, LJ]. The word is stronger than the word previously used to describe the mystery when he said that it was οὐκ ἐγνωρίσθη 'not made known' (3:5). The revelation of this mystery does not constitute a change in God's character and will, but only reveals what had always been there [Can, LJ].

QUESTION—What is meant by ἀπὸ τῶν αἰώνων 'from the ages'?
1. Αἰώνων is temporal and refers to the successive periods of time in the past [Alf, Can, DNTT, Ea, EBC, ECWB, EGT, El, Ho, ICC, ISBE, ISBE2, LJ, Lns, MNTC, My, NCBC, NIC, NTC, Rob, TD, TH, WBC, We, WeBC]: which was hidden from previous ages. This phrase states the temporal limit from which the concealment dated [Alf, Ea, EGT, El]. While the decree itself took place before time began [DNTT, EGT, El, My], it was kept concealed since the ages of the world began [EGT, El, My]. It covers the period of time from the commencement of time [Ea, EBC, Ho, ISBE2, Rob, TH, We], or from the time when intelligent beings, from whom it could be concealed, were created [El, My], until the time of its revelation [ISBE2], the period of Paul's commission [Ea].
2. Αἰώνων refers to supernatural persons [BAGD (4. p. 28), IB]: which was hidden from the supernatural beings who rule the spheres, the Aeons. The phrase may be interpreted in the personal sense as in 1 Cor. 2:7–8, and as

the equivalent of the ταῖς ἀρχαῖς καὶ ταῖς ἐξουσίαις 'principalities and powers' in 3:10, the spiritual beings who rule the spheres [IB].

QUESTION—What is meant by saying this hiding was done ἐν τῷ θεῷ 'in God'?

Ἐν τῷ θεῷ 'in God' has a locative sense [WBC]. It means this purpose of God secretly existed in the mind of God [Alf, Can, EBC, ECWB, EGT, LJ, Lns, MNTC, NCBC, TH, WBC, We]. It was in his mind from the time of his primal counsels, from the foundation of the world (1:4) [Alf, Can, EBC, ECWB, El, LJ, Lns, NCBC, WBC, We]. It has been concealed until the Gospel dispensation in God's bosom [Alf, Ba, Ea, LJ]. When God created everything he included in the one creative thought all the matters concerning his creation [We]. In the final analysis, it makes little difference whether it is translated 'in God' or 'by God' since, in both cases, God does the hiding [TH].

the (one) having-created[a] all-things,

TEXT—Some manuscripts contain the phrase διὰ Ἰησοῦ Χριστοῦ 'through Christ Jesus'. GNT does not note the variant. This phrase is accepted by Cal, Si, and KJV.

LEXICON—a. aorist act. participle of κτίζω (LN **42.35**) (BAGD p. 455): 'to create' [BAGD, El, LN, Lns, NTC, Rob, TH, WBC, We; KJV, NASB, NIV, NRSV]. This verb is also translated as a noun: 'creator' [AB, NIC; NAB, NJB, REB, TEV, TNT]. It denotes the creation of something which has not existed before [LN].

QUESTION—What is the function of this participial clause?

1. The clause indicates that the content of the μυστήριον 'secret' has always been at the center of God's purpose in creation [AB, Alf, Ba, Can, Ea, EBC, ECWB, EGT, El, IB, LJ, Lns, MNTC, My, NCBC, NIC, Rob, TNTC, WBC, WeBC]. The purpose may be to show that God is not abandoning his first creation for the new one [AB], but that from the start, the redemption of all things in Christ [WeBC], salvation, life, and unity in Christ, have always been the purpose in the creation of heaven and earth [AB, Alf, Ba, Can, Ea, EBC, ECWB, EGT, El, IB, LJ, MNTC, My, NIC, Rob, TNTC, WeBC], so that this new revelation, the mystery that all men, Gentile as well as Jew, are to be united in Christ, has always been in the heart of God [AB, Alf, Ba, Can, Ea, EBC, MNTC, My, NIC], has always been under his control [Ba, Ea, LJ, MNTC], and will certainly complete his purpose. In the context of the ensuing mention of the principalities and authorities, the clause serves as a reminder that God is able, because he is the creator, to bring about his purpose of salvation as it effects all creation, including the powers in rebellion against him [WBC]. The fact that God is creator of all things involves his perfect right to dispose of the course of world history and the progress of his kingdom according to his own wisdom and will [Alf, Cal, Can, ICC, NTC] without the need to account for any actions connected therewith to mankind [Cal, NTC]. The

writer is saying that God, as creator, necessarily has a plan of arrangements for things to take place, and that each part is revealed at the fitting time for its revelation [Ea, TNTC]. Paul is saying that, at the fittest times, God created both the human material on which redemption was to work, and the peculiar and varied mechanism by which the purposes of redemption were to be achieved [Ea]. This mystery, which was in God's mind and the purpose he had in view when he created all things, is the mystery which Paul is to preach! [EGT] The τὰ πάντα 'all things' shows that the Gentiles are also God's creatures, and the Creator of all has always acted and will always act with due reference to all his intelligent creatures [Lns].
2. The clause is merely an expression of reverence [Ho]. The reference to God as creator may be accounted for as merely an expression of reverence without any intention of special reference to the topic under discussion. This is a common phenomena of speech.

QUESTION—What is the meaning of τὰ πάντα 'all things'?
1. It should be understood as referring to the first, or physical, creation [AB, Alf, Ea, ECWB, EGT, El, Ho, IB, ICC, LJ, Lns, MNTC, My, NCBC, NIC, NTC, Rob, St, TD, TH, TNTC, WBC, WeBC]. It is to be interpreted in the widest sense, taking in physical and spiritual things alike, all that exists [Alf, My], the world [TH], the universe [Ho]. The phrase is in a position of emphasis [Alf, Ea, EGT, El, ICC].
2. It should be interpreted of the new spiritual creation [Cal]. Context requires us to understand 'all things' as referring to the spiritual renewal which is part of the blessings of redemption.

DISCOURSE UNIT: 3:10–13 [ICC]. The topic is the disclosure of God's wisdom to the angelic powers.

3:10 in-order-that[a] it-might-be-made-known[b] now

LEXICON—a. ἵνα (LN 89.59): 'in order that' [LN, Lns, NIC, NTC, WBC; NASB, REB, TEV, TNT], 'in order to' [TH], 'for the purpose of' [LN], 'so that' [LN; NRSV], 'to the intent that' [El, Rob, We; KJV], 'therefore' [NAB], not explicit [AB]. Some start a new sentence here with an indication of purpose or intent: 'His intent was that' [NIV], 'The purpose of this was that' [NJB].
b. aorist pass. subj. of γνωρίζω (LN 28.26) (BAGD 1. p. 163): 'to be made known' [AB, BAGD, El, LN, Lns, NIC, NTC, Rob, TH, WBC, We; NAB, NASB, NIV, NRSV, REB], 'to be known' [KJV], 'to be revealed' [BAGD]. This passive verb is also translated as an active verb: 'to learn' [NJB, TEV], 'to make known' [TNT].

QUESTION—What relationship is indicated by ἵνα 'in order that'?
1. It indicates the purpose of the contents of 3:8–9 as a whole [Alf, Cal, Can, Ea, EGT, El, Ho, Lns, MNTC, NTC, TD, WBC, We; KJV]

EPHESIANS 3:10 223

1.1 It makes this verse the end purpose of the grace that was given to Paul (3:8) [Alf, EGT]: to me was this grace given…in order that the manifold wisdom of God might now be made known to the rulers and authorities.

1.2 It makes this verse the end purpose of the two infinitive clauses of 3:8–9 [Ea, El, Ho, Lns, NTC, WBC]: to me was this grace given, to preach to the Gentiles…and to enlighten all men…in order that the manifold wisdom of God might now be made known to the rulers and authorities. The ἵνα 'in order that' indicates a final purpose, not the grand object, but still an important minor design. It winds up the entire preceding paragraph, and discloses a grand reason for God's method of procedure [Ea].

2. t indicates the result of the contents of 3:8–9 [NAB]: Now, therefore, through the church, the manifold wisdom of God is being made known to the principalities and powers in the heavenly places.

3. It indicates the purpose of the creation of the universe [Ba, IB]: who created all things in order that the manifold wisdom of God might now be made known to the rulers and authorities.

4. It indicates the purpose of 'hidden…in God' (3:9) [EBC, ICC, My, TH; REB, TEV, TNT]: hidden in God in order that now the manifold wisdom of God might be made known to the rulers and authorities through the church.

5. It indicates the purpose of the infinitive clause of 3:9 [Rob]: to enlighten all men as to what the administration of the secret is…in order that now, through the church, the manifold wisdom of God might be made known to the principalities and powers in the heavenly places.

6. It indicates the result of the infinitive clause of 3:9 [LJ]: to enlighten all men as to what the administration of the secret is…so that now, through the church, the manifold wisdom of God is being made known to the principalities and powers in the heavenly places.

7. It explains how the secret (3:9) is going to be administered [AB]: and to make all men see how the Messiah is going to administer the secret, to wit: the manifold wisdom of God.

QUESTION—Who is the actor in the passive verb γνωρισθῇ 'might be made known' and how does this affect the interpretation of the prepositional phrase διὰ τῆς ἐκκλησίας 'through/by means of the church'?

1. God is the actor and therefore the preposition διὰ 'by means of' signals means or instrumentality [Alf, Ba, Cal, Can, DNTT, EBC, EGT, El, ICC, Lns, MNTC, St, TD, WBC, WeBC]: in order that God might make known, by means of the church, his manifold wisdom to the rulers and authorities in the heavenly places. By means of the formation of the Church, God reveals the consequences of Christ's victory to these evil powers [WBC]. It refers to what these supernatural beings observe concerning the formation, growth, character, and blessedness of the community of believers in Jesus which has been gathered together out of all the nations of mankind [Can].

2. The church is the actor and therefore the διά 'through' primarily signals agency [AB, CBC, Ea, NIC, TD, TH, TNTC, We] and secondarily, instrumentality [AB]: in order that the church might now make known the manifold wisdom of God to the rulers and authorities in the heavenly places. As a lighthouse of God (5:8), it shines brightly among the powers of the world as a proof of the triumph of God's goodness (2:7; 3:10) [AB]. By virtue of its very existence [AB, TD], the church reveals the wisdom of God [TD] serving as a 'theater' for God's works.
3. Paul is the actor and therefore the preposition διά 'by means of' signals means or instrumentality [Ho, LJ, My]: in order that, by means of the church, I might make known the manifold wisdom of God to the rulers and authorities in the heavenly places. This statement of purpose stands in significant relationship to the vocation of Paul, through whom this making known to the heavenly powers was *partly* effected, that is to say, Paul shared this distinction with others who also preached to the Gentiles [My]. It is through the results of the message entrusted to Paul, especially that concerning the nature of the Church, that these principalities and powers have been able to see the manifold wisdom of God [LJ].

QUESTION—What is the force of the νῦν 'now'?

This time particle carries a secondary emphasis [Alf] and stands in opposition to ἀπὸ τῶν αἰώνων 'from the ages' of 3:9 [Alf, Ea, EBC, EGT, El, Ho, Lns, My, WBC]. It means 'now, since the Messiah has come, now under the Christian dispensation, this revelation is to be made' [Ba, WBC]. It refers to that period known as the fullness of time [We]. It contrasts the past time of concealment with the present time of disclosure [TD].

to-the rulers[a] and the authorities[b] in heavenly-places,[c] through[d] the church

LEXICON—a. ἀρχή: 'rulers'. See this word at 1:21.
  b. ἐξουσία: 'authorities'. See this word at 1:21.
  c. ἐπουράνιος: 'heavenly places'. See this word at 1:3.
  d. διά with genitive object (LN 90.4): 'through' [AB, El, LN, Lns, NIC, NTC, Rob, TH, WBC, We; all versions except KJV, TEV], 'by' [LN; KJV], 'by means of' [TEV]. This is a marker of intermediate agent with a causative agent implicitly or explicitly supplied [LN].

QUESTION—What is meant by ταῖς ἀρχαῖς καὶ ταῖς ἐξουσίαις ἐν τοῖς ἐπουρανίοις 'to the rulers and the authorities in the heavenly places'?

1. These are good supernatural beings [Alf, Ba, Cal, Can, Ea, EBC, ECWB, EGT, El, Ho, LJ, Lns, My, NTC, Si, TH, TNTC, We (probably)]: to the good spirits who rule in the realm of the heavens. This is clearly a reference back to 1:21 and the angels over whom Christ has been exalted [Can]. These angels are called ἀρχαί 'rulers' and ἐξουσίαι 'authorities' because these are names of dignity which are appropriate here, in accordance with the greatness of Paul's commission [EGT]. Paul does not call them angels because this name would relate to their office and work with regard to men. What he is interested in focusing upon by using ταῖς

ἀρχαῖς καὶ ταῖς ἐξουσίαις 'to the rulers and authorities' is their power and rank in the heavenly world [Lns, My]. As in 1:21, the two nouns refer to different ranks, even though, in this verse, only two ranks are indicated, unlike 1:21 [Lns].
2. These are supernatural beings who oppose God and Christ [CBC, DNTT, IB, ISBE, ISBE2, MNTC, NCBC, TD, WBC; NJB (note), TNT (note)]: to the evil spirits who rule in the realm of the heavens.
3. These are the ruling supernatural beings, both the good and the evil [AB, BAGD, ICC, Rob, Si-ed, St]: to all the spirits who rule in the realm of the heavens. The church is to be an example to all creation, and so this includes an assignment concerning the intangible powers, the evil and the good, that govern all human life (see the discussion on these terms at 1:21) and make their spiritual dominion felt from their 'heavenly' places [AB].
4. These are all created intelligent beings, both evil and good, heavenly and earthly [NIC, WeBC]: to all created intelligent beings in the heavenly places. In a context such as this, these is no need to limit this phrase to hostile forces [NIC]. This possibly includes the ruling powers on earth as well as the angel and demon personalities [WeBC].

QUESTION—To what is ἐν τοῖς ἐπουρανίοις 'in the heavenly places' connected and what does it mean?

It is connected to ταῖς ἀρχαῖς καὶ ταῖς ἐξουσίαις 'to the rulers and authorities' [AB, Alf, DNTT, EGT, El, IB, ICC, LJ, Lns, MNTC, My, NCBC, NIC, NTC, St, TD, TH, TNTC, WBC, We, WeBC; all versions except NJB]: to the rulers and authorities who rule in the heavenly places. The words ἐν τοῖς ἐπουρανίοις 'in the heavenly places' describe a sphere in which evil as well as good forces are at work [NCBC; TNT (note)]. Since Satan and his hosts have been banished from God's heaven, the phrase primarily has reference to the earth's atmosphere, or firmament [DNTT, TD], the lower heavens where these beings are said to dwell [TD; TNT (note)]. The phrase is the full equivalent of the simpler ἐν τοῖς οὐρανοῖς 'in the heavens'. It takes the plerophoric form ἐν τοῖς ἐπουρανίοις from cultic pagan terminology because of a growing liturgical and apologetic interest [TD].

the manifold[a] wisdom[b] of-God,

LEXICON—a. πολυποίκιλος (LN **58.46**) (BAGD p. 687): 'manifold' [AB, El, LN, Lns, NIC, Rob, TH, WBC, We; KJV, NAB NASB, NIV], 'in all its different forms' [TEV], 'in its many different forms' [**LN**], 'in its rich variety' [NRSV], 'in its infinite variety' [REB], 'many-sided' [LN; NJB, TNT], '(very) many sided' [BAGD], 'many and diverse' [LN], 'iridescent' [NTC]. This term pertains to something that is different in a number of ways [LN].

b. σοφία (LN 32.32) (BAGD 3.b. p.760): 'wisdom' [AB, BAGD, El, LN, Lns, NIC, NTC, Rob, TH, WBC, We; all versions]. It usage here designates God's wisdom [BAGD]. This term denotes the capacity to understand with the result that one acts wisely [LN]. See this word at 1:8, 17.

QUESTION—What is meant by ἡ πολυποίκιλος σοφία τοῦ θεοῦ 'the manifold wisdom of God'?

1. This has reference to the whole of God's plan of redemption in general [Can, Ho, ICC, NIC, NTC, Si, TD, TH, TNTC, WeBC; NAB (note)]: in order that God's manifold wisdom, shown in all the various parts of his plan for redemption, might be made known. This wisdom is God's plan of salvation in Christ [NAB (note)]. This wisdom is the content of the soteriological 'mystery' and so identical with 'the riches of Christ' of 3:8 [TD]. According to Scripture, the aspect of the divine character of which these superhuman intelligent beings have no direct knowledge is God's grace and mercy, which, to them, might seem inconsistent with his holiness and justice, but when they see how, in the salvation of sinners through Christ, God's righteousness no less than his love is satisfied, we can understand how wisdom is the attribute specially observed [Can]. The word πολυποίκιλος 'manifold' must refer to the application of wisdom to different areas of experience so the phrase 'in everything' can be an adequate equivalent [TH].

2. This has particular reference to the formation of the church [Cal, Ea, EGT, El, IB, LJ, Lns, MNTC, My, NCBC, St, WBC, We]: in order that God's manifold wisdom, shown in uniting Jews and Gentiles into one redeemed body, may be made known. Wisdom is that quality that has to do with the use of knowledge to bring about desired goals [LJ], so that we can define the wisdom of God as that attribute by which he arranges his purposes and plans, and arranges the means to bring forth the results that he purposes [LJ, Lns, NCBC]. The wisdom shown cannot be said to be that of the general plan of redemption, the manner in which God was able to show mercy and reconcile grace and justice [Ea], but has special reference to God's plan for incorporating the Gentiles into his church and so extending salvation to all men [Ea, EGT, El, LJ, Lns]. In the church all the strands of human history come together to reveal a spiritual purpose for creation and each strand has contributed in its own way to the divine purpose [IB, We]. By being placed last, the words are emphatic [Lns, WBC].

3:11 according-to[a] (the) purpose[b] of-the ages[c] which he-formed/carried out[d] in[e] the Christ Jesus our Lord,

LEXICON—a. κατά with accusative object (LN 89.8): 'according to' [BAGD, El, Lns, NTC, Rob, TH, WBC, We; KJV, NIV, NJB, TEV], 'in accord with' [NAB], 'in accordance with' [LN; NASB, NRSV], 'in relation to' [LN], not explicit [AB, NIC]. This preposition is also translated as a verb: 'to accord with' [REB], 'to fulfill' [TNT]. This is a marker of a relation showing similarity of process [LN].

b. πρόθεσις (LN 30.63) (BAGD 2.b. p. 706): 'purpose' [BAGD, El, LN, Lns, NIC, NTC, Rob, TH, WBC, We; all versions except NJB], 'plan' [BAGD, LN; NJB], 'design' [AB], 'resolve, will' [BAGD]. This term denotes that which is planned or purposed in advance [LN].

c. αἰών (LN 67.143) (BAGD 1.b. p. 27): 'age' [AB, El, LN, Rob, TH, We], 'eternity' [NJB], 'eon' [Lns], 'era' [LN]. Some translate this noun as an adjective modifying πρόθεσιν 'purpose': 'eternal' [BAGD, NIC, NTC, WBC, We; KJV, NASB, NIV, NRSV, TEV, TNT], 'age-long' [REB], 'age-old' [NAB]. This term denotes a unit of time as a particular period or stage of history [LN].

d. aorist act. indic. of ποιέω (LN 90.45) (BAGD I.1.b.δ. p. 681): 'to form' [Lns, NIC, NTC; NJB], 'to make' [BAGD, El, TH], 'to do' [BAGD, TH], 'to purpose' [Rob; KJV], 'to achieve' [TEV], 'to carry out' [AB; NAB, NASB, NRSV], 'to accomplish' [WBC, We; NIV, REB, TNT]. In this reference, ποιέω is used with the noun πρόθεσιν 'purpose' as a periphrasis for a simple verb of doing [BAGD].

e. ἐν with dative object (LN 90.6): 'in' [AB, El, Lns, NIC, NTC, Rob, TH, WBC, We; all versions except TEV], 'through' [TEV]. This is a marker of agency. Often this implies that the agent is also used as an instrument [LN].

QUESTION—What relationship is indicated by κατά 'according to'?

1. It joins this verse to γνωρισθῇ 'might be made known' at the beginning of 3:10 [Alf, Ea, EGT, El, Ho, Lns, My, NTC, Si, St, TH, WBC]: the manifold wisdom of God might be made known according to the purpose of the ages. This disclosure of God's manifold wisdom to the rulers and authorities in the heavenly places is in accordance with the purpose of the ages [Alf, Ea, EGT, El, Ho, NTC]. In its period and instruments it is in unison with God's own eternal plan, which has been wrought out in Christ [Ea].

2. It joins this verse to ἡ πολυποίκιλος σοφία τοῦ θεοῦ 'the manifold wisdom of God' [Can, TNTC, We]: the manifold wisdom of God, (which is) according to the purpose of the ages. The connection of this verse is probably not so much that the declaration to the angels of God's manifold wisdom is according to the eternal purpose of God, as that the wisdom of God is concerned with the eternal purpose which God formed in Christ [TNTC]. The verse teaches that the wisdom of God, while much variegated and acting differently at different times, is not like the wisdom of men, changing with varying circumstances, but is constantly carrying out one great plan, formed before these ages began to roll and steadfastly held throughout all their changing course [Can].

QUESTION—What is the meaning of the genitive construction πρόθεσιν τῶν αἰώνων 'the purpose of the ages'?

1. The genitive τῶν αἰώνων 'of the ages' is one of the object or contents and presupposes that all ages are planned and instituted by God [AB]: the purpose concerning the ages.

2. This genitive serves to define the general relation of time to God's purpose [El]. Those who follow or reflect this interpretation assume that the genitive construction here is used as an equivalent of the adjective αἰώνιος 'eternal' [Alf, Ba, Ea, ECWB, EGT, Ho, ICC, NCBC, NIC, NTC, Rob, WBC, We]: God's eternal purpose. This interpretation implies that God's decision was made before all times [AB, El, Ho, NCBC, NIC, Rob, St, WBC], or spans all times [NTC, St], and therefore is 'eternal' in nature [AB, Ho, NCBC, NIC, NTC, Rob, St, WBC]. According to most, this genitive focuses more upon the ages, with the implication that the purpose was being worked on throughout these ages [Alf, Can, Ea, EBC, Ho, IB, ICC, Lns, MNTC, NTC, Rob, We]: the purpose throughout the ages, or, the purpose that ran through the ages [ICC, MNTC, My, Rob]. According to others, this genitive focuses more upon the decree of purpose, with the implication that the purposing took place before or at the commencement of the ages [Ba, EGT, El, Ho, NCBC, NIC, TH, WBC]: the purpose of ages, or, the purpose which existed, or was determined upon, in the ages. The Apostle is not speaking of God's purpose in regard to different times or dispensations [El, WBC], but that it is before all time and therefore eternal [WBC].

QUESTION—What is the meaning of the verb ἐποίησιν 'he formed/carried out'?

1. It means 'to make or form (a plan or purpose)' [Alf, Ba, BAGD, Cal, ICC, Lns, MNTC, NIC, NTC, Rob, Si, TD, TNTC]: according to the plan which he formed.
2. It means 'to achieve or carry out (a plan or purpose)' [AB, Can, Ea, EBC, ECWB, EGT, El, Ho, IB, My, NCBC, St, TD, WBC, We]: according to the plan which he carried out. After stressing the eternal decision in 1:4–5 and 10, chapters 2 and 3 describe the execution of God's will [AB]. The addition 'in Christ Jesus' clearly points to the carrying out of God's purpose in Jesus Christ, the word made flesh [El, Ho, My]. Also, the mention of Christ's lordship implies the carrying out of God's purpose [WBC].

QUESTION—What is the meaning of the preposition ἐν 'in'?

1. It means 'by' or 'through', denoting agency [TH, TNTC; TEV]. Christ is the agent of God's purpose [TNTC].
2. It means 'in', denoting the sphere or element in which the action of the verb takes effect [Ea]: which he accomplished in Christ.
3. It means 'with reference to' Christ, or 'which were to be executed through' Christ. The eternal plan had respect to Christ, and was to be executed by his coming and work [Ba].

QUESTION—How is τῷ Χριστῷ 'the Christ' used here?

1. It is simply used as part of Jesus' name [Ba, Cal, Ea, ECWB, EGT, El, Ho, IB, Lns, MNTC, NIC, NTC, TH; all versions]: in Christ Jesus our Lord. From eternity God's plan or purpose centered on the one we now call 'Christ Jesus our Lord' [NTC].

2. It specifies the messianic office of our Lord [AB, Alf, Can, ICC, My, NCBC, Rob, TNTC, We]: in the Messiah, Jesus, our Lord. 'Jesus' may be added to 'Messiah' and 'Lord' to draw attention to the ministry of the incarnate and crucified person (cf. 2:13–18) rather than the function of the preexistent person [AB, Can]. It was in his Messiah [Alf], or Christ [ICC], that God formed the purpose, and that Messiah [Alf], or Christ [ICC], is Jesus our Lord [Alf, ICC].

3:12 in[a] whom we-have the boldness[b] and access[c] in[d] confidence[e]

TEXT—Some manuscripts of the Textus Receptus tradition have the definite article before προσαγωγήν 'access' as well as with παρρησίαν 'boldness' thus making them separate concepts from each other. GNT does not note this variant reading. Those who support the reading with both articles are Alf, Ea, ECWB, El, and My. Commentators from both groups state that the presence of the article before προσαγωγήν 'access' is superfluous [EGT, Lns, My].

LEXICON—a. ἐν with dative object (LN 89.26): 'in' [AB, El, Lns, NIC, NTC, Rob, TH, WBC, We; all versions except TEV, TNT], 'in union with' [TEV, TNT], 'because of' [LN (89.26, **33.72**)], 'on account of, by reason of' [LN].

  b. παρρησία (LN 25.158) (BAGD 3.b. p. 630): 'boldness' [BAGD, El, LN (25.158), Lns, Rob, TH, WBC; KJV, NASB, NRSV, TEV], 'courage' [BAGD, LN, NTC], 'confidence, fearlessness' [BAGD], 'freedom' [NIC; NIV, REB], 'freedom of address' [We]. The phrase ἔχομεν τὴν παρρησίαν 'we have the boldness' is translated 'we can speak freely' [NAB, TNT], 'we are bold enough' [NJB]. It is also translated as an adjective modifying προσαγωγήν 'access': 'free access' [AB]. This word denotes fearlessness in the presence of persons of high rank. Used in relation to being in the presence of God, it denotes a joyousness and confidence as the result or accompaniment of faith [BAGD].

  c. προσαγωγή (LN **33.72**) (BAGD p. 711): 'access' [AB, BAGD, LN, Lns, NIC, NTC, Rob, TH, WBC, We; KJV, NASB, NRSV, REB], 'approach' [BAGD, LN], 'admission' [El]. This noun is also translated as a verb: 'to draw near' [NAB, TNT], 'to approach' [NIV, NJB], 'to go into (God's) presence' [TEV] 'to address' [**LN**]. This noun denotes the right or opportunity to address someone, with the implication that the person addressed is of higher rank or status [LN]. See this word at 2:18.

  d. ἐν with dative object (LN 89.80): 'in' [El, Lns, TH, We; NJB, NRSV], 'with' [LN (89.80, **33.72**), NIC, Rob; KJV, NAB, NIV, REB, TEV], 'while at the same time' [LN (89.80)]. The whole phrase ἐν πεποιθήσει 'in confidence' is treated as an adverb modifying ἔχομεν 'we have': 'confidently' [AB; TNT], or as an adjective modifying προσαγωγήν 'access': 'confident access' [NTC, WBC; NASB]. This is a marker of attendant circumstances and often also carries the implication of means [LN (89.80)].

e. πεποίθησις (LN 31.82) (BAGD 1. p. 643): 'confidence' [BAGD, El, LN (31.82, **33.72**), Lns, NIC, Rob, TH, We; KJV, NAB, NIV, NRSV, REB], 'complete confidence' [NJB], 'all confidence' [TEV], 'trust' [BAGD, LN]. Some treat the whole phrase ἐν πεποιθήσει 'in confidence' as an adverb modifying ἔχομεν 'we have': 'confidently' [AB; TNT], or as an adjective modifying προσαγωγήν 'access': 'confident access' [NTC, WBC; NASB]. This noun denotes trust or confidence in others. This noun denotes the belief in something or someone to the extent of placing trust and reliance upon or in them [LN].

QUESTION—How does this verse relate to the context?

Paul has finished with his lofty statement on the transcendent purpose of God and returns to speak once more of the actual experience of Christians in this life [Can, TNTC] and so links the ultimate divine purpose of creation to the human experience of communion with God in Christ [IB]. He does so by presenting the consequence of the accomplished purpose spoken of in 3:11 [Ho, Rob] in the form of a practical conclusion [EBC] or an indirect appeal [EGT] drawn from the considerations of the centrality of Christ to God's eternal purpose [EBC], which has a bearing on the practical life of believers [EBC, ECWB, EGT]. The verse returns to the thought of 2:18 [ECWB, Lns, NIC, Rob, TH] and speaks of the nearness and intimacy which believers now have with God in a remarkable fullness of expression. It is in Christ, of whom glorious things have just been spoken, that they have this nearness and intimacy [Can, IB]. Since Christ has this infinite significance, they may rely upon him with absolute trust [MNTC].

QUESTION—What is the significance of the phrase ἐν ᾧ 'in whom'?

Since the antecedent is ἐν τῷ Χριστῷ Ἰησοῦ τῷ κυρίῳ ἡμῶν 'in Christ Jesus our Lord', it indicates Christ as the sphere [Ea] or the element and condition of the believer's boldness and access to God [Alf], as well as the objective ground of the possession of these [Alf, EGT, El, My, TD, WBC]. The relative pronoun ᾧ 'whom' here seems to have a slight demonstrative force, nearly equivalent to ἐν αὐτῷ γάρ 'for in him' [EGT, El]. The phrase introduces the experimentally confirmatory proof for what has been stated in the previous verse as ἣν ἐποίησεν 'which he has fulfilled' in Christ Jesus [My].

QUESTION—What is the relationship between the two nouns παρρησίαν 'boldness' and προσαγωγήν 'access'?

1. These two nouns form one concept, even a hendiadys [AB, DNTT, EGT, Ho, ICC, Lns, NIC, NTC, TD, TH, WBC; NIV, NJB, NRSV, REB, TEV]: we have free access, access with freeness of speech. The meaning is 'boldness to enter' [TH]. Παρρησίαν 'boldness' and προσαγωγήν ἐν πεποιθήσει 'access in confidence' are synonymous expressions, in keeping with the tendency of Ephesians to heap up synonymous words or phrases [TD]. Παρρησίαν 'boldness' is the lesser or auxiliary term and serves to amplify προσαγωγήν 'access' [Lns]. Παρρησίαν 'boldness' is

defined by the words καὶ προσαγωγὴν ἐν πεποιθήσει 'and confidence of access', the καί 'and' being epexegetic [DNTT].
   2. These two nouns are treated as separate concepts [Alf, Ba, Cal, Can, Ea, ECWB, El, IB, LJ, My, NCBC, TNTC, We; KJV, NAB, NASB, TNT]: we have boldness and access. The textual variant with a definite article before each noun distinguishes them as twin elements of a distinctive and possessed privilege [Ea]. The single article before παρρησίαν 'boldness' couples both terms together as parts of the right of personal communion with God [We].

QUESTION—What is meant by παρρησίαν 'boldness'?
   1. It refers to freeness of speech [Ba, Can, Ea, EBC, ECWB, IB, ICC, Lns, We, WeBC; NAB, TNT]: we have freedom to speak to God. Here it seems to mean 'freedom of utterance' [Ba] and it indicates that believers may now come to God in prayer [Ba, Ea, IB] with confidence through the Lord Jesus [Ba]. It means believers may say all that is in their heart without fear [Can, Lns] or shame, the privilege of all who are reconciled to God [Can].
   2. It refers to a confident attitude [AB, Alf, Cal, EGT, El, Ho, LJ, My, NCBC, NIC, NTC, Rob, TD, TH, TNTC, WBC]: we have boldness before God. It refers to the state of mind [Alf], a cheerful boldness [Alf, El], a freedom of spirit [El], which may underlie a liberty of speech [Alf]. It is 'fearlessness' [Ho, LJ, TNTC, WBC], freedom from the fear of rejection or of evil [Ho, LJ], freedom from shame [TD, WBC], which are elements belonging to the attitude of those who have nothing to conceal because they are assured of God's gracious disposition toward them in Christ [WBC]. The context indicates that the apostle is speaking of the Christian's experimental consciousness, the free joyful mood of those reconciled to God [My]. It is arbitrary to restrict this to prayer [El, My], though the term was especially used in this context in Hellenistic Judaism [WBC].

QUESTION—To what is the phrase ἐν πεποιθήσει 'in confidence' attached, and what is its significance?

Ἐν πεποιθήσει 'in confidence' is used adjectivally ('full of confidence') [TD]. It refers to the assurance the believer has that his prayers will be heard [Ba] or that God accepts him in a father-child relationship [Can, Ea, ECWB, Ho, Lns, WeBC]. It indicates the proper manner in which God is called upon [Cal].
   1. This phrase goes with both the nouns παρρησίαν 'boldness' and προσαγωγήν 'access' [AB, Ea, EGT, ICC, Lns, My, NIC, TH, We; REB]: we have boldness and access, both with confidence, or, we have freedom of access with confidence. The phrase strengthens the idea of boldness: 'we have the boldness to enter confidently' [TH].
   2. This phrase only goes with προσαγωγήν 'access' [Alf, Cal, Can, DNTT, ECWB, El, Ho, LJ, NCBC, NTC, TD, TNTC, WBC, WeBC; NAB, NASB, NIV, NJB, NRSV, TEV, TNT]: we have boldness and confident

access. The phrase ἐν πεποιθήσει 'in confidence' strengthens the idea already resident in προσαγωγήν 'access' [NTC, WBC]. 'Access with confidence' is a thought very similar to 'boldness', but is more personal [TNTC].

through/because-of[a] the faith/faithfulness[b] in/of-him.
LEXICON—a. διά with genitive object (LN 89.26, 89.76) (BAGD A.III.1.d. p. 180): 'through' [BAGD, El, LN (89.76), NIC, NTC, TH, WBC, We; NAB, NASB, NIV, NJB, NRSV, TEV, TNT], 'by means of' [BAGD, LN (89.76), Lns], 'by' [BAGD, LN (89.76), Rob; KJV], 'because of' [AB, LN (89.26)], 'born of' [REB]. The preposition in this reference denotes the efficient cause [BAGD].
b. πίστις (LN 31.85) (BAGD 2.b.β. p. 663): 'faith' [BAGD, El, LN, Lns, NIC, NTC, Rob, TH, WBC, We; all versions except REB], 'trust' [LN; REB], 'faithfulness' [AB].
QUESTION—What relationship is indicated by διά 'through/because of'?
   1. It indicates means [Ea, WBC; all versions except REB]: we have boldness and access by means of faith in him. It is the means by which believers appropriate for themselves the new situation God has brought about in and through Christ [WBC].
   2. It indicates reason [My, TH]: we have boldness and access because of faith in him.
   1. It indicates the means by which believers have boldness and access to God [Alf, Ba, Cal, Can, Ea, EGT, El, Ho, ICC, LJ, Lns, MNTC, My, NIC, NTC, Rob, St, TNTC, WBC, We; all versions except REB]: we have boldness and access by means of faith in him. It indicates the instrumental cause for ἔχομεν... 'we have, etc.' [My], the subjective means [Lns, My] for its appropriation and continued possession [My]. It is the means by which believers appropriate for themselves the new situation God has brought about in and through Christ [WBC].
   2. It indicates the reason that believers have boldness and access to God [AB, BAGD (A.III.1.d. p. 180), EBC, TH]: we have boldness and access because of faith in him. Both of the phrases 'in whom' and 'through faith in him' state the basis for the boldness which believers may have in entering into God's presence. This relationship is often expressed as a type of cause [TH]. It is in Christ and on the ground of faith in him that believers can enter into God's presence (Eph. 2:18) without the inhibitions that stem from any kind of self-reliance or self-consciousness [EBC].
QUESTION—What relationship is shown by the genitive construction πίστεως αὐτοῦ 'faith of him'?
   1. Christ is the object of the faith [Alf, BAGD, Cal, Can, Ea, ECWB, EGT, El, Ho, ICC, LJ, Lns, MNTC, My, NIC, NTC, Rob, TD, TH, TNTC, Tu, WBC, We, WeBC; all versions except KJV]: through faith in him. That this is faith in Christ is clearly indicated by the objective genitive [BAGD]. There is nothing more implied in the genitive αὐτοῦ 'of him'

than in the usual εἰς αὐτόν 'in him' construction [El, My]. The article before πίστεως 'faith' is parallel to the article before παρρησίαν 'boldness' [Rob] so that the meaning is '*our* faith in him' [Rob, We].
2. Christ is the one producing the action denoted by πίστις 'faith/faithfulness' [AB, NCBC]: by his faith/faithfulness. Paul usually uses the formulae 'faith into Christ' (εἰς Χριστόν) or 'faith upon Christ' (ἐπὶ Χριστῷ) when he speaks of the believer's faith in Christ. The formula used here differs only in the presence of the article from the parallel passages in Gal. 2:16; 3:22; Rom. 3:22; and Phil. 3:8. These texts speak of the 'faith of Christ' which in Eph. 2:13–18 was described as the means of opening the door to God. In such a case, the words 'through his faithfulness' are synonyms for 'in Christ's blood', 'in his flesh' etc. in Eph. 2:13–18. While a man may approach God 'in confidence', as this text indicates, such a confidence is an accompaniment of access, not an instrument. In Eph. 2:18, where προσαγωγή 'access' occurred previously, it was shown that all emphasis is put upon him who makes the introduction, Jesus Christ the Mediator [AB].

DISCOURSE UNIT: 3:13–21 [Ba]. The topic is the apostle's prayer that his readers might avail themselves fully of the doctrine of the Gentiles' place in the purpose of God and be able to appreciate fully the advantages which this was intended to confer.

DISCOURSE UNIT: 3:13–19 [Ba]. The topic is the apostle's wish that they should comprehend the glory of this plan of salvation.

3:13 Therefore[a] I-ask[b] (that you/I) not to-lose-heart[c] in[d] my tribulations[e] on-behalf[f] of-you,

LEXICON—a. διό (LN 89.47): 'therefore' [AB, LN, NIC, NTC, WBC; NASB, NIV, NRSV], 'wherefore' [El, Lns, Rob, We; KJV], 'for this reason' [LN], 'hence' [NAB], 'so then' [LN], 'then' [REB, TEV], 'so' [NJB, TNT]. This is a relatively emphatic marker of result, based upon what has preceded, and usually denotes that the inference is self-evident [LN].
  b. pres. mid. indic. of αἰτέω (LN 33.163) (BAGD p. 26): 'to ask' [AB, BAGD, LN, Lns, NTC, Rob; NASB, NIV], 'to desire' [KJV], 'to beg' [NIC, WBC, We; NAB, NJB, REB, TEV, TNT], 'to plead for' [LN], 'to entreat' [El], 'to pray' [NRSV]. This verb denotes an urgency of request, even to the point of making a demand [Ho, LN]. Here, the verb has the simple sense of 'asking' (not 'demanding') and the middle voice has the full reflexive sense of 'asking for oneself' [EGT].
  c. pres. act. infin. of ἐγκακέω (LN **25.288**) (BAGD 2. p. 215) or ἐκκακέω (BAGD p. 240): 'to lose heart' [AB, BAGD (both listings), El, LN, Lns, NIC, NTC; NASB, NRSV, REB], 'to despair' [BAGD (2. p. 215)], 'to let (something) make (one) waver' [NJB], 'to give up' [**LN**], 'to faint' [Rob, We; KJV], 'to be disheartened' [NAB], 'to be/become discouraged' [LN, WBC; NIV, TEV, TNT]. This verb denotes the loss of motivation in the

accomplishment of some valid goal [LN]. The verb has the connotation of 'to be a coward' [Ba, Can, ECWB, My, NCBC, Rob].

d. ἐν with dative object (LN 89.26): 'in' [El, Lns], 'at' [NIC, Rob, We; KJV, NASB], 'over' [AB, NTC; NRSV, REB], 'by' [NAB], 'because' [TEV], 'because of' [LN, WBC; NIV, TNT], 'on account of, by reason of' [LN], not explicit [NJB].

e. θλῖψις (LN 22.2) (BAGD 1. p. 362): 'tribulation' [El, Lns, Rob, We; KJV, NASB], 'trouble and suffering' [LN], 'suffering' [LN, WBC; NIV, NRSV, REB, TNT], 'affliction' [BAGD, NIC], 'persecution' [LN]. This noun is also translated as a verb: 'to suffer' [TEV], 'to suffer difficulties' [LN (25.288)], 'to suffer tribulations' [AB], 'to suffer (something)' [NTC], 'to endure trials' [NAB], 'to go through hardships' [NJB]. This usage of the noun denotes distress that is brought about through outward circumstances [BAGD].

f. ὑπέρ with genitive object (LN 90.36) (BAGD 1.a.ε. p. 838): 'in/on behalf of' [BAGD, LN, Lns, NIC, WBC; NASB, TNT], 'for the sake of' [BAGD, LN], 'on account of' [NJB], 'for' [AB, BAGD, El, LN, NTC, Rob, We; KJV, NAB, NIV, NRSV, REB, TEV]. This preposition marks someone who is benefited by an event or in whose behalf an event takes place [LN].

QUESTION—What relationship is indicated by διό 'therefore'?

1. It indicates a conclusion drawn from the whole digression of 3:2–12 [AB, Alf, Ba, Cal, Can, EBC, EGT, El, IB, Lns, My, NIC, NTC, TNTC, WBC, We] or, from 3:8–12 [Ea, ECWB, ICC]: in light of the important ministry God has given me and the great spiritual privileges we have, I therefore ask that you not lose heart. The logical reference is to the preceding description of the great plan which Paul was appointed to serve [AB, Alf]. This has special reference to Paul's own part in it [Alf]. These readers were not to be discouraged over a system of religion which caused such calamities to happen to its spokesmen, but, rather to hold to it because this religion had so many benefits for them [Ba]. They should not desert such a great cause merely because its spokesman was imprisoned [Can].

2. It indicates a conclusion drawn from the previous verse [Ho, MNTC, TH]: because we enjoy this access to God, I therefore ask that you not lose heart. Διό 'therefore' introduces the logical consequence of the 'boldness' and 'confidence' spoken of in the last verse. The readers should not lose their boldness and confidence because of the writer's suffering on their behalf [TH].

QUESTION—Who are the participants of the verbs in this clause?

1. I (Paul) ask you (Ephesians) not to lose heart [AB, Alf, Ba, Cal, Can, Ea, EBC, ECWB, EGT, El, Ho, IB, ICC, LN (25.288), Lns, MNTC, My, NCBC, NIC, NTC, Rob, St, TD, TNTC, WBC, We, WeBC; all versions].

2. I ask God that you not lose heart [AB, DNTT; NRSV].

3. I ask God that I not lose heart [TD]. Paul's request in prayer is that he should not fail to discharge his ministry in this situation [TD]. TH reports

this interpretation to be held in modern times by the authors, Dodd, Goodspeed, and it is the margin reading of the RSV.

QUESTION—What did these Gentile believers face that might cause them to lose heart?

The idea is not that they might give up their own faith in the Gospel [Lns], but that they might lose heart over the great cause of the Gentiles since Paul, their apostle and leading spokesman, had been imprisoned for some four years, and his work among the Gentiles was apparently at an end [ECWB, Lns, Rob].

QUESTION—What relationship is indicated by ἐν 'in' in the phrase ἐν ταῖς θλίψεσιν 'in my tribulations'?

1. It indicates the reason or cause of the possible discouragement or loss of heart [AB, Can, NTC, Rob, TH, TNTC, WBC, We; KJV, NAB, NASB, NIV, NJB, NRSV, REB, TEV, TNT]: not to lose heart because of my tribulations.
2. It indicates the sphere, circumstances, or relation in which the discouragement would be shown [Alf, Ea, EGT, El, ICC, Lns, My]: not to lose heart in my tribulations. Ἐν 'in' has the proper force of 'in', not 'at', and points to the sphere [Alf, EGT, El], circumstances [EGT, ICC], or relation [Ea, EGT, My] in which the faint-heartedness might show itself. Ἐν 'in' is not properly 'on account of' as many think, but rather it represents the close and sympathizing relationship in which Paul and his readers stood. His afflictions had become theirs [Ea]. The ἐν 'in' denotes the subsisting relation 'in which' their courage is not to fail [My].

QUESTION—What is meant by θλίψεσιν 'tribulations'?

The immediate reference is to Paul's imprisonment (3:1) [AB, Cal, CBC, Ea, EBC, ECWB, IB, Lns, MNTC, NCBC, NIC, NTC, Rob, St, TD, TH, TNTC, We, WeBC]. It designates all those sufferings which came upon him because he was the Apostle to the Gentiles [ICC, My, WBC]. His desire to bring the Gospel to the Gentiles was the cause of his punishment [NCBC, TNTC, We, WeBC].

QUESTION—What is the function of the phrase ὑπὲρ ὑμῶν 'on your behalf'?

It takes up the phrase ὑπὲρ ὑμῶν ἐθνῶν 'on behalf of you Gentiles' of 3:1 and the εἰς ὑμᾶς 'for you' of 3:2, so closing this section as it began, by recalling to the Gentile Christian readers their intimate links with the apostle [WBC].

which is your glory.[a]

LEXICON—a. δόξα (LN 25.205, 87.4): 'glory' [El, LN (87.23), Lns, NIC, NTC, Rob, WBC, We; KJV, NAB, NASB, NIV, NJB, NRSV, REB], 'glorification' [AB], 'benefit' [TEV], 'respect, honor' [LN (87.4)], 'pride' [LN (25.205)]. One translates this noun as a verb: 'to be proud' [TNT]. This noun may denote something which is a basis for legitimate pride [LN (25.205)], or it may denote honor as an assignment of status to a person [LN (87.4)].

QUESTION—What is the antecedent of the indefinite feminine relative pronoun ἥτις 'which'?

1. The antecedent is ταῖς θλίψεσίν μου 'my tribulations' [AB, Cal, Can, CBC, Ea, EBC, ECWB, EGT, El, Ho, IB, ICC, Lns, MNTC, My, NIC, NTC, Rob, St, TH, TNTC, WBC, We, WeBC; all versions except, possibly, KJV]: my tribulations are your glory. Paul's sufferings for the Gentile churches were vicarious [AB, IB, NIC, WBC]. His very afflictions which tended to dishearten them were an honor to them [Can, Ea, TNTC]. The indefinite relative pronoun ἥτις 'which' is used by attraction to the following predicate δόξα 'glory' [Ea, EGT, El, HG, Lns, My, NIC, We], taking both its number [EGT, HG, Lns, NIC] and gender [EGT, El, Lns, NIC] from that noun, however its antecedent is the ταῖς θλίψεσίν μου 'my tribulations' [Ea, EGT, El, HG, Lns, My, NIC, We].
2. The antecedent is the whole preceding statement relative to not losing heart [NCBC]: your not losing heart is your glory. This refers to the thought of the whole preceding sentence. The readers finding courage from the circumstances of Paul's ordeals will be their glory.

QUESTION—What is the force of the indefinite feminine relative pronoun ἥτις 'which'?

The pronoun has the force of an explanation, meaning 'inasmuch as', 'for', or 'indeed' [AB, Alf, Ea, EGT, El, HG, Ho, Lns, My, NIC, We; NASB, REB]: not to lose heart in my tribulations for you, inasmuch as they are your glory. Here the meaning is: 'since this is such a thing as to be your glory' [Lns]. The clause gives the readers a reason or motive for not losing heart [EGT, Ho, ICC, My]. It states how the things Paul is suffering ὑπέρ ὑμῶν 'in your behalf' will benefit the Ephesians [Lns]. It implies that what is predicated ('glory') belongs to the nature of the thing ('my tribulations') [ICC, My].

QUESTION—What is meant by δόξα ὑμῶν 'your glory'?

1. It refers to some temporal benefit the church has or will gain [Alf, Ba, Can, EBC, EGT, El, IB, ICC, Lns, My, NTC, TD, TNTC, WeBC].
  1.1 It refers to the worth God and/or Paul place upon these Gentile believers as recipients of salvation [Alf, Can, EBC (probably), EGT, El, ICC, Lns, My, NTC, TD]. It shows how much Paul thinks of them that he suffers so for them [Can, NTC]. All this suffering by the apostle on their behalf reveals the worth God places on these Gentile churches [NTC]. The greater the office of the one suffering on their behalf, the greater would be the honor which the sufferings would bring to them [EGT, ICC, My].
  1.2 It refers to the honor the church possesses as the repository of the glorious gospel of truth [Cal, Ea, ECWB, IB, MNTC, NCBC, TD, TNTC, We]. Paul's sufferings show the grandeur of the truth which the church has received [NCBC, We] and ratify the substance of their faith [Cal, Ea]. Paul's readers are to consider that out of the sacrifice of his sufferings God will bring some great blessing for the Church. Jew and Roman were only the instruments of Christ, who had imposed this

imprisonment on his servant for some purpose of his own. This purpose could only help forward the work among the Gentiles, though how was not immediately evident. They would find in the end that all this would turn out to be an honor to them [MNTC].

2. It refers to their final glorification [AB, CBC, DNTT, NIC, TD, TH, WBC]. The apostle's sufferings in prison will hasten the time when they will all share in the 'glory' of God's Kingdom [CBC]. Apostolic suffering is seen as helping to make up the quota of messianic suffering prior to the consummation of salvation in glory, so that, in this way, apostolic suffering mediates salvation to others, bringing to these Gentile believers the experience of glory [NIC, WBC].

DISCOURSE UNIT: 3:14–21 [AB, CBC, EBC, Ho, Lns, NCBC, NTC, Rob, St, TH, TNTC, WBC, WeBC; NAB, NIV, NJB, TEV]. The topic is Paul's prayer [AB, CBC, Lns, TH, TNTC, WBC, WeBC; NAB, NIV, NJB] on behalf of the Church [WeBC] for the perfection of his readers [AB], for knowledge [EBC, Rob, TH] and fullness [EBC], and that Christ will make his home in them [TH]. It is adoration of the church glorious for its lofty goal of knowing the love of Christ [NTC], confidence in God's power [St], the love of Christ [NCBC; TEV].

DISCOURSE UNIT: 3:14–19 [Alf, ECWB, EGT, El, IB, ICC, MNTC, My, NCBC, NIC, Rob, Si, We]. The topic is Paul's prayer for his readers [Alf, ECWB, EGT, IB, ICC, MNTC, NCBC, Rob, Si, We] in regards to their advancement to spiritual fulfillment [IB], their being enabled to discharge their office for the whole body [Alf, We], their advancement to perfect faith and knowledge [MNTC], their knowledge of the mystery, already described, in all its fullness [ECWB, IB, MNTC], their becoming strong in the power of the Spirit [Alf, EGT, El, ICC, My, NIC], the presence of Christ in them [ECWB, EGT, El, ICC], their growth in the knowledge of the love of Christ [ECWB, EGT, El, ICC, My, NIC, Rob], and the realization in themselves of growth into the 'fullness of God' [ECWB, El, My], i.e. the Divine perfections [EGT].

3:14 (For) this reason[a] I-bow[b] my knees to[c] the Father,

TEXT—Some manuscripts add the words τοῦ κυρίου ἡμῶν Ἰησοῦ Χριστοῦ 'of our Lord Jesus Christ' after πατέρα 'Father'. GNT omits these words with a B rating, indicating that the omission is almost certain. The addition is accepted by only Ba, Cal, Ho, and KJV.

LEXICON—a. χάριν: 'reason'. See this phrase at 3:1.

b. pres. act. indic. of κάμπτω (LN 53.61) (BAGD 1. p. 402): 'to bow' [AB, BAGD, El, Lns, Rob, We; KJV, NASB, NRSV], 'to bend' [BAGD, NIC, NTC, TH], 'to fall on' [TEV]. Some combine this verb with its object γόνατα 'knees': 'to kneel' [WBC; NAB, NIV], 'to kneel in prayer' [REB, TNT], 'to pray, kneeling' [NJB], 'to bow before, to worship' [LN]. 'Knees' is a metonymy standing for the person [LN (fn. 8, p. 541)] and for a person 'to bend or bow' means that he is worshipping [BAGD, LN].

c. πρός with accusative object (LN 84.18): 'to' [LN, Lns, NIC, NTC, TH; REB, TNT], 'unto' [El, Rob, We; KJV], 'before' [AB, BAGD, WBC; NAB, NASB, NIV, NJB, NRSV, TEV].

QUESTION—What is the meaning and referent of τοῦτο χάριν 'for this reason'?

1. The phrase indicates reason or cause [AB, Alf, Bu, Can, Ea, EBC, ECWB, EGT, El, Ho, ICC, LJ, Lns, MNTC, NCBC, NIC, NTC, Rob, St, TH, TNTC, WBC, We, WeBC; all versions except NJB]. Most commentators regard τοῦτο χάριν 'for this reason' as resuming the τοῦτο χάριν 'for this reason' of 3:1 [AB, Alf, Bu, Ea, EBC, ECWB, EGT, El, HG, Ho, ICC, LJ, Lns, MNTC, NCBC, NIC, NTC, Rob, St, TH, TNTC, We; TNT (note)].

1.1 This refers both to the material of 3:2–13 and the material of chapter 2 [TNTC, WBC], or of the last part of chapter 2 [AB, Alf, El, Lns, MNTC, NTC, Rob, TH]: Because you are united together with us Jews in God's church and have such a place in God's great plan, I bow my knees to the Father. It refers to the train of thought at the end of chapter 2 as well as to the ideas parallel to it in the digression of 3:2–13 [El, WBC]. Paul is led to prayer by the thought of Christ's grace in raising to life those who were dead in sin, by the realization of the unity of Jew and Gentile in one household, by the contemplation of the whole purpose of God, and, finally, by the temptation of his followers to lose heart [TNTC]. With τοῦτο χάριν 'for this reason' resuming the τοῦτο χάριν 'for this reason' of 3:1 [AB, Alf, WBC], the following prayer justifies the long and solemn parenthesis of 3:2–13 [Alf]. The reference is the same as the referent in 3:1, but the intervening material, 3:2–13, has added another reason to the reason of 3:1, that is, God's wonderful dealings with Paul himself, dealings that have given Paul confidence in prayer. What the apostle means by using this phrase is this: It is because God has dealt so kindly with you, Ephesians, and me, Paul, that I have the courage of confident access to pray to the Father for you [NTC].

1.2 This refers primarily [EGT, ICC] or only [Ea, EBC, Ho, LJ] to the concluding section of chapter 2 [Ea, EBC, EGT, Ho, ICC, LJ]: Because you are built into the spiritual temple, I bow my knees to the Father. It is because the Gentile Christians now are incorporated into the body of Christ that Paul asks the Father that they may fully appropriate their spiritual privileges [EBC].

1.3 This refers primarily to the parenthetical material just discussed, 3:2–13 [St]: Because of God's revealed purpose for you, I bow my knees to the Father.

1.4 This refers only to 3:13 [Can]: Because it will not be easy for you to remain steadfast in regard to my sufferings for you, I bow my knees to the Father.

1.5 This refers to all of the preceding parts of the Epistle [NCBC, WeBC]: Because of everything I've written so far, I bow my knees to the Father.

EPHESIANS 3:14

2. The phrase indicates purpose [Ba, LN (89.60), My].
2.1 This refers to what immediately precedes [Ba]: Therefore, in order that God's great purpose may be carried on and that the purposes of my sufferings on your behalf may be answered to your benefit and glory, I bow my knees to the Father.
2.2 This refers to 3:13 only [My]: Therefore, in order that you may not become disheartened, I bow my knees to the Father.

QUESTION—What is the significance of κάμπτω τὸ γόνατά μου 'I bow my knees'?

This is metonymy, the bodily attitude associated with prayer being put for the exercise of praying itself [Cal, Ea, Ho, ICC, LN (53.61), My, TD]. It does not indicate that Paul actually knelt as he wrote [EGT, ICC, LJ, My], but it does indicate that this was the normal, literal posture he used when he prayed, as seen from the present tense of the verb [Lns].

1. The posture is significant as expressing a special earnestness and humility in this prayer [AB, Can, DNTT, EGT, El, ICC, Rob, St, TNTC, WBC, WeBC].
1.1 This was the Eastern posture of prostration [AB, DNTT, Rob, TD, WeBC]. Equivalent expressions indicate that no distinction is intended between kneeling and complete prostration [TD]. This posture is not the upright kneeling the Western Church is familiar with, but kneeling with the head touching the ground (Luke 22:41 and Matt. 26:39) [AB, DNTT, Rob], the Eastern prostration [Rob, WeBC].
1.2 This was a posture of kneeling accepted in the Church [ICC, St, TNTC, WeBC]. Kneeling for prayer was the posture customarily used by the early Christians [WeBC] and it has become the accepted Christian attitude in prayer [TNTC].
2. This posture has no special significance as it was a proper and usual posture used in prayer [Ba, Cal, Ea, EBC, ISBE2, LJ, Lns, NCBC, NTC]. Kneeling as a posture in prayer is distinct from prostration [ISBE2]. While standing was the posture commonly used by the Jews, kneeling was not unknown to them, and it was the common posture for Christians [EBC]. The posture indicates solemnity, adoration, and submissiveness [EBC, LJ, NTC]. Such a posture indicates reverence [Ba, Cal, LJ, Lns] and could [NTC], or should [Ba], be assumed when we pray to God [Ba, NTC], especially in matters of continued prayer [Cal]. The posture is the instinctive expression of homage, humility, and petition [Ea, Lns, NCBC].

3:15 from[a] whom the-whole/every[b] family/fatherhood[c] in (the) heavens[d] and on earth is-named,[e]

LEXICON—a. ἐκ with genitive object (LN 89.3): 'from' [AB, El, LN, Lns, NIC, NTC, TH, WBC, We; all versions except KJV] 'of' [Rob; KJV]. This is a marker of the source from which something or someone is physically or psychologically derived [LN]. The preposition ἐκ 'from'

240　　　　　　　　　　　　EPHESIANS 3:15

conveys a more direct idea of origination than the preposition ἀπό 'from' would [EGT, El].
b. πᾶς (LN 59.23): 'every' [El, LN, TH, WBC, We; NAB, NASB, NJB, NRSV, REB, TEV, TNT], 'each' [AB, LN], 'the whole' [LN, NTC; KJV, NIV], 'all' [LN, Lns, NIC, Rob]. This denotes the totality of any object, mass, collective, or extension [LN].
c. πατριά (LN 10.24, 11.56) (BAGD 3. p. 636): 'family' [AB, BAGD, Lns, NTC, TH, WBC, We; all versions except NJB], 'family line, lineage' [LN (10.24)], 'nation, people' [LN (11.56)], 'a division of a nation' [BAGD], 'race' [El], 'fatherhood' [NIC, Rob; NJB]. This noun denotes persons of successive generations who are related by birth [LN (10.24)], or it denotes a relatively large group of people who constitute a sociopolitical unit that shares a presumed biological descent [LN (11.56)].
d. οὐρανός (LN 1.11) (BAGD 2.c. p. 595): 'heaven' [AB, BAGD, El, LN, NIC, NTC, Rob, TH, WBC, We; all versions], 'heavens' [Lns]. This noun here denotes heaven as the abode of the angels [BAGD]. This noun denotes heaven as the dwelling place of God [LN, TD] and other heavenly beings [LN]. There is no difference of meaning between the singular and plural forms [LN].
e. pres. pass. indic. of ὀνομάζω (LN 33.127) (BAGD 1. p. 574): 'to be named' [BAGD, El, Lns, Rob, TH; KJV], 'to be called, to be given a name' [BAGD, LN]. Most translate this passive verb as active: 'to take a name' [NIC; NAB, NJB, NRSV, REB], 'to receive a name' [AB, BAGD], 'to receive a true name' [TEV], 'to receive a name and a nature' [TNT], 'to derive a name' [NTC, WBC, We; NASB, NIV].

QUESTION—How does this verse relate to its context?

This verse is a description of the 'Father' to whom Paul prays [Can, Ho, IB, LJ, Lns, MNTC, NCBC, NTC, WBC]. The preposition ἐκ 'from' points to the source from which the name πατριά 'family/fatherhood' is derived [EGT, El, My]. The primary reason for this expansion is simply to stress the Father's greatness, reminding the readers that he is praying to a very great God [WBC].

QUESTION—What is the meaning of πᾶσα 'the whole/every'?
1. It means 'every, each' [AB, Alf, Can, CBC, DNTT, Ea, ECWB, EGT, El, HG, ICC, MNTC, My, My-ed, NCBC, TD, TH, TNTC, WBC, We; NAB, NASB, NJB, NRSV, REB, TEV, TNT]: every family. The qualifying phrase ἐν οὐρανοῖς καὶ ἐπὶ γῆς 'in heaven and on earth' makes it quite improbable that 'the whole family' is meant [TH]. Grammatically, the anarthrous πᾶσα πατριά 'every family' cannot mean 'the whole family' [EGT, El, ICC, TNTC, WBC] so that all such ideas that angels and men, or the blessed in heaven and the believing on earth, are viewed as forming one great family, are excluded. What is taught is that the various classes of men on earth and the various classes of angels in heaven, each by itself, gets the significant name πατριά 'family, community' only as each order is related to God, the common Father [EGT].

2. It means 'all, the whole' [Alf-ed, Ba, Cal, EBC, Ho, LJ, Lns, Mo, NIC, NTC, Rob, St, WeBC; KJV, NIV]: the whole family. There is something inherently inappropriate in a reference to a multiplicity of families here [St]. The emphasis of the epistle has been on the oneness, the unity, of the body, rather than on plurality. So the context favors this interpretation [EBC, Ho, LJ, Lns, NTC, St]. He is encouraging them to no longer think of themselves as Gentiles but as members of the one family [LJ], and it is to the head of this one great family that Paul is about to pray on their behalf [LJ, NTC].

QUESTION—What is the relationship between the noun πατήρ 'father' in the preceding verse and πατριά 'family/fatherhood' here?

There is a deliberate play upon the words due to their cognate construction [Alf, Can, CBC, Ea, EBC, ECWB, EGT, El, Lns, MNTC, My, NCBC, NIC, NTC, Rob, St, TD, TH, WBC]. It is from the name πατήρ 'father' that every πατριά 'family' derives its appellation [El]. The classes of beings referred to by the apostle have each become a πατριά 'family' from their relation to the πατήρ 'father' [Ea].

QUESTION—What is meant by πατριά 'family/fatherhood'?
1. It means 'family, lineage' [AB, Alf, Ba, BAGD, Can, Ea, EBC, ECWB, Ho, LJ, Lns, MNTC, NCBC, NTC, TD, TH, WBC, We, WeBC; all versions except NJB]: every family. The word denotes people who have a common πατήρ 'father' [Alf, Ea, ECWB, Ho, NCBC, NTC, Rob, WBC, We], immediate or remote [Ho]. Here it should be taken as a general reference to family groupings, and so to the basic relationship structures of human life [WBC]. The usage of the term presupposes a societal, 'family' structure that exists within the group so named, and here focus is placed upon that structure [AB].
2. It means 'tribe, race, people, nation' [BAGD, EGT, El, IB, ICC, My, TH]: every race. Here the widest sense of 'class', 'order', 'nation', or 'community' is indicated since the proper sense of 'family' is not applicable to angels, who are indicated by the phrase ἐν οὐρανοῖς 'in (the) heavens' [EGT, My]. The earthly families the writer has in mind are the nations which ascribe their unity to some common ancestor, such as the Jews from Judah, the son of Jacob, and the Greeks from Hellen, the son of Deucalion [IB].
3. It means 'fatherhood' [NIC, Rob, Si, St, TNTC; NJB]: every fatherhood. Strictly speaking πατριά cannot be translated 'fatherhood' but, by context and derivation, this idea is here [TNTC]. The relationship between πατήρ 'father' and πατριά 'family' is deliberate and should be preserved in translation; the translation 'fatherhood' for πατριά 'family' is justified [NIC]. The whole point of the apostle's play on words here is to show that the Greek word for family is named from the Greek word for 'father'. But in English the 'family' is not named from the 'father', so in order to make Paul's point and to reproduce the play on words a paraphrase in English is necessary as, 'the Father, of whom all fatherhood is named' [Rob].

QUESTION—What does ἐν οὐρανοῖς καὶ ἐπὶ γῆς 'in heaven and on earth' mean?
  1. It refers to the same entities as the τὰ πάντα 'all things' used elsewhere in the Epistle [AB, WBC]. It refers to every societal structure among the angelic and demonic powers in heaven and families on earth [AB, WBC].
  2. It refers to 'family' groups of men on earth and of angelic hosts in heaven [Alf, Cal, Can, CBC, DNTT, Ea, EGT, ICC, My, NIC, Si, TD, TH,]. The term 'father' was used with great latitude in ancient times. Since πατριά may be the equivalent of the Hebrew 'father's house', Paul may conceive of the angels as belonging to the regular rule of order of God's house, as principalities and powers under the Father's dominion [Can]. The πατριά 'families' on earth are, no doubt, the nations [IB, ICC], with their fundamental divisions into Jews and Gentiles [ICC]. The πατριά 'families' in heaven are the angels, regarded as belonging to certain groups, or 'tribes' [CBC, ICC, TD] with no implication of descent being necessary [TD].
  3. It refers to the society of redeemed men on earth and of redeemed saints in heaven [Alf-ed, Ba, Ho, LJ, Lns, NCBC, NTC, St, WeBC]. Those who are seen as children here, then, are those who are by Jesus Christ brought into a spiritual relationship with God. The portion of the πατριά 'family' designated by ἐν οὐρανοῖς 'in (the) heavens' then are not the angels, but the redeemed already saved, while those designated by ἐπὶ γῆς 'on the earth' are the company of believers still living [Ho, LJ, Lns]. The emphasis on the unity of the church in this epistle ties in with the idea that the church militant on earth and the church triumphant in heaven is still *one* church [NTC].
  4. It refers to redeemed men in both heaven and earth and to the angelic hosts [EBC].

QUESTION—What is meant by ὀνομάζεται 'is named'?
  1. This verb refers to assigning the names of the ancestors or fathers to the various families and clans that are found in heaven and earth [Alf, Can, DNTT, ECWB, IB, My-ed, WBC]. It refers to whatever group is united under one common fatherhood and bears the name, as in a family or clan, of the common ancestor [ECWB]. The fathers whose names these families bear are the imperfect representatives of God, and the families, with their heads, are the types in miniature of the whole society of spiritual beings united in sonship to the Heavenly Father. Therefore, it is ultimately from God that every group derives the name of πατριά 'family', and by that very name are witnesses to the Divine Fatherhood which the apostle is stressing [ECWB]. It means that every family reflects in its name (and constitution, though this is not focused upon here) the being and source of the great Father himself [Alf]. The verb evokes some OT connotations as to 'naming' in terms of bringing into existence and exercising dominion. The Father is Creator and Lord of all family groupings. Their existence and significance depends upon him [WBC]. God names each family in

heaven and earth, so he is Father of them all [DNTT, TD], for it is the prerogative of a father to give names [TD].
2. This verb refers to associating the name 'God' with this family [Ho, LJ, Lns, MNTC]. Just as children derive their name from their father and their relationship to him is determined from that, ὀνομάζεται 'is named' means that the family of God derives its name from him and are known and recognized as his children [Ho]. The family name that is on us is the name of God [LJ]. Paul thinks of the inhabitants of heaven and earth as divided into countless races and groups, all of them acknowledging God as their 'Father', and by this common relation to him, they are all bound together [MNTC].
3. This verb refers to the actual cognate construction between πατήρ 'father' and πατριά 'family/fatherhood', so the name (or title) involved is πατριά in the sense of 'fatherhood' [Rob, St] or 'family' [Ea, ICC, My, TD, We]. Πατήρ 'father' is named in πατριά 'family/fatherhood' [My]. If proper regard is given to the etymological play on the words πατήρ 'father' and πατριά 'family' and to the preposition ἐξ 'from', it will be evident that the meaning is not that God is the name-giver, but that every πατριά 'family' is so named after the πατήρ 'Father' [TD]. It may be that Paul is saying that the very notion of fatherhood is derived from the fatherhood of God [St].
4. It means the same as 'is', 'is constituted', or 'exists' [Ba, Cal, CBC (probably), TH, TNTC (probably)] and the name involved, as agent, is 'Christ' [Ba, Cal] or 'Father' [TH, TNTC]. This refers to the whole community as being constituted into one family, all bearing the name of the head of the family, not that all are actually called by the same name, nor that angels are called Christians, but all constitute one great and glorious brotherhood in Christ [Ba]. 'Name' here stands for identity and character. The main point that Paul is making is that God is the Father of all animate beings; there is no group that does not owe its existence to him. Accordingly, the whole clause may be rendered effectively as 'who causes every group in heaven and earth to exist' [TH].

3:16 that[a] he-might-give[b] you according-to[c] the riches[d] of-his glory[e]

LEXICON—a. ἵνα (LN 90.22): 'that' [AB, El, LN, Lns, NIC, NTC, Rob, TH, We; all versions except NJB, TEV], 'in order that' [WBC], not explicit [NJB, TEV]. This is a marker of the content of discourse, especially if purpose is implied [LN].
  b. aorist act. subj. of δίδωμι (LN 57.71): 'to give' [LN, Lns, TH; TEV], 'to grant' [AB, El, NIC, NTC, Rob, WBC, We; KJV, NASB, NRSV, REB, TNT], 'to bestow gifts' [NAB], 'to enable' [NJB]. The phrase 'to give to be strengthened' is translated 'to strengthen' [NIV]. This verb denotes the act of giving and usually implies some value in the item given [LN].
  c. κατά with accusative object (LN 89.8): 'according to' [El, Lns, NIC, NTC, Rob, TH, WBC, We; KJV, NASB, NRSV], 'in accordance with'

[LN], 'in keeping with' [NAB], 'in' [NJB], 'from' [TEV], 'out of' [NAB, NIV, REB, TNT], not explicit [AB]. This preposition marks a relation involving similarity of process [LN].

d. πλοῦτος: 'riches'. See this word at 1:7, 18; 2:7; 3:8.

e. δόξα: 'glory'. See this word at 1:6, 12, 14, 17, 18.

QUESTION—What is the function of ἵνα 'that'?

The non-final ἵνα 'that' with the subjunctive δῷ 'may give' introduces the content of the prayer [EBC, EGT, El, ICC, Lns, Mo, My, NTC]. This is the first of three occurrences of this particle (3:16, 18, 19b) which mark the introduction of each petition [EBC]. Another commentator regards this as the main petition of the prayer, the other ἵνα 'that' particles only being developments of this petition [Lns]. The purpose of the prayer and its content are blended in this particle [Alf, EGT, El, My].

QUESTION—How is the genitive construction τὸ πλοῦτος τῆς δόξης 'the riches of the glory' to be interpreted?

Whether the genitive means 'the wealth of the glory' or 'the glorious riches' is academic here, since the infinite resources of God's wisdom, power, and love can be spoken of as his 'glory' or as his 'wealth' [NIC].

1. The genitive τῆς δόξης 'of the glory' is used adjectivally, modifying τὸ πλοῦτος 'the riches' [Ba, EBC, NCBC; NIV, TNT]: the glorious riches. The riches are the resources of divine grace [NCBC].

2. The genitive τῆς δόξης 'of the glory' is used substantively [AB, Alf, Cal, Can, Ea, ECWB, EGT, El, Ho, ICC, Lns, MNTC, My, NIC, NTC, Rob, St, TH, WBC, We, WeBC; all versions except NIV, TNT]: the wealth of the glory.

QUESTION—What is meant by δόξα 'glory'?

1. The noun denotes the Divine fullness, perfection, or resources [AB, Alf, Can, DNTT, Ea, EBC, EGT, El, Ho, IB, ICC, LJ, Lns, My, NIC, NTC, TH, WBC, We]. This is the whole of the revealed perfections of God [EGT, Ho, ICC, LJ, Lns, My, NTC, We], everything in God that makes him glorious, the proper object of adoration [Ho, NTC], not just the mercy or power of God [EGT, Ho, My, NTC]. Here the noun incorporates elements of both radiance and power, conveying the perfection of God's activity [WBC]. The noun expresses the divine character of God as seen in his majesty [DNTT], power [DNTT, MNTC], and goodness [MNTC]. These attributes are seen as belonging to God's fatherhood and as being possessed in infinite measure [MNTC].

2. Here the noun stands for 'mercy' [Ba, Cal].

with-power[a] to-be-strengthened[b] through[c] his Spirit[d] in/into/in-reference-to[e] the inner[f] man,[g]

LEXICON—a. δύναμις (LN 76.1) (BAGD 1. p. 207): 'power' [AB, BAGD, LN, Lns, NIC, NTC, Rob, TH, WBC, We; NASB, NIV, NJB, NRSV, REB, TEV, TNT], 'might' [BAGD, El; KJV], 'strength, force' [BAGD]. This noun is also translated as an adverb modifying the infinitive κραταιωθῆναι 'to be strengthened': 'mightily' [BAGD]. It is also conflated with this infinitive and translated as an active verb [NAB], see b. below. Here the noun designates the power of the Holy Spirit [BAGD]. This noun denotes the potential of an entity to exert force in the performance of some function [LN].

b. aorist pass. infin. of κραταιόω (LN **76.10**) (BAGD p. 448): 'to be strengthened' [BAGD, El, Lns, NIC, NTC, Rob, TH, WBC, We; KJV, NASB, NRSV], 'to become strong' [BAGD, LN], 'to become strengthened' [**LN**], 'to be strong' [TEV], 'to be fortified' [AB]. This passive verb is also translated as an active verb: 'to strengthen' [NIV], 'to grow firm' [NJB]. It is also conflated with the noun δύναμις 'power' and translated as an active verb: 'to strengthen' [NAB]. This verb is also translated as a noun coordinate with δύναμις 'power' and made one of the direct objects of δίδωμι 'to give': 'strength' [REB, TNT]. This verb denotes becoming strong psychologically [LN]. The aorist tense is used here to denote the decisive act by which the blessing is conveyed [We].

c. διά with genitive object (LN 90.4): 'through' [AB, El, LN, NIC, NTC, TH, WBC, We; all versions except KJV], 'by' [LN, Rob; KJV], 'by means of' [Lns]. This preposition marks the intermediate agent through which the causative agent, mentioned either explicitly or implicitly, brings an event or state into being [LN].

d. πνεῦμα (LN 12.18) (BAGD 5.a. p. 676): 'Spirit' [AB, El, LN, Lns, NIC, NTC, Rob, TH, WBC, We; all versions]. Here, this noun denotes the spirit of God [BAGD, LN].

e. εἰς with accusative object (LN 83.13): 'in' [El, LN, Lns, NIC, NTC, Rob, TH, WBC, We; KJV, NASB, NIV, NRSV, TEV, TNT], 'within, inside' [LN], 'with regard to' [NJB], 'toward' [AB]. The whole phrase εἰς τὸν ἔσω ἄνθρωπον 'in the inner man' is also translated as an adverb 'inwardly' [NAB], 'inward' [REB].

f. ἔσω (LN 26.1) (BAGD 2. p. 314): 'inner' [AB, El, Lns, NTC, Rob, TH, WBC; KJV, NASB], 'inward' [We] 'inside, within' [BAGD]. This adverb of place is also translated in conjunction with the noun ἄνθρωπος 'man': 'the inner nature' [BAGD], 'inner being' [LN, NIC; NIV, NRSV], 'inmost being' [LN; TNT], 'inner self' [NJB, TEV]. It is also translated in conjunction with the whole phrase in which it occurs [NAB, REB], see e. above. Used in conjunction with ἄνθρωπος 'man' this becomes an idiom designating the inner person, the psychological faculty of man, including the intellectual, emotional, and spiritual aspects as contrasted to the purely physical aspects of human existence [LN]. This adverb is used adjectivally in Eph. 3:16 [HG].

g. ἄνθρωπος (LN 26.1) (BAGD 2.c.α. p. 68): 'man' [AB, BAGD, El, Lns, NTC, Rob, TH, We; KJV, NASB], 'being' [TNT], 'person' [WBC]. This noun is also translated in conjunction with the adverb of place, ἔσω 'inner' [BAGD, LN, NIC; NIV, NJB, NRSV, TEV, TNT], see f. above. It is also translated in conjunction with the whole phrase in which it occurs

[NAB, REB], see e. above. When combined with ἔσω 'inner' this noun denotes man in his spiritual, immortal aspects, as striving towards God [BAGD].

QUESTION—What do the words δυνάμει κραταιωθῆναι διὰ τοῦ πνεύματος αὐτοῦ 'to be strengthened with power through his Spirit' have to do with this prayer?

These words denote the gift requested, the infinitive κραταιωθῆναι 'to be strengthened' acting as the object of the verb δῷ 'may give' [Lns, TH]. Others regard these words as containing the first request [Can, EBC, TD, TNTC] or an elaboration on the first main request reflected in the verb δῷ 'may give' [WBC].

QUESTION—How is the dative case form of δυνάμει 'with power' to be understood?

1. The dative is to be understood in the instrumental sense [AB, Alf, Can, Ea, EGT, El, Ho, ICC, Lns, My, NCBC, NIC, NTC, TH, TNTC, WBC, We; KJV, NASB, NIV, NJB, NRSV]: to be strengthened with power. The process described by κραταιωθῆναι 'to be strengthened' is accomplished by the infusion of power into the man within [Ea, EGT, El]. The dative indicates the means by which these people were to be strengthened—by means of power [EGT, Lns]. It cannot be the dative of reference because it was not one particular faculty that was to be strengthened, but the whole inner man [El, Ho, My]. To take it adverbially would direct the thought more toward the strengthener rather than the subject in whom the strength is to be infused [El, My].
2. The dative is to be understood adverbially [Ba]: to be strengthened mightily, or powerfully.
3. The dative is translated as a coordinate substantive [REB, TEV, TNT]: may he give to you strength and power.

QUESTION—What is meant by κραταιωθῆναι 'to be strengthened'?

This refers to the ordinary, constant strengthening ministry of the Spirit of God to the believer [AB, Can, Ea, EBC, MNTC, My, NIC, TNTC, We, WeBC]. This empowering takes place through the indwelling of the Holy Spirit within the believer [TNTC, WeBC]. The request is that Paul's readers may be equipped with the power that enables them to live and work for Christ and to stand firm in him [TNTC]. Strength of mind and heart is what will be required of Paul's readers if they are to withstand danger and temptation, and not faint [Can]. Strength will be necessary for these Christians to comprehend the dimensions of God's wisdom [AB, LJ] and hold on to it in knowledge [AB]. According to others, it refers to strengthening these Christians for the mighty effort that is required of them in order to obtain the true knowledge of God, to which the unaided faculties of man are not equal [MNTC, NIC]. Strength is imparted to the 'inner man' by the Spirit applying those truths which have a tendency to cheer and sustain.

QUESTION—What is meant by διὰ τοῦ πνεύματος αὐτοῦ 'through his Spirit'?

The words designate the Spirit of God [AB, Alf, Can, Ea, EBC, El, Ho, IB, ICC, LJ, Lns, MNTC, My, NCBC, NIC, NTC, TH, TNTC, WBC, We, WeBC; all versions] and indicate that this strength is given by [Alf, Can, Ea, LJ, Lns] or through him [AB, EGT, IB, NCBC, NIC, TH, We] as the causal medium [El, Lns] or agent in this invigoration [Ea, EBC]. The πνεῦμα 'Spirit' is the mode in which God communicates himself to people [NCBC].

QUESTION—What is the function of the preposition εἰς 'in' in the phrase εἰς τὸν ἔσω ἄνθρωπον 'in the inner man'?

1. This preposition marks the goal or destination of δυνάμει κραταιωθῆναι 'to be strengthened with power' [AB, Alf, Ea, EGT, El, ICC, TD, TH]: into the inner man, or, (to grow) toward the inner man.
2. This preposition means 'in' [Ba, Cal, Can, EBC, HG, Lns, NIC, NTC, Rob, TD, Tu, WBC]: to be strengthened in the inner man. The preposition may be used in place of the dative case [TD]. The preposition (meaning literally 'into') suggests the depth of the penetration by the Spirit [EBC]. The preposition is static, 'in' [HG, Lns], although it may also be translated 'with respect to' [Lns]. Within the NT, εἰς 'into' frequently takes the place of ἐν 'in' in a local sense [WBC]. The Pauline epistles do not often confuse the local use of ἐν 'in' and εἰς 'into', but Eph. 3:16 is probably the only case where Paul does confuse them [Tu].
3. This preposition means 'in reference to, with regard to' [My; NJB]: to be strengthened in reference to the inner man. This gives a more precise definition of the relation [My].

QUESTION—What is the ἔσω ἄνθρωπον 'inner man'?

1. This designates the mental, moral, spiritual part of man [Alf, Ba, BAGD, Cal, Can, EBC, ECWB, EGT, El, Ho, IB, ICC, IDB, ISBE, ISBE2, LJ, LN (26.1), Lns, MNTC, My, My-ed, NCBC, NIC, NTC, Rob, St, TD, TH, TNTC, WBC, We]: to be strengthened in the spiritual part of your being.

1.1 While the context is concerned with the Christian, the term denotes a faculty that, considered in itself, is common to both regenerate and unregenerate persons [Alf, Ba, BAGD, Cal, Ea, EGT, El, IB (probably), ICC, IDB, ISBE, ISBE2, LN (26.1), MNTC, My, My-ed, NTC, St, TD, TH, WBC]. This is the spiritual part of man [Alf, Cal, ECWB, TD], including all the faculties which make up the spiritual nature of man, the intellectual, emotional, and moral [ECWB, ICC, LN (26.1), TD]. In the unregenerate person this is kept under subjection to the flesh [Alf, EGT, ICC, ISBE, MNTC, My, My-ed, WBC], but in the regenerated man it is renewed [Alf, ICC, ISBE, My, TD, WBC] or regenerated [EGT, El] by the Spirit of God [Alf, EGT, ICC, ISBE, My, WBC] and so becomes 'the new man' [EGT]. This is the higher moral and rational part of man's nature [EGT, IB, ICC, ISBE, My, TD], by which he is able to grasp the nature of eternal things and to acknowledge the goodness of what is good, even though he lacks the power to act upon it [IB, ICC,

My]. It is the part of man that is accessible to divine revelation and so is open to its claim [TD]. It is not identical with 'the new man' [Ea, EGT, El, IB, ICC, ISBE, My, My-ed, WBC], but rather the sphere in which that renewal takes effect [Ea, EGT, El, ISBE, My-ed, WBC]. However, by synecdoche the term is applied so as to designate 'the new man', the internal nature of the regenerate man [My-ed]. The term designates primarily the mind of man [Ea, EGT, El, IDB, MNTC, My, WBC], or his heart [El, ISBE2, NTC, St, TH, WBC]. The term designates a faculty that includes more than just man's mind, reason, or heart [Alf, BAGD, Cal, ECWB, IB, ISBE, LN (26.1)]. It is man's higher nature [ISBE], including the intellectual [ISBE, LN], emotional [LN], moral [ISBE], and spiritual [BAGD, ISBE, LN].

1.2 The term refers to a faculty that only the regenerate possess [Ho, LJ, Lns, NIC, TNTC]. This is the spiritual part of the regenerate man, including his soul, spirit, heart, mind [LJ, Lns]. The unregenerate man has no 'inner man' [LJ]. This is the interior principle of spiritual life, the product of the Spirit of God [Ho], or the soul as the organ and temple of God [Ho]. This is identical with 'the hidden man of the heart' in 1 Pet. 3:4 [NIC], it is the new creation [Ho, NIC], the immortal personality [NIC].

2. This designates Christ who indwells each individual believer [AB]: (to grow) toward the Inner Man, the Messiah, who dwells within each of you. The context of 3:16 speaks about the impact and effect of Messiah's coming. There is not only an advent of Christ among mankind and a presence of Christ in the congregation, treated earlier in the epistle, but, according to 3:17 (which is an interpretative comment on the ἔσω ἄνθρωπον 'inner man', rather than a new and additional thought), he also comes into individual men in order to dwell there. He proves present and effective by creating faith, love, and knowledge [AB].

3:17 to-dwell[a] the Christ through[b] the faith[c] in[d] your hearts,[e]

LEXICON—a. aorist act. infin. of κατοικέω (LN 85.69) (BAGD 1.b. p. 424): 'to dwell' [AB, BAGD, El, LN, Lns, NIC, NTC, Rob, TH, WBC, We; all versions except NJB, TEV], 'to live' [BAGD, LN; NJB], 'to reside' [BAGD, LN], 'to make a home' [TEV], 'to settle (down)' [BAGD]. This verb denotes the living or dwelling in a place in an established or settled manner [LN]. This is the intransitive meaning, and is used here of the possession of human beings by Christ [BAGD]. While the indwelling of Christ is continual, the aorist tense marks full possession of Christ [Lns], or the decisive act which conveys the blessing [We]. The aorist tense carries the meaning of something that happens once and forever, so Paul is praying for a specific blessing upon these readers [LJ].

b. διά with genitive object (LN 89.76) (BAGD A.III.1.d. p. 180): 'through' [AB, BAGD, LN, Lns, NIC, NTC, Rob, TH, WBC, We; all versions except KJV], 'by' [El, LN; KJV], 'by means of' [BAGD, LN], 'with'

[BAGD]. This preposition denotes the efficient cause [BAGD]. It is a marker of the means by which one event makes another event possible [LN].

c. πίστις (LN 31.85) (BAGD 2.d.α. p. 663): 'faith' [AB, BAGD, El, LN, Lns, NIC, NTC, Rob, TH, WBC, We; all versions], 'trust' [LN]. This denotes trust or confidence in Christ as true piety or genuine religion which, in the Christian literature of the period, means being a Christian [BAGD]. This noun denotes belief in someone or something to the extent of complete trust and reliance [LN].

d. ἐν with dative object (LN 83.13): 'in' [AB, El, LN, Lns, NIC, NTC, Rob, TH, WBC, We; all versions], 'within, inside' [LN]. This preposition defines a position as being within certain limits [LN].

e. καρδία (LN 26.3) (BAGD 1.b.θ. p. 404): 'hearts' [AB, BAGD, El, LN, Lns, NIC, NTC, Rob, TH, WBC, We; all versions], 'inner selves, minds' [LN]. This is a figurative use of the literal term. It denotes the source of a person's psychological life in various aspects, but chiefly it focuses upon the thoughts [LN].

QUESTION—What relationship is indicated by the use of the infinitive κατοικῆσαι 'to dwell'?

1. This clause presents a second, parallel petition [IB, WeBC; TEV]: I pray that the Father may give to you...to be strengthened with power in the inner man through his Spirit, and that Christ may dwell in your hearts by faith. It is not a definition of the preceding infinitive clause, but a second means for the inward preparation for the increase of knowledge and love [IB]. This request is the insurance of their inner strengthening requested in the previous petition. The faith by which Christ abides in their hearts works by the love for which Paul prays in the next petition [WeBC].

2. This clause is in form a separate petition, parallel to the previous infinitive κραταιωθῆναι 'to be strengthened' and the clause it governs (3:16b), but is at the same time a definition or elaboration of that infinitive clause [Can, ICC, MNTC, My, NIC, St, TD, TNTC, WBC, We]: I pray that the Father may give to you...to be strengthened with power in the inner man through his Spirit, (which is to say that I am also praying) that Christ may dwell in your hearts by faith. While the indwelling of Christ in the heart is no different from being strengthened through the Spirit [MNTC, My, NIC, St, TNTC, WBC], the form makes this a parallel petition [My, NIC, St, TD, WBC; and probably MNTC, TNTC]. As to the construction, this is the second of three petitions.

3. This clause is a definition of the previous infinitive κραταιωθῆναι 'to be strengthened' and the clause it governs (3:16b) [AB, Cal, ECWB, Ho, NCBC, NTC]: I pray that the Father may give to you...to be strengthened with power in the inner man through his Spirit, that is, that Christ may dwell in your hearts by faith. This clause indicates the source or nature of the spiritual strength spoken of in the first clause [Ho]. The indwelling of Christ is not a consequence of the work of the Spirit; it is identical with it.

4. This clause gives the purpose or contemplated result of the previous infinitive κραταιωθῆναι 'to be strengthened' and the clause it governs (3:16b) [Alf, CBC, Ea, EBC, EGT, El, HG, LJ (probably), Lns, NIC (translation), TH; NASB, NIV, NJB, REB, TNT]: I pray that the Father may give to you...to be strengthened with power in the inner man through his Spirit, with the result that Christ may dwell in your hearts.

QUESTION—What does διὰ τῆς πίστεως 'through faith' mean?

This states the means by which Christ dwells in our hearts [Cal, EGT, TH, WeBC]. This is the condition of receptivity [EGT, TNTC] or trust [TH, WBC] which must exist on our side [EGT, TH]. Faith induces and also realizes Christ's presence with us [Can, Ea, Ho].

QUESTION—What is meant by καρδία 'heart'?

This indicates what was meant by τὸν ἔσω ἄνθρωπον 'the inner man' [ISBE, NCBC, NTC, St, TH, WBC]. It is that part of the individual's psyche where he interacts with God or the power of evil [IDB, ISBE2]. It is the seat and center of the moral life as viewed on the side of the affections [El]. If Christ dwells in the heart, it means he controls that which directs moral conduct [TD] and the whole course of a person's life [NCBC, St, WBC]. This describes man's total identity and existence under the aspects of his vitality, intelligence, will, and decision [AB, IDB, ISBE, ISBE2]. The heart is the inner shrine of emotion and power, the center of the spiritual life [Ea, ISBE]. The heart is where mind, feeling, and will reside [EBC, EGT, LJ, Lns, WBC], especially the will [ISBE2, Lns]. It frequently stands by synecdoche for the total personality of the believer [EBC, IDB, ISBE2], the whole soul [Ho, ISBE], the man himself [ISBE]. The use of this term indicates that the indwelling of Christ is within individual hearts, not just within the church [ICC].

in[a] love[b] having-been-rooted[c] and having-been-grounded,[d]

LEXICON—a. ἐν with dative object (LN 89.5, 89.141): 'in' [El, LN (89.5, 89.141), Lns, NIC, NTC, Rob, TH, WBC, We; all versions except NAB], 'with regard to, in the case of' [LN (89.5)], 'of, consisting of' [LN (89.141)]. Two commentators incorporate nouns into the translation of the two participles and interpret this preposition as stating love as the substance of these nouns (cf. LN (89.141)): to stand firm on the root and foundation of love [AB], love is to be the root and foundation of life [NAB]. One uses 'love' twice with the two participles and translates ἐν by 'in' with one of them and by 'on' with the other [NJB]. This preposition marks an area of activity which bears a relation to something else [LN (89.5)]. The preposition marks that of which something consists [LN (89.141)].

b. ἀγάπη: 'love'. See this word at 1:4, 15; 2:4.

c. perf. pass. participle of ῥιζόω, ῥιζόομαι (LN 74.18) (BAGD p. 736): 'to be rooted' [El, LN, Lns, NIC, NTC, Rob, TH, WBC, We; KJV, NASB, NIV, NRSV, TNT], 'to be firmly rooted, to be fixed' [BAGD], 'to be

planted' [NJB], 'to be strengthened' [LN]. This verb is also translated in part or in the main as a noun: 'root' [AB; NAB], 'roots' [TEV], 'deep roots' [REB]. This is a figurative usage of a verb that means 'to cause to take root' [BAGD]. It denotes becoming strengthened, with focus upon the source of the strength [LN]. The perfect tense means that this event happened in the past and the state brought about by that event continues to exist in a stable and constant condition [Lns, NCBC].
  d. perf. pass. participle of θεμελιόω (LN 7.42, 31.94) (BAGD 2.a. p. 356): 'to be grounded' [El, WBC, We; KJV, NASB, NRSV, TNT], 'to be founded' [LN (7.42), Lns, NTC, Rob], 'to be well founded' [NIC], 'to be firmly founded' [TH], 'to be established' [BAGD; NIV], 'to be strengthened' [BAGD], 'to be caused to be steadfast in, to be provided a basis or foundation for' [LN (31.94)], 'to be built' [NJB]. This verb is also translated in part or in the main as a noun: 'foundation' [AB; NAB, TEV], 'firm foundation' [REB]. This is a figurative usage in respect to believers whom God establishes [BAGD]. This verb denotes the laying or construction of a foundation [LN (7.42)]. It denotes the provision of a firm basis for belief or practice [LN (31.94)]. The perfect tense means that this event happened in the past and the state brought about by that event continues to exist in a stable and constant condition [Lns, NCBC, We].

QUESTION—To what is the prepositional phrase ἐν ἀγάπῃ 'in love' attached?
  1. It is attached to the preceding infinitive clause [Rob; REB]: that by faith Christ may dwell in your hearts in love. We must remember that these words are written to Gentiles. It is 'through faith' that they are made partakers of Christ, and it is 'in love' that they are united to all other believers, Jew and Gentile [Rob].
  2. It is attached to the two nominative participles [AB, Alf, Ba, Bu, Cal, Can, Ea, EBC, ECWB, EGT, El, Ho, IB, ICC, ISBE2, LJ, Lns, MNTC, My, NCBC, NTC, St, TD, TH, TNTC, WBC, We, WeBC; all versions except REB]: that you being rooted and grounded in love. The phrase ἐν ἀγάπῃ 'in love' is in a position of emphasis, and the fact that two participles are used instead of one, strengthens this emphasis [Lns]. It supplies the key to the meaning of the two participles, which accounts for this emphasis [MNTC]. Our love is not the root or foundation [Can, ECWB], but it is the sentiment [Can] or condition [ECWB] in which we are to be steady and always growing [Can, ECWB]. It is idle to infer from these words that love is the root and foundation of our salvation. Paul does not inquire here upon what our salvation is founded, but rather he is concerned with what firmness and constancy we ought to continue in the exercise of love. Our roots ought to be so deeply planted and our foundations so firmly laid in love that nothing will be able to shake us [Cal]. Love was to be the sole basis and foundation on which they were to be enabled to realize all the majestic proportions of Christ's surpassing love to man [Alf, ISBE2].

252 EPHESIANS 3:17

QUESTION—Who is the subject and object of this love?
1. This is both God and Christ's love for us and our love for them and each other [AB, TH, WBC]. God's love and man's love are not alternatives in the interpretation of these verses [AB, WBC]. Our love for God and Christ and each other is but a reflection of God and Christ's love for us [AB].
2. It is Christians' love as a principle [Can, El] or the grace of Christian love [Ea, EGT, Ho, ICC, My, My-ed] with no object specified. The fact that ἀγάπη 'love' is used without any modifying genitive points to love as a Christian grace or principle here [EGT, El, ICC, My, My-ed]. This is primarily our love to the Redeemer, but also love to each other and all [Ba, Can, Ea, Ho, LJ, Lns, My-ed, NTC]. Others state only that this is Christian brotherly love [My, NCBC, NIC, St].

QUESTION—How are the two participles ἐρριζωμένοι 'being rooted' and τεθεμελιωμένοι 'being grounded' related to the surrounding statements?
1. They are joined to the preceding infinitive clause or clauses [Alf, Cal, Can, EGT, El, ICC, LJ, NCBC, WBC, WeBC; NAB, NRSV].
  1.1 They express the purpose or intended result of the preceding infinitive clause [Cal, EGT, El, ICC, LJ, NCBC, WeBC; NAB]: so that you have been rooted and grounded in love. The perfect tenses of the participles correctly expresses the *state* which would result from the indwelling of Christ [EGT, El], which state must be realized before the ability for comprehending the love of Christ can be acquired [EGT, El].
  1.2 They express a further, subsidiary request [WBC]: that you may be rooted and grounded in love.
  1.3 They express the condition and means of the infinitive clauses [Can]: (that) having been rooted and grounded in love, Christ may dwell by faith in your hearts.
  1.4 They express a circumstance coincident with the action of the preceding infinitive clause [NRSV]: that Christ may dwell by faith in your hearts as you are being rooted and grounded in love.
  1.5 They express the second part of a compound request in this verse [NAB]: may Christ dwell in your hearts by faith and may you be rooted and grounded in love.
2. They are connected to the following ἵνα 'in order that' clause and state the ground upon or the circumstance in which the action of that clause takes place [Bu, Ho, IB, Lns, My, NIC, NTC, TNTC, We; KJV, NASB, NIV, NJB, REB, TEV, TNT]: in order that you, having been rooted and grounded in love, may have strength to comprehend, etc. These nominative participles *govern* the following clause. While this participial clause does further express what is meant by the infinitive κραταιωθῆναι 'to be strengthened' (3:16) [My], or shows the purpose of both the strengthening and the indwelling [NTC], this clause is, nevertheless, attached to the following ἵνα 'in order that' clause [My, NTC]. It is prefixed to this clause, rather than included within it, in order to

emphasize the idea that it is the loving soul that is in a position to recognize the love of Christ [My, We].

QUESTION—What modal force are these participles meant to convey?
1. They have an imperative force, expressing a command [AB, BD, Tu2, Tu3]: continue to be rooted and grounded in love. The perfect tenses of these two participles describe the result of the meanings of their verb stems ('rooting' and 'grounding'), not the process, therefore the exhortation is concerned with maintaining the acquired status described by the perfect tenses [AB].
2. They have an optative force expressing a wish or prayer [Mou, TD, WBC, WeBC; NAB, TEV, TNT]: I wish, or pray, that you may be rooted and grounded in love.
3. They have a subjunctive or indicative force appropriate to their place and function in the clause to which they are assigned, as already discussed above [Alf, Ba, Cal, Can, Ea, ECWB, EGT, El, Ho, IB, ICC, Lns, MNTC, My, NCBC, NIC, NTC, Rob, St, TNTC, We; all versions except NAB, TEV, TNT]: having been rooted and grounded.

QUESTION—What are the metaphors which these two participles bring to mind?

Ἐρριζωμένοι 'having been rooted' brings to mind a tree or vine firmly planted in the ground and τεθεμελιωμένοι 'to be grounded' brings to mind the foundation upon which a building rests [AB, Bu, CBC, EBC, ECWB, Ho, IB, ISBE, LJ, Lns, My, NCBC, NIC, NTC, Si-ed, St, TH, TNTC, We, WeBC]. The second part of the metaphor, 'grounded', refers back to 2:21–22, the foundation of the temple [WeBC]. Another, while acknowledging a double metaphor, nevertheless links the participle ἐρριζωμένοι 'having been rooted' to 2:20 ff. also [TD]. The metaphors have to do with the steadfastness of the believers [Ba, CBC, Ea, Ho, Lns, My, NTC, St, We, WeBC], as well as with life [We, WeBC], fruit-bearing [NTC], and growth [NTC, WeBC]. Paul's prayer is that Christians may be like a mature tree with deep roots thrust down, or like a building with a solid deep-dug foundation [CBC, Ho, Lns, St, TNTC]. The power bestowed on us is to make us like a solidly rooted tree that is growing to be massive and strong and like a solidly founded building that is rising high and imposing [Lns]. Love is the foundation of Christian character, as all advancement is connected with its exercise. It works by keeping Christ, its object, enshrined in the mind, and changing its subject into the image and likeness of Christ [Ea]. The comparison is: just as a tree is firmly established by its network of strong roots in the ground and as a building is steadfast by reason of the strong foundation upon which it rests, so you should be strongly established in love. The point of comparison is the strength of the network of roots and the strength of the foundation of the building. The nonfigurative statement would be: you should be strongly established in love.

QUESTION—Could this be just a single metaphor?

Some commentators argue for a single metaphor [Alf, Ea, EGT, El] or even none at all [ICC]. They state that ῥιζόω 'to cause to take root' was so constantly used in the figurative sense of 'to fix firmly' that the original botanical image dropped away [Alf, EGT, El], and that it was used, sometimes in conjunction with θεμελιόω 'to lay a foundation' [Alf], with an architectural, rather than botanical, meaning [BAGD, Ea, EGT, El]. One argues that the single metaphor of a building is more natural than the double metaphor, the allusion being to the spiritual temple mentioned at the end of chapter 2 [Ea]. Another argues that the metaphors are very dead, that Paul used the words in their applied meanings with no intention of bringing metaphorical images to their minds, even though this same commentator uses the metaphor in his comments [ICC].

3:18 in-order-that/that[a] you-may-be-able[b] to-comprehend[c] with all the saints[d]

LEXICON—a. ἵνα (LN 89.49, 89.59, 90.22): 'in order that' [Lns, NTC, WBC], 'in order to, for the purpose of' [LN (89.59)], 'to the end that' [We], 'that' [El, LN (89.49, 90.22), Rob; KJV, NASB, NIV, NRSV]; 'so that' [LN (89.49, 89.59), TH; TEV, TNT], 'and then' [NJB], 'thus' [NAB], 'so as a result' [LN (89.49)], 'while' [NIC], not explicit [AB; REB]. This is a marker of result, although in some cases there may be an implication of underlying or indirect purpose [LN (89.49)]. This is a marker of purpose [LN (89.59)]. This is a marker denoting the content of discourse, particularly when or if purpose is implied [LN (90.22)].

b. aorist act. sub. of ἐξισχύω (LN **74.10**) (BAGD p. 276): 'to be able' [BAGD, Rob; KJV, NAB, NASB], 'to be fully able' [El, **LN**; TNT], 'to be completely able' [LN], 'to have strength' [TH; NJB], 'to have power' [NIV, NRSV, TEV], 'to be strong' [Lns, NTC; REB], 'to be strong enough' [AB, BAGD, We], 'to prevail' [NIC]. This active verb is also translated as passive: 'to be empowered' [WBC]. Some say or imply that the ἐκ- prefix on the verb intensifies it [EGT, Ho, LJ, LN, My, TH] but others disagree [EBC] or are doubtful of this [MM].

c. aorist mid. infin. of καταλαμβάνω (LN 32.18) (BAGD 2. p. 413): 'to comprehend' [El, LN, NIC, Rob; KJV, NASB, NRSV], 'to understand' [BAGD, LN; TEV], 'to apprehend' [We], 'to grasp' [AB, BAGD, LN, Lns, NTC, TH, WBC; NIV, NJB, REB, TNT], 'to grasp fully' [NAB], 'to realize' [LN]. Some commentators emphasize the reflexive force of the middle voice and say it means 'to grasp for oneself' [ICC, Lns, TD], but others reject the reflexive force, saying that it means 'to comprehend' [Ea, EBC, EGT, El, Rob].

d. ἅγιος: 'saints'. See this word at 1:4, 15, 18; 2:19; 3:8.

QUESTION—What relationship is indicated by ἵνα 'in order that/that'?

1. It indicates an intended result of the infinitive clause of 3:17 [Cal, El]: that Christ may dwell in your hearts so that you may be able to comprehend,

etc. The second fruit of Christ's dwelling in their hearts is that they should perceive the greatness of Christ's love to men (the first fruit being their having been rooted and grounded in love) [Cal, El].

2. It indicates the grand purpose which the preceding petitions had in view [Ea, Ho, LJ, Lns, NIC, NTC, Rob, TH]: all this is in order that you may be able to comprehend, etc. This is not to be regarded as parallel to the ἵνα 'in order that' clause of 3:16 ('that he might give to you') as though it were a second object clause of 'I bow my knees to the Father' (3:14). This is a purpose clause, most immediately of 'that Christ may dwell in your hearts by faith', but through that clause also to 'that you might be strengthened with power etc.' [Lns]. The clause depends on the preceding participles, but has further reference to the infinitive clause of 3:16 'to be strengthened with power etc.' [Rob].

3. It indicates the second major petition of the prayer [AB, EBC, WBC]: (I pray) that you may be able to comprehend, etc. This second major request presupposes the first request and builds upon it [WBC].

QUESTION—To what does the strengthening inherent in ἐξισχύσητε 'you may be able' have reference?

This strengthening is in reference to the ability of the believer, and the effort he must make, to understand this subject [AB, Can, Ea, Ho, LJ, Lns, MNTC, NIC, Rob, St, TNTC, WBC]. The verb ἐξισχύσητε means more than just 'to be able' for it is not the usual word indicating mere possibility, but an unusual one which suggests that some vigor is necessary [Can]. It can mean 'to acquire power' [Si-ed].

QUESTION—What is the import of σὺν πᾶσιν τοῖς ἁγίοις 'with all the saints'?

This means that this is a knowledge which only God's people may acquire [Ho, LJ], a knowledge in which all of them may share. It is not a private or peculiar experience for especially favored individuals [Can, EGT, IB, NIC, Si, TH, TNTC, We]. Paul wants his readers to be equal with all other believers in this attainment [Can, Lns, My]. Some also feel that Paul implies that this is not a knowledge which can be gained in isolation, apart from others but, if it is to be attained, must be attained *with others* [AB, IB, MNTC, My, NTC, St, TH, TNTC, WBC, We] only as they share in the life of the community [IB, WBC], united in fellowship with their brethren [MNTC, My], each using the varying gifts of the Spirit for the edification of the body (4:7) [TNTC]. It is a corporate experience [TH], the cooperation of all being required for the attainment of the full conception [We]. The thought of this shared insight will be developed further in 4:1–16, particularly 4:13 [WBC]

what (is) the breadth[a] and length[b] and height[c] and depth,[d]

TEXT—Some manuscripts reverse the order of ὕψος 'height' and βάθος 'depth': 'depth and height' [Ba, Cal, Ea, EGT, El, Ho, LJ, MNTC, My, TNTC; KJV]. GNT takes no notice of this variant reading.

LEXICON—a. πλάτος (LN 81.15) (BAGD 1. p. 666): 'breadth' [AB, BAGD, El, LN, Lns, NIC, NTC, Rob, WBC, We; all versions except NIV, TEV], 'width' [BAGD, LN, TH], '(how) wide' [NIV], (how) 'broad' [TEV].
b. μῆκος (LN 81.12) (BAGD p. 518): 'length' [AB, BAGD, El, LN, Lns, NIC, NTC, Rob, TH, WBC, We; all versions except NIV, TEV], '(how) long' [NIV, TEV].
c. ὕψος (LN **81.3**) (BAGD 1.a. p. 850): 'height' [AB, BAGD, El, LN, Lns, NIC, NTC, Rob, TH, WBC, We; all versions except NIV, TEV], '(how) high' [NIV, TEV]. In this verse, this term, along with the other three terms designating the dimensions of space, are used figuratively, and taken together they mean 'that which is all-encompassing' [LN].
d. βάθος (LN 81.8) (BAGD 1. p. 130): 'depth' [AB, BAGD, El, LN, Lns, NIC, NTC, Rob, TH, WBC, We; all versions except NIV, TEV], '(how) deep' [LN; NIV, TEV]. This term designates the distance beneath a surface [LN].

QUESTION—What is the object of these four dimensions?

1. These dimensions refer to Christ's or God's love for us [Ba, Can, CBC, DNTT, EBC, EGT, El, Ho, ICC, ISBE, ISBE2, LJ, Lns, MNTC, My, NCBC, NTC, Si, St, TD, TH, TNTC, WBC; NAB, NIV, NJB (note), REB, TEV, TNT]: that you might be able to fully understand the love of Christ. It is probable that the same object is meant here as in the following clause, namely, the love of Christ [Can, EGT, El, Ho, MNTC, WBC]. The τε 'and' of the following clause is not contrary to this interpretation since this particle expresses a close, internal relationship [ICC, WBC] between the clauses it links [WBC].
2. These dimensions refer to the mystery in 3:9 [AB, Alf, ECWB, IB, NIC, Rob, We] as containing the wisdom of God [AB, NIC, We], or as incorporating all that God has revealed to us and done in and for us [Alf]: that you might be able to comprehend with all the saints the vastness of God's wisdom in all that he has done for us.
3. These dimensions refer to salvation in Christ [DNTT]: that you might be able to comprehend with all the saints the comprehensiveness of God's grace and salvation in Christ.
4. These dimensions refer to man's pursuit of wisdom, to be found in Christ's love [Cal]: that you may be able to comprehend the love of Christ, which is the length and the breadth, the depth and the height, that is, the complete perfection of wisdom.
5. These dimensions refer to the size and glory of the church as the spiritual temple of 2:19–22 which is still before the apostles mind [Ea]: that you may be able to comprehend the vast dimensions of the church.
6. These dimensions represent the comprehensiveness of the heavenly inheritance, or the vastness of the heavenly city (Rev. 21:16) [TD]: that you may be able to comprehend with all the saints the comprehensiveness of your heavenly inheritance.

QUESTION—What is the meaning of this list of dimensions?
1. Each of these dimensions is regarded as having some particular reference [AB, Can, Ea, EBC, LJ, Si, St, WeBC]. These dimensions are usually made to denote the places where the metaphorical search for the extent of God's wisdom takes place: heaven, a depth greater than *sheol* (the grave), water or the sea, and some reference to earth (e.g.: Job 11:7–9, Amos 9:2–3, etc.) [AB]. This clause mentions the extent of Christ's love in all directions [Can, EBC, LJ]. Πλάτος 'breadth' refers to its reaching over the whole world, to all races and classes of mankind [Can, EBC, LJ, Si, St, WeBC], μῆκος 'length' to its reaching from eternity to eternity [Can, EBC, LJ, Si, St], or from a man's birth to his death [WeBC], ὕψος 'height' to its reaching up to the very throne of God [Can, EBC], or, more specifically, to the height to which the redeemed are destined to be exalted [LJ, St], or to the most exalted among men [WeBC], and βάθος 'depth' to its reaching down to the lowest degree of our sin and misery [Can, EBC, LJ, Si, St], or to the most morally depraved among men [WeBC].
2. These dimensions are interpreted together in a collective sense to express the immensity of the subject [Ba, Cal, DNTT, El, HG, IB, ICC, ISBE, ISBE2, My, NIC, NTC, Rob, TD, TH, TNTC, WBC, We]. These dimensions must not be interpreted individually, but have a collective sense [NTC, TNTC, We].

3:19 and^a to-know^b the love^c of-Christ surpassing^d of-knowledge,^e

LEXICON—a. τέ (LN 89.88) (BAGD 1.b. p. 807): 'and' [AB, BAGD, El, LN, Lns, NIC, NTC, Rob, TH, WBC, We; all versions except NJB, TNT], 'and then' [LN], 'yes' [TEV], not explicit [NJB, TNT]. One translation starts a new sentence here in a manner indicating that this clause is another request [TNT]. Used alone, there is a somewhat rare usage where this conjunction connects single concepts, parts of clauses or words. Here it connects infinitives [BAGD]. In this usage, τέ 'and' is a marker of a close relationship between sequential events and states [LN]. The τέ 'and' marks a closer connection than the more common καί 'and' would do [EGT]. It marks an adjunctive rather than a conjunctive connection [El]. It makes its clause parallel to the clause containing καταλαβέσθαι 'to comprehend', marking a harmonious symmetrical relation of these parts, yet not after the manner of a climax [My].

b. aorist act. infin. of γινώσκω (LN 27.18): 'to know' [AB, El, LN, Lns, NIC, NTC, Rob, TH, WBC, We; all versions except NAB, TEV], 'to experience' [NAB], 'to come to know' [TEV], 'to become acquainted with, to be familiar with' [LN]. This verb denotes the learning to know a person through direct personal experience, and it implies a continuity of relationship [Can, EGT, El, Ho, LJ, LN, Lns, My, NIC, TH, TNTC, WBC].

c. ἀγάπη: 'love'. See this word at 2:4.

d. pres. act. participle of ὑπερβάλλω (LN 78.33) (BAGD p. 840): 'to surpass' [AB, BAGD, NIC, NTC, WBC; NAB, NASB, NIV, NRSV], 'to exceed' [Lns], 'to pass' [El, Rob, We; KJV], 'to lie beyond' [TNT] 'to go beyond, to outdo' [BAGD] This verb is also translated as an adjective: 'beyond' [TH; NJB, REB], 'extraordinary, supreme, to a far greater degree' [LN]. It is also translated as an adverbial litotes: '(to) never (be) fully (known)' [TEV]. It is also translated as a verbal phrase: 'to lie beyond' [TNT]. This term indicates a degree which extraordinarily exceeds a point on an implied or overt scale of extent [LN]. This participle has the adjectival force of a comparative in this occurrence [EGT, El, HG, ICC, My], and accounts for the following noun γνῶσις 'knowledge' occurring in the genitive case [EGT, ICC, My, Rob].

e. γνῶσις (LN 28.17): 'knowledge' [AB, El, Lns, NIC, NTC, Rob, TH, WBC, We; all versions except TEV], 'what is known' [LN]. This noun is also translated as a verb: 'to be known' [TEV].

QUESTION—How is this clause related to the context?

1. It forms the second part of the compound request started in 3:18 [Ea, EGT, El, My, WBC, WeBC; NIV, REB]: and (I pray) that you will be able to comprehend with all the saints, etc. and to know the love of Christ which surpasses knowledge. The τέ introduces a climactically parallel clause which both explains and advances on the vaguer rhetorical language of the previous one [WBC].
2. It forms the second part of the compound purpose or goal [Rob, TNTC (probably), We] or result [NAB] started in 3:18: so that you may be able to comprehend with all the saints, etc. and know the love of Christ which surpasses knowledge.
3. This forms another, separate request [TNT]: (I pray) that you will know the love of Christ which surpasses knowledge.
4. It is subordinate to and explanatory of the preceding infinitive clause [AB, Alf, Bu, Can, TH; TEV]: and even to know the love of Christ though it surpasses knowledge. The TEV uses the word 'yes' to show that the writer is continuing his prayer and is emphasizing what he said in the last verse about his readers' comprehending the love of Christ [TH].
5. This is subordinate to the following clause [NJB]: so that, knowing the love of Christ which surpasses knowledge, you may be filled, etc.

QUESTION—What is the meaning of γνῶναι 'to know'?

The tense expresses cognition in a particular case so Paul seems to be praying that they may know from time to time, as each opportunity arises, what the love of Christ reveals, finding new depth still to be fathomed, even though they will never understand it in its entirety [ECWB]. This is a relative knowledge which increases in proportion as the believer is filled with the spirit of Christ and is thereby 'rooted and grounded in love' [ICC, My]. Paul's statement does not mean that these readers have not known Christ's love yet, but is a prayer for a greater knowledge of it [LJ]. To know the love of Christ is to know Christ himself in an ever continuing experience and, as a result, to have this love reproduced in oneself [NIC].

QUESTION—What is meant by ὑπερβάλλουσαν τῆς γνώσεως 'surpassing of knowledge'?

This is best regarded as a parenthetical statement describing Christ's love [TH]. This states that the love of Christ for mankind is infinite [Ba, Can, Ea, Ho, NTC] and therefore transcends finite, human comprehension [Ba, Can, Ea, ECWB, Ho, IB, LJ, NCBC, NIC, NTC, TH]. Together with the infinitive γνῶναι 'to know', this participial phrase forms a figure of speech called oxymoron or paradox, where the two elements of the figure seemingly contradict one another [AB, Ba, Can, Ea, EBC, ECWB, El, ICC, LJ, Lns, My, NIC, TH, TNTC, WBC, We, WeBC]. Paul uses this figure to emphasize the vastness of Christ's love [AB, Ba, Can, ICC, LJ, Lns, TH, WBC]. Though it cannot be fully known, Paul wants his readers to understand this love as much as possible [Ba, Ea, EBC, ECWB].

QUESTION—What is the genitive relationship in the phrase τὴν ἀγάπην τοῦ Χριστοῦ 'the love of Christ'?

The person designated by the genitive Χριστοῦ 'of Christ' produces the action designated by the noun ἀγάπην 'love' [AB, Alf, Ba, Can, Ea, ECWB, EGT, El, Ho, ICC, LJ, Lns, My, NCBC, NIC, NTC, Rob, TH, WBC, We, WeBC]. Some commentators report Luther as interpreting it as an objective genitive, our love for Christ [ICC, My]. Others see it as Divine love acting through us: His love for us and, through our response to that love, our love for him, and others for his sake [DNTT, Ds2, TNTC].

in-order-that/that[a] you-may be filled[b] to[c] all[d] the fullness[e] of-God.

LEXICON—a. ἵνα (LN 89.49, 89.59, 90.22): 'in order that' [Lns, NTC, WBC], 'that' [El, LN (89.49), Rob, We; KJV, NASB, NIV], 'so that' [LN (89.49), NIC, TH; NAB, NJB, NRSV], 'so' [REB], 'and so' [TEV, TNT], not explicit [AB].

b. aorist pass. subj. of πληρόω (LN 59.37) (BAGD1.b. p. 671): 'to be filled' [LN, Lns, NTC, Rob, TH, We; KJV, NIV, NJB, NRSV, REB, TNT], 'to be filled up' [El, NIC, WBC; NASB], 'to be completely filled' [TEV]. This passive verb is also translated actively: 'to attain' [AB; NAB].

c. εἰς with accusative object (LN 90.23) (BAGD 4.e. p. 229): 'to' [AB, BAGD, El, NIC, NTC, WBC; NAB, NASB], 'unto' [Rob, We], 'in, into' [TH], 'to the measure' [NIV], 'with' [KJV, NJB, NRSV, REB, TEV, TNT], 'with respect to' [LN, Lns], 'with reference to' [LN], 'so that' [BAGD]. This preposition is used to denote the goal, specifying the result of an action or condition [BAGD]. This preposition is a marker of content as a means of denoting a particular referent [LN].

d. πᾶς (LN 63.2) (BAGD 1.c.α. p. 631): 'all' [BAGD, El, Lns, NIC, NTC, Rob, WBC, We; KJV, NASB, NIV, NRSV, TNT], 'utter' [NJB], 'the very' [REB, TEV], 'the whole' [BAGD], 'whole, entire, total' [LN], 'full' [AB], not explicit [TH; NAB]. One translation represents the force of πᾶς 'all' with the words 'of God himself' [NAB]. When this term occurs with the definite article, the meaning pertains to being entire or whole, so that the focus is on the totality of the thing named [LN].

e. πλήρωμα (LN 59.32) (BAGD 3.b. p. 672): 'fullness' [BAGD, El, LN, Lns, NIC, NTC, Rob, TH, WBC, We; all versions except TEV, TNT], 'full measure, totality, completeness' [LN], 'sum total' [BAGD], 'perfection' [AB], 'perfect fullness' [TNT], 'nature' [TEV]. This noun denotes a total quantity with an emphasis upon completeness [LN].

QUESTION—What relationship is indicated by ἵνα 'in order that, that'?

1. It indicates the purpose of the preceding clause [Can, ICC, TH; NRSV, TEV, TNT]: to know the love of Christ so that you may be filled with all the fullness of God. Paul adds this clause to show that knowledge of whatever kind is not the ultimate end [ICC].
2. It indicates the final purpose of the request that Christ might dwell in their hearts (3:17) [ECWB, Lns; NAB]: May Christ dwell in your hearts by faith so that you may attain to all the fullness of God. This clause forms the climax of Paul's prayer.
3. It indicates the purpose of 3:18 [El, Ho, LJ, My; NJB]: you will be able to comprehend, etc., so that you may be filled with all the fullness of God. He has asked that they may be strengthened in order to comprehend Christ's infinite love; and that they might comprehend Christ's love in order that they might be filled to the measure of God's fullness [Ho].
4. It indicates the purpose of all the preceding requests of this prayer [Ea, IB, Rob; NIV, REB]: So may you be filled with all the fullness of God. This clause depicts the grand purpose and result of the whole prayer, the climax of the whole supplication [Ea].
5. It indicates the final petition of Paul's prayer [AB, EBC, St, TD, TNTC, WBC, WeBC]: (I pray) that you may be filled with all the fullness of God. This is Paul's fourth and last petition [St]. It is preferable to regard this as the climax and final item in Paul's prayer [EBC, WBC] rather than as a consequence of the preceding clause [EBC]. The ἵνα 'that' clause in Eph. 3:19 gathers together the petitions of 3:16–19a [TD, WBC]: that you may be filled completely, that the whole fullness, given by God, may be yours, especially in respect to the knowledge of the love of Christ [TD].

QUESTION—What is meant by 'being filled with all the fullness of God'?

1. This refers to the Divine perfections, to a filling of such as God himself is full (or fills himself) [Alf, EGT, El, Ho, IB, ISBE2, LJ, Lns, NIC, NTC, Si, St, TH, WBC, WeBC]: may you be filled with all the fullness of God as he himself is full. The words indicate a filling with divine wisdom and love even as God is said to be full, yet each in one's own degree, and all to the utmost capacity [Alf, LJ, Lns]. This is expressive of the Divine perfections [EGT, El, Ho, LJ, NTC, St]. The believer is to seek to attain to absolute perfection. He must try to be perfect as man, as God is perfect as God, and perfection for man consists of being full of God [Ho, LJ]. The fact that this can never be attained in this life is no valid objection, since

this is a statement of Paul's desire for these believers, an *ideal* [EGT], much as is the injunction to be perfect as our Father in heaven is perfect (Matt. 5:48) [EGT, Ho, LJ, St, WeBC]. It is the language of hyperbole [NIC].
2. This refers to a filling with the gifts of grace [My, NCBC, TD] or the riches of God [ICC]: may you be filled with the gift of God's riches. These riches of God are all that is spiritually communicable to the saints as the partakers of the Divine nature [ICC]. This fullness is the operation of grace in the believer, the charismatic fullness bestowed by God, the divine gifts of grace. It is not the perfection of God, since this cannot be attained by man in this temporal life [My]. These gifts are inward strength from the gift of the Spirit, the indwelling of Christ in the heart which creates an enduring love for others, and a sense of the reality and adequacy of Christ's love for the individual believer [NCBC].
3. This refers to the fulfillment of the Divine purpose [ISBE2, Rob, St, We]: may you fully attain to the fulfillment of God's purpose. This is the perfect consummation of created beings according to the Divine idea [We]. Paul uses the word πλήρωμα 'fullness' or 'fulfillment' and its verb πληροῦμαι 'to be filled' or 'fulfilled' in various ways to express the complete attainment of God's ultimate purpose for the whole universe in Christ and through the Church (Eph. 1:10; 3:10), a thought that occurs again and again in both Colossians and Ephesians. The words convey the thought of perfection or completeness as opposed to imperfection or incompleteness [Rob]. (This interpretation is not inconsistent with 1. above, as ISBE2 and St hold both).
4. This refers to the idea of Christian maturity [EBC, IDB, ISBE2]: may you fully attain to the maturity God has ordained for you. The thought is that there is a completeness, a maturity of character that is ordained by God, both for each individually and for the church corporately, and this is the goal toward which we press, and for which the author prays [IDB]. A footnote of the New English Bible gives an alternative translation: 'the fullness which God requires'. This fullness which God requires is related to Christian maturity as measured by the full stature of Christ (Eph. 4:13). This cannot mean a fullness such as God himself possesses, for this is not possible to a finite creature [EBC]. (This interpretation is not inconsistent with 1. and 3. above, since ISBE2 incorporates elements of all three into its interpretation, but focuses more on this one).

QUESTION—What is the meaning of the preposition εἰς 'to'?
1. This preposition should be translated as 'with' [Ba; KJV, NJB, NRSV, REB, TEV, TNT]: with all the fullness of God.
2. This preposition indicates the direction or goal of the Christian's growth or perfection (πληρωθῆτε 'you may be filled') [AB, Alf, BAGD, Can, Ea, EBC, ECWB, EGT, El, Ho, IB, ICC, IDB, LJ, Lns, My, NIC, NTC, Rob, St, TH, TNTC, WBC, WeBC; NAB, NASB, NIV]: toward the measure of all the fullness of God. The preposition does not mean 'with' [Ea, EGT,

El, Ho, LJ, NIC, St, WBC], but rather 'for' or 'into' [Ea], 'unto' [EGT, Ho, St, WeBC], 'up to' [El; NASB], 'with respect to' [LJ, Lns], 'to the measure of' [NIV], or 'up to the measure of' [Rob]. It looks at a filling up to an end quantitatively considered [Can, Ea, El, My, St, TNTC]. It expresses the measure up to which the filling is to be, or the limit of the filling, or the goal it has before it [EGT, WBC, WeBC]. It expresses the standard which is to be reached [Ho, St]. It does not indicate a static state of fullness, but a progressive filling toward the goal of the complete fullness of Christ (Eph. 4:13) [WBC, WeBC].

DISCOURSE UNIT: 3:20–21 [AB, Alf, Ba, CBC, EBC, ECWB, EGT, El, IB, ICC, LJ, Lns, MNTC, My, NCBC, NIC, NTC, Rob, Si, St, TH, WBC, We, WeBC]. The topic is praise to God for his faithfulness and power with regard to his church [AB, Alf]; for what his foreordaining love and grace has accomplished already in these Gentiles [ECWB, EGT, LJ, NIC, NTC, Si], for the power that is already at work in these believers, far in excess of what they can even imagine [WBC], and for the greater things of the future for which this grace destines them [EGT, WeBC], far beyond what they can even imagine [My, Rob, St]; particularly in regards to his cosmic purpose in Christ [IB, Rob].

3:20 Now[a] to-the (one) being-able[b] beyond[c] all-things to-do superabundantly[d] of-what we-ask or we-think

LEXICON—a. δέ (LN 89.87): 'now' [El, Lns, NIC, NTC, Rob, WBC, We; KJV, NASB, NIV, NRSV, REB], 'and' [LN], not explicit [AB; NJB, TEV, TNT]. This particle marks a sequence of closely related events [LN].

b. pres. pass. participle of δύναμαι (LN 74.5): 'to be able' [AB, El, LN, Lns, NTC, Rob, WBC, We; KJV, NASB, NIV, NRSV, REB, TEV], 'can' [LN]. Some translate this full verb as an auxiliary verb with the infinitive ποιῆσαι 'to do' later in the verse: 'can do' [NIC; NAB, NJB, TNT]. The verb forms a play on words with its cognate noun form, δῆναμιν 'power', which occurs later in the verse [AB, WBC].

c. ὑπέρ with accusative object (LN 78.29) (BAGD 2. p. 839): 'beyond' [BAGD, El, LN, Lns, We; NASB], 'above' [Rob, WBC; KJV], 'more than' [BAGD, LN, NTC; NAB, NIV, NJB, REB, TEV, TNT], 'greater than' [BAGD], 'to a greater degree than' [LN], 'above and beyond' [BAGD]. The phrase ὑπὲρ πάντα ποιῆσαι 'beyond all things to do' is translated 'to outdo' [AB]. Some combine this preposition with ὑπερεκπερισσοῦ 'superabundantly': 'far more abundantly than' [NIC], 'abundantly far more than' [NRSV]. In this usage this preposition indicates a degree which is beyond that of the scale of extent with which it is compared [LN].

d. ὑπερεκπερισσοῦ (LN 78.34) (BAGD p. 840): 'superabundantly' [AB, El], 'exceeding abundantly' [Lns, Rob, We; KJV, NASB], 'most exceedingly' [MM], 'infinitely' [BAGD, NTC; NJB, TNT], 'infinitely more abundantly' [WBC], 'so much' [TEV], 'immeasurably' [NAB, NIV,

REB], 'quite beyond all measure' [BAGD], 'to an extreme degree, to a very great degree' [LN]. Some combine this term with the preposition ὑπέρ 'beyond' (see c. above) [NIC; NRSV]. This term expresses the highest form of comparison imaginable [BAGD, WBC]. It indicates a degree considerably in excess over what would be expected [LN]. This is one of the double-compound words that were favorites of Paul [AB].
- e. pres. act. indic. of νοέω (LN **31.6**) (BAGD 3. p. 540): 'to think' [BAGD, El, NIC, Rob, WBC, We; KJV, NASB, TNT], 'to think of' [TEV], 'to imagine' [AB, BAGD, LN, NTC; NAB, NIV, NJB, NRSV], 'to conceive' [Lns; REB], 'to be able to form an idea' [LN]. In this verse, it is also possible to understand the verb as meaning merely 'to hold a particular view' so that the translation here could be 'far beyond what we think to be the case' [LN].

QUESTION—What relationship is indicated by δέ 'now'?

It marks a transition to a different subject [AB, Ea, El, Lns, NIC, NTC, Rob, We; all versions] and some translate it as 'now' [Ea, EGT, El, Lns, NIC, NTC, Rob, We; KJV, NASB, NIV, NRSV, REB], though some do not explicitly mark this transition by translating the particle [AB; NAB, NJB, TEV, TNT]. Some state that the particle also has some contrastive force, though slight [Alf, EGT, El]. One even translates it 'but' [Alf]. With this particle he makes a transition from recipients to the Giver [Ea]. The δέ 'now' brings out a slight contrast in this verse to what has just preceded, namely, in the preceding verses, between *ourselves* [Alf, El], and our need of strength and our growth in knowledge and fullness [Alf], and God, who is the subject of the present verse [El]. However, another sees the contrast as between the Giver of the grace and the grace given [EGT].

QUESTION—What relationships are indicated by ὑπέρ 'beyond' and ὑπερεκπερισσοῦ 'superabundantly', and to what are they connected?
1. These two terms go together to form an emphatic phrase expressing Paul's exulting thoughts [AB, Cal, Can, MNTC, NIC, NTC, TD, WBC; all versions]. This comparative term ὑπερεκπερισσοῦ 'superabundantly', compounded with two prepositions, forms a phrase with the preceding ὑπέρ 'beyond', 'superabundantly above all', that expresses the exulting thoughts of Paul, who heaps one comparative upon another in defiance of strict grammar [Can].
   1.1 Together they govern πάντα 'all things', forming a prepositional phrase that modifies the relative clause ὧν αἰτούμεθα ἢ νοοῦμεν 'that which we ask or think' as an adverb [Cal, Can, ECWB, NIC, NTC, St, TD, WBC; all versions except NAB, NJB, TEV]: who is able to do superabundantly beyond all that we ask or think. Ὑπερεκπερισσοῦ modifies the preposition ὑπέρ 'beyond' [Can, WBC]: 'superabundantly above all'. There is a comparative idea that is drawn from the context [TD], and so ὑπέρ means 'more than' [NIC, NTC, St, TD; NRSV, REB]: 'who can do more than all we may ask or think' [TD].

1.2 Together they form an adverbial phrase of comparison modifying the relative clause ὧν αἰτούμεθα ἢ νοοῦμεν 'that which we ask or think' [MNTC; NAB, NJB, TEV]: who is able to do all things, superabundantly beyond what we ask or think. The accusative πάντα 'all things' functions as the object of the infinitive ποιῆσαι 'to do' rather than as the object of the preposition and ὑπέρ 'beyond' reiterates the adverb ὑπερεκπερισσοῦ 'superabundantly' [MNTC, Mo (though expressing no preference for either this interpretation or 2.)].

1.3 Together they form an adverbial phrase modifying the infinitive ποιῆσαι 'to do' (πάντα 'all' with the relative clause being the object) [AB]: who is able to outdo superabundantly all that we ask or think. The resulting statement serves to buttress the oxymoron of 3:19a 'to know the knowledge surpassing love of Christ' [AB].

2. These two terms are not immediately related to each other. Ὑπέρ 'beyond' goes with πάντα 'all things' and has its normal prepositional function. Ὑπερεκπερισσοῦ likewise functions as a preposition with the meaning 'far beyond' and modifies the relative clause ὧν αἰτούμεθα ἢ νοοῦμεν 'that which we ask or think' [Alf, Ea, EGT, El, Ho, ICC, LJ, Lns, My, Rob, We]: who is able to do beyond all things, far beyond that which we ask or think. Ὑπερεκπερισσοῦ 'far beyond', with the clause it modifies, repeats the clause containing ὑπέρ 'beyond' in a more detailed and specific form [Alf, EGT, El, My].

QUESTION—What relationship is shown by the genitive case of the relative pronoun ὧν 'of which'?

This relative pronoun depends upon ὑπερεκπερισσοῦ 'superabundantly' [ICC, We]. It is in the genitive case because of the idea of comparison in ὑπέρ 'beyond' in the double-compound comparative ὑπερεκπερισσοῦ 'superabundantly' [Alf, BD, Ea, EGT, El, ICC, Lns, Mo, My]. Another explanation is that ὧν 'of which' is attracted to the case of an omitted antecedent [HG].

QUESTION—To what does the clause ὧν αἰτούμεθα ἢ νοοῦμεν 'of which we ask or think' refer?

1. It has particular or specific reference to the petitions just made in 3:16–19 [AB, Ba, Can, Ea, EGT, Ho, IB, ICC, MNTC, My, Rob, TNTC, WBC]. Paul has prayed that God would grant a blessing which transcends man's knowledge, and he is confident that even such a request as this will be granted [MNTC]. God was not only able to do what Paul had asked, but infinitely more than he knew how to ask or even to think [Ho, TNTC].

2. The reference is wider than just to the petitions of 3:16–19 and may apply to other petitions a believer may make [Cal, EBC, El, LJ, Lns, NCBC, NIC, NTC, Si, St, We, WeBC]. Believers ought always to connect God's ability with the power working within them when the petition concerns the promises made to them and their own salvation [Cal]. God's capability of meeting his people's spiritual needs far exceeds anything they can ask in prayer or conceive in their anticipation [EBC]. There is no need nor

legitimate desire that Christians can ask for or even think of that God cannot supply superabundantly [WeBC].

QUESTION—What is the significance of the shift from the first person singular (3:14) to the first person plural in the verbs αἰτούμεθα 'we ask' and νοοῦμεν 'we think'?

Since this clause refers particularly to Paul's petitions, some use the third person singular in their comments, possibly indicating they regard the first person plural of the verbs in this clause as an editorial 'we' referring to the writer himself [Ho, Rob, TD, TNTC]. The writer shifts to the first person plural to draw the readers into sharing in his prayer concerns and into the breadth of his vision of God's power [WBC].

QUESTION—What idea is Paul expressing by using the words ὧν αἰτούμεθα ἢ νοοῦμεν 'of which we ask or think'?

He is saying God's ability to answer prayer far transcends not only the spoken petitions offered, but even such thoughts as are too deep to utter due to their very vastness [Ea, EGT, El, Ho, WBC]. Whatever expectations are formed concerning Divine blessings, the infinite goodness of God will exceed all wishes and thoughts [Cal]. This clause is saying that God is not restricted by the feebleness of men's prayers or the narrowness of their knowledge [Ho, ICC]. God's power, not men's prayers nor their highest conceptions, is the measure against which Paul puts his anticipations and desires [Ho]. The verb νοοῦμεν 'we think' has the meaning of 'to ponder, consider' [EGT] or 'to conceive, imagine' [TD]. It may designate those thoughts that occur to us, yet are not shaped into petitions [We, WeBC].

according-to[a] the power[b] the-(one that) is-working[c] in[d] us,

LEXICON—a. κατά with accusative object (LN 89.8): 'according to' [El, Lns, NIC, NTC, Rob, We; KJV, NASB, NIV], 'in accordance with' [LN, WBC], 'in relation to' [LN], 'by' [AB; NRSV], 'by means of' [TEV], 'through' [REB, TNT]. Some translate the prepositional phrase κατὰ τὴν δύναμιν 'according to the power' as a relative pronoun possessive phrase: 'whose power' [NAB, NJB]. This usage of the preposition indicates a relation involving a correspondence or similarity of process [LN].

b. δύναμις: 'power'. See this word at 1:19; 3:7, 16. This noun takes up the idea expressed in the previously occurring cognate participle δυναμένῳ 'being able' forming a play on words [AB].

c. pres. mid. or pass. participle of ἐνεργέω (LN 42.3) (BAGD 1.b. p. 265): 'to work' [BAGD, El, LN, Rob, We; KJV, NASB, NJB, TEV], 'to be at work' [LN, NTC, WBC; NAB, NIV, NRSV, REB, TNT], 'to function' [LN], 'to operate' [Lns, NIC], 'to exert' [AB]. See this word at 1:11, 20; 2:2.

d. ἐν with dative object (LN 83.13): 'in' [AB, El, LN, Lns, NIC, Rob, We; KJV, NAB, NJB, TEV, TNT], 'within' [LN, NTC, WBC; NASB, NIV, NRSV], 'among' [REB].

QUESTION—To what δύναμις 'power' does this clause refer?

This is the power that he had prayed his readers might come to know (1:19) [Can, Ea, Ho, LJ, NCBC, NIC, NTC, WBC], the power that had actually been at work within Christ 1:20 [WBC], the power that he had described as working in them in their quickening and conversion (2:1–10) [Can, Ea, Ho, LJ, Lns, NCBC, NTC, St, WBC] and the forming of one new humanity out of Jewish and Gentile believers [WBC], and the power the writer has described as operative in the ministry of the apostle (3:7) [WBC]. The power is the might of the Holy Spirit who indwells us [Alf, EGT, El, NCBC, NIC], just referred to in 3:16 [El, NCBC].

QUESTION—What is the voice of the participle ἐνεργουμένην 'is working'?
1. This is the middle voice [Alf, Ea, EBC, EGT, El, Ho, ICC, LJ, Lns, MNTC, My, NIC, Si-ed, WBC, We, WeBC]: the power which is working in us. This is not passive [Alf, EGT, El, ICC, My]. The middle voice is used instead of the active when there is an impersonal subject [Ea, EBC, El, ICC]. This seems to be the standard NT usage of this verb [EBC].
2. This is the passive voice [AB, Rob]: the power that is exerted, or is made to work, in us. The passive voice here serves to remind us that this power working in us is not self-originated [Rob].

QUESTION—What is the significance of the present tense of this participle?

It shows this power as continually at work within the lives of believers [EBC, IB, MNTC], continually enlightening and endowing the inner man [My], however much it exceeds in scope our desires or imaginations [IB]. Another sees it as having reference to the possibilities of God's future dealings with Christians [EGT].

QUESTION—What is the force of the phrase ἐν ἡμῖν 'in us'?

This means 'in our souls' [El] or 'in our minds' [My]. Ἐν ἡμῖν 'in us' is an appeal to the consciousness of our experience [EGT, LJ, My]. The power that we know to be working in us is a witness to the nature of the power that governs the universe and brings everything to its appointed end [IB] and to God's ability to accomplish superabundantly more than we ask or think [EGT]. It is the certainty of the Divine power already working that fills Paul with this exultant confidence [Rob]. Another view is that it means 'among us', within our group [REB].

3:21 to-him (be) the glory[a] in[b] the church and in[c] Christ Jesus to/from[d] all the generations[e] of-the age[f] of-the ages. Amen.[g]

TEXT—Some manuscripts of the Textus Receptus tradition omit καί 'and', suggesting the translation 'in the church through, by Christ Jesus' is possible. GNT make no mention of this alternative reading. The alternative reading is followed by Ea, ECWB, Ho, LJ, My, Si, KJV, and TNT.

LEXICON—a. δόξα (LN 33.357): 'glory' [AB, El, Lns, NIC, NTC, Rob, WBC, We; all versions], 'praise' [LN]. This is the speaking of something as being unusually fine and deserving of honor [LN].

b. ἐν with dative object (LN 89.76, 90.6): 'in' [AB, El, Lns, NIC, NTC, Rob, WBC, We; all versions], 'through, by means of' [LN (89.76)], 'by' [LN (89.76, 90.6)], 'from' [LN (90.6), TH]. This is a marker of the means by which one event makes another event possible [LN (89.76)]. This is a marker of the agent and often has the implication that the agent is also the instrument [LN (90.6)].

c. ἐν with dative object (LN 89.76, 89.119, 90.6): 'in' [AB, El, LN (89.119), Lns, NIC, NTC, Rob, WBC, We; all versions except KJV, TNT], 'by' [LN (89.76, 90.6); KJV], 'through, by means of' [LN (89.76)], 'in union with, joined closely to' [LN (89.119)], 'through our union with' [TNT], 'from' [LN (90.6)]. See LN 89.76 and 90.6 entries in b. above. This is the marker of a close personal association [LN (89.119)].

d. εἰς with accusative object (LN **67.95**): 'to' [El, NIC, NTC; NASB, NRSV], 'unto' [We], 'from' [AB; NJB, REB, TNT], 'through' [NAB], 'throughout' [Rob, WBC; KJV, NIV], 'for' [LN, Lns; TEV]. LN lists this as part of a variant of a set phrase. See entry g. below.

e. γενεά (LN **67.95**, 67.144) (BAGD 3.b. p. 154): 'generation' [AB, BAGD, El, Lns, NIC, NTC, WBC, We; all versions except KJV, TEV], 'age' [BAGD, LN (**67.95**, 67.144), Rob; KJV], 'epoch' [LN (67.144)], 'period of time' [BAGD], 'time' [TEV]. See this word at 3:5.

f. αἰών (LN **67.95**) (BAGD 1.b. p. 27): 'age' [BAGD, El, We], 'eon' [Lns]. The phrase αἰῶνος τῶν αἰώνων 'age of the ages' is translated 'eternity' [NIC], 'forever and ever' [AB, NTC; NASB, NIV, NJB, NRSV, TEV, TNT], 'forevermore, for evermore' [BAGD, WBC; REB], 'world without end' [Rob; KJV, NAB], 'for all ages forever and ever' [LN]. The word can be used of time to come which, if used in the sense of having no end, is the same as 'eternity' [BAGD]. It is used as part of the variant of a set phrase, εἰς πάσας τὰς γενεὰς τοῦ αἰῶνος τῶν αἰώνων 'to, or from, all the generations of the age of the ages'. This phrase designates an unlimited duration of time with particular focus upon the future. [LN].

g. ἀμήν (LN 72.6) (BAGD 1. p. 45): 'amen' [AB, BAGD, El, Lns, NIC, NTC, Rob, WBC; all versions], 'so let it be' [BAGD], 'truly' [BAGD, LN], 'indeed, it is true that' [LN], not explicit [We]. This is a Hebrew term, usually translated in the LXX by γένοιτο 'let it be', and was taken over into Christian vocabulary [BAGD]. The term is a strong affirmation of something that is declared [LN].

QUESTION—What is the force of αὐτῷ 'to him' and to whom does it refer?

This is a rhetorical repetition with the pronoun of the τῷ δυναμένῳ 'to him who is able' of 3:20 [El, My, WBC], or it repeats all that has been said about God the Father in 3:14 [Lns]. The pronoun is emphatic by position [Ea, EGT, El, Lns] and refers to God [AB, Alf, Ba, Can, Ea, EBC, EGT, El, Ho, LJ, Lns, MNTC, NCBC, NIC, TNTC, WBC]. The rhetorical repetition is necessary because like the previous intercessory prayer-report where the writer started a digression with a description of God's awesome power, here he has used a rhetorical flourish to again describe it and he must use the pronoun αὐτῷ 'to him' to return to the introductory object of his doxology [WBC].

QUESTION—Is the ellipsed verb in the phrase αὐτῷ ἡ δόξα 'to him (be) the glory' indicative or optative?

1. The verb to be supplied in this phrase should be in the indicative mode (ἐστί 'is') [Can, TNTC, WBC]: to him (is) the glory. It is best to regard ascriptions of glory which simply employ a noun as predicative possessive statements rather than as wishes, so the indicative mode is preferred [WBC]. The indicative mode is preferable because in the next clause this glory is said to be alike in the Church and in Christ [Can].
2. The verb to be supplied in this phrase should be in the optative mode (εἴη 'be') [Alf, Ba, Ea, EGT, El, Ho, ICC, ISBE, MNTC, My, NIC, NTC, Rob, St, TH, We, WeBC; all versions]: to him (be) the glory. Because αὐτῷ stands first in the sentence, the optative is to be supplied [EGT].

QUESTION—What is meant by δόξα 'glory'?

1. This means praise to God [DNTT, Ea, El, IDB, ISBE, ISBE2, Lns, MNTC, My, NCBC, TD, TH, WBC]. As used in doxologies, δόξαν διδόναι 'to give glory' and its variants does not imply the addition of something which is not already present, but is rather a predication, the extolling of what is [TD]. This is the glory that is due to him [El], and redounds to him from his gracious dealing with us [El, ISBE2]. His glory is recognized and acknowledged by the church [Lns]. This is the recognition of what God has done and will do, with the result being praise to him [NCBC]. Being a human acknowledgment and ascription of praise of what properly belongs to God, δόξα 'glory' denotes the splendor of God's exalted status or honor, but the other connotations of his radiance and power would not be missing entirely [WBC].
2. This refers to the manifestation of the perfections of God [AB, Can, ICC, LJ, Rob, St]. The meaning is not simply that the Church and Christ Jesus both give praise to God, for while that could be the meaning of ἐν τῇ ἐκκλησίᾳ 'in the Church', it could hardly be the meaning of ἐν Χριστῷ Ἰησοῦ 'in Christ Jesus'. Rather it is that both the Church and its Head are to the glory of God because in both are revealed most fully the Divine perfections [Can]. This 'glory' refers primarily to God's power [LJ, St], manifested in the formation of the church and its unity in Christ Jesus as its head, as has been described in chapters 2–3, and to be marveled at eternally by the 'principalities and powers' [LJ].
3. Both of the above ideas are included [Alf, Ba, Can, EGT, IB, NIC, NTC, TNTC]. The idea is that praise is to be given to God and his glorious perfections are to be shown forth both in the church as the body and in Christ Jesus as the Head [EGT]. The splendor of God's amazing attributes, power, wisdom, mercy, love, grace, etc., is manifested both in the church and in Christ Jesus, and because of this may praise and adoration be rendered to him [NTC].

QUESTION—What is the meaning of the prepositions ἐν 'in' in the compound phrase ἐν τῇ ἐκκλησίᾳ καὶ ἐν Χριστῷ Ἰησοῦ 'in the church and in Christ Jesus'?

1. The meaning is 'in the church through Christ Jesus' [AB, Ba, Ho, LJ; KJV]. Both the church and the Messiah are given equal dignity in this statement and both are mentioned as the means of God's glorification. [AB]. Not only is the church the means by which God's praise is celebrated, it is also the means by which his glory is to be manifested, 3:10 [Ba]. Glory is rendered to God in the church and in and through Christ Jesus, as its head and representative [Ho].
2. The meaning is 'in the church in union with Christ Jesus' [Ea, Lns, TH; TNT]. The words define the spirit in which praise is presented to God. It is offered 'in the church' but it is presented by the members in the consciousness of their union with Christ and, consequently, in a spirit of dependence on him. The glory is sung by the members, but the spirit of the song is inspired by oneness with Christ. Translating the second ἐν 'in' with 'by' or 'through' is not in accordance with the ordinary meaning of the preposition [Ea]. The ἐν 'in' in reference to the church refers to the hearts of believers and is therefore subjective. The ἐν 'in' in connection with Christ Jesus refers to our union with him and so is objective. Thus all the glory that is due to God is connected solely and alone with Christ Jesus, the name denoting both his office and his person [Lns].
3. The prepositions have similar meaning in both parts of the phrase [Alf, Can, ECWB, EGT, El, IB, ICC, MNTC, My, NTC, Rob, St, TNTC, WBC, We, WeBC; all versions except KJV, TNT]: in the church and in Christ Jesus. The church is the medium by which the greatness and perfection of God's glory is exhibited, as it is also exhibited in Christ Jesus [ICC, Rob, We]. The double phrase is to be understood in light of the fact that the church and Christ are complementary parts of one organism, as head and body [Can, EGT, IB, NTC, St, WBC, WeBC]. Together they form the sphere through which God manifests his glory [IB, NTC, WBC] and the medium through which creation is to praise its Creator [IB]. The church is also seen as the present, outer, visible, external sphere of praise to God, while Christ Jesus is seen as the inner, spiritual sphere of this praise [Alf, El, My, WBC], the true element alone in which praise is duly to be ascribed to God [Alf, El, My], so the sense is: 'in the church and thus in Christ Jesus' [Alf]. Others see the parallelism of these phrases as implying the great idea of the Epistle—the unity of the Church in Christ [ECWB, TNTC]. All that is 'in the Church' is 'in Christ Jesus'. The visible unity of the Church represents the invisible unity with God in Christ, as it also depends upon him [ECWB]. Others see the church and Christ as together being the sphere for the outworking of the purposes of God [MNTC, TNTC].

QUESTION—What is meant by ἐκκλησία 'church'?

This is the company of redeemed mankind, both here on earth and in heaven [Ho, TNTC]. Another sees 'the church' as the redeemed in their final, glorified state [LJ] while another sees 'the church' as referring to the redeemed here on earth [Lns]. It combines both aspects. God is glorified in the cultic acts (worship) of the church as well as in the fact of its existence. But he will only be perfectly glorified in the Church when it fully shares in his glory, so there is an eschatological aspect to this also [WBC].

QUESTION—What is meant by πάσας τὰς γενεὰς τοῦ αἰῶνος τῶν αἰώνων 'all the generations of the age of the ages'?

1. The expression has exclusive reference to the everlasting future [Alf, Ba, Can, DNTT, Ea, Ho, LJ, Lns, My-ed, NIC, TD]. It means, in the strongest sense, FOR EVER [Ba, Ea]. The probable meaning is that eternity is conceived as containing ages, as ages contain years, and then those ages are thought of as made up of or measured by generations [Alf, Can, Ea, My-ed, NIC]. The various biblical expressions of eternity do not convey substantially different meanings, but each expression is used in accordance with the tone of feeling in the writer's mind and the particular feature of eternity which he wishes to emphasize, whether its final and conclusive character (best suggested by a brief form), or the immense extension of it, as here, to which the longer forms are more suitable [Can, Ho].

2. The expression presents eternity as consisting of all time, past, present, and future, and extending into and throughout eternity future [ECWB, EGT, ICC (probably), MNTC, My, St, WBC]. This age would be the messianic age, which opens with the Coming of Christ, and brings all other αἰῶνος 'ages' with all their γενεαί 'generations' to their end, and will itself endure forever. Thus the glory to be given to God is to endure not only up to the Coming of Christ, but ever onward from generation to generation in the messianic age [EGT, My]. The whole of time and eternity is thought of as one age, which is divided into many ages, and each of these into generations [MNTC]. Γενεὰς 'generations' refers to history and τοῦ αἰῶνος τῶν αἰώνων 'of the age of the ages' refers to eternity [St]. The phrase incorporates both history and eternity, the meaning being that praise is due to God for generations to come and as one age follows on another into infinity [WBC].

QUESTION—What is the meaning of γενεάς 'generations' in this expression?

1. It primarily denotes a span of time [AB, DNTT, Ea, El (probably), ISBE, ISBE2, My, My-ed, NIC, NTC, WeBC]. It is needless to understand γενεάς 'generations' as referring to successive generations of living creatures. Often the word simply indicates a period of time measured by the average life span of a man [Ea], about 33 years [DNTT, ISBE, My]. The term covers the time between the birth of parents and the birth of their children. This denotes a chronological aspect of time and the phrase τοῦ αἰῶνος τῶν αἰώνων 'of the age of the ages' reinforces this [NTC]. The term is here applied figuratively as an expression of duration in eternity

[ISBE]. The Hebrews regarded a generation as a century while the Greeks regarded it as a third of a century [WeBC].
2. It primarily denotes the intelligent creatures living within a span of time [Can, ECWB, Lns, TD]. The whole expression is emphatic and peculiar. The singular αἰών 'age' in the expression is the culmination of all the ages we can reckon or conceive, so that the concept is of each generation, in each of the ages, of all the ages, adding its own peculiar thanksgiving to the great chorus of praise which fills eternity [ECWB]. Another believes the reference to be the death of each generation of believers as each generation passes into the great age of eternity [Lns]. The use of πατριά 'family/fatherhood' at the beginning of this prayer, in 3:15, could cause γενεάς 'generations' here to refer to the generations and races of intelligence creatures of which God is Father, thus these 'generations' would receive their enlightenment through the church in line with the teaching of 3:10 [TD].

QUESTION—What is the significance of the ἀμήν 'amen'?

This was the Hebrew expression used in the OT when the people gave assent to declarations made at their solemn assemblies [DNTT, EGT] and it was also used as their response to the prayers offered in the synagogue [AB, DNTT, EGT, NIC, TD]. In Rabbinic Judaism anyone who said 'amen' to a doxology or prayer made it his own [DNTT], making the validity of it binding upon himself [TD]. It expresses hearty approval [NTC] or confirmation [DNTT, TD] and has the sense of 'so be it' [EGT, TH]. Paul is probably putting himself in the place of the congregation he is addressing, acting as their spokesman in this act of praise [AB, WeBC]. The readers are expected to confirm to themselves this glory that belongs to God [WBC].

DISCOURSE UNIT: 4:1–6:24 [Ba, Cal, EGT, IB, Lns, NCBC, NIC, Si, TNTC, WBC]. The topic is the practical applications of the epistle to the Christian life [Ba, Cal, EGT, IB, WBC], the obligations of membership in the one holy church [Lns], the responsibilities of the Christian [NCBC], how glory is to be rendered to God now in the church [TNTC].

DISCOURSE UNIT: 4:1–6:22 [AB]. The topic is ethical and practical teachings related to the Christian life.

DISCOURSE UNIT: 4:1–6:20 [Alf, EBC, My, NIC, TH, WBC, We, WeBC]. The topic is an exhortation to practical applications of the epistle to the Christian life [Alf, EBC, My, NIC, TH, WBC, We].

DISCOURSE UNIT: 4:1–5:20 [St; REB]. The topic is the new standards which are expected from the new society [St], Christian conduct [REB].

DISCOURSE UNIT: 4:1–5:2 [Si]. The topic is the traits of Christian manhood.

DISCOURSE UNIT: 4:1–32 [Ba, Ea, Ho, WeBC]. The topic is an exhortation to unity, holiness, and to specific virtues [Ba, Ea, Ho], the Church's calling in Christ and the need for their conduct to measure up to that calling [WeBC].

DISCOURSE UNIT: 4:1–24 [We]. The topic is the ground, growth, and character of the Christian life.

DISCOURSE UNIT: 4:1–16 [AB, Alf, Ba, Can, Ea, EBC, ECWB, EGT, Ho, IB, LJ, Lns, MNTC, My, NCBC, NTC, Rob, St, TH, TNTC, WBC, WeBC; NAB, NASB, NIV, NJB, TEV]. The topic is the ground of the Christian's duties [Alf], the final summary of doctrine [ECWB], a call to spiritual maturity [WeBC], an exhortation to the readers to conduct their lives in a manner worthy their divine calling [EGT, My, NCBC], to humility [EGT, NCBC] and unity in the church [Alf, Ba, Can, Ea, EBC, ECWB, EGT, Ho, LJ, Lns, MNTC, My, NCBC, NTC, Rob, St, TH, TNTC; NAB (note), NASB, NIV, NJB, TEV], the constitution of the church [AB].

DISCOURSE UNIT: 4:1–10 [El, Si]. The topic is an exhortation to live worthy of the divine calling [El].

DISCOURSE UNIT: 4:1–6 [Alf, Ba, CBC, ECWB, IB, Lns, Rob, TNTC, WBC; NAB]. The topic is an exhortation to unity [Ba, CBC, Lns, TNTC; NAB], the ground of the unity of the Body of Christ [Alf, WBC], the doctrine of one Spirit, one Lord, and one God and Father of all [ECWB], the need for consecration [IB].

DISCOURSE UNIT: 4:1–3 [Ho, ICC, LJ, Lns, My, NIC, Si, WBC, We]. The topic is an admonition to keep the unity of the Spirit in the bond of peace [Lns, My, NIC], an exhortation to walk worthily of their calling [Ho, ICC, My, WBC], in a manner that corresponds to the Christian faith [We].

4:1 I beseech/admonish[a] you therefore[b] I the prisoner[c] in[d] the-Lord
LEXICON—a. pres. act. indic. of παρακαλέω (LN 33.168) (BAGD 2. p. 617): 'to beseech' [AB, NIC, Rob, We; KJV], 'to entreat' [NTC; NASB], 'to beg' [LN; NRSV, TNT], 'to urge' [BAGD; NIV, NJB, TEV], 'to plead (for, with)' [LN; NAB], 'to implore' [REB], 'to admonish' [Lns], 'to appeal to' [BAGD, LN], 'to exhort' [BAGD, El, WBC], 'to encourage' [BAGD], 'to request, to earnestly ask for' [LN].
b. οὖν (LN 89.50) (BAGD 1.a. p. 593): 'therefore' [AB, BAGD, El, LN, NIC, NTC, Rob, WBC, We; KJV, NASB, NJB, NRSV], 'then' [BAGD, LN; NAB, NIV, REB, TEV, TNT], 'accordingly' [BAGD, LN, Lns], 'so, consequently' [BAGD, LN], 'so then' [LN].
c. δέσμιος (LN 37.117) (BAGD p. 176): 'prisoner' [AB, BAGD, El, LN, Lns, NIC, NTC, Rob, WBC, We; all versions].
d. ἐν with dative object (LN 89.26, 89.119) (BAGD I.5.d. p. 260): 'in' [AB, BAGD, El, LN (89.119), Lns, NIC, NTC, Rob, WBC, We; NJB, NRSV], 'for' [NAB, NIV], 'for the sake of' [REB, TNT], 'of' [KJV, NASB], 'because of, on account of, by reason of' [LN (89.26)]. This preposition is also translated as a dependent clause: 'because I serve' [TEV].

QUESTION—What is meant by παρακαλῶ 'I beseech/admonish'?
1. It means to beseech or entreat [AB, Ba, Ho, ICC, LN, NCBC, NIC, NTC, Rob, TH, TNTC, We; KJV, NAB, NASB, NRSV, REB, TNT]. Since it is to an absolute duty that he calls them, more than exhortation is implied [ICC].
2. It means to exhort, admonish, or encourage [Alf, BAGD, Can, DNTT, Ea, EBC, EGT, El, Lns, My, TD, WBC; NIV, NJB, TEV]. This appeal covers all the precepts that follow, though its immediate object ('to walk worthily') is the statement of a principle that ought to rule all Christian conduct [Can].

QUESTION—What relationship is indicated by οὖν 'therefore'?
1. It indicates an exhortation based on the immediately preceding 3:21 [My]. A walk in keeping with the vocation by which one belongs to the church is what is practically in keeping with the praise of God in the church [My].
2. It indicates an exhortation based on the previous chapter [Ea, Rob] especially from 3:6 onwards [EGT, El].
3. It indicates an exhortation based on the whole of the preceding three chapters [AB, Alf, Ba, Can, CBC, ICC, LJ, Lns, NCBC, NIC, NTC, St, TH, TNTC, WBC, We].
4. It indicates an exhortation based on only certain references in the first three chapters [EBC]. The opening of chapter 4 marks the principal transition of the entire epistle. Paul has in mind certain references in these chapters to spiritual privileges and the Christian calling (3:6, 12, 14–19) [EBC].

QUESTION—What is meant by ἐν κυρίῳ 'in the Lord'?
It denotes a sphere of identification or existence [AB, Alf, BAGD, Can, Ea, EGT, El, NCBC, NIC, TD, Tu2; NJB, NRSV]: in the Lord. This is the mystical use of ἐν 'in' [Tu2] and denotes the mystical union or identification of the subject with Christ or the Lord [IB, NCBC, NIC, Tu2]. In addition, some interpret it as designating a sphere of activity: in the Lord's service [AB, Alf, EGT, TD]. The formula ἐν κυρίῳ 'in the Lord' designates a state or activity as Christian (Eph. 4:1) [TD]. Some see, or also see, a causal [Ba, LJ, LN, TH; TEV] or benefactive [Alf, Ea; NAB, NIV, REB, TNT] element expressed in this preposition: because I serve the Lord, or, for the sake of the Lord's cause. He was in confinement in the cause of the Lord [Alf, Ba]. He was a prisoner because the Lord had so willed it and because it was his service [Ba]. Only the KJV and NASB interpret it as possessive: of the Lord.

to-walk[a] worthily[b] of-the calling[c] of-which you-were-called,[d]
LEXICON—a. aorist act infin. of περιπατέω (LN 41.11) (BAGD 2.a.α. p. 649): 'to walk' [BAGD, El, Lns, Rob, We; KJV, NASB], 'to live' [BAGD, LN], 'to live lives' [NTC; TNT], 'to live a life' [NAB, NIV, TEV], 'to lead a life' [WBC; NJB, NRSV], 'to lead lives' [NIC], 'to conduct (oneself)' [AB, BAGD], 'to behave, to go about doing' [LN]. The

phrase 'to walk worthily' is translated 'to live up to' [REB]. The aorist tense is used when the *new* life of the Christian is meant, corresponding to the divine call which causes a new beginning (Eph. 4:1) [BD]. This is the constantive aorist which views the walk of the Ephesians as a whole [Lns]. This verb denotes the living or behaving in a customary manner with a possible focus upon the continuity of that action [LN, WBC].

b. ἀξίως (LN **66.6**) (BAGD p. 78): 'worthily' [BAGD, Lns, We], 'worthy of' [AB, El, LN, NIC, NTC, Rob, WBC; all versions except NASB, REB, TEV], 'that measures up to' [TEV], 'in a manner worthy of' [BAGD; NASB], 'suitably' [BAGD], 'properly, fitting' [LN]. This adverb is also translated as a verb: 'that corresponds to' [LN]. This adverb denotes that which pertains to being fitting or proper in correspondence to what should be expected [LN].

c. κλῆσις (LN **33.313**) (BAGD 1. p. 435): 'calling' [BAGD, El, LN, Lns, NIC, NTC, Rob, WBC, We; NAB, NASB, NIV, NRSV, REB], 'call' [BAGD; TNT], 'vocation' [AB; KJV, NJB], 'invitation' [BAGD]. This noun is also translated as a clause: 'the standard (God) set' [LN (**66.6**); TEV]. In Christian literature this term is used almost exclusively in the religious sense of a divine call to salvation [BAGD, MM].

d. aorist pass. indic. of καλέω (LN 33.312) (BAGD 2. p. 399): 'to be called' [AB, BAGD, El, LN, Lns, NIC, NTC, Rob, WBC, We; KJV, NASB, NJB, NRSV], 'to be called to a task' [LN]. This passive verb is also translated actively: 'to receive' [NAB, NIV, TNT]. This verb is also translated as a clause: 'when he called you' [LN (**66.6**); TEV], '(God) has called you' [LN (**33.313**); REB]. This verb denotes the urgent invitation to someone to accept responsibilities for a particular task and implies a new relationship to the person who issues the invitation [LN].

QUESTION—What does the adverb ἀξίως 'worthily' mean?

It has the sense of 'in harmony with' [Ea]. It introduces the standard or criterion to which the readers' lives are expected to conform [TH, WBC]. Paul wants them to always seek to do what is most in keeping with their vocation [EBC, LJ, NIC]. The lives of Christians must correspond to this call [IB, Rob]. The word also has the idea of what is becoming to a thing, or what is suited to it, what matches it [LJ], what is fitting or in accord with something [DNTT].

QUESTION—What is the force of the noun κλῆσις 'calling' with its cognate verb ἐκλήθητε 'you were called'?

This is a play on words [Bu, Tu3] where words of similar sound [Bu, HG, Tu3], appearance [Bu], and meaning [HG, Tu3] are used. But the writer is not attempting to lay a double stress upon the idea of the divine calling [IB]. The figure serves to call attention to a solemn or important statement that might otherwise be passed over without notice [Bu].

QUESTION—What is meant by the noun κλῆσις 'calling'?

This genitive noun supplies the standard or measure to which the adverb ἀξίως 'worthily' points [TH]. The noun κλῆσις 'calling' refers to the position of status, honor, and responsibility that God has entrusted to his saints. This calling is the same for all saints, despite the diversity of the spiritual gifts they are given, therefore in biblical diction this noun is never used in the plural [AB]. Κλῆσις 'calling' is the summons to salvation [ISBE, TH], to glory and virtue [Ea], or to unity and purity [St]. Others state this calling as being to sonship, which requires holiness, humility, mutual forbearance, and brotherly love, which he immediately takes up with the phrases in 4:2 [Ho, NTC]. Others state this calling as being to the place which God has appointed for them in his plan of the ages [IB], or, to the unity in Christ which God's ultimate plan for the ages requires [Rob].

QUESTION—What is the force of the passive verb ἐκλήθητε 'you were called'?

This is a divine passive that underlines the idea inherent in the call: God has taken the initiative in bringing humanity back to the goal he intended it to fulfill [Can, NCBC, WBC]. The aorist tense of the verb looks back particularly to the regeneration of the readers on their reception of the gospel [Can, Lns, My, WBC, We] and of the Spirit, referred to in 1:13 [WBC]. This calling takes place through the agency of the Holy Spirit and consists essentially of the Spirit influencing the mind to turn to God. But though it takes place through the agency of the Spirit, this does not preclude the employment of various means [Ba].

4:2 with[a] all[b] humility[c] and meekness,[d]

LEXICON—a. μετά with genitive object (LN 89.79) (BAGD A.III.1. p. 509): 'with' [BAGD, El, Lns, NIC, NTC, Rob, WBC, We; KJV, NAB, NASB, NJB, NRSV]. Some omit this preposition and make ταπεινοφροσύνης 'humility' and πραΰτητος 'meekness' the objects of an implied imperative verb: 'be humble and gentle' [AB, LN (**88.59**); NIV, REB, TEV, TNT]. This denotes the attendant circumstances of something that takes place. Here, of the state of mind that is attendant to the worthy walk [BAGD].

b. πᾶς (LN 78.44) (BAGD 1.a.δ. p. 631): 'all' [BAGD, El, Lns, NIC, NTC, Rob, WBC, We; KJV, NASB, NJB, NRSV], 'altogether' [AB], 'always' [REB, TEV, TNT], 'perfect' [NAB], 'complete' [LN], 'completely' [LN; NIV], 'full, greatest' [BAGD]. This term denotes the highest degree of something [BAGD]. It denotes a degree of completeness [LN].

c. ταπεινοφροσύνη (LN 88.53) (BAGD p. 804): 'humility' [BAGD, LN, Lns, NIC, WBC; NAB, NASB, NJB, NRSV], '(to be) humble' [AB, LN (**88.59**); NIV, REB, TEV, TNT], 'humble attitude, without arrogance' [LN], 'lowliness' [El, NTC, Rob, We; KJV], 'modesty' [BAGD].

d. πραΰτης (LN **88.59**) (BAGD p. 699): 'meekness' [BAGD, El, LN, Lns, NTC, Rob, We; KJV, NAB], '(to be) meek' [**LN**], 'gentleness' [BAGD, LN, NIC, WBC; NASB, NJB, NRSV], '(to be) gentle' [AB; NIV, REB, TEV, TNT], 'humility, considerateness, courtesy' [BAGD], 'mildness'

[LN]. This denotes gentleness in attitude and behavior, in contrast to harshness, in one's dealings with others [LN].

QUESTION—To what is the phrase μετὰ πάσης ταπεινοφροσύνης καὶ πραΰτητος 'with all humility and meekness' connected?

1. It goes with the infinitive clause of 4:1, 'to walk worthily etc.' [Ea, EGT, El, Ho, ICC, Lns, My, NCBC, NIC, NTC, Rob, St, TNTC, WBC, We, WeBC; KJV, NAB, NASB, NRSV]: I beseech you to walk worthily, with all humility and meekness. The phrase specifies the dispositions with which the moral walk is to be associated [El, ICC, My, TNTC, WeBC]. The preposition μετά 'with' expresses accompaniment [Ea, EGT, El, ICC], association [EGT], visible manifestation [Ea].
2. It goes with the following nominative participle ἀνεχόμενοι 'enduring' [NJB]: With all humility and meekness, with patience, endure one another in love.
3. It is taken as an imperative statement and so equivalent to a new principle verb [AB; NIV, REB, TEV, TNT]: be always humble and meek, and patient too.

QUESTION—What is the force of the πάσης 'all' and what does it qualify?

Πάσης, having no article, has elative significance. It means 'full, supreme, total, pure' [TD]. It means 'all possible' [EGT, LJ], 'every kind of' [EGT, LJ], 'in all situations, at all times' [LJ], but not 'the greatest' [EGT].

1. Πάσης 'all' qualifies the first ethical quality of this verse [EGT, TNTC; REB]: with all humility. This term emphasizes the noun ταπεινοφροσύνης 'humility' [TNTC].
2. Πάσης 'all' qualifies the first two ethical qualities of this verse [ICC, LJ, Lns, My, NTC, WBC, We]: with all humility and meekness. 'All humility and meekness' is the opposite of any attitude or conduct that would manifest these virtues only in part [Lns].

QUESTION—What is meant by ταπεινοφροσύνη 'humility'?

It stands in contrast with a high-minded or haughty attitude [Can, EBC, ECWB, Ho, ISBE, ISBE2, St, WBC, We, WeBC]. It recognizes the fact that we are intended to be dependent upon God and to do his will [CBC, ISBE2, We]. It is the quality which does not seek prominence for one's self, nor insists on one's rights [NCBC]. It recognizes the worth of other people [St], seeing all as equal in God's sight [TH].

QUESTION—What is meant by πραΰτης 'meekness'?

It stands opposed to resentment, retaliation, or revenge at injustices [Ba, Can, EGT, ICC]. It involves an attitude of courtesy, considerateness [CBC, EBC, St, WBC, We], and a willingness to waive one's own rights [NTC, St, WBC, We]. This attitude comes from a desire for the common good, without concern for personal reputation or gain [WBC]. The term does not suggest timidity or lack of courage [CBC, EBC, NCBC, St], but of restrained or controlled strength [EBC, NCBC, St, TNTC], i.e., self control [WeBC]. It is gentleness [NIC, TH, TNTC].

with^a patience,^b
LEXICON—a. μετά with genitive object (LN 89.123) (BAGD A.II.6. p. 509): 'with' [BAGD, El, LN, Lns, NIC, NTC, Rob, WBC, We; KJV, NASB, NRSV], 'combined with' [LN], 'and with' [NJB], 'and' [NAB, TEV, TNT], 'and...too' [REB], not explicit [AB; NIV].

  b. μακροθυμία (LN 25.167) (BAGD 2.a. p. 488): 'patience' [LN, NIC, WBC; NAB, NASB, NJB, NRSV], '(to be) patient' [NIV, REB, TEV, TNT], 'long-suffering' [El, Lns, NTC, Rob, We; KJV], 'forbearance, patience toward others' [BAGD]. The phrase μετά μακροθυμίας 'with patience' is translated 'patiently' [AB]. It is also translated as the direct object of an implied imperative verb: 'be patient' [NIV]. This term denotes a state of emotional calm when confronted with provocation or misfortune, and this without complaint or irritation [LN].

QUESTION—To what is this μετά 'with' phrase connected?

  1. It is parallel with the preceding μετά 'with' phrase and adds another quality to the two preceding ones [Alf, Ea, EGT, El, Ho, ICC, LJ, My, WBC; NAB, NASB, NRSV, REB, TEV, TNT]: with humility and meekness, and with patience. The first two nouns are introduced with a single preposition because they are closely associated in meaning [Ea, ICC]. But this third noun is a special and distinct virtue, a peculiar result of the first two qualities, and so it is introduced with the preposition repeated [Ea]. This phrase is further developed in the following clause 'enduring one another in love' [EGT, El, My].

  2. It qualifies the participle ἀνεχόμενοι 'enduring' [AB; NJB]: patiently endure one another in love.

  3. It is interpreted as an imperative verb and made an independent clause, with the participial clause 'enduring one another in love' subordinate to it [NIV]: be patient, enduring one another in love.

QUESTION—What is meant by μακροθυμία 'patience'?

It means the attitude of forbearance [AB, Alf, ECWB, EGT, Ho, ICC, ISBE, NCBC, NIC, TNTC, WBC, WeBC], the reluctance to avenge wrongs [EBC, EGT, Ho, ICC, TNTC, WeBC], as seen by the addition of the following words 'enduring one another in love' [AB, ICC, NCBC, WBC]. It includes patience in all kinds of disappointments [We]. This term designates the continued and patient exercise of 'meekness' [Can, ECWB, WeBC], and is exercised in 'enduring one another' [Can, EBC, EGT, El, ICC, Lns, TNTC, WeBC].

enduring^a one-another in^b love,^c
LEXICON—a. pres. mid. participle of ἀνέχω, ἀνέχομαι (LN **25.171**) (BAGD 1.a. p. 65): 'to endure' [BAGD, NTC], 'to forbear' [El, Rob, We; KJV], 'to show forbearance to' [NASB], 'to bear' [AB], 'to bear with' [BAGD, NIC, WBC; NAB, NIV, NRSV], 'to bear up with' [Lns], 'to put up with' [BAGD], 'to put up with failings' [REB], 'to be patient with' [**LN**], 'to have patience' [LN], 'to support' [NJB], 'to be tolerant with' [TEV,

TNT]. This verb denotes being patient with someone in the sense of enduring possible difficulty with them [LN].
b. ἐν with dative object (LN 89.76, 89.84): 'in' [AB, El, Lns, NIC, NTC, Rob, WBC, We; KJV, NASB, NIV, NJB, NRSV, REB], 'with' [LN (89.84)], 'by, by means of, through' [LN (89.76)]. The phrase ἐν ἀγάπῃ 'in love' is translated 'lovingly' [NAB], 'to show love by' [TEV, TNT].
c. ἀγάπη: 'love'. See this word at 1:4, 15; 2:4; 3:17, 19.

QUESTION—What is the connection and function of the nominative participle ἀνεχόμενοι 'enduring'?

1. It connects with the accusative ὑμᾶς 'you' of 4:1 and indicates the further content of παρακαλῶ 'I beseech' [IB]: I beseech you...be enduring one another. The shift from the accusative to the nominative gives the participle the force of the imperative mood, as well as bringing it into close relationship to the participle σπουδάζοντες 'making every effort' in the next clause [IB].
2. It connects with all the preceding prepositional phrases as part of the listing of qualities which accompany the Christians' κλήσεως 'calling' [Ho]: I beseech you to walk worthily of your calling with all humility, meekness, and patience, that is, enduring one another in love.
3. It connects with the preceding μετὰ μακροθυμίας 'with patience' with a more remote connection to the subject of the κλήσεως 'calling' in 4:1 [Rob, TNTC]: I beseech you to walk worthy of your calling...with patient forbearance of one another. The connection is by anacolouthon [Rob]. It is the practical outworking of patience [TNTC].
4. It connects with the three preceding prepositional phrases, each being the outgrowth of the preceding, and 'enduring one another' being the outgrowth of 'with patience', with a more remote connection with 'to walk worthily' [WeBC]: I beseech you to walk worthily of your calling...with humility producing meekness, and meekness producing patience, and patience producing endurance of one another in love. This participial clause is thus the product of the three antecedent virtues.
5. It defines the phrase μετὰ μακροθυμίας 'with patience' [Alf, Ea, EBC, EGT, El, ICC, LJ, Lns, My, NCBC], or forms a natural pair with it [St], yet it is more remotely connected with ἀξίως περιπατῆσαι 'to walk worthily' [Alf, Ea, El, LJ, Lns, My, NCBC, St] in a generic-specific relationship [Alf, El, LJ, Lns]: I beseech you to walk worthily...with patience, enduring one another. This participial clause more fully elucidates 'with patience' [EGT, El, ICC], being the natural expansion of this phrase [El], yet not so closely that it forms one clause with it [EGT, El, Lns, My] (i.e., not 'patiently enduring one another' nor 'enduring one another with patience' because this would destroy the symmetry between the participial clauses [Lns]).
6. It indicates an imperative construction [BD, Mo, Mou, TH, Tu, Tu2, Tu3, We; NJB, TEV, TNT]: Be enduring one another in love.

QUESTION—What relationship is indicated by ἐν 'in'?
1. The phrase ἐν ἀγάπῃ 'in love' is attached only to the preceding participial clause [AB, Alf, Can, CBC, Ea, EGT, El, Ho, LJ, Lns, My, NTC, We (probably); NAB, TEV, TNT].
   1.1. The preposition ἐν 'in' indicates the manner in which they are to endure one another [Ea (probably), EBC, EGT, LJ (probably); NAB]: lovingly endure one another.
   1.2. The preposition ἐν 'in' indicates the means by which they are to endure one another [Lns, TH, WBC]: endure one another by means of loving one another.
   1.3. The preposition ἐν 'in' indicates the reason for enduring one another [Can, Ho]: endure one another because you love one another.
   1.4. The preposition ἐν 'in' indicates the quality which is the goal of the readers enduring one another [CBC (probably); TEV, TNT]: show your love by enduring one another.
2. The phrase is attached to all of the preceding material [IB, NCBC, NIC, St, TNTC]: with all humility and meekness, and with patience, enduring one another; doing all this in love.
3. The preposition ἐν 'in' indicates a final quality, completing this list of virtues [IB, Rob, St]: with all humility and meekness, with patience, endurance for one another, and love. The phrase is the climax of the list of virtues [IB, Rob, St] and is emphatic by virtue of its position at the end of this list of virtues It gives the list of virtues a positive content, which, in themselves, essentially consist in abnegation [IB].

DISCOURSE UNIT: 4:3–6 [St]. The topic is Christian unity arising from the unity of God.

4:3 making-every-effort[a] to-keep[b] the unity[c] of-the Spirit[d] in[e] the bond[f] of-the peace;[g]

LEXICON—a. pres. act. participle of σπουδάζω (LN **68.63**) (BAGD 2. p. 763): 'to make every effort' [BAGD, NIC, NTC, WBC; NAB, NIV, NRSV], 'to spare no effort' [REB], 'to take every care' [NJB], 'to take pains' [AB, BAGD], 'to do one's best' [**LN**; TEV], 'to try one's best' [TNT], 'to endeavor' [LN; KJV], 'to work hard' [LN], 'to be diligent' [Lns; NASB], 'to give diligence' [El, Rob, We], 'to be eager' [BAGD], 'to be zealous' [BAGD]. The present tense indicates that this action should be done continuously [Lns, NTC, St]. This verb denotes the doing of something with intense effort and motivation [LN].

b. pres. act. infin. of τηρέω (LN 13.32) (BAGD 3. p. 815): 'to keep' [BAGD, El, LN, Lns, Rob, We; KJV, NIV], 'to preserve' [NIC, NTC; NAB, NASB, NJB, TEV, TNT], 'to maintain' [AB, WBC; NRSV], 'to retain, to cause to continue' [LN], 'to make fast' [REB]. This verb denotes the causing of a state to continue [LN]. It means to maintain something with watchful care [EGT], to 'hold fast' [DNTT].

c. ἑνότης (LN **63.3**) (BAGD p. 267): 'unity' [AB, BAGD, El, LN, Lns, NIC, NTC, Rob, WBC, We; all versions], 'oneness' [LN].
d. πνεῦμα (LN 12.18) (BAGD 5.d.α. p. 677): 'Spirit' [AB, BAGD, El, LN, Lns, NIC, NTC, Rob, WBC; all versions], 'Spirit of God, Holy Spirit' [LN], 'spirit' [We].
e. ἐν (LN 89.76): 'in' [El, Lns, NIC, Rob, We; KJV, NASB, NRSV], 'by' [LN, WBC; NJB, TNT], 'by means of' [LN, NTC; TEV], 'through' [AB, LN; NIV], 'with' [REB], 'as' [NAB].
f. σύνδεσμος (LN 63.7) (BAGD 1.b. p. 785): 'bond' [AB, BAGD, El, Lns, NIC, NTC, Rob, WBC, We; KJV, NASB, NIV, NRSV], 'bonds' [REB], 'binding force' [NAB]. This noun is also translated as a verb: 'to bind together' [LN; NJB, TEV], 'to bring together, to unite' [LN]. The phrase ἐν τῷ συνδέσμῳ τῆς εἰρήνης 'in the bond of peace' is translated 'by living peacefully together with one another' [TNT].
g. εἰρήνη (LN 22.42) (BAGD 1.b. p. 227): 'peace' [AB, BAGD, El, LN, Lns, NIC, NTC, Rob, WBC, We; all versions except TNT], 'tranquility' [LN], 'harmony' [BAGD], 'peacefully' [TNT].

QUESTION—How does this verse relate to the context?

This verse is a participial clause that is parallel to the preceding participial clause [Ea, El, Ho, My, WBC]. This verse is a further description of the mutual forbearance expressed in the preceding clause, and further, introduces the larger, fundamental idea of unity [EGT]. It gives the motive [Ea, IB, NCBC] and accompanying (simultaneous) effort behind the preceding ἀνεχόμενοι 'enduring' participial clause [Ea]. It gives the inward feelings that characterize the preceding participle, ἀνεχόμενοι 'enduring' [El] and the inward efforts by which it is to be promoted [El, My]. Some implicitly [ICC, LJ] or explicitly [Lns] recognize a greater focus upon this participial clause over the preceding one when they state that this clause expresses the end to be reached by practicing the virtues named in the preceding verse [ICC, LJ, Lns]. The participle has an imperative force [AB, HG, Mo, Mou, WBC] and suggests that maintaining unity is of the utmost importance and urgency [AB, St, WBC].

QUESTION—What is meant by τὴν ἑνότητα τοῦ πνεύματος 'the unity of the Spirit'?

This is not just the congeniality of a social group, but that unity which the Holy Spirit gives [AB, LJ, Lns, My, NCBC, WBC]. Being given, this unity is not a human achievement, but must nevertheless be preserved and protected [AB, ECWB, LJ, TNTC, WBC]. This is presented as something that already exists, but is in danger of being broken if believers do not conduct themselves with the lowliness, meekness, and loving forbearance that befits their calling [Can, Ea, EBC, LJ, Lns]. It is a Spirit-produced, Christian community spirit; a unity of affection, confidence, and love; a harmony of views [Ba, Cal, We].

EPHESIANS 4:3

QUESTION—What relationship is indicated by ἐν 'in'?
1. It indicates the means by which the readers are to maintain unity [AB, Ba, Cal, Ho, LJ, MNTC, NCBC, St, TD, TNTC, WBC, We, WeBC; KJV, NASB, NIV, NJB, REB, TNT]: making every effort through the bond of peace to keep the unity of the Spirit. Peace is not an end in itself, rather it is the means by which the greater end of the unity of the Spirit is continually preserved [NCBC].
2. It indicates the element [Ea, El], sphere [EGT, El, Lns], or ethical relation [Lns, My] in which unity is preserved and demonstrated: making every effort in the bond of peace to keep the unity of the Spirit. Peace is not the instrument by which the unity of the Spirit is kept [ICC, Lns, My]. Rather, it is the unity of the Spirit that maintains the peace. Ἐν 'in' is parallel to the ἐν 'in' before ἀγάπῃ 'love' in the previous verse [ICC, Lns, My], so its meaning must be similar to that [My].
3. It indicates the means by which the Spirit establishes unity in the church [NTC, TH; NAB, TEV]: making every effort to keep the unity which the Spirit gives by means of the bond of peace. Peace promotes unity [NTC].
4. It indicates the element or sphere within which the Spirit works in order to establish unity in the church [Can]: making every effort to keep the unity which the Spirit gives within the bond of peace. Peace is the bond in which the unity of believers consists [Can].

QUESTION—What is the relationship between the two nouns in the genitive construction τῷ συνδέσμῳ τῆς εἰρήνης 'the bond of peace'?
1. The genitive εἰρήνης 'of peace' is in apposition to συνδέσμῳ 'bond' [Alf, Bu, Can, Ea, EGT, El, IB, ICC, LJ, Lns, MNTC, My, NTC, TH, We], or is otherwise expressed as epexegetical [BAGD (1.b. p. 785)] or as the genitive of identity [El]: peace which is the (uniting) bond. Peace is the bond by which the unity of believers is preserved [Can, Ea], or to be more precise, in which the unity of believers consists [BAGD, Can, NTC].
2. The bond produces peace [ECWB]: the bond of love which brings about peace.

QUESTION—What is meant by εἰρήνη 'peace'?
The peace is between Christians [AB, Ba, Cal, Can, DNTT, Ea, EGT, IDB, LJ, Lns, My, NTC, St, TD, TNTC, WBC], between Jewish and Gentile Christians [NIC, TD], or between God and man [CBC, ISBE2].

DISCOURSE UNIT: 4:4–11 [ICC]. The topic is the essential unity of the Church.

DISCOURSE UNIT: 4:4–6 [AB, IB, Lns, My, NIC, NTC, Si, TH, WBC, We]. According to some commentators these three verses contain a confession or hymn [AB, CBC, DNTT, TNTC], the topic of which is the fact and the content of the church's confession [AB]. According to another, they include one or two pieces of creedal material the writer has incorporated into his own rhetoric, setting forth the unifying realities upon which the appeal to unity is based [WBC].

4:4 (There is) one[a] body[b] and one Spirit/spirit,

LEXICON—a. ἕν (LN 63.4) (BAGD 2.a. p.231): 'one' [AB, El, LN, Lns, NIC, NTC, Rob, WBC, We; all versions except NAB], 'but one' [NAB], 'one and the same' [BAGD]. This term designates that which is united as one as contrasted with being divided or consisting of separate parts [LN]. The term is used emphatically [BAGD].

b. σῶμα (LN 11.34) (BAGD 5 p. 800): 'body' [AB, BAGD, El, Lns, NIC, NTC, Rob, WBC, We; all versions except NJB], 'Body' [NJB], 'church, congregation, Christian group' [LN]. It designates believers in Christ as being joined together as a single group, and may carry the implication that each person has a distinctive function within that group [LN]. This term is used in reference to the church as a unified σῶμα 'body' [BAGD].

QUESTION—How is this verse related to the preceding context?

1. This verse is an explanation [MNTC, My, NCBC, TD, TNTC] or illustration [Ea, El] of the unity mentioned in the previous verse: Unity means that there is one body, etc. The fervent style of the apostle accounts for the asyndeton [Ea] which abruptly introduces an assertatory illustration of the preceding statement of unity [Ea, El]. This verse, together with the next two, expresses the spiritual realities that unite the church, which transcend all differences of background [TNTC], or which guarantees the unity [TD].
2. This verse gives the grounds for the exhortation to keep the unity of the Spirit [DNTT, EBC, EGT, Ho, ICC, LJ, Lns, TH]: making every effort to keep the unity of the Spirit because there is one body, etc.
3. The phrase ἓν σῶμα καὶ ἓν πνεῦμα 'one body and one spirit' is in apposition to the nominative participles of 4:2–3 [Rob]: enduring one another in love, making every effort to keep the unity—that is, being one body and one spirit.
4. In effect, this verse is an exhortation to unity [Ba, Cal]: Be one body and one spirit. The union ought to be such that we all are as one body and one soul—a complete man. This is then supported by a powerful argument: 'as you have been called in one hope of your calling' [Cal].

QUESTION—What is the significance of the numeral ἕν 'one' in this and the other verses of this unit?

The repetition of the numeral 'one' lends emphasis to each occurrence [BAGD (2.a. p. 231), Cal, NIC]. The apostle plays on the term 'one' to stress the essential unity of the Church. In these three verses the term occurs seven times, three times in the first triad of nouns, three times in the second triad, and, finally, once in the reference to God in 4:6, who is a summary of all the unities in himself. It should be noticed that each of these three groups of one's is grouped around a reference to each of the three Persons of the Trinity [LJ]. Because this usage of ἕν 'one' is intimately tied in with the connotations inherent in the phrase εἷς θεός 'one God', see the treatment of this phrase in 4:6.

QUESTION—What is meant by the term σῶμα 'body', and how is it related to the other members of the triad in this verse?

The word has reference to the church [Ba, Cal, Can, CBC, Ea, EBC, ECWB, EGT, El, Ho, IB, ICC, LJ, Lns, MNTC, My, NCBC, NIC, NTC, Rob, Si, St, TD, TH, TNTC, WBC, We, WeBC], Christ's mystical [Alf, Can, EGT, El, Ho, ISBE, LJ, My] or corporate Body [IDB, NIC, TD, We]. The usage is metaphorical with the fact of the Spirit inhabiting and animating this body implied [Cal, Can, CBC, Ea, ICC, LJ, Lns, My, NCBC, NIC, NTC, Rob, St, TD, TH, TNTC, We]. The comparison is: just as a person's body, though composed of many parts, is a single whole with one spirit animating it, so the Church, though composed of many individuals, distributed throughout many congregations throughout many ages and places, is a single whole with the one Spirit of God animating it [Can, Ea, EBC, El, Ho, ICC, LJ, WBC]. The point of comparison is the natural body as it is animated by a single spirit or soul [Cal, EBC, ECWB, Ho, LJ, Lns, MNTC, TD, We] (with one, and possibly two, commentators restricting the point of comparison to Christ's own earthly body [NCBC, TD (possibly)]). The nonfigurative statement would be: the Church, though consisting of many individuals and forming many congregations in many places and ages, is still a single entity governed by the one Spirit of God.

QUESTION—What is meant by the noun πνεῦμα 'Spirit/spirit'?

1. This refers to the Holy Spirit [AB, Alf, Ba, BAGD, Can, CBC, Ea, EBC, ECWB, EGT, El, Ho, ICC, LJ, Lns, My, NCBC, NIC, NTC, Rob, Si, St, TD, TH, TNTC, WBC, WeBC; all versions]. The Holy Spirit is a Person and so indivisible. This forms the basis for everything the apostle has to say here [LJ, Lns]. This first triad centers in the 'one Spirit' [Lns, NIC], the 'one Church' having its source in him [LJ, NCBC, NIC, NTC, Si, St, TNTC] as does also the 'one hope' [ECWB, LJ, My, NTC].
2. This refers to the communal spirit of the believers [Cal, IB, Rob, We]. One commentator translates πνεῦμα 'spirit' as 'soul' and says that the words 'body' and 'soul' refer to the whole man [Cal]. Another commentator adopts the first interpretation in his expository section and this interpretation in his exegetical section [Rob].

just-as[a] also you-were-called[b] in[c] one hope[d] of-the calling[e] of-you;

LEXICON—a. καθώς (LN 64.14): 'just as' [AB, LN, NTC, WBC; all versions except KJV], 'even as' [El, Lns, Rob, We; KJV], 'as' [NIC].
b. aorist pass. indic. of καλέω: 'to be called'. See this word at 4:1.
c. ἐν with dative object (LN 89.5, 89.80, 90.10): 'in' [El, LN (89.5), Lns, NIC, NTC, Rob, We; KJV, NASB, REB], 'to' [AB, WBC; NIV, NRSV, TEV] 'with regard to' [LN (89.5)], 'with' [LN (89.80, 90.10)], 'by' [LN (90.10)]. Some do not specify this preposition and make ἐλπίδι 'hope' the subject of an implied 'to be' verb, a predicate nominative of an implied 'to be' verb, or as an object of another implied verb: 'one hope is the goal of

your calling' [NJB], 'there is one hope' [AB; NAB, TEV], 'to share one hope' [TNT].
d. ἐλπίς: 'hope'. See this word at 1:18.
e. κλῆσις: 'calling'. See this word at 1:18 and 4:1.

QUESTION—What relationship is indicated by καθώς 'just as'?

It illustrates and enforces the unity as being entirely in accordance with their calling [EGT, El, My, We]. This is a confirmation by illustrative proof that the one Spirit dwells in all the members of the Body: since all the members have a single, common hope [Can, Ea, EGT, Ho]. The sense is: 'there is one body and one spirit; in like manner there is one hope resulting from your calling' [Ba]. The emphasis in this καθώς 'just as' clause is upon the phrase 'one hope' [Lns].

QUESTION—What is the function of καί 'also' here?

The καί 'also' marks this as a second thought suggested by the first [EGT]. It marks the accordance of the calling with the previously stated unity [El].

QUESTION—What relationship is indicated by ἐν 'in'?

1. It indicates the element, condition, or sphere in which they were called to live and move [Alf, Ea, EGT, El, Lns, Tu]: you were called to live in the sphere, or condition, of the hope that belongs to your calling. The preposition points to the element [Ea, EGT] or ethical domain [EGT] in which their calling took place. The Christian experience of hope is the state in which the believer moves [Tu].
2. It indicates the instrument by which the calling took place [My]: you were called by the hope of your calling. The calling took place by the fact that *one* hope was communicated to them [My].
3. It indicates that hope was the essential accompaniment of their calling [EBC, ICC]: you were called with hope accompanying that calling.

QUESTION—What is meant by the genitive construction ἐλπίδι τῆς κλήσεως 'hope of (your) calling'?

1. Their calling produced their hope [Ba, CBC, EGT, El, Ho, NTC, Rob]: the hope that results from your calling.
2. Their calling is characterized by hope [Alf, BAGD (2. p. 399), Ea, ICC, We (probably)]: the hope which characterizes your calling. Hope is what belonged to the call and what characterized it when they received it [Ea]. The hope is coincident with the calling but not consequent upon it [We].

QUESTION—What is meant by ἐλπίς 'hope'?

This hope is the same as 'the hope of his calling' in 1:18 [AB, Can, EBC, LJ, NIC, TH, TNTC, WBC, WeBC]. Ἐλπίς 'hope' signifies the substance of hope [AB, TH, WeBC]. It means the expectation of future good with the objective sense necessarily implied [Ho]. The content of the hope is the ultimate cosmic reunification of all things in Christ (1:9–10 and 3:9–10), the evidence for which may be seen already in the unification of Jew and Gentile into the one body of the Church [WBC]. It is the hope of being made fellow-citizens of the saints, and of the household of God [Can]. The hope is the outworking of God's purposes for the world [CBC], obtaining glory in eternity with Christ [Ea, EBC, WeBC], the perfect unity of heaven [ECWB], receiving eternal salvation [Lns]. The writer recognizes that what his readers hope for in the end will determine their conduct in the present [WBC].

4:5 one Lord,[a] one faith,[b] one baptism,[c]

LEXICON—a. κύριος (LN 12.9): 'Lord' [AB, El, LN, Lns, NIC, NTC, Rob, WBC, We; all versions], 'Ruler, One who commands' [LN]. This noun is used as a title for God and for Christ and denotes one who exercises supernatural authority over mankind [LN].

b. πίστις (LN 31.102) (BAGD 2.d.α. p. 663): 'faith' [AB, BAGD, El, Lns, NIC, NTC, Rob, WBC, We; all versions], 'Christian faith' [LN]. This usage of the noun denotes true piety, genuine religion, which means being a Christian [BAGD].

c. βάπτισμα (LN 53.41) (BAGD 2. p. 132): 'baptism' [AB, BAGD, El, LN, Lns, NIC, NTC, Rob, WBC, We; all versions]. This noun denotes the employment of water in a religious ceremony, the purpose of which is to symbolize purification and initiation through repentance [LN]. This is a passive noun in which the focus is not upon the action described by the verb βαπτίζω 'to dip', but on the object or result of that act [TH]. Βάπτισμα 'baptism', as opposed to βαπτισμός 'baptism' (which signifies the act alone), stands for the act together with the result, and therefore means the institution [TD].

QUESTION—Who is referred to by the term κύριος 'Lord'?

This refers to Christ [AB, Alf, Ba, Cal, Can, CBC, DNTT, Ea, ECWB, EGT, El, Ho, ICC, LJ, Lns, MNTC, My, NCBC, NIC, NTC, Rob, Si, St, TH, TNTC, WBC, We, WeBC] as Head of the Church [Alf, El, LJ, Rob]. The 'Spirit' has been mentioned in 4:4 and the 'Father' will be mentioned in 4:6 [Ba].

QUESTION—To what does πίστις 'faith' refer here?

1. It primarily refers to the act of believing [Alf, Can, CBC, Ea, EGT, El, IB, ICC, MNTC, My, My-ed, NIC, NTC, St, TH]. This subjective faith has the κύριος 'Lord' just mentioned as its object [Alf, EGT, El, ICC, NIC, St]. Both the circumcised and the uncircumcised are alike justified on the common ground of belief in Christ [NIC].

2. It primarily refers to what is believed, the substance or content of the faith [AB, Bu, ECWB, LJ, Lns, TD, WBC, We]. This is metonymy, 'faith' being put for the doctrine believed [Bu]. Some commentators think it has specific reference to the baptismal confession of Jesus as Lord [ECWB, WBC]. Others believe it refers to belief in the essence of the gospel, the doctrine of justification by faith, for which Paul contended during a good part of his ministry [LJ].

3. Both subjective and objective senses are prominent [Ba, DNTT, EBC, Ho, NCBC, WeBC]. The word denotes both the subjective act of believing and the content of that belief, the latter either in the sense of the common body of doctrine [Ba], or the same body of doctrine concerned with Christ

[WeBC], or simply the affirmation of allegiance to Christ as Lord [EBC, NCBC].

QUESTION—To what does βάπτισμα 'baptism' refer?

1. It refers to the rite of water baptism [AB, Alf, Ba, Cal, Can, CBC, DNTT, Ea, EBC, EGT, El, Ho, IB, ICC, IDB, ISBE, ISBE2, Lns, MNTC, NCBC, NTC, Si, TD, TH, TNTC, WBC]. The argument here is that all have been consecrated to the Father, Son, and Holy Spirit by the application of water as the symbol of the purifying influences of the Holy Spirit [Ba, Can]. If some were consecrated by circumcision and others by baptism, this would constitute a difference such as existed between Jews and proselytes, and not unity [Can]. The baptism is one, not because it had only one form [Ba, TH, WBC], or was to be administered on only one occasion [Cal, ISBE2, TH, WBC], but because it is initiation into Christ, into the one body. All members of the one body had undergone the one, common baptism and, as such, it is a unifying factor [Ba, Ea, EBC, EGT, ISBE2, TH, TNTC, WBC]. All had been 'baptized into Christ', not into various leaders in the church nor various churches [TNTC]. It may be proper to translate 'one purpose for which we are all baptized' or 'one person in whose name we are baptized' [TH].

2. It refers to the spiritual reality of which water baptism is a sign [LJ]. This refers to the action of the Holy Spirit by which he incorporates each believer into the body of Christ. It signifies that each believer has been put into the sphere and influence of Christ and is completely identified with him in his death and burial, and as he was resurrected, so each believer walks in newness of life [LJ].

4:6 one God and Father of-all, the (one) over[a] all and through[b] all and in[c] all.

TEXT—Instead of ἐν πᾶσιν 'in all', some manuscripts have ἐν πᾶσιν ὑμῖν 'in you all'. GNT assigns an A rating to the reading ἐν πᾶσιν 'in all', indicating the reading is certain. The reading ἐν πᾶσιν ὑμῖν 'in you all' is taken by Ba, LJ, and KJV.

LEXICON—a. ἐπί with genitive object (LN 37.9) (BAGD I.1.b.α. p. 286): 'over' [AB, BAGD, El, LN, Lns, NIC, NTC, We; NAB, NASB, NIV, NJB, REB, TNT], 'above' [Rob, WBC; KJV, NRSV], 'Lord of' [TEV]. This usage of the preposition marks an object or person over which somebody exercises power, control, or authority [BAGD, LN].

b. διά with genitive object (LN 84.29): 'through' [AB, El, LN, Lns, NIC, NTC, Rob, WBC, We; all versions except NAB, TEV, TNT]. This preposition is also translated as a verbal phrase: 'to work through' [NAB, TEV, TNT].

c. ἐν with dative object (LN 83.13, 84.22, 89.119): 'in' [AB, El, Lns, NIC, NTC, Rob, WBC, We; all versions except NJB], 'within' [NJB].

QUESTION—Are the four occurrences of 'all' here neuter or masculine, and to what do they refer?
1. Each 'all' is neuter in gender and denotes creation or nature as a whole [AB, CBC, ECWB, IB, Rob, WBC]. This passage is a continuation of the Epistle's concern with cosmic matters from 1:10, 22, 23 and 3:9 and which will show up again in 4:10 [WBC]. Moreover, as recently as 3:14–15, the writer has used the term 'Father' in reference to every family in heaven and earth [AB, Rob, WBC]. The occurrences of 'all' apply to all of God's rational creation, and in a lower sense, even to his creatures [ECWB], or the total range of things [Rob], though the context shows that the primary concern is with the members of the church [ECWB, Rob, WeBC], which inherits, by special gift, what is the birthright of all humanity [ECWB].
2. Each 'all' is masculine in gender and refers to persons [Alf, Cal, Can, Ea, EGT, El, Ho, ICC, LJ, Lns, MNTC, My, NIC, NTC, Si, St, TH, We]. In the first clause it must be persons of whom God is said to be related as 'Father'. This would indicate that it is persons that are referred to in the following phrases as well [Can].
2.1 The reference is universal to all persons [El, ICC, TH, We]. The power of the church's missionary activity is the universal Fatherhood of God, for the church can appeal to men because they are in a true sense God's children [We].
2.2 The reference is restricted to redeemed people, the church [Cal, Can, EBC, EGT, Ho, LJ, Lns, MNTC, My, NIC, NTC, Si, St]. That the references are all restricted to the church is indicated by the fact that the immediate context is bracketed by first and second person references, 4:4 speaks of 'your calling' [Can] and 4:7 refers to 'each one of us' [Can, Lns, My].
2.3 The first occurrence refers particularly to the church and the last three are more universalistic in reference to persons [Alf].
2.4 The first and last occurrences refer particularly to the church, while the second and third seem more universalistic in their tone [Ea].
3. Masculine and neuter genders are apparently mixed with the first and last occurrences referring to the church while the second and third occurrences are universalistic in scope [Ba, NCBC]. The distinctive name by which Christians spoke of the one true God was 'Father'. God is 'above all', supreme and transcendent. 'Through all' indicates that he is actively at work throughout his creation. 'In all' indicates that God comes to us in Christ to make our lives his dwelling place [NCBC].

QUESTION—What is meant by ἐπὶ πάντων 'over all'?
This preposition indicates God's transcendence [IB, Rob]. This refers to God's sovereignty over all people [Alf, ECWB, El, ICC, TH, We]. It refers to the Father's sovereignty or transcendency over the church [Can, Ea, EBC, EGT, Ho, LJ, Lns, My, NIC, NTC, Si].

QUESTION—What is meant by διὰ πάντων 'through all'?
This refers to the co-extensiveness of the Son's work of redemption in the whole nature of man [Alf, El, Lns]. It denotes God's activity in using redeemed men as his instruments or agents [Can, LJ, Lns, NIC], working out his purposes, and revealing his character and will through them [Can, LJ]. This refers to the notion of God's immanence [EGT, Si], the pervading, controlling, animating presence of the Father [EGT]. The διά 'through' expresses diffusion, indicating that, in respect of believers, God pervades all, abides in all [Ho] and rules all [My]. This is God working through all things—the notion of providence, a pervading, sustaining and working presence [Ea, ICC, LJ, Rob]. God works 'through' all in his creative activity [EBC]. It has reference to God's omnipresence [IB].

QUESTION—What is meant by ἐν πᾶσιν 'in all'?
This refers to a kind of indwelling of all people by the Spirit [Alf, El, Lns], or of redeemed people by God [Ba, Can, LJ, Lns, My, NCBC, Si] through the Spirit [EGT, Lns, My, Si] or Christ [NCBC]. It is to be understood of Christians collectively, on the grounds that were the individual sense meant, Christ or the Spirit would be the subject [NIC]. The idea conveyed by this preposition is an intimate and special union and inhabitation [Ea, Lns]. This preposition indicates God's pervasive immanence [EBC, IB, Rob, TD]. It denotes God indwelling the individual for both creating and sustaining the physical life, and regenerating the spiritual life [ECWB]. It denotes God's sustaining activity [We].

DISCOURSE UNIT: 4:7–16 [Ba, Can, CBC, El, Ho, IB, LJ, Lns, NCBC, NIC, Rob, TNTC, WBC, We; NAB, NRSV, TNT]. This unit consists of a single long sentence in Greek [NCBC, WBC]. The topic is the diversity of gifts providing for the building up and growth of the church in love and unity [Can, WBC], unity being served by diversities of gifts [IB, LJ, Lns, NCBC], the very diversity of gifts in the membership serving to keep and maintain unity by means of the common goal [Lns], the Lord's provision for spiritual health and growth [Ba, NIC].

DISCOURSE UNIT: 4:7–14 [Rob]. The topic is the diversity of gifts that lead to the goal of unity.

DISCOURSE UNIT: 4:7–13 [Alf]. The topic is the manifold grace which is given to each member of the church.

DISCOURSE UNIT: 4:7–12 [AB, St, WeBC]. The topic is the exalted Christ himself giving diverse gifts to the church [AB], unity being enriched by the diversity of gifts [St], spiritual gifts as evidence of spiritual maturity in the church [WeBC].

DISCOURSE UNIT: 4:7–11 [ECWB, TH, We]. The topic is the types of ministry with which the membership of the church is endowed [ECWB], the affirmation and strengthening of the body by the variety of gifts bestowed on individual Christians by the church's one Lord [TH], the unity of the Christian community due to the combination and ministry of all its members [We].

DISCOURSE UNIT: 4:7–10 [El, LJ, My, Si, St]. The topic is Christ giving grace in measure to each member of his church as proven by the testimony of Scripture [El, My], the ascended Christ as the giver of spiritual gifts [St].

4:7 But/Now[a] to-each one of-us was-given[b] the grace[c] according-to[d] the measure[e] of-the gift[f] of Christ.

TEXT—Some texts omit the article before χάρις 'grace'. With the article ἡ 'the', the word may express *the* grace which the writer and his fellow believers had experienced [EGT] or *the* unspeakable grace [Alf]; without the article, 'grace' in the absolute or generic sense could be meant [Alf]. GNT does not mention the variant. Those who accept, or whose work reflects the reading with the article by giving a sense of definiteness to 'grace', are AB, Alf, Cal, Can, Ea, EGT, El, GNT, Ho, ICC, LJ, Lns, MNTC, My, NIC, NTC, Rob, TH, WBC, We; NJB (note), REB, TEV, TNT. Those who do not reflect the presence of the article in this way are Ba, WeBC; KJV, NAB, NASB, NIV, and NRSV.

LEXICON—a. δέ (LN 89.94, 89.124): 'but' [El, LN (89.124), NIC, NTC, Rob, We; KJV, NASB, NIV, NRSV, REB], 'however' [WBC], 'now' [Lns], 'and yet' [TNT], 'and' [LN (89.94)], not explicit [AB; NAB, NJB, TEV].

b. aorist pass. indic. of δίδωμι (LN 57.71): 'to be given' [AB, El, LN, Lns, NIC, NTC, Rob, WBC, We; KJV, NASB, NIV, NRSV, REB], 'to be bestowed' [NJB]. This passive verb is also translated actively: 'to give' [TNT], 'to receive' [NAB, TEV]. The aorist tense of this verb is gnomic, expressing the idea of a general truth and fixing attention upon the actual bestowal of the gift [IB].

c. χάρις: 'grace'. See this word at 3:2, 7, 8.

d. κατά with accusative object (LN 89.8) (BAGD II.5.a.γ. p. 407): 'according to' [BAGD, El, Lns, NIC, Rob, We; KJV, NASB, NRSV], 'in accordance with' [BAGD, LN], 'in conformity with, corresponding to' [BAGD], 'in relation to' [LN], 'in the proportion' [WBC], 'in whatever way' [NJB], 'after which' [AB]. This preposition is not specified by some and the phrase is handled in various other ways: it is placed in apposition to χάρις 'grace' [REB]; μέτρον 'measure' is conflated with this preposition and made the direct object of ἐδόθη 'was given': 'a due portion' [TNT]; the preposition and μέτρον 'measure' are conflated and translated by the phrases 'within the limits' [NTC], 'in proportion to what' [TEV], 'in the measure in which' [NAB]. This preposition is also conflated with the compound genitive phrase τὸ μέτρον τῆς δωρεᾶς τοῦ Χριστοῦ 'the measure of the gift of Christ' and translated as a clause of comparison: 'as Christ apportioned it' [NIV]. This preposition is a marker of a relationship involving similarity of process [LN]. This preposition indicates a standard with which something conforms [BAGD].

e. μέτρον (LN 81.1) (BAGD 2.b. p. 515): 'measure' [AB, BAGD, El, LN, Lns, NIC, Rob, We; KJV, NAB, NASB, NRSV], 'quantity, number' [BAGD], 'a particular share' [REB]. This noun is also translated as a verb: 'to allot' [WBC]. This noun is also conflated with κατά 'according to': see d. above. It is also conflated with τῆς δωρεᾶς 'of the gift' and translated as a verb: 'to apportion' [NTC; NIV], 'to allot' [NJB].

f. δωρεά (LN 57.84) (BAGD p. 210): 'gift' [AB, BAGD, El, LN, Lns, NIC, Rob, We; KJV, NASB, NRSV], 'present' [LN], 'bounty' [BAGD; REB, TNT]. This noun is also translated as a verb: 'to give' [BAGD (2.b. p. 515), WBC; TEV], 'to bestow' [NAB].

QUESTION—What relationship is indicated by δέ 'but'?
1. It indicates contrast [Alf, EGT, El, St]: but. It contrasts the general ἐν πᾶσιν 'in all' (4:6) with the particular ἑνὶ ἑκάστῳ 'to each' of this verse. With this verse the apostle is qualifying what he has said about the church's unity [St].
2. It indicates transition as well as contrast [Ea, Ho, LJ, My, WBC; TNT]: Now, to each one of us, however, grace was given. This marks a transitional contrast from the theme of unity to individual varieties of gifts necessary to maintain this unity [Ea, My]. The force of δέ 'but' is 'but not withstanding the unity of the church…' [Ho]. It implies a contrast but at the same time it refers back to what has gone before. He is going to look at another aspect of the subject of unity [LJ]. It forms the transition from the four occurrences of 'all' in the previous verse to each individual among the Christians [My]. The sense is 'no single one, however…' [My, WBC]. The argument is: although there is unity, yet each has individual gifts given to him [TNT (note)].
3. Its function is purely transitional [Lns, TH; NAB, NJB, TEV]: now. It introduces a new subject and does not set one term against another. It connects with the four occurrences of 'all' in 4:6 and proceeds to take up the differences found in individuals [Lns]. The sudden change of subject in 4:7 is not easy to account for, but having spoken of the unity of the church in the preceding verses, the writer now wishes to show that the variety and multiplicity of gifts in the church is Christ's own doing and each such gift has its part to play within the body as a whole. Many translations show this switch simply by starting a new paragraph [TH].

QUESTION—Who is the actor of the passive verb ἐδόθη 'was given'?
1. Christ is the actor in this verb [Alf, Ea, EBC, El, Ho, Lns, My, NIC, TD, TH, WBC; NAB, NASB, NJB, TNT]. Christ is the implied agent of this verb as he is the subject of the following verses [TH]. He gave these gifts at the time of his exaltation [Alf], i.e., after his ascension [El, NIC]. This verb is explained by the ἔδωκε 'he gave' of 4:8 [Ea].
2. God is the actor in this verb [AB, Ba, Cal, EGT, NCBC, WeBC]. God bestows his gifts upon believers without restraint [WeBC].

QUESTION—What is meant by χάρις 'grace'?
1. This is a gift or gifts for a particular ministry or ministries [AB, BAGD (4 p. 878), Cal, CBC, DNTT, Ea, LJ, Lns, MNTC, NIC, NTC, St, TH; NJB (note), TNT (note)]. The following verses indicate that this is gift in connection with not only personal privilege and honor, but official rank and function as well [Ea].
2. This designates, not a gift itself, but what lies behind it [Alf, EBC, EGT, El, Ho, ISBE, My, NCBC, Rob, TD, TNTC, WBC]. This is the privilege of having a special calling in God's service [TNTC]. This is enabling grace [EBC, NCBC]. Χάρις 'grace' here is not equated with χάρισμα 'grace-gift' but the grace provided for [EBC], and manifested in the gift [EBC, El, My] through its energizing force [El]. Since what the writer has in view here is the outworking of grace in a variety of ways in individual believers, χάρις 'grace' here is equivalent to χάρισμα 'grace-gift' [WBC]. This is the subjective grace that works within the believer and shows itself in the result [EGT].
3. This is the grace necessary to live the Christian life [Ba]. The χάρις 'grace' referred to here is the gracious influence of the Holy Spirit given to all true Christians to enable them to live a life of holiness. All are not given the same grace nor in the same amount, but each is given enough to enable him to live as he ought to live [Ba].
4. This is salvation [Can, WeBC]. This is the favor or blessing of being made members of the spiritual body of Christ. This occurs upon the regeneration of the individual. Besides this common grace given to all, there are particular graces given to individuals at the same time, which differ in kind and measure [Can]. The gift of God's saving grace to the individual believer forms the foundation for all other divine gifts to that person. This is the greatest of God's gifts to men; the giving of all the other gifts depends on receiving it [WeBC].
5. This is a combination of interpretations 3 and 4 above [ECWB]. This is given in the Divine purpose in the regeneration of the whole body even though each receives it separately and makes it his own gradually in the course of life [ECWB].

QUESTION—What is the meaning of τὸ μέτρον 'the measure'?
The interpretation chosen here will depend in part upon the interpretation taken in regard to the meaning of χάρις 'grace' above.
1. It means that this grace is distributed in varying amounts to different individuals according to the decision of Christ or God [Ba, Cal, Can, Ea, EBC, ECWB, EGT, El, Ho, IB, LJ, Lns, MNTC, My, NIC, NTC, Rob, St, TD, TNTC, WBC, We]. It is given in a certain measure [Ba, Cal, Can, Ea, EGT, Ho, MNTC, NIC, NTC, Rob, St, TNTC, WBC] so that all are not absolutely alike in gifts and functions [Can, Ho, MNTC]. It is not unlimited, yet each has enough for the purpose for which he was called into the Kingdom of God [Ba]. Christ's giving himself on the cross in full measure and without restraint is the 'measure' of his gift. Christ gives it to each

individual according to that individual's capacity to receive it in faith [ECWB].
2. It means that this grace is distributed to all in accordance with Christ's or God's generosity [NCBC, TH, WeBC]. The degree of God's generous endowment to individuals is compared with the grace that was given to Christ (John 3:34, Rom. 8:32), i.e., without measure or limit [NCBC]. As Christ gave himself without restraint and in full measure, so God gives his gifts to believing men without restraint 'according to the measure of the gift of Christ' [WeBC]. The gift each Christian has is determined by Christ's generosity. We are dealing here with the attribute of generosity and not with a fixed proportion between countable objects. Μέτρον 'measure' may be expressed by 'how great is' or 'the great size' [TH].

QUESTION—What is the relationship between the nouns in the genitive construction τὸ μέτρον τῆς δωρεᾶς τοῦ Χριστοῦ 'the measure of the gift of Christ'?

1. Christ gave or distributed the δωρεᾶς 'gift' [Alf, BAGD (2.b. p. 515), Can, CBC, Ea, EBC, ECWB, EGT, El, Ho, IB, ICC, LJ, MNTC, My, NIC, NTC, Rob, St, TD, TH, TNTC, WBC, We, WeBC]: the gift that Christ gave. The ἔδοκεν δόματα 'he gave gifts' in 4:8 explains this τῆς δωρεᾶς τοῦ Χριστοῦ 'of the gift of Christ' [EGT, My]. The gift is measured and given by Christ [Alf, Ea, EGT, My]. As a witness to the church's belief that Jesus is the central point in human life, the Risen Jesus gives to each member of his church a gift suitable for making a contribution to God's service [CBC]. Christ gave himself on the cross for man's salvation [WeBC].
    1.1. Δωρεᾶς 'gift' acts as the subject of the noun μέτρον 'measure' [Alf, Ea, EGT, My]: the gift is measured (by Christ).
    1.2. Δωρεᾶς 'gift' is the possessor of the μέτρον 'measure' [El, WeBC (probably)]: the measure of the gift, or the gift's largesse. The meaning is the measure which the gift has, which belongs to and defines the gift [El]. Christ's giving himself on the cross in full measure and without restraint is the 'measure' of his gift [WeBC].
    1.3. The noun χάρις 'grace' in the genitive is implied following μέτρον 'measure' so that it acts as possessor or object of 'measure' [BAGD (2.b. p. 515)]: according to the measure of grace, or according to the grace measured.
2. The phrase τῆς δωρεᾶς τοῦ Χριστοῦ 'the gift of Christ' is in apposition to the noun μέτρον 'measure' and Χριστοῦ 'Christ' is in apposition to δωρεᾶς 'gift', he himself constituting the gift from God [AB]: The gift consisting of the Messiah is the measure according to which grace is given to each one of us. Although the following verses clearly describe the Messiah as the donor, in this verse he is God's great gift. In this case he is manifested in the various gifts received by the church since he distributes 'grace' (3:8). In so doing he proves to be the plenipotent

'administrator' (1:10) of that grace which, according to 1:6, 8; 3:2, 7, God himself bestows [AB].
3. Christ is the intermediate agent of the action implied in δωρεᾶς 'gift' and μέτρον 'measure' is in apposition to δωρεᾶς 'gift' [Ba]: the measure of grace is the gift given to us in or through Christ. The gift is what he purchased by his merits. It comes to us through him [Ba].
4. Christ is the object of the giving [Lns, NCBC]: the grace given to Christ. Our endowment corresponds with the measure of the gift bestowed upon Christ [Lns].

DISCOURSE UNIT: 4:8–10 [AB, LJ, NTC, We]. The topic is the gifts bestowed upon the Church by the ascended Messiah [AB, LJ, NTC, We].

4:8 **Therefore**[a] **he/it says,**
LEXICON—a. διό (LN 89.47): 'therefore' [AB, LN, NIC, NTC, WBC; NASB, NRSV], 'wherefore' [El, Lns, Rob, We; KJV], 'as' [TEV], 'this (or that) is why' [NIV, NJB, REB, TNT], 'for this reason, for this very reason, so then' [LN], 'thus you find' [NAB]. This particle is a relatively emphatic marker expressing result and usually denotes the fact that the inference it makes is self-evident [LN].
QUESTION—What relationship is indicated by διό 'therefore'?
1. It indicates the grounds for the assertion he has just made in 4:7 about Christ giving out gifts of grace by measure to the members of his church [Alf, Ba, Ea, EBC, EGT, El, Ho, LJ, MNTC, My, NCBC, NIC, Si, St, TH, WBC].
2. It indicates the reason why Christ is the one who dispenses the gifts. It is because he has achieved dominion over all powers from the lowest to the highest [TD].
QUESTION—Who or what is the implied subject of λέγει 'he/it says' and what is its role?
1. God is the subject [AB, Alf, Cal, DNTT, Ea, EGT, El, HG, ISBE, LJ, MNTC, My, NCBC, NTC, Si-ed]: God says. God, whose word the Scriptures are, is the natural subject [El, My].
2. The Psalmist is the subject [We]: The Psalmist says. The subject is either 'Scripture' generally, or, more simply, 'the Psalmist' [We].
3. Scripture is the subject [ICC, Rob, WBC; NAB, REB, TEV, TNT]: Scripture says.
4. The subject is impersonal [Ba, Lns, TD; NASB, NIV, NJB, NRSV]: it says. It is equivalent to the passive formula 'it is said' [Ba; NRSV].

"Having-ascended[a] **into**[b] **(the) heights**[c] **he-led-captive**[d] **captivity,**[e]
LEXICON—a. aorist act. participle of ἀναβαίνω (LN 15.101) (BAGD 1.a.β. p. 50): 'to ascend' [AB, BAGD, El, LN, NIC, NTC, WBC, We; NAB, NASB, NIV, TNT], 'to ascend up' [Rob; KJV], 'to go up' [BAGD, LN (15.101, **1.13, 55.24**), Lns; NJB, TEV].

b. εἰς (LN 84.22): 'into' [LN], 'to' [AB, LN (**55.24**); NJB, TEV, TNT], not explicit, or conflated with ὕψος and translated 'on high' [El, LN (**1.13**), Lns, NIC, NTC, Rob, WBC, We; KJV, NAB, NASB, NIV].
c. ὕψος (LN **1.13**) (BAGD 1.b. p. 850): 'heights' [NJB, TNT], 'the very heights' [LN (**55.24**); TEV], 'height' [AB, BAGD], 'high' [LN], 'on high' [El, LN (**1.13**), Lns, NIC, NTC, Rob, WBC, We; KJV, NAB, NASB, NIV], 'world above, sky' [LN], 'heaven' [BAGD, LN].
d. aorist act. indic. of αἰχμαλωτεύω (LN **55.24**) (BAGD p. 27): 'to lead captive' [El, NIC, NTC, Rob, WBC; KJV, NASB], 'to capture' [AB, BAGD], 'to make captive' [LN, Lns; NRSV], 'to take captive' [LN], 'to capture someone in war' [LN], 'to take captive in war' [BAGD]. The clause ᾐχμαλώτευσεν αἰχμαλωσίαν 'he led captive a host of captives' is translated 'to lead captives in train' [We; NIV], 'to take a host of captives' [NAB], 'to take a host of captives with (him)' [TNT], 'to take captives' [NJB], 'to take many captives with (him)' [TEV], 'to take captives into captivity' [REB]. In Eph. 4:8 the cognate noun αἰχμαλωσία 'captivity' is added redundantly to this verb following Semitic usage. This Hebraism simply means 'to take many captives' [LN].
e. αἰχμαλωσία (LN 55.23) (BAGD 2. p. 26): 'captivity' [El, LN, Lns, NIC, Rob; KJV, NRSV], 'captives' [NIV, NJB, TEV], 'many captives' [LN (**55.24**)], 'a host of captives, prisoners' [NTC, WBC, We; NAB, NASB, TNT], 'a catch of prisoners' [AB], 'prisoners of war' [BAGD]. This noun is also translated as a prepositional phrase: 'into captivity' [REB].

QUESTION—What is the function of this quotation?

The varied gifts given by the exalted Christ calls to the apostle's mind the metaphor incorporated in this Psalm [Rob]. It is the connection between Christ's ascension and the gifts he bestows that the apostle wants to emphasize [DNTT, Rob, TD, TH, WBC; NJB (note)]. The only words of the quotation he will comment upon in the following verses are ἀναβάς 'having ascended' and ἔδωκε δόματα 'he gave gifts' [Rob; NJB (note), TNT (note)]. This quotation confirms the assertion just made about Christ distributing the various spiritual gifts to his church [Ea, EBC, El, Ho, LJ, MNTC, My, Si, TH], or otherwise serves to enforce the assertion made in 4:7 [St, TNTC, WBC]. Paul can apply this quotation to Christ on the principle that what is said about Yahweh in the OT may be applied to Christ in the NT because the persons are the same [Ho, LJ, NTC].

QUESTION—What is meant by ἀναβάς εἰς ὕψος 'ascending to the heights'?

The writer refers this to Christ's ascent to heaven [AB, Alf, Ba, Cal, Can, CBC, DNTT, Ea, ECWB, EGT, El, Ho, IB, Leu, LJ, LN (1.13), Lns, MNTC, My, NCBC, NIC, NTC, Rob, Si, Sp, St, TD, TNTC, WBC, We, WeBC; NAB (note), NJB (note), TNT (note)]. In Psalm 68:18, however, this referred to God [Cal, Can, Da, Del, DNTT, EGT, Ho, Leu, LJ, Lns, Mac, MNTC, My, NCBC, NTC, TD, TNTC, WBC, We, Wei; NAB (note)], or to God as present in the Ark of the Covenant [Alf, Ba, ECWB, Kid, NIC, Si, Sp, St], or to the temporal king [AB, Rob, TH; TNT (note)], ascending to Mt. Zion (or

Mt. Sinai [Da]) in triumph [Ag, Alf, Ba, Del, ECWB, EGT, Kid, Leu, Mac, My, NCBC, NIC, Rob, Si, Sp, St, TD, TH, TNTC, WBC, We, Wei; NAB (note), TNT (note)], or for an enthronement celebration [AB]. Some commentators see a reference to a Jewish king ascending the newly conquered Mt. Zion in Jerusalem with his spoil in this psalm [CBC, Rob, TH]. The writer sees the partial triumphs in Jewish history, which this psalm celebrates, as prefiguring the universal and eternal triumph of Christ [Alf, Ea, Ho, My]. Some see the ascent in the psalm as a metaphorical description of Yahweh's victorious ascent to his throne in heaven again after coming down to earth to deliver his people from their enemies [Can, DNTT, Ea, EGT, Ho, Lns, NTC, TNTC]. Others see it as a metaphor of the victorious king marching up to the opened gate of the stronghold he has won to receive tribute from his vanquished enemies [Del, MNTC]. If the phrase ἀναβὰς εἰς ὕψος is taken to mean he went up on a mountain or high building, it would be better to translate it 'when he went up to heaven' [LN (1.13)]. Yet translating this as 'heaven' here makes the writer's discussion in 4:9–10 meaningless [TH].

QUESTION—How does the action of the participle ἀναβάς 'having ascended' relate to the principle verb ἔδωκεν 'he gave'?

1. This aorist participle denotes an action simultaneous and parallel to that of the principle verb [AB, Alf]: ascending he gave gifts.
2. This aorist participle denotes an action preceding that of the principle verb [Ea, EGT, El]: having ascended he gave gifts. It indicates Christ's ascension had taken place before he distributed these gifts [EGT, ISBE2, MNTC]. The ascension of Christ secures our salvation and his enthronement is the source of abundant blessing because, as the enthroned king, he gives gifts to men [ISBE2].

QUESTION—What is the meaning of the short clause ᾐχμαλώτευσεν αἰχμαλωσίαν 'he led captivity captive'?

The clause means no more than 'he made captives' [EGT; NJB] or 'he took many captives' [TH; NAB, TEV, TNT]. In any case, in 4:8 it is subordinated to the principle idea in the next clause of the victorious Christ distributing gifts to men [EGT, Ho, Rob]. This is a metaphor of a triumphant conqueror [AB, Alf, Ba, Can, CBC, Da, Del, Ea, ECWB, EGT, El, Ho, ICC, Kid, Leu, LJ, Lns, MNTC, My, NIC, NTC, Rob, Sp, St, TH, TNTC, We, WeBC]. The captives constitute the proof of his victory [ISBE]. According to some this reference in the psalm represents Yahweh as having descended from heaven to earth to help his people and is now ascending again in a triumphal march leading the great host of captives he has captured [Can, Ea, LJ, TNTC]. On the principle that all former divine deliverances are foreshadowings and types of the great salvation wrought by Christ, Paul applies this reference to Christ's work [Can, Ea, LJ, My, Sp, We].

QUESTION—What is meant by the noun αἰχμαλωσίαν 'captivity'?

This term expresses the state of being taken captive as a prisoner of war and being kept a captive [LN]. This is a collective [Cal, NIC], abstract [Alf,

BAGD, Ea, EGT, El, Ho, ICC, My] term standing for concrete prisoners of war [Alf, BAGD, Ea, EGT, El, Ho, ICC, My, NIC].
1. These captives are the spiritual beings Christ has triumphed over—the demonic principalities and powers that oppose him [AB, Alf, Can, CBC, DNTT, ECWB, Ho, IB, LJ, Lns, MNTC, St, TD, WBC].
2. These captives are all the forces of evil that Christ has triumphed over, including Satan and his hosts, evil men, and sin and death [Ea, El, ICC, My, My-ed, Sp].
3. These captives are the souls of people he has rescued [NTC, TNTC, We]. Christ's erstwhile captive foes are, like the apostle himself, Christ's gifts to his church [TNTC, We].
4. These captives are not only Satan and the principalities and powers that opposed Christ, but also those people who were held captive by them [Ba, Cal, Sp, WeBC]. 'Captivity' is a collective noun for captive enemies. The plain meaning is that God reduced his enemies to subjection. These enemies also include the obstinacy of our natures [Cal]. The imagery is that of a Roman triumphal procession where the Roman conqueror not only leads the enemy he has conquered in triumph but also the captives that enemy had held [Ba].

he-gave^a gifts^b to-men."^{c}

TEXT—Some manuscripts begin this clause with καί 'and'. GNT gives the reading without καί 'and' a B rating, indicating that this reading is almost certain. Those who include an 'and' between these clauses are Alf, Bu, Cal, Ea, ICC, Lns, NTC, Rob, We, KJV, NAB, NASB, and NIV. (There is no conjunction here in either the LXX or Hebrew texts of this psalm.)

LEXICON—a. aorist act. indic. of δίδωμι (LN 57.71) (BAGD 1.b.β. p. 193): 'to give' [AB, BAGD, El, LN, Lns, NIC, NTC, Rob, WBC, We; all versions], 'to grant' [BAGD].
b. δόμα (LN 57.73) (BAGD p. 203): 'gifts' [AB, BAGD, El, LN, Lns, NIC, NTC, Rob, WBC, We; all versions].
c. ἄνθρωπος (LN 9.1): 'men' [AB, El, Lns, NTC, Rob, WBC, We; all versions except NJB, NRSV, TEV], 'mankind' [LN, NIC; TEV], 'humanity' [NJB], 'people' [LN; NRSV], 'persons' [LN]. When used in the plural, this noun has a generic meaning [LN].

QUESTION—Why does the author alter this clause from the original psalm?
In this clause the writer uses a different verb than is used in the Greek version (LXX) of the psalm, and which also has a somewhat different meaning from the verb used in the Hebrew text. The writer substitutes ἔδωκεν 'he gave' for the LXX's ἔλαβες 'you received' (the change of person being a purely formal change that does not affect the meaning at all [Can, Ea, IB, Lns, NTC]) and capable of carrying the meaning of 'to receive in order to distribute' or 'to bring' or 'to pass on' [AB, Alf, Bu, Cal, Ea, ECWB, EGT, Ho, My, St]. The reasons the commentators give for the writer incorporating this change are not necessarily mutually exclusive.

1. The author is focusing attention upon one aspect of the meaning of 'to receive (in order to give)' [AB, Alf, Bu, Ea, ECWB, Ho, LJ, Lns, My, St]. Christ's *giving* of Eph. 4:8 presupposes his *receiving* these gifts from the hands of his Father [LJ, Lns]. The word ἔλαβε 'he received' is ellipsed: 'and *receiving* gifts gave them to men'. Here the sense originally intended by the Holy Spirit is preserved though the word used varies from the original [Bu].
2. The author is following a rabbinic interpretation or paraphrase of the passage [AB, CBC, DNTT, EBC, IB, ICC, IDB, MNTC, NIC, Rob, Si, St, TH, TNTC, WBC, We; NJB (probably)] or making a free translation [ECWB]. The writer is using an interpretative gloss to contrast what God is doing for the Church *now* with what he did at the time of the psalm, i.e. a reversal of the situation has taken place by Christ's ascension, instead of the victor receiving gifts from the vanquished, gifts are now given [DNTT]. The author uses a form of text current among the rabbinical schools and follows it with an arbitrary midrashic interpretation (4:9 ff.) in which he transfers to Christ what had been applied to Moses [IB, WBC].
3. The author follows the inspiration of the Spirit of God in making the change because the messianic character of this passage incorporated this meaning [EGT, El, My, My-ed, NTC, Si-ed]. In the original the Lord *receives* gifts of homage from men. In Paul's meaning the Lord *gives* gifts to men [My]. Both the words and the ideas are changed—so much so that it goes beyond the free translation commonly seen in other OT quotations in the NT [EGT, My].
4. The author quotes only the previous words from the psalm. The words ἔδωκεν δόματα τοῖς ἀνθρώποις 'he gave gifts to men' are his own words [Ba, Cal, Kid]. The author is using the language of the psalm in an emblematic manner to express the idea he wants to put across without really intending to say that the words of the psalm actually said this [Ba, ICC (though in support of 2. above)].
5. The author unintentionally misquotes this citation [NCBC]. The author's overwhelming sense of wonder at the gifts Christ gives causes him to recall the psalmist's words in a form more congenial to his overflowing gratitude [NCBC].

QUESTION—What are the gifts given to men?

In the original psalm the gifts were the captured booty shared out among the people (Ps. 68:12) [AB, Can, Ea, Kid, Lns, NIC, NTC, Rob, St, TNTC], or gifts of homage given to the victorious king by his subjects [EGT, My, NCBC, Rob, Wei], or tributary gifts from the vanquished [Da, Del, ICC, Kid, Leu, Mac, MNTC, NIC, Rob, Sp, Wei], or, possibly, the receiving of the captured prisoners themselves [Ag, EGT, ICC], regarded as gifts or offerings [EGT, ICC]. Here the gifts are eternal life and both the ordinary and extraordinary gifts of the Spirit [WeBC]. They are all the spiritual endowments with which men may be blessed [Si-ed]. They are the various spiritual gifts [El, MNTC, My] discussed in this section [El, St, TNTC], especially the gifts of administration of the church [Ba, Ea, Sp] listed in 4:11 [NCBC]. They are the qualities necessary for the mission Christ has given his followers on earth [Lns]. A few think that the gifts are the gifted persons given to the Church [AB, My-ed, NTC, We] (who formerly were among the captives led in the train of the Conqueror [My-ed, NTC, We]).

QUESTION—To whom does τοῖς ἀνθρώποις 'to men' refer?

This refers to mankind collectively, both here and in the original psalm [Alf]. Some commentators on the psalm refer 'among men' principally to the captives [Ag, Del, Kid]. In Jewish interpretive tradition of this psalm, it referred to Israel, or the merits of the Great Man (Abraham), or it was left unspecified [AB]. In Eph. 4:8, 'men' are the members of the church [Kid, LJ, My-ed, NTC, Sp, TNTC]. One commentator cites the occurrence in the psalm of the singular Hebrew noun with the definite article 'in the man', and refers this to Christ's human nature [Bu], i.e. his status as 'Son of Man' [Bu]. Another cites the same opinion in respect of the Greek plural used by Paul, τοῖς ἀνθρώποις 'to men', that the reception of these gifts referred to those who received Christ as mediator [Si-ed].

4:9 Now[a] the (word) "he-ascended,"[b] what does-it-mean[c] except that also he-descended[d] into[e] the lower[f] regions[g] of-the-earth?[h]

TEXT—Some manuscripts contain the word πρῶτον 'first' after κατέβη 'he descended'. GNT omits it with an A rating, indicating that the shorter reading is certain. Πρῶτον 'first' is included by Ho, KJV, NAB, and TEV. In any case, πρῶτον 'first' only expresses what is implied in the text [NIC, TNTC].

TEXT—Some manuscripts omit μέρη 'regions'. GNT includes it with a C rating, indicating uncertainty as to whether or not it should be included. It is omitted by AB, El, My, and WBC, although two of these include in their translation the word 'parts' or 'regions' for clarity [El, WBC].

LEXICON—a. δέ (LN 89.94): 'now' [El, Lns, NIC, NTC, Rob, WBC, We; KJV, NASB, REB, TEV], 'and' [LN]. This relationship is also indicated by juxtaposition [AB; NAB, NIV, NRSV, TNT], or by a new paragraph [NJB].

b. aorist act. indic. of ἀναβαίνω: 'to ascend'. See this word at 4:8.

c. pres. act. indic. of εἰμί (LN 13.4) (BAGD II.3. p. 224): 'to mean' [BAGD, NIC, NTC; NAB, NASB, NIV, NJB, NRSV, TEV, TNT], 'to imply' [AB, El, WBC; REB], 'to be' [LN, Lns, Rob, We; KJV]. As a copula and following verbs of asking, recognizing, knowing, or not knowing, εἰμί 'to be' is explanatory, meaning 'is a representation of, the equivalent of' and is usually translated 'to mean' [BAGD].

d. aorist act. indic. of καταβαίνω (LN 15.107) (BAGD 1.a.δ. p. 408): 'to descend' [AB, El, LN, Lns, NIC, NTC, Rob, WBC, We; all versions except NJB, TEV], 'to go down' [BAGD, LN; NJB], 'to come down' [BAGD, LN; TEV].

e. εἰς with accusative object (LN 84.22): 'into' [El, LN, Lns, NIC, NTC, Rob, We; KJV, NAB, NASB, NRSV, TNT], 'to' [AB, WBC; NIV, NJB, REB, TEV].
f. κατώτερος (LN **83.54**) (BAGD p. 425): 'lower' [El, LN, Lns, NIC, NTC, Rob, WBC, We; KJV, NAB, NASB, NIV, NRSV], 'lowest' [REB, TEV], 'deepest' [NJB], 'below' [TNT]. This term is also joined with the preposition εἰς and both terms are translated as 'down to' [AB]. This pertains to being in a position below a point of orientation [LN (**83.54**)]. The phrase κατώτερα μέρη τῆς γῆς 'lower parts of the earth' may refer to 'the world below'. However, some scholars interpret this expression in reference to the earth being low in contrast to heaven. On that basis Eph. 4:9 could be translated as 'he came down to earth itself' [LN (**1.18**)].
g. μέρος (LN 1.79) (BAGD 1.b.γ. p. 506): 'regions' [BAGD, LN, NTC, WBC; NAB, NIV, TNT], 'territory' [LN], 'parts' [BAGD, El, Lns, NIC, Rob, We; KJV, NASB, NRSV], 'levels' [NJB], 'level' [REB], 'depths' [TEV]. It may be that this word is also assimilated into the translation of γῆ 'earth' [AB]. This is used in reference to regions of the earth that stand in relation to some ethnic group or geographical center, but does not necessarily imply any governmental administration [LN].
h. γῆ (LN1.39): 'earth' [AB, El, LN, Lns, NIC, NTC, Rob, WBC, We; all versions except NIV, REB], 'world' [LN], 'very earth' [REB]. This noun is also translated as an adjective modifying 'regions': 'earthly' [NIV]. This term designates the surface of the earth as the place where mankind dwells, in contrast to the heavens above and the world below [LN].

QUESTION—What relationship is indicated by δέ 'now'?

The particle δέ introduces an inference or a transitional explanation [Ea, EGT, El] carrying forward the argument [My]. It introduces Paul's exposition [Lns], his comments on ἀνέβη 'he ascended' [Si-ed]. This verse is part of a parenthetical aside consisting of 4:9–10 [ECWB, IB, MNTC, TH]. The writer argues that the statement in the psalm regarding the ascent of God implies a previous descent [Can, El, Lns, My, NTC] or humiliation [Cal]. The Deity and heavenly abode of Christ are clearly presupposed in the writer's interpretation [Ba, Ea, EGT, El, IB, ICC, My, NTC]. As Deity, he could never be said to have ascended unless he had formerly come down, and in the quote just cited that descent implies such a warfare and victory as belongs only to the incarnate Redeemer [Ea].

1. The purpose of this verse is to prove that Psalm 68:18 refers to Christ [EGT, Ho, IB, LJ, TH, TNTC] and to stress the relationship of the distribution of spiritual gifts to the Church [Can, My, We]. The pervading idea of the epistle is that the Divine humanity of Christ will fill all things and that all things will be gathered into himself [ECWB, MNTC, TNTC]. The writer will use this argument of Christ's descent to stress the grace which lies behind the distribution of gifts to the Church by the Savior [Can, My], but especially how the distribution of these gifts is necessarily connected with Christ's general position of filling the whole universe

[My]. Because Christ is sovereign over all existence, he is in position to give the great variety of gifts that have been observed in the Church [MNTC].
2. The purpose of the verse is to identify Christ, who ascended, with the Spirit in his subsequent descent to reside in his Church and impart necessary gifts to it [ICC, WBC]. The movement of thought in this verse from Christ's ascent to heaven to the giving of gifts to the Church requires a descent in the Spirit. This is consistent with the close association, and even virtual interchange, of Christ and the Spirit seen elsewhere in Ephesians [WBC].

QUESTION—What is the function of the question τί ἐστιν 'what does it mean?' in this context?

This is a rhetorical question to which Paul will give the answer in the following clause introduced by εἰ μὴ ὅτι 'except that' [EGT]. The purpose of this question is to call attention to the word ἀνέβη 'he ascended' [TH].

QUESTION—What does κατέβη εἰς τὰ κατώτερα μέρη τῆς γῆς 'he descended into the lower regions of the earth' mean?
1. This has reference to Christ's descent into Hades following his death [Alf, BD, Can, ECWB, El, HG, IB, Lns, MNTC, My, My-ed, Rob, TD, TH, Tu2; NJB (note), TNT (note)]. This contrast shows that he has traversed all things from the place of the dead to the right hand of God and his superiority rests on this fact, implying, as it does, that he fills all things. Moreover, if αἰχμαλωσίαν 'captivity' in 4:8 refers to Satan and his hosts, then the warfare in which this captivity took place may be most naturally conceived in all its extent as reaching even to their habitation itself [Alf, My-ed].
2. This has reference to Christ's coming to earth as opposed to heaven, from which he came [AB, Ba, Bu, Cal, Ea, EBC (probably), EGT, Ho, ICC, IDB, ISBE2, LJ, NCBC, NIC, NTC, St, TD, WBC; NIV, REB].
   2.1 This refers to Christ's Incarnation as man [Ba, Cal, EBC (probably), EGT, Ho, IDB, LJ, NCBC, NIC, NTC, Si, Si-ed, St, TD, TNTC; NAB (note)] and to his humiliation in death [Cal, EBC (probably), EGT, NTC, Si, Si-ed, St, TNTC]. The Redeemer not only came to earth but stooped to the most humble condition of humanity here [Ba].
   2.2 This refers to Christ's coming in the Spirit to reside in his Church subsequent to his ascension to heaven [ICC, WBC]. The movement of thought in this verse from Christ's ascent to heaven to the giving of gifts to the Church requires a descent in the Spirit. This is also consistent with the close association, and even virtual interchange, of Christ and the Spirit seen elsewhere in Ephesians [WBC].
3. This refers to Christ's descent to live a human life and experience a human death [CBC, We]. This refers to Christ's descent in Incarnation to live through all stages of life common to men including their death and fate after death. This means he shared men's fate in Hades. This is indicated in the fact that the phrase τὰ κατώτερα μέρη τῆς γῆς 'the lower

regions of the earth' would be very unlikely to be used to describe the earth itself. But, in light of the prevailing cosmology, it could be used in reference to Hades (Ps. 63:10 LXX) [We].
4. This refers to Christ's death and burial [WeBC].

4:10 **The (one) who-descended he-himself is also the (one) who-ascended far-above[a] all the heavens,[b]**

LEXICON—a. ὑπεράνω (LN 83.49, 87.31) (BAGD p. 840): 'far above' [AB, LN (87.31), Lns, WBC, We; KJV, NASB, NRSV, REB, TNT], 'above and beyond' [TEV], 'high above' [BAGD, NIC; NAB], 'above' [El, LN (83.49), Rob; NJB], 'higher than' [NTC; NIV], 'over' [LN (83.49)]. This denotes a position above another irrespective of contact [LN (83.49)]. This is a marker of superior status and suggests an additional factor of degree [LN (87.31)].

b. οὐρανός (LN 1.11) (BAGD 1.e. p. 594): 'heavens' [AB, BAGD, El, LN, Lns, NIC, NTC, Rob, WBC; all versions]. There seems to be no semantic distinction in the NT between the singular and plural forms. Both denote the supernatural dwelling place of God and other heavenly beings. There is a semantic component in this word of 'above' or 'in the sky' but the element of 'abode' is more significant than location above the earth [LN]. This involves the Jewish concept of more than one heaven [Alf, BAGD, Can, CBC, EBC, EGT, ICC, My, NCBC, Rob, TH, Tu, Tu3, WBC].

QUESTION—What is the function of this verse?

This verse expresses the result of 4:9 [My] or its conclusion [El]. It stresses the identity of the person who descended with that of the person who ascended [Alf, Ba, Can, Ea, EBC, EGT, El, Ho, ICC, Lns, My, NCBC, NTC, TNTC, WBC, We], the one who is the source of the church's gifts [EGT]. Rather than stressing the identity of the Messiah, it focuses on the continuation and crowning of his humiliation by his exaltation [AB]. This verse employs the imagery of a king who establishes his rule by visiting all parts of his realm [AB, My].

QUESTION—What is the function of the pronoun αὐτός 'he himself'?

The pronoun is emphatic [Alf, El, ICC, My] and it is the subject, not the predicate [Alf]. It means 'he and no other' [Alf, Ea, EGT] or 'he precisely' [My]. The absence of an article preceding αὐτός 'himself' prevents this pronoun from having the meaning 'the same' (as translated in the KJV) [AB, El, ICC, We], though substantially that is the sense of the use of the pronoun here [We].

QUESTION—What is the force of the καί 'also' in this verse?

Some think that it indicates that the descent was subsequent to the ascent [ICC, WBC]. However, there is no reason why καί 'also' here does not have any more than its familiar *additive* force [EGT].

QUESTION—What is the meaning of the phrase ὑπεράνω πάντων τῶν οὐρανῶν 'far above all the heavens'?

This phrase explains the εἰς ὕψος 'into the heights' in the quotation of the psalm in 4:8 [Lns, My, WBC]. The word πάντων 'all' indicates that a plurality of heavens is definitely in view [WBC]. Some associate the plural 'heavens' here with the three heavens Paul mentions in Corinthians [CBC, Ea, EGT, Ho, Lns, NCBC, TH], or with the concept of seven heavens [Alf, Ea, EBC, EGT, Ho, ICC, My, NCBC, Rob, TH, Tu, Tu3, WBC]. However, a number of commentators also say the point is not the number of heavens, but the fact that Christ is exalted above anything that can be called heaven [Alf, Can, Ea, EGT, El, WBC]. What is being asserted is that Christ is Yahweh, the high God of the OT and, as there, these heavens cannot contain him [WBC].

1. The compound term ὑπεράνω 'far above' denotes primarily a local setting [ICC, NCBC, TH, WBC]: He himself is also the one who ascended to a locality far above the heavens. In this case 'heaven', according to one commentator, may denote not the home of God, but the abode of the spiritual forces which are intermediate between men and God [NCBC]. Another states that defining heaven as the abode of God would then place Christ above God himself [TH]. However, another thinks that this is paradoxical language. Christ is viewed both locally as being in heaven, but at the same time as being above the heavens, the heavens not being able to contain him [WBC].
2. The compound term ὑπεράνω 'far above' primarily denotes superior status [Alf, Can, Ea, EGT, El, Ho, Lns, My, NTC, St]: He himself is also the one who ascended to an office far superior to any created being. This interpretation does not entirely exclude the local sense [My].

in-order-that[a] he-might-fill[b] all[c] (things).

LEXICON—a. ἵνα (LN 89.59): 'in order that' [NTC, WBC], 'that' [El, Rob, We; KJV, NAB, NASB, TNT], 'in order to' [AB, LN, Lns, NIC; NIV], 'so that' [LN; NRSV, REB], 'for the purpose of' [LN]. This conjunction is also coalesced into the infinitive of the verb 'to fill' [NJB, TEV].
b. aorist act. subj. of πληρόω (LN 59.37) (BAGD 1.a. p.671): 'to fill' [AB, BAGD, El, LN, Lns, NIC, NTC, Rob, WBC; all versions except NAB, TEV, TNT], 'to make full' [BAGD], 'to bring to completeness' [We], 'to fill with gifts' [NAB], 'to fill with his presence' [TEV, TNT].
c. πᾶς (LN 59.23, 63.2) (BAGD 2.b.β. p. 633): 'all things' [AB, BAGD, El, Lns, NTC, Rob, We; KJV, NASB, NJB, NRSV], 'all men' [NAB], 'the universe' [BAGD, NIC; REB], 'the whole universe' [NIV, TEV, TNT], 'the cosmos' [WBC], 'all' [LN (59.23)], 'whole, total' [LN (63.2)]. This denotes the whole of creation [BAGD].

QUESTION—What is the meaning of this purpose clause?

The ἵνα 'in order that' with the aorist subjunctive πληρώσῃ 'he might fill' following the aorist participles in this sentence gives a present and enduring meaning to the verb [Alf, Ea, EGT, El]. The ascension is past, but this purpose of it still remains, or is still the present result [Ea]. As the two participles are aorists and denote definite historical acts in the past, so πληρώσῃ 'might fill', also an aorist denoting a past historical act, expresses an act which is simultaneous with the exaltation and of permanent effect. The purpose was attained: namely, he then filled all things and continues to do so now [Lns].

1. Filling denotes the presence of the person of Christ throughout the universe [AB, Alf, Ba, Cal, Can, DNTT, Ea, EBC, ECWB, EGT, El, Ho, My, NCBC, NIC, St, TD, TNTC, WBC, WeBC]. The variations within this main interpretation are based on commentators' emphases and are not necessarily mutually exclusive.

1.1 This presence involves the exercise of his sovereign authority [AB, CBC, Ea, ECWB, EGT, Ho, TNTC, WBC], his sustaining and ruling power [El, My, TD], or influence [Ba]. The thought is that the object of his ascension was that Christ might enter into his regal relation with the whole world and by virtue of that position and prerogative bestow his gifts as he willed and as they were needed [EGT, My]. In particular, this purpose clause points back to the bestowal of grace expressed in 4:7 and prophetically confirmed in 4:8 as expressing the universal relation into which Christ has entered towards the whole world, which relation necessitates the bestowal of grace on all individuals [My]. He was exalted that he might fill the universe with his activity as its sovereign governor and his Church with his presence as its head [EGT]. Both here and in 1:23 the reference is more particularly to the fullness of his grace as it extends from his glorified humanity to all his members [ECWB]. What is expressed here is that Christ, as God clothed in our nature, exercises universal dominion [Ho].

1.2 This presence involves his working by the Spirit [Alf, Cal, St, TNTC, WBC, WeBC]. Though, as deity, Christ was formerly everywhere present, yet, since his entering into the possession of his kingdom, the power of his Spirit has been exerted differently. Wherever the right hand of God is displayed, Christ is spiritually present by his infinite power [Cal]. He is active in the Spirit in giving gifts to the Church and equipping it for its role. As Käsemann indicates, the presupposition is the principle that the Giver is not separated from his gift, but is really present in it [WBC]. The outpouring of himself in the Spirit removed his self-imposed physical limitations with regard to physical place or space, enabling him to assume again the divine prerogative of omnipresence [WeBC].

1.3 This presence involves his character as Savior [Can]. By his descent Christ became our Savior and, by ascending 'far above all the heavens', Christ becomes everywhere present in that character, in the grace, love, and saving power that are manifested in his incarnation on earth and his death on the cross [Can].

1.4 This presence involves his attribute of omnipresence [NCBC, TD]. The ascension of Christ is thought of as that which sets him free from anything which might localize him. It makes him totally available everywhere to all men at all times [NCBC].

1.5 This presence involves particularly his supplying the Church with the gifts necessary to promote its growth until it matches his own fullness [AB, NIC, TD]. The distribution of the gifts is the mode by which the Messiah makes himself present [AB].

2. Filling denotes not the personal omnipresence of his human nature in all regions of the universe but the action of bringing all things into subjection to himself by his redeeming power [IB, Lns]. This is the so-called ubiquity of the human nature of Christ which is defined in terms of the omnipotence that is bestowed on that nature. It is not connected with an absolute presence, but with his universal dominion [Lns].

3. Filling denotes not being omnipresent in all regions of the universe, but the action of filling the entire universe with his gifts, salvation, and the services of the offices of the Church which proclaim it [NTC].

4. Πληρώσῃ would better be translated as 'might fulfill' [ISBE, MNTC, Rob, We]. Christ can hardly be said to fill all the spheres of the universe merely by having visited them. Rather, Paul's idea is that he had accomplished his mission in bringing all things within the compass of God's plan, reuniting all things in himself [MNTC]. The presence of Christ is the means by which he brings all things to their completeness [We].

QUESTION—What is meant by τὰ πάντα 'all things'?

The τὰ πάντα 'all things' denotes the entire universe [Alf, Can, EGT, El, Ho, Lns, MNTC, My, St, TD], which includes both heaven and earth, principalities and powers, and the church [AB].

DISCOURSE UNIT: 4:11–16 [My]. The topic is Christ giving different teachers to the church so that dependence on false teaching may cease and the truth be acknowledged in love, and so that all may grow in relation to Christ.

4:11 And he-himself gave/appointed[a] some (to be) apostles,[b] some prophets,[c] some evangelists,[d] some pastors[e] and teachers,[f]

LEXICON—a. aorist act. indic. of δίδωμι (LN 37.98) (BAGD 5. p. 193): 'to give to be' [El, NTC; NIV, REB, TNT], 'to give as' [Lns, NIC, TH, We; NASB], 'to give' [Rob, WBC; KJV, NAB], 'to appoint, to appoint to be' [AB, BAGD, LN; TEV], 'to assign' [LN]. This verb is also translated as a clause: 'his gift was that they should be' [NJB], 'he gave gifts to be' [NRSV]. This verb denotes the assignment of a person to a task as a special benefit to others [LN].

b. ἀπόστολος: 'apostle'. See this word at 3:5.

c. προφήτης: 'prophet'. See this word at 3:5.

d. εὐαγγελιστής (LN 53.76) (BAGD p. 318): 'evangelist' [AB, BAGD, El, LN, Lns, NIC, NTC, Rob, TH, WBC, We; all versions], 'preacher of the gospel' [BAGD]. This term denotes one who announces the gospel. Early usage suggests this term often implies the semantic component of travel from place to place in order to announce this good news [LN].

e. ποιμήν (LN **53.72**) (BAGD 2.b.γ. p. 684): 'pastor' [BAGD, El, LN, NIC, NTC, Rob, WBC, We; all versions], 'minister' [LN], 'shepherd' [AB, Lns, TH]. This is a figurative extension of the meaning 'shepherd' and denotes one who leads a Christian congregation and is responsible for its care and guidance [BAGD, LN].

f. διδάσκαλος (LN 33. 243) (BAGD p. 191): 'teacher' [BAGD, El, LN, Lns, NIC, NTC, Rob, TH, WBC, We; all versions], 'instructor' [LN]. This noun is also translated as an adjective modifying 'pastors': 'teaching' [AB]. The term denotes an official of the Christian church [BAGD].

QUESTION—How is this verse related to the context?

The object of the verse is to show that the Lord has made ample provision for the extension and edification of the Church [Ba].

1. This verse resumes the subject left off at the end of 4:7 [Alf, Ea, EBC, EGT, LJ, Lns, My]. This verse resumes the subject [Alf, Ea, EBC, EGT, LJ], which seems to have belonged at the end of 4:7 [Ea, EBC, EGT, LJ], that is the diversity of gifts bestowed by Christ as a motive to unity [Alf, LJ]. With a retrospective glance at 4:7, the apostle now brings into prominence, in reference to the Church, the special point he made in the general ἵνα πληρώσῃ τὰ πάντα 'that he might fill all things' in 4:10, in order to give the clinching argument to his exhortation to keep the unity of the Spirit [My].

2. This verse refers back to the ἔδωκεν 'he gave' of 4:8 [CBC, IB, Rob, Si, TH, WBC; TEV, TNT] and explains what those gifts are [CBC, IB, MNTC, Si, WBC]. Having commented on ἀναβάς 'he ascended' in the quotation in 4:8, the writer goes on to comment on the ἔδωκεν 'he gave' in that quotation. In each case it is Christ who fulfills this ancient hymn [Rob].

QUESTION—What is the function of the pronoun αὐτός 'he himself'?

This pronoun is emphatic [Ea, ECWB, El, LJ, Lns, My, Rob, St, TH] and refers to the same pronoun in 4:10 [Ea, ECWB, El, LJ, Lns, My, WBC]. It has the effect of repeating the force of the pronoun in 4:10: this Jesus who ascended—this Jesus and no other, is the sovereign donor of these gifts [Ea, ECWB, ICC, My, Rob, WBC]. Referring back to 4:10 as it does, this pronoun prevents treating either 4:8–10 or 4:9–10 as parenthetical material [My].

QUESTION—What is the meaning of ἔδωκεν 'he gave'?

1. The verb means 'to give' [Alf, Ba, Cal, Can, Ea, ECWB, EGT, El, Ho, IB, ICC, Lns, MNTC, My, NIC, NTC, Rob, TH, TNTC, WBC, We; KJV, NAB, NASB, NIV, NJB, NRSV, REB, TNT]: he gave some persons as apostles to the church. The author wishes his readers to think of these officers more as gifts than as functionaries [Ea]. He gave them to the Church [Cal, Can, Ho, IB, LJ, Lns, My, TNTC, WBC, We, WeBC], and through it, ultimately, the whole of mankind (4:8) [AB, Can].

2. The verb here means 'to appoint' [AB, BAGD; TEV]: he appointed some to be apostles.

QUESTION—What is distinctive about this list of officers?

This list of officers is not meant to be exhaustive [Can, LJ, NTC, St]. The writer only used it to illustrate, from the personal acquaintance of his readers with these offices, his theme that there are different offices and gifts that all lead to the same end of unity [LJ]. They are listed in order of their importance [Can, Ea, EGT, Ho, IB, IDB, ISBE2, LJ, Si-ed] or rank [Cal, NTC]. They are all persons, not just ministries, (though some commentators lay more stress on the *charisma* or abilities which qualified them for the office as the gift [LJ, MNTC, NCBC]) so that the persons are seen as the gift [AB, Alf, Can, Ea, EGT, ICC, Lns, My, NTC, Rob, Si, WBC, We] as well as [AB, Alf, ICC, We] or more than [Ea, NTC] their office. Another view is that, despite the concrete nature of the terms used, the persons are not the gifts, but the abilities the persons possess [NCBC, TH].

QUESTION—What were the ἀποστόλους 'apostles'?

1. The term designates only the original twelve disciples and Paul [AB, Ba, Cal, Ea, ECWB, El, Lns, NTC].
2. The term designates a wider circle of officers than the twelve and Paul [EGT, ICC, ISBE, My, Rob, St, TNTC, We]. It refers to a large class of men who discharged the functions of a prophetic ministry as God's envoys to the unbelieving world [ISBE]. The term includes the original twelve plus also all those named in the NT as apostles, such as Barnabas and James, the Lord's brother [My].

QUESTION—What were the εὐαγγελιστάς 'evangelists'?

Evangelists were missionaries who brought the gospel into new regions [AB, Cal, Can, Ea, EBC, ECWB, Ho, Lns, MNTC, NTC, Rob, TD, TNTC, WBC, WeBC] and established churches [ECWB, TD, TNTC, WBC]. Some commentators give a more general account of their ministry, stating that it was concerned with presenting the gospel to those outside the Church generally [ISBE, NCBC, NIC, St, We]. They were like the apostles [AB, Can, ECWB, El], whom they assisted [DNTT, EGT, ICC, LJ, My, Si, TD, TNTC, WeBC], and whose work they continued after the apostles died [AB, Can, ECWB, NIC, Rob, TD, WBC]. They were subordinate to the apostles [Cal, DNTT, EGT, El, ICC, My, NTC, Si, TD]. They were itinerant preachers [Alf, ISBE, LJ, My], usually sent on a special mission [Alf, LJ] by an apostle, sometimes to precede, but usually to follow, the apostle's ministry of founding and establishing churches [LJ].

QUESTION—Who were the ποιμένας 'pastors'?

These were probably the officers named as ἐπίσκοποι 'bishops' or πρεσβύτεροι 'elders' elsewhere in the NT [AB, Can, CBC, DNTT, Ea, EBC, EGT, Ho, ICC, LJ, Lns, My, NCBC, NIC, WBC].

QUESTION—What were the διδασκάλους 'teachers'?

The teachers were the persons whose particular function it was to explain the truths of Christianity [Ea, NCBC, NIC, TH, WBC] and the application of this wisdom and knowledge to conduct [WBC]. The διδασκάλους 'teachers' differed from the εὐαγγελιστάς 'evangelists' in that they taught people who were already Christians [Ho, NCBC]. They differed from the προφήτας 'prophets' in that what prophets uttered came immediately from the Spirit, whereas what the διδασκάλους 'teachers' taught came from their understanding of truths previously given to the church [ICC, TD]. Like prophets, the ministry of teachers was in itinerant one [IDB].

QUESTION—Do 'pastors' and 'teachers' form one class of officers or two?

Commentators on both sides of the question note that these two nouns are grouped together to set them off as officers of established congregations as opposed to the apostles, prophets, and evangelists, who all had an itinerate ministry that was related to the Church at large [AB, Alf, Ea, EBC, EGT, El, IB, ICC, ISBE2, NTC, Rob, TD, TH, WBC, We], some giving it as the, or one of the, reason(s) for the listing as one group [AB, Alf, Ea, EBC, EGT, El, IB, ICC, ISBE2, Rob, TD, TH, WBC].

1. They are grouped together because they are both titles for one office [AB, Alf, Bu, Can, Ea, EGT, Ho, ICC, LJ, LN (**53.72**), Lns, My, NIC, NTC, Rob, TD, TH, TNTC, We, WeBC], the office of pastor-teacher [AB, Alf, Bu, Can, Ea, ECWB, EGT, El (probably), Ho, LJ, LN (**53.72**), Lns, My, Rob, TNTC, WeBC], not other offices that also have a teaching function [AB, My; and probably El, LJ]. These two roles were complementary [Ho, LN (**53.72**)] and (often [Can]) resided in the same persons [Alf, Bu, Can, EGT, El, Ho, LJ, My, TH, TNTC]. While there were men who were teachers, but not pastors [El, LJ, My, St], and while they constituted a distinct group of men, they can scarcely be said to have formed a distinct class of officers [El, ICC], for the gift of teaching was a special endowment, which even ordinary church members might possess [My]. The two titles form an hendiadys, 'teaching shepherds' [AB], 'teaching overseers' [NTC], or either 'shepherds who also feed', or 'teachers who also shepherd' [Bu].
2. They form two classes of officers [Cal, CBC, EBC, IDB, ISBE2, MNTC, NCBC, WBC]. Though Paul appears here to speak indiscriminately of pastors and teachers as belonging to one and the same class, and teaching is, to some extent, applicable to all pastors, still, a man may be a teacher and yet not qualified to preach [Cal, WBC].

DISCOURSE UNIT: 4:12–16 [ECWB, ICC, LJ, We]. The topic is the singleness of purpose in giving the many gifts, namely the perfecting of individual believers in the likeness of Christ, and the resultant building up of the whole Church in unity with Christ [ECWB, LJ, We].

4:12 for[a] the equipping/perfecting[b] of-the saints for[c] (the) work[d] of-ministry,[e]

LEXICON—a. πρός (LN 89.60) (BAGD III.3.a. p. 710): 'for' [BAGD, Rob, TH, WBC; KJV, NASB], 'in order to' [LN, NTC], 'for the sake of' [LN], 'for the purpose of' [BAGD, LN], 'in view of' [Lns], 'with a view to' [El,

We]. This preposition is also conflated with καταρτισμός 'perfecting' and translated as an infinitive of purpose (see next entry) [AB; NIV, NJB, NRSV, REB]. These phrases are also translated as a unit: 'in roles of service for the faithful' [NAB]. Some begin a new sentence here: 'He gave them to equip...' [NIC], 'He did this to...' [TEV], 'Their task was to...' [TNT].

b. καταρτισμός (LN **75.5**) (BAGD p. 418): 'equipping' [BAGD; NASB], 'equipment' [BAGD], 'preparation' [TH], 'training, discipline' [BAGD], 'the complete outfitting' [Lns], 'service' [NAB], 'perfecting' [El, Rob, We; KJV], not explicit [NAB]. This noun is also translated as a verb: 'to knit together' [NJB], 'to equip' [AB, BAGD, NIC; NRSV, REB], 'to fully equip' [NTC], 'to prepare' [NIV, TEV], 'to train' [TNT], 'to make fully qualified' [LN], 'to bring to completion' [WBC]. This noun denotes the making of someone to be completely adequate or sufficient for something [LN]. The noun is used metaphorically in Eph. 4:12 [MM].

c. εἰς (LN 89.57, 90.23): 'for' [AB, El, LN (**75.5**), Lns, NIC, NTC, Rob, TH, WBC, We; all versions except NAB], 'for the purpose of, in order to' [LN (89.57)], 'with respect to, with reference to' [LN (90.23)], not explicit [NAB].

d. ἔργον (LN 42.42) (BAGD 1.b. p. 308): 'work' [AB, BAGD, El, LN, Lns, NIC, NTC, Rob, TH, WBC, We; all versions except NAB, NIV], 'works' [NIV], 'task' [LN], not explicit [NAB]. As part of the genitive phrase ἔργον διακονίας 'the work of ministry', this noun is also translated as an adjective modifying 'ministry': 'practical service' [BAGD (1. p. 184)]. This word denotes that which a person normally does [LN].

e. διακονία (LN 35.19) (BAGD 1. p. 184): 'ministry' [NIC, NTC, Rob; KJV, NRSV], 'ministration' [El], 'service' [AB, BAGD, LN, TH, WBC; NAB, NASB, NIV, NJB, REB, TNT], 'Christian service' [TEV]. This noun is also translated as a gerund: 'ministering' [We]. As part of the genitive phrase ἔργον διακονίας 'the work of ministry', this noun is also translated as an adjective modifying 'work': 'ministration work' [Lns]. This noun denotes the rendering of assistance or help by the performance of certain duties which are often of a humble nature [LN].

QUESTION—What relationship is indicated by πρός 'for', and the two occurrences of εἰς 'for'?

Πρός 'for' indicates Christ's purpose for giving or appointing the classes of people mentioned in 4:11 [AB, Alf, Alf-ed, Ba, Cal, Can, CBC, Ea, EBC, EGT, El, Ho, IB, ICC, LJ, My, NCBC, NIC, NTC, Rob, St, TH, TNTC, WBC, We, WeBC; all versions]: he gave apostles and others in order that they equip/perfect the saints.

1. The apostles, prophets, evangelists, pastors, and teachers are to equip/perfect the saints so that they (the saints) may do the work of ministry so that the body of Christ be built up [AB, Alf-ed, Can, EBC, EGT, IB, NCBC, NIC, NTC, Rob, St, TH, TNTC, We, WeBC].

1.1 Each prepositional phrase is the means for the accomplishment of the following phrase [AB, Can, EBC, EGT, IB, Lns, TNTC] and each indicates a slightly different set of actors [AB, Alf-ed, EBC, EGT, IB, NIC, NTC, Rob, St, TH, TNTC, We]: Christ gave the apostles, prophets, evangelists, pastors, and teachers to the church so that (πρός 'for') these may equip/perfect the saints, so that (εἰς 'for') these saints may do the work of ministry, so that (εἰς 'for') all the members of the church (both officers and laity) build up the body of Christ. With this construction, those possessing the gifts mentioned in 4:11 equip the saints, who do the work of ministry [AB, Alf-ed, Can, EBC, NIC, NTC, Rob, St, TH, TNTC, We], and so all members together build up the body of Christ [AB, Alf-ed, TNTC, We].

1.2 The first prepositional phrase with πρός 'for the perfecting/equipping of the saints', indicates the purpose for which Christ gave apostles, prophets, evangelists, pastors, and teachers to the church, while the two succeeding phrases with πρός 'for the work of ministry' and 'for the building up of the body of Christ', indicate the function of these officers, consequently, the actors in the first and last prepositional phrases are the same, with the actors in the second prepositional phrase being the saints [NCBC, WeBC]: (Christ gave the apostles, prophets, evangelists, pastors, and teachers to the church) so that (πρός 'for') these may equip/perfect the saints so that (εἰς 'for') these saints may do the work of ministry, so that (εἰς 'for') the apostles, prophets, etc., build up the body of Christ.

2. The apostles, prophets, evangelists, pastors, and teachers are to equip/perfect the saints, do the work of ministry, and so build up the body of Christ [Alf, Ba, Cal, Ea, El, Ho, ICC, LJ, My, WBC; KJV]. This verse gives three purposes for the gift of the ministries mentioned in 4:11 with the actors in all three phrases being the ministers mentioned in 4:11 [Alf, Ba, Cal, Ea, ECWB, ICC, LJ, My, WBC; KJV].

2.1 The three prepositional phrases are coordinate and parallel with each other [WBC; KJV]: (Christ gave the apostles, etc., to the church) to equip/perfect the saints, to do the work of the ministry, and to build up of the body of Christ.

2.2 The first prepositional phrase with πρός 'for the perfecting/equipping of the saints', gives the more remote, ultimate purpose and the following two phrases with εἰς, 'for the work of ministry' and 'for the building up of the body of Christ', give intermediate purposes, the order of thought in these two phrases being inverted [Alf, Cal, Ea, El, Ho, ICC, LJ, My]: Christ gave these apostles, etc., to the church for the work of the ministry, to build up the body of Christ, in order that the saints might be perfected. The order of thought is inverted, the logical order being: he has given teachers for (εἰς) the work of the ministry, for (εἰς) the edifying of his body, in order to (πρός) the perfecting of his saints [Ea, El].

2.3 The first two prepositional phrases give the immediate purpose and are inverted, and the third gives the ultimate purpose [ECWB]: Christ gave these apostles, etc., to the church for the work of the ministry, with a view to perfecting the saints, unto building up the body of Christ [ECWB].

QUESTION—What is meant by τὸν καταρτισμόν τῶν ἁγίων 'the perfecting/equipping of the saints'?

1. This refers to the equipping, preparing, conditioning, or training of the saints [AB, Can, DNTT, EGT, IB, ISBE2, Lns, MNTC, NCBC, NIC, NTC, Si-ed, St, TD, TH; NASB, NIV, NRSV, REB, TEV, TNT]: to prepare the saints. The noun refers to the preparation for perfection, but not to the perfection itself [DNTT].
2. This refers to completing or perfecting imperfect Christians [Alf, Ba, Cal, Ea, ECWB, El, Ho, ICC, LJ, My, Rob, TNTC, WBC, We; KJV, NJB]: to perfecting the saints. The notion of completion also includes the area of meaning of the first interpretation, making complete by restoration or training [WBC]. The idea is the perfect and harmonious development of each power for active service in due connection with the other powers [We].
    2.1 This refers to making the church complete in love, knowledge, and order [Ba].
    2.2 This refers to the administration of the church [Cal, Ea; NJB]: to the administration of the saints. The word means 'perfection' so what Paul is expressing is a just and orderly arrangement, the orderly administration of divine law [Cal].
    2.3 This refers to the ultimate perfection of the saints [Alf, El, My]: in order to ultimately bring the saints to perfection. The nature of this perfecting is explained in 4:13 [El].

QUESTION—What is meant by διακονία 'ministry'?

1. This word refers to service of an official kind in the Church, that of ministerial service, the ministry [El, Ho, ICC, LJ, My, TD].
2. This word refers to a more general sense of service [DNTT, EGT, IB, Lns, MNTC, NCBC, NIC, NTC, Rob, St, TD, TH, TNTC, WBC]. The fact that this word occurs without the article points to the more general sense [EGT, Lns]. The noun refers to all services performed within the Christian community [DNTT, TD] for its edification [TD]. The service these saints are to perform is ministering to one another [Lns, NCBC]. This corresponds to 'the grace given to every one of us' (4:7), which is the topic of this section [Rob].

for[a] (the) building-up[b] of-the body[c] of-the Christ,

LEXICON—a. εἰς (LN 89.57): 'for' [AB, El, Lns, NIC, Rob; KJV, NRSV, REB, TNT], 'with a view to' [NTC], 'in order to' [LN; TEV], 'for the purpose of' [LN], 'so that' [NIV], 'to' [TH; NASB]. This preposition is conflated with 'building' and translated as an infinitive: 'to build up'

[NAB, NJB]. The preposition denotes the direction of an action to its specific end [TD].
b. οἰκοδομή (LN **42.34**) (BAGD 1.b.β. p. 559): 'the building up' [El, NIC, NTC, TH, WBC; NASB, REB, TNT], 'upbuilding' [Lns], 'the building' [Rob], 'the edifying' [KJV]. This noun is also translated as a gerund: 'building' [AB], 'building up' [We; NRSV]; as a verb: 'to build up' [LN; NAB, NJB, TEV], 'to be built up' [BAGD; NIV], 'to receive edification, to be edified' [BAGD]. This noun may focus either upon the event of building up or upon the result of that event [LN]; here it is used figuratively of the process of building, construction, and has reference to spiritual strengthening [BAGD].
c. σῶμα (LN **11.34**) (BAGD 5. p. 800): 'body' [AB, BAGD, El, Lns, NIC, NTC, Rob, TH, WBC; all versions except NJB], 'Body' [We; NJB], 'the church which is like a body' [LN].

QUESTION—What is meant by οἰκοδομήν 'building up' and how does it conflate with σῶμα 'body'?

1. This is a dead metaphor and means 'edifying, edification' [Cal, EBC (probably), Ho, ICC; KJV]: for the edification of the body of Christ. This is the same thing as what was called 'the perfecting of the saints' in the first phrase. It consists in our being united (or consolidated [EBC]) in the one body of Christ through the preaching of the word [Cal].
2. The metaphor is retained and οἰκοδομήν means 'building up' [AB, Alf, Ba, Can, Ea, ECWB, EGT, El, IB, ISBE, LJ, Lns, MNTC, NCBC, NIC, NTC, Rob, Si-ed, St, TH, TNTC, WBC, We, WeBC; all versions except KJV]: for the building up of the body of Christ. The noun οἰκοδομή is figurative speech for spiritual edification, which refers to everything that develops our spiritual life [Lns]. The word carries the image of the addition of each element which is needed for the completion of the body of Christ [We]. Whereas the word denoted the edifice in 2:21, here the word denotes the process of erection [Ea]. The two metaphors of the Church as a building and as a body are mixed here [AB, DNTT, EGT, LJ, My, Rob, Si-ed, TD, TH], but the controlling idea is the body [LJ, Rob, Si-ed, TD] because this image is more adequate for what he wants to say respecting the growth and unity of the Church [TNTC] whereas, in 2:21, the controlling idea was an edifice (the temple) and the thought of biological growth was introduced [DNTT, Rob, Si-ed, TD, WBC]. Conflation of metaphors may indicate an insufficiency of any one figure of speech to convey the intended image exactly. Actually, in this verse, the diverse metaphors are mutually corrective. To speak merely of the growth of the body would convey nothing more than the further development of an organism according to the laws of internal cellular processes. On the other hand, a building metaphor alone would depict the church as a mechanical composite [AB].

4:13 until[a] all we-attain[b] to[c] the unity[d] of-the faith and the knowledge[e] of-the Son of-God,

LEXICON—a. μέχρι (LN 67.119) (BAGD 2 p. 515): 'until' [AB, BAGD, LN, Lns, NIC, NTC, TH, WBC; NASB, NIV, NJB, NRSV, REB], 'till' [El, Rob, We; KJV, NAB], 'until in the end' [TNT], 'and so' [TEV]. This term denotes the continuous extent of time up to a given point [LN].

    b. aorist act. subj. of καταντάω (LN **13.16**) (BAGD 2.a. p.415): 'to attain (to)' [BAGD, **LN**, NIC, NTC, TH, WBC, We; NASB, REB], 'to arrive at' [BAGD, El, Lns], 'to reach' [NIV, NJB], 'to achieve, to come to be' [LN], 'to come (to)' [Rob; KJV, NRSV], 'to come to meet' [AB], 'to become' [NAB, TNT], 'to come together' [TEV]. The subjunctive mode is used here to indicate the indefinite future [HG], or a punctiliarly conceived future event [Tu]. It indicates the eventual, expected, and contemplated result of ἔδωκεν 'he gave' in 4:11 [Alf, Ea, EBC, EGT, El]. The subjunctive mode also carries a perfective sense: 'shall have attained' [EGT].

    c. εἰς with accusative object (LN 84.16): 'to' [LN, NTC, Rob, TH, WBC; NASB, NRSV, REB, TEV], 'unto' [We], 'at' [El, Lns], 'in' [KJV], not explicit [AB, NIC; NAB, NIV, NJB, TNT]. The preposition is omitted by making 'unity of the faith' the direct object of the verb 'to attain' [AB, NIC; NAB, NIV, NJB, TNT].

    d. ἑνότης (LN **63.3**) (BAGD p. 267): 'unity' [BAGD, El, LN, NIC, NTC, Rob, WBC, We; KJV, NASB, NIV, NJB, NRSV, REB], 'oneness' [LN, Lns, TH; TEV], 'one' [NAB]. This is also translated as an adjective modifying 'faith': 'unifying' [AB]. The clause καταντήσωμεν εἰς τὴν ἑνότητα τῆς πίστεως 'we shall attain to the unity of the faith' is translated 'we become one in that unity which comes through believing' [TNT].

    e. ἐπίγνωσις (LN 28.2) (BAGD p. 291): 'knowledge' [AB, BAGD, Lns, NIC, Rob, TH, WBC, We; all versions except TNT], 'full knowledge' [El], 'clear knowledge' [NTC], 'knowledge about' [LN]. This noun is also translated as a verb: 'to know' [TNT].

QUESTION—What relationship is indicated by μέχρι 'until'?

This conjunction introduces a temporal clause which defines the building up of the Church in terms of all its members attaining a goal described by three prepositional phrases with εἰς 'unto' that explain this goal from three aspects. This conjunction has both a prospective [Alf, Can, Ea, El, My, NCBC, WBC] and a final [TH, WBC] force. The ministers are to carry out their work both until and in order that the Church will reach this goal [WBC]. This conjunction expresses the final goal, the ultimate result, of all that has preceded from 4:11 [TH]. It indicates the duration of the offices of ministry mentioned in 4:11 [Alf, Can, Ea] (in fact, of *all* the ministerial work of the Church [NCBC]) or the time up to which this arrangement will last [El, My]. They will last until all Christians arrive at the state of complete unity and entire perfection [Ba, Can], that is, so long as the Church is in the world [Cal, My]. This does not mean the particular ministerial offices mentioned in 4:11 are permanent, but that the ministerial nature of these offices will continue until the Church reaches its goal [Ho].

QUESTION—What is the relationship in this verse between the three phrases each beginning with the preposition εἰς 'to'?

1. The three prepositions are parallel and dependent upon the verb [AB, Rob, TH, WBC, We].
   1.1 The prepositions introduce three coordinate phrases describing the nature of the church's goal of maturity [Rob, TH, WBC, We]: until we all attain to the unity of faith, until we attain to the mature man, and until we attain to the measure of the stature of the fullness of Christ. The first describes the intellectual goal [We] as the Church's unity in faith and knowledge [WBC, We]. The last two describe the goal in terms of the Church's completed state [WBC], one as maturity, and the last as conformity to the standard of Christ [We].
   1.2 The prepositions introduce the goal toward which the church is moving by introducing three parallel utterances about Christ [AB]: until we all come to meet the Son of God in his unifying faithfulness and knowledge, the Perfect Man, the Messiah in his perfection as the standard of manhood. The whole of 4:13 presents one goal in three steps: that the Messiah is in person the perfection of believers. When the church meets this man, Christ, these three goals will be attained in a simultaneous manner [AB].
2. The prepositions introduce three phrases, the first two being parallel to each other and dependent upon the verb, and indicating two goals for which the ministerial offices of the Church are intended. The third phrase describes the second [Ba, Can, EBC, ECWB, LJ, TD; NAB, NIV, NJB, REB, TEV, TNT]: until we all attain to the unity of faith and the state of the perfect man, that is, the measure of the stature of the fullness of Christ. The first goal is unity of faith and knowledge of the Son of God, the second is that of the full-grown man, the formation of Christ in the soul up to the stature of Christ's own fullness [Can, ECWB, LJ]. The first phrase is the means of the second and the third explains the second. By unity of faith and knowledge of Christ as the Son of God, the church reaches maturity. The third phrase explains the ultimate end in view [EBC, LJ].
3. The prepositions introduce three phrases, the second phrase in apposition with the first phrase and the third phrase in apposition with the second [Alf, Ea, EGT, El, Ho, IB, Lns, My, St; NASB, NRSV]: until we all attain to the unity of faith, that is, the mature man, which is the measure of the stature of the fullness of Christ.

QUESTION—What is indicated by the genitive construction τὴν ἑνότητα τῆς πίστεως καὶ τῆς ἐπιγνώσεως τοῦ υἱοῦ τοῦ θεου 'the unity of the faith and of the knowledge of the Son of God'?

1. The unity of the faith refers to the act of believing and the knowledge refers to acquaintance or experience with the Son of God [Alf, Cal, Can, ECWB, EGT, El, Ho, Lns, St, TH, TNTC].

1.1 'Faith' and 'knowledge' both express the source or means of the unity [EGT, Ho, St, TH]: believers are to be united together by believing in the Son of God and by personal experience or acquaintance with the Son of God. This does not mean 'to a point where we all agree about our faith and about our knowledge concerning the Son of God'. The passage is not about different doctrines and heresies, but about the unity of believers. It means 'being like one in the way we trust Christ and in the way we experience the Son of God' [TH].

1.2 'Knowledge' is used epexegetically to explain faith [Cal, TNTC]: believers are to be united together by believing in the Son of God, that is, by knowing the Son of God. 'Knowledge' was added to 'the unity of the faith' to explain the nature of true faith and of what it consists [Cal]. The addition of 'knowledge' emphasizes the fact that faith is more than just the acceptance of a collection of doctrine, it is unity in 'the knowledge of the Son of God', which also comes from the deepest possible fellowship with that Person [TNTC].

1.3 'Knowledge' gives the result of 'the unity of the faith' [Alf, ECWB, El, Lns]: believers are to be united together by believing in the Son of God, resulting in their further knowing the Son of God.

1.4 'Knowledge' is only associated with 'the unity of the faith' as another quality necessary for maturity (ἄνδρα τέλειον 'mature man') to be achieved [Can]: believers are to be united by believing in the Son of God in association with full acquaintance with him.

2. 'The unity of the faith' refers to the act of believing and 'the knowledge' is doctrine concerning the Son of God [Ea]: believers are to be united together by believing in the Son of God and by a unity in their doctrine about the Son of God. 'Unity of knowledge' is also specified by the apostle, for some are not fully informed in some areas of truth and are ignorant and erring in other areas, while others excel in different areas of truth. All are to be characterized by completeness and harmony in their perception of truth concerning the Savior [Ea]. We are to arrive at oneness both in regards to our faith and our knowledge [Ea (and Lns, My, WBC in support of 1. above and 4. below)]. Some knowledge is necessary to faith and faith, in its turn, produces more knowledge. Unity of faith with knowledge is implied in this interpretation, but is not the prominent idea [Ea].

3. 'The unity of the faith' is that believers realize they have a common experience in believing and 'the knowledge' refers to acquaintance or experience [EBC, NIC, NTC, Rob].

3.1 Τοῦ υἱοῦ τοῦ θεοῦ 'the Son of God' is attached to ἐπιγνώσεως 'knowledge' only [EBC]: believers are to be united together by the realization of their common experience of believing and by their personal experience of knowing the Son of God. The realization of unity will come from an increasing knowledge of Christ as the Son of God in both personal and corporate experience [EBC].

3.2 Τοῦ υἱοῦ τοῦ θεοῦ 'the Son of God' is attached to both τὴν ἑνότητα τῆς πίστεως 'the unity of the faith' and τῆς ἐπιγνώσεως 'the knowledge' [NIC, NTC, Rob]: believers are to be united together by the realization of their common experience of believing in and being united with the Son of God, and by their personal experience of knowing him. The 'unity of faith' is virtually the same as the previously mentioned 'unity of the Spirit' [NIC]. When unity is ultimately reached by all the saints, it will be a spiritual oneness, not an intellectual one. It will be a consciously realized unity produced by faith in and knowledge of the Son of God. Though we are one now, then we shall know ourselves to be one [Rob].

4. 'The unity of the faith' is doctrine and practice held in common and 'the knowledge' is personal experience or acquaintance with the Son of God [CBC, IB, ICC, My, NCBC, WBC].

4.1 'The Son of God' is attached to 'knowledge' only, with 'knowledge' indicating that knowledge is also a source or means of unity [NCBC, WBC]: believers are to be united together by their body of doctrine and by the knowledge of the Son of God. Syntactically, the repetition of the definite article with 'knowledge' makes it likely that 'the Son of God' goes only with 'knowledge' [WBC]. 'The unity of the faith' is the consequence of believers' deep awareness of Christ as the Son of God. The 'unity of the faith' is the 'one faith' mentioned in 4:5. As it was there, it is also likely here that 'faith' is used absolutely [NCBC]. This knowledge is that referred to in 1:17–19 and 3:16–19. Such knowledge of what is given in the 'one Lord' (4:5) will also have the quality of oneness [WBC].

4.2 'The Son of God' is attached to both 'the unity of the faith' and 'the knowledge' as its source or means [CBC, IB, ICC, My]: believers are to be united together by their body of doctrine concerning the Son of God and by their knowing the Son of God. In 4:3 this unity was viewed objectively as 'the unity of the Spirit' in terms of its source and sphere. Here it is viewed subjectively in terms of its thought content and experience [IB]. 'Knowledge' does not just explain 'faith' [ICC], but is a condition of it, and is presented as a distinct notion [ICC, My].

5. 'The unity of the faith' refers to both the act of believing and the body of doctrine and practice held in common, and 'the knowledge' is acquaintance or experience with the Son of God [Ba, LJ]. 'Knowledge' is not intellectual knowledge and apprehension; it is knowledge based upon a personal relationship [LJ].

5.1 'The faith' and 'the knowledge' both produce unity among believers [LJ]: believers are to be united together by believing the body of truth about the person of the Son of God and by personal experience or acquaintance with the Son of God.

5.2 'Knowledge' gives the purpose of 'the unity of the faith' [Ba]: believers are to be united together by believing the same truths and having the

same confidence in the Son of God, in order to have the same acquaintance with the Son of God.
6. 'The unity' refers to a unity between 'faith' and 'knowledge' [MNTC, TD]: believers will be united when their body of faith and knowledge about the Son of God become one. The goal of the community is growth toward unity and ripeness of knowledge, which is a certain knowledge of divine truth in contrast to the variety and changeableness of human opinion. The unity guarantees the security and solidity of faith, its one basis being the unity and the historicity of the person of Christ. This goal is the task of the divine word and the Church's ministry [TD].
7. The phrase refers to the Son of God's unity of his faithfulness and his knowledge [AB]: until we all come to meet the Son of God's own unifying faithfulness and knowledge. The next phrases explain this faith and knowledge as qualities inherent in the Perfect Man and in Messiah's perfection. The noun πίστις 'faith' here refers to Christ's faithfulness to God and consequently to his faithfulness to his people. Therefore the phrase ἑνότητα τῆς πίστεως 'unity of faith' refers to the total, integral and comprehensive relationship to both God and man, in which the Son of God lives united with God. The noun ἐπιγνώσεως 'knowledge' refers to the Son of God's knowledge both of the bride and of God [AB].

to[a] a mature/perfect[b] man,[c]

LEXICON—a. εἰς with accusative object (LN 84.16): 'to' [LN, NTC, Rob, TH, WBC; NASB, NRSV, REB], 'unto' [El, We; KJV], 'at' [Lns], not explicit [AB]. It is omitted by making 'man' appositional to the 'Son of God' [AB]. This preposition is also translated as a verb: 'to become' [NIV, TEV], 'to form' [NAB, NJB]. It is also translated as a clause: 'reaching the dimensions of' [NIC], 'then we shall have achieved' [TNT].

b. τέλειος (LN **88.100**) (BAGD 2.a.α p. 809): 'mature' [BAGD, LN, TH, WBC; NASB, NIV, REB, TEV], 'fully mature' [NIC], 'maturity' [NRSV], 'perfect' [AB, Rob; KJV, NAB, NJB, TNT], 'full-grown' [BAGD, El, Lns, NTC, We], 'grownup' [LN], 'adult' [BAGD]. This usage of the term focuses upon maturity in behavior [LN].

c. ἀνήρ (LN 9.1) (BAGD 2. p. 66): 'man' [El, LN, Lns, NIC, NTC, Rob, TH, We; KJV, NAB, NASB], 'Man' [AB; NJB], 'manhood' [REB, TNT], 'person' [LN, WBC], 'human being, individual' [LN], 'people' [TEV], not explicit [NIV, NRSV]. It is conflated into 'mature' [NIV, NRSV]. This noun does not refer to a generic 'mankind' [AB, Lns, Rob, TH], but rather denotes an adult male [AB, BAGD, LN, Lns, Rob, TH, WBC].

QUESTION—What is meant by ἄνδρα τέλειον 'a mature/perfect man'?
1. This is a metaphorical reference to the church in its attainment of the state of spiritual maturity [Alf, Ba, Cal, Can, CBC, DNTT, Ea, EBC, ECWB, EGT, El, Ho, IB, ICC, LJ, MNTC, My, NIC, Rob, St, TD, TH, TNTC, WBC, WeBC; NJB (note)]. This describes the attainment of faith and knowledge as a coming to maturity [Can, Ho, IB, My, NIC, St, TNTC].

The singular number indicates that the corporate nature of the passage is being continued [IB, St, TH, TNTC, WBC], even emphasized [TH]. It indicates the unity of which the apostle has been speaking [Alf, Ea, EGT, El]. It refers to the summation of all believers in the one perfect Man, Christ Jesus [Alf, DNTT, TD, WBC; NJB (note)], Christ as the head and Christians as forming the body [DNTT, LJ, TD; NJB (note)]. The maturity of the 'perfect man' is contrasted with the childlikeness which follows [Alf, Ba, DNTT, Ea, EGT, El, ICC, My, Rob, TH, TNTC, WBC].

1.1 The image, at this point, is nonspecific, it refers to any mature man [Ba, Cal, Ea, El, Ho, IB, My]: to a mature man. Reference is to the complete man, the man who has reached his full growth and is in a state of strength, vigor, and wisdom [Ba]. Whoever is in Christ is in all respects, fully, a perfect man [Cal]. The singular suggests the idea of the holy personality into which they are united and consummated [El], forming one, ethical person [My].

1.2 The image involves not only the maturity of any full-grown man, but also the image of the corporate body of Christ [Can, DNTT, EBC, EGT, ICC, LJ, MNTC, NIC, Rob, St, TD, TH, TNTC, WBC; NJB (note)]: to the maturing of us as the body of Christ. This is a reiteration of the church as the 'one new man' in 2:15 [EBC, EGT, ICC, Rob, St, TD, TH, TNTC, WBC; NJB (note)], Christ as the head and Christians as forming the body [DNTT, LJ, TD; NJB (note)]. Believers are to grow out of their individualism into the corporate oneness of the full-grown man [Rob].

1.3 The image is the person of Christ himself as the standard of the Church's maturity [CBC]: to the maturity of Christ himself. The mature manhood demanded of believers is that of Christ's perfection in his earthly life [CBC].

2. This is a metaphorical reference to a state of spiritual maturity by the individual believer [Lns, NCBC, NTC, Si, We]: to a mature man. Since οἱ πάντες 'we all' form the church, it is incongruous to make the singular ἄνδρα τέλειον 'a mature man' the Church. Neither can it refer to the body of Christ [Lns]. It is difficult to apply such a personal phrase as ἄνδρα τέλειον 'a mature man' to a community [NCBC].

3. This is a reference to the person of Christ [AB]: the Perfect Man. This differs somewhat from 1.3 above, in that AB interprets this passage as referring to the Church *meeting* Christ, the Perfect Man, at his Coming, rather than having primary reference to the attainment of a standard. The adjective means 'perfect' in the sense of 'sinless' [AB].

to[a] (the) measure[b] of-(the)-maturity/stature[c] of-the fullness[d] of-the Christ,

LEXICON—a. εἰς with accusative object (LN 84.16): 'to' [LN, NTC, Rob, TH, WBC; NASB, NRSV], 'unto' [El, We; KJV], 'at' [Lns], not explicit [AB, NIC; NAB, NJB, REB, TNT]. The preposition is omitted by relating 'measure' to the previous context in various ways: it is placed in apposition to 'unity of faith' [AB]; it is placed in apposition to 'we' [NJB]; it is placed in apposition to 'a mature man' [NIC]; it is made into a clause modifying 'the mature man' [NAB, REB, TNT]. This preposition is also translated as a verb: 'to attain to' [NIV], 'to reach to' [TEV].

b. μέτρον (LN 81.1) (BAGD 2.b. p. 515): 'measure' [BAGD, El, LN, Lns, NIC, NTC, Rob, TH, WBC, We; KJV, NASB, NRSV], 'whole measure' [NIV], 'standard' [AB], not explicit [NJB, TNT]. This noun is also translated as a verb: 'to measure' [REB], 'to come' [NAB], and as a verbal phrase 'to reach to the very height of' [TEV]. See this word at 4:7.

c. ἡλικία (LN 67.156, 81.4) (BAGD 1.c.α. (preferred), or 2. p. 345): 'stature' [BAGD (2.), El, LN (81.4), NIC, NTC, Rob, TH, WBC, We; KJV, NAB, NASB, NRSV, REB, TEV], 'bodily stature' [BAGD (2.)], 'height' [LN (81.4)], 'age' [BAGD (1.c.α.), Lns], 'prime, of age, mature' [LN (67.156)], 'maturity' [BAGD (1.c.α.), TNT], 'fully mature' [NJB], 'manhood' [AB], not explicit [NIV]. It is omitted by conflating it with 'measure': 'whole measure' [NIV]. This noun denotes the period of life when a person is at his prime and mature [LN (67.156)], the age of strength [BAGD (1.c.α.)], or it may denote height as a dimension of the stature of a living object [BAGD (2.), LN (81.4)].

d. πλήρωμα (LN 59.32) (BAGD 3.b. p. 672): 'fullness' [BAGD, El, LN, Lns, NIC, NTC, Rob, TH, WBC, We; KJV, NASB, NIV, NJB], 'full measure, completeness' [LN], 'perfection' [AB], 'sum total' [BAGD]. This noun is also translated as an adjective modifying 'stature': 'full' [NAB, NRSV, REB, TEV, TNT]. As the dependent genitive it follows ἡλικίας 'maturity/stature', modifying it [Tu].

QUESTION—What is meant by the genitive construction μέτρον ἡλικίας τοῦ πληρώματος τοῦ Χριστοῦ 'measure of the maturity/stature of the fullness of Christ'?

1. Christ is the one who possesses the 'measure of stature of the fullness' [Alf, Ba, Cal, Can, CBC, Ea, EBC, ECWB, EGT, El, Ho, IB, ICC, IDB, ISBE2, Lns, NCBC, NIC, NTC, St, TH, WBC; NAB, NASB, NJB, NRSV, REB, TEV, TNT]: the measure of the stature of Christ's fullness. This expression explains what the apostle means by 'perfect manhood' [Ea, ECWB, EGT, El, Ho, IB, NCBC, St, TH]. This pictures the body of Christ as having a gradual growth, like a natural body, and coming at last to full and complete stature. The measure of this body's perfection is that it is to be the fullness of Christ, that in order to fit its head [Can]. But each can partake of it only up to the 'measure' which God grants him. When he so partakes of it he is relatively (not absolutely) perfect [ECWB]. It refers to the maturity level God or Christ has set for the Church in order to accomplish his purpose for it [ISBE2, TH].

1.1 Christ's πληρώματος 'fullness' possesses the qualities specified by the other two nouns in this chain [Ba, Can, ECWB, EGT, El, IDB, ISBE2, NCBC, WBC; NASB]: the measure of the stature of Christ's fullness. The genitive phrase τοῦ πληρώματος τοῦ Χριστοῦ 'the fullness of Christ' is possessive [El], i.e., 'the measure of the stature belonging to

Christ's fullness'. It has reference to the completeness, the maturity of character which Christ has realized, both as an individual and as the Body of which Christians are members [IDB]. 'Fullness' has reference to the attainment of piety and knowledge, so that believers become like Christ in this respect [Ba, Can] and have no more need for ministers to teach them [Can]. 'Fullness' has reference to all the graces and gifts that fill God or Christ [EGT, ISBE2, WBC], which dwell in the Church, and which the Church is to seek through increased maturity so as to give more room for these attributes and powers to dwell in it [WBC]. It means total Christlikeness [NCBC].

 1.2 Πληρώματος 'fullness' modifies μέτρον 'measure' [EBC]: the full measure of Christ's perfection.

 1.3 Πληρώματος 'fullness' modifies ἡλικίας 'maturity/stature' [Cal, CBC, Ea, Ho, ICC, Lns, NIC, NTC, TH, Tu; NAB, NRSV, REB, TEV, TNT]: the measure of Christ's full stature. 'The fullness of Christ' marks the measure of this stature [Lns, NTC]. The maturity is that to which belongs the fullness of Christ, the full possession of the gifts of Christ [ICC]. It denotes Christ's full manhood [NIC].

2. Christ is the one who fills and ἡλικίας 'stature, manhood' is synonymous with πληρώματος 'fullness, perfection' or serves as an explication of it [AB, My]: Christ who perfects us and is himself the standard of perfection/manhood. The Messiah makes the church perfect and full rather than she him [AB]. The ἡλικίας 'stature' is characterized by πληρώματος 'fullness, perfection', πληρώματος defining the age as that to which the fullness of Christ is peculiar. Πληρώματος 'fullness, perfection' refers to all the gifts of grace that Christ communicates [My].

3. Christ is the one who is fulfilled when the Church achieves the full stature intended for it [ISBE, MNTC, Rob, We]: to the measure of the stature of the fulfilled Christ. It refers to the Church as Christ's larger incarnation and to the maturity level God or Christ has set for the Church in order for it to accomplish his purpose for it. When the Church attains such a development or stature, Christ will have his fulfillment in the Church [MNTC]. When all the saints have reached the goal of unity, Christ will have been fulfilled [ISBE, Rob]. Christ and the Church together are ultimately the one Christ—the Christ that is to be [Rob]. The Church is also the fullness of Christ here, πληρώματος 'fullness' referring to the presence, power, agency, and riches of Christ in the Church [ISBE].

QUESTION—Does this phrase refer to Christ in his present, glorified state or to his earthly life?

 1. This refers to Christ's perfection in his glorified state [AB, Ba, Can, EBC, ECWB (probably), EGT, Ho, IDB, LJ, Lns, NIC, Rob, WBC]. This image of Christ in 'fullness' is the absolutely perfect humanity, through which is manifested the image of God [ECWB]. It looks at Christ as embodying the sum of the qualities which reside in him as Head of the Church [EGT].

2. This refers to Christ's perfection in his earthly life [CBC, NTC]. The 'full stature of Christ' was his perfection in his earthly life and consisted in his unwavering belief that the cause of God would triumph and in his complete obedience to God's will [CBC]. This is a fullness of him who completely fulfilled the earthly mission for which he had been anointed [NTC].

QUESTION—What is meant by ἡλικίας 'maturity/stature'?
  1. It means 'maturity' [AB, Cal, DNTT, ICC, ISBE2, Lns, My, My-ed, TD, TNTC]. It refers to full or mature age, but does not mean 'old', for this word implies a vigor of spiritual life that is continually advancing [Cal]. The context deals with maturity, not physical stature [ICC, My]. Even if 'stature' were unambiguously expressed, it could only be understood as a mark of the mature man [ICC].
  2. It means 'stature' [Alf, Ba, Can, Ea, ECWB, EGT, El, Ho, ISBE, MNTC, NIC, WBC, We]. It refers here to 'stature' more than 'age' because the phrase of which it is a part is parallel to (in apposition to [EGT]) ἀνὴρ τέλειος 'perfect man' (a man of mature stature), and because the following verses, especially 4:16, are given the prominent idea of growth, not age [Ea, ECWB, EGT, El]. The word ἡλικίας 'stature' indicates that Christ is the standard for moral character, he is the measure to be reached [Ba].
  3. It means both, i.e., 'manhood, a full-grown man' [LJ, TH]. Ultimately both 'age' and 'stature' are involved [LJ, TH], for the picture involved is the development of a child into manhood [LJ].

QUESTION—When will the goal expressed in this verse be obtained?
  The point of whether this can be achieved in this life is irrelevant; the point is that this is the Christian's ambition [TNTC].
  1. It will be obtained only in heaven [AB, Ba, Cal, Can, Ho, LJ, TD, We]. The ministers of the church are needed so long as we remain on earth for weakness and ignorance are always with us. We shall never reach the unity to which we aspire until our flesh is laid aside [Cal]. Though the goal is eschatological, the ministers of the Church are to strive toward meeting this goal [TD].
  2. It may be obtainable while on earth [DNTT, Ea, ECWB, EGT, El, ICC, ISBE2, Lns, My, NCBC, WeBC]. This goal is achieved when believers are no longer carried about by every wind of doctrine (4:14) [DNTT, ISBE2]. Perfection in an absolute sense will not be obtained while we are still on earth, but the apostle is writing about the results of the ministry as exercised in the church below [Ea, WeBC]. Each believer is expected to arrive at spiritual maturity, in turn, as he comes on the scene. Some mature much faster than others [Lns]. The Church will reach this state in a period of time just preceding the *Parousia* of Christ [My].

DISCOURSE UNIT: 4:14–16 [AB, Alf, Rob, Si]. The topic is spiritual discernment and growth [Si], the goal of the Christian's duties as a member of the Church—to come to perfection in Christ [Alf].

4:14 so-that^a no-longer we-should-be children,^b

LEXICON—a. ἵνα (LN 89.49, 89.59): 'so that' [LN (89.49, 89.59), Lns, NTC, TH, WBC], 'that' [El, LN (89.49), Rob, We; KJV], 'as a result' [NASB], 'so as a result' [LN (89.49)], 'then' [NAB, NIV, NJB, TEV], 'in order that, for the purpose of' [LN (89.59)], not explicit [AB, NIC; NRSV, REB, TNT]. The relationship indicated by ἵνα...ὦμεν 'so that...we may be' is also translated by starting a new sentence [AB, NIC; NRSV, REB, TNT] with purpose/result and cohortative constructions: 'we are to be' [AB; REB], 'we shall be' [TNT], 'let us be' [NIC], 'we must be' [NRSV]. This is a marker of result, but in some cases it implies an underlying or indirect purpose [LN (89.49)]. This is a purpose marker for states or events [LN (89.59)].

b. νήπιος (LN 9.43) (BAGD 1.b.α. p. 537): 'child' [El, NTC, Rob, TH, WBC, We; KJV, NAB, NASB, NJB, NRSV, REB, TEV], 'little child' [TNT], 'small child' [LN], 'babe' [AB], 'infant' [BAGD, Lns, NIC; NIV]. This denotes a small child, older than a helpless infant, but probably no older than about three or four years of age [LN]. This is used figuratively of an immature Christian who views spiritual things from the viewpoint of a child [BAGD].

QUESTION—What relationship is indicated by ἵνα 'so that'?

1. It indicates another purpose for the giving of the gifts of 4:11 [Alf, Can, Ho, TD, WBC, We], yet subordinate to the purposes expressed in 4:12 [Alf, Ho]: he gave these ministries for the equipping of the saints, etc., in order that we should no longer be children. This verse is coordinate with 4:13 and not dependent upon it [We].
2. It indicates the purpose of setting the goal given in 4:13 before the readers [Ea, EGT, El, My]: until we all attain to the fullness of Christ in order that we may no longer be children. It is subordinate to the immediately preceding statement [EGT, El, My] and remotely dependent upon 4:11–12 [El]. As 4:13 set forth the limit put upon the bestowal of these gifts from Christ and the goal they were intended to reach, this verse now gives the purpose of setting such a goal before us and of the giving of the gifts of apostles, prophets, etc. [EGT, El]. In order to arrive at full maturity, they must first emerge out of the state of childhood [My].
3. It indicates an explanation of what the attainment of 4:13 means [EBC, ECWB, LJ, MNTC, NCBC, NIC, NTC]: until we all attain to the fullness of Christ, that is, that we should no longer be children. These verses characterize the ideal of full Christian maturity [NTC].
4. It indicates the actual result of the goal expressed in 4:13 [Lns]: until we all attain to the mature man with the result that we are no longer children.

This is the actual negative result of arriving at the goal; 4:15 will give the positive result [Lns].

QUESTION—What is meant by μηκέτι ὦμεν νήπιοι 'no longer may we be children'?

The negative μηκέτι 'no longer' implies something different from the condition of immaturity existing at the moment of writing [EGT, My]. The verb indicates progress between the states of childhood and manhood [Cal, Ea]. Since manhood is not achieved in this life and we are to move beyond childhood, the state of this life of progress is implied to be likened to youth [Cal].

being-tossed-to-and-fro-by/like-waves[a] and being-carried-about[b] by-every wind[c] of-teaching[d] in/caused-by/from[e] the trickery[f] of-men,

LEXICON—a. pres. mid./pass. participle of κλυδωνίζομαι (LN 16.12) (BAGD p. 436): 'to be tossed to and fro by waves' [Lns, NTC], 'to be tossed about by the waves' [LN; REB], 'to be tossed here and there by waves' [BAGD; NASB], 'to be tossed back and forth by the waves' [WBC; NIV], 'to be carried by the waves' [TEV], 'to be tossed by the waves' [AB; TNT], 'to be buffeted by waves' [TH], 'to be tossed to and fro' [El, Rob; KJV, NRSV], 'to be tossed here and there' [NAB], 'to be tossed one way and another' [NJB], 'to be tossed about' [NIC], 'to be storm-tossed' [We]. The imagery in this verse is based upon a person in a boat being tossed about by the waves [LN].

b. pres. pass. participle of περιφέρω (LN 15.190) (BAGD 2. p. 653): 'to be carried about' [LN, Lns, Rob, We; KJV, NAB, NASB], 'to be carried around' [LN, NIC], 'to be carried hither and thither' [NJB], 'to be carried here and there' [BAGD], 'to be carried' [TH], 'to be borne about' [El], 'to be whirled about' [AB], 'to be whirled around' [NTC; REB], 'to be blown about' [NRSV, TEV, TNT], 'to be blown here and there' [NIV], 'to be gusted here and there' [WBC]. This denotes being carried around from one place to another [LN]. It is possible that the figure here is that of a weathervane so that the meaning would then be 'to be turned around' [BAGD].

c. ἄνεμος (LN 14.4) (BAGD 2. p. 64): 'wind' [BAGD, El, LN, Lns, NIC, Rob, TH, WBC, We; KJV, NAB, NASB, NIV, NRSV, TNT], 'shifting wind' [TEV], 'gust' [AB, NTC], 'new gust' [NJB], 'fresh gust' [REB].

d. διδασκαλία (LN 33.224, 33.236) (BAGD 2. p. 191): 'teaching' [BAGD, LN (33.224, 33.236), Lns, NIC, TH, WBC; NIV, NJB, REB, TEV], 'false teaching' [TNT], 'doctrine' [El, LN (33.236), NTC, Rob, We; KJV, NAB, NASB, NRSV], 'what is taught' [LN (33.236)]. This noun is also translated as an adjective modifying ἀνέμῳ 'wind': 'doctrinal gust' [AB]. This noun denotes the provision of instruction in either a formal or informal setting [LN (33.224)]. It denotes the content of what is taught [BAGD, LN (33.236)].

e. ἐν with dative object (LN 89.26, 89.76, 90.6): 'in' [El, Lns, TH], 'by' [LN (89.76, 90.6), NTC, Rob, WBC; KJV, NASB, NIV, NRSV, TEV], 'through' [LN (89.76), NIC], 'because of' [LN (89.26)]. This preposition is also translated as a phrase: 'dupes of' [REB], 'victims of' [We], 'at the mercy of' [NJB, TNT]. It is also translated as a clause: 'caught in' [AB], 'that originates in' [NAB]. This is a marker of cause or reason with the focus being upon the instrument [LN (89.26)]. This is a marker of the means by which one event makes possible the occurrence of another event [LN (89.76)]. This is a marker of agency, sometimes implying the agent is used as an instrument [LN (90.6)].

f. κυβεία (LN **88.157**) (BAGD p. 456): 'trickery' [AB, BAGD, **LN**, NTC; NAB, NASB, NRSV], 'cunning' [WBC; NIV], 'craftiness' [BAGD, LN, NIC], 'deceit' [TH], 'fraud' [We], 'sleight' [El, Rob; KJV], 'gambling' [Lns]. This noun is also translated as an adjective modifying ἀνθρώπων 'men': 'cunning rogues' [REB], 'cunning men' [TNT], 'deceitful men' [TEV]. The phrase ἐν τῇ κυβείᾳ τῶν ἀνθρώπων 'in the trickery of men' is translated 'at the mercy of all the tricks people play' [NJB]. This noun denotes the trickery that results from craftiness [LN].

QUESTION—What is meant by the metaphorical use of the participles?

The sudden change of metaphor suggests the former metaphor of childishness was not really vivid to the writer [IB]. The metaphor portrays what Paul meant by ὦμεν νήπιοι 'we be children' [My, NIC]. These metaphors portray the helplessness just referred to [Lns]. They portray uncertainty [ISBE], or the instability and fickleness which is characteristic of childhood [Ea, EBC, Ho, NCBC, St]. They portray the distressing hesitation of those who do not place absolute reliance upon the word of God [Cal]. They may be separate metaphors or they may form a single metaphor [Ho].

QUESTION—How are these metaphors related?

1. The image of the waves and the image of the wind form separate metaphors [Cal, EBC, EGT, El, LJ]. There is disagreement concerning the image of the first metaphor. The second metaphor is that of straw or other light substances, being driven by the wind, often in opposite directions [Cal, Ho]. The metaphors portray the changefulness and agitation which are the results of unthinking submission to false teaching [EGT]. The second metaphor portrays the liability of the child to be misled and deceived because of its ignorance and gullibility [LJ].
    1.1 The first metaphor is that of being tossed *like* waves [Alf, El, Ho, LJ]. This is the meaning of the passive verb, it is not to be translated 'tossed about *by* the waves'. Thus the metaphor does not involve a ship [El]. This metaphor portrays the unstable, changeable nature of a child to react in excessive and extreme ways to things that happen to it [LJ].
    1.2 The first metaphor is that of a small ship upon the open sea, guided neither by skill nor design, but carried about by the force of the tempest [Cal].

2. The image of the waves and the image of the wind together form a single metaphor [AB, Ba, Ea, ECWB, Ho, IB, ICC, Lns, MNTC, My, NCBC, NIC, Rob, Si, St, TH, TNTC, WBC].
   2.1 The metaphor is about waves being tossed and carried about by the wind [AB, Ea, ICC, Rob]. Since ἀνέμῳ 'wind' and περιφερόμενοι 'carried about' are both most naturally connected with it [ICC, Rob], 'tossed about like the waves' is the better translation (corresponding to James 1:8) [ICC]. The image is that of the wind driving the waves [AB (probably), Ea].
   2.2 The metaphor is about a ship being tossed by waves and carried about by the wind [Ba, ECWB, Ho, IB, Lns, MNTC, My, NIC, Rob, Si, St, TH, TNTC, WBC] or flotsam and jetsam [NCBC, WBC] drifting at the mercy of a storm. This metaphor of confusion and lack of direction contrasts sharply with the goal-oriented language of 4:13 [WBC]. The erratic course of the ship suggests the tendency to seize eagerly upon any new opinion that is suggested from any quarter [IB].
3. The images of children, waves, and wind all form a single metaphor [NTC]. The picture is of children in a storm-tossed boat which they cannot control [NTC].

QUESTION—What relationship is indicated by the genitive construction παντὶ ἀνέμῳ τῆς διδασκαλίας 'every wind of teaching'?

The genitive διδασκαλίας 'teaching' defines what the image ἀνέμῳ 'wind' is intended to portray [DNTT, Ea, LJ, Lns, My, NCBC, NIC, TH, WBC]. The metaphor is applied to τῆς διδασκαλίας 'the teaching' to indicate the impulsive power that 'the teaching' possesses, not to portray its emptiness [Ea]. Others think that what is meant is changeableness [ICC, LJ, TH, TNTC] or instability [WBC].

1. 'Teaching' has an abstract reference [EGT, El, ICC, My, Rob]. The article τῆς indicates that doctrine in the abstract sense is intended [EGT, El, ICC, My, Rob]—every kind and every degree of it [EGT, El, WBC]. The almost technical sense that the singular διδασκαλία 'teaching' with the article has in the Pastorals does not apply here. This is a reference to false teaching in the guise of various religious philosophies that threatened to assimilate, and so to dilute or undermine, the Pauline teaching [WBC].
2. 'Teaching' has a definite reference [TD]. The author is thinking of a single διδασκαλία 'teaching', and this can only refer to the historically guaranteed witness concerning Jesus (4:1–11) being followed in the community. The fact that πάντι 'every' is attached to ἀνέμῳ 'wind', and not to διδασκαλίας 'teaching', indicates that Paul is cautioning his readers against being swayed by each variable wind that comes as representing itself as part of the community's doctrine and so claiming to be a revelation of the will of God [TD].

QUESTION—What relationship is indicated by the phrase ἐν τῇ κυβείᾳ 'in the trickery'?
1. It indicates the sphere within which the varying currents of doctrine exert their force [AB, Alf, EGT, El] or within which the doctrines are encompassed [We]: teaching that operates in the trickery of men, or teaching that is encompassed in the trickery of men. To make this instrumental would be a repetition of παντὶ ἀνέμῳ 'with every wind' [Alf, El] and mar the parallelism with the following ἐν ἀγάπῃ 'in love' (4:15) [El]. The contrast with the following ἐν ἀγάπῃ 'in love' (4:15) indicates that the preposition ἐν has its usual meaning of 'in' here [EGT]. The phrase stands in contrast to τῆς πίστεως καὶ τῆς ἐπιγνώσεως τοῦ υἱοῦ τοῦ θεοῦ 'the faith and knowledge of the Son of God' (4:13) [EGT, El].
2. It indicates the instrumental cause of the teaching [Ea, Ho, Rob, WBC; KJV] or the 'being carried about by every wind of teaching' [ICC, MNTC, My; NASB, NIV, NRSV, TEV, TNT]: being tossed by waves and carried about by every wind of teaching that is caused by the trickery of men. The phrase is attached to the whole clause governed by the participles κλυδωνιζόμενοι 'tossed about like the waves' and περιφερόμενοι 'being carried about', not just to περιφερόμενοι 'being carried about' [ICC, My]. Thus the instrumental sense is not pleonastic [ICC].
3. It indicates the source of the teaching [EBC; NAB]: teaching that comes from the trickery of men.

QUESTION—What is meant by κυβείᾳ 'trickery'?
1. It denotes deliberate trickery and fraud [AB, Alf, Cal, Can, Ea, EBC, ECWB, EGT, El, Ho, ICC, LJ, MM, MNTC, My, NIC, NTC, Rob, Si, St, TH, TNTC, WBC, We]. The word came to denote sleight of hand or deception because of the practice of using dice to cheat [Cal, Can, ECWB, El, Ho, ICC, MM, TH, TNTC, WBC, We]. Their dice are loaded [Si]. The phrase ἐν τῇ κυβείᾳ τῶν ἀνθρώπων 'in the trickery of men' indicates a second characteristic of childhood [Ea, ECWB], instability [ECWB], or the liability of being imposed upon [Ea] and deceived [EGT, Ho].
2. It denotes the element of chance [Ba, Lns] or fickleness [IB]. Up to this point the idea is the element of chance. Paul adds the element of deception and cheating with the next words, ἐν πανουργίᾳ 'in craftiness'. The lack of an article with πανουργίᾳ 'craftiness' indicates it is attached to ἐν τῇ κυβείᾳ τῶν ἀνθρώπων 'in the trickery of men' [Lns]. It suggests the fickleness of the dice rather than the cheating that frequently accompanies dice playing; therefore it involves no reference to trickery, but to men's fickleness [IB]. This term denotes a person whose opinions are the result of mere chance. He finds one person holding one opinion and another holding another opinion and allows himself to be influenced by them without any settled principles [Ba].

in[a] craftiness[b] for/in/in-accordance-with[c] the scheming[d] of-error,[e]

LEXICON—a. ἐν with dative object (LN 89.26, 89.76, 90.6): 'in' [El, Lns, TH], 'by' [LN (89.76, 90.6), NTC, Rob, WBC; NASB, NRSV], 'because of' [LN (89.26)], 'victims of' [We]. Not explicit [AB, NIC; KJV, NAB, NIV, NJB, REB, TEV, TNT].

  b. πανουργία (LN 88.270) (BAGD p. 608): 'craftiness' [BAGD, El, LN, Lns, WBC, We; NASB, NIV, NRSV], 'treachery' [LN], 'unscrupulousness' [NJB], '(evil) cunning' [BAGD], 'cunning' [TH], 'cunning craftiness' [KJV], 'trickery' [BAGD, NIC], 'talent' [NTC], 'skill' [NAB], 'experts' [AB]. This noun is conflated with μεθοδείαν 'scheming': 'schemes' [REB], 'wickedly plotting' [TNT]. It is combined with μεθοδείαν 'scheming' and translated as a clause: 'the tricks they invent' [TEV]. This noun denotes trickery that involves evil cunning [LN].

  c. πρός with accusative object (LN 89.7, 89.9, 89.60): 'for' [NTC], 'in' [AB, LN (89.7), WBC; NAB, NASB, NIV, NJB, NRSV], 'by' [TEV], 'for the purpose of' [LN (89.60)], 'after' [Lns], 'according to' [LN (89.9), Rob], 'in accordance with' [LN (89.9), TH], not explicit [REB, TEV, TNT]. This preposition is also translated by a relative pronoun: 'whereby' [KJV], 'which' [NIC]. It is also translated as a verb or verb phrase: 'to tend to' [El], 'to direct to further' [We]. This preposition is omitted and πανουργία 'craftiness' and μεθοδείαν 'scheming' are conflated into: 'schemes' [REB], 'tricks' [TEV].

  d. μεθοδεία (LN 88.158) (BAGD p. 499): 'scheming' [AB, BAGD, LN, MM, NTC, TH, WBC; NASB, NIV, NRSV], 'wiles' [Rob, We], 'craftiness' [BAGD, MM; KJV], 'deceit' [LN], 'expert method' [Lns], 'settled system' [El]. This noun is also translated as an adjective: 'deliberate' [NJB]. It is also translated as a verb: 'to scheme' [NIC], 'to propose' [NAB]. It is also translated as a phrase (combined with ἐν πανουργίᾳ 'by craftiness'): 'by the tricks they invent' [TEV], 'wickedly plotting' [TNT]. It is also conflated with πανουργία 'craftiness' into: 'schemes' [REB]. The genitive phrase τὴν μεθοδείαν τῆς πλάνης 'the scheming of error' is also translated 'they lie in wait to deceive' [KJV]. This noun denotes a crafty scheming done with intent to deceive [LN]. It indicates a deliberate, systematic plan [ECWB, El, LJ, MM, Rob] with a definite view to undermining the truth of God [EBC, LJ, TNTC].

  e. πλάνη (LN 31.8, 31.10) (BAGD p. 665): 'error' [BAGD, El, LN (31.10), Rob, TH, WBC, We; NAB], 'misleading belief, deceptive belief, mistaken view' [LN (31.10)], 'deception' [BAGD, LN (31.8), Lns; NJB], 'deceit, delusion' [BAGD]. This noun is also translated as an adjective modifying μεθοδείαν 'scheming': 'deceitful scheming' [AB, NTC; NASB, NIV, NRSV], 'deceitful schemes' [REB]. It is also translated as a verb: 'to deceive' [KJV]. It is also translated as a clause: 'to lead people/us astray' [NIC; TNT], 'who lead others into error' [TEV]. This noun denotes the action of causing someone to hold a wrong view. It may refer to more than just mistaken notions and involve deception of a behavioral nature

[LN (31.8, 31.10)]. This noun denotes the content of that which misleads or deceives [LN (31.10)]. This noun is used in Christian literature only in a figurative sense of wandering from the path of truth [BAGD].

QUESTION—What are the relationships between the terms πανουργία 'craftiness', μεθοδείαν 'scheming', and πλάνης 'error'?

This false teaching, πλάνης 'error', has a systematic process of deception that is peculiar to itself, μεθοδείαν 'scheming'. In order that this scheming may not fail or scare away its victims by an unguarded revealing of its nature and purpose, it is brought about by a special maneuver, πανουργία 'craftiness' [Ea]. The μεθοδείαν τῆς πλάνης 'scheming of error' is that which the πανουργία 'craftiness' has in view and to which it is naturally disposed [El].

QUESTION—What relationship is indicated by πρός 'in'?

1. It indicates the direction and purpose of πανουργία 'craftiness' [Alf, Can, Ea, EGT, El, ICC, Lns, My, NIC, NTC, TD, We]: in craftiness for carrying out the scheming of error.
2. It indicates the area or sphere in which πανουργία 'craftiness' operates [AB, WBC; NAB, NASB, NIV, NJB, NRSV]: in craftiness which operates in the scheming of error.
3. It indicates a standard of reference [Mo, Rob, TH]: by craftiness in accordance with the scheming of error.
4. It indicates the means by which the craftiness is carried out [KJV, TEV]: in craftiness by the scheming of error.

QUESTION—What is indicated by the genitive construction τὴν μεθοδείαν τῆς πλάνης 'the scheming of error'?

1. The genitive πλάνης 'of error' has adjectival force, describing τὴν μεθοδείαν 'the scheming' [AB, NTC, St, TNTC]: deceitful scheming.
2. The genitive πλάνης 'of error' acts as the subject of this phrase [Alf, Can, Ea, El, ICC, LJ, Lns, My, Rob (probably)]: the error that uses scheming. As the subject of this phrase, it forms a parallel with the preceding genitive τῇ κυβείᾳ τῶν ἀνθρώπων 'the trickery of men' [El]. The schemes are those that error adopts [Alf, Can, El], the article with πλάνης 'of error' almost personifying it [Can, El, ICC] as a dangerous opponent who lays a snare consisting of the mistakes and sophistries of men into which the immature believers are driven [Can]. The article personifies πλάνης 'of error' in the abstract (i.e., not to the extent of forming a metaphor for Satan) [El, My] and so renders the contrast to truth, expressed in the following ἀληθεύοντες 'speaking truth' (4:15) [El, Rob, WBC], more forcible and significant [El].
3. The genitive πλάνης 'of error' indicates the purpose [NIC] or result [EGT, WBC] of the μεθοδείαν 'scheming': the error that is the result of scheming. The genitive is personified by its article [EGT].

4:15 but[a] speaking/living-truth[b] in[c] love[d] let-us-grow-up[e] into[f] him in-all-(things), who is the head,[g] Christ,

LEXICON—a. δέ (LN 89.124) (BAGD 1.d. p. 171): 'but' [BAGD, El, LN, Lns, NIC, NTC, Rob, TH, We; KJV, NASB, NRSV], 'rather' [AB, BAGD; NAB, REB], 'but rather' [WBC], 'instead' [NIV, TEV], 'on the other hand' [LN], not explicit [NJB]. This is also translated as a negative affirmation: 'no' [TNT]. This particle is used to emphasize a contrast [BAGD].

b. pres. act. participle of ἀληθεύω (LN 33.251) (BAGD p. 36): 'to speak the truth' [AB, LN, Lns, NIC, TH, WBC; KJV, NASB, NIV, NRSV, TEV], 'to profess the truth' [NAB], 'to tell the truth' [BAGD, LN], 'to be truthful' [BAGD], 'to live the truth' [We], 'to live by the truth' [NJB], 'to adhere to the truth' [NTC], 'to hold the truth' [El], 'to maintain the truth' [Rob; REB], 'to base our lives on truth' [TNT]. The verb may mean 'to cherish, maintain, say, do, or live the truth' [AB, NTC, Rob, St].

c. ἐν with dative object (LN 89.84): 'in' [AB, El, Lns, NTC, Rob, TH, WBC, We; all versions except TNT], 'with' [NIC], 'on' [TNT].

d. ἀγάπη: 'love'. See this word at 4:2.

e. aorist act. subj. of αὐξάνω (LN 59.62) (BAGD 3. p. 121): 'to grow up' [BAGD, El, NIC, NTC, Rob, WBC, We; all versions except NJB, REB], 'to fully grow up' [REB], 'to get grown up' [Lns], 'to grow' [AB, LN; NAB], 'to grow completely' [TH; NJB], 'to increase' [LN]. The mode in which this verb occurs indicates an exhortation [TH].

f. εἰς with accusative object (LN 90.23): 'into' [El, NTC, Rob, TH, We; KJV, NASB, NIV, NJB, NRSV, REB], 'to' [NIC, WBC; NAB, TEV], 'toward' [AB], 'with respect to' [LN, Lns], 'into a perfect union with' [TNT].

g. κεφαλή (LN **87.51**) (BAGD 2.a. p.430): 'head' [AB, BAGD, El, LN, Lns, NIC, NTC, Rob, TH, WBC, We; all versions]. It denotes one who is superior in rank [BAGD] and status because of his authority to command [LN].

QUESTION—What relationship is indicated by δέ 'but'?

This particle introduces the following positive clauses as being in contrast with the state of childishness indicated in 4:14 [Alf, Ea, EGT, El, Ho, LJ, MNTC, NCBC, NIC, NTC, St, TH]. It contrasts heresy's deception with the gospel's integrity [EBC], or the integrity of those who hold the truth [NTC, Rob]. Being in contrast, the material in this verse is still governed by the ἵνα 'in order that, so that' (4:14) indicating purpose [Ea, EGT, El, My, WBC] or further result [Lns]. This contrast takes the form of chiasmus with ἀληθεύοντες 'speaking the truth' opposed to τῆς πλάνης 'of error' and ἐν ἀγάπῃ 'in love' opposed to ἐν πανουργίᾳ 'in craftiness' [WBC].

QUESTION—What relationship is indicated by the participle ἀληθεύοντες 'speaking/living the truth'?

This participle modifies the following clause governed by the verb αὐχήσωμεν 'let us grow up' [Cal, Ea, EGT, El, Lns, NCBC, WBC] and marks the primary and permanent means of growth: by holding the truth [Ea, NCBC, NTC, TH, TNTC, WBC; TEV]. Growth takes place as believers speak the truth in love [WBC]. Truth and love are put forth here as the twin conditions for growth [Rob, St].

QUESTION—What is meant by ἀληθεύοντες 'speaking/living the truth'?

1. The verb refers to verbal testimony [AB, Ba, BAGD, EGT, ISBE2, LN, Lns, My, NIC, TH, WBC; KJV, NAB, NASB, NIV, NRSV, TEV]: to speak the truth. The context deals with the confession, the ministers of the Word, true and false teaching, and lying, all of which indicate a verbal testimony is intended here [AB].

1.1 It refers to the confession held by the church [AB, EGT, Lns, My, WBC]. The passage calls upon the church and all its members to be a confessing church. Paul is talking about a confession that incorporates God's love, mutual love for one another, and an edifying enthusiasm for missionary endeavor. The truth entrusted to the congregation is that of love that conquers all [AB].

1.2 It refers to daily, ordinary truth-telling among believers [Ba, NIC]. This is an OT expression used to denote fidelity between two parties. It is applicable to the confession of the Christian faith [NIC].

2. The verb has a more general reference [Alf, Cal, Can, CBC, DNTT, Ea, EBC, ECWB, El, Fd, Ho, IB, ICC, LJ, MNTC, NCBC, NTC, Rob, Si, St, TD, TH, TNTC, We; NJB, REB, TNT]: to follow the truth. Since it is not the false teachers that are addressed, but their victims, holding the truth is more naturally inculcated on them [Ea, ICC].

2.1 The truth refers generally to integrity of life [Cal, DNTT, EBC, Fd, IB, ICC, NTC, Rob, Si, TD]. This is the practice of integrity, truthfulness in acts and speech [NTC]. The concern for truth is the secret of maturity in the Church [EBC]. It means 'to be sincere in love', or 'to live by true faith in love' [TD].

2.2 The truth refers primarily to the gospel [CBC, ECWB, Ho, TH] or Christian doctrine [Ea, LJ, MNTC, NCBC, TH]. The 'truth' is the standard by which we judge all other teachings [LJ]. It is primary [LJ, NCBC], not to be replaced by love, which indicates the way in which we hold the truth [LJ]. This is 'being true' and incorporates speaking truly to and acting honestly towards others as well as loving the truth (the Christian doctrine) and clinging to it at all costs. Particularly this latter element is what stands in contrast to the childishness of 4:14 [ECWB].

QUESTION—To what is ἐν ἀγάπῃ 'in love' connected?

1. It is connected to ἀληθεύοντες 'speaking/living the truth' [AB, Alf, Ba, Cal, Can, DNTT, ECWB, Ho, LJ, Lns, MNTC, NCBC, NIC, NTC, Rob, St, TD, TNTC, WBC, We; all versions]: speaking/living the truth in love. Orthodox teaching is capable of being promoted at the expense of love. This must not happen [AB, Alf, Ba, Can, LJ, MNTC, NCBC, NIC, Si, St, WBC]. Where there is no love, the truth God has revealed is denied [AB,

Alf]. This phrase does not mark a limitation, but a characteristic of Christian conduct [ICC]. This love denotes the temper of love in general and is not especially directed toward God, or Christ [Can, My], or our fellows, but goes out in all directions [Can].
- 1.1 The preposition indicates the element or sphere within which the truth operates [Alf, Si, WBC]: in love. The phrase describes the sphere of growth, but the meaning is not that believers are to grow in love, as if that was the virtue in which they were to make progress, but that in love they are to grow in reference to everything. Love is the means and the sphere of their advancement [Ea]. It is the proper environment of truth and the source of its persuasive power [Si].
- 1.2 The preposition indicates the manner in which truth should be applied [Ba, BAGD, Cal, LJ, NIC, TNTC]: with love. It means 'to speak the truth in such a way that the spirit of love is maintained' [BAGD (ἀληθεύω)].
- 2. It is connected to αὐξήσωμεν 'let us grow up' [Ea, EGT, El, IDB, My]: in love let us grow up into him in every way. The phrase marks the chief element, the peculiar temperament in which Christian growth is accelerated and achieved [Ea].
- 3. It is connected to both [ICC]: living the truth in love, let us in love grow up into him. It is more natural to connect ἐν ἀγάπῃ 'in love' with the participle than with the verb which is fully defined by the words which follow it. Probably, however, Paul intended to connect the phrase to both ideas since his thought proceeds from truth to love to growth [ICC].

QUESTION—What is meant by αὐξήσωμεν...τὰ πάντα 'let us grow up...in all things'?
- 1. The verb is intransitive and τὰ πάντα 'all things' is adverbial [AB, Alf, Ba, BAGD, Cal, Can, CBC, DNTT, Ea, EBC, ECWB, EGT, El, Ho, IB, ICC, LJ, Lns, MNTC, My, NCBC, NIC, NTC, Rob, Si, St, TD, TH, TNTC, WBC, We; all versions]: let us grow up in every way. The verb continues the metaphor of infants and of the mature man in 4:13–14. Its subjunctive mode and aorist tense in combination with the negated present subjunctive μήκετι ὦμεν (νήπιοι) 'no longer should we be (children)' (4:14) means that the verb is to be interpreted as punctiliar and ingressive: 'get grown up' [Lns]. Yet, another commentator states this combination indicates the *progressive* development of the Christian life [My]. Truthful dealing promotes growth in all respects, particularly in the faith and knowledge mentioned (4:13) [Can]. To grow up into Christ means acquiring an ever deepening understanding of how Christ and all that he has told us of God apply to our situation and our present lives [CBC]. As the accusative of specification, τὰ πάντα 'all things' is almost like an adverb [BAGD (2.b.β. p. 633)]. Others say that the accusative is that of reference [Alf] or relationship [TD]. Others say that the accusative defines the extent of growing into Christ—in all the parts of our growth [EGT, El, ICC, Lns].

2. The verb is transitive with the accusative τὰ πάντα 'all things' as its object. Τὰ πάντα 'all things' refers to the universe [TD]: let us make all things grow toward Christ. This must be interpreted in light of the statement in 1:22 where the Lord is given to the totality of creation just as he is given to the Church as its head. When we speak the truth in love, the church plays its part in causing this totality to grow into Christ, κεφαλή 'head' expressing the claim of Christ and the church to the world. This is also reflected in 1:10 where the created world comes to fulfillment in Christ [TD].

QUESTION—What relationship is indicated by εἰς 'into (him)'?
1. The preposition εἰς indicates direction or goal [AB, Alf, DNTT, EBC, EGT, El, Ho, ICC, LJ, MNTC, NIC, TD, TH, WBC; NAB, TEV]: let us grow up to him. This preposition often occurs where the preposition ἐν 'in' might be expected, i.e., staying in a place may be regarded as the result of movement towards it [TD]. This is an increase towards the measure of the stature of the perfect man (4:13) [Alf, Ba, DNTT, EGT, Ho, LJ, MNTC, NIC, Rob, TD]. The growth or maturity of Christians is directed toward the goal of what Christ is, to become like him and become completely incorporated in him 'in every way' [TH]. It is into Christ as the head that the body grows [EBC]. The verb αὐξήσωμεν 'let us grow up' with εἰς 'into' indicates both the ideas of 'unto' and 'into'. The growth of Christians bears relation to Christ both as to its center (*in* him) and as to its standard (as defined by 'the stature of the fullness of Christ' 4:13) [El]. This marks the ascending direction of our growth to the head, whereas the following verse will mark the descending direction [ICC, My (though supporting 2. below)]. We are to grow to correspond to our head [LJ, MNTC, NIC].
2. The preposition indicates reference [Lns, My]: let us grow up with respect to him. 'With respect to' or 'in relation to' is the only interpretation which fits the metaphor. The body does not grow *toward* the head, nor *into* union with the head, but only *with respect to* (in correspondence with) the head [Lns, My].
3. The preposition indicates union [BAGD, Can, IB, NTC, Rob, TH; TNT]: let us grow up in union with him. As Christians become more and more of one mind and heart, they move into ever closer and more vital union with Christ [Can, IB, TH]. BAGD (αὐξάνω p. 121) indicates this preposition means 'in union with'. This interpretation may include 1. above as well [TH].

4:16 from[a] whom all the body being-fitted-together[b] and being-held-together[c] by[d] every joint/ligament/connection/feeling[e] of-supply[f]

LEXICON—a. ἐκ with genitive object (LN 89.3, 89.25, 89.77, 90.16): 'from' [El, LN (89.3, 89.77, 90.16), Lns, NIC, NTC, Rob, TH, WBC, We; KJV, NASB, NIV, NRSV], 'by' [LN (90.16); NJB], 'by means of' [LN (89.77)], 'through' [NAB], 'under control' [TEV], 'because of' [LN

(89.25)], not explicit [AB]. This preposition is also translated as a verb: 'to depend on, upon' [REB, TNT]. It is also combined with the translation of ἐνέργειαν 'working' later in the verse: 'he is at work' [AB].
b. pres. pass. participle of συναρμολογέω (συναρμολογέομαι LN **62.1**) (BAGD p. 785): 'to be fitted together' [BAGD, MM, NIC; NASB, NJB], 'to be harmoniously fitted together' [NTC], 'to be joined together' [BAGD, LN, TH, WBC; NIV, NRSV], 'to be fitly joined together' [KJV], 'to be framed together' [Lns], 'to be fitly framed together' [El, Rob, We], 'to be bonded together' [REB]. This passive verb is also translated actively: 'to fit together' [AB, LN; TEV]. This participle is also conflated with the next participle: 'to be held together' [TNT], 'to join firmly together' [NAB]. The present tense indicates that this process is not yet complete but is still going on [Alf, EGT, El, ICC, My, We]. This verb denotes the fitting of something together in a coherent and compatible manner. The gloss 'to be joined together' does not suggest this verb is to be understood as a causative passive. It simply refers to the state of being joined together [LN]. The preposition συν- 'with' refers both to the inner relationships within the community and also to the relationship between the community and Christ [TD]. See this word at 2:21.
c. pres. pass. participle of συμβιβάζω (LN **63.5**) (BAGD 1.a. p. 777): 'to be held together' [NIC, NTC; NASB, NIV, REB, TEV], 'to be knit together' [Lns, TH, We; NRSV], 'to be joined together' [NJB], 'to be brought together' [BAGD, LN, MM, WBC], 'to be combined, to be caused to be a unit' [LN], 'to be compacted' [El, MM, Rob; KJV], 'to be united' [BAGD, **LN**]. This passive verb is also translated actively: 'to join together' [AB]. This participle is also conflated with the previous participle (see b. above). The present tense indicates that this process is still going on [EGT, El, ICC, My].
d. διά with genitive object (LN 89.76): 'by' [LN, NTC, Rob, WBC; all versions except NJB], 'by means of' [El, LN, Lns], 'through' [AB, LN, NIC, TH, We].
e. ἁφή (LN **8.60**) (BAGD p. 125): 'joint' [BAGD, El, Lns, NTC, Rob, TH; KJV, NASB, NJB, REB, TEV], 'ligament' [BAGD, LN, MM, NIC, WBC; NAB, NIV, NRSV], 'ligaments' [TNT], 'connection' [BAGD], 'contact' [AB, We]. This noun denotes the part of the joints which binds the different parts of the body together [LN].
f. ἐπιχορηγία (LN 35.31) (BAGD p. 305): 'supply' [Lns, Rob, TH], 'spiritual supply' [El], 'strength' [NJB], 'support' [BAGD, LN], 'provision' [LN]. This noun is translated as an adjective modifying ἁφῆς 'joint': 'supporting' [NIC, NTC; NAB, NIV], 'constituent' [REB]. It is also translated as a phrase: 'with which it is equipped/provided/supplied' [NRSV, TEV, TNT]. It is translated as a clause: 'he provides sustenance' [AB], 'adding strength' [NJB], 'that serves for support' [BAGD], 'which gives supply' [WBC], 'that which is supplied' [We], 'that which supplies' [KJV, NASB].

QUESTION—How is the phrase ἐξ οὗ 'from whom' connected?

It refers back to the immediately preceding Χριστός 'Christ' in 4:15 [AB, Ea, EBC, EGT, Ho, IB, LJ, Lns, MNTC, NIC, NTC, Rob, St, TH, We], and it connects, as subject, with the periphrastic verb construction τὴν αὔξησιν…ποιεῖται 'it makes its growth' later in the present verse [Alf, El, ICC, LJ, NIC, Rob, TH, We]. The preposition ἐκ 'from' marks the source of the body's growth [AB, Ea, EGT, El, Ho, Lns, We]. It denotes the causal going forth of the influences from the head [My]. This corresponds with εἰς αὐτόν 'unto him' in 4:15 [Ea, EBC, St] indicating that Christ is seen as both the goal and the source of the church's growth in these two verses [WBC]. This verse appropriately closes the paragraph by summing up all of its exhortations to unity by metaphorically drawing upon the growth and vigor of a healthy human body [Can, Ea, LJ, Lns, Si, WBC].

QUESTION—What is meant by the passive participles συναρμολογούμενον 'being fitted together' and συμβιβαζόμενον 'being held together' and who is the agent involved in their action?

The agent of these passive participles is Christ [AB, My, NIC, Rob, St, TD] or the servants of Christ, the ministers of 4:11 [MNTC, WBC]. The 'joints' or 'ligaments' are the means [Ea, EGT, Lns, NIC].

1. These participles are fully synonymous with each other [IB (probably), MNTC, NIC, WBC; NAB, TNT]: joined firmly together. Christ, as head, imparts cohesion to this body [IB]. The participles form a doublet [NIC]. They are virtually synonymous, and when taken together underline forcefully that for the unified growth of the body to take place the members must be involved in a process of continued adjustment to each other [WBC].
2. There is a discernible distinction in meaning between the two synonyms [AB, Alf, Ba, Ea, EBC, ECWB, EGT, El, Ho, ICC, LJ, Lns, My, NTC, Rob, TNTC, We; TEV]: being fitted and kept together.
   2.1 The first participle, συναρμολογούμενον 'being fitted together', indicates the vertical relationship of the members to the head, while the second, συμβιβαζόμενον 'being held together' indicates the horizontal relationship of the members to each other, they are kept together [AB; TEV].
   2.2 The first participle relates to the preparation of the component parts, their harmonious fitting to each other, the second relates to the combining of these parts together into a firm, solid structure [Alf, Ea, EBC].
   2.3 The first participle συναρμολογούμενον 'being fitted together' relates to the mechanical assembly of parts, the structure of the image, the second συμβιβαζόμενον 'being held together' relates more to the representation of the reality, the unity of an organic body [ECWB, EGT, El, Ho, ICC, LJ, Lns, My, Rob, We]. Both participles refer to a union of parts fitted to each other, a σῶμα 'body' concept [Ho, ICC, Lns, My, Rob, TNTC], but the second is used of bringing persons together for reconciliation or friendship [Ho, ICC, Lns, My, Rob, TNTC, WBC

(though supporting 1. above)]. The second participle strengthens the idea of uniting that is indicated in the first participle [EGT, Ho, LJ, Lns, TNTC]. The second participle serves to explain the first [Ho]. The second participle, συμβιβαζόμενον 'being held together', is often used figuratively to denote a kind of mental unity or concord [LJ]. The distinction consists chiefly in this, that the first participle relates to the image portrayed, the second more to the reality represented, as consisting of persons [Ho, Lns, My]. At most, the differences between the two do not go beyond the ideas of 'joining' and 'coalescence' [EGT].

QUESTION—To what is the phrase διὰ πάσης ἁφῆς τῆς ἐπιχορηγίας 'by every joint of supply' connected?

1. It is connected to the two preceding participles [Ba, Ea, EBC, EGT, El, Ho, ICC, LJ, LN (**8.60**), Lns, MNTC, NCBC, NIC, NTC, Rob, TD, TH, WBC; KJV, NAB, NASB, NIV, NJB, NRSV, REB, TNT]: being fitted and held together by every joint of supply. This phrase expresses the instrumentality or means by which the symmetry and compactness expressed in the participles are secured [Ea, EGT, Lns, NIC].
2. It is connected to the second participle συμβιβαζόμεμον 'being held together' [TEV]: the whole body being held together by every joint with which it is supplied.
3. It is connected to the following κατ' ἐνέργειαν κ.τ.λ. 'according to the working, etc.' [AB]: according to God's working through every connection of supply.
4. It is connected to τὴν αὔξησιν...ποιεῖται 'it makes its growth' [Alf, ECWB, My, TNTC]: by every joint of supply it makes its growth. Because ἐπιχορηγίας 'supply' relates to the growth of the body more than its joining together, it seems better to join this phrase with τὴν αὔξησιν...ποιεῖται 'it makes its growth' [ECWB, My]. This phrase indicates the source [ECWB] or means [TNTC] of the growth.

QUESTION—What is meant by ἁφῆς 'joint, ligament, connection'?

1. This means 'joint' [Alf, Ba, BAGD, CBC, DNTT, Ea, EGT, El, Ho, Lns, My-ed, NCBC, NTC, Rob, TH, TNTC; KJV, NASB, NJB, REB, TEV]: every joint of supply. The NT only uses the word in the sense of 'joint' as the point of binding or junction, or even, in Eph. 4:16 and Col. 2:19, 'that which effects the binding' [DNTT]. This word does not refer to the joint in the sense in which we commonly use it [Ba, TH]. It incorporates anything that unites or fastens together the different parts of the body—the blood vessels, tendons, cords, muscles [Ba, Lns], and bones [Lns]. By 'joints' is meant the nerves and tissues which bind the different parts into one [CBC, Rob]. The joints are the points of connection and communication between member and member and the supply that comes from the head as in the parallel, Col. 2:19 [EGT]. The ἁφαί 'joints' are the various spiritual gifts and offices that are the channels of supply for

the divine influences from the head, specifically those parts related to the dissemination of the Word of God, the ministry (4:11) [Ho].
2. This means 'ligament' [BAGD, EBC, LN (**8.60**), MM, MNTC, NIC, TD, WBC; NAB, NIV, NRSV, TNT]: every ligament of supply. These ligaments are the nerves and tissues which not only bind all the parts together like cords, but also serve as channels by which the body receives its nourishment [MNTC, WBC]. These ligaments refer to the ministers of 4:11 [WBC].
3. This means 'connection, band' or 'contact' [AB, BAGD, ECWB, IB, ICC, LJ, TD, TH, We]: every connection of supply. It is obvious that anatomical exactness is not to be expected here [TD]. The meaning 'contact' best fits the context, both here and in Col. 2:19 [ICC]. It is not the function of 'joints' or 'ligaments' to supply nourishment to the body [ICC, LJ, TH]. This refers to both the vascular system which supplies blood to the body, and the nervous system which is connected through the spinal cord to the brain [LJ]. The apostle seems to be saying that individual church members, by their mutual dependence and communication, are tools of the head for communicating nourishment, vitality, unity, and solidity to the body as a whole [AB, Ba, IB].
4. This means the feeling or perception of vital energy [Bu, My]: sensation of the supply. This expression very appropriately points to the growth *from within outward* through the influence of Christ [My].

QUESTION—What is meant by ἐπιχορηγίας 'supply' and what is the significance of its genitive case?
1. The genitive gives an active sense to the noun whereby every ἀφῆς 'joint' performs some function [AB, Alf, Ba, BAGD, Bu, Cal, Can, CBC, Ea, EBC, ECWB, EGT, Ho, IB, LJ, Lns, MNTC, NIC, NTC, Rob, Si, TD, WBC, We; KJV, NAB, NASB, NIV, NJB].
1.1 The active sense refers to every ἀφῆς 'joint' as supplying or transferring something on to the rest of the body [AB, Alf, Ba, Bu, Cal, Can, ECWB, El, Ho, IB, LJ, Lns, NIC, WBC, We; KJV]: every joint which transfers life or sustenance. The thought is not so much that each part shares in the life which comes from the head [IB, MNTC, TH], but that each part is a channel which receives and passes on this life [AB, Cal, Ho, IB, MNTC, NIC, TH] (by means of the gifts given to each member [AB]). Whenever one part comes into close contact with another, it communicates what it has to give, the ἐπιχορηγίας 'supply' not being a definite force, but varying with each different part [We]. The word is almost a technical one [ECWB] for the abundant supply of strength and nervous energy from the head in the form of nutriment or sustenance [AB, ECWB, IB, LJ]. As applied to the church, the body of Christ, this refers to the supply of the Spirit [ECWB, Ho] or spiritual life [AB, Ho, LJ, My (supporting 2.1 below), WBC]. The genitive defines what is the predominant use or purpose of the joints [El], or the genitive is objective, meaning 'every joint or sensation for the purpose of supply' [Bu].

1.2 The active sense refers to the function of every ἀφῆς 'joint' in holding the body together [BAGD (p. 305), CBC, Ea, EBC, NTC, Rob, TD; NAB, NIV, NJB]: every joint which holds the body together. It means 'each link which serves to support it'. Ἐπιχορηγίας 'supply' is the assistance the joints give in compacting and organizing the body [Ea]. The passive participle of Col. 2:19 indicates that the body is supplied by the bands and ligaments, whose function it is to keep the limbs in position and check the play of the muscles. It is not by nutriment which is not their function and which is not indicated either here or in Colossians. Order and unity are the conditions of growth which the Apostle is indicating [Rob].

1.3 Both of the above are meant [EGT, MNTC, Si]: every joint which transfers life and sustenance and holds the body together. The joints or ligaments are the constituents of union in the body and the media of the impartation of life received by the members from the head [EGT, MNTC]. This is the sense also in the Col. 2:19 parallel [EGT].

2. The genitive gives a passive sense to the noun [ICC, My, NCBC, TH, TNTC; NRSV, REB, TEV, TNT].

2.1 The passive sense refers to something which is supplied to every ἀφῆς 'joint' [ICC, My]: every joint to which sustenance is supplied. The meaning of this phrase may well be 'through each part being in touch with the ministration (from the head)' [ICC]. Another says the genitive is objective, denoting every feeling (ἀφῆς 'joint') in which the supply from Christ is experienced or perceived [My].

2.2 The passive sense refers to every ἀφῆς 'joint' as supplied to the body [NCBC, TH, TNTC; NRSV, REB, TEV, TNT]: every joint supplied to the body. The reference to every joint with which the body is furnished [NCBC, TNTC]. All the parts are held together by joints and muscles and so enable each to fulfill its function within the whole [NCBC].

according-to[a] (the) working[b] in[c] measure[d] of-each individual[e] part[f]

LEXICON—a. κατά with accusative object (LN 67.33, 89.8): 'according to' [El, Lns, NTC, Rob, TH, WBC, We; KJV, NASB], 'in accordance with, in relation to' [LN (89.8)], 'for' [NJB], 'through' [REB], 'as' [NIV, NRSV], 'and with' [NAB], 'when' [LN (67.33)], 'so when' [TEV], not explicit [AB; TNT].

b. ἐνέργεια (LN 42.3) (BAGD 1. p. 265): 'working' [BAGD, LN, Lns, TH; NASB], 'active working' [El], 'effectual working' [Rob; KJV], 'effective working' [We], 'functioning' [NAB, REB], 'activity' [WBC], 'operation, action' [BAGD], 'practice' [LN], 'energy' [NTC]. This noun is also translated as a verb: 'to work' [NJB, TEV], 'to do work' [NIV, TNT], 'to be working' [NRSV]. The phrase κατ' ἐνέργειαν 'according to the working' is also translated as a series of verbs: 'to be at work...to provide (sustenance)...to enable' [AB]. The phrase is also translated as an adverb modifying ποιεῖται 'grows': 'effectively' [NIC].

c. ἐν with dative object (LN. 89.84) (BAGD III.2. p. 261): 'in' [El, Lns, Rob, TH, We; KJV], 'according to' [AB, BAGD, NIC; NJB], 'that corresponds to' [NTC], 'with' [LN], not explicit [NIV, TNT]. The phrase ἐν μέτρῳ 'in measure' is translated as an adjective: 'proper' [NAB, NASB, REB], 'commensurate with' [El, WBC]; as a possessive: 'its own (work)' [TNT]; as an adverb: 'properly' [NRSV]; as a comparative phrase: 'as it should' [TEV]. This usage of the preposition denotes a norm [BAGD] or standard of judgment (= κατά 'according to' with the accusative case) [DNTT].

d. μέτρον (LN 81.1) (BAGD 2.b. p. 515): 'measure' [BAGD, El, LN, Lns, Rob, TH; KJV], 'due measure' [NIC, We], 'capacity' [NTC], 'needs' [AB], 'function' [NJB], not explicit [NIV, TNT]. The phrase ἐν μέτρῳ 'in measure' is translated in different ways. See c. above. This usage of the term denotes 'measure' as the result of measuring [BAGD]. This noun denotes a unit of measurement of either length or volume [LN].

e. ἕκαστος (LN 59.27): 'each' [AB, El, LN, Lns, NIC, NTC, Rob, WBC, We; all versions except KJV, NAB], 'every' [TH; KJV]. This word is also translated by pluralizing μέρος 'part': 'members' [NAB]. This term denotes each item of a totality in a distributive sense [LN].

f. μέρος (LN 63.14) (BAGD 1.b.β. p. 506): 'part' [AB, El, LN, Lns, NIC, NTC, Rob, TH, WBC, We; all versions except NAB], 'component part, element' [BAGD], 'members' [NAB].

QUESTION—What relationship is indicated by κατά 'according to'?

1. It indicates correspondence with the preceding participles [AB, NTC; NAB]: all the body is harmoniously fitted together and held together according to the energy that corresponds to the capacity of each individual part.
2. It indicates correspondence with the preceding phrase 'by every connection of supply' [Ho, LJ, Lns, TD, We]: a supply which corresponds to the working of each individual part. The phrase is in apposition to διὰ πάσης ἁφῆς τῆς ἐπιχορηγίας 'by every joint of supply', and explains how the joint's supply operates in fitting together and holding together the parts of the body, 'by every joint's supply, that is, according to the working of each single part's portion' [Lns]. It is more natural to say that the divine influence from the head is according to the capacity and function of each part than to say 'the growth is according to the working etc.' The growth of the body is due to the living influence which pervades it, and not to the efficiency of the parts [Ho]. The bonds (ἁφαί 'joints') have different powers assigned to them and, according to the measure of the power they have received, they must contribute to the building up of the entire body [TD].
3. It indicates simultaneous action with the event noun ἐπιχορηγίας 'supply' [EBC, IB]: by every joint of supply when each part works properly. It is only when each individual part works properly that the body receives its needed support [EBC].

4. Κατά 'according to' indicates correspondence with the following phrase 'it makes the growth of the body' [Alf, Ea, ECWB, EGT, El, MNTC, My, Rob, TH, WBC]: according to the working by measure to each individual part the body makes its growth. Like the preceding phrase, this is also joined to 'it makes the growth of the body' [ECWB], and indicates the method of the body's growth [ECWB, EGT, El]. It denotes the relations of the body's growth [My, Rob]. It describes this growth as occurring in accordance with an inward operation that adapts itself to the nature and function of each individual part and gives to each its proper measure [EGT, El].
5. It indicates simultaneous action with the verb phrase 'it makes...the growth' [NIV, NRSV, TEV]: as/when each part works properly it makes the growth of the body.
6. It indicates the means of the body's growth [REB]: the body grows through the proper working of each part.

QUESTION—To what is ἐν μέτρῳ 'in measure' connected?

1. It is connected with the preceding κατ' ἐνέργειαν 'according to the working' [Cal, CBC, Ea, EBC, EGT, El, ICC, MNTC, My, NCBC, NTC, TD, WBC; NAB, NASB, NRSV, REB, TEV, TNT]: according to the energy measured out to each individual part, or, according to the proportionate working of each individual part. It qualifies ἐνέργειαν 'working' and this is then defined by the following genitive ἑνὸς ἑκάστου 'of each one'. It is as if the writer had intended to say κατ' ἐνέργειαν ἑνὸς ἑκάστου 'according to the working of each one' but then recalled the thought of 4:7 and inserted ἐν μέτρῳ 'in measure' [ICC]. This phrase, together with the κατ' ἐνέργειαν 'according to the working' preceding it, indicates that each part of the body receives the energizing power it needs, and the growth of the body as a whole is in proportion to and adapted to each part. It recalls the unity in diversity thrust earlier in the section [WBC].
2. It is connected with the following ἑνὸς ἑκάστου μέρους 'of each individual part' [AB, Ba, ECWB, Ho, IB, LJ, Lns, Rob, TD, TNTC]: according to the working of each individual part in its measure. The meaning is 'in accordance with function in the full measure of each individual part', or 'as each part duly fulfills its appropriate function' [Rob]. It means each part receives all it needs 'according to the measure of its capacity' [LJ].
3. It is connected with the periphrastic verb construction τὴν αὔξησιν... ποιεῖται 'it makes its growth' [NIC]: it grows effectively according to the measure of each individual part.
4. It is connected with τῆς ἐπιχορηγίας of the supply [We]: according to the working of the service rendered (i.e., supply) in due measure by every part.

QUESTION—What is meant by ἐν μέτρῳ 'in measure'?

1. The phrase is used absolutely [AB, Ba, Cal, Can, DNTT, Ea, ECWB, EGT, El, Ho, IB, ICC, LJ, Lns, MNTC, My, NIC, NTC, Rob, TD, TNTC, We]: in the measure of each part.

EPHESIANS 4:16 339

1.1 This focuses on the provision that each part receives [AB, Cal, DNTT, Ea, EGT, El, Ho, ICC, LJ, My, NTC, Si, TD]. This means that each part receives exactly and specifically what it needs [AB, Ea, El, LJ, My], the equable apportionment of life [Si]. This statement refers to the gifts given to each individual saint (4:7, 12) [AB, Ea, ICC, TD], implying their diversity and manifoldness [TD]. Others state the implied reference is to the gifts given for the ministry (4:11) [Ho, TD].

1.2 This focuses on the function each part performs [Ba, Can, DNTT, ECWB, IB, Lns, MNTC, NIC, Rob, TNTC, We]. The support needed and furnished to each part is in exact proportion to its strength. Each works according to the 'measure' of its strength [Ba]. It indicates correct capacity [ECWB]. This phrase refers back to the phrase κατὰ τὸ μέτρον τῆς δορεᾶς τοῦ Χριστοῦ 'according to the measure of Christ's gift' in 4:7. It means 'in its appointed measure' [IB].

2. The phrase is used attributively [NCBC, TD, TH, WBC; NAB, NASB, NRSV, REB, TEV]: proper working, or working properly. This is used as an adjective to modify ἐνέργειαν 'working' [TD, WBC; NAB, NASB, REB] or adverbially to modify the verbal idea in that noun [NCBC; NRSV, TEV] and means 'appropriate to, proper, properly, as it should' [NCBC, TH; NAB, NASB, NRSV, REB, TEV], referring to the function each part performs [TD, TH].

QUESTION—What is the difference between μέρους 'part' and the ἁφῆς 'joint' earlier in the verse?

1. The μέρους 'part' is the same as the ἁφῆς 'joint' mentioned earlier [AB, Ba, Can, CBC, Ea, EGT, IB, LJ, Lns, NTC, Si, TD, TNTC, We]. Both ἁφῆς 'joint' and μέρους 'part' refer to the class of ministers with their associated gifts mentioned in 4:11 [CBC, TD]. Others treat both ἁφῆς 'joint' and μέρους 'part' without distinction, as referring to every member in the body [AB, Ba, Can, Ea, EGT, IB, LJ, Lns, NTC, Si, TNTC, We]. Πάσης ἁφῆς 'every joint' and ἑνὸς ἑκάστου μέρους 'every single part' are practically the same, with ἁφῆς 'joint' referring to the living juncture with other joints and μέρους 'part' only to the general relation to the body as a whole [Lns].

2. The μέρους 'part' and the ἁφῆς 'joint' mentioned earlier refer to different entities in the body [Ho, MNTC, WBC]. The πάσης ἁφῆς 'every joint' refers to the ministerial class of 4:11 while μέρους 'part' refers to the rest of the members [Ho, MNTC, WBC].

makes[a] the growth[b] of-the body[c] unto[d] (the) building up[e] of-itself in love.

LEXICON—a. pres. mid. indic. of ποιέω (LN 13.9, 42.7) (BAGD II.1. p. 683): 'to make' [AB, BAGD, LN (13.9), Rob, TH, WBC; KJV, TNT], 'to make for itself' [We], 'to produce' [Lns], 'to promote' [El; NRSV], 'to bring about' [LN (13.9), NTC], 'to cause' [NASB], 'to cause to be' [LN (13.9)], 'to do (something)' [BAGD, LN (42.7)]. This verb is conflated with αὔξησιν 'growth': 'to grow' [NIC; NAB, NIV, NJB, REB, TEV]. The middle voice stresses the body's involvement in the growth [AB, Ea, EGT, ICC, Lns, My, St, TH, WBC], or it strengthens the sense, speaking of the energy with which the process is carried out [Ea, EGT, El]. The present tense indicates that the growth is always going on [Lns]. The middle voice is mostly used as a periphrasis for the simple verbal idea of doing something for oneself or of oneself [BAGD].

b. αὔξησις (LN 23.188) (BAGD p. 122): 'growth' [AB, BAGD, LN, Lns, NTC, TH, WBC, We; NASB, NRSV], 'increase' [BAGD, El, Rob; KJV]. This noun is also translated as a verb: 'to grow' [NIC; NAB, NIV, NJB, REB, TEV, TNT]. This noun is placed in front of the verb ποιεῖται 'makes' for emphasis [Lns].

c. σῶμα (LN 11.34) (BAGD 5. p. 800): 'body' [AB, BAGD, El, Lns, Rob, TH, We; KJV, NASB, NJB, NRSV, TNT], 'whole frame' [REB], 'whole body' [TEV]. This noun is also translated as an adjective modifying αὔξησιν 'growth': 'bodily' [NTC, WBC]. It is also incorporated into the translation of σῶμα 'body' earlier in the verse [NIC; NAB] or into the translation of ἑαυτοῦ 'of itself' later in the verse [NIV]. This is a figurative extension of the meaning of σῶμα 'body' (8.1) [LN] and is used of the Christian community, the church as a unified body [BAGD, LN]. It carries the implication of each member having a distinctive function within the group [LN].

d. εἰς with accusative object (LN 67.119, 89.57): 'unto' [Rob, We; KJV], 'to' [LN (67.119), TH], 'with a view to' [NTC], 'in' [NRSV], 'for' [El, Lns; NASB], 'for the purpose of' [LN (89.57), WBC], 'so that' [AB, NIC], 'until' [LN (67.119); NJB], 'and so' [TNT], not explicit [NAB, NIV, REB, TEV]. This preposition marks intent, often implying the expected result [LN (89.57)].

e. οἰκοδομή (LN 42.34) (BAGD 1.b.β. p. 559): 'building up' [El, WBC, We; NASB, NRSV], 'upbuilding' [Lns, NTC], 'building' [Rob, TH], 'construction' [LN], 'edification' [BAGD], 'edifying' [KJV]. This noun is also translated as a verb: 'to build up' [AB, LN; NAB, NIV, NJB, REB, TEV, TNT], 'to be built up' [NIC]. The noun is used figuratively of spiritual strengthening [BAGD]. The noun here denotes the act of building [TD]. See this word at 4:12.

QUESTION—What is the subject of the periphrastic construction τὴν αὔξησιν...ποιεῖται 'makes the growth'?

The subject is the nominative σῶμα 'body' at the beginning of the verse, so the sense is 'all the body makes the growth of the body' i.e., 'the body makes its own growth' [Ea, El, Ho, Lns, TH]. Due to the two occurrences of 'the body' in the verse, 'the body' is both the subject and object of this verb [NIC].

QUESTION—What relationship is indicated by εἰς 'unto'?

This preposition indicates intended result or purpose [AB, Alf, Ea, EGT, El, LJ, Lns, My, NIC, TNTC, WBC]: so that the body makes its own growth, building itself up in love, or, it makes the growth of the body for building itself up in love. Again, this describes the church in relation to her destiny of becoming a completed house of God [AB].

QUESTION—To what is the phrase ἐν ἀγάπῃ 'in love' attached?

1. It is attached to the noun οἰκοδομήν 'building up' [AB, Alf, Ba, Cal, DNTT, ECWB, EGT, Ho, ICC, LJ, Lns, MNTC, NCBC, NIC, NTC, Rob, TD, TNTC, WBC, We; NAB, NASB, NJB, REB]: for the building up of itself in love. This phrase serves to recall the opening exhortation to love in 4:2 [WBC, We]. It gives the means by which the οἰκοδομήν 'building up' is to take place [WBC]. It denotes the condition in which the completion of the church takes place [EGT]. It is the bond that unites the members with one another, so that only by love can the body be built up to Christ's stature [NIC]. This love is love for one another [Lns, WBC].

2. It is attached to the whole of the clause τὴν αὔξησιν τοῦ σώματος ποιτεῖται εἰς οἰκοδομὴν ἑαυτοῦ 'it makes the growth of the body for the building up of itself' [My, TH]: in love it makes the growth of the body for the building up of itself. Because of 4:15, the connection with the whole clause is more in keeping with the context than just a connection with εἰς οἰκοδομὴν ἑαυτοῦ 'for the building up of itself' [My]. Love for one another is the ethical sphere within which the growth for the building up of itself by the whole body proceeds [My, TH].

DISCOURSE UNIT: 4:17–6:20 [LJ]. The topic is practical answers to how Christians are to maintain the unity of the Spirit in the bond of peace. This is the third and last main division in the epistle and it consists of a series of short statements of doctrine followed by illustrations of implications for practical conduct.

DISCOURSE UNIT: 4:17–6:9 [Alf, NTC]. The topic is an exhortation to glorious renewal through Spirit-born total transformation [NTC], exhortations to a course of life grounded in the teaching just laid down [Alf].

DISCOURSE UNIT: 4:17–5:21 [Alf, Can, ECWB, Lns, NTC, TNTC; NIV]. The topic is four admonitions to the church generally [Lns], general duties of Christians as united to Christ their Head [Alf], exhortation to Christian living [Can], glorious renewal upon all with the putting off of the old man and putting on the new [NTC], personal standards [TNTC], living as children of light [NIV].

DISCOURSE UNIT: 4:17–5:20 [IB, NIC, TH; NJB]. The topic is general admonitions on the new life in Christ [TH; NJB], Christian conduct [NIC], an exhortation against pagan ways [IB].

DISCOURSE UNIT: 4:17–5:17 [LJ]. The topic is darkness and light.

DISCOURSE UNIT: 4:17–5:4 [St]. The topic is a new set of clothes. Their new status as God's new society involved a new lifestyle. The description is that of the typical pagan life.

342   EPHESIANS 4:17

DISCOURSE UNIT: 4:17–5:2 [Ho, NCBC]. The topic is a general exhortation to holiness and specific instances of conduct that correspond to it [Ho], an injunction to abandon non-Christian characteristics [NCBC].

DISCOURSE UNIT: 4:17–32 [AB, Ea, NCBC, TH; NASB, TEV]. The topic is the Christian's new life in Christ [AB, NCBC, TH]. This second half of the chapter is concerned with the ethics of the saints [AB].

DISCOURSE UNIT: 4:17–24 [Ba, CBC, EBC, ECWB, EGT, El, Ho, IB, ICC, LJ, Lns, MNTC, NIC, NTC, Rob, St, TH, TNTC, WBC, We, WeBC; NAB]. The topic is an exhortation to put off the old life and put on the new [ECWB, EGT, El, LJ, Lns, MNTC, NIC, NTC, Rob, TH, TNTC, WBC, We, WeBC], the church against the heathen world [MNTC], an exhortation to holiness [Ba, Ho, St], a different life for the Christian [EBC], the Christian revolution [CBC].

DISCOURSE UNIT: 4:17–19 [AB, LJ, My, Si, St, WBC, We]. The topic is the injunction not to walk like Gentiles [AB, My, WBC], discarding old traits and cherishing the new [Si], sin in a pagan world [LJ], the old, pagan life [St, We].

4:17 This therefore/now^a I-say^b and testify/insist-upon^c in^d (the) Lord,
LEXICON—a. οὖν (LN 89.50) (BAGD 1.a. p. 593): 'therefore' [BAGD, LN, Lns, NTC, Rob, We; KJV, NASB], 'then' [BAGD, El, LN, NIC, WBC; REB, TEV, TNT], 'so' [BAGD, LN; NIV, NJB], 'now' [AB; NRSV], 'consequently, accordingly' [BAGD, LN], 'so then' [LN], not explicit [NAB].
   b. pres. act. indic. of λέγω (LN 33.69): 'to say' [AB, El, NIC, NTC, Rob, We; KJV, NASB, NJB], 'to tell' [NIV, TNT], 'to declare' [Lns; NAB], 'to affirm' [NRSV], not explicit [WBC; TEV]. This verb is also translated '(this) is my word to you' [REB].
   c. pres. mid. indic. of μαρτύρομαι (LN 33.223, 33.319) (BAGD 2. p. 494): 'to testify' [El, LN (33.223), Lns, NTC, Rob; KJV], 'to declare, to assert' [LN (33.223)], 'to attest' [NJB], 'to solemnly attest' [NAB], 'to solemnly declare' [WBC], 'to affirm' [BAGD, NIC; NASB], 'to insist (on, upon)' [AB, BAGD, LN (33.319); NIV, NRSV, TNT], 'to urge' [REB], 'to implore' [BAGD], 'to solemnly charge' [MM], 'to adjure' [We], 'to warn' [TEV]. This verb denotes a serious declaration given on the basis of a presumed personal knowledge [LN (33.223)] or it denotes the emphatic stating of an opinion or a desire [LN (33.319)].
   d. ἐν with dative object (LN 89.5, 89.119, 90.6, 90.30) (BAGD I.5.d. p. 259): 'in' [AB, BAGD, El, LN (89.5, 89.119), Lns, NIC, NTC, Rob, WBC, We; all versions except NASB], 'with regard to' [LN (89.5)], 'in union with' [LN (89.119)], 'together with' [NASB], 'by' [LN (90.30)].
QUESTION—What relationship is indicated by οὖν 'therefore'?
   1. It indicates exhortation to conduct that is incumbent upon those who ascribe to the doctrine just presented in 4:1–16 [Cal, Ho, IB, LJ, Lns, MNTC, NCBC, NTC, Si, St; all versions except NAB, NRSV]: therefore. The government which Christ has appointed to govern the growth of his

church has now been considered, so he next turns to consider the conduct which doctrine should facilitate in the lives of Christians [Cal]. This particle introduces the third main section of this epistle which continues through 6:20 so it introduces a practical and detailed answer to the implied question of how Christians are to achieve the state of unity and life discussed in 4:1–16 [LJ].
2. It resumes the ethical instruction begun in 4:1–3 [AB, Alf, Can, Ea, EBC, EGT, El, ICC, My, NIC, Rob, TNTC, WBC, We, WeBC; NRSV]: now. The μηκέτι ὑμᾶς περιπατεῖν 'no longer are you to walk' of the present verse gives the negative side of ἀξίως περιπατῆσαι 'to walk worthily' in 4:1–3 [Alf, EGT, El, ICC, My], and therefore subordinate to it [Alf]. The particle resumes the ethical paraenesis which was begun at 4:1 and broken off at 4:3 by the digression on the one body [NIC] or on the nature of the church's unity [Rob].

QUESTION—What is the referent of τοῦτο 'this'?

Τοῦτο 'this' refers to the following subject matter [Alf, Ea, EGT, ICC, Lns, My, WBC; all versions], specifically the μηκέτι περιπατεῖν 'no longer to walk' to which it is in apposition [HG].

QUESTION—What is meant by μαρτύρομαι 'I testify/insist upon'?

1. The verb makes a solemn declaration [Alf, Ba, Ea, ECWB, EGT, El, IB, Lns, MNTC, My, NTC, TNTC, WBC; KJV, NAB, NASB, NJB]: I testify, solemnly declare. It asserts that he is ministering by the authority of Christ [Ba, ECWB, NTC, WBC]. The moral appeal is a matter of testimony; the teacher witnesses to the truth which has been committed to him [IB]. The purpose of this assertion is the exhortation in the following words [Ba]. The imperatival sense lies in the following context [Alf, ICC].
2. The verb makes an injunction [AB, EBC, ICC, NCBC, Rob, TD, TH, We; NIV, NRSV, REB, TEV, TNT]: I insist upon, urge, adjure, protest. The verb originally meant 'to call to witness', then 'to affirm' [AB], 'asservate' [Rob], or 'to protest' [Rob], 'to protest with finality' [AB]. Here it makes an emphatic demand, though the translation 'adjure' strikes a false note since there is no thought of calling upon God to give force to the injunction [TD]. From its background from the law courts, the word in ordinary language came to mean 'to insist upon' [NCBC].
3. The verb contains both meanings [Can, Ho, LJ]: I solemnly declare and urge. The verb means he speaks what he personally knows to be the mind of Christ [Can, Ho]. But it is not to be limited to the declaration of a matter of personal knowledge, but also includes the meaning to protest (as in Gal. 5:3), to make a solemn appeal as in the sight of God. The use of the term marks a most emphatic and solemn form of protest [Can]. The verb is used here to call God as a witness to the truth of what he will say [Ho, LJ].

QUESTION—What is meant by ἐν 'in'?

1. It refers to Paul's position in Christ [Can, EGT, El, Ho, IB, LJ, My, We] as the source of Paul's authority [AB, Cal, CBC, ECWB, EGT, NCBC,

NTC, St, TH, WBC; REB, TEV, TNT]: I say and testify/insist upon as being united with the Lord. It identifies the writer with Christ and presents the exhortation as one made by Christ himself [EGT]. It means 'in communion with the Lord' [Ho, LJ, We], in the mystical unity of life with Christ [IB]. Some think that Paul is telling his readers that he speaks as Christ's ambassador or apostle, that the Lord is giving this exhortation through him [AB, LJ], and that if they reject this instruction they must one day give account to Christ [Cal, LJ]. Others think that it does not mean 'on the Lord's authority' nor 'by the Lord' [EGT, El].

2. It refers to the common position both Paul and his readers occupy in Christ [EBC, ICC, Lns, MNTC, Rob, TNTC]: I say and testify/insist upon as being united together with all of you in the Lord. The phrase εἶναι ἔν τινι 'to be in someone' is classical, meaning 'to completely depend on someone'. In the NT the expression takes on new significance with the idea of fellowship and union with Christ and God. Whatever the believer does ἐν κυρίῳ 'in the Lord' is done from a sense of dependence on him and union with him. Here, because an apostolic precept is concerned, it is implied that he speaks with authority. But it would not have been appropriate to use the phrase had he not been addressing those, who like himself, were united to and in fellowship with the Lord [ICC]. The phrase indicates both the motive behind Paul's admonition and the motive to which he appeals in his hearers for their obedience [Lns].

3. The phrase refers to a joint action performed by Paul and Christ [NASB]: I say and testify together with the Lord.

no longer[a] (are) you to-walk,[b] as also the Gentiles[c] walk in[d] (the) futility[e] of their minds,[f]

TEXT—Some manuscripts insert λοιπά 'other' before ἔθνη 'Gentiles'. GNT does not note this variant reading. The reading with λοιπά 'other' is accepted by only Ba, Cal, Ea, LJ, My, and KJV.

LEXICON—a. μηκέτι (LN 67.130) (BAGD 4. p. 518): 'no longer' [AB, BAGD, El, LN, Lns, NIC, NTC, Rob, WBC, We; NAB, NASB, NIV, NRSV], 'not from now on' [BAGD], 'henceforth...not' [KJV]. This word is also translated as an imperative: 'give up' [REB], 'you must give up' [TNT]. The words μηκέτι ὑμᾶς περιπατεῖν 'no longer are you to walk' are translated: 'do not go on living' [NJB], 'do not continue to live' [TEV]. This temporal negative implies that at one time these converts had walked in typical Gentile fashion, but they are now no longer to do so [LJ, Lns, NCBC].

b. pres. act. infin. of περιπατέω: 'to walk'. See this word at 2:2.

c. τὰ ἔθνη: 'Gentiles'. See this word at 2:11; 3:1, 6, 8.

d. ἐν with dative object (LN 13.8, 89.84): 'in' [AB, El, LN (13.8), Lns, NIC, NTC, Rob, WBC, We; KJV, NASB, NIV, NRSV, TNT], 'with' [LN (13.8, 89.84); REB], not explicit [NAB, NJB, TEV]. This preposition serves as a marker of a state or condition [LN (13.8)] or it serves as a marker of the manner in which an event occurs [LN (89.84)].

e. ματαιότης (LN **65.37**) (BAGD p. 495): 'futility' [AB, BAGD, LN, NIC, NTC, WBC; NASB, NIV, NRSV], 'vanity' [El, Lns, Rob, We; KJV] 'emptiness, purposelessness' [BAGD]. This noun is also translated as an adjective: 'empty' [LN; NAB], 'worthless' [TEV], 'futile' [BAGD, LN; REB], 'useless' [LN], 'empty' [NJB, TNT]. This noun suggests either absence of purpose or the failure to attain any true purpose [MM, Rob].

f. νοῦς (LN 26.14, 30.5) (BAGD 3.a. p. 544): 'minds' [BAGD, NIC, WBC; NAB, NRSV], 'mind' [AB, BAGD, El, LN (26.14), Lns, NTC, Rob, We; KJV, NASB], 'thoughts' [TEV], 'thinking' [NIV], 'notions' [REB], 'attitude, way of thinking' [BAGD, LN (30.5)], 'disposition, manner of thought' [LN (30.5)]. This noun is also conflated with ματαιότης 'futility' and translated as an adjective: 'empty-headed' [NJB], 'empty-minded' [TNT]. This noun denotes the whole of the mental and moral state of being as a sum total [BAGD]. It denotes the psychological faculty of understanding, reasoning, thinking, and deciding [Cal, Ea, IDB, ISBE2, LJ, LN (26.14), My], or it denotes a particular way of thinking [LN (30.5)].

QUESTION—What is the function of καί 'also' here?

It introduces a comparison or a gentle contrast between the ὑμᾶς 'you' and the ἔθνη 'Gentiles' of which they had lately formed a part [El]. It has its reference in the former walk of the readers [My]. It emphasizes the words that follow [We].

QUESTION—What is meant by ἐν ματαιότητι τοῦ νοὸς αὐτῶν 'in the futility of their minds'?

1. The noun ματαιότητι 'futility' causes the phrase to carry an implication of the Gentiles' connection with idolatry [AB, CBC, IB, NIC, We, WeBC].
2. The occurrence of the noun here is not presented as giving the phrase a specific connection with Gentile idolatry [Alf, Cal, Can, DNTT, Ea, EBC, ECWB, EGT, El, Ho, ICC, IDB, LJ, Lns, MNTC, My, NCBC, NTC, Rob, Si, St, TH, TNTC, WBC]. It means that their thinking, their reasoning, was worthless [TH]. It states the *waste* of the whole of the rational powers on worthless goals [Alf, Ea, LJ, Lns]. The noun implies a goal and aim of the νοός 'mind'. The thoughts aim to bring the person to the right goal, but this turns out to be vacuity, emptiness and delusion [Lns]. The noun includes everything in the following verses concerning the blindness and depravity of the heathen [Ho].

QUESTION—What relationship is indicated by ἐν 'in'?

This indicates the element [Alf] or sphere [Ea, El, My] of the Gentiles' moral walk [El].

QUESTION—What is meant by νοός 'minds'?

This noun may denote the mental faculty of the mind itself, or it may denote its use and application. The latter is the more appropriate meaning here, since ματαιότητι 'futility' is ascribed to it [Can]. It is not just the intellect [Ea, EGT, Ho, LJ]. In the meaning of 'mind, disposition' it expresses the inner orientation or moral attitude of a person [TD]. It stands for that portion of man's spiritual nature whose function it is to comprehend and relish Divine truth [Ea, EGT, IDB]. It is the same as the 'inner man', the spiritual intuition of the principles of truth and right, which is the true humanity [ECWB]. Here it stands for the whole human soul [Ho, LJ].

4:18 darkened[a] in-the understanding[b] being, having-been-alienated[c] (from) the life of God

LEXICON—a. perf. pass. participle of σκοτόω (σκοτόομαι LN **32.44**) (BAGD 2. p. 758): 'to be darkened' [BAGD, El, **LN**, Lns, NIC, NTC, Rob, WBC, We; KJV, NAB, NASB, NIV, NRSV, TNT], 'to be in the dark' [NJB, TEV], 'to be blacked out' [AB], 'to be closed' [REB], 'to be incapable of perceiving, to be not able to understand' [LN].

b. διάνοια (LN **26.14**) (BAGD 1. p. 187): 'understanding' [BAGD, El, Lns, NIC, NTC, Rob, We; KJV, NAB, NASB, NIV, NRSV, TNT], 'thinking' [WBC], 'intelligence' [BAGD], 'minds' [BAGD, LN; REB, TEV]. This noun is also translated as an adverb: 'intellectually' [AB; NJB]. This is the psychological faculty of understanding, reasoning, thinking, and deciding [LN].

c. perf. pass. participle of ἀπαλλοτριόω, ἀπαλλοτριόομαι (LN 11.75) (BAGD p. 80): 'to be alienated from' [El, Lns, NIC, NTC, Rob, We; KJV, NRSV, REB], 'to be estranged from' [BAGD; NAB, NJB], 'to be strangers to' [LN; TNT], 'to be excluded from' [AB; NASB], 'to be separated from' [WBC; NASB, NIV]. This passive verb is also translated actively: 'to have no part in' [TEV]. Here the verb implies hostility and enmity [TD].

QUESTION—How does this verse relate to the context and what is the significance and structure of the two participial clauses comprising it?

The two participial clauses are emphatic by position [ICC, My]. Emphasis is put upon ἐσκοτωμένοι 'darkened' first, then on ἀπηλλοτρωμένοι 'alienated' [EGT]. The unnamed agent of these perfect passive participles is Satan [Lns].

1. This verse gives the reason or reasons for the 'futility of their mind', mentioned in the preceding clause [Can, Ea, EBC, Ho, MNTC, My, NTC].

1.1 The two perfect participles indicate the two reasons for the 'futility of their mind' [Can, Ea, EBC, LJ, My, NTC]: the Gentiles walk in the futility of their minds because their understanding has been darkened and because they have been alienated from God.

1.2 The first perfect participle gives the reason for the ματαιότητι τοῦ νοὸς αὐτῶν 'the futility of their mind' while the second perfect participle is an ultimate consequence of the first [Ho, MNTC]: the Gentiles walk in the futility of their minds because they are darkened as to the understanding, so that they are alienated from the life of God because of the ignorance that is in them and their hardness of heart. The logical and theological order of this statement is: darkness of mind is the cause of ignorance which, in turn, is the cause of hardness of heart which, with ignorance, are two causes of alienation from God [Ho].

2. This verse gives the results of the 'futility of their mind' mentioned in the preceding clause [ECWB, NCBC]. The first result is intellectual, 'darkened in the understanding' and this leads to the second, 'having been alienated from the life of God', which is moral. The two διά 'because of' clauses are connected to this second result and indicate the causes of this alienation [ECWB].

3. This verse defines and explains the 'futility of their mind', mentioned in the preceding clause [EGT, El, Ho, ICC, LJ, Lns, WBC]. It gives a further description of the walk of the Gentiles. Their walk is what it is because of the condition indicated by the two participles [EGT, LJ]. The two διά 'because of' clauses following the participial clauses indicate only the cause of 'having been alienated' [LJ].

3.1 The two perfect participles are coordinate [El, WBC]. The second perfect participle, 'having been alienated', indicates an accompanying condition to the condition indicated in the first perfect participle, 'darkened' [WBC]. The occurrence of the present participles, ὄντες 'being' in the first participial clause and οὖσαν 'is' in the second, points to the apparent parallel nature of the clauses in this verse [El].

3.2 The second perfect participle, 'having been alienated', is the result of the first, 'having been darkened' [EGT, Lns]: their being darkened in understanding has resulted in their being alienated from the life of God. The participle 'being darkened' implicitly indicates the cause of 'having been alienated'. Being in a state of moral darkness they also become separated from the true life [EGT, Lns]. The διά 'because of' clause following the participial clauses indicates the cause of both perfect participles, the second διά 'because of' clause explains the first διά 'because of' clause [Lns].

3.3 The second perfect participle, 'having been alienated', is the reason for the first, 'being darkened' [Ba]: their understanding has been darkened because they have been alienated from the life of God. Their understanding is darkened because they were alienated from the true God, and particularly because their hearts are hardened [Ba].

4. This verse lists further details about the Gentiles' life style [Rob, St, TH, TNTC, WeBC; KJV, NIV, NRSV, REB]. Some of these commentators treat the two perfect participles as parallel to 'the futility of their mind' in the last verse [Rob, TH]. Two of them understand the second perfect participle 'having been alienated' as being the result of the first, 'darkened' [St, TNTC]. One suggests the first, 'darkened' is the result of the second, 'having been alienated' [WeBC]. Another supplies a logical progression of ideas as mostly in reverse to that given in the text: hardness

of heart produces ignorance, ignorance produces darkened understanding, the consequence of which is alienation from the life of God. These characteristics are seen as the cause of the attributes listed in 4:19 [St].
5. The first participle, 'darkened', is a comment related to 'the futility of their mind' in 4:17, while the second participle, 'alienated', makes a further comment about the Gentiles' state [NAB, NJB, TEV, TNT]: no longer walk as the pagans do in the vanity of their minds—their understanding darkened. They are alienated from the life of God because of the ignorance that is in them and the hardness of their hearts.

QUESTION—What is meant by ἐσκοτωμένοι 'darkened'?

This refers to their state of moral darkness [El, MNTC]. It refers to the effect that indulgence in sin and vice has upon the mental powers [LJ, MNTC, NCBC], nullifying the sense of right and wrong [My-ed, NCBC], and ultimately causing a noticeable stupor [Ba, Si-ed] and rendering the person unfit for high intellectual effort [Ba]. This participle prepares the way for the subsequent figure of insensibility (πώρωσιν 'hardness') [Si-ed]. The perfect passive participle ἐσκοτωμένοι 'darkened' functions as the equivalent of an adjective and is a metaphorical synonym for ἄγνοιαν 'ignorance' later in the verse [AB]. The condition it portrays is the opposite of that of the perfect participle πεφωτισμένους 'having been enlightened' in 1:18 [AB, Can, IB, ICC, Rob, WBC, We]. It consists in the mind being beclouded with false ideas and prejudices [Can]. It emphasizes the inability of the heathen to understand spiritual truth [TH, WBC].

QUESTION—What is meant by the noun διανοίᾳ 'understanding' and what relationship is indicated by its dative case?

The dative case indicates the sphere [Alf, Ea, EGT, El] or element to which the darkness is limited [El]. It is also said to indicate the dative in its ethical use [EGT]. The dative case indicates a more subjective evaluation than an accusative would give [Alf]. It may stress that the darkness has its seat *in* the mind, as opposed to an accusative of reference which would stress its influence over the mind [El].
1. This refers to the perceptive faculty, intellectual discernment [Alf, Cal, DNTT, Ea, El, Ho, ICC, ISBE2, LJ, Lns, MNTC, My, NTC, TD, TH, WBC]. This is apparent from the figurative term connected with it as well as from the language of the following clause [Ea]. It refers to the intellect because it is distinguished from νοός 'mind' in 4:17 and from καρδίας 'heart' in the final clause in this verse [Ho]. Being in the singular, this refers to the thinking faculty [Cal], the activity and product of the mind [Lns]. This refers to the power of discursive reasoning [NTC]. It refers to the faculty of religious discernment [DNTT], the faculty of moral and spiritual understanding [ISBE2, TD]. It implies the ability to apply knowledge as well as to acquire it [ISBE2].
2. This refers to both the faculties of thinking and feeling [EGT].

QUESTION—To what is the present participle ὄντες 'being' attached and how does it affect the meaning?
- 1. It is attached to the perfect participle ἐσκοτωμένοι 'darkened' [AB, Alf, Ba, Cal, Can, EGT, El, GNT, HG, Ho, ICC, My, NTC, WBC, We]: the understanding being darkened. The present participle ὄντες 'being' which is attached to ἐσκοτωμένοι 'darkened' serves to emphasize the present, durative status of the darkening [AB, HG] rather than the moment or mode of its origin [AB]. It marks their permanent and enduring state [El]. The rhythm of the sentence is decisive for this construction despite the parallel passage in Col. 1:21 [We].
- 2. It is attached to the perfect participle ἀπηλλοτριωμένοι 'alienated' [BD, Ea, Rob]: being alienated.
- 3. It is attached to both perfect participles [Lns]: the understanding being darkened and being alienated from the life of God. The perfect tense of the participles indicates a past act in each case with present and enduring results. The present periphrastic construction, brought about by attaching the present participle ὄντες 'being' to them, stresses the continuing condition indicated in the perfect participles. The agent of these passive participles is Satan [Lns].

QUESTION—What is meant by τῆς ζωῆς τοῦ θεοῦ 'the life of God'?
- 1. This is another term for salvation or regeneration [AB, Cal, Ea, EBC, ECWB, EGT, El, Ho, IB, ICC, LJ, Lns, My, NCBC, NTC, Rob, TH, WBC, We]. This is life which corresponds to the nature of God and which he communicates to his children [We]. The noun ζωῆς 'life' denotes the element or principle of Divine life within us [Ea, LJ, Lns, My, NCBC], or the principle of life as opposed to death [EGT, El, ICC, My]. It does not mean a godly life or conduct [AB, Ea, EGT, El, My, NCBC]. It is the life from God that existed in unfallen man, and now re-exists in all those who are in fellowship with God, the life which results from the operation and indwelling of God's Spirit [Ea, LJ]. Regeneration is called here, by way of eminence, τῆς ζωῆς τοῦ θεοῦ 'the life of God' because when God governs us by his Spirit, he does truly live in us. Of this, all men who are not new creatures in Christ are destitute [Cal].
- 2. This indicates life as the original created state of man [Alf, Can, MNTC]. This is life as opposed to death [Alf]. This is the life that God lives in men, the relationship in which men ought to do by nature the things of the law [Can]. Because Paul speaks of it as a life they once had or might have had [Can], it is not life as regenerated in the believer so much as it is life in man's original created state, when God was his life and light before he fell by sinning [Alf, Can].
- 3. This indicates the daily Christian walk [Ba, CBC]. It refers to a life like that of God, a life of which he is the source and author, a life which pleases him, as opposed to a life unlike God [Ba]. It is being attuned to God and giving obedience to him [CBC].

because-of[a] **the ignorance**[b] **being in them,**

LEXICON—a. διά with accusative object (LN 89.26): 'because of' [AB, El, LN, Lns, NIC, NTC, WBC, We; NAB, NASB, NIV, NJB, NRSV], 'because' [REB, TNT], 'on account of, by reason of' [LN], 'through' [Rob; KJV], 'for' [TEV].

b. ἄγνοια (LN 28.13) (BAGD 2. p. 11): 'ignorance' [BAGD, El, LN, Lns, NTC, Rob, WBC, We; KJV, NAB, NASB, NIV, NJB, NRSV, REB]. The phrase τὴν ἄγνοιαν τὴν οὖσαν ἐν αὐτοῖς 'the ignorance being in them' is translated 'deep-rooted ignorance' [NIC], 'inherent refusal to know' [AB], 'to be completely ignorant' [TEV], 'to be utterly ignorant' [TNT]. This is used in a religious sense and is almost the equivalent of 'sin' [BAGD].

QUESTION—What relationship is indicated by διά 'because of'?

1. It indicates the reason for their alienation from the life of God [AB, Alf, Cal, Ea, ECWB, EGT, El, Ho, ICC, LJ, My, NIC, NTC, WBC, WeBC; KJV, NAB, NRSV, TEV]: having been alienated from the life of God because of the ignorance that is in them. As knowledge of God is the true life of the soul, so ignorance of God is the death of it [Cal].
2. It indicates the reason for being darkened in understanding [St]: being darkened in understanding because of the ignorance that is in them.
3. It indicates a reason for both the darkening of their understanding and their alienation from the life of God [Can, EBC, IB, Lns, MNTC, My-ed; NASB, NIV, NJB, REB, TNT]: because of the ignorance that is in them and the hardening of their hearts, their understanding is darkened and they have been alienated from the life of God. This state of darkness and deadness is traced back to ignorance [Can, EBC] which is due to the hardening of their heart [Can]. There is no difficulty in tracing their habitual ignorance to repeated acts of excluding the light of truth. An effort to be ignorant results in a complete darkening of the understanding. For the two-fold condition of darkening and alienation, the apostle gives a two-fold ground, whose members mutually condition one another [My-ed].

QUESTION—What is meant by the clause τὴν ἄγνοιαν τὴν οὖσαν ἐν αὐτοῖς 'the ignorance that is in them'?

Usually the noun ἄγνοιαν 'ignorance' denotes lack of knowledge or inability to comprehend. Here the religious sense is meant [AB, ISBE2] which carries the implication that the ignorance is willful, an ignoring and repudiation of the truth [AB, Alf, CBC, ISBE, Lns, MNTC, NCBC, TH, TNTC, WBC]. This is reinforced by the following prepositional clause [IB, My-ed, NCBC, TH, WBC]. The implied object of this ignorance is God [AB, Alf, Can, IDB, ISBE, LJ, Lns, NCBC, WBC] and/or of Divine things [EGT, ISBE, LJ, MNTC, NCBC]. The words τὴν οὖσαν ἐν αὐτοῖς 'that is in them' are emphatic [AB, Can] (*contra* Rob who states it is not emphatic) and state that the origin of this ignorance is inherent in the human psyche itself [AB, EGT, LJ, Lns], that it is a habitual state [Can], that it is indwelling [El, LJ] and deep-seated [Ea, El, LJ, NIC]. Another states this present participle indicates the cause of the ignorance [Rob].

because-of[a] their hardness[b] of-the-heart,

LEXICON—a. διά with accusative object (LN 89.26): 'because of' [El, LN, Lns, NIC, Rob, WBC, We; KJV, NASB], 'due to' [NTC; NIV], 'the consequence of' [NJB], 'on account of, by reason of' [LN]. This is also conflated or partially conflated with the previous occurrence of the preposition by the use of a conjunction: 'and of' [AB], 'and' [NAB, NRSV, REB, TEV, TNT].

b. πώρωσις (LN 27.52) (BAGD p. 732): 'hardness' [El, NTC; NASB, NRSV], 'hardening' [BAGD, NIC, WBC, We; NIV], 'dulling' [BAGD], 'petrification' [AB, Lns], 'unwillingness to learn, mental stubbornness' [LN], 'blindness' [Rob; KJV]. This noun is also translated as a verb phrase: 'to grow hard as stone' [REB]. The phrase τὴν πώρωσιν τῆς καρδίας αὐτῶν 'their hardness of heart' is translated 'their resistance' [NAB], 'closed minds' [LN; NJB], 'to be stubborn' [TEV], 'to be insensitive' [TNT]. The word is used in Christian literature only with a figurative meaning, 'dullness, insensibility, obstinacy' [BAGD].

QUESTION—What relationship is indicated by διά 'because of'?

1. It indicates the reason for their ignorance [Cal, CBC, ICC, Lns, My, NTC, Rob, St, WBC, We; NIV, NJB]: the ignorance that is in them is caused by their hardness of heart. The ignorance of God has its root in the blindness of their hearts [Cal] and is the spring of all error [We]. The ignorance due to the hardness of their hearts is culpable [ICC, NTC, St].

2. It indicates the reason for their ignorance as well as the darkening of their understanding and their alienation from God [Can, MNTC]: because their hearts are hardened, there is an ignorance in them that has caused their understanding to be darkened and has alienated them from the life of God. This preposition is more immediately connected with the preceding ἄγνοιαν 'ignorance' but, at the same time, it is parallel to the preceding διά 'because of' [Can].

3. The preposition indicates a second reason for their alienation from God [AB, Alf, Ea, ECWB, EGT, El, Ho, LJ; NAB, NRSV, TEV]. This preposition is coordinate with [Ea, EGT, El, LJ, TH], but somewhat explanatory or causal of, the previous διά 'because of' [Ea, El, LJ]. This prepositional phrase is subordinate to ἀπηλλοτριωμένοι τῆς ζωῆς τοῦ θεοῦ 'having been alienated from the life of God' [Alf].

4. The preposition indicates a reason for both the darkening of their understanding and their alienation from God [Ba, My-ed, TH; NASB, REB, TNT]: their understanding has been darkened and they have been alienated from the life of God because of their hardness of heart.

5. The preposition indicates a second reason for their alienation from the life of God, the darkening of their understanding, and the futility of their minds [IB, NCBC]. This prepositional clause is not said to be the cause of

the ignorance that is in them, for the two prepositional clauses are parallel [IB]. This preposition indicates the underlying cause of all the trouble with unconverted Gentiles [NCBC].
6. The preposition indicates the result of ἀπηλλοτριωμένοι τῆς ζωῆς τοῦ θεοῦ 'having been alienated from God's life' [WeBC]: because of the ignorance that is in them, they have been alienated from the life of God which resulted in the hardening of their hearts.
7. The preposition indicates the reason for having been darkened in the understanding [KJV]: being darkened in the understanding because of the hardness (blindness (KJV)) of their heart.

QUESTION—What is meant by πώρωσιν τῆς καρδίας 'hardness of heart'?
1. The noun πώρωσιν indicates a hardening or hardness [AB, Alf, Ba, Can, Ea, EBC, ECWB, EGT, El, Ho, IB, ICC, ISBE2, LJ, Lns, MNTC, My, My-ed, NCBC, NIC, NTC, Si-ed, St, TD, TH, TNTC, WBC, We, WeBC; NASB, NIV, NRSV, REB].
    1.1 The noun πώρωσιν indicates hardness in the sense of insensibility [Ba, ECWB, EGT, ICC, LJ, MNTC, NCBC, Si-ed, TD, TNTC, WeBC; TNT].
    1.2 The noun indicates hardness in the sense of obduracy, stubbornness [Alf, CBC, El, ISBE2, NIC, St; NAB, NJB, TEV]: stubborn hearts.
    1.3 The noun carries both senses [AB, Can, Ea, EBC, IB, NTC, TH, WBC]. It does not indicate insensibility to all feeling and all desire, but only to what was good and uplifting and to that which would bring them into closer harmony with the will of God [NTC]. It describes insensibility to what would cause others acute pain, lack of susceptibility to impressions on the mind and conscience, lack of shame or remorse for wrong-doing, and lack of gratitude for kindness [Can]. 'Hardening' is a way of describing the ignorance as a refusal or stubbornness to recognize the voice of God [CBC, LJ, NTC, TH, WBC] or of conscience [NIC, NTC].
2. The noun indicates a blindness [Cal, Rob; KJV]. This blindness which covers the heart of men is the punishment of original sin [Cal]. The word could be used in connection with the eyes, so that the meaning of insensibility passed over into that of blindness, with accompanying carry-over into figurative language. The problem with translating it as 'hardening' is that this may be taken to denote obstinacy or hardening of the will [Rob].

QUESTION—What is meant by καρδίας 'heart'?
This noun, in the distributive singular, indicates that it is something that belongs to each person in a group [Tu].
1. This denotes the personal center of a person's being, the seat of intellect, will [DNTT, Lns, TD, WBC, WeBC], and emotions [DNTT, Lns, WBC].
2. This denotes, in this context, sensibility to feeling [Can, LJ, MNTC, NTC; TNT].

4:19 who having-become-callous[a] they-gave-over[b] themselves to-licentiousness[c] for (the) practice[d] of uncleanness[e] of all (kinds) with greediness/covetousness.[f]

TEXT—Instead of ἀπηλγηκότες 'having become callous', some manuscripts have ἀπηλπικότες or ἀφηλπικότες, both meaning 'having become hopeless, despairing'. None of our sources support these alternative readings. GNT assigns ἀπηλγηκότες 'having become callous' an A rating, indicating this reading is certain.

LEXICON—a. perf. act. participle of ἀπαλγέω (LN **25.197**) (BAGD p. 80): 'to become callous' [BAGD, LN, MM, NTC; NASB], 'to lose all sensitivity' [NIV, NRSV], 'to lose all moral sensitivity' [NIC], 'to lose all feeling of shame' [LN; TEV], 'to lose compunction' [Lns], 'to lose feeling' [We], 'to be past feeling' [El, Rob; KJV], 'to be dead to all feeling' [REB], 'to be dead to all feeling of shame' [TNT]. This verb is also translated adverbially as a phrase: 'without remorse' [NAB], 'in their insensitive state' [AB]. It is also translated as a clause: 'their moral sensitivity having become dulled' [WBC], 'their sense of right and wrong once dulled' [NJB].

b. aorist act. indic. of παραδίδωμι (LN 57.77) (BAGD 1.b. p. 615): 'to give over' [AB, BAGD, El, LN, Lns, NIC, Rob, WBC; KJV, NASB, NIV, TEV], 'to abandon' [NTC; NAB, NJB, NRSV, REB], 'to give up' [BAGD, We; TNT], 'to hand over' [BAGD, LN], 'to turn over' [BAGD].

c. ἀσέλγεια (LN 88.272) (BAGD p. 114): 'licentiousness' [BAGD, NTC; NRSV, TNT], 'licentious behavior, extreme immorality' [LN], 'lasciviousness' [Rob, We; KJV], 'sensuality' [BAGD; NASB, NIV], 'debauchery' [AB, BAGD, NIC, WBC], 'lust' [NAB], 'vice' [REB, TEV], 'excess' [Lns], 'wantonness' [El]. This noun is also translated in conjunction with the verb παραδίδωμι 'to give over': 'to abandon all self control' [NJB]. This noun denotes behavior that is totally lacking in moral restraint. It usually carries the implication of sexual licentiousness [LN].

d. ἐργασία (LN **41.20**) (BAGD 1. p. 307): 'practice' [BAGD, NIC, NTC; NASB, TNT], 'practicing' [Lns], 'working' [El], 'pursuit' [BAGD], 'indulgence' [NAB], 'behavior' [LN]. This noun is also translated as a verb: 'to practice' [**LN**; NRSV, REB], 'to indulge' [NIV], 'to pursue' [WBC; NJB], 'to work' [Rob, We; KJV], 'to do' [AB; TEV], 'to engage in' [LN].

e. ἀκαθαρσία (LN 88.261) (BAGD 2. p. 29): 'uncleanness' [El, Lns, Rob, We; KJV, NJB], 'impurity' [NIC, NTC, WBC; NASB, NIV, NRSV, TNT], 'immorality' [BAGD], 'filthy things' [AB], 'lewd conduct' [NAB], 'indecency' [REB], 'indecent things' [TEV]. This noun is used of the state of moral impurity [LN]. It is used in a figurative sense of unnatural vices [BAGD] particularly those of a sexual nature [BAGD, LN].

f. πλεονεξία (LN 25.22) (BAGD p. 667): 'greediness' [BAGD, El, Lns, Rob; KJV, NASB], 'greed' [LN], 'insatiableness' [BAGD], 'avarice' [BAGD, LN], 'covetousness' [BAGD, LN, NIC, WBC], 'selfishness'

[We], 'a continual lust for more' [NIV], 'to excess' [NJB], 'without restraint' [TEV], not explicit [NAB, REB]. This noun is also translated as a verb: 'to still ask for more' [AB]. It is also translated as an adjective and as an adverb modifying ἐργασία 'practice': 'greedy' [NTC], 'unrestrained' [TNT], 'greedy (to practice)' [NRSV].

QUESTION—What is the purpose of this verse in the context?

1. This verse is connected with the Gentiles' spiritual condition in 4:18 [AB, Alf, Cal, Can, Ea, ECWB, EGT, Ho, IB, LJ, My, NCBC, NIC, NTC, Rob, St, TH, TNTC, We]. The vices described in this verse are the active counterparts of the passive 'ignorance' in the last verse, bred by recklessness [Rob].
  1.1 This verse indicates the result of their ignorance and/or hardness of heart [AB, Alf, Cal, Can, Ea, ECWB, EGT, Ho, IB, LJ, NCBC, NIC, NTC, St, TNTC, We]. The commission of evil deeds and captivity in wickedness are the result of their refusal to know God [AB]. The heart that has been so hardened so as to become 'callused' offers no resistance to the worst excesses of evil conduct presented to it [IB].
  1.2 This verse is the grounds, through observable experience, for the assertion of the last verse that the Gentiles are alienated from the life of God [My].
2. This verse is explanatory of τὰ ἔθνη περιπατεῖ ἐν ματαιότητι τοῦ νοὸς αὐτῶν 'the Gentiles walk in the futility of their minds' in 4:17 [Lns]. The relative clause of this verse is parallel to the perfect participles of the last verse, and like them, have both causal and qualitative force. This verse, with 4:18, indicates how the Gentiles walk in futility of mind [Lns].

QUESTION—What is meant by the relative pronoun οἵτινες 'who'?

This is not the simple relative pronoun οἵ 'who' [Ho], but οἵτινες 'such who', which has an explanatory force [EGT, El, Ho] equivalent to 'who as' [Ea, EGT], 'such as who' [Ho, My, We], or 'being persons who' [ICC]. The pronoun denotes a class of sinners [Ea]. Paul does not mean to denote every last Gentile as guilty of the whole gamut of the evils listed [LJ], but it is used to describe Gentile life as a whole [LJ, Lns]. One commentator states it has causative as well as qualitative force: the Gentiles walk in futility of mind because they are such as who have given themselves over to licentiousness [Lns].

QUESTION—What is meant by ἀπηλγηκότες 'having become callous'?

This shows a total lack of all emotions on moral matters; the person is wholly hardened in sin [Ba, EBC], beyond remorse [Ea, EBC, LJ], reckless [Rob]. This is moral insensibility, the deadness that occurs when the heart has stopped being sensitive to the prickings of conscience [EGT, El, Ho, LJ, Lns, My, NCBC, NTC, TNTC], the lack of any feeling of shame [TH].

QUESTION—What is meant by τῇ ἀσελγείᾳ 'to licentiousness'?

1. This indicates open, unrestrained lust [Ea, LJ], shameless, outrageous sensuality [EGT, MNTC], devoid of any sense of decency. It was reckless and grossly animal-like [ECWB]. In the NT, the word primarily refers to

sexual excesses [Ea, EBC, ECWB, EGT, LJ, MNTC, My, NCBC, NTC, TH, WBC, We]. It is the attitude that regards sex as nothing more than a means of pleasure, with no accompanying sense of responsibility [NCBC]. The sins listed in this verse are mainly, though not exclusively, sexual [TH].

2. This noun has here its general meaning and is not restricted to its sexual connotation [AB, Cal, CBC, Ho, IDB, Lns, NIC, Rob, TD, TNTC]. This word means lewdness [AB, Rob], outrageous lasciviousness, licentiousness [AB], debauchery [IDB, TD], or voluptuousness [TD]. It is the open practice of uncleanness, such as to shock public decency [Rob]. It alludes to sexual depravity, but is not restricted to it. It was used to describe the deliberate neglect of limits and measures, and the refusal to follow any distinct way or order [AB]. Consequently it has a notion of violence in it [AB, TNTC]. Like the other two principal nouns in this verse, its meaning is meant to be comprehensive in character to denote man's total determination to vice [AB]. The noun ἀσελγείᾳ 'licentiousness, lasciviousness' denotes the wantonness with which they indulge in intemperance and licentiousness [Cal]. This is 'vice', the ruthless attitude that seeks its own ends at any cost [CBC], the throwing off of all restraint and with no regard for public decency or the rights and feelings of others [NIC]. The word means 'excess' [Ho, Lns].

QUESTION—What is meant by εἰς ἐργασίαν 'for the practice'?

The preposition εἰς 'for' indicates the object or purpose [AB, Alf, Ea, EGT, El], the conscious aim of the verb παρέδωκαν 'they gave (themselves) over' [Alf, EGT, El, My], not just an incidental result [Alf].

1. The word indicates an almost total preoccupation with something [Alf, Can, EBC, ICC, ISBE, TNTC, We; NJB]. The word indicates the working at something as though it were a trade or business [Alf, Can, ICC, ISBE, TNTC, We]. It suggests they made a business of ἀκαθαρσίας 'uncleanness', but it should not be understood of a literal trading in impurity [ICC]. It indicates that their pursuit of all kinds of uncleanness has become an 'occupation' or an 'earnest pursuit' [TNTC].

2. The word is simply the equivalent of τὸ ἐργάζεσθαι 'the doing, working' [Ea, EGT, El, TH; KJV, TEV], or 'performance, practice' [Lns, Rob, WBC; NASB, NRSV, REB, TNT].

QUESTION—What is meant by ἀκαθαρσίας 'uncleanness'?

1. This word indicates moral uncleanness in the widest sense [Cal, CBC, EGT, ISBE2, Lns, NIC, TD, WeBC]. This is all manner of moral evil [Lns, NIC], 'vice' [Lns]. It stands for any wayward moral behavior that keeps man from fellowship with God. It covers such sins as licentiousness, covetousness, and sexual abuses [ISBE2]. It stands for scandalous enormities of all kinds [Cal]. It denotes all those desires that lead to low and unworthy conduct, and includes sexual lusts [CBC]. Rom. 1:18–32 indicates the range of meaning of ἀκαθαρσίας 'uncleanness', which includes idolatry, sexual sins of all kinds, and the final complete reversal

of values in which their evil conduct becomes the accepted and approved social norm [WeBC].
2. The word refers especially or primarily to sexual sins [Ea, LJ, My, TD, TH, WBC]. This word usually denotes, in the NT, the special sin of lewdness or unchastity [Ea, LJ].
3. This word connotes an association with idolatry [AB]. The word includes, but is not restricted to sexual sins. To the Jewish mind, the word expressed a religious attitude on the part of pagans that was often associated with sexual sins. But any act connected with idolatry was regarded as unclean [AB].

QUESTION—To what is the phrase ἐν πλεονεξίᾳ 'with greediness/covetousness' connected?
1. This phrase is connected to both ἀσελγείᾳ 'licentiousness' and ἀκαθαρσίας 'uncleanness' [AB, Cal, Ea, EBC, IB, LJ; NIV]: they have given themselves over insatiably both to licentiousness and the working of all kinds of uncleanness. It indicates the spirit or atmosphere in which the vices that precede it in the text are carried out [AB, Ea, IB].
2. This phrase is more immediately connected to ἀκαθαρσίας 'uncleanness' [Can, ECWB, EGT, Lns, MNTC, My, NCBC, TH, TNTC, WeBC; NAB, NJB, TEV]: they have given themselves over to licentiousness, to the working of all kinds of uncleanness insatiably. This describes the prevailing state or frame of mind in which they committed the ἀκαθαρσίας 'uncleanness' [EGT, El]. The result of ἀσελγείᾳ 'licentiousness' is not just the working out of uncleanness of every kind, but that the practice of uncleanness is done with greediness, with a reckless delight in uncleanness for its own sake [ECWB]. The two great heathen vices were ἀκαθαρσίας 'uncleanness' and πλεονεξίᾳ 'greediness' [EGT, MNTC, My].
3. This phrase is connected to ἐργασίαν 'practice' [NTC, TD; NRSV, TNT]: for the greedy practice of every kind of uncleanness. The possibility must be considered that ἐν πλεονεξίᾳ 'with greediness/covetousness' is used modally with ἐργασίαν 'practice' to indicate unlawful enrichment through practicing all conceivable uncleanness. If not, then it is appended loosely with ἀκαθαρσίας 'uncleanness', the writer not taking into account the preceding construction because of the slowness of letter writing in antiquity [TD] (which virtually equates to the absolute usage below).
4. This phrase is used absolutely, indicating the greed for gain as yet another vice to which they have given themselves [Ho, NIC, WBC]: they have given themselves over to licentiousness, to the working of all kinds of uncleanness and greediness. The phrase ἐν πλεονεξίᾳ means 'together with covetousness'. The heathen have given themselves up to uncleanness and covetousness [Ho].

QUESTION—What is meant by πλεονεξία 'greediness/covetousness'?
1. It means 'greediness' [AB, Alf, Cal, Can, DNTT, Ea, EBC, ECWB, EGT, El, IB, IDB, ISBE2, Lns, MNTC, NTC, Rob, TH, TNTC, We, WeBC; KJV, NASB, NIV, NJB, NRSV, TEV, TNT]. This is the desire for always having more, a wider vice than mere covetousness [Alf, MNTC, TNTC], although covetousness is usually the form in which it is manifested [Alf, MNTC]. Except for its occurrence in 2 Cor. 2:11, it always appears to be directed toward material gain [DNTT]. It is self-seeking or greed in whatever direction this central tendency extends itself. As here, it may include within itself, as an element, lustful sins though it never equates to 'lasciviousness' [Alf]. This is the spirit of covetous extortion that has self as its prevailing power. The gathering of all possible objects and enjoyments for one's self [Ea, EBC, IB] is its absorbing occupation [Ea]. This indicates a reckless delight in foulness for its own sake [ECWB]. Greediness is the key to the viciousness of pagan life, as love is to the goodness of Christian life [IB].
2. It means 'covetousness' [Ho, ICC, LJ, My, NCBC, NIC, WBC]. It indicates covetousness, extortion, and the attitude that nothing matters but the gratification of self [LJ]. This is the ruthless appetite for more and more of what you want [NCBC].

DISCOURSE UNIT: 4:20–24 [IB, WBC, WeBC]. The topic is that the truth, as it is in Jesus, requires putting off the old man and putting on the new [IB], the call to a transformation from the old way of life to a new way of life in Christ [WeBC].

DISCOURSE UNIT: 4:20–21b [AB, LJ]. The topic is Messiah's school, in which Christians have learned better ways than those of the Gentiles [AB], the knowledge of the truth through hearing and learning Christ [LJ].

4:20 But^a you not so^b have-learned^c Christ,
LEXICON—a. δέ (LN 89.124): 'but' [AB, El, LN, Lns, NIC, Rob, WBC, We; KJV, NASB, REB, TNT], 'however' [NTC; NIV], 'now' [NJB], not explicit [NAB, NRSV, TEV].
b. οὕτως (LN 61.9): 'so' [El, LN, NTC, Rob, We; KJV], 'thus' [LN, Lns], 'in this way' [LN; NASB], 'that/this way' [AB; NIV], 'along these lines' [TNT], 'that' [NIC]. The negative adverbial phrase οὐχ οὕτως ἐμάθετε 'you have not so learned' is also translated 'that is not the way you learned' [WBC; NRSV], 'that is not what you learned when you learned' [NAB], 'that is hardly the way you have learnt' [NJB], 'that is not how you learned' [REB], 'that was not what you learned' [TEV].
c. aorist act. indic. of μανθάνω (LN 27.12, 32.14) (BAGD 1. p. 490): 'to learn' [BAGD, El, LN (27.12), Lns, NTC, Rob, WBC, We; KJV, NAB, NASB, NJB, NRSV, REB, TEV], 'to be taught, to be instructed' [LN (27.12)], 'to learn of' [TNT], 'to come to know' [NIV], 'to become student of' [AB], 'to understand' [LN (32.14)]. This verb is also translated

as a clause: you learned the lesson in the school (of Christ) [NIC]. This verb occurs with the thing learned in the accusative case, here 'Christ' which is equivalent to Christian teaching [BAGD].

QUESTION—What relationship is indicated by δέ 'but'?

This particle introduces a contrast that sets the conduct of Christians against the conduct just attributed to the pagan life style in the previous verses [Cal, LJ, MNTC, WBC] and takes up again the μηκέτι ὑμᾶς κ.τ.λ. 'no longer should you, etc.' of 4:17 [We].

QUESTION—What is significant about the plural pronoun ὑμεῖς 'you'?

The pronoun is emphatic by position [Alf, Ea, El, LJ, NTC, TNTC]. It stands in contrast to the yet unconverted and unfeeling heathen [EBC, EGT, El, LJ, My].

QUESTION—What is meant by οὐχ οὕτως 'not so'?

The negative particle with the adverb results in the formation of a litotes that suggests more than is expressed [EGT, El, ICC, LJ, Lns, My]. Litotes serves to bring out the positive emphasis. It means that the very suggestion of living like pagans is utterly impossible [LJ]. It means they did not learn Christ under teaching that was characteristic of, or taught prospects for, living a life of vanity and ignorance of God [Alf, Ea]. Their knowledge of Christ is such that it has not led them to live as the heathen [Ho, Lns, My]. The three infinitives which follow in verses 22, 23, and 24 indicate the litotes here implies a positive ellipsis which is the counterpart of this negative statement because these infinitives can depend only loosely on the negated verb ἐμάθετε 'you learned' and really require a *positive* affirmation. The complete thought would be: 'you have not so learned Christ so as to continue to live like the heathen; you have learned him so as to put off the old nature, etc.' [IB]. The adverb is emphatic [LJ]. It may imply that there were those who taught a Christian lifestyle that permitted them to continue their former Gentile lifestyle [Can, TH].

QUESTION—What is meant by the phrase ἐμάθετε τὸν Χριστόν 'you have learned Christ'?

It means the same as knowing Christ in a personal way [AB, Alf, Can, Ea, EBC, ECWB, EGT, El, Ho, LJ, NCBC, NTC, Si, St, TD, TNTC, WBC, WeBC].

1. The name Χριστόν 'Christ' is a metonymy that designates Christ, not just his person, but also his mission, as the object and/or content of the instruction [ECWB, EGT, El, ICC, LJ, Lns, MNTC, My, NTC, St, TH, TNTC, WBC, We]. Christ himself is put as the sum of the gospel [EGT, We]. Christ is both the object of the learning and the content [El, ICC, LJ]. To learn Christ is to believe and embrace the preaching and teaching they have heard about Christ [Lns]. The name Χριστόν 'Christ' here is emphatic and stands in distinction from the name Ἰησοῦ 'Jesus' at the end of 4:21. It indicates the true nature of the office of Messiah [EGT] as Anointed Priest, Prophet, and King, or as the Mediator, in whom Christians escape from the guilt and bondage of the sins just mentioned

[ECWB]. It stands for all that makes him Christ [Lns]. It indicates also the moral content of Christ's message, which stands in sharp contrast to the sexual sins just mentioned [TH].
2. The name Χριστόν 'Christ' is a metonymy that stands for the Christian way of life [NCBC, NIC]. It stands for a way of life [NCBC, NIC] that is in sharp contrast to the licentiousness which has just been condemned [NCBC].

QUESTION—What is indicated by the aorist tense of the verb ἐμάθετε 'you learned'?

The aorist tense points back to the definite time of their conversion [EGT, ICC], or the aorist tense of the verbs at this point are not to be pressed to indicate the time of conversion, but the past without further definition. As the context does not fix upon a particular moment, they may be translated in English as simple past tenses, or, more preferably and naturally, by the perfect tense [Rob]. Although the aorist is used, it denotes a process of learning [AB, NTC, WBC].

4:21 if indeed^a you-heard^b him and in^c him were-taught,

LEXICON—a. γέ (LN 91.6) (BAGD 3.a. p. 152). The two particles εἴ γε 'if indeed' are translated 'if indeed' [BAGD, El, Lns; NASB], 'if so be' [Rob; KJV], 'if at least' [We], 'assuming' [AB], 'assuming that' [WBC], 'inasmuch as' [BAGD], 'for surely' [NTC; NRSV], 'surely' [NIV], 'certainly' [TEV, TNT]. These particles are also translated by a conjunction combined with a verb or rhetorical questions: 'unless you failed' [NJB], 'for I take it' [NIC], 'for were you not told about him, were you not taught the truth?' [REB]. They are also translated by a verb in combination with an expression denoting expectation: 'I am supposing, of course' [NAB].

b. aorist act. indic. of ἀκούω (LN 36.14): 'to hear' [El, Lns, Rob, We; KJV, NASB, TNT], 'to hear of/about' [NIC, NTC, WBC; NIV, NRSV, TEV], 'to hear properly' [NJB], 'to listen' [AB], 'to pay attention to and obey' [LN]. This active verb is also translated passively: 'to be told about' [REB], 'to be preached' [NAB]. This verb denotes paying attention to and being in conformity with what a person advises or commands [LN].

c. ἐν with dative object (LN 89.84, 89.119): 'in' [AB, El, LN (89.119), NIC, NTC, Rob, WBC, We; NASB, NIV, NRSV], 'in union with' [LN (89.119)], 'in connection with' [Lns], 'by' [KJV], not explicit [NAB, NJB]. The phrase ἐν αὐτῷ 'in him' is translated: 'as Christians' [REB, TNT], 'as his followers' [TEV].

QUESTION—What is the relationship of this clause to the context?

This clause is a closer specification of the preceding clause, ἐμάθετε τὸν Χριστόν 'you learned Christ' [Can, MNTC, TNTC, WBC]. The writer states the supposition upon which 'learning Christ' consists [Can]. The verses which follow are an expansion and explanation of ἐμάθετε τὸν Χριστόν 'you learned Christ' [MNTC, WBC]. This clause stands in a parenthetical relationship to the clause ἐμάθετε τὸν Χριστόν 'you learned Christ' [IB, LJ, Lns].

QUESTION—What is meant by the εἴ γε 'if indeed'?

1. This implies a slight or polite doubt about how well they had learned Christ [Ba; NJB]. They imply a slight and delicate doubt about how attentively they had listened and learned [Ba].
2. This expresses Paul's assumption that they had indeed learned Christ [AB, Alf, Can, Ea, EGT, El, Ho, IB, ICC, LJ, Lns, My, NCBC, NIC, TH, TNTC, WBC; NAB, NIV, NRSV, REB]. It introduces a gentle irony that calls upon the readers to verify the statement that it was Christ they had heard and in whom they had been taught [TNTC]. It does not directly assert what is assumed to be true [Ea]. This is a restrictive conjunction which is used because the writer is writing a circular type letter, does not personally know all the recipients, and/or was not personally present when the gospel was first preached to them [AB, ICC, NIC, TH]. (Others, however, state Paul had evangelized and taught the Ephesian believers himself [LJ, My, TD]). He intends to appeal to them through their thorough acquaintance with the gospel which was gained through evangelists other than himself. So he is expressing his trust in the quality of their instruction through the hands of others [AB]. These two particles do not absolutely assume that after their conversion the readers had genuinely received Paul's teachings, but that he believes and trusts that it was so [Alf]. With a delicate supposition, the writer takes it as certain that they had heard Christ's teachings [EGT, NCBC].
3. This emphasizes that they had learned Christ [Cal, EBC, ECWB, NTC, Rob; TEV, TNT]. The particles εἴ γε 'if indeed' does not imply doubt, but gives emphasis [Rob]. The tone of doubt here is not real doubt, but that rhetorical doubt that indicates strong affirmation [ECWB]. He not only tells them they had heard Christ, but uses a stronger expression as if to tell them this doctrine had not been just slightly pointed out, but had been faithfully delivered and explained [Cal].

QUESTION—What is meant by the two verbs ἠκούσατε 'you heard' and ἐδιδάχθητε 'you were taught'?

These verbs express the content of the assumption expressed in εἴ γε 'if indeed'. The meaning is 'if you genuinely heard him and if you genuinely were taught in him'. The two clauses to which they belong are included in the ἐμάθετε τὸν Χριστόν 'you learned Christ' of the previous verse [Alf, Can, El, ICC, LJ, Lns, My, Rob, TNTC]. The verb ἠκούσατε 'you heard' refers to the hearing of Christ's voice in the presentation of the gospel [AB, Can, EBC, El, ICC, LJ, My, NCBC, NTC, TH, WBC] (i.e., as the central figure in the gospel [CBC, LJ, NTC]) and their first believing in Christ [Can, ECWB, LJ, NCBC, WBC]. The fact that the accusative αὐτόν 'him' is used with it indicates that the meaning of the verb is 'to hear about' (to hear someone's actual words requires the genitive case) [WBC]. The verb means more than just hearing; it means 'to attend to' with the sense of obedience to what is heard [LJ]. The second verb, ἐδιδάχθητε 'you were taught', refers to the teaching they had received following their conversion [Alf, Can, EBC, ECWB, EGT, El, ICC, LJ, My, NCBC, WBC]. The agent of the passive verb ἐδιδάχθητε 'you were taught' is the Spirit [Ba, LJ], and/or the appointed ministers [Ba, ECWB, LJ, Lns, TH, WBC].

QUESTION—What relationship is indicated by the phrase ἐν αὐτῷ 'in him'?
Like the preceding αὐτόν 'him', this phrase is emphatic by its position before its verb [Lns, My].
  1. The ἐν 'in' indicates union with Christ [Alf, Ea, EBC, ECWB, EGT, El, HG, Ho, ICC, LJ, Lns, MNTC, We]. It indicates the spiritual sphere or condition in which they were taught. Being united with him in spirit, they were effectually taught and fitted to become one with him in mind as well [Ea]. The phrase expresses the unity with Christ and the atmosphere of Christ's presence which embraced both teachers and pupils in the teaching [ECWB]. It means 'in communion with him' [Ho, ICC, We]. The phrase means that inward union with the divine Teacher is to become possessed of his mind and will [MNTC]. The sense is 'if it was in vital union with Christ that after your conversion you received my teaching' [Alf]. The phrase does not mean 'by him' [Ea, EGT, El, ICC, LJ] nor 'about him' [Ea, EGT], nor 'in his name' [EGT].
  2. The ἐν 'in' indicates the manner of their instruction. They had been taught as members of Christ's church, 'as Christians' [CBC, My, NIC, NTC, TH; REB, TEV, TNT]. The whole atmosphere of their instruction had been Christian [NTC].
  3. The ἐν 'in' indicates the sphere of their instruction [AB, Rob, St, TNTC]. Christ was the sphere within, the foundation upon, or the administration under which their teaching and learning took place [AB]. Christ was the context, even the atmosphere in which their instruction was given [St].

DISCOURSE UNIT: 4:21b–24 [AB]. The topic is the instruction these readers received when they learned Christ, i.e., to be totally renewed by putting off subservience to the Old Man and letting the New Man take over.

4:21b as[a] (the) truth[b] is in Jesus,
LEXICON—a. καθώς (LN 64.14, 89.34): 'as' [El, NIC, Rob, WBC; KJV, NRSV, REB, TNT]. 'even as' [Lns, We], 'just as' [AB, LN (64.14), NTC; NASB], 'in accordance with' [NIV], 'in accord with' [NAB], 'what' [NJB], 'that' [TEV], 'inasmuch as, because' [LN (89.34)].
  b. ἀλήθεια (LN 72.2) (BAGD 2.b. p. 36): 'truth' [AB, BAGD, El, LN, Lns, NTC, Rob, WBC, We; all versions], 'the way of truth' [NIC]. It is especially used of the content of Christianity as the absolute truth [BAGD].
QUESTION—What relationship is indicated by καθώς 'as'?
  1. It indicates congruence [AB, Alf, Ea, EGT, El, Lns, My, WBC; NAB, NASB, NIV, REB, TNT].

1.1 The congruence is with regard to manner or standard [Alf, Ea, EGT, El, Lns, My, WBC; NAB, NASB, NIV]: in him you were taught in accordance with the way truth is in Jesus. This is a predicate of manner or standard attached to the preceding verb ἐδιδάχθητε 'you were taught' [Alf, Ea, EGT, El, Lns, WBC], or both ἠκούσατε 'you heard' and ἐδιδάχθητε 'you were taught' [My], and has the force of 'in this way' [Alf] or 'according to' [Alf, El, WBC; NAB, NIV]. It indicates the quality of the teaching they had received [Alf]. It tells the kind of teaching which they had enjoyed [Ea, EGT, El]. It stands in contrast to οὐχ οὕτως 'not so' in 4:20 [Ea, Lns, My, WBC] so that it now states positively what was previously stated negatively [My, WBC].

1.2 The congruence is with regard to comparison [REB, TNT]: you were taught the truth as it is in Jesus.

1.3 The congruence is indicated by a quotation [AB]: you were taught just as it is in the instruction, 'Truth in Jesus!...' Because 'just as' is not here followed by 'so also', it does not introduce a comparison, but rather a quotation. It is likely that the words καθώς ἐστιν 'just as is' introduce an ellipsis where a participle meaning 'attested', 'affirmed', or 'said' has been omitted and a quotation follows, beginning with 'Truth in Jesus' and extending through 4:24 where, at 4:25, the conjunction διό 'therefore' occurs, indicating the author is resuming his own composition and train of thought. Other indications of a possible quotation here are the sandwich construction indicated by ἀλήθεια 'truth' here and in the final clause of 4:25, the parallelisms that are characteristic of Hebrew poetry, and, unusual for Paul, the occurrence of the single name 'Jesus' [AB].

2. It indicates the reason they were taught in Christ [Ho; NRSV]: you were taught in him because truth is in Jesus.

3. It indicates the contents of what they had been taught [NJB, TEV]: you were taught the truth that is in Jesus.

QUESTION—What is meant by ἀλήθεια 'truth'?

What the ἀλήθεια 'truth' consisted of is spelled out in the following verses [Ba, Ea, My-ed, St].

1. The noun ἀλήθεια 'truth' indicates, in general, the spiritual reality which Christ's mission on earth demonstrated [Alf, Ba, Cal, Can, CBC, Ea, EBC, Ho, ICC, LJ, Lns, MNTC, My-ed, TNTC]. The noun ἀληθεία 'truth' indicates spiritual reality in any sense [Lns].

1.1 This is mainly propositional truth [Alf, Ba, Can, Ea, EBC, My-ed]. The noun ἀλήθεια 'truth' refers to the fact that Jesus was God's Son and the Savior of the world as proved by his resurrection from the dead [EBC]. The noun ἀλήθεια 'truth' indicates the true nature of what Christ taught [Alf, Ba, Can, Ea, My-ed].

1.2 This is referring to moral truth or excellence [Cal, Ho, ICC]. The noun ἀλήθεια 'truth' stands opposed to ἀπάτης 'deceit' in 4:22 and has the sense of 'true teaching'. This was concerned with obedience to practical

teaching [ICC]. He indicates that any knowledge of Jesus that does not result in the mortification of the flesh is untrue and insincere. It indicates a reproof of any superficial and spurious knowledge which would leave them unacquainted with newness of life [Cal].
1.3 This includes both propositional and moral truth [AB, CBC, LJ, MNTC, TNTC].
2. The noun ἀλήθεια 'truth' refers to a body of formal, recognized instruction [NCBC, NIC, NTC, WBC]. This refers to the content of the gospel as well as to the apostolic tradition through which it is transmitted [WBC]. It refers to the body of catechetical instruction that was given in preparation for baptism [NCBC, WBC] and/or to the διδαχή 'teaching', the body of apostolic tradition [NIC, NTC] which was first articulated by Jesus [NIC] or is viewed as summed up in him [WBC].
3. The noun ἀλήθεια 'truth' means 'true' [ISBE, ISBE2, My, TD]. The word appears to be used in the OT sense of what is true, of what is firm, solid, or valid [TD], of that which has certainty and force [ISBE2, TD], so that 'as the truth is in Jesus' = 'as this is so in Jesus' [TD]. Its use in Eph. 4:21 designates a valid norm [ISBE2]. This is logical truth, the correspondence of concepts with facts and is found in Scripture in such passages as deal with practical religious applications, such as Eph. 4:21 [ISBE]. The word thus interpreted and its connection with the following words give the sense of 'it is truth (true) that in Jesus you are to put aside the old man' [My].

DISCOURSE UNIT: 4:22–24 [LJ]. The topic is what they had learned in Christ.

4:22 you (are) to-put-off[a] in-regard-to[b] the former way-of-life[c] the old man[d] which is-corrupted[e] according-to[f] the lusts of-deceit,[g]

LEXICON—a. aorist mid. infin. of ἀποτίθημι (ἀποτίθεμαι LN **68.37**, 85.44) (BAGD 1.b. p. 101): 'to put off' [El, NIC, NTC, Rob, WBC; KJV, NIV], 'to put aside' [NJB], 'to put away' [LN (85.44), We; NRSV], 'to put away from oneself once for all' [Lns], 'to lay aside' [BAGD; NAB, NASB], 'to renounce...to lay aside' [REB], 'to get rid of' [TEV], 'to rid oneself' [BAGD], 'to strip off' [AB], 'to remove' [LN (85.44)], 'to finish with' [TNT], 'to stop [**LN** (68.37)], to cease' [LN (68.37)]. This is a figurative extension of meaning of ἀποτίθεμαι 'to put off' [LN (85.44)], denoting the cessation from what one is in the habit of doing [LN (68.37)]. The aorist tense implies an action variously described as single, once-for-all, decisive, definite, concluding [AB, Alf, Ea, ECWB, El, IB, ICC, LJ, Lns, St, TH, TNTC, We], or summarizing [NTC]. The middle voice shows the self-interest of the Christian in this matter [Lns].

b. κατά with accusative object (LN 89.4): 'with regard to' [LN; NIV], 'as regards' [WBC], 'with respect to' [NTC], 'in reference to' [NASB], 'in relation to' [LN], 'as concerning' [Lns, Rob], 'as concerns' [El], 'concerning' [KJV], 'what fits' [AB], not explicit [TNT]. This preposition is also translated as a verb: 'to have regard to' [We] 'to belong to' [NJB]. It is also translated by making the words 'the former way of life' the direct object of the verb 'to put off': 'to put off your former way of life' [NIC], 'to put away your former way of life' [NRSV], 'to lay aside your former way of life' [NAB], 'renouncing your former way of life' [REB]. The words κατὰ τὴν προτέραν ἀναστροφήν 'with regard to the former way of life' are translated as a relative clause: 'which made you live as you used to' [TEV].

c. ἀναστροφή (LN 41.3) (BAGD p. 61): 'way of life' [BAGD, NIC, WBC; NAB, NIV, NJB, NRSV, REB, TNT], 'manner of life' [NTC, Rob; NASB], 'mode of life' [Lns], 'behavior' [AB, BAGD, LN (41.3)], 'conduct' [BAGD, LN (41.3)], 'conversation' [El, We; KJV]. This noun is also translated as a verb: 'to live' [TEV]. This noun denotes personal conduct, focusing upon overt daily behavior [LN].

d. παλαιὸς ἄνθρωπος (LN **41.43**) (BAGD 2.c. β. p. 68, 2. p. 605): 'old man' [AB, BAGD, El, Lns, NIC, NTC, Rob, We; KJV], 'old self' [**LN**; all versions except KJV, REB], 'old person' [WBC], 'old pattern of life' [LN], 'old human nature' [REB]. This is an idiom, literally meaning 'old person' or 'former person' and denotes the old, former pattern of behavior in contrast to the new pattern to which people are to conform [LN]. This phrase is used in Pauline and Post-Pauline thought to differentiate between two sides of human nature, the earlier, old, unregenerate nature as contrasted with the new [BAGD].

e. pres. pass. participle of φθείρω (LN 20.39, 88.266) (BAGD 2.a. p. 857): 'to be corrupted' [BAGD, NIC, NTC, WBC; NASB, NIV, NJB], 'to be corrupt' [Rob; KJV, NRSV], 'to be in process of corruption' [Lns], 'to be in process of decay' [REB], 'to wax corrupt' [El, We], 'to be destroyed' [LN (20.39); TEV], 'to be ruined' [BAGD, LN (88.266)]. This verb is also translated actively: 'to rot' [AB], 'to deteriorate' [NAB]. It is also translated as an adjective: 'self-destructive' [TNT]. The present tense indicates continuous process [Can, Ea, EBC, ECWB, EGT, El, IB, ICC, Lns]. This verb denotes the inner corruption (in the realm of morals and religion) of someone by erroneous teaching or immorality [BAGD]. This verb denotes the ruination or destruction of something by causing it to be corrupt and so to cease to exist [LN (20.39)], or it denotes a type of moral destruction by causing someone to become perverse or depraved [LN (88.266)].

f. κατά with accusative object (LN 89.8, 89.113): 'according to' [El, Rob; KJV], 'in accordance with' [LN (89.8); NASB], 'in accord with' [Lns], 'after' [We], 'because of' [WBC], 'in' [AB], 'through' [NTC; NAB], 'by' [NIC; NIV, NJB, NRSV, REB, TEV], 'with' [LN (89.113); TNT].

g. ἀπάτη (LN 31.12) (BAGD 1. p. 82): 'deceit' [El, Lns, Rob, We; NASB], 'deception' [BAGD, LN], 'deceitfulness' [BAGD], 'pleasure' [TNT], 'illusion' [NAB]. This noun is also translated as an adjective: 'deceitful' [AB, NIC, NTC; KJV, NIV, TEV], 'deceptive' [BAGD], 'illusory' [NJB].

This noun is also translated as a verb: 'to be deluded' [NRSV, REB]. It is also translated as a relative clause: 'which come from deceit' [WBC].

QUESTION—To what are the three infinitives ἀποθέσθαι 'to put off', ἀνανεοῦσθαι 'to be renewed', and ἐνδύσασθαι 'to put on' of 4:22–24 connected and what is their force?

1. They are connected to the passive verb ἐδιδάχθητε 'you were taught' in 4:21 [AB, Alf, Ea, EBC, ECWB, EGT, El, HG, Ho, IB, Lns, Mo, NIC, NTC, Rob, TD, TH, Tu, WBC, We; NIV, NRSV, TEV, TNT]. The pronoun ὑμᾶς 'you' is used here simply for lucidity [EGT] to resume the subject after the parenthetical καθώς 'just as' clause at the end of 4:21 [Alf, HG, Lns, NTC, Tu]. The pronoun is emphatic, 'you as Christians' [We].

1.1 These verses express the contents of the passive verb ἐδιδάχθητε 'you were taught' in 4:21 [AB, Alf, Ea, EBC, ECWB, EGT, El, HG, Ho, Lns, Mo, NTC, TD, WBC, We; NIV, NRSV] or epexegetical of it [IB, NIC, Rob]: you were taught to put off..., to be renewed..., to put on...

1.2 These verses are exhortations based on what they were taught [TEV, TNT]: you were taught in him, therefore put off..., be renewed..., put on...

2. They are connected to the noun ἀλήθεια 'truth' in 4:21 [Ba, ICC, My, St; NAB]: just as the truth in Jesus is this: to put off...to be renewed...to put on. This and the following verses state what the truth was that the Lord Jesus taught [Ba, My, St]. Both the occurrence of the pronoun ὑμᾶς 'you' as subject of the infinitive and the unsuitableness of ἀνανεοῦσθαι 'to be renewed' to be taken with ἐδιδάχθητε 'you were taught' are in favor of this interpretation [ICC].

3. They are connected to the verb ἐμάθετε 'you learned' in 4:20 [LJ, MNTC]: you did not so learn Christ: to put off..., to be renewed..., to put on... After reminding them that Christ had been their teacher, he refers what they had learned [MNTC].

QUESTION—What is meant by the infinitive ἀποθέσθαι 'to put off'?

The meaning is to lay aside or renounce [Ba, Ho, LJ, MNTC; NAB, NASB, REB]. The use of this term, which must be considered with the corresponding terms ἐνδύσασθαι 'to put on' in 4:24 (and to which it is a contrastive parallel [EGT, El, LJ, NTC, Rob, TNTC, WeBC]) and ἀνανεοῦσθαι 'to be renewed' (which indicates the internal motivation for the change) in 4:23 [AB, LJ], involves a clothing metaphor [AB, Alf, Cal, CBC, Ea, EBC, EGT, El, Ho, IB, ICC, LJ, My, NCBC, NIC, NTC, Rob, St, TH, TNTC, WBC] which emphasizes the grace by which the act is achieved as well as the ensuing radical change of life and conduct [AB, St, WBC], or character [IB, NCBC]. The infinitive ἀποθέσθαι 'to put off' is better translated as 'to strip off' since this implies a violent effort which includes the abandonment, if not the destruction, of the old garment [AB]. The clothing metaphor carried by these three infinitives involves the symbolism of a change of clothing as indicating of a person's change of status and membership in a new community, as when he becomes a soldier and puts on military attire and weapons, or becomes a priest, or other high official, and dons the appropriate garb for this position [AB, St]. Such a change of clothes involves an exchange of personalities or identities and the transmission of power [AB, St, WBC].

QUESTION—How does the aorist tense of this infinitive relate to the experience of Christian life?

Some commentators think that the action initially occurred at the moment of conversion and so the time relates to this [Can, Lns, St], but the old man continues to cling to the Christian even after the decisive break at conversion and must be put off again and again (accounting for the occurrence of the iterative present infinitive ἀνανεοῦσθαι 'to be renewed' in 4:23). Paul's view is one definite, decisive break and then a continuous renewal [Lns, Rob]. The aorist tenses mark a fresh act of the will [Rob]. The process is viewed as momentary in regard to a change of garments, but in regard to an altered life, it is viewed as continuous (ἀνανεοῦσθαι 'to be renewed' 4:23) [Rob]. Others think that since the focus of this passage is an ethical one, the time of this change of clothing is every hour of a person's life [AB, LJ, NTC, WBC, WeBC]. Each time it must be a once for all, complete decision, with no reservations, even though, in experience, the 'putting off' must be repeated many times [LJ]. Another commentator says that the injunction is not an exhortation to repeat what was done at conversion and baptism, but to continue to live out its significance by giving up on the old person that they were [WBC]. The action indicated in this infinitive is coordinate with the action in the infinitive ἐνδύσασθαι 'put on' in 4:24; the old man is put off as the new one is put on. Either action is impossible without the other [Lns, NTC, Si, St]. This 'putting off the old man' is the process of sanctification [Ho, LJ], the practical 'learning of Christ' which is growth in spiritual communion with him [ECWB].

QUESTION—What relationship is indicated by κατά 'in regard to' in the phrase κατὰ τὴν προτέραν ἀναστροφήν 'in regard to the former way of life'?

1. It is connected to the infinitive ἀποθέσθαι 'to put off' [AB, Alf, Ea, EGT, El, Ho, ICC, LN (41.43), My, NIC, NTC, Rob, WBC, We; KJV, NAB, NASB, NRSV, REB, TNT]: to put off, as concerns the former way of life, the old man. Some translate 'the former way of life' as the object of the verb 'to put off', but place it in apposition to 'the old man' [AB, NIC; NRSV, TNT]. It defines in what respect the 'putting off' is to take effect, and so means 'in reference to' rather than 'in conformity with' [EGT, El, My]. However, LN (**41.43**), in treating παλαιὸς ἄνθρωπος 'old man', translates this preposition as 'in accordance with', and AB uses 'what fits'. The old nature is not to be put away only with regard to its former manifestations, but entirely [Ho].

2. It is connected to the verb ἐδιδάχθητε 'you were taught' in 4:21 [NIV]: you were taught, with regard to your former way of life, to put off the old man.

3. It is connected to the phrase τὸν παλαιὸν ἄνθρωπον 'the old man' [NCBC, TH; NJB, TEV]: to put off the old man which belongs to your former way of life.

QUESTION—What is meant by τὸν παλαιὸν ἄνθρωπον 'the old man'?

1. This term designates the presence of the old sinful nature in each individual believer [Alf, Ba, Can, DNTT, EBC, ECWB, EGT, El, ICC, ISBE, LN (**41.43**), MNTC, My, NCBC, NIC, NTC, Rob, St, TD, TH, TNTC, WBC, We]: put off from yourselves your old sinful ways. This is the former pattern of behavior as contrasted to the new pattern to which people should conform [LN (**41.43**)]. The 'old man' is the person living under the dominion of the present evil age and its powers [WBC]. It is the old ethical individuality, the pre-Christian moral personality, but does not include original sin which cannot be laid aside. It incorporates the moral habits typical of unregenerate man under the dominion of the sin-principle [My]. It refers to the whole character as representing the former self [We]. It means your former unconverted selves [Alf, Can, EBC, ECWB, EGT, El, ISBE, LN (**41.43**), St, TD], their own evil will that had led them astray [MNTC]. The phrase is a personification [El, My] of our whole sinful condition before regeneration [El]. It denotes the personality, extending to every part of our nature, the entire thinking, feeling, and acting that made up our old corrupted personality [Can, NIC]. The use of the noun ἄνθρωπον 'man' in the expression indicates that the change effects the whole personality, not just some particulars of it [ICC]. The phrase contrasts with τὸν καινὸν ἄνθρωπον 'the new man' in 4:24 [EGT, El, ISBE, Rob, St, TD].

2. This term designates the presence of the old, corporate, sinful nature as inherited from Adam as the head of the race of sinful humanity [AB, Cal, CBC, Ea, ISBE2, LJ, Lns, My-ed, Si-ed]: put off from yourselves the rulership typical of the old sinful Adamic humanity. It stands for all we have in common with Adam [Cal, CBC, ISBE2, LJ, Lns, My-ed], who, in Genesis 3, made 'self' his god [CBC]. This interpretation incorporates the first interpretation and gives greater meaning to the title. In Ephesians, every time the singular noun 'man' is used, a specific relationship to Christ is indicated [AB], so the 'old man' must always be thought of in terms of our new relationship to God [AB, LJ]. Since τὸν παλαιὸν ἄνθρωπον 'the old man' is the antithesis of τὸν καινὸν ἄνθρωπον 'the new man', Christ (4:24) [AB, ISBE2, LJ, My-ed, Si-ed], the referent of τὸν παλαιὸν ἄνθρωπον 'the old man' is Adam, his antitype [AB, Si-ed]. The term has a definite ethical connotation [AB]. The phrase does not mean φύσις 'nature' in its essential meaning, but τῆς ἁμαρτίας ἐνέργεια 'working of sin' [Ea]. The adjective παλαιὸν 'old' refers not to 'old in sin' as some imagine [Ea], but to the former unconverted state [Ea, Ho, LJ, LN (**67.18**)] because it is corrupt [Ho].

QUESTION—What is meant by φθειρόμενον 'corrupted'?

This participle denotes the inward or moral corruption that was taking place in the old man [Alf, BAGD, Can, EBC, El, IB, NCBC, NTC, Rob, St, TD, WBC, We], though this is denied by one commentator [My]. This corruption is a process [Can, Ea, EBC, ECWB, EGT, El, IB, ICC, LJ, Lns, MNTC, NCBC, NTC, Rob, WBC, We, WeBC] in which the man is becoming more and more unsound and rotten [Can, Ea, LJ, WBC, We] in affections, conscience, intellect, and even, perhaps, in his very physical constitution [Can]. It marks both disintegration or decay and corruption [El, LJ, Rob, TNTC]. It denotes both corruption and destruction or ruin [DNTT, EGT, Ho, LJ, Lns, My, NCBC, NIC, Rob, St, TNTC, WBC, WeBC; TEV, TNT]. It not only denotes pollution but also disintegration and a moving onward toward the final destruction [LJ]. This destruction is the external one, judgment, the final destruction of the soul in perdition [My].

QUESTION—What is the time reference in this durative participle?

1. The present tense should be translated as representing the present tendency to corruption in the 'old man' [AB, Alf, Cal, Can, Ea, EBC, ECWB, EGT, El, Ho, IB, ICC, LJ, Lns, MNTC, My, NIC, NTC, Rob, WBC, We; KJV, NAB, NASB, NIV, NJB, REB]: which is being corrupted according to the lusts of deceit. The present tense is employed because this is the constant condition and characteristic of the 'old man' [Ea].

2. The present tense should be translated as having the force of the imperfect, i.e., durative action in past time [NCBC, TH; TEV]: which was being corrupted according to the lusts of deceit. The author does not intend to say that the old nature lingers on within the new one, causing all sorts of the former evils to reappear even though this is a common human experience [NCBC].

QUESTION—What relationship is indicated by κατά 'in regard to' in the phrase κατὰ τὰς ἐπιθυμίας τῆς ἀπάτης 'according to the lusts of deceit'?

This preposition does not seem to indicate any causality [Ea] (*contra* WBC) or instrumentality [El] but has its usual meaning of indicating conformity or harmony with something [Alf, Ea, EGT, El, ICC, Lns]. The process of corruption was going on according to the lusts of deceit [Can, EGT, El]. It might be paraphrased 'as might be expected under the guidance of (the lusts of deceit)' [Alf], implying this is the nature of the lusts [ICC].

QUESTION—What is meant by τὰς ἐπιθυμίας τῆς ἀπάτης 'the lusts of deceit'?

1. The genitive is one of quality [Bu, IB, NCBC, NIC, NTC, TH, TNTC; KJV, NIV, NJB, TEV]: deceitful lusts. They are lusts which deceive, and are the instruments of deceit [Bu]. The 'lusts of deceit' are the governing principle of the decay [IB]. These tyrannous desires swamp every faculty of discernment [NCBC]. 'Deceitful' characterizes these lusts as misleading and corrupting those who yield to them [TH].

2. The genitive indicates that the lusts do the deceiving [Alf, Ba, Can, CBC, Ea, EBC, EGT, El, Ho, ICC, LJ, Lns, MNTC, My, We; NRSV, REB]: the lusts which deceive. The genitive τῆς ἀπάτης 'of deceit' is personified [Alf, Ea, My], or nearly so [EBC, EGT, El, ICC] (by the article giving it the abstract force approaching personification [EGT, El, ICC] and by attributing ἐπιθυμίας 'lusts' to ἀπάτης 'deceit' [ICC]), and contrasts with ἀληθείας 'truth' in 4:24 [Alf, Ea, EGT, El, My, St]. It is as though the lusts are the servants or instruments of deceit [Alf, EGT]. 'Lusts' deceive a person into thinking self-satisfaction is what matters in life [CBC]. Deceit manipulates the lusts and lusts manipulate the man [LJ].
3. The genitive indicates that the ἀπάτης 'deceit' (or 'pleasure') is the object of these lusts [TNT]: lust for pleasure.
4. The genitive is descriptive of these lusts [ECWB]: the lusts, those of the spirit of delusion. These lusts also blind the soul which yields to them [ECWB].
5. The genitive is one of source [WBC]: the lusts which come from deceit.

QUESTION—What is meant by ἐπιθυμίας 'lusts'?

The Greek word denotes any passion or propensity of the heart [Ba]. The word covers not only the desires which are generally acknowledged to be base, but those that are sometimes applauded, such as ambition and cunning [Cal], in fact, every strong and excessive desire that proceeds from self-love [Cal, Ea, LJ] or lack of confidence in God [Cal]. It is an anxious self-seeking that carries with it an impulse or a motion of the will [TD]. The use of the word here indicates that the old man is controlled, not by reason and good sense, but by his passions and desires [Ba]. The noun expresses the driving power in man's *flesh*, the ruling power of sin [DNTT]; these desires are all he has to guide him [Can]. The phrase κατὰ τὰς ἐπιθυμίας 'according to the lusts' contrasts with κατὰ θεόν 'according to God' in 4:24 [Ea].

4:23 and to-be-renewed/to-be-made-new[a] in/by-the spirit/Spirit[b] of-the-mind[c] of-you

LEXICON—a. pres. pass. infin. of ἀνανεόω (LN **58.72**) (BAGD 1. p. 58): 'to be or become renewed' [BAGD, El, NIC, NTC, Rob, WBC, We; KJV, NASB, NJB, NRSV, REB, TNT], 'to get oneself renewed' [BAGD], 'to be made new' [LN; NIV], 'to be made completely new' [TEV], 'to continue to be renewed' [Lns]. This passive verb is also translated actively: 'to acquire something fresh' [NAB], 'to become new' [AB]. The present tense implies a continuous, repeated renewal [AB, Alf, Can, Ea, EBC, ECWB, IB, LJ, Lns, Rob, St, TD, TNTC, We, WeBC]. Christ, God, or the Spirit of God, is the agent of this passive verb [Alf, Can, DNTT, Ho, LJ, Lns, My, TD, TNTC].

b. πνεῦμα (LN 12.18, 26.9, 30.6) (BAGD 3.c. p.675): 'spirit' [AB, LN (26.9), Lns, NIC, NTC, Rob, WBC, We; KJV, NASB, NJB, NRSV, REB], 'spiritual nature, inner being' [LN (26.9)], 'heart' [TEV], 'attitude' [LN (30.6); NIV], 'spiritual state, state of mind' [BAGD], 'disposition'

[BAGD, LN (30.6)], 'way of thinking' [LN (30.6)], 'Spirit' [El, LN (12.18)]. This noun is also translated as an adjective: 'spiritual' [NAB]. It is also conflated with νοὸς 'mind' and translated as an adverb modifying ἀνανεοῦσθαι 'to be renewed': 'spiritually' [TNT]. This noun denotes the non-material, psychological faculty of man which is potentially sensitive and responsive to God [LN (26.9)] or it denotes an attitude or disposition which reflects the way a person thinks about something or deals with some matter [LN (30.6)]. Alternatively, this noun may indicate the third person of the Trinity, the Holy Spirit [LN (12.18)].

c. νοῦς (LN 26.14, 30.5) (BAGD 3.a. p. 544): 'mind' [AB, BAGD, El, LN (26.14), Lns, NIC, Rob, WBC, We; KJV, NASB, NJB, REB], 'minds' [NTC; NIV, NRSV, TEV], 'way of thinking' [BAGD, LN (30.5); NAB], 'manner of thought' [LN (30.5)], 'attitude' [BAGD, LN (30.5)], 'disposition' [LN (30.5)]. It is also conflated with πνεύματι 'spirit' and translated as an adverb modifying ἀνανεοῦσθαι 'to be renewed': 'spiritually' [TNT]. This noun denotes the psychological faculty of reasoning, thinking, understanding, and deciding [LN (26.14)] or it denotes a particular manner or way of thinking [LN (30.5)]. It denotes the sum total of every person's whole mental and moral state of being [BAGD]. It is the seat of right understanding [DNTT, EGT], feeling, and volition [EGT]. It is the center of a person's thinking [TNTC]. See this word also at 4:17.

QUESTION—What relationship is indicated by δέ 'and'?

The conjunction δέ 'and' connects the infinitive ἀνανεοῦσθαι 'to be renewed' to elements in 4:20 or 21 (cf. the relevant Question in 4:22), as a second complement [Ea, ECWB, El, My, St, TD, WBC, We]. The conjunction indicates the introduction of the positive aspect of things as the writer switches from the contrasting negative aspect [Ea, EGT, El, Ho, Lns, My, We]. This verse, properly speaking, is the transition statement between the negative exhortation of the previous verse to put off the old man and the positive exhortation of the next verse to put on the new man [LJ].

QUESTION—What is meant by ἀνανεοῦσθαι 'to be renewed'?

1. The word refers to a renovation, reformation, or a restoration [Ea, EBC, ECWB, El, ISBE2, LJ, TD, TH, TNTC, WBC]. This verb focuses upon the transformation of the spirit and mind, not upon a replacement or substitution [TH]. The preposition ἀνά 'again', as a constituent component in this infinitive, means 'again' or 'back' [Ea, ISBE2], and refers to a moral renovation to a previously existing state [Ea, EBC, El], or it may only express change. The image of God was impaired by the fall of man, but in the new creation is fully reinstated [EBC].

2. The word refers to regeneration, a creation of something new [AB, Ba, LN (**58.72**), My, NCBC; NIV, TEV]. This word refers to more than a rejuvenation, such as 'to renew' might suggest; it refers to a whole new creation of a person's spirit, so that 'to become new' is the preferred translation [AB]. The verb means 'to make new' and refers to the work of regeneration [Ba]. This is a renewal into moral freedom and might which

the human spirit receives in the act of regeneration by means of the Holy Spirit, enabling the spirit to put the νοῦς 'mind' at the service of God's will and to contend always against the σάρξ 'flesh' principle that still remains in the Christian [My].

QUESTION—What is meant by τῷ πνεύματι 'the spirit'?
1. This refers to the inner being of a person [AB, Alf, Bu, Cal, Ea, ECWB, EGT, Ho, IB, ICC, Lns, My, NCBC, Rob, TH, WBC, We]: be renewed in your spirit and mind. This πνεύματι 'spirit' is the restored and divinely-informed leading principle of their νοῦς 'mind' [Alf, Ea, ECWB, EGT, My], the moral personality whose organ is the mind or reason, the faculty in man that makes him most akin to God [EGT], and through which he is to fellowship with God [EGT, IB, Lns, My, TH, We]. This contrasts with 4:17 where it is said the children of the world are walking in the ματαιότης 'futility' of *their* minds [Alf, Lns, Rob, We].
2. This refers to a person's attitude or way of thinking [Ba, BAGD, CBC, DNTT, EBC, ISBE2, LJ, MNTC, NTC, St; NIV, TEV]: be renewed in the spirit of your mind. Paul does not say the Christian is to be renewed in his mind only, but in the spirit of his mind. He is not talking about our spirits but about a power interior to the mind itself that governs and controls it, the fundamental way of thinking and reasoning, the disposition or direction [LJ], the new outlook on things [LJ, St] which governs the way the mind thinks and reasons [LJ].
3. This refers to the Holy Spirit of God [Can, El, TD]: be renewed by the Spirit of your mind. Τῷ πνεύματι 'the spirit' does not refer exclusively to the Holy Spirit *per se*, but to the gracious union he forms with the human spirit [El]. Instead of the futility of mind in which the unregenerate walk (4:17), the Christian's mind is so animated by the Spirit of God that he is gradually filled with fresh, new, youthful strength and vigorous life which lends zest and interest to all his thoughts [Can].

QUESTION—What is indicated by the genitive construction τῷ πνεύματι τοῦ νοὸς ὑμῶν 'the spirit of the mind of you'?

Some connect ὑμῶν 'of you' only with ναός 'mind' [EGT; KJV, NASB, NIV, NJB, NRSV]: your mind. Some of those who take πνεύματι 'spirit' to refer to the human spirit connect ὑμῶν 'of you' with both 'spirit' and 'mind' [Alf, TH; REB, TEV, TNT]: your spirit and mind.
1. This is an appositional genitive [AB, Ba, BAGD, ISBE2, LN (**58.72**), NCBC, WBC; REB, TEV]: your spirit, that is, your mind. It is a way of piling up synonyms [BAGD, ISBE2, WBC] that is characteristic of Ephesians [WBC]. If 'spirit' here means the human spirit, it is pointless to ask how 'spirit' differs from 'mind' [NCBC]. They are used together to indicate the innermost self [NCBC, WBC], showing that the change does not refer to just superficial conduct, but to the very springs of a person's being [NCBC]. Others think the synonyms indicate the attitude, nature, or temper of the new man [Ba, BAGD].

2. This is a partitive genitive [Ea]: the part of the spirit that controls itself. What τῷ πνεύματι 'the spirit' refers to is the highest part of the inner nature which, when referred to in its aspect of thought and emotion, is called νοῦς 'mind' [Ea].
3. This is a subjective genitive [EGT, My]: the spirit that controls the mind. The spirit, the *ego* of man's higher life-principle, has the νοῦς 'mind' as the organ of its moral operation, that is, reason in its ethical quality and operation, to subject the mind itself to serve the divine will [My].
4. This is a possessive genitive [Alf, ECWB, El]. This contrasts with the 'futility' which exists in the mind of the pagans in 4:17 [Alf, El].
    4.1 'The spirit' is the spiritual nature of the inner man [Alf, ECWB].
    4.2 'The Spirit' here is the Holy Spirit with which the νοός 'mind' is endued through his union with the human spirit, and so becomes the agent of the mind's renewal (Rom. 12:2) and the seat of his working [El].

QUESTION—What relationship is indicated by the dative case of τῷ πνεύματι 'the spirit'?
1. The dative case indicates location [AB, Ba, Cal, Ea, EBC, ECWB, TNTC]: in the spirit of your mind. The dative indicates the special seat of the moral renovation—in the spirit [Ea]. The place of this constant renewal or rejuvenation is in the spirit of the mind [TNTC].
2. The dative indicates reference or respect [EGT, Lns, My, WBC]: in respect of the spirit of your mind.
3. The dative case indicates agency [Alf, Can]: through the spirit/Spirit of your mind. The omission here of the preposition ἐν 'in' points to the fact that agency is in view [Alf].
4. The dative case indicates instrumentality [El, TD]: with your Spirit-aided mind. This is probably an instrumental dative in which νοός 'mind' indicates where God's Spirit is at work [TD].

4:24 and to-put-on[a] the new[b] man the-one created in-accordance-with[c] God

LEXICON—a. aorist mid. infin. of ἐνδύω (LN 49.1) (BAGD 2.b. p. 264): 'to put on' [AB, BAGD, El, LN, NIC, NTC, Rob, WBC, We; all versions except NRSV], 'to put on once for all' [Lns], 'to clothe yourselves' [NRSV], 'to clothe, to dress' [LN]. The aorist tense implies an once-for-all act [EGT, ICC, Lns, My, NIC, TH]. This verb is very often used in the figurative sense of taking on characteristics, virtues, intentions, etc. [BAGD].
b. καινός: 'new'. See this word at 2:15.
c. κατά with accusative object (LN 89.8) (BAGD II.5.b.α. p. 407): 'in accordance with' [BAGD, LN], 'in accord with' [Lns], 'according to' [NIC], 'similarly to' [BAGD], 'in relation to' [LN], 'after' [Rob, We; KJV], 'according to the likeness of' [NRSV], 'after the likeness of' [NTC], 'in the likeness of' [NASB, TNT]. This preposition is also

translated as a verb phrase: 'to be like' [NIV]. The phrase κατὰ θεόν 'in accordance with God' is translated as a unit: 'after God's image' [AB, El], 'in God's image' [NAB], 'on God's principles' [NJB], 'in God's likeness' [WBC; REB, TEV].

QUESTION—What relationship is indicated by καί 'and'?

The infinitive ἐνδύσασθαι 'to put on' is connected to one of the elements in 4:20 or 21 (cf. ἀποθέσθαι 'to put off' in 4:22) as the third and final complement and contrasts with the infinitive ἀποθέσθαι 'to put off' [El, Ho, LJ, NIC, TD, TH].

1. This verse states the basis and beginning of the renewing process described in 4:23 [AB, DNTT, El, Ho, ISBE2, LJ, Lns, NCBC, NTC, St, TD, TH, TNTC, WBC, WeBC]. In relation to the last verse, this aorist infinitive, as indicated by the καί 'and' [Lns], gives a further and more distinct statement of man's renewal on the positive side [El, Ho, LJ, Lns]. It is another way of expressing this renewal [NCBC, NIC]. They had done this when they had given their hearts to Christ [NTC, St] and professed him openly at baptism [NTC, TH, WBC]. For Paul, putting on the new nature is the beginning of sharing Christ's nature [DNTT].

2. This verse states the culmination of the renewing process [Ea, My]. In relation to the last verse, this aorist infinitive gives a further and more distinct statement of man's renewal on the positive side (expressed in the last verse in the present tense, denoting a continual process) as it is realized in the moment of its completion by the putting on of the new man, so that it is the result or accompaniment of the renewal [Ea]. The laying aside of the old man is the negative commencement of the change and is therefore represented as a momentary act (aorist tense). Then the becoming renewed is presented as an enduring process (present tense). The finishing act (aorist tense) of this is the putting on of the new man, correlative to the 'putting off' of 4:22 [My]. It stands to renewal as regeneration stands to sanctification [Ea].

QUESTION—What is meant by ἐνδύσασθαι 'to put on'?

This is an aorist middle infinitive and it refers to a direct reflexive act which the Christian is expected to perform upon himself [Alf, Ea, LJ], as contrasted to the present passive infinitive ἀνανεοῦσθαι 'to be renewed' (4:23) which is a continuing process performed upon him [Alf, EGT, ICC, LJ] and a continuing way of life [NIC]. It corresponds to the other aorist infinitive, ἀποθέσθαι 'to put off' (4:22), as denoting a single, instantaneous act [EGT, ICC, LJ, Lns, NIC, TH] (probably baptismal [NIC, NTC, TD, TH]) and the action described by it is simultaneous with that of ἀποθέσθαι 'to put off' (4:22) [AB, LJ, Lns, NTC]. It has an imperatival sense [NIC, TD]. It provides a contrasting metaphor to that of ἀποθέσθαι 'to put off' [Ho, LJ, NCBC, TH]. As there we are called on to put off the old nature as we put off ragged and filthy garments, so here we are to put on the new nature as a garment [Ho, LJ, NTC, TH] of light [Ho]. In ethical contexts such as this one, the garment to be 'put on' consists of good works or of spiritual armaments [AB, LJ, Lns]. It refers to an appropriation of the new identity in such a way that its ethical dimensions become apparent [WBC].

QUESTION—What is meant by τὸν καινὸν ἄνθρωπον 'the new man'?

1. This refers to the Christian's new nature or the new self [Alf, Ba, Can, CBC, Ea, EBC, Ho, ISBE, ISBE2, LJ, Lns, MNTC, My, NCBC, NTC, St, TD, TH, TNTC, WeBC; NJB (note)]: and put on the new self. This contrasts with τὸν παλαιὸν ἄνθρωπον 'the old man' (4:22) which is to be put off [Alf, Can, Ea, EBC, TD]. It is the effect of regeneration on a person and, in other contexts, is called the 'new creation' [Ba, LJ, WeBC; NJB (note)]. The τὸν καινὸν ἄνθρωπον 'the new man' is more than a new set of habits, rather it is the new life principle itself which produces the new set of habits [Lns].

2. This refers to the new humanity [EGT, El, WBC] consisting of Jew and Gentile (2:15) [EGT, WBC]: and put on the new humanity. The aorist κτισθέντα 'created' suggests the 'new man' is not regarded here as a new nature created for the individual, but as the new and holy form of human life created once and for all in and by Christ and in which the individual convert participates [EGT]. For the author of Ephesians, τὸν καινὸν ἄνθρωπον 'the new man' has both corporate and individual connotations. As in 2:15, he is a member of the new humanity composed of Jews and Gentiles. But as the τὸν παλαιὸν ἄνθρωπον 'the old man' is under the dominion of this present age, so τὸν καινὸν ἄνθρωπον 'the new man' is under the dominion of the new creation and its life and must be 'put on' by each individual [WBC].

3. This refers to Christ as the prototype of the new humanity [AB, ECWB, NIC, We]: and put on Christ. This is the same as 'to put on Christ' (Gal. 3:27) [DNTT, ECWB, NIC] for Christ is 'the new man' [ECWB, We], 'the second Adam' [ECWB]. The 'new man' is essentially the Lord Jesus Christ, or at least as his life is lived out in his people, who have been incorporated into the new humanity of which he is the head [NIC]. Through his Divine personality Christ makes his human nature effective in due measure for every believer [We].

QUESTION—What is meant by τὸν κατὰ θεὸν κτισθέντα 'the one created in accordance with God'?

1. This refers to the restoration of God's image [Ba, Ea, EBC, Ho, ISBE, LJ, Lns, My, NCBC, NTC, TNTC, WBC; NAB, NASB, NIV, NRSV, REB, TEV, TNT]. Man is restored to the divine image in the soul which was lost in Adam's sin [Ba, LJ, NCBC, NTC]. It refers to the recovery of original holiness. The moral image of God reproduces itself in man [Ea, LJ]. The fact that the phrase ἐν δικαιοσύνῃ καὶ ὁσιότητι τῆς ἀληθείας 'in righteousness and holiness of the truth' immediately follows the word κτισθέντα 'created' makes it very likely that the writer intended to present the righteousness and holiness he mentions as primarily of God's creation, making the point that the new humanity has been recreated to be like God because these are characteristics of God [WBC].

2. This refers to far more than Adam's original likeness to God's image [AB, Alf, Cal, Can, DNTT, IDB, MNTC, TD]. It refers to the fact that man was originally created in God's image [Alf, Cal, Can], but at the same time indicates that the image of God in which Adam was originally created was far less glorious than that which is granted to us in Christ [Alf]. The new creation in Christ of the divine image in man restores and perfects the original image of God in man [Can]. There is a far more rich and powerful manifestation of Divine grace in the second creation than in the first, even though the image of God, both in the first creation and in the second, is uniformly represented to us as conformity and resemblance to God [Cal]. At the least, it implies that the character with which man was originally created has been restored to him in Christ. But there may be a subtler idea—that man's life in Eden was only a foreshadowing of what God intended that man become, and that this promise of a higher nature has now been realized in 'the new man' [MNTC].

QUESTION—What is meant by the aorist passive participle κτισθέντα 'created'?

It reminds us that the creation of the new nature is God's doing, not ours [NCBC]. It indicates either that God called the pattern or ideal of renewed life into being in Christ [Can, My] or that he created, by regeneration, in each individual Christian a new life [Can, LJ]. The aorist participle κτισθέντα 'created' in this clause refers to a once-for-all act [Alf, El]. It is not likely that an act of ongoing creation is meant [AB]. This tense points to the past creation of this new humanity in Christ [AB, El, NIC]; it points to the preexistence of the 'New Man' [AB, We]. In the case of each individual Christian, τὸν καινὸν ἄνθρωπον 'the new man' is not created again, but is 'put on' [Alf, El] or personally appropriated [We].

QUESTION—What relationship is indicated by κατά 'in accordance with'?

1. It indicates a correspondence to God's image [AB, Alf, Ba, BAGD, Can, DNTT, Ea, EBC, EGT, El, Ho, ISBE, ISBE2, LJ, Lns, MNTC, Mo, My, NIC, NTC, Rob, TH, TNTC, Tu, WBC, We; KJV, NASB, NIV, NRSV, REB, TEV, TNT]: created in accordance with God's image. God is both the author and the pattern of this image [EBC, Lns, WBC].

2. It indicates a reference to the will of God [ICC, NCBC]: created according to the will of God. The preposition by itself in that phrase in Colossians means 'after the manner of' and if given that meaning here would imply that the similitude is in the verb, i.e. that God was κτισθείς 'created'. But the phrase κατὰ θεόν 'in accordance with God' also occurs three times in 2 Cor. 7:9–11 where it means 'in a godly manner', which suggests that, in the present verse, this phrase means 'according to the will of God' [ICC].

in righteousness[a] and holiness[b] of-the truth.

LEXICON—a. δικαιοσύνη (LN 88.13): 'righteousness' [El, LN, Lns, NIC, NTC, Rob, WBC, We; KJV, NASB, NIV, NRSV, TNT], 'uprightness' [NJB], 'justice' [NAB]. This noun is also translated as an adjective:

'upright' [REB, TEV]. It means doing what God requires, doing what is right [LN].
b. ὁσιότης (LN 53.45, 88.25) (BAGD p. 585): 'holiness' [BAGD, El, LN (88.25), Lns, NIC, NTC, Rob, WBC, We; all versions except REB, TEV], 'piety' [AB, BAGD], 'devoutness' [BAGD], 'dedication, consecration' [LN (53.45)]. This noun is also translated as an adjective: 'holy' [TEV], 'devout' [REB]. This noun designates the state resulting from being dedicated to the service of God [LN (53.45)], or it denotes the quality of holiness as an expression of the divine in contrast with the human [LN (88.25)].

QUESTION—What relationship is indicated by ἐν 'in'?
1. It indicates the element or sphere in which the character of τὸν καινὸν ἄνθρωπον 'the new man' is created [Alf, Ea]. The preposition indicates the elements in which the new man is manifested [Ea].
2. It indicates the quality or ethical condition or state in which the creation was realized [EGT, El, Ho, LJ, Lns, NCBC]. It specifies the things in which the new man was created and in which the likeness between him and God consists [EGT, El, Lns]. It gives the elements of which the image of God consists. It does not consist merely of a rational nature, immortality, nor dominion, but of righteousness in all principles, devout affections for God, and possession of true knowledge about God [Ho, LJ].

QUESTION—How are the nouns related in the genitive construction δικαιοσύνῃ καὶ ὁσιότητι τῆς ἀληθείας 'righteousness and holiness of the truth'?
1. Truth modifies both 'righteousness' and 'holiness' as an adjective [AB, Bu, Cal, IB, NTC; NIV, NRSV]: in true righteousness and holiness. If this interpretation is followed, τῆς ἀληθείας 'of the truth' denotes sincerity [AB, Cal] or genuineness [Bu, NTC]. The emphasis falls on 'true' [Bu].
2. Truth modifies only 'holiness' as an adjective [Ba, Can, NIC; KJV]: in righteousness and true holiness. It is called 'piety of the truth' in order to indicate that it is not the mere feeling that may arise from instinct or habit, but the affection that is rooted in the knowledge of the Christian's true relations to God and man, which the term ὁσιότητι 'holiness' indicates [Can]. The phrase ὁσιότητι τῆς ἀληθείας 'holiness of truth' stands in contrast to τὰς ἐπιθυμίας τῆς ἀπάτης 'the lusts of deceit' in 4:22 [Ba].
3. Truth is the source of righteousness and holiness [BAGD (probably), EGT, Ho, LJ, MNTC, Rob, TH, TNTC, WBC, We; NAB, REB, TNT], or it possesses righteousness and holiness [ECWB, Ho, Lns]: in the righteousness and holiness which truth has. It means that righteousness and holiness which truth has or produces. Righteousness and holiness, morality and religion, are the products of truth, and without truth they cannot exist [Ho]. Truth is strongly practical and expresses itself in virtues like righteousness and holiness [BAGD]. As the corrupting and beguiling lusts belong to the spirit of deceit, so righteousness and holiness belong to Christ, 'the truth' [ECWB]. In contrast to the lusts or passions of deceit, 'righteousness and holiness' are of the 'truth' [MNTC, Rob], they spring

from God's Spirit and keep restoring man's higher nature rather than tainting and destroying it [MNTC].
4. 'Righteousness' and 'holiness' modify the truth, which contains an implied reference to life [CBC; TEV]: in the upright and holy true life. Such a life is called 'just' because it faces God's demands, and 'devout' because it makes him its center [CBC].

QUESTION—What is meant by δικαιοσύνῃ καὶ ὁσιότητι 'righteousness and holiness'?
1. The two nouns are synonyms with no real distinction in meaning [ICC, WBC]. In the NT each of these terms has both moral and religious connotations [WBC] and their meanings tend to overlap [ICC]. They may be understood here as used together in synonymous parallelism to present a summary of human virtue [WBC].
2. They retain here distinctions similar to the ones they had in Classical Greek [AB, Ba, Cal, Can, Ea, EGT, Ho, MNTC, My, NIC, NTC, Rob, TH, TNTC]. 'Righteousness' refers to right attitudes or integrity towards men [AB, Ba, Cal, Can, EGT, Ho, MNTC, My, NIC, NTC, Rob, TH, TNTC] and 'holiness' refers to obedience and right attitudes or purity towards God [AB, Ba, Cal, Ea, EGT, Ho, MNTC, My, NIC, NTC, Rob, TH, TNTC], though some are not certain that this distinction is wholly preserved here [Ba, EGT, El, WBC]. The first noun defines what its possessor should be to every other creature in the universe while the second states man's primary relationship to God who has first claim on man's affection and loyalty [Ea].
3. They are basically similar to 2., but each has additional implications which relate to the inward part of man's life, as well as outwardly [Alf, LJ]. The first noun, δικαιοσύνῃ 'righteousness', denotes a just relation, both inwardly between the powers of the Christian's soul and outwardly towards men and duties [Alf, LJ]. The second noun, ὁσιότητι 'holiness', denotes the integrity of the Christian's spiritual life [Alf] and the piety towards God [Alf, TD] which is its condition [Alf]. The two nouns together complete the idea of the moral perfection of τὸν καινὸν ἄνθρωπον 'the new man' [Alf, LJ].
4. Other statements [Can, EBC, ECWB, Lns, NCBC, WeBC]. The first noun relates to the fulfillment of our duties to equal love for all our fellows, while the second denotes not only what we term 'godliness', but dutiful affection to parents and kindred [Can]. The first noun is moral obedience to the will of God [NCBC, TD], the second denotes the quality of life that is appropriate to one who lives in total obedience to God [NCBC]. The first is goodness shown to others, both to man and to God while the second is goodness in itself, as it exists in God [ECWB]. The first denotes a love for what is right, while the second denotes an aversion to sin and means 'free from contamination' [EBC, Lns]. The first justifies the sinner before God and changes his relationship to Christ, the second changes a

man's inward nature and sanctifies him, purifying his desires and putting them in alignment with God's will [WeBC].

QUESTION—What is meant by ἀληθείας 'truth'?

The noun ἀληθείας 'truth' refers to God's essence [Alf], or to the divine essence of things in contrast to earthly appearances [MNTC], or to Christ himself as the manifestation of the fullness of the Godhead [ECWB], and stands opposed to ἀπάτης 'deceit' in 4:22 [Alf, Ea, ECWB, EGT, Ho, IB, LJ, Lns, St, TNTC, WBC]. Since ἀληθείας 'truth' has the definite article [Ho, TNTC], it may mean 'the truth' *par excellence*, the evangelical message, the objective truth given in the gospel [CBC, EGT, Ho, LJ, Lns, My, TH, TNTC, WBC], the content of Christianity which is the absolute truth [BAGD]. It is spiritual knowledge of God that came by Jesus Christ and which illuminates the understanding and sanctifies the heart [Ho, LJ]. Others believe it means 'sincere' [AB, Cal] or 'genuine' as opposed to deceptive [NTC]. It warns us that both our righteousness and our holiness must be sincere because we have to do with God whom it is impossible to deceive [Cal]. It implies a reference to believers' discrimination between the truth given in Christ and the false claims made by others [AB]. A leading thought of this section is truth as it applies to conduct [Rob].

DISCOURSE UNIT: 4:25–6:20 [We]. The topic is the outward manifestation of the Christian life, personal and social.

DISCOURSE UNIT: 4:25–5:20 [Ba]. The topic is an exhortation to particular virtues.

DISCOURSE UNIT: 4:25–5:14 [We]. The topic is special features of the Christian character.

DISCOURSE UNIT: 4:25–5:7 [NAB]. The topic is vices to be avoided.

DISCOURSE UNIT: 4:25–5:5 [Rob]. The topic is precepts for the new life.

DISCOURSE UNIT: 4:25–5:4 [St]. The topic is six concrete examples of putting off the old life and putting on the new.

DISCOURSE UNIT: 4:25–5:2 [CBC, EBC, Ho, IB, MNTC, NTC, Rob, TNTC, WBC]. The topic is advice for Christian living [CBC], Christian behavior patterns [EBC], special injunctions [IB, WBC] which illustrate putting off the old humanity and putting on the new [WBC], obligations for the new life [MNTC], replacing falsehood and bitterness by truth and love [TNTC].

DISCOURSE UNIT: 4:25–32 [AB, EGT, El, ICC, Lns, My, NIC, TH, We, WeBC; NAB]. The topic is a series of detached, practical exhortations arising out of the charge to put off the old man and put on the new [EGT], special exhortations [My], warning against special sins [ICC], negative and positive precepts [NIC], some rules for the new life [TH], obligations of Christians to Christians [We], principles and practices of the new way of life in Christ

[WeBC], examples that illustrate the change from the old to the new [AB], vices to be avoided [NAB].

DISCOURSE UNIT: 4:25-30 [ECWB]. The topic is the power of the new life in the conquest of sin generally [ECWB].

DISCOURSE UNIT: 4:25-29 [LJ]. The topic is practical illustrations of putting off the old man and putting on the new.

4:25 Therefore[a] putting-off/having-put-off[b] the falsehood/lying[c]

LEXICON—a. διό (LN 89.47): 'therefore' [AB, LN, NIC, NTC, WBC; NASB, NIV], 'wherefore' [El, Lns, Rob, We; KJV], 'then' [NAB, REB, TEV], 'so' [NJB, TNT], 'so then' [LN; NRSV], 'for this reason' [LN].
  b. aorist mid. participle of ἀποτίθημι: 'to put off'. The aorist tense of this participle here implies a once-for-all action [Alf, EGT, El, ICC, Lns]. See this word at 4:22.
  c. ψεῦδος (LN 33.254) (BAGD p. 892): 'falsehood' [BAGD, El, LN, Lns, NIC, NTC, WBC, We; NASB, NIV, NRSV, REB], 'lie' [AB, BAGD, LN], 'lies' [NJB]. This noun is also translated as a gerund: 'lying' [Rob; KJV, NAB, TEV, TNT]. This noun denotes the content of a false utterance [LN].

QUESTION—What relationship is indicated by διό 'therefore'?

This conjunction makes an inference from the image of the old man versus the new [AB, Cal, Can, Ea, EBC, El, IB, Lns, My, NTC, Rob, TH, WBC] or from the general obligation to be conformed to the image of God [Ho, WBC]: therefore, since the old man is to be put off, put off lying. It introduces a collection of seven sentences (4:25-5:2) containing injunction and motivating clauses that all refer back to 4:22-24 with its injunctions to put off the old humanity and put on the new [AB, WBC]. It introduces a deduction in the form of an application [Ea, NCBC, WBC]. Given that the old man and all its lusts are to be abandoned and the new man created in righteousness and holiness of the truth is to be assumed, ψεῦδος 'lying', the vice and habit of falsehood, must be dropped [Ea]. The apostle now starts a series of detailed warnings about what deceitful desires (4:22) produce. Διό 'therefore' makes the connection between principle and practice [EBC].

QUESTION—What is meant by ἀποθέμενοι τὸ ψεῦδος 'putting off/having put off the falsehood'?

This participial clause, with its use of the same verb as in 4:22, is a reference back to the admonition to put off the old man [AB, CBC, DNTT, Ho, Lns, My, NCBC, NTC, Rob, TH, WBC, We] and utilizes the same metaphor of laying aside worn-out, useless clothing [AB, DNTT, Ho, My] (though another commentator says the metaphor has been dropped [Rob]). Some commentators understand the verb ἀποτίθημι 'to put off' to be part of a set formula used in the moral teaching of the early church [CBC]. Falsehood, or the lie, is mentioned first in this unit because of the emphasis on truth in the previous unit [AB, ICC, LJ, Lns] (4:21c, and especially because of the just previously mentioned ἀλήθεια 'truth' ending 4:24 [LJ, Lns, My, NTC, Rob, TNTC, WBC] where it is presented as related to the image of God [LJ]), as well as being parallel to τὰς ἐπιθυμίας τῆς ἀπάτης 'the lusts of deceit' in 4:22 [AB, LJ, Lns], and because lying, or falsehood, is central to the sinful human condition [LJ], springing naturally from selfishness which is the essence of all sin [El, LJ].

1. Τὸ ψεῦδος 'lying, falsehood' refers abstractly to all forms of falsehood in general [Alf, Cal, Can, CBC, EBC, EGT, El, ICC, LJ, NIC, NTC, We]. 'Lying' is a synecdoche in which one aspect of dishonesty, lying, is put for the whole spectrum of dishonest, deceitful dealings [Cal, CBC, EBC, LJ], falsehood in all its forms as contrasted with 'the truth as it is in Jesus' (4:21) and 'true righteousness and holiness' (4:24) [EBC]. 'Falsehood' is more comprehensive than 'lying' [Can, ICC] because it includes not only knowingly speaking an untruth [Can], but every kind of false pretense or appearance [Can, CBC], all of which are to be done away with as part of the old man [Can]. Falsehood in every form [El, ICC] is the chief characteristic of the παλαιὸς ἄνθρωπος 'old man' [El, LJ], the most universal of all sins [LJ].

2. Τὸ ψεῦδος means 'lying' [Ba, Cal, CBC, Ea, EBC, Ho, ISBE2, MNTC, My, NCBC, Rob, TH, TNTC, WBC; KJV, NAB, NJB, TEV, TNT]. Here the focus seems to be on spoken falsehood, 'lying' [NCBC, TNTC, WBC], though it is not restricted to this [TNTC]. The singular τὸ ψεῦδος 'the lie' is frequently used collectively for 'lies' and, with the parallel Col. 3:8–9, argues against the interpretation that it denotes deception as a way of life [WBC]. The next clause indicates that 'lying', not falsehood in general, is meant [Rob]. It is the very root of all offenses against brotherhood [MNTC]. The reference is to willful falsehood, for a person may himself be deceived and unwittingly pass on the deception to others [Ea].

3. Τὸ ψεῦδος 'the lie, the falsehood' is specific to the deception mentioned in the previous unit, the great deception under which unregenerated men live [AB, Lns, St]. It is not 'lying' nor does it mark a course of conduct, but it is the great lie by which unredeemed men are darkened in their minds and blinded and alienated from God (4:18–19). It is the same as τῆς ἀπάτης 'the deceit' in 4:22 and τὴν μεθοδείαν τῆς πλάνης 'the scheming of error' in 4:14, the opposite of ἀλήθεια 'truth' in 4:21, 24 [Lns]. It is possible this is the great lie of idolatry, the supreme falsehood of paganism, the chief symptom of a futile and darkened mind (4:17–18). Along with it they are to forsake all lesser lies and speak the truth [St]. The noun ψεῦδος 'lie' is used to characterize as a lie the whole former existence of the saints when they were yet pagans (cf. Col. 3:9 which specifies lying as the main characteristic of life under the old man). Paul is implying that any Christian who continues to speak, act, or live as if Christ had not yet come and made peace by 'creating one new man' (2:14–18) is living a lie [AB].

QUESTION—What relationship is indicated by the aorist participle ἀποθέμενοι 'putting off, having put off'?
1. The participle indicates an action going on concurrently with λαλεῖτε ἀλήθειαν 'speak the truth' and introduces a second command [AB, EBC, ICC, NTC, Rob, TH, WBC, We; all versions]: put off the lie/lying and let each person speak the truth with his neighbor. Putting off falsehood and telling the truth are two sides of the same coin [EBC, NTC]. Translating 'having put away' would imply a separation in time between the actions of the participle and the imperative verb [ICC, NTC]. The participle is aorist because the falsehood is to be put away once and for all. 'Putting away' is the best rendering in English [ICC]. The occurrence of the infinitive form of this verb, with imperative force, in the writer's previous argument for putting off the old man (4:22), makes it the more likely that this participle here also has imperative force. The specific act of putting away lying is not so much something that has been accomplished in the past, but is seen as something that is still incumbent upon the readers [WBC].
2. The participle indicates an action that precedes λαλεῖτε ἀλήθειαν 'speak the truth' [Alf, Ea, EGT, El, Lns, St]: since you have put off lying, let each person speak the truth with his neighbor. The Apostle could have used the present participle here, but he prefers the aorist, with its implication of a past tense, because a man must have once for all put off falsehood as a characteristic before he can begin the habit of speaking truth [Alf]. The aorist tense has its proper force of expressing an action understood to be done [EGT, El], finally and completely [Lns].

speak[a] truth[b] each with[c] his neighbor,[d]

LEXICON—a. pres. act. imper. of λαλέω (LN 33.70) (BAGD 2.b. p. 463): 'to speak' [AB, BAGD, El, LN, Lns, NIC, NTC, Rob, WBC, We; all versions except TEV], 'to tell' [LN; TEV]. The present tense denotes a continuous action [EGT, Lns].
b. ἀλήθεια (LN 72.2) (BAGD 2.a. p. 35): 'truth' [AB, BAGD, El, LN, Lns, NIC, NTC, Rob, WBC, We; all versions except NIV]. This noun is also translated as an adverb: 'truthfully' [NIV]. This noun denotes the content of that which is true and so in accordance with what actually happened [LN].
c. μετά with genitive object (LN 89.108): 'with' [El, LN, Lns, NIC, NTC, Rob, WBC, We; KJV, NASB, TNT], 'to' [AB; NAB, NIV, NJB, NRSV, REB, TEV].
d. πλησίον (LN 11.89) (BAGD 1.b. p. 672): 'neighbor' [AB, BAGD, El, LN, Lns, NIC, NTC, Rob, WBC, We; KJV, NAB, NASB, NIV, TNT], 'neighbors' [NRSV], 'one another' [NJB], 'each other' [REB], 'the other believer' [TEV], 'the one who is near or close by, the fellow man' [BAGD]. This noun denotes a person who lives close besides others and implies that the person is of the same ethnic and cultural background, i.e.,

of the same 'in-group' as another [LN]. The context makes it clear that the substantive is used here in reference to fellow-Christians [BAGD, Ea, EGT, Ho, ISBE2, My, NTC, TD, TH, WBC].

QUESTION—Is this a quotation from Zechariah 8:16?
1. It is a quotation [GNT, NCBC, NTC, Rob; NASB, NJB, TNT]. It lends added authority to the writer's words [NCBC, NTC, Rob].
2. This may not be an intentional quote from the OT [Can, WBC]. The fact that there is no citation formula with this quotation points to the writer's acquaintance with words of both the LXX and Hebrew texts and the facility with which his mind used biblical language. He may not have intended to make a formal quote here [Can].

QUESTION—What is meant by ἀλήθειαν 'truth'?
The use of ἀλήθειαν 'truth' here is a resumption of the usage from 4:21, 24 and points to the fact that the present verse was composed as an interpretation and application of the quote given in 4:21c–24 [AB]. As τὸ ψεῦδος 'the lie/lying' was put for all manner of deceit, hypocrisy, and cunning (synecdoche), so ἀλήθειαν 'truth' here stands for honest dealing and every kind of sincere communication [Cal], the avoidance of all underhanded and deceitful dealing with fellow human beings [CBC, Rob]. It is socio-moral honesty [WeBC], openhearted candor [NIC]. The Hebrew concept of 'truth' embraces 'faithfulness' and even 'righteousness', so that this command 'to speak the truth' includes the responsibility to be a witness to revelation, to follow Christ, to show unselfish love, and to build up one's fellow man to be his best [AB]. Others assume simple honesty and veracity in speech or communication is the meaning here [Ba, BAGD, DNTT, Ea, EGT, LJ, Lns, MNTC, NTC, St, TH, TNTC, WBC]. It means a person's statements must correspond with the facts [Ba, TH].

because[a] we-are parts[b] of-one-another.[c]

LEXICON—a. ὅτι (LN 89.33): 'because' [El, LN, Lns, NIC, We; TEV, TNT], 'for' [AB, LN, NTC, Rob, WBC; all versions except NJB, TEV, TNT], 'since' [LN; NJB], 'in view of the fact that' [LN].

b. μέλος (LN 63.17) (BAGD 3. p. 501): 'parts' [BAGD; NJB], 'parts of one body' [REB], 'members' [BAGD, El, LN, Lns, NIC, NTC, Rob, WBC, We; KJV, NAB, NASB, NRSV]. This is conflated with the following ἀλλήλων 'one another' and translated as a unit: 'one body' [AB; NIV], 'members together in the body of Christ' [TEV]. The clause ἐσμὲν ἀλληλῶν μέλη 'we are parts of one another' is translated: 'as one body we all belong to one another' [TNT]. This noun denotes a part as a member of a unit. It involves a figure of speech based upon the relationship of parts to the body (LN 8.9) [BAGD, LN].

c. ἀλλήλων (LN 92.26) (BAGD p. 39): 'one another' [BAGD, LN, NIC, NTC, WBC; NAB, NASB, NJB, NRSV, REB], 'each other' [BAGD, LN], 'one of another' [El, Lns, Rob, We; KJV]. This is also conflated with the preceding μέλη 'parts' and translated as a unit: 'one body' [AB;

NIV], 'members together in the body of Christ' [TEV]. This is a pronoun that marks a reciprocal relationship between entities [LN].

QUESTION—What relationship is indicated by ὅτι 'because'?

It indicates the grounds for putting away lying and speaking truth [AB, Can, CBC, ECWB, EGT, Ho, IB, LJ, My, NCBC, Rob, St, TH, TNTC, WBC]. The idea is that falsehood destroys fellowship [LJ, Lns, MNTC, St, TNTC, WBC] and loosens the bonds of unity [Ba, ECWB, Ho, LJ, MNTC, NTC, TH, TNTC, WBC, WeBC], as also do the other vices listed in this unit, anger, stealing, and foul language [IB, Lns, MNTC, St].

DISCOURSE UNIT: 4:26–27 [ECWB, St]. The topic for this unit is not losing one's temper, but ensuring that one's anger is righteous [St].

4:26 **Be angry**[a] **and (do) not sin;**[b] **(let) not the sun set upon**[c] **your anger,**[d]

LEXICON—a. pres. act. imper. of ὀργίζω, ὀργίζομαι (LN 88.174) (BAGD p. 579): 'to be angry' [BAGD, El, LN, Lns, NIC, NTC, Rob, We; KJV, NASB, NRSV], 'to be full of anger, to be furious' [LN]. This imperative is also translated as a condition: 'if you are angry' [AB, WBC; NAB, REB], 'even if you are angry' [NJB], 'if you become angry' [TEV], 'if you have cause to be angry' [TNT]. It is also translated as a prepositional phrase: 'in your anger' [NIV]. This imperative, as well as the following negative imperative μὴ ἁμαρτάνετε 'do not sin', is an iterative present [Lns].

b. pres. act. imper. of ἁμαρτάνω (LN 88.289) (BAGD 1. p. 42): 'to sin' [AB, BAGD, El, LN, Lns, NIC, NTC, Rob, WBC, We; KJV, NASB, NIV, NJB, NRSV], 'to transgress, to do wrong' [BAGD], 'to engage in wrongdoing' [LN], 'to lead into sin' [TEV]. This active verb is also translated as passive: 'to be led into sin' [REB]. This negated imperative is also translated as a hortatory clause 'let it be without sin' [NAB], 'do not turn it into sinful anger' [TNT]. The negative particle μή 'not' with the present imperative has to do with a course of action and may have the force of 'keep from', implying the imminent peril of sin [HG, Mou], or it may imply the cessation of an action already started [Tu], i.e., 'stop sinning'.

c. ἐπί with dative object (LN 67.33, 67.136) (BAGD II.2. p. 288): 'upon' [El, Lns, Rob, We; KJV], 'on' [AB, NIC, NTC, WBC; NAB, NASB, NJB, NRSV], 'at, in' [BAGD], 'at the time of' [BAGD, LN (67.33)], 'when' [LN (67.33)], 'during' [BAGD, LN (67.136)], 'during the course of' [LN (67.136)]. The prepositional phrase ἐπὶ παροργισμῷ ὑμῶν 'upon your anger' is also translated as a temporal clause: 'while you are still angry' [NIV]. The clause within which this preposition occurs is translated 'do not let sunset find you nursing your anger' [REB], 'do not stay angry all day' [TEV], 'calm down before sunset' [TNT]. This is a marker which is simultaneous with or overlaps another point of time [LN (67.33)], or it marks the extent of time within a unit of time [LN (67.136)].

384   EPHESIANS 4:26

d. παροργισμός (LN **88.176**) (BAGD p. 629): 'anger' [BAGD, LN, NIC, WBC; NASB, NJB, NRSV, REB, TNT], 'wrath' [MM, Rob; KJV, NAB], 'temper' [AB], 'angry mood' [BAGD, NTC], 'angered mood' [El], 'exasperation' [Lns], 'sense of provocation' [We], 'being provoked' [LN]. This noun is also translated as a negated imperative verb: 'do not stay angry' [**LN**; TEV]. The prepositional phrase ἐπὶ παροργισμῷ ὑμῶν 'upon your anger' is also translated as a temporal clause: 'while you are still angry' [NIV]. This noun denotes a state of provocation [MM], a state of being quite angry and upset about something [LN].

QUESTION—How does the quotation ὀργίζεσθε καὶ μὴ ἁμαρτάνετε 'be angry and do not sin' differ from the Hebrew original?

This quotation is an exact wording of the LXX of Psalm 4:4. Some commentators mention that it differs from the Hebrew text 'be troubled (or tremble, stand in awe) and do not sin' (Ps. 4:5) [AB, Ag, Alf, El, Mac, MNTC, My, Si-ed, TD, TH, WBC, WeBC; KJV, NRSV, REB], but others maintain that the Hebrew word 'be troubled' does denote anger and so it is not substantially different [Del, Ea, EBC, ICC, Lns, NIC, Rob, TNTC; NIV, TEV]. Some feel that since the quote is not offered in proof of anything [Can], the question is not really relevant [Can, ICC, WBC].

QUESTION—What is meant by the imperative ὀργίζεσθε 'be angry'?

This is a very different anger from that prohibited in 4:31 [El, Ho, My, St] for that context will show that the apostle speaks of malicious anger. Others, however, think 4:26 prohibits all anger, though recognizing its inevitability [ISBE2, TD, WBC]. The same generic feeling of anger may be holy if mixed with holy affections and springs from a holy mind, but sinful if malicious [Ho, ISBE, My]. Christ himself experienced anger (Mark 3:5) [Can, DNTT, EBC, ECWB, EGT, Ho, ICC, ISBE, LJ, Lns, MNTC, My-ed, NCBC, NTC, St, TNTC]. The verb ὀργίζεσθε 'be angry' assumes a just occasion for the anger [We, WeBC]. Yet other commentators believe justifiable anger aroused by cruelty or vileness is not the subject in this verse [IB, Si], on the grounds that if anger is righteous it should be sustained until the evil which caused it has been removed [IB].

1. The Greek imperative here indicates a condition and/or is permissive or concessional [AB, Alf, Ba, BD, Cal, DNTT, HG, Ho, ISBE2, NCBC, St, TD, TH, WBC; NAB, NIV, NJB, REB, TEV, TNT]: if you are angry, or be angry (if you must). This is a Hebrew idiom that permits anger (and then restricts it) rather than actually commanding it [St]. Another commentator denies it even gives permission to express anger [WBC]. This is not a command to righteous indignation [AB, NCBC], but it concedes that people do become angry over injustices [AB, ISBE2, NCBC, WBC]. The apostle speaks of an anger that is a weakness in the human condition, but by cherishing it, it becomes a sin [Alf]. The sense is: 'Anger should be avoided at all costs, but if you do get angry over something, refuse to indulge it, otherwise you sin' [WBC], or 'As far as I

am concerned, you may be angry (if you can't help it) but, in doing so, do not sin' [BD].
2. The Greek imperative here indicates a duty to be angry on the proper occasion [Can, Ea, EBC, ECWB, EGT, El, ICC (probably), ISBE, LJ, Lns, My, My-ed, NIC, NTC, Rob, WeBC; KJV, NASB, NRSV]: be angry. It is sometimes a duty to be angry at what is wrong, at men who are ungodly, false, and cruel [Can, EGT, El, LJ, WeBC] and therefore this imperative marks more than a concession [Can].

QUESTION—What is the function of καί 'and' in this statement?

It has the force of softening any antitheses in meaning between the two imperatives [EBC] and joins them closely together so that the two imperatives are not to be regarded as separate [EBC, Lns, MNTC, NTC], but together mean 'Do not let your anger be mixed with sin' [EBC, NTC] or 'do not sin in your anger' [MNTC, My, St; NIV]. (Two versions also adopt this close joining of the two imperatives in their translation of the Hebrew text of the Psalm [NRSV, REB]). This conjunction has a rhetorical force that adds something to the statement that seems to be not quite consistent with the preceding or that serves to qualify it in some way. Its sense is 'and yet' [EGT].

QUESTION—What is meant by the negative imperative μὴ ἁμαρτάνετε 'do not sin'?

This imperative forbids every kind of sinning to which anger may lead [My]. This imperative has the main force in the quote [Alf, Ea, EGT, El, My]. It implies there are limits within which anger must remain and if it goes beyond these limits, it becomes sinful [Ba, Cal, Can, ECWB, MNTC]. The first flush of anger is an involuntary self protective reaction that is not sinful in itself [Ba, Ea, ICC, ISBE, LJ], but if it is excited without cause, transcends the cause [Ba, Cal, Ea, ICC, LJ], focuses upon the person rather than the offense [Ba, Cal, LJ, WeBC], seeks revenge [Ba, Cal, LJ], is increased by reflection upon the cause [Ba, Cal, CBC, LJ], or is accompanied by an unforgiving spirit [Ba, Cal, LJ], it becomes sinful [Ba, Cal, CBC, Ea, ICC, LJ, WeBC]. This is the first of two limits which Paul places upon anger [Cal].

QUESTION—What is meant by the negative imperative clause ὁ ἥλιος μὴ ἐπιδυέτω ἐπὶ τῷ παροργισμῷ ὑμῶν 'do not let the sun set upon your anger'?
1. This clause indicates nothing more than a speedy abandonment of anger [EGT, El, ICC, My, TD]. The clause simply means 'before evening let your irritation be over' [El, My] and teaches the very speedy and undelayed abandonment of anger [My].
2. This clause implies more than just the speedy abandonment of anger [AB, Alf, Ba, Cal, Can, DNTT, EBC, ECWB, Ho, LJ, Lns, NCBC, NIC, NTC, Rob, St, TH, TNTC, WBC, We, WeBC]. The following implications are not mutually exclusive.
   2.1 This clause implies a prohibition against nourishing anger [Ba, Cal, ECWB, Ho, NCBC, NIC, Rob, St, TH, TNTC, WBC, We, WeBC]. This

is the practical enforcement of the command μὴ ἁμαρτάνετε 'do not sin' [ECWB, WBC] and places two safeguards against even righteous anger [ECWB, Lns]—(1) it sets a time limit upon anger [Alf, Cal, Can, Ea, EBC, ECWB, Lns, NIC] and (2) it prevents the stimulation or strengthening of anger [Cal, ECWB, Lns, NCBC, NIC] by nursing it [NIC] or brooding over it [ECWB]. It is directed against overindulgence in even justifiable anger [Lns]. Sleeping on anger leads to cherishing it [Ba, Ho] and thoughts of revenge [Ba].

2.2 This clause implies day's end is the time for being at peace [Alf, Can, DNTT (probably), LJ, NCBC, NIC, NTC, St, TNTC, We, WeBC] by means of giving and seeking forgiveness [Alf (probably), LJ, NIC, NTC, WeBC] at the time of evening prayer [LJ, NIC, WeBC].

2.3 This clause implies it belongs to a class of social obligations which were to be fulfilled by sunset [AB, EBC, Rob, St, WBC]. The admonition is parallel to other social obligations in Deuteronomy having to do with rendering to others what is owed to them, such as the paying of the day's wages to workers, the return of a cloak held as surety, the burial of a malefactor put to death, all of which were likewise to be fulfilled by the day's end [AB, EBC, Rob].

QUESTION—What is meant by the noun παροργισμῷ 'anger'?

1. This noun means the same as ὀργή 'anger' and is translated 'anger' [WBC; NASB, NJB, NRSV, REB, TNT]. No real difference from ὀργή 'anger' is indicated in this noun and stylistic difference accounts for its occurrence here [WBC].

2. This noun has a different meaning than ὀργή 'anger' [AB, EBC, EGT, El, ICC, LJ, My, TD, We].

2.1 This composite noun indicates something less permanent than settled, deep-rooted wrath [AB, EGT, El, ICC, My, TD, We]. The change from the verb form of ὀργή 'anger' to παροργισμῷ 'anger' is surely intentional with παροργισμῷ 'anger' meaning an angry outburst that threatens to become lasting bitterness [TD].

2.1.1 This noun denotes the 'arousing of wrath', which is different from ὀργή 'anger' which expresses a lasting mood [My, We]. This noun denotes what provokes the wrath, not the feeling of wrath itself [We]. The first sense of the provocation must not be cherished [We].

2.1.2 This noun denotes a state or a mood [AB, BAGD, EBC, EGT, El, LN, MM, NTC, St, TNTC]. Παροργισμῷ 'anger' denotes a state of provocation [EBC, EGT, LN, MM], an angry mood [BAGD, El, NTC], a fit of indignation or exasperation [Ea, EGT, El, My, My-ed], a spirit of resentment [NTC, St, TNTC], or a violent irritation which is expressed in hiding oneself from others, flaming looks, harmful words, or inconsiderate actions [AB], but it does not denote anger as a permanent state [ICC], a lasting mood or the disposition to anger [EGT, El].

2.2 This composite noun indicates a permanent, settled wrath [LJ]. This is a stronger word than ὀργή 'anger'. It means 'exasperation', an anger roused and nursed until it becomes a settled, permanent condition, spawning hatred, bitterness of spirit, and vindictiveness [LJ].

4:27 neither give place^a to the devil.

LEXICON—a. τόπος (LN 71.6) (BAGD 2.c. p. 823): 'place' [Rob, We; KJV], 'room' [Lns], 'foothold' [NTC; NIV, NJB, REB], 'chance' [BAGD, LN; TEV, TNT], 'opportunity' [AB, BAGD, LN, NIC, WBC; NASB], 'possibility' [BAGD, LN]. This noun is also translated as 'a chance to exert influence' [BAGD], 'a chance to work on you' [NAB]. The words δίδοτε τόπον 'give place' are translated 'make room' [NRSV].

QUESTION—What is the connection of this clause with the preceding?

1. This clause is to be interpreted with the preceding injunction [AB, Alf, Cal, Ea, El, IB, LJ, Lns, My, NCBC, NIC, NTC, Si, TNTC, WBC, We, WeBC; NJB]: neither (in nursing your anger) give place to the devil. This clause provides the motivation for the two preceding prohibitions [AB, WBC]. The clause marks a slight climax [Alf]. The μηδέ 'neither' marks a close connection with the preceding exhortation [Ea, Lns, TNTC] (in contrast to El, who says it should not be described as 'closely connected'), not logically or as a developed thought, but as an allied injunction [Ea]. This is done on the principle that δέ 'and' in negative sentences often has much the same conjunctive force as καί 'and' in affirmative sentences [El, Lns]. Nursing wrath affords an opportunity for the devil [IB, NCBC, NIC]. This clause sums up 4:26–27 as teaching that the Devil will take possession of the heart if wrath endures [AB, Cal].
2. This clause is to be interpreted as a general command [TH]: Don't do anything to give the devil a chance to make you sin. Despite the fact that this clause continues on from 4:26 without a break, it can be understood as a general command and not restricted to the anger of that verse [TH].

QUESTION—What is meant by the words δίδοτε τόπον 'give place'?

This noun is used metaphorically here [AB, TD] to mean providing an opportunity [AB, Alf, Ba, EGT, El, My, TD, TNTC, WBC] for the devil to become active [My]. 'To give place to' is to get out of the way of [Ho], to allow free scope to [Ho, Rob, Si-ed]. The present imperative verb δίδοτε 'give' is ingressive: 'don't begin to give place to the devil' [Lns].

1. The danger of giving place to the devil is primarily directed against the Church's unity and fellowship [Ba, Can, ECWB, NIC, Rob, TH, WBC]. The connection seems to be the danger to the Christian community as a whole, for anything that interrupts the unity and concord that should prevail among the brethren opens up a breach that will be used by Satan for his own purposes [Can, ECWB]. What is implied is that when wrath is cherished, the devil will use it as an opportunity to keep up a spirit of resentment among brethren [Ba, NIC].

2. The danger of giving place to the devil is primarily directed against the individual himself [AB, Cal, Ea, LJ, Lns, My, NCBC, NTC, WeBC]. Christians are not to give place to the devil even in a point, for if wrath gains an empire in the heart, it lays it open to him and the feelings of envy, cunning, and malice, which are especially identified with his presence and operations, and in a short time he will cover the platform of the whole soul [Ea]. Cherished anger gives the devil great power over us because it furnishes us a motive to yield to his suggestions [Ho]. Cherished anger mean loss of control over everything that makes a person human [LJ]. One loses control over reason. He is no longer able to think and evaluate things in a balanced manner [LJ, My]. All this gives the devil his greatest opportunity [LJ].
3. The danger of giving place to the devil is directed both against the group and against the individual himself [MNTC, TNTC]. Indignation nursed as a grievance will let the devil lead his victim on to unkind thoughts, words, and actions that will work havoc with personal relationships. His activity poses a danger alike to the individual's spiritual life and the welfare of the fellowship [TNTC]. If the mischief that arises out of quarrels does not end in some deadly hostility, it at least wrecks havoc in a man's own soul [MNTC].

4:28 The (one) stealing^a no-longer let-(him)-steal,

LEXICON—a. pres. act. participle of κλέπτω (LN 57.232) (BAGD p. 434): 'to steal' [BAGD, LN, NTC, We; NASB]. This participle is also translated as a noun: 'thief' [AB, NIC, WBC; REB, TNT], 'thieves' [NRSV], 'stealer' [El, Lns]. This present participle is translated as a present perfect tense: 'who has been stealing' [NAB, NIV]. It is also translated as a past tense: 'that stole' [Rob; KJV], 'who was a thief' [NJB], 'used to rob' [TEV]. This includes, in stealing, every way of obtaining unjustly what is not one's own [Cal, Can, EBC, Ho, LJ, Lns, My, WeBC], even if not covered under the laws of men [Cal, Ho, LJ]. The force of the participle here is iterative [HG, Mo] or durative [Mo, NTC, Tu]. Some commentators say that the present participle is not used for the past [Alf, Ea, EGT, El, Ho, My, NTC, We]. However, another commentator, while retaining the present tense, acknowledges that it really applies to actions prior to conversion [NTC]. Other commentators see a force similar to the imperfect tense here [BD, Mo, Tu] because it represents action prior to that of the main verb μηκέτι κλεπτέτω 'let him no longer steal' [BD, Mo, Tu].

QUESTION—How does this verse relate to the context and the theme of this unit?

This unit is concerned with practical illustrations arising out of the previous discussions of growing into the perfect man and maintaining the unity of the Spirit in the bond of peace [LJ]. Stealing is a disruptive force, resulting in the creation of chaos, and making unity and fellowship impossible [LJ, Si, TD], arising as it does out of utter selfishness [LJ, NTC, TD] and disrespect for the persons and property of others [LJ, Si, WeBC], and striking at mutual trust and fellowship [LJ, MNTC, Si, TD]. The prohibition of stealing and the encouragement of industriousness and generosity is another one of the items, along with lying and anger, which Paul saw as being of vital and pivotal importance to the Christian life and the unity and growth of the Christian community [LJ]. The writer selected stealing as another item that was a traditional topic in paraenetic material of the time and could serve as another typical activity of the old sinful nature which believers were to put off [WBC]. It is not necessary to infer that pilfering was a common vice in the church [Ba], but theft is common in the pagan life style [Ba, LJ, Lns] and these converts are cautioned not to fall into their old ways again [Ba, Lns]. Some think that this vice probably existed among the readers [Can, Ea, EBC, EGT, LJ, My].

but rather let-him-labor[a] working with-his-own hands the good[b] (thing),

TEXT—Ancient texts contain numerous variations of the reading ταῖς ἰδίαις χερσὶν τὸ ἀγαθόν 'with his own hands the good' adopted by GNT. Some vary the sequence of the words, so placing either ταῖς ἰδίαις χερσὶν 'his own hands', or τὸ ἀγαθόν 'the good' in emphasis [AB]. (The natural position that scribes would have assigned to τὸ ἀγαθόν 'the good' would have been next to the participle ἐργαζόμενος 'working' [WBC]). Others omit either of these or ἰδίαις 'his own' [AB]. GNT assigns a C rating to their reading, indicating the committee had difficulty in deciding which variant they would place in their text. Those who support the reading given in GNT are: AB, Ea, EBC, ECWB, EGT, El, ICC, Lns, NCBC, NTC, TD, TH, WBC; NASB, NIV, NJB, NRSV, TEV, TNT. Those who support a reading omitting ἰδίαις 'his own' or who do not translate this pronominal adjective are: Alf, Cal, Ho, MNTC, My, Rob, TNTC; KJV, NAB, REB.

LEXICON—a. pres. act. imper. of κοπιάω (LN 23.78, 42.47) (BAGD 2. p. 443): 'to labor' [El, LN (42.47), NIC, NTC, Rob, We; KJV, NASB, NRSV], 'to be laboring' [Lns], 'to work' [NIV], 'to work hard' [AB, BAGD, LN (42.47), WBC; REB], 'to start working' [TEV], 'to toil' [BAGD, LN (42.47)], 'to strive' [BAGD], 'to be tired, weary' [LN (23.78)]. This active verb is also translated as a reflexive: 'to exert oneself' [NJB]. This verb is also translated as a noun: 'labor' [NAB]. It is also translated as an adjective modifying 'honest work': 'hard honest work' [TNT]. This verb denotes engagement in hard work, implying difficulties and trouble [LN (42.47)] or it denotes being tired or weary, as the result of hard or difficult work [EBC, LN (23.78)], working to the point of fatigue [LJ, Lns, TD, TNTC]. The present tense of this imperative, and of the participle ἐργαζόμενος 'working' as well, expresses steady labor and work as a rule of life [Lns].

b. ἀγαθός (LN 88.1) (BAGD 2.a.α. p. 3): 'good' [BAGD, LN, WBC], 'good act' [LN], 'what is good' [BAGD, NTC; NASB], 'the thing that (or which) is good' [El, Rob, We; KJV], 'that which is good' [Lns], 'useful' [NIV]. This noun is also translated as an adverb modifying 'work': 'to work honestly' [AB; NRSV]. It is also translated as an adjective modifying an implied noun: 'at honest labor' [NAB], 'an honest job' [NIC; NJB], 'an honest living' [REB, TEV], 'honest work' [TNT]. This noun denotes positive moral qualities of the most general nature [LN]. Used as a pure substantive, this noun denotes what is intrinsically valuable or morally good. Here it is used in reference to honest work [BAGD].

QUESTION—What is the force of the contrastive μᾶλλον δέ 'but rather'?

This is not simply stating the opposite, but indicates a wider and freer contrast [Lns]. It has a *corrective* force [EGT, El, My], even indicating a preference [Ea], something that is far better than what has just been stated [Lns].

QUESTION—What is meant by ἐργαζόμενος ταῖς ἰδίαις χερσίν 'working with his own hands'?

This participial clause implies a contrast to the former idleness [Alf, EGT] as well as the bad use of those hands [Alf, EBC, EGT, My, WBC]. The reference is to manual labor [AB, Ea, EBC, WBC], manual labor being the most common type of employment in those times [Ea]. Some commentators feel the phrase probably is not meant to specify that the work *must* be manual [NCBC, TH], it simply means 'to work hard' [TH].

QUESTION—What is meant by τὸ ἀγαθόν 'the good'?

1. This refers to the preceding ἐργαζόμενος ταῖς ἰδίαις χερσίν 'working with his own hands' [BAGD, Cal, Can, Ea, EBC, EGT, El, Ho, ICC, LJ, MNTC, NIC, NTC, TH; NAB, NIV, NJB, NRSV, REB, TEV, TNT]. 'The good' denotes that which belongs to the category of the good and honest. It may *perhaps* also include the notion of what is beneficial instead of detrimental to others [El].
    1.1 It connotes honest work [BAGD, Can, EGT, El, Ho, MNTC, NIC, NTC, TH; NAB, NJB, NRSV, REB, TEV, TNT]. This refers to manual labor as intrinsically and morally good. Here it is used in reference to honest work [BAGD].
    1.2 It connotes useful work [Cal, Ea, EBC; NIV]. Useful employment is that which benefits others in the community. A Christian must not follow an employment that tends to harm or degrade others [Ba, Cal].
    1.3 It connotes work that is both honest and useful [Can]. The need and desire for earthly goods finds its legitimate satisfaction in work that is honest and that produces something useful [Can].
2. This refers to the following clause [ECWB]. There is in 'the good' a peculiar harmony with the doctrine of unity discussed in this chapter, for the sense of unity will always manifest itself as working what is 'good' or *gracious* for the sake of the one who is needy [ECWB].
3. This refers to both the preceding clause and the following clause [AB, Ba, Lns]. This refers to honest [AB, Lns] or useful [Ba] employment and, as

well, is defined by what is expressed in the following clause [AB, Ba, Lns].

in-order-that he-may-have-(something)/be-able[a] **to-share**[b] **with-the-one-who has need.**
LEXICON—a. pres. subj. act. of ἔχω (LN 57.1, **74.12**) (BAGD I.6.a. p. 333): 'to have' [AB, El, LN (57.1), Lns, NIC, NTC, Rob, WBC, We; all versions except TEV], 'to possess' [LN (57.1)], 'to be able to' [BAGD, LN (**74.12**); TEV], 'to have the capacity to' [LN (74.12)]. The present tense means 'may continue to have' [Lns].
   b. pres. act. infin. of μεταδίδωμι (LN 57.96) (BAGD p. 511): 'to share' [AB, BAGD, LN, Lns, NIC, NTC, Rob, WBC; all versions except KJV, TEV], 'to give' [BAGD, El, LN, We; KJV], 'to help' [TEV]. It means to distribute personally rather than through some agent or official [EBC]. The present tense is iterative, 'to share with at any time a needy one appears' [Lns].
QUESTION—What relationship is indicated by ἵνα 'in order that'?
Paul is not content just to admonish abstinence from what is definitely wrong. He sets over it the good that Christians should do [Cal, Can, ECWB, LJ]. This purpose clause [WBC] gives the reason [Alf, LJ] or motivation [AB, Can, Ho, TNTC, WBC] for the prohibition of theft [AB, Alf, LJ] or for honest labor [Ho, TNTC, WBC]. It introduces the result of doing something useful [EBC]. It introduces a higher motive for labor than just providing self-support [Ea, TNTC], as well introducing the thief's truest restitution [Ea, EGT, Lns]. The sharing of goods with the needy, earned by one's own efforts, is given as the rationale for, or the object of, honest work [AB, Alf, EGT, El, Ho, LJ, TNTC, WBC, We, WeBC], not self-satisfaction manifested in creativeness, productiveness, or anything else [AB]. The motive is communal well-being [WBC]. Honest labor is needful if the needy are to live [AB, Ba]. At the same time, working for what one may gain for oneself is not excluded [AB, Ba].
QUESTION—What is meant by ἔχῃ 'he may have/be able to'?
  1. This verb denotes the possession of something [AB, DNTT, El, Lns, NIC, NTC, Rob, TH, TNTC, WBC, We, WeBC; all versions except TEV]: he may have something to share.
  2. This verb denotes a capacity to perform a given function [BAGD, LN (**74.12**), MNTC; TEV]: he may be able to share.
QUESTION—Who is referred to as τῷ χρείαν ἔχοντι 'to the one having need'?
  1. This is universal, referring to whoever is poor and needy, not just to the poor and needy in the Church [AB, TD]. Universality of concern is a characteristic of Ephesians [AB]. Giving from the fruit of one's labor serves the Christian community indirectly in respect of its good repute in the world [TD].

2. This refers to the poor and needy within the Christian community [Cal, ECWB, MNTC, TH, WBC]. This applies primarily to the poor in the Christian fellowship [TH, WBC] but not necessarily exclusively [WBC].

DISCOURSE UNIT: 4:29–30 [ECWB, St]. The topic is using the mouth for good, not evil [St].

4:29 **Every unwholesome/harmful/useless[a] word out of your mouth let it not proceed,**

LEXICON—a. σαπρός (LN **20.14**) (BAGD 2. p. 742): 'unwholesome' [BAGD, LN; NASB, NIV], 'foul' [AB; NJB, TNT], 'corrupt' [El, NIC, NTC, Rob, We; KJV], 'bad' [BAGD], 'evil' [BAGD, WBC; NAB, NRSV], 'offensive' [REB], 'harmful' [LN; TEV], 'worthless' [Lns]. This term denotes that which is harmful due to the fact that it is used to describe what is unwholesome and corrupting. In this verse the term takes its meaning from the contrast with ἀγαθός 'good' which describes what is good for building up what is necessary, and so means 'helpful'. By contrast, then, σαπρός denotes that which is 'harmful' [LN (20.14)].

QUESTION—How does this verse fit into the context?

Paul proceeds from a warning against doing harm to others by dishonest deeds to doing harm to them by evil and corrupt speech [Can, MNTC, TD, WBC, We]. This is apparent from the linkage with the previous verse supplied by ἀγαθός 'good' and χρεία 'need' [TD, WBC]. Another says Paul proceeds from an improper attitude toward material things to an improper use of the tongue [NTC]. Like the lying, wrath, and dishonesty of the preceding verses, the sin spoken of in this verse is directed against the unity of the Church in God [ECWB, LJ, NIC, Rob, WBC] and the harm that evil and unwholesome words cause in communal life [WBC]. Another commentator simply sees a shift here to more general and comprehensive exhortations after the three definite exhortations of 4:25, 26, and 28 [My].

QUESTION—What is meant by the adjective σαπρός 'unwholesome, harmful, useless'?

1. The writer has unwholesome speech in mind, which tends to defile others [AB, Ba, Cal, Can, DNTT, Ea, ECWB, LJ, NTC, Rob, Si, TNTC, WeBC]. Paul is condemning any use of the faculty of speech that is morally unhealthy [Can, LJ], that suggests impure thoughts [Cal, Can, LJ], light views of sin, irreverence towards God, or trifles with serious things [Can]. Profanity and obscenity, as well as careless or light speech, profane religious and sacred concepts which results in a nullification of sacred ideas conveyed by language, which is man's most powerful weapon for influencing the thoughts and lives of his fellows [WeBC].
2. The writer has harmful speech in mind [EBC, MNTC, NCBC]. This is more than just bad language; it is malicious gossip and slander—whatever injures others and incites dissension [EBC]. The adjective is applied to anything worthless, so the reference here is to any kind of words that may produce mischief [MNTC].

3. The writer has a broad definition in mind, covering both interpretations 1 and 2 [Ho, ICC, NIC, St, TH, WBC].
4. The writer has useless speech in mind [EGT, El, LN (20.14), Lns, My]. The word σαπρός 'worthless' here is dependent upon the contrasting ἀγαθόν 'good', which specifies words which edify. The adjective σαπρός, therefore, means words which lack this quality [LN (20.14), My, TD]. It does not mean 'filthy' here but, as suggested by ἀγαθόν 'good' in the next clause, 'profitless' [EGT, El], 'worthless' [Lns, My], 'bad, of no good to anyone' [EGT].

but if such (is) good for edification/building-up[a] of-the need/use,[b]
TEXT—Some manuscripts have πίστεως 'of faith' in place of χρείας 'of need'. This clause would then read: 'but such as are good for edification of the faith'. GNT assigns the reading containing χρείας 'of need' an A rating, indicating that this reading is certain. None of the commentators used in this compilation of exegetical opinion supported the alternative reading.
LEXICON—a. οἰκοδομή: 'building up'. See this word at 4:12, 16.
  b. χρεία (LN 57.40) (BAGD 3. p.885): 'need' [El, LN], 'lack' [LN], 'use' [KJV], not explicit [TNT]. This noun is also translated as a verb: 'to need' [NAB]. Most use an explanatory phrase or clause to translate this word: 'that which is needed' [We], 'what is needed' [LN], 'the thing that is lacking and (therefore) necessary' [BAGD], 'where necessary' [Lns], 'where it is necessary' [BAGD], 'as the need may arise' [NIC] 'as the need arises' [WBC], 'as fits the need' [NTC], 'as need may be' [Rob], 'according to the need of the moment' [NASB], 'according to (their) needs' [NIV], 'as occasion offers' [NJB], 'as there is need' [NRSV], 'to provide what is needed' [TEV]. The prepositional phrase πρὸς οἰκοδομὴν τῆς χρείας 'for the edification of the need/use' is also translated: 'for meeting a need constructively' [AB], 'what is helpful to the occasion' [REB]. This noun denotes that which is lacking and is particularly needed [Alf, Ho, LN].
QUESTION—What is meant by the term ἀγαθός 'good'?
1. This adjective means 'fit, capable, useful' [Ba, BAGD (1.a.β. p. 2), Can (probably), HG, Ho; NRSV], 'suitable, serviceable' [Ea, EGT, El, My], 'beneficial' [Lns, TH], or 'helpful' [TH]: useful or serviceable to edification. Such words as are adapted to instruct, counsel, and comfort others [Ba]. The adjective ἀγαθός 'good' followed by the preposition πρός 'for' (the preposition providing the sense of 'fit' [HG] or indication of purpose [TD, Tu]) signifies 'good' in the sense of 'suitable' or 'serviceable' [Ea, EGT, El, My].
2. This adjective means 'graciousness' or 'full of sympathy' [ECWB]. A person with this quality quickly notes what the need of each is and hastens to speak accordingly so as to meet that need [ECWB].
3. The adjective means 'morally good' [Rob, WBC]. It does not just mean 'good for a purpose' since this would be expressed by εὔθετος [Rob].

This specifies speech which is morally good for what builds up others rather than tearing them down [WBC].

QUESTION—What is meant by the genitive construction οἰκοδομὴν τῆς χρείας 'edification/building up of the need/use'?

The noun οἰκοδομήν 'edification' is also translated 'building up' [AB, Can, DNTT, EBC, ECWB, NCBC, NIC, NTC, Rob, Si-ed, St, TD, TH, WBC, We; NIV, NRSV, TEV] and is used here in a metaphorical sense [Cal]. Here it denotes the act or process of building, in distinction from a completed structure [TD]. One commentator feels 'edification' has become hackneyed as a definition and should be avoided [Rob]. Since the word here refers back to its two other metaphorical occurrences in this chapter (4:12, 16), some commentators prefer 'building up' [Rob, WBC]. The writer is talking about speech which helps those who hear to build up their character into the likeness of Christ [Can].

1. The noun χρείας means 'need' [AB, Alf, BAGD, Can, Ea, EBC, ECWB, EGT, El, Fd, Ho, ISBE2, LJ, Lns, MNTC, My, NIC, NTC, Rob, Si-ed, TD, TH, WBC, We; all versions except KJV, NJB, REB, TNT], 'necessity' [Ho, Lns, NTC], 'occasion' [Can, Fd, Ho, ICC, LJ, MNTC, Rob, St, TH, TNTC; NJB, REB] or 'matter in hand' [Fd, Rob, TNTC] and denotes the *lack* of edification [AB, Alf, BAGD, Ea, EBC, ECWB, EGT, El, Fd, Ho, ISBE2, LJ, Lns, MNTC, My, NIC, NTC, Rob, Si-ed, TD, TH, TNTC, WBC, We]. The word 'need' focuses on each individual occasion of need [Can, EBC, Ho, ICC, LJ, MNTC, My, Rob, Si-ed, St, TH, TNTC, WBC; NASB, NJB, NRSV, REB]. It can be a need that is pressing and continuous [Ea]. The noun χρείας 'need' is used here because its occurrence in 4:28 suggested its use here also [WBC].
    1.1 'Building up' specifies the 'need' [AB, Ho]: the need for edification. The need consists of the lack of building up [AB]. This phrase means the edification that the necessity calls for [Ho].
    1.2 'Need' is the object of the 'building up' [Alf, BAGD, Ea, ECWB, Fd, ICC, LJ, My, NTC, TH, TNTC, We; REB, TEV]: edifying the particular need at the time. The actual 'need' or 'occasion' is that which requires the edifying influence of the words [ICC]. The sense is 'for the improvement of the occasion' [Fd, ICC, TH].
    1.3 'Need' is the more remote reference or the point of view of 'building up' [Can, El; NASB, NIV]: building up in respect to (or, according to) the need. Edification, or building up, fellow Christians is to be done with reference to the need of the occasion [Can].
    1.4 'Need' is an attribute of 'building up' [WBC; NAB]: the needed edification. They are to say the good things that people need to hear [NAB].
2. The noun χρείας means 'use' [Ba, Bu, Cal; KJV].
    2.1 'Use' is an attribute of 'building up' [Ba]: for useful edification.
    2.2 'Building up' denotes the purpose to which the implied word (λόγος) is to be put [Can; KJV]: the use of building up. It means 'the edification of

use' or 'the edifying use' and denotes the progress of the Christian's edification [Cal].

2.3 'Use' is the object of edification [Bu]: the building up of use. The figure of speech called *antiptosis*, in which the governing noun becomes the adjective, applies here. The meaning is 'edifying use' [Bu].

in-order-that/that-is it-might-give grace[a] to-those-who-hear.

LEXICON—a. χάρις (LN 88.66) (BAGD 3.a. p. 878): 'grace' [LN, Lns, NTC, Rob, We; KJV, NASB, NRSV], 'kindness, graciousness' [LN], 'gracious deed or gift, benefaction' [BAGD]. The phrase δῷ χάριν 'give grace' is translated 'to help' [NAB], 'to benefit' [WBC; NIV], 'to do good to' [AB; NJB, TEV], 'to bring a blessing to' [REB], 'to minister a blessing to' [El], 'to minister grace to' [NIC], 'to be blessed' [TNT]. The noun denotes a spiritual benefit [Ea] or favor [ICC] for the hearer.

QUESTION—What relationship is indicated by ἵνα 'in order that'?

1. It indicates purpose [Ho, LJ, Lns, My, NCBC, WBC] following the pattern of all the other exhortations in this unit [WBC]: let words proceed from your mouth which are good for building up in order that such words might give grace to those who hear. This is the aim of the πᾶς λόγος ἐκ τοῦ στόματος ὑμῶν ἐκπορευέσθω 'let every word proceed out of your mouth' [My] which is conceived as supplied in the ἀλλὰ εἴ τις 'but if such (is)' [My, WBC]. This is the first motivation for profitable discourse, the second being reverence for the Holy Spirit (4:30) [Ho].

2. It introduces an explanation of the preceding positive injunction to edifying speech [Cal]: let words proceed from your mouth which are good for building up, that is, words that might give grace to those who hear. To explain the manner in which edification takes place, the writer adds 'that it might impart grace to the hearers' [Cal].

3. This is an elliptical imperative use of ἵνα 'that' [HG]. This use of ἵνα 'that' is not purely purpose, and not result. It indicates an elliptical imperative [HG].

QUESTION—What is meant by χάριν 'grace'?

1. The noun χάριν 'grace' here denotes the conveying of the grace of God through human speech to the hearer [Alf, EBC, EGT, El, ICC, LJ, Lns, My, NCBC, NTC, TD, TH, TNTC, We]. What is said elsewhere to be a Divine prerogative is here attributed to human speech [We]. Combined with the verb δῷ 'might give' [EGT, El, My], the noun χάριν 'grace' always means 'to confer a kindness' [EGT, My] or 'a blessing' [EBC, EGT, El, My], whether temporal [EBC], or spiritual [EBC, El]. Due to the change of meaning in χάριν 'grace' in the NT, the most exact translation here is 'blessing', since it hints at the theological meaning but does not wholly obscure the classical and idiomatic meaning of διδόναι χάριν 'to give a favor or benefit' [El]. Paul does not say *we* are to give grace, but *that which we speak* is to give edifying grace, and therefore divine grace, to those who hear us [Lns]. Since the ultimate source of all blessings is

God himself and the channel here is human, even the everyday conversation of Christians becomes a means of grace to others [EBC].
2. The noun χάριν 'grace' here denotes kindness done by us [Can, WBC]. The word does not denote here the favor of God, but only kindness or good done by the speaker [Can]. The force of δῷ χάριν 'may give grace' is 'to do a favor' or 'to confer a benefit'. Human words may be carriers of divine grace, but that should not be assumed here [WBC].
3. The noun χάριν 'grace' here denotes both speech that is gracious and pleasurable, and speech that is a means of grace or religiously helpful [MNTC, NIC, Rob]. There is a play upon words here. Paul uses the classical meaning of 'pleasant speech' to carry his deeper, Christian meaning. This play cannot be reproduced in English [Rob]. A Christian's conversation should both serve as a means of God's grace to another individual, helping to build up the common life in Christ, and, according to J. A. Findlay, leave a pleasant impression on those who listen to it [NIC].

DISCOURSE UNIT: 4:30–32 [LJ]. The topic is a statement of the doctrine of the sealing of the Spirit with its practical obligations.

4:30 and (do) not grieve/insult[a] the Spirit the holy (one) of God, in whom you-were-sealed[b] for/until/for-the-purpose-of[c] (the) day of redemption.
LEXICON—a. pres. act. imper. of λυπέω (LN **25.275**) (BAGD 1. p. 481): 'to grieve' [AB, BAGD, El, Lns, NIC, NTC, Rob, WBC, We; KJV, NASB, NIV, NJB, NRSV, REB, TNT], 'to make sad' [**LN**; TEV], 'to sadden' [LN; NAB], 'to pain' [BAGD], 'to vex, to irritate, to offend, to insult' [BAGD]. This verb denotes causing someone to be sad, sorrowful, or distressed [LN]. The imperative is present tense and implies an iterative action that matches πᾶς λόγος σαπρός 'every worthless statement' in 4:29. The apostle does not mean 'stop grieving', for he in no way implies his readers were doing that. He is warning against a sin that has not yet been committed by his readers [Lns].
b. aorist pass. indic. of σφραγίζω: 'to be sealed'. See this word at 1:13.
c. εἰς with accusative object (LN 67.117, 67.119, 89.57) (BAGD 2.a.β. p. 228): 'for' [AB, BAGD, El, LN (67.117), Lns, NTC, WBC; NASB, NIV, NRSV, REB], 'until' [LN (67.119)], 'on' [BAGD; TNT], 'unto' [Rob, We; KJV], 'to' [LN (67.119)], 'at' [LN (67.117)] 'in' [LN (67.117)], 'against' [NIC; NAB], 'in order to, for the purpose of' [LN (89.57)]. This preposition is translated as a verb: 'to be ready for' [NJB]. It is also translated as a noun phrase indicating purpose: 'a guarantee that' [TEV]. This preposition is a marker of the extent of time [LN (67.117)], or it marks the continuous extent of time, up to an indicated point [LN (67.119)], or it marks intent, often implying an expected result [LN (89.57)]. See this word at 1:14.

QUESTION—What is the function of the initial καί 'and' in this verse, and how does this verse relate to the context?

1. This verse is linked to 4:29 [Alf, Cal, Can, Ea, EBC, EGT, El, Ho, ICC, Lns, My, NIC, Rob, St, TD, TH, TNTC, WBC, WeBC]. The Spirit especially claims to express himself in the utterances of Christians [Rob, TNTC], so the misuse of the organ of speech is a wrong done to and felt by the Spirit who claims to control it [Rob, TNTC, WBC]. It is not a prohibition to grieve the Spirit in general, but an exhortation not to grieve him by worthless speech in particular [Lns]. Reverence for the Holy Spirit is a motive for enjoining profitable speech [Ho]. This verse is obviously a strengthening of the admonition of 4:29 to guard against corrupt speech [Can, TD]. The Spirit manifests his work in men through the various gifts of utterance that he bestows. Nothing can be more abhorrent to him than to witness corrupt speech coming out of the same mouths into which he has given such gifts of utterance [Can].
2. This verse is linked to all of the preceding prohibitions and commands of 4:25–29 [AB, Ba, ECWB, IB, NTC]. This general exhortation fitly serves to close this discourse unit (4:25–30), which warns against typical sins, and is at the same time exhaustive of the general sins against men. By doing so, it refers to all the practical commands that have just been discussed. The four cardinal sins forbidden above are regarded as 'grieving' the Holy Spirit. The verse relates to the theme of the unity of the Church in this chapter because that unity is always in God, through the Holy Spirit working the image of Christ into each individual [ECWB].
3. This verse constitutes another independent prohibition [MNTC]. The prohibitions now take a wider sweep. Paul is thinking of the Spirit here both as the regenerating power in the believer and as the unifying principle in the Church. Both functions go together, for the more an individual is renewed, the more causes of discord and enmity disappear from the Church [MNTC].
4. This verse is linked to 4:31 [LJ, NCBC] and serves as an introduction to another discourse unit [LJ]. This verse is an introduction to material that is to come rather than a summing up and enforcing of that which has gone before. Nevertheless, there is a connection with the preceding material. It serves as a kind of center or focus of all that is said regarding the particulars [LJ]. The faults of 4:31 both grieve the Spirit and disrupt the harmony of the fellowship [NCBC].

QUESTION—What is meant by the negative imperative μὴ λυπεῖτε 'do not grieve'?

1. This is used figuratively [Ba, Bu, Cal]: do not, so to speak, grieve the Holy Spirit of God. We are not to think that the Spirit literally endures grief and pain. This is an anthropomorphism which describes what *men* endure [Ba, Bu] and is applied to the Spirit [Ba, Bu, Cal] to show the kind of conduct that is *fitted* to cause grief [Ba].

2. This is used in its literal sense [AB, Alf, Can, CBC, EBC, ECWB, EGT, El, Ho, IB, ICC, ISBE, LJ, Lns, My, NCBC, NTC, Si, St, TD, TH, TNTC, WBC, WeBC]: do not grieve the Holy Spirit of God. When the Spirit is 'grieved', his holiness is offended and his love is wounded [Ho]. In both Testaments, God is himself said to be susceptible to grief [ISBE].
  2.1 The verb means 'to grieve' [AB, Alf, Can, Ea, EBC, ECWB, EGT, El, Ho, ISBE, LJ, Lns, My, NCBC, NTC, Si, St, TH, TNTC, WBC, WeBC]. The word means to disappoint and sadden the Spirit [LJ].
  2.2 The verb means 'to insult' [BAGD, TD], 'to offend' [BAGD, CBC, IB], 'to wound' [TD]. The verb can also have the sense of 'to vex, irritate, offend, insult'. [BAGD]. These sins against fellow Christians are also an offense against the Holy Spirit who inhabits them [IB].

QUESTION—Why is the construction τὸ πνεῦμα τὸ ἅγιον τοῦ θεοῦ 'the Spirit the holy (one) of the God' used?

The repetition of the articles in this construction gives it solemnity [Alf, Ea, El] and emphasis [Alf, Can, Ea, El, NIC, NTC, WBC]. This is the full title for the Holy Spirit [EBC, NTC]. This title, together with the moving anthropomorphism 'grieve', serve to give a special gravity to the prohibition [EBC]. It renders the enormity of such action most palpable [My]. The entire divine majesty is thrown into the scales in order to persuade us not to grieve the Spirit [Lns]. But not only is the majesty of the Spirit stressed [NTC, WBC], but also his holiness and sanctifying power [NTC, TNTC, WBC]. This title not only specifies the object of the grieving but introduces the motivation for not grieving him as well. The following relative cause intensifies this motivation [Lns].

QUESTION—What is the function of the clause ἐν ᾧ ἐσφραγίσθητε εἰς ἡμέραν ἀπολυτρώσεως 'in whom you were sealed for the day of redemption'?

This clause provides the motivation [AB, Ea, LJ, My, NIC, WBC] or grounds [EBC, ICC] for not grieving the Holy Spirit. It is an enhancement of the warning not to grieve the Spirit by recalling the blessing that the readers have received from the Holy Spirit [El, My]. The consideration that their security rests in the Holy Spirit and their assurance of reaching the day when their redemption will reach final completion constitutes an additional reason for avoiding anything out of harmony with the Holy Spirit's holy being and action [EGT].

QUESTION—What relationship is indicated by the prepositional phrase ἐν ᾧ 'in whom'?

  1. This phrase indicates that the Holy Spirit is the instrument of the sealing [AB, Cal, NIC, Rob, St, TD; KJV, NAB, NIV, NRSV, REB, TEV (probably), TNT]: with whom you were sealed. The phrase has a predominately instrumental sense [TD]. God has sealed us by his Spirit, the Spirit being the seal by which we are distinguished from the wicked and impressed as sure evidence of adoption [Cal]. (Cal, NIC, and TNT use 'by' but appear to be referring to an instrumental meaning.)

2. This phrase indicates that the Holy Spirit is the environment of the sealing, or the sphere or element in which it takes effect [Alf, Can, Ea, ECWB, EGT, El, NTC, WBC, We, WeBC]: in whom you are sealed. It means 'in whom' [Alf, Can, Ea, ECWB, EGT, El, NTC, WBC, We], not 'by whom' [Alf, EGT] nor 'whereby' [ECWB, EGT]. This phrase marks the element or condition of the sealing. The action of sealing is performed by the Father, the Holy Spirit being the seal itself (1:13) [Alf]. In contrast to 1:13, where the simple dative case means 'by', here it means 'in'. If there is an intended significance to the difference, it may be that here we are said to be encompassed about by the Holy Spirit, taken into his embrace, so to speak, and so stamped with the likeness of God [Can].
3. This phrase indicates that the Holy Spirit is the agent of the sealing [Ho, MNTC, TH, TNTC; NASB, NJB]: by whom you were sealed. The Greek means 'in' or 'by'. The whole clause could be translated 'by whom you are kept secure until the Day of complete salvation' [TH].
4. This phrase indicates that the sealing is with regard to the Holy Spirit [EBC, Lns]: in connection with whom you were sealed. The simple dative of 1:13 is here changed into a distinctly personal phrase 'in connection with whom' [Lns].

QUESTION—What is meant by the passive verb ἐσφραγίσθητε 'you were sealed'?

The reference to this truth in this context is emphatic [ECWB]. It emphasizes the obligation upon Christians to revere the Spirit as the pledge of their glorious destiny. Present conduct must be worthy of the inheritance upon which they have begun to enter [IB]. The aorist tense implies a once-for-all action [ICC]. God is the agent of this passive verb [Lns]. See the discussion in 1:13 for the imagery and meaning involved in this verb.

QUESTION—What is meant by ἡμέραν ἀπολυτρώσεως 'day of redemption'?

This is a reference back to the ἀπολύτρωσιν τῆς περιποιήσεως 'redemption of the possession' in 1:14 [AB, Alf, Cal, Ea, NIC, NTC, Rob, WBC, We].

1. This refers to a future eschatological day when Christ returns to complete the salvation process [AB, Alf, Can, CBC, DNTT, Ea, EBC, EGT, El, ICC, ISBE2, LJ, Lns, MNTC, My, NIC, NTC, TD, TH, TNTC, WBC, We, WeBC]. The genitive indicates a temporal relation [EGT, El, WBC], the day on which redemption will manifest itself [EGT] and will be fully realized [El]. The motivation for the prohibition, to not grieve the Spirit, lies in an event to be consummated in the future, but of which, in the present time, the Spirit's presence and operation in believers is a guarantee. This contrasts with the previous injunctions of this unit in which their motivational clauses have had reference to the realities and opportunities of the present [AB]. Despite the future perspective inherent in this statement, the emphasis still remains on the believers' present relationship to the Spirit, who guarantees their future and whom, therefore, they should not grieve [WBC].

2. This refers to the state the believer enters after death [NCBC]. It refers to the final completion of salvation beyond the death of the believer [NCBC].

DISCOURSE UNIT: 4:31–5:21 [ECWB]. The topic is the power of the new life against special besetting sins.

DISCOURSE UNIT: 4:31–5:2 [ECWB, St]. The topic is bitterness and malignity as unworthy of the love of God which has been manifested to us in Christ [ECWB].

DISCOURSE UNIT: 4:31–32 [AB]. The topic is a summary admonition consisting of two brief catalogues of opposite actions that are characteristic of the Old and New Man respectively. Their sum adds up to the theme 'live as people who are forgiven'.

4:31 (Let) all bitterness[a] and wrath[b] and anger[c] and clamor[d] and slander[e] be-put-away[f] from you with all malice/evil.[g]

LEXICON—a. πικρία (LN **88.201**) (BAGD 2. p. 657): 'bitterness' [AB, BAGD, El, **LN**, Lns, NTC, Rob, WBC, We; all versions except REB], 'bitter resentment' [LN], 'animosity' [BAGD], 'anger' [BAGD], 'harshness' [BAGD, NIC], 'spite' [LN; REB]. This term denotes a state of sharp, intense hate or resentment [LN]. It is an embittered and resentful spirit which refuses to be reconciled [ICC, MM, Rob, St, TH, TNTC]. It includes within it animosity, resentment, anger, and harshness [DNTT, Ea, EGT, NTC, TD] and especially focuses upon the feelings and disposition [EGT, El] as opposed to just speech [EGT].

b. θυμός (LN 88.178) (BAGD 2. p. 365): 'wrath' [BAGD, El, LN, NIC, Rob, We; KJV, NASB, NRSV], 'anger' [BAGD, LN, NTC], 'fury' [LN], 'rage' [BAGD, LN, WBC; NIV], 'exasperation' [Lns], 'bad temper' [NJB, REB], 'passion' [AB; NAB, TEV], 'outbursts of temper' [TNT]. This noun denotes a state of intense anger and carries the implication of passionate outbursts [LN].

c. ὀργή (LN 88.173) (BAGD 1. p. 578): 'anger' [AB, BAGD, El, LN, Lns, NIC, Rob, WBC, We; all versions except REB], 'indignation' [BAGD], 'wrath' [BAGD, NTC], 'fury' [LN], 'rage' [REB]. This noun denotes a relative state of anger [LN].

d. κραυγή (LN 33.84) (BAGD 1.a. p. 449): 'clamor' [BAGD, El, NIC, Rob, We; KJV, NASB], 'yelling' [Lns], 'brawling' [NTC; NIV], 'harsh words' [NAB], 'insults' [REB], 'shouting' [AB, WBC; NJB, TEV], 'wrangling' [NRSV], 'shout, scream, cry' [LN], 'bawling' [TNT]. This noun denotes the sound of a loud shout or scream [LN].

e. βλασφημία (LN 33.400, 33.401) (BAGD 1. p. 143): 'slander' [BAGD, NIC, NTC, WBC; NAB, NASB, NIV, NRSV, REB, TNT], 'defamation' [BAGD], 'reviling' [LN (33.400)], 'railing' [We], 'blasphemy' [BAGD, LN (33.401), Lns], 'evil speaking' [El, Rob; KJV], 'cursing' [AB], 'abuse' [NJB], 'insults' [TEV], 'serious insult' [LN (33.401)]. This noun denotes the action of speaking against someone so as to harm their reputation. This may be directed both against persons and divine beings [LN (33.400)], or it denotes the content of a defamation [LN (33.401)]. The religious connotation of blasphemy against Deity, which is predominate in this word, is present even where it is not expressed, such as where the root βλασφημ- occurs in lists of offenses [TD].

f. aorist pass. imper. of αἴρω (LN 90.96) (BAGD 4. p. 24): 'to be put away' [El, Lns, NIC, NTC, Rob; KJV, NASB], 'to be taken away from' [AB, BAGD, LN, We], 'to be removed from' [BAGD, LN, WBC], 'to be far removed from' [NJB]. This passive verb is also translated actively: 'to get rid of' [NAB, NIV, TEV], 'to put away from' [NRSV], 'to have done with' [REB], '(to do) away with' [TNT]. This verb denotes causing someone to no longer experience something [LN]. The verb denotes a once-for-all action [LJ].

g. κακία (LN 88.105, **88.199**) (BAGD 1.b. p. 397): 'malice' [AB, BAGD, El, NIC, NTC, Rob, WBC, We; all versions except REB, TEV], 'ill will' [BAGD], 'hateful feeling' [LN (88.199); TEV], 'malignity' [BAGD], 'baseness' [Lns], 'evil' [LN (88.105); REB], 'wickedness, badness' [LN (88.105)]. This term denotes a special kind of moral inferiority [BAGD]. It denotes a feeling of strong dislike and hostility. It also possibly implies a desire to do harm [LN (88.199)], or it denotes the quality of wickedness, implying it is harmful and damaging [LN (88.105)].

QUESTION—How is this verse connected in the context?

1. This verse is connected to the previous verse as showing the manner in which the Holy Spirit is grieved [LJ, MNTC, NIC]. This verse actually reinforces the idea of the regenerating and unifying power of the Spirit presented in the last verse by showing how the Spirit is vexed by every offense against the full brotherhood that should ideally prevail in the Church [MNTC]. Unworthy speech is clearly in view when grieving the Holy Spirit is mentioned. This verse shows of what such speech may consist. It is speech which has some quality of malice in it [NIC]. The list of vices in this verse remind us of the ones treated in 4:25–29, yet the Apostle is not repeating himself here. Though the terms are the same in certain respects, yet they have an essential difference which has been brought in by the last verse. In 4:25–29 Paul has looked at conduct in general, but after 4:30 he is much more concerned with the state of our spirits. This verse, with its negative aspect, and the next, with its positive, are therefore a kind of practical exposition of what we are to avoid if we are not to grieve the Holy Spirit who lives within us [LJ].

2. This verse is a separate injunction [AB, ECWB, NTC, Rob, Si, St, TH, TNTC, WBC, We] connected with the following verse [AB, WBC] or verses [ECWB, St, We]. This is the fifth injunction, enforced by the following verse [Rob]. With it the author passes from sins in word to sins which are often expressed in word [We]. The author lists six sins which must be done away with [TH, TNTC]. It is used as a way of summing up

the counsel he has been giving on putting off the Old Adam [Si]. It is a recapitulation of the sins of the tongue (4:25–29) [NTC, Rob, TNTC], or it has a connection with 4:22–24 and 4:26, emphasizing the dangers of anger in a fresh and decisive way [WBC].

QUESTION—Is there any significance to the order in which this catalogue of sins characteristic of the Old Man occurs?

The sequence of the conjunction καί 'and' adds one term to another and indicates that each term in this list is distinct from the preceding one [Lns]. The occurrences of καί 'and' constitute a figure of speech called *polysyndeton* (many 'ands') which serves to point to the climax in 4:32, signaled by occurrences of *asyndeton* (no 'ands') [Bu].

1. Each is the result of the preceding vice, all of them having their source in κακία 'malice' [Ea, ECWB, ICC, Lns]. Bitterness produces exasperation, which produces anger, which produces yelling, which produces blasphemy and cursing [Lns]. Bitterness produces wrath and anger, (anger being both the effect and cause of wrath) while clamor and slander represent the final stage, clamor corresponding to wrath, as both of these relate to emotional outbursts, and slander, corresponding to anger, as both of these relate to more settled feelings and actions [ECWB].
2. θυμός 'wrath' and ὀργή 'anger' are the result of πικρία 'bitterness' [Alf, EGT, El, LJ], and κραυγή 'clamor' and βλασφημία 'slander' are the result of both θυμός 'wrath' and ὀργή 'anger' [EGT, El, LJ], all of them having their source in κακία 'malice' [El].
3. θυμός 'wrath' is the result of πικρία 'bitterness', while κραυγή 'clamor' and βλασφημία 'slander' are the result of ὀργή 'anger' [EBC, Ho].

QUESTION—What is meant by θυμός 'wrath' and ὀργή 'anger'?

1. These two nouns are materially the same in meaning [Ba, DNTT, TH]. As in the LXX, θυμός 'wrath' often stands alongside ὀργή 'anger' without any perceptible difference in meaning [DNTT]. The words are practically synonyms, though some commentators see a difference of duration in the words [TH].
2. There is a difference between θυμός 'wrath' and ὀργή 'anger' [AB, Cal, Can, DNTT, Ea, ECWB, EGT, El, Ho, ICC, LJ, LN (88.178), Lns, MNTC, NCBC, NIC, NTC, Rob, St, TD, TNTC, WBC, We]. The Stoics wrote that wrath carries the implication of passionate outbursts [Can, DNTT, ECWB, EGT, El, LJ, LN (88.178), NCBC, NTC, Rob, St, TNTC, WBC] of a temporary nature [ICC] while anger denotes a lingering, settled animosity [Can, ECWB, EGT, El, ICC, LJ, NCBC, NTC, Rob, St, TNTC, WBC] or deliberate thought [DNTT]. Wrath is an excitement that indicates an outburst of anger or fury is about to take place [AB]. Wrath denotes the mind in the commotion of passion, while anger is the passion itself [Ho]. Wrath is the mental excitement and commotion that is the result of bitterness, while anger is settled hostility [Ea, El, LJ, We]. Wrath is anger that is sullen; anger is passionate anger [MNTC]. One commentator seems to reverse the distinction of duration, saying wrath denotes the

power, anger denotes the act, but here, the major difference is that anger is a more sudden attack [Cal]. Both may blaze up and subside, and both may endure, but wrath is still inward while anger is its outward manifestation [Lns]. These two words overlap in meaning [NIC] and are often found conjoined [EGT, Lns].

QUESTION—What is meant by κραυγή 'clamor' and what relationship, if any, does it have with the following term, βλασφημία 'slander'?

Κραυγή 'clamor' is noise, disorder, and high words, such as men use in a brawl [Ba, Ea, LJ, NIC, NTC] or when they are excited [AB, Ba, Ea, St], the fierce and impetuous invective that is characteristic of a person in a towering rage [Ea], the shouting characteristic of quarreling [NCBC, NIC, NTC, St, TH]. It leads to βλασφημία 'slander' [ICC], or βλασφημία 'slander' serves as a closer definition of κραυγή 'clamor', being the chronic form in which κραυγή 'clamor' is displayed [Alf, WBC]. Another commentator sees βλασφημία 'slander' as the result, or one phase of the κραυγή 'clamor', for anger leads to calumny and scandal [Ea]. Others say that βλασφημία 'slander' is abusive speech spoken about other people in their absence [NCBC, St], whereas the preceding noun, κραυγή 'clamor', is abusive speech hurled in their face [NCBC]. The implied object of βλασφημία 'slander' is the Christian brother [AB, DNTT, EGT, El, Ho, LJ, My, NTC, TH] but, by using this term, the Apostle is implying that by saying evil things about one another, Christians are essentially also blaspheming God [AB, LJ], (or causing others to blaspheme God's name [DNTT, TD]) since man is made in the image of God [LJ]. Yet, another commentator maintains that these are not words that injure God's honor, but evil-speaking that is directed against Christian brethren [My]. The slander or reviling is not by an outbreak of verbal abuse, but the insidious undermining of evil surmise and slander [Alf]. Βλασφημία 'slander' is more than just 'slander', it is any form of speech, arising from anger, that is intended to wound or injure others [Ho, LJ].

QUESTION—What is indicated in the passive voice of the verb ἀρθήτω 'Let (something) be put away from'?

The passive is used even though the person who receives the command is himself to be the agent of the verb [DNTT, LJ, MNTC, TH, WBC; NAB, NIV, NRSV, REB, TEV, TNT]. The usage is stylistic [TH, WBC]. Paul is telling these Ephesians to put these evils away from themselves [LJ]. The passive voice serves to make the personal element in the command a little less direct [TH]. Only one commentator believes the passive is used because God is the unstated agent. He states that the passive implies the putting away of this catalogue of sins is not done by any Herculean efforts of man, but it is the responsibility of man not to resist God's action [AB].

QUESTION—What is meant by σὺν πάσῃ κακίᾳ 'with all malice/evil'?

This means 'together with every kind of malice' [AB, Ea, EBC]. The term κακία 'malice' is not a sixth vice added to the other five preceding the verb ἀρθήτω 'let (these vices) be put away from'. Rather, it is a summary concept which includes the previous five kinds of wickedness. The use of the term κακία 'malice' here is a way of acknowledging the incompleteness of the listing, the sample character of the things the writer had in mind, and so is the equivalent of the English 'etc.' The sense of this phrase is 'together with every kind of malice, etc.' [AB].

QUESTION—What is meant by κακία 'malice/evil'?
1. This noun means 'malice' [AB, Alf, BAGD, Cal, Can, Ea, EBC, ECWB, EGT, El, Ho, IB, ICC, ISBE2, LJ, MNTC, My, NCBC, NIC, NTC, Rob, St, TH, TNTC, WBC, We; all versions except REB] or 'hate, hateful feeling' [TH,; TEV]: all malice. As distinguished from its synonym πονηρία 'evil', κακία 'malice' points to the evil habit of the mind, while πονηρία 'evil' points to its outworking [El]. This is the more general expression for malevolent affections [Can]. It is used to gather up in one word all that has been specified in the preceding list [NCBC, NTC, St]. It is uncharitableness in all its forms [El], the general disposition which is the opposite of goodness, graciousness, and sympathy [ECWB]. It is bad-heartedness, opposed to εὔσπλαγχνοι 'tenderhearted' in 4:32 [Ea], and the root of all the previous vices [Alf, Ea, EBC, ECWB, MNTC, We]. The context indicates that it means 'malevolence', the desire or determination to injure [Ho, LJ, NIC, NTC, St, WBC]. The removal of κακία 'malice' will greatly aid the correction of the other vices which are offenses that usually accompany it [Cal].
2. This noun means 'evil' [Ba; REB], 'baseness' [Lns], standing for what is morally deficient or inferior [ISBE2, Lns, TD]: all evil. Every kind of evil is to be put away [Ba]. It does not mean malicious, but 'base' [Lns], bad, or morally inferior [Lns, TD].

DISCOURSE UNIT: 4:32–5:2 [ICC]. The topic is an exhortation to be tenderhearted and forgiving after the pattern of God's forgiveness in Christ [ICC].

4:32 **But/And be kind/good/generous[a] to one-another, tenderhearted,[b] forgiving/ being-generous-with[c] each-another, just-as also God in[d] Christ forgave/ was-generous-with you.**

TEXT—Some manuscripts omit the conjunction δέ 'but/and' and a few others substitute οὖν 'therefore, then' in place of δέ 'but/and' [Alf, EGT, El, My, NIC]. GNT places δέ 'but/and' in brackets in its text to acknowledge the disputed omission, but does not assign a rating to it in the critical apparatus. The reading with δέ 'but/and' is supported by Alf, Ea, EGT, El, ICC, Lns, My, NIC, NTC, Rob, We; KJV, NAB, NASB, NRSV, and TEV. A conjunction is not translated by AB, WBC, NIV, NJB, REB, or TNT.

LEXICON—a. χρηστός (LN 88.68) (BAGD 1.b.α. p. 886): 'kind' [BAGD, El, LN, NIC, NTC, Rob, WBC, We; all versions except NJB, REB], 'good' [AB], 'loving, benevolent' [BAGD], 'gracious' [LN], 'benignant' [Lns], 'generous' [NJB, REB].
  b. εὔσπλαγχνος (LN 25.51) (BAGD p. 326): 'tenderhearted' [BAGD, El, Lns, NIC, NTC, Rob, We; KJV, NASB, NRSV, REB, TEV], 'warm-

hearted' [AB], 'compassionate' [BAGD, LN, WBC; NAB, NIV, TNT], 'sympathetic' [NJB].
- c. pres. mid. (deponent = active) participle of χαρίζομαι (LN 40.10, 57.102) (BAGD 2. p. 876): 'to forgive' [AB, BAGD, El, LN (40.10), Lns, NIC, NTC, Rob, WBC, We; all versions except TNT], 'to remit, to pardon' [BAGD], 'to deal generously with' [TNT], 'to give, to grant, to bestow generously' [LN (57.102)]. This verb denotes forgiveness on the basis of a gracious attitude towards someone [LN (40.10)], or it denotes giving or granting something graciously and generously, implying good will on the part of the giver [LN (57.102)].
- d. ἐν with dative object (LN 89.26, 89.76, 89.119, 90.6): 'in' [AB, El, LN (89.119), Lns, NIC, NTC, Rob, WBC, We; all versions except KJV, TEV], 'in union with' [LN (89.119)], 'for the sake of' [KJV], 'through' [LN (89.76); TEV], 'by means of' [LN (89.76)], 'by' [LN (89.76, 90.6)], 'because of, on account of' [LN (89.26)].

QUESTION—What relationship is indicated by δέ 'but'?

It indicates contrast: 'but' [Alf, Ea, EGT, El, NIC], 'in place of these' [NAB], 'on the other hand' [Lns], 'instead' [TEV], 'and' [NTC, Rob; KJV, NASB, NRSV]. This verse is the positive counterpart of the negative injunction given in the previous verse [Ho, IB, ICC, LJ, NCBC, NIC, NTC, TNTC, WBC, WeBC]. The contrast here is both in the qualities involved [Lns, WBC, WeBC] (the previous verse listing vices destructive to harmonious relationships, the present one listing virtues conducive to communal living [WBC]) and also in the tenses of the imperative verbs, the aorist of 4:31 versus the present of this verse. The style is also contrastive. Whereas the previous verse used *polysyndeton* (cumulative καί 'and') to indicate a build up of climax—one quality overflowing to bring on the next, this verse uses *asyndeton* to indicate that the three qualities it lists are not climactic, but they simply stand side by side [Lns].

QUESTION—What is meant by χρηστοί 'kind/good/generous'?

1. This adjective means 'kind' [Alf, BAGD, EBC, ECWB, EGT, El, Ho, ICC, LJ, LN, Lns, My, NIC, NTC, Rob, St, TNTC, WBC, We, WeBC; all versions except NJB, REB]. This indicates the showing of a sweet [EBC, El] and generous [EBC] disposition. It is gentleness in dealing with wrong [ECWB]. Kindness entails consideration of the needs and interests of others [WBC] so it means to be disposed to do good [Ho, TH], to be helpful [LJ, Lns, TH] or useful to others, as the origin of the word indicates [LJ]. It is love in practical action [TNTC].
2. This adjective means 'courteous, polite' [Ba, Cal, Ea, NCBC]. This means kindness in the sense of being considerate to others and willing to accommodate oneself to the interests of others [NCBC]. Christianity produces true courteousness. It does not make its followers disposed to violate the rules of social intercourse. The secret of true politeness is kindness, benevolence, or a desire to make others happy [Ba]. This is 'kindness' or gentleness of countenance, language, and manners [Cal].

This is benign courtesy, the bland and generous exchange of good deeds with the earnest desire for reciprocal obligations [Ea].
3. This adjective means 'good' [AB, NTC]. The English term 'kind' is not a good word with which to translate χρηστοί because it may have the connotation of condescension or softness, which is not as appropriate here as a term that describes a reliable and firm attitude. The presupposition is that God himself is the model of goodness, because in 5:1 he exhorts his readers to be imitators of God [AB]. This is Spirit-imparted goodness of heart, the opposite of 'malice' in 4:31 [NTC].
4. This adjective means 'generous' [NJB, REB].

QUESTION—What is meant by εὔσπλαγχνοι 'tenderhearted'?

This word describes very deep feelings of love and pity [NTC]. It is being disposed to pity and compassion [Ba, Cal, Ho, ISBE, LJ, NCBC]. It is directed to persons who are suffering any kind of distress. Paul does not state the action which will follow this feeling for this is understood [Lns]. This term calls upon Christians to sympathize with the needs and afflictions of others [Cal, WBC, WeBC] and to be affected by them in the same manner and to the same degree as though it were happening to themselves [Cal]. It means a deep and mellow affection and sympathy in contrast to the wrath and anger which they are exhorted to abandon [Ea]. This is the attitude of heart which must lie behind the kindness just mentioned [TNTC].

QUESTION—What is meant by χαριζόμενοι 'forgiving/being generous with', and what is the significance in the change of tense between the two occurrences of this verb in this verse?
1. This verb means 'to forgive' [AB, Alf, Ba, BAGD, Cal, Can, DNTT, Ea, ECWB, EGT, El, Ho, IB, ICC, LJ, Lns, My, NIC, NTC, Rob, TD, TH, WBC, WeBC; all versions except TNT]: forgiving each other. The verb χαρίζομαι 'to forgive' has a connotation of favor and cheerfulness which it retains from its original meaning. As such, it is especially appropriate to designate the forgiveness which is to characterize relationships within the circle of the saints, since forgiveness is a form of love which is to find manifestation and rule within that circle. The verb does have a sense of restriction here. The change of tense between the first occurrence of the verb as a present participle and the second occurrence as an aorist finite verb indicates that in the second occurrence, God forgave the saints as a past [AB], once-for-all action [AB, Alf, TNTC] on the occasion of the atoning death of Christ [EBC, EGT, El], whereas in the first occurrence, where the present participle carries an imperative meaning, the saints are ever being called upon anew to forgive one another [AB]. The action of the participle χαριζόμενοι 'forgiving' is contemporaneous with the action implied in the χρηστοί 'kind' and εὔσπλαγχνοι 'tenderhearted' and, at the same time, is the special form or manner in which these qualities were to manifest themselves [EGT, El], i.e., it is their product [ECWB].

2. This verb means 'to act in grace', 'to be beneficent', or 'to be generous' [NCBC, St, We; TNT]: being generous with each other. This word has an area of meaning which is much wider than just 'to forgive' [NCBC, We], it means 'to deal graciously with' [We (even so, this commentator uses 'forgiving' in his translation)]. It is derived from the noun χάρις 'grace' and it means Christians are to treat others with the same grace or generosity with which God has treated them [NCBC, St]. It describes a treatment of others that is generous to the point of being uncalculating and free of all limitations which may be imposed by considerations of ill-feeling or self-interest. The aorist tense of the finite verb indicates a particular time in the past when they realized they had been accepted by God, reconciled to him, and forgiven. This was either at their conversion or baptism [NCBC].

QUESTION—What is the difference between the reciprocal pronoun ἀλλήλους 'one another', used in the first clause, and the reflexive pronoun ἑαυτοῖς 'each other', used in the second?

1. There is no difference in meaning [AB, BAGD (3. p.212), El, LN (**92.26**), My]. This is only a rhetorical device to avoid monotonous repetition [AB]. Both ἀλλήλους 'one another' and ἑαυτοῖς 'each other' are pronouns that denote a reciprocal reference between entities [LN]. The reciprocal pronoun ἑαυτοῖς 'each other' is used for the reciprocal pronoun ἀλλήλους 'one another' [BAGD, El].
2. The change in pronouns implies a subtle difference in meaning or force [Can, Ea, EGT, ICC, Rob, WBC, We].
2.1 The idea is that Christian unity is such that an act of kindness or forgiveness done to a brother is really done to oneself [Can, Ea]. The pronoun ἑαυτοῖς 'each other' is really stronger word than ἀλλήλους 'one another' and a 2nd person reciprocal pronoun rather than 3rd person, so this clause literally means 'forgiving yourselves' [Can].
2.2 The reflexive pronoun ἑαυτοῖς 'each other' has a stronger idea of fellowship and corporate unity than ἀλλήλους 'one another' [EGT, ICC, Rob, WBC, We] so that ἑαυτοῖς 'each other' is more appropriate to the second clause than ἀλλήλους 'one another' would be [Rob].

QUESTION—What relationship is indicated by the words καθώς καί 'just as also'?

1. These words make a comparison between God's action in forgiving and the saints' forgiving, as well as introducing the norm of forgiveness [Alf, Ba, Cal, Can, CBC, Ea, EBC, ECWB, EGT, El, Ho, ICC, ISBE, ISBE2, LJ, Lns, My, NIC, NTC, TD, TH, TNTC, WBC]. This is the motivation clause for the exhortation contained in 4:31–32. Καθώς 'just as' has both comparative and causal force here [WBC]. The words draw a parallel as to manner [LJ, Lns]. Whereas the καθώς 'just as' points to God's example (and also has a slightly argumentative force [El]), the καί 'also' sets the two instances (the Divine and the human) over against one another [EGT] in a comparison. But the two combined do more than simply compare [El]. They argue from example [Alf, Cal, Can, Ea, El,

NTC, TNTC]. This clause gives the rule, the measure, and the motive for universal forgiveness on the part of Christians [Ea]. The clause introduced by this conjunction argues the case for the saints to forgive each other from God's own example [Alf, Cal, Can, Ea, El, TNTC], whom they ought to resemble, as well as from mingled motives of justice and gratitude [Alf]. What God has done in Christ on behalf of the believer was the theme of the first half of the epistle, and this now provides both the ground and the norm for believers' behavior toward each other [WBC]. The lesson and motive presented is the same as that taught by Christ in the parable of the unmerciful servant (Matt. 18:15–35) [Can, Ea, EBC, ICC, LJ, NTC, TD].

2. These words also serve to introduce a quotation [AB]. This verse does more than just make a comparison between God's and the saints' forgiveness and make explicit the source and norm of the saints' mutual forgiveness. The conjunction may also introduce a quotation here, just as it does elsewhere in Ephesians. If this is indeed the case, another conjunction, οὖν 'therefore' at 5:1 marks the resumption of Paul's own words [AB].

QUESTION—What is meant by the phrase ὁ θεὸς ἐν χριστῷ 'God in Christ'?

1. The phrase ἐν χριστῷ 'in Christ' here indicates the sphere, element, or condition of God's action [Alf, Can, Ea, EGT, El, Ho, ICC, Lns, NCBC, NIC, TD, TH, WBC (probably), We]: God, acting in Christ, forgave you. The phrase ἐν χριστῷ 'in Christ' here does not mean 'for Christ's sake' [Alf, Can, EGT, El, ICC], nor 'on account of' or 'by means of Christ' [Ea]. Rather the preposition ἐν 'in' indicates that Christ was the sphere or the conditional element in which God's act of forgiveness took place [Alf]. The phrase means God is revealed in Christ, acts in him, and speaks in him [Ea, EGT, ICC, TD]. The thought is a comprehensive one: God is the source or author of forgiveness of sins; it comes from him as a free gift of pure grace; God bestows it upon us in Christ [Can], by making him to be the propitiation for our sins [Can, El].

2. The phrase ἐν χριστῷ 'in Christ' here indicates the cause of God's action [Ba]: God, on account of what Christ has suffered and done, forgave you.

3. The phrase ἐν χριστῷ 'in Christ' here indicates the means or agency of God's action [Cal; TEV]: God, through Christ, forgave you.

4. The phrase ἐν χριστῷ 'in Christ' here indicates that God's forgiveness of our sins was in Christ's behalf [LJ; KJV]: God, for Christ's sake, forgave you.

DISCOURSE UNIT: 5:1–21 [WeBC; NASB]. The topic is the church's walk in Christ [WeBC], being imitators of God [NASB].

DISCOURSE UNIT: 5:1–20 [AB, NCBC, TH; TEV]. The topic is light against darkness [AB], putting the new life into practice [NCBC].

EPHESIANS 5:1 409

DISCOURSE UNIT: 5:1–14 [EGT, Lns]. The topic is an admonition against filthiness [Lns], the imitation of God in the walk of love and purity [EGT].

DISCOURSE UNIT: 5:1–7 [WeBC]. The topic is the believers' walk in love instead of lust.

DISCOURSE UNIT: 5:1–6 [We]. The topic is the self-sacrifice of Christ which is to be our pattern as contrasted to the life of selfish indulgence which is liable to the wrath of God.

DISCOURSE UNIT: 5:1–5 [TH]. The topic is purity of life.

DISCOURSE UNIT: 5:1–2 [AB, Alf, Ba, Cal, El, LJ, My, NIC]. The topic is imitating God [AB, Ba, Cal, El, LJ, My, NIC], and walking in love as Christ did [AB, Ba, Cal, El, My].

5:1 Be therefore imitators[a] of-God as children beloved

LEXICON—a. μιμητής (LN 41.45) (BAGD 1 p. 522): 'imitator' [AB, BAGD, LN, Lns, NIC, NTC, WBC, We; NAB, NASB, NIV, NRSV], 'follower' [El, Rob; KJV]. The phrase γίνεσθε μιμηταί 'be imitators' is translated 'take (God) as your pattern' [NJB], 'you must be like' [REB], 'you must try to be like' [TEV], 'try to be like' [TNT]. It refers to likeness and similarity, not to complete duplication [Lns].

QUESTION—What relationship is indicated by οὖν 'therefore'?

1. It indicates a conclusion based on what precedes [Can, CBC, Ea, EBC, ECWB, Ho, ICC, TH, WBC]. It is the application of the preceding injunction to forbearance and forgiveness [Can, ECWB, WBC] as well as being an expansion of it [ECWB, Ho]. The reference of οὖν 'therefore' is just to the preceding verse, not to the whole foregoing subject [ICC].
2. It indicates a transition to a new train of thought which is developed in 5:3ff [AB, Alf, IB, LJ, Lns, MNTC, NCBC, NTC, Rob, Si].
2.1 This transition is part of the preceding passage [IB, MNTC, NTC,]. The οὖν 'therefore' now makes the last clause a point of departure for wider thoughts [IB, MNTC].
2.2 This transition is part of the following passage [AB, EGT, Lns, NCBC]. This inferential particle refers back to the fact of God's forgiveness in the preceding clause [EGT]. This verse introduces a wider application of the thought of 4:32 in the form of a more general principle of conduct [NCBC]. The admonitions of 4:1, 17, 25 all begin with οὖν 'therefore' and rest upon and connect with the previous admonition. So also here [Lns]. The οὖν 'therefore' introduces a statement which departs from the pattern of the previous verses which introduced their injunctions by negative prohibitions. Paul chooses strictly positive terms with which to summarize the preceding passage and introduce a new train of thought [AB].

2.3 This transition is a short paragraph in itself [Alf, LJ, Rob, Si]. The two verses which οὖν 'therefore' introduces must be viewed as transitional [Alf].

QUESTION—What is meant by being μιμηταὶ τοῦ θεοῦ 'imitators of God'?

In this verse the imitation of God is especially relevant in the area of mercifulness or forgiveness (4:32) [AB, Ba, Can, Ea, ICC, NIC, Rob, WBC] and is limited to this particular duty, not to the whole of the long, foregoing paragraph [Ea, ICC]. From the context of 5:2, the imitation is the broader one of walking in love [Alf, CBC, DNTT, ECWB, EGT, El, Ho, IB, LJ, My, NTC, TH, WeBC] but with special reference to the showing of mercy [ECWB] or forgiveness [DNTT, EGT, IB], with primary reference to fellow Christians [IB]. Another view is that what is to be imitated is Christ's obedience to the Father's will which was shown in love and forgiveness [DNTT]. The concept involved is really that of following God, i.e., obedience or discipleship [Cal, DNTT, ISBE2, TD; KJV].

QUESTION—What relationship is indicated by the comparative ὡς 'as'?

The ὡς 'as' introduces the characteristic quality of a person who is referred to in the context [BAGD (III.1.a. p. 898)]. It gives this phrase the sense of 'in accordance with your relation to God as his beloved children' [My]. It introduces the reason [EGT, LJ, Lns], and motive [Can, Lns], as well as the manner in which the imitation of God is to take place [EGT], strengthening the injunction to imitation [NTC, TD], and leading the way for the further injunction of 5:2 [Rob]. It is patterned after the way a beloved child imitates its father [AB, Ba, Can, CBC, Ea, EBC, ECWB, EGT, IB, LJ, NIC, NTC, St, TH, WBC, WeBC].

QUESTION—What is meant by τέκνα ἀγαπητά 'beloved children'?

This means children whom God loves [Ba, Can, Ea, ECWB, EGT, El, ICC, LJ, My, NTC]. It indicates these are children who share God's nature [Can, NCBC, We] and are conscious of his love [We]. Children who revel in their father's love, and love in him return, are naturally keen to imitate their father [Ba, LJ, Lns, NTC].

5:2 and walk in love, just-as Christ also loved us and gave-up[a] himself for[b] us

TEXT—Instead of ἡμᾶς '(loved) us', some manuscripts read ὑμᾶς 'you'. GNT assigns the ἡμᾶς 'us' reading a B rating, indicating that this reading is almost certain. Others who support this reading are AB, Cal, Ea, EBC, ECWB, El, Ho, LJ, My, NCBC, NIC, St, TH, WBC; KJV, NIV, NRSV, TEV, TNT. Those who support the variant reading ὑμᾶς 'you' are Alf, Can, EGT, ICC, Lns, MNTC, NTC, Rob, We; NAB, NASB, NJB, REB.

TEXT—Instead of ἡμῶν '(for) us', some manuscripts read ὑμῶν 'you'. GNT assigns the reading ἡμῶν 'us' an A rating, indicating that this reading is certain. Only Alf, MNTC, and Rob support the variant reading.

LEXICON—a. aorist act. indic. of παραδίδωμι (LN 37.111) (BAGD 1.b. p. 615): 'to give up' [NIC, NTC, WBC, We; NASB, NIV, NJB, NRSV,

REB], 'to give' [AB, El, Lns, Rob; KJV, NAB, TNT], 'to hand over, to turn over to' [LN], 'to hand over to suffering, death, punishment' [BAGD], 'to give one's life' [TEV].

b. ὑπέρ with genitive object (LN 90.36) (BAGD 1.a.γ. p. 838): 'for' [AB, BAGD, El, LN, Lns, NIC, NTC, Rob, WBC, We; all versions except REB], 'in behalf of' [BAGD, LN; REB], 'for the sake of' [BAGD, LN]. This preposition marks benefaction, indicating a participant has been benefited by an event, or that it was in his behalf that an event took place [LN].

QUESTION—How is this verse related to the preceding context?

This verse, along with 5:1 [AB], is a restatement of the thought in 4:32 [AB, TD]. The apostle first invoked the Divine example in regard to forgiveness [Rob, TNTC, WBC], now he defines how the command to imitate God in the previous verse is to be understood [AB, DNTT, Ea, EGT, El, ICC, LJ, MNTC, My, NCBC, NIC, NTC, Rob, TNTC, WBC] with reference to the wider command to walk in love [Rob, WBC], the καὶ 'and' explaining the previous verse by connecting and adding the following material [EGT, El, My]. This verse gives the specific application of the command to imitate God (5:1) [TH, WeBC].

QUESTION—Who is the implied object of the event word ἀγάπη 'love' in the clause 'walk in love'?

1. The implied object is fellow Christians [AB, Ba, Cal, Can, ECWB, Ho, IB, ICC, IDB, MNTC, NIC, Rob, TNTC, WBC] and/or others in general [Ea, EBC, LJ, NCBC, NIC, Rob, Si, St, TH], including enemies [CBC, NIC].
2. The implied object is God [Lns].
3. The implied object is both God and man [WeBC].

QUESTION—What relationship is indicated by καθώς 'just as'?

As in 4:32 this conjunction indicates a comparison [Ba, IB, LJ, Lns, NIC, Rob, St, TNTC, We, WeBC]. As Christ loved us so we also are to love one another [Ba, LJ]. The scope and quality of the love we are to emulate is illustrated by the example of Christ [IB]. This conjunction indicates a standard of comparison together with particular practical applications of the love illustrated that are to be followed by Christians [TNTC]. Just as Christ 'delivered himself up', we are to deliver ourselves up to love. And just as Christ's self-sacrificing love was a 'fragrant offering and sacrifice to God', so ours will be also, because such self-giving for others is pleasing to God [St, WeBC]. This also gives a reason for walking in love [Ho, WBC]. It indicates a comparison and a reason by introducing a quotation from a contemporary hymn or confession. The quotation consists of the rest of the verse, the diction of which is raised to a poetic level involving parallelisms such as occur elsewhere in Pauline writings when the offering of Christ is mentioned [AB].

QUESTION—What is meant by παρέδωκεν ἑαυτόν 'delivered himself up'?
The verb implies Christ's full, voluntary, self surrender [Ea, LJ, My, NTC], done on his own initiative [TH]. It properly means to deliver up to the power of someone [Ho] and has no sacrificial connotations [Ho, My]. The words are used absolutely [Alf, We] and are not to be joined to τῷ θεῷ 'to God' [Alf, EBC, We]. It is implied that what Christ 'delivered himself up' to is death [Ea, EGT, El, Ho], as is implied in Pauline declarations elsewhere when he uses this verb [EGT, El]. These words are added to show what the writer means by ὁ χριτὸς ἠγάπησεν ἡμᾶς 'Christ loved us' [Ba, Can, Ea, El, ICC, Lns, MNTC, My], the καί 'and' being epexegetical [Ea, El, Lns], or having an ascensive force [EGT]. The words imply that Christians should be willing to sacrifice their lives for their brethren also [Ba].

QUESTION—What is meant by the preposition ὑπέρ 'for'?
1. This preposition is benefactive, 'for, in behalf of' [AB, Alf, BAGD, Can, DNTT, Ea, ECWB, EGT, Ho, ICC, My, NTC, Rob, TD, TH, WBC; REB]: Christ delivered himself up in our/your behalf. In delivering himself up, Christ acted as the believers' representative, i.e., on their behalf, but sometimes the idea of representation also involves that of substitution [WBC].
2. This preposition is substitutional, 'instead of' [EBC, LJ]: Christ delivered himself up instead of us/you. The context and the use of the term θυσίαν 'sacrifice' give ὑπέρ 'for' the meaning 'in our stead, in our room, in our place' [LJ].
3. This preposition is both benefactive and substitutional [El, Lns]: Christ delivered himself up for, and in our stead. It incorporates both the ideas of benefaction and substitution, because one cannot act 'for' someone unless one also acts 'in his stead' [Lns].

(as) an offering[a] and a sacrifice[b] to-God for an aroma[c] of-fragrance.[d]
LEXICON—a. προσφορά (LN 53.16) (BAGD 2. p. 720): 'offering' [AB, BAGD, El, LN, Lns, NIC, NTC, Rob, WBC, We; all versions], 'sacrifice' [LN].
b. θυσία (LN **53.20**) (BAGD 2.a. p. 366): 'sacrifice' [AB, BAGD, El, LN, NIC, NTC, Rob, WBC, We; all versions except NAB], 'offering' [BAGD], 'slaughter sacrifice' [Lns], 'gift' [NAB].
c. ὀσμή (LN 79.45) (BAGD 2. p. 586): 'aroma' [NASB], 'odor' [LN, Lns, NIC, NTC, We], 'smell, scent' [LN], 'savor' [El, Rob; KJV], 'fragrance' [NAB], 'fragrant offering' [BAGD], not explicit [WBC; NIV, NJB, NRSV, TNT]. This is the scent or odor of a substance, either agreeable or disagreeable [LN]. The words τῷ θεῷ εἰς ὀσμὴν εὐωδίας 'to God for an aroma of fragrance' is translated 'whose fragrance is pleasing to God' [AB; REB], 'yielding a fragrant odor' [NIC], 'as a sweet-smelling (offering and sacrifice) that pleases God' [TEV].
d. εὐωδία (LN 79.46) (BAGD p. 329): 'fragrance' [AB, LN, We; REB], 'fragrant' [NIC, NTC, WBC; NASB, NIV, NRSV], 'fragrant odor'

[BAGD], 'aroma' [LN], 'sweet smell' [El, Lns], 'sweet-smelling' [Rob; KJV, NJB, TEV, TNT], 'pleasing' [NAB]. This denotes a pleasant or sweet-smelling odor. In many languages this usage may seem strange when it is used in reference to sacrifice because burning flesh is not normally regarded as fragrant or pleasant [LN].

QUESTION—What is meant by the phrase προσφοράν καὶ θυσίαν 'an offering and a sacrifice'?

The original Hebrew noun underlying προσφοράν 'offering' is 'meal offering' [AB, DNTT, Ea, EBC, EGT, My, TH]. This was the offering made without blood, an offering made of grain or fruit which was presented to the Lord in the sanctuary for the support of the priests. The worshipper presented this offering as symbolizing his life of obedience [AB]. The commentaries are somewhat divided on the Hebrew noun which underlies θυσίαν 'sacrifice', but agree that it usually represents a blood offering [AB, Ea, EBC, EGT, LJ, My, TH]. Some indicate that the 'whole burnt-offering' is meant [AB, DNTT, LJ]. This was the offering which symbolized atoning death [AB, LJ]. Others believe the 'peace-offering' [Ea, EBC, EGT, My, TD], and/or the 'sin-offering', portions of which were burnt on the altar, are particularly in view [Ea, EBC, EGT]. Eventually, about the time of the exile, or just previous to it, the sharp differentiation between the two words with respect to bloody and unbloody sacrifices was no longer made [AB] and either or both terms could be used for the animal or the meal offerings [AB, Ea, EGT, WBC].

1. These two nouns form an hendiadys [AB, DNTT, ICC (probably), WBC]: a sacrificial offering. It is probable that Paul here uses the two nouns without any technical differentiation [AB, ICC] just as in Rom. 12:1 and Phil. 4:18 θυσία 'sacrifice' is used for an unbloody sacrifice while, in Phil. 2:17, it denotes the death of the victim. Neither does the author of Hebrews, though thoroughly acquainted with sacrificial matters, use either προσφοράν 'offering' or θυσίαν 'sacrifice' in their original meanings [AB]. The words appear to be taken from Ps. 40:6 where together they refer to all kinds of ceremonial offerings [ICC].

2. These two nouns form a generic-specific doublet [Alf, Ea, El, Ho, LJ, Lns (probably), My; NAB, TNT]: an offering, in fact, a sacrifice. The two terms together present the whole idea of the sacrifice, as both a voluntary gift and an expiatory sacrifice [Ea, Ho, LJ, Lns, My]. The prominent idea here is the *one* sacrifice which Christ made [Alf], whether that of the offering of a perfectly righteous and obedient life or the sacrifice he made at his death [Alf, El].

3. Each noun is used in its own distinctive meaning [Ba, EBC, ECWB, EGT, NTC, Si, TH, We]: an offering and a sacrifice to God. The προσφοράν 'offering' denotes anything which is offered to God in any way. In Scripture the word commonly refers to an offering made without blood, such as the thank-offering. It means Christ regarded himself as such an offering. The other noun, θυσίαν 'sacrifice', properly refers to the bloody oblation

[Ba, ECWB] offered as atonement for sin, signifying the giving up of the life which is resident in the blood of the victim as just retribution for a person's sin [Ba]. They describe the two great classes of bloody and unbloody offerings [EGT, TH]. The προσφοράν 'offering' was Christ offering himself humbly in complete obedience and the θυσίαν 'sacrifice' was Christ's completion of that offering by his sacrificial death on the cross [ECWB, We].

QUESTION—To what is τῷ θεῷ 'to God' connected?
1. This is connected to παρέδωκεν ἑαυτόν 'he delivered himself up' [Can, My]: he delivered himself up to God.
2. This is connected to προσφοράν καὶ θυσίαν 'an offering and a sacrifice' [Alf, Ba, EBC, EGT, El, ICC, LJ, Lns, NCBC, NIC, NTC, Rob, St, WBC, We; all versions except NAB, REB, TNT]: He delivered himself up for us as an offering and a sacrifice to God.
3. This is connected only with προσφοράν 'offering' [NAB]: He delivered himself up as an offering to God, a gift of an aroma of fragrance.
4. This is connected only with θυσίαν 'sacrifice' and its modifying phrase [Cal; TNT]: He delivered himself up for us as an offering, a fragrant sacrifice to God.
5. This is connected with εἰς ὀσμὴν εὐωδίας 'for an aroma of fragrance' [AB, Ho, MNTC; REB]: He delivered himself up for us as an offering and a sacrifice for an aroma of fragrance to God.

QUESTION—What is meant by the phrase εἰς ὀσμὴν εὐωδίας 'for an aroma of fragrance'?

The genitive εὐωδίας 'of fragrance' denotes the characterizing quality of the ὀσμήν 'aroma' [El]. The material object (implied), though not the grammatical one, is τῷ θεῷ 'to God' [TD]. Originally it expressed an anthropomorphism, the pleasure Deity was thought to experience in the smell of roasted meat [AB, CBC, EGT, ICC, IDB, ISBE, NCBC] mixed with incense [Can, Lns] (or, as though it were incense [Ba, Si]). The phrase then also had the specific meaning of a sacrifice acceptable and pleasing to God [AB, Ba, Cal, CBC, EBC, ECWB, EGT, ISBE, ISBE2, LJ, Lns, NCBC, TD, TNTC, WBC, WeBC], not because it is properly performed, but because God is pleased with the character or conduct of the person offering it [AB, ISBE, Lns]. In this context the person whose sacrifice is pleasing to God and whom God accepts is Christ, not the saints directly [AB, EBC, LJ, Lns, NTC, Rob, Si, TD, TNTC, WBC, WeBC], and then, by implication, the saints through him [AB, DNTT, EBC, NTC, Rob, St, TNTC, WBC, WeBC] who imitate the love shown in Christ's sacrificial love [Ba, Cal, Can, DNTT, NTC, Rob, St, TNTC, WBC, WeBC] as well as the holiness, obedience, and love for God that this sacrifice manifested [Can, NIC].

QUESTION—To what is εἰς ὀσμὴν εὐωδίας 'for an aroma of fragrance' connected?
1. It is connected to both προσφοράν 'offering' and θυσίαν 'sacrifice' [AB, Alf, Ba, EBC, Ho, LJ, MNTC, NCBC, NIC, NTC, St, TH, WBC; KJV,

NASB, NIV, NRSV, TEV]: as an offering and a sacrifice for an aroma of fragrance.
2. It is connected primarily with θυσίαν 'sacrifice' [Cal, ECWB, EGT, Lns; NAB, NJB, REB, TNT]: as an offering and a fragrant sacrifice.

DISCOURSE UNIT: 5:3–21 [Alf]. The topic is an exhortation against things that are unbecoming to the holiness of life of those who are children and imitators of God.

DISCOURSE UNIT: 5:3–20 [EBC, Ho, NCBC]. The topic is living as children of light in the Lord [EBC], specific admonitions relative to sins against ourselves [Ho], wrong attitudes to be discarded [NCBC].

DISCOURSE UNIT: 5:3–17 [Ba]. The topic is the breaking off from vices of the surrounding heathen society and which the readers themselves had practiced before their conversion.

DISCOURSE UNIT: 5:3–14 [ECWB, El, IB, ICC, MNTC, NIC, NTC, TNTC, WBC]. The topic is light against darkness [IB, TNTC], going from darkness to light [AB, NIC, WBC], warning against sins of uncleanness [ECWB, ICC], self-indulgence [NTC], or sensuality [MNTC], which are incompatible to those who are children of light [ECWB].

DISCOURSE UNIT: 5:3–11 [ICC]. The topic is special warnings against sins which make a person impure.

DISCOURSE UNIT: 5:3–7 [AB, Cal, Si]. The topic is church discipline [AB], a call to purity [Si], forbidding compromise with conduct that is typical of past pagan speech and conduct [AB].

DISCOURSE UNIT: 5:3–6 [WBC]. The topic is the prohibition of talk about sexual vices and the dire consequences of those who practice such vices.

DISCOURSE UNIT: 5:3–5 [CBC, LJ, My]. The topic is things to avoid [CBC], warning against vices [My].

5:3 **But fornication[a] and uncleanness (of)-every-(kind) or covetousness not-even let-it-be-named[b] among you, as it-is-fitting[c] to-saints,**

LEXICON—a. πορνεία (LN 88.271) (BAGD 1. p. 693): 'fornication' [AB, BAGD, El, LN, Lns, NIC, Rob, WBC, We; KJV, NRSV, REB], 'unchastity' [BAGD], 'prostitution' [BAGD, LN], 'immorality' [NTC; NASB], 'sexual immorality' [LN; NIV, TEV], 'sexual vice' [BAGD (2. p. 574); NJB, TNT], 'lewd conduct' [NAB]. This noun denotes every kind of unlawful sexual intercourse [BAGD, LN] and often implies prostitution [LN].

b. pres. pass. impera. of ὀνομάζω (LN **33.93**) (BAGD 2. p. 574): 'to be named' [BAGD, El, Lns, NIC, Rob, We; KJV, NASB], 'to be mentioned' [AB, BAGD, **LN**, NTC, WBC; NAB, NRSV, REB, TEV], 'to be spoken about' [LN]. This passive verb is also translated actively: 'to mention'

[TNT]. The clause μηδὲ ὀνομαζέσθω ἐν ὑμῖν 'don't let it even be named among you' is also translated as 'there must not be even a hint among you' [NIV], 'there must (not even) be a mention' [NJB]. The clause implies the thought 'much less be actually practiced' [BAGD]. This verb denotes the speaking of something by mentioning the name of it. However, the text does not mean that one should not even use a term such as πλεονεξία 'covetousness', but that there should never be a reason to have to speak of greed, since no one in the congregation should be guilty of such a thing [LN].

c. pres. act. indic. (impersonal) of πρέπω (πρέπει LN **66.1**) (BAGD 2. p. 699): 'to be fitting' [AB, BAGD, **LN**, NIC, NTC], 'to befit' [Lns, WBC; REB], 'to be seemly' [BAGD], 'to be proper' [NASB, NRSV], 'to be becoming' [El, Rob, We; KJV], 'to be right' [LN; TEV], 'to be suitable' [BAGD]. This verb denotes that which is fitting or right and carries the implication of possible moral judgment [LN]. The clause καθὼς πρέπει ἁγίοις 'as it is fitting to saints' is also combined with the negative of the previous clause and translated 'your holiness forbids this' [NAB], 'because these are improper for God's holy people' [NIV], 'this would scarcely become the holy people of God' [NJB], 'such talk is out of place' [TNT].

QUESTION—What relationship is indicated by δέ 'but'?

It indicates both contrast and transition [Alf, Ea, El]. The glorious renewal of which the larger unit is speaking requires not only the imitation of Christ in self-sacrifice but the avoidance of self-indulgence with which this verse and this subunit is concerned [NTC, St, TNTC]. The δέ 'but' indicates the move from the topic of a self-sacrificial love to that of self-indulgent sensual lust [WBC]. It is contrastive with reference to the mention of πορνεία 'fornication' and other vices immediately after the mention of Christ's sweet-smelling sacrifice of love and obedience [Alf, LJ]. It is transitional in that the apostle returns to the subject of vices prevalent in the pagan world [Ea, EGT, El, Lns, My, WBC] and marks a gentle transition to another part of the exhortation [El, My]. The component of obedience and love to God implied in εἰς ὀσμὴν εὐωδίας 'for an aroma of fragrance' in the previous verse is what accounts for a natural transition to the seemingly abrupt topics of impurity with which this verse begins [Can, Lns].

QUESTION—What is meant by pairing πορνεία 'fornication' with ἀκαθαρσία 'uncleanness'?

Together, the terms cover every kind of sexual sin [St]. Πορνεία 'fornication' may denote not only promiscuous behavior of both unmarried and married people as well as those sexual activities and relations that are prohibited in the Pentateuch, including incest, adultery, and homosexuality. But with ἀκαθαρσία 'uncleanness' joined to it, the meaning appears to be restricted to promiscuity and adultery, with ἀκαθαρσία 'uncleanness' or 'filth' denoting the wider range of wild or putrid sexual behavior [AB]. Πορνεία 'fornication' covers sexual perversion of every description while ἀκαθαρσία 'uncleanness' indicates not only unclean deeds, but the words, thoughts, desires, passions, and intents of the heart [NTC]. Πορνεία 'fornication' pertains to adultery and intercourse with prostitutes while ἀκαθαρσία 'uncleanness', with its modifying πᾶσα 'every kind of', widens the prohibition to any and all kinds of impurity [WBC]. Others believe πορνεία 'fornication' stands for every kind of unlawful sexual intercourse [BAGD, DNTT, EGT, TH], and that ἀκαθαρσία 'uncleanness' is a stronger term and may mean 'perversion' [TH].

QUESTION—What is meant by πλεονεξία 'covetousness'?

1. This word focuses on a greedy desire for material gain: avarice [AB, Ba, Cal, CBC, DNTT, Ea, EBC, El, Ho, IDB, ISBE, ISBE2, LJ, Lns, My, Rob, Si, Si-ed, TD, TH, WeBC; all versions except NAB, TNT]. This is the desire to get as much as one can at the expense of others [CBC].
2. This word focuses on a greedy desire for sensual pleasure [Alf, Can, EGT, IB, ICC, MNTC, NCBC, NTC, St, TNTC, WBC, We; NAB, TNT]. As in 4:19, πλεονεξία 'covetousness' here probably relates to the greedy desire for sensual pleasure such as πορνεία 'fornication' and ἀκαθαρσία 'uncleanness' provide, rather than the desire for material gain [Can, IB, MNTC], the thought of avarice being foreign to this context [IB].
3. This word is broad enough to fully include both of the above meanings in this context [ECWB]. The constant connection of πλεονεξία 'covetousness' to ἀκαθαρσία 'uncleanness' suggests the two kinds of coveting which are united in the Tenth Commandment. The desire for sensual pleasure would be especially relevant to the youth, the desire for material gain to old age [ECWB].

QUESTION—What is meant by the negative clause μηδὲ ὀνομαζέσθω ἐν ὑμῖν 'don't let it even be named among you' and with what is it connected?

Most do not question that this clause is in primary reference to the sins listed in this verse, and then, by extension, also to those that follow in the next [AB, Ba, Cal, CBC, DNTT, Ea, EBC, El, Ho, IB, LJ, MNTC, My, NCBC, NTC, St, TD, TH, TNTC, WBC, We, WeBC; all versions except KJV], yet LN in two separate instances (33.93, 66.1) seems to cite this clause as being restricted to πλεονεξία 'covetousness'. The force of the negative imperative singular, μηδὲ ὀνομαζέσθω 'don't let it be named', is that it is directed to each of the sins mentioned [WeBC].

1. This means the topics listed by the writer are not even to be mentioned in conversation among God's people [AB, Alf, CBC, DNTT, Ea, EGT, El, Ho, IB, ICC, LJ, MNTC, My, NCBC, NIC, Rob, St, TD, TNTC, WBC, We]. Not only were such sins to be entirely avoided, but they should be so universally absent from the Christian community that there would be no occasion even to refer to them [Ea, Ho], or no room even to discuss them as being permissible for Christians [IB]. The meaning is that if such things were talked about, such conversation would be unbecoming of saints [Alf, El, LJ], the very words themselves being disgraceful for saints to utter

[My]. While the very mention of these sins is depreciated, it does not mean that Christians should not call things what they are [NIC].

2. This means these things are not to occur among God's people so they cannot be known or rumored to be present among Christians [Ba, Cal, LN (33.93), Lns, NTC, TH; NIV]. Paul cannot mean these terms cannot be mentioned in conversation for the purpose of rebuking or cautioning against such conduct because he himself does this here and elsewhere [Ba, Lns, NTC]. But he is saying not to let these sins exist among you so that none will have occasion to speak of these things as existing among you [Ba, LN, Lns, NTC].

QUESTION—What is meant by the clause καθὼς πρέπει ἁγίοις 'as it is fitting to saints'?

This is the grounds for avoiding the aforementioned sins [CBC, WBC]. The use of ἁγίοις 'saints' in this clause is intentional, contrasting the previously listed sins with the purity and self-consecration of the Christian life [Ea]. The meaning of separation to God in ἁγίοις 'saints' has full moral significance here [EGT, Ho, IB, ISBE, LJ, MNTC, TNTC, WBC] as is indicated by the absence of the definite article with the noun, thus indicating stress on the qualitative aspects of the word, the holiness of those set apart for God's service [WBC]. The verb πρέπει 'it is fitting' implies voluntary compliance to a standard which could not be legalistically codified [AB].

5:4 and filthiness/filthy-speech[a] and foolish-talking[b] or wittiness/coarse-joking,[c] which (are) not proper,[d]

LEXICON—a. αἰσχρότης (LN **88.149**) (BAGD p. 25): 'filthiness' [El, NTC, Rob, We; KJV, NASB], 'indecent behavior' [**LN**], 'shameful deed' [LN], 'indecency' [Lns], 'ugliness, wickedness' [BAGD], 'obscenity' [WBC; NIV], 'shameless (talk)' [AB], 'shameful talk' [NIC], 'obscene (talk)' [NAB, NRSV], 'obscene (language)' [TEV], 'foul (talk)' [NJB], 'coarse (talk)' [REB], 'coarse (language)' [TNT]. This noun denotes action which is in defiance of social and moral standards together with the resulting shame, disgrace, and embarrassment [LN].

b. μωρολογία (LN **33.379**) (BAGD p. 531): 'foolish talking' [El, MM, Rob, We; KJV], 'foolish talk' [BAGD, LN, WBC; NIV], 'foolish speech' [NIC], 'foolish (words)' [**LN**], 'foolish (language)' [TNT], 'silly talk' [AB, BAGD, Lns, NTC; NAB, NASB, NRSV], 'stupid talk' [LN; REB], 'salacious talk' [NJB], 'profane (language)' [TEV].

c. εὐτραπελία (LN **33.34**) (BAGD p. 327): 'wittiness' [Lns], 'jesting' [El, Rob, We; KJV], 'levity' [NIC], 'flippant talk' [REB], 'coarse jesting' [BAGD; NASB], 'coarse joking' [NIV], 'coarse jokes' [NJB], 'buffoonery' [BAGD], 'vulgar language' [**LN**; TEV], 'vulgar speech, indecent talk' [LN], 'vulgar talk' [NRSV], 'ribald talk' [AB], 'suggestive talk' [NAB], 'suggestive language' [TNT]. This noun is also translated by a descriptive phrase: 'wittiness in telling coarse jokes' [NTC]. This noun

denotes coarse joking which involves vulgar expressions and indecent content [LN].
d. imperfect act. indic. (impersonal) of ἀνήκω (LN **66.1**) (BAGD 2. p. 66): 'to be proper' [BAGD, Lns], 'to be fitting' [BAGD, **LN**, NIC, WBC; NASB, TEV], 'to befit' [Rob, We], 'to be right' [LN], 'to be convenient' [KJV]. The negated verb οὐκ ἀνῆκεν 'it is not proper' is also translated 'to be improper' [AB, NTC], 'to be unbecoming' [El], 'to be out of place' [NAB, NIV, REB], 'to be entirely out of place' [NRSV], 'to be no room for' [TNT], 'to be wrong' [NJB]. The relative clause ἃ οὐκ ἀνῆκεν 'which are not proper' is translated: 'all this is wrong for you' [NJB], 'these things are out of place' [REB].

QUESTION—What is meant by αἰσχρότης 'filthiness/filthy speech'?
1. It refers to filthy conduct in general [Alf, BAGD, Cal, Ea, EGT, El, Ho, IB, ICC, ISBE, ISBE2, LJ, LN (88.149), My, My-ed, NCBC, NTC, Rob, TNTC, We; KJV, NASB]: obscene behavior. It refers, in general, to shameless, immoral conduct [EGT, ISBE2], ethical uncleanness [ISBE2], or to anything that is morally hateful or disgusting, in either speech or conduct [Ho, LJ]. It refers to anything which opposes the purity of the believer [Ea], anything that is indecent [Cal, Ea], anything that is inconsistent with the modesty of believers [Cal]. The context obviously limits the reference of this noun to uncleanness and sins of the flesh [El].
2. It refers to filthy speech [AB, Ba, CBC, EBC, ECWB, LN (**33.34, 33.379**), Lns, MNTC, NIC, Rob, St, TD, TH, WBC, WeBC; all versions except KJV, NASB]: obscene talk. The fact that this term is separated from the vices of 5:3 [ECWB] and is connected to the two sins of speech here [ECWB, TD, WBC, WeBC] indicates that Paul uses it as equivalent to αἰσχρολογία 'obscene speech' [ECWB, TD, TH, WBC, WeBC]. The noun αἰσχρότης 'filthy speech' can be used as a synonym of αἰσχρολογία 'obscene speech' [AB, EBC]. The last two vices illuminate the αἰσχρότης 'filthy speech', showing that it is not general conduct [WBC], but obscene conversation which the word here denotes, as the Col. 3:8 parallel with its αἰσχρολογία 'obscene speech' suggests [WBC, WeBC].

QUESTION—What is meant by μωρολογία 'foolish talk'?
1. This noun refers to idle 'chit-chat' or frivolity [Ba, Ho, LJ, Lns, My, NIC, WBC]. This is talk which is not suited to instruct, edify, or profit anyone [Ba]. The context indicates that both μωρολογία 'foolish talk' and the following noun, εὐτραπελία 'wittiness/coarse joking', have sexual connotations [Lns, WBC]. This is the frivolous, senseless talk of fools [Ho], empty thoughtless chatter [LJ].
2. This noun refers to talk characteristic of those the Bible describes as fools [Alf, Ea, ECWB, My-ed, NCBC, TD]. This refers to any talk which is offensive to Christian decency and sobriety [Ea]. The 'fool', as the Bible presents him, is a man who acknowledges no standards of morality and rejects belief in God [NCBC]. It is talk which no longer discerns between

right and wrong, foolish and wise, or noble and base [ECWB, NCBC]. It is a reference to false teaching [TD].
3. This noun refers to both of the above kinds of talk [Cal, El]. This refers to talk which is either unprofitable or wickedly foolish [Cal]. Trench is probably right in adding to the ordinary meaning of idle, aimless, foolish talk a reference to the sin and vanity of spirit which is typical of the talk of fools [El].
4. This noun refers to stupid chatter or silly twaddle [EBC, NTC, TH, TNTC]. This is the kind of talk one would expect to hear from a drunkard or a fool [NTC, TH, TNTC].

QUESTION—What is the function of the particle ἤ 'or'?
1. This disjunctive particle sets off εὐτραπελία 'wittiness/coarse joking' as a different kind of speech from μωρολογία 'foolish talk' [AB, Alf, Ea, El, Rob]. The particle helps prepare the way for the play on words in the contrast of εὐτραπελία 'wittiness/coarse joking' and εὐχαριστία 'thanksgiving' [Rob].
2. This sets off εὐτραπελία 'wittiness/coarse joking' as a species of μωρολογία 'foolish talk' [Ba, Cal, Can, EBC, ECWB, Lns, St, We]. The force of the ἤ 'or' between these two nouns may be paraphrased as 'foolish talking' or 'ready wit' [We].

QUESTION—What is meant by εὐτραπελία 'wittiness/coarse joking'?
1. This is used in what pagans regarded as the good sense of the term [Alf, Ba, Cal, ECWB, El, Ho, NIC, Rob, TD, TNTC, We, WeBC]: wittiness or jesting. The meaning here is evidently 'jesting' or 'levity', the reference being to that which is light and trifling in conversation [Ba] and which could lead, all too often, to the borderline of impropriety [Rob, TNTC]. Still, the word itself, here, appears untainted [Rob]. The Greek term εὐτραπελία 'wit' was often used by pagan writers for that ready and ingenious pleasantry in which intelligent and able men properly indulge. But as idle talk is frequently concealed under the garb of jesting or wit, the apostle condemns it as a part of μωρολογία 'foolish talk' [Cal]. This is a kind of 'joking' which is versatile and finds occasion for wit or levity in anything, however sacred. Where μωρολογία 'foolish talk' is coarse and brutal, εὐτραπελία 'wittiness' is refined and deadly [ECWB].
2. This is used in the bad sense of the term [AB, BAGD, Can, Ea, EBC, EGT, IB, ICC, ISBE, LJ, LN, Lns, MNTC, My, My-ed, NCBC, NTC, Si, St, TH, WBC]: coarse or vulgar joking. Both μωρολογία 'foolish talk' and εὐτραπελία 'wittiness' are probably allusions to coarse joking, the cheapest kind of wit [St]. This is clever, polished, witty talk which has a tendency to be harmful and sinful. It can be suggestive, ribald [LJ], and scurrilous [LJ, My]. The determinative content of 5:3 [EBC] indicates the apostle seems to refer to wit in connection with licentious speech [ICC, Lns], lewdness and coarse joking [Ea, EBC, LJ, Lns, My-ed, NCBC, TH, WBC], or double entendre [Ea, EBC, LJ, My-ed, TH, WBC]. The writer

is not condemning good clean merriment [IB, My-ed], but to the practice of making jokes of indecency [IB].

QUESTION—What is meant by the negative verb phrase οὐκ ἀνῆκεν 'it is not proper' and to what is it connected?

The phrase means these things are inconsistent with Christian duty [Cal] or out of character for the Christian [ECWB, LJ], and specifies what does not belong. It can be seen as standing in contrast to καθὼς πρέπει ἁγίοις 'as it is proper for saints' at the end of 5:3 [TD] or as a milder repetition of it. It is perhaps suggested by the ambiguous use of εὐτραπελία 'wittiness' [ECWB]. Such conversation is described as not fitting, and again, the reason seems to be that the treating of sexual matters as topics of amusement is not to take them seriously and may lead to the situation in which the actual practice of sexual vices is accepted all too easily [WBC].

1. It is in apposition with the three vices mentioned in this verse [AB, Cal, ISBE2, LJ (probably), Lns, NTC, TD]. If the articular participial clause, τὰ οὐκ ἀνήκοντα '(as) things which are not proper' is the correct reading, this is a neuter participle in apposition with the preceding feminine nouns [Lns]. The reason why this short clause is inserted after εὐτραπελία 'wittiness/coarse joking' may be that it was intended to carry an insinuation such as 'even that form of speech regarded as humorous and well accepted by pagans is radically opposed to Christian conduct' [AB].

2. It is in apposition, chiefly, with the last two vices [Ba, Ea, EGT, El, Ho, My]. Through correspondence with the last clause of the previous verse, this certainly refers to the last two vices mentioned in this one, and may include all three [Ea]. This short clause is in apposition to the two nouns μωρολογία 'foolish talk' and εὐτραπελία 'wittiness/coarse joking' since these oral sins form the direct contrast to εὐχαριστία 'thanksgiving' [EGT, El, My].

but rather thanksgiving/gracious-speech.[a]

LEXICON—a. εὐχαριστία (LN 33.349) (BAGD 2. p. 328): 'thanksgiving' [AB, BAGD, LN, NIC, WBC; NIV, NJB, NRSV, TNT], 'thankfulness' [LN], 'the expression of thankfulness' [NTC]. It is also translated as an active verb: 'to give thanks' [El, Lns, Rob, We; KJV, NAB, NASB], 'to render thanks' [BAGD], 'to thank God' [REB], 'to give thanks to God' [TEV]. This noun denotes the expression of gratitude for benefits or blessings [LN].

QUESTION—What is meant by εὐχαριστία 'thanksgiving, gracious speech'?

1. It means 'thanksgiving' [AB, Alf, Ba, Can, CBC, Ea, EBC, ECWB, EGT, El, Ho, IB, ICC, ISBE2, LJ, Lns, My, NCBC, NIC, NTC, St, TD, TH, TNTC, WBC, We, WeBC]. The noun denotes the oral expression of the inward feeling of gratefulness [El]. Our speech is much better employed in thanking God. If we are grateful to God, then we try to live a life worthy of him [CBC, LJ]. The remembrance of the goodness of God

which has been lavished upon Christians provides an impenetrable barrier to filthiness of every kind [IB]. This is giving joyful praise to God for his good gifts and the temperate, pure-hearted enjoyment of them [Can]. In setting vulgarity and thanksgiving against each other, Paul reflects the difference between pagan and Christian attitudes to sex. All God's gifts, including sex, are subjects for gratitude, rather than jokes [St].
2. It means 'gracious speech' [Cal]. The context calls for something of a general character which displays itself in all our communications with each other. But if εὐχαριστία is translated 'thanksgiving', this limits the exhortation too much. It is also possible to translate this Greek word as 'grace', so that the apostle is saying all our conversations ought to be sweet and graceful. This will be achieved if useful speech and agreeable speech are properly mingled [Cal].
3. It includes both meanings [MNTC, Rob]. The apostle expresses himself with a play on words. To a Greek reader εὐχαριστία would suggest 'well-graced talk', a conversation befitting a gentleman. But it is also the word Christians used for 'thanksgiving', so Paul uses it to convey this meaning as well as the other [MNTC]. Paul chose the word εὐχαριστία 'thanksgiving' because of the double meaning its corresponding adjective, εὐχάριστος 'agreeable, thankful', had for a Greek reader [Rob].

QUESTION—To what is εὐχαριστία 'thanksgiving' in opposition?
1. It opposes all six of the vices mentioned in 5:3–4 [ISBE2, LJ, Lns, NTC, Rob, St, WBC, WeBC]. The whole emphasis of the apostle is that the Christian is to have nothing to do with these evil things, and the positive way to accomplish this is through thanksgiving. However, the joyfulness of thanksgiving stands particularly in contrast to the bright, breezy, back-slapping, thoughtless humor of the unregenerate person. The apostle is not telling us here how we are to talk and conduct ourselves among non-Christians, but in the church of God [LJ]. The striking thing is that Paul only lists one virtue in contrast to all these vices. Thanksgiving for God's love to us, his children, lifts us above the vileness of the world [Lns]. In itself thanksgiving, being God-centered, is not an obvious substitute for vulgarity, since the latter is obviously self-centered. But, whereas sexual impurity and covetousness both express self-centered acquisitiveness, thanksgiving, as recognizing God's generosity, is the exact opposite, and so, it is the antidote required [St, WBC].
2. It opposes the three vices mentioned in this verse [Ba, Cal, EBC, IB, Si, TH, TNTC; TNT]. Paul would have men assemble together for the purpose of praising God rather than engaging in idle, trifling, and indelicate conversation [Ba].
3. It opposes μωρολογία 'foolish talking' and εὐτραπελία 'wittiness/coarse joking' [Ea, ECWB, EGT, El, Ho, My, We]. The 'foolish talking' and 'joking' aim at the mirth and play of the mind. Paul does not austerely condemn such light-heartedness, but he would find a wholesome channel for it in the habitual expression of thanksgiving to God, which proceeds

from a natural and childlike cheerfulness [ECWB]. Foolish talking and jesting are not the ways that Christian cheerfulness should express itself, but rather in thanksgiving [Ho].

DISCOURSE UNIT: 5:5–21 [St]. The topic is further incentives to righteousness. Though Paul continues the topic of sex, discussed in 5:3–4, he moves on from the models of Christian behavior to a new unit dealing with four motivations for holiness.

DISCOURSE UNIT: 5:5–7 [St]. The topic is the first motivation for Christian behavior, the certainty of judgment.

5:5 For[a] this you-know[b] knowing,[c] that every sexually-immoral-person or unclean-person or covetous/lustful-person, which is an-idolater,[d]

TEXT—Instead of ὅ 'which', some manuscripts have the variant reading ὅς 'who'. GNT does not note this variant reading. Those who support the variant reading ὅς 'who' are Ea, El, My, KJV (probably), and NASB.

LEXICON—a. γάρ (LN 89.23): 'for' [AB, El, LN, Lns, NTC, Rob, WBC, We; KJV, NASB, NIV, NJB, REB, TNT], 'because' [LN], not explicit [NIC; NAB, NRSV, TEV].

b. pres. act. indic. or impera. of οἶδα (LN 28.1, 29.6, 32.4): 'to know' [El, LN (28.1), Lns], 'to know about, to have knowledge of, to be acquainted with' [LN (28.1)], 'to understand, comprehend' [LN (32.4)], 'to remember, to recall, to recollect' [LN (29.6)]. This is also translated in conjunction with the immediately following synonymous present participle γινώσκοντες 'knowing' (cf. c. below): 'to know' [KJV], 'to keep in mind' [AB], 'to be well aware' [NIC], 'to be sure' [NIV, NRSV, TEV, TNT], 'to be very sure' [NTC, WBC; REB], 'to know of a surety' [Rob], 'to know with certainty' [NASB], 'to be quite certain' [NJB], 'to know by what one observes' [We], 'to make no mistake' [NAB].

c. pres. act. participle of γινώσκω (LN 27.2, 28.1, 31.27, 32.16) (BAGD 6.c. p. 161): 'to know' [BAGD, LN (28.1)], 'to know about, to have knowledge of, to be acquainted with' [LN (28.1)], 'to come to know' [BAGD], 'to acknowledge' [LN (31.27)], 'to come to understand, to perceive, to comprehend' [LN (32.16)], 'to learn' [LN (27.2)], 'to be aware' [El], 'to realize' [Lns]. This is also translated in conjunction with the immediately preceding synonymous ἴστε 'you know' (cf. b. above). This participle is more immediately joined with ὅτι 'that' and seems to be used with a slight causative force that serves to elucidate and justify the appeal to the knowledge of the readers [El].

d. εἰδωλολάτρης (LN 53.64) (BAGD p. 221): 'idolater' [BAGD, El, LN, Lns, NIC, NTC, Rob, WBC, We; KJV, NAB, NASB, NIV, NRSV], 'worshiper of idols' [LN], 'worshipping a false god' [NJB] 'a form of idolatry' [TEV, TNT]. The clause ὅ ἐστιν εἰδωλολάτρης 'which is an idolater' is translated 'who worships an idol' [AB], 'which makes an idol of gain' [REB]. In the NT, where the term 'idolatry' does not denote the worship of alien gods, it is used figuratively for undue obsession with anything that is less than God [IDB].

QUESTION—What relationship is indicated by γάρ 'for'?

It indicates the grounds for the emphatic command he has given in the preceding injunctions [Can, Ea, EGT, My], especially 5:3 [Ho]. Those injunctions are here confirmed or enforced by referring to the readers' own knowledge [EGT, El, Ho]. What he asserts in repeating the worst forms of the sins he has been writing about is that none guilty of them has any part in Christ's kingdom [Can].

QUESTION—What is meant by τοῦτο ἴστε γινώσκοντες 'this you know knowing'?

1. This clause involves a construction in which two synonyms are joined and translated as an intensive verb [AB, Ba, BD, MNTC, NCBC, NIC, NTC, Rob, Si-ed, St, TH, Tu, Tu3, WBC; all versions except KJV]. This construction is a Hebraism which utilizes two synonymous verbs to introduce an emphatic statement [AB, BD, NTC, TH, Tu, WBC], thus drawing attention to the statement that follows [NTC].

    1.1 This is to be translated as an indicative [NIC, NTC, Rob, Si-ed; NASB, NIV, NJB, TEV]: this you surely know.

    1.2 This is to be translated as an imperative [AB, Ba, BD, MNTC, NCBC, St, TH, Tu, WBC; NAB, NRSV, REB, TNT]: be very sure of this. This introduction reminds its readers of what they ought to be able to remember [AB].

2. Each verb in this clause is to be translated separately as indicatives [Alf, Can, Ea, ECWB, EGT, El, Ho, ICC, Lns, My, We]: this you know, being aware that, etc. Together they seem to say 'For this you know, learning it afresh so as to know it better', i.e., this statement is certain and admits of an ever-growing certainty [ECWB]. What has been taught by a teacher (ἴστε 'you know') is confirmed by actual experience (γινώσκοντες 'knowing') [We]. This is an appeal to their awareness that such sins are incompatible with any inheritance in the Kingdom of God [EGT, El].

    2.1 The finite verb ἴστε 'you know' refers back to 5:3 while the participle γινώσκοντες 'knowing' refers to the facts of the following clause introduced by ὅτι 'that' [Ho]: For you know (that such vices should not be named among you), knowing that no fornicator, etc.

    2.2 Both the finite verb and the participle refer to the following clause introduced by ὅτι 'that' [ECWB, ICC, Lns, My]: For this you know, learning it afresh so as to know it better, that no fornicator, etc. Paul wants the force of both verbs included in this statement. The ἴστε 'you know' from οἶδα refers to simple knowledge and the participle γινώσκοντες 'being aware' carries the idea of personal realization: 'this you know, as realizing that no fornicator, etc.' [Lns]. The present participle indicates the way and manner of the knowing indicated by the finite verb [My].

QUESTION—What is meant by πλεονέκτης 'covetous person/lustful person'?
1. This has reference to a person's greedy acquisition of wealth [Ba, Cal, Can, DNTT, Ea, El, Ho, ICC, Lns, My, NCBC, NIC, NTC, Si, Si-ed, TD; all versions except NAB, TNT].
2. This has reference to a sensual, immoral person [IB, MNTC, Rob, St, TNTC, WBC, We; NAB, TNT]. The word has the wider sense of someone who lives for the selfish satisfaction of his own appetites [MNTC, We] at the expense of others [We]. The person who is characterized by unrestrained sexual greed elevates the desired object, whether his own or another person's satisfaction, to the center of life, which is antithetical to the thanksgiving which recognizes God as the center [WBC]. The equation of πλεονέκτης 'covetous/sensual person' with εἰδωλολάτρης 'idolater' goes back to the OT prophets who spoke of Israel's idolatry as adultery. Here the figure is reversed [IB].

QUESTION—What is the meaning of the phrase ὅ ἐστιν εἰδωλολάτρης 'which is an idolater' and what is its referent?

Most translate the words ὅ ἐστιν 'which is' (or the alternate reading ὅς ἐστιν 'who is') as an assertion [Ba, Cal, Can, EBC, EGT, El, MNTC, My, NIC, NTC, TH, WBC, We; NIV, NJB, TEV, TNT]: such a person is an idolater. Others regard them as a definition, 'that is to say' [AB, Alf, BD, Lns; NAB, NRSV, REB]: that is to say, an idolater.
1. The referent is πλεονέκτης 'covetous person/lustful person' alone [Alf, Ba, Cal, Can, CBC, DNTT, Ea, EBC, ECWB, EGT, El, Ho, ICC, IDB, ISBE2, Lns, MNTC, My, NCBC, NIC, NTC, Si, TD, TH, TNTC, WBC; NRSV, REB, TEV, TNT]. The parallel passage, Col. 3:5, shows unambiguously that the referent is the covetous person here [Alf, EGT, WBC]. Such a person is an idolater because he bestows on wealth the love and reverence he owes to God [Ba, Can, Ea, El, IDB, NIC], or because greed is the worship of the self [CBC, ISBE2, NTC, WBC].
2. The referent is the three nouns, πόρνος 'sexually immoral person', ἀκάθαρτος 'unclean person', and πλεονέκτης 'covetous person/lustful person' [AB, BAGD, Mo, St, We; NAB, NIV, NJB (note)]. A neuter relative pronoun may be used where, strictly speaking, a masculine or feminine might be expected. In such cases the reference is presumably to the whole idea of the preceding clause rather than to just the single word which is the relative pronoun's immediate antecedent [Mo]. What is in focus is the evil man who reveals his sin against God in evil deeds against men, deeds which are multi-dimensional [AB]. Uncontrolled desires give things, especially wealth, a worship due to God alone and so turn them into idols [NJB (note)].

(does) not have an-inheritance[a] in the kingdom of-Christ and God.
LEXICON—a. κληρονομία 'inheritance'. See this word at 1:14, 18.

QUESTION—What is meant by 'not having an inheritance in the kingdom of Christ and God'?

1. This clause refers to the present aspects of the kingdom of Christ and God [AB, Alf]. The verb ἔχει 'have' describes the status of possessing the gifts and privileges that have been handed out to the saints, not just the mere possibility of gaining forgiveness and access to God. This is about losing what has already been granted, i.e., adoption, resurrection, enthronement, access, and freedom, so that this is not parallel to Synoptic statements about entering the kingdom of God [AB].
2. This clause refers to the future aspect of the kingdom of Christ and God [BAGD, Can, EBC, ICC (probably), IDB, ISBE2, My, NCBC, TH]. The present tense of ἔχει 'have' indicates the certain future relation to this kingdom as though it was a present reality [My]. It is best to refer the present statement to the future consummation of the hopes of Christians [Can].
3. This clause incorporates both aspects of this kingdom [Ho, Lns, MNTC, NIC, NTC, TD, WBC]. This kingdom is the rule of God's grace on earth and glory in heaven. It extends from creation into all eternity [Lns]. The genitive τοῦ Χριστοῦ 'of Christ' refers to the present aspects of the Kingdom, while the genitive θεοῦ '(of) God' refers to the future aspect of it [MNTC, NIC]. No idea of successive kingdoms, such as is presented in 1 Cor. 15:24–28, is presented here. Rather, they are identified as a single kingdom in terms of their time and their nature [WBC].

QUESTION—What is meant by the phrase τῇ βασιλείᾳ τοῦ Χριστοῦ καὶ θεοῦ 'the kingdom of Christ and God'?

1. The genitive phrase τοῦ Χριστοῦ καὶ θεοῦ 'of Christ and God' ascribes the βασιλεία 'kingdom' to Christ and to God jointly [AB, Alf, Can, DNTT, Ea, EBC, ECWB, EGT, El, IB, ICC, LJ, My, NIC, Rob, TD, TH, TNTC, WBC, We]. The words Χριστοῦ καὶ θεοῦ 'of Christ and God' are in the closest union to each other [Alf, Can, EBC, ECWB, El, Rob] and are presented under a single conception [El, ICC]. They are in no way to be distinguished from each other [Alf], so that a translation such as 'of Christ and also of God' is out of order [Alf, El, ICC]. Rather, the force is 'being the kingdom of Christ, it is the kingdom of God' [ICC], i.e., the rule of Christ and the rule of God are identical [DNTT], one reign [AB]. The genitive θεοῦ 'of God' shows the nature of this kingdom, while τοῦ Χριστου 'of the Christ' refers to the Messiah as the king of this kingdom [AB, IB, Rob].
2. The genitive phrase τοῦ Χριστοῦ καὶ θεοῦ 'of Christ and God' is an assertion of the Lord's deity [Bu, Ho, Lns, St, Tu2]. Since Paul everywhere supports the deity of Christ, it should be recognized that this is but another instance of this recognition and the grammatical rules supporting this recognition acknowledged [Ho, Lns], the plea that θεός 'God' often does not take the article notwithstanding [Lns]. One states that serious consideration must be given to departing from the current

English versions by translating this 'in the kingdom of Christ who is God' [Tu2]. Another agrees with this translation, but grounds it in an assertion that this genitive phrase is an hendiadys [Bu].

DISCOURSE UNIT: 5:6–21 [Rob]. The topic is darkness and folly vs. light and wisdom.

DISCOURSE UNIT: 5:6–20 [TH]. The topic is living in the light [TH].

DISCOURSE UNIT: 5:6–17 [LJ]. The topic is a warning against false and specious arguments that would keep them from living a Christian life.

DISCOURSE UNIT: 5:6–14 [CBC, My]. The topic is having no fellowship with darkness [My], the light of the world [CBC].

5:6 No-one let-deceive^a you with-empty words;

LEXICON—a. pres. act. impera. of ἀπατάω (LN **31.12**) (BAGD p. 82): 'to deceive' [AB, BAGD, El, LN, Lns, NTC, Rob, WBC, We; all versions], 'to mislead' [BAGD, **LN**], 'to beguile' [NIC]. This verb denotes causing someone to have erroneous or misleading views of the truth [LN].

QUESTION—What is the significance of the anacolouthon here?

The lack of any connecting particle gives the solemn warning in this verse more emphasis [EGT, El]. This verse underlines the motivation of 5:5 [WBC]. Paul's purpose was not only to show his readers the inconsistency of the preceding vices with their participation in the kingdom of God, but he wishes them to be on guard against plausible sounding arguments which might lead them to think lightly of these vices [Can]. He has urged them to acknowledge the truth of divine judgment upon these sins in the previous verse, now he warns them against the empty words of false teachers who would persuade them to believe otherwise [St].

QUESTION—Who are the people who would try to deceive them?

1. This refers to persons within the church [AB, Alf, ECWB, ICC, LJ, MNTC (probably), St (probably)]. These are probably the 'experts in deceitful scheming' referred to in 4:14, teachers within the church who, through their promises, doctrines, arguments, and counsels, made light of sin and encouraged others to lead a permissive or licentious life [AB]. Christians were separate from unbelieving heathen and the Epistle gives no reason to think they would need to be warned against teaching coming in from the unbelieving world. Rather, we must think of persons among them who took sins of impurity lightly [ICC]. It seems likely these are people who were the precursors of the later antinomian Gnostics, who held that, because of the nature of the body, it being made of and in contact with evil matter, things done in the body could have no effect upon the soul [ECWB, MNTC, NCBC, St], just as in Colossians it was the more ascetic form of Gnosticism which Paul warned against [ECWB].

2. This refers to persons in the surrounding pagan society [Ba, Ea, Lns, My, WBC, We]. It probably refers to Gentiles who justified their vices as

matters of indifference [WBC]. This may refer both to the justifications of heathen philosophers who defended these vices [Ba], as well as social pressures from heathen friends to conform to the norms of the surrounding society [Ba, Ea, My, We]. The ὑμᾶς 'you' is emphatic here. Its force is 'let no one deceive you who have learnt the truth' [We].

3. This refers to any and all sources of such deceit [Can, EBC, EGT, El, Ho].

QUESTION—What is meant by κενοῖς λόγοις 'empty words'?

The adjective κενοῖς 'empty' may refer to either the contents of the words, or to their effect. In the first case, these words would be void of substance and truth. In the second, they would be characterized as idle, ineffectual, witless, or pretentious words. Probably it refers to both here [AB, DNTT, St]. Their words are empty [BAGD, DNTT, St] and their teaching ineffective [DNTT] and deceitful [St]. This phrase stands in opposition to the edifying words of grace mentioned in 4:29 [AB]. Most interpret the adjective as describing the words as to their contents [Alf, BAGD, Can, CBC, Ea, EGT, Ho, LJ, MNTC, My, NIC, NTC, TH, WBC]. These words have no truth [Alf, BAGD, Ea, Ho, My, NTC, TH, WBC], no underlying facts behind them [Alf, BAGD]. They have a tendency to perniciousness [Ea, MNTC], and tend to mislead [Ea]. Arguments for living for one's self are shallow because they do not take God into account [CBC].

for because-of these-things the wrath of-God is-coming upon[a] the sons of-disobedience.[b]

LEXICON—a. ἐπί with accusative object (LN 90.57) (BAGD III.1.b.γ. p. 289): 'upon' [AB, BAGD, El, Lns, NTC, Rob, WBC, We; KJV, NASB, TEV], 'on' [BAGD, LN, NIC; NAB, NIV, NJB, NRSV, REB, TNT], 'to' [BAGD, LN]. This figurative use of the preposition is used of the powers, conditions, influences, etc. that come upon someone [BAGD]. It marks the one who experiences something, often implying an action by a superior force or agency [LN].

b. ἀπείθεια (LN **36.23**) (BAGD p. 82): 'disobedience' [BAGD, El, LN, Lns, NTC, Rob, We; KJV, NASB]. The phrase τοὺς υἱοὺς τῆς ἀπειθείας 'the sons of disobedience' is translated: 'the rebellious' [AB], 'the disobedient' [NIC; NAB], 'God's rebel subjects' [REB], 'those who are disobedient' [WBC; NIV, NRSV], 'those who do not obey (God)' [**LN**; TEV], 'those who disobey (God)' [TNT], 'those who rebel against (God)' [NJB]. This noun denotes an unwillingness or refusal to obey the demands of some authority [LN]. In Christian literature this noun is used to denote disobedience towards God [BAGD, DNTT, TD].

QUESTION—What relationship is denoted by γάρ 'for'?

It indicates the reason for not listening to unbelievers [Lns].

QUESTION—What is the referent of διὰ ταῦτα 'because of these things'?

The author is thinking of the above mentioned evil works here rather than the immediately preceding κενοῖς λόγοις 'empty words' [AB, Alf, Can, Ea, EBC, EGT, El, Ho, IB, ICC, LJ, MNTC, My, NIC, NTC, St, TH]. It is

EPHESIANS 5:6 429

indeed these abuses of the sensual life for which men shall chiefly answer at the Judgment [MNTC].

QUESTION—What is meant by the words ἔρχεται ἡ ὀργὴ τοῦ θεοῦ 'the wrath of God is coming', and what is its time reference?

The verb ἔρχεται 'is coming' is emphatic by position, being placed before its subject [Lns]. Paul's purpose in mentioning this judgment is not to threaten his readers with judgment [AB, Cal], for this is stated to be against unbelievers, but to cause them to consider fellowship with the ungodly in their sinful works in light of the judgment which is to fall upon the ungodly world [Cal]. The primary motive for obedience is not to be fear of judgment, for in 5:8 Paul will describe that which enables God's people to walk on the road of obedience and love [AB]. But others believe the writer is warning his readers about the possibility of sharing this judgment [ECWB, NTC] so that repentance is his object [NTC]. The noun ὀργή 'wrath' indicates God's settled displeasure with and opposition to sin [ISBE].

1. These words refer primarily to judgments in the present age [AB, Alf (probably), Cal, Ho, NCBC]. The present tense of the verb denotes an indefinite time reference, and shows that the reference is to the ordinary judgments of God on these sins which Paul's readers may witness with their own eyes [Cal].
2. These words refer primarily to the judgments of the eschatological future [BAGD, DNTT, Ea, EBC, EGT, El, IDB, MNTC, My, NTC, TD, WBC]. The present tense of ἔρχεται 'is coming' often has a future reference [DNTT, WBC], so much so that it can be classed as an eschatological term [TD]. The verb refers to the fact that though the judgment will be particularly felt in the future, yet it is already appointed [Ea, EBC, El, NTC] and so it can be spoken of as descending at the present time [Ea, EBC, NTC]. It is so certain that it is as if it had already arrived [NTC].
3. These words refer equally to both aspects [Can, IB, ICC, LJ, Lns, St, We (probably)]. The tense of ἔρχεται 'is coming' is the continuous or iterative present and definitely points to the present time as well as the future [LJ, Lns]. The present judgments of God consist of a guilty conscience, the natural consequences of sin, both upon the individual committing it and upon society that tolerates it, and specific active judgments more immediately from God's own hand. But the apostle also has in mind, as well, the final eschatological judgment and punishment the individual must undergo [LJ].

QUESTION—What is meant by τοὺς υἱοὺς τῆς ἀπειθείας 'the sons of disobedience'?

These are non-Christians, the same people as are denoted by this Hebrew idiom in 2:2–3 [AB, DNTT, EBC, ECWB, EGT, Ho, ICC, ISBE2, Lns, NCBC, NIC, Rob, Si, St, TD, TH, WBC, We]. This is a disobedience to the principles and practices of the Gospel [EGT, El, NIC], whether as codified law or as a principle written on their hearts [NIC], a refusal to believe the gospel [My]. The idiom 'sons of' denotes these people's *practice* of disobedience [Lns]. This phrase stands in contrast to the phrase τέκνα φωτός 'children of light' in 5:8 [DNTT].

DISCOURSE UNIT: 5:7–14 [We]. The topic is the familiar contrast of darkness and light, under which the foregoing lessons are now gathered together.

5:7 Therefore (do) not be/become sharers-together[a] with-them;
LEXICON—a. συμμέτοχος: 'sharer together'. See this word at 3:6.
QUESTION—What relationship is indicated by οὖν 'therefore'?

It indicates an exhortation grounded upon the previous statement [Alf, Ba, Ea, EGT, El, LJ, My, TNTC, WBC, We; TEV]: God's wrath is coming upon the sons of disobedience, therefore do not be sharers together with them. This verse supplies the connection between 5:3–6, dealing with the prohibition of sexual vices and those who practice them, and 5:8–14, which treat the images of light and darkness [WBC]. The apostle has just stated a doctrine concerning God's wrath, now he draws an argument from it which he will begin developing in the next verse, that of walking in the light [LJ, NTC]. Having completed his list of special prohibitions, the apostle now returns to his general principle of not being like the Gentiles [Rob].

QUESTION—What is meant by μὴ γίνεσθε 'do not be'?

1. The verb γίνεσθε means 'to be' [Alf, Lns, NTC, Rob; KJV, NASB, NIV, NRSV]: do not be sharers together with them. There is no idea of a gradual 'becoming' like them, but a 'being' like them, which the writer is discouraging [Alf]. The present tense of this verb is iterative: do not at any time be sharers together with them [Lns].
2. The verb γίνεσθε means 'to become' [Ea, EGT, El, NIC, WBC]: do not become sharers together with them. The verb means 'to become'. It is not the equivalent of ἐστε 'be' [EGT]. What is prohibited is falling back into the ways which, by grace, they have forsaken [EGT, El].

QUESTION—What is meant by συμμέτοχοι 'sharers together'?

1. The noun means being an associate or partner in something [AB, BAGD (p. 778), Ea, EBC, Ho, IB, Lns, My, NCBC, NIC, NTC, Rob, St, TNTC, WBC, We, WeBC; NIV, NRSV], of supporting and abetting the sons of disobedience in their sins [Lns]. For Christians to be joint-partakers with 'the sons of disobedience' would be a moral impossibility, because children of light would have to be in fellowship with children of darkness [NIC]. Christians fall from the state of reconciliation and become co-partners with the 'sons of disobedience' and share in the coming wrath if they practice the same sins [My]. The word refers to joint participation in something [NIC, St, WeBC], not to social contact or association [St, WeBC] (though TH; NAB, REB, TEV and TNT seem to disagree). The word does not denote a general distancing from all aspects of life in the Gentile world, but a separation, in particular, from its immoral aspects [AB, WBC].
2. In this verse the noun simply denotes those who participate in something [ECWB, EGT, Mo]. While in 3:6 this noun means a 'co-participant', here

it means little more than 'participant' [Mo]. This is a *participation* with the disobedient in their vices [EGT].

QUESTION—To what does the pronoun αὐτῶν 'them' refer?
1. This refers to the preceding τοὺς υἱοὺς τῆς ἀπειθείας 'the sons of disobedience' [Alf, Can, Ea, EBC, ECWB, EGT, El, Ho, ICC, Lns, MNTC, My, NCBC, NIC, NTC, Rob, St, TNTC, WBC, We; NASB, NIV, NJB, TEV, TNT].
    1.1 The reference is to the present practice of the sins characteristic of the sons of disobedience [Alf, Ea, EGT, El, NCBC]: do not be sharers together with the sons of disobedience in their sins.
    1.2 The reference is to both the sins of the sons of disobedience and their doom [Can, ECWB, Ho, ICC, My, NIC, NTC, St, TNTC, WBC, We]: do not be sharers together with the sons of disobedience in their sins, and so of their doom.
2. This refers to μηδεὶς ὑμᾶς ἀπατάτω 'let no one deceive you' at the beginning of 5:6 [TH]: do not be sharers together with those who would deceive you.
3. This refers to the evil works which this chapter has been discussing [AB, Ba, IB; NAB]: do not be partakers of these evil works upon which the wrath of God is coming. The pronoun αὐτῶν 'them' is in the genitive case, which would indicate the deeds in which participation is taken [IB]. This interpretation seems to be supported by 5:11–14 where it is stated that saints must not be associated with deeds which are done in darkness [AB].

DISCOURSE UNIT: 5:8–21 [Si]. The topic is light versus darkness.

DISCOURSE UNIT: 5:8–14 [AB, Cal, St, WeBC]. The topic is the believers' walk in light rather than in darkness [WeBC], the victorious power of the light of Christ [AB], the fruit of light [St].

5:8 **for you-were formerly darkness,[a] but now light[b] in (the) Lord;**

LEXICON—a. σκότος (LN 88.125) (BAGD 2.b. p. 758): 'darkness' [AB, BAGD, El, LN, Lns, NIC, NTC, Rob, WBC, We; all versions except TEV, TNT], 'evil world, realm of evil' [LN]. This noun is also translated as a phrase: 'in the darkness' [TEV]. The clause ἦτε ποτε σκότος 'you were darkness' is translated 'you used to be completely one with darkness' [TNT]. This is one of several occurrences of the figurative usage of σκότος 'darkness' which has the sense of a 'bearer' or 'victim' or an 'instrument of darkness' [BAGD].

b. φῶς (LN 14.36) (BAGD 3.a,c. p. 872): 'light' [AB, BAGD, El, LN, Lns, NIC, NTC, Rob, WBC, We; all versions except TEV, TNT]. This noun is also translated as a phrase: 'in the light' [TEV], 'as the light itself' [TNT]. 'Light' is a metonymy for redeemed persons whose lives are illuminated by and conformed to Christian truth [BAGD (3.c. p. 872)].

QUESTION—What relationship is indicated by γάρ 'for'?

It indicates the reason these readers should not be sharers with the υἱοὺς τῆς ἀπειθείας 'sons of disobedience' [Ea, St], the readers' present state being totally different from theirs [Alf, Ea, EGT, Lns, St]. At the same time it proves and confirms the preceding warning [EGT, El, Ho, WBC].

QUESTION—What is the significance of ἦτε 'you were'?

Standing as the first word of this verse, ἦτε 'you were' is emphatic by position [Alf, Ea, EGT, El, My] and by its imperfect (past) tense [Lns]. It places the emphasis on the time past [ICC]. It stresses the fact that their former Gentile state is now behind them [EGT, El].

QUESTION—What is meant by ἦτε σκότος 'you were darkness'?

The word σκότος 'darkness' is a metonymy [Bu] in which an abstract noun is used to refer to persons [Bu, Ea, EGT, El, Lns, My, Si]. This is a stronger statement than ἐν σκότει 'in darkness' would be [Alf, Ea, EBC, El, LJ, NCBC, NTC, Rob, Si, St, TNTC, WBC, We] because the use of the abstract identifies these readers with their respective environments [DNTT, Si]. The writer is saying his readers were formerly darkness itself [Alf, Can, Ea, EBC, ECWB, EGT, El, LJ, NTC, Rob, St, TNTC, WBC]. The metaphor of darkness stands for spiritual and moral conditions [TH, WeBC] (as does the metaphor of light in the next clause [TH]), yet the thought is not predominately that of individual character [We], but of social influence [AB, We]. The outward element of darkness (as also light in the following clause) is presented as pervading the inner nature of the soul [ECWB, EGT, ICC, LJ, Si]. They were formerly blinded by Satan [Si], having been engulfed in the same ignorance and having practiced the same abominations [Ba, IB, LJ, NCBC, Si], had gloried in their shame [Si], and had themselves been new sources of dissemination of that darkness which hates and quenches light in themselves and others [ECWB]. The Jews used 'darkness' to refer to being outside of the will and purpose of God and subject to the power of the forces that oppose God [CBC, IDB]. 'Darkness' refers to the heathen world of which they had been a part [Can, IB, NCBC, NTC]. It refers to the whole nature of man apart from regeneration [Cal, LJ]. 'Darkness' suggests Satan [NCBC], evil and badness [CBC, IDB, NCBC, St, TH], ignorance of Divine truth [Bu, Ea, Ho, IDB, My, NTC, St, WBC], the immorality just described [WBC], and depravity [Ea, NTC] which produce sin and unhappiness [Ho, NTC], their state of being lost, and death [TH].

QUESTION—What is the significance of the omission of the verb ἐστέ 'you are' in the contrastive νῦν δὲ φῶς 'but now light' clause?

The omission serves to give emphasis to this clause, as well as to prepare for the coming exhortation, by showing these readers not only what they *ought* to be, but *were* by profession [Alf]. The words 'You are' are supplied in all versions.

QUESTION—What is meant by φῶς 'light'?

This is another occurrence of metonymy of the abstract being used for the concrete [BAGD, Bu, Lns, Si]. They themselves are now light, not only being enlightened themselves, but as giving light to others [DNTT, IB, ICC, ISBE, LJ, NTC, TNTC]. The contrast of light and darkness is so absolute that it serves to point out the lesson that they are antithetical to darkness and their conduct is to be in harmony with their transformation [Ea, EGT, LJ]. Light is the symbol of God [IDB, NCBC, TH, TNTC], of his glory, holiness, and wisdom [TNTC], of goodness [NCBC, TH], of truth and righteousness [St], of knowledge of Divine truth [AB, Ba, Ea, Ho, My, NTC, WBC], of holiness [Ba, Ea, Ho, NTC, WBC], of happiness [AB, Ba, Ho, NTC] (the knowledge producing holiness and happiness [Ho]), life and their status of being saved [AB, TH].

QUESTION—What relationship is indicated by the preposition in the phrase ἐν κυρίῳ 'in the Lord'?

1. It indicates means or instrument [Ba, NCBC]: you are light through the Lord. The change from darkness to light is accomplished by the power of the Lord in bringing men to conversion [NCBC]. The meaning is that they had been enlightened by the Lord to see the evil of their practices [Ba].
2. It indicates identification [Alf, Ea, EBC, ECWB, EGT, El, Ho, ICC, LJ, Lns, My, St, TD, TH, WBC, We; REB, TEV]: you are light in union with the Lord. The preposition means 'in union with' [Alf, EBC, ECWB, Ho, LJ, Lns, St, TH] and indicates the conditioning element of their new state [Alf]. They have become identified as light because they are identified with Christ [WBC]. It is Christ within the Christian who fills him with life, light, and power, and makes him light himself [LJ]. Some translate this relationship 'in fellowship with' [Ea, EGT, El, ICC, My, TD, We] or 'as Christians' [REB]. Others use a statement of possession: 'since/now that you belong to the Lord' [TH; TNT], 'since you have become the Lord's people' [TEV].
3. It indicates source [ISBE]: you are light from the Lord. The phrase 'light in the Lord' indicates the source of light [ISBE].

walk as children of-light

QUESTION—What is the significance of the omission of a connecting particle such as οὖν 'therefore' with this final clause of the verse?

The omission of an οὖν 'therefore' introducing this clause makes the inference of a logical conclusion more forcible [Alf, Ea, EGT, My]. The preceding use of abstract nouns in place of concrete persons has also added to the force of this conclusion [El]. The intent of this reference is that his readers might exercise an influence for good on those among whom they live, as is indicated in the following context [Can, EGT, El], therefore they are to pursue a moral walk in accordance with this privilege [El]. Their behavior must correspond with their new identity [AB, St].

QUESTION—What is the significance in the use of περιπατεῖτε 'walk' here?

The ground for this imperative verb rests upon the preceding (implied) indicative, ἐστέ 'you are' [AB, TD, WBC]. Having spoken of these readers as being 'light', the apostle now comes to speak of their conduct and so he returns to his metaphor of 'walking' [Rob]. Their daily lives are to be in accord with their new nature [TNTC] since it is the nature of light to shine in darkness [ISBE2]. The apostle has used this same verb in the preceding context (5:2) in connection with love [Ea, LJ]. These occurrences set out different aspects of the same holiness or purity [Ea]. It means 'doing the will of God' [AB, NIC] and so the saints are given their area of responsibility in the present and future acknowledgment and execution of God's will, a responsibility they are to fulfill voluntarily and enthusiastically through their gratitude and jubilation [AB].

QUESTION—What is meant by τέκνα φωτός 'children of light'?

The phrase τέκνα φωτός 'children of light' is translated: 'people who belong to the light' [TEV], 'those who belong to the light' [TNT], or 'people who belong to God' [LN (**11.14**)]. The second occurrence of φῶς 'light' in this verse is a figurative usage in which such persons are said to be τέκνα φωτός 'children of light' [BAGD (3.a. p. 872)]. The phrase τέκνα φωτός 'children of light' denotes persons to whom God's truth has been revealed and whose lives presumably are lived in accordance with that truth [LN (11.14)]. This is a Hebraism meaning 'enlightened people' [Bu, Cal, NCBC]. This phrase denotes such men as those whose essential nature is light [IB, TNTC]. It stands in contrast to τοὺς υἱοὺς τῆς ἀπειθίας 'the sons of disobedience' in 5:6 [WBC]. As in the preceding section (5:1) where Christians are regarded as the beloved children of the God of love, here they are designated as children of the God of light [WeBC]. The noun τέκνα 'children' indicates a community [DNTT, We] of nature as υἱός 'son' indicates privilege [We].

1. The genitive φωτός 'of light' indicates the source of these τέκνα 'children' [Bu (probably), Ea, NTC]: children born of light. It presents these readers as being the very offspring of him who is light [NTC].
2. The genitive φωτός 'of light' indicates possession [Lns, TH; TEV]: children belonging to light. The genitive is either ethical or that of possession [Lns].
3. The genitive φωτός 'of light' indicates association [Mo]: people associated with light.

5:9 —**for the fruit[a] of-the light (is) in all goodness[b] and righteousness and truth**—

TEXT—Instead of φωτός 'light', some manuscripts have πνεύματος 'Spirit'. GNT assigns an A rating to the reading with φωτός 'light', indicating that this reading is certain. The word πνεύματος 'Spirit' is read only by Ba and KJV.

LEXICON—a. καρπος (LN 42.13) (BAGD 2.a. p. 404): 'fruit' [AB, El, Lns, NIC, NTC, Rob, WBC, We; KJV, NASB, NIV, NRSV], 'harvest' [REB], 'result, outcome, product' [BAGD], 'effects' [NJB], 'deed, activity, result of deeds' [LN]. The words ὁ καρπὸς τοῦ φωτός 'the fruit of the light'

are translated 'light produces' [NAB, TNT], 'where light is, there is a harvest' [REB], 'light brings a rich harvest' [TEV].
b. ἀγαθωσύνη (LN 88.1) (BAGD p. 3): 'goodness' [BAGD, El, LN, Lns, NIC, NTC, Rob, WBC, We; all versions except NRSV], 'uprightness' [BAGD], 'good' [AB, LN; NRSV], 'good act' [LN]. This noun denotes positive moral qualities of the most general kind [LN].

QUESTION—What relationship is indicated by γάρ 'for'?

It indicates the reason for the preceding comparison clause [Alf, EGT], and a confirmation of it [Ea, EGT, El]. It confirms the propriety of using the term περιπατεῖτε 'walk' in the last clause and also supplies its fuller explanation [El]. This is given in the form of a parenthetical statement [Alf, Cal, Can, Ea, EBC, EGT, El, LJ, Lns, My, Rob, TH, TNTC, WBC, We; KJV, NASB, NIV] (in sense, though not fully so in form [El]), explaining what the will of God is (expressed in the figure of walking in the light) [Cal, Can, Ea, EBC, Lns, WBC] and adding an inducement to the duty [Ea, EGT, El, My]. In this way this verse joins the περιπατεῖτε 'walk' of the last clause with the modal participle δοκιμάζοντες 'proving' in the following clause [El, My]. The noun καρπός 'fruit' is a collective [Lns, My], summarizing what περιπατεῖτε 'walk' means [Lns], or summarizing the aggregate of moral effects which is the result of Christian enlightenment [My].

QUESTION—What is meant by ὁ καρπὸς τοῦ φωτός 'the fruit of the light'?

1. The metaphor focuses upon the naturalness of a particular kind of plant generating fruit in accordance with its kind [AB, DNTT, LJ, NCBC, Si, TNTC, We (probably)]. The result of spiritual light is compared with the product of a fruit-bearing plant. The point of the comparison is the naturalness of the fruit to the type of plant which produces it. A nonfigurative statement would be: the natural result of conducting yourselves in accordance with what Christ has taught you is to be good, righteous, and true in every way, since this comes out of your very nature as Christians.
2. The metaphor focuses upon the role of sunlight in the production of fruit [St, TH, WBC; TEV]. Paul is likening the fruits of the light given by Christ in this verse and the next ('goodness', 'righteousness', 'truth', and 'what is pleasing to the Lord') to a natural harvest ripening under the sun [St, TH; TEV]. The comparison is the result of spiritual enlightenment upon the believer just as sunlight produces the harvest in the natural world. The point of the comparison is the effect of the sunlight: the production of ripe fruit. The nonfigurative statement would be: the result of conducting yourselves in accordance with what Christ has taught you is to be good, righteous, and true in every way, since it is Christ who produces this in you.

QUESTION—What relationship is indicated by ἐν 'in'?

1. This preposition indicates the sphere with which ὁ καρπὸς τοῦ φωτός 'the fruit of the light' is associated [Alf, Ea, Lns], i.e., the element and condition in which it is manifested [Alf, Ea]: the fruit of the light is characterized by all goodness, righteousness, and truth. It indicates that

the three qualities listed are within the sphere of the fruit of light. This is not the same as saying that the fruit of the light consists in all goodness, etc., but that it is always associated with these qualities as its element and sphere. These qualities characterize its fruits [Ea].
2. The ἐν 'in' (understood with an implied 'is') has the sense of 'consists of' [AB, Ba, Bu, El, Ho, MNTC, My, NTC, TD, WBC], or more exactly, it imparts the idea of containment [El, My]: the fruit of the light consists of all goodness, righteousness, and truth. The fruit is seen in the production of all kinds of goodness [Ba].

QUESTION—What force does πάσῃ 'all' have?

This πάσῃ 'all' has the force of 'all forms of, every form of' [EGT, El, We, WeBC] or 'every kind of' [ICC]. It indicates the whole of the sphere indicated by the preposition ἐν 'in' [Lns].

QUESTION—What is the purpose for the listing of the three nouns, ἀγαθωσύνῃ 'goodness', δικαιοσύνῃ 'righteousness', and ἀληθείᾳ 'truth'?

The whole of Christian morality is presented in its three great forms: the good, the right, and the true [EGT, El, My, We]. These sum up all forms of piety and virtue [Ho]. The first quality, ἀγαθωσύνῃ 'goodness', covers personal character; the second, δικαιοσύνῃ 'righteousness', social dealings; the third, ἀληθείᾳ 'truth', ruling principles. Together the three virtues mark our obligation to self, neighbors, and God [We]. The first two qualities relate to the Christian's treatment of others, while ἀληθείᾳ 'truth' relates to loyalty to his own conscience [MNTC]. The latter two qualities, δικαιοσύνῃ 'righteousness' and ἀληθείᾳ 'truth', are more specific definitions of ἀγαθωσύνῃ 'goodness' [NTC], or they add character, strength, and veracity to 'goodness' [Si].

QUESTION—What is meant by ἀγαθωσύνῃ 'goodness'?

It is the pure opposite of evil [WeBC]. It is kindness [Can, NCBC, Si], benevolence [Can, EBC, Ho, ICC, LJ], active goodness and beneficence [EGT, Ho], or genuine moral excellence [Ea, Lns, TD] that comes out of religious principles [Ea] and results in kindness [Ea, ECWB], generosity, or goodness [Ea]. This noun stands in opposition to κακία 'malice' (4:31) [Ea, EBC, NTC, TNTC].

QUESTION—What is meant by δικαιοσύνῃ 'righteousness'?

It expresses the qualities of 'goodness' not only as they are directed toward men but more particularly as they are directed toward God [Lns]. 'Righteousness' is a narrower term than 'goodness', and has legal connotations. This describes a person who not only conforms to the letter of the law, but its spirit also, who wants to know what is right, and just, and equitable, and to conform to it [LJ]. It is doing what is right [IDB], having equal love and regard to our fellows [Can, CBC], and giving everyone their due [EBC, WeBC]. It means justice [CBC], fairness [EBC, LJ], integrity [Ea], probity [EGT], freedom from what is morally wrong or imperfect [EGT, NCBC], moral rectitude [Ea, EGT, Ho, My] which rules itself according to Divine law [Ea, Ho, LJ, Lns, NTC].

QUESTION—What is meant by ἀληθείᾳ 'truth'?

This term describes a person who is open and has nothing to hide, one whose life is characterized by truth in all its varied manifestations [LJ]. It means religious truth [Ho], or moral truth [EGT, Ho, My]. It is straightforward dealing with others [CBC]. It is genuineness and honesty [EBC, NCBC, TH], sincerity and integrity [EGT, LJ, Lns, My, NCBC, NTC]. It stands in contrast to the ψεῦδος 'falsehood' of 4:25 [NIC], and the deceit mentioned in 5:6, and the things done in secret which will be mentioned in 5:12 [LJ].

5:10 proving/approving[a] what is pleasing[b] to-the Lord,

LEXICON—a. pres. act. participle of δοκιμάζω (LN 27.45, 30.98, 30.114) (BAGD 1. p. 202): 'to prove' [El, Rob, We; KJV], 'to verify' [NTC], 'to test' [LN (27.45)], 'to put to the test' [BAGD], 'to examine' [BAGD, LN (27.45)], 'to test out' [Lns], 'to try to learn' [NASB], 'to discover' [WBC], 'to judge to be genuine, to judge as good, to approve' [LN (30.114)], 'to regard as worthwhile, to think of as appropriate' [LN (30.98)]. This participle is also translated as an imperative or imperative clause: 'approve' [NIC], 'find out' [NIV], 'try to discover' [NJB], 'try to learn' [BAGD; TEV], 'try to find out' [NRSV, TNT], 'find out by experience' [AB], 'learn to judge for yourselves' [REB], 'be correct in your judgment' [NAB].

b. εὐάρεστος (LN 25.94) (BAGD 1. p. 318): 'pleasing' [AB, BAGD, LN, NTC, WBC; NASB, NRSV, REB, TNT], 'well-pleasing' [El, Lns, NIC, We], 'acceptable' [BAGD, Rob; KJV]. This adverb is also translated as a verb: 'to please' [NAB, NIV, TEV]. The clause τί ἐστιν εὐάρεστον τῷ κυρίῳ 'what is pleasing to the Lord' is translated 'what the Lord wants of you' [NJB].

QUESTION—What relationship is indicated by the use of the participle δοκιμάζοντες 'proving/approving'?

1. This participle is connected to the imperative περιπατεῖτε 'walk' in 5:8 [Alf, Ba, Ea, EBC, EGT, El, Ho, ICC (probably), LJ, Lns, MNTC, My, NIC, NTC, Rob, TD, TH, TNTC, WBC, We, WeBC; KJV, NASB] and defines the manner in which this walk is to take place [EGT, El, WBC]: walk as children of the light, proving what pleases the Lord. The participle functions as the modal predicate of the imperative περιπατεῖτε 'walk' in 5:8 [Alf, Ba, Ea, EGT, El, My]. The participle should not be taken as an imperative [ICC, WBC; KJV, NASB], since this as not natural because it stands between two verbs marked as imperatives [ICC].

2. This participle is regarded as another imperative verb [AB, BAGD, NIC (probably); all versions except KJV, NASB]. It is linked to περιπατεῖτε 'walk' by supplying a conjunctive 'and' in a coordinate construction [NIC; NIV]: walk as children of light and prove what is pleasing to the Lord. One commentator links the participle to the imperative περιπατεῖτε 'walk' in 5:8, stating that while it has imperative force it still contains the first explanation of what it means to walk as children of light [AB].

QUESTION—What is meant by δοκιμάζοντες 'proving/approving'?
1. This focuses upon the process of investigation [AB, Alf, BAGD, CBC, DNTT, Ea, EBC, ECWB, EGT, El, Ho, IB, ICC, ISBE, ISBE2, LJ, Lns, MNTC, My, NCBC, Rob, TD, TH, WBC, We; KJV, NASB, NIV, NJB, REB, TEV]: trying to find out what is pleasing to the Lord. We try to find out the Lord's will by doing it [MNTC]. It refers to finding out in the circumstances what is the ethically correct course of action. Paul believes that believers are able to discover God's will in specific situations as they place the whole of their beings at God's disposal [WBC], and this discovery is accomplished through the Holy Spirit renewing and acting upon the believer's powers of judgment [TD]. The whole course of his life is to be a continual testing of what the Lord's will is, a continual investigation of what pleases the Lord [Alf, CBC, Ea, EBC, El, IB], not what pleases himself [Alf, Ea, TNTC]. The verb here means to try to find out in each situation what is in accord with the will of God by examining carefully one's heart and action as directed by God's word [ECWB].
2. This focuses upon the result of the investigative process [Ba, NTC; NAB]: verifying what is pleasing to the Lord. This verb means to prove or verify by means of testing [NTC].
3. This focuses upon the consent of the mind to the result of the investigative process [Can, NIC, Si-ed, TNTC]: approving what is pleasing to the Lord. It means 'approving as befitting' [Si-ed]. The verb makes plain the demand for careful thought and consideration [TNTC]. Christians see clearly what is pleasing to the Lord, make proof of it by practicing it, and so commend it to others [Can]. Christians not only try to learn what is pleasing to the Lord, but having their minds so in tune with his that when they have learned what pleases him, they approve it [NIC].
4. This includes all of the above [St, WeBC]: testing, discerning, and approving what is pleasing to the Lord.

QUESTION—What is the referent of τί 'what'?
Some commentators refer τί 'what' to the ἀγαθωσύνη 'goodness', δικαιοσύνη 'righteousness', and ἀληθεία 'truth' of the last verse, showing what is well pleasing to the Lord [Can, LJ, MNTC]. The tenor of the remarks of others indicates they take this verse as referring, in general, to whatever action shows obedience to the Lord's will rather than just to something mentioned in the immediate context [Ea, EBC, EGT, Ho, IB, NCBC, NTC, TH].

QUESTION—Which person of the Godhead is designated by κυρίῳ 'Lord'?
1. It refers to Christ [Can, CBC, Ho, IB, LJ, My, NCBC, NIC]. In the previous reference to κυρίῳ 'Lord' in this sentence (5:8), the reference is clearly Christ [Ho].
2. It refers to God the Father [EBC, MNTC, NTC, TH]. Because of the use of the adjective εὐάρεστον 'pleasing' in reference to the OT sacrifices, κυρίῳ 'Lord' here probably refers to God [TH].

DISCOURSE UNIT: 5:11–12 [Can, NCBC, TH, WBC, WeBC]. The topic is the reproval of the world's evil by the light of believers' lives [WeBC].

5:11 and not have-fellowship-with/take-part-in[a] the unfruitful[b] works of-(the) darkness, but rather even rebuke/expose[c] (them).

LEXICON—a. pres. act. impera. of συγκοινωνέω (LN **34.4**) (BAGD 1. p. 774): 'to have fellowship with' [El, Lns, NIC, Rob, We; KJV], 'to have to do with' [AB; NIV, TEV, TNT], 'to associate with' [**LN**], 'to take part in' [NTC, WBC; NAB, NJB, NRSV, REB], 'to participate with' [LN], 'to participate in' with someone [BAGD; NASB], 'to be in partnership with' [LN], 'to be connected with' something [BAGD]. This verb denotes being in association with some joint activity and implies, in some contexts, that this association is a somewhat enduring relationship [LN]. In this verse, the verb has the meaning of actually taking part in something [BAGD].

b. ἄκαρπος (LN **65.34**) (BAGD 2. p.29): 'unfruitful' [El, Lns, NIC, NTC, Rob, We; KJV, NASB, NRSV], 'fruitless' [AB, WBC; NIV], 'unproductive' [BAGD, **LN**], 'worthless' [TEV], 'useless' [BAGD, LN], 'vain' [NAB], 'futile' [NJB], 'barren' [REB]. The phrase τοῖς ἔργοις τοῖς ἀκάρποις 'the unfruitful works' is translated 'those useless people' [TNT]. The term 'unfruitful' indicates that there is no lasting or permanent benefit or value [Cal, Can, IB, LJ, St], it is sterile or barren [NIC, NTC, St, WBC], with no profitable gain or blessing [EGT, St]. It refers to enjoyments that perish with the using [Can], having effects which are positively harmful [Cal]. It refers to things that contribute nothing to a person's mental abilities, nor to his knowledge and understanding, nor do they add to his purity or moral cleanliness, nor uplift or inspire him to high achievement, nor ennoble him in any way [LJ], nor lead him to contribute in any beneficial way to others [LJ, TH], but rather consume his resources and wreck his life [LJ].

c. pres. act. impera. of ἐλέγχω (LN **33.417, fn 72**) (BAGD 1. p. 249): 'to rebuke' [**LN**], 'to reproach' [LN], 'to reprove' [El, Lns; KJV], 'to condemn' [NAB], 'to show the true nature (to convict)' [We], 'to show (them) up for what (they) are' [NJB, REB], 'to bring to light' [BAGD], 'to expose' [BAGD, MM, NIC, NTC, Rob, WBC; NASB, NIV, NRSV, TNT], 'to expose by words' [LN (fn 72)], 'to set forth' [BAGD, MM], 'to bring out to the light' [TEV], 'to disprove (by conduct)' [AB]. This verb denotes making a statement that someone has done wrong and implies that adequate proof of that wrongdoing exists [LN].

QUESTION—What relationship is indicated by καί 'and'?

It connects this verse to the imperative περιπατεῖτε 'walk' [Ea, My], adding another exhortation to that of 5:8 [EBC, My]. Whereas the apostle insisted on the duty of Christians in 5:10 to walk so as to show they were subjects of divine illumination [Ho, LJ], here he adds a statement of their attitude or duty relative to the sins of those who were still in darkness [Ho, LJ, Lns, St, TNTC].

QUESTION—What is meant by μὴ συγκοινωνεῖτε 'have no fellowship with/ take part in'?

1. Συγκοινωνεῖτε means 'to fellowship with' someone [Alf, Cal, Ea, ECWB, El, Ho, IB, ICC, My, NIC, Rob, We; TNT]. In this word the idea of personal fellowship prevails over that of participation in something outward, though the phrase τοῖς ἔργοις τοῖς ἀκάρποις τοῦ σκότους 'the unfruitful works of darkness' places the emphasis upon the unfruitful works [We]. The phrase τοῖς ἔργοις τοῖς ἀκάρποις τοῦ σκότους 'the unfruitful works of darkness' understood as metonymy for those who commit these works [Alf, Cal, ECWB (probably), Ho (probably), IB, My (probably), We; TNT]: have fellowship with no one in the unfruitful works of darkness. The believer must beware of joining or in any way assisting those who do evil. The giving of consent, advice, approbation, or assistance constitutes fellowship with those who carry out the evil deed [Cal].

2. Συγκοινωνεῖτε means 'to participate in' something [AB, DNTT, EBC, NTC, St, TD, TH, TNTC, WBC; all versions except TNT]. It means 'to share with someone in something' [TD]. This verse defines 5:7 by showing that not being partners with the sons of disobedience means not taking part in their vices [AB, WBC]. Christians are not to be involved in these works. Notice that it is the deeds which are to be shunned here, not the doers. Paul is not supporting a pharisaical separatism. The believer refuses to accept the standards of the world or follow its ways [EBC]. The translator must be careful to translate this phrase in such a way that the focus remains upon the deeds, not the doer [TH].

QUESTION—What is meant by τοῖς ἔργοις τοῖς ἀκάρποις τοῦ σκότους 'the unfruitful works of darkness'?

The phrase is literally 'the works, the unfruitful (ones) of the darkness', a construction which emphasizes 'the unfruitful ones of darkness' [Lns, We]. The genitive τοῦ σκότους 'of darkness' may be either subjective ('produced by the darkness') [Lns] or possessive ('belonging to the darkness') [Lns, TH]. The 'works of darkness' are those that spring from ignorance of God [Ho, LJ, My] and opposition to him [My]. These are such sins that the apostle has been writing about since 4:25 [NTC]. The 'fruit' of these works are death and shame [Ea, LJ]. Most regard those who commit these acts as unbelieving pagans [Ba, Cal, Can, CBC, Ea, EBC, EGT, El, Ho, ICC, LJ, Lns, NCBC, NTC, St, TNTC, WBC, WeBC], though other authorities regard these works as being committed by erring believers [AB, ECWB, IB, IDB].

QUESTION—What is the function of the formula μᾶλλον δὲ καί 'but rather even'?

This is a formula which gives special intensity to the antithesis which follows [Ea]. It combines the effects of the corrective μᾶλλον 'rather', the adversative δέ 'but', and the ascensive καί 'and' [EGT, El]. Its import is to emphasize the idea that it is not enough for believers to simply abstain from such works, but they must go further and reprove them [Ea, EGT, El, My].

Another view of καί is that it is not ascensive and means 'also'. The force of the whole expression is that administering reproof for these works is not something to be reluctantly added to that of avoiding fellowship, but is to be added with zest [Lns].

QUESTION—What is meant by the imperative ἐλέγχετε 'to rebuke/ expose'?

This is the positive duty of Christians toward the evil works of the world [CBC, Ea, IB, St]. The question of whether the stronger or the weaker sense of ἐλέγχετε 'to rebuke/expose' is indicated here depends upon whether its object, the phrase τοῖς ἔργοις τοῖς ἀκάρποις τοῦ σκότους 'the unfruitful works of darkness', is interpreted as a metonymy for 'those who have done the unfruitful works of darkness' or focuses upon the deeds themselves. If it is understood as a metonymy, the meaning is 'to rebuke'. If the focus is upon the deeds themselves, the meaning is 'to expose' [LN (33.417 fn 72)].

1. This has the stronger sense of 'to rebuke' [Alf, Can, CBC, Ea, ECWB, EGT, El, LN (**33.417**), Lns, My; KJV, NAB]: but rather even rebuke them. The object of the reproof is to bring their heathen neighbors to understand their depravity and forsake such deeds [EGT, El, My]. The verb describes a double function: (1) that of 'convincing' the sinner himself, and (2) if that fails, of 'convicting' him before men and angels. Both functions are urged here. To 'have no fellowship' with such men constitutes a tacit reproof, but this is not enough. Open reproof in word and deed is to be added, subject to the contents of the next verse (5:12) [ECWB]. Christians 'show up' the evil ideals which surround them by the example of their lives, the refusal to conform to such standards, and by vocal protest [CBC]. There was not simply to be negative separation, but positive rebuke [Ea].

2. This has the weaker sense of 'to expose' [AB, BAGD, EBC, Ho, IB, ICC, LJ, MM, MNTC, NCBC, NIC, NTC, Rob, St, TD, TH, TNTC, WBC, We, WeBC; NASB, NIV, NJB, NRSV, REB, TEV, TNT]: but rather even expose them. These unfruitful works will be corrected by Christians showing them to be vile and destructive [Ho, LJ]. This exposure or reproof takes place through the example of Christian life, conduct [Ba, Cal, LJ, NTC], and teaching [Ho, LJ]; in short, by the attractive power of holiness, after the pattern of Christ [LJ]. In the NT the use of this verb is restricted. It means to correct or set right, in the sense of 'to point away from sin to repentance'. It implies educational discipline. Here it is used in reference to a private matter between two people [TD].

DISCOURSE UNIT: 5:12–14 [IB, ICC, Si]. The topic is the effect light has upon those who practice the works of darkness [IB].

5:12 For the (things) being-done in-secret[a] by them are shameful[b] even to-speak-of,

LEXICON—a. κρυφῇ (LN **28.71**) (BAGD p. 454): 'in secret' [AB, BAGD, El, LN, Lns, NTC, Rob, WBC, We; all versions except NRSV], 'secretly' [LN, MM; NRSV], 'in private, privately' [LN]. This adverb is also

translated as an adjective modifying γινόμενα 'being done': 'secret (actions)' [NIC].
b. αἰσχρός (LN 88.150) (BAGD p. 25): 'shameful' [AB, BAGD, LN, Lns, NIC, WBC; NAB, NIV, NJB, NRSV, REB, TNT], 'really too shameful' [TEV], 'shame' [El, NTC, Rob, We; KJV], 'disgraceful' [LN; NASB], 'base' [BAGD].

QUESTION—What relationship is indicated by γάρ 'for'?
1. The connection is with the ἐλέγχετε 'rebuke/expose' in 5:11 [Alf, Ea, EGT, El, Ho, Lns, My, Rob].
   1.1 It indicates the grounds for the preceding charge to rebuke sins [Alf, EGT, El, Ho, Lns, My]: rebuke them because the things done in secret by them are shameful even to speak of. Rebuke them because to have the least part in them, even in speaking of them, is shameful, i.e., let your only connection with such evil works be that which ἐλέγχετε 'rebuke' makes necessary [Alf]. Rebuke them, for to speak of the things they do in secret brings them to a sense of shame [Lns].
   1.2 It makes a contrast with the command to rebuke them [TH]: On the other hand some things done in secret are really too shameful to mention. This verse seems to be a contradiction to the command at the end of 5:11, so it may be necessary to employ a contrastive device such as 'on the other hand' or 'but' [TH]. (ICC notes that such a contrastive meaning for γάρ 'for' is impossible.) This verse is a parenthetical comment since the flow of thought skips from 5:11 to 5:13 [TH].
2. It gives the grounds for both the negative and positive parts of 5:11 [WBC].

QUESTION—What is meant by τὰ κρυφῇ γινόμενα 'the things being done in secret'?
1. This has general reference to deeds that are commonly done by pagans [Ba, Cal, Can, Ea, EBC, EGT, El, LJ, Lns, MNTC, My, NCBC, NIC, NTC, Rob, Si, TH, WBC] or by Christians who have returned to their pagan ways [AB]. These words form a special interpretation of τὰ ἔργα τοῦ σκότους 'the works of darkness' [Rob]. These are not exactly equivalent to τοῖς ἔργοις τοῖς ἀκάρποις τοῦ σκότους 'the unfruitful works of darkness' in 5:11 [Ea, EGT, El, ICC, Lns, My, Si], for many of these are practiced openly [Ea, ICC, Lns, My], but are a specific subclass of them [Ea, EGT, El, Lns, My, Si]. It is not certain what these sins are [TH], but the context seems to point to those referred to in 4:3–5 [TH, WBC], especially the sexual sins [WBC]. Sexual vices are particular examples of sins practiced in private, while covetousness may be more open [Lns].
2. This has reference to things that were done in religious rites [IB]. The writer is not referring to the pagan mystery religions, but he is referring to Christian sects which imitated them. He probably has no exact knowledge of what went on in such gatherings, but is put off by their secretive nature because it serves as a cover for shameful deeds. By contrast, he implies everything in Christianity must be done openly and aboveboard [IB].

QUESTION—What is the referent of ὑπ' αὐτῶν 'by them'?

This refers back to the τοὺς υἱοὺς τῆς ἀπειθείας 'the sons of disobedience' in 5:6 [El, NCBC, WBC] or, obliquely, to those in 5:11 who are τοῦ σκότους 'of the darkness' [BAGD (3.b. p. 123) (probably), BD, Tu, WBC], who are the same persons.

QUESTION—What is meant by αἰσχρόν ἐστιν καὶ λέγειν 'it is shameful even to speak of'?

Interpretations as to the meaning of this expression are connected to the problem of how ἐλέγχετε 'rebuke/expose' is interpreted in 5:11.

1. The sense of shame is that felt by a speaker when he mentions these sins [AB, Alf, Ba, Can, Ea, EBC, ECWB, EGT, El, MNTC, My, NCBC, NIC, NTC, TD, TH, WBC, We, WeBC]. This verse is similar to, or reiterates, 5:3 [EBC, ECWB, NCBC, TNTC, WBC]. Christians naturally shrink from discussing such sins [We].

1.1 It means that these sins are not to be mentioned at all [AB, CBC, EBC, MNTC, NCBC, NTC, Si, TH, WBC]. The apostle feels that the mention of some of these practices would only cause their evil influence to spread [CBC, EBC] by playing on people's interest in the sordid and scandalous [CBC]. Christians are not to drag out into the limelight things which have been done under the cover of darkness. It is bad enough that these things happen, but their effect can only be worsened when garrulous tongues and self-righteous ears feed on them [AB, EBC].

1.2 It means that these sins can be mentioned only in a general manner and briefly for purposes of denunciation [Alf, Ba, ECWB].

1.3 The phrase must be taken as a description of the nature of these sins, and not as a command to Christians not to mention them, and so serves to strengthen the final clause of 5:11 [Ea, EGT, El, My, Rob].

2. The sense of shame is that felt by the perpetrators of the sins [Cal, Ho, LJ, Lns]. Just to state the things done is shameful, not for the believer who makes the statement, but for those who do the works of darkness. The idea that Paul means that it makes the believer blush just to mention these things is not indicated [Lns]. Just the fact that these sins must be done under cover of darkness indicates the sense of shame that operates within the perpetrator [Cal, LJ].

DISCOURSE UNIT: 5:13–14 [TH, WeBC]. The topic is the light from Christians' lives transforming the darkness [WeBC].

5:13 **but all-(things) being-rebuked/exposed[a] by the light are being-revealed,[b]**

LEXICON—a. pres. pass. participle of ἐλέγχω: 'to rebuke, to expose'. See this word at 5:11.

b. pres. pass. indic. of φανερόω (LN 24.19, 28.36) (BAGD 1.b. p. 852): 'to be revealed' [AB, BAGD, LN (28.36), NIC], 'to be clearly revealed' [TEV], 'to be made manifest' [El, Rob, We; KJV], 'to be made to appear, to be caused to be seen' [LN (24.19)], 'to be made visible' [LN (24.19), NTC], 'to become visible' [BAGD; NASB, NIV, NRSV], 'to be seen' [NAB], 'to become illumined' [WBC], 'to be illuminated' [NJB], 'to be exposed' [REB], 'to be shown up for what it truly is' [TNT], 'to be made public' [Lns], 'to be made known' [LN (28.36)], 'to become known' [BAGD], 'to be made plain, to be brought to the light, to be disclosed' [LN (28.36)].

QUESTION—What relationship is indicated by δέ 'but'?
1. It indicates contrast [Alf, Ea, EBC, EGT, El, My, NIC, WBC; all versions except TEV, TNT]. These things are done in secret but they may and should be exposed [Alf, Ea, EGT, El, MNTC]. Thus this whole sentence (consisting of this verse and the first clause of the next) becomes a further grounds for ἐλέγχετε 'reprove' (5:11) [EGT, El, Ho, My].
2. It indicates transition [Lns, TH; TEV]. This verse is a parenthetical remark in regard to the application of the light [Lns]. The particle continues the thought [Lns, TH].

QUESTION—What is the referent of τὰ πάντα 'all things'?
1. The reference is to τὰ κρυφῇ γινόμενα 'the things being done in secret' in 5:12 [Ea, EGT, El, Ho, Lns, My, NIC; NAB]: for the things done in secret, being reproved/exposed, are revealed by the light.
2. The reference is to τοῖς ἔργοις τοῖς ἀκάρποις τοῦ σκότους 'the unfruitful works of darkness' in 5:11 [Alf, Can, NTC (probably)]: for the unfruitful works of darkness, being reproved/exposed, are revealed by the light. The reference is not just to τὰ κρυφῇ γινόμενα 'the things being done in secret', but must be broader, because the apostle is speaking about the detecting power of light in general, as is indicated by the resumptive πᾶν 'all' in 5:14 [Alf].
3. The reference is unrestricted, i.e., any and all things [Ba, EBC, ECWB, LJ, NCBC, Rob, St, TH, WBC, We; NASB, TEV]: for whatever is reproved/exposed is revealed by the light.

QUESTION—What relationship is indicated by the use of the participle ἐλεγ-χόμενα 'being rebuked/exposed' here?
1. This participle is temporal [EGT, El, My, NCBC, NTC, Rob, St, We; NAB, NASB, TEV]: when they are rebuked/exposed. The absence of the definite article with this participle indicates that it is not an epithet, but a secondary predicate. It is either a predication of manner or of time appended to τὰ πάντα 'all things'. Its meaning must be the same as that of the finite verb form in 5:12 [El].
2. This participle is attributive to τὰ πάντα 'all things' [Lns, TH, WBC; KJV, NIV, NJB, NRSV, TNT]: all things that are rebuked/exposed by the light.

QUESTION—What is meant by the phrase ὑπὸ τοῦ φωτός 'by the light' and to what is it connected?

Most regard this phrase to be metaphorical [Ba, Cal, Can, DNTT, Ea, EGT, El, Ho, Lns, My, Rob, St, WBC, WeBC; NAB], based upon the function of physical light in the natural world [EBC; NAB]. It must be remembered that by φωτός 'light' is meant not mere knowledge or moral teaching [Can], but salvation and conduct as reflected in Christ's followers [Can, DNTT, NTC, WBC, WeBC], or the word of God [Cal, Lns], divine truth [Ho], the gospel [Ba, Ea]. Its reference is the *Christian* light previously referred to [EGT, My].

1. It is connected to the participle ἐλεγχόμενα 'being exposed' [Lns, NCBC, NTC, Rob, St, TH, We; all versions except KJV, NAB, REB]: all things being exposed by the light are being revealed. The point to be focused upon is that these things must be reproved by the light. The fact that they are also φανεροῦται 'being revealed' by the light is self-evident [Lns]. Just as the parallel phrase ὑπ᾽ αὐτῶν 'by them' in 5:12 goes with the participle γινόμενα 'being done', so here ὑπὸ τοῦ φωτός 'by the light' modifies the participle ἐλεγχόμενα 'being rebuked/exposed' [NTC].
2. It is connected to the finite verb φανεροῦται 'are being revealed' [AB, Alf, Ba, Ea, EBC, EGT, El, Ho, IB, LJ, My, NIC, WBC; KJV, NAB, REB]: all things being rebuked/exposed are being revealed by the light. This interpretation is required by the following clause, πᾶν γὰρ τὸ φανερούμενον φῶς ἐστιν 'for everything that is revealed is light' [Ho].

QUESTION—What is meant by φανεροῦται 'are being revealed'?

1. This verb is in the passive voice [AB, Alf, BAGD, ECWB, EGT, El, Ho, ICC, MNTC, My, NIC, NTC, Rob, St, TH, WBC, We; all versions]: all things being exposed by the light are manifested (or become visible).
1.1. This verb means 'to be revealed, to be made manifest' [AB, Alf, BAGD, EGT, Ho, ICC, My, NIC, NTC, Rob, St, TH, We; KJV, NAB, NASB, NIV, NRSV, REB, TEV, TNT]. Like its synonym ἀποκαλύπτω 'to reveal' (denoting the general and outward aspect of revelation, while φανερόω 'to reveal' gives the more special and inward aspect [ISBE]). The meaning of this verse, together with the first clause of 5:14 which is connected to it, is 'the light of your Christian life which will be shed upon these works of darkness by your reproof of them, will bring them out of the category of darkness into that of light'. The apostle's readers themselves had once been darkness, but having been reproved by the Spirit had themselves become light in the Lord (5:8) [Alf]. The use of this verb indicates that the light of the gospel allows us to see the true nature of actions [Ba].
1.2. This verb means, more accurately, 'to be illumined' [ECWB, El, MNTC, WBC; NJB]. Because of the relation in this context of this verb to τοῦ φωτος 'the light', this verb means 'to become visible through being lit up', i.e., 'to become illumined' [WBC]. Reproving something in the Christian way means to bring it into the full light of Christ's truth. The effect of this is not only reproval but to illuminate it by the innate power of the light [ECWB].
2. This verb is in the middle voice [Si-ed]: all things being exposed by the light manifest themselves. Most commentators would constrain us to the

passive meaning, but it seems possible that this verb, both here and in its participial form in the next clause, should be understood in the sense of the middle voice [Si-ed].

5:14 for everything that is-revealing/is-being-revealed is light.

QUESTION—What relationship is indicated by γάρ 'for'?

It indicates the grounds for the statement of the preceding clause concerning the power ascribed to 'light' [Ea, EBC, EGT, El, Lns, MNTC, My, NTC]. Confirmation is made by referring to a general proposition about the connection that exists between *manifestation* and *light* [EGT, My], i.e., that it cannot come from any other source than from the light [My]. It explains that everything that is so made public is light [Lns].

QUESTION—What is meant by this clause?

1. The participle φανερούμενον 'is revealing' is middle voice, but with the force of the active [Ba, Cal, Ea, ICC, LJ, Si-ed, Tu; KJV, NAB, NASB, NIV, NRSV]: light is what reveals everything. Anything which will reveal the real form and nature of an object deserves to be called light. Therefore, the gospel should be considered a system of light and truth [Ba]. Φῶς 'light' is a metaphor for the causative agent of this revealing, the gospel, the word of God [Ba, Cal, Ea, LJ]. Paul has enjoined his readers to reprove the evil works of unbelievers, and so to drag them out of the darkness, and now he adds that what he has enjoined them to do is the proper business and function of light [Cal, Ea].

2. The participle φανερούμενον 'is being revealed' is passive voice [AB, Alf, Can, EBC, ECWB, EGT, El, Ho, IB, Lns, MNTC, Mo, My, My-ed, NCBC, NIC, NTC, Rob, Si, St, TH, TNTC, WBC, We; NJB, REB, TEV, TNT]. This is a proverbial saying [NIC].

   2.1 This clause is a statement of a general truth in support of the preceding particular affirmation [EBC (probably), EGT, El, Lns, MNTC, My, NTC]: everything that is revealed becomes light. It means that 'whatever is illumined is light', i.e., becomes daylight [El], or is of the nature of light [El, MNTC, NTC]. The logic of the relationship between the two clauses is based upon the reasoning: what it is in effect (φῶς ἐστιν 'is light'), it ought to be in cause (ὑπὸ τοῦ φωτός 'by the light' (5:13)) [El, My], i.e., if the general truth expressed in this clause is warranted, so must be the Christian truth expressed in the preceding clause [My]. The meaning is that everything that is finally seen in its true colors is no longer secret, but instead takes on the nature of light [EGT]. Φῶς 'light' is a metaphor for the reality or truth of what is revealed, the result of exposure to spiritual truth [EBC, El, Lns, MNTC, NTC, Si].

   2.2 This clause is a statement about the transforming power of salvation, with φῶς 'light' as a metaphor expressing that transformation [AB, Alf, Can, CBC, ECWB, Ho, IB, Mo, My-ed, NCBC, NIC, Rob, Si, St, TH, TNTC, WBC, We, WeBC; TNT (note)]: everything that is being revealed is transformed as the effect of the light. Light is the salvation brought by Christ and reflected by his followers [Can]. Light is the complete change that takes place in the person as the effect of revelation [AB, WBC]. In Paul's mind 'to become manifest' is to cease to be darkness, and to become a partaker of light's very nature [Rob]. This clause seems to say that when light penetrates a dark place, the darkness disappears and, in a manner of speaking, is transformed into light [TH]. The apostle is not speaking about the nature of spiritual light, but about its effects. It illuminates or turns into light all it comes into contact with, or wherever it penetrates. Spiritual truth has an illuminating, corrective, and sanctifying effect in those in whom it dwells. Though 'light' does not of itself transform, it is preparatory and necessary to that transformation [Ho]. The apostle explains here what he means by illumination (φανεροῦται 'is illumined', last clause) [ECWB]. This is the catching of the light and reflecting it so that the object illuminated becomes a new source of light [ECWB, My-ed, TNTC; TNT (note)]; the newly baptized Christian becomes a beacon to others, exposing the shallowness of much that goes on around him [CBC]. Thus understood, this clause is the culmination of the explanation of a three step process by which people are transformed. First, they, or their works, are dragged out of darkness into light, then they are illuminated [ECWB, My-ed, TNTC], and then they become light in themselves and light-givers to others [ECWB, My-ed, TNTC, WBC; TNT (note)]. There are the exceptions to this but, as the following quote will demonstrate, Paul is not thinking about these [ECWB, Si]. The whole metaphor is based upon the ability of natural light, not only to illuminate, but to change and to foster life [ECWB].

Therefore it says, Get-up, O sleeper,[a] and rise[b] from-among the dead,
LEXICON—a. pres. act. participle of καθεύδω (LN 23.104) (BAGD 2.b. p. 388): 'to sleep'. This articular participle is translated as a substantive: 'O sleeper' [BAGD, WBC; NAB, NIV], 'you sleeper' [AB, Lns], 'sleeper' [NTC; NASB, NJB, NRSV, REB, TEV, TNT]. It is also translated as a short clause: 'you who sleep' [El, Rob, We; KJV], 'O you who sleep' [NIC]. This verb is also translated figuratively as 'to be dead' [LN]. This verb is used here figuratively for spiritual laziness and indifference [BAGD].
b. aorist act. impera. of ἀνίστημι (LN 23.94) (BAGD 2.a. p. 70): 'to rise' [AB, BAGD, WBC; NIV, NJB, NRSV, REB, TEV, TNT], 'to arise' [BAGD, El, Lns, NTC, Rob, We; KJV, NAB, NASB], 'to raise to life, to make live again' [LN], 'to arouse' [NIC]. This verb is used here figuratively of a spiritual reawakening [BAGD], of causing someone to live again after having died [LN]. The abbreviated form of the imperative used here is ἀνάστα 'rise', the regular form of the imperative being ἀνάστηθι.

The abbreviated form is compatible with short exclamations, as used here [AB].

QUESTION—What relationship is indicated by διό 'therefore'?
1. It indicates an conclusion based on 5:3–14a [AB, NIC].
2. It indicates an conclusion based on 5:8–14a [NCBC, St]. The occurrence of the verb ἐπιφαύσει 'will shine upon' in the third stanza demonstrates that the link up of this quotation is with the material from 5:8 onward [NCBC]. The material quoted forms a natural conclusion to this section [St].
3. It indicates an conclusion based on the need for the ἔλεγξις 'reproof' just discussed in 5:11–14a [EGT, El, Lns, My, NTC]. Since this ἔλεγξις 'reproof' is so urgent and necessary and its nature has just been described, the following quotation holds true [El, My]. It introduces a sample of the way in which the reproof is to be offered. The aim is always the sinner's conversion [Lns].
4. It indicates an conclusion based on 5:14a [Alf, Can, Ho, IB, MNTC, TH, WBC, We]. Since light is efficacious and accessible, the Scriptures call even upon the sleeping and the dead to arise and partake of its life-giving beams [Ho]. The διό 'therefore' is linked most immediately with the clause of 5:14a, but also with 5:8 where the writer's chain of thought began [WBC].

QUESTION—What is the source of the quoted material here?
1. This material comes from an early Christian hymn [AB, Alf-ed, BAGD, CBC, EBC, ECWB, IB, ICC, ISBE2, Lns, MNTC, NCBC, NIC, Rob, Si-ed, TD, TH, TNTC, WBC, We; NJB (note), TNT] or a liturgical text [TD].
2. This material is from an OT passage or passages [Alf, Ea, EGT, El, Ho, ISBE, My-ed, NTC]. The material in Isa. 60:1–2 matches the requirements of this context [Alf, El, Ho, My-ed, NTC], though the apostle's quote is expressed in a condensed and summary form, and presents the spiritual meaning of the passage [El, Ho, My-ed]. But this is only a paraphrase of that passage, as shown by the occurrence of ὁ Χριστός 'the Christ' [Alf, Ea], which indicates clearly that the apostle is appropriately citing the language of prophecy in the light of the fulfillment of prophecy [Alf]. The subject of 'says' is God [Alf, Ba, DNTT, EGT, El, ISBE, My, NCBC, NTC] or Scripture [Ho].
3. This material is Paul's own composition [Ba]. This appears to be Paul speaking as an inspired man. In this context of telling them to avoid the vices of the pagans around them the message is: come out from among them and be separate. Awake from false security, arouse from the death of sin, and Christ will enlighten you [Ba].
4. This material comes from an otherwise unrecorded saying of Jesus [Can] or the general tenor of the message being preached by Christ's ministers [Cal]. Paul represents Christ as speaking through his ministers, alluding to the language of Isa. 60:1 to call upon his followers to reprove pagans and

EPHESIANS 5:14 449

bring them to the light. The intent of these verses is that which is preached by Christ's ministers every day [Cal].
5. This material comes from an unknown apocryphal source [My, TD]. Paul meant to quote OT Scripture, but by a lapse of memory mistook this fragment of an apocryphal saying, now unknown to us, for canonical Scripture [My].

QUESTION—What is meant by the present articular participle ὁ καθεύδων 'O sleeper'?

From the καθεύδων 'sleeper' it appears that the quote is not directed at the church, but at recent converts or those who do not yet believe [ICC, My, NCBC]. The whole context from 5:3 onward, including the present quotation, is directed toward Christians who are still living in paganism [NTC]. Given that this context deals with the effects of a faithful ἔλεγξις 'reproof' (5:11, 13), the point of this quote is not only to enforce the need to encourage the church to reprove pagan practices, but also to point out the need of the surrounding pagan population to respond to the saving light of Christ's truth [EGT].
1. This is a euphemism for spiritual death [AB, Alf, Cal, ISBE2, Lns]. The NT often uses the idea of sleep to refer to natural death, but also extends this concept to refer to spiritual death, as in the hymn in Eph. 5:14 [ISBE2].
2. This is a metaphor for spiritual sluggishness or torpor [Ba, BAGD, Can, ECWB, ISBE, My, NCBC, TD, TNTC, WBC, WeBC]. If a distinction is to be drawn between this clause and the next, this clause relates to awakening out of a state of lethargy and carelessness [ECWB]. Sleep is the condition of forgetfulness and drunkenness which is part of spiritual darkness [WBC]. The meaning of τῶν νεκρῶν 'the dead' is identical to that of νεκρούς 'dead' in 2:1 [Ba, Ea, TNTC, WBC] and refers to deadness in sin [ECWB, NCBC, TD, TNTC, WBC] and moral insensibility [Ba, My].

QUESTION—What is the relationship between the first two imperative clauses?

The two clauses utilize a rhetorical device in which they have similar sounding endings, καθεύδων 'sleeper' and νεκρῶν 'dead'. They follow a Semitic style with the imperative verbs placed at the beginning of the line, and linked by καί 'and'. These two lines are a synthetic parallelism and constitute a summons to ethical awareness [WBC]. The first imperative, ἔγειρε 'get up', serves to intensify the second, ἀνάστα 'rise', and so means 'Up and arise' [Lns]. The two stanzas form a climactic couplet, giving a twofold description of the natural state of man under the dominion of sin. Just as the physical life is suppressed and gone both in the sleeping person and in the dead one, so the moral, vital activity of the true spiritual life is missing in the natural man [My]. The assumption behind the use of these two imperatives is that a dead man, like a sleeper, may be aroused from his state by the appropriate call (Mark 5:41; John 5:25, 11:43; Acts 9:40; 1 Thess. 4:16). This verse implies that the action of standing up follows Christ's creative awakening call. The conjoining καί 'and' supports the idea that the awakening precedes the rising. Nevertheless, these two stanzas should not be understood as implying that the dead possess a hearing ear and the ability to obey! [AB]. On the other hand, another commentator thinks that the summons in the second imperative to arise from the dead implies that the sleeper in the first clause has awakened in response to the first call and at this point has the ability to obey [WeBC].

and Christ will-shine-upon[a] you.

LEXICON—a. pres. act. indic. of ἐπιφαύσκω (LN **14.39**) (BAGD p. 304): 'to shine upon, on' [AB, BAGD, El, **LN**, NIC, NTC, Rob, WBC, We; all versions except KJV, NAB], 'to shine forth upon' [Lns], 'to illuminate' [LN], 'to give light' [KJV, NAB]. This verb denotes the act of causing light to shine upon some object with the purpose of illuminating it. This verb occurs only here in the NT and is used figuratively [LN].

QUESTION—What relationship is indicated by καί 'and'?

1. The καί 'and' introduces an action subsequent to the actions indicated by the imperatives in the preceding stanzas [Ba, NCBC, WBC]. If the non-Christian will turn from his vain and worthless life of evil, Christ will give him light [NCBC].
2. The καί 'and' introduces an action concurrent with the actions indicated by the imperatives in the preceding stanzas [AB, Cal, NTC]. The conjunction with the future tense of the verb ἐπιφαύσει 'will shine upon' should *not* be understood as indicating that only *after* the call of the Messiah which raises the hearer from the dead will the light of the Messiah prove effective. Rather the conjunction here serves to introduce an interpretation relating to the previous two stanzas without implying any sequence of events. When Christ illuminates the believer, he arises to new life [AB, Cal]. The imperatives, and the obedience they engender, presuppose the light of the Messiah [AB]. When, by divine power, the sinner puts off the old nature and puts on the new, and more and more awakens and arises from his dead state, the light of Christ shines upon him illuminating his entire life with Christ's loving presence [NTC].

QUESTION—What is meant by the future verb ἐπιφαύσει 'will shine upon'?

It recalls OT passages such as Ps. 27:1; Isa. 9:2, 60:1–2; Mal. 4:2, in which God's glory, or light, is conceived of appearing over Israel and exerted life-giving power (cf. also Rom. 6:4 where God's glory is the agent of resurrection). The verb indicates that the Messiah, by shining upon the dead, communicates something of his own essence to those illuminated [AB]. In his light they themselves become light (5:8) [AB, CBC], so confirming the statement about light in the previous clause. This final stanza means that Christ will shine upon the believing person with the light of his truth and bring him out of the ignorance and immorality that characterize pagan darkness [EGT, My]. The subject and verb of this stanza are transposed, thus emphasizing both [Lns].

DISCOURSE UNIT: 5:15–6:9 [WBC, We]. The topic is cardinal social relationships [We], wise and Spirit-filled living in worship and household relationships [WBC].

DISCOURSE UNIT: 5:15–33 [Rob]. The topic is a return to practical precepts of conduct appropriate to the saints' participation in the conflict between light and darkness.

DISCOURSE UNIT: 5:15–21 [CBC, ECWB, EGT, El, ICC, Lns, NTC, TNTC, We, WeBC; TNT]. The topic is the correct use of the present time [CBC], specific things which belong to the correctness and consistency of the Christian walk [EGT], an admonition to exercise Christian wisdom [Lns], wisdom replacing folly among believers [TNTC], the believers' walk in wisdom as opposed to folly [WeBC], the temper of Christian social relationships in general [We].

DISCOURSE UNIT: 5:15–20 [Cal, IB, MNTC, NIC, WBC; NRSV]. The topic is a brief summary of what has been written concerning the distinctive elements of the Christian life [IB], being filled with the Spirit [NIC], wise and Spirit-filled living [WBC], general exhortations [MNTC].

DISCOURSE UNIT: 5:15–18a [AB]. The topic is making good and wise use of the allotted time until the Day of the Lord.

DISCOURSE UNIT: 5:15–17 [My, Si, St]. The topic is Christians being careful in their walk as wise persons [My], the nature of wisdom [St].

DISCOURSE UNIT: 5:15–16 [Ho]. The topic is Christians being wise and making the most of every opportunity to do good even though surrounded by evil.

5:15 Then watch[a] carefully[b] how you-walk not as unwise[c] but as wise,[d]

TEXT—The order given in GNT is ἀκριβῶς πῶς 'carefully how', in which ἀκριβῶς 'carefully' modifies the preceding imperative verb βλέπετε 'watch': 'watch carefully how you walk'. GNT give this a B rating, indicating that this reading is almost certain. Those supporting this reading are AB, EBC, EGT (probably), GNT, ICC, MNTC, NIC, NTC, Rob, St, TH, TNTC, WBC, We; all versions except KJV. Other manuscripts contain a reading in which the order of ἀκριβῶς 'carefully' and πῶς 'how' is transposed so that ἀκριβῶς modifies the following present active verb περιπατεῖτε 'you walk': 'watch how carefully you walk'. Those supporting this reading are Alf, Ba, Can, Ea, ECWB, El, Ho, LJ, Lns, My, Si-ed; KJV. Whichever reading is preferred, the general sense of the clause is not greatly affected [IB]. However, this textual problem does affect the interpretation of the last clause of this verse.

LEXICON—a. pres. act. impera. of βλέπω (LN 27.58, 30.1) (BAGD 4.c. p. 143): 'to watch' [AB], 'to watch out for' [LN (27.58)], 'to see' [Lns; KJV], 'to look' [We], 'to take heed' [El, Rob] 'to keep watch' [NAB], 'to be careful' [NIC, NTC; all versions except KJV, NAB, REB], 'to take care' [REB], 'to pay attention to' [LN (27.58), WBC], 'to direct one's attention to a matter, to note' [BAGD], 'to beware of' [LN (27.58)], 'to think about' [LN (30.1)], 'to consider' [BAGD, LN (30.1)]. This verb denotes being ready to learn about future needs and dangers and implies being prepared to respond appropriately [LN (28.58)] or it denotes the processing of information through giving consideration to various aspects of a matter [LN (30.1)].

b. ἀκριβῶς (LN 72.19) (BAGD p. 33): 'carefully' [AB, BAGD, We], 'careful' [Rob, WBC; NAB], 'accurately' [BAGD, LN, Lns], 'accurate' [LN], 'circumspectly' [KJV], 'with strictness' [El], 'strict, strictly' [LN], 'well' [BAGD]. The phrase βλέπετε ἀκριβῶς 'watch carefully' is translated 'be careful' [NIC; NASB, NRSV, TEV], 'be most careful' [NTC], 'be very careful' [NIV, NJB, TNT], 'take great care' [REB]. This adverb denotes strict conformity to a norm or standard and involves both detail and completeness [LN].

c. ἄσοφος (LN **32.54**) (BAGD p. 116): 'unwise' [BAGD, LN, Lns, NTC, Rob, We; NIV], 'unwise person' [**LN**, WBC; NRSV], 'unwise man' [NASB], 'fool' [AB, El; KJV], 'foolish' [BAGD], 'senseless person' [NJB], 'ignorant person' [TEV]. This adjective is also translated as an adverb modifying περιπατεῖτε 'you walk': 'unwisely' [NIC]. It is also translated as a negative adverb phrase: 'not foolishly' [TNT]. It is also translated as a comparative negative phrase: 'not like simpletons' [REB]. It is also translated as a clause: 'do not act like fools' [NAB], 'don't live like ignorant people' [TEV].

d. σοφός (LN **32.33**) (BAGD 3. p. 760): 'wise' [BAGD, El, LN, Lns, NTC, Rob, WBC, We; KJV, NASB, NIV, NRSV], 'wise man' [AB], 'wise person' [NIC], 'intelligent' [NJB], 'prudent, understanding' [LN]. This adjective is also translated as a verb phrase: 'act sensibly' [REB], 'behave sensibly' [TNT]. It is also translated as a comparative phrase: 'like thoughtful men' [NAB], 'like wise people' [TEV], 'like people who are wise' [**LN**].

QUESTION—What relationship is indicated by οὖν 'then'?

Three admonitory sections have been introduced (4:17, 4:25, 5:1), each with its connective linking it to its preceding material, so forming one whole chain. This οὖν 'then' introduces the last of four specific admonitions which constitute one group [Lns].

1. It indicates a resumption [Alf, Can, EBC, EGT, El, Ho, ICC, Lns, My, NCBC, Rob, St, TH].

1.1 The resumption is from 5:8 [Alf, Can, EBC, EGT, El, ICC, My, NCBC, Rob, St, TH]: walking as children of light then, watch how you walk, etc. The occurrence of περιπατεῖτε 'you walk' in this verse resumes its last occurrence in 5:8 [Rob]. The writer passes from the statement he has just made in 5:11–14 about reproving the unfruitful works of darkness [EGT, My] to take up again the exhortation of 5:8 to walk as children of light [Alf, Can, EBC, EGT, ICC, My], defining it more exactly by pointing out the wisdom needed for this walk [Can]. He had digressed to discuss the purity that becomes this walk and, after having shown what the blessed effect of that could be, he infers from this consideration that they should not only have the moral abhorrence of evil, but also Christian wisdom to carefully guide their conduct [Can].

1.2 The resumption is from 5:10–11 [Cal, Ho, Lns]: having no fellowship with the fruitless works of darkness and even reproving them, then watch how you walk, etc. The exhortation contained in this verse and the next most naturally connects with the subject matter of 5:10–11 [Ho]. If believers must not neglect to reprove the works of darkness, much less can they be blind to their own conduct [Cal, Lns].

2. It indicates a logical conclusion or summary [AB, Cal, CBC, Ea, LJ, Lns, TNTC, WBC, We, WeBC]: we conclude then, that you must watch how you walk, etc. The last verse is especially present in the apostle's mind as he makes this transition [Ea, LJ] even though the connection is also with the whole paragraph dealing with the subject of light [LJ, WBC].

QUESTION—To what is the adverb ἀκριβῶς 'carefully' attached and what is meant by it?

1. It is attached to the preceding imperative verb βλέπτε 'watch' and means 'accurately, carefully' [AB, EBC, EGT (probably), GNT, ICC, MNTC, NIC, NTC, Rob, St, TNTC, WBC, We; all versions except KJV]. Attached to βλέπτε 'watch' (the common Pauline expression for 'see to it'), this adverb stresses the importance and urgency of a person to give the utmost concentration to leading an irreproachable life [EBC, WBC].

2. It is attached to the following indicative verb περιπατεῖτε 'you walk' [Alf, Ba, Cal, Can, Ea, ECWB, El, Ho, LJ, Lns, My, Si-ed, WeBC; KJV] and means 'accurately, strictly, correctly, carefully' [Ea, ECWB, El, Ho, LJ, Lns, My, Si-ed]. Connected to περιπατεῖτε 'you walk', the adverb means to walk strictly by rule, not deviating by a hair's breadth [Ho]. The word is generally used in the NT of intellectual accuracy and thoroughness, but only here and in Acts 26:5 is it used with a moral sense [ECWB]. The word here may be extended to mean 'circumspectly', as in the KJV, because this meaning is virtually involved in the concept of accuracy since the accuracy or perfection of the believer's walk has special reference to observers [Ea, LJ]. While the adverb ἀκριβῶς 'carefully' draws attention to the strict, exact nature of the Christian walk being enjoined here [Alf], the immediately following πῶς 'how' directs attention to the sort of strictness that walk is [Alf, Lns].

QUESTION—How is the negative clause μὴ ὡς ἄσοφοι ἀλλ᾽ ὡς σοφοί 'not as unwise but as wise' related to its context and what is meant by it?

The clause replaces the metaphorical contrast between light and darkness in the previous verses [Cal, EBC] with a contrast between wisdom and folly [EBC]. To live wisely is not just to have knowledge, but to have skill in living. This requires ethical insight into the will of the Lord (5:17) [WBC].

The meaning of ἄσοφοι 'unwise' in this context relates to the previous discussion of how the people of this world live in their indulgence of foolish desires and pleasures [Ba, LJ]. Because of the preceding discussion involving the metaphors of light and darkness, σοφοί 'wise' is equivalent to those who have been enlightened, ἄσοφοι 'unwise' to those in darkness [Ho]. The σοφοί 'wise' are those who can anticipate the consequences of their actions and so act to avoid what will bring trouble and regret [NCBC].

1. This negative clause is dependent upon πῶς ἀκριβῶς περιπατεῖτε 'how carefully you walk' [Alf, Ea, El, Lns] and explains it [Alf, El, LJ, Lns, My]: watch, therefore, how you walk—carefully, that is, not as unwise, but as wise. More immediately, this clause serves to explain ἀκριβῶς 'carefully' [ECWB, El, Lns, My] both positively and negatively [El, Lns, My] because wisdom is the practical knowledge of the true end and purpose of life and folly is the absence of it [ECWB]. The negative μή 'not' is not subjective, but is due to the implied participle ὤν 'being' in this clause: 'not as being unwise' [Lns].

2. This negative clause explains πῶς 'how' and therefore, like it, is dependent upon the imperative βλέπετε 'watch' [EGT, ICC]: watch carefully, therefore, how you walk, that is, not as unwise, but as wise. The subjective negative particle μή 'not' is particularly in point because the whole sentence is dependent upon the imperative βλέπετε 'watch' [EGT, ICC]. The antithetic parallelism of this negative clause places the nature of the walk, that is to be consistently followed, in a strong light [EGT].

3. This negative clause is dependent upon the implied command μὴ περιπατεῖτε 'walk not' [We]: Watch carefully, therefore, how you walk. Walk not as unwise, but as wise. The negative construction of this clause is determined by the implied command [We].

5:16 buying-up/redeeming[a] the time/opportunity,[b] because the days are evil.

LEXICON—a. pres. mid. participle of ἐξαγοράζω (LN 37.131) (BAGD 2. p. 271) or ἐξαγοράζομαι (LN 65.42, **68.73**): 'to buy up' [El, Lns, NIC, We], 'to buy out' [LN (65.42)], 'to pay a price' [LN (37.131)], 'to buy back' [MM], 'to redeem' [AB, LN (37.131, 68.73), Rob; KJV] 'to make the most of' [BAGD, NTC, WBC; NAB, NASB, NIV, NRSV], 'to make the best of' [NJB], 'to make full use of' [TNT], 'to use to the full' [REB], 'to make good use of' [LN (65.42); TEV], 'to take advantage of' [LN (65.42)]. It means 'to buy off' claims against something so as to satisfy the claims [BAGD], to cause the release or freedom of someone by something which is costly to the individual effecting the release [LN (37.131)]. 'Redeeming the time' is an idiom meaning to do everything with urgency [LN (68.73)] or to take full advantage of any opportunity [LN (65.42, 68.73)]. The verb means 'to purchase'; 'to buy up' from the power or possession of any one; and then 'to redeem', 'to set free'. Here in this clause it means to rescue or recover our time from waste and improve it for great and important purposes [Ba]. The middle voice of the verb gives it a reflexive meaning [Alf, Ea, EGT, El], intimating that the purchase is for one's own personal benefit [Ea, EGT, El, LJ, My].

b. καιρός (LN 22.45, 65.42, **68.73**) (BAGD 2. p. 395): 'time' [AB, BAGD, Rob, WBC; KJV, NASB, NRSV, TNT], 'present time' [NJB], 'opportunity' [BAGD, El, LN (22.45), Lns, NTC, We], 'every opportunity' [LN (65.42, 68.73); NIV, TEV], 'present opportunity' [NIC; NAB, REB], 'every chance' [LN (65.42)], 'good occasion' [LN (22.45)]. This usage of the noun denotes a favorable opportunity or occasion in light of propitious circumstances [LN (22.45)]. The idea of 'fitting season' or 'opportunity' is especially associated with this word [MM]. It denotes the right, proper, or favorable time [BAGD].

QUESTION—What relationship is indicated by the participle ἐξαγοραζόμενοι 'buying up, redeeming'?

1. The metaphor involved is that of buying in the market place [Alf, Can, CBC, DNTT, Ea, EBC, ECWB, EGT, El, ICC, LJ, Lns, My, My-ed, NIC (probably), NTC (probably), Si, Si-ed, TD, WBC, We (probably), WeBC]. The figure is that of a merchant whose foresight enables him to use all things for his own purposes [Ea, EBC]. The καιρόν 'time/opportunity' is pictured as in some other's possession and you buy it [Ea, My, WeBC]. You make it your own by purchase [Ea, WeBC], giving in exchange those pleasures or that indolence which would have made you forego such a bargain [Ea], or the careful heed and effort that is expended on the walk [EGT, ICC, Lns, WeBC], the effort of doing of that for which the opportunity is fitted, being thought of as the purchase price [My, TD]. The meaning, then, is to make use of [Lns, My] or make the most of every opportunity [Ea, EBC]. As merchants carefully looking out for the best bargains, believers are to buy up these opportunities and make them their own [Alf, El, LJ]. As applied to opportunity in this context, the verb has only the connotations of making a sacrifice to obtain it, quickness in seizing it, and sagacity in using it to the utmost, whatever its nature and the appropriate response [ECWB]. As in the parallel passage in Col. 4:5, the clause has special reference to Christian witness in the world [Can, CBC, ICC, LJ, NCBC (in support of 3. below), NIC], though others think the reference is to the Christian's moral life in general [IB (in support of 3. below), Lns, My, NTC, WBC, WeBC], the total conduct of the Christian [WBC, WeBC]. The participle is modal, modifying the indicative verb περιπατεῖτε 'you walk' in 5:15 [Can], or the ὡς σοφοί 'as wise' clause [EGT, El, IB, LJ, My, NTC, WBC].

2. The metaphor involved is that of redemption [AB, Cal, MM, Rob]. The simple form of the verb, ἀγοράζω 'to buy' is used of the purchase of slaves and the similar use of the compound ἐξαγοράζω in Gal. 3:13, 4:5 suggests a meaning in Eph. 5:16 of buying back (at the expense of personal watchfulness and self denial) the present time, which is now being used for evil and godless purposes [MM]. Such corruption has

infected the age, and the devil appears to have obtained such tyrannical sway, that time cannot be dedicated to God without being in some way redeemed. The price of its redemption is the withdrawal from the endless allurements which would easily lead us astray, from the cares and pleasures of the world, and abandoning everything that would hinder us [Cal].
- 2.1 The participle modifies the imperative βλέπετε 'watch' in 5:15 and derives its imperative sense from it [AB]: watch carefully how you walk..., redeem the time!
- 2.2 The participle modifies the indicative verb περιπατεῖτε 'you walk' in 5:15 [Cal]. The apostle enforces his injunction to regulate their lives circumspectly as wise men by a consideration of the time [Cal].
- 3. No metaphor is intended and it means 'to make the most of' [IDB, MNTC, NCBC, St; NAB, NASB, NIV, NJB, NRSV], 'to make good use of' [TH; TEV], 'to avail oneself of', 'to improve for good' [Ho], 'to put to profit' [IB], or 'to use to the full' [LN (**68.73**), TNTC; REB, TNT]. The participle is modal, modifying ὡς σοφοί 'as wise' and showing the characteristic of this wisdom [Ho, NCBC, St, TNTC]. Christians are told to seize and use every opportunity for carrying on their Christian witness [TH, TNTC]. Christians are to put to profit the fleeting opportunities that occur [IB, TNTC]. The injunction here is in general reference to the Christian's moral life, while in Col. 4:5 it has specific reference to relations with non-Christians [IB]. The verb may have lost its connotation with marketing and simply mean 'to use to the full' with the prefix ἐξ- only having an intensifying force [TNTC].
- 4. It means 'to buy off' [BAGD (2. p. 271)]. While it could mean 'to make the most of the time', the earliest occurrence of this compound verb suggests a different meaning for this verb when it is used with the accusative, which is to buy off the claims of an injured man in order to satisfy the one who has been wronged and avoid punishment. As applied to the present passage, this would mean the evil days bring wrathful demands from God that must be satisfied [BAGD].

QUESTION—What is the relationship between καιρόν 'time/opportunity' here, and ἡμέραι 'days' in the next clause?
1. Καιρόν 'time' is coextensive with ἡμέραι 'days' [AB, Ba, Cal, DNTT, ISBE2 (probably), MNTC, Rob, WeBC; NJB].
2. Καιρόν 'opportunities' and ἡμέραι 'days' are not coextensive, but καιρόν refers to individual opportunities that occur on occasion during these ἡμέραι 'days' [Alf, BAGD (2. p. 395), Can, Ea, EBC, ECWB, EGT, El, Ho, IB, ICC, LJ, LN (**68.73**), Lns, My, NCBC, NIC, NTC, St, TD, TH, TNTC, WBC, We; NAB, NIV, REB, TEV].

QUESTION—What relationship is indicated by ὅτι 'because'?
It indicates the reason why the opportunity must be bought up [Ea, ECWB, El, Lns, NCBC]. It refers to the fact that moments for sowing on receptive soil in such evil days are so few that they must be seized upon when they

occur [ICC, Lns, NCBC, NIC]. Paul's meaning is not that the more wickedness there is, the more opportunity there is to buy up. Wickedness reduces the opportunities, but it is the reason why every opportunity that is still offered must be bought out completely [Lns]. Our lives are brief and present only so much opportunity [Lns, We]. The words may carry the implication that the days are under God's judgment and so 'the time is short' (1 Cor. 7:29) so that each opportunity must be grasped before it is too late [TNTC].

QUESTION—In what way are the days evil?

The clause contains a metonymy in which 'days' are put for what transpires in them [Bu]. Πονηραί 'evil' is used here in a moral sense [BAGD (1.b.β. p. 691), EBC, EGT, El, Ho, ICC, My, NCBC, TD] and not necessarily of hardship and distress [EBC, El, ICC], though that might accompany the moral evil [EBC]. It means viciously, actively wicked [Lns]. On the other hand, other commentators believe 'evil' here refers to the times of persecution that was shortly to fall upon the church [WeBC] or the trouble and distress which mankind, and particularly Israel, have to endure in the last days [IDB]. Everything around us tends to corrupt and mislead so that it is difficult for godly persons, as people walking along a very thorny path, to escape unhurt [Cal].

5:17 Because-of this (do) not be foolish,[a] but understand[b] what the will of-the Lord (is).

TEXT—Instead of the imperative συνίετε 'understand', some manuscripts read the present act. participle συνιέντες 'understanding'. Others read συνιόντες (present act. participle of σύνειμι 'to be with') 'being with'. GNT does not note these variant readings. The reading συνιέντες 'understanding' is taken by Cal, Ea, El, Ho, LJ, and KJV. The reading συνιόντες 'being with' is taken by only My (though he translates it as 'understanding').

LEXICON—a. ἄφρων (LN 32.52) (BAGD p. 127): 'foolish' [BAGD, **LN**, Lns, NIC, NTC, WBC, We; NASB, NIV, NRSV, REB], 'senseless' [AB, LN], 'unwise' [El, LN; KJV], 'ignorant' [BAGD], 'thoughtless' [NJB], 'stupid' [TNT]. This adjective is also translated as a noun: 'fool' [Rob; TEV]. It is also translated as a prepositional phrase: 'in ignorance' [NAB]. This adjective pertains to not using one's understanding, especially in practical matters [LN], being without reason, senseless, lacking moral intelligence [EGT], not seeing things in their true light [Ho], not making a correct use of one's understanding [Ho, Lns], and not estimating things according to their relative importance [Ho]. It is undisciplined behavior [DNTT]. It is a stronger word than ἄσοφοι 'unwise' in 5:15 [EBC, ECWB] because it alludes to stupid imprudence or senseless foolishness in action [EBC], moral stupidity in action [TNTC], lack of practical understanding or judgment [My, We], though one commentator states ἄσοφοι 'unwise' and ἄφρονες 'foolish' are practically the same in meaning [Lns] and others say ἄφρονες 'foolish' is only a variation on the preceding ἄσοφοι

'unwise' [WBC], including within it and particularizing the ἄσοφοι 'unwise' [TD].
   b. pres. indic. or impera. act. of συνίημι (LN 32.5, 32.26) (BAGD p. 790): 'to understand' [BAGD, El, LN (32.5, 32.26), Lns, NTC, Rob, WBC, We; KJV, NASB, NIV, NRSV, REB, TNT], 'to comprehend' [BAGD, LN (32.5)], 'to learn to comprehend' [AB], 'to be able to comprehend' [LN (32.26)], 'to discern' [NIC], 'to try to discern' [NAB], 'to try to find out' [TEV], 'to perceive' [LN (32.5)], 'to recognize' [NJB], 'to have insight into' [LN (32.5)], 'to gain an insight into' something [BAGD], 'to be intelligent' [LN (32.26)]. This verb denotes using one's understanding to arrive at insight [LN (32.5)] or it denotes being able to understand something and to evaluate it [LN (32.26)].

QUESTION—To what does τοῦτο 'this' refer?
1. This connects this verse to 5:15–16 [Alf, Ba, CBC, Ea, EBC, ECWB, EGT, El, Ho, ICC, LJ, My, NTC, Si, TH, TNTC, WBC, We]: because you must watch carefully how you walk and buy up your opportunities, you must not be foolish. Understanding the Lord's will for the present time and avoiding foolishness means the reader must recognize the times in which he lives and make the most of opportunities for good [WBC]. Διὰ τοῦτο 'because of this' resumes the exhortation of 5:15 to be wise [EBC, NTC] and to walk precisely [EGT, El, ICC, My, NTC].
2. This connects with the preceding clause only [Cal, Can, Lns, MNTC]: because the days are evil, you must not be foolish. The next verse contrasts with this in showing how the unregenerate seek to cheer themselves and others when they feel the days are evil, but which leads to folly and senselessness [Can].

QUESTION—What is meant by the negative imperative μὴ γίνεσθε ἄφρονες 'do not be foolish'?
1. The negative imperative μὴ γίνεσθε means 'do not be' [AB, Alf, Cal, Can, Ho, LJ, Lns, NIC, NTC, TH, WBC; all versions except NAB] or 'do not show yourselves' [ICC, We]: do not be foolish.
2. The negative imperative μὴ γίνεσθε means 'do not continue' [NAB]: do not continue in foolishness.
3. The negative imperative μὴ γίνεσθε means 'do not become' [Ea, EGT, El, My, TNTC]: do not become foolish. The γίνεσθε 'be' must not be reduced to the idea of ἐστε 'you are'. It means 'do (not) become' [EGT]. The apostle regards his readers as having begun, as Christians, to act with integrity and good sense. They are not to slip back into their former conduct of foolishness [EGT, TNTC].

QUESTION—What is the point of the clause introduced by ἀλλά 'but'?
This clause is at the heart of the writer's definition of wisdom, 'understanding what the will of the Lord is' [Ba, Cal, ECWB, MNTC, WBC], or how wisdom is to be obtained [Can]. If these readers are to buy up their opportunities, their earnest quest each day must be to have a practical understanding of what the will of the Lord is [TD, TNTC].

QUESTION—What is meant by τὸ θέλημα τοῦ κυρίου 'the will of the Lord'?

It is the same as δοκιμάζοντες τί ἐστιν εὐάρεστον τῷ κυρίῳ 'approving what is acceptable to the Lord' in 5:10 [IB, LJ, NCBC, NIC, Rob, TNTC]. Τὸ θέλημα τοῦ κυρίου 'the will of the Lord' refers to the will of Christ [EBC, EGT, Ho, Lns, My, NIC, NTC, TH, WBC, WeBC] or of God [AB, Cal, CBC, NCBC, St, TD, TNTC] and is used here as equivalent to the more common τὸ θέλημα τοῦ θεοῦ 'the will of God' [IB].

1. This refers to the general will of the Lord, particularly with regard to the salvation and sanctification, or holy living, of his people [Cal, Can, EBC, ECWB, Ho, ISBE2, LJ, Lns, NIC, NTC, TNTC]. It means to know his purpose towards us and towards the world and, therefore, to know the real purpose of our life [ECWB].
2. This refers to the particular will of the Lord in given circumstances [CBC, Ea, MNTC, Si, St, TD, WBC, We]. Because of the crucial importance of the times in which they were living, these readers must keep all their senses alert so they will be able to know on every occasion what God would have them do [MNTC, WBC]. This is directed particularly at how an opportunity may be used in the most sensible and positive way for God [CBC, Ea].
3. This refers to both the general and specific will of the Lord [AB, WeBC]. This refers to the will of Christ for man and the world, with the specific and individual will of God always being understood in relation to his general and corporate will [WeBC]. This is accomplished by acts of learning and doing God's will in which the total life of man is involved, as is shown in Paul's use of the verb δοκιμάζω 'to prove, to approve' in contexts treating this subject [AB].

DISCOURSE UNIT: 5:18–6:9 [LJ]. The topic is life in the Spirit in marriage, home, and work.

DISCOURSE UNIT: 5:18–21 [LJ, St]. The topic is new life in the Spirit [LJ], the fullness of the Holy Spirit [St].

DISCOURSE UNIT: 5:18–20 [AB, Ba, My]. The topic is an injunction to be filled with the Spirit [My], an injunction against the misuse of wine and exhortations to be filled with the Spirit and to worship God with songs of praise and thanksgiving [Ba]. This unit serves to sum up the preceding subsections [AB].

5:18 And (do) not get-drunk[a] with wine, in[b] which is debauchery,[c]

LEXICON—a. pres. pass. impera. of μεθύσκω (μεθύσκομαι LN **88.285**) (BAGD p. 499): 'to get drunk' [AB, BAGD, **LN**, NTC, WBC; NASB, NIV, NJB, NRSV], 'to be drunk' [Lns, Rob; KJV], 'to be drunken' [We], 'to be made drunk' [El], 'to be intoxicated' [NIC], 'to become intoxicated' [BAGD, LN]. The negative imperative μὴ μεθύσκεσθε 'do not get drunk' is translated 'avoid getting drunk' [NAB]. The clause μὴ μεθύσκεσθε οἴνῳ 'do not get drunk with wine' is translated 'do not give way to drunkenness' [REB], 'give up drinking too much' [TNT]. The present tense implies giving up a bad habit [TNT (note)].

b. ἐν with dative object (LN 89.26, 89.141): 'in' [LN (89.141)], 'of' [LN (89.141)], 'consisting of' [LN (89.141)], 'because of, on account of, by reason of' [LN (89.26)]. The phrase ἐν ᾧ 'in which' is translated 'that' [AB], 'wherein' [El, Lns, Rob, We; KJV]. The words ἐν ᾧ ἐστιν 'in which is' is translated 'for with that comes' [NIC], 'which is associated with' [NTC], 'leading to' [WBC], 'that leads to' [NAB], 'which leads to' [NIV], 'for that is' [NASB, NRSV]. The clause ἐν ᾧ ἐστιν ἀσωτία 'in which is debauchery' is translated 'this is simply dissipation' [NJB], 'the ruin that goes with it' [REB], 'which will only ruin you' [TEV], 'you will ruin your whole lives' [TNT].

c. ἀσωτία (LN **88.96**) (BAGD p. 119): 'debauchery' [BAGD; NAB, NIV, NRSV], 'dissipation' [BAGD, NIC, WBC; NASB, NJB], 'dissoluteness' [El, Lns], 'profligacy' [AB, BAGD], 'excess' [Rob; KJV], 'reckless deeds' [**LN**], 'senseless deeds, recklessness' [LN], 'unrestrained living' [NTC], 'riot' [We], 'ruin' [REB]. This noun is also translated as a verb: 'to ruin' [TEV, TNT].

QUESTION—What relationship is indicated by καί 'and'?

It indicates a transition from something general to a particular instance [AB, Alf, Ea, EBC, ECWB, EGT, El, Ho, ICC, Lns, My, NTC, TNTC, We], the injunction it introduces thus becomes climactic [Ea] or prominent [TNTC]. It introduces the final negative imperative—positive imperative contrast in the series which leads into the chain of participles, all of which are subordinate to and give the consequences of the second half of this verse (the πληροῦσθε ἐν πνεύματι 'be filled with the Spirit') [WBC]. From the general idea of reckless levity, Paul passes on to the special sin of drunkenness [ECWB]. The connection seems to be that after the injunction in the preceding verse, given in the form of an antithesis, μὴ γίνεσθε ἄφρονες, ἀλλὰ συνίετε κ.τ.λ. 'do not be foolish, but understand, etc.', the apostle proceeds to give one prominent instance [Alf, My], retaining the same antithetical form [Alf].

QUESTION—What is the reason for the citation of drunkenness here as a vice to be avoided?

Drunkenness is not introduced only as a foil for spiritual exhilaration. It is introduced as one concrete example of worldly folly in wicked days. It is a sample of how fools cause themselves to be utterly incapable of wisdom, sound judgment, and real understanding [Lns]. The injunction μὴ μεθύσκεσθε οἴνῳ 'do not get drunk with wine' condemns excessive and immoderate drinking of every description [Ba, Cal, Lns, WeBC]; it is not restricted to wine [Ba]. Wine here, as the most common drink of the times [Ea, Lns], is named as the means of intoxication [Ea, HG, Lns, Tu]. Drunkenness was a problem to which some of these saints were exposed, both as to their personal habits [AB, Ba, Can, Ea, EBC, HG, ISBE, Mou, My-ed, NCBC, NTC, Si, TNTC, Tu] and, possibly, as to the religious rites which were prevalent in the region [AB, Ba, DNTT, Ea, ECWB, IB, MNTC, NTC, Si, TD, TH]. Drunkenness is introduced for the sake of its antithesis πληροῦσθε ἐν πνεύματι 'be filled with/in the Spirit/spirit' [LJ, NIC, St] and because of the link in the context of the basic contrast between folly and wisdom [WBC, WeBC], and behind that, of darkness and light [WBC]. It continues the contrast drawn in the first part of this section between the unwise conduct of unbelievers and the wise conduct of believers [WBC, WeBC]. Drunkenness is introduced to form a parallel, both of similarity and contrast [LJ, St], of the difference between the old life and the new one. The reason for the strange and surprising introduction of drunkenness is that (1) nothing was more characteristic of the gentile world in our Lord and Paul's time than drunkenness and its accompanying vices, and (2) to provide a vehicle to show, by means of both the similarities and the contrasts with drunkenness, what the characteristic quality of the new life under the influence of the Spirit of God was like [LJ]. As to the similarity, in both drunkenness and life in the Spirit, the life is under the control of or 'filled' by an agent to which the person yields himself [LJ, WBC]. Both also lead to a sense of exhilaration. As to the differences, drunkenness, while it excites, at the same time really depresses the faculties and takes a person's control of his life from him [LJ, St, WeBC], leading to an addiction which ends in the waste, misery, and destruction of the life (ἐν ᾧ ἐστιν ἀσωτία 'in which is debauchery') [LJ, WeBC]. Life filled with the Spirit, on the other hand, enhances a person's faculties [LJ, NIC, St, WBC] to understand Christ's will [WBC], gives him the power to control his appetites [LJ, St], and brings true joy (5:19–20) [LJ] together with other qualities of the fruit of the Spirit (Gal. 5:22–23) [LJ, St].

QUESTION—What is the significance of the present tenses in the verbs μεθύσκεσθε 'to get drunk' and πληροῦσθε 'to be filled'?
1. These present tenses denote continuous actions or states of being [Can, EBC, EGT, El, HG, IB, ICC, LJ, Mou, TNTC, Tu, WBC]. Some regard the negative imperative μὴ μεθύσκεσθε 'do not get drunk' as a command to cease an activity already being engaged in [HG, TH, Tu; TNT]. In general, μή 'not' with the present imperative forbids what one is already doing [HG, Mou, Tu]. See material below on πληροῦσθε ἐν πνεύματι 'be filled with the Spirit/spirit' for supporting statements on that verb.
2. These present tenses are aorist presents [Lns]. The verbs simply state what to shun and what to do [Lns].

QUESTION—What relationship is indicated by the clause ἐν ᾧ ἐστιν ἀσωτία 'in which is debauchery'?
This clause states the *misuse* of wine [AB, Alf, DNTT, ECWB, EGT, ISBE, Lns, NTC, TD]. It does not teach total abstinence from it [AB, Alf, DNTT, ECWB, ISBE, LJ, Lns, NTC, TNTC] (*contra* Ba, WeBC). The antecedent of ᾧ 'which' is not οἴνῳ 'wine' but the whole negative injunction [Ea, EGT, ICC, Lns, My, TH].

1. This clause is a definition or explanation of the preceding negative injunction [AB, Alf, Can, ECWB, LJ, NCBC; NASB, NJB, NRSV]. This passage is defining drunkenness as a waste [AB, ECWB, LJ]. Drunkenness is both the effect and the cause of debauchery [ECWB].
2. This clause states the result of drunkenness [Ba, EBC, ECWB, NIC, NTC, Rob, St, TH, WBC; NAB, NIV] or that which accompanies it [NIC, NTC; REB]. Drunkenness induces debauchery [EBC, NTC]. Since this follows the use of wine, it is not proper that Christians should be in the habit of drinking it [Ba].
3. This clause is a deterring remark [My; TEV, TNT], giving the specific objection to drunkenness [TNTC] and giving the reason to abstain from intoxicants [WeBC].

QUESTION—What is meant by ἀσωτία 'debauchery'?

The noun ἀσωτία 'debauchery' was rarely used, but it could denote the intemperate spending that licentious behavior entailed [AB]. Since spendthrifts are self-indulgent and reckless [Alf, ECWB], the noun took on the meaning of 'dissoluteness, dissipation, debauchery [Alf, EBC], profligacy' [Alf, EBC, ECWB]. In classical Greek it described extravagant squandering, both of money and of the physical appetites [EBC]. It presents drunkenness as a waste [AB, LJ, TNTC]. The noun stands for all that is implied in a wanton and dissolute life [Cal, LJ]. It describes the diminished sense of responsibility which accompanies this life style [NCBC], drunkards very quickly throwing off every restraint of modesty or shame [Cal, NCBC]. It denotes one who is given up to a destructive course of life [Ho, IB, LJ], 'reckless, wild, disorderly, unrestrained living' [ISBE2, NTC, TD, TH].

but be-filled with/in[a] (the) Spirit/spirit,[b]

LEXICON—a. ἐν with dative object (LN 89.5, 89.76, 90.6): 'with' [AB, El, NIC, NTC, Rob, WBC; all versions except REB, TNT], 'in' [LN (89.5), Lns, We], not explicit [REB, TNT], 'with regard to' [LN (89.5)], 'by means of, through' [LN (89.76)], 'by' [LN (89.76, 90.6)].

b. πνεῦμα (LN 12.18, 26.9) (BAGD 5.d.β. p. 677): 'Spirit' [AB, BAGD, El, LN (12.18), NIC, NTC, Rob, WBC; all versions except REB], 'Holy Spirit' [REB], 'spirit' [LN (26.9), Lns, We], 'inner being' [LN (26.9)]. The imperative clause πληροῦσθε ἐν πνεύματι 'be filled with/in the Spirit/ spirit' is translated 'let the (Holy) Spirit fill you' [REB, TNT].

QUESTION—What is meant by this command?

1. Πνεύματι 'Spirit' refers to the Holy Spirit of God [AB, Alf, BAGD, Cal, Can, CBC, DNTT, Ea, EBC, EGT, El, Ho, ISBE2, LJ, MNTC, Mo, My, NCBC, NIC, NTC, Rob, Si, St, TD, TNTC, WBC, WeBC; all versions], or his operations [Bu, ISBE] and gifts [Bu]. This is the Spirit of God dwelling in, and informing, the man's own spirit [Alf]. It means to 'find your overflow of soul in the rapture which the Spirit gives' [MNTC], or 'let your fullness be that which comes through the Spirit' [Rob]. When a person is in this state he is truly lifted out of himself [MNTC], he is in that

higher mood in which he can commune with God and understand his will [MNTC, NTC]. Others infer this filling with the Spirit is another way of describing the reception of the Spirit [NCBC] or the baptism of the Spirit [WeBC]. Yet Paul is not for a moment implying that the Spirit is a substance with which men can fill their personalities as they do their bodies with wine [EBC, LJ, NIC, WeBC]. Such a supposed implication ignores the personality of the Spirit. Rather the idea is that we are to be filled with the influence of a living Person [LJ, NIC, WeBC]. This clause is unusual in form, in that the verb πληροῦσθε 'be filled' is passive and is followed by the preposition ἐν 'in' with the dative object [Ea, EBC] when the meaning of the passive verb is obviously 'to be filled' rather than 'to be made complete' [EBC]. This may indicate that ἐν πνεύματι 'in (the) Spirit' indicates the element [Ea] or sphere [EBC] of the filling and not the instrument [Ea, EBC] (*contra* EGT, El, My, NIC, Rob who call it instrumental, though El, NTC, Rob, TH, and WBC concede ἐν 'in' has the meanings of both 'in' and 'by', since the fullness which comes through the Spirit and the fullness which consists of being full of the Spirit [Rob, TH] is hard to distinguish in this clause, the Spirit being at once both the inspirer and the inspiration [Rob]). The implied comparison is with men who sought to fill themselves with wine [Ea, EBC, LJ, My-ed] and so stimulate themselves away from their sense of unhappiness or sorrow of heart [Ea, ECWB, My-ed, NCBC, NTC]. Some think the peculiar form of πληροῦσθε ἐν πνεύματι 'be filled with (the) Spirit' may have been used to indicate that the Spirit is not only to be an influence within us, but we are to be in him also [Alf, Can, DNTT, Ea], but another says this distinction is a needless refinement [EGT]. The present tense of the imperative verb indicates this does not refer to a once-for-all reception of the Spirit, but rather points to a continuous [EBC, LJ, St, TNTC, WBC] or a repeated [TNTC] experience.

1.1 This clause contrasts with the clause μὴ μεθύσκεσθε οἴνῳ 'do not get drunk with wine' [Cal, Can, CBC, Ea, EBC, ECWB, EGT, El, Ho, IB, ICC, ISBE2, LJ, My, NCBC, St, TNTC, WBC, WeBC]. The nouns πνεύματι 'Spirit' and οἴνῳ 'wine' are not simply contrasted, but the clauses are placed in antithesis to each other [Ea, EGT, My]. The contrast is not between the *instruments* of exhilaration but between the *states*, one due to wine, the other to the inspiration and enlightenment of the Spirit [EGT, El, LJ, My]. The writer presents, as the opposite of intoxication and exhilaration with drink, the holy state of being filled and exhilarated with the Spirit of God [Cal, Can, LJ, St, WBC]. The fact that πληροῦσθε ἐν πνεύματι 'be filled with the Spirit' contrasts with μὴ μεθύσκεσθε οἴνῳ 'do not get drunk with wine' does not justify a conclusion that when we are filled with the Spirit we lose control of ourselves just as when we are drunk. After all, the final quality of the fruit of the Spirit in Gal. 5:22–23 is ἐγκράτεια 'self control' [St].

1.2 This clause contrasts the imperative πληροῦσθε 'be filled' with the negative imperative μὴ μεθύσκεσθε 'do not be drunk' and ἐν πνεύματι 'with the Spirit' with οἴνῳ 'with wine' [AB, Ba, NIC, NTC]. This clause was added to contrast with the preceding clause, both as to the effects of drunkenness and inspiration, and as to the filling materials themselves [AB].

1.3 This clause contrasts the imperative πληροῦσθε 'be filled' with the negative imperative clause μὴ μεθύσκεσθε οἴνῳ 'do not become drunk with wine' [Alf], and ἐν πνεύματι 'in the Spirit' with ἐν ᾧ ἐστιν ἀσωτία 'in which is debauchery' [Alf, Si, TD]. Πληροῦσθε 'be filled' is contrasted with μὴ μεθύσκεσθε οἴνῳ 'do not become drunk with wine', not with μὴ μεθύσκεσθε 'do not be drunk' alone. The point of the contrast is to place the joy which comes from being filled with the Spirit, and the expression of this joy through Christian hymns and thanksgiving (5:19), in contrast with the joy of debauchery and its expression in the singing of drunken songs [Alf]. In contrast with the profligacy and all its vicious concomitants, the apostle contrasts the picture of a Pentecostal infilling of the Holy Spirit, infinitely purer than the wasteful indulgence denoted by ἀσωτία 'debauchery' and as salutary as it was noxious [Si].

2. Πνεύματι 'spirit' refers to the spiritual component of man's nonmaterial makeup and the clause contrasts with the clause μὴ μεθύσκεσθε οἴνῳ 'do not get drunk with wine' [IB, ICC, Lns, We]. The imperative clause πληροῦσθε ἐν πνεύματι 'be filled in spirit' means 'let the utmost capacities of your highest faculty be rightly satisfied' so that its special powers may be brought into play. The passage assumes that only the Spirit of God can satisfy the spirit of man. In its contrast with the preceding negative imperative, this clause expresses, in the most striking way, the necessity of carefully guarding complete self-control in the times when men are a state of highest exaltation. The real contrast to ἐν πνεύματι 'in spirit' is the unstated ἐν σαρκί 'in the flesh' [We]. Paul would not combine wine that is used for the purpose of getting drunk with the Holy Spirit. The expression πληροῦσθε ἐν πνεύματι 'be filled in spirit' refers to the richness and abundance of spiritual life in our own spirits [Lns]. That this is due to the Holy Spirit is self-evident [Lns]. The contrast is not between the *instruments* of exhilaration but between the *states*, one due to wine, the other to the progressive fulfillment of the spiritual life [IB, ICC]. The contrast is not between the nouns, οἴνῳ 'wine' and πνεύματι 'in spirit', but between the verbs and, for this reason, both the verbs in the contrasting clauses are placed forward for emphasis. There is no stated contrast to οἴνῳ 'wine', this must be inferred from the context, and that is shown to be spiritual joy and thankfulness expressed in psalms, hymns, etc. [Lns]. The signification of the verb πληροῦσθε 'be filled' is middle voice because obviously those who are to be filled must cooperate in the process. But the use of ἐν 'in' with this

verb to express the content with which a thing is to be filled is without any corroborating example; the meaning of ἐν is not suitable to the idea of 'filled with'. Where the material is only regarded as the means of making full, it might conceivably be spoken of as the instrument but, in this case, the agent must be expressed which would be quite inappropriate to the Holy Spirit. For these reasons πνεύματι is best interpreted as referring to the spiritual part of man [ICC].

5:19 speaking to-yourselves/one-another in psalms^a and hymns^b and spiritual songs,^c

TEXT—Some manuscripts omit πνευματικαῖς 'spiritual' after ᾠδαῖς 'songs'. GNT assigns the reading ᾠδαῖς πνευματικαῖς 'spiritual/Spirit-inspired songs' a B rating, indicating that this reading is almost certain. Only REB supports the variant reading which omits πνευματικαῖς 'spiritual'.

LEXICON—a. ψαλμός (LN 33.112) (BAGD 2. p. 891): 'psalm' [AB, BAGD, El, LN, Lns, MM, NIC, NTC, Rob, WBC, We; all versions], 'song of praise' [BAGD, LN]. This refers here to Christian songs of praise rather than to the OT Psalms [BAGD]. This denotes a song or psalm sung to the accompaniment of a harp [MM].
  b. ὕμνος (LN **33.114**) (BAGD p. 836): 'hymn' [AB, BAGD, El, **LN**, Lns, NIC, NTC, Rob, WBC, We; all versions], 'song of praise' [BAGD]. This denotes a song having religious content [LN].
  c. ᾠδή (LN 33.110) (BAGD p. 895): 'song' [AB, BAGD, El, LN, MM, NIC, NTC, Rob, WBC, We; all versions], 'ode' [Lns]. This denotes a particular melodic pattern having a verbal content [LN]. In early Christian literature this refers only to sacred songs, to songs of praise to God [BAGD].

QUESTION—What is the implied social setting of this verse?
  This may refer to Christian worship services [AB, Alf (probably), Ba, CBC, Ea, EBC, ECWB, Ho, ISBE2, Lns, MNTC, NCBC, NIC, St, WBC] (involving small groups of people rather than large congregations [NCBC]), Christian social meetings in general [Can, Rob], or both [El, We]. Some specify the ancient Christian love-suppers [Rob], or fellowship gatherings [WeBC] which, for believers, took the place of the Greek public feasts, from which Christians would be excluded by reason of the idolatrous rites accompanying those feasts [Rob]. Some state that it refers to daily Christian intercourse [EGT, IB, ISBE]. The first participle implies a great degree of congregational participation [NCBC].

QUESTION—What relationship is indicated by the participle λαλοῦντες 'speaking'?
  This is the first of a series of participles which qualify the preceding imperative clause μὴ μεθύσκεσθε οἴνῳ κ.τ.λ. 'be not drunk with wine, etc.' [Alf] or, more specifically, πληροῦσθε ἐν πνεύματι 'be filled with the spirit' [Ea, EBC, El, Ho, My, TH, WBC, We], presenting the results of that filling [Bu, Cal, CBC, Ea, EBC, ECWB, EGT, El, Ho, Lns, My, NTC, WBC]. Because the participles modify the subject of that imperative [Lns] they show, as

well, the condition of those who are so filled [EBC, EGT, Lns, MNTC], or the test or measure of being so filled [Bu]. The participles take on an imperative sense [Ba, EBC, Lns, NTC, TH] from their attachment to the imperative πληροῦσθε 'be filled' [EBC, Lns, NTC]. It is noticeable that each of these participles is connected with the expression of praise [EBC].

QUESTION—What is meant by λαλοῦντες 'speaking'?
1. The verb means 'to speak' or 'to recite' [Can, NTC, TH; TEV]. It may refer to the recital of the words of psalms, hymns, and spiritual songs [TH; TEV], though another says that this was not to be the mere recital of memorized words but the communication of thanksgiving with feeling [NTC].
2. The verb indicates more than conversational speech; it may indicate singing or congregational antiphonal speech [AB, Ea, EBC, Ho, IB, Lns, MNTC, My, NIC, Si-ed, St, TD]. This verb is not confined to normal speaking, but covers utterances of any kind so that it is applicable to the medium of the types of songs mentioned in this clause [EBC]. Paul has in mind a Christian worship service in which one believer utters a lyrical song on some theme of the Christian life and is then answered in turn, in like fashion, by another [MNTC]. It may refer to speaking antiphonally in chorus [AB, Ea, ECWB, My, NIC, Si-ed, St, TD, WBC, We].

QUESTION—What is meant by the pronoun ἑαυτοῖς 'yourselves/one another'?
1. This means 'to yourselves' [Bu, Lns, Rob; KJV]: speaking to yourselves. This is to be done 'to yourselves', 'in your hearts', 'admonishing yourselves' as is evident from the parallel passage in Col. 3:16. The pronoun is reflexive, 'for your own sakes' [Lns]. It is not equivalent to ἀλλήλοις 'to one another' [Bu, Lns], so that we are not commanded to listen to the songs of another or others, however exquisite it may be, but are ourselves to sing as worshippers [Bu].
2. This means 'among yourselves' [Ba, Cal, Ea, TH; NJB, NRSV] or 'to one another' [AB, Alf, Can, ECWB, EGT, El, Ho, ICC, MNTC, My, NCBC, NIC, NTC, St, TD, TNTC, WBC; NAB, NASB, NIV, REB, TEV, TNT]: speaking to one another. The pronoun is used in a reciprocal sense [EGT, TD] and is used in place of ἀλλήλοις 'one another' [Ea, EGT, El, HG, Ho, MNTC, TNTC, Tu]. Speaking among yourselves means endeavoring to edify one another [Ba, NCBC], to promote purity of heart by songs of praise [Ba]. The pronoun indicates the singer's private pleasure alone is not the purpose of the singing [AB]. With the common punctuation of these clauses, the pronoun does not run smoothly, for men do not speak to one another in psalms and hymns, but to God. With another punctuation (see the next Question, interpretation 2), however, the pronoun naturally refers to 'one another' [Can].

QUESTION—What relationship is indicated by the preposition ἐν 'in'?
1. This connects the words ψαλμοῖς 'psalms', ὕμνοις 'hymns' and ᾠδαῖς πνευματικαῖς 'spiritual songs' with the participle λαλοῦντες 'speaking' [AB, Alf, Ba, BAGD, Bu, Cal, Ea, EBC, ECWB, EGT, El, Ho, ICC, LN

(12.21, 33.114), Lns, MNTC, My, NCBC, NIC, NTC, Rob, Si-ed, St, TH, TNTC, WBC, We, WeBC; all versions]. This has the function of more closely defining the speaking [BAGD (2.ε. p. 463)].

2. This connects the words ψαλμοῖς 'psalms', ὕμνοις 'hymns' and ᾠδαῖς πνευματικαῖς 'spiritual songs' with the following participle ᾄδοντες 'singing' [Can]. Connecting these words with the participle ᾄδοντες 'singing' is more natural because these words denoting songs go more naturally with singing than with speaking. The punctuation of the relevant clauses would then be: 'but be filled with the Spirit, speaking to one another in psalms and hymns and spiritual songs singing; and making melody in your heart to the Lord. Thus the sequences of thought are first to the walk of the Christians as pervaded by the Spirit, then to the expression of their feelings through song, and then to the accompanying melody of heart [Can].

QUESTION—What is the relationship of the three synonymous nouns ψαλμοῖς 'psalms', ὕμνοις 'hymns' and ᾠδαῖς 'songs'?

1. These are synonymous repetitions [EGT, El, ISBE, My, NCBC, NIC, Si-ed, TD, WBC] and are meant to have a cumulative effect [EGT, My, WBC] characteristic of urgent and animated discourse [My]. In NT times, at least, they were used indiscriminately [ISBE]. The three nouns are used together for rhetorical force [EGT, WBC] and it is futile or precarious to build an interpretation upon supposed differences between them [EGT, NCBC, NIC, Si-ed, WBC].

2. Each noun denotes a particular type of song [Alf, Ba, Bu, Cal, Can, CBC, Ea, EBC, ECWB, Ho, ICC, IDB, ISBE, Lns, NTC, Rob, St, TNTC, WeBC]. They are not to be confined strictly to their derivational meanings [Alf, Ea, Ho, IDB, NTC].

    2.1 The noun ψαλμοῖς 'psalms' properly refers to sacred songs which were accompanied by musical instruments [Alf, Bu, Ea, ECWB, Ho, ICC, Rob, St, TNTC] though some indicate that, in the NT and the early Church, musical instruments probably were no longer used [Bu, Ea]. The word is not confined to designating just the OT Psalms [Alf, BAGD, Ea, Ho, ISBE, NTC, TNTC (*contra* Ba, Bu, Can, CBC, EBC, ECWB, Lns, TH, WeBC)] though mainly this would be the case [NTC]. For Jews in these congregations at Ephesus, the OT Psalms would be the natural reference [Ea].

    2.2 The noun ὕμνοις 'hymns' denotes songs sung in praise of God [Ba, Bu, Can, Ea, EBC, ECWB, Ho, ICC, ISBE2, LN, Lns, NTC, Rob, TH]. Some differentiate this noun from ψαλμοῖς 'psalms' by stating that, though it is difficult to determine precisely the difference between the terms [Ba, Cal], 'hymns' (in both pagan and Christian usage) were songs sung in honor of deity [Ba, Bu, Can, Ea, EBC, ECWB, Ho, ICC, LN, Lns, NTC, TNTC], while ψαλμοῖς 'psalms' referred mainly to the Psalms of the OT [Ba, Bu, Can, EBC, ECWB, Lns, NTC], or ὕμνοις 'hymns' and ᾠδαῖς πνευματικαῖς 'spiritual songs' are synonymous, designating Christian compositions generally, while ψαλμοῖς 'psalms' were those from the OT Psalter [CBC, TH] or similar in composition [TNTC]. After Christians adopted the use of the noun [Bu], it was confined strictly to denote songs of praise and glory *directly addressed to God* [Bu, Can, NTC].

    2.3 The noun ᾠδαῖς 'songs' properly referred in secular literature to all lyrical poetry [Alf, ECWB, ICC, ISBE]. It is a more general term than the preceding nouns [Can, Ea, ECWB, ISBE, Lns, Rob], may have the connotation of improvisation and marks the natural outburst of the excited heart [Ea]. The noun ᾠδαῖς 'songs' refers to spiritual songs which dwelt on themes other than direct praise to God or Christ [NTC]. Others say it refers to sacred songs of praise to God [BAGD, ECWB], perhaps spontaneously composed [ECWB, TH] and sung by the composer only. It would be more varied and elaborate than the other two [ECWB]. Another states that spiritual songs were more suited to personal, private, or family use in worship, though they were used also in public worship [ISBE].

QUESTION—What is meant by πνευματικαῖς 'spiritual' and to what is it connected?

    1. This adjective modifies ᾠδαῖς 'songs' [AB, Alf, Ba, BAGD (2.β. p. 679), Bu, Cal, Can, DNTT, Ea, EBC, ECWB, EGT, El, Ho, ISBE, LN (12.21), Lns, MNTC, My, NIC, NTC, Rob, Si, Si-ed, St, TD, TH; all versions except REB]. It modifies ᾠδαῖς 'songs' to distinguish it from profane heathen ᾠδαῖς 'songs' [Bu, Cal, Can, EBC, EGT, Ho (probably), Lns, My, Rob]. The nouns ψαλμοῖς 'psalms' and ὕμνοις 'hymns' were already recognized as denoting consecrated music and needed no such designation [Ea, Lns]. It designates the song as derived from or inspired by the Spirit [Alf, DNTT, Ea, EBC, EGT, El, ISBE, LN, My, NIC, TD, TH; NAB, NJB] as indicated by the last clause of the previous verse [El]. Some say it also [Ea, ISBE, LN, TD], or only, means 'spiritual' [BAGD (2.β. p. 679), Bu, Can, Ho, NTC, Rob, St; KJV, NASB, NIV, NRSV, TNT]. If this be the case, then it would designate the songs as sacred or religious [Can, EGT, ISBE, ISBE2, LN, TD; TEV], as expressing spiritual thoughts and feelings [Ho], or as songs of the spiritual life [MNTC]. It affects the whole passage by presenting the spiritual counterpart of worldly revelry, in which jesting, wine, song, and music were the sources of enjoyment [Cal, Can, Lns, My, Si, TD].

    2. This adjective modifies all three of the preceding nouns [ICC, WBC]. While the adjective agrees in gender only with the ᾠδαῖς 'songs', the fact of the synonymity of these three nouns makes it likely that the adjective actually goes with all three. The adjective denotes inspiration from the Spirit but this does not necessarily mean spontaneity [WBC].

singing[a] and making-melody[b] in-your heart to-the Lord,

LEXICON—a. pres. act. participle of ᾄδω (LN 33.109) (BAGD p. 19): 'to sing' [BAGD, El, LN, Lns, NIC, NTC, Rob, WBC, We; KJV, NASB, NJB, NRSV]. This participle is also translated as an imperative: 'sing' [AB; NIV, REB, TNT] and is also conjoined with the following ψάλλοντες 'making/playing music/melody' and translated as an imperative clause: 'sing praise' [NAB], 'sing hymns and psalms' [TEV]. This verb denotes the action of uttering words in a melodic pattern [LN].

b. pres. act. participle of ψάλλω (LN 33.111) (BAGD p. 891): 'to make melody' [BAGD, El, NIC, NTC, Rob, We; KJV, NASB, NRSV], 'to make music' [WBC], 'to play' [Lns], 'to chant' [NJB], 'to sing, to sing praise(s)' [BAGD, LN], 'to sing a psalm, to sing a song of praise' [LN], 'to sing a hymn' [MM]. This participle is also translated as an imperative: 'play' [AB], 'make music' [NIV, REB, TNT]. It is also conjoined with the preceding ᾄδοντες 'singing' and translated as an imperative: 'sing praise' [NAB], 'sing hymns and psalms' [TEV]. This verb carries the possible implication of accompanying songs of praise with musical instruments [LN]. The verb originally meant 'to pluck, to play' a stringed instrument, but after the time of Lucian, and in the LXX, the verb meant 'to sing', usually without musical accompaniment [BAGD]. It denotes making music in any way, whether playing an instrument, singing with instrumental accompaniment [Ho, Lns, NTC, St], or chanting [Ho]. It may be taken as a synonymous doublet with the preceding participle [AB, Ho, TD]. However, if they are to be distinguished from each other, then ψάλλοντες 'making melody' may have its original meaning of plucking a stringed instrument [AB, Ba, EGT] (in a figurative sense [TD]) and this verse may be interpreted as encouraging the use of musical instruments in corporate worship [AB].

QUESTION—What relationship is indicated by the two participles ᾄδοντες 'singing' and ψάλλοντες 'making melody'?

1. These two participles are coordinate with λαλοῦντες 'speaking' [Alf, Ea, EBC, ECWB, EGT, El, My, WBC (probably), We (probably), WeBC]. This clause specifies a second kind of praise [EGT, El, My], that of unvoiced praise [EGT, My] and inward worship, in addition to that specified by the λαλοῦντες κ.τ.λ. 'speaking, etc.' [EGT, El]. It refers to the inner music of the person's heart which accompanies audible praise [EBC, ECWB, EGT, El, We]. The participles correspond to the preceding nouns ψαλμοῖς 'psalms' and ὕμνοις 'hymns' [Alf, ECWB, WBC]. While the previous clause directed attention to the corporate and horizontal level, to ἑαυτοῖς 'one another', this clause is concerned with an individual and vertical dimension, τῇ καρδίᾳ ὑμῶν 'in your heart' and τῷ κυρίῳ 'to the Lord' [WBC].

2. These two participles are subordinate to λαλοῦντες 'speaking' [Ho, Lns, NTC, TH (probably)]. The participles define the kind of singing required

in λαλοῦντες ἑαυτοῖς ἐν ψαλμοῖς κ.τ.λ. 'speaking to one another in psalms, etc.' [Ho, Lns].

QUESTION—What is meant by τῇ καρδίᾳ ὑμῶν 'in your heart'?
1. The phrase denotes the place in which the singing is to be done [AB, Alf, Ba, Cal, Can, CBC, Ea, EBC, EGT, El, Ho, My, NIC, St; all versions except NAB, NASB, REB] or the source from which it springs [Cal, NTC, TD; REB]: singing in/from your heart. It qualifies the participle ψάλλοντες 'making melody/music', transforming it to denote the inner music of the heart [EBC, EGT, El], not necessarily audible expression [EBC], but not meaning silent singing either. What is meant is the engagement of the heart in the singing [TD]. It indicates that the heart is to be full of thanksgiving [CBC], or of such sentiments as are expressed in these songs [Cal, Can]. This phrase indicates that the mind and will of man, if not the whole man, is to be engaged in the worship of God in this form [AB, Ba].
2. This phrase denotes the manner in which the singing is to be done, 'heartily, enthusiastically' [MNTC, TH; NAB]: sing with all your hearts. Paul desires that this singing should correspond with heartfelt emotion [MNTC].
3. This phrase denotes the instrument with which the singing is to be done [Lns, NCBC; NASB]: sing with your heart. It contrasts with the mechanical instruments with which the singing and making music is to be done, the lips and the fingers. The singing and making music is to be done with the heart [Lns]. The outward singing is to be the expression of what is felt deeply in one's heart [NCBC].

QUESTION—To whom does τῷ κυρίῳ 'the Lord' refer?
This refers to Christ [AB, Alf, Ea, Ho, IB, My, NIC, Si-ed, TD, TH, WBC] or to God and Christ [Ba]. The end of this verse (τῷ κυρίῳ 'to the Lord') is balanced with the end of the next (τῷ θεῷ καὶ πατρί 'to the God and Father') [TD].

5:20 giving-thanks[a] always[b] for/on-behalf-of all-things/men in[c] (the) name[d] of-our Lord Jesus Christ to-the God and/even (the) Father.

LEXICON—a. pres. act. participle of εὐχαριστέω (LN 25.100, 33.349) (BAGD 2. p. 328): 'to give thanks' [BAGD, El, Lns, NIC, NTC, Rob, WBC, We; KJV, NASB, NIV, NJB, NRSV], 'to render, return thanks' [BAGD], 'to thank' [LN (33.349)], 'to be thankful, to be grateful' [LN (25.100)]. This participle is also translated as an imperative: 'give thanks' [AB; NAB, REB, TEV, TNT]. This verb denotes being thankful on the basis of some received benefit [LN (25.100)] or it denotes expressing gratitude for benefits or blessings [LN (33.349)].
b. πάντοτε (LN 67.88): 'always' [AB, El, LN, Lns, NTC, Rob, WBC, We; KJV, NAB, NASB, NIV, NJB, TEV, TNT], 'at all times' [LN, NIC; NRSV], 'on every occasion' [LN], 'every day' [REB].

EPHESIANS 5:20 471

    c. ἐν with dative object (LN 89.80, 89.119): 'in' [AB, El, LN (89.119), Lns, NIC, NTC, Rob, WBC, We; all versions], 'in union with, joined closely to' [LN (89.119)], 'while at the same time' [LN (89.80)].

    d. ὄνομα (LN 33.126, 58.22) (BAGD I.4.c.γ. p. 572): 'name' [AB, El, LN (33.126), Lns, NIC, NTC, Rob, WBC, We; all versions], 'category of, being of the type that' [LN (58.22)]. This noun designates a category or kind which is based upon an implied designation of a class of entities [LN (58.22)], (i.e., here, 'to give thanks under the category of people who belong to our Lord Jesus Christ'). With ἐν 'in', ὄνομα 'name', in reference to God or Christ, means in the great majority of occurrences 'with mention of the name', 'while naming', or 'while calling on the name' [BAGD].

QUESTION—How is this verse related to the context?

    1. This is connected to the imperative μὴ μεθύσκεσθε οἴνῳ κ.τ.λ. 'be not drunk with wine etc.' [Alf] or, more specifically, to πληροῦσθε ἐν πνεύματι 'be filled with the Spirit' in 5:18 [AB, DNTT, Ea, EBC, EGT, El, Ho, IB, My, NCBC, St, TD, WBC, WeBC]. It is a third, coordinate clause, giving another particular way in which being filled with the Spirit will find its expression [EBC, EGT, El, My]. It makes prominent [My] a special form of praise, an attitude of thanksgiving [EGT, My] which serves to prepare the way for the further duty to be expressed in the next verse [El]. It is connected with πληροῦσθε ἐν πνεύματι 'be filled with the Spirit' and gives a further description of its results and accompaniments [Ea]. The participle εὐχαριστοῦντες 'giving thanks' takes up 5:18ff. by way of summary [DNTT].

    2. This is more immediately connected to 5:19 [Ba, ECWB, Lns, NTC, We]. This indicates that the proper subject for psalms and hymns is thanksgiving and praise [Ba, ECWB]. It defines the singing and playing in another direction [Lns]. This verse gives the chief element in which the activities of the previous verse takes place [We], the previous verse being the means by which believers reveal their gratitude to God [NTC].

QUESTION—What is the significance of the words πάντοτε ὑπὲρ πάντων 'always for all things'?

These words form an emphatic juxtaposition [My]. It indicates that an attitude of constant thanksgiving is to be a basic and lasting characteristic of the Spirit-filled Christian [DNTT, NCBC, WeBC]. Christians will give thanks, not just sometimes for some things, but always for everything [WBC]. These words take this verse from its primary application to thanksgiving in public worship [DNTT, ISBE2, WBC] and extends it to the believers' whole lives [WBC]. These words sum up 'whatever you do in words or deeds, do it all in the name, etc.' of the parallel passage in Col. 3:17 [NIC].

QUESTION—What is meant by ὑπὲρ πάντων 'for all things'?

    1. Πάντων 'all things' is interpreted as neuter in gender, with its preposition ὑπέρ 'for' having a causal meaning, i.e., thanks is to be given for all

things generally [AB, Alf, Cal, Can, Ea, EBC, ECWB, EGT, El, Ho, IB, ICC, Lns, My, NCBC, NIC, Rob, Si, St, TH, TNTC, WeBC; all versions except NJB]: give thanks always for all things. The phrase relates to events rather than things [TH]. This is the cause of the gratitude expressed in the giving of thanks [Lns]. This is parallel to the ἐν παντί 'in all things' of 1 Thess. 5:18 [AB, ECWB].

- 1.1 It indicates thanks is to be given to God for both favorable and adverse happenings [AB, Ea, EBC, El, Lns, NCBC, NTC, Si, TNTC]. Even afflictions are attended with enough mercies to cause the saints to engage in blessed giving of thanks [Ea].
- 1.2 It indicates that the focus is on blessings for which thanks is to be given to God [EGT, Ho, IB, ICC, My, St]. The epistle does not particularly discuss the sufferings of the Christian [EGT], so it is most concordant with the context to interpret this as referring to all the *blessings* the Christian receives [EGT, Ho, IB, ICC, My], the total good that he receives from God [EGT].
2. Πάντων 'all things' is interpreted as masculine in gender, with its preposition ὑπέρ meaning 'in behalf of' i.e., thanks is to be given in behalf of all men [Ba]: give thanks always in behalf of all men. We are to praise God for his general mercy to the human race. Such a general mandate includes within it also the giving of thanks for all his dealings with us, both for his mercies and for the afflictions which he sees as needful for our good [Ba].
3. Πάντων 'all things' is interpreted to mean 'everywhere' [NJB]: giving thanks always and everywhere to God who is our Father in the name, etc.

QUESTION—What is meant by the formula ἐν ονόματι τοῦ κυρίου ἡμῶν Ἰησοῦ Χριστοῦ 'in the name of our Lord Jesus Christ'?

1. The phrase denotes an action done by Christ's authority and warrant [DNTT, Ea, Ho, IB, TH, WeBC]. It means as living under Christ's authority and owing our access to God to his mediation [IB]. By Christ's warrant, thanks are offered and for his sake they are accepted [Ea, WeBC]. The phrase is an acknowledgment of Christ's Lordship and of believers as his disciples [TH].
2. The phrase denotes dependence upon Christ [EGT, Ho, ICC], and regard for who he is [EGT, MNTC]. The action of thanksgiving has significance only in reference to him [ICC]. The idea is that through Christ we know God as Father and so are assured of his goodness. Therefore all thanksgiving must be inspired by the remembrance of Christ [MNTC].
3. The phrase denotes the revelation which has taken place through Christ [EBC, Lns, St]. The noun ὄνομα 'name' always signifies revelation [Lns] and so thanks is to be given in Christ's name because as the Son he is the one who fully reveals God [EBC, Lns, St].
4. The phrase denotes identification with Christ [Ba, Can, ECWB, NTC, Rob]. The blessings for which we give thanks are given through the intervention of Christ on our behalf, so that even the gratitude we return

for them can only be pleasing and acceptable to God through Christ's merits [Ba, Can, NTC]. Christ purifies our thanksgivings [NTC]. Since the ground of our thanksgiving is the relationship God has with us as our adoptive father through Christ, so we are to give thanks in his name to identify ourselves with him in perfect unity [ECWB].
5. The phrase indicates that the power to give thanks comes through Christ [IDB].
6. The phrase stands for the event of salvation connected with the name of the Lord Jesus Christ, for which thanks is given [TD].

QUESTION—What relationship is indicated by the καί 'and/even' preceding πατρί 'Father'?
1. This καί should be translated 'and' [Alf, Can, Ea, EGT, El, Lns, NIC, NTC, Rob, WBC; KJV, REB]: to the God and Father. This states that God is both our God and our Father through Jesus Christ our Lord [Can]. The definite article with θεῷ 'God', its absence with πατρί 'Father', and the καί 'and' all indicate but another epithet of him who is named under the term θεῷ 'God' [Ea]. It designates one who is God and at the same time the Father [EGT, Rob] so that the καί 'and' here may well have more emphasis than a simply exegetical καί [WBC].
2. This καὶ should be translated 'even' [Ba, Ho; NASB]: to God, even the Father. This does not distinguish the Father from God, as if the two were separate. The meaning is that thanks is to be given especially to God the Father [Ba].
3. This καί is not explicitly translated [AB; NAB, NIV, NJB, NRSV, TEV, TNT]: to God the Father (or, to God who is our Father [NJB]).

QUESTION—Does God's fatherhood, here indicated by καὶ πατρί 'and father', extend here only to Christ, or to both believers and Christ?
1. It extends to both [Ea, EBC, ECWB, El, ICC, Lns, MNTC, NIC, NTC, TD (probably), TH, WeBC]. The word appears to be applied in a general sense so that it covers the paternal character of God both toward Christ and toward all his adopted human children [Ea, ECWB]. It also implies an emphasis on obedience to his sovereign will [TD].
2. It extends primarily to Christ [EGT, Ho, My]. The phrase ἐν τῷ ὀνόματι 'in the name' suggests that the relationship of Father is primarily to Christ [EGT]. 'God the Father of our Lord Jesus Christ' is the covenant title of God under the new dispensation. As such, it presents the only ground upon which we can approach him as our Father [Ho].

DISCOURSE UNIT: 5:21–6:24 [St]. The topic is new relationships.

DISCOURSE UNIT: 5:21–6:9 [AB, IB, NCBC, NIC, TH; NJB, REB]. The topic is the third exhortation, that of mutual subordination in the Christian household [IB], Christ's rule in all realms [AB], Christian counsel to particular groups [NCBC], being subject [NIC], the new life in Christ: family relations [TH], the morals of the home [NJB], Christian relationships [REB].

DISCOURSE UNIT: 5:21–33 [AB, Ba, EBC, Ho, IB, MNTC, St, WBC; TEV]. The topic is Christ's rule over husband and wife [AB], the Christian relationship of marriage [EBC], husbands and wives and their marriage as a symbol of Christ's relationship with the Church [IB], relationships within the family: marriage [MNTC], husbands and wives [Ho, St, TH; TEV], household relationships—wives and husbands [WBC].

DISCOURSE UNIT: 5:21–24 [Ba, My]. The topic is wives being subject to their husbands [Ba, My].

DISCOURSE UNIT: 5:21 [NIC; NRSV]. The topic is mutual submission [NIC].

5:21 Being-subject[a] to-one-another in/because-of[b] (the) fear/reverence[c] of-Christ,

TEXT—Instead of Χριστοῦ 'of Christ', many manuscripts read θεοῦ 'of God'. GNT does not note the variant reading. Only KJV supports the variant reading θεοῦ 'of God'.

LEXICON—a. pres. mid. or pass. participle of ὑποτάσσω (ὑποτάσσομαι LN 36.18) (BAGD 1.b.β. p. 848): 'to be subject to' [NIC; NASB, NJB, NRSV, REB], 'to be subjected' [BAGD], 'to subject oneself' [BAGD, Lns, NTC, We], 'to be subordinate' [AB], 'to be subordinated' [BAGD], 'to submit to' [El, LN, WBC; NIV], 'to submit oneself' [Rob; KJV, TEV], 'to obey' [LN], 'to defer to' [NAB], 'to be ready to give way to' [TNT]. This verb denotes submission to the orders or directives of another [LN]. Here the verb indicates submission in the sense of voluntary yielding in love [BAGD].

b. ἐν with dative object (LN 89.5, 89.26, 89.84): 'in' [El, LN (89.5), Lns, NIC, Rob, WBC, We; KJV, NASB], 'with regard to' [LN (89.5)], 'because, because of' [AB, LN (89.26); TEV], 'on account of, by reason of' [LN (89.26)], 'out of' [NTC; NAB, NIV, NJB, NRSV, REB, TNT], 'with' [LN (89.84)].

c. φόβος (LN 53.59) (BAGD 2.b.α. p. 864): 'fear' [AB, El, Lns, NIC, Rob, WBC, We; KJV, NASB], 'reverence' [BAGD, LN (53.59), NTC; NAB, NIV, NJB, NRSV, REB, TNT], 'respect' [BAGD], 'awe' [LN (53.59)]. This noun denotes profound respect and awe for deity [LN (53.59)].

QUESTION—How is this verse related to the context?

1. It is joined to the preceding section [Alf, Ba, Can, CBC, Ea, ECWB, EGT, El, LJ, Lns, My, NTC, Si, St, TNTC, We, WeBC; NAB, NASB, NIV]. The participle ὑποτασσόμενοι 'being subject to' adds a fourth additional clause to μὴ μεθύσκεσθε οἴνῳ κ.τ.λ. 'be not drunk with wine etc.' [Alf, LJ], or, more specifically, to πληροῦσθε ἐν πνεύματι 'be filled with the Spirit' [Ba, Can, CBC, Ea, ECWB, EGT, El, LJ, Lns, NTC, St] and then out of this general injunction come all the particular applications of it to life relationships as given in 5:22–6:9 [Alf, Ba, Ea, ECWB, LJ, NTC, TNTC, WeBC].

1.1 The participle is coordinate with the preceding participles [Alf, Ea, EGT, El, LJ, My, St].
1.2 The participle is subordinate to the preceding εὐχαριστοῦντες 'giving thanks' [Can, Lns, NTC]. The participle refers to mutual subjection to one another [Lns].
1.3 The participle is translated as an independent imperative [NAB, NASB, NIV, TNT].
2. It is joined to the following verses [AB, Ba, Cal, EBC, GNT, Ho, IB, ICC, MNTC, NCBC, NIC, St, TH, WBC; NJB, REB, TEV]. The writer now turns from the theme of the contrast between Christian and pagan morality to the application of Christian principles to all the personal relationships of domestic life. He uses a single phrase to define the fundamental attitude: a mutual subjection which is based upon reverence for Christ [IB]. The words serve most naturally as the introduction to what follows [MNTC].
2.1 The participle is taken as an independent imperative [AB, Cal, IB, MNTC (probably), NCBC, NIC (probably), TH, WBC; NJB, REB, TEV] or a nominative absolute [ICC]: Be subject to one another.
2.2 The participle is taken as modifying an implied imperative verb of the same root in the following verse [Ho]: Being subject to one another in the fear of Christ, you wives be subject to your own husbands as to the Lord.

QUESTION—What is meant by ὑποτασσόμενοι ἀλλήλοις 'being subject to one another'?

1. This clause focuses on an attitude of reciprocal or mutual subjection to one another [AB, Can, CBC, DNTT, Ho, IB, ISBE2, LJ, Lns, MNTC, NCBC, NIC, NTC, Si, St, TD, TH, TNTC, WBC, WeBC (probably)]. This is an attitude of meekness, gentleness, and humility toward one another [St]. There must be within the Christian community a willingness to serve, learn from, and be corrected by any other believer, regardless of age, sex, class, or any other division [TNTC]. Paul is talking about reciprocal subjection within the fellowship of the church [AB, Ho, Lns, NCBC, NIC, NTC], even though, in the following verses, submission is only applied to three of the six groups mentioned, namely wives, children, and slaves [AB, Lns, NCBC, NTC]. This subordination consists of a willingness to respect and honor the needs of others [CBC, ISBE2, NCBC, NIC, TD], even taking precedence over one's own needs [ISBE2, NCBC, TD].
2. This clause focuses not so much on a reciprocal subjection of Christian to Christian, but on voluntary subjection to the various areas of constituted authority in life [Alf (probably), Ba, EBC, ECWB, EGT, El, Rob]. In the Divine ordering of human life one person is to be subject to another, but this must not be pressed into meaning that even the highest is, in some sense, subject to those beneath him. The husband, in the following verses, is not told to be subject to his wife, nor parents to their children [Rob].

Rather husbands, parents, and masters are told to use their authority in a proper manner, with no abuse of their power [Ba].

3. This clause covers both reciprocal subjection of Christian to Christian as well as to all constituted authority [Cal, Ea]. Where love reigns, believers will mutually minister to each other. Even the authority of kings and governors is held for the service of the community. It is highly proper that all should be exhorted to be subject to each other in their turn [Cal].

QUESTION—What relationship is indicated by ἐν 'in/because'?

It indicates a reason for being subject to one another [AB, Cal, EBC, LJ, NTC, St, TH, WBC; NAB, NIV, NJB, NRSV, REB, TEV]. Some mention that it gives the spirit *in* which the duty of subjection was to be fulfilled [EGT, El]. It indicates both the motive and manner of Christian conduct [DNTT].

QUESTION—What is meant by φόβῳ Χριστοῦ 'the fear of Christ'?

1. The noun is used in the sense of 'respect' or 'reverence' [BAGD, Can, CBC, Ea, EBC, EGT, Ho, IB, ICC, ISBE, ISBE2, Lns, NIC, NTC, St, TH, WBC, WeBC; NAB, NIV, NJB, NRSV, REB, TNT]: in the reverence for Christ. In the NT the lower sense of dread in the fear of God is removed, but there remains a filial fear and sense of awe and of the greatness of the issues involved, as in Eph. 5:21 and other passages [ISBE]. This is not slavish terror [CBC, Ea, WBC], but the solemn awe which the authority of Christ inspires [Ea, WBC], reverence for Christ who is our supreme Lord and Head, as one whom we are afraid to displease [Can]. The motive is reverence for Christ and a regard to his will and his glory, because Christ, to whom we are responsible for all our conduct, is God [Ho].
2. The notions of terror, horror, trembling, and turning to flight inherent in this noun are not to be excluded here [AB, DNTT, LJ, My, NCBC]. Though the believer's relationship to Christ is one governed by love, so that he has a fear of hurting, grieving, or disappointing Christ, who loves him so much and has done so much for him, yet passages such as 2 Cor. 5:9, Phil. 2:12–13, and Heb. 12:28–29 indicate that the elements of fear, trembling, and shame involved in the believer losing his reward are not to be excluded from this fear [LJ]. The fear is of Christ as judge [LJ, My, NCBC, WBC (in support of 1. above)].

DISCOURSE UNIT: 5:22–6:9 [Alf, Can, ECWB, LJ, Lns, NTC, Rob, Si, TNTC, WeBC]. The topic is exhortation to mutual subjection [Can], life in the Spirit governing all relationships [LJ], relationships [TNTC], relative duties [Si], four admonitions for four special classes of members [Lns], the urging of glorious renewal upon special groups [NTC], the Church's family life in Christ [WeBC], the bearing of the truth of unity on the three great relationships of life [ECWB].

DISCOURSE UNIT: 5:22–33 [Alf, ECWB, EGT, El, ICC, LJ, NIC, NTC, Rob, Si, TNTC, We; NAB, NASB, NIV]. The topic is marriage [LJ], the duties of wives and husbands [Alf, ECWB, EGT], wives and husbands [El, NIC, Rob, TNTC, We], the sanctity of the nuptial bond as a type [Si].

DISCOURSE UNIT: 5:22–24 [CBC, Lns, St, We, WeBC; NRSV, TNT]. The topic is the admonition for wives [Lns], the duty of wives [CBC, St], the type of the wife's subjection [We], the Christian relationship of wives to their husbands [WeBC].

5:22 the wives to their/their-own husbands as to the Lord,

TEXT—Some manuscripts place ὑποτάσσεσθε 'be subject to' or ὑποτασσέσθωσαν 'let them be subject to' after either γυναῖκες 'wives' or ἀνδράσιν 'husbands'. GNT supports the reading without these verb forms with a B rating, indicating that this reading is almost certain. Those who appear to support a variant reading with ὑποτάσσεσθε 'be subject to' are: Ba, Cal, Ho, NCBC.

QUESTION—What relationship is indicated by this verbless clause?

This clause is dependent upon the preceding participial clause, therefore the 2nd. pers. sing. imperative ὑποτάσσεσθε 'be subject to' is implied [AB, Alf, Can, Ea, EBC, EGT, El, HG, LJ, Lns, Mou, My, NIC, NTC, Rob, St, TH, TNTC, WBC, We, WeBC]. The continuity of the apostle's style did not require a verb here [Ea], so that the idea conveyed in the participle in the previous clause guides the meaning of this one. Wives are exhorted to be dutiful to their husbands in the spirit of the preceding participle [Ea, LJ]. The argument is: if you are submissive to one another in the fear of Christ, how much more should wives be submissive to those to whom they naturally owe submission (and likewise with children and slaves) [LJ]. Some commentators note that the structure of this clause in relation to 5:21 indicates an example of the preceding command, given in the participle ὑποτασσόμενοι 'being subject to', now being presented in the text [AB, WeBC]. The example of the subordination of wives is the same mutual subordination which is also shown by the love of the husband, the obedience of the children, the parent's responsibility for their children, and the slaves' and masters' attitude toward each other [AB].

QUESTION—What is meant by ἰδίοις 'their own'?

1. This pronoun is used for the ordinary possessive pronoun [NIC, Rob, WBC; all versions except KJV, NASB]: their husbands. The pronoun carries no special emphasis here [NIC, Rob, WBC]. It could be inserted or omitted with indifference where the context made the meaning clear [Rob]. Its presence here may be explained by the fact that it was a common feature in the household codes of the time [NIC].
2. This pronoun is used because of the additional emphasis it carries [AB, Alf, Ea, EBC, EGT, ICC, LJ, Lns, My, NTC, We; KJV, NASB]: their own husbands. This intensive pronoun is used to intensify the recognition of the relationship of the wife to her husband [AB, Alf, EGT, ICC] and to suggest its duties [Alf]. The word indicates a peculiar relationship of the closeness of possession and relation [Ea]. It indicates that the husbands, as

such, are peculiarly and exclusively theirs [EGT], yet does not imply an antithesis to other men [ICC].

QUESTION—What is meant by ὡς τῷ κυρίῳ 'as to the Lord'?
1. The adverb ὡς 'as' does not express the same degree of similarity or resemblance on the wife's subjection to her husband as to Christ [Alf, Ba, Can, Ea, EGT, El, Ho, IB, LJ, My, NIC, NTC, TH, TNTC, WBC, WeBC]. The adverb ὡς 'as' is not to be understood in the strictest sense [TH]. It presents the character [Ea] or the aspect [El] of the submission that is enjoined on the wife. It does not express similarity [EGT, El, Ho, My] or in the same manner [ICC, LJ] as though the obedience of the wife to her husband is as devout and unconditional as that which she is to render to her Lord [Ho, LJ]. The point of the ὡς 'as' is that the wife is to regard her obedience to her husband as an obedience to Christ [EGT, LJ, NIC, NTC, WBC]. This phrase explains the essence of the submission required of Christian wives [Ea]. It means 'in obeying your husband, obey the Lord' [Alf, Ba, Can, EBC], not because in all things she is to have regard to Christ, but because the husband stands peculiarly in Christ's place, but not so as to be identified in power with Christ nor, in nature, with the obedience owed to him [Alf].
2. The adverb ὡς 'as' implies a close degree of resemblance or similarity [NCBC]. The wives are told to give the same obedience to their husbands as they give to Christ. This seems to assign a degree of wisdom and authority to the husband that is not reasonable [NCBC].

5:23 because (the) husband is head of-the wife as also Christ (is) head of-the church,

QUESTION—What relationship is indicated by ὅτι 'because'?

The ὅτι 'because' introduces the reason [Cal, Ea, EGT, ICC, LJ, Lns, My, WBC, WeBC] or ground [Ho, IB] for the wife's submission ὡς τῷ κυρίῳ 'as to the Lord'. The writer is laying the foundation for his analogy [IB]. It introduces an explanation of how the submission of the wife is to be 'as to the Lord' [Can, Ea].

QUESTION—What is the significance of the lack of the definite article with ἀνήρ 'husband' and its presence with γυναικός 'wife'?

The lack of the definite article with ἀνήρ 'husband' (literally 'man') indicates any ἀνήρ 'man' that belongs to the class of husbands [EGT, El], any husband, taken as an example [Alf] or it gives the noun qualitative force [HG]. The article with γυναικός 'wife' performs the function of a possessive pronoun 'his' [Ea, EGT, El, Lns], pointing out the special relationship to ἀνήρ 'husband' [Ea, El, Rob].

QUESTION—What is meant by κεφαλή 'head'?
1. This refers to the right to rule, direct, and control the 'body' [Alf, Ba, BAGD, Ho, IB, ISBE2, My, NCBC, NIC, Rob, TH, TNTC, WBC]. The word κεφαλή 'head' is equivalent to κύριος 'lord' [NCBC]. The ground of the wife's submission to her husband is the gifts and attributes which

are his by nature of his masculinity, which enable and entitle him to lead and command [Ho]. The following clause is added to fill in what is lacking in the metaphor of headship as regards the fuller expression of Christ's relationship to the church, his body [Rob, TH].
2. This refers not only to the head's authority, but to the function of providing unity [AB, Ea, ECWB, IDB, Lns, MNTC, NTC, TD, We, WeBC], i.e., nurturing the 'body' [AB, Ea, IDB, MNTC, NTC, TD], and directing its growth and life [AB, MNTC, TD]. The husband is head of the wife not only because of the authority God has given to him but, as shown by the comparison with Christ, by virtue of the fact that he is vitally interested in her welfare. He is her protector [NTC].
3. This refers to multiple functions of the 'head' [CBC, LJ, St]. The husband is head of the wife by virtue of the fact that the male was created before the female, and by virtue of the fact that God appointed him head over the woman (as well as all created things on earth) and gave him the gifts and abilities suited to exercising that leadership. The woman was made from him, to be a complement to him, to exercise other gifts that complemented his [LJ, St], to help him function as the lord of creation, as God's representative in this world. He is also head over the wife in order that, as a married unit, they may function together in an organic, intimate, vital unity, yielding a corporate result [LJ].
4. This refers to the leader of a family or household [Can, IDB]. The starting point of this image is the OT use of the word 'head' for the leading person of a community [IDB].

QUESTION—What relationship is indicated by the words ὡς καί 'as also'?

The καί 'also' introduces identity of category [Alf] or sameness in the relation of κεφαλή 'head' [Ea]. The words introduce a comparison of the headship God has given the husband over his wife with the headship he has given Christ over the church [Cal, EGT, El, Ho, IB, LJ, Lns, MNTC, My, NCBC, NTC, WBC]. The ὡς καί 'as also' indicates the point which is common to the two subjects. Each is head, though they are head of different objects [EGT, El]. Here ὡς 'as' introduces more than just a comparison. It introduces a dependent clause that provides a reason for the content of the preceding main clause. The accompanying καί means more than 'also', it serves to emphasize and clarify the force of ὡς 'as' and the uniqueness of the Messiah. The force of the two words together conveys an understanding something like 'the husband is head of the wife, only because, and in the same way that, the Messiah is head of the church'. Thus this introduces the husband's role as head of his wife, not in an absolute sense, but in a very restricted and qualified sense [AB].

he-himself (being the) savior/Savior[a] of-the body;

LEXICON—a. σωτήρ (LN 21.22, 21.31) (BAGD 2. p. 801): 'savior' [AB, El, LN (21.22), Lns, NIC, Rob; KJV, NAB, REB], 'deliverer, rescuer' [LN (21.22)], 'Savior' [BAGD, LN (21.31), Lns, NTC, WBC, We; NASB,

NIV, NRSV, TEV, TNT]. This noun is also translated as a verb 'to save' [NJB].

QUESTION—How is this clause related to its context?

The emphatic pronoun αὐτός 'he himself' placed at the beginning of this clause indicates that the author is not expounding κεφαλὴ τῆς ἐκκλησίας 'head of the church' but wishes to make a new point [NIC, TD]. The pronoun αὐτός 'he himself' is singular in number and only refers back to Χριστός 'Christ' [AB, ICC, My]. In the introduction of the analogy of the relationship of Christ and the church, the writer has primarily the concept of headship in mind and only provides this additional thought as a further description which applies to Christ as head of the church [WBC]. It explains why and in what sense Christ is head of the church. His authority over the church is the result of his having saved it [TH].

1. This statement is only applicable to Christ [AB, Alf, Can, Ea, ECWB, EGT, El, Ho, IB, ICC, Lns, My, TH, WBC, We, WeBC]. This is an independent clause [EGT, Ho, My] which states definitely and emphatically the way in which Christ, while resembling the husband in the matter of headship, is at the same time different from him [EGT]. Though there is a point of comparison with the husband in the term κεφαλή 'head' in the preceding clause [Ea], there is none in the term σωτήρ 'savior' in this one, because the love and protection a husband is able to give to his wife can never be called σωτηρία 'salvation', and does not resemble the salvation Christ provides [Ea, WeBC].

2. This statement has implications applicable to the husband [Ba, Cal, EBC, LJ, MNTC, NIC (probably), NTC, Rob, St, TD, TNTC]. The pronoun αὐτός 'he himself' naturally refers to Christ. But in this point, as in the others, the resemblance still ought to hold [Cal, NTC]. The metaphor of headship does not fully explain Christ's relationship to the church, his body, so Paul adds this clause to show that it is the function of the head to plan for the safety of the body and to provide for its welfare. This clause links the responsibility to protect with the right to rule [Rob]. The idea here seems to be that as Christ gave himself to save his body, the church, and made it the object of intense solicitude to preserve it, so the husband is to regard himself as his wife's natural protector and to save her from want, affliction, and pain [Ba]. Paul regards the husband, even if to an infinitely lesser degree, the protector of his wife [EBC, Rob, TNTC].

QUESTION—What is meant by σωτὴρ τοῦ σώματος 'Savior/savior of the body'?

1. Σωτήρ 'Savior' is used primarily in its restricted, soteriological sense (assuming that the initial capitalization in the English 'Savior' indicates the soteriological sense) [Alf, Ba, BAGD, Cal, DNTT, Ea, EBC, ECWB, EGT, El (probably), Ho, ICC, ISBE, Lns, My, NTC, TD, TH, TNTC, WBC, We, WeBC (probably); NASB, NIV, NRSV, TEV, TNT]. The noun σωτήρ 'savior' indicates Christ is not only the church's redeemer by

the act of atonement, but its continued deliverer, preserver, and benefactor, and so is deservedly the church's head [Ea].
2. Σωτήρ 'savior' is used in a wider sense, including the meanings of 'preserver, protector, benefactor' [AB, Can, CBC, DNTT, IB, NCBC, NIC (probably), Rob, St; KJV, NAB, REB] which also includes the soteriological meaning above [AB]. When applied to Jesus, he is understood to be the true and lasting benefactor of mankind [CBC]. Here 'savior' appears to be used, not as a title for Christ, but as a description of his function in protecting and preserving the church from the assaults of her spiritual foes and the disintegrating effects of sin [IB].

5:24 **but/now/therefore**[a] **as the church is-subject/subjects-itself to-the Christ, so also the wives to-their husbands in everything.**

LEXICON—a. ἀλλά (LN 89.125, 91.2) (BAGD 6. p. 39): 'but' [LN (89.125), NIC, Rob, WBC, We; NASB, REB, TNT], 'instead, on the contrary' [LN (89.125)], 'nevertheless' [El, Lns], 'yet' [LN (91.2)], 'now' [BAGD; NIV], 'and' [LN (90.1); NJB, TEV], 'then' [BAGD, NTC] 'therefore' [KJV], not explicit [NAB, NRSV]. This conjunction is also translated: 'the difference notwithstanding' [AB].

QUESTION—What relationship is indicated by ἀλλά 'but/now/therefore'?
1. It indicates contrast [AB, Alf, Ea, ECWB, EGT, El, Ho, IB, ICC, Lns, My, WBC, We, WeBC; NASB, REB, TNT]: but.
    1.1 The contrast is with an implied statement derived from the preceding clause [AB, Alf, ECWB, EGT, El, Ho, IB, ICC, Lns, My, WBC, We, WeBC]: (Husbands cannot be saviors to their wives as Christ is savior to the church), but the wives should be subject to their husbands as the church is subject to Christ. The ἀλλά 'but' refers to the limitation just placed upon the analogy [AB, IB].
    1.2 The contrast is with an implied statement derived from the context of the marital relationship [Ea]: (Do not disallow the marital headship, because it is a divine institution), but as the church is subject to Christ, so let the wife be subject to her husband.
2. This conjunction is resumptive [BAGD, Cal, EBC, LJ, NIC, NTC, Rob, TD (probably), TNTC; NAB, NIV, NJB, NRSV]: now. The apostle checks himself from further remarking on the last clause and resumes his main line of thought [NIC, Rob, TD]. Before taking up the point of sacrificial love which the husband owes to his wife after the pattern of Christ, to which the preceding clause alluded, the apostle stresses again the wife's duty [TD, TNTC]. The conjunction ἀλλά 'then' substantiates the analogy given in 5:23a. The apostle is developing a likeness rather than pointing out a difference, as seen in the adverbs ὡς 'as' and οὕτως 'so' [EBC]. This conjunction may be used with an imperative or a subjunctive to strengthen a command [BAGD, LJ].
3. This conjunction indicates an inference from the preceding material and means 'therefore' [CBC; KJV, TEV]: therefore the wives must be subject

to their husbands. If the parallel between the church and the wife holds true, then the woman must be subject to the husband in everything [CBC].

QUESTION—What is the voice of the verb ὑποτάσσεται 'is subject to', and what would be the voice of the ellipsed verb in the part concerning the wife?

1. This is to be taken as the middle voice with reflexive force [AB, Lns, MNTC, TD, TH; TEV]: as the church subjects itself to Christ, so also should the wives (or, so let the wives) subject themselves to their husbands. The verb carries with it the idea of willing submission. The church puts itself under the control of Christ [Lns, MNTC].
2. This is to be taken as the passive voice [Alf, Cal, Can, CBC, Ea, ECWB, EGT, El, HG, Ho, LJ, My, NIC, NTC; all versions except NAB, NIV, TEV]: as the church is subject to Christ, so also should the wives (or so let the wives) be subject to their husbands. The subjection of the church to Christ is a voluntary subjection [Ea, ECWB, LJ, NTC], arising out of faith in his absolute wisdom and goodness, and love for his unspeakable love [ECWB], and from the affection and softness of the wife's nature [Ea].
3. This is taken as the equivalent of an active voice [WBC; NAB, NIV]: as the church submits to Christ, so also should the wives submit to their husbands.

QUESTION—What is meant by the phrase ἐν παντί 'in everything'?

1. The phrase is unrestricted [My (probably), NIC, TH, WBC, We]. This states the ideal [We]. The analogy between the church's attitude and that of the Christian wife is exact [TH]. She must submit to her husband in everything [TH, WBC]. It is presupposed that the right to command on the part of the husbands is in keeping with their position of representing Christ towards the wife, so that what is commanded will be after the manner of making rules for the godly [My]. In this ideal picture of Christian marriage the writer does not even consider the possibility that the wives' submission to their husbands might conflict with their submission to Christ [NIC, WBC].
2. The phrase is restricted to 'everything' within a given sphere of authority [Can, EGT, Lns]. It means everything that is within the husband's domain of authority [Can, Ea], everything that pertains to the marriage relationship [EGT, Lns], everything that belongs to family and household life [Can, Lns].
3. The phrase is unrestricted as to spheres of social life, but restricted as to degree [AB (probably), Ba, ECWB, Ho, LJ (probably), NTC (probably)]. It means in everything that is not contrary to the will of God [Ba, Ho, NTC]. The context, especially 4:25–5:20, has shown that godly conduct is the type of 'everything' which Paul means [AB].
4. The phrase describes the priority which the wife is to assign to her husband and family life over against other commitments she may take upon herself [TNTC]. Her marriage and her family must be her first concern [TNTC].

DISCOURSE UNIT: 5:25–33 [Ba, CBC, LJ, Lns, My]. The topic is the duties of husbands [CBC, Lns], an injunction for husbands to love their wives [Ba, My].

5:25 **The husbands, love your wives, just-as also Christ loved the church and gave-up himself for[a] her,**

TEXT—Some manuscripts have the intensive possessive pronoun ἑαυτῶν 'your own' following γυναῖκας 'wives'. GNT does not note the variant reading. Only Ea includes the variant ἑαυτῶν 'your own'.

LEXICON—a. ὑπέρ with genitive object (LN 90.36) (BAGD 1.a.ε. p. 838): 'for' [AB, El, LN, Lns, NIC, NTC, Rob, WBC, We; all versions], 'in behalf of' [BAGD, LN], 'for the sake of' [LN].

QUESTION—What is the function of this verse?

This verse begins to define what Paul means by ὑποτασσόμενοι ἀλλήλοις 'being subject to one another' (5:21) as it applies to husbands [AB]. Its purpose is to show that the exhortation for wives to submit is not to be separated from the call for husbands to give themselves in love for their wives, and that the exercise of headship by the husband is not to be made through self-assertion, but through self-sacrifice [WBC].

QUESTION—What is meant by ἀγαπᾶτε τὰς γυναῖκας 'love your wives'?

Paul picks out, on each of the two sides, the chief contribution that each must make to achieve peace, harmony, and unity in the marriage relationship—submission on the part of the wife, love on the part of the husband [LJ]. Love prompts to acts of kindness and service, so that the one who does such deeds to another is subjecting himself [Can, NCBC, TNTC, WBC] and his own pleasure and advantage for the greatest good of another [NCBC, TNTC, WBC]. The main characteristic of this love is that it is spontaneous [NTC] and self-sacrificing [NTC, WBC]. However, another commentator notes that the idea of self-sacrifice is not inherent in the verb ἀγαπᾶτε 'love' itself, but in the context [NIC].

QUESTION—What relationship is indicated by καθώς 'just as'?

1. It indicates a comparison [Alf, Ba, Cal, Can, CBC, DNTT, EBC, ECWB, EGT, Lns, NIC, NTC, St, TH, TNTC]. The comparison that is drawn includes both the measure and the manner of Christ's love for the church [EGT]. Paul holds up the conduct of the Redeemer towards his church as the model for a husband to follow as regards his wife [Ba]. This is the highest possible example of self-sacrificing love that Paul can point to [Can, Lns].
2. It indicates both a comparison and the grounds for the command to love their wives [AB, Ea, Ho, LJ, WBC], as well as introducing a quotation [AB, TD]. It has causal force in addition to the primary comparative force. Christ's love for the church is not only the model for the husband's love for his wife, but also provides the grounds for it [WBC]. Moreover, the poetic form of 5:25b–27 indicates either that Paul himself composed 'a

psalm' at this point or, more likely, that this material is quoted from a hymn [AB] or confession known to the readers [AB, TD].

QUESTION—What is the significance of the aorist tense of the verb ἠγάπησεν 'he loved'?

The aorist tense points to the definite action in the past that is defined by the following verb, παρέδωκεν 'he gave (himself) up' [NCBC, WBC]. It does not mean his love is confined to this action [NCBC], nor that his love for the church is not continuous [NCBC, TH], but rather that its quality and extent is seen in his action of voluntarily giving himself up to die on the cross [NCBC]. Standing as it does before the following clause καὶ ἑαυτὸν παρέδωκεν ὑπὲρ αὐτῆς 'and gave himself up for her', the verb seems to look back to his eternal pre-existent state in which he set his love upon his people and determined to come and save them [St]. This is a retrospective way, for the then-present church, of talking about the significance of Christ's love. It looks at the particular point in history when that love was demonstrated and when that loving relationship began. It does not necessarily imply that the church was in existence at the time of Christ's death [WBC].

QUESTION—What is meant by ἑαυτὸν παρέδωκεν ὑπὲρ αὐτῆς 'he gave himself up for her'?

As in 5:2, which contains similar wording, this clause introduces how Christ's love was preeminently shown [El, My, NTC]. Christ gave himself up to death to redeem his church [Ba, Cal, DNTT, Ea, EBC, EGT, El, LJ, NCBC, St] as proof and expression of his love [Ea]. The main point in expressions such as ἑαυτὸν παρέδωκεν 'he gave himself up' is self-sacrificial love, the willingness to die [TD]. The verb indicates that Christ gave his life for the church of his own accord [NCBC]. As in 5:2, the preposition ὑπέρ 'for' may have substitutionary overtones [EBC, El, Lns], meaning 'in her stead' [El], though another commentator lists this as one of a number of verses in which the substitutionary aspect is difficult to determine [DNTT].

1. This is a model of imitation for the husband [Ba, Cal, CBC, Ea, EBC, EGT, Ho, LJ, Lns, NIC, NTC, St, TNTC, WBC, WeBC]. The husband is to have the same spirit of self sacrifice for the welfare of his wife that Christ has for his church [Ba, Cal, Ea, LJ]. The one peculiar consequence of Christ's giving himself up for the church, that of redeeming it (and in the regenerating and cleansing effect of that sacrifice [ECWB]), is impossible for men to imitate [Cal, ECWB]. But a man may be said to give himself for his wife, in a lower sense, by taking the chief share of the burden of life for her, and in that sense imitate the love of Christ [ECWB].
2. This is not a model of imitation for the husband [AB]. As in the clause αὐτὸς σωτὴρ τοῦ σώματος 'he himself the savior of the body' in 5:23, the apostle is never suggesting that the husband become a duplicate of Christ and consider himself as his wife's 'savior' [AB].

5:26 in-order-that he might-sanctify[a] her having-cleansed[b] (her) with-the washing[c] of the water[d]

LEXICON—a. aorist subj. act. of ἁγιάζω (LN 53.44, 88.26) (BAGD 2. p. 8): 'to sanctify' [BAGD, El, Lns, NIC, NTC, Rob, TH, WBC, We; KJV, NASB, TNT], 'to consecrate' [BAGD, LN (53.44); REB], 'to make holy' [AB, LN (88.26); NAB, NIV, NJB, NRSV], 'to dedicate' [BAGD], 'to dedicate to God' [LN (53.44); TEV]. This verb denotes the inclusion of something within the circle of what is holy, in both the religious and moral uses of the word [BAGD]. It means to dedicate something or someone to the service of and to loyalty to a deity [LN (53.44)], or it means to cause someone to have the quality of holiness [LN (88.26)].

b. aorist act. participle of καθαρίζω (LN 79.49) (BAGD 2.b.α. p. 387): 'to cleanse' [BAGD, El, LN, Lns, NTC, Rob, TH, WBC, We; KJV, NASB, NIV, NRSV, REB, TNT], 'to clean' [AB, LN], 'to make clean' [LN; TEV], 'to purify' [BAGD, NIC; NAB]. This participle is also translated as an adjective modifying ὕδατος 'water': 'cleansing water' [NJB].

c. λουτρόν (LN **53.43**) (BAGD p. 480): 'washing' [BAGD, **LN**, MM, NIC, NTC, Rob, TH, WBC; KJV, NASB, NIV, NRSV], 'bath' [AB, BAGD, Lns, We; NAB], 'laver' [El]. This noun is also translated as a participial phrase: 'by washing her/it' [NJB, TEV]. This noun is coalesced with the participle καθαρίσας 'having cleansed' [REB, TNT].

d. ὕδωρ (LN 2.7) (BAGD 1. p. 833): 'water' [AB, BAGD, El, LN, Lns, NIC, NTC, Rob, TH, WBC, We; all versions].

QUESTION—What relationship is indicated by ἵνα 'in order that'?

This is the first of three ἵνα 'in order that' clauses that give the purpose of Christ's expression of love for the church [WBC]. In this verse and the next Paul explains the purpose of Christ's atonement in relation to the church [EBC, EGT, Ho, NTC, TNTC, WeBC]. Specifically, the telic ἵνα 'in order that' in this verse introduces the nearer purpose [Alf, Ea, EGT, El, Ho, ICC, Lns, NCBC, NTC], while that in the next verse introduces the ulterior design of Christ's love and death [Ea, Ho, Lns, NTC].

QUESTION—What is meant by ἁγιάσῃ 'he might sanctify'?

1. This denotes Christ's separation of the church to himself [Cal, Ea, EBC, EGT, LJ, Lns, MNTC, NTC, TH, TNTC, WBC, We; REB, TEV]: in order that he might consecrate her. The verb means to separate her to himself [Cal, EBC, EGT, LJ, WBC], and this is accomplished by Christ's death on her behalf [WBC], by the forgiveness of sins and regeneration by the Spirit [Cal, Lns]. Sanctification, in light of its OT background, involves a setting apart in order to bring about a condition and state of moral purity. By Christ's death believers have been separated from the sinful world and transferred into the sphere of God's holiness [WBC]. The action of this verb points to a single, definite act [EGT, TNTC], and this applies to the church as a whole [EGT]. Others, nevertheless, state that this separation is a life-long process [EBC, LJ, NTC]. Actually this involves not only the consecration of the church to himself but also her moral or spiritual

purification, the first idea being prominent [Ea, LJ]. If the participle καθαρίσας 'having cleansed' refers, as it does, to spiritual purification, then it can scarcely be thought that the apostle would express the same idea in the preceding ἁγιάσῃ 'he might sanctify'. The meaning is that having purified her he might consecrate her to himself, the idea of consecration being suspended until it is brought out with special emphasis in the next verse [Ea].

2. This denotes the moral or spiritual purification of the church [AB, CBC, ECWB, El, Ho, ICC, IDB, My, NCBC, NIC, St, TH, WeBC; NAB, NIV, NJB (note), NRSV]: in order that he might make her holy or morally pure. The verb has a double meaning: (1) to mark something off as belonging wholly to God, and (2) moral goodness, or a quality of life that is appropriate to someone living under God's control [NCBC]. The verb ἁγιάσῃ 'he might sanctify' does not stand here for simple consecration, but denotes the communication and infusion of holiness and moral purity [El, ICC], the complete absence of sin, as described in the following verse [TH]. The moral and spiritual fitness of the church is progressive, a gradual process which is not complete at the original calling of the converts. It is due to Christ's action of cherishing the church, and not to her own self-culture [IDB].

QUESTION—What relationship is indicated by the aorist participle καθαρίσας 'having cleansed'?

Some commentators think that καθαρίσας 'having cleansed' refers to the act of actual spiritual regeneration and purification [Alf, Ba, Cal, Ea, EBC, LJ, NTC, WBC]. Others think that it refers to purification from guilt based upon an expiatory sacrifice [EGT, Ho, My, St]. One thinks that it refers to both of the above, stating that it is not necessary to distinguish here between cleansing from the guilt of sin by forgiveness and from its power by regeneration since both happen coincidentally [Can]. Many commentators think that the reference involves a reference to the cleansing involved in or symbolized by the act of baptism [Alf, Ba, Cal, Ea, EBC, IB, St, TD, TH, TNTC, WBC, We].

1. The action of the participle precedes that of the subjunctive verb ἁγιάσῃ 'he might sanctify' [Alf, Can, Ea, ECWB, El, Ho, My, St; NASB, TEV]: in order that having cleansed her he might then sanctify her. The cleansing is the initial act, followed by the work of sanctification [Can]. Some indicate that the finite verb and the participle express the two results of Christ's love and sacrificial death in 5:25, seeming to regard these verb forms as separate notions [Can, Ea, My, St].

1.1 The participle indicates the means by which Christ sanctifies the church [ECWB]: in order that in order that by washing her, he might then sanctify her.

1.2 The participle indicates the negative counterpart of the positive action made by ἁγιάσῃ 'he might sanctify' [My]: in order that he might sanctify her, that is, after having first cleansed her.

1.3 The participle indicates a coordinate circumstance with the finite subjunctive verb ἁγιάσῃ 'he might sanctify' [Alf, (probably), El, Ho, St; NASB, TEV]: in order that he might sanctify her, having cleansed her.
2. The action of the participle is concurrent with the action of the preceding subjunctive verb ἁγιάσῃ 'he might sanctify' [AB, Ba, Cal, CBC (probably), EBC, EGT, IB, ICC, LJ, Lns, MNTC, NIC, NTC, Rob, TD, TH, TNTC, WBC, We; all versions except NASB, TEV]: in order that he might sanctify her as he cleanses her. The aorist tense is used instead of the present because the thought bears upon the definitive 'cleansing' of baptism rather than upon the progressive purification of the soul [IB]. Since the moment of purification is the same as the moment of sanctification the actions of the two verbs are concurrent, even though, logically, the notion of cleansing precedes that of sanctifying [AB, EBC, ICC]. Some state that the cleansing by the washing of water is the outward symbol of the sanctification that is taking place in the heart [Ba, Cal, TNTC].
2.1 The participle indicates the means by which Christ sanctifies the church [Cal, EBC, EGT, LJ, Lns, MNTC, NIC, Rob, TD, TH, TNTC, WBC, We; NJB, NRSV]: in order that he might sanctify her by cleansing her as he does so. The action of the participle specifies the way in which the sanctifying takes effect [EBC, EGT], or it specifies the means by which the sanctification takes place [NIC, Rob, TD, WBC].
2.2 The participle indicates a negative restatement of the positive statement made by ἁγιάσῃ 'he might sanctify' [ICC, Lns, NTC, TH]: in order that he might sanctify her, that is, he might cleanse her. The verb ἁγιάσῃ 'he might sanctify' presents the positive aspect of the church's purification, separating her to God [Lns], or actually infusing her with holiness [ICC]; while the participle καθαρίσας 'having cleansed' presents the negative aspect, the removal of sin and guilt [ICC, Lns, NTC, TH].
2.3 The participle indicates a coordinate circumstance with the finite subjunctive verb ἁγιάσῃ 'he might sanctify' [AB]: in order that he might sanctify and cleanse her. This participle introduces a parenthetical clause with the preceding subjunctive verb ἁγιάσῃ 'he might sanctify': 'to make (her) holy and clean'. Both verbs have an original cultic meaning, often denote the same thing, and are used interchangeably [AB].

QUESTION—What is meant by τῷ λουτρῷ 'the washing'?
1. It means the act of washing and refers to the rite of baptism [Ba, BAGD, Cal, DNTT, EBC, Ho, IB, ISBE, ISBE2, LJ, LN, MM, NCBC, NIC, NTC, Rob, Si, St, TH, TNTC, WBC, WeBC; KJV, NASB, NIV, NJB, NRSV, TEV]: the washing in/with water. The definite article indicates a specific event and the readers would have taken this only as a reference to their experience of baptism [WBC]. In Eph. 5:26 the joining of this noun with the phrase τοῦ ὕδατος 'of water' has usually been interpreted as a reference to baptism, because the literal washing of an object with water

would not be a means of ritual purification in the sense in which the church is said to be consecrated or dedicated to God [LN]. This washing, or baptism, is a sacrament, or a sign, invalid and ineffective in itself, that is given by God [Cal, LJ, TNTC] as an accommodation to the weakness of human capacity, which needs an external confirmation, or pledge, that God is at work within the soul [Cal, LJ]. Its whole efficacy as a sign of the washing which God performs upon the human soul by the blood of Christ is due to the activity of God's Spirit [Cal]. Baptism symbolizes not only a washing from the guilt of sin, but the progressive cleansing from sin's pollution of the human soul [LJ].
2. It means 'bath' [AB, BAGD, EGT, ICC, Lns, MNTC, TD, We; NAB] or 'laver' [Alf, Can, Ea, ECWB, El, IDB, ISBE]: the bath of water.
2.1 The reference is to the rite of baptism [Alf, Can, Ea, ECWB, EGT, El, ICC, IDB, ISBE, Lns, MNTC, TD]. The reference is to baptism [Alf, Can, Ea, ECWB, EGT, El, ICC], involving also the imagery of the purifying bath of the bride previous to marriage [Alf, El, ICC] and it refers to the basin or bath in which the washing took place [Can, ICC] as well as the action of bathing [ICC]. The occurrence of the article with both λουτρῷ 'laver' and ὕδατος 'water' gives equal prominence to both [Ea]. They mark the λουτρόν as the well-known bath of the baptismal water [EGT, El]. This phrase defines the nature of the purification. The washing of water in baptism was the sacrament which expressed purification. The dative case (λουτρῷ 'laver') refers to the instrument [Ea, El, Lns] and the genitive case (ὕδατος 'of water') denotes the material [Ea, EGT, El, Lns].
2.2 The reference is not to the rite of baptism [AB]. Baptism in water can only be applied to individuals, not to the church as a whole. The phrase τῷ λουτρῷ τοῦ ὕδατος 'the bath of the water' is a metaphor for either the cleansing of sin through the blood of Christ or the activity of the Holy Spirit in regeneration. The basis for understanding this as a metaphor was laid down in the OT passages, such as Ezek. 36:25–27 where the 'clean water' with which the Lord will sprinkle Israel is the new heart and the new Spirit he will put within them. This is taken up by the Gospel of John (4:14, for example, where the Spirit given by the Messiah is the 'springs of water'), and Mark 1:8 where the Messiah baptizes with the Spirit, or Heb. ch. 9–10 and Rev. 7:14, where the blood of Christ is the only proper means of washing and purification [AB].

in/with/by[a] (the) word,[b]

LEXICON—a. ἐν with dative object (LN 89.5, 89.26, 89.76, 89.80, 90.10): 'in' [El, LN (89.5)], 'by' [AB, LN (89.76, 90.10), TH; KJV, NAB, NRSV, REB, TEV], 'through' [LN (89.76), WBC; NIV], 'by means of' [LN (89.76)], 'in connection with' [Lns, NTC], 'with regard to' [LN (89.5)],

'with' [LN (89.80, 90.10), NIC, Rob; NASB, NJB, TNT], 'accompanied by' [We], 'because of, by reason of, on account of' [LN (89.26)].
b. ῥῆμα (LN 33.98) (BAGD 1. p. 735): 'word' [AB, BAGD, El, LN, NIC, Rob, TH, WBC; KJV, NASB, NIV, NRSV, TEV, TNT], 'spoken word' [Lns, NTC], 'a form of words' [NJB], 'a confession of faith' [We], 'saying' [BAGD, LN], 'message' [LN], 'expression, that which is said' [BAGD], 'the power of the word' [NAB]. This noun denotes that which has been stated or said, and primarily focuses upon the content of the communication. In this usage it is fully synonymous with the similar usage of λόγος 'word', the difference being only a matter of style [LN]. Generally, the singular form is used to bring together all the divine teachings as a unified whole, meaning 'gospel' or 'confession' [BAGD].

QUESTION—To what is ἐν ῥήματι 'in word' connected and what is meant by it?

1. This phrase is attached to the whole of the preceding part of the verse [AB, Ba, Can (probably), El, My-ed; REB, TNT]: in order that by the word he might sanctify and cleanse her in the washing of water.
   1.1 The ῥήματι 'word' refers to the gospel, the truth, the divine word, preached and received [Ba, Can, El, My-ed].
      1.1.1 The preposition ἐν 'with, by' denotes the means or instrument [AB, Ba, Can, My-ed]: in order that by means of the gospel he might sanctify and cleanse her in the washing of water.
      1.1.2 The preposition ἐν 'in connection with' denotes the accompanying circumstance [El]: in order that in connection with the gospel he might sanctify and cleanse her in the washing of water.
   1.2 The ῥήματι 'word' refers to the open confession of the candidate for baptism of his faith or the prebaptismal teaching he received and the preposition ἐν 'with' denotes the means or instrument [TNT (note)]: in order that by the baptismal confession he might sanctify and cleanse her in the washing of water.
   1.3 The ῥήματι 'word' refers to the pronouncement by the Bridegroom which legally binds the bride to himself, with the preposition ἐν 'by' denoting the means or instrument [AB]: in order that by his word of acquisition he might sanctify and cleanse her in the washing of water. In Jewish culture the 'word' by which a man validly betrothed a woman to himself and made her his wife had many forms, but its substance was 'I love you' [AB, St (in support of 3.4 below)]. The nearest equivalent here would be the covenant formula 'I will be your God and you shall be my people' [AB].
2. This phrase is attached to the verb ἁγιάσῃ 'he might sanctify' [My, TH; TEV] and ῥήματι 'word' is the gospel, the truth, the divine word, preached and received [My, TH] and the preposition ἐν 'by, by means of' denotes the means or instrument [My, TH; TEV]: in order that he might sanctify her by the gospel. Sanctification by the word must of necessity be something other than the cleansing by baptism. The phrase belongs to

ἁγιάσῃ 'he might sanctify', but is not immediately joined to it because the author wishes to place the two verbs, ἁγιάσῃ 'he might sanctify' and καθαρίσας 'having cleansed', in parallel, and likewise the two instrumental phrases τῷ λουτρῷ τοῦ ὕδατος 'the washing/bath of the water' and ἐν ῥήματι 'in word', thereby arranging the structure of the verse with emphatic distinctiveness and purpose [My].

3. This phrase is attached to the participle καθαρίσας 'having cleansed' [Alf, CBC, Ea, EBC, ECWB, EGT, ICC, LJ, NCBC, NIC (probably), Si, St, TD, TNTC, We; NAB, NIV, NJB (probably)]: having cleansed her by the word and by the washing in water. This phrase is then coordinate with, not subordinate to, τῷ λουτρῷ τοῦ ὕδατος 'the washing/bath of the water' [ECWB, TNTC], both the agencies of τῷ λουτρῷ τοῦ ὕδατος 'the washing/bath of the water' and the ῥήματι 'word' making possible this καθαρίσας 'cleansing' [TNTC]. 'Water' and 'word' are both administered to the candidate for baptism [St]. It defines the καθαρισμός 'cleansing' as one that does not take place by means of the τῷ λουτρῷ τοῦ ὕδατος 'the washing/bath of the water' in and of itself, but by that only as administered in the *power* of or on the *ground* of the preached Word or Gospel [EGT].

3.1 The ῥήματι 'word' refers to the gospel, the truth, the divine word, preached and received [Alf, Ea, EGT, LJ, Si, TNTC].

3.1.1 The preposition ἐν 'with, by' denotes the means or instrument [Alf, Ea, LJ, Si]: having cleansed her by the gospel. While baptism has its sacramental symbol in the washing of water, it has its special instrument in the word [Ea].

3.1.2 The preposition ἐν 'in accordance with' denotes conformity to a standard [EGT]: having cleansed her in accordance with the gospel.

3.2 The ῥήματι 'word' refers to the open confession of the candidate for baptism of his faith that Jesus is Lord [CBC, NCBC, NIC, We]. The simple creed κύριος Ἰησοῦς 'Jesus is Lord' is itself involved in the baptismal formula, implying the acceptance of this confession [We].

3.2.1 The preposition ἐν 'with, by' denotes the means or instrument [NCBC, NIC]: having cleansed her by the baptismal confession.

3.2.2 The preposition ἐν 'in connection with' denotes the accompanying circumstance [We]: having cleansed her in connection with the baptismal confession. The change from the instrumental dative case with τῷ λουτρῷ τοῦ ὕδατος 'the washing/bath of the water' to the preposition ἐν 'accompanied by' with ῥήματι 'word' points to the different relations of the effect of the material act of baptism and the spiritual accompaniment of the word involved in the cleansing [We].

3.3 The ῥήματι 'word' refers to the baptismal formula spoken at the moment of baptism [EBC, ECWB, ICC, TD (probably); NJB (note)]. The Greek term ῥῆμα 'word' means something spoken [EBC, ECWB]. This was probably the trinitarian formula used at the moment of baptism [EBC, ECWB, ICC] (the invocation of the name of Christ making the washing the act of baptism [TD]), yet this is suggested not by ῥήματι 'word' itself, which retains its indefinite meaning, but by its connection here with the language of baptism, which defines what ῥῆμα 'word' is intended [ICC]. Implied, also, is the acceptance of the faith on the part of man and the grace-giving blessing of God [ECWB, Ho (in support of 4.3. below)], so that ῥῆμα 'word' includes the whole spiritual element of baptism [ECWB].

3.3.1 The preposition ἐν 'by' denotes the means [TD]: cleansing her by means of the baptismal formula with the bath of the water. The cleansing takes place through the specified bath (note the double article) by means of the word [TD].

3.3.2 The preposition ἐν 'in connection with' denotes the accompanying circumstances [EBC, ICC]: having cleansed her in connection with the baptismal formula with the washing of the water. This is neither strictly instrumental nor modal, but rather denotes either the accompaniment or the element of the action of the verb [EBC].

3.4 The ῥήματι 'word' refers to the pronouncement by the Bridegroom which legally binds the bride to himself, with the preposition ἐν 'by' denoting the means or instrument [St]: having cleansed her by his word of acquisition. See 1.3. above.

4. This phrase is attached to the phrase τῷ λουτρῷ τοῦ ὕδατος 'the washing/bath of the water' [Cal, DNTT (probably), Ho, IB, MNTC, NTC, Rob, TD; NASB (probably)] with the preposition ἐν 'in connection with' denoting the accompanying circumstance [Ho, IB (probably), MNTC, NTC, Rob]: the washing/bath of the water in connection with the word. The idea, then, is that this washing with water is one connected with the word of God, either as the trinitarian formula used in the rite of baptism or as the promise of remission of sins and regeneration, of which baptism is the sign and seal [Ho]. The rite of baptism with water does not save anyone. Rather it is the 'washing of water in connection with the spoken word' by which sanctification and cleansing take place [NTC].

4.1 The ῥήματι 'word' refers to the gospel, the truth, the divine word, preached and received [NTC]: the washing of the water in connection with the gospel.

4.2 The ῥήματι 'word' refers to the open confession of the candidate for baptism of his faith that Jesus is Lord [DNTT, MNTC, Rob]: the washing of the water in connection with the baptismal confession of faith. The ceremony of baptism itself was nothing without the 'word', the confession which expressed a vital faith [MNTC]. The rite of baptism enshrines the gospel, and this is expressed in the confession 'Jesus is Lord' [DNTT].

4.3 The ῥήματι 'word' refers to the baptismal formula spoken at the moment of baptism [Ho, Rob, TD]: the washing of the water in connection with the baptismal formula. It means 'with a word which is appropriate to this washing' [Rob]. This was probably the trinitarian

formula used at the moment of baptism [Ho], or any baptismal formula involving a reference to Christ [Rob].
5. The phrase ἐν ῥήματι 'in word' is attached to both the participle καθαρίσας 'having cleansed' and λουτρῷ 'washing' and denotes the means of the cleansing and the washing [TD]: and cleanse her (through the word) with the washing of water through the word.
6. The phrase ἐν ῥήματι 'in word' is attached to the genitive τοῦ ὕδατος 'of the water', the ῥήματι 'word' refers to the baptismal formula, and the preposition ἐν 'in connection with' refers to the accompanying circumstance [Lns]: the water connected with the baptismal formula.

5:27 in-order-that he-himself might-present/raise-up[a] the church to-himself glorious,[b] not having spot[c] nor wrinkle[d] nor any such-things,[e]

TEXT—Instead of the masculine nominative intensive pronoun αὐτός 'he himself' as object of the verb παραστήσῃ 'he might present', some manuscripts have the feminine accusative pronoun αὐτήν 'her, it'. GNT does not note this variant reading. Only KJV and NIV support the variant reading αὐτήν 'her, it'.

LEXICON—a. aorist subj. act. of παρίστημι or παριστάνω (LN **13.83**, 57.81) (BAGD 1.c. p. 628): 'to present to' [AB, El, LN (57.81), Lns, NIC, NTC, Rob, TH, WBC, We; all versions except NJB], 'to render' [BAGD], 'to make' [BAGD], 'to provide' [LN (13.83, 57.81)], 'to raise up (for oneself)' [LN (**13.83**)], 'to cause to exist' [LN (13.83)]. The clause ἵνα παραστήσῃ αὐτὸς ἑαυτῷ...τὴν ἐκκλησίαν 'in order that he might present the church to himself' is translated 'so that when he took the Church to himself' [NJB]. The meaning 'to present' (BAGD 1.b.) becomes almost equivalent to 'to make, to render, to set up, to place' [BAGD, DNTT, EBC]. This verb denotes causing something to come into existence [LN (13.83)].

b. ἔνδοξος (LN **79.19**) (BAGD 2. p. 263): 'glorious' [BAGD, LN, Lns, TH, We; KJV, NAB], 'all-glorious' [Rob; REB], 'splendid' [BAGD, LN], 'resplendent' [AB], 'radiant' [NIV]. This adjective is also translated as a prepositional phrase: 'in splendor' [LN, WBC; NRSV], 'in all its splendor' [**LN**], 'in glorious beauty' [El], 'in all her glory' [NASB], 'in all the glory' [TNT], 'in all its beauty' [TEV]. It is also translated 'brilliant in purity' [NTC], 'invested with glory' [NIC], 'to be glorious' [NJB]. In referring to the church here, the adjective denotes brilliance in purity [BAGD].

c. σπίλος (LN **79.57**) (BAGD p. 762): 'spot' [BAGD, El, **LN**, MM, NTC, Rob, TH, We; KJV, NASB], 'stain' [BAGD, LN, Lns, MM; NAB, NIV], 'blemish' [BAGD]. The participial clause μὴ ἔχουσαν σπίλον 'not having spot' is translated 'free from spot' [AB, NIC], 'without spot' [WBC; TEV], 'without a spot' [NRSV], 'with no speck' [NJB], 'with no stain' [REB]. The clause μὴ ἔχουσαν σπίλον ἢ ῥυτίδα ἤ τι τῶν τοιούτων 'not having spot nor wrinkle nor any such things' is translated

'in (all the glory of) her perfect beauty' [TNT]. Put beside ῥυτίς 'wrinkle', σπίλος refers to a spot on the body [BAGD].
d. ῥυτίς (LN **8.54**) (BAGD p. 738): 'wrinkle' [AB, BAGD, El, **LN**, Lns, MM, NIC, NTC, Rob, TH, WBC, We; all versions except TNT]. This noun denotes lines or creases in the skin, and in this passage is used symbolically as a type of imperfection, though in some languages this taken as indicative of age and so of seniority and even wisdom [LN].
e. τοιοῦτος (LN 92.31) (BAGD 3.a.β. p. 821): 'such things' [BAGD, TH], 'such thing' [AB, El, Lns, NTC, Rob, WBC, We; KJV, NASB], 'similar things, things like that' [BAGD], 'of such a kind, of a kind such as this' [LN]. The words τι τῶν τοιούτων 'any such things' are translated 'anything of the sort' [NIC; REB], 'anything of that sort' [NAB], 'anything like that' [NJB], 'anything of the kind' [NRSV], 'any other blemish' [NIV], 'any other imperfection' [TEV].

QUESTION—What relationship is indicated by ἵνα 'in order that'?
1. It indicates the further purpose of the clause καὶ ἑαυτὸν παρέδωκεν ὑπὲρ αὐτῆς 'and gave himself for her' in 5:25 [Alf, Ea, EBC, EGT, El, Lns, NTC, WBC]. This verse declares the ultimate purpose of the love and death of Christ for the church [Ea, El].
2. It indicates the purpose of 5:26 [Cal, NIC, TD, TH; TEV, TNT]. Paul declares the design of baptism and of our being washed. It is that we may live in a holy and blameless manner of life before God [Cal].
3. It indicates the ultimate purpose (or result [NJB, REB]) of both καὶ ἑαυτὸν παρέδωκεν ὑπὲρ αὐτῆς 'and gave himself for her' in 5:25 and of the ἵνα 'in order that' clause in 5:26 [Ho, ICC, LJ, My; NJB, NRSV, REB]. The clause gives the remoter object of παρέδωκεν 'he gave' and depends upon ἁγιάσῃ 'he might sanctify' [ICC]. The ἵνα παραστήσῃ 'in order that he may present' is dependent upon the immediately preceding participle καθαρίσας 'having cleansed': 'having purified it that he might present it' [Ho].

QUESTION—What is meant by the clause παραστήσῃ αὐτὸς ἑαυτῷ 'he himself might present to himself'?
The language is strange because one does not normally present something to oneself [TH]. The aorist form of the verb παραστήσῃ 'he himself might present' points to a single definite act [EGT, Lns]. This statement emphasizes the exclusive agency of Christ in the preparation of the church for her bridal presentation to himself [Alf, Can, Ea, El, NTC]. In both secular and biblical Greek παρίστημι 'to present' meant 'to set before, to introduce, to place at someone's disposal' as well as, in certain other NT contexts, 'to produce'. Usually the person to whom the 'presentation' is made is an official of some sort, with an intermediary participating in the 'presentation' and interceding for the person presented. In religious contexts where a person presented himself and his sacrifice to God, this was the priest. In the context of a Judean wedding, it was the function of a male friend of the bride to present the bride to the bridegroom, much in the fashion of the bride's

father in American custom, though others state, citing John 3:29, that this was the responsibility of the friend of the bridegroom [EBC, ECWB, NIC, TH, WBC]. Christ himself fills both the roles of bridegroom and the one who presents the bride [AB, EBC, ECWB, Ho, IB, LJ, NIC, Rob, TD, TH, WBC], much as in the parable in Ezek. 16:3–14 [AB]. Paul does this as a way of emphasizing that the whole of salvation is the work of the Lord [LJ, NTC].

1. This refers to the future eschatological presentation of the church as it will be perfected in sanctification [AB, Alf, Ba, Can, Ea, EBC, ECWB, EGT, El, Ho, ISBE2, LJ, Lns, My, NIC, NTC, Si, St, TD, TNTC]. This presentation is clearly that future one at the Lord's coming [Alf, Ba, El, LJ, NTC], not the present progressive sanctification of the present life [Alf, El]. The words ἵνα παραστήσῃ 'in order that he may present' refer to the consummation of the age [TD]. The presentation is not contemporary with the consecration in 5:25 but is posterior to it and does not finally and formally take place on earth. This presentation, therefore, takes place during the period of the second coming [Ea]. The church is to be an object of admiration to all intelligent beings because of its absolute perfection, free from all defect [Ho].
2. This is a presentation that refers to the present, positional sanctification of the church as it is taking place in this present age [Cal, CBC, DNTT, IB, ICC, NCBC, WBC]. By his self sacrifice Christ has presented the church with the splendor of a bride [DNTT]. There are no grounds for assuming that this verse awaits the parousia of Christ for its fulfillment. Such a claim ignores the fact that in 5:32 the 'one flesh' marriage union is applied to the present relationship of Christ and the church, and that throughout this context, the past and present relationship of Christ and the church is the model for husbands and wives to follow in their marriages. The writer's realized eschatology as presented in this epistle accounts for the glory and holiness being seen as present attributes of the church. Christ's activity in endowing the church with these qualities is a present and continuing one. What is important in this context is the nature of Christ's love, and the elaboration on sanctification here illustrates this but, as in 5:23c, cannot itself apply to the husband's responsibility for his wife [WBC]. Paul writes that the Lord presents the church to himself, not that he might show it off before others, even though the fruits of the church's hidden purity are manifested afterwards in its outward works. It is not Paul's purpose to state here what the Lord has accomplished, as though perfection in righteousness is achievable in this life, but for what purpose Christ has cleansed his church [Cal]. Christ's aim for the church is that its members should be completely Christian in outward appearance as well as inward faith [NCBC]. The picture is possibly that of Jesus the King receiving acceptable people into his court, but it could equally well be translated 'to make the church all glorious for himself'. The language used in this verse refers to things required of the church. The adjective

ἔνδοξον 'glorious' means 'bright with God's glory' and refers to the church as a center of light reflecting God's will and purpose, ἁγία 'holy' means set apart for God's service, and ἄμωμος 'blameless' refers to the perfect obedience required of Christians [CBC].
3. This is a presentation that refers to a moment of baptism [MNTC]. For the moment Paul has turned away from the marriage image. If there is any metaphor it is contained in the phrase αὐτὸς ἑαυτῷ 'he himself to himself'. In baptism, as we know it, everything is done by the celebrant who presents the convert to Christ. But Paul is thinking of a baptism which is administered by Christ in his own person. He takes the whole church under his protection, purifies it to make it worthy of himself, and presents it to himself [MNTC].
4. This means to raise up the church with no reference to a bridal image [LN (13.38)].

QUESTION—What is meant by ἔνδοξον 'glorious'?

This prefixed form of the adjective is emphatic [Alf]. This adjective is formed on the noun δόξα 'glory', which came to be used for the weighty, awe-inspiring, irresistible appearance of God in storm clouds or in radiant light, and the manifestation of himself in mighty and wonderful acts in which he proved himself the savior of men. As applied to the adjective ἔνδοξον 'glorious' in the present context, this means that the splendor attributed to the Messiah's bride is a gift of God or the Messiah and which makes the church conformed to the image of Christ. In the present metaphorical context, ἔνδοξον 'glorious' is specifically related to the dress of the bride [AB, St] (literally referring to being 'arrayed in glory' [Can]). All this attention to the bride's dress and adornment is given on the grounds that it would not be fitting for the King and Bridegroom [AB, Lns], who is presented in both Testaments as 'riding forth in majesty' [AB], to have a queen and bride who lacks glory [AB, Lns]. Another commentator states that the meaning of ἔνδοξον here has reference to the bride's honorable estate and so should be rendered 'honorable' rather than 'glorious'. The bride is 'honorable' by virtue of not having spot nor wrinkle nor any such things and being holy and blameless [TD].

1. This adjective is in the predicative position [AB, CBC, Ea, ECWB, EGT, El, IB, ICC, Lns, NIC, NTC, Rob, TD, TH, WBC; NASB, NJB, NRSV, REB, TEV, TNT]: in order that he might present to himself the church as glorious. The adjective is placed emphatically forward before its substantive [Ea, El, ICC, My]. This verse attributes qualities to his bride which she does not possess on her own [AB].
2. This adjective is in the attributive position [Can, Ho, LJ, TNTC, We; KJV, NAB, NIV]: in order that he might present to himself the glorious church.

QUESTION—What is meant by the participial clause μὴ ἔχουσαν σπίλον ἢ ῥυτίδα ἤ τι τῶν τοιούτων 'not having spot nor wrinkle nor any such things'?

This clause, together with the following ἵνα 'in order that' clause, defines what the writer means by ἔνδοξον 'glorious' [Can, Ea, EGT, El, Ho, LJ, Lns, WBC], this participial clause doing so negatively [Ea, EGT, Lns, My]. The nouns σπίλον 'spot', ῥυτίδα 'wrinkle' and the phrase τι τῶν τοιούτων 'any such things' are taken from physical beauty, health, and symmetry, to denote spiritual perfection [Ea, LJ, WBC]. The combination of the two nouns, σπίλον 'spot' and ῥυτίδα 'wrinkle', stresses the fact that when the church is presented she will have no moral or spiritual stain whatever [NTC].

1. This is a metaphorical reference to cleaning away the marks of neglect and abandonment and to purifying of the church [AB, ISBE, ISBE2]. The noun σπίλος 'spot' is used figuratively here of moral defects [ISBE]. The spots and wrinkles which, it is implied, Christ removes in his bride is most likely the effect of neglect, loneliness [AB], and/or sin [AB, ISBE, ISBE2], not of old age [AB, ISBE2].
2. This is a metaphorical reference to the youthful appearance of the bride [Ba, EBC, Ho, ISBE, Rob, St, WBC]. The noun σπίλον 'spot', in combination with ῥυτίδα 'wrinkle', refers to a blemish of the skin, not something that can be washed off, so that the notion is not that of purifying something, but of the image of a young and lovely bride with no physical blemish [WBC].
3. This refers to the lack of any mark of defilement or of age [IB, LJ, TH, TNTC, We]. The bride is seen as beautiful, young, and completely pure [TH]. The noun σπίλον 'spot' denotes the stains of sin, and the noun ῥυτίδα 'wrinkle' denotes the decadence of age [TNTC].

but in-order-that it-might-be holy and blameless.
QUESTION—What is meant by this description?

This clause lays aside the wedding metaphor and states plainly the purpose for which Christ has reconciled the church [Cal, Ho, WBC], i.e., the literal [My] ethical meaning [El]. It makes clear that this bride's beauty is moral [WBC]. This clause shows that what is figuratively true of the external appearance of the bride is also literally true of her internally [LJ, Lns]. This marks the future eschatological perfection of the church, not a present status or possession [AB, Ea, Lns]. This refers to complete moral beauty, fully devoted to God in both body and soul, without fault of any kind [Can]. This phrase states the moral beauty of the bride first positively and then negatively [LJ, TH]. Positively, she partakes of God's own holiness (ἁγία 'holy'), which is not to be described as mere absence of sin, but positive righteousness, truth, beauty, and everything that in all its essence is glorious, as it is in God. Then, she is also described negatively as 'without blame' (ἄμωμος 'blameless') [LJ]. In the NT ἄμωμος 'blameless' is used of the perfect moral and religious piety to which believers are obligated by virtue of their membership in the holy community of the last time [TD].

5:28 Likewise also the husbands ought[a] to-love their-own wives as their-own bodies.

LEXICON—a. pres. act. indic. of ὀφείλω (LN 71.25, 71.35) (BAGD 2.a.β. p. 599): 'ought' [BAGD, El, LN (71.25), Lns, NIC, NTC, Rob, We; KJV, NASB, NIV, REB, TEV], 'should' [WBC; NAB, NRSV, TNT], 'to be under obligation' [LN (71.25)], 'to be obligated' [BAGD], 'to owe' [AB], 'to have to, to be necessary' [LN (71.35)], 'must' [BAGD, LN (71.35); NJB]. This verb denotes a moral obligation [Alf, Ba, Can, Ea, EBC, EGT, Ho, LJ, Lns, NIC, NTC, Rob, TH, WBC].

QUESTION—What relationship is indicated by οὕτως 'likewise'?

1. It refers back to the reference to Christ's love for the church [AB, Can, DNTT, Ea, EBC, ECWB, EGT, El, Ho, IB, ICC, Lns, MNTC, My, NCBC, NIC (probably), NTC, Rob, TD, TNTC, WBC, We, WeBC]: just as Christ loved the church, likewise the husbands ought also to love their own wives.

   1.1 The ὡς 'as' preceding τὰ ἑαυτῶν σώματα 'their own bodies' introduces a qualitative affirmation [Ea, EBC, ECWB, EGT, El, Ho, IB, ICC, Lns, My, NTC, Rob, We]: husbands ought to love their wives as being their own bodies. The wife is a part of their total self, not as another person external to themselves [IB]. This phrase makes an absolute identification of the husband with his wife as being 'one flesh' [ECWB]. It does not say that husband and wife are not distinct individuals, as though they were the same substance. Rather, it infers that the one complements the other to the extent that each nature needs the other for its full development in the present life [Ho]. They are complementary parts of one personality [IB]. Some state that ὡς 'as' is argumentative [Ho] or semi-argumentative in force [El]. In this hortatory application the ὡς 'as' must have a semi-argumentative force, otherwise there would be two comparisons in this verse, one introduced by οὕτως 'likewise' and the other by ὡς 'as', which would mar the perspicuity of the passage [El].

   1.2 The ὡς 'as' preceding τὰ ἑαυτῶν σώματα 'their own bodies' introduces a logical conclusion [AB]: husbands ought to love their wives since their wives are their own bodies.

   1.3 The ὡς 'as, like' preceding τὰ ἑαυτῶν σώματα 'their own bodies' introduces a comparison [NCBC, WBC]: just as Christ loved the church, so husbands ought to love their wives like they love their own bodies.

2. It refers forward to the ὡς τὰ ἑαυτῶν σώματα 'as their own bodies' [Alf, Ba, BAGD, CBC, TH]: the husbands also ought to love their own wives *in such a way* as they love their own bodies. Up to this point the appeal to husbands to love their wives has been based upon the love of Christ for the church. But here an additional reason is given—the idea of self love. A man's wife is part of himself [CBC]. The καί 'also' preceding οἱ ἄνδρες 'the husbands' refers to Christ's action of loving his body, the church. The ἑαυτῶν 'their own' is emphatic [Alf].

The one-who-loves his-own wife loves himself.
QUESTION—What is the function of this clause?
  The change to the singular here in contrast to the plurals of the previous clause brings the point home to every individual husband. This statement is terse and axiomatic [Lns]. The change in number should also be noted in areas where polygamy is practiced [TH].
  1. This statement is an inference from the preceding clause [Ea, IB, My, NIC, NTC, Rob]. The words ἑαυτῶν ἀγαπᾷ 'loves himself' are not identical with the formula of the preceding clause ἀγαπᾶν...ὡς τὰ ἑαυτῶν σώματα 'love...as their own bodies', it is an inference from it. If the husband as head of his wife, loves her as being his own body, it is a plain inference that he is only loving himself [Ea].
  2. This statement is an explanation of the preceding clause [EBC, El, ICC, Lns] or an affirmation that the obligation of the husband complies with that universal law of nature by which we all love ourselves [Alf, Cal, CBC, ECWB, EGT, MNTC]. This clause explains the preceding ὡς τὰ ἑαυτῶν σώματα 'as their own bodies' [El, ICC]. It is not identical with the preceding clause, nor an inference from it [ICC]. Lest the staggering implication of the previous clause be lost to the reader [EBC], Paul puts it another way to avoid any ambiguity [EBC, Lns] and to make it emphatic [Lns]. A man and his wife are fused into a single entity. She is an extension of his own personality and so part of himself [EBC]. Paul's argument rests on the axiom that a man's wife is a part of his very self [El]. He loves himself as he loves his wife because she is part of himself [Cal, CBC, ECWB]. It is a love not only of duty or obligation, but of nature [EGT, El].
  3. This statement provides a motive for the preceding clause [NCBC, TNTC (probably)]. The apostle is not exhorting husbands to love their wives as an extension of self love. This is shown by the use of the verb forms of ἀγαπάω 'to love' in this clause, which implies a seeking of one's highest spiritual welfare. As a man should seek his own highest spiritual welfare, so he is to seek the same for his wife [TNTC].
  4. This statement indicates the result of true love for the wife [AB]. The logic of Paul's argument is not based upon natural man's selfish inclination to do himself good. The direction of the argument in this section (5:25–33) is not from love of self to love of one's wife to love of Christ. Rather it is from the love shown by Christ to the love shown for his wife to the love he shows for himself. Proper self-love is the result of giving love to others, not the basis upon which one may love others [AB].

5:29 For no-one ever hated[a] his-own flesh but he-nourishes/brings-up/takes-care-of[b] and cherishes/clothes/takes-care-of[c] it/her, just-as also the Christ (does with) the church,

TEXT—Instead of ὁ Χριστός 'the Christ' in the second clause, some manuscripts have ὁ κύριος 'the Lord'. GNT does not note this variant reading. The variant reading is taken only by KJV.

LEXICON—a. aorist act. indic. of μισέω (LN 88.198) (BAGD 2. p. 522): 'to hate' [AB, BAGD, El, LN, Lns, NIC, NTC, Rob, WBC, We; all versions], 'to detest' [BAGD, LN]. This verb denotes strongly disliking someone or something, with the implication of aversion and hostility [LN]. The aorist tense of this verb is gnomic in force [AB, Lns (probably)], which generalizes or makes the statement proverbial in form [AB].

b. pres. act. indic. of ἐκτρέφω (LN **23.6**) (BAGD 1. p. 246): 'to nourish' [BAGD, El, Lns, NIC, NTC, Rob, WBC, We; KJV, NAB, NASB, NRSV, TNT], 'to keep nourished' [REB], 'to feed' [**LN**; NIV, NJB, TEV], 'to provide food for, to give food to someone to eat' [LN], 'to provide' [AB]. The implication of this verb is that food is provided for an extended period of time and that it provides adequate nourishment. The prefixed form, ἐκτρέφω, may be somewhat more emphatic in meaning than the unprefixed τρέφω, but this cannot be determined for certain from existing contexts [LN]. Some say the prefix ἐκ- in this verb points to the result [Ea], the careful, continued nourishing from one stage to another [EGT], the evolution and development produced by the τρέφω 'nourishing' [El, My].

c. pres. act. indic. of θάλπω (LN **35.36**) (BAGD p. 350): 'to cherish' [BAGD, El, NIC, NTC, Rob, WBC, We; KJV, NASB], 'to take care of' [**LN**; NAB, TEV, TNT], 'to care for' [AB; NIV], 'to tenderly care for' [NRSV], 'to look after' [NJB], 'to comfort' [BAGD], 'to warm' [Lns], 'to keep warm' [REB]. This verb literally means 'to keep warm', but it is figuratively applied to comforting or cherishing someone [BAGD]. This verb denotes taking care of something, implying cherishing and concern for the object [LN].

QUESTION—What is the situation assumed by this verse?

The statement made in this verse is clearly applicable to the normal course of things [AB, Can, Ea, My, NIC, Si, WBC], exceptional cases not entering into consideration [My]. Cases of insanity and despair are left out of consideration [Can, Si]. No one in his right mind has ever hated his own flesh. Such a thing is contrary to nature and only occurs when nature is entirely disordered [Can].

QUESTION—What relationship is indicated by γάρ 'for'?

1. The γάρ 'for' indicates a further explanation of the preceding statement [CBC, MNTC, NCBC, TD, TH, TNTC; TEV]. This is regarded as a restatement, in different words, of the preceding clause [CBC]. Paul develops this thought a little further [TD, TNTC] and comes closer to the

actual terms used in Gen. 2:24 when he says 'For no man ever yet hated his own flesh' [TNTC].

2. The γάρ 'for' indicates grounds for the preceding statement [Ba, Ea (probably), EBC, EGT, El, Ho (probably), Lns, My, NIC, WBC; NAB, NIV]. The γάρ 'for' shows how self evident the statement just made is [EBC, Lns, NIC]. First, the preceding statement is ultimately based on a general law of nature, then it is suggested by the example of Christ in the καθώς 'just as' clause [El]. This statement is intended to impel the husbands to exercise self love which results in love for his wife. The connection of thought is: he who loves his wife, loves himself; for, if he did not love her, he would hate his own flesh, which is so repugnant to nature that no one has ever yet done it, etc. [My].

QUESTION—What is the connotation of σάρκα 'flesh' here?

It refers to the body apart from its ruin by sin [AB, Ea, EGT, My, NIC]. The connotation of σάρκα 'flesh' here is neutral [AB], nonethical [EGT]. Paul is referring to the normal and natural behavior of a man toward his body [AB, EGT]. Paul has changed from σῶμα 'body' (5:28) to σάρξ 'flesh' here in anticipation of his quote from Gen. 2:24 in 5:31 [AB, Ea, El, ICC, NIC, TH, We], so preparing the way for it [Rob, WBC]. Texts which speak about the Christian's need to battle against the desires of the body are irrelevant here [AB].

QUESTION—What is meant by ἀλλὰ ἐκτρέφει καὶ θάλπει αὐτήν 'but he nourishes and cherishes it'?

This is the positive counterpart of the negative ἐμίσησεν 'hated' [Lns]. Ἕκατος 'each one' is understood before the two verbs [Ea]. Most understand αὐτήν 'it/her' (and consequently the antecedent, ἑαυτοῦ σάρκα 'his own flesh') to refer to the husband's own body [AB, Alf, Ba, Cal, Can, Ea, EBC, ECWB, EGT, El, Ho, LJ, LN, Lns, MNTC, My, NCBC, NIC, NTC, Rob, Si, St, TH, TNTC, WBC]. However, one commentator understands it to refer directly to the husband's wife. He says the thought is compressed from 'the one who has learned to think of his wife as his own flesh, as he ought, will nourish and cherish her as Christ does the church' [IB].

1. The two verbs refer to the feeding [Alf, EGT, El, LJ, LN, Lns, My, NIC, NTC, St, TH, We; all versions], and the clothing [Alf, LN, Lns, My, NIC, St, We] or other needs of the body [EGT, El, LJ, NTC, TH; NAB, NIV, NJB, REB, TEV, TNT], respectively. One's physical body needs two essential things for existence—food to nourish it and warmth to make it reasonably comfortable [Lns]. The verb ἐκτρέφει 'he nourishes' refers to providing nourishment for the body all the way up through its various stages to maturity [Alf, EGT]. The verb looks at the outward growth and development of the body [El]. It denotes the development that is brought about by nourishment [El, My]. Properly the second verb, θάλπει 'he cherishes', means 'to warm' [Alf, Ba, EGT, Lns, My; REB; as well as some supporters of other interpretations below: Ea, EBC, ECWB, ISBE].

1.1 The verb θάλπει 'he cherishes' refers to providing both clothing and shelter for the body [NTC; REB]. REB translates θάλπει as 'he keeps (it) warm'.

1.2 The verb θάλπει 'he cherishes' refers to the fostering warmth of the breast [EGT (probably), El].

1.3 The verb θάλπει 'he cherishes' refers to care for the body in general [LJ, TH; NAB, NIV, NJB, NRSV, TEV, TNT].

2. The two verbs respectively refer to the treatment of the body as the proper rearing of a child [Ba, ECWB], and to the providing of clothing [Ba], or other needs [ECWB] for it. The verb ἐκτρέφει 'he nourishes' refers to the rearing up of the body from childhood [Ba, ECWB]. It means to properly bring up a child. The sense is that a person provides for his body and guards it from exposure and want [Ba]. The verb θάλπει 'he cherishes' refers to providing the body with all it needs for health, comfort, and life [ECWB].

3. The verbs are synonyms and refer to the treatment of the body as the proper rearing of a child [ISBE, ISBE2, WBC]. The analogy may be the consideration of the church as a child-bride who is being brought to maturity by the bridegroom's care. More directly relevant to this verse is the occurrence of the two verbs in reverse order in an extra-biblical marriage contract where the duties of the husband are 'to cherish and nourish and clothe' his wife [WBC].

4. The two verbs together are understood in a general fashion of all the loving attention we show to our own bodies [AB (probably), Can, CBC, Ea, EBC, Ho, NCBC, TNTC]. This may refer to food and clothing, but these two verbs are really a rather general expression for all the loving attention that a husband should show to his wife [Can]. Both terms express tenderness and solicitude and so are both suited to express the care by which every man provides for the wants and comfort of his own body [Ho]. A man's care over his body is that of a nursing-mother over a child [AB, Ea].

QUESTION—What relationship is indicated by καθώς 'just as'?

1. This comparative clause refers to Christ's nourishing and cherishing of the church as a parallel to the last clause [Alf, ECWB, EGT, Ho, My, TD, TH, WBC]. The nourishing and cherishing implied in this clause must be understood metaphorically, in keeping with its subject. To bring into the interpretation any two particular elements is arbitrary [My]. This is a broad statement of Christ's loving care for the church [EGT]. The idea of the natural rearing and cherishing of the body suggests the thought of the tender care Christ provides as he 'rears up' his church from weak infancy to full maturity in heaven, all the while 'cherishing' it 'as a nurse cherishes her children' [ECWB].

2. This comparative clause refers to the general idea of Christ's love and care for the church rather than as a strict parallel to the last clause [Ba, Cal, CBC, Ea, EBC, El, NCBC, NIC, St, TNTC].

5:30 **because we-are members of his body.**

TEXT—Some manuscripts contain additions to the end of this verse following τοῦ σώματος αὐτοῦ 'his body'. Some add καὶ ἐκ τῶν ὀσέων αὐτοῦ 'and of his bones', others add ἐκ τῆς σαρκὸς αὐτοῦ καὶ ἐκ τῶν ὀσέων αὐτοῦ 'of his flesh and of his bones'. Others have minor variations of these two longer variant readings [GNT]. GNT gives the short reading (ending with τοῦ σώματος αὐτοῦ 'his body') an A rating, indicating that the text is virtually certain. The addition ἐκ τῆς σαρκὸς αὐτοῦ καὶ ἐκ τῶν ὀσέων αὐτοῦ 'of his flesh and of his bones' is supported by Alf, Ba, Cal, Ea, ECWB, El, Ho, LJ, My, Si, and KJV.

QUESTION—What relationship is indicated by ὅτι 'because'?

1. This indicates the reason for Christ's implied actions (nourishing and cherishing) in the previous clause [Alf (probably), CBC, DNTT, Ea, EBC, EGT, El, Ho, Lns, My, NCBC, NIC; NASB, NIV, NJB, REB]: just as Christ does the church, the reason being that we are members of his body. The reason is that the church is part of him [EGT] and stands in the nearest and dearest relation to him [Ea]. Following 'church' in the preceding clause is an implied linking phrase 'which is his body' [Ho], or 'which is married to him' [Alf].
2. This gives the grounds for Christ's implied actions (nourishing and cherishing) in the previous clause [TH, We]: just as Christ does the church, as we know he does since we are members of his body. This should not be translated as though this is the reason for Christ's nourishing and cherishing the church, rather it is the basis for this declaration [TH]. Paul appeals to the knowledge of these readers' own personal experience [We].

QUESTION—What is meant by μέλη ἐσμὲν τοῦ σώματος αὐτοῦ 'we are members of his body'?

1. This clause refers to the corporate or mystical body of Christ, the church [AB, Ba, Ea, EBC, EGT, El, Ho, ICC, ISBE2, LJ, Lns, MNTC, My, NCBC, NIC, NTC, Si, St, TD, TH, TNTC, WBC, We, WeBC].
   1.1 This implies the unity of the members of the body with Christ [Ba, CBC, ICC, TNTC]. There is a close and intimate union between Christians and the Savior, so much so that they may be spoken of as *one* [Ba]. Paul returns to this concept to stress that the church is part of the very being of the risen Jesus, and as such he loves and cares for it [CBC].
   1.2 This implies not only the unity of the members of the body with Christ, but of the marriage analogy as well [AB (probably), El, ISBE2, Si, St, TD]. This phrase refers both to the union the members of the church have with Christ as members of his mystical body, the church, and to the more mysterious marital relationship in which Christ in his natural and now glorified body stands to his church [El]. This statement fuses the two analogies Paul has been using for the church, the church as Christ's body and the church as Christ's bride [St].

1.3 This implies not only the unity of the members of the body with Christ, but of the source of their spiritual existence as members of the church as well [Ea, EGT, El, Ho, LJ, My].
2. This clause refers to the physical body of Christ [Alf, Can, ECWB].
2.1 The reference is to Christ's body as now glorified [Alf, ECWB]. This means that members of the church, as spiritually united with him, are parts and members of his glorified body [Alf, ECWB].
2.2 The reference is to Christ's physical body as expressive of his incarnation in human nature [Can]. See comments by Can in the next QUESTION.

QUESTION—If the words ἐκ τῆς σαρκὸς αὐτοῦ καὶ ἐκ τῶν ὀσέτων αὐτοῦ 'of his flesh and of his bones' really belong in the text, what is meant by them?

A major problem with these words is how we as members of the church are derived ἐκ τῆς σαρκὸς αὐτοῦ καὶ ἐκ τῶν ὀσέτων αὐτοῦ 'of his flesh and of his bones' [Lns, WBC], the phrase ἐκ τῶν ὀσέτων αὐτοῦ 'of his bones', especially being a problem, for no one has been able adequately to explain what it means to be 'members of his bones' [ICC, WBC]. No one has been able to explain how this language is appropriate to the figurative or mystical body of Christ, unless the words are proverbial in form, but there is no evidence they were ever used that way. The utmost that can be said about the whole phrase ἐκ τῆς σαρκὸς αὐτοῦ καὶ ἐκ τῶν ὀσέτων αὐτοῦ 'of his flesh and of his bones' is that it expresses an intimate connection [ICC]. Others, however, state that with σάρξ 'flesh', ὀστέον 'bone' is a metaphor, in Gen. 2:23, 2 Sam. 5:1, and other passages for kinship [DNTT, IDB, ISBE], for having the same nature as another [ISBE], and that here, in this variant reading, this phrase expresses affection [ISBE], kinship between Christians and Christ [DNTT], and that the phrase expresses the essence of a man [IDB]. The whole idea of a mystical derivation from the glorified flesh and bones of Christ is unbiblical. Mystical derivation is not mystical union [Lns].

5:31 Because[a] of-this a-man shall-leave[b] his father and his mother and shall-be-joined[c] to his wife, and the two shall-become[d] one flesh.

TEXT—Some manuscripts omit the definite articles before πατέρα 'father' and μητέρα 'mother'. GNT does not note these variant readings, though it does place the definite articles in brackets in its text. Those who support the variant readings omitting the articles are AB, Alf, EGT, El, and My.

LEXICON—a. ἀντί with genitive object (LN **89.24**) (BAGD 3. p. 73): 'because' [LN]. The phrase ἀντί τούτου is translated 'because of this' [**LN**], 'for this reason' [AB, BAGD, LN, WBC; NAB, NIV, NRSV, TEV, TNT], 'for this cause' [El, Lns, Rob, We; KJV, NASB], 'this is why' [NIC; NJB, REB], 'therefore' [NTC]. This preposition is a marker of reason and may possibly imply purpose as well [LN].

b. fut. act. indic. of καταλείπω (LN **34.40**) (BAGD 1.a. p. 413): 'to leave' [AB, El, **LN**, Lns, NIC, NTC, Rob, WBC, We; all versions except NJB], 'to leave someone behind' (when a place is left) [BAGD], 'to no longer relate to' [LN]. This future tense verb is also translated as a customary present tense: 'leaves' [NJB]. This verb denotes a causing of a particular relationship to cease. In translating this verse, any expression which suggests abandonment or desertion should be avoided, since what is involved is the limitation of a particular relationship [LN].

- c. fut. pass. indic. of προσκολλάω (προσκολλάομαι LN **34.22**) (BAGD p. 716): 'to be joined to' [AB, BAGD, El, **LN**, MM, NIC, Rob, WBC; KJV, NRSV, TNT], 'to join oneself to' [LN], 'to become a part of' [LN], 'to be united to' [NIV, REB], 'to unite with' [TEV], 'to adhere closely to' [BAGD], 'to be faithfully devoted to' [BAGD], 'to be glued to' [Lns], 'to cleave to' [MM, NTC, We; NASB], 'to cling to' [NAB], 'to stick to' [MM]. This future tense verb is also translated as customary present tense: 'becomes attached to' [NJB].
- d. εἰς with accusative object and fut. act. indic. of εἰμί 'to be' (LN 13.51): 'to become' [AB, LN, NIC, NTC, WBC, We; all versions except KJV, NAB, NJB], 'to be' [El, Lns, Rob; KJV], 'to change' [LN] 'to be made into' [NAB]. The future tense of this construction is also translated as customary present tense: 'become' [NJB]. The idiom εἰμί εἰς literally means 'to be into' and denotes a change from one state to another [LN].

QUESTION—What relationship is indicated by ἀντὶ τούτου 'because of this'?

1. This phrase connects to a previous reference in Genesis [Cal, EBC, Lns, NTC, TH]. Though Paul substitutes a slightly different connective here than the LXX has, it is meant as part of the quote from Gen. 2:24 and does not connect to anything in Paul's preceding statements [Lns, NTC, TH]. Early Christians would have understood that the connection was with Gen. 2:23. The words are Adam's [Lns]. It is not clear whether Moses used these words as part of Adam's quoted speech or to introduce his own inference regarding the creation of man, nor is it all that important, for in either case it is an announcement from God regarding the duties that men owe their wives [Cal]. The connection in Genesis is with the idea of the bond which exists between man and his wife by virtue of creation, expressed in Gen. 2:23 [EBC, NTC] by Adam's words 'bone of my bone and flesh of my flesh' [EBC]. The meaning of Paul's ἀντὶ τούτου 'because of this' is the same as the ἕνεκεν τοῦτο of the LXX [NTC].
2. This phrase connects to a previous reference in Ephesians [AB, Alf, Ba, Can, CBC, Ea, ECWB, EGT, Ho, IB, LJ, MNTC, My, NCBC, NIC, Rob, St, TH, WBC, We].
2.1 The connection is with 5:25–30 [AB], or 5:28–30 [IB], but principally with 5:30 [AB, Alf, Ba, Can, CBC, Ea, El, Ho, LJ, MNTC, My, NCBC, St, WBC]: so ought the husband to love his own wife as his own body...for we are members of his body; because of this, (it is said) a man shall leave, etc. The connection is with the thought of the Christo-soteriological origin of the church and its unifying effect, as described in 5:25–30 [AB], i.e., that Christians are members of Christ [Alf, Ba]. Paul's connection of ideas is: 'corresponding to this, that is, that we are

members of Christ's body, shall a man...cleave unto his wife'. A man leaves his father and mother so as to cleave to his wife and become one flesh with her stands over against, or is the counterpart to, Christ's making us members of his body. That the one union is parallel to the other is Paul's thought here [Can]. Just as Eve was formed out of the body of Adam and therefore it is said that a man shall leave his father and mother and be joined to his wife and they two shall become one flesh, so since we are members of Christ's body, therefore Christ and the church are also one flesh [Ho]. This connection presupposes the question: why has it been written that 'a man will leave...be joined...become one'? The answer is that in the great event in which the Messiah proved to be the 'savior of his body' (5:23), all that was said of Adam and Eve in Genesis 2 was fulfilled. This accords with the statement given in 5:32 that Gen. 2:24 refers to Christ and the church [AB].

2.2 The connection is with 5:28–9a, b [ECWB, EGT, NIC (probably), Rob, We]: the husband ought to love his own wife as his own body...; because of this, a man shall leave, etc. It seems far simpler to consider the words of 5:29c–30, 'even as the Lord...his bones', as parenthetical and refer this quotation back to 5:28–29, for the Lord quotes this verse from Genesis in exactly the same way to show the indissoluble character of the marriage bond. But here the similarity of connection with the original passage is even stronger: because a man's wife is as his own body, 'for this cause shall a man', etc. To connect this quotation with the words immediately preceding in 5:30 is possible, but yields a meaning that is too mystical even for this passage [ECWB].

2.3 The connection is with 5:28 only [Rob; TEV]: the one who loves his own wife loves himself. Because of this a man shall leave, etc. Paul uses this quote to justify his statement that 'he that loves his own wife loves himself' [Rob]. The TEV places 5:29–30 in parentheses to make clear that it regards this quote as supporting the statement made in 5:28, not of 5:29–30.

QUESTION—What is the significance of the future tense forms of the verbs in this verse?

1. The future tense forms here do not have future meaning, but are gnomic or proverbial futures [AB, Alf, Can (probably), WBC; NJB (probably)]. They point to the past, present, and future aspects which constitute Christ's union to his bride, the church: his leaving his father's side, which is past, his gradual preparation of the union, which is present, and his full consummation of it, which is future [Alf].
2. The future tenses are predictive of the future impulse and acting of the human race [Ea, EGT, El, ICC (probably), Lns]. The words are Adam's. He had no father or mother, and he uttered them while still in the Garden of Eden. They are prophetic of what young men would later do [Lns]. They are ethical futures, expressing what can, should, or must be [EGT].

3. The future tenses are predictive of Christ [AB, El, My]. That these future tenses indicate something positively future, in no way invalidates their force as ethical futures, indicating what will, shall, and ought to happen [AB, El].

3.1 They predict Christ's coming in the flesh, i.e., the incarnation [El].

3.2 They predict Christ's second coming [My, TD]. This refers to the union at the end of the age when the church, the Bride of Christ actually becomes his wife [My, TD]. Paul uses the future tenses, not because they are present in the LXX of Gen. 2:24, but because he is using the words of Gen. 2:24 *as his own words*, and the event he is applying them to is still future to his time [My].

QUESTION—What is meant by καταλείψει 'he shall leave'?

This verb is to be interpreted relatively and not absolutely. It is altogether a question of degree [Cal]. When a person marries, he or she enters a relationship which breaks the former relationships and supersedes them [DNTT, LJ, TNTC]. The love that a man bears his father and mother is surmounted by a more powerful attachment [Ea]. He must learn to think of himself no longer as the son of his parents, but as the husband of his wife. The leaving of the father and mother is essentially this: that he must not allow his father and mother to control him as hitherto they have done [LJ, TNTC]. It is important *to avoid* translating this verb with any implication of abandonment or desertion [TH]. In Paul's implied analogy, Christ leaves his father's side in heaven to come and be joined to his bride, the church [AB, DNTT, LJ, My, TD]. But others say this verb and the following one cannot be applied to Christ's relationship with the church [Ho, IB, ICC, WBC], as though he left his Father in heaven to be joined to the church, because the idea that his union with the church could be conceived as closer than his unity with the Father is unacceptable [IB].

QUESTION—What is meant by προσκολληθήσεται 'he shall be joined to'?

The Hebrew qabfD 'to be attached to, to be joined' and its Greek equivalents describe a voluntary, passionate, intimate relationship which involves a man's soul and body [AB]. Literally, the Greek verb προσκολληθήσεται means 'will be glued to' [EBC, EGT, ISBE, Lns], and when taken in conjunction with the reference to σάρκα μίαν 'one flesh', refers only to sexual intercourse as hallowed by God himself [EBC, Lns, TD, TH]. It designates the closest form of personal union [ISBE]. It signifies an underlying sense of belonging or commitment [ISBE2]. This verb is used figuratively [BAGD, MM] to denote the attachment a husband feels for his wife in LXX Gen. 2:24 and parallels [BAGD]. It denotes the beginning of an association with someone, whether permanent or temporary. In this verse the translator should avoid a term which denotes only sexual relations, since the focus of this verb is upon interpersonal relationships [LN (34.22)].

QUESTION—What is meant by ἔσονται οἱ δύο εἰς σάρκα μίαν 'the two shall become one flesh'?
1. The author views the union of Christ and the church as a further illustration of the meaning of σάρκα μίαν 'one flesh' in Gen. 2:24, i.e., Gen. 2:24 is properly a statement concerning the human marriage relationship [Ba, Cal, Can, DNTT, Ea, ECWB, EGT, IB, ICC, NCBC, NTC, St, We]. There is no evidence that the marriage connection was originally designed to symbolize or typify this union. However it may be used to illustrate that connection and to show the strength of the attachment that exists between Christ and his people [Ba]. Paul uses this clause to cover two subjects, the common law of marriage and the spiritual union between Christ and his church, the first as the illustration of the latter [Cal]. The words of this quotation are to be understood simply of human marriage. They are used to show why language from Gen. 2:23 was used in the preceding verse to depict the union of Christ and the church. The allegory that Paul draws is not in the quotation itself, i.e., he does not allegorize this verse directly, but he implies it in the nuptial figure and language as he applies it to Christ and the church. The quotation is used to show the source and authority for this allegory [Ea]. Paul simply uses the words of Genesis to describe the fact of human marriage [Can, DNTT, EGT, NCBC, NTC]. He does not say that marriage was instituted because of the union of Christ and the church [Can]. But he does use the words to illustrate their highest ideal, the church's relation to Christ [EGT, NCBC, NTC]. The words basically refer to the sexual union of male and female, but Paul looks at the love standing behind this union and finds that the love of Christ for his church is the highest pattern and ideal for married love [NTC, St].
2. The author views the union of Christ and the church as the basis for the meaning of σάρκα μίαν 'one flesh' in Gen. 2:24, i.e., this clause in Gen. 2:24 is prophetic of Christ's coming [AB, Alf, CBC, EBC, El, Ho, MNTC, My, TD, TH, WBC]. From the beginning God intended that the human marriage bond would typify the supreme union between Christ and the church, and as marriage superseded all previous relationships, so the union with Christ supersedes all other relationships [MNTC]. This expression covers more than just the human couple's sexual union. It also implies a psychic and spiritual unity, and their life together. It does not mean that they are no longer different personalities, but it does denote a new social unit which is separate from other units, and which is nuclear. As applied to Christ and the church, this expression means that he has elected the church to be his own, that he is joined to the church as 'head' to her 'body', in a relationship that itself points on to the renewal of all things in Christ. The sole basis of Gen. 2:24 is the shining model of the Christ-church relationship, the benefits of which the saints may enjoy even now [AB]. The clause means that Christ and the church will form one *ethical* person, just as married persons, by virtue of their sexual union,

become a physical unity [My]. This whole verse is said in 5:32 to refer not to human marriages but to the relationship of Christ and the church [Alf, CBC].

3. The author views the union of Christ and the church as leading to spiritual procreation [WeBC]. It is evident that the sexual union of husband and wife does not weld them into one person in the real and permanent sense of the word. But this union does lead to one actual new person when a child is born as the result. Thus the deeper truth revealed in this Genesis quotation is that the union of believers with Christ as their head is intended to spell out the higher purpose for the church, which is spiritual procreation [WeBC].

5:32 This mystery is great;[a] but I speak about[b] Christ and about[b] the church.

LEXICON—a. μέγας (LN 87.22) (BAGD 2.b.β. p. 498): 'great' [BAGD, El, LN, Lns, NTC, Rob, WBC, We; KJV, NAB, NASB, NRSV, REB, TNT], '(has) great significance' [NJB], 'important' [BAGD, LN] 'eminent' [AB], 'deep' [NIC; TEV], 'profound' [NIV], 'sublime' [BAGD].

b. εἰς with accusative object (LN 90.23): 'about' [LN, WBC; NIV], 'concerning' [LN, Rob; KJV], 'with respect to' [LN], 'with reference to' [LN, NTC; NASB], 'in reference to' [El, NIC], 'as relating to' [AB], 'in regard to' [Lns]. This preposition is also translated as an adverbial phrase modifying λέγω 'I speak': 'looking to' [We]. It is also translated as a clause: 'it refers to' [NAB]. The words λέγω εἰς 'I speak about' are translated 'I am applying it to' [NJB, NRSV], 'which I take to refer to' [REB], 'which I understand as applying to' [TEV], 'in my view it has to do with' [TNT].

QUESTION—What is meant by τὸ μυστήριον τοῦτο μέγα ἐστίν 'this mystery is great'?

This is an explanatory comment on the preceding verse [El, My] giving the apostle's interpretation of the preceding quote [My]. The noun μυστήριον 'mystery' is generally used in the plural of divine truths in other epistles, but may occur in the singular, as here, [TNTC] to indicate some particular deep truth which has been revealed in the divine plan [EBC, TNTC, WBC]. The adjective μέγας 'great' is in the predicate position to τὸ μυστήριον τοῦτο 'this mystery' [IB, TH]. It means 'great' in the sense of grandeur and importance [EGT], or 'deep' [El], 'of profound significance' [IB, NCBC].

1. The noun μυστήριον 'mystery', as elsewhere in Ephesians, refers to a revealed secret, something which hitherto had not been made known, and is not discoverable by unaided human reason [Ba, Can, CBC, Ea, EBC, ECWB, EGT, El, IB, ICC, Lns, MNTC, My, NIC, NTC, St, TNTC, WBC, We].

1.1 The reference is to the relationship of husband and wife in human marriage [EGT, El, IB, TNTC, We]: the mystery of being 'one in the flesh' in marriage is great. The present verse presents the mystery of the conjugal relationship in itself, and still more in its typical application to Christ and the church [El, IB]. To refer this to a comparison of the relation of husband and wife with that of Christ and the church causes the following ἐγὼ δὲ λέγω 'but I say' to lose its point [EGT, El]. Neither does it refer only to the spiritual union of Christ and the church. The sense, in relation to the following clause, is: 'the truth of which I have spoken with regard to the relation of husband and wife as one flesh is a revelation of profound importance, but in speaking of it as I have done, I wish to explain that I, for my part, understand it as clearly pointing beyond itself to some transcendental, eternal reality [IB] and that my intention is to direct your thoughts to that higher relation between Christ and his church [EGT, El, IB], which in its likeness to human marriage, its greatest significance lies' [EGT, El]. After writing the words of this clause, the apostle then contemplates the manifold applications of the primitive marriage ordinance [TNTC, We]. He sees that, in the final union, humanity will reach its consummation [We] and then states the greatest mystery of them all [TNTC, We].

1.2 The reference is to the relationship between Christ and the church [Ba, Can, CBC, Ea, EBC, My, WBC]: the mystery of the bond of unity between Christ and the church is great. Paul is saying that Gen. 2:24 enunciates a more profound truth than was realized until Christ actually came to win his bride [EBC]. This does not mean that the union between Christ and the church is incomprehensible [Ba, Can, Ea] when it is disclosed, but that it is not known to those uninitiated into this truth [Ba, Ea].

1.3 The reference is both to the relationship of husband and wife in human marriage and to the relationship between Christ and the church [ECWB, MNTC, St]: the mystery of oneness, both that which takes place between husband and wife and that between Christ and the church, is great. The words apply to the type as well as to the antitype. All history shows that the indissoluble and sacred nature of marriage is a 'mystery' contained in God's law and fully revealed in Christ alone, but it is clear from the next clause that Paul's thought has passed from the type to focus upon the antitype. Yet the two cannot really be separated because the type brings out features of the antitype which no other comparison can make clear. The noun μυστήριον 'mystery' is a secret of God's law which has been fully revealed in Christ alone [ECWB].

1.4 The reference is to the comparison of human marriage with the union of Christ and the church [ICC, Lns, NIC, NTC]: the revelation of this comparison with and the application of human marriage to the union of Christ and his church is great. The meaning of this clause is 'this revelation, that the institution of human marriage, revealed in Genesis, is applicable to Christ and the church, is an important or profound doctrine' [ICC].

2. The noun μυστήριον 'mystery' has a special meaning here [AB, Alf, BAGD (2. p. 530), Cal, DNTT, Ho, IDB, ISBE, ISBE2, LJ, NCBC, Rob, TD (probably), TH].
  2.1 It means something which is beyond complete human comprehension [BAGD (2. p. 530), Cal, Ho, LJ, NCBC].
    2.1.1 The reference is to the relationship of husband and wife in human marriage [NCBC]: the mystery of being 'one in the flesh' in marriage is great.
    2.1.2 The reference is to the relationship between Christ and the church [BAGD (2. p. 530), Cal, Ho]: the mystery of the bond of unity between Christ and the church is great. The spiritual union between Christ and the church is presented as something surpassing human comprehension [Cal, Ho].
    2.1.3 The reference is both to the relationship of husband and wife in human marriage and to the relationship between Christ and the church [LJ]: the mystery of oneness, both that which takes place between husband and wife and that between Christ and the church is great.
  2.2 It has a secret mystical, typological, or allegorical meaning and the reference is to the relationship between Christ and the church [AB, Alf, DNTT, IDB, ISBE, ISBE2, Rob, TD, TH]: the mystery of the bond of unity between Christ and the church is great. The noun μυστήριον 'mystery' is used in the sense of a hidden meaning in the Genesis text which can only be properly understood when it is interpreted in a typological or allegorical manner [TH].

QUESTION—What is affirmed in the clause ἐγὼ δὲ λέγω εἰς Χριστὸν καὶ εἰς τὴν ἐκκλησίαν 'but I speak about Christ and the church'?

This clause is added to make clear that the reference of τὸ μυστήριον τοῦτο 'this mystery' is to Christ and the church and not just to the institution of marriage [Alf, Cal, Can, Ea, ICC]. Another commentator says this clause applies the words of Genesis to Christ and the church in a secondary manner, but not as its primary interpretation [NCBC]. The δέ 'but' is not simply explicative, but having a contrastive meaning, as though the writer supposed his phraseology might be interpreted in another and different way [AB, DNTT, Ea, El, IB, MNTC, My, NIC, WBC].

5:33 Nevertheless[a] you also the-(one) by one, each so let-him-love his-own wife as himself,

LEXICON—a. πλήν (LN 89.130) (BAGD 1.c. p. 669): 'nevertheless' [El, LN, NTC, Rob; KJV, NASB], 'however' [BAGD, We; NIV, NRSV], 'in any case' [AB, BAGD, WBC; NAB], 'to sum up' [NJB], 'well then' [Lns], 'but' [BAGD, LN, NIC], 'only' [BAGD], 'except' [LN]. This particle is also translated as a clause: 'but it applies to' [REB, TEV], 'but it has to do with' [TNT]. This is a marker of contrast, and implies the validity of something despite other considerations [LN]. Coming at the beginning of

EPHESIANS 5:33 511

a sentence or clause, this particle may be used to break off a discussion and emphasize what is important [BAGD].

QUESTION—What relationship is indicated by πλήν 'nevertheless'?

1. This particle breaks off the preceding discussion and emphasizes the important points, 'nevertheless', 'in summary' [Alf, Ba, BAGD, Cal, Can, Ea, EGT, El, HG, IB, ICC, Lns, MNTC, My, NCBC, NIC, Rob, TNTC, WBC, We, WeBC; KJV, NASB, NIV, NJB, NRSV].

    1.1 It indicates a return from a digression [Ba, Cal, ICC, MNTC, NCBC, Rob, TNTC, WBC, WeBC]. Paul resumes the subject which he had been discussing [Ba, ICC] in 5:21–29 before his diversion by the subject of the Redeemer's love for his church [Ba]. In conclusion, the Apostle returns to the practical part of his lesson which is the duty of his readers to practice in daily life [Rob]. The writer brings his readers back to the gist of his exhortation on marriage. The particle rounds off the discussion and accentuates the main point [WBC].

    1.2 It indicates a return to a startling thought [Ea, El (probably)]. The πλήν 'nevertheless' does not indicate a return from a digression [Ea, El, Lns, My], but indicates a comparative force [El]. The preceding verses have not been a digression, but an interlinked and extended illustration. The πλήν 'nevertheless' has the sense of 'yet apart from this'; that is, apart from the illustration of the conjugal relationship of Christ with his church. It indicates a return to the startling thought that the love of the husband for his wife is based upon that of Christ for his church [Ea].

2. This particle introduces a contrast or an exception to the Genesis quotation, 'howbeit', 'in any case' [AB, CBC, EBC, ECWB, Ho, LN, TH; NAB, REB, TEV, TNT]. The particle is strongly adversative [TH]. Paul uses this particle to return his readers' thoughts to the literal and commonly accepted interpretation of Gen. 2:24 [AB, CBC, EBC (probably), ECWB, Ho, TH], indicating that he did not forget it or deny it in stating his opinion of its figurative sense [AB]. They are at least to get hold of the essential instructions he has been trying to convey [EBC] and understand that the literal sense of Gen. 2:24 applies to each husband [TH; TEV, TNT (note)]. This interpretation of the connection is to be preferred because of the words καὶ ὑμεῖς 'you also' which presuppose the connection is to what immediately precedes [Ho].

QUESTION—To whom does the καί 'also' refer in the phrase καὶ ὑμεῖς 'you also'?

It refers to Christ, 'you also (as well as Christ)' [Alf]. The καί 'also' conjoins the ὑμεῖς 'you' with Christ, meaning 'love is to be fulfilled in you also, as in Christ' [EGT, El, My].

QUESTION—Who is referred to in ὑμεῖς οἱ καθ' ἕνα 'you one by one'?

1. It refers to the husbands [AB, Ba, Can, Ea, EBC, EGT, El, Ho, Lns, My, NCBC, NTC, WBC; KJV, NAB, NASB, NIV, NJB, NRSV]. The distributive phrase οἱ καθ' ἕνα 'one by one' individualizes the ὑμεῖς

'you' [EGT, El, HG, Lns, Mo, Tu], emphatically including every husband [WBC], and excluding all exceptions [EGT, Lns, NTC].
2. It refers to both husbands and wives [REB, TEV, TNT]. These translations follow their translation of ὑμεῖς οἱ καθ' ἕνα 'you one by one' with a colon, indicating that they understand that the address is directed to both the husband and the wife.

QUESTION—What is meant by the imperative clause ἕκαστος τὴν ἑαυτοῦ γυναῖκα οὕτως ἀγαπάτω ὡς ἑαυτόν 'each one must so love his own wife as himself'?

The injunction to husbands to love their wives reiterates not only the argument from 5:28 about loving their wives as their own bodies, but also incorporates that of 5:25 about loving the wife as Christ loves the church [NCBC, WBC]. The imperative verb ἀγαπάτω 'must love' interprets the verbs καταλείψει 'shall leave', προσκολληθήσεται 'shall be joined to', and the clause ἔσονται οἱ δύο εἰς σάρκα μίαν 'the two shall become one flesh' in the preceding quote from Genesis. As such, the verb includes in its meaning the element of sexual love [AB]. The ἕκαστος 'each one' reinforces the preceding οἱ καθ' ἕνα 'one by one' [My] expressing still more emphatically a duty from which no single husband is exempt [EGT, Lns, My, NTC]. The adverb οὕτως 'so' indicates the manner of what each is to do, that is, each is to love his own wife in a manner that is in keeping with the ideal of Christ presented in this 'mystery' [My]. The combination of οὕτως 'so' with ὡς 'as' reinforces the comparative construction [WBC]. The imperative verb ἀγαπάτω 'must love' is singular in number, in agreement with ἕκαστος 'each one' rather than ὑμεῖς 'you (pl.)' [Alf, Ea, EGT, El, Ho, My] which is the real subject [Ho, My]. Its present tense is durative, indicating constant love [NTC].

1. The phrase ὡς ἑαυτόν 'as himself' is an implied reference to Lev. 19:18, 34 [AB, NCBC, NIC, WBC]. It shows that the husband's love for his wife is but an extension of the command given to Israel to love the neighbor and the stranger 'as oneself' [AB]. The wife is the husband's primary and exemplary neighbor [WBC]. But the phrase does not point to a comparison of the measure of love (i.e., 'as much as' oneself) so much as it does to the reason and result of love. The one who loves another ends up loving himself simply because one receives by giving. This is true even in this context in the case of the Messiah and his love for the church. The bounty of love spent falls back upon the lover [AB].
2. The phrase ὡς ἑαυτόν 'as himself' means 'as being himself' [Ea, EBC, EGT, El, Ho, ICC, Lns, We]. It means as being one flesh with him (5:28, 31) [Ea, EGT, Ho, Lns].

and the wife that[a] she-may-fear/respect[b] her husband.
LEXICON—a. ἵνα (LN 90.22) (BAGD III.2. p.378): 'that' [LN, Lns], not explicit [LN; NAB, NRSV]. This particle is also represented by ellipsis ('...') [AB]. The particle ἵνα 'that', under the influence of the following

subjunctive verb, is also translated 'see to it that' [NTC; NASB], 'see that' [Rob, We; KJV], 'must' [NIV, REB, TEV], 'let' (the wife...) [El, NIC, WBC; NJB, TNT]. The particle ἵνα 'that' is a marker of the content of discourse, particularly if purpose is implied. In this verse an expression of command is implied, and therefore this clause with ἵνα 'that' may be interpreted as being a matter of content [LN]. With a subjunctive verb it may be used elliptically as a periphrasis for the imperative, 'is to' (respect her husband) [BAGD].

b. pres. sub. mid. of φοβέω (φοβέομαι LN 25.252, 87.14) (BAGD 2.b. p. 863): 'to fear' [AB, LN (25.252, 87.14), WBC, We], 'to be afraid' [LN (25.252)], 'to respect' [BAGD, Lns, NTC; NASB, NIV, NJB, NRSV, TEV], 'to show respect' [NAB, TNT], 'to show great respect for' [LN (87.14)], 'to reverence' [El, NIC, Rob; KJV], 'to have reverence' [BAGD], 'to show reverence' [REB], 'to show great reverence for' [LN (87.14)]. This verb may denote being in a state of fear [LN (25.252)], or it may denote having such a sense of awe or respect for a person that a measure of fear is involved [LN (87.14)].

QUESTION—What is the force of the words ἡ δὲ γυνή 'and the wife'?

This is a nominative absolute construction [Ea, Ho, ICC] which is emphatic by position [EGT, El, My] and leads to an anacolouthon, a broken sentence, with the onset of the following ἵνα 'that' clause [AB, My]. It indicates a second and indirect address to the wife, in contrast to the emphatic and direct address to the husband. This address to the wife closes a broad chiastic structure which began with 5:21 [WBC].

QUESTION—What relationship is indicated by ἵνα 'that'?

1. It indicates Paul's hope or expectation [AB, My; NAB, NRSV]: and the wife—she ought to fear her husband. After the mention of the wife (ἡ δὲ γύνη 'and the woman'), Paul hesitates, then continues with a broken sentence: ἵνα φοβῆται τὸν ἄνδρα 'may she fear her husband' [AB].
   1.1 Φοβῆται means 'she ought to reverence' or 'should respect' [My; NAB, NRSV].
   1.2 Φοβῆται means 'may she fear' [AB]. Paul's final statement regarding the wife expresses his hope that, in consequence of the husband loving his wife after the pattern of Christ's love for the church, the wife will fear her husband [AB].
2. It indicates Paul's command [Alf, Ba, BAGD, Cal, Can (probably), CBC (probably), Ea, EBC, ECWB, EGT, El, HG, Ho, IB, ICC, LJ, LN, Lns, Mo, Mou, NCBC, NIC, NTC, Rob, St, TD (probably), TH, Tu, WBC; all versions except NAB, NRSV]: and the wife, (let her see) that she fears her husband. The ἵνα 'that' depends upon an implied imperative verb (required for the resolution of the nominative absolute γυνή 'wife' into smoother English [Ea, Ho, ICC]), such as 'I command' or 'let her see' [Ea, El, Ho, ICC, We].
   2.1 The subjunctive φοβῆται means 'respect, reverence' [BAGD, Cal, Can, CBC, Ea, EBC, EGT, El, ICC, LJ, Lns, NIC, NTC, Rob, TH, TNTC; all

versions except NAB, NRSV]. It means 'reverential obedience' [LJ]. This is the kind of fear that is based upon reverence and respect, not fearfulness [TNTC].

2.2 The subjunctive φοβῆται means 'fear' [Ba, ECWB, IB, NCBC, TD, WBC, We]. It denotes the obedience that is demanded by the superior authority of masters or husbands as lords. It is a sign of complete dependence upon the power of the stronger [TD]. The wife's fear of her husband is modeled upon the church's fear of Christ, which certainly includes respect, but is much stronger than this, though not the fear of the slave. Fear involves observance of the proper authority structures in society [WBC].

DISCOURSE UNIT: 6:1–9 [Ea, Ho, ICC, My, Rob, St; NASB]. The topic is the duties of parents and children and of masters and slaves [Ho, St], the principles of reverence and love in the whole sphere of family life [Rob], family relationships [NASB], special injunctions to children and fathers, slaves and masters [ICC], the conduct of children, fathers, slaves, and masters [My].

DISCOURSE UNIT: 6:1–4 [AB, Alf, Cal, CBC, EBC, ECWB, EGT, El, IB, LJ, Lns, MNTC, NIC, NTC, Rob, Si, TH, TNTC, WBC, We, WeBC; NAB, NIV, TEV, TNT]. The topic is the relation of parents and children [AB, Alf, ECWB, IB, MNTC, NIC, Rob, TNTC, We], advice to children and fathers [CBC], parent-child relationships in the home [LJ], children and parents in household relationships [WBC], the third admonition, that for children and fathers [Lns], parenthood in Christian relationships [EBC], the Christian relationship of children to their parents [WeBC], the new life in Christ for parents and children [TH], the parental bond [Si], children are to obey their parents, and fathers are not to provoke their children, but to educate them in a holy manner [El].

DISCOURSE UNIT: 6:1–3 [Ba, St; NRSV]. The topic is an exhortation to children to obey their parents [Ba, St], with a promise of the blessing that will follow such obedience [Ba].

6:1 Children, obey[a] your parents[b] in/in-association-with/because-of[c] (the) Lord; for this is right/righteous.[d]

TEXT—Some manuscripts do not contain the words ἐν κυρίῳ 'in the Lord'. GNT includes these words with a C rating, indicating difficulty in deciding which variant to place in the text. The reading which omits the phrase is taken only by REB.

LEXICON—a. pres. act. impera. of ὑπακούω (LN 36.15) (BAGD 1. p. 837): 'to obey' [AB, BAGD, El, LN, NIC, NTC, Rob, WBC, We; all versions except NJB], 'to be obedient' [NJB], 'to keep obeying' [Lns], 'to be subject to' [BAGD]. Obedience consists of listening to the advice given by parents [EBC] or readiness to hear [EGT].

b. γονεύς (LN 10.18) (BAGD p. 165): 'parents' [AB, BAGD, El, LN, Lns, NIC, NTC, Rob, WBC, We; all versions].

c. ἐν with dative object (LN 89.26, 89.84, 89.119) (BAGD 1.5.d. p. 259): 'in' [El, LN (89.119), Lns, NIC, NTC, Rob, WBC, We; all versions except REB, TEV, TNT], 'because of' [AB, LN (89.26)], 'on account of, by reason of' [LN (89.26)] 'in union with, joined closely to' [LN (89.119)], omitted for textual reasons [REB]. The phrase ἐν κυρίῳ 'in the Lord' is translated 'it is your Christian duty' [TEV], 'this is your Christian duty' [TNT].

d. δίκαιος (LN 66.5, 88.12) (BAGD 5. p. 196): 'right' [AB, BAGD, El, LN (66.5), NIC, NTC, Rob, WBC; KJV, NASB, NIV, NRSV], 'proper' [LN (66.5)], 'righteous' [LN (88.12), Lns], 'just' [LN (88.12), We]. The clause τοῦτο ἐστιν δίκαιον 'this is right' is translated 'that is what is expected of you' [NAB], 'that is what uprightness demands' [NJB], 'it is only right that you should' [REB], 'this is the right thing to do' [TEV]. This clause is also coalesced with the phrase ἐν κυρίῳ 'in the Lord' and translated 'this is your Christian duty' [TNT].

QUESTION—How is this verse related to the context?

Paul now turns to a second relationship in which the duties of being filled with the Spirit (5:18) [LJ, WBC] and of mutual subjection (5:21) is illustrated [Can, Ea, Ho, LJ, St, TNTC, WBC]. As in the earlier set of instructions (5:22), the naturally subordinate group is addressed first [LJ, St, TNTC, WBC]. This section plainly implies that the apostle assumed the presence of children in the congregation as this epistle was read [CBC, DNTT, Ea, EBC, Lns, My-ed, NTC, St, TD, WBC] and is directly addressed to these children [DNTT, Ea, EBC, NTC, St, WBC].

QUESTION—What is meant by τέκνα 'children'?

The term denotes children who were not of age and were still under the care and government of their parents [Ba]. It includes children from the time they were old enough to understand the precept until they were no longer under parental authority [Can, WBC] (though always owing filial duty) [Can]. The children in view here have attained the age of discretion [TD]. They are older children, perhaps teenagers, who were old enough to be conscious of a relationship to their Lord and to be appealed to on its basis, yet young enough to be still in the process of being reared [NCBC, WBC]. It was customary for grown children to live in one household with their parents where the father remained head of the household until his death and such children are here addressed [BB]. The application of this passage will vary according to culture as to whether, or at what age, a child is regarded to be independent of direct parental control [St].

QUESTION—What relationship is indicated by the phrase ἐν κυρίῳ 'in the Lord'?

The κυρίῳ 'Lord' here is Christ [AB, Alf, Can, Ea, EBC, ECWB, EGT, El, Ho, IB, LJ, Lns, My, NCBC, NTC, St, TNTC, WBC, We; and probably TD, TH, WeBC], or God [Ba, Cal]. This phrase is connected to the imperative verb ὑπακούετε 'obey' [AB, Alf, Ba, Cal, Can, Ea, EBC, ECWB, EGT, El, Ho, IB, ICC, LJ, Lns, MNTC, My, NCBC, NIC, NTC, St, TH, TNTC, WBC,

We, WeBC; TEV, TNT]. Some claim that this restricts the requirement of obedience to commands that are in compliance with the Lord's will [Ba, Cal, NCBC, St, WeBC]. But others say the apostle is not really addressing what the reaction of children should be to commands that are contrary to it [Alf, Can, EBC, IB, ICC, Lns, NIC, WBC].

1. The preposition ἐν 'in' indicates the sphere within which the action of obedience is to take place [Alf, Ea, EBC, EGT, El, WBC, WeBC; and probably Ho, LJ, St]: obey your parents in an attitude of obedience to the Lord. The preposition describes the element or sphere in which children are to obey their parents [Alf, Ea, EBC, EGT, El, WBC, WeBC] and defines the quality of that obedience as being fulfilled in communion with Christ [EGT] or within a Christian context [WeBC]. Not merely natural instinct, but religious motive should prompt children to obedience [Ea, Ho, LJ].
2. The preposition ἐν 'in' indicates the close personal union with the Lord upon which the action of obedience depends [BAGD, Can, ECWB, IB, Lns]: in close association with the Lord, obey your parents. The phrase indicates the unity which binds all within the Christian community to Christ. To 'obey in the Lord' is to obey in the light and grace of that unity, the result of which is to transfigure all natural relations to a diviner glory [ECWB]. The words denote the mystic union of the believer with the Lord [Can, IB], and even this aspect of obedience that arises out of that union is not beyond the capacity of the child to understand. It means to obey as being surrounded by the love of Christ and trusting and relying upon his grace and strength for the ability to obey [Can].
3. The preposition ἐν 'in' indicates the manner in which the obedience is to be rendered [TH; and probably TD; TEV, TNT]: as Christians obey your parents. The phrase here characterizes the action as Christian [TD].
4. The preposition ἐν 'in' indicates the reason or motivation behind the action of obedience [AB, St]: obey your parents because of the Lord.

QUESTION—What is meant by τοῦτο γάρ ἐστιν δίκαιον 'for this is right/righteous'?

This is the grounds for requiring children to obey their parents [Can, Ho, LJ, NCBC, TNTC, WBC, WeBC]. This clause reinforces the concept of the obligation inherent in ἐν κυρίῳ 'in the Lord' [St, TH, WBC].

1. Δίκαιον 'right' denotes what is correct or right action in the eyes of society [AB (probably), Alf, Can, Ea, ECWB, El, Ho, IDB (probably), St, WBC, We, WeBC; REB]. It is the natural sense of what is right. The next verse will give an additional reason by appealing to the Word of God [Can, El, St, WBC]. The meaning is not that obedience is 'right' because it is according to the Scriptures [Ea], but that it has its foundation in the natural relationship which exists between parents and children [Ea, Ho, St, TNTC, We (probably)], a relationship which is consistent with our notions of right and moral obligation, and which Scripture also enjoins [Ea, ECWB, St, TNTC].

2. Δίκαιον 'right, righteous' denotes what is righteous action in the eyes of God [Ba, Cal, EBC, EGT, IB, ICC, ISBE2, LJ, Lns, MNTC, My, NCBC (probably), NTC, Rob, TD; NJB, TNT (probably)]. The presence of the phrase ἐν κυρίῳ 'in the Lord' in this verse and the appeal to God's authority in the scripture quotation in the next indicate the appeal here is to a religious standard of what is righteous [Cal, LJ, Rob], a standard higher than just that of natural law [LJ]. Δίκαιον 'right, righteous' is a forensic term and implies the Lord as righteous judge who pronounces his verdict upon every child's conduct in accordance with his divine norm of right [Lns].

6:2 Honor[a] your father and mother,

LEXICON—a. pres. act. impera. of τιμάω (LN 87.8) (BAGD 2. p. 817): 'to honor' [AB, BAGD, El, LN, Lns, NIC, NTC, Rob, WBC, We; all versions except TEV], 'to respect' [LN; TEV].

QUESTION—What is the purpose for introducing the LXX quotation from Ex. 20:12 and Deut. 5:16 contained in 6:2–3?

1. This quotation confirms [EBC, El, Ho, NTC], gives the reason [El, WBC] or the ground [ECWB, IB, LJ, My, NIC, TH, TNTC, We, WeBC], and the motivation [Cal, Can, EGT, Lns (probably), WBC] for the injunction of 6:1. The children's Christian education had begun with the decalogue [EBC, NTC, TNTC], so Paul appeals to what they had already learned [EBC].
2. This quotation is another form of the injunction of 6:1 [Ea]. Whereas the injunction of 6:1 is based upon δίκαιον 'right', natural right, the quotation of the fifth commandment is based upon divine authority [Ea].

QUESTION—What is meant by τίμα 'honor'?

It means to respect, reverence [Ea, EBC, Ho, LJ, Lns, NTC, St, TH, WeBC], love, and obey one's parents [Cal, Ea, EBC, EGT, LJ, Lns, My, NTC, St, TD, TH, WeBC]. Τίμα 'honor' is the frame of mind or *disposition* from which the obedience demanded of the children proceeds [EGT, My]. The fifth commandment of the decalogue concerns the appropriate care of aged parents [BB, NCBC]. For young children, still living in the father's house it meant obedience to parents. For older children it meant a respectful attitude and caring for their parents' physical needs when they become old [NCBC, WBC].

which is (the) first/foremost[a] commandment[b] with/because-of[c] (a) promise,

LEXICON—a. πρῶτος (LN 60.46, 65.52, 87.45) (BAGD 1.c.α. p. 726): 'first' [BAGD, El, LN (60.46), NIC, Rob, WBC, We; all versions], 'foremost' [BAGD, LN (87.45), Lns], 'great, important, prominent' [LN (87.45)], 'most important' [BAGD, LN (65.52)], 'of foremost significance' [NTC], 'basic' [AB].
 b. ἐντολή: 'commandment'. See this word at 2:15.
 c. ἐν with dative object (LN 89.5, 89.26, 89.80, 90.23): 'with' [LN (89.80), Rob, WBC, We; KJV, NASB, NIV, NRSV], 'in connection with' [Lns],

'in regard of' [El], 'with regard to' [LN (89.5)], 'with respect to, concerning, with respect to' [LN (90.23)]. This preposition is also translated as a verb: 'to contain' [AB; TNT], 'to be accompanied by' [NIC]. The phrase ἐν ἐπαγγελίᾳ 'with a promise' is translated 'with a promise attached' [NTC], 'to carry a promise with it' [NAB, REB], 'that has a promise attached to it' [NJB], 'that has a promise added' [TEV].

QUESTION—What relationship is indicated by ἥτις 'which'?

This relative pronoun explains [Ea, EGT, El, Lns] or expresses the reason for honoring parents [Ea, EGT, My, TH, WBC]. The writer inserts this comment in the midst of the quotation to show that it is in the interests of the children to respect their parents [TH]. As parallel to the *general* motive to morality given in the preceding verse in τοῦτο γάρ ἐστι δίκαιον 'for this is right', the relative clause introduced by ἥτις 'which' here provides a *particular* motive, which results in a climactic construction with the previous verse [My].

QUESTION—What is meant by ἐντολὴ πρώτη 'the first/foremost commandment'?

    1. This means the first (in sequence) commandment which has a promise attached to it [Alf, Ba, Cal, Can, Ea, ECWB, EGT, El, ICC, MNTC, Mo, My, NCBC, Rob, St, TH, WBC; TEV, TNT]: the first commandment which has a promise attached to it. The reference is to its position within the Decalogue [Alf, Ba, Cal, Ea, MNTC, NCBC, TH; TNT (note)], or in the Decalogue as the introduction to the whole of the Law [Can, ECWB, EGT, El, My, Rob, St, WBC], which contains similar promises [ECWB, Rob]. This is not saying that the observance of the first four commandments in the Decalogue would have no blessings attached to them, but that those blessings are general, whereas here, with this commandment, the blessing is specific [Ba]. Since it is the only commandment in the Decalogue with a specific promise attached to it, πρώτη 'first' must imply all of God's commandments, not just those of the Decalogue [El, My, Rob, St].

    2. This means the first commandment which a child learns [ICC].

    3. This means the commandment which is first in importance [AB, BAGD, EBC, Ho, IB, LJ, Lns, NTC, TNTC, WeBC] as far as children are concerned [IB, TD, TNTC]. It is basic [AB]. It may be that the absence of an article with πρώτη 'first' means that it is a primary commandment [EBC, NTC, TNTC], one of foremost significance. The rabbis considered this commandment the weightiest of all [EBC]. It is probable that it means first in importance relating to our social duties [Ho, LJ, Lns]. It is a law, that when neglected, leads to the collapse of society [LJ, Lns].

QUESTION—What relationship is indicated by ἐν 'with/because of'?

    1. It indicates in what respect the commandment is first [AB, Alf, Ba, BAGD (1.c.α. p. 726), Cal, Can, Ea, EGT, El, Ho, ICC, LJ, Lns, MNTC, My, NCBC, NIC, Rob, St, TH, TNTC, WBC, We; all versions]: the first commandment with a promise attached. The prepopsition ἐν 'with' means

'accompanied with' [Alf, NIC]. It expresses the exact point in which the predication of πρώτη 'first' is to be understood [El, My].
2. It indicates the reason the commandment is foremost [TD]: a special commandment by reason of the promise annexed to it.
3. It adds a further thought to the fact that the promise is first in importance [EBC, IB, NTC]: it is the foremost commandment and it has a promise attached.

6:3 in-order-that it-may-be well[a] with-you and you-shall-be (a) long-time[b] upon/in the earth/land.

LEXICON—a. εὖ (LN 65.23, 88.6) (BAGD p. 317): 'well' [AB, BAGD, El, LN (65.23), Lns, NTC, Rob, We; KJV, NASB, NRSV, REB, TNT], 'fine, excellent' [LN (65.23)], 'good' [LN (65.23, 88.6)], 'beneficial' [LN (88.6)]. The clause εὖ σοι γένηται 'it may be well with you' is translated 'you may prosper' [BAGD; NJB], 'it may go well with you' [NIC, WBC; NAB, NIV, TEV]. This adverb denotes events that measure up to their intended purpose [LN (65.23)], or that which is good, beneficial [LN (88.6)].

b. μακροχρόνιος (LN **67.89**) (BAGD p. 488): 'long time' [LN, Lns, NTC]. The clause ἔσῃ μακροχρόνιος 'you may be a long time' is translated 'you may live a long time' [**LN**, NIC; TEV] 'you may have a long life' [BAGD; NAB, NJB], 'you may enjoy long life' [NIV], 'you may live long' [AB, El, Rob, WBC; KJV, NASB, NRSV, REB], 'you shall live long' [We], 'you will live long' [TNT].

QUESTION—What relationship is indicated by ἵνα 'in order that'?
This continues the quotation and indicates the purpose, or intended result, of honoring one's father and mother [BD, Ea, EBC, El, My (probably), St, We]: honor your father and mother in order that it may be well with you and you shall be a long time on the earth. Both motivating clauses are introduced by a single ἵνα 'in order that' [WBC]. In the LXX texts of Exod. 20:12 and Deut. 5:16, the particle ἵνα 'in order that' occurs with each clause [Ea, El], and in the Hebrew text of Deut. 5:16 a like particle meaning 'that, so that' also precedes each clause. The longevity is the temporal result and development of εὖ σοι γένηται 'it may be well with you' [Ea, El, St].

QUESTION—What is meant by εὖ σοι γένηται 'it may be well with you'?
This clause promises temporal blessings [EGT] or material prosperity such as safety, health, and good harvests [St], permanent well being under God's constant blessing [Lns], or prosperity [NIC]. This clause means that by obeying their parents children will be more happy, useful, and virtuous than if they disobey them [Ba].

QUESTION—What is meant by ἔσῃ μακροχρόνιος ἐπὶ τῆς γῆς 'you shall be a long time upon/in the earth/land'?
1. The words ἐπὶ τῆς γῆς 'upon the earth' refer here in a general sense to long life upon the earth [AB, Alf, Ba, Cal, Can, Ea, EBC, ECWB, El, Ho, ICC (probably), LJ, Lns, MNTC, NCBC, NIC, NTC, Rob (probably), St,

TH, TNTC, WBC], or in the land where one lives [EGT]. The relative clause 'which the Lord your God will give to you' follows this phrase in the original commandment. The apostle adapts this promise to his Christian readers [Alf, Ba, EBC, ECWB, LJ, Lns, NCBC, NIC, St, WBC] by removing from it the reference to the land of Canaan [Ba, Cal, Can, CBC, Ea, EBC, El, Ho, IB, LJ, Lns, NCBC, NIC, NTC, St, TH, WBC], a promise which was special and peculiar to the Jewish people [Alf, Cal, Can, CBC, Ea, EBC, Lns, NCBC], less suited [ECWB, ICC, NIC] or not applicable to those under the new covenant [Cal, Can, EBC, St (probably), TNTC]. This promises children who honor their parents a long life upon the earth [Ba, Ea, ECWB, Ho, IB, LJ, NTC, WBC] or in the land where their Christian lot is cast [EGT]. Other things being equal, obedience to parents is conducive to length of life [Ba, Ea, Ho, NTC] for it implies the possession of principles of restraint, sobriety, and industry [Ea], and other good characteristics [Ba] which tend to secure a lengthened existence [Ba, Ea]. Yet, the promise is not to be regarded as absolute [Can, Ea, LJ, NTC] in a mathematical or statistical sense [Can], but holds true as a principle of Divine administration and indicates the usual course of providence [Ea, Ho]. The Hebrews regarded a long life as a great blessing [Ba, Cal].
2. The words ἐπὶ τῆς γῆς 'in the land' are restricted, even in this passage, to the land of Canaan [My; probably NJB, TEV, TNT]. There is no explanation how Paul uses an implied reference to Palestine in his argument here.
3. The words ἐπὶ τῆς γῆς 'upon the earth' are spiritualized in a general sense to mean eternal life [CBC, IB, WeBC]. In the OT God used the temporal promise of long life in the Promised Land to teach the concept of immortality. Here he may be saying that there is a relationship between the lesson of obedience of children to their parents and their obedience to God in respect to inheriting eternal life. Those who are not obedient to parents have a hard time practicing obedience to God as well as practicing good temporal citizenship [WeBC]. The inheritance of the ancient Israelite was the land of Palestine; the Christian's inheritance is being right with God [CBC].

6:4 And the fathers/parents, (do) not make-angry[a] your children but raise[b] them in/by (the) training/discipline[c] and admonition[d] of-(the)-Lord.

LEXICON—a. pres. act. impera. of παροργίζω (LN 88.177) (BAGD p. 629): 'to make angry' [BAGD, LN, NIC, WBC], 'to anger' [NAB], 'to cause to be provoked' [LN], 'to provoke to anger' [Lns, MM; NASB, NRSV], 'to provoke to wrath' [El, Rob, We; KJV], 'to provoke the wrath of' [AB], 'to goad to resentment' [REB], 'to make resentful' [TNT], 'to exasperate' [NIV], 'to drive to resentment' [NJB], 'to treat in such a way as to make angry' [TEV]. The present imperative refers to iterative action: do not again and again provoke to anger [Lns].
b. pres. act. impera. of ἐκτρέφω (LN **35.51**) (BAGD 2. p. 246): 'to raise' [**LN**; TEV], 'to bring up' [AB, BAGD, El, LN, NIC, Rob, WBC; all

versions except TEV], 'to rear' [BAGD, LN], 'to rear tenderly' [NTC], 'to nourish' [Lns], 'to nurture' [We], 'to nurse' [MM]. This verb denotes the raising of a child to maturity by the provision of physical and psychological needs [LN]. The present tense indicates a steady course of nourishing [Lns].

c. παιδεία (LN 33.226, **36.10**) (BAGD 1. p. 603): 'training' [BAGD, LN (36.10), NIC, WBC; NIV], 'upbringing' [BAGD], 'teaching' [LN (33.226)], 'instruction' [BAGD, LN (33.226)], 'nurture' [KJV], 'discipline' [BAGD, El, LN (**36.10**), Lns, MM, NTC, Rob, We; NASB, NRSV, REB]. The phrase ἐν παιδείᾳ καὶ νουθεσίᾳ κυρίου 'in the discipline and admonition of the Lord' is translated 'the way the Lord disciplines and corrects you' [AB], 'with Christian discipline and instruction' [TEV], 'in Christian discipline and training' [TNT], 'with the training and instruction befitting the Lord' [NAB], 'with correction and advice inspired by the Lord' [NJB].

d. νουθεσία (LN **33.231**, 33.424) (BAGD p. 544): 'admonition' [BAGD, El, Lns, NTC, Rob, WBC, We; KJV], 'instruction' [BAGD, LN (**33.231**), NIC; NAB, NASB, NIV, NRSV, REB, TEV], 'teaching' [LN (33.231)], 'warning' [BAGD, LN (33.424)], 'advice' [NJB], 'training' [TNT]. This noun is also translated as a verb 'to correct' [AB]. This noun denotes the provision of instruction as to what constitutes correct behavior and belief [LN (33.231)], or it denotes the advising of a person concerning the dangerous consequences of some event or action [LN (33.424)]. Joined to κυρίου 'Lord', this means Christian instruction [BAGD].

QUESTION—What relationship is indicated by καί 'and'?

This connective continues the statement of this domestic topic [EGT] by closely connecting the injunction contained in this verse as parallel or complementary to the preceding injunction [Ea, NTC, We] and introducing the corresponding duty of parents to their children [Can, EGT, El, NTC, TNTC, We]. The obedience of children to their parents is to be reciprocated by the parents in kindness to their children [DNTT]. The καί 'and' underlines the linkage between the exhortations to both halves of the pairing, children and fathers [WBC], the article with πατέρες 'fathers/parents' serving to distinguish the class of πατέρες 'fathers/parents' from the corresponding class of τὰ τέκνα 'the children' (6:1) [HG].

QUESTION—What is meant by οἱ πατέρες 'fathers/parents'?

In Greek, the plural noun πατέρες 'fathers' may designate both parents, father and mother [BAGD (1.a. p. 635), BB, Can, St, TH, WBC].

1. The noun πατέρες here means 'fathers', because it refers to them particularly [Ba, EBC, EGT, El, Ho, LJ, Lns, NCBC, NTC, Si, WeBC, and probably MNTC, St, TD] or explicitly [Ea, ISBE, ISBE2, My, TH, WBC, We]. This command is addressed particularly to fathers because they are the head of the family [Ba, EBC, EGT, El, My, WBC, We, WeBC] and the government, education, and discipline of the family is especially committed to them [Ba, Ea, El, My, NTC, WBC, We, WeBC]. The plural

form here has the same meaning as the singular form had in the quotation in 6:2. The father represents both parents here [Ho, St, WeBC]. What is said to the fathers also applies to the mothers [LJ, Lns, St, WeBC].
2. The noun πατέρες here means 'parents' [AB, Alf, BAGD (1.a. p. 635), BB, Cal, Can, CBC, NIC, Rob (probably), Si-ed (probably), TNTC; TEV]. This actually refers to both parents, not just the father [Alf, TNTC]. That this includes both parents is evident from the quotation in 6:2 [Can].

QUESTION—What is meant by μὴ παροργίζετε τὰ τέκνα ὑμῶν 'do not make your children angry'?

It refers to the exasperation produced by arbitrary, capricious, or unsympathetic rule, and the like [ECWB, LJ, Lns, My, NCBC, Rob, St, TNTC, WBC]. It refers to vexatious commands and unreasonable blame [Alf, El, LJ, My, NCBC] in the course of everyday interaction with the children [Alf, EBC, El]. It refers to unreasonable and severe commands that are hard to obey [Ba, EBC, Ho, TH, WBC], and to discipline done in a spirit of anger and superior power [Ba, NTC], rather than discipline exercised because it is correct for the situation [Ba]. It refers to harsh and unreasonable treatment or undue partiality or favoritism [Ea, Ho, LJ, NTC, St, WBC], the type of discipline that causes resentment [CBC, EBC, WeBC].

QUESTION—What is meant by the verb ἐκτρέφετε 'raise'?

It refers to the child's education in its entirety [EBC]. The child's bringing up or rearing [AB, BAGD, El, LN (35.51), NIC, NTC, Rob, WBC; all versions] is in view rather than just material support [Ea, EGT]. It has an extended sense of nourishment [Can, LJ, TH, TNTC], with the idea of supplying whatever is needful for life and growth [Can, LJ, TH], including here, mental and spiritual preparation for life [LJ]. The verb actually came to be used not only for bodily nourishment, but for the nurture of body, mind, and soul [TNTC]. The verb unquestionably has a connotation of gentleness and forbearance [Cal, EBC, NTC, Si, TNTC].

QUESTION—What is meant by ἐν 'in/by'?
1. It indicates the sphere [Alf, EGT, El, WBC] or the regulative element in which the training and admonition are to take place [My]: raise them in the sphere of Christian discipline and admonition.
2. It is instrumental [Ho]: raise them by Christian discipline and admonition.
3. It indicates the manner in which children are to be raised [AB]: raise them the way the Lord disciplines you.

QUESTION—What is meant by παιδεία καὶ νουθεσία 'the training/discipline and admonition'?
1. The conjunction καί 'and' joins the two nouns παιδεία 'training/discipline' and νουθεσία 'admonition' in a coordinate relationship [AB, Alf, Ba, BAGD, Cal, Can, CBC, DNTT, EBC, ECWB, El, IB, IDB, ISBE, ISBE2, LJ, LN, Lns, MNTC, My-ed, NCBC, NTC, Rob, Si, St, TH, We, WeBC; all versions]: in the training/discipline and admonition of the Lord. The two nouns in this phrase denote the two aspects of the domestic

education which ἐκτρέφετε 'raise' calls for [EBC, ECWB, El]. The two nouns specify two methods in the Christian education of children [El, LJ].

1.1 Παιδεία refers to childhood 'training, education' in general [Ba, Can, IB, IDB, ISBE2, LJ, LN, NCBC, NIC, We; NAB, NIV]. In its usage in the NT there is little emphasis on chastisement [IDB]. It means discipline, or education in general [Can, IDB, LJ, We], literally the training of children [Ba, Can, IDB], and it is evident that Paul intends it in this sense here [Can]. Παιδεία 'training' has a more general meaning than νουθεσία 'admonition'. It stands for the totality of nurturing, rearing, bringing up a child, including discipline, and focuses particularly upon the parents' actions. It includes, in general, the whole process of the cultivation of the mind and the spirit, the morals and moral behavior, the whole personality of the child [LJ]. The distinction between παιδεία 'training' and νουθεσία 'admonition' may be that παιδεία 'training' has reference to training by means of deeds, while νουθεσία 'admonition' complements this by training by means of words [ISBE2]. This term focuses upon inculcating into the child patterns of behavior worthy of a Christian [NCBC].

1.2 Παιδεία refers specifically to childhood 'discipline, chastisement', the idea of corrective punishment being included as a prominent feature in its meaning [AB, Alf, BAGD, Cal, CBC, DNTT (probably), EBC, ECWB, EGT, El, ISBE, Lns, MNTC, My-ed, NTC, Rob, Si, St, TH, WeBC]. This term denotes the active sense of 'upbringing, education, training, instruction' particularly as it is attained by 'discipline' or 'correction' [ECWB, EGT]. This discipline involves both punishment (chastisement) and nurturing (training or upbringing) [TH].

2. The conjunction καί 'and' joins the two nouns παιδεία 'training' and νουθεσία 'admonition' in a generic-specific relationship [Ea, Ho, ICC, My, WBC]: in the training, that is, specifically, the admonition of the Lord. Παιδεία 'training' has here, as in classical writers, its more general meaning [ICC, My, WBC] and νουθεσία is more specifically instruction and admonition [ICC]. Παιδεία refers to childhood 'training, education' in general [Ea, Ho, ICC, My, WBC]. The meaning of the noun is not restricted to discipline. It signifies the entire circuit of education and upbringing [Ea, WBC] which a child requires, of which discipline is the necessary and prominent element [Ea]. It is the general term, designating the training of children as a whole [My]. Νουθεσία 'admonition' is one special element or aspect of the παιδεία 'training' [Ea, WBC], the verbal admonition [WBC]. It is included under the more general παιδεία 'discipline' [Ho], νουθεσία 'admonition' more specially designating the reproof which aims at changing conduct, whether this admonition takes place by word or actual punishment [My].

3. The conjunction καί 'and' joins the two nouns παιδεία 'training' and νουθεσία 'admonition' into an hendiadys [DNTT, TD]: in the admonitory

training of the Lord. The two nouns in this phrase are essentially identical in meaning [DNTT, TD].

QUESTION—What relationship is indicated by the genitive κυρίου 'of the Lord'?

Some state or imply that this usage of κυρίου 'of the Lord' is a way of characterizing this discipline and admonition as Christian [BAGD, DNTT, EGT, IDB, MNTC, NCBC, TH, WBC, WeBC; TEV, TNT]. Most say that κυρίου 'the Lord' refers to Christ [AB, Can, CBC, Ea, EGT, El, Ho, LJ, MNTC, My, NCBC, NIC, NTC (probably), Si, TH, WBC], but some understand that God is referred to here [DNTT, ISBE2].

1. The genitive κυρίου 'of the Lord' has a subjective sense, 'such as the Lord prescribes, approves' [AB, Ba, Can, CBC (probably), Ea, EGT, El, Ho, ICC, ISBE2, MNTC, My, NCBC, NTC, Rob (probably), Si, St, TD, TNTC, We; NJB]: in discipline and admonition approved by the Lord. The genitive κυρίου 'of the Lord' is juxtaposed with ἐν κυρίῳ 'in the Lord' in 6:1, 'obedience in the Lord', as the duty of the child, relates to 'discipline of the Lord', as the duty of the parent [Rob]. Fathers are enjoined to heed the discipline which the Lord himself exerts over them [AB]. The force of the genitive is such that the Lord himself is seen as inspiring, prescribing, administering or guiding the discipline and admonition [Ea, EGT, ICC, My, St, TNTC, We], i.e., as training and teaching the child by means of the father or parents [Can, St, TD, TNTC, We] through his Spirit acting in the father [My]. This is divine discipline, exercised through the father who acts for God in the training of his children [ISBE2].

2. The genitive κυρίου 'of the Lord' has an objective sense [DNTT, IB, LJ, NIC; NAB]: in discipline and admonition appropriate to followers of the Lord. The correct way to bring up children is not determined by the use or nonuse of certain educational helps, but by whether or not the training is directed towards the Lord. It is not the educational method, but the purpose to which it is applied, that determines whether the upbringing is Christian or not [DNTT]. Children are to be brought up in the knowledge of the Lord Jesus Christ as their Savior and Lord [LJ]. The training and instruction of the Lord refers to following Christ's example [NIC].

3. The genitive κυρίου 'of the Lord' has a qualifying sense [Lns, WBC]: such discipline and admonition that has the Lord as its reference point. The two nouns this genitive modifies are without articles and are made definite by the genitive. This allows the genitive to have a qualifying force [Lns].

DISCOURSE UNIT: 6:5–9 [AB, Alf, Cal, CBC, EBC, ECWB, EGT, IB, Lns, MNTC, NIC, NTC, Rob, Si, TH, TNTC, WBC, We; NAB, NASB, NIV, NJB, TEV, TNT]. The topic is the hardest form of subjection, that of slaves to masters [ECWB], advice to slaves and masters [CBC], the duties of masters and slaves [Alf], Christian relationships and employment [EBC], the mutual relationships of Christian servants and masters [We, WeBC], the dignity of service [Si], slaves and masters [AB, IB, Lns, NIC, Rob, TH, WBC; NAB, NIV], servants and masters [EGT, MNTC, TNTC].

DISCOURSE UNIT: 6:5-8 [Ba, Si, St; NRSV, REB, TEV]. The topic is the duty of servants to their masters [Ba, St].

6:5 **The slaves, obey those (who) according-to (the) flesh[a] (are) masters[b] with fear and trembling[c] in singleness[d] of-the heart of-you as to-Christ,**

TEXT—Instead of τοῖς κατὰ σάρκα κυρίοις 'those (who) according to the flesh (are) masters', some manuscripts have the order τοῖς κυρίοις κατὰ σάρκα 'the masters according to the flesh'. GNT does not note this variant word order. Those who support this variant word order are Alf, Ea, El, My; KJV, and NASB.

LEXICON—a. σάρξ (LN 26.7) (BAGD 6. p. 744): 'flesh' [El, NTC, Rob, We; KJV, NASB], 'human standards' [BAGD], 'human reckoning' [NJB], 'human nature, human aspects' [LN], 'the external side of life' [BAGD]. The prepositional phrase κατὰ σάρκα 'according to the flesh' is translated: 'earthly' [AB, NIC, WBC; NIV, NRSV, REB], 'bodily' [Lns], 'human' [NAB, TEV, TNT].

b. κύριος (LN 57.12) (BAGD 1.a.β. p. 459): 'master' [BAGD, El, LN, Lns, NIC, NTC, Rob, WBC, We; all versions], 'lord' [AB, BAGD, LN], 'owner' [BAGD, LN]. This noun denotes one who owns and controls property, especially servants and slaves [BAGD, LN, TD] and the noun has important semantic components of high status and respect as well [LN]. This was the normal word to designate a slave owner [NCBC].

c. τρόμος (LN 16.6) (BAGD p. 827): 'trembling' [AB, BAGD, El, LN, Lns, NIC, NTC, Rob, WBC, We; all versions except NAB, NIV, NJB], 'quivering' [BAGD], 'awe' [NAB], 'fear' [NIV]. The words φόβου καὶ τρόμου 'fear and trembling' are translated 'deep respect' [NJB]. This noun denotes a shaking or trembling, and often implies fear [BAGD, LN] and/or consternation [LN].

d. ἁπλότης (LN 88.44) (BAGD 1. p. 85): 'singleness' [El, Lns, Rob, WBC, We; KJV, NRSV], 'simplicity, uprightness, frankness' [BAGD], 'sincerity' [BAGD, LN, NIC, NTC; NASB, NIV], 'purity of motive' [LN]. The phrase ἐν ἁπλότητι τῆς καρδίας 'in the sincerity of (your) heart' is translated 'whole-heartedly' [AB], 'sincerity' [NAB], 'sincere loyalty' [NJB], 'with a sincere heart' [BAGD; TEV]. This phrase is also translated as an adjective modifying a nominal idea in the verb ὑπακούετε 'obey': 'give single-minded obedience' [REB, TNT]. This noun denotes the quality of sincerity as it expresses singleness of purpose or motivation [LN].

QUESTION—How is this verse related to the context?

This section, along with those dealing with husbands and wives and children and parents, still falls under the general control of the exhortation in 5:18 to be filled with the Spirit [LJ, WBC], and more particularly that of 5:21, to be subject to one another in the fear of Christ [LJ, Rob, TNTC, WBC]. Again, those whose natural position in life is recognized to be subservient to someone else, here the slaves, are addressed first [LJ, WBC].

QUESTION—What is meant by κατὰ σάρκα 'according to the flesh'?

1. The phrase refers to human attitudes, standards, or modes of thought prevalent in society [AB, BAGD, Cal, Can, EBC, ECWB, EGT, El, Ho, IB, LJ, Lns, My, NCBC, NIC, TD, WBC, We (probably), WeBC; NAB, NIV, NRSV, REB, TEV, TNT]. This phrase sets up an implicit contrast with another sort of master, and since that other master is identified in 6:9 as in heaven, the gloss 'earthly' becomes an appropriate translation for the phrase here used of the relationship to human masters [WBC]. The phrase recognizes a limit to the authority of their earthly masters [WBC, We]. It asserts that their earthly κύριοι 'masters' are only their masters in matters of earthly relations and material interests [EGT].
2. The phrase refers to the slaves' control over their own bodies [Ba]. This phrase is used to limit their obligation to obedience. Though this class were not 'lords' over their spirits, they controlled their bodies and could command the service which their bodies should render [Ba].

QUESTION—What is meant by μετὰ φόβου καὶ τρόμου 'with fear and trembling'?

The preposition μετά 'with' means 'connected with' [TD], showing these emotions were to be the regular accompaniment of obedience [Ea].

1. This refers to their attitude to serving Christ in their condition as slaves [Alf, CBC, ECWB, Ho, IB, LJ, MNTC, NIC, NTC, St, WeBC; and probably EBC, EGT, El, ICC, Lns, My, Si, Si-ed]. This attitude is to arise, not from dread of their condition as slaves [Alf, CBC, Ho, ICC, LJ, MNTC], but from anxiety to fulfill their duty to Christ [Alf, CBC, Ho, LJ, MNTC]. The use of this phrase in 1 Cor. 2:3, 2 Cor. 7:15, and Phil. 2:12 is enough to show that nothing more is intended here than a solicitous zeal [EGT, ICC, My], and anxious care not to come short in the discharge of their duty [EGT, El, ICC, My, WeBC]. The phrase has been softened with usage and probably was used here as hyperbole [Si-ed], meaning no more than meekness and diffidence [Si, Si-ed]. These nouns are not to be confused with an attitude of craven servility [EBC, LJ, MNTC, WeBC], but represent a keen sense of their shortcomings and a consequent anxiety not to make any mistake [EBC, MNTC]. The slaves are not to fear the anger of their earthly masters, but the disapproval of Christ, who is never pleased with service poorly performed [MNTC].
2. This refers to their respect for their earthly masters [Cal, Can, Ea, ISBE2, TD, TH, WBC] and their fear of offending them [Ba, We]. 'Fear' can denote the obedience demanded by the superior authority of husbands and masters as lords. This fear is a sign of the entire dependence of the subordinate upon the power of the stronger and requires humility from the slave even to the point of unjust treatment (1 Pet. 2:18). Yet this is not mere dissimulation for the sake of appearance because, in the end, it is

shown to God himself whose authority is seen in the claims of these masters. This also applies to wives [TD]. The phrase functions here to intensify the attitude of respect which slaves are to have for the authority of their masters. It emphasizes the obedience they owe their human masters, not God or Christ [WBC]. The context indicates that the respect and fear they are to show toward their earthly masters is enforced by the higher authority of God's will [Cal].

3. This refers to both of the above [NCBC]. Not only could disobedience to their earthly master be punished with the utmost severity, but good performance on their part would reflect favorably on their allegiance to Christ [NCBC].

QUESTION—What is meant by ὑπακούετε...ἐν ἁπλότητι τῆς καρδίας ὑμῶν 'obey...in singleness of your heart'?

This clause states the spirit in which the obedience was to be given [EGT, El] or in which the μετὰ φόβου καὶ τρόμου 'with fear and trembling' was to take place [My]. Καρδίας 'heart' here refers to the inner center of a person which determines his attitudes and actions [TD, WBC], especially here, as it ought to be [TD]. Despite its plural reference, the noun καρδίας 'heart' is singular and is used according to the Hebrew and Aramaic idiom where the singular is used distributively of every person in the group [Tu]. The phrase emphasizes the purity of their motive [TD, WBC]. It refers to a simple, sincere desire to do what should be done [Ba, NCBC], to the performance of the slaves' duties with no duplicity of mind [Can, Ea, EBC, ECWB, El, Ho, IDB, LJ, Lns, My, NTC, Si, St, TH, We] or deception or divided loyalty [IB, ICC, ISBE, LJ, My, Rob, We], but with singleness of purpose [WBC] and genuine good will [ICC, IDB] and the wholehearted desire of doing their duty to Christ [Can, CBC, El, Ho, IDB, NCBC, Si, St, TNTC] by giving undivided effort and attention to their tasks [Ea, LJ, Lns]. It contains also the idea of uprightness and integrity [BAGD, IDB, NIC (probably), NTC, TH, TNTC, WBC] and may imply a willingness to give of one's self without reservation, i.e., generous service [IDB, TNTC]. It implies openness [EBC, ISBE, LJ, NCBC] and concentration of purpose, the slave having only one goal before him: to serve his earthly master as an expression of his commitment to his divine Lord [EBC, LJ, NCBC]. The participial clauses ποιοῦντες τὸ θέλημα τοῦ θεοῦ ἐκ ψυχῆς, 'doing the will of God from the heart (lit. 'soul')' (6:6) and μετ' εὐνοίας δουλεύοντες ὡς τῷ κυρίῳ 'serving with good will/zeal as to the Lord' (6:7) serve to further define this term [IDB]. The apostle is aware that good work can only be produced when the worker's heart is in it and, in giving this advice, it is his desire to help these slaves find a good way to live and to make their position more tolerable through the fulfilling of their part in the common responsibility of all for the establishment of good social order [AB].

QUESTION—What is meant by ὡς τῷ Χριστῷ 'as to Christ'?

This phrase shows that the rendering of proper service to masters is, in fact, service to the Lord [Ba, Cal, Can, CBC, Ea, EGT, Ho, IB, ICC, LJ, Lns, My,

NIC, NTC, Rob, Si, St, TH, TNTC, WBC, WeBC], though it does not necessarily go so far as to imply that earthly masters stand as Christ's representatives to their slaves (*contra* St) [WBC]. The phrase indicates that obedience to Christ is the standard by which obedience to their human masters is to be measured [TH]. They are perform their work as if they were doing it for Christ [TH, TNTC, WBC; NIV, NJB, NRSV, REB, TEV, TNT].

6:6 not according-to eye-service^a as men-pleasers^b

LEXICON—a. ὀφθαλμοδουλία (LN 35.29) (BAGD p. 599): 'eye-service' [BAGD, El, LN, Lns, NIC, NTC, Rob, We; KJV, NASB]. This noun is also translated as verbal clause: 'to serve in order to call attention to oneself' [LN], 'to put on a show' [AB], 'to catch their/the eye' [WBC; TNT], 'to render service for appearance only' [NAB]. The phrase μὴ κατ' ὀφθαλμοδουλίαν 'not according to eye-service' is translated: 'not only to win their favor' [NIV], 'not only when you are under their eye' [NIV], 'not only while being watched' [NRSV], 'not merely to catch their eye' [REB], 'not only when they are watching you' [TEV]. This noun denotes service with a view to impressing others [LN]. It refers to service that is performed solely to attract attention, not for its own sake, nor to please God, nor one's own conscience [BAGD].

b. ἀνθρωπάρεσκος (LN **25.98**) (BAGD p. 67): 'men-pleaser' [BAGD, El, **LN**, Lns, MM, NIC, NTC, Rob, We; KJV, NASB], 'pleasing people' [LN], 'those who please men' [WBC], 'who want to please men' [TNT]. This noun is also translated as a verb phrase: 'to please men' [NAB], 'to seek to please people' [AB]. The phrase ὡς ἀνθρωπάρεσκοι 'as men-pleasers' is translated 'when their eye is on you' [NIV], 'as if you had only to please human beings' [NJB], 'in order to please them' [NRSV], 'curry favor with them' [REB], 'because you want to gain their approval' [TEV]. This noun denotes causing people to be pleased, implying that principle is sacrificed in doing so [BAGD, LN], so that such action is seen as contrary to the will of God [LN].

QUESTION—What part does this verse play in the context?

This verse (together with the next [Ho]) is an explanation [Ho, WBC], more precise description [Lns, My], further specification [El], or an expansion [ECWB] of the idea of ἁπλότητι τῆς καρδίας 'singleness of heart' (6:5) [ECWB, El, Ho, My, WBC] or of the phrase ὡς τῷ Χριστῷ 'as to Christ' [Lns]. It illustrates negatively and positively what is meant by the phrase [Can, Ea, WBC].

QUESTION—What is meant by κατ' ὀφθαλμοδουλίαν 'according to eye-service'?

There is probably no significant difference in meaning between the preposition κατά 'according to' here and the preposition ἐν 'in' used in the parallel passage ἐν οφθαλμοδουλίᾳ 'in eye-service' in Col. 3:22 [NIC]. This refers to a δουλεία 'service' of Christian slaves which, though outwardly correct, is performed without dedication and with no sense of inner obligation to the master for the sake of God and Christ. The reference to ὀφθαλμοί 'eyes' in this compound noun refers to the deceived 'eyes' of the master and contrasts with the deceitful ψυχή 'soul' of the slave referred to at the end of the verse [TD]. It refers to performing service or working hard only when the slave is under the direct observation of his master [Ba, Can, EBC, EGT, Ho, IB, ISBE, LJ, Lns, My, NCBC, NTC, St, TH, TNTC, WBC, WeBC] to escape punishment [ISBE, WeBC] or to save appearances and gain undeserved approval [EGT, ISBE, LJ, Lns, My, NTC, St, WBC], a service rendered not out of a pure heart, but adopting only a resemblance to it [Alf, My, TD]. The implication is that acceptable service ceases when the slave feels he is no longer under his master's observation [EGT, LJ, My, WBC, WeBC].

QUESTION—What is meant by ἀνθρωπάρεσκοι 'men-pleasers'?

It continues the notion implicit in ὀφθαλμοδουλίαν 'eye-service' of currying favor with the masters [WBC]. The men whom the slaves endeavor to please are their masters. The fault with this lies in the fact that such an attitude is not conditioned by the higher motive of serving Christ and doing the will of God. It has human approval as its only aim [My]. It describes one who does not take God into account and so makes it his purpose to satisfy men [EBC, TD] and is the opposite of an incipient θεάρεσκος 'God-pleaser' [EBC, TD, TH]. The real purpose of the Christian slave's service, in his station in life, is to please and honor God [Ba, Can, Ho, IB], to be as faithful in their master's absence as in his presence [Ho]. It is not enough that their obedience satisfy the eyes of men; God desires truth and sincerity of heart [Cal].

but as slaves of-Christ doing the will of-the God from (the) soul,[a]

LEXICON—a. ψυχή (LN **26.4**) (BAGD 1.b.γ. p. 893): 'soul' [BAGD, El, Lns], 'heart' [BAGD, **LN**, NTC, We; KJV, NASB, NIV, NRSV], 'whole being' [**LN**], 'inner self, mind, thoughts, feelings, being' [LN]. The phrase ἐκ ψυχῆς 'from the soul' is translated: 'from the bottom of your heart' [AB], 'with your whole heart' [NAB], 'with all your heart' [TEV]; and as adverbs: 'gladly' [BAGD], 'heartily' [NIC, Rob], 'wholeheartedly' [WBC; NJB, REB, TNT].

QUESTION—What is meant by δοῦλοι Χριστοῦ 'slaves of Christ'?

All believers were formerly δοῦλοι 'slaves' of sin, uncleanness, lusts, lawlessness, etc. before they were converted and the δουλεία 'subservience' the slave renders is that of obedience to the will of a master. When Christ liberates men from this δουλεία 'subservience' to sin, they do not become autonomous beings in relation to sin and to God, but are placed in the position of υἱοθεσία 'adoption as sons'. This results in an attitude of obedience to him, leading to the idea of this obedience as δουλεία 'subservience' so that the noun δοῦλοι 'slaves' comes to be used as an expression of obligation to Christ, but with a somewhat different sense from the earlier usage in relation to sin [TD]. The slave usually has no higher motive than to please him who has the power of punishment or sale over him. His sole motive, whether through deception or an ingenious show of obedience, is to prevent his master from being displeased with him. But the apostle supplies another and deeper inducement [Ea], that the Christian slave should regard himself as the slave of Christ, which will lead to honest and punctual work, done to please the Lord in heaven (an echo of 5:10 [WBC]) [Ea, WBC, WeBC], whose eye is everywhere [Ho, St].

QUESTION—What is meant by ποιοῦντες τὸ θέλημα τοῦ θεου 'doing the will of God'?

This is a definition or explanation of ὡς δοῦλοι Χριστοῦ 'as slaves of Christ' [Alf, EGT, El, Ho, Lns, My, NCBC] as opposed to ἀνθρωπάρεσκοι 'men-pleasers' [Ho, My], with the present participle ποιοῦντες 'doing' receiving the emphasis [EGT]. This present participle, together with the following one, δουλεύοντες 'serving' in 6:7, define what such slaves do and how they do it [Lns]. It means that it is God's will that Christian slaves obey their masters, and since these Christian slaves are really Christ's slaves, they are obligated to do God's will. In this epistle, it is assumed that the slave masters here are fellow Christians [TH]. It means that God expects industry, fidelity, conscientiousness, submission, and obedience in the situation in life where they are placed [Ba]. Such workers will take care that their work is honest and thorough [Can]. In faithfully serving their masters, they are serving God [Cal].

QUESTION—What is meant by ἐκ ψυχῆς 'from the soul' and to what is it attached?

This phrase means 'heartily' [Ea, LJ] and stands in contrast to the earlier κατ' ὀφθαλμοδουλίαν 'according to eye-service' [Ea, TD, WBC]. It shows that the principle of obedience is nothing external [Ho], but springs from the whole inner being of the person [Ho, WBC]. It indicates that they do the will of God from free choice, gladly, and spontaneously [NCBC], with energy and enthusiasm [NTC]. It is the equivalent of 'with all your soul' in Matt. 22.37 and Mark 12:30 [DNTT, Ho, WBC]. The phrase describes man's total commitment with reference to the powers of his soul rather than of his physical powers [TD].

1. It is attached to the preceding clause ποιοῦντες τὸ θέλημα τοῦ θεοῦ 'doing the will of God' [AB, Ba, Can, Ea, EBC, ECWB, El, Ho, IB, LJ, Lns, My, NCBC, NIC, NTC, St, TD, TH, TNTC, WBC; all versions]: doing the will of God from the soul. Attaching this phrase to the preceding participial clause does not result in tautology [EGT, El] because, to be true to the character of δοῦλοι Χριστοῦ 'slaves of Christ', it is not enough just to do God's will, but to do it with hearty readiness [EGT].

2. It is attached to the following clause (verse 7) [Alf, ICC, Rob, We]: from the soul with good will/zeal serving as to the Lord. Taking it so does not result in tautology with μετ' εὐνοίας 'with good will/zeal' [Alf, ICC] because ἐκ ψυχῆς 'from the soul' expresses the source within him to

show how the slave feels towards his work, while μετ' εὐνοίας 'with good will/zeal' expresses his feeling toward his master [Alf, ICC, We].

6:7 with good-will/zeal[a] serving[b] as to-the Lord and not to-men,

LEXICON—a. εὔνοια (LN **25.72**) (BAGD 2. p. 323): 'good will' [El, NIC, Rob, We; KJV, NASB], 'zeal' [BAGD], 'eagerness' [LN], 'enthusiasm' [BAGD, WBC; NRSV], 'fervor' [AB], 'wholeheartedness' [LN], 'ready mind' [Lns, NTC]. The phrase μετ' εὐνοίας 'with good will/zeal' is also translated as an adjective: 'cheerful' (service) [REB]. It is also translated as an adverb: 'wholeheartedly' [**LN**; NIV], 'willingly' [NAB, NJB], 'cheerfully' [TEV], 'gladly' [TNT].

b. pres. act. participle of δουλεύω (LN 35.27) (BAGD 2.a. p. 205): 'to serve' [BAGD, LN, WBC; NIV], 'to do service' [El, Rob, We; KJV], 'to render service' [AB, BAGD, NIC, NTC; NASB, NRSV], 'to give service' [NAB, REB, TNT], 'to perform the duties of a slave' [BAGD], 'to do work as slaves' [TEV], 'to slave' [Lns], 'to work' [NJB], 'to obey' [BAGD].

QUESTION—What is the function of this verse in the context?

This verse constitutes a further explanation of what is meant by being δοῦλοι Χριστοῦ 'slaves of Christ' [EGT, El]. It sums up the whole character of the obedience of the slave [Ho]. This verse largely repeats, for emphasis, the substance of the previous verse [NCBC, WBC].

QUESTION—What is meant by εὐνοίας 'good will/zeal'?

1. It means a benevolent attitude, 'good will' [Alf, Can, CBC, Ea, EBC, ECWB, EGT, El, Ho, IB, LJ, Lns, My, NCBC, NIC, NTC, Rob, St, TD, TH, TNTC, We; all versions except NIV, NRSV]. They should be well disposed to their masters, having his interests at heart, and desiring to do him good [Can, EGT]. It means 'good-will', 'affection' [TD]. This phrase also implies a measure of zeal, an eagerness for service [Ea, EBC, ECWB, NCBC, NIC, Rob, St, TH].
2. It means an enthusiastic attitude, 'zeal' [AB, BAGD, LN, WBC; NIV, NRSV].

QUESTION—What is meant by ὡς τῷ κυρίῳ καὶ οὐκ ἀνθρώποις 'as to the Lord and not to men'?

The ὡς 'as' does not imply any fiction, but rather the reality that they do serve the Lord rather than men [EBC]. It indicates the subjective motivation of the subject of the discourse or action [BD, Tu]. This phrase is in contrast with ἀνθρωπάρεσκοι 'men-pleasers' in 6:6 [Ea]. The words τῷ κυρίῳ 'to the Lord' stress the thought of the Lord's sovereignty [We]. The negative phrase οὐκ ἀνθρώποις 'not to men' is a repetition of the negative idea in ἀνθρωπάρεσκοι 'men-pleasers'. It is given for emphasis [LJ].

6:8 knowing that each whatever good[a] he-may-do/shall-have-done, the-same he-will-receive[b] from (the) Lord whether slave or free.[c]

TEXT—Instead of ὅτι ἕκαστος ἐάν τι ποιήσῃ 'that each whatever (good) he may do/shall have done' (supported by Alf, EGT, GNT, Rob, WBC, We), other texts contain the reading ὅτι ἕκαστος ὃ ἐάν (or ἄν) ποιήσῃ 'that each whatsoever (good) he may do/shall have done' (supported by ICC, EBC). The Textus Receptus tradition contains the reading ὅτι ὃ ἐάν τι ἕκαστος ποιήσῃ 'that whatsoever each may do/shall have done' (supported by Bu, Ea, El, Ho, My; and probably KJV). Also reported are the readings ὅτι ἐάν ποιήσῃ ἕκαστος 'that if each should do' (the easiest and therefore most suspicious reading [El]) and ὅτι ἐάν τι ἕκαστος ποιήσῃ 'that whatever each may do', and other minor variations [Alf, EGT, El, ICC]. GNT does not note any of these alternate readings. Some of these readings affect the interpretation of the particle ἐάν 'if' [EBC, EGT].

LEXICON—a. ἀγαθός: 'good'. See this word at 4:28.
  b. fut. mid. indic. of κομίζω (κομίζομαι—LN 57.136) (BAGD 2.a. p. 443): 'to receive' [AB, BAGD, El, NIC, Rob; KJV], 'to receive a recompense' [BAGD], 'to receive back' [LN, Lns, MM, NTC; NASB], 'to receive again' [We; NRSV], 'to get back' [LN], 'to recover' [MM]. This middle voice verb is also translated as a passive: 'to be paid back' [LN], 'to be repaid' [NAB, REB], 'to be recompensed' [WBC], 'to be rewarded' [NJB]. It is also translated actively with 'Lord' as its subject: 'to reward' [NIV, TEV, TNT].
  c. ἐλεύθερος (LN 87.84) (BAGD 1. p. 250): 'free' [AB, BAGD, El, Lns, NTC, Rob, WBC, We; all versions except NJB], 'free person' [LN, NIC], 'free man' [LN; NJB]. This noun refers to a person who is not a slave, whether or not he has ever been a slave, or was formerly a slave but is one no longer [LN]. This term denotes political or social freedom [BAGD].

QUESTION—What relationship is indicated by the participle εἰδότες?
  It indicates the grounds [EBC, EGT, El, Ho, WBC] and motive [LJ] for the injunctions given in 6:5–7 and introduces the concluding part of this encouragement to the slaves [El, Ho]. In contrast to contemporary household codes which encouraged slaves by hopes of better treatment and material rewards from the master, this one provides motivation to Christian slaves by holding up before them the prospect of eschatological reward [WBC]. It assumes such knowledge on the part of the Christian slaves, 'seeing you know' [Alf, Ea, EGT, El, LJ, NIC].

QUESTION—What is meant by ἕκαστος ἐάν τι ποιήσῃ ἀγαθόν 'whatever good each may do/shall have done'?
  Ἕκαστος 'each' is positioned forward for emphasis [NTC, WBC]. The ἀγαθόν 'good' is intrinsic good [NTC]; it is whatever a person does that is right [Ba]. Whatever this is, the Lord will appropriately reward each person in the future world [Ba, Can]. The ἀγαθόν 'good' is the conduct the apostle has been enjoining on slaves [Cal, Can (probably) Ea]. In contrast to the parallel in Col. 3:24–25, only the good is mentioned here [NTC, TH, TNTC, WBC, We], and this may be because the apostle is giving encouragement and not warning [NTC, TNTC, WBC]. The adjective ἀγαθόν 'good' is emphasized by being held over until the end of the clause [Bu].

1. The subjunctive aorist verb ποιήσῃ is translated as a past perfect tense, 'shall have done' [Alf, EBC, EGT; NJB, TNT]: 'whatever good each shall have done'. The verb looks back at actions done from the perspective of the Lord's second coming [Alf]. The ποιήσῃ, as followed by the future κομίσεται 'shall receive', is best translated 'shall have done' [EGT].
2. The subjunctive aorist verb ποιήσῃ is translated as a present tense, 'may do' [AB, Ba, Can, LJ, MNTC, NIC, NTC, Rob, WBC, We; all versions except NJB, TNT]: whatever good each may do.
3. The subjunctive aorist verb ποιήσῃ 'may do' is translated as a future tense [El, Lns]: whatever good each shall do.

QUESTION—What is meant by τοῦτο κομίσεται παρὰ κυρίου 'the same he will receive from the Lord'?

The τοῦτο 'the same' is emphatic [Alf]. It means 'this in full' or 'this exactly' [Alf], 'this' and not something else [Ea]. The author speaks of reciprocity, the good that a person does is returned in kind, or in the same manner [TH]. The verb κομίζομαι 'to receive' is used most often in the NT in the sense of 'obtaining' something or of 'receiving back' or 'recovering' what is one's own [EGT, We].

1. The reference of the future tense of κομίσεται 'he will receive' is to the time of judgment at Christ's second coming [AB, Alf, Ba, Can, CBC, Ea, EBC, EGT, El, Ho, LJ, MNTC, My, NIC, NTC, TNTC, WBC, We]. The future verb κομίσεται 'he will receive' looks forward to the final judgment [AB, EBC, EGT] and introduces a currency metaphor. It has the sense of receiving something in the value as then estimated—changed, so to speak, into the currency of the new and final state which will take place at Christ's second coming [Alf]. The reward may be the Lord's approval in the day of judgment [CBC].
2. The reference of the future tense of κομίσεται 'he will receive' is to heaven [IB].
3. The reference of the future tense of κομίσεται 'he will receive' is both to the time of judgment at Christ's second coming and to the judgments of the present life [ECWB, Lns, WeBC]. How and when the slave gets his reward back depends upon the Lord. Often it will be, in part, in this life [Lns]. The reward will certainly be received, in part, in this life, if nothing more than a good conscience and the favor and blessing of God. But its full payment will be in the life to come [WeBC].

QUESTION—What is the significance of the nominal clause εἴτε δοῦλος εἴτε ἐλεύθερος 'whether slave or free'?

The Lord's rewards for righteous acts are given irrespective of the outward station a person occupies in life [Cal, EGT, LJ], the same principle of recompense applying to both slave and freeman. They will in no way be influenced by the person's social status [EBC], but take into consideration only *spiritual* [EGT] or *moral* states [El, My]. This clause gives emphasis to the teaching in this passage of equal standing of slave and free at the future judgment [WBC] and provides a transition to the exhortation to masters in 6:9 [TNTC, WBC].

DISCOURSE UNIT: 6:9 [Ba, Si, St; NRSV, REB, TEV]. The topic is the duties of masters to their servants [Ba, St], the accountability of masters to their Overlord [Si].

6:9 **And the masters, do the same-things to them, stopping[a] the threatening,[b] knowing that both their and your master is in heaven and (there) is no partiality[c] with him.**

TEXT—Instead of καὶ αὐτῶν καὶ ὑμῶν κυριός 'both their and your master', some manuscripts contain other variant readings, the most important one being καὶ ὑμῶν αὐτῶν κυριός 'your master also'. GNT does not note these variant readings. The reading 'your master also' is taken only by LJ and KJV.

LEXICON—a. pres. act. participle of ἀνίημι (LN **68.43**) (BAGD p. 69): 'to stop' [**LN**, NTC; NAB] 'to give up' [BAGD, El, LN, NIC; NASB], 'to refrain from' [Lns], 'to forbear' [Rob, We; KJV], 'to quit' [LN], 'to cease from' [BAGD], 'to abandon the use of' [WBC]. The participial clause ἀνιέντες τὴν ἀπειλήν 'stopping the threatening' is translated as an imperative clause: 'do not threaten (them)' [NIV], 'do without threats' [NJB], 'stop threatening (them)' [NRSV], 'stop using threats' [AB; TEV], 'give up using threats' [REB, TNT]. The present participle has durative force, 'always refraining from' [Lns].

b. ἀπειλή (LN **33.291**) (BAGD p. 83): 'threatening' [BAGD, El, **LN**, NIC, NTC, Rob, We; KJV, NAB, NASB], 'threat' [AB, BAGD, LN, Lns, WBC; REB, TEV, TNT].

c. προσωπολημψία (LN 88.238) (BAGD p. 720): 'partiality' [BAGD, LN, MM, NTC, WBC; NASB, NRSV], 'favoritism' [NIC; NIV, NJB, REB], 'respect of person(s)' [El, Lns, Rob, We; KJV], 'undue favor' [MM]. The clause προσωπολημψία οὐκ ἔστιν παρ' αὐτῷ 'there is no partiality with him' is translated 'he who fosters no favoritism' [AB], 'who plays no favorites' [NAB], 'he has no favorites' [TNT], 'who judges everyone by the same standard' [TEV].

QUESTION—What relationship is indicated by καί 'and'?

The initial καί 'and' indicates an immediate connection with the preceding verses [Ea, My, WBC], because the duties enjoined in this verse are reciprocal to those enjoined in the previous verses [Ea, EGT]. As the admonition that was directed to slaves (6:5–8) was full of implied significance for their masters also, the exhortation directed in this verse specifically to their masters could be brief [NTC]. Its force is 'Not only slaves have their duties, but you masters have your special obligations' [Ho]. The καί 'and' indicates that obligations are not all on the side of the slaves [ICC, LJ].

QUESTION—What is meant by τὰ αὐτὰ ποιεῖτε πρὸς αὐτούς 'do the same things to them'?

1. Τὰ αὐτά 'the same things' refers back to the contents of 6:5–8 [Ba, Can, Ea, Ho, IB, LJ, Lns, NIC, NTC, Rob, St, TNTC, WeBC; and probably ICC, TH, WBC, We]. It is not necessary to seek the verbal antecedent of τὰ αὐτά 'these things'; it is used *ad sensum* [Lns]. It expresses identity of spirit, not outward action [We]. The phrase τὰ αὐτά 'the same things' refers to contents of the previous verses [Ba, Can, Ea, Ho], to the general εὔνοια 'good will' manifested in these verses [Can, El, ICC (probably)]. As the slaves were exhorted to doing the will of God in a spirit of kindness and faithfulness with due regard to the genuine welfare of their master, so the master is to deal similarly with his slaves with a view to their welfare [Ba], remembering that the eye of God is upon them, that they serve God in this life in the role of masters, and will render account to him [Ba]. The duty just taught to the slaves was earnest, conscientious, religious service. The duty being taught to masters is earnest, conscientious, religious government. The elements of service are those also of proprietorship. It is possible to confine and weaken the meaning by specifying too minutely the reference of τὰ αὐτά 'the same things' [Ea]. Literal exactness is not meant [Can, Rob, TH], for it is not the duty of masters to obey their slaves, but the good will enjoined upon the slaves in the previous verses is applicable to the masters [Can, TH] in the fullest and strictest sense. As the slaves are to benefit their master by their labor, so the master is to benefit his slaves by his care and supervision [Can].
2. Τὰ αὐτά 'the same things' refers back particularly to the participial clause ποιοῦντες τὸ θέλημα τοῦ θεοῦ 'doing the will of God' in 6:6 [EBC].
3. Τὰ αὐτά 'the same things' refers back particularly to the phrase μετ' εὐνοίας 'with good will/zeal' in 6:7 [EGT, My]. The meaning is that masters are to act toward their slaves in the same Christian way that the slaves have been called upon to act toward them, in the same consideration and goodwill [EGT, My].
4. Τὰ αὐτά 'the same things' refers back particularly to the participial clause δουλεύοντες ὡς τῷ κυρίῳ καὶ οὐκ ἀνθρώποις 'serving as to the Lord and not to man' in 6:7 [NCBC]. Slaves have been exhorted to make it their aim in all their work to please Christ, and to do this with cheerfulness and goodwill. Masters are likewise exhorted to please Christ by treating their slaves with cheerfulness and courtesy [NCBC].

QUESTION—What is meant by ἀνιέντες τὴν ἀπειλήν 'stopping the threatening'?

This is a negative modal definition of the preceding τὰ αὐτὰ ποιεῖτε πρὸς αὐτούς 'do the same things to them' [My]. This refers to the customary practice of slave owners of seeking to extort the last ounce of effort from their slaves by the threat of punishing them [NCBC]. Paul singles out the prevailing vice and most customary form of bad feeling evinced by slave owners with this explanatory participial clause. In forbidding the use of threats, he naturally includes in this every similar form of harshness [El, LJ]. It does not mean they were to remit punishment when it was just [Ba], legitimate and necessary [St], but they were to govern their slaves by love rather than by terror [Ba, Cal, Can, CBC].

QUESTION—What relationship is indicated by the participle εἰδότες 'knowing'?

It indicates the grounds [EGT, El, Ho, St, WBC] or the motive by which Paul enforces his injunctions [Can, Ea, El, LJ, MNTC, My]. The participle εἰδότες 'knowing' is said by one commentator to be punctiliar in force, 'having come to know' [Lns]. Another gives it durative force, 'continually be aware of the fact that' [TH]. It assumes the knowledge by the subject of the material presented in the remainder of the clause [Alf, LJ]. The positioning of the genitive phrase (καὶ αὐτῶν καὶ ὑμῶν 'both theirs and yours') before the noun it modifies (ὁ κύριος 'master') makes this phrase emphatic by position [HG, Lns]. The occurrence of both possessive pronouns in the phrase καὶ αὐτῶν καὶ ὑμῶν 'both theirs and yours' has the effect of making both the master and the slave feel that, in a most important sense, they are equal before God [Ba]. The phrase shows that, in this verse, both masters and slaves are clearly Christians [NCBC, NIC].

QUESTION—Who is ὁ κύριος 'the master'?

1. Ὁ κύριος 'master' refers to God [Ba, Cal, Can, EBC, TD, TH]. In the day of judgment God will not show favoritism or partiality [TH].
2. Ὁ κύριος 'master' refers to Christ [AB, CBC, Ea, Ho, LJ, MNTC, My, NCBC, NIC, St, TD, TNTC, WBC, WeBC]. This is the exalted Christ [My], the coming Lord [AB].

QUESTION—What is meant by προσωπολημψία 'partiality'?

The meaning is that God will not be influenced in the distribution of rewards and punishments by the rank or external condition of the master and the slave [Ba, Can]. Both will be treated according to their essential character [Ba, Can, ISBE]. God does not form his opinion of a person, as men do, on a person's relationships, beauty, wealth, rank, friendship, or anything of that sort [Cal, LJ, NCBC]. Paul reminds these masters that they are mistaken if they think that God will have little regard for their slaves because they appear to be of little account before men [Cal, LJ]. The master's attitude, as the slave's, is not to be determined by standards of different social status, but by the relationship to Christ before whom master and slave stand on equal footing [IB, LJ]. The warning, implicit in this clause, is for both masters and slaves [MNTC], but is particularly appropriate to masters because the higher up in social status a person is the more likely he is to expect special consideration [NCBC, NIC, WBC]. A reference to the last judgment may be implicit in this clause, but its function is more to make masters conscious of their present accountability [WBC].

DISCOURSE UNIT: 6:10–24 [Ea, ECWB, Ho, NTC, TNTC; NASB]. The topic is the conclusion [ECWB, TNTC], the armor of God [NASB], an exhortation to all to put on the Church's God-given effective armor, and conclusion [NTC], the image of a spiritual warfare, the mission of Tychicus, and valedictory blessing [Ea], directions in reference to the spiritual conflict and prayer, the mission of Tychicus, and invocation of divine blessings upon the brethren [Ho].

DISCOURSE UNIT: 6:10–22 [NCBC]. The topic is God's equipment for the Christian.

DISCOURSE UNIT: 6:10–20 [AB, Alf, Ba, Can, CBC, EBC, EGT, El, LJ, Lns, NCBC, NTC, Rob, St, TH, TNTC, WBC, We, WeBC; NASB, NIV, NJB, REB, TEV, TNT]. The topic is the superior power [AB], principalities and powers [St], the Christian warfare [Ba, TH, We], the Christian conflict [TNTC], the spiritual war [NJB], the call to arms against spiritual foes [Can], the Christian warfare with evil [CBC], into battle [EBC], the Christian soldier [LJ], the spiritual warrior in God's armor [Rob], putting on the full armor of God [NTC], the whole armor of God [TEV], the armor of God [NIV], the Christian armory [REB], a general exhortation to the spiritual conflict and prayer [Alf], concluding appeal to stand firm in the battle against spiritual powers [WBC], the Church's spiritual victory in Christ [WeBC], a general concluding exhortation expressed in terms of the Christian's spiritual warfare, the powers of evil against which he contends, and the weapons with which he is to arm himself [EGT], closing admonition for all to stand against the great enemies of the church [Lns], final exhortation [NCBC].

DISCOURSE UNIT: 6:10–18 [IB]. The topic is the fourth exhortation: to put on God's armor.

DISCOURSE UNIT: 6:10–17 [ECWB, MNTC, My, NIC, Si, WBC; NAB, NRSV]. The topic is warfare [MNTC], putting on the armor of God [My], being strong in the Lord [NIC], the Christian panoply [Si], the Christian warfare [NAB], the final exhortation, to put on the whole armor of God in order to stand fast in the struggle against unearthly powers of evil [ECWB].

DISCOURSE UNIT: 6:10–13 [Cal, LJ, WBC]. The topic is the Christian warfare [LJ], the necessity for putting on God's full armor in order to be strong and to stand against the spiritual powers [WBC].

DISCOURSE UNIT: 6:10–12 [ICC, We]. The topic is the Christian position [We], an exhortation to prepare for the spiritual combat by arming themselves with the panoply of God [ICC].

DISCOURSE UNIT: 6:10–11a [LJ, WeBC]. The topic is the source of the believers' spiritual strength [WeBC].

6:10 Finally/in-the-future,[a] be-strong[b] in (the) Lord and in the strength[c] of-the might[d] of-him.

TEXT—Instead of the genitive τοῦ λοιποῦ 'finally/in the future', some manuscripts have the absolute accusative τὸ λοιπόν 'finally'. GNT does not note this variant reading. The reading with the accusative is taken by Ea, El, Ho, My, Si-ed; KJV; and probably Ba, ICC, TNTC.

TEXT—Some manuscripts insert ἀδελφοί μου 'my brothers' between the accusative τὸ λοιπόν 'finally' and ἐνδυναμοῦσθε 'be strong'. GNT does not note this addition. This addition is included by KJV and probably TNTC.

LEXICON—a. λοιπόν, λοιπός (LN 61.14) (BAGD 3.a.β. p. 480): 'finally' [BAGD, El, LN, Lns, NTC, Rob, WBC; all versions], 'in summary, beyond that, at last' [LN], 'for the rest' [NIC], 'for the remaining time' [AB], 'in the future' [BAGD, We]. It means 'henceforward' [Alf, EGT, St].

b. pres. mid. or pass. impera. of ἐνδυναμόομαι, ἐνδυναμόω (LN **74.7**) (BAGD 2.b. p. 263): 'to be strong' [NIC, Rob, WBC; KJV, NASB, NIV, NRSV], 'to become strong' [AB, BAGD], 'to grow strong' [NJB], 'to build up strength' [TEV], 'to be powerful' [Lns], 'to find strength' [REB], 'to draw strength from' [NAB], 'to become capable' [**LN**], 'to become able' [LN], 'to be strengthened' [El], 'to be made powerful' [We]. This imperative is also translated as a clause: 'find your source of power' [NTC]. The Greek clause ἐνδυναμοῦσθε ἐν κυρίῳ καὶ ἐν τῷ κράτει τῆς ἰσχύος αὐτοῦ 'be strong in the Lord and in the strength of his might' is translated 'draw upon the Lord's power and let him supply you with his mighty strength' [TNT]. The present tense of this imperative is durative [Lns, NCBC, TNTC].

c. κράτος: 'strength'. See this word at 1:19.

d. ἰσχύς: 'might'. See this word at 1:19.

QUESTION—What is meant by τοῦ λοιποῦ 'finally/in the future'?

1. It has a logical force [Ba, BAGD, Can, DNTT, Ea, EBC, El, Ho, ICC, LJ, Lns, MNTC, Mo, My, NCBC, NIC, NTC, Rob, Si-ed, TH, TNTC, WBC, WeBC; all versions]: finally. This is the meaning when the accusative absolute reading τὸ λοιπόν is taken. Τοῦ λοιποῦ is equivalent to τὸ λοιπόν 'finally' [Rob, WBC], or practically so [NTC]. It means 'for the rest' [Can, EBC, LJ, MNTC, My], i.e., 'for the rest of what I have to say to you; all that I have now to add is this one exhortation' [Can].

    1.1 This term indicates a final point to be made in relation to all the preceding material in this epistle [Ho, LJ, Rob, Si, TH, WeBC]. This term indicates more than an afterthought [LJ]. It introduces the final part of the outworking of the apostle's theme concerning salvation and calling, a part closely connected with all he has written previously in the epistle [LJ, Rob]. This term introduces the conclusion of this epistle, containing directions for the struggle necessary to secure the salvation which the epistle has proclaimed [Ho].

    1.2 This term indicates a final point to be made in relation to the preceding section of the epistle, to which it forms the conclusion [Ba, WBC]. Paul was aware that the discharge of the duties laid upon his readers in the previous sections would require strength from above against supernatural foes [Ba, WBC].

EPHESIANS 6:10 539

1.3 This term indicates a final point to be made, particularly in relation to 5:3–20 where actions relating to darkness and shame were discussed, or even further back to 4:25–31 where the reader is exhorted not to give any opportunity to the devil [NCBC]. The reader is little prepared for the sudden change of tone from the sedate treatment of household matters to a rousing call to preparedness for battle [NCBC].

2. It has temporal force [AB, Alf, EGT, IB, St, Tu, We]: in the future. The apostle is indicating that the whole of the period between the Lord's first coming and his second will be characterized by conflict [St]. Paul has a limited time period in mind. Its beginning is probably the making of peace between Jews and Gentiles through the cross and the resurrection and it will terminate on the day the Bridegroom meets the Bride and the Lord sits in judgment over all [AB].

QUESTION—What is meant by ἐνδυναμοῦσθε ἐν κυρίῳ 'be strong in the Lord'?

The preposition ἐν 'in' means 'in union with' [Ea, ECWB, EGT, IB, Lns, MNTC, TH, TNTC; TEV], and, at the same time, indicates means [IB, TH]: 'by being joined to the Lord' [TH]. Another commentator states that it indicates the element of our spiritual life [El]. Others, that it indicates the source of the strengthening [WBC, WeBC; NAB]. The wording of this clause is reminiscent of such OT passages as 1 Sam. 30:6 and Zech. 10:12 [WBC], but here 'the Lord' is Christ [TD, WBC], or 'Lord' is God [Cal, DNTT].

1. This is the middle voice of this imperative [Ba (probably), Ho (probably), Lns, NTC, TH; NAB, REB, TEV, TNT]: strengthen yourselves in the Lord. The first exhortation is to muster strength for the conflict and to seek that strength from the right source [Ho]. 'To be strong in the Lord' is (1) to be strong or courageous in his cause, and (2) to feel that he is our strength and to rely upon him and his promises [Ba]. The question is academic since both 'strengthen yourselves' and 'be strengthened' coalesce because of the modifying phrase ἐν κυρίῳ 'in the Lord' [NTC].

2. This is the passive voice of this imperative [AB, Alf, BAGD, Can, Ea, ECWB, EGT, El, HG, IB, ICC, My, NCBC, NIC, Rob, St, TNTC, WBC, We]: 'be made strong by the Lord'. It means 'to become strong, to gain strength' [My]. It means to summon up courage and vigor [Cal]. People cannot strengthen themselves, they must be empowered, and that constantly [TNTC]. The passive form shows that the strength needed does not lie within ourselves [Can, WBC], but is received from without, from the Lord [AB, Cal, Can, WBC].

QUESTION—What is meant by καὶ ἐν τῷ κράτει τῆς ἰσχύος αὐτοῦ 'and in the strength of his might'?

The καί 'and' appends this clause to the previous one, explaining it [Ea, EGT, El, Lns] and specifying the principle in which our strength is to be sought and in which it dwelt [Ea, El]. It is not explicative, but annexes the

effective principle of the strengthening that is to take place to the element in which it occurs [My].
1. The two nouns in this genitive construction form an hendiadys [NCBC, NIC, TD (probably), TH, WBC; NAB, NIV, REB, TEV, TNT]: in his mighty strength. The two words are almost synonyms [NCBC] and have already occurred together in combination at 1:19 [NCBC, NIC, WBC]. Paul prayed his readers might experience this same power in 3:16 [NIC, WBC]. Here they are told one way this power can take effect in their lives [NIC].
2. The two nouns in this genitive construction retain their individual meanings [AB, Alf, Can, Ea, EGT, El, Ho, IB (probably), ICC, LJ, Lns, NTC, Rob, TNTC, We; KJV, NASB, NJB, NRSV]: in the strength of his might. The phrase means 'in the vigor derived from his strength' [Ho]. Κράτος 'strength', on the other hand, is the manifestation of that ἰσχύς 'might' in action [LJ], or as abundantly effective in view of the purpose to which it is applied [We].

QUESTION—What is meant by the preposition ἐν 'in' in this phrase?
1. It indicates the means of the strengthening [AB, Cal, Can, IB, My, NIC, TH, We; NJB, TEV]: by means of the strength of his might. This phrase implies 'through fellowship with him' [We].
2. It indicates the principle or element in which the increase of strength is to be sought and in which it dwells [El] or in which it is to realize itself [EGT]: in the strength of his might.
3. It indicates the source of the strengthening [WBC, WeBC; NAB]: from the strength of his might. This is the second of a combination of two prepositional phrases that indicate the source of this strengthening. The believers' relationship to Christ gives them access to his power [WBC].

DISCOURSE UNIT: 6:11–13 [AB]. The topic is God's power, presented as God's own imposing armor, which is made available to the saints for an imminent battle against superhuman opposing forces, which they are to resist and hold out against.

6:11 **Put-on[a] the full-armor/armor[b] of-God**

LEXICON—a. aorist mid. impera. of ἐνδύω: 'to put on'. See this word at 4:24.
  b. πανοπλία (LN **6.30**) (BAGD 2. p. 608): 'full armor' [BAGD, NTC, WBC; NASB, NIV, NJB, REB], 'whole armor' [El, Lns, We; KJV, NRSV], 'all the armor' [**LN**; TEV], 'weapons and armor' [LN], 'panoply' [BAGD, NIC], 'splendid armor' [AB], 'armor' [MM, Rob; NAB, TNT]. This noun denotes a complete set of the implements used in defensive or offensive warfare, usually with emphasis upon defensive armament that includes helmet, shield, and breastplate. It is used figuratively in this passage of the virtues of Christian character that are to be used in the strife with evil [LN].

QUESTION—What is the function of this verse in the context?

This verse is a further explanation of what is to be done in order to become strong enough to meet all enemies [EGT, Lns, My, TD, TNTC]. It is a more specific parallel to the injunction of 6:10 [St]. While the previous verse has shown that the primary need is for strength to abide in Christ, this one shows the need for defense and gives us the means by which this is to be accomplished [Can, Ho, WeBC]. The previous verse dealt with strength and courage, this one with preparation to meet the enemy [Ea].

QUESTION—What is meant by ἐνδύσασθε 'put on' the armor?

The aorist imperative ἐνδύσασθε 'put on' is military language [Lns, TD] and is a command such as a general gives to his troops, denoting one decisive act [Lns]. Passages in the OT where qualities such as strength, honor, majesty, righteousness, salvation, beauty, glory, shame, etc., were to be 'put on' indicate the same kind of thought pattern as is occurring in this metaphorical context [AB]. The comparison in the metaphor is just as a heavily armed soldier of the line uses the various items of his battle equipment to protect himself against the enemies arrayed against him and to wage war against them, so the Christian believer must use the spiritual qualities God has provided him against the spiritual powers of evil that are bent upon his defeat and destruction. The point of comparison is the various items of a soldier's battle equipment that are designed to protect the various parts of his body and enable him to successfully battle against his enemy. A nonfigurative statement would be: use the spiritual qualities God has given you to counter the temptations and trials your spiritual enemies will bring against you to cause you to quit serving God.

QUESTION—What is meant by τὴν πανοπλίαν 'the whole armor'?

1. Πανοπλίαν 'whole armor' or 'full armor' denotes the completeness of the equipment [Alf, Ba, BAGD, Cal, Can, CBC, DNTT, Ea, EBC, ECWB, EGT, El, Ho, ICC, IDB, ISBE (probably), ISBE2, LJ, LN (6.30), Lns, MNTC, My, NCBC, NIC, NTC, Si, TD, TH, TNTC, WBC, We, WeBC; all versions except NAB, TEV, TNT]. This term denoted the total military equipment worn by the Roman soldier as he went into battle [CBC, LJ, NCBC, NIC, TH], or at least the essential pieces of the Roman soldier's equipment [ISBE]. Some commentators state that the armor here is both offensive and defensive [Alf, Ba, DNTT, EBC, El, Ho, ISBE2, LJ, LN, NCBC, NIC, WBC, WeBC], implying the Christian warrior is to attack his spiritual enemies as well as defend himself from them [Ho, LJ, NCBC], while others state it is defensive [Cal, TD], or mainly so [TD]. The use of this term implies believers are to use all the armor God provides us, not utilizing one piece while neglecting another [Ba, Cal, Ea, ECWB, EGT, IDB, LJ, MNTC, NTC, Si, WeBC]. If any item is lacking, defeat may be the consequence [Ba, ECWB, LJ, Si, WeBC].

2. Πανοπλίαν 'armor' denotes the quality of the armor rather than the completeness of the listing [AB, Rob, St] and just denotes 'armor' [IB, Rob; NAB, TNT]. The noun is the collective term for 'armor' and is not

substantially different from the term ὅπλα 'armor' [IB]. The emphasis of the passage is not upon the completeness of the armor, but upon the fact that it is divine armor [Rob, St].

QUESTION—What is meant by the genitive construction τὴν πανοπλίαν τοῦ θεοῦ 'the whole armor of God'?

The genitive τοῦ θεοῦ 'of God' does not mean armor that God wears [Ba, Ea], but means 'as supplied, provided, by God' [Alf, Ba, Ea, EBC, ECWB, EGT, El, Ho, ICC, IDB, LJ, Lns, My, NTC, TD, TH, TNTC, WBC, We, WeBC; REB, TEV]. It is modeled on what God himself wears (Isa. 11:5, 59:17; Wisd. of Sol. 5:17–20) [EBC], which passages form the background for this phrase [EBC, EGT, Lns, My, St, TD, TNTC, WBC; NJB (note)]. Some state that the genitive phrase implies it is armor that has been made by God [MNTC, NTC] or designed by him for the believer's protection [LJ, WeBC]. Others state that, in light of the OT background of this term, it is difficult to escape the impression that this phrase also refers to the armor God himself is pictured as wearing [AB, IB, Rob, St, TD, TNTC, WBC; NJB (note)]. The picture is that God gives parts of his own personal armor to the believer [TD].

DISCOURSE UNIT: 6:11b–13 [WeBC]. The topic is the need for believers to have spiritual strength.

6:11b in-order-that you may-be-able to-stand[a] against the schemes[b] of-the devil;

LEXICON—a. aorist act. infin. of ἵσταμαι, ἵστημι (LN 13.29) (BAGD II.1.c. p. 382): 'to stand' [El, Lns, NIC, Rob, WBC, We; KJV, NRSV], 'to stand firm' [AB, NTC; NAB, NASB, REB], 'to stand up' [TEV], 'to take (one's) stand' [NIV], 'to make a stand' [TNT], 'to offer resistance' [BAGD], 'to resist' [NJB], 'to firmly remain, to continue steadfastly' [LN].

b. μεθοδεία: 'scheme'. See this word at 4:14.

QUESTION—What relationship is indicated by πρός 'in order that'?

It indicates purpose [Ea, EGT, El, HG, Ho, ICC, Lns, MNTC, MT, St, Tu] in providing the equipment [El, Ho, LJ, MNTC, St], as well as the purpose of the ἐνδυναμοῦσθε 'be strong' of 6:10 [LJ, TD].

QUESTION—What is meant by στῆναι πρός 'to stand against' the schemes of the devil?

This is a military phrase [Ea, EGT, El, ICC, My, TH] meaning to stand in front of, with the intention of opposing [Ea, WBC], to stand one's ground [EGT, El, ICC, My, NCBC, NTC, WBC] as opposed to running away [EGT]. The verb points to a primarily defensive situation [TH]. It means to hold on to a position [EBC, WBC, We]. The word στῆναι 'stand' is a key one in this context (6:13, 14) [EBC, TNTC]. The task of the warring believer here is not to win, but to stand—to preserve and maintain what has already been won decisively by God in Christ [WBC].

QUESTION—What is meant by τὰς μεθοδείας τοῦ διαβόλου 'the schemes of the devil'?

The plural here denotes the various concrete instances of the abstract quality of μεθόδεια 'scheming' [Alf, Ea, EGT, El, ICC, My, We], or it denotes the placing of this abstract subject in a class, here meaning 'astuteness' [Tu]. It refers to cunning or deceptive stratagems [Ba, Can, ECWB, EGT, MNTC, TD, WeBC], devised by a great and unscrupulous wisdom [Can], through which Satan attempts to delude and destroy believers and drag them down to perdition [Ba]. It suggests designs and aims which are carefully thought out for the planned attack [WeBC]. Satan approaches believers so as to lay down some plausible teaching, some seemingly harmless temptation that does not immediately repel them [Ba]. It means the manifold temptations to unbelief, to sin, and to conformity to the surrounding pagan world [IB]. In the context of Ephesians, these stratagems are likely to have been attempts to destroy the unity of the church (3:14–22; 4:1–16, 27) through the introduction of false doctrine and the fomenting of dissension (4:2, 21, 31, 32; 5:6) [EBC].

6:12 because our wrestling/struggle^a is not against blood and flesh, but against the rulers,^b against the authorities,^c

LEXICON—a. πάλη (LN 39.29) (BAGD p. 606): 'wrestling' [BAGD, El, Lns, MM, NTC, We], 'struggle' [BAGD; NASB, NIV, NRSV, REB], 'battle' [WBC; NAB]. This noun is also translated as a verb: 'we wrestle' [NIC, Rob; KJV], 'we are wrestling' [AB], 'we have to struggle' [NJB], 'we are fighting' [TEV, TNT]. The clause οὐκ ἔστιν ἡμῖν ἡ πλάνη πρὸς αἷμα καὶ σάρκα 'our struggle is not against blood and flesh' is translated 'it is not against human beings that we fight' [**LN**]. This noun denotes engaging in an intense struggle against strong opposition. The struggle involves either physical or nonphysical force [LN].

b. ἀρχή: 'ruler'. See this word at 1:21.

c. ἐξουσία: 'authority'. See this word at 1:21.

QUESTION—What relationship is indicated by ὅτι 'because'?

1. It indicates the grounds for mentioning the schemes of the devil (6:11) [Alf, Ea, EGT, Ho, My, NCBC, WeBC]. It gives the reason for the mention of τὰς μεθοδείας τοῦ διαβόλου 'the schemes of the devil' as dangers that the Christian is to stand his ground against [EGT, El].
2. It indicates the grounds for giving the command ἐνδύσασθε τὴν πανοπλίαν τοῦ θεοῦ 'put on the full armor of God' [LJ, Lns, WBC] as well as for the command of 6:10, 'be strong in the Lord' [LJ].

QUESTION—What is meant by ἡ πάλη 'wrestling/struggle'?

1. Πάλη 'wrestling' is used in reference to a sporting contest [AB, Alf, Ba, EGT, El, IB, ICC, ISBE, ISBE2, LJ, Lns, MM, My, NIC, NTC, Pf, Rob, Si, TNTC, We, WeBC; KJV]. The author may be mixing his metaphors in this passage [AB, Alf, Ba, EGT, IB, LJ, NTC, TNTC, We]. No doubt this context speaks of a spiritual war and spiritual weapons, yet Paul has not chosen to use the term πόλεμος 'war' here, but rather chooses to mix the

metaphors of sport and of war, as other ancient writers did, and use a word that originally denoted the activity of an athlete [AB]. The noun πάλη 'wrestling' is understood in its literal sense of a hand-to-hand battle in which the combatants close and wrestle for the mastery [Alf, EGT] so that the figure of the panoply is left for the moment to bring in the figure of the wrestler and the idea of an individual encounter at close quarters that it conveys [EGT, LJ, NTC, TNTC, We]. The struggle against these spiritual forces of evil is presented on the one hand as a 'wrestling' which, against a human opponent in the arena, would not require any kind of armor; and, on the other hand, as a warfare for which armor is necessary [IB, LJ]. He is making the point that the believer's battle with these spirits is not merely a human wrestling match [ISBE2 (probably), Lns, My, Pf], no mere game in which our opponent struggles only to throw us and pin our back to the floor. No, believers face a tremendous army consisting of all the evil forces of the supernatural world [Lns]. This enemy is not like 'blood and flesh' that may be seen and grappled with. This enemy is all the more dangerous because he cannot be seen [Pf]. The article with this noun expresses generally the *kind* of conflict which the Christian is *not* engaged in [My].

2. Πάλη 'struggle' is used in reference to fighting in general [Ea, EBC, Ho, **LN**, MNTC, NCBC (probably), TD, TH, WBC; all versions except KJV]. The apostle here uses this noun in the more general sense of 'conflict' [Ho, TD] (and was so used in Greek tragedy [TD]), 'struggle, fight' [TH]. Πάλη 'struggle' could be transferred out of the arena and applied to a military context [WBC]. It denotes a personal encounter [Ea]. In the context it is inappropriate to use the specific term for 'wrestling' in a picture of a soldier armed for combat, a more general term is called for [TH].

QUESTION—What is meant by οὐκ...πρὸς αἷμα καὶ σάρκα 'not against blood and flesh'?

The negative in this clause is not a comparative negative [EGT] and so is not to be softened into the sense of 'not so much as' [Alf, Ea, EGT, El, My] or 'not only' [Ea]. The form of this clause points to an absolute negation [Alf, EGT, El, My] (the following affirmation which is also absolute [El]) meaning that the conflict is *not* with men [Alf, EGT]. It is not with men that the source and origin of all the saints' spiritual conflicts arise [Ba]. In the synecdoche αἷμα καὶ σάρκα 'blood and flesh', the usual order σάρκα καὶ αἷμα 'flesh and blood' is reversed [AB, EBC, ECWB, EGT, IB, ICC, LJ, Lns, My, NIC, NTC, TD, Tu3, WBC, We] but the reason is not known [AB], unless it is merely accidental [My, Tu3]. The phrase is neutral here, not having any connotation of human corruption [Ea, EGT, Ho, LJ, Lns, My], but only pointing out humanity's ordinary condition and form [DNTT, Ea, LJ, Lns, WBC]. It means 'feeble humanity' [DNTT, EGT, My, NTC, TD, WBC], 'mortal humanity' [NIC, St], or 'human nature' [IDB, NCBC], or 'other people' [Bu, NCBC, TH]. The point is that the Christian believers'

EPHESIANS 6:12 545

difficulties are far greater than if their conflict was just with men [Cal]. They are such that no human power can withstand them [Cal, LJ].

QUESTION—Who are the entities referred to in the contrastive ἀλλά 'but' clause?

These are evil superhuman powers [AB, Ba, Can, CBC, El, Ho, Lns, NIC, Rob, St, TD, WBC, WeBC] of the highest rank and position [Ea, WeBC] who are opposing God for control of the world [CBC]. They stand in contrast to the αἷμα καὶ σάρκα 'blood and flesh', the merely human powers just mentioned [Can, Ea, ECWB, IB, ICC, Lns, WBC]. The writer lists these beings, not for classification purposes, or for completeness, but to indicate the variety and comprehensiveness of the power the devil has at his disposal [WBC]. The repetition of πρός 'against' before each of these substantives is rhetorical [EGT, El, My], designed to emphasize the enumeration [El, LJ, Lns], call attention to the fact that each of these must be dealt with individually [TNTC, We], and emphasize that the believer's conflict is spiritual [Bu].

1. These four designations of spirit beings represent all evil spirits in general [LJ, Lns, MNTC, NTC, TD, WeBC; and probably NCBC, NIC, St, TNTC]. Paul is not enumerating different classes of warriors among evil spirits [Lns, TD], but uses more or less synonymous designations of the devil's forces which are arrayed against Christian believers [TD]. The phrases are appositions, each one parading the entire army of demons before us. Four views of it are given for the sake of completeness. Each demon has his 'rule' in which he exercises his 'authority'. They are all 'world tyrants of this darkness' and 'spiritual forces of wickedness'. The first two abstract titles are thus defined by concrete titles [Lns].

2. These four designations of spirit beings represent two different classes of spirits [Can, Ea, ECWB, Ho, My]. The definite articles attached to the nouns ἀρχάς 'rulers', ἐξουσίας 'authorities', κοσμοκράτορας 'world rulers' and πνευματικά 'spiritual forces' point back to the mention of the superhuman powers mentioned previously in 1:21, who are put under the feet of Christ, and in 3:10, who are learning through the church the manifold wisdom of Christ. They are listed here (1) according to their rank in the scale of being, not as having the right to command the obedience of the believer, but as to the formidability of their order and organization, (2) in reference to the sway they actually exercise, as dominating the ungodly world as it is in its present state of darkness regarding its ignorance of God and of Christ, and (3) in reference to the subtlety of their assaults, as 'spiritual hosts of wickedness' [Can]. As to their position, these are foes of the highest rank, the nobility and chieftains of the fallen spirit-world; as to their office, their domain is τοῦ σκότους τούτου 'this darkness', in which they hold dictatorial sway; as to their essence, they are πνευματικά 'spiritual' or 'spirits', unencumbered by an animal frame; and as to their character, they are πονηρίας 'wicked' or 'evil', their appetite for evil being only exceeded by their capacity for producing it [Ea]. With the terms ἀρχάς 'rulers' and

ἐξουσίας 'authorities' Paul describes them simply as angelic (or demonic [My]) powers [ECWB, My], with probable reference to the relation of rank and order among themselves [Ho, My]. But the following two phrases describe these beings with reference to the evil they produce from two different aspects [ECWB, My], as to their *sphere* [My], i.e., their relationship to the world, as those whose dominion in this world is worldwide [Ho, My], reigning over the existing state of ignorance and alienation from God [Ho], and as to their *ethical* character [My], i.e., their wicked moral nature [ECWB, Ho, My].

3. These four designations of spirit beings represent three different types of spirits [IB, TH, We]. The ἀρχάς 'rulers' and ἐξουσίας 'authorities' are two of the orders of spirits which in the astrological thinking of the time were thought to hold dominion over human life. To these are now added a third class, τοὺς κοσμοκράτορας τοῦ σκότους τούτου 'the world rulers of this darkness' [IB]. The three classes distinguished all belong to τοῦ σκότους τούτου 'this darkness' [We]. The fourth designation, τὰ πνευματικὰ τῆς πονηρίας 'the spiritual forces of wickedness', is a comprehensive designation of all the classes of hostile spirits against which the Christian believer must contend [IB, We].

QUESTION—What is meant by the terms τὰς ἀρχάς 'the rulers' and τὰς ἐξουσίας 'the authorities'?

They are called ἀρχάς 'rulers' or 'princes', as those who are first or high in rank, and ἐξουσίας 'authorities' or 'potentates', as those invested with authority [Ho, My]. The two nouns which were used to describe the classes and orders of the good powers in Rom. 13:1, 3 and Eph. 1:21 are used here to describe their evil counterparts [El, ISBE2, My]. Paul's point is that not merely spiritual agencies are set against us, but the most powerful of them [MNTC], powers second only to that of God himself [LJ]. The meaning of the nouns in these phrases have been presented in the Lexicon and Question sections of 1:21.

against the world-rulers[a] of-this darkness, against the spiritual-forces[b] of-(the) wickedness in the heavenly (places).

TEXT—Some manuscripts include the words τοῦ αἰῶνος 'of the age' between τοῦ σκότους 'of the darkness' and τούτου 'this'. GNT does not note this variant reading. The addition is accepted by Bu, Cal, and KJV. The apparent support of NAB, NIV, NJB, REB, TEV, TNT for this variant is probably a translation of their interpretation of τούτου 'this'.

LEXICON—a. κοσμοκράτωρ (LN **12.44, 37.73**) (BAGD p. 445): 'world-ruler' [BAGD, El, LN (**37.73**), NIC, NTC, WBC, We; TNT], 'world tyrant' [Lns], 'world force' [NASB], 'cosmic power' [LN (**12.44**); NRSV, TEV]. The phrase τοὺς κοσμοκράτορας τοῦ σκότους τούτου 'the world-rulers of this darkness' is translated: 'the overlords of this dark world' [AB], 'the powers of this dark world' [NIV], 'the rulers of the darkness of this world' [Rob; KJV], 'the rulers of this world of darkness' [NAB]. The contrastive clause ἀλλὰ πρὸς τὰς ἀρχάς, πρὸς τὰς ἐξουσίας, πρὸς τοὺς κοσμοκράτορας τοῦ σκότους τούτου 'but against the rulers, against the authorities, against the world rulers of this darkness' is translated: 'but against the principalities and the ruling forces who are masters of the darkness in this world' [NJB], 'but against cosmic powers, against the authorities and potentates of this dark age' [REB]. This noun refers to one who rules over the entire world. Most commentators interpret this to mean a supernatural power [LN (12.44)], though it is possible to understand it in this context to refer to a human ruler [LN (37.73)]. This is one of a number of titles denoting supernatural forces and powers which have some particular role in controlling the activities and destinies of human beings [LN (12.44)]. In the literature of the time, this term referred to spirit beings who were regarded as having parts of the cosmos under their control [BAGD].

b. πνευματικός (LN **12.44**, 79.3) (BAGD 3. p. 679): 'spiritual force' [Lns, NIC, NTC, WBC, We; NASB, NIV, NRSV], 'spirit-force' [BAGD; TNT], 'spiritual host' [AB, El, Rob], 'superhuman force' [REB], 'spiritual, not physical, not material' [LN (79.3)]. The phrase τὰ πνευματικὰ τῆς πονηρίας 'the spiritual forces of wickedness' is translated: 'wicked spiritual forces' [LN (**12.44**); TEV], 'spiritual wickedness' [KJV], 'evil spirits' [NAB] 'spirits of evil' [NJB].

QUESTION—What is meant by τοὺς κοσμοκράτορας τοῦ σκότους τούτου 'the world rulers of this darkness'?

The genitive phrase τοῦ σκότους τούτου 'of this darkness', and the genitive phrase τῆς πονηρίας 'of wickedness' in the following phrase, may either be taken also with the first two designations, τὰς ἀρχάς 'the rulers' and τὰς ἐξουσίας 'the authorities' [AB; REB, TEV] as well as with the last two designations, τοὺς κοσμοκράτορας 'the world rulers' and τὰ πνευματικὰ 'the spiritual forces', or only with these last two designations [AB].

1. The phrase τοὺς κοσμοκράτορας τοῦ σκότους τούτου 'the world rulers of this darkness' presents these spirits as presiding over, if not directly causing, the darkness of the pagan world [AB, Alf, Ba, Cal, Ea, EBC (probably), EGT, Ho, ICC, ISBE2, LJ, LN (37.73), Lns, MNTC, My, NCBC, NIC, NTC, Rob, St, TD, TH, TNTC, WBC, We]. This refers to the malignant spirits who are responsible for the regions of ignorance and sin with which the earth abounds [Ba, Ea, LJ], σκότους 'darkness' being the symbol of ignorance [Ba, Cal, Ea, LJ, NTC], misery and sin [Ba, Cal, Ea, NTC]. The phrase τοῦ σκότους τούτου 'of this darkness' refers to 'this state of darkness' [Alf, WBC], or to the present condition of the world [NCBC, NIC, WBC], or 'this age of darkness' [My, We]; or it is a case of the abstract being used for the concrete, so that it refers to those in darkness, i.e., those who constitute the kingdom of darkness [Ho].

   1.1 This noun refers to worldwide rule [Ea, EBC, ICC, LN (37.73), My, NIC, TD, TH, We]. The devil's forces are called rulers of the world in order to bring out the terrifying power their influence has, and to show the comprehensiveness of their plans, so emphasizing the seriousness of the situation [TD].

1.2 This noun refers only to the world of darkness [Rob; and probably EGT, LJ]. It is not worldwide rule of which the apostle speaks here, but of the rule of this world, as is made clear by the addition of 'of this darkness' [Rob]. The phrase τοῦ σκότους τούτου 'of this darkness' limits the domain of these κοσμοκράτορας 'world rulers' to this world [EGT, Rob] as it now lies in the darkness of its ignorance [EGT]. The noun κόσμος 'world' which is a part of the compound noun κοσμοκράτωρ 'world ruler' refers to the world as that system which is organized and set in opposition to the laws and government of God. It does not mean just the material universe [LJ].

2. The phrase τοὺς κοσμοκράτορας τοῦ σκότους τούτου 'the world rulers of this darkness' presents these spirits as unable to dispel the moral and spiritual darkness in which the pagan world lies outside of Christ [IB]. The title κοσμοκράτωρ 'world ruler' was applied to a number of savior-gods in the Roman world, especially in the relationship each sustained to the sun-god Helios. The phrase τοὺς κοσμοκράτορας τοῦ σκότους τούτου 'the world rulers of this darkness' describes these savior-gods as malignant and unable to dispel the darkness which enshrouds human life apart from Christ [IB].

QUESTION—What is meant by τὰ πνευματικὰ τῆς πονηρίας 'the spiritual forces of wickedness'?

The genitive τῆς πονηρίας 'of wickedness' means those spirit-forces whose essential character is wickedness [EGT, El, My].

1. The adjective πνευματικά 'spiritual' denotes the abstract idea of elements or aspects of evil [EGT, HG, ICC, We; KJV]: against the elements of wickedness. The phrase τὰ πνευματικὰ τῆς πονηρίας 'the spiritual forces of wickedness' sums up in an abstract form all the powers of evil which are at work in the unseen world order [We].

2. The adjective πνευματικά 'spiritual' denotes evil spirits collectively [Alf, BAGD, Bu, Cal, DNTT, Ea, EBC, ECWB, El, Ho, IB, ISBE, ISBE2, LJ, Lns, MNTC, My, NCBC, NTC, Rob, St, TD, TH, TNTC, WBC; NAB, NJB, TNT]: against the spirits of evil. The phrase τὰ πνευματικὰ τῆς πονηρίας 'the spiritual forces of wickedness' does not designate a separate class of evil spirits so much as provide a general term for all such powers. It is equivalent to the term 'evil spirits' [WBC]. The adjective πνευματικά 'spiritual' has reference, not to their character or moral quality, but to their nature or essence [ISBE], as invisible [Cal]. Πονηρίας 'wickedness' denotes the malignity and cruelty of the devil, while the term πνευματικά 'spiritual' is used to point to the invisible [Cal, TD], and hence more dangerous, nature of the enemy [Cal].

3. The adjective πνευματικά 'spiritual' denotes both the evil spirits and the attitudes and movements they produce [AB, Can]: against the evil spirits

and all that they do. The reference is not merely to immaterial beings, but also to those movements, attitudes, or other impulses which tend to lead astray, and which point to a consistent system of evil to which, if we yield at any one point, we are in danger of becoming entirely enslaved [Can].

QUESTION—To what is ἐν τοῖς ἐπουρανίοις 'in the heavenly places' attached?

For the presentation of the meaning of this phrase, see 1:20.

1. This phrase is joined to the immediately preceding τὰ πνευματικὰ τῆς πονηρίας 'the spiritual forces of evil' [AB, Alf, Ba, CBC, Ea, EBC, ECWB, EGT, El, Ho, ICC, ISBE2, LJ, LN (1.12), Lns, MNTC, My, NCBC, NIC, NTC, Rob, TD, TH, WBC, WeBC; all versions]: (our wrestling is) against the spiritual forces of evil which are in the heavenly places.

   1.1 The reference is to heaven [CBC, Ea, Ho, LN (1.12), TD, WBC]. It refers to the world to which God and Christ also belong [TD]. It refers to the sphere of the evil powers, not to that in which the believers are fighting. The phrase is used to indicate the formidability of these evil forces [WBC]. The reference is to the celestial position of the church which these spirits have invaded in their attempt to pollute, divide, secularize, and overthrow it, and in which this combat is taking place [Ea]. All intelligent beings are either terrestrial or celestial, with good and bad in each class. These superhuman beings are not earthly magnates, but belong to the order of celestial intelligences and are therefore the more to be dreaded. This interpretation indicates the connection with the next verse [Ho].

   1.2 The reference is to the lower heavens [Alf (probably), Ba, EGT, El, ICC, My, NTC, TD; NJB (note), TNT (note)], or the sky and the air [Ba, DNTT, NTC, TD]. This is the space between the surface of the earth and the heaven where God lives [NJB (note)]. The phrase denotes the domain of these spirit-forces and means much the same as the ἀήρ 'air' in 2:2 [Alf, EGT, El, NTC, TD], but Paul uses ἐν τοῖς ἐπουρανίοις 'in the heavenly places' here to emphasize as strongly as possible the superhuman and superterrestrial nature of these forces [EGT, My].

   1.3 The reference is to the spiritual realm as opposed to the earthly realm [ECWB, ISBE, ISBE2, LJ, Lns, MNTC, NCBC, NIC, Rob, WeBC]. The term refers to the unseen spiritual world [ISBE], the non-physical [ISBE2]. It is meant to present a contrast with the earth. The believers' wrestling is essentially in the spiritual realm [LJ]. These spiritual hosts are described as fighting in the region above the earth (i.e., 1.2 above). But the meaning underlying this figure is that the power of evil is directly from spiritual sources [ECWB, NIC] and not acting through physical and human agency, attacking a believer's spirit in that higher aspect in which it contemplates heavenly things and ascends to communion with God [ECWB].

2. This phrase is joined to ἔστιν ἡμῖν ἡ πάλη 'our wrestling is' [Can; and probably TNTC, We] and refers to spiritual position [Cal, Can, TNTC, We]: our wrestling is for heavenly things. So far from being identified with the air, this phrase, in its other occurrences, seems to be distinguished from it [Can]. Man's conflict in his life is partly on earth and partly 'in the heavenly realm'. We are not to conceive of this heavenly realm as properly local, even though the requirements of language place some constraint upon us to represent it so. The phrase represents a mode of existence rather than a place. There is no force in the combination of ἐν τοῖς ἐπουρανίοις 'in the heavenly places' with τὰ πνευματικὰ τῆς πονηρίας 'the spiritual forces of wickedness' as if the heavenly realms were their dwelling place [We]. It seems, rather to denote spiritual position so that, while the Christian is seated with Christ in a higher spiritual position than these superhuman powers, they may attack us there [Can, TNTC] and seek to throw us down [Can]. The phrase points to the elevated position from which the attack is made [Cal].

DISCOURSE UNIT: 6:13–18 [ICC]. The topic is a detailed description of the spiritual armor.

DISCOURSE UNIT: 6:13–17 [We]. The topic is the Christian armor.

6:13 Therefore take-up[a] the full-armor of-God, in-order-that you-may-be-able to-withstand[b] in the evil/wicked day and having-done/having-conquered[c] all to-stand/stand-victorious.

LEXICON—a. aorist act. impera. of ἀναλαμβάνω (LN 15.203) (BAGD 2. p. 56): 'to take up' [AB, BAGD, El, Lns, NIC, NTC, WBC, We; NASB, NJB, NRSV, REB, TNT], 'to take unto oneself' [Rob; KJV], 'to lift up and carry' [LN], 'to put on' [NAB, NIV, TEV].
  b. aorist act. infin. of ἀνθίστημι (LN **39.18**) (BAGD 3. p. 67): 'to withstand' [BAGD, El, Lns, NIC, Rob, WBC, We; KJV, NRSV, REB], 'to resist' [BAGD, **LN**; NAB, NASB, TNT], 'to put up resistance' [AB; NJB], 'to resist the enemy's attacks' [TEV], 'to stand one's ground' [BAGD, NTC; NIV], 'to oppose, to set oneself against' [BAGD].
  c. aorist mid. (deponent = act.) participle of κατεργάζομαι (LN **42.17**, 77.6, 90.47) (BAGD 1. or 4. p. 421): 'to do' [LN (90.47), NIC, NTC, Rob; KJV, NASB, NIV, NRSV], 'to do fully' [El], 'to do what duty requires' [NAB], 'to perform' [LN (90.47)], 'to accomplish' [BAGD (1. p. 421), LN (**42.17**), Lns, WBC, We], 'to achieve' [BAGD (1. p. 421)], 'to perform successfully, to do thoroughly' [LN (42.17)], 'to carry out' [AB], 'to prove victorious, to conquer, to overpower, to subdue' [BAGD (4. p. 421)], 'to prepare, to make ready' [LN (77.6)]. The participial clause ἅπαντα κατεργασάμενοι 'having done all' is translated 'even though you exert yourselves to the full' [NJB], 'after doing your utmost' [REB], 'after fighting to the end' [TEV], 'when you can do no more' [TNT].

QUESTION—What is the referent of διὰ τοῦτο 'therefore'?

The τοῦτο 'this' part of the expression διὰ τοῦτο 'therefore' (literally, 'because of this') refers back to the contents of 6:12 [Lns]. The imperative command in 6:11 to put on God's full armor has been justified in 6:11b–12. Now that justification serves as the ground on which the earlier imperative is repeated in slightly different form [WBC]. This refers to the fact that the conflict is essentially spiritual [We]. It refers back to the fact that the Christian's spiritual foes, in dwelling around and above him, are too strong for him [Alf, EBC, NTC] and so the command to take up the full armor of God is reiterated from 6:11 [EBC, NTC]. The need for God's panoply is very pointedly deduced from the nature and power of the foes the Christian is called upon to meet [Can, Ea, El, NCBC]. The force of the expression is 'because your enemies are such as these' [EGT, Ho, My], 'because you must meet this terrific assault' [MNTC].

QUESTION—What is meant by ἀναλάβετε τὴν πανοπλίαν τοῦ θεοῦ 'take up the full armor of God'?

The verb ἀναλάβετε 'take up' is the regular word for equipping oneself with or putting on weapons [CBC, Ea, EGT, El, My, TD] and is taken from military language [TD]. It describes the final step taken for preparation before the actual battle [AB]. This clause takes up the exhortation in 6:11 again in almost the same words. The result is a bracketing of the last verse, with its description of the great power of the enemy host, with two exhortations to become armed with God's panoply [Lns]. Such repetition indicates great emphasis [LJ, Lns]. The metaphor of 6:11 is not only resumed, but further developed [NTC, Rob]. The aorist tense of this, and all the rest of the verbs in this verse, should be noted. They all convey an incisive urgency of command [NTC]. Another commentator thinks that they convey the ring of victory [Lns]. For the meaning of τὴν πανοπλίαν τοῦ θεοῦ 'the full armor of God', see 6:11.

QUESTION—What is meant by ἵνα δυνηθῆτε ἀντιστῆναι 'in order that you may be able to withstand'?

This purpose clause is the intermediate goal of taking up the full armor of God [Can, ECWB, Lns, NTC]. It implies an imminent conflict [We]. It conveys the idea of bravery and activity [ECWB] and implies the promise of victory [Cal]. The infinitive ἀντιστῆναι 'to withstand' implies a stand against great opposition [TNTC]. The implied object of the infinitive ἀντιστῆναι 'to withstand' is the powers of evil [EGT], the assaults of the demons [My]. The common idea of passively waiting for the attack is to be avoided; these soldiers are drawn up in battle array and are rushing into the fight [NTC]. They are both defending themselves and attacking [NTC, Si].

QUESTION—What is meant by τῇ ἡμέρᾳ τῇ πονηρᾷ 'the evil day'?

This is the time of the τὰς μεθοδείας τοῦ διαβόλου 'schemes of the devil' (6:11) [EBC, TD]. The repetition of the definite article with the adjective πονηρᾷ 'evil' is a means of emphasizing the adjective: 'in the day, the evil one' [Lns]. In this construction both the substantive and the adjective receive

emphasis, with the adjective being added as a sort of climax in apposition with a second article [HG].
1. The reference is to any time of particular trial or temptation in the life of the individual believer [Ba, Cal, Can, CBC, Ea, EBC, ECWB, EGT, El, Ho, ICC, Lns, MNTC, NCBC, NIC, NTC, St, TD, TH, We, WeBC; and probably BAGD (4.a. p. 347), DNTT, Si].
  1.1 The adjective πονηρᾷ has an ethical sense, 'wicked' [BAGD (1.b.β. p. 691), Lns].
  1.2 The adjective πονηρᾷ 'evil' describes difficult events which occur during this time [Ea, TD, TH, WeBC]. It describes not the character of the day as morally evil as such [TD, TH], but the events which take place in it, events which are destructive and bad [TH]. It is 'evil' because of the possibility of sad consequences from failure or being unprepared [Ea].
2. The reference is to the astrological horoscope [IB]. The author was battling the surrounding pagan influence of astrology here and the 'evil day' is the time when an individual's horoscope reveals that his 'unlucky star' is in the ascendancy. The point is not that the author believed in astrology, but that many of the Christians of that time had formerly believed in it and were not yet totally liberated from the influences of their pagan upbringing and influences [IB].
3. The reference is to the eschatological 'last days' [AB, My, My-ed, TNTC].
  3.1 The adjective πονηρᾷ 'evil' has an ethical or moral sense, 'wicked' [My]. The believers were to arm themselves for a single, *preeminently* morally evil day, well known to them, in which the satanic powers put forth their last and greatest efforts. Paul expected such a time shortly before Christ's Parousia [My].
  3.2 The adjective πονηρᾷ 'evil' describes harmful events which occur during these eschatological days [AB].
  3.3 The adjective πονηρᾷ 'evil' describes both the moral aspect of this time as well as the trials it contains [TNTC]. It indicates a time of severe conflict due to persecution from without and trials from within the Christian fellowship [TNTC].
4. The reference is both to the present age and to the particularly evil days which signal the end of history [WBC]. The present and future perspectives overlap. The readers are to realize that they already live in the evil days (5:16), but that these will culminate in an even greater evil day, when they must especially resist the devil's forces [WBC].

QUESTION—What is meant by ἅπαντα κατεργασάμενοι 'having done/conquered all'?
  1. The aorist participle means 'having done' [Ea, ECWB, El, MNTC, NCBC, NIC, NTC, Rob, TD, TH; KJV, NAB, NASB, NIV, NRSV, REB, TNT] or 'having accomplished' [AB, Alf, Can, EBC, EGT, El, ICC, LN (**42.17**), Lns, My, Rob, Si-ed, TH, TNTC, WBC, We], with the following

aorist infinitive στῆναι 'to stand', either retaining the same meaning it had in 6:11 [Ea, El, MNTC, NCBC, NIC, NTC, TD (probably), TNTC, WBC, We; NAB, NJB, REB, TNT], taking on the sense of 'to stand ready' for another assault from the enemy [TH], or being changed to the sense of 'to stand victoriously' at one's post [EGT, Lns, My] (cf. next QUESTION).

1.1 This aorist participle refers to the preparation for battle [AB, TD (probably), WBC]. Having accomplished all that is necessary to prepare for the battle and in being fully armed for it, believers are to stand firm [WBC]. It has specific reference to having put on the spiritual armor described in 6:14ff. [TD].

1.2 This aorist participle refers to doing all that is requisite to the struggle [Alf, Can, Ea, EBC, ECWB, EGT, El, ICC, MNTC, My, NIC, NTC, TH, We; NAB, NJB, REB, TNT]. The participle refers to the Christian soldier having accomplished everything requisite to the combat [Alf, Ea, EGT, El, MNTC, My], or that duty requires [ICC, NIC, Rob, We; NAB], and having 'withstood' the foes [Can, ECWB], i.e. to being fully equipped and having bravely fought [Alf]. The context seems to be talking about a series of constant battles with the enemy, not the final eschatological battle. With this interpretation, the participial clause would mean that after fighting each battle to the finish, the Christian warrior will still be on his feet, ready for the next skirmish [TH].

2. The aorist participle means 'having conquered' and refers to the result of the battle [Ba, CBC, Ho; TEV] with the meaning of the following aorist infinitive στῆναι 'to stand' being changed from the meaning it had in 6:11 to 'to stand victorious' [TEV]. It means to have met every challenge [CBC]. After the conflict is over the believers will maintain their ground as victors [Ho].

QUESTION—What is meant by the infinitive στῆναι 'to stand'?

This is the final goal of taking up the full armor of God [Can, ECWB]. The implication is that when the Christian has done all that is humanly possible (ἅπαντα κατεργασάμενοι 'having done all') God will enable him to hold on in the fight against evil [TNT (note)]. Others state it is the final result [EGT, My, NTC] and give it the connotation of a victorious stance [EGT, My]. It corresponds to the preceding ἀντιστῆναι 'to withstand' of which it is the result [My]. The ability of ἀντιστῆναι 'to withstand' is to be sought with a view to being found holding one's position when the conflict is finished [EGT], not dislodged, or fallen, but *standing* victorious at one's post [EGT, My]. The infinitive here conveys the idea of calm, well-balanced, steadfastness [ECWB].

DISCOURSE UNIT: 6:14–20 [Alf]. The topic is the particulars of the armor and the attitude of the soldier.

DISCOURSE UNIT: 6:14–17 [AB]. The topic is the six pieces that form the Christian soldier's armor.

6:14 **Stand therefore having-girded[a] your waist[b] with truth**
LEXICON—a. aorist mid. participle of περιζώννυμαι, περιζώννυμι (LN 49.15, **77.5**) (BAGD 2.c. p. 647): 'to gird oneself' [BAGD, LN (49.15), Lns, We; NASB], 'to gird oneself about' [El, Rob; KJV], 'to fasten a belt around oneself' [NTC, WBC], 'to be girded' [AB, LN (49.15)], 'to be tied around' [LN (49.15)]. The participial clause περιζωσάμενοι τὴν ὀσφὺν ὑμῶν 'having your waist girded about' is translated as an idiom for causing oneself to be in a state of readiness: 'ready' [LN (**77.5**)], 'to get ready, to prepare oneself' [LN (77.5)]. The clause περιζωσάμενοι τὴν ὀσφὺν ὑμῶν ἐν ἀληθείᾳ 'having girded your waist with truth' is translated as a prepositional phrase: 'with the girdle of truth round your waist' [NIC], 'with the belt of truth buckled around your waist' [NIV], 'with the truth as the belt around your waist' [NAB], 'with truth a belt around your waist' [NJB], 'with truth as a belt tight around your waist' [TEV]. This participial clause is also translated as an imperative clause: 'fasten the belt of truth around your waist' [NRSV], 'fasten on the belt of truth' [REB], 'make truth the belt round your waist' [TNT]. The verb denotes that the action of girding was the soldier's own act [EGT, LJ, Lns]. This verb denotes having a belt or sash around oneself. It appears to differ from its synonym ζώννυμι 'to gird, fasten one's belt' in that it emphasizes that a strip of cloth is placed around the middle part of the body [LN (49.15, note 8)].
   b. ὀσφῦς (LN 8.42) (BAGD 1. p. 587): 'waist' [AB, BAGD, LN, NIC, NTC, WBC; all versions except KJV, NASB, REB], 'loins' [BAGD, El, Lns, Rob, We; KJV, NASB], not explicit [REB]. This noun denotes the part of the human body between the chest and the hips [LN]. It denotes the place on the human body where a belt or girdle was worn [BAGD]. The singular noun with ὑμῶν 'your (pl)' is used distributively here according to Semitic idiom [BD, HG, Tu] where one would expect the plural [HG].
QUESTION—What relationship is indicated by οὖν 'therefore'?
   This particle indicates a moving on in the discourse to describe the various pieces of armor after the repeated call to put on this armor [WBC].
QUESTION—What is meant by the aorist imperative στῆτε 'stand'?
   This imperative, as considered with the remainder of this section, indicates the *manner* in which the Christian soldier is *to stand forth* [My]. Whether this is interpreted as 'stand ready for the fight' or 'stand in the fight' matters little [Alf]. The imperative repeats the emphasis in 6:11 and 13 for immovable steadfastness [EBC] but, whereas 6:13 talked about standing firm in the midst of battle, here it refers to standing firm in anticipation of it [EBC, El, ICC, My]. Another commentator states that the verb has the same meaning throughout its occurrences in this context [WBC]. The imperative is best rendered 'take your stand', the definite act being in view [EGT]. The aorist is constative: 'stand once for all' [Lns]. In 6:13 the soldier has already stood

and won, here he stands ready for a further assault, with the following sentences explaining what must be done if he is so to stand [EGT].

QUESTION—How are the aorist participles in 6:14–16 related to the aorist imperative στῆτε 'stand'?

The aorist participles in this sentence are all antecedent in time to the command στῆτε 'stand' [Alf, Ea, Lns]. They explain what has to be done *before* the soldier takes up his stand [EBC, EGT, El, ICC]. Further, they are all indirect middles, calling attention to definite acts the Christian is to perform himself [EBC, Lns, TNTC].

QUESTION—What was the girdle that is implied in the verb περιζωσάμενοι 'having girded (yourself)'?

1. This girdle was a functional component of the soldier's armor [Alf, Ba, Cal, Can, DNTT, Ea, EBC, ECWB, EGT, El, ICC, LJ, Lns, MNTC, My, NCBC, NIC, NTC, Si, St, TD, TH, TNTC, WBC, We]. The allusion is to Isa. 11:5 [Can, DNTT, Ea, EBC, EGT, El, Ho, IB, ICC, ISBE2, MNTC, My, NCBC, NIC, NTC, Rob, TD, WBC, We, WeBC]. The girdle was the first item put on [EBC, ECWB, El, LJ, Lns, My, NTC, TNTC, WBC], as all the items of armor listed in 6:14–17 are listed in the order in which they were put on [EBC, ECWB, TNTC] (*contra* NTC who states the order is defensive armament first, then the sword as offensive). In the case of the Roman soldier, the girdle was a leather belt [ISBE, St] that gathered in his short tunic [EBC, Lns, NTC, St, WeBC] and helped keep the breastplate in place when it was put on [EBC, Lns, NTC], as well as holding the scabbard for his sword [EBC, El, ICC, ISBE, Lns, NTC, St, WeBC]. With some soldiers the girdle seems to have been a cincture of iron or steel [Ba, Ea], and was designed to keep every part of his armor in place [Ba, Ea, EGT, El, LJ]. Others, however, think that, since the metal studded belt worn over the armor cannot be the girdle because it obviously could not be put on first, the girdle must refer to a leather apron that the Roman soldier wore under his armor like breeches [TD, WBC].

2. The girdle was a symbol of the wearer's rank [AB]. This was a special sash or belt that designated an officer or high official. The allusion is to Isa. 11:5 where the girdle of righteousness is the distinctive sign of the high office of the Messiah. The saints form an army in which each one bears the insignia of supreme dignity [AB].

QUESTION—What is meant by ἐν ἀληθείᾳ 'with truth'?

The meaning of the preposition ἐν here is 'with' [Alf] (*contra* Lns, who prefers 'in'), even though the sense is local, not instrumental [Alf, Lns]. The girded soldier is pictured as surrounded by the girdle [Alf, Lns], even though English still requires this to be expressed by 'with' [Alf]. Others state ἐν here is instrumental, 'with' [DNTT, Ea, EGT, El, ICC, My, TD] and may imply, as well, that other parts of the equipment were *within* the girdle also [EGT].

1. The ἀληθείᾳ 'truth' here is subjective truth [Alf, Cal, Can, DNTT, ECWB (probably), EGT, IB, ICC, MNTC, NCBC, NIC, NTC, TD, TH, TNTC,

WBC, We]. Truth as an ethical quality is meant, though the truth of doctrine is not unrelated to ethical quality [NIC]. This is truth in its widest sense [ICC] as making up an element of the Christian's character [ICC, NCBC, WBC]. The comparison in this metaphor is between the soldier's girdle and the Christian believer's truthfulness, faithfulness, and/or sincerity. The point of comparison is that as the girdle keeps all the other armor in place so the Christian believer's truthfulness is essential to the operation of the other qualities listed [Alf, EGT, MNTC], without which they would all simply be a hindrance [Alf, TNTC]. A nonfigurative statement could be: be truthful, sincere, or faithful, for this is essential to the operation of the other graces.

1.1 This is truth shown as sincerity or integrity [Alf, Cal, Can, DNTT, ECWB (probably), EGT, ICC, MNTC, NCBC, NTC, TNTC, We]. Sincerity or truthfulness has been mentioned before in this epistle (4:15–25) as a means of Christian growth and perfection [Can, NTC], in contrast to the *deceitfulness* of the unregenerate man [NTC]. Here, making truth a habit is given to us as a means of defense [Can].

1.2 This is truth shown as faithfulness [IB, TH, WBC]. In Isa. 11:5 the Hebrew word refers to faithfulness [IB, WBC; (also AB, EBC, TNTC, which support interpretations above and below)], and loyalty [WBC].

2. The ἀληθείᾳ 'truth' here is objective truth [AB, Ba, CBC, EBC, Lns, TD]. This is knowledge of God's nature and his plan for human life, which was revealed in Jesus [CBC], and the knowledge of the gospel [EBC, Lns]. The absence of an article with the noun stresses the quality of the term [Lns]. Another view is that divine reality is meant since an article would be expected if the reference was to the gospel [TD]. The comparison in this metaphor is between the soldier's girdle and the Christian believer's sense of truth. The comparison is that as the girdle's function was to keep all the soldier's other armor in place, with the result that he could consistently and firmly oppose the enemy, so the Christian's grasp of God's truth is essential to the operation of the spiritual qualities that are portrayed in the metaphor. A nonfigurative statement could be: know the truth of God's Word for it will show you how to use the spiritual qualities God gives you, and so you will be consistent and firm in your conduct.

3. This is the subjective realization of objective truth, the awareness that one knows God's truth [Ea, El, Ho, LJ, My, Si, St, WeBC]. It probably indicates both the truth of doctrine and the sincerity of character, or faithfulness, that doctrinal truth produces [Si, St]. The comparison is the same as in 2. above. A nonfigurative statement could be: be certain you conform to the truth as revealed in God's Word for it will give you assurance, consistency, and firmness in your conduct.

and having-put-on the breastplate[a] of-righteousness

LEXICON—a. θώραξ (LN 6.39) (BAGD 1. p. 367): 'breastplate' [BAGD, El, LN, Lns, NIC, NTC, Rob, WBC, We; all versions], 'cuirass' [AB]. This noun denotes a piece of a soldier's armor that covered his chest to protect it from blows and arrows [LN].

QUESTION—What is meant by τὸν θώρακα τῆς δικαιοσύνης 'the breastplate of righteousness'?

The allusion is to Isa. 59:17 [AB, Can, Ea, EBC, EGT, El, Ho, IB, ICC, ISBE, ISBE2, MNTC, My, NCBC, NIC, NTC, Rob, TD, TH, TNTC, WBC, We, WeBC], which figure is more fully worked out in the OT apocryphal book *The Wisdom of Solomon* 5:17 ff. [AB, Alf, EBC, ICC, MNTC, My, NCBC, NIC, Rob, TD, WBC, We]. The genitive construction τὸν θώρακα τῆς δικαιοσύνης 'the breastplate of righteousness' is that of apposition, i.e., righteousness is the breastplate [Alf, Bu, Ea, EGT, El, ICC, Lns, My, We]. The breastplate was the ancient cuirass or coat of mail (1 Sam. 17:5) [Ba, Si]. It covered the body from the neck to the thighs [AB, Ba, EBC, Ho, LJ, NTC] or the chest area [Ea, EGT]. It consisted of two parts, one covering the body from the front, the other from the back [AB, Ba, Ea, Ho, ISBE2, NTC, St, TH] though, properly speaking, the θώραξ 'breastplate' refers to just the front piece [DNTT, EBC, ISBE2, WBC]. Since Paul has a Roman soldier in mind as his metaphorical model, the θώραξ 'breastplate' he has in mind is probably the coat of chain mail [AB, DNTT, Ea, EBC] or the leather or bronze two-piece model [Ea, EBC]. However, only the richest officers could afford the coat of chain mail [AB, EBC, IB]. It was made of metal rings or overlapping plates or scales [AB, Ba], fastened together to be flexible [Ba], yet protecting the body from sword, spear, or arrow [Ba, Can].

1. The focus of δικαιοσύνη 'righteousness' here is imparted righteousness, the believer's experiential righteousness, the purity and uprightness which is produced in his life by the Spirit of Christ [Alf, Ba, Cal, Can, EBC, EGT, El, ICC, My, NCBC, NIC, NTC, TD, TH, TNTC, WBC, We, WeBC; NJB, REB]. This is truth applied to our relationships with others, illuminated, purified, and strengthened by Christ's grace [We]. This is a blameless life or holy life [Cal, NTC], uprightness and integrity of character [EBC, TNTC; NJB, REB] resulting directly from the appropriation of Christ's righteousness [EBC], loyalty both in principle and action to God's holy law [TNTC]. It is total obedience to the known will of God [NCBC]. The point of comparison is the protection which the breastplate afforded the soldier's vital organs. A nonfigurative statement could be: protect the integrity of your spiritual life with the righteousness which the Spirit of Christ produces within you.

2. The focus of δικαιοσύνη 'righteousness' here is that which is imputed to the believer [AB, Bu (probably), CBC, DNTT, Ea, ECWB, Ho, LJ, Lns, My-ed, Si, TD], but implies as well the experiential righteousness which is its result [AB, ECWB, LJ, Si, TD]. It is the 'righteousness of God' through which man is justified by grace alone (Rom. 3:21–31) [AB, Ea,

Ho, LJ, TD], as indicated by the definite article accompanying it [Ea]. Subjective righteousness is not very well adapted to be called an item in the τὴν πανοπλίαν τοῦ θεοῦ 'full armor of God' and the aorist participle does not fit this interpretation either, but it is something which rightly used is adapted to Christians as an adequate protection against temptation, and therefore must refer to righteousness by faith in Christ (Rom. 3:22) [TD]. The comparison and point of comparison with this interpretation is the same as in 1. above. A nonfigurative statement could be: protect the integrity of your spiritual life with Christ's own righteousness which God has provided for you.

3. Both aspects of righteousness seems to be equally stressed [St]. The completeness of God's pardon for past offenses and the integrity of character that goes with such a justified life, together form a coat of mail that cannot be penetrated [St].

6:15 **and having-fitted-(shoes)-on[a] the feet with (the) preparation/ steadfastness/ equipment[b] of-the gospel of-the peace,**

LEXICON—a. aorist mid. participle of ὑποδέομαι, ὑποδέω (LN 49.17) (BAGD p. 844): 'to be fitted' [WBC; NIV], 'to be shod' [El, Lns, NIC, NTC, Rob, We; KJV, NASB], 'to put shoes on' [BAGD], 'to put on' [BAGD, LN, MM], 'to wear' [LN], 'to wear for shoes' [NJB], 'to tie beneath, to bind beneath' [BAGD], 'to bind under' [MM], 'to be strapped under' [AB], 'to tie on' [LN]. The participial clause ὑποδησάμενοι τοὺς πόδας 'having put shoes on the feet' is translated: 'as your footgear' [NAB], 'as your shoes' [TEV], 'as shoes for your feet' [TNT], 'as shoes for your feet put on' [NRSV], 'let the shoes on your feet be (the Gospel)' [REB].

b. ἑτοιμασία (LN **77.1**) (BAGD 316): 'preparation' [BAGD, Lns, NIC, Rob; KJV, NASB], 'preparedness' [El, We], 'readiness' [BAGD, **LN**, NTC, WBC; NIV], 'zeal to propagate' [NAB], 'eagerness to spread' [NJB], 'readiness to announce' [TEV], 'readiness to preach' [TNT]. This noun is also translated 'being ready to' [LN], 'steadfast' [AB], 'to give you firm footing' [REB], 'whatever will make you ready to proclaim' [NRSV].

QUESTION—What is meant by this metaphor?

The OT reference the writer has in mind here is Isa. 52:7 [DNTT, EBC, EGT, IB, MNTC, NIC, Rob, St, TD, WBC, WeBC] (*contra* AB, ISBE2, LJ, who argue that the messenger of Isaiah would have been running barefoot with a victory-message, not wearing military footwear [AB, ISBE2]). The writer probably has the Roman *caliga* in mind [AB, Alf, EBC, EGT, ICC, ISBE2, MNTC, NIC, Si, St, TD, TNTC] (*contra* El, who thinks it may be any strong military sandal). It was a half-boot [AB, ISBE2] or leather sandal tied to the ankles and shins with straps [AB, LJ, St]. It had soles heavily studded with nails [AB, Ea, EBC, ECWB, ISBE2, LJ, NTC, St, WBC]. These boots equipped the soldier for long, quick marches [AB, MNTC,

NTC, Si, St, WBC] and gave him a solid stance [AB, ISBE2, St] as he hurled his spears, used his sword, or shielded himself against stones, lances, and arrows [AB, St].

1. Ἐτοιμασία means 'readiness' or 'preparedness' [Alf, Ba, BAGD, Cal, Can, Ea, EGT, El, Ho, ICC, ISBE, **LN**, Lns, MNTC, My, NTC, Rob, Si, St, TD, TH, WBC, WeBC; KJV, NAB, NASB, NIV, NJB, NRSV, TEV, TNT]. The preposition ἐν 'in' is local, meaning 'with' [Alf], or instrumental [Ea, EGT, El, My, TD]. The definite article may be omitted when it would follow the preposition ἐν 'with' [Alf].

1.1 The genitive construction ἑτοιμασίᾳ τοῦ εὐαγγελίου 'preparation of the gospel' indicates the preparation or preparedness produced by the gospel [Alf, Ba, Cal, Can, Ea, EBC, ECWB, EGT, El, Ho, ICC, ISBE, Lns, My, NTC, Si, WBC; NIV]: with the readiness that comes from the gospel, whose message and spirit is peace. It is the readiness and zeal to plunge into the fight which the gospel of peace gives us [ICC, Lns, My, NTC, Si]. The principles provided by the peaceful and pure Gospel were to do for the Christian what the greaves and iron-spiked sandals did for the soldier, namely to aid him in his marches and to cause him to be firm in his foot-tread, and to protect him in the conflict with his foes [Ba]. As soldiers covered their feet and legs with greaves to protect them against injuries, so the Christian must be shod with the gospel if he is to pass unhurt through the world [Cal]. The noun ἑτοιμασία 'preparation' refers to the effect of the gospel, for it enjoins us to lay aside every hindrance and to be prepared both for journey and for war [Cal, Si]. The point of comparison in this metaphor is the readiness for marching or combat which the footwear provided the soldier with the readiness of mind for participating in God's service which the gospel provides the Christian. A nonfigurative statement would be: let the good news about peace with God prepare your minds to serve him in opposing the evil spiritual forces.

1.2 The genitive construction indicates something which is done to the gospel [**LN**, MNTC, St, TD, TH; NAB, NJB, NRSV, TEV, TNT; and probably BAGD, Rob]: readiness to announce the gospel of peace. Readiness for the propagation of the gospel is the most effective means of combating satanic powers. Paul is evidently thinking of the joyful proclamation of the gospel in the messianic NT period [TD], the missionary spirit, the readiness to carry the gospel everywhere [MNTC, St]. The point of comparison in this metaphor is the readiness for marching or combat which the footwear provided the soldier with the believer's readiness to participate in the proclamation of the gospel of peace. A nonfigurative statement would be: get yourselves ready to proclaim the good news about peace with God as you oppose the evil spiritual forces.

2. Ἐτοιμασία means 'steadfastness' and indicates a firmness of foundation. The genitive construction ἑτοιμασίᾳ τοῦ εὐαγγελίου 'steadfastness of

the gospel' indicates that steadfastness is produced by the gospel [AB, EBC, ECWB, NIC, TNTC, We; REB]. The gospel of peace with God gives the believer a firm foothold [EBC, We] and alacrity [We] in his campaign against the forces of evil because it gives him firm assurance of God's love. The preposition ἐν 'in' is not instrumental, but probably indicates the ground upon which the saints stand or the well-established realm in which they live [AB]. The point of comparison is the firm footing which the footwear provided the soldier in combat with the firm assurance of God's love which the good news of peace with God provides the believer in his battle with evil. A nonfigurative statement would be: be firmly assured of God's love for you which the good news about peace with God provides as you strive against evil spiritual forces.

3. Ἑτοιμασία means 'equipment' and indicates that the gospel is the equipment which the Christian believer wears [DNTT, IB, ISBE2, LJ, NCBC, Si-ed]. This verse has reference to the believer's readying himself by 'being shod with the equipment of the gospel of peace' [DNTT]. 'Equipment' includes both the ideas of readiness and stability or steadfastness. The gospel provides the Christian with the teachings and doctrines which, in turn, give him the assurance and stability he needs in his battle with the hosts of evil [LJ]. The genitive construction ἑτοιμασίᾳ τοῦ εὐαγγελίου 'equipment of the gospel' is that of apposition [IB]: with the equipment which is the gospel of peace. The point of comparison in this metaphor is the footwear with which the soldier is equipped, which prepares him for physical stability and mobility in combat, with the gospel of peace with which the Christian is equipped which, with its doctrinal teaching, prepares him with mental stability and mobility in his spiritual battle with evil. A nonfigurative statement would be: furnish yourself with the gospel of peace which will give you mental and spiritual stability and mobility as you strive against evil spiritual forces.

QUESTION—What is meant by the genitive construction τοῦ εὐαγγελίου τῆς εἰρήνης 'the gospel of peace'?

This genitive 'of peace' is that of content or substance [Ea, EGT, El]. This is the gospel which has peace as its message [DNTT, TD] and brings peace [TD]. Εἰρήνης 'peace' is clearly emphatic here [ECWB]. There is a paradox in the picture of the warrior in the midst of battle being equipped with the gospel of peace [IB, ICC, Lns, TD, WBC]; but to establish the peace of God in the universe, the believer must do battle against the spiritual evil which disturbs that peace [IB, Si, WBC].

1. Εἰρήνης 'peace' means peace with God [Cal, Can, CBC, Ea, EBC, ECWB, EGT, El, Ho, IB, ICC, My, NTC, TH, TNTC; and probably DNTT, St]. This is not merely peace with one another, but with God [El, ICC]. It is a peace that can only be secured and enjoyed if we war against his enemies [El]. It is called the gospel of peace from its effects because it is the message of our reconciliation with God which gives peace to our conscience [Cal, NTC] and gives to our mind a peculiar and continuous

preparedness for action and movement [Ea, Ho]. It is God's peace-making activity in reconciling us to himself that enables us to stand firmly in our warfare with evil [CBC].

2. Εἰρήνης 'peace' means both peace among men and between man and God [ISBE2, NCBC].

3. Εἰρήνης 'peace' means the messianic salvation [AB, BAGD (3. p. 227), TD]. This is the messianic peace described in 2:13–18 that unites and draws ever closer together 'those far' and 'those near', and in so doing gives the strength to resist nonhuman, demonic attacks [AB]. Christian thought in the NT frequently regards the proclamation of εἰρήνη 'peace' as nearly synonymous with messianic salvation [BAGD].

6:16 in all-things having-taken-up the shield[a] of-the faith, with which you-will-be-able-to-extinguish[b] all the arrows[c] of-the wicked-one which have-been-set-on-fire;[d]

TEXT—Instead of ἐν πᾶσιν 'in all-things', some manuscripts have ἐπὶ πᾶσιν 'besides all things'. GNT does not note this variant reading. Those who support the alternate reading are Ba, BD, Ea, EBC, El, Ho, Lns, My (and hesitantly Alf, EGT).

LEXICON—a. θυρεός (LN **6.40**) (BAGD p. 366): 'shield' [AB, BAGD, El, **LN**, MM, NIC, NTC, Rob, WBC, We; all versions except REB], 'great shield' [REB], 'long-shield' [Lns]. This is the large, heavy, oblong [Alf, Ba, Can, EGT, El, Ho, ICC, ISBE, LJ, MNTC, My, NCBC, NTC, St, TH, WBC, We, WeBC] or rectangular [AB, CBC, DNTT, ISBE, ISBE2, TD] shield that could protect most of the body [Can, DNTT, ECWB, Ho, ISBE, ISBE2, LJ, MNTC, NCBC, St, TD, TH, TNTC, WBC, We, WeBC], as opposed to the smaller, lighter, circular ἀσπίς 'buckler or target shield' [AB, Alf, DNTT, EGT, El, ICC, My, NCBC, WBC]. It measured about 4 by 2_ feet [Ea, Ho, ICC, LJ, Lns, My, NCBC, St, TD, WBC, WeBC] and protected the body from the level of the eyes to the top of the greaves at the knees [Lns]. It was usually made of light wood, or formed on a rim of metal, and covered with several layers of stout hide [AB, Ba, DNTT, El, MNTC, My, TNTC, WBC]. Sometimes it had a metal boss on the front at the center [AB, DNTT]. The shield was normally carried on the left arm [Ba, TH] and on the inside surface had straps through which the arm was passed [Ba]. Others state it was made of two layers of wood, glued together, covered with linen, or canvas, then with hide [EBC, IB, NIC, Rob, St, TD, TH, WeBC], and bound with iron [EBC, Rob, St] at the top and bottom [Rob, St], and in addition had an iron boss attached [Rob, TD].

b. aorist act. infin. of σβέννυμι (LN 14.70) (BAGD 1. p. 745): 'to extinguish' [BAGD, LN, Lns, NTC, WBC; NAB, NASB, NIV], 'to put out' [BAGD, LN; TEV, TNT], 'to quench' [AB, El, NIC, Rob, We; KJV, NJB, NRSV, REB].

c. βέλος (LN **6.36**) (BAGD p. 139): 'arrow' [BAGD, **LN**, Lns, WBC; NIV, NJB, NRSV, REB, TEV], 'dart' [El, **LN**, NIC, Rob, We; KJV, NAB, TNT], 'missile' [AB, MM (probably), NTC; NASB]. This noun denotes a missile, and includes arrows that are launched by a bow and darts that are hurled by hand [LN]. The arrows were made of cane [Alf, Ba, TD], or metal [TD] with a head in the form of a distaff filled with an inflammable material which is ignited before launch [Alf, TD]. They were arrows that had been wrapped with coarse fiber, then soaked with pitch, and set afire before launching them [AB, DNTT, EBC, EGT, IB, ICC, LJ, MNTC, My, NTC, St, TD, TH, TNTC, WBC, WeBC].

d. perf. pass. participle of πυρόομαι, πυρόω (LN 14.63) (BAGD 1.a. p. 731): 'to be set on fire' [BAGD, LN, Lns, We], 'to burn' [LN]. This passive participle is usually translated as an adjective modifying βέλη 'arrows, darts, missiles': 'flaming' [BAGD (p. 139), NTC; NASB, NIV, NRSV], 'burning' [WBC; NJB, REB, TEV], 'fiery' [El, Rob; KJV, NAB], 'fire-tipped' [NIC; TNT]. It is also translated as the first element of a compound noun: 'fire-missiles' [AB].

QUESTION—What is meant by ἐν πᾶσιν 'in all things'?

1. It means 'in addition to' [AB, Alf, BD, Can, CBC, Ea, EBC, ECWB, EGT, El, HG, Ho, IB, ICC, LJ, Lns, My, NIC, NTC, Rob, St, TD, WBC; NASB, NIV, NRSV, REB] or 'among' [EGT]: in addition to all else (or amongst this other equipment), having taken up the shield of faith, etc. It refers to the other equipment listed [AB, El, St]. Even more armor is necessary [WBC]. It indicates an accompanying circumstance [HG]. The action of taking up the shield is to be taken in addition to putting on the other items of equipment [Can, LJ, NIC]. Whereas the previous three items have been fastened to the body, this refers to the three items of armor yet to be taken up: the shield, the helmet, and the sword [LJ, My].

2. It means 'on all occasions' [Mo, TH; NAB, NJB, TEV, TNT]: on all occasions having taken up the shield of faith, etc. This means 'always, at all times' [TH], 'in all circumstances' [Mo, TH]. It means 'let faith be the constant shield' [TNT]. The meaning 'in addition to all' would be appropriate only if this was the final item of the soldier's equipment that the writer was about to describe [TH].

3. It means 'above all' in the sense of importance [NCBC; KJV]: more important than all, having taken up the shield of faith, etc. Faith is more important than integrity, uprightness, and the knowledge that we bear great good news [NCBC].

4. It means 'furthermore' [Si-ed]: furthermore, having taken up the shield of faith, etc. Alternatively, it may be understood figuratively as covering the rest of the armor [Si-ed].

5. It means 'above all' and refers to the position of the shield as covering the rest of the equipment [Ba, MNTC, TNTC]: having taken up the shield of faith (and hold it up) above all your equipment. It means 'to cover all the rest' or perhaps, 'along with all these' [MNTC].

QUESTION—What is meant by the participle ἀναλαβόντες 'having taken up'?
The participle ἀναλαβόντες 'having taken up', as in 6:13, is a military term [AB, TD]. The previous participles in this sentence have been specific to the way each item of armor is fastened upon the body. But the shield, helmet, and sword have no special fastening; they are simply taken up or assumed, and so they are covered by this general participle and the imperative verb in 6:17, δέξασθε 'take' [Ea, LJ].

QUESTION—How are the nouns related in the genitive construction τὸν θυρεὸν τῆς πίστεως 'the shield of the faith'?
The genitive is appositional, the shield being the symbol of faith [Alf, Ea, EGT, El, IB, ICC, Lns, MNTC, My, NCBC, TH, TNTC]: take up the shield, that is, faith. One commentator translates it 'faith's shield', the shield which faith possesses and uses [Bu].

QUESTION—What is meant by πίστεως 'the faith'?
1. Πίστεως 'faith' focuses on the subjective aspect, the act of believing [AB, Alf, Ba, Cal, Can, CBC, DNTT, Ea, EBC, ECWB, EGT, Ho, ICC, LJ, My, NCBC, NTC, Si, St, TD, TH, WBC, WeBC]. It is belief and confidence in God or Christ [AB, Can, Ea, Ho, LJ, NCBC, NTC, Si, St, TH, WBC], or in the promises contained in his Word [Cal, LJ, Si, St], by which we lay hold of him. Faith is confidence in the rightness and final victory of God's cause [CBC]. In this metaphor, the shield is compared with faith. The point of comparison is the fact that the shield formed the primary armor of the soldier, the previous mentioned items being supplemental. The shield had the capability, in contrast to the other body armor, of being large enough for the body to hide behind, and maneuverable enough to give coverage for the body from the specific direction of immediate threat. The act of trusting in God is presented as being similar in function on the spiritual level. A nonfigurative statement would be: use your capability for trust in God to allow him to protect you from particularly dangerous temptations from the devil.
2. Πίστεως 'faith' focuses on the objective aspect, what is believed [IDB, Lns]. The presence of the definite article here points to the objective use of πίστις 'faith', i.e., that which is believed. But belief in that which is believed also implies the subjective element of faith. When Jesus faced these fierce temptations in the wilderness, he did not quench them with 'I believe' but 'it is written'. Everything depends upon *what* you believe. The participle δυνήσεσθε 'you will be able' contains the subjective factor of faith [Lns]. The comparison and point of comparison is much the same as in 1. above, except that the body of faith is substituted. A nonfigurative statement would be: use the teaching and doctrines in which you believe to protect yourself from particularly dangerous temptations from the devil.
3. Πίστεως 'faith' focuses on 'faithfulness', being loyal to God [NIC]. The comparison and point of comparison is much the same as in 1. above, except that the faithfulness to God is substituted. A nonfigurative

statement would be: use your faithfulness to God to protect yourself from particularly dangerous temptations from the devil.

QUESTION—What relationship is indicated by ἐν 'with'?

The construction ἐν ᾧ 'with which' gives a definite instrumental force to this clause, specifying the defensive implement by which the fire-tipped arrows will be extinguished [El]. The ἐν ᾧ 'with which' implies the shield is being held in the proper position, i.e., in front of the body [My].

QUESTION—How were the fiery arrows extinguished?

1. The infinitive σβέσαι 'to extinguish' refers to the direct effect the shield itself had upon the fiery arrows [AB, Ba, DNTT, EGT, IB, MNTC, My, NCBC, NTC, TH, WBC]. It refers to the flaming arrow being extinguished by impact with the shield, as a candle is extinguished when it is struck against something [Ba, NTC] or, as it fastened itself to a leather-covered shield, it burnt itself out harmlessly [EGT, IB, MNTC, My, NCBC]. Some state that the shield, being made of leather, was soaked in water before battle and so in that way was effective in extinguishing the flames of arrows that were embedded in the shield [AB, DNTT, NCBC, TH, WBC].

2. The infinitive σβέσαι 'to extinguish' refers to the indirect effect the shield had upon the fiery arrows [Ea, Lns, NIC, TD]. As the arrows glanced off the shield, they were quickly extinguished on the ground [Ea] or ineffectively burned themselves out there. In this way the infinitive is said to describe the final result of glancing off the shield, rather than any direct effect of the shield itself [TD]. A few commentators believe the writer deliberately uses σβέσαι 'to extinguish' here to show an incongruity with actual physical warfare [Cal, Lns; and probably NIC, TD] in order to demonstrate the superiority of the spiritual shield of faith.

QUESTION—What is meant by the metaphor of the τὰ βέλη...[τὰ] πεπυρωμένα 'arrows which have been set on fire'?

The metaphor refers to setting the mind on fire with lies [LJ, Lns, Si]. As the burning arrow or dart was a special danger to the soldier of old, so particular temptations such as fear, complaining against God, anger, evil desire, doubt, despair, etc., [Ba, Can, Ea, ECWB, Ho, LJ, NTC, Si, St, TNTC] are capable of kindling a flame of passion which may rage throughout a believer's whole nature [Can, Ho] even to the point of destroying him [Ho]. Qumran parallels indicate that here the flaming arrows are external temptations imposed from without by persecutions and pressures from religious, cultural, and political forces [AB]. These arrows represent every type of assault from the evil one, from temptation, to unloving conduct, to heretical teachings [WBC]. Others think that it is not necessary [ICC] or appropriate [My] to go beyond fierce temptations as symbolized by these fiery arrows [ICC, My] by trying to identify them as burning desires, despair, or the like [My], or to restrict them to any particular form of temptation, other than especially dangerous ones [Ho].

QUESTION—What is meant by τοῦ πονηροῦ 'the wicked one'?

Used absolutely like this, this designates the evil one, Satan [DNTT]. This designates, preeminently [Ba, Ea, My], the great enemy of the people of God [Ba], the morally evil one [My], the Devil [AB, CBC, EGT, El, Ho, My, TD, TH], Satan [Cal, IB, TH]. This expression either designates a proper person or the leader and representative of the foes described in 6:12 [Ea] since the conflict is personal [Alf, EGT, El, LJ] and individual [El, LJ]; this adversary is a concrete person, not an abstract principle [Alf, LJ]. The fact that it is singular does not mean that Satan alone shoots these fiery arrows; they are attributable to him no matter who shoots them. The term recalls 6:12 and 13 [Lns].

6:17 and take[a] the helmet[b] of-the salvation[c]

LEXICON—a. aorist mid. (deponent = act.) impera. of δέχομαι (LN 18.1) (BAGD 2. p. 177): 'to take' [AB, Lns, NIC, NTC, Rob; all versions except REB, TEV], 'to take hold of' [LN], 'to take in hand' [BAGD], 'to grasp' [BAGD, LN], 'to grab' [LN], 'to receive' [El, WBC, We], 'to accept' [REB, TEV].

b. περικεφαλαία (LN **6.38**) (BAGD p. 648): 'helmet' [AB, BAGD, El, **LN**, Lns, NIC, NTC, Rob, WBC, We; all versions]. The helmet of the ancient warrior was a cap made of thick leather [AB, Ba, DNTT, Ea, IDB, LJ, NTC, TH], and strengthened with metal plates or bosses [LJ]. In some cases it was made of brass [AB, Ba, DNTT, NTC, St, TH] or iron [AB]. The model worn by Roman soldiers was made of bronze and had protecting cheek pieces [AB, IDB, WBC]. An inside lining of felt or sponge made the weight bearable [AB, DNTT, IDB, St]. It usually had a plume or crest of some kind as an ornament [Ba, Ea, Ho, IDB St]. The function of the helmet was to protect the head from blows by sword, war club, or battle-ax [Ba, TH] and nothing but an ax or hammer could pierce it [AB, St].

c. σωτήριος (LN 21.29, 29.30) (BAGD 2. p. 802): 'salvation' [AB, BAGD, El, LN (21.29), Lns, NIC, NTC, Rob, WBC, We; all versions except TNT], 'the gift of salvation' [TNT], 'the message of salvation, the message about being saved' [LN (21.30)], 'deliverance, means of deliverance' [BAGD], 'the way of saving, the manner of saving' [LN (21.29)]. In Christian literature, this term refers to messianic salvation and the one who mediates it [BAGD]. This substantive denotes the means by which people experience divine salvation [LN (21.29)] or it denotes the message of salvation itself [LN (21.30)].

QUESTION—What is the function of καί 'and'?

This καί 'and' joins the two groups of armor. Until the present verse, the armor presented is that of a list of virtues which involve a certain degree of human effort. With this verse the items listed are gifts in the purest sense. The shift from the participial constructions of 6:14–16 to a finite imperative verb marks this division [WBC]. The change from a participial construction to the imperative δέξασθε 'take' marks a more rapid and vivid depiction of the extended metaphor that is being used [EGT, El, IB, ICC, My]. It adds to the vividness of the picture [IB, ICC, My], as does the forefronting of τὴν περικεφαλαίαν τοῦ σωτηρίου 'the helmet of salvation' [ICC, My].

QUESTION—What is the significance of the imperative verb δέξασθε 'take'?

As a soldier prepared for battle, his armor would have been laid out in order on the ground before him [EBC, IB]. After he had taken it up and put it on [EBC, IB], he would normally be holding his shield with his left arm [EGT, My, WBC]. Then an attendant, or armor-bearer would hand him his helmet, and then his sword [EBC, IB]. So the occurrence of the verb δέξασθε 'take, receive' is appropriate to the metaphor [EBC, EGT, IB, WBC], and appropriate also to the concept of salvation, which is to be 'taken' or 'received' as a gift from God [Ea, ECWB, EGT, IB, NIC, TH, TNTC]. In the LXX of Isa. 59:17, from which this figure is taken, the verb used is περιέθετο 'he strapped on', the technical term for securing the helmet to the head [AB].

QUESTION—What is meant by the phrase τὴν περικεφαλαίαν τοῦ σωτηρίου 'the helmet of salvation'?

The forefronting of this phrase marks an emphasis [Lns]. The genitive construction is appositional [Alf, EGT, El, Ho, IB, Lns, My, TNTC]. The NT parallel is 1 Thess. 5:8 [AB, Alf, Ba, Cal, Can, EBC, EGT, ICC, NTC, Rob, TD, TNTC, We]. The OT background for this figure comes from Isa. 59:17 [AB, Can, DNTT, EBC, EGT, El, IB, ICC, ISBE2, Lns, MNTC, NIC, NTC, Rob, TD, TNTC, WBC, We].

QUESTION—What is meant by the use of the neuter noun σωτηρίου 'salvation'?

The noun σωτηρίου 'salvation' is the neuter gender, meaning 'salvation' or 'deliverance' [AB, Alf, Ba, BAGD, Cal, Can, CBC, Ea, EBC, ECWB, EGT, El, Ho, IB, ICC, LJ, Lns, MNTC, My, NCBC, NIC, NTC, Rob, Si, St, TD, TH, TNTC, Tu, WBC, We; all versions]. This is not the usual word; σωτήρια 'salvation' (feminine gender) is used in the NT to denote salvation [ECWB, EGT, El, Lns, TD, TH, WBC] in the abstract [ECWB], but the neuter form is the word that occurs in the LXX of Isa. 59:17, which probably accounts for its occurrence here [Alf, ECWB, El, ICC, Lns, My, Rob, TD, WBC]. The comparison in this metaphor is the helmet of the ancient soldier with the assurance of salvation. The point of comparison is the protective power of each. A nonfigurative statement would be: use the certainty of your of salvation to protect your soul from the temptations and trials the Devil will place upon you.

1. The salvation spoken of here is futuristic, the hope of salvation [Ba, Cal, IB, TD]. A soldier does not fight well without a hope of victory and the Christian cannot contend against the devil without the hope of final salvation [Ba]. Putting on this helmet means that, trusting in this salvation, one can and should fully commit oneself to the commencing struggle against the powers which seek to prevent salvation [TD].

2. The salvation spoken of here has reference to its present aspects [Alf, Can, CBC, Ea, EGT, El, Ho, Lns, MNTC (probably), My, NCBC, NIC, TH, WBC, We]. This is salvation appropriated by faith [Alf, El]. It consists in the awareness that what ultimately protects believers is the fact that God has already delivered them from bondage to Satan and seated them with Christ in the heavenly realms (2:1–10) [WBC]. It is the glad awareness that one has been put right with God, together with the inward sense of peace (as 'wholeness') and vitality which this brings [NCBC].
3. Both the present and future aspects of salvation apply here [AB, EBC, ECWB, LJ, NTC, Si, St, TNTC]. In 1 Thess. 5:8 the helmet is the hope of full salvation [EBC, LJ, NTC]. Salvation is a present deliverance from the power of sin and this will be consummated in eternity [EBC, LJ, NTC, TNTC] by complete deliverance from every kind of evil [EBC, LJ]. The present assurance of future full salvation and ultimate victory is what keeps a Christian from giving up the fight in times of persecution or tremendous discouragement [LJ, NTC].

and the sword[a] of-the Spirit, which is (the) word of-God.

LEXICON—a. μάχαιρα (LN 6.33) (BAGD 2. p. 496): 'sword' [AB, BAGD, El, LN, Lns, NIC, NTC, Rob, WBC, We; all versions]. The sword was short [AB, Ba, EBC, Lns, NTC, St], usually two-edged [Ba, EBC], and resembled a dagger [AB, Ba]. It was used for cutting and stabbing [EBC, LN] and Roman soldiers used it as their crucial offensive weapon in close combat [WBC].

QUESTION—What is meant by τὴν μάχαιραν τοῦ πνεύματος 'the sword of the Spirit'?

Here the apostle passes on to the only offensive weapon of the Christian [CBC, Ea, EBC, ECWB, EGT, Ho, Lns, TH, WBC], though others think the sword is both defensive and offensive [LJ, NCBC, St, WeBC], or defensive only [TD, TNTC]. The comparison of speech to a sword is frequent in the OT [Rob, TNTC], but the passage the writer has in mind here is Is. 11:4 [Rob, TD, WBC] and what is said about the Messiah in this passage, who will smite the earth with the word of his mouth, is transferable to the Christian [WBC].

1. This genitive construction is either that of possession [Bu, EBC, IB, NIC, TH, WBC (probably)] or it indicates τοῦ πνεύματος 'the Spirit' as the origin or source of τὴν μάχαιραν 'the sword' [AB, Alf, Ba, CBC, DNTT, Ea, EBC, EGT, El, Ho, ICC, LJ, Lns, My, NCBC, NIC, NTC, St (probably), TD, TH, TNTC, We, WeBC; REB, TEV, TNT]: take the sword which the Spirit provides, which is the word of God. It is the sword which has been forged [Alf], or furnished, by the Spirit [AB, Alf, Ba, CBC, Ea, EBC, EGT, El, Ho, ICC, LJ, NCBC, NTC, TH, TNTC, We], or used by the Spirit [EBC, IB, NCBC, NTC, TH, We, WeBC]. The Spirit is not so much the one who supplies the sword, as the one who gives it its effectiveness, who is its cutting edge [WBC]. The temptation of Christ

(Matt. 4:4, 7, 10) gives the pattern for the way the Christian soldier is to use this sword [Alf, Ba, Ea, EBC, LJ, NIC, St, TNTC, WeBC] in resisting temptation [St, TNTC]. The comparison in this metaphor is the sword of the Roman soldier with the word of God. The point of comparison is being on the offense. A nonfigurative statement would be: use God's words, inspired by the Spirit himself, to repel and destroy evil ideas.

2. This genitive construction is appositional, the μάχαιραν 'sword' being used figuratively for the πνεύματος 'Spirit' [Can, MNTC]: take the Spirit as your sword, which is the word of God. In this interpretation the three ideas of Spirit, sword, and word are identified together [Can]. The comparison in this metaphor is the sword of the Roman soldier with the Holy Spirit and the words which he generates. The point of comparison is being on the offense. A nonfigurative statement would be: use God's own Spirit and the words that come from him to repel and destroy evil and falsehood.

QUESTION—What is meant by the relative clause ὅ ἐστιν ῥῆμα θεοῦ 'which is the word of God'?

The μάχαιραν 'sword' is identified as the ῥῆμα θεοῦ 'word of God' [AB, Alf, Ba, Bu, CBC, DNTT, Ea, EBC, ECWB, EGT, El, HG, Ho, IB, ICC, IDB, ISBE, LJ, Lns, MNTC, MT, My, NCBC, NIC, NTC, Rob, Si, Si-ed, St, TD, TH, TNTC, WBC, We, WeBC]. The ῥῆμα θεοῦ 'word of God' is a definite utterance of God [We].

1. It refers to Scripture [Ba, CBC, Ea, EBC, ECWB, EGT, El, Ho, ICC (probably), ISBE, LJ, Lns, My, NCBC, NIC, NTC, Si, Si-ed, St, TD, TH, WBC, WeBC], whether as recorded [EBC, Ho, LJ, NCBC, St, TD], or as proclaimed in spoken words [Ba, ECWB, EGT, NCBC, NIC, NTC, TD, TH, WBC], or as marking its source—having proceeded from God's mouth [Lns]. This phrase refers to the OT word in part or in whole [TD]. It is the gospel [Ea, El, My, NCBC, WBC], the revealed will of God [Ea], and for us it is, in effect, Holy Scripture [Ea, Ho, NTC, St]. It is the detailed knowledge of Scripture [LJ], the use of specific divine sayings which the Spirit leads us to use in specific situations, as demonstrated in the temptation of Christ [LJ, TD]. This 'word of God' differs from the belt of truth in 6:14, which is knowledge of the central truth of salvation, the scheme of salvation as a whole [LJ]. The ῥῆμα θεοῦ 'word of God' differs from the λόγος τοῦ θεοῦ 'word of God' in that λόγος 'word' indicates *substance*, whereas ῥῆμα 'word' indicates an *utterance* of God. The phrase may apply to the utterances of the NT prophets or to Spirit-given answers Christians may give as a witness or as under interrogation (Matt. 10:19–20) [NCBC]. This is the gospel of Christ, however and wherever spoken, but the phrase cannot be limited to the written Holy Scripture in general [ECWB, EGT].

2. This is any spoken utterance which has the Holy Spirit as its source [AB, DNTT, IB, TNTC]. The word ῥῆμα 'word' in Pauline diction means a specifically weighty and binding pronouncement. Because of the paren-

thetic context, especially 4:25, 29; 5:13, 18–19 [AB], the ῥῆμα θεοῦ 'word of God' referring to prophetic speech, the singing of spiritual hymns, or prayer cannot be excluded. In addition the phrase is used of the words of God that are used in the OT, or of the words of the Lord later gathered up into the Gospels [AB, DNTT]. But in the immediate context Paul will speak of prayer (6:18) [AB, MNTC] and of the proclamation of the mystery of the gospel (6:19), so it is probable that the ῥῆμα θεοῦ 'word of God' which Paul calls a μάχαιραν 'sword' has to do with prayer and the preaching of the gospel. According to 6:18–20 the particular mode in which the saints are to wield this 'sword' is in the prayer of the saints to God and the proclamation of good news to the world. Whatever the reference, whether a traditional or freshly inspired saying, this ῥῆμα 'word' can be called the cutting edge of the Spirit. But the phrase cannot be limited to the mere quotation of Bible texts [AB]. The word of God is never used in the NT to refer to the Holy Scripture generally. It means 'the word which God gives us to speak', especially in times of crisis (cf. Matt. 10:19), and was also specifically used sometimes of the gospel message (1 Pet. 1:25) [IB]. The reference is to all words that come from the Spirit of God, though it is natural for believers today to think primarily of the Bible [TNTC].

3. The ῥῆμα θεοῦ 'word of God' is identified as τοῦ πνεύματος 'the Spirit' and utterances that have him as their source [Can, MNTC]. The relative pronoun ὅ 'which' is in the neuter gender and more properly points back to τοῦ πνεύματος 'of the Spirit' than it does to the feminine τὴν μάχαιραν 'the sword', though it is possible the gender of the relative pronoun could be explained by attraction forward to the similar gender of ῥῆμα 'word'. As salvation is not different from the helmet, but symbolized by it, so the sword here is not something distinct from the Spirit, but is simply his figurative name; and the Spirit as the sword of the Christian soldier is explained to be the word of God. It is not the repetition by rote of God's word, but the speaking from the filling of the Spirit, of which the ῥῆμα θεοῦ 'word of God' is his utterance, and so applied in the ways and for the purposes for which God's word was designed [Can]. Prayer is called the sword of the Spirit because the Spirit accompanies it and gives it force [MNTC].

DISCOURSE UNIT: 6:18–20 [AB, Ba, MNTC, My, NIC, Si, We; NAB, NRSV]. The topic is an exhortation for the saints to be vigilant in prayer for each other and for Paul's ministry of proclaiming the gospel [AB, Ba, MNTC, My] in which they participate by intercession [AB], a description of the spirit of the Christian warrior as he directs the vital powers of his armor to unceasing prayer for all his fellow believers [We], exhortation to watch and pray [NIC], the dynamism of prayer [Si], the power of prayer in Christian warfare [WeBC], assiduous prayer [NAB].

6:18 **By-means-of/with**[a] **every prayer and petition**[b] **praying**[c] **on every occasion in the Spirit/spirit,**

LEXICON—a. διά with genitive object (LN 89.76, 90.8) (BAGD A.III.1.b. p. 180): 'by means of' [LN (89.76, 90.8), Lns, NTC], 'through' [AB, LN (89.76, 90.8), WBC], 'by' [LN (89.76)]. 'with' [BAGD, El, LN (89.76, 90.8), NIC, Rob; KJV, NASB, NIV], 'in' [We; NJB, NRSV, REB], not explicit [TNT]. This preposition is also translated as a verb: 'using' [NAB]. The words διὰ πάσης προσευχῆς 'by means of/with every prayer' are translated 'do all this in prayer' [TEV].

b. δέησις (LN 33.171) (BAGD p. 172): 'petition' [AB, Lns, WBC; NAB, NASB], 'entreaty' [BAGD; NJB], 'supplication' [El, NIC, NTC, Rob, We; KJV, NRSV], 'prayer' [BAGD, LN], 'request' [LN; NIV], 'plea' [LN]. The words πάσης προσευχῆς καὶ δεήσεως 'every prayer and petition' are translated: 'constantly ask God's help in prayer' [REB], 'do all this in prayer, asking God's help' [TEV], 'always keep on praying and asking for God's help' [TNT]. In the second occurrence of this noun in this verse, its translation is changed to 'intercession' [AB], or this noun is changed to an infinitive, 'to pray' [NJB], or to an imperative verb, 'pray' [NAB, TEV], or to a participle, 'interceding' [REB], 'praying' [TNT]. This noun denotes asking for something which is presumably needed, and doing so with urgency [LN]. When used with προσευχή 'prayer', δέησις 'petition' denotes a more specific supplication [BAGD].

c. pres. mid. (deponent = active) participle of προσεύχομαι (LN 33.178) (BAGD p. 714): 'to pray' [BAGD, El, LN, Lns, NTC, Rob, WBC, We; KJV], 'to speak to God, to ask God for' [LN]. This participle is also translated as an imperative: 'pray' [AB, NIC; all versions except KJV, NJB, REB], 'keep praying' [NJB], 'pray always' [REB].

QUESTION—How is this verse connected to the preceding context?
1. The connection is through the preposition διά 'by means of, with' [Alf, Can, Ho, IB (probably), ICC, NTC, Rob, St, TH; TEV].
    1.1 Διά 'by means of, with' connects with 6:14–17 [Alf, Can, Ho, IB (probably), ICC, TH; TEV]. This is connected with the στῆτε οὖν 'stand therefore' of 6:14 [Alf, Ho, IB, ICC].
        1.1.1 Διά 'by means of, through' indicates the means by which the believer fulfills the command to stand equipped and ready for battle (6:14) [Alf, Can]: stand therefore, by means of having put on all these pieces of armor through every prayer and petition. All the Christian habits that are symbolized by the pieces of the foregoing armor are attained by prayer, and this is especially true of the sword of the Spirit [Can].
        1.1.2 Διά 'with' indicates the condition or attendant circumstances of fulfilling the command to stand equipped and ready for battle (6:14) [Ho, IB (probably), ICC, TH; TEV]: stand therefore, having put on all these pieces of armor with every prayer and petition.
    1.2 Διά 'with' connects with the τὴν μάχαιραν τοῦ πνεύματος 'the sword of the Spirit' in 6:17 and indicates the attendant circumstances of

acquiring this sword [NTC, Rob, St]: and take the sword of the Spirit, which is the Word of God, with every kind of prayer and petition. Though prayer is to pervade all of our spiritual warfare, scripture and prayer belong together as the two chief weapons with which the Spirit equips us [St].

2. The connection is through the participle προσευχόμενοι 'praying' [Ba, Ea, ECWB, EGT (probably), El, LJ, Lns, NIC, TNTC, WBC; KJV]. The style of the writer in this epistle is towards the tautological [WBC].

2.1 This participle indicates an additional means of being empowered in the Lord (6:10). It indicates a command which is parallel to the one in 6:13 to take up the whole armor of God [LJ]: be empowered in the Lord and in the strength of his might, taking up all the armor of God and, as you do so, continually praying on each occasion in the spirit with every kind of prayer and petition.

2.2 This participle connects with 6:13–17 and gives a further description of the Christians' armor [Lns]. Prayer is also a part of the Christian armor, forming the seventh piece [CBC, Lns]. The preposition διά 'by means of' denotes the means by which the action of the present durative participle προσευχόμενοι 'praying' is to be accomplished [Lns].

2.3 This participle connects with 6:14–17 [Ba (probably), Ea, ECWB, EGT, El, NIC, TNTC, WBC]. The participle προσευχόμενοι 'praying' [Ea, EGT, El], or even both participles, προσευχόμενοι 'praying' and ἀγρυπνοῦντες 'keeping alert' [WBC], is probably a part of the series of participles connected with the verb στῆτε 'stand' in the main exhortation at 6:14 [Ea, EGT, El, NIC, WBC]. Prayer is the great weapon of the Christian warrior's armor [Ba].

2.3.1 The participle describes the means by which the armor is put on [ECWB, WBC] and διά 'by means of, through' denotes the means of praying [WBC]: stand therefore having put on all of the armor of God by praying on each occasion in the Spirit through all kinds of prayer and petition.

2.3.2 The participle describes the manner in which the armor is to be put on [Ba (probably), Ea, EGT, El]: stand therefore having put on all of the armor of God, and as you do so, praying on every occasion in the Spirit with all kinds of prayer and petition. No matter how well outfitted with armor, or how skilled in its use, we will be defeated without prayer, but our victory is assured if our battle is accompanied by prayer [Ba].

2.3.2.1 Διά 'by means of' denotes the formal cause, the manner in which the praying is to be done [Ea, EGT].

2.3.2.2 Διά 'with' indicates the attendant circumstances, or mode, or condition of their praying [El (probably)].

3. The connection is to 6:14–17 through both the preposition διά 'with' and the participle προσευχόμενοι 'praying' [My]: stand therefore, having taken up the whole armor of God with every kind of prayer and petition,

praying on each occasion in the Spirit. The prepositional phrase and the participle mark two parallel specifications of mode. The prepositional phrase is independent of the following participle, otherwise it would result in a tautological redundancy of expression, and the preposition denotes the condition in which something is done, e.g., 'stand therefore...while you are engaged in every kind of prayer and petition'.
4. The participle προσευχόμενοι 'praying' (together with the participle ἀγρυπνοῦντες 'keeping alert') starts a new trend of thought with this verse [AB, Cal, MNTC, NCBC, We, WeBC; NAB, NASB, NIV, NJB, NRSV, TNT (probably)]: be praying on each occasion in the Spirit by means of/with every kind of prayer and petition. This section, 6:18–20, marks a skillfully made transition to the usual personal notices and final greetings with which the apostle usually ends his epistles [MNTC]. A very strong emphasis on the need for prayer follows the description of the fighting equipment of the Christian warrior [NCBC].
4.1 Διά 'by means of, through' indicates the means of praying [AB; NAB].
4.2 Διά 'with' indicates the accompanying circumstances or condition of the praying [Cal, MNTC, NCBC, We, WeBC; NASB, NIV, NJB, NRSV].

QUESTION—What is meant by πάσης προσευχῆς καὶ δεήσεως 'every prayer and petition'?
1. This is an hendiadys [AB, Rob, Si]: every kind of petitioning prayer. To differentiate between these two synonyms seems hypercritical [Si]. Δεήσεως 'petition' is joined with προσευχῆς 'prayer' for the sake of fullness of expression [Rob]. Both nouns in this phrase form an hendiadys and express adoration [AB].
2. This is a generic-specific doublet [Alf, Cal, Can, DNTT, Ea, EBC, ECWB, EGT, El, Ho, ICC, ISBE2, LJ, Lns, My, NCBC, NIC, NTC, Si-ed, TH, WBC, We, WeBC; REB, TEV, TNT]: every kind of prayer, that is, petitions. In this phrase the two terms are employed together primarily for the purpose of intensification, but the remainder of the verse takes up these two forms and develops them separately, προσευχῆς 'prayer' in προσευχόμενοι ἐν παντὶ καιρῷ ἐν πνεύματι 'praying on each occasion in the Spirit' and δεήσεως 'petition' in εἰς αὐτὸ ἀγρυπνοῦντες ἐν πάσῃ προσκαρτερήσει καὶ δεήσει περὶ πάντων τῶν ἁγίων 'to this end keeping alert in all perseverance and petition for all the saints' [WBC]. The πάσης 'every' means 'every kind of' [Alf, Ba, Ea, EGT, Ho, LJ, My, NTC, WeBC], supplication for ourselves, intercession for others, prayer alone, prayer in the family, in the social meeting, in the great assembly, prayer at the usual hours, prayer at special times, etc. [Ba, Ea, Ho, LJ, WeBC]. It includes all the elements of prayer, adoration, confession, thanksgiving, petition [Can, LJ, NTC]. It describes prayer as to its variety and earnestness [EGT, El].

QUESTION—What is meant by προσευχόμενοι ἐν παντὶ καιρῷ 'praying on every occasion'?

This phrase must not be understood as indicating the constant act of formal prayer [TH, WeBC] which is not practical in the Christian life [WeBC]. Since prayer is the expression of all the believer's feelings and desires which terminate in God, it is possible that a man should pray almost literally without ceasing [Ho]. Prayer is to be made in every season, in times of prosperity or adversity, because in each we have need of the help and blessing of God [Cal, Can], not in just times of felt need [Cal, NTC]. The universal concern expressed here by παντὶ 'every' is for man's whole lifetime, in all its years, days, hours, and minutes [AB]. It describes prayer as to its constancy [EGT, El, Ho]. The phrase ἐν παντὶ καιρῷ 'on every occasion' elucidates the phrase πάσης προσευχῆς 'every prayer' since the different kinds of prayer, in respect to contents and form, are to be appropriate to the different circumstances of time [My].

QUESTION—For whom are they to pray?

The implied indirect object of προσευχόμενοι 'praying' is 'for yourselves' [Ea, El, LJ, MNTC] since this participial clause is somewhat parallel to the next one dealing with being alert to pray for all the saints [Ea], though another commentator states that περι πάντων τῶν ἁγίων 'for all the saints' at the end of this verse is closely connected to this participle as well (stating that the intervening words define prayer as constant, spiritual, resolute, and manifold) [We]. The force of the two clauses is that, in praying for themselves, they were to uniformly blend supplications for all the saints [Ea, El].

QUESTION—What is meant by ἐν πνεύματι 'in the Spirit/spirit'?

1. This refers to the Holy Spirit [AB, Alf, Ba, Can, CBC, DNTT, Ea, EBC, ECWB, EGT, El, Ho, IB, ICC, ISBE, ISBE2, LJ, My, My-ed, NCBC, NIC, NTC, Rob, Si, St, TD, TH, TNTC, WBC, WeBC; all versions]: praying in the Spirit. This is praying in communion with [EBC, IB] and with the aid of the Holy Spirit [Ba, El, Ho, NCBC, NIC, TNTC], either following his guidance and inspiration in praying for the right things [CBC, Ea, Ho, St; TEV] (the teaching of Rom. 8:26–27 being perhaps what is particularly meant here [Alf, DNTT, Ea, ECWB, EGT, El, Ho, LJ, My, NCBC, TNTC, WeBC]), or being empowered by him to pray as one should [REB, TNT] or both [Can, LJ, TH, WBC].

2. This refers to the human spirit [DNTT, Lns, We]: praying in spirit. Prayer is not to be offered in form or in word only, but in that part of our being by which we hold communion with God. The activity of the Holy Spirit here is not precluded [We]. The use of the anarthrous πνεύματι 'spirit' in Gal. 5:16–25 and 6:8 and elsewhere indicates that the reference here is not primarily to the Spirit, but to our spirit. The Holy Spirit is still implied here for one cannot truly pray in spirit without the Spirit's help [Lns].

and to this-(end) keeping-alert[a] with all perseverance[b] and petition for all the saints

LEXICON—a. pres. act. participle of ἀγρυπνέω (LN **27.57**) (BAGD 2. p. 14): 'to keep alert' [WBC], 'to be on the alert' [NTC], 'to be vigilant' [LN, Lns], 'to be on the lookout for' [LN], 'to guard, to care for' [BAGD], 'to watch' [El, Rob, We; KJV]. This participle is translated as an imperative phrase: 'stay awake' [AB], 'keep awake' [NIC], 'keep watch' [REB], 'be alert' [**LN**; NIV], 'be on the alert' [NASB], 'keep alert' [NRSV, TEV], 'keep at it day and night' [TNT]. This verb is also translated as an adverb modifying an imperative 'pray': 'pray attentively' [NAB]. It is also conjoined to the noun προσκαρτερήσει 'perseverance' and translated as an imperative phrase: 'never get tired of staying awake' [NJB].

b. προσκαρτέρησις (LN **68.68**) (BAGD p. 715): 'perseverance' [BAGD, El, NIC, NTC, Rob, WBC, We; KJV, NASB], 'patience' [BAGD], 'constancy' [MM], 'steadfastness' [Lns]. This noun is also translated as an imperative or imperative phrase: 'persevere' [NRSV, REB], 'keep on' [LN; NIV], 'never give up' [TEV], 'never get tired of' [NJB]. It is also translated as an adjective modifying δεήσει 'petition': 'persevering intercession' [AB]. It is also translated as an adverb modifying a participle 'praying' or an imperative 'pray': 'pray constantly' [NAB], 'persistently praying' [TNT]. It means holding out against fatigue and difficulty [ECWB]. It means never becoming discouraged and disheartened [Ba].

QUESTION—What is meant by καὶ εἰς αὐτό 'and to this end'?

'This end' refers to praying at all times in the Spirit [Alf, Ea, EGT, El, Ho, My, WBC, WeBC] or in spirit [Lns]. The καί 'and' introduces the transition to a new element of prayer, that of intercession for all Christians and for the apostle himself [My]. The purpose of staying awake is praying [AB, Alf, LJ, MNTC, WBC, WeBC], specifically, intercession for others [EGT, LJ, MNTC].

QUESTION—What is meant by ἀγρυπνοῦντες 'keeping alert'?

This refers both to watching for opportunities for prayer [Ba, Can, WeBC] and keeping watch against everything which would hinder prayer [Ba], such as being overcome with sleep or drowsiness when there is a special call or opportunity for prayer [Can]. The participle is used figuratively and refers to remaining sensitive to the Spirit's promptings to prayer [TH]. This participle does not describe an act separate from the preceding participle. Both participles refer to the same action [Lns].

1. The verb has the military connotation of a soldier on the alert [ECWB, IB, NCBC, Rob, St; and probably Lns]. It is possible that this phrase sustains the military image [ECWB, Rob]. The Christian should never be caught off guard [IB, Lns, NCBC] with his armor laid aside for comfort. Here the Christian's own self-discipline is stressed. He is to provide watchful alertness against every approach of evil [NCBC]. The participle ἀγρυπνοῦντες 'keeping alert' may have some reference to the soldier

being on guard. If so, it means that, in the direct exhortation of this verse, the metaphor has not been completely dropped [ECWB].
2. The verb has no military connotations [AB, TH]. The writer has left the military imagery and is speaking directly to the need of believers to pray constantly [TH]. Nevertheless, the participle here does have metaphorical force, for it denotes not physical alertness (the literal application being hard to justify in light of the eschatological context, since abstinence from physical sleep could hardly be a remedy against either temptation or a demonstration of eschatological preparedness for the Messiah's final advent), but to spiritual alertness. Accordingly, it refers to being totally oriented toward what is coming and toward readily responding to the Messiah who is coming. This being the case it also influences the parallel charge to 'pray...with all prayers'. This will not apply exclusively to formalized prayers, offered either in solitude or in community, but to their whole life and being, offered as a prayer to God. This verse, then, portrays the life of the individual saint as one uninterrupted address and response to God [AB].

QUESTION—What is meant by πάσῃ 'all'?

Most translate it as 'all' [El, Lns, NIC, NTC, Rob, TD, WBC, We; KJV, NASB]. One commentator states that it has elative significance here [TD]. The force of πάσῃ 'all' here is 'with every possible perseverance and petition' [Mo]. Some take it only with the latter noun δεήσει 'petition', translating it 'always' and translating that noun in verbal form [NIV, NRSV, REB, TEV]. The universal concern expressed by the πάσῃ 'every' preceding προσκαρτερήσει 'perseverance' is for the whole mental, emotional, and physical range of a person's personal existence and the energies present in him or to be received and used in the head, heart, and limbs [AB].

QUESTION—What is meant by πάσῃ προσκαρτερήσει καὶ δεήσει 'all perseverance and petition'?
1. The words πάσῃ προσκαρτερήσει καὶ δεήσει 'all perseverance and petition' form a hendiadys [Bu, ISBE2] or a virtual one [Ea, EGT, El, Ho, ICC, and probably AB, ECWB]: with every persevering petition for all the saints. In the NT the verb corresponding to προσκαρτερήσει 'perseverance' is usually used for adherence with unshakable tenacity to prayer [AB, ECWB]. Προσκαρτερήσει 'perseverance' does not indicate a mechanical attachment, but such as an ever new decision and passionate fidelity would produce [AB]. The meaning of δεήσει 'petition' in this phrase is 'intercession' [AB, EGT (probably)]. Προσκαρτερήσει 'perseverance' so clearly receives its explanation from δεήσει 'petition' that this may be considered a *contextual* hendiadys [El]. The words indicate that perseverance is to be characterized by prayer, each noun having a blended, though distinct signification [Ea].
2. Προσκαρτερήσει 'perseverance' focuses on the attribute with which the δεήσει 'petition' is to be made [Ba, Cal, LJ, MNTC, NTC, TD, WBC]: keeping alert to pray with all kinds of perseverance in every petition for

all the saints. Προσκαρτερήσει 'perseverance' means every tendency to weariness must be counteracted by a cheerful performance of the duty of prayer, even though the petition requested is not immediately obtained [Cal, MNTC], for this is evidence of a faith that will not be discouraged [MNTC]. Salvation is corporate, not just private and personal.
3. Δεήσει 'petition' receives the focus as being an amplification of προσκαρτερήσει 'perseverance' [Alf, My]: keeping alert with all perseverance, that is, as to the making of every petition (in prayer) for all the saints. The second substantive explains the former one without losing its force from being coupled to it: importunity accompanied by and exemplified by supplication [Alf]. The προσκαρτερήσει 'perseverance' is perseverance in prayer, and so corresponds to the διὰ πάσης προσευχῆς 'with every kind of prayer' at the beginning of the verse, then the καὶ δεήσει 'and petition' is attached to the προσκαρτερήσει 'perseverance' with the phrase περὶ πάντων τῶν ἁγίων 'for all the saints' as a nearer definition, with περὶ πάντων τῶν ἁγίων 'for all the saints' going only with δεήσει 'petition' [My].
4. The two substantives bear no particular relationship to each other [Lns, NCBC]. Προσκαρτερήσει is better translated 'steadfastness' than 'perseverance' and means more than constancy in prayer. It refers to the steadfastness of these soldiers in their entire battle and is virtually the same thing as the command στῆτε οὖν 'stand therefore'. Προσκαρτερήσει 'steadfastness' and δεήσει 'petition' are different things. The one is a virtue and quality of the spirit, the other a begging prayer [Lns]. Προσκαρτερήσει 'perseverance' applies to the soldier wearing his armor at all times, recognizing that it is easy to grow tired and slack and so expose himself to attacks for which he is unprepared, and δεήσει 'petition' relates to supplication for all saints [NCBC].

DISCOURSE UNIT: 6:19–20 [IB, ICC, We; NIV]. The topic is an appeal for prayers [IB], the apostle's request for their prayers for himself with respect to freedom of speech to proclaim the gospel [ICC, We].

6:19 and for me, that/in-order-that to me may-be-given speech[a] in (the) opening[b] of-my mouth, with boldness[c] to-make-known the mystery of-the gospel,

LEXICON—a. λόγος (LN 33.98, 33.99) (BAGD 1.a.β. p. 477): 'speech' [LN (33.99)], 'speaking' [BAGD, LN (33.99)], 'utterance' [El, NIC, Rob, We; KJV, NASB], 'word' [AB, LN (33.98), WBC; NAB, NIV, TNT], 'the right words' [REB], 'message' [LN (33.98), NTC; NRSV, TEV], 'saying, statement' [LN (33.98)], 'opportunity' [NJB]. The words ἵνα μοι δοθῇ λόγος 'in order that to me may be given speech' is translated 'that to me may be given the floor' [Lns].

b. ἄνοιξις (LN **33.29**) (BAGD p. 71): 'opening' [BAGD, El, Lns, Rob, We; NASB]. The phrase ἐν ἀνοίξει τοῦ στόματός 'in the opening of the mouth' is translated as a verb: 'to open' [AB, NIC, NTC; KJV, NJB], 'to address, to start speaking, to begin to speak' [LN]. The phrase is also translated as a temporal phrase: 'when, whenever I open my mouth' [WBC; NIV], 'when I speak' [NRSV, REB, TNT]. The words λόγος ἐν ἀνοίξει τοῦ στόματός μου 'speech in the opening of my mouth' are translated 'a message when I open my mouth' [BAGD], 'a message to utter, a message to announce' [**LN**]. The purpose clause ἵνα μοι δοθῇ λόγος ἐν ἀνοίξει τοῦ στόματός μου 'in order that to me may be given speech in the opening of my mouth' is translated 'that God may put his word on my lips' [NAB], 'that God will give me a message when I am ready to speak' [TEV]. The idiom ἄνοιξις τοῦ στόματός 'opening of the mouth' is a Semitic idiom [LN, Tu3], which denotes beginning to speak in a somewhat systematic and formal manner [LN].

c. παρρησία: 'boldness'. See this word at 3:12.

QUESTION—How is this verse related to the context?

This verse continues on from the last verse as a continuation of the sentence which began in 6:17 [TH]. Up to this point Paul has asked prayer for others, now he cannot help but ask prayer for himself in light of the great responsibility he bears in making known the mystery of the gospel [TNTC].

QUESTION—What is the difference, if any, between the phrase περὶ πάντων τῶν ἁγίων 'for all the saints' in the last verse and the καὶ ὑπὲρ ἐμοῦ 'and for me' here?

1. There is a distinction between περί 'for' and the occurrence of καί 'and' with ὑπέρ 'for' that must be noted here [AB, Alf, Can (probably), Ea, ECWB, EGT, El, ICC, My, TD, TH, We; NASB]: keeping alert to pray with all perseverance and petition for all the saints and especially for me. When καί 'and' joins a part to the whole [Ea], a particular to the general, it has adjunctive force [EGT], adding intensive or climactic force [Ea]. It marks a special case [AB, EGT, El, ICC]. While these two prepositions can often be substituted for each other (the distinctions between them having been lost in the Hellenistic period), here the occurrence of ὑπέρ 'for' where another περί 'for' could have been used serves to emphasize the ὑπὲρ ἐμοῦ 'for me' [TD].

1.1 There is little difference in the meaning of the prepositions themselves [Alf, El, ICC, My].

1.2 There is a significant difference in the meaning of the prepositions [AB, Ea, ECWB, We]. The intensive or climactic force introduced by καί 'and' is also marked in the change of preposition [AB, Ea]. The preposition ὑπέρ 'for, on behalf of' has a more direct and definite meaning than does περί 'for' in the last verse [We]. Περί 'for' properly denotes 'touching all saints' [ECWB]. It ideally encircles all the saints with their supplications [Ea]. The prayer for the apostle, on the other hand, was more direct and personal so ὑπέρ 'for' was used where the blessing prayed for was clearly specified [AB, Ea]. It means 'on behalf of'. The change expresses a greater earnestness in the request for their prayers in reference to the need expressed in the remainder of this verse and the next [ECWB]. To translate the two prepositions as having the same meaning seems to suggest that Paul's request for prayer for himself was an afterthought [AB].

2. There is no significant difference of meaning in these prepositions [Ba, DNTT, HG, Lns, MNTC, Mo, NCBC, NIC, NTC, Rob, Tu, WBC], nor, apparently, any special force to καί 'and' [Ba, Lns, MNTC, NCBC, NIC, NTC, Rob, WBC; all versions except NASB]: keeping alert to pray with all perseverance and petition for all the saints and for me. While the change in prepositions helps mark the introduction of a special request [Rob], there is no real difference in their meaning [HG, Rob].

QUESTION—What relationship is indicated by ἵνα 'in order that, that'?

It indicates the purpose of Paul's request that they pray for him [Alf, Ea, EGT, El]. Others say that it is nonfinal or epexegetical, indicating the contents of the prayer that he wants them to pray for him [AB, ECWB, Ho, Lns, NIC, Tu, WBC]. Another commentator states that it indicates both the aim of the ὑπὲρ ἐμοῦ 'for me' as well as the content of the intercession for the apostle [My].

QUESTION—What is the significance of the passive verb δοθῇ 'may be given'?

The passive form indicates that this gift is sought from God, the passive form being used to avoid mentioning the divine name unnecessarily [AB, TH], as was the Jewish custom [AB]. Δοθῇ 'may be given' is given a position of special emphasis (*contra* Alf) stressing what Paul desires in this verse as being a gift from God [EBC, EGT, El, My].

QUESTION—What is meant by λόγος 'speech'?

1. Λόγος 'speech' denotes a 'message' [Cal (probably), CBC, ECWB, ICC, My, NCBC, NIC, TH, TNTC, WBC; NAB, NIV, NRSV, REB, TEV, TNT]: that God will tell me what to say. What Paul desires is that which he ought to speak when he opens his mouth [My]. He desires the words that will make the gospel intelligible to those who hear him [NCBC].
2. Λόγος 'speech' denotes facility or fluency in speaking [EBC, Ho, LJ, Si, St]: that God will enable me to speak fluently. Λόγος 'speech' denotes the power of ready speech [Ea, EBC, Ho, LJ], the freedom of utterance [Ho, LJ, Si], with a focus upon clarity of communication [St]. It must not be forgotten that Paul was never a good natural speaker (1 Cor. 2:1; 2 Cor. 10:10, 11:6) [LJ].
3. Λόγος 'speech' denotes the opportunity to speak [Lns; NJB]: that God will give me an opportunity to open my mouth. The occurrence of πρεσβεύω 'I am an ambassador' in the next verse points to the fact that λόγος 'speech' here is used as a parliamentary, forensic, and a court term and that it refers to being given the right to speak, the opportunity to make his defense and present his message, to be given the floor [Lns].
4. Λόγος 'speech' denotes both a message and facility in delivering it [AB, Ea, LJ]: that God will tell me what to say and enable me to say it fluently.

QUESTION—How is the phrase ἐν ἀνοίξει τοῦ στόματός μου 'in the opening of my mouth' connected?
1. The phrase is connected to the preceding ἵνα μοι δοθῇ λόγος 'in order that to me may be given speech' [AB, Alf, Ea, EBC, ECWB, EGT, El, Ho, MNTC, My, NIC, NTC, TH, TNTC, WBC, We; all versions except KJV]. The infinitive clause γνωρίσαι τὸ μυστήριον τοῦ εὐαγγελίου 'to make known the mystery of the gospel' marks the purpose of the gift of the λόγος ἐν ἀνοίξει τοῦ στόματός μου 'speech in the opening of my mouth' [Alf, TH]. It, with the attached ἐν παρρησίᾳ 'in boldness', either explains the preceding clause [Ea] or indicates its contemplated result [Ea, ECWB, El]. A decision as to whether ἐν παρρησίᾳ 'in boldness' is connected with the preceding clause or with the following one cannot be made on philological grounds alone [AB].
2. The phrase ἐν ἀνοίξει τοῦ στόματός μου 'in the opening of my mouth' is a supplementary clause, further explaining ἵνα μοι δοθῇ λόγος 'in order that to me may be given speech', and is more closely connected to the following infinitive clause γνωρίσαι τὸ μυστήριον τοῦ εὐαγγελίου 'to make known the mystery of the gospel' [Ba, ICC, LJ, Lns, Rob; KJV]. With this interpretation the phrase ἐν ἀνοίξει τοῦ στόματός μου 'in the opening of my mouth' gives a fullness of expression to the idea of ἵνα μοι δοθῇ λόγος 'in order that to me may be given speech', which corresponds to the gravity of the thought. The phrase completes from the subjective side what is expressed on the objective side by ἵνα μοι δοθῇ λόγος 'in order that to me may be given speech'. Taking the phrase with the preceding ἵνα 'in order that' clause makes the phrase superfluous and trivial [ICC].

QUESTION—What is meant by the phrase ἐν ἀνοίξει τοῦ στόματός μου 'in the opening of my mouth'?
This phrase indicates the beginning of an act of speaking [Ea, EGT, Ho, LJ, My, NIC, NTC, TH, WBC, We; NIV, NRSV, REB, TEV, TNT]. The phrase denotes no more than opening the mouth to speak [My]. The phrase means 'when I open my mouth to speak' or similar translations [Ea, EGT, Ho, LJ, WBC, We; NIV, NRSV, REB, TEV, TNT] or 'when I am ready to speak' with not much emphasis upon 'being ready' [TH]. The ἐν 'in, with' marks the *occasion* of the action, and the action itself is the gift of Divine help which is sought [EGT, El]. 'Opening the mouth' is a common expression in the Bible for proclaiming God's word [WBC].
1. This phrase indicates the ability to speak clearly and boldly [Cal], or to speak joyfully and with great confidence about good things [ISBE]. To open the mouth means to speak with perfect freedom, free from the smallest dread. He was so ardent in his zeal that he was never satisfied with his exertions for spreading the gospel [Cal].
2. This phrase indicates the beginning of a solemn and deliberate announcement or speech [AB, Can, Ea, EBC, ECWB, EGT, El, ICC, Lns, NIC, TD, We]. The phrase ἐν ἀνοίξει τοῦ στόματός 'in the opening of

the mouth' is always used of solemn and deliberate utterance [ECWB, El, ICC]. The idea here is based upon the OT idea of God's word being put into the mouth of the prophets [AB, TD]. Combined with λόγος 'word, speech', this phrase denotes inspiration [AB]. God also caused the missionary word, the evangelical message to go out to the nations through the mouths of the apostles [TD].

QUESTION—What relationship is indicated by ἐν 'with (boldness)'
1. It indicates the manner in which he opens his mouth [Alf, Ba, Cal, LJ, Lns; KJV]: opening my mouth with boldness.
2. It indicates the manner in which he will make known the mystery of the gospel [AB, Can, Ea, EBC, ECWB, EGT, El, Ho, ICC, MNTC, My, NIC, NTC, Rob, TH, TNTC, WBC, We; all versions except KJV]: with boldness making known the mystery of the gospel. The ἐν 'in, with' denotes an adverbial relationship for this phrase, 'boldly, freely' [Ho].

QUESTION—What is meant by παρρησίᾳ 'boldness'?
It characterizes the presentation of the gospel as being bold and open [AB, DNTT, Ea, My] or courageous [DNTT, St, WeBC]. It literally means 'uninhibited speech' [NCBC] or 'freedom of speech' [MNTC, WeBC] and suggests this idea as well as that of boldness in general [MNTC, NCBC]. It means frankness of speech [EBC, Ho, LJ, My], an uninhibited openness of speech [EBC, NIC, TD], plainness of speech [ECWB], keeping nothing back and not compromising the gospel in any way out of concern for his own reputation or safety [LJ, NCBC, NIC, Si, St] or out of undue shyness or lack of confidence [NCBC].

QUESTION—What is meant by γνωρίσαι 'to make known'?
The meaning of this verb in both the LXX and the NT is the immediate proclamation of the divine will [DNTT] and carries the implication of a revelatory character that corresponds to that of μυστήριον 'mystery' here [DNTT, TD], the revelation of the μυστήριον 'mystery' taking place in the apostle's action of γνωρίσαι 'to make known' [TD]. This infinitive should not be translated as 'to proclaim' because this is misleading. The verb is not the ordinary one for preaching, but rather refers to elucidating a message in such a manner as to make sure it is understood [NCBC]. The infinitive indicates the hypothetical or conceived result [HG].

QUESTION—What relationship is indicated by the genitive construction τὸ μυστήριον τοῦ εὐαγγελίου 'the mystery of the gospel'?
While the μυστήριον 'mystery' may refer to the unexpected way in which God's purpose has been worked out in the reconciliation of Jews and Gentiles into a Christian community, it may, on the other hand, have its more general force of 'the unbelievable truth' of the gospel [NCBC].
1. The genitive construction τὸ μυστήριον τοῦ εὐαγγελίου 'the mystery of the gospel' denotes the mystery, secret, or revelation that is contained in the gospel [AB, Alf, EGT, ISBE, My, NTC, TH, We]. The genitive construction indicates that the substance of the gospel [AB, EGT, ISBE, TH], God's world-embracing purpose of redemption through Christ

[ISBE], or the intention of drawing the Gentiles into God's house through Jesus Christ, was a formerly hidden divine truth [AB, TH] and is now the means by which this purpose is carried out [AB]. It refers to the mystery that forms the content of the gospel [My]. It means 'the revelation contained in the gospel' [We].

2. The genitive construction τὸ μυστήριον τοῦ εὐαγγελίου 'the mystery of the gospel' denotes the fact that the whole of the gospel was a divine secret [Ea, El, Ho, NIC, WBC]. The apostle assigns the name μυστήριον 'mystery' to the gospel, for it is a whole system which remained a secret until God's time came for revealing it [Ea]. It denotes the mystery that the gospel involves [El]. The gospel *is* the mystery [NIC, WBC].

6:20 on-behalf of-which I am-an-ambassador[a] in a-chain,[b]

TEXT—Instead of ἐν αὐτῷ 'in it', some manuscripts contain the reading αὐτό 'it', pointing more explicitly to τὸ μυστήριον 'the mystery' in the last verse as its antecedent [NIC]. GNT assigns the reading ἐν αὐτῷ 'in it' a C ranking, indicating difficulty in deciding which reading to place in the text. It is possible that NAB, NIV, NRSV follow the reading αὐτό 'it' since they translate this pronoun as the direct object of either the verb παρρησιάσωμαι 'I may be bold' or the infinitive λαλῆσαι 'to speak'.

LEXICON—a. pres. act. indic. of πρεσβεύω (LN 37.88) (BAGD p. 699): 'to be an ambassador' [AB, BAGD, El, LN, Lns, MM, NIC, NTC, Rob, WBC, We; all versions except TNT], 'to be an envoy' [BAGD], 'to serve as an ambassador' [TNT], 'to work as an ambassador or envoy' [BAGD], 'to be a representative of' [LN].

b. ἅλυσις (LN 6.16, **37.115**) (BAGD 2. p. 41): 'chain' [AB, El, LN (6.16), Lns, NIC, NTC, WBC, We; NAB, NASB, NIV, NJB, NRSV, REB], 'imprisonment' [BAGD, LN (37.115)]. Literally, this noun denotes a chain, but generally it is used of imprisonment. The phrase ἐν ἁλύσει 'with a chain' is translated 'in prison' [LN (**37.115**)], 'in bonds' [Rob; KJV], or it is translated as a verb phrase: 'though now I am in prison' [LN (**37.115**); TEV], 'prisoner though I am' [TNT]. The phrase ἐν ἁλύσει 'with a chain' equates with 'as a prisoner' [BAGD].

QUESTION—What relationship is indicated by ὑπὲρ οὗ 'on behalf of which'?

The referent of the relative pronoun οὗ 'which' is τὸ μυστήριον τοῦ εὐαγγελίου 'the mystery of the gospel' [AB, Alf, Ba, BAGD, DNTT, Ea, EBC, EGT, El, NIC, NTC, Rob, WBC; KJV, NASB, NJB, REB, TEV, TNT], more specifically the μυστήριον 'mystery' than the εὐαγγελίου 'gospel' [EGT, ICC, My] since this was properly the object of γνωρίσαι 'to make known' in the last clause to which the verb πρεσβεύω 'I am an ambassador' is connected in substance [Alf, EGT, El, ICC, My]. Others, however, indicate the reference is to the preceding genitive τοῦ εὐαγγελίου 'the gospel' [Ho, MNTC, NCBC, NIC, TD].

QUESTION—What is meant by πρεσβεύω 'ambassador'?

Ambassadors were sacred persons [Ba, Ea, My]. They were inviolable by the law of nations [AB, Can, CBC, Ea, EBC, ECWB, My, WBC], so that 'an ambassador in chains' would seem to be a contradiction in terms [Can]. They could be snubbed or expelled [AB], but not imprisoned [AB, My, WBC]. Paul does not have in mind so much that his privilege has been violated, as that his embassy must be carried on despite his wrongful confinement [Can]. The verb πρεσβεύω ἐν ἁλύσει 'I am an ambassador' has τοῦ Χριστοῦ 'of Christ' [Alf, My, TH] or ὑπέρ Χριστοῦ 'on behalf of Christ' [AB, EGT, TH] as its implied supplement [AB, Alf, EGT, My, TH]. Here, the verb expresses the official character of the message of reconciliation which the apostle bears [DNTT]. It is not so much his office, as his work that he has in mind [Can]. Those to whom he is sent is understood [Alf, My]; it is not just to the governmental powers of Rome, but his office is as coextensive as his apostolic commission [EGT]—it is to all the Gentiles [EGT, My].

QUESTION—What is meant by ἐν ἁλύσει 'in a chain'?

1. The phrase refers to the apostle being chained to his Roman guard [EBC, ECWB, EGT, IB, ICC, ISBE, Lns, NTC, Rob, Si, St]. This term is used in the plural with the term πέδαις 'fetters' in Mark 5:4 and Luke 8:29, the latter referring to binding the feet, so that ἁλύσεσιν 'chains' there must refer to 'manacles' binding the hands [ECWB]. The reference here is to the custom of chaining a prisoner by his hand to the soldier who guarded him [ECWB, Lns, St]. The singular form here is probably to be taken literally [ECWB]. Another commentator states that ἁλύσει 'chain' here refers to the leg iron which bound the apostle to the soldier who guarded him [IB]. The reference cannot be shown to refer exclusively to his Roman captivity, though it is probable, since he was confined with a chain in Caesarea also (*contra* Lns who states a chain was *not* used on him in Caesarea) [EGT]. The collective use of this noun is not clearly shown anywhere in the NT [EGT, ICC].

2. The phrase ἐν ἁλύσει 'in a chain' does not necessarily refer to his being chained to his Roman guard [AB, Can, Ea, El, MNTC, My, TH, TNTC; TEV, TNT]. It indicates 'being in custody' [MNTC] or 'in prison' [TH; TEV, TNT]. It is not necessary to press the singular ἁλύσει 'chain' to refer to the chain to which he was bound to his Roman guard [Alf, Can, Ea], or to any historical instance in which he was held in military custody [El, My], though it is not improbable [Can, Ea, El]. Such singulars are often used collectively [Alf, Can, Ea, El].

that/in-order-that in[a] it I-may-be bold[b] as I ought[c] to-speak.

LEXICON—a. ἐν with dative object (LN 67.33, 67.136) (BAGD II.3. p. 260): 'in' [BAGD, Lns, We], 'when' [BAGD, LN (67.33)], 'while' [BAGD], 'during' [BAGD, LN (67.136)], 'at the time of' [LN (67.33)], 'within, for, in the course of' [LN (67.136)], not explicit [NAB, NIV,

NRSV]. The phrase ἐν αὐτῷ 'in it' is translated 'therein' [El, Rob; KJV], 'of it' [WBC; REB], 'in this matter' [NIC], 'when I proclaim it' [NTC], 'in proclaiming it' [NASB, NJB], 'about the gospel' [TEV], 'in making it known' [TNT]. The phrase is also coalesced with the infinitive λαλῆσαι 'to speak' and translated 'in my proclamation' [AB].

b. aorist mid. (deponent = act.) subj. of παρρησιάζομαι (LN 25.159, 33.90) (BAGD 1. p. 631): 'to be bold' [LN (25.159); TEV], 'to become frank and bold' [AB], 'to have courage' [LN (25.159); NAB], 'to enjoy liberty' [NIC], 'to speak boldly' [El, LN (33.90), Lns, Rob, We; KJV, NASB], 'to speak openly' [BAGD, LN (33.90)], 'to speak freely, fearlessly' [BAGD], 'to speak with courage' [NTC], 'to talk boldly and openly' [WBC], 'to declare boldly' [NRSV], 'to express oneself freely' [BAGD]. This verb is also translated as an adverb modifying the following infinitive λαλῆσαι 'to speak': 'fearlessly' [NIV, NJB], 'boldly' [REB, TNT]. This verb denotes having courage or boldness in the face of danger or opposition [LN (25.159)], or it denotes speaking openly about something with complete confidence [LN (33.90)]. The usage of this verb in the NT is confined to the free and bold proclamation of the gospel, which is both the privilege and the right of the servant of Christ [MM].

c. pres. act. impersonal δεῖ (LN 71.21): 'ought, should, to have to do' [LN], 'to be necessary' [Lns]. The phrase ὡς δεῖ με 'as I ought' is translated 'as I ought' [El, NIC, NTC, Rob, WBC, We; KJV, NAB, NASB, NJB, TNT], 'as I should' [NIV, TEV], 'as I must' [NRSV], 'as is my duty' [REB], 'for this I must be' [AB]. This impersonal verb denotes being something which should be done as the result of compulsion, whether it is internal, as a matter of duty, or external, as a matter of law, custom, or circumstances [LN].

QUESTION—What relationship is denoted by the ἵνα 'that, in order that' clause?

This clause is parallel with ἵνα μοι δοθῇ λόγος 'in order that to me may be given speech' in 6:19 [Alf, Ea, EGT, El, Ho, ICC, My, We] and, as well, more precisely defines the thought already expressed there, as the final clause ὡς δεῖ με λαλῆσαι 'as I ought to speak' indicates [My]. This clause is a virtual repetition, for the sake of emphasis, of what he said in the preceding verse [NTC].

1. This indicates the content of the prayer [AB, Can (probably), ECWB, Ho]: (pray this) that I may speak boldly. This is how he prays and desires their prayers [Can]. This clause serves to enforce the reference in the previous verse to plainness of speech [ECWB].

2. This indicates purpose or anticipated result [Alf, Ea, EBC, EGT, El, Lns, My]: (pray) in order that I may speak boldly. It indicates a second purpose [EGT, El] of the προσευχόμενοι 'praying' [EGT] and ἀγρυπνοῦντες 'keeping alert' in 6:18 [EGT, El]. This purpose clause is parallel to the infinitive λαλῆσαι 'to speak' in the final clause of this verse (note that Lns has classified the ἵνα 'that' in 6:19 as indicating the content of the

prayer) [Lns]. This part of the verse resumes the purpose of the prayer, and dwells upon the same thought as the whole of the previous verse [Ea], or upon the gift of a conditioned παρρησία 'boldness' [El].
3. This indicates both the content of the prayer and the purpose [WBC]. The two ἵνα 'that' clauses in 6:19–20 indicate the content of this prayer of intercession. The purpose clause at the end of verse 20, ἵνα ἐν αὐτῷ παρρησιάσωμαι ὡς δεῖ με λαλῆσαι 'that in it I may speak boldly, as I ought to speak', underscores the writer's stress on boldness and openness despite his imprisonment [WBC].

QUESTION—What is meant by ἐν αὐτῷ 'in it'?

The referent of ἐν αὐτῷ 'in it' is the ὑπὲρ οὗ 'on behalf of which' which, in turn, refers to infinitive clause γνωρίσαι τὸ μυστήριον τοῦ εὐαγγελίου 'to make known the mystery of the gospel' in 6:19 [AB, Ba, BAGD, Cal, Can, Ea, EBC, EGT, El, My NIC, NTC, Rob, WBC; KJV, NASB, NJB, REB, TEV, TNT]. The ἐν 'in' of this phrase marks the sphere of the boldness, not its ground [Ea], though other commentators understand it as noting that *in* which one is busied, i.e., 'occupied in proclaiming that mystery' [EGT, El, My]. The apostle's earnest wish was that his imprisonment might not have any dispiriting effect on him and cause him to compromise his message and so betray his high calling as an ambassador for Christ [Ea]. Another commentator understands the ἐν αὐτῷ 'in it' to refer to Christ, and so designating the verb παρρησιάσωμαι 'I may be bold' as a Christian activity [TD].

QUESTION—What is meant by παρρησιάσωμαι 'I may be bold'?
1. It refers to the apostle's conduct in speech [BAGD, Can, Ea, EGT, El, LJ, Lns, MM, My, NIC, NTC, Pf, Rob, St, TH, TNTC, WBC, We; all versions]: that I may speak boldly. It means to speak boldly, keeping back nothing through favor or out of the fear of man [Can, LJ, TNTC], but declaring fully the whole counsel of God [Can]. This verb expresses the joyful and fearless courage with which the early proclamation of the message concerning the Risen Christ was accompanied [Pf]. Twice in this request for prayer Paul expresses his desire to be given liberty of speech as he makes the gospel known. Liberty of speech cannot be separated from the inward liberty of spirit which enables a person to speak from the heart [NIC].
2. It refers also to the apostle's general conduct [AB, DNTT]: that I may be bold. The boldness and courage represented by this term were qualities, along with perseverance, that were demanded of the apostle even in prison. These were special qualities of such a character that they were regarded as not being under the control of the person himself, but were a fruit of the Spirit and had to be sought repeatedly [DNTT]. Παρρησιάζομαι originally denoted a boldness shown in speech, but eventually came to denote frank and bold behavior in all ways. In an accurate English translation, both of these meanings must be made explicit because the occurrence of the infinitive λαλῆσαι 'to speak',

though separated from παρρησιάσωμαι 'I may be bold', is nevertheless related to it [AB].

QUESTION—What relationship does the clause ὡς δεῖ με λαλῆσαι 'as I ought to speak' sustain to the preceding clause?

This last clause is a further qualification of the παρρησία 'boldness' in 6:19. With the idea of speaking already partially understood in the παρρησία 'boldness', the λαλῆσαι 'to speak' merely refers back to it [Alf], more precisely defining it [My]. The ὡς δεῖ με does not mean just 'as I ought', but 'in the fashion as I ought' [Si-ed]. The δεῖ 'I ought' expresses all kinds of necessity or obligation according to context. Here it indicates that it befits an ambassador of Christ to be unhampered by fear in speaking the message (the gospel) that he is to deliver even to kings [Lns]. Paul's manner of speech demonstrates what he is, his total freedom despite his chains. Paul must be bold in speaking, otherwise his frank and courageous manner of speaking would be refuted by his manner of life [AB].

DISCOURSE UNIT: 6:21–24 [AB, Alf, Ba, Cal, Can, CBC, EBC, ECWB, ICC, Lns, NIC, NTC, Rob, Si, St, TH, TNTC, WBC, WeBC; NAB, NIV, NJB, NRSV, REB, TEV]. The topic is the conclusion [AB, Alf, Ba, Can, EBC, ECWB, Lns, NTC, St; NAB], letter-closing [NIC], closing words [Rob], postscript [WBC], final greetings [NIV, TEV], personal news and final salutation [NJB], final message and greeting [TNTC], the personal commendation of Tychicus who bears this letter, and final benediction [ICC].

DISCOURSE UNIT: 6:21–22 [EGT, El, IB, MNTC, My, NCBC, NIC, WBC, We, WeBC; NASB, TNT]. The topic is the sending of Tychicus to tell of the apostle's state and to encourage the readers [EGT, El], the commendation of Tychicus as the bearer of this epistle [IB], the messenger Tychicus [MNTC], the sending of Tychicus [My], the mission of Tychicus [WeBC], personal notes [NIC], personal tidings [We].

6:21 Now/but in-order-that you also may-know the (things) with-respect-to[a] me, what/how I-am-doing/faring,[b]

LEXICON—a. κατά with accusative object (LN 89.4) (BAGD II.6. p. 407): 'with respect to' [BAGD], 'in relation to' [BAGD, LN], 'with regard to' [LN], 'about' [AB; TEV]. The words τὰ κατ' ἐμέ, 'the things with respect to me' are translated 'the things concerning me' [Lns], 'my condition' [El], 'my affairs' [NIC, NTC, Rob; KJV], 'about my affairs' [TNT], 'my circumstances' [WBC, We; NASB], 'how I am' [NAB, NIV, NRSV, REB], 'what is happening to me' [NJB]. The vague τὰ κατ' ἐμέ, 'the things with respect to me' is a customary formula [BB] and seems to refer to the matters relating to the state of Paul's trial before the emperor's court [AB].

b. pres. act. indic. of πράσσω (LN 42.8, **90.76**) (BAGD 1.a. or 2.b. p. 698): 'to do' [BAGD (1.a. p.698), LN (42.8); NAB, NIV, NJB, NRSV, REB], 'to carry out/perform' [LN (42.8)], 'to fare, to experience' [LN (90.76)], 'to be, to be situated' [BAGD (2.b. p. 698)]. The clause τί πράσσω 'what I am doing/experiencing' is translated 'how I am getting along' [BAGD (2.b. p. 698), LN (**90.76**), NTC, WBC; TEV], 'how I am getting on' [NIC], 'how I am making out' [LN (**90.76**)], 'how I am faring' [LN (**90.76**), Lns], 'how I fare' [El, We], 'how I am doing' [NASB], 'how I am' [TNT], 'how I do' [Rob; KJV], 'the state of my affairs' [AB]. This verb denotes carrying out some activity and may possibly focus upon the procedures involved [LN (42.8)], or it denotes experiencing events or engaging in them [LN (90.76)].

QUESTION—What relationship is indicated by δέ 'but/now'?

Δέ 'but/now' marks a transition to a different subject [Alf, Ea, EGT, El, My, WBC], but still indicates a contrast between the more solemn occupations of which the apostle has just spoken and his personal welfare [Alf].

QUESTION—What relationship is indicated by ἵνα 'in order that'?

It indicates that Paul's purpose in sending Tychicus with personal news about him was to prevent the danger of uncertain or false rumors concerning Paul from unsettling the minds of the Ephesians [Cal, Ho, TNTC, We].

QUESTION—What is meant by καί 'also'?

1. The καί 'also' refers to the concerns of these Ephesian readers [AB, Alf, TNTC]: now, as to your kind concern about my personal affairs, in order that you may know all the details, Tychicus will make everything known to you. The καί 'also' may mark a shift from the apostle's concern about matters concerning his reader's spiritual state which he has been treating in this epistle to a concern that they might also want to know something about his welfare [Alf], or perhaps Paul had received a letter from the Ephesian church or in some other way had heard news from their church and now Paul recognizes that they are entitled to receive news from him about his affairs [AB, TNTC].

2. The καί 'also' implies other groups who either know or to whom the apostle is sending news of his affairs [Can, Ea, ECWB, EGT, El, Ho, ICC, Lns, MNTC, My, NIC, NTC, Rob, TH, We]: now, in order you also (just as others) may know of my affairs, Tychicus will make everything known to you. This implies that other readers either possessed or desired knowledge of the apostle's affairs [EGT, El, Ho, ICC, MNTC, My, NIC, TH], or it refers especially to the readers of the epistle to Colossae [Can, Ea, ECWB, Lns, My, NTC], being a reference to Col. 4:7 [My], showing that Ephesians was written after Colossians (*contra* AB who believes Ephesians was written before Colossians) [Can, Ea, ECWB, My, NTC], and was intended to be read also by the Colossians [Ea]. It has the sense of 'just as others' [My]. This would be the natural meaning of the καί 'also' if Colossians and Ephesians were written and sent at the same time [NIC, TNTC (supporting 1. above)], so this interpretation is rendered more probable by the nearly identical wording of these two verses with Col. 4:7–8 [Rob].

3. The καί 'also' serves simply to emphasize the accompanying ὑμεῖς 'you' (pl.) [WBC]: now in order that *you* may know the things with respect to me. One commentator thinks the above interpretations all read too much into the καί 'also' and states that it is employed loosely and that only to emphasize the accompanying nominative pronoun ὑμεῖς 'you' (pl.) [WBC].

QUESTION—What is meant by τί πράσσω 'what/how I am doing/faring'?

The clause τί πράσσω 'what/how I am doing/I fare' explains the idiom τὰ κατ' ἐμέ, 'the things with respect to me' [Ea, EGT, El, ICC, Lns, My].

1. The clause τί πράσσω means 'what I am doing', i.e., concerning the apostle's activities [Ba, BAGD (1.a. p. 698), EBC; NAB, NIV, NJB, NRSV, REB]. This clause relates to how the apostle was employed, whereas τὰ κατ' ἐμέ, 'the things with respect to me' inquires not only about the things in which he was engaged, but about his condition, his feelings [Ba].

2. The clause τί πράσσω means 'how I am faring', i.e., concerning the apostle's condition [AB, Alf, BAGD (2.b. p. 698), Can, DNTT, Ea, EGT, El, Ho, ICC, LN (**90.76**), Lns, My, NIC, NTC, Rob, Si-ed, TD, WBC, We; KJV, NASB, TEV, TNT]. This indirect question asks not what the apostle is doing [Alf, Ho], but the state of his welfare [Ea, Ho]. Asking what the apostle was doing would be pointless, because they already knew that [Alf, Ho].

Tychicus the beloved brother and faithful servant[a] in (the) Lord will-make-known everything to-you,

LEXICON—a. διάκονος: 'servant'. See this word at 3:7.

QUESTION—Who is Tychicus?

Tychicus is named in the list of Paul's companions who accompanied him from Corinth to Asia (Acts 20:4), and is said to be from the province of Asia [Alf, Can, CBC, ECWB, EGT, El, Ho, ICC, IDB, ISBE, ISBE2, Lns, My, NTC, Rob, Si, St, WBC, WeBC], that is, Asia Minor, of which Ephesus was the capital [Ba]. He also carried the epistle to the Colossians [Alf, Ba, Can, CBC, EBC, ECWB, EGT, El, Ho, ISBE, ISBE2, My, Si, St, WBC, WeBC]. Later Paul also sent him to Crete to succeed Titus [Alf, Ba, Can, CBC, EBC, EGT, El, Ho, IDB, ISBE, ISBE2, My, Rob]. It is not improbable that he was from Ephesus itself [Ba, EGT, ISBE2, St] and was well known to the church there [Ba, El, St, WBC, WeBC], but not, probably, to the Colossians [El]. An inclusive possessive pronoun, 'our brother', is implied [TH].

QUESTION—What is meant by διάκονος 'servant'?

1. This refers to an official office that Tychicus was appointed to by the church and means 'minister' [Cal, Ho]. The next verse indicates Tychicus was capable not only of comforting the Ephesian readers in respect of their concern for Paul, but of administering the higher consolations of the gospel. This argues that he was a minister of Christ and the gospel [Ho].

2. This does not refer to an official office in the church [BAGD (1.b. p. 184), Can, CBC, DNTT, Ea, ECWB, EGT, El, IDB, ISBE, ISBE2, My, TD, TNTC, WBC; and probably EBC, Lns, Rob, TH] and means 'minister' in the general sense [Can, EGT, El, TNTC; and probably Lns, Rob] or 'servant, helper' [Alf, BAGD, CBC, DNTT, EBC, EGT, IDB, TH, WBC; NIV, NJB, REB, TEV, TNT]. This refers to the service Tychicus rendered to the cause of Christ [Can, CBC, EGT] by his journeys [Can] and the personal assistance he provided to Paul [Can, EGT, El]. He, like Mark, was useful to the apostle for general service [Ea].

QUESTION—What is meant by ἐν κυρίῳ 'in the Lord'?

The phrase ἐν κυρίῳ 'in the Lord' is connected only to 'servant/minister', not to both ἀδελφός 'brother' and διάκονος 'servant/minister' [Alf, Ea, EGT, ICC, Lns, My, NTC, St, TH; NJB, REB, TEV, TNT], Christ's work being the field or sphere in which Tychicus' labor was bestowed [Alf, Ea, El, My; REB, TEV, TNT]. The phrase ἐν κυρίῳ 'in the Lord' characterizes a state or activity as 'Christian' [TD]. One commentator disagrees and attaches ἐν κυρίῳ 'in the Lord' to both nouns, stating that this is more consonant with Paul's usual manner [We].

QUESTION—What is meant by πάντα γνωρίσει ὑμῖν 'will make everything known to you'?

This clause is the central statement of 6:21–22 [WBC]. This probably indicates that Paul, following his usual custom had intended to add some personal notes at the end of this epistle, but considered that the many details of his matters could better be handled in a personal way by Tychicus, the carrier of this epistle [AB], who would have personal acquaintance with Paul's situation [AB, NTC]. The verb γνωρίσει 'will make known to you' is used in both the OT and NT in language associated with the immediate proclamation of the divine will [DNTT]. It implies here that Paul saw his suffering and imprisonment as the fulfillment of his commission to proclaim the gospel (even though BB states that it is not a technical word in Pauline writings for the promulgation of the gospel) [BB].

6:22 whom I-have-sent[a] to you for this very (purpose), in-order-that you-may-know the (things) concerning us and (that) he-may-encourage[b] your hearts.

LEXICON—a. aorist act. indic. of πέμπω (LN 15.66) (BAGD 1. pp. 641-2): 'to send' [AB, BAGD, El, LN, Lns, NIC, NTC, Rob, WBC, We; all versions]. In this reference, ἔπεμψα 'I have sent' is an epistolary aorist [BAGD, BB, EGT, HG, Lns, Mo, Mou, MT, Tu, WBC], the writer writing from the standpoint of the receivers of the letter, that when they have received it and read it, the sending of Tychicus will at that point be properly a past tense [BB, EGT, Mo, MT, Tu, WBC].

b. aorist act. subj. of παρακαλέω (LN **25.150**) (BAGD 4. p. 617): 'to encourage' [BAGD, **LN**, NIC, WBC; NIV, NRSV, TEV, TNT], 'to comfort' [BAGD, El, Lns, Rob, We; KJV, NASB], 'to cheer up' [BAGD], 'to console' [LN], 'to reassure' [AB], 'to strengthen' [NTC]. This verb is also translated as a noun: 'consolation' [NAB]. The clause καὶ παρακαλέσῃ τὰς καρδίας ὑμῶν 'and (that) he may encourage your hearts' is translated: 'and encourage you thoroughly' [NJB], 'and to put fresh heart into you' [REB].

QUESTION—What is meant by ὃν ἔπεμψα πρὸς ὑμᾶς εἰς αὐτὸ τοῦτο, 'whom I have sent to you for this very purpose'?

This asserts that it is Tychicus' mission to impart the very knowledge of Paul's condition that he has mentioned in 6:21 and asserts again in the ἵνα 'in order that' clause following the express purpose indicator εἰς αὐτὸ τοῦτο 'for this very purpose' [EBC, My, TH]. Most commentators assume that Tychicus was sent to the Ephesians from Rome where this epistle was written, there being no statements to the contrary. One commentator, however, states that it refers to Tychicus' instructions to go on to Ephesus from Colossae [My]. The reference of the purpose phrase εἰς αὐτὸ τοῦτο 'for this very purpose' is forward to the contents of the following ἵνα 'in order that' clause [El, ICC]. Paul felt it proper to send a special messenger to provide information about his condition and to give them consolation in their various trials [Ba, EGT] of which concern about his own imprisonment and pending trial was certainly one [Ba, Cal, EBC, EGT, Ho, Si, St, TNTC, We].

QUESTION—What is meant by ἵνα γνῶτε τὰ περὶ ἡμῶν καὶ παρακαλέσῃ τὰς καρδίας ὑμῶν 'in order that you may know the things concerning us and that he may encourage your hearts'?

The ἵνα 'in order that' is in apposition with the preceding εἰς αὐτὸ τοῦτο 'for this very purpose' [HG], and the clause ἵνα γνῶτε τὰ περὶ ἡμῶν 'in order that you may know the things concerning us' is a restatement of the first clause of 6:21, ἵνα δὲ εἰδῆτε καὶ ὑμεῖς τὰ κατ' ἐμέ, 'now, in order that you may know the things with respect to me' [EGT, El, TH], but with the difference that here Paul includes the welfare of his coworkers with his own (ἡμῶν 'us' (exclusive [TH])) [BB, Ea, EGT, El, Lns, My, TH, We]. The difference between the εἰδῆτε 'you may know' of that clause and the γνῶτε 'you may know' of this clause is that εἰδῆτε 'you may know' relates to knowledge of the facts of a case, whereas γνῶτε 'you may know' relates to the relationship existing between the subject and the object, conveying the idea of personal interest and concern of the Ephesians regarding the facts. The following clause bears this out [Lns].

QUESTION—In what way would he encourage their hearts?

1. The reference is general [Alf, El]: that he may encourage your hearts wherever such encouragement is needed. The reference of παρακαλέσῃ 'he may encourage' is best left generally to their particular need for comfort or encouragement [Alf, El], since we do not know the exact state of the church [El].

2. The reference is particularly to the reader's concern over Paul's imprisonment and pending imperial trial [Ba, Cal, Can, Ea, EBC, ECWB, EGT, Lns, My, NTC, We, WeBC]: that he may encourage your hearts

concerning my welfare. The occurrence of the clause καὶ παρακαλέσῃ τὰς καρδίας ὑμῶν 'and (that) he may encourage your hearts' is a plain reference back to 3:13 where his readers are said to be in danger of being discouraged because of his sufferings [Ea, EBC, ECWB, EGT, My, NTC, We] and implies that things were going well for Paul at this point [Can, ECWB, Lns, WeBC], and the personal notices in the epistles to Philemon and to the church at Philippi, written about the same time as Ephesians, bear this out [Can, ECWB]. He expected his trial to issue in a decision favorable to the progress of the gospel, and he expected to be released shortly and to visit Philemon and, presumably, other friends. News such as this would have encouraged the readers [Can].

DISCOURSE UNIT: 6:23–24 [EGT, El, IB, MNTC, My, NCBC, NIC, WBC, We, WeBC; NASB, TNT]. The topic is the closing benediction [EGT, IB, MNTC, NCBC, NIC, WeBC], concluding wishes [My], double salutation and blessing [We], the two closing epistolary elements—the wish for peace and grace-benediction [WBC], peace to the brethren and grace to all true Christians [El].

6:23 **Peace/prosperity to the brethren and love with/by-means-of[a] faith from God (the) Father and (the) Lord Jesus Christ.**

LEXICON—a. μετά with genitive object (LN 89.78, **89.123**) (BAGD A.II.6. p. 509): 'with' [BAGD, El, LN (89.78, 89.109, **89.123**), NIC, NTC, Rob, WBC, We; KJV, NASB, NIV, NRSV, REB, TEV], 'by means of, through' [LN (89.78)], 'combined with' [LN (**89.123**)], 'and above all' [AB], 'in company with' [Lns], 'and' [NAB, NJB, TNT].

QUESTION—What is the function of this verse?

This verse is the first part of a double apostolic blessing [Alf, Can, EBC, My, We] addressed to the brethren (6:23) [Alf, Can] and to all real lovers of the Lord Jesus Christ (6:24) [Alf] everywhere [Can]. The third person references in this conclusion, as opposed to the use of the second person in the conclusions of other epistles, is somewhat accounted for by the facts that this epistle is encyclical in nature [Can, ECWB, EGT, IB, ICC, NIC, Rob, WBC], it would not come to the readers all gathered together in one group [Can], and the apostle would have each of the churches, as they read it in turn, to know that this blessing is intended for all alike [Can, Rob]. The slightly more distant nature of third person references are due to the lack of personal acquaintance between Paul and these readers [AB].

QUESTION—What is meant by εἰρήνη 'peace'?

1. Εἰρήνη 'peace' is regarded as the result of man's reconciliation to God [Can, CBC, Ea (probably), EGT, El, Ho] and refers to all the benefits of χάρις 'grace', or favor with God, which reconciliation to God brings [CBC, Ho].
   1.1 It means 'prosperity' [Ea]. Coming from a Christian it means 'all that is good for them here and hereafter' [Ea].

1.2 It means 'tranquility, concord' [Can]. It is peace with God, bringing with it peace of conscience and heart, for which the apostle prays [Can].
1.3 It means both 'prosperity' and 'tranquility, concord' [EGT, El]. It equates with the Hebrew greeting, *shalom* 'peace, prosperity'. This greeting has the Christian connotation of well-being as mental peace and good due to reconciliation with God [EGT]. This is a prayer for the calm tranquility and prosperity of soul which is the result of reconciliation and the special gift of God's Spirit [El].
2. Εἰρήνη 'peace' is regarded as the result of men's reconciliation with each other [Cal (probably), EBC, IB, NTC, St, TH]. This is more than a farewell greeting. This is a prayer for reconciliation. Paul longs to see the whole brotherhood, Jews and Gentiles alike, at peace with each other [EBC].
2.1 It means 'prosperity' [NTC]. As in 1:2, it is true spiritual wholeness and prosperity [NTC].
2.2 It means 'tranquility, concord' [EBC (probably)].
2.3 It means both of the above [Cal]. He wishes the Ephesians to be peaceable and quiet among themselves [Cal].
3. Εἰρήνη 'peace' is regarded as the result of both man's reconciliation to God and their reconciliation with one another [AB, ECWB, ISBE2, TNTC, WBC].
3.1 It means 'prosperity' [AB, ISBE2]. It is the pronouncement of peace with all the implications that the terms 'messianic peace' or the 'God of peace' possess [AB]. Εἰρήνη 'peace' in the NT has the broader connotations of the Hebrew *shalom* 'peace, prosperity', i.e., well being, completeness, inner satisfaction, the contentment and serenity that comes from living a full life [ISBE2].
3.2 It means 'tranquility, concord' [ECWB, TNTC]. Peace is first with God in the thankful receiving of his mercy. From this naturally arises 'love with faith' towards God, and then peace and love towards men [ECWB].
3.3 It means both of the above [WBC]. At this stage of the letter, the notion of peace has connotations beyond that of general well-being for Christians. It recalls to the reader the earlier emphasis on the peace God has given as a result of reconciliation to himself and with each other [WBC].

QUESTION—What relationship is indicated by μετά 'with, by means of'?
1. It indicates that faith accompanies ἀγάπη 'love' [Alf, BAGD, ECWB, EGT, El, ICC, Lns, NIC, Rob, St, TD, WBC]: peace to the brethren and love with faith. Μετά 'with' is used to indicate a close connection between two nouns, the first of which is the one being emphasized [BAGD], e.g., especially love with faith. It has the simple idea of *accompanying* [EGT, Lns, NIC], as the fruit accompanies the tree, love being the fruit of faith [Lns]. This occurrence of 'faith' with 'love' may refer back to 1:15 [NIC, Rob, WBC] where the apostle praises the readers for their faith and the love they show to all the saints. At the end of this letter he is

saying he hopes these qualities will continue to characterize his readers [NIC]. The faith is somewhat presupposed as already being theirs [Alf, EGT, El, St, WBC], and he prays that love may always accompany it [Alf, St]. This is *brotherly* love which shows itself where faith is, and by which faith works [EGT]. Faith is represented as the perpetual *concomitant* of a true love [El], which is the characteristic of a true faith [El, ICC] and the medium by which the energy of faith is displayed [El].

2. It indicates that faith accompanies both εἰρήνη 'peace' and ἀγάπη 'love' [AB, Cal, We]. The phrase is taken with both εἰρήνη 'peace' and ἀγάπη 'love' since ἀπὸ θεοῦ 'from God' belongs to both. Peace and love are God's gifts, and faith is the condition under which they are appropriated [We]. 'Love with faith' is the means by which 'peace' or 'harmony' is achieved, for this is brotherly *love* and agreement in *faith* [Cal]. Paul now concludes by averring that no other εἰρήνη 'peace' and ἀγάπη 'love' is meant than those that create and sustain πίστεως 'faith', and, in turn, are received and confessed by it [AB].

3. The phrase μετὰ πίστεως 'with faith' is interpreted absolutely, with all three nouns receiving essentially equal emphasis [IDB, TH; NAB, NJB, TNT]: peace, love, and faith to the brethren. Πίστεως 'faith' is not mutual confidence in one another, but faith in God. The phrase is an unusual expression. The writer has mentioned his knowledge of their faith and love in 1:15, but here its relationship to ἀγάπη 'love' is obscure. It may be best expressed 'together with confidence in God' or even put it in a separate sentence [TH].

4. It indicates that ἀγάπη 'love' is combined with πίστεως 'faith' [Ea, EBC, Ho, LN (**89.123**), My, WeBC]: peace to the brethren and love combined with faith. The phrase ἀγάπη μετὰ πίστεως 'love with faith' is conceived of as one object wished for, with the emphasis placed on ἀγάπη 'love' [My]. This is love in union with faith [Ea, Ho]. He does not ask for love and faith. They already had faith [Ho, My]. What he desires is that their faith might issue in brotherly love [Ho]. This is not God's love for man, but man's love for his fellow man, and this 'with faith' as its accompaniment, is inseparably combined with it, because faith works by love [Ea]. Peace with one another in the body of Christ will only happen through mutual love combined with faith from which it is derived [EBC].

5. It indicates that love comes by means of faith [Ba, Can, IB, TNTC]: peace to the brethren and love by means of their faith. The preposition μετά 'with' indicates that faith springs from love [TNTC], or faith works by love [Ba, Can, IB]. The apostle is desiring that his readers not only have faith [Ba], but the faith which works by love [Ba, Can]. Without union with Christ through faith, love cannot begin to grow [TNTC].

QUESTION—What relationship is indicated by the prepositional phrase ἀπὸ θεοῦ πατρὸς καὶ κυρίου Ἰησοῦ Χριστοῦ 'from God the Father and the Lord Jesus Christ'?

Paul joins the first cause (God the Father) with the second (the Lord Jesus Christ) [My]. The only difference between this phrase and its occurrence in 1:2 is the occurrence of the preposition ἡμῶν 'our' with πατρός 'Father' in 1:2 [Ea, EGT], yet the phrase means the same here as it does there [Ea]. Another commentator, however, feels the absence of the ἡμῶν 'our' here places more focus on the relation of God to Christ with respect to their joint bestowal of spiritual blessings [EGT].

1. This phrase is attached both to εἰρήνη τοῖς ἀδελφοῖς 'peace to the brethren' and ἀγάπη μετὰ πίστεως 'love with faith' [AB, Ba, Cal, CBC, EBC, ECWB, EGT, Ho, Lns, NIC, NTC, St, WBC, We, WeBC]. The ultimate source of peace, love, and faith, is from God himself [EBC, WBC]. These are the three essential features of Christian community life [EBC]. Here the name of Christ the Son occurs in perfect equality with that of God the Father [EBC, NTC], one preposition governing both names [NTC]. The Father and the Son are united as objects of worship and the source of saving and spiritual blessing [Ho]. As in the opening greeting of this epistle (1:2) [CBC], the gifts the apostle prays for are seen as coming from both the Father and the Lord Jesus Christ [CBC, ECWB, Lns]. Peace and love are regarded as coming equally from both the Father and the Son [Ba, Cal, Lns].
2. This phrase is attached to ἀγάπη μετὰ πίστεως 'love with faith' [Can]. The apostle prays that his readers may have, from God the Father and the Lord Jesus Christ, that love which is the fruit and evidence of faith [Can].

6:24 **Grace (be) with all who are-loving our Lord Jesus Christ in incorruptibility/immortality/sincerity.**[a]

TEXT—Some manuscripts add ἀμήν 'amen' at the end of this sentence. GNT assigns an A rating to the reading without the closing ἀμήν 'amen', indicating that this reading is certain. Only KJV follows the reading with ἀμήν 'amen'.

LEXICON—a. ἀφθαρσία (LN 23.127, **68.57**) (BAGD p. 125): 'incorruptibility' [BAGD, Rob], 'incorruption' [El, Lns, We], 'immortality' [BAGD, LN (23.127), NIC, WBC], 'unceasing, always, eternally, undying' [LN (68.57)], 'eternity' [AB], 'sincerity' [KJV]. The phrase ἐν ἀφθαρσίᾳ 'in incorruptibility' is translated as an adverb modifying ἀγαπώντων 'are loving': 'unceasingly' [LN (**68.57**)]. It is also translated as an adjective modifying a supplied noun 'love': 'imperishable' [NTC], 'unfailing' [NAB], 'incorruptible' [NASB], 'undying' [NIV, NRSV, REB, TEV, TNT]; modifying a supplied noun 'life': 'imperishable' [NJB]. The meaning in this passage refers either to those who love the Lord, and because of this are even now partakers of the future life, or it refers to the Lord himself, who reigns in immortal glory [BAGD].

QUESTION—What is the function of this verse?

This verse closes the epistle with a general benediction pronounced upon all who love Christ [Alf, Ho]. It is a second and more general benediction [Ea, EGT, El, Lns, My]. The words ἡ χάρις μετὰ πάντων 'grace be with all' is essentially a prayer [TH]. Χάρις 'grace' is the parting wish with which, in some form, the apostle closes all his epistles. But in this one alone, the prayer for grace has a wider scope. The reason for this is the focus of the apostle's mind upon the one great body in which Christ has reconciled both Jews and Gentiles alike to God and to one another, and this great unity has been showing itself to him as a reality, not just as a mere ideal or theory. This thought moves him to invoke this blessing not only upon the great body as a whole of which he has been thinking, but upon the dear men and women who compose this body [Can]. Paul's greetings and benedictions are not personal ones as is evident from the fact that he uses the same ones in letter to churches he has not personally visited as for those he has. At the same time, neither are they mere formulas, for Paul intends his greetings and farewells to be serious invocations of the grace that has come, and continues to come, from the resurrected Lord Jesus Christ [ISBE2].

QUESTION—What is meant by ἡ χάρις 'the grace'?

The emphasis in this verse falls upon this term as the emphasis in the last verse fell upon the term εἰρήνη 'peace'. As the word *par excellence* that Paul uses for the generous giving of God [NCBC], the recipients of this epistle would find this grace-benediction highly appropriate for a letter which has laid so much stress on the undeserved favor the recipients have received from God and Christ [WBC]. It differs from the introductory salutation (1:2) only in that here the definite article occurs with it and this holds true for introductory and concluding prayers in his other epistles also [TNTC]. This article may denote the grace of Christ who is mentioned both before and after ἡ χάρις 'the grace' [EBC, El], or it may refer to the grace about which Paul has written so much in this epistle [EBC, NTC, TNTC]. It is '*the* grace' [EGT], pre-eminent grace [My], the grace besides which there is none other, of which Christians have had experience [EGT]. Another commentator suggests that the grace that is meant is the grace which has given the gifts of peace and love with faith mentioned in the previous verse [TD]. Or, it might show the influence of a liturgical form of closing prayer in use even at this early time in Christian worship [TNTC]. Another commentator suggests that the reason for the article is that χάρις 'grace' is not followed by the preposition ἀπό 'from' as in the introductory greeting. He also suggests that χάρις 'grace' here means daily forgiveness and all the gifts that come to us through Christ [Lns].

QUESTION—What is meant by the participial clause τῶν ἀγαπώντων τὸν κύριον 'who are loving the Lord'?

This is a Christological adaptation [WBC] of a traditional formula describing the people who fear God, serve him, and keep his commandments [AB, WBC]. It is parallel to and describes the same people denoted by τοῖς ἀδελφοῖς 'the brethren' in 6:23 [AB, NCBC]. The combination of both terms makes the diction ponderous [AB]. Others, however, state that τοῖς ἀδελφοῖς 'the brethren' of the last verse denotes the readers [My], Christians in Ephesus [Ea, El, Lns] or Asia [EGT], while τῶν ἀγαπώντων τὸν κύριον 'who are loving the Lord' is more general [Ea, EGT, El, Lns, My], denoting all Christians [EGT, Lns]. This love, while not necessarily ecstatic, must control the Christian. It includes an adoring admiration for his person, desire for his presence, zeal for his glory, and devotion to his service [Ho].

QUESTION—What relationship is indicated by the phrase ἐν ἀφθαρσίᾳ 'in incorruptibility/immortality/sincerity'?

    1. The phrase is connected with χάρις 'grace' [Lns, NCBC, NIC, WBC; and probably NJB].

    1.1 With ἀφθαρσίᾳ meaning 'incorruptibility' and interpreted as 'immortality' [NCBC, NIC, WBC]: grace and immortality be with all who are loving our Lord Jesus Christ.

    1.1.1 'Immortality' or immortal life is an accompaniment of χάρις 'grace' [NIC, WBC]: grace and immortality be with all who are loving our Lord Jesus Christ.

    1.1.2 'Immortality' is a quality of χάρις 'grace' [NCBC]: undying grace be with all who are loving our Lord Jesus Christ.

    1.1.3 'Immortality' is both a quality of χάρις 'grace' and its accompaniment [TD]: undying grace and immortality be with all who are loving our Lord Jesus Christ.

    1.2 With ἀφθαρσίᾳ meaning 'incorruption' [Lns]: grace in connection with incorruption be with all who love our Lord Jesus Christ.

    2. The phrase is connected with the articular present participle τῶν ἀγαπώντων 'who are loving' [Alf, Ba, BAGD, Cal, Can, CBC, Ea, EBC, ECWB, EGT, El, Ho, ICC, LJ, LN (68.57), MNTC, Mo (probably), My, NTC, Rob, Si, Si-ed, St, TD, TH, TNTC, We, WeBC; all versions except NJB]. The phrase ἐν ἀφθαρσίᾳ 'in incorruptibility' denotes the element [Alf, EGT, El], conditioning sphere, [Alf, El] or manner [Can, Ea, ECWB, EGT, El, My] of the love.

    2.1 With ἀφθαρσίᾳ meaning 'incorruptibility, incorruptness, imperishable' [Alf, BAGD, Ea, ECWB, EGT, El, ICC, My, NTC, Rob, Si, Si-ed, St, We] and interpreted as 'immortality, unceasing, undying' [BAGD, CBC, EBC, LN (68.57), MNTC, NTC, Rob, St, TH, WeBC; NIV, NRSV, REB, TEV, TNT].

    2.1.1 It describes Christians as being those who already possess immortal life [BAGD, EBC, Rob]: grace be with all who are loving our Lord Jesus Christ, who already possess immortality. (BAGD lists this as one possible interpretation with 3 below, as another possibility, stating no preference.)

    2.1.2 It indicates a quality of Christian love and means that Christian love will never end [Alf, EBC, EGT, El, ICC, LN (68.57), MNTC, My,

NTC, Rob, WeBC; NIV, NRSV, REB, TEV, TNT]: grace be with all who are loving our Lord Jesus Christ with an undying love.

2.1.3 It indicates that Christian love will result in immortality [CBC]: grace be with all who are loving our Lord Jesus Christ with a love that results in immortality. This is a love that results in *immortality*. This relationship of love with the risen Christ has a lasting quality about it and can survive all setbacks, Rom. 8:38–39, and results in the full life that awaits Christians when God has fulfilled his purposes and is all in all (1 Cor. 15:51) [CBC].

2.2 With ἀφθαρσία 'incorruptibility' interpreted as 'sincerity' [Ba, Cal, LJ, TD; KJV]: grace be with all who are sincerely loving our Lord Jesus Christ. This means love with a pure heart, without dissembling, without hypocrisy [Ba]. It means to love with the whole heart, without any admixture, without any ulterior motives [LJ].

2.3 With ἀφθαρσία 'incorruptibility' interpreted as both 'immortality' and 'sincerity' [Can, Ho, Mo, TNTC]: grace be with all who are sincerely loving our Lord Jesus Christ with an undying love. It denotes a Christian love that is not only sincere and free from unworthy motives, but constant, not to be overcome by allurements or quenched by difficulties or dangers [Can]. This may be an instance where a double meaning is intended in the words [Mo].

3. The phrase is connected with τὸν κύριον ἡμῶν Ἰησοῦν Χριστόν 'our Lord Jesus Christ' [BAGD, DNTT, TD] with ἀφθαρσία meaning 'incorruptibility' [TD] and interpreted as 'immortality' [BAGD, DNTT]: grace be with all who are loving our Lord Jesus Christ in his incorruptibility. (BAGD lists this as one possible interpretation with 2.1.1 above as another possibility, stating no preference. An article in TD simply translates the verse in this way.)

4. The phrase is connected to the whole verse [AB, IB] and each of its parts [AB], with ἀφθαρσία 'incorruptibility' interpreted as 'eternity' [AB] or 'forever' [IB]: grace be with all who are loving our Lord Jesus Christ forever. Their present life is embedded in God's eternity, and their love for the Lord demonstrates their awareness of this salvation as well as their gratitude for the good life given to them [AB].

www.ingramcontent.com/pod-product-compliance
Lightning Source LLC
Chambersburg PA
CBHW052013040526
R18239600001BA/R182396PG44108CBX00012BA/23